The Music Machine

edited by Curtis Roads

The Music Machine

Selected Readings from *Computer Music Journal*

The MIT Press
Cambridge, Massachusetts
London, England

Printed and bound by Halliday Lithograph
in the United States of America.

Library of Congress Cataloging-in-Publication Data

The Music machine : selected readings from Computer
music journal / edited by Curtis Roads.

    p.   cm.
  Includes index.
  ISBN 0-262-18131-2
  1. Computer music—History and criticism. I. Roads,
Curtis. II. Computer music journal.
ML 1093.M88 1989   88-9208
789.9′9—dc19

Contents

Curtis Roads

Preface

The "music machine" is an ancient idea, embodied in automatic instruments from the Aeolian harp (powered by gusts of wind) to music boxes and orchestrions (powered by springs or steam) to today's digital signal processing engines (powered by the flow of electrical current through millions of logic gates). The deeply rooted impulse to create music machines—for performance, composition, music printing, and scholarship—seems destined to last, if we are lucky, far into the future.

The digital electronic computer is the music machine of the present. As computer music expands to become more a part of everyday musical life, the need for information about it continues to grow. The community of interest is a broad group that includes composers, performing musicians, media artists, scientists, educators, students, scholars, researchers, musical engineers, software developers, entrepreneurs, and audiences. This community needs direct access to primary-source articles on the art, the science, and the technology of computer music. The MIT Press asked me to prepare *The Music Machine* with this goal in mind.

Computer Music Journal has, since 1977, served as a chronicle of international activity in the field of computer music and digital audio. In its pages have appeared articles by and interviews with most of the major figures in computer music. This book brings together a selection of articles from volumes 4 through 9, which include the 24 issues I edited from 1980 through 1985. In addition, it presents a valuable new survey of MIDI (Musical Instrument Digital Interface) software, written by Christopher Yavelow.

Besides assembling these fine papers in one place, the book offers overviews (one for each of the seven parts) that place the papers in perspective and relate them to current work. The overviews and the index should help readers who are just beginning to learn about the field.

The Music Machine follows an earlier volume, edited by John Strawn and me, called *Foundations of Computer Music* (MIT Press, 1985). *Foundations* drew its content from the journal's first three volumes (1977 through 1979). Reflecting the expansion of the field in the 1980s, *The Music Machine* adds

four parts to the scheme of the earlier book: one made up of interviews with prominent figures in the field, one on composition techniques, one exploring musical applications of artificial intelligence, and one devoted to MIDI.

The most important development in computer music in the 1980s is the proliferation of powerful and inexpensive personal computers and digital synthesizers. Activity in computer music has spread far beyond the laboratories of academic and research institutions. The technology is now so accessible that virtually any musician can set up a home studio for research, composition, or playing. We see more and more computers on stage in concert halls and in nightclubs. Sophisticated digital music systems for live performance are no further than the local musical instrument store.

A lively industry has grown up around the idea of delivering computer-based tools for music-making and sound processing. With millions of musicians and personal computer users as a market, tiny and enormous companies compete side by side. Individual, academic, and industrial research efforts all contribute to the constantly shifting mix of technologies and musical possibilities.

Virtually all styles of music—even folk idioms—have been "computerized." Digital synthesis and MIDI technology now dominate popular music, and a healthy diversity of styles coexist in the various new music scenes. It has often been pointed out that "computer music" is not a style in itself; rather, it is a generalized means of music production. But this is not to say that its effect is neutral; far from it. Each new technical advance seems to spawn a series of pieces that exploit the new effect. Technology pushes the music, which pulls the technology along with it. The popular MIDI specification, for example, has generated a host of performance possibilities and applications that were never part of the original conception of MIDI. This rapidly evolving situation poses a special challenge to music educators, who must adapt their very concept of music to a changing technical and musical environment. The 54 articles selected for *The Music Machine* serve as a contribution to this vital reeducation process.

Acknowledgments

I greatly appreciate the comments of Judy Backman and John Strawn, who were kind enough to review my overviews and provide much helpful feedback. The overviews were greatly improved by their criticisms. I also thank everyone in the journals division of The MIT Press—especially Christine Lamb, Journals Manager—for their support and encouragement throughout the past nine years of work on *Computer Music Journal*.

Editor's Note
Several of the articles refer to "sound examples." These were included on soundsheets (thin analog records) bound into *Computer Music Journal*. It was not possible to reissue the soundsheets with this book; however, many libraries retain copies of these disks.

I

Interviews

Curtis Roads

Overview

Interviews are an effective means of communication; they tend to bring out ideas, emotions, opinions, and contradictions that would be difficult to present in another format. This collection of interviews intermingles musical and technical discussions, and conveys much of historical interest along the way.

It is fitting that this book begin with an interview with the father of computer-generated sound, Max V. Mathews. Through the years, he has explored virtually every aspect of computer music, from sound synthesis to algorithmic composition and real-time performance. In this interview, Mathews reveals the path that led to the development of his sound synthesis programs Music IV and Music V, which are still in use twenty years after the publication of his book *The Technology of Computer Music* (Mathews 1969). The final part of the interview explores his more recent work with the Sequential Drum, an instrument for real-time performance that has lately been outfitted with a MIDI interface.

As a technical "wizard" at Stanford University during the early 1970s, James "Andy" Moorer helped to make the Center for Computer Research in Music and Acoustics (CCRMA) one of the most influential institutes for computer music. The second interview focuses on many of the research issues he has investigated in the course of his unusually productive career, including automatic music transcription, signal-processing software, the phase vocoder, linear predictive coding, music languages, and the design of digital audio processing systems. The Lucasfilm Audio Signal Processor (also known, later, as the SoundDroid), discussed in the latter part of this interview, is described in more detail in article 47.

Clarence Barlow is—partly as a result of his theoretical writings (Barlow 1987) and his teaching positions at Cologne, Amsterdam, Darmstadt, and elsewhere—one of the most prominent composers in Europe. The third interview, conducted by the late Stephan Kaske, traces Barlow's path to computers and their application in his often complex pieces. In expressing his ambivalence about working with computers, Barlow speaks for many composers who feel that the transformation of computers into effective musical workstations has only begun.

The composer and performer David Rosenboom directs the Center for Contemporary Music (CCM) at Mills College in Oakland, California. In the fourth interview, Larry Polansky, his colleague at Mills, engages Rosenboom in a discussion about instruments and the aesthetic issues they present in his compositions. Toward the end of the interview, Rosenboom outlines his vision of CCM as a mecca for research and performance.

A generation of experimental composers have passed through the University of California at San Diego. Richard Boulanger, while a doctoral candidate there, interviewed two composers who were members of the faculty—Joji Yuasa and Roger Reynolds—along with the visiting composer Charles Wuorinen. To Reynolds, the compositional act involves "a necessary schizophrenia" between planning and reacting to "unexpected developments." For both Yuasa and Reynolds, the computer's ability to precisely manipulate sounds in space is one of its primary attractions as a compositional medium. Wuorinen conveys strongly held views on various topics, ranging from the use of compositional algorithms to the problems of composing for electronic media. His eye-opening recollections of the RCA synthesizer (installed at the Columbia-Princeton studios in the 1950s and 1960s) put the brave composers who used this difficult instrument in a new light.

The postmodern movement in computer music, characterized by lush naturalistic timbres and a return to traditional means of expression such as metered rhythms and tonal harmony, is represented here by Paul Lansky. But that label only begins to describe the breadth of Lansky's output, which even in a single piece (such as *Six Fantasies on a Poem by Thomas Campion* [1979]) can range from known musical styles to experimental procedures and unorthodox sounds. Perhaps the best explanation is that Lansky is a master of musical vernacular. He applies this skill, in conjunction with other means, whenever it suits his musical impulse.

References

Barlow, S. 1987. "Two Essays on Theory." *Computer Music Journal* 11(1): 44–60.

Mathews, M. 1969. *The Technology of Computer Music.* Cambridge, Mass.: MIT Press.

Roads, C. 1978. "An Interview with Gottfried Michael Koenig." *Computer Music Journal* 2(3): 11–15. Reprinted in C. Roads and J. Strawn, eds., *Foundations of Computer Music* (Cambridge, Mass.: MIT Press, 1985).

1

C. Roads

Interview with Max Mathews

Introduction

Max Mathews is a pioneer in computer music, having developed the first sound synthesis programs in the late 1950s at Bell Laboratories. He is the author of the classic text on the subject, *The Technology of Computer Music* (1969, The MIT Press), and of numerous papers on the application of computer technology to music and acoustics.

This interview took place in Cambridge, Massachusetts in late June 1980. Dr. Mathews had recently returned from a research visit to Institute de Recherche et Coordination Acoustique/Musique (IRCAM) in Paris, where he and Curtis Abbott had worked with his Sequential Drum and its interconnection to the 4C Machine.

Background

Roads: First, I'd like to ask you a little about your background; where you went to school, what you studied, and how you got interested in computer music.

Mathews: I studied electrical engineering in all my schools; Cal Tech first, and then M.I.T. I eventually got a Doctor's degree in electrical engineering. At that time and ever since I've been interested in large, complex systems and in computers; first in analog computers and then, when they became practical, in digital computers. Leaving M.I.T., I went to Bell Labs for my working career. I worked in the Acoustics Research Department applying digital techniques to speech transmission problems and, eventually, to music. I've always enjoyed music as an amateur musician.

Roads: I noticed in your demonstration and performance out at Stanford that you at some point

Computer Music Journal, Vol. 4, No. 4, Winter 1980

learned to play the violin. Did you study violin as a child?

Mathews: I studied violin through high school and have continued to play it ever since, taking a few lessons but not many. I like the instrument very much personally, although I call it an "inefficient" music instrument in that you have to practice more to achieve a given musical performance than with almost any other instrument. Anyway I'm stuck with the violin; I'm certainly not going to learn any other instruments except the computer and new instruments I might invent myself!

Music I

Roads: It must have been in the early and mid-1950s that you started applying computers toward musical goals. Can you tell us a little about your experiences with the program Music I? You brought that up on an IBM 704 computer?

Mathews: That was the only computer we had that was capable of doing sound processing.

Roads: That was at Bell Labs?

Mathews: Actually the 704 computer was in New York City at IBM World Headquarters on Madison Avenue. We used to go in there and run our programs and bring a digital magnetic tape back to Bell Labs. The digital-to-analog converter was at Bell Labs.

Roads: What was the converter like?

Mathews: We had a 12-bit vacuum tube converter; it was quite a nice machine. It was made by a company called Epsco, I believe.

Roads: Music I was capable of playing melodies, was it not?

Mathews: It generated one waveform, an equilateral triangular waveform, with the same rise as decay characteristics. You could specify a pitch, and an amplitude and a duration for each note and that was it.

memory. Some hardware synthesizers today seem to give you this.

Mathews: True. The hardware synthesizers probably have to repeat the trajectory of the software programs.

Roads: That must have been 1958. Was this still on the 704 computer?

Mathews: By that time we had moved to the IBM 7094 at Bell Labs. That was a very, very effective machine. We used it for almost a decade, not only for musical purposes, but for our great preponderance of computations at Bell Labs in speech processing and visual signal processing. That was a fine machine and some of the notable early operating systems were developed for that machine, including Bellsys 1 and Bellsys 2.

Roads: Had you heard of anyone else doing anything similar at around that time?

Mathews: No. There were some people, Lejaren Hiller in particular, who had done a bit with composing music—compositional algorithms—but as far as I know there were no attempts to perform music with a computer. In fact, we were the only ones in the world at the time who had the right kind of digital-to-analog converter hooked up to a digital tape transport that would play a computer tape. So we had a monopoly, if you will, on this process.

Roads: This was 1957?

Mathews: Yes.

Roads: Some people made compositions with Music I, is that not true?

Mathews: One brave soul, a psychologist named Newman Guttman, made one composition. But it was not hard to realize that we could do better. Music I sounded terrible and was very limited. It was clear that if we were going to get better music out we had to do better. It wasn't hard to see things that could be added and changed.

Music II

Roads: So you developed Music II. As I recall, Music II was capable of four independent voices of sound, and a choice of 16 waveforms stored in

Music III

Roads: In Music III, which you introduced in 1960, you introduced also the concept of the *unit generator*, which is certainly one of the major conceptual advances which has made computer music possible today. Can you describe why that became a necessary concept?

Mathews: I too think it's a very important concept, and more subtle than it appears on the surface. I wanted to give the musician a great deal of power and generality in making the musical sounds, but at the same time I wanted as simple a program as possible; I wanted the complexity of the program to vary with the complexity of the musician's desires. If the musician wanted to do something simple, he or she shouldn't have to do very much in order to achieve it. If the musician wanted something very elaborate there was the option of working harder to do the elaborate thing. The only answer I could see was not to make the instruments myself—not to impose my taste and ideas about instruments on the musicians—but rather to make a set of fairly universal building blocks and give the musician both the task and the freedom to put these together into his or her instruments. I made my building blocks correspond to many of the functions of the new analog synthesizers.

I wouldn't say that I copied the analog synthesizer building blocks; I think we actually developed them fairly simultaneously. In any case, that was an advantage because a musician who knew how to patch together Moog synthesizer units would have a pretty good idea how to put together unit generators in the computer.

Music IV

Roads: Yes. Music IV followed Music III in 1963. What was the advantage of Music IV over Music III?

Mathews: Music IV was simply a response to a change in the language and the computer. It had some technical advantages from a computer programming standpoint. It made heavy use of a macro assembly program which existed at the time.

Roads: So up until that point you had been programming in assembly language without a macro facility?

Mathews: Macro assemblers were just invented at that time. Indeed, Music IV debugged a lot of the macro assembler that was used at Bell Labs. It made very heavy and rather sophisticated use of the macro facilities, and I discovered a lot of bugs in them that the designers hadn't anticipated, and that they were glad to fix.

So in essence Music IV was musically no more powerful than Music III and was only a little more convenient to use, but it was computationally quite a bit more sophisticated.

Roads: From Music IV a number of people made their own versions, like at Princeton.

Mathews: Music IVB and IVBF and things like this were developed at least with the inspiration of Music IV.

Music V

Roads: Was the need to get these programs out into the world part of the motivation for developing a machine-independent version of Music IV, that is, Music V?

Mathews: Certainly. There were several motivations. One was that again we'd changed computers.

So I had to contemplate rewriting the program once more and I wanted to make a universal program. Also, I wanted to make it as universally available as possible. At that time the Fortran compiler was available and was the most widely used compiler. I was able to work out what I still believe was a very ingenious technique so as to have almost all of the complexity of the program encoded in Fortran statements which are portable, but have the inner loops of the unit generators, which are computationally rather simple but get executed so many times that they put a heavy load on the computer, programmed in machine language. So the overall program was both simple in terms of the amount of coding required to put it on a new and different machine, and efficient in terms of running rapidly.

Roads: Even though you had developed Music V as a means of spreading computer music out into the world, a number of musicians had already got wind of what was going on at Bell Labs and were starting to go there to find out more about what you were up to. Some of your colleagues, including F. R. Moore, Jean-Claude Risset, and James Tenney, were able to do some very significant work at Bell Labs around that time. Can you describe the atmosphere at Bell Labs? Were composers visiting?

Mathews: When we first made these music programs the original users were not composers, they were the psychologist Guttman and John Pierce and myself, who are fundamentally scientists. We wanted to have musicians try the system to see if they could learn the language and express themselves with it. So we looked for adventurous musicians and composers who were willing to experiment. The first one was David Lewin, who was at Harvard at the time. We corresponded and he did a composition mostly by mail, which was a brave thing to do. Then John Pierce met Jim Tenney at the University of Illinois, where Tenney was studying with Hiller. Pierce was very much impressed with Tenney's music and his interest in computers. He invited Tenney to take a temporary job at the Laboratories to try out the music programs. Tenney took the job and developed some timbres of his own and also some pieces. To my mind, the most interesting music he did at the Laboratories involved the use of random noises of various sorts.

Roads: Yes, his *Noise Studies*.

Mathews: Then after Tenney, Jean-Claude Risset was sent to the Laboratories on a French scholarship to do a thesis in physics. Risset has a Ph.D. in physics. His thesis involved analyzing the timbre of the trumpet and developing a new technique for analysis called *analysis by synthesis*, which is still, I think, the most powerful technique for analyzing natural music sounds.

Early Reaction to Computer Music

Roads: Computer music today seems to be gaining acceptance at least in some limited quarters. There are computer music centers established, and modern composers recognize that some form of computer literacy is an important part of their compositional training. But what was the early reaction both of the public and musicians to your demonstrations of computer music? It must have been quite a shock to some people.

Mathews: The reaction amongst all but a handful of people was a combination of skepticism, fear, and a complete lack of comprehension. Amongst musicians, the group that was the most interested in the computer was the composers, while the group that was the most antagonistic to the computer was the performers. The group that understood the computer the least was "the general audience." The rock and popular musicians were willing to think about the possibilities, but they also have the same difficulties anyone dealing with a well-established musical technique has. They are used to well-known and hence powerful methods for making sounds. They're not very patient with "new" techniques which are quite weak and tedious to use, and which certainly require much more experimentation.

Graphics Interaction

Roads: That leads to my next question. When I look back over your work, I see a very logical progression. You developed this series of flexible sound synthesis programs culminating in Music V, which

is still in use today and which essentially has not been surpassed in terms of flexibility. But there was another rigid aspect that was part of the Music V process which was the input process. I know that you turned to graphical systems of interaction at one point. What led you to that?

Mathews: I was led to it by a desire to broaden and make more facile the techniques for specifying compositions. I think my graphical experiments were very interesting; they did not, though, lead to a language which is as universally understood as the Music V language is. In some sense, I think today the Music V language is much more important than the Music V program, in that almost anyone involved in computer music can read a Music V score or read a description of a Music V instrument with unit generators and understand it, and translate it into whatever language he or she is using, whether it be Music 11, Music 10, or Music 360. It provides a well-documented and universally understood way of describing a sequence of notes and their interpretation and musical instruments.

The graphic languages didn't get to that level of generality. I could describe an accelerando with a single line, where the ordinate value of the line was the tempo, so if it sloped upward the tempo was increasing and if it sloped down it was decreasing, and that was quite a nice, easy way of making accelerandos. I had some experiments for drawing melodic lines; that made graphical sense.

GROOVE

Roads: After you developed this flexible sound synthesis system and a means of graphic interaction with this system, what did you turn to then?

Mathews: I got into graphics at the end of Music IV's history, and I did Music V as the next thing. My graphical input work was at the very end of the life of the 7094 computer. I spent a time getting Music V in operation, then Risset carried out the brunt of Music V work at Bell Labs. He worked on analysis-by-synthesis techniques and a catalog of computer-generated sound. After Music V I got interested in real-time work and developed the

GROOVE system. That was quite a different direction.

Roads: That was with F. R. Moore?

Mathews: Yes, he had come to Bell Labs by that time.

Roads: The GROOVE system, as I recall, was a hybrid system consisting of a minicomputer connected to an analog sound synthesis system, with a number of input devices such as joysticks and knobs for conducting a score which had been prepared beforehand and input to the computer. It also incorporated graphics, did it not?

Mathews: It had graphical displays. The point about GROOVE was that it looked upon the score as a recording of the control functions for the analog synthesizer. These are the functions of time which specify the way the frequencies and all the other things one controls in an analog synthesizer change with time to make music. Now, it basically recorded these time functions in sampled form at about 100 to 200 Hz, fast enough to record human gestures, and would store this on disk. The program was a flexible way of playing back these functions and combining them with other functions of time that were generated by the performer playing on the *sensors* of the instrument. These combined functions were then used to control the analog synthesizer. In addition, the program had very good editing facilities so you could go back to these stored functions and change them. You could change one sample of a single function without affecting anything else.

Roads: So you could get a display or printout of these functions, allowing musicians to perfect what they had done in real-time—edited improvisations, so to speak.

Mathews: Exactly. The functions were displayed on a scope and you could move to a particular sample in the function and you would hear the resulting sound as a sustained sound and you could flip the editing switch on and change the value of the function at that point and hear what it was doing to the sound.

Roads: Yes, editing with real-time feedback. As far as I know the most extensive use that was made of this machine was by Emmanual Ghent. Was there anyone else who worked with this machine?

Mathews: You're certainly right that Ghent worked with it more than anyone else. F. R. Moore made plenty of compositions with it. Boulez and I worked with it on the Conductor program which was based on the GROOVE system.

Roads: When was that?

Mathews: That was 1975 and 1976.

Roads: The GROOVE system, which was developed in 1968, ran, as far as I know, up until 1979, didn't it?

Mathews: Yes, eventually we couldn't maintain the computer it ran on. I haven't reprogrammed it because I think one should now use a digital synthesizer. Also I think a different way of storing the score is better and more appropriate now, such as the way Curtis Abbott has used at IRCAM.

The Sequential Drum and 4CED

Roads: I understand that you have recently returned from IRCAM, where you attached a new instrument called the Sequential Drum to the 4C digital synthesizer.

Mathews: Yes. The Sequential Drum is another sensor which you hit like a drum. The sensor sends three signals to the computer. One of these is a pulse which tells the computer when the drum is hit and how hard it's been hit, and the other two say *where* you hit the drum in terms of x and y coordinates. The computer and the synthesizer use these three pieces of information to synthesize a sound. The musician decides how to use this information in controlling the sound.

In my case, I tried an interesting principle in which the pitches to be played are a sequence in the computer memory. Each time you hit the drum you automatically get the next pitch in the sequence. I did this because most traditional music has a very rigid pitch line and the musician is not allowed to deviate from the composer's intention.

I actually built two drums; one I used at Bell Labs and the more recent one I took to Paris. The computer there was the PDP-11/34 and the synthesizer was the 4C Machine. I was very fortunate that Curtis Abbott had written a program which I could adapt to this sequential principle. It's a program one can do many things on. It is one of the first general real-time programs. I think it's a good program partly because it resembles Music V and Music 10. If you've learned these languages it becomes quite easy to learn Abbott's program. It's also a good program because he has figured out the right structure for describing a series of complex events in a score and for synchronizing and controlling events which are determined by a score with events determined by the input sensors like the drum.

Roads: As I understand it, in Curtis Abbott's program, wherein a traditional *pfield* in a language like Music 11 might specify a value which would be typed in by a composer, in the 4CED program an instrument, instead of being fed by a pfield would be fed by an external event which might occur at any time.

Mathews: That's right. A note can be initiated by a performer or by a score.

Roads: These scores themselves can be structured into rather complex entities. One score event might trigger a whole series of score events. One can, for instance, attach a subscore to a particular event. So not only do you have this complex instrument connection to real-time, you also have a complex score connection to real-time, as I understand it.

Mathews: That's quite correct. The score controls the real-time processing of events in the 11/34 computer. It allows one to put together a whole series of events in a treelike structure where one starts going up the trunk and when one reaches a side branch that branch starts whatever it is doing and at the same time one proceeds on up the trunk perhaps starting other side branches. So you can get a lot of things going simultaneously. The side branches all end, and the trunk continues on, so the overall synchronization is quite simple since it all depends on how fast you climb the trunk.

Electronic Violins

Roads: This Sequential Drum is only one in a number of new musical instruments you've developed, including a new violin.

Mathews: Yes, I've made a number of electronic violins. Some of them are closely related to normal violins, in that I've worked very carefully on the resonances of normal violins, and made electronic circuits which introduce these same resonances into the electronic violins. The electronic instruments all have regular violin strings and they all have bows. So the source of the vibrations is the same as in a regular violin. But thereafter the sound gets modified electronically. It is possible to tune the resonances very accurately, and it is, of course, possible to have as much energy as you want in the sound. It also makes it possible to use some of the things we know about timbres to change completely the timbre of the violin. Notably, we can make it sound like a brass instrument or like a human voice. The other thing I've most recently done is incorporate *volume expansion* to increase the dynamic range of the violin. The normal violin I think suffers from having a very narrow dynamic range. One can expand the entire spectrum of the violin, but it's more interesting to expand only a portion of the spectrum. This way you not only get a change in the dynamic range, but you get a marked change in the spectrum.

I've also made some physical changes in the violin. My latest instruments are played in a vertical position, as one plays a cello. I've learned to play the violin that way myself, and I'm convinced that that's a superior physiological position. In short, I'm going back to the old style of the viols. I've introduced some other human-engineering changes— some very low frets which one feels with the fingers but which do not constrain the pitch of the string to the pitch of the fret. So one can do vibrato or a glissando and for that matter, one can tune the scale to whatever variations one might want.

Intelligent Instruments

Roads: Do you see a time when families of instruments such as the ones you've developed would be used in concert for a new kind of musical performance—an orchestra of intelligent instruments?

Mathews: In truth, I don't know whether the intelligent instruments will be used in concert form or whether they'll be used in the home, or whether

both will happen. Certainly one could use the increased capabilities to enhance performances by virtuosos. One could also use the capabilities to make a wider range of music available to the amateur player.

Roads: Do you also see new kinds of musical interaction resulting from the use of intelligent musical instruments? One of the implications of your Sequential Drum is that the performer is in a new kind of relationship with both the score and the instrument.

Mathews: That's certainly true. With the intelligent instruments both the score and the control from the player form separate inputs to the instrument. The score does not have to pass through the performer as it does with traditional instruments. Also, the score doesn't stand between the musician and the instrument, as with Music V. So I think this is a much more powerful and flexible arrangement.

Also, we will have very interesting situations when we have several intelligent instruments and several performers interacting with one another, where part of the interaction flows directly from one instrument to the other. That's a very pregnant situation.

Roads: This implies that these intelligent instruments will be in some way cognizant of each other. Do you foresee a day when these instruments will actually be able to listen to one another the way that musicians listen to achieve ensemble quality?

Mathews: I don't think they'll listen with microphones. I think the basic information of what each instrument is doing will be transmitted to the other instruments over a digital channel. This gets into another important question of how one makes multiple, independent computers work together on a single problem. That's one of the most interesting unsolved computational problems today.

Experiments with Inharmonic Timbres

Roads: You've recently concluded a series of experiments dealing with "stretched" inharmonic tones. What was the motivation behind that project, and what were the results?

Mathews: It's clear that inharmonic timbres are one of the richest sources of new sounds. At the same time they are a veritable jungle of possibilities so that some order has to be brought out of this rich chaos before it is to be musically useful. So John Pierce and I have been studying one small class of inharmonic sounds, those which have overtones like normal sounds except that the overtones are stretched farther apart than normal overtones or compressed closer together than normal overtones.

Roads: So the relationship of a pseudooctave might be 2.2/1 or 2.3/1, not 2/1?

Mathews: Exactly. Our initial experiments were aimed at finding out what properties of normal harmonic music carried over to music that was made with stretched overtones. We found some things carried over and some things did not. The sense of "key" carried over better than we expected.

Roads: So you can actually detect "keys" in sequences of completely inharmonic sounds.

Mathews: That's right. You play two samples and a person can reliably say whether they're in the same or a different key.

Other properties do not carry over. The sense of finality in a traditional cadence does not carry over. A person who hears a cadence with unstretched tones says, "That sounds very final to me." When he hears the same cadence played with stretched tones, he'll say, "That doesn't sound especially final." But we have been able to make other inharmonic materials which do convey a sense of cadence.

Roads: Yes, very strongly so in the one's I've heard. These modified sounds relied on the critical-band phenomenon, as I recall.

Mathews: They were related to a theory of the critical band and how it affects the consonance and dissonance of sounds, which was primarily developed by Plomp and Levelt.

Roads: If we can detect "keys" and some form of finality within a cadence or progressions within inharmonic tones, then some of the theories of harmony in the past must not be as cogent as some of their proponents have thought them to be.

Mathews: Our results are contradictory. We looked at two theories. One was the Rameau theory of the fundamental bass, and the other was the Helmholtz and Plomp theory of the consonance and dissonance of overtones. The destruction of the cadence would support the Rameau theory and the persistence of the sense of key would support the Helmholtz and Plomp theory. So we have one result which supports one theory and one which supports the other, with the overall conclusion that the world is a more complicated place than we had perhaps hoped it was. We will have to dig deeper before we can say what is causing the various perceptions we find meaningful to music. But unanswered questions such as these make life interesting.

2

C. Roads

A Conversation with James A. Moorer

Introduction

James Andersen Moorer was born in November 1945 in Hollywood, Florida. He has been involved with computer music since the early 1970s, when he first experimented with algorithmic music composition (Moorer 1972). His subsequent work has spanned a number of disciplines, including digital signal processing, synthesizer architecture, and composition. A Fellow of the Audio Engineering Society, Dr. Moorer became the director of the digital audio project at Lucasfilm Ltd. in 1980. This interview was recorded in the early afternoon of 26 April 1982 at Lucasfilm in San Rafael, California.

Background

Roads: Could you tell us a little about your background?
Moorer: I graduated from M.I.T. a couple of times, having nothing better to do—once in electrical engineering, and once in applied mathematics. I then took a job at the Stanford Artificial Intelligence Laboratory (SAIL). The climate at SAIL was marvelous. John Chowning once described it as a kind of Socratean abode. There were people of different disciplines, all quite good at them, meeting around a common instrument—the computer. There were doctors, astronomers, physicists, mathematicians, electrical engineers, programmers, musicians, and curiously enough, even some artificial intelligence researchers! I worked there for several years, and was drawn into computer music along the way.

I have always been interested in music, and in technology and the arts. I started taking piano lessons when I was four years old. My father still plays the trumpet semiprofessionally. During my college years, I spent a great deal of time and money build-

Computer Music Journal, Vol. 6, No. 4, Winter 1982

ing devices for my guitar and amplifier. Some of them worked. Most of them didn't, but it was fun and it was an important learning period. I decided I wanted to commit myself to technology and the arts, though I didn't have a clear idea of how to do that.

At Stanford, that idea became much clearer because John Chowning and Leland Smith were there, along with Loren Rush. Through watching what they were doing, I became more and more interested in computer music. I saw that some of the talent and training I had matched the talent and training they had. They were in dire need of technological help. That was when the alliance between us was made. I decided to do my thesis in music transcription by computer, which is somewhere in between artificial intelligence, music, and signal processing. In the process of doing the thesis work I learned a lot about signal processing and I developed ideas for how to apply it to music.
Roads: Would you describe your thesis work in more detail?
Moorer: Yes. The thesis was a preliminary study in techniques for transcribing musical sound by computer (Moorer 1975). By *transcription*, I mean that you play a piece into a microphone, and the sound is digitized and fed into a computer. The computer listens to it and prints out a notated score. It was known that for the single-voiced case this was fairly easy to do. For the polyphonic case, it was not known whether it was even possible, much less how it could be done. Through the thesis work, I demonstrated that it was possible, though the system I developed required stupendous amounts of computer power. It was so terribly noise-sensitive that I could not consider it to be a functional system. It was an existence proof that the computer could take musical dictation at about the same level as a sophomore music student. That is, it could hear two instruments well, while three and four instruments confused it. It would start to miss notes.

In the course of this work I came across a num-

Fig. 1. James A. Moorer
with the Lucasfilm Audio
Signal Processor.

ber of interesting questions concerning how people hear. For instance, there is the notes and octaves problem. As we know, a single tone from an orchestral instrument can be represented in terms of its harmonic series. There is the fundamental—usually the pitch being played—the second harmonic an octave higher, the third harmonic an octave and fifth higher, and the fourth harmonic two octaves higher. Consider the problem of two instruments playing an octave apart. The harmonic series of the upper instrument falls directly on the even harmonics of the lower instrument. So mathematically it looks to the computer like a single instrument playing with particularly strong even harmonics. To complicate things, there are instruments with strong even harmonics, such as flutes played in the lower register. There is something the ear is doing to resolve the two tones. We still don't know for sure what it is, but the suspicion is that there are several interlocking factors, including the timing of the attack, and the phase-locked frequency jitter from the harmonics of a given instrument. Since the harmonics of instruments are synchronized to different core phases, we should be able to discriminate two instruments playing at octaves by correlating the phases of the harmonics. My colleagues at Stanford, including Andy Schloss and Joseph Rockmore, are presently exploring some of these topics.

Signal Processing Software

Roads: What were some of your other activities at the Stanford lab?

Moorer: I wrote a large set of numerical and graphic signal processing routines to run in the SAIL environment. This is what the music people at CCRMA [Center for Computer Research in Music and Acoustics, Stanford University] are using to this day (Moorer 1977).

Roads: What was in this package?

Moorer: Well, although I do not propose them as a paradigm of programming style or of how I would do things now, I do consider many of the programs to be a minimal set that anyone pursuing serious numerical analysis must have. The core programs were the Fourier Transform and inverse transform programs, including the phase vocoder analysis, and the estimation theoretical programs: linear prediction, analysis, and synthesis. There was a host of filter design and filter application programs and also some special reverberation programs. One of the most useful programs is called S. S is an interactive, graphics sound-exploring program. It allows you to look forward or backward over a sound file. You can look at the sound file with the sound samples in the top half of the screen and the Fourier Transform of those samples in the bottom half of the screen. S is absolutely invaluable for seeing what is happening inside a sound. You can use S to see what went wrong in your last music synthesis run. Quite often, you are able to see such things as exactly 128 samples missing from the middle of the sound file. You can also easily see aliasing components.

Anything that allows you to look at the sound is immensely useful. I do not understand how people can do computer music without graphics aids.

Roads: Could you describe a typical use of S?

Moorer: Michael McNabb wanted a vowel sound for a composition, so he recorded a soprano singing that vowel and used S to find graphically the beginning and ending sample numbers of one period of it. Within S, he wrote out that segment onto another file. Then he read the new file into a wavetable of the music synthesis program. Instantly, he could synthesize that vowel, with no analysis, no Fourier Transforms, and no magic.

In computer music we seem to have spent so much time trying to synthesize natural-sounding instrument tones with limited results. This kind of sound-editing tool, however clumsy it is, gives the musician this kind of capability. We have more sophisticated means, but this is a working tool, and like all working tools its use has extended far beyond what its inventor ever intended for it. As I said, I cannot imagine doing computer music without a lot of graphics.

The Phase Vocoder

Roads: After completing your signal processing package, you turned to analysis/synthesis techniques. Out of that research came two papers on linear prediction and the phase vocoder in the *Journal of the Audio Engineering Society* (Moorer 1978*b*; 1979*a*).

Moorer: That's correct. Curiously enough, we use the phase vocoder analysis for an entirely different purpose from that for which it was developed. It was intended as a kind of channel vocoder for encoding speech.

Roads: Could you give us a description of the phase vocoder?

Moorer: The idea of a channel vocoder is quite straightforward. There are several commercial vocoders on the market. The basic vocoder is a bank of bandpass filters that break up the incoming waveform into a number of separate frequency domains. Each domain typically covers one-third of an octave. There are at least two ways to reconstruct the signal. In the trivial way, you take the signal that comes out of each channel and you add them up. In a more sophisticated system, you detect the pitch with essentially equal-amplitude harmonics. You then modulate each frequency band of the new signal with the energy in each frequency band of the original signal. The global spectrum of the new signal follows that of the original. The extent to which this works is the extent to which the new source [an oscillator] models the original source. For speech this can be done fairly well; for other things, not so well.

The idea of the phase vocoder takes this one step further. The phase vocoder produces not only the magnitudes of each channel, but the phases—a complex number for each channel. This gives you all the information you need to reconstruct the signal both theoretically and practically. This has a certain intuitive appeal. You know that in the absence of modification the phase vocoder is an identity—the numbers you get out are the same as the numbers you put in, to 17 places or as many as you can stand. The test of any analysis/synthesis system is how little it distorts the signal. The phase vocoder, or *short-term Fourier system*, as it is also called, is capable of zero distortion. One of the things we do is code the signal in between the signals that are coming out of each channel. A simple way to code these signals involves using a density of analysis channels such that the harmonic of the original waveform (if it is periodic) falls into a unique channel. Consequently, what comes out of each channel is a pure sinusoid. We can measure its frequency, phase, and amplitude. Thus, we can recreate the signal exactly by producing a new sinusoid of that frequency, phase, and amplitude.

In the electronic music literature this is called *additive synthesis*. Needless to say, when the assumption is violated, and the input signal is something like white noise, the output of each channel is not a sinusoid and cannot be represented with only phase, frequency, and magnitude data. You must use a different representation. But for harmonic sounds in which the pitch and amplitude are not changing, categorizing the signal by these three numbers yields a system which is an identity. (The three numbers can be generalized to two: magnitude and continuous or unwrapped phase.) It's a damn good approximation even when the pitch and amplitude are changing relatively slowly. We use it to give a compact representation for harmonic sounds. This representation has uses in music synthesis, in that it provides a way to synthesize sound with uncanny accuracy, although the intermediate representations can be bulky and difficult to deal with. It gives a method for psychoacousticians to determine what aspects of a sound are perceptually relevant. You can go through the intermediate representation and start deleting things, or smoothing things, or reducing the data, and then ask, Does it sound the same?

Another application of the phase vocoder is in categorizing sounds in a systematic manner. Categorizing sound is absolutely essential to the computer musician. There is, in a way, too much freedom. In the old orchestral days you had only 30 to 40 different kinds of instruments from which to choose. In the computer domain there are more like 30,000 perceptually distinct kinds of instruments. We have to develop some way of systematizing this huge universe of sounds. Techniques like phase vocoder analysis can be useful for this kind of task.

Roads: To what kinds of compositional uses has the phase vocoder been applied?

Moorer: The phase vocoder has been most useful in synthesizing the notes in between notes, giving a smooth transition between, say, a bassoon tone and a trombone tone. It can fill in the range of instruments that are numerically between the two. Sometimes they are also perceptually in between; at other times they are not.

Roads: Can it also be used for such compositional tasks as time/rate changing?

Moorer: Yes. Some of the recent work by Portnoff and Holtzman published in their dissertations at M.I.T. indicates that the short-term Fourier technique can be an extremely powerful method of doing time/rate changing. Their work shows that it can be applied over a wide variety of sounds, not just quasi-periodic ones.

Linear Prediction Synthesis

Roads: You also developed a system for high-quality linear predictive synthesis of sound, did you not?

Moorer: Yes. I used speech research from Santa Barbara, M.I.T., and Bell Laboratories, but I applied it to the musical domain. The original idea was to get a handle on the synthesis of the human voice. In the musical case, what you typically want to do is produce new and different sounds or modify the voice beyond what a human being could do.

Roads: Could you give us a capsule description of the linear prediction technique?

Moorer: The idea is as follows. Linear prediction models the sound as a kind of excitation—either periodic or noiselike—which is filtered through a series of resonant chambers. Presumably, this models the human vocal tract. The filters model the nasal cavities and the throat, and the excitation models the glottis. It works quite well for speech. In applying it to music, we found that since most of the research had been done in the communications industry, the general quality of speech produced by linear prediction was much lower than that acceptable in the musical domain. Raising the quality of the linear prediction system for music turned out to be a tremendous amount of work.

Roads: So this is the area in which you concentrated?

Moorer: Yes. I should mention that my linear prediction software package is coded in PDP-10 assembly language, and is thus not very portable. The package by Kenneth Steiglitz being used by Paul Lansky at Princeton is also available, but it is written in Fortran. It embodies many of the same principles for high-quality speech and music modification.

Converters for Music

Roads: You were in residency at the Paris music and acoustics research center, IRCAM [Institut de Recherche et Coordination Acoustique/Musique]. Could you describe some of your experiences there?

Moorer: Yes. I spent two years as a technical advisor to IRCAM, from the summer of 1977 to the summer of 1979. IRCAM was in a preliminary stage then. We had just gotten our computer and we were just starting to get our programs up on it. I did several things there, including a study on digital reverberation (Moorer 1978a). I brought up most of the Stanford software on their PDP-10. Presumably, they are now going off in their own direction, but that gave them a head start in making music very quickly. Another thing I did was commission the building of a set of analog-to-digital and digital-to-analog converters [ADCs and DACs]. They are in use all over IRCAM in various projects.

Roads: Who built them, and what are the features of these converters?

Moorer: They were built by Tim Orr in London. When you look at the market, you can buy various converter chips, but it is still difficult to buy a complete music conversion system. There were only a few companies that marketed them in 1977. Three Rivers Corporation did for a while, but they no longer do. Digital Sound Corporation now markets them, but they were not available in 1977.

To anyone who wants to attach a converter to a computer, I would just say, It's harder than you think! It is not a matter of buying a converter, a sample-and-hold unit, and an op-amp and sticking them together to make sound. Every person who has ever tried it has spent a great deal of time trying to get the quality up to musical standards. Achieving a level of quality similar to that of a good analog tape recorder is very hard. Going beyond that to gain all the intrinsic advantages of digital audio (greater precision, higher sound quality) is immensely difficult.

Roads: Why is that the case?

Moorer: That's a good question! The problem is that sources of noise are ubiquitous and subtle. It does not take much noise to corrupt the signal. If you think about it, the 20-V peak-to-peak audio output of a DAC divided into 64,000 parts [for a 16-bit converter] means that noise down in the range of hundreds of microvolts is enough to swamp the low-order bit. This is the first problem. In digital logic, you typically tolerate noise of $\frac{1}{2}-1$ V at huge currents. For instance, in bringing 16 bits onto a board with line drivers and receivers on each end, fully terminated, you are dumping half an ampere onto a board. If this board has as little as 1 mΩ of resistance in the ground plane, you have already lost the low-order bit, simply from ground currents.

The next problem is sample-and-hold units. Most of these units were designed for instrumentation purposes. That is, they are designed to converge to within a certain accuracy in a given time period without regard to how, electronically, they get from one level to another. There are nonlinearities within them, in the signal processing sense, such

that if you put two sine waves into them, you get them plus a third tone out. It is very difficult to build a sample-and-hold amplifier that exhibits a purely exponential decay. There is not a single sample-and-hold unit you can buy that is suitable for musical use. They all have to be modified. This will change, because the digital audio industry is about to break into the consumer market in a huge way. Within a few years there will be a large demand for inexpensive, high-quality music conversion systems.

There is an interesting research problem here for prospective doctoral students in engineering. The conversion systems we are now seeing keep all distortion products 90 db down. How do we break the 100-db barrier?

Digital Audio Standards

Roads: One of the subjects one can read about in publications dealing with audio is the controversy around standards for digital audio. Some people are arguing that 16-bit samples are not wide enough to represent digital audio information. They are suggesting that 20 or even 24 bits with error correction may be preferable. What is your view on this issue?

Moorer: Part of the controversy stems from the inability to make one size fit all. We are envisaging several uses for digital audio as an industry. One of these is now established, namely, digital audio for tape recorders in recording studios. In the future, we will see other devices in the studio replaced by digital means. In the professional studio, 16 bits is a minimum. In digital audio processing, for example in mixing or equalization, you must have more than 16 bits. Twenty bits are an absolute minimum, and 24 bits seem to be the standard toward which people are tending. There is even some talk of establishing a 32-bit floating-point representation for digital audio processing.

For the consumer market, with digital audio adapters on videocassette recorders, there is some feeling that 14-bit companding DACs are an adequate standard. I have no opinion on this one way or the other, since I am involved with professional applications.

Roads: Didn't you do some studies on data reduction for digital audio?

Moorer: Indeed. While I was at IRCAM, one of the studies I did concerned different forms of data reduction for professional audio (Moorer 1979b). One of the things we explored was a differential floating-point scheme, called *ADPCM* [adaptive differential pulse-code modulation]. We coded up 16-bit or more samples into a 12-bit sample, using 4 bits of exponent and 8 bits of mantissa. The output samples were synthesized by converting this into an integer and adding it to an output accumulator register—a differential scheme. With ADPCM, there is an error in the signal, that is, the output samples are not identical bit-for-bit with the input samples, but the error curve falls below the threshold of perceptibility. The problem was that the noise curve was too close to the threshold of perceptibility. If you did any further processing of the signal, the error would be raised above the threshold. Now I would favor a 16-bit differential scheme, with 12 bits of mantissa. This yields a huge dynamic range—about 22 bits' worth—and it covers almost the full dynamic range of human hearing. An immense amount of processing can be performed on the signal without audibly deteriorating the sound.

Languages for Computer Music

Roads: How will the development of standards for digital audio and music instruments affect the musician?

Moorer: That is an interesting question. We are arguing worldwide about what the standards for digital audio recording should be. This is an ugly issue, because it determines whether the tape you record at home will be compatible in your neighbor's house.

I think there is a more important matter. Although it will not affect us this year or next, it will become more important toward the end of the century. Common musical notation, which was developed over several hundred years, is not sufficient for specifying digital music synthesis. Not only does the note concept have its limitations in representing such musical gestures as freely sliding pitches, microtones, clusters, and timbral nuances, but classical music notation is completely inadequate for specifying the acoustics of a particular sound. What must be developed is a new musical language, a new notation. There are already a number of languages for computer sound synthesis, typically divided into a score language and an orchestra language. The score language specifies a queue of events turning on and off, while the instrument language represents the signal flow through audio processing modules. We have already seen an explosion of languages for computer music, with no standardization, despite the efforts of some to bludgeon others into using their system. I have not yet seen a music language with a rich enough structure to support all the things we have been doing in music synthesis over the past 10 years.

Roads: A current trend is the idea of embedding a music language within a general-purpose language such as C or Lisp.

Moorer: Indeed. My philosophy all along has been that better programming languages make better music languages. As soon as musicians achieve a certain degree of sophistication with the computer, they immediately need all the power of a general-purpose programming language. Restriction to some subset without adequate control structures or subroutines is used to make the implementation easier. It makes it nearly impossible for the musician to go beyond a certain level of programming sophistication. This is one of the frustrations that musicians currently working with computer music feel. They can take the language so far and no further. The language should be extensible in any direction. In computer science, people have known how to do this for quite a few years now.

Encouraging Breadth

Roads: Besides pursuing all of this research, some of which we have not touched upon, you have had the time to complete some pieces.

Moorer: Yes. I have two short pieces that are currently circulating: *Perfect Days* and *Lions Are Growing*. There are several other perpetually unfinished pieces that will perhaps emerge at some point. I don't have the musical creativity to spend all my time making music. I am obligated to express creativity in other domains.

The notion of interdisciplinary people is beginning to be accepted again now, especially in America. This includes people who are skilled in both technology and music. There has been an unfortunate tendency in the past to categorize people as either musicians or engineers. In computer music, and in some other domains, there has been some rationalization of this in statements such as, "Composers don't know anything about computers; therefore, they need their musical input languages to be simple and trivial." This is easy to do, but at the expense of trivializing musical expression, restricting the composer to very limited forms.

The other side of this is trivializing the engineer, assuming that engineers cannot possibly know anything about music. There are people with broad musical backgrounds in the engineering community. I think we should pay more attention to encouraging and developing that kind of breadth. Interdisciplinary training is essential for the development of computer music.

The Future of Digital Audio Processing

Roads: When will the technology of computer music be fully accepted by the musical establishment?
Moorer: This question has the implication, When will the older composers use the new technology? The answer is, of course, only when the new technology offers them something relevant to what they are doing. It has to be something so attractive and so tempting that they are lured into it. Until computer music can provide those attractions, it will be relegated to only a few outposts of academia.

In computer music it has been relatively difficult to provide a friendly and attractive environment for the composer, not because it is so technical, but because we have not spent a lot of time working on the human interface. We have been busy just making sound. This is starting to change. Projects like Bill Buxton's SSSP system at Toronto and Ornstein

and Maxwell's Mockingbird system at Xerox PARC [Palo Alto Research Center] are first steps in giving composers access to this attractive computing power.
Roads: What would you say is the future of digital music hardware?
Moorer: I believe the key to the future of computer music is the digital audio processing station. The reason I say this is that, although general-purpose computers are getting faster, they are still terribly slow compared to specialized number-crunching devices. General-purpose computers are too slow for real-time music synthesis, by two orders of magnitude, for a typical computer that a composer could afford and that had some degree of musical sophistication. So the only hope is special-purpose digital hardware. There are a number of these devices in existence, including the Systems Concepts digital synthesizer by Samson, the 4C and 4X machines by diGiugno at IRCAM (Moorer 1981; Moorer et al. 1979), and several other commercial products. These devices are so attractive that as soon as they appeared in computer music studios, everyone wanted to use them. No one wants to use the software synthesis approach. The MUS10 program at Stanford, which was the main means of synthesizing sound there up until 1978, is now only rarely used.
Roads: You seem to be saying that software synthesis is obsolete.
Moorer: Software synthesis is either dead or dying. It is still marginally useful, but on the way out. I am hoping its demise will be quick and relatively painless.

Although many people had hoped the new microprocessors could be used for synthesis, they are still terribly slow by music synthesis standards. To give an example, just to do the operations of an eight-channel mixing desk with equalization and gain controls and some processing items like reverberation, with a few oscillators thrown in, about 18 million multiply-adds per second are needed for high-quality sound. A typical microprocessor today can execute about 10,000–15,000 multiply-adds per second. To give you an idea how many operations 18 million per second is, the Cray-1 supercomputer, in one of its vector modes, hits about 33 million operations per second. The Cray-1 would make a perfectly adequate music synthesizer, but it is a $7.5 million computer, which unfortunately puts it beyond the reach of most computer musicians.

The Cray-1 has a general-purpose architecture. If we switch to a special-purpose signal processing architecture, we can achieve similar performance at much less cost. For example, the Systems Concepts digital synthesizer hits about 10 million multiply-adds per second with 20-bit integer arithmetic, and its price tag is around $120,000.

Roads: This solves the problem for the major institutions, but what about the independent musician?
Moorer: This is coming, but slowly. Over the next decade we will see VLSI [very-large-scale-integration] chips made strictly for processing digital audio. This will come from the digital audio industry. For example, if you want a gain control on your digital tape recorder, you will need 50,000 multiply-adds per second—beyond the limits of today's general-purpose microprocessors. So it has to be done with special-purpose hardware. The Yamaha GS-1 digital music synthesizer uses a number of special-purpose synthesis chips. We will see more and more of this.

Parallel Processing for Music

Roads: In the research laboratories there is some speculation that, of signal processing tasks involving numerical computation and for artificial intelligence tasks involving symbolic computation, computers with hundreds or thousands of processing elements may be needed, programmed with parallel programming languages.
Moorer: Right. We talk about this all the time. It keeps popping up, though no one as yet has been able to make much use of it. No one knows how to program so many elements, and some of the parallel programming languages make it difficult to exploit the parallelism of the hardware. Often, the problem at hand has been to reorganize and reprogram for the particular network being used. The algorithm, as it flows from the programmer's mind, is usually stupendously inefficient in a multiple-processor environment and has to be recoded for that environment. An example of this is the Cm* project at Carnegie-Mellon University. There is not yet any automatic technique for reorganizing programs for parallel environments.
Roads: So you see the development of such reorganization techniques as a stepping-stone to fully exploiting parallel processing?
Moorer: Yes. Dataflow languages have the advantage that computation is expressed fundamentally as a dataflow graph. So some of the algorithms for dividing up a graph into cut sets, that is, separating a program into a number of discrete running entities, might have an application in computer music. The music domain is a rich environment for computer scientists, and this is marvelous computer science question. It has applications outside the task of synthesizing music. The questions we inevitably face in designing musical software and hardware are computer science questions, and they must be answered if we are to make progress.

The Design of Digital Sound Synthesizers

Roads: How would you evaluate the contemporary crop of digital music synthesizers?
Moorer: I see two major traps which should be avoided at all costs. One is this. The engineer has built a device that performs functions A, B, and C (e.g., oscillators, ring modulators, and envelope ramps) but not D and E (e.g., filters and reverberators). This is an unfortunate trend. It is to some extent modeled after analog synthesizers, in that if you wanted an oscillator, you bought an oscillator module; if you wanted a filter, you bought a filter module. But digital hardware is so much more versatile than that!

Building a synthesizer that isn't programmable is idiotic. It is so easy to allow the programmer to get at such things as the control memories. An alternative, coming in the future, will be high-speed, general-purpose synthesizers with pipelined arithmetic processors. These will be horizontally microcoded such that the user can get at all the features of the machine. For example, in reverberation we do not want to use the usual power-of-two-length wavetables, but rather prime-length tables.

Roads: In order to avoid possible confusion, could you explain the difference between a general-purpose synthesizer and a general-purpose computer?

Moorer: A digital synthesizer will typically execute the same program for every sample. The program changes only every few thousand samples or so. Typically, the user will set up a "patch," that is, some processing sequence that will last, say, 2000 samples. Then you have to change 100–1000 instructions in the time interval of a single sample. Technically, the processing engine should have the same generality as a standard computer, meaning it should be a Turing machine. However, I feel very strongly that the traits of musical sound, in particular the fact that the same program generates a number of samples in a long sequence, can be exploited to make these processors fast and cheap.

The second trap to be avoided in digital synthesizers concerns software. An idiosyncratic processor requires an idiosyncratic language. The language that you use for machine A cannot be used on machine B. The reason is that the instrument definition is directly related to the microcode, to the architecture of the machine. Certain numerical techniques cannot be transported from machine to machine. We need to develop the concept of a signal processing language such that a numerical algorithm for music production can be translated into a number of different realizations for different synthesizers. The synthesizers have to be made general enough to support such a signal processing language. If we do not do this, musicians will not be able to communicate and share ideas. Sharing of instrument designs is important to the musical development of computer music.

Roads: Are there not commercial considerations that work against this notion of interchangeability? Some manufacturers tend to make their products idiosyncratic so that their features stay proprietary.

Moorer: That's right, and this has been a barrier. We have the possibility of surmounting this barrier, but commercial pressures work against this. It is sometimes commercially advantageous for a company to be the sole developer of supplied software and updates.

The Digital Audio Project at Lucasfilm

Roads: What kinds of projects are you involved in at Lucasfilm?

Moorer: I was hired to lead the digital audio project, which includes Curtis Abbott and Jim Lawson in programming and John Snell in console design. Right now I am planning the project and doing the hardware design and construction. I hope the hardware construction will be completed within the year. Then I will get back to helping to program the devices we have constructed.

Roads: Could you briefly describe what it is you have built?

Moorer: We are building a number of audio processing stations (Moorer 1982; Snell 1982). Each station consists of a number of computers controlled by a Motorola MC68000 processor running the Unix operating system. Each station has a large-scale digital audio processor. This audio processor is capable of performing about 18 million operations per second, in a minimal configuration. We intend to use the stations in three capacities: sound-effects mixing and editing for films, general music mixing, and sound synthesis.

Roads: So for the sound-effects mixing you will have a library of sound stored on disk which you can retrieve to mix and edit?

Moorer: Exactly. We are currently storing our sound library on industry-standard, 300-Mbyte disk packs. A single audio processor can, in real time, transfer eight channels of high-quality audio from these disks, treat it, and forward it to up to eight DACs. The audio processor is programmable, meaning that what is done with the sound is up to the user. Initially, we will install features that sound-effects editors regularly use. More advanced applications include sound synthesis algorithms, such that the sound-effects editor can synthesize new sounds or process prerecorded sounds—the *musique concrète* idea.

The advantage of using this system as a general

music-mixing console is that, at any time, you can drop into sound synthesis mode and apply arbitrary processing techniques such as pitch-shifting and reverberation. This gives the music mixer a great deal of freedom. It blurs the distinction between the editing phase and the mixing phase. This is important in the film industry, because the sound-effects editor, the dialogue editor, and the music editor never hear the combined product of their labor until very close to when the movie is released. They may find out that the sound effects obscure the dialogue, so they have to attenuate the effects even though it sounds artificial. If the problem had been anticipated, different sound effects might have been used. A different spectral mix of effects might have been chosen; for example, high- and low-frequency sounds that do not interfere with the dialogue. As another case, there might be a cymbal crash in the music at a point where off-screen dialogue is supposed to be heard, and it is too late for anything but an unaesthetic solution.

Roads: What are the special features of this audio processing station?

Moorer: First, the device is modular, with from one to eight audio signal processors and total compute power of 140 million operations per second. All the data buses have been designed to handle this kind of traffic. We pipe the disks directly into the signal processor. We do not go across a backplane or through a bus. The reason is that most buses restrict us to a single disk access, and most buses cannot support eight disks running full blast into the signal processor.

The MC68000 control processors can be replicated if need be. Formatting commands for the signal processor may consume an entire control processor, so we have a provision for up to eight control processors—one for each signal processing element. There might also be several consoles or keyboards attached to one machine. Two entire stations can be linked together if necessary.

There are two other points, one of which concerns bandwidth, the other of which concerns updating. Each device is capable of continuous processing while huge amounts of data are flowing into and out of it. This large throughput is generic

to digital audio. As an example, you might be reading eight channels from the disks and two channels from the ADCs, while sending six channels out to the DACs. Each one of these channels represents 100,000 bytes per second. The total bandwidth is tens of millions of bytes flowing into and out of the machine simultaneously with whatever sound processing might be happening. Our device is designed to handle that kind of bandwidth. Fifteen to twenty percent of the hardware is devoted to buffer memories and FIFO [first in, first out] queues.

As for updating, you have to realize that we cannot halt the machine to load a new program every few thousand samples. The flow of data through it must be continuous. So what we have done is generalize a feature of the Systems Concepts digital synthesizer—the idea of an update queue. Each signal processor has a 255-element, time-ordered queue for updates. The control computers enter things into this queue at their leisure. At the exact sample where the change is to take place, the processor is stopped and the microinstruction memories are updated at the full machine rate, which is, of course, 20 times faster than the instruction rate of the controlling computer. Still within the space of one sample period, the machine picks up again without breaking the audio flow. This allows us to update the machine in bursts, on a sample, without waiting for the control computer.

Roads: How is the Lucasfilm audio processing station different from the digital mixing desk introduced recently by the Neve company in Great Britain?

Moorer: They have not attempted to solve either the storage problem or the update problem. They have chosen only to solve the numerical computation problem. For storage, they actually rely on standard tape recorders, either analog or digital. The intercommunication among each of their processing elements is extremely limited, to the point where it is infeasible to break up one large computation like linear prediction among several processors. Their elements are designed to perform a single task, like equalization or compression. Likewise, you have to stop the machine to load up a program. They are not designed for simultaneous input and output. The Neve unit still represents a significant advance over the state-of-the-art in mixing desks, and it will of course have utility.

Our approach has been to leapfrog to the next generation, to move directly to what I consider the most promising direction for the future, more general-purpose signal processors.

Roads: Will these signal processing stations become available to outsiders?

Moorer: We will probably have one visiting scholar per year here in the future, but this is not a particularly general way of allowing the signal processors to be used. We would like to license the processor to someone else to produce. If it were reengineered for manufacturing, it would come out at about the same price as a minicomputer system. So university studios and recording studios could afford it. Since we are not a factory, we are interested in making contacts in the industry to have it manufactured.

Long-term Plans

Roads: What are your long-term plans for research?

Moorer: There are a number of things I would like to do. For instance, now that we are finishing up the construction of these signal processing stations at Lucasfilm, I would like to play with them! I see several years of exploring their possibilities. There is a lot of music in them. I would also like to evaluate these machines, and assess their strong and weak points, to learn how to improve future designs. For me, the big thing to avoid at all cost in the future is trying to build another system like this! It was a very difficult and tedious process.

Roads: How long did it take to develop this system?

Moorer: We just got sound out of the machine recently, so from the day I sat down with pencil and paper to the day we got sound it was a full two years. The bulk of the labor was last year—the actual construction, wirewrapping, debugging, writing the simulator, and so on. So I now look forward to implementing various ideas I have had for it over the past two years.

Roads: What are some of these ideas?

Moorer: For instance, the problem of equalizing audio environments pops up in the film industry when some of the dialogue is recorded in the studio, and some of it is recorded on the original set. Quite often it is necessary to intermix studio-recorded and set-recorded dialogue. To date, getting them to sound similar has been a very ad hoc process. But isn't there some digital signal processing technique we could use? For instance, we could play a maximal length sequence through a speaker at the set and capture the impulse response of the set. Then we could deconvolve the impulse response of the studio from the studio-recorded dialogue and apply the impulse response of the set to it. Is there some way this could be done exactly and in high fidelity? Typically, the problem with the maximal-length-sequence scheme is that the impulse response estimate is somewhat noisy. I'd like to look into ways of improving this.

There are other projects, like overlapping dialogue where you want to replace one voice but not the other. This pops up in multiple-performer music. If you have two microphones, one for musician A and one for musician B, you invariably get crosstalk. Are there any good ways to diminish this effect with digital means? There are, with estimation-theory techniques. I'd like to see how far one could take this, that is, how much reduction one could get. Ten to fifteen decibels would be enough, but we don't know if this is possible.

Along the lines of some of the speech processing techniques I've worked with, there are more mathematical aspects of speech processing into which I would like to dig.

Roads: Such as?

Moorer: The techniques we are currently using in linear prediction, such as Burg's algorithm and the covariance method, are numerically unstable. To accumulate a covariance matrix on an integer processor requires 48-bit arithmetic. To actually compute the linear prediction coefficients, I have to use up to sextuple precision: six 24-bit words to represent an intermediate result. That's because the computation itself is numerically unstable: errors accumulate. Each stage of the filter is optimized separately. So a tiny error in optimizing one stage of a filter makes a huge difference in the error or residue signal coming out of it. Consequently, the next filter stage is extremely sensitive to errors in the previous stage. Is there any better way to do this? Currently, linear predictive analysis is so time-consuming that even with the most powerful signal processors it cannot be done in real time. There are things that I would like to investigate, for example, adaptive multiple-band systems, that might have lower noise ratios.

I would also like to build on the phase vocoder research done by Portnoff and Holtzman for changing pitches and durations of musical tones. Their research indicates that there is a robust framework. What are its limitations? How can it be made even more robust? These are questions I would like to answer.

There is another musical project we have talked about but never done. It is an enormous project, the fabled "Lexicon of Analyzed Tones" (Moorer, Grey, and Strawn 1977a; 1977b; 1978). One could make the argument that cataloging orchestral instruments is an obsolete sort of thing to do. However, I could make the counterclaim that the orchestral instruments give us immediately a wide variety of musically interesting timbres. I would like to see someone go through the entire pitch range of each orchestral instrument at several dynamics and articulation styles and analyze and categorize each tone. I would like to give several synthesis algorithms for each instrument; that is, a frequency modulation algorithm, an additive synthesis algorithm, a wavetable synthesis algorithm, and so on. This lexicon would be the kind of Rosetta stone for computer music we have all been looking for. Most of the computer musician's time is spent looking for sounds, and the lexicon would help to reduce that effort.

In the very long run I would like to write a graduate-level textbook giving the advanced technical basis for each sound synthesis and processing technique. This would be carried through on a sound mathematical basis.

References

Moorer, J. 1972. "Music and Computer Composition." *Communications of the Association for Computing Machinery* 15(2):104–113.

Moorer, J. 1975. "On the Segmentation and Analysis of Continuous Musical Sound." Report STAN-M-3. Stanford: Stanford University Department of Music.

Moorer, J. 1977. "Signal Processing Aspects of Computer Music." *Proceedings of the IEEE* 65(8):1108–1137. (Revised and updated version in C. Roads and J. Strawn, eds. Forthcoming. *Computer Music*. Cambridge, Massachusetts: MIT Press.)

Moorer, J. 1978a. "About This Reverberation Business." *Computer Music Journal* 3(2):13–28.

Moorer, J. 1978b. "The Use of the Phase Vocoder in Computer Music Applications." *Journal of the Audio Engineering Society* 26(1/2):42–45.

Moorer, J. 1979a. "The Use of Linear Prediction of Speech in Computer Music Applications." *Journal of the Audio Engineering Society* 27(3):134–140.

Moorer, J. 1979b. "The Digital Coding of High-Quality Musical Sound." *Journal of the Audio Engineering Society* 27(9):657–666.

Moorer, J. 1981. "Synthesizers I Have Known and Loved." *Computer Music Journal* 5(1):4–12.

Moorer, J. 1982. "The Lucasfilm Audio Signal Processor." *Computer Music Journal* 6(3):22–32.

Moorer, J., J. Grey, and J. Strawn. 1977a. "Lexicon of Analyzed Tones (Part 1: A Violin Tone)." *Computer Music Journal* 1(2):39–45.

Moorer, J., J. Grey, and J. Strawn. 1977b. "Lexicon of Analyzed Tones (Part 2: Clarinet and Oboe Tones)." *Computer Music Journal* 1(3):12–29.

Moorer, J., J. Grey, and J. Strawn. 1978. "Lexicon of Analyzed Tones (Part 3: The Trumpet)." *Computer Music Journal* 2(2):23–31.

Moorer, J. et al. 1979. "The 4C Machine." *Computer Music Journal* 3(3):16–24.

Snell, J. 1982. "The Lucasfilm Real-time Console for Recording Studios and Performance of Computer Music." *Computer Music Journal* 6(3):33–45.

3

Stephan Kaske

A Conversation with Clarence Barlow

Introduction

Clarence Barlow was born in 1945 into Calcutta's English minority. After studies in mathematics and physics he moved to Cologne, West Germany, in 1968, where he has lived and worked ever since. In 1971 he began to apply stochastic compositional processes and finally to use computers for his music. His tremendously complex piano composition *Çoğluoautobüsişletmesi* (1978–79, Wergo Records, 60098, reviewed by Curtis Abbott in *Computer Music Journal* 7(4):66–70) proves Barlow to be one of the most individual and interesting composers of contemporary music. This interview took place on the afternoon of 11 August 1984 in Munich, Federal Republic of Germany.

Background

Kaske: Could you tell us a little bit about your compositional background? Why did you start to work with computers?
Barlow: I found it necessary to work with computers because I began to write complex structurally organized pieces in the early 1970s. This was probably due to the fact that I was always interested in mathematics and physics and such things and actually studied mathematics at college.

But let's put it another way. You asked me about my compositional background. When I started seriously, my music was somewhere around 1780 in style. I very gradually developed through the nineteenth century, writing music in the style of Haydn, Schubert, and later Sibelius, whose music became a great influence. Then I went in a rather Russian direction: Tchaikovsky and Rachmaninov. After about seven years of composition, I finally crossed the threshold into the twentieth century. I then wrote music in the style of Bartok, Hindemith to a

Computer Music Journal, Vol. 9, No. 1,
Spring 1985

certain extent, Prokofiev, and finally I was writing twelve-tone music in 1965.

The first time I ever used a computer was due to my plan to write a piece for cello, trombone, vibraphone, and percussion. This was a kind of homework given to me by Bernd Alois Zimmermann, which I began writing after his death (he never saw the composition, unfortunately). I heard a cello repeatedly playing a low C in my imagination and then gradually moving up through the range. I tried to write it down until I found that I really did not know how many Cs to write before the first D-flat came in. I now knew I needed a strong structure, a strong system by which to develop it. I had never written any algebraic rules for composition until then. My music had been highly serial. I had specified rows and rows of parameters for different aspects, but in this case I realized that I would have to adopt a stochastic approach. I formulated the rules accordingly. For example, the lowest note should remain constant and the highest note should move up in a sort of sinusoidal curve. First very slowly, then a little faster, and then again slowly reaching the top note of the range. I also wanted the most frequent note to form a parabola, somewhat moving between these two. The distribution of the frequency of occurrence would be also a kind of parabola in the third dimension. Having conceived this model I then started to throw dice and coins and realized that I would have to work for about six months several hours a day in order to get two or three minutes of music. So it was after about two months of despair that I suddenly realized that computers could do this. You see, it was not so much that I saw a computer and said "Ah, what can I do with this?" It was just the other way around. I had a musical problem and I did not know what to do with it, until it suddenly hit me one morning lying in bed before I got up that a computer could do it.

Then I found a couple of people that could program computers, and they tried to solve this problem for me. They did not succeed. I never thought that I wanted to become a computer programmer,

but then I was forced to, because these people did not succeed. So I learned Fortran and within one week I had my piece.

Kaske: Did you consider this a breakthrough in your compositional development, or did it follow more or less a linear progression?

Barlow: It was a turning point, but long before I even dreamt of a computer. The fact that I came up with an algebraic model for composition was the turning point—the fact that I wrote stochastic music. The computer entered about three months later.

Kaske: Where did you work at this time and where did you have access to computers?

Barlow: The second of the programmers I approached was a student of Cologne University. He told me that I could attend a computer course in the Easter holidays, which I did. So that is where I used the computer for the next two years: the big Siemens 4004 with 100 Kbytes of memory.

About Computers

Kaske: How did you proceed from this point? Did the computer become a more important part in your compositional thinking after this?

Barlow: I think it obviously had an effect on my compositional methods, in that I knew that it was available, but I can swear that every single piece that I have composed since then was begun without thinking about the computer. In 1971, at about the same time I started computer programming, I wrote a piano composition that was a piece actually only explicit in the form of instructions, *Text-music*. And it was about a year later that I had the idea of writing a program to install all the mechanisms of the piece. Now there are 15 versions of the piece, seven done by other people, and maybe a total of seven or eight are the result of this program. That is one example. Then I started to write an electronic piece in Cologne's Music Academy (Musikhochschule Köln) in the electronic studio there, which used an ARP synthesizer, no computer. The plan was very clear. But I realized that I would have to work for two years on that ARP synthesizer using all the available time, as the only one in the studio, to do that piece. That's again where I realized, a computer could do the piece much better. So I went to the EMS studio in Stockholm and did it there. Computers made my pieces available, made them possible for me. But I think the fact that I never thought of the computer at all for any of these pieces, shows that it was just my structural thinking that led to my "habit" of using the computer finally.

Kaske: So for you using a computer does not have a purpose in itself?

Barlow: I hate the computer.

Kaske: That is a surprise. Maybe you do not want to say that you hate the computer, but you hate programming?

Barlow: I hate having to sit at night for hours and hours in a terribly inhuman environment, pushing little keys and getting bugs all the time and having to debug the whole thing, just because I want a result that is clear to me but that I cannot work out because it is so difficult to get all the details together. I've even bought my own computer now, because I did not see any way out. Obviously it is fascinating to find, when you have obtained the result, that you created it. You type the name of the program and type "return" and it starts off and you get your menu on the screen. It gives you whatever you want. That's wonderful, but it is not that which fascinates me so much as having this result. If one day biophysicists or whatever reach the point where they are able to tune into our brainwaves and to structure our minds with something like a feedback so that we can just sit there and not have to work in a slavelike fashion, I think I'll probably switch my computer to this new medium.

Kaske: It is definitely a problem of the musician/ machine interface in this case that bothers you.

Barlow: Obviously I exaggerated a bit when I said that I hate computers, but I never wanted to use them. And now, in the process of writing my second piano trio I have just started to think about the technique of composition—I knew months before what it was going to sound like—and I am beginning to realize now—with a sinking heart—that I will probably have to program a part of it, because there is such a lot to manage at one time.

Çoğluotobüsişletmesi

Kaske: Let us talk about your piece *Çoğluotobüsişletmesi*, which is your most popular composition. Wergo published a record including two versions of the piece, the first played by the pianist Herbert Henck omitting parts of the original score, since it is virtually mechanically impossible for one pianist to play the piece alone. The second version was realized on a DEC computer using the 4X synthesizer at IRCAM in Paris. Why are there two versions?

Barlow: The composition in its original shape is a piano piece containing all the notes in the score. Now, in fact no single pianist can tackle all these notes and come out alive, I imagine. So I decided to thin out the score a bit for Herbert Henck, not only just to give the poor man a break but for the simple reason that I thought, through inaccuracy of human execution a lot of the subtle details might get lost. It might help the piece to loosen up the structure and make some of the textures more transparent. Of course, once I decided to obliterate part of the score, I put a new dimension into the piece by obliterating more and more, until there are large, total absences, general pauses towards the end, this process stop-

ping just before the last three minutes. So that gives it a new angle, and the advantage of it is that the texture for example around the twentieth minute is so transparent, that it really becomes very exciting when the pianist plays it. You have these little snaps entering in one tempo and in another key overlapping and disappearing, little bits of threads that have been cut off at both ends. So that's why I have this piano version. But if I do meet this phenomenal pianist one day who is able to play the whole score, that would be it. Or if a piano duo—which is much more realizable—were willing to sit down at one piano and play the piece, I'd be very, very happy. This is why I took the trouble to notate the entire score, including all these obliterated bits as well in the shape of crossed heads.

In order to be able to hear the whole piece, the way it is, I had to resort to a computer. The B side of the record gives you the piece as it is scored, but in a very sterile digitally-synthesized realization. The pianist, on the other hand, gives me a very musical interpretation, but less perfect.

Kaske: Tell us a little bit more about the compositional techniques you developed in the *autobus*. Maybe you can give us a very short outline of the theory behind this piece.

Barlow: Let me put it this way. Every piece I have composed in recent years is the result of a musical inspiration. It is not the result of a desire to fumble with formulas. My inspiration for the *autobus* piece came to me in a bus sitting in Eastern Anatolia on the 11th of May, 1975. I imagined a tremendously virtuoso piece with a high degree of polyphony. After analyzing this first idea I began to see that the piece consisted of several streams of music, each of which could be a chordal stream instead of being monodic; in each stream tonality and metricism would play an important role in that these phenomena would increase or decrease as I would like. There might be bits where three or four of the streams would be atonal and the remaining ones strongly tonal or maybe half tonal, the same going for metricism, that is, a strong or a weak feeling for metricism. In other words what I wanted to do was to create and manipulate fields of tonal and metric strength. In order to do that I had to understand what tonality is. So I reduced the problem to the

interval, the building block of the mode, the tonal field. I went back to the old Pythagorean idea that the smaller the number, the more harmonic the interval. I discovered that this was not sufficient, because the number 7 is smaller than 8 and 9, but not used at all in classical music theory. I realized, as many others have done before me, that the divisibility of the numbers is also important. So I was forced to develop an algebraic coefficient for numbers that contained both aspects, the concept of smallness and of divisibility, which I call the *indigestibility* of the number. Using this algebraic formula I was able to develop a harmonicity coefficient for any desired interval given its frequency ratio.

For metricism I also worked on what I call the *indispensability of attack* on any given pulse of the meter on any given level, be it on the 16th-note level or the 32nd-note level. The harmonicity and indispensability ratings enabled me to develop a priority system in the sense that the more support given to the field desired, the more probable the event would be. This brought me to the domain of stochastic procedures and consequentially to the computer. I found it impossible to write this piece by hand. I wanted to write it in four different streams running at the same time and I'd developed eight different parameters for each of these streams, so I used a computer, which meant several months of programming.

Digital Sound Synthesis and Computer Fetishism

Kaske: The computer version of your *autobus* is the first time—except for an electronic composition [*Sinophony II*] done at EMS, Stockholm, in 1973—you have used computer sound synthesis in your compositions. You have not considered computer sound synthesis a timbre source for your music so far. Will you continue using the computer as an algebraic device for your compositional structures incorporating sound synthesis only very occasionally, or will computer sound synthesis become an important part of your work in the future?

Barlow: At the time of composing *Sinophony II*, I had a musical approach which was very anti-aesthetic, if you like, or anaesthetic. It was not important to me to produce sounds like "Wow," but I put them together through constructivist and structuralist thinking. I had about 400 sine tones together at the thickest part of the piece and they form groups. The groups are so arranged that they work a bit like overtone spectra, except that these overtone spectra are a little squashed, the whole octave compressed into a fifth, and the whole spectrum is squashed correspondingly. But in spite of that they blend surprisingly well to form a kind of timbre.

This timbre, as you see, was the result of a mechanistic kind of thinking. It was not something I aimed at, it was not a sound I envisaged. It was the result of mathematical manipulation. That's the way I used to think in those days. Now I am in a phase of composition, where I have certainly returned to a type of music that has to really sound well, it has to please me. I am not satisfied with the general run-of-the-mill electronic synthesis. Most synthesizers that I have heard sound so clinical, so artificial and so clichéd. They sound like everything coming out of the East and West Coast studios in America. They all have the same kind of general scheme and I do not want that. I want something different, but the computer cannot give me what I want, at least not those computers to which I have access. For example, if a computer could give me perfect piano timbre so good that I couldn't tell it from the real thing—not that I want to use that—then I would go on, and I would ask: Can it give me perfect voice

timbre? And if it could do that, then I would believe that it would be worth my working with it. If it could do all that, I would go on and make other sounds with it.

I prefer to work with instrumental timbres because they sound so much more alive and exciting. If I could understand the stochastic aspects of what makes instrumental timbres so alive, then I would create my own timbres and instruments like that. I am not averse to using an instrument as limited as, for example, the Yamaha DX-7 for synthesis in the case of pure-pitch music. I write much music that doesn't depend on timbre so much. Pitch and rhythm have been of great importance to me. That is the reason why I would not be averse to using a DX-7. But if I wanted to use the whole paraphernalia of computer synthesis, then I would much prefer to write something really exciting in timbre. So I would use the DX-7 or the most fantastic computer music studio on earth, but anything in between seems to me to be too large for the results that it can provide and not sufficient for timbral composition. So I am not terribly interested in that direction yet.

Of course it could also be the fact that I live in Europe, where you are not seduced by sound synthesis techniques at a very early stage. We began to use the computer very early—look at Xenakis—but mainly for composition, and we remained there for a while, since we were quite happy with what it was giving us. I said earlier that I used a computer only when I had a problem. I never had the need except in the case of difficult pieces. I have realized three compositions up to now synthetically: *Sinophony II*, *Relationships Version 4* for two pianos, which is very difficult to play, so I have a computer realization of that, and the third is *Çoğluotobüsişletmesi*, the computer version.

Kaske: How do you explain the phenomenon that one can tell the origin of computer music pieces being produced at US studios by their timbres? Pieces from Stanford's Center for Computer Research in Music and Acoustics, for example, cannot be mistaken for M.I.T. pieces and vice versa. They have their very own atmosphere of sound. Do you believe that this phenomenon originates in the different hardware and software facilities of these studios? Are certain synthesis techniques favored by the different hardware and software of these studios? Most composers have only limited time to complete a piece so they resort to the appropriately "fastest" techniques. Or do you think that many American computer music composers are simply sound fetishists?

Barlow: The latter. I think it's not the hardware or software but the compositional techniques in which composers tend to immerse themselves that are so uniform. Composers just can't break away, their imagination obviously doesn't reach the point where they could write something completely different from everybody else around them. I mean, look at European composers of instrumental music. You find certain cities where everyone writes the same. People living in Cologne tend to have more or less all the same sound in general, this postserial approach that was first presented in Darmstadt in the 1950s and 1960s. Obviously there are exceptions. In Paris you have this tremendous love for instrumental timbre and there is a kind of neo-impressionist music coming out of that city. It's not that much the hardware, it's the composers' brains. It's obviously their inability to stretch their imagination.

Computer Music

Kaske: Is that the reason why—according to our observation—you did not attend the computer music conferences in the past?

Barlow: No. For one thing I must say that I am terribly misinformed about everything. I never read any magazines, any lists of important events and I miss everything. I heard about the Venice conference after it was practically over. I might have attended the Rochester event, but then it was a long way to go and I was also discouraged by the fact that my piano piece *Çoğluotobüsişletmesi* had been refused for presentation and for lecturing purposes. If it had been accepted, I might have crossed the ocean. It might be of interest to you that I have never been in America. But I do hope to change that, maybe next year.

Kaske: A large group of programmers come into computer music without being musicians. On the other hand there's a lot of young composers who have no idea how to program, but who are prepared to face new challenges. And there are the established composers who doubt if they should risk the challenge of programming. It looks as if you are almost an outsider. You work with computers but you do not consider yourself a part of the computer music community.

Barlow: That's because I don't believe that computer music really exists. Is my music computer music? To my knowledge I was probably the first person in Germany to work with computers and for many years the only one. But I never thought of myself as a computer composer. I was a composer who occasionally resorted to a computer just as I might well use a pencil. I didn't make a great fetish or aesthetic out of it. Whenever I give a lecture on what they call computer music, I usually open it by saying that it doesn't exist. Algorithmic composition and digital sound synthesis exist but neither the one nor the other has any aesthetic implications.

Kaske: So in your opinion there is no such thing as computer music as a genre?

Barlow: No, but it does of course happen that if there is computer music it's because all the composers who use computers tend to have the same aesthetic, the same way of composing. If I had a reason to go to M.I.T. or to Stanford or San Diego and do a piece at one of these places, I think it would sound quite different.

Kaske: . . . which is true for quite a few European composers doing a piece at an American studio.

Barlow: You see, that belies the hypothesis that it could be the hardware. Okay, everything has the same sort of scheme there, as I said before, the same luster or the same sound in general. That may be a result of the hardware. But if the musical composition styles could diverge a little bit more, could be more individual, then I think one would forgive the general overall sound. After all, the piano music of Chopin, Scriabin, and Mozart also have the same timbre, and that of Bartok and Stockhausen. But we forgive that fact, because the music is so different. We don't mind the fact that Stockhausen's piano pieces are for piano.

Kaske: Why is there such a thing in America that calls itself the computer music community?

Barlow: Just for the same reason that suddenly people get fascinated by the double bass and all decide to use it, and there will be a double bass scene. Computers are one of those fads of our time. Every twelve-year-old boy today wants a computer. You have this machine. So you come and you sit and you drum your fingers a little, saying: "Now, what can I do with it?" And you get an idea to program, not the other way around. It is not a tool any more, it's a fetish.

The IRCAM Experience

Kaske: You worked at IRCAM in Paris. How would you compare your experiences there with your feelings about American studios?

Barlow: Well, IRCAM is really in America, as far as I can feel and see, even though I have never been in America. It was certainly nice working there, but then, what really is a bit bothersome, is the fact that it is after all in France. There is this French bureaucracy on the first floor that is pretty damaging to creativity.

But it's a fun place to work if one avoids going upstairs and if one realizes that one will not get much support or cooperation. Also if one can put up with working in an artificially lighted underground cellar situation. Almost everything I know about American computer music stems from IRCAM. Many of the American composers I met there write rather academic music, but it was fun to go out and have wine with them. Come to think of it, I think that I liked those best who were slow, who didn't write much.

Computer Music in West Germany

Kaske: Let us come back to Germany. Why has the impulse of electronic music, which was created in the 1950s by Stockhausen and his colleagues, not been pursued by other German composers in such a way that computers were used for the solution of compositional problems. Three German composers, Brün, Koenig, and Laske went abroad to pursue their compositional projects, and young composers

have to go to the United States to study the techniques of computer music. Germany is an "underdeveloped country," as you called it once. Do you see any chance for computer music here, and if not, why?

Barlow: I think something is happening, but very slowly. Germany always tended to wait until other people have done something to make sure that it's good and then copy it like mad. So I think there will be a great revolution here in a very short time and there will be studios all over the place. I know a lot of composers whose music is very structural. They would really profit by using a computer. But they've been hesitant and they've thought it would take some of the control of the composition out of their hands. This is the way they've been thinking. Now they are beginning to realize that something can be done with computers after all. Let me give you an example: Cologne Music Academy. Seven years ago I approached them; I needed money. I offered them my services in teaching "computer music." And they said: "Do you really believe that one can make music with computers?" I said, "Sure, Xenakis has, I have," but they didn't even want to listen to it. But suddenly a month ago I received a phone call. They want me to teach computer music there. It's this German desire for uniformity that makes it start now all over the place at the same time.

January at the Nile

Kaske: Let us talk about your most recent piece, *January at the Nile*. Which new aspects entered into your theoretical considerations?

Barlow: In the piece *January at the Nile* my original inspiration was a melody that I thought to be in a vaguely D-major tonality that repeats itself, getting more and more burdened as time goes on, becoming richer by more neighbor notes and passing notes until it breaks down because of its sheer weight. That is the feeling I had in 1981. It was not only a verbal feeling but I actually heard this in warm cello sounds. The technique I employed was of having all the notes of one generation of the melody carried over into the next. In other words, the melody repeats itself again and again, but in each

Fig. 3. Excerpt from the score of Im Januar am Nil (January at the Nile) by Clarence Barlow. The score was printed under the control of a computer program called *SC developed by the composer. Certain comments were added by hand.

Kaske

new generation a whole string of new neighbor notes enter, which are then carried over into the next generation. Their harmonic importance increases as time goes on, so that they begin to gradually form their own tonal fields, and they get their own neighbor notes. At the beginning these neighbor notes support a given key. At the end each of them has its own key moving very rapidly in succession. So you end up in a feeling of multitonality which becomes so rapid that it becomes atonal. That is a totally different approach than my work on the *autobus*.

Kaske: There are also aspects of sound synthesis incorporated in the piece. Patterns and chordlike structures are created that resemble human voices or something like a speaking pulse.

Barlow: This is an almost peripheral aspect which, however, cost me most of the time. I think eighty percent of my time went on this orchestrational aspect of the piece. I had the idea at some point of having the first three minutes not played explicitly—the range of the melody by the way is all around the open C string of the cello. I decided to just have the overtones of the melody played, upwards from middle C. This gave me, of course, the freedom to shape the timbre of the imagined result in sound. I hoped that one would hear the residual tone clearly if one would play sufficient overtones. I decided to generate these overtones through natural harmonics and shape them dynamically in such a way that a timbre would result. Since I find speech timbre very interesting, I decided to make it sound like speech.

Kaske: But cello tones are very complex sound events and their single partials are very hard to control or to predict. Were you able to create speech sound by simply applying an "additive synthesis" technique to cello sounds? Did you make any experiments, for instance by adding sine tones, before that?

Barlow: Yes. I generated the resultant score using sinusoids and it does resemble speech sounds to a high degree. The natural harmonics of instruments I hoped would be close enough to sinusoids to give me this result. I don't think that this is why it doesn't work that well; I think it's rather the inac-

curacies of the amplitude, the attack, and the playing together. I have heard the computer synthesis of the first three minutes very many times; and recently while lecturing on a performance of the piece I was suddenly able to hear speech at the beginning. It was a result of constant conditioning. I knew where to look for the proper phonemes and I now heard them, much to my own surprise. For this piece I chose 200 words from the German language that did not contain any noise spectra and created sentences using these. I spoke them on tape, analyzed them using Fast Fourier Analysis and wrote a series of programs that finally gave me a printed score using scordatura on the strings.

Future Projects

Kaske: What are your future projects?

Barlow: My most immediate big project is the real-time installation of the *autobus* algorithms. I would like to be able to one day sit on the stage and raise the tonality potentiometer and hear the music getting more tonal. And do the same with the metricism parameter, the melodicity parameter, and the rhythmicity or syncopation parameter. Dynamics and articulation would be other parameters. Even consonance and dissonance that is a physiological phenomenon and not so much a psychological one—it has to do with the roughness of sound and is independent of tonality—I would like to install this parameter as well.

Kaske: This is certainly a dream of every composer. But the improvement of the musician/machine interface, making the programming environment more comfortable, might call for a machine that knows something about all these things.

Barlow: Yes, I'll have to do a mass of programming.

Kaske: And you might have to apply artificial intelligence techniques to these programs to make them more knowledgeable. I understand that you want to be able to shift from one stage of a parameter to another without intermediate steps. Tell us a little bit more about this musical scenario.

Barlow: I would like to be able to become a freely

improvising musician sitting on the stage with a really relevant music coming out which you can very clearly hear. Those people who like my *autobus* piece are the public for whom I would like to do something spontaneously. The *autobus*, for example, is a fixed piece in which I laid down all the parts in advance. But I'd like to decide on the spot in a hall: "Oh, this is nice. I'd like to stay here for a while." Or: "Let me move over to that mode." Or:

"Oh, I never thought of that mode. Let me type it in quickly." And then I would have the computer evaluate it and modulate into it. I don't know enough about artificial intelligence. I am a little wary of it. My formulas for this piece are algebraic in nature. I see no other way for me than writing these formulas as algorithms. And those should be as efficient as possible.

4

C. Roads

Interview with Paul Lansky

Paul Lansky was born in 1944 in New York City. He is presently an associate professor in the Department of Music at Princeton University. This interview was recorded on the afternoon of 14 March 1983 in Cambridge, Massachusetts.

Musical Background

Roads: Could you tell us a little about your musical background?

Lansky: I started studying music when I was in grade school. I went through several instruments, finally settling on the French horn, which I took quite seriously. For a long time I had planned to become a professional French horn player, and I did play professionally after college, with the Dorian Wind Quintet. I was moving toward composition during high school, and there came a point later where it was clear that I had no alternative but to stop playing the horn professionally and take up composition full-time.

Roads: How would you say your instrumental background has influenced your composition?

Lansky: It was in large part responsible for my turn to computer music because I was very interested in performing. In electronic music I think of myself as a performer. Making my own noises creates a similar kind of satisfaction to the feeling one gets from being one's own boss, which is part of the thrill of performing.

Roads: Where did you study music?

Lansky: My musical studies got serious at the High School of Music and Art in New York. I worked a great deal in composition and theory at Queens College [City University of New York], and then I went to Princeton as a graduate student.

I studied with many different people, never really with one person. I was a bad composition student, in the sense that I didn't take advice well and

Computer Music Journal, Vol. 7, No. 3, Fall 1983

worked in a rather single-minded way, though this created an early sense of self-sufficiency, for which I am glad.

The Path to Computer Music

Roads: What was your first major piece?

Lansky: I suppose the piece which opened the most interesting territory was called *Piano Piece in Three Parts* [1968]. In it I began to experiment with harmonic relations and ideas that eventually led me into computer music in an oblique way.

Roads: How is that?

Lansky: When I first went to Princeton in 1966, Jim Randall, Godfrey Winham, Tuck Howe, and others had been running Music IV on the old IBM 7094 for a few years, and there was a lot of activity. Max Mathews had gotten us started and Bell Laboratories was providing sound conversion. I started working with computer synthesis after having taken Milton Babbitt's classic course in 12-tone theory. I thought this would be an interesting way to explore that area. I worked on a computer piece [1966–1967] which attempted to project 12-tone relations in spectral terms. I think I succeeded in projecting those relations but I don't think it was a very successful piece, and I was quite discouraged about the computer.

Then the piano piece led me to begin to experiment with George Perle's 12-tone modal system. Perle, with whom I had studied at Queens College, had very carefully refrained from talking about any of his own music with his students, with the result that one became much more interested in what he was doing. Beginning in 1969, Perle and I collaborated for a period of about three or four years on extending this system. He ultimately wrote his book *Twelve-tone Tonality* [1977, University of California Press] and I used the computer to help me deal with all this and also integrated it into my dissertation ["Affine Music," 1973, Department of Music, Princeton University].

Again, I had the feeling that the computer could

right to left and from top to bottom, in one case in terms of bandwidths and indices of frequency modulation, and in another case in terms of specially designed filters in which the formant frequencies could be manipulated.

Roads: How was this related to the pitch structure?

Lansky: The pitch and timbre arrays would work in parallel. At the source, which was the "Tristan chord" and its inversion, I would have a very simple timbre. As the cycles folded outward, the timbres would become more and more complex.

I think in a sense this experiment failed, in that I was not convinced that the results were a real reflection of local pitch relations in terms of timbre. I was generating a context in which there was interesting differentiation among sounds, and an interesting piece, but nothing more.

help me come to grips with the wealth of relations described by this approach. This led to my first real computer piece *mild und leise* [1974]. There were two things I wanted to experiment with in this piece. First, I was becoming dissatisfied with pitch-class, rather than pitch, as a conceptual basis, both in serial music and in the work that Perle and I were doing. I wanted to experiment with specific pitch configurations, and second, I wanted to see if I could do something with timbre which would relate to these systematic ideas in interesting ways.

Roads: Could you discuss these timbral experiments?

Lansky: Essentially, the system Perle and I were working on is based on multidimensional cyclic arrays. The point is that you are not so concerned with ordering, as you are in the 12-tone system, but more concerned with the context that a given bunch of notes may have in this universe of pitch cycles in many dimensions.

A given pitch-pair relation, for example C and G, can occur in many different contexts in these cyclic arrays. Different C's and G's will have different meanings depending on where they are found. I became very interested in trying to reflect the syntax of pitches in the timbre.

The timbral structures that I used were based on moving timbres in a two-dimensional array from

Instrumental Versus Computer Works

Roads: When I look at your list of works I see an almost equal division between works for chamber groups and pieces for computer sound. Could you talk about the differences between the two media?

Lansky: For a long time, I assumed that if I wrote two computer pieces in a row they would be essentially the same piece.

Roads: Why is that?

Lansky: Because in the way I work on a computer piece (and I think this is probably true for most people), the issue of instrument design and programming is intimately connected with the compositional process. For example, with *mild und leise*, the way in which I constructed an instrument had a lot to do with the way I was thinking compositionally.

Roads: So do you try to alternate between works for traditional instruments and works for computer sound?

Lansky: Yes, but I think that is easing now because very interesting things started happening to my mind in contemplating musical issues in terms of the computer. I found that I would work on a computer piece and then compose an instrumental piece as a way to freshen myself up for another computer piece.

In my instrumental composing, I began to move further and further away from pitch-centered concepts, and more and more toward ideas that are not really designed for traditional instruments.

Roads: Such as?

Lansky: After *mild und leise* I composed *Crossworks* [1975] for chamber ensemble. I was very intent on deriving a compositional concept as a sonic object in itself, rather than basing it on a chart of pitch classes or any sort of list. *Crossworks* was based on some observations I had made about some implicit ideas in Schönberg's *Opus 16, No. 2.* I then noticed that in preparing for compositions I had been looking for objects which were already laden with musical implications, for example, the "Tristan chord" or ideas from Schönberg, rather than using my own arrays or charts. This led to my next computer piece, in which I began to work with linear prediction, basing it on a line from Shakespeare's *Tempest.* The main idea of the piece was to be a simple tune, and the way the piece would progress would be only in terms of that tune and its possible transformations.

Roads: This was the text setting *Artifice* (on Ferdinand's reflection) [1976].

Lansky: Yes. The line was "This music passed by me upon the waters." My concerns there were not so much with the semantic content of speech, but rather with the sonic surface of those words. I wanted to start with something very simple and make it complex. A simple tune—C, D-flat, B-flat, C, A—becomes much more complicated into a labyrinth until it becomes almost hypnotic. The purpose of the speech synthesis was mainly to provide timbral and dramatic colorations for the motivic transformations. I seemed to be following a path with these pieces which led to a point at which *musique concrète* was becoming more and more suggestive.

From Serial Music to *Musique Concrète*

Roads: How would you say your musical environment shaped you as a composer?

Lansky: I grew up in the 1950s and 1960s, and I first came upon composition when serial music was in full bloom. Stravinsky had begun to use serial

procedures, and Princeton was a marvelous place to be. However, I found myself moving further and further away from it. The only 12-tone piece I ever wrote was my first computer piece, which I started in 1966. It told me that I was not going to be a very good 12-tone composer.

In getting involved with computer music, one of the most interesting things to happen to me is one that I expected the least. There was an assumption that many of the practices of serial music would be ideally suited for the machine. I found that this was probably true in a certain sense, but in working with computers I was drawn to things that one might assume the machine would be least useful for. I rediscovered the beauty and complexity of human sound and the sounds of the real world, which are, after all, wonderfully rich and complicated. This began when I first started to fool with speech synthesis.

Artifice was a hesitant attempt to deal with words in music. I had tried writing songs and I felt that, for me, setting a text was a sort of arbitrary and pointless act. I also noticed that I had grown up listening to European opera and vocal music, and like many Americans, I did not understand the words most of the time. I also noticed that there was a great deal of music around me in which the words were right up front, the cutting edge of the music, as it were, in jazz, folk, and popular music. So I decided I would use the machine to deal with this issue. If I had just written a piece for soprano and piano, I had the feeling I would reinvent someone else's wheel.

To deal with this I decided to write a piece in which the sound of speech was to become a musical object. This was the *Six Fantasies on a Poem by Thomas Campion* [1979].

Roads: So was this piece a kind of turning point in your compositional development?

Lansky: Yes. I would say it was an eye opener. My objective, which I feel I have accomplished, is to take something that sounds like someone talking, and place the listeners in a perspective in which they are forced to perceive the contours, shapes, and rhythms of speech as musical objects. The idea was to isolate the different aspects of speech, the pitch contour, the sound of syllables and plosives, and the mouthing of the words. I noticed that I was dealing with a very interesting kind of *musique concrète*, and I began to appreciate the brilliance of that concept. One of the most interesting results of doing this piece was that I noticed that my view of the machine was changing, and that I was beginning to think of it as a way to "photograph" and transform musical reality.

The Computer as Camera

Roads: How would you liken computer sound processing to photography?

Lansky: I notice, for example, that as I start to deal more and more with manipulation of sounds from the real world, my position as a composer changes.

Roads: You are acting much more in the role of an interpreter, in the same way that a photographer is. You have to choose what to photograph and then decide how you will process it.

Lansky: That's exactly the point. I noticed after I finished the *Six Fantasies* that it would be interesting to try to look at some intrinsically musical sound in the same way that I had looked at speech. In *Folk Images* [1981], I started to play around with linear prediction on violin sources and began dealing with folklike material.

Composers since the dawn of music have set folk songs, but I wanted to do it from a *musique concrète* point of view. Previously I had regarded myself—coming out of this heady musical environment at Princeton—as someone who was inventing very complicated musical notions. Now I was confronting objects, photographing them, as it were, that were already heavily laden with musical connotations and history. Many of the folk songs I dealt with had been sung for generations and existed in many different versions. I found that my experience in dealing with them was a lot like dealing with text.

Roads: In some pieces of *musique concrète* and text sound, the material is so laden with connotations that the original content of the material takes precedence over the way the composer structures it. How did you deal with this problem?

Lansky: There is an interesting question concerning the ego of the person constructing these art works. I found, for example, that it was very liberat-

ing, in setting these folk songs, to not even regard myself as a composer. I suppose a photographer has problems similar to what you describe. He is certainly not inventing visual relationships. All he is doing is noticing them and showing them to other people. His are the eyes through which others see reality. Similarly, I wanted mine to be the ears through which others would hear this folk music.

Roads: This reminds me of something Gottfried Michael Koenig said about the composer as a selector. He uses it in a different context—interpretation of the output of computer programs—but in both cases the material is given. In your case it is given through a microphone, through a recording of a sound. In his case it is through a computer program which generates score material. Do you see a commonality there?

Lansky: Of course. On the other hand, when you begin to think of any period of music history in which there is a sense of "musical style," you can take the following point of view. What a composer is doing in order to create idiosyncrasy and peculiarity, something most composers are interested in doing, is interpreting familiar objects. When Mozart wrote a piece, he was interpreting objects and relations which were very familiar to him. He was certainly selecting. In his hands, however, these objects become utterly idiosyncratic. The view I've always assumed was that these objects were basically grammatical concepts, and that composition meant infusing them with contextual meaning. More recently, however, I'm becoming more interested in the idea that separating musical syntax and semantics is a peculiar and uncomfortable activity.

A strong assumption in my earlier thinking was that the development of my music was moving me toward inventing objects (or grammars) rather than responding to things. My own compositional psychotherapy now involves seeing what it's like to respond to objects and put them in new perspectives.

Audience Response

Roads: How do you imagine the audience responds to these new objects?

Lansky: The *Six Fantasies* are objects created by a

machine and could only have been created by a machine. The interest that people seem to have in them sometimes comes from the ways in which the sounds undergo original and unusual manipulations. The computer is certainly a big help in this respect since it so radically changes the physical and social environment of the music, thus freeing listeners from long-ingrained patterns of association.

Roads: So there is a kind of novelty effect.

Lansky: I think so. I hope that computer music will outwear this sense, but certainly people respond to the novelty. (It would be nice in the future if the description of the piece's hardware and software resources became as relevant as an assertion that a pianist played on a Baldwin or a Steinway.) There is something very special about the sound of the human voice, however, that helps transcend categories.

In *Folk Images* there is an entirely different sense. It is conceivable that these pieces could be performed on traditional instruments. One of my reasons for realizing these pieces was so that I could perform them and put them in idiosyncratic contexts, "photograph" them from peculiar angles, in a sense.

Harmony

Roads: One of the most striking aspects of your compositions is your sense of harmony. Could you tell us where you acquired it and where you see it in the context of contemporary music?

Lansky: That's an interesting question. My concept of harmony is ambiguous at this point.

Roads: It is even ambiguous in your compositions. One finds, on the one hand, an entire *Fantasy* done in an unabashed tonal style, and then you seem to take an opposite tack and work completely in an inharmonic timbral domain for another *Fantasy*. So there seems to be a kind of tension between working with lush, harmonic textures and working with rich, timbral textures.

Lansky: Yes. I am taking advantage of the freedom that I find in being my own boss. The inconsistencies you notice are entirely the result of my enjoy-

ment of the freedom the machine gives me. Self-indulgent experimentation is probably the best term for it. I have the sense that, had I scored the *Folk Images* for traditional instruments, it would exist in a strange performance domain. It would have little attraction to new music groups, and if I did what I wanted to do with the piece, it would probably have little appeal to "old" music groups as well.

As If

Roads: You have just completed a composition for string trio and computer-synthesized sound, entitled *As If* [1982]. Could you tell us about this piece?

Lansky: This was commissioned by the Columbia-Princeton Electronic Music Center for the Speculum Musicae in New York. One thing that I have recently become interested in and that I touched lightly in this piece is the concept of the position of a piece with respect to a listener. (The combination of "analog" and "digital" music raises this because they have such different senses of performance in relation to the listener.) There is, for example, a great difference between listening and overhearing. This does not have to do so much with the quality of the sound, but rather with the position the listener is in with respect to the performer and the flow of the music. In this piece I was interested in writing music in which the listener experiences different modes of perception, for example, the sound of someone practicing an instrument.

Roads: Is this the "overhearing" mode of perception?

Lansky: Exactly. The way in which the music develops is not tied to a linear and logical continuity. Rather, it is a continuity that one would perceive in overhearing someone work something out. The third movement starts out with a tape of a synthesized violin working in a hesitant and fragmented way. Then I respond to that with the live string trio playing in a very straightforward way. The piece goes back and forth between the straightforward "concert" mode of performance and a kind of "oblique" mode of performance on the tape, where the listener is in a different position, thus gaining a perspective on both modes of performance.

Roads: It is interesting that you are concerned with modes of hearing, especially after discussing the concept of *musique concrète*. One of the fundamental tenets of *musique concrète*, as espoused by Pierre Schaeffer in his *Traité des objets musicaux*, is that listening to *musique concrète* is an entirely different mode of hearing than listening to traditional music. In his view, in listening to *musique concrète* you are not encumbered by extant musical language. It is not your task, as it is in conventional music, to parse the input, or decode its conventional meanings (e.g., anticipating a harmonic resolution by hearing a cadential formula). To Schaeffer, this is an almost indirect form of hearing. By contrast, in *musique concrète* you are placed up against sound in a mode of "direct hearing" without reference to a conventional language.

Lansky: That is an interesting point of view. My view is that these two modes of hearing are only points in a spectrum containing many modes of hearing. For example, I am interested in crossing these modes of perception. In the *Six Fantasies* I distilled the sound of speech into something that was noiselike, or songlike, or musiclike. It also works the other way around. I have heard interesting works in which composers have, for example, attempted to infuse speechlike gestures into instrumental music. I probably disagree with Schaeffer in that what I seem to be trying to do is to infuse "direct hearing" with the encumbrances of "musical" thinking.

Roads: *As If* uses digitized and resynthesized extracts from a jazz saxophone performance. What role do these extracts play in the piece?

Lansky: One of the wonderful things about great saxophone playing lies in the special qualities of the instrument with respect to phrasing. I wanted to create a context in which you would notice the specialness of these saxophone objects. That's not to say that when you listen to a great saxophonist perform you are not impressed at every point. But when you take these gestures out of their original context and contrast them with other modes of expression, they exhibit an unmistakably special quality.

Again, this was an attempt to deal with modes of hearing and perception through juxtaposition. I am interested in "photographing" sounds associated with human behavior, rather than merely arbitrary world sounds, and good jazz playing always seemed to me to be full of musical personality. Given a recording of four saxophone players, for example, you can usually tell in an instant who is playing at any given time.

Roads: Phrasing is certainly something you have concentrated on in both the *Six Fantasies* and in *Folk Images*.

Lansky: Yes, although I would prefer not to think of phrasing in terms of virtue. That is, I do not believe there is such a thing as good or bad phrasing. Phrasing is the way you articulate a thought. I can imagine a wonderful piece in which every note would have the same envelope and amplitude. I see no way to distinguish that as the determining factor in the quality of the piece.

Roads: It surprises me to hear you say that.

Lansky: Let me say it the other way around. I can similarly imagine an utterly vacuous piece that is elegantly phrased. "Musical phrasing" is not a repository of musical virtue. It's certainly a familiar experience to hear someone express a vacuous thought very eloquently, or on the other hand utter deep thoughts with great hesitation and difficulty.

Musical Illusions and Animation

Roads: The notion of phrasing is certainly related to the notion of gesture. Some composers, notably Pierre Boulez and Luciano Berio, have spoken of their concern with preserving the gesture of the instrumentalist in working with computer music. They feel the subtle spontaneity of instrumental gestures is very important, and they feel it is difficult to capture with current technology. This is why they have turned to digital processing of instruments in performance rather than work exclusively with synthetic sounds.

Lansky: That's a very interesting point. When one listens to natural sounds emanating from loudspeakers, there is an illusion that the sound is emerging from some context. By contrast, there is a strange conceptual basis to purely synthetic sounds emanating from loudspeakers. Yet this has been a fundamental assertion of computer music.

I can easily imagine a music in which one perceives a "mode of behavior" which establishes a context. If may be the behavior of natural sounds, or it may be the behavior of some synthetic but coherent acoustic context, such as a simulated room or street.

Roads: You're saying that when we listen to the sound of a violin playing, we build a kind of physical model in our mind about how the sound is being made when the violinist strikes the string with the bow. We construct an expectation of what is possible and what is impossible on this instrument. You see to be asking, When composers use synthetic instruments, what expectations can the listener construct?

Lansky: Yes. The design of illusions is important in computer music. With much synthetic sound, the dimensions of the illusion are very limited. The sound is emanating directly from speakers rather than from a model of a real environment.

Roads: How does one achieve the same kind of animation in computer music that one achieves in live performance?

Lansky: The sense in which the sound one hears is "real" is related to the extent to which one can imagine its environment. One of the lively illusions one hears discussed in computer music is a kind of "outer space" quality. People construct a mental outer space scenario in listening to such sounds.

I'm very interested in creating a human scenario, a human illusion. I want to create an illusion that the sound you're hearing has a human basis in a particular acoustic space. In other words, it might sound like a recording of a sound emanating somewhere along a tree of transformations from a real-world source.

I hope more composers will be taking this approach to computer music in the future. The computer is the first musical instrument capable of modeling so many aspects of real-world sound. Lots of electronic music machines can modulate sine waves, but so far it is only the computer that can observe, imitate, and transform world sounds.

The Social Situation of the Composer

Roads: What is the difference between the musical life of the computer music composer and the composer of orchestral music?

Lansky: I love this question. I found it ironic that computer music led me more deeply into the realm of what human beings do when they make sound. It also strikes me as interesting that the social and musical life of a computer musician is different than what one would expect. For example, you might assume that someone who is writing for a machine has given up on human beings and doesn't give a damn whether the music is played.

My experience in writing computer music is that as you work with it you're playing it for your friends. They are responding to what you are doing. There is no hiding from what you are doing in your notation. You can't say, "It should sound good when it's well performed." In computer music, what you play is what you get. The virtue is that you are representing yourself in terms which you are responsible for and which, presumably, you are satisfied with.

At Princeton we have a wonderful time playing our sounds for each other while our pieces are in progress. This is very different from a situation in which a composer is holed up in a room for a year writing a piece and nobody sees or hears any of it until he's done.

You do give up one thing in computer music. You are giving up the role of the playwright. You are no longer scripting a performance. For some composers this is the whole point. They really want to deal with performers and the subtleties and ambiguities of notation. For me, this is an odd choice.

Composers and Programming

Roads: How important is it for a computer music composer to learn to program?

Lansky: I certainly grew up entirely in a musical environment. My mathematical background is no more than that of any other musician who went to a college instead of a conservatory. There is a certain attitude that one shouldn't make these poor composers learn to program. I think this is a misconception. Composing is enormously difficult, and composers in general tend to be a very intelligent community. I have rarely met a composer who has dabbled with computer music who couldn't learn to program. Just as sculptors, painters, and filmmakers routinely become involved with the chemistry of their materials, so I think composers should learn something about acoustics and the nature of sound. Computer programming is certainly an interesting way to do this.

Criticisms of Computer Music

Roads: What, in your view, is the worst cliché of computer music?

Lansky: I have trouble with Bessel functions at this point.

Roads: You're referring to the technique of frequency modulation.

Lansky: I'm very impressed with how far it can be extended. But very simple frequency modulation wears me down. Since my particular interests have to do with reprocessing sounds rather than building up sounds from scratch, I tend to find some purely synthetic pieces to be less interesting.

But overall, I find the community of computer music composers to be an interesting group. I think this has to do largely with the fact that these people are listening to what they are doing, and developing good ears in the process. They also have a lot of patience and high resistance to frustration.

Roads: What, in your view, is the most unhealthy aspect of computer music?

Lansky: It is the extent to which there is an obsession with the machine rather than with what it produces. I have heard too many discussions among computer music people who were only concerned with software and hardware without even considering what kinds of pieces they were producing. For my money you can write wonderful pieces on primitive machines with terrible software, and you can write execrable pieces with super machines and brilliant software. Good machines and better soft-

ware certainly make life easier, but there is not a one-to-one correlation between the quality of pieces and the tools used to make them. Often, systems which are too easy to use encourage thoughtlessness.

Roads: Do you see any danger in hardware systems for digital sound synthesis?

Lansky: What I do see as a danger is that the design of the machine creates preconceptions about the way in which the instrument is to be used.

Roads: Isn't that also true about software synthesis, though?

Lansky: Yes, it is absolutely true. From my point of view, the best approach to designing software is to make it as low level as possible, without forcing the composer to write too much code (particularly operating system software), but giving him the responsibility for imagining and designing things with the greatest degree of generality.

One of the things that often happens in music software is that programmers first design a language for the specification of the pitch in terms of a 12-part division of the octave, for example. Immediately, the first thing someone learns in computer music is to specify pitch in terms of equal temperament. This is certainly an obvious thing to implement, but right away the structure of the language is encouraging conceptions which channel one's thinking along a certain line.

Roads: What would you do differently?

Lansky: One of the things I do is to initially avoid describing the computer in terms of an analog synthesizer, with oscillators and the rest. I have students learn to use it first as a sound processor. I give them tapes of sounds, and routines to edit, mix, and filter them. This develops a sense of the machine as a powerful signal processor. I like to design projects in which the structure of the objects they manipulate is different from the objects they're familiar with. For example, the first thing they do may not be to synthesize "Twinkle, Twinkle Little Star," but rather to synthesize glissandi or experiment with different tuning systems.

These kinds of concerns worry me a lot because I see much energy being poured into real-time synthesizer design in which the main input device is a keyboard, or in which the input language is designed to look as familiar as possible to musicians. A keyboard is a powerful device, but immediately composers are put into a situation in which their entire musical background is brought heavily to bear on the interaction with the machine. This is not good if it limits the composer's conceptions. One way out of this is to put composers into a position where they are responsible for a great deal of programming.

This sounds like an absurd point of view in that presumably you do want to take advantage of musical background, but I regard the real power of computer synthesis to lie in its ability to be responsive to the most utterly idiosyncratic compositional frames of mind on an ad hoc and arbitrary basis. I am interested to see if the next generation of music machines will be as powerful in this respect as some current software-based music systems are. I hope they will be, and I think the future of computer music depends on the fact that composers should settle for nothing less. The computer is the first real instrument of the imagination, and the main energy in developing systems should be put into constructing a working environment where this remains true, and in avoiding the imposition of the designer's musical imagination on that of the composer.

Compositions by Paul Lansky

Piano Piece in Three Parts (1968). Publisher: Boelke-Bomart, Inc., Hillsdale, New York, 1978, 12 pages

Two Studies for Wind Quintet (1969)

Modal Studies (piano), (1970)

Modal Fantasy (piano), (1970). Publisher: Columbia University Press, New York, 1975, 20 pages. Recording: Robert Miller, CRI SD-342, 1975

String Quartet #2 (1971, rev. 1977). Publisher: Boelke-Bomart, Inc., Hillsdale, New York, 1978, 21 pages. Recording: Pro-Arte String Quartet, CRI SD-402, 1979

Affine Study (piano), (1972)

mild und leise (computer-synthesized tape), (1973–1974). Recording: Columbia-Odyssey Y34149, 1976

Crossworks (chamber ensemble), (1974–1975). Publisher: Boelke-Bomart, Inc., Hillsdale, New York, 1978, 27 pages. Recording: Boston Musica Viva, Nonesuch H-71351, 1978

Artifice (*on Ferdinand's reflection*) (computer-synthesized tape), (1975–1976)

Fanfare (two French horns). Publisher: Perspectives of New Music, vol. 14/2, 1976, page 235

Dance Suite (piano), (1977). Publisher: Boelke-Bomart, Inc., Hillsdale, New York, 1978, 16 pages

Serenade (violin, viola, piano), (1978)

Six Fantasies on a Poem by Thomas Campion (computer-synthesized tape), (1978–1979). Recording: CRI SD-456, 1982

Folk Images (computer-synthesized tape), (1980–1981)

As If (string trio and computer-synthesized tape), (1981–1982)

5

Larry Polansky

Center for Contemporary Music
Mills College
Oakland, California 94613

Interview with
David Rosenboom

Introduction

David Rosenboom, currently Coordinator of the
Center for Contemporary Music at Mills College in
Oakland, has long been an innovator in American
experimental music. He has done significant work
in composition, performance (as a pianist, violist,
violinist, tablist, and electronic instrumentalist),
theory, and instrument design. Among other things,
Rosenboom pioneered the use of computers in live
performance and the integration of biofeedback
techniques in compositional environments. I took
this opportunity to interview him not about his
past, but about current and future trends in his
work. I have supplied a brief discography at the end
for those interested in listening to Rosenboom's
work.

Mental Models of Evolution

Polansky: The theme of evolution—of the artist
and of the artist and society together—seems to be
consistent in your work, for instance, in *On Being
Invisible* and in the "In the Beginning" series [8
pieces for various media, including instruments,
electronics, film, and text]. Is this a conscious
development?
Rosenboom: Interesting point. It's very much related to what I'm doing right now. I seem to have
this cycle of about four years where I come to a
place in which I have to evaluate myself, or the
idea I've been interested in, and start over. I feel
that I'm at that stage right now. Consequently, I'm
standing back and looking at a lot of my work from
over the years, and one reason that I do distance
myself is that I see consistencies that I didn't know
were there. And now, I'm especially looking at some
pieces from quite far back, some pieces from the

Computer Music Journal, Volume 7, No. 4,
Winter, 1983

[University of] Illinois days, some early electronic
pieces, and a lot of percussion pieces. I can identify
themes and consistencies that I hadn't before. One
of these is a kind of cosmological point of view;
that is, my music is very much derived from thinking about nature and about modeling the universe.
I'm one of those people who likes to try and develop a coherent mental model of the universe.
Polansky: What Jim Tenney calls amateur
cosmology.
Rosenboom: Right. But I do think that one can be a
cosmologist no matter what one's discipline. One
can come to visions of the universe that are quite
strong, that one then begins to articulate. I'm sure
that Einstein had a vision of the universe which he
found a way to express mathematically, but I'm
sure that the vision was there long before the expression of it. For me this is true in music. To that
extent, evolution plays an important part, because
I'm interested in how the universe evolves, how we
evolve, and how cultures evolve. So you're right, a
lot of my music has more or less consciously dealt
with the process of evolution. In the recent series,
"In the Beginning," there has been a kind of concern with modeling. Since the proportional modeling is very abstract, I reached a point in one piece,
#5 (subtitled "The Story"), where I decided to talk
about the whole idea of modeling in itself. For me,
the personification of the model was the concept of
the double. When Bob Hughes asked me for a piece
for the Arch Ensemble, I also had the idea that I
wanted to use a film, and that I wanted the film to
contain images, very abstract scenes that depicted
this strange preoccupation with the idea of modeling. Then, in order to make the scenes more meaningful, I wrote the text, and then I decided to just
do them all at the same time—play the piece, show
the film, and talk.
Polansky: Did you make the film?
Rosenboom: I made it with George Manupelli—
whom I asked because he's such a great filmmaker,
and the kinds of scenes I wanted were well suited
to his camera technique. The text depicts a scene in

which there are three characters talking, two of them are the spirit characters, which represent the polar opposites of humanity—maleness/femaleness, hard/soft, etcetera. These characters further represent the polar aspects of a single consciousness to which humans have evolved after some cataclysmic event—be it natural or unnatural, we don't know—but a sort of cusp in catastrophe theory terms. These creatures are waking up, the first waking forms of this new evolutionary form. At first they're discussing the phenomenon of their own survival, and then they discover the double, and by this I mean all the forms of the double—the idea of humanity copying itself, the robotic forms (mechanistic synthetic copies), religious copies in the forms of inventions of gods that look like humans, the Don Juan (spirit) form—because I saw in the double a fundamental basis for the idea of modeling. They talk to the double, and the big question to them is, How in the world did *it* survive? For in *their* minds they created it. Did it have enough motivation to prepare for its own survival? The conversation goes on, the film happens, and the music, which is the model that I made, is underneath.

Feedback

Polansky: By reading your book, *Biofeedback and the Arts* [1976. Vancouver: A.R.C. Press], which is several years old, I had the feeling that in that period you had some concept of the artist as an evolutionary model for humanity.
Rosenboom: I saw the arts as a kind of science of intuitive thought. Artists can conceive of these radical approaches to evolutionary processes, and they are a certain natural and necessary part of evolution—artists are products of natural forces.
Polansky: It's not our fault we're here.
Rosenboom: Right. It's built in. I was very involved in the idea of the feedback model, and the notion that we could enhance our naturally self-organizing qualities by creating even more feedback paths than we already have, and this could lead to possibilities for global feedback.

I saw the idea of monitoring the brain state of an individual, and making that audible, and making

that something that organizes musical form, as a model for the notion that humanity must evolve in order to survive itself and what it's doing to Earth. [Humanity] must evolve to a state of consciousness in which it conceives of itself as a single organism that lives on the Earth. Of course, it's politically naive and can be criticized on the same basis that everybody tore down Buckminster Fuller, but at the same time these things are worth pursuing, worth educating people to think about.

On Being Invisible, which is perhaps the most elaborate of all the feedback pieces that I did, deals with the evolution of a system, of which the person is a part, that goes through its own tendencies toward and away from order. It begins from either precomposed order or from a stochastic, randomly generated beginning. The natural shifts of attention that the person goes through, or volitionally manipulates, sensed by the computer measurement of brain signals, organize the musical form. Other pieces were generated collaboratively, like some of the pieces of the Maple Sugar group in Toronto that we were a part of, which were really involved with the view of artists in their surroundings—artists as creatures of social context, and how a group can work as a group.

Virtuosity

Polansky: It seems that a common thread in your work is the use of a very interesting idea of virtuosity, whether it's in the use of high-speed machines capable of complex decisions to restructure your own thought processes, or other performers who can make almost unhumanly quick and complex decisions. People like [pianist and composer] J. B. Floyd, or [master mrdangam player] Trichy Sankaran, people who can do things almost on the order of machines, stretching motor and physiological limits.
Rosenboom: The reason is that these people tend to assume consciousness of a number of higher levels of the organization of the music they create. The ability to give the "go" signal to a generative system that's in your brain that goes to your arm that makes something happen almost without

thinking, is somehow correlated with the ability to think in real time on rather high levels of musical information. Sankaran is particularly amazing in this. He's kind of like a high-speed correlation computer, in that he can sense the tiniest rhythmic suggestion and build a huge rhythmic composition on it immediately with his drumming technique. That's something that Richard Teitelbaum exploited in one of his brainwave pieces with Sankaran and Barbara Mayfield (who did Tai Chi). Sankaran would hear patterns in Barbara's brainwaves, and he would instantly mushroom them into fantastic rhythmic ideas.

Computer Instruments

Polansky: Since a lot of your work has been in either practical or conceptual instrument design, you've been interested in the development of unusually complex interactions between yourself and the machine. The newest of these experiments is the Touché keyboard instrument, and your computer language Foil [Far Out Instrument Language]. Would you talk about these a little?

Rosenboom: The Touché is an instrument created in collaboration with Don Buchla. It was conceived as a keyboard-performance tool that would eventually allow for the implementation of real-time algorithmic composition, and which would also contain some of the more interesting advances of computer synthesis in a portable package that could be taken on stage. It consists of three special-purpose processors: one for digitally generating waveforms, one for controlling the slower-moving musical parameters in an analog manner, and one for making the stimulus/response mapping of the system between the inputs and the outputs. The software is Foil. Foil is based on the notion of *instrument definition,* a package of data that at any one time completely describes the stimulus/response characteristics of the instrument and all of its time-varying functions. One can have a library of these, available for instant access, and also edit and load them. I'm currently working on some enhancements of this as well—to make it run

faster, and also to make possible the real-time algorithmic composition in which the performance execution routines will be linked to a "metacompiler." One can then experiment with language structures by entering syntactically based descriptions of languages, and then use these languages to make music. (This will be written with the aid of a compiler called Meta 3.)

Concept Spaces

Polansky: Two things you have talked about a lot lately are the development of formal languages and the idea of concept spaces.

Rosenboom: *Concept spaces* result from another consistency in my compositions. I'm always making representations of multidimensional spaces in which I consider the elements of a given universe (piece) to be related. They're related by their closeness in that space in some way. There's a piece that I wrote for percussionists Alan O'Connor and William Youhass in 1966, when I was very involved in proportional relationships in music, that involved relating everything to long time units. I would, for instance, take the length of a piece as a fundamental and then, by dividing it up "ad absurdum," derive everything else in the piece—including the color of the lights in the hall. Not that I thought that this relationship would be necessarily organic or perceivable, but I used it to build a unifying model. In that space, I worked with spatial mappings of rhythmic ratios, and I worked out a set of compositional invariants, in the serial sense, that appeared in the form of sets of simple ratios and additive sequences.

Polansky: What was the name of that piece?

Rosenboom: It is called *A Precipice in Time* (1966) and is dedicated to Ornette Coleman. It is a very bombastic piece. Another piece that I did in Buffalo [1967] for Lucas Foss's group was one where I made a circular mapping of parametric opposites, and the musicians had to relate to each other through that. The score was composed of a set of symbols that had a dictionary of specific performance actions. That was actually influenced by the semantic differential.

Polansky: The Osgood thing?

Rosenboom: Right, which I had studied in psychology classes at Illinois, because he was at Illinois. I got exposed to it through Kenneth Gaburo's class in systems theory there, which was a wonderful class.

Osgood's book [*The Measurement of Meaning*] is a good example of a concept space model, and I've been thinking about that ever since. As it's developed, it's proved to be such a useful tool that I think it can be built into formal languages, and of course appears in neurological modeling. I think of perception as a hierarchical system, but it's important to understand that it's fully parallel. That is, information on one level is available to all other levels, not just the next level up, which is a fundamentally different approach than the straightforward tree structure. But given that, the sensory mechanisms create some segmentation of the perceptual space, and those become elements. These are mapped into a higher-level space, which has a different set of axes. Once those are mapped, changes from one to another are contours in that space. Contours become recognized as features, and shapes in a space on that given level become points in the next-higher-level space. So the transformation from one shape to another becomes represented as a contour of points in a higher-level space. This continues to go up the feature-extraction ladder in the neurological mechanism.

These ideas have been useful to me compositionally. I'm interested in embedding such a structure in a compositional or an analytical language that has flexibility for users of the language, who can parameterize that space any way they want. This structure is fundamental to our perception and is therefore not stylistically based.

Recordings

Polansky: What about your latest record?

Rosenboom: I made a 45-RPM single, which was an electronic version of the University of Michigan fight song.

Polansky: Did they like it?

Rosenboom: They liked it! Talk about cultural discontinuity! Some producer had this idea to make this record when Michigan was going to play football in the Rose Bowl against UCLA. Somehow he heard my record [*Future Travel*], and he went to Jose Cruz (the producer of *Future Travel*) and asked him. At first I didn't want to do it, but then as a favor to Jose, who had been so generous in making *Future Travel*, I did it. It was a busy time for me, but I had a four-track and my instruments, so one Saturday afternoon I just made the piece. And they loved it. It came out on a 45 single and sold really well right away, and then they lost to UCLA! It's on the shelf now, but they'll probably bring it out again next year.

Polansky: Can you talk a little about *Future Travel* [reviewed in *Computer Music Journal* 7(1):76–77]?

Rosenboom: *Future Travel* is made entirely on the Touché, with the exception of some percussion instruments here and there, and some violin and piano. The music is a result of the modeling process, once again from the "In the Beginning" series, and especially from a part of that process that deals with melody. A melody is represented there as simply a shape—a plot on a graph, which is applied to various pitch sets. These pitch sets come from that proportional idea I worked out. I made a program in which I could access different shapes and apply them to different pitch sets, causing them to be played in various proportional rhythmic relationships, in real time. That is, by touching a key, I would pick a fundamental, and all the pitch sets would be derived, in complex ways, from the undertone or overtone series of that. Then I would pick a shape by touching another key, and that would become a melody. I used rhythmic structures that consisted of cross rhythms based on irreducible ratios: 9/4, 7/6, etcetera, and I could stop and start these. I found that I could produce such a broad range of musics that had such a wide range of stylistic referents, that I was quite shocked. I could pick certain proportional sets that could produce a blues, or something I'd never heard before. I was so amazed that it worked that I decided that I would just go into the studio, and gamble that I could create bed tracks with this system that would suggest tunes to me, which I would then orchestrate into pieces. It was a gamble, since the studio time was expensive, but I was pleased with the result. Kathy Morton, the recording engineer, was instrumental in making it work.

The Center for Contemporary Music

Polansky: The last thing I want to talk about is your current job as coordinator of the Mills College Center for Contemporary Music [CCM]. What kind of plans do you have there?

Rosenboom: The position is one of the most difficult jobs I've ever had, because there is such tremendous historical weight attached to the place. There have been so many incarnations (radically different aesthetics and styles) there. When you step into a situation like that, you have so many people to think about and so much to consider. I have basically tried to make the CCM a place where people could continue to experiment in as free a way as possible—with new aesthetics and new musical styles—and to try to substantiate the studios and enhance the facilities. There's always been experimentation with electronic media, and I've tried to find ways to continue that by keeping the CCM abreast of new developments and by finding ways that the Center could contribute in a unique way to the field. I wouldn't like it to become just another electronic or computer music studio. We've tried to figure out areas where we could do things that aren't being done other places.

Polansky: What are some of those areas?

Rosenboom: In particular, the development of an approach to languages for use in computer music systems, which you and I have both tried to think about, in a way that's quite distinct from what's happening in other computer music centers. That's well under way, moving the facilities in the direction of programmable media in general. We need to continue to substantiate the intense use that is made of advanced recording processes in the creation of pieces, and the CCM's relationships to other media, for example, video and film. Those are all more or less obvious. What's not so obvious are the things that one does to try and keep the Center alive by showing a variety of communities that it has value, to many different people and different ways of working. I think it's a free environment in

which people can keep experimenting. It's also a demanding environment, in that there's a certain expectation of quality, and of innovation. This we should continue to live up to. And there's an imperative that it continue to support the experimental music community. It's fundamental that it remain experimental, and I believe that it has, which makes it an exciting place to work—a place where people don't have to worry about whether their work will be accepted or not—that is, provided they're serious. So that's what we're trying to do, and in that respect we're trying to continue a performance program that presents both new names in music and experimental directions, and also some "landmarks" that we're interested in, including those that haven't been too well exposed on the West Coast.

Polansky: Like Xenakis, and Salvatore Martirano?

Rosenboom: Right, and also support young artists who aren't that well known yet.

Polansky: What do you see as the future of the CCM? Are there any major projects or changes you'd like to make?

Rosenboom: Well, I'd like to reorganize and update the studios and get the performance program to be a little more self-producing. I'd like to recruit even more students. We have a great group of students there now, but we can handle more. I'd like to continue to develop positive and productive interfaces with other parts of Mills College—the other arts departments, computer science, and other disciplines. I'd like to continue to see the Public Access program thrive as an important part of the community, and I'd like it to be a strong archival center for documentation and recordings about experimental music.

Discography

Brainwave Music. A.R.C. Records 1002.
Suitable for Framing, with J. B. Floyd and Trichy Sankaran. A.R.C. Records 1000.
On Being Invisible. Music Gallery Editions Records, Vol. 4.
My New Music. J. Jasmine (Jacqueline Humbert and David Rosenboom). A.R.C. Records.
And out come the night ears, with Don Buchla. 1750 Arch Street Records 1774.
Future Travel. Street Records SRA-002.

6

Richard Boulanger
Computer Audio Research Laboratory
Center for Music Experiment, Q-037
University of California, San Diego
La Jolla, California 92093 USA

Interview with Roger Reynolds, Joji Yuasa, and Charles Wuorinen

Introduction

This interview took place on 9 March 1984 at the University of California, San Diego's Center for Music Experiment (CME). At the time of the interview all three composers were in residence at CME, each completing the computer-generated tape portions of compositions utilizing the resources of the center's Computer Audio Research Lab (CARL). The three compositions were premiered on the New York Philharmonic's Horizons '84 festival. [See the article by Brooke Wentz in this issue—Ed.]

During the past two decades each of these three composers has been creatively involved with the electronic medium—with analog electronics in their earlier compositions and with the computer in their recent ones. The first part of the interview focuses on issues that faced the composers in three of their early works—Yuasa's *Icon* (1966–67: NHK Studio), Wuorinen's *Time's Encomium* (1968–69: Columbia-Princeton Electronic Music Center), and Reynolds's *Voicespace* (1975–80: CME and Stanford University). The second part deals with "state of the art" issues manifest in their most recent CARL compositions—Yuasa's *Beyond the Midnight Sun*, Wuorinen's *Bamboula Squared*, and Reynolds's *Transfigured Wind*. The underlying questions was: How has the changing technology been reflected in their changing compositional concerns?

Early Involvement with Tape Music

Boulanger: What was it about the electronic medium which first attracted you to it?
Reynolds: I began working with tape in the early sixties. What most attracted me was the opportunity to transfer particularly attractive sound materials into a formal musical context. My concern was not with structural precision, but rather with enlarging what I felt to be the range of musical experience.

The range of inference that one can draw from a repeatable experience is certainly one of the things that I find most delightful about art. Although many of the extraordinary experiences we have during our lives are unrepeatable, musical experience—the flow of information involving the listener in the act of anticipation and reflection—is repeatable in at least some form. The magic that a composer might find in his or her daily experience can now be represented (and possibly enhanced) in a formal musical work and thereby not lost as the work ends. The relations and interrelations—the interaction of the sounds themselves—can be recreated; and this extraordinary content can be sought (and possibly found) again.

Yuasa: I began working with tape in 1953, making *musique concrète* pieces. I became involved with "pure" electronic music, so to speak, in 1963. I saw the new sonic possibilities as quite important; but what most attracted me was (and still is) the expressive potential of this new "instrument." It offered the composer an opportunity for the creation and exploration of new and unique forms of expression. Just as composers must think deeply of the function and the character of any acoustic instrument for which they write, so too must they think of the tape or electronic medium not only as a source of new sounds but as a new means of expression.

Wuorinen: It so happened that I was present for the early developments of "tape music" in New York during the 1950s because teachers and colleagues of mine were involved with it. At that time I did a couple of things, but without a great deal of conviction about the use of the medium. Indeed, *Time's Encomium* would probably not exist were it not for the fact that the commission involved specified that it be purely electronic.

Computer Music Journal, Vol. 8, No. 4,
Winter 1984

There have always been things about the electronic medium that bothered me. In making a work for tape, one makes a commitment to a configuration of detail which (at least until now) has been essentially unalterable. In other words, there is a precision of choice much celebrated by Milton Babbitt (a dear friend and colleague), but a precision of choice that I think is a liability rather than an asset. My belief is that compositional choices tend to be made specific, in traditional terms, by clusters of possibilities that may look very precise on the page but which (as we all know) are capable of an infinite number of modes of realization. With the electronic medium there is a very different situation. One is obliged to be specific whether one wants to be specific or not. In any event, this is an aspect that has always strongly differentiated electronic music from music that is to be performed. Since I have spent a great deal of my life as a performer and conductor, I am extremely concerned with the process that takes place in the realization of a written mute silent page in sound by a performer. This whole area has been a preoccupation of mine for a long time and has made me, up until recently, reluctant to commit any sizable amount of my time to the production of electronic music.

However, even from the early 1960s I saw in the computer a very different animal. In it, the possibility of multiple realizations of the same essential information existed in a way that would have been laborious to the point of impossibility with tape. Moreover, it seemed to me that the written record left by the process of making a computer piece could stand very well in relation to the not particularly degradable information that exists in a conventional score. I had been quite concerned at the time, about what was going to happen to all those tapes after 25 or 50 years.

Recently, with the very impressive development of digital synthesis and other applications of the computer to the production of electronic music, my attitude and interest have somewhat changed. When I make use of the computer, I am as interested in the implementation of certain compositional algorithms to produce musical structures as I am in its ability to produce actual sounds.

Use of Space

Boulanger: One of the primary features of *Icon*, the *Voicespace* pieces, and *Time's Encomium* is the movement of sound. Each of you, though, seems to have a slightly different view on how this "spatial" parameter might function structurally. Could you describe what techniques you used to create the localization effects in these pieces and what structural role, if any, they played in the composition itself?

Yuasa: The sound source for *Icon* was white noise. The one-channel source master resulted from filtering white noise in various ways and with various devices. This monaural source master was distributed among five channels. It was possible to control the timing and amplitude levels of each of the five channels with the help of a primitive computer and thereby to position and move the sound anywhere within the listening field. The computer system used punched tape for controlling the gating of the sound and a special device built for transitions. This device would make the rise and fall time proportional to the total gate time.

As far as my use of space was concerned, I was interested in creating a unique sound environment or "sound-space" in which the listener would be totally involved in the spiral movement of the sound. I also wanted to use sounds not only as points but also as surfaces. These surfaces, which would cover certain regions of the listening area, were free to move and alter their direction and speed. I was interested in creating spaces which would submerge the listener in a sonic environment characterized by and contributing to a totally different sense of space and time.

Reynolds: My primary interest in the *Voicespace* pieces was still to gain access to and utilize sonic materials, and to potentially create musical experiences that were not likely to be available to us. In the case of *Still* (1974–75) that sonic source was the focal *fry*—controlled successions of glottal pulses. The exploration of this source involved the timbral evolution of the oral cavity by the reconfiguration of the vocal apparatus associated with the controlled recitation of the text. These pulses were so faint and so subtle that the microphone had to be literally inside the singer's mouth in order to get the kind of dynamic range and clarity of timbre that I was after.

As concerns the spatial component of the work, I attempted to explore the ways in which relationships among spatially distinct gestures such as discontinuous sounds in succession, continuous sound that rotated, sounds that went into the distance, or sounds that grew more massive or more singular with time, could lead to a motivic mapping of the sonic space. This is something, of course, that has interested composers a long while. It's been intuitively clear, if not musically practical, that sounds have as distinct a position perceptually as they do a distinct loudness for example. There is probably a great deal more precision in our ability to discriminate position and changes in position than loudness and changes in loudness. Even the more sacred parameters of sound might be less precisely perceived.

In *Still* I employed a template of ten positions in quadraphonic space. The template was used to map the paths of successive sounds. A gating mechanism was constructed whereby glottal pulses advanced a sequencer that placed the sounds in specific locations and controlled the relative amplitude of the four channels. The tape was subsequently processed in order to include information about reverberation and the spectral character associated with the proximity of the source. This procedure was applied to both discontinuous and continuous paths. In some instances the source changed from a point to a volume, back to a point, and so on. My effort was to see, with a very limited stencil, whether rotating it, moving it left and right, using portions of it, and reversing its direction would be sufficiently memorable.

In the case of digital devices it is now possible to go much further not only to use distinct position and the evolution of source size, but also to control such crucial cues as changing velocity. My long term aim, then, is the development of a vocabulary of spatial motives.

Wuorinen: Although I am quite enchanted with antiphony and spatial distribution of musical information in other people's music, somehow in my own it never seems to be a particularly significant issue. In the case of *Time's Encomium*, as with certain more recent efforts of mine, the principle use of channel distribution is simply to separate musical materials from each other. I am less concerned with the actual spatial origin of the sound source than I am with its integrity or independence from its neighbors.

In *Time's Encomium* reverberation was used in part to distinguish the basic material from its modifications. This is a very simple-minded and crude utilization but nevertheless a palpable one. It does introduce a sense of distance and a locational difference when one compares or hears the two kinds of material side by side.

Thus, the use of channel distribution, reverberation, and sense of relative distance in *Time's Encomium* is actually a good example of a compositional attitude that pervades most of my efforts. Basic structural/formal compositional processes, which are essentially undetectable by the listener, have extremely obvious sonic manifestations in the result. If I decide that I want to make a distinction between primary and secondary material by reverberating the secondary material, what strikes the ear as a result is the difference in the perceived distance from the hearer of the two kinds of material. But seeking the creation of that sense of distance is not something that motivates me in the first instance.

The RCA Synthesizer

Boulanger: Improvements in digital signal processing technology are making it easier to do very complex things and at the same time making it possible for a larger number of composers to access some very powerful systems. Might you describe what it was like working in the "good old days" with the RCA synthesizer?

Wuorinen: About 10 years ago I gave a brief interview in which I presented such a description. Somehow, before it was broadcast, this interview came to the attention of both Babbitt and Ussachevsky who were then very much involved. They, with great alacrity, caused the interview to be suppressed because they were afraid that a few true words on the subject would cause RCA (which had only lent the giant monster to the Columbia-Princeton Electronic Music Center) to take their synthesizer away in a huff. I think enough rust has probably accumulated on that machine by this point that one can say without any fear of damaging anyone that working on it was a perfect nightmare.

It was (and still is) a 750-vacuum-tube affair in which information was encoded by a fiendish combination of 4-bit binary switches, banks on the walls and console of this nearly room-sized machine, and two particularly clever paper drives, each of which would encompass two channels of information. Holes were punched in the paper that then passed over a metal roller to which contact was made by a set of brushes. The brushes were arranged so that they would lie over the holes that passed beneath, making continuous contact. Time was represented on the machine as the number of holes at a certain rate of the paper drive. Pitch and other information was represented in binary numbers by a combination of preset switches and banks of holes in the paper.

Now all of this so far is merely tedious. But of course, the paper drives were far from perfect, the paper not impervious to tearing, and the brushes not resistant to bending. For example, if one were to crank back a few feet of the punched paper, without remembering to lift the brushes from the roller (an act not always automatic) a great many of them would be bent. This would then require dismantling the entire apparatus and taking tweezers to straighten out the brushes, putting it back together and so forth. The brushes also got dirty and contact was not always as good as it needed to be.

The actual range and capacity of the machine are a little dim in my memory, but I do recall that anything but the most simple kinds of timbral manipulations were extremely difficult. When I began to use the machine I restricted both my rhythmic and timbral expectations to a very limited palette because I knew that I would be spending the rest of my life there if I didn't. This explains why the entirety of *Time's Encomium* is not synthesized. Only the core material of the composition is. This

core was then subjected to much looser kinds of analog studio transformations.

The RCA synthesizer was distinctly transitional. It was, I believe, designed in the late 1940s, built sometime in the early 1950s. It came to the Columbia-Princeton Electronic Music Center only around 1959 or 1960. It has never been very much used. Babbitt, of course, is the composer who has spent by far the most time and certainly achieved the most impressive results with it. But I know, from both my own experience and from his, that it is a tremendous amount of labor of a very frustrating sort.

Interaction with Sound

Boulanger: Substantial portions of both *Icon* and *Time's Encomium* were composed before entering the studio. The same is true of Wourinen's more recent *Bamboula Squared*. Yet Yuasa has stated elsewhere that some of the sections of *Icon* are characterized by "free improvisation," and one would assume that the studio processing of the pre-composed "core" material of *Time's Encomium*, might represent an instance of (in Wourinen's own words) a composer's "intuitive response to his compositional design." The production of these pieces suggests to me an interactive compositional relationship with the emerging work. Would you identify this interactive process as a unique characteristic of working with the medium? If not, how does the medium's relatively instantaneous feedback affect your decision-making process during the formative stages of a composition in a way which might differ when compared to your composing for purely instrumental resources?

Wuorinen: There's no difference—it's all very simple. If I like the results I keep them; if I don't, I either change them or throw them out. The fact that one is able to hear, electronically, the physical manifestation of one's work sooner than with ordinary instruments has never made any difference to me since I have never had any difficulty in knowing precisely what my instrumental work is going to sound like. I cannot recall the last time I have been surprised in a rehearsal.

The delay actually constitutes no disadvantage from my point of view. I prefer the delay involved in composition for ordinary instruments and voices because the presence of the actual physical sound that I am making electronically is often a distraction. It often involves one on a level of detail that may be inappropriate for a certain stage of composition. This is not, therefore, necessarily an advantage. It is simply a characteristic of the medium—you hear things sooner. I must say, though, that if one had a real-time system with which the results of any compositional decision were immediately receivable, that might alter the picture considerably. But in what way, I can't really say.

Boulanger: Roger, how, if at all, does the sonic feedback which you receive during the various stages of the compositional process affect and possibly redirect your original notions about the piece?

Reynolds: I find that composition involves a certain necessary schizophrenia. That is to say, I have at the same time to maintain a complete confidence in the correctness and the force of my initial decisions while at the same time withhold final agreement until I've found the various portions of the totality. I must begin with an extremely firm sense of my source materials, my structural intention, and my "tools"—a set of techniques, devices, and strategies for exploration.

I am rarely surprised by the relationship between what I plan and what happens. On the other hand, if what I plan always resulted in something that I expected, I would find work in music unpleasant and unchallenging. I like to put myself in the position where, although I maintain this confident exterior, there is some fairly substantial element of doubt left as the process of generating both instrumental and digitally processed materials evolves. I maintain a firm hold on the overall picture but I want there to be unexpected developments.

I think it is imperative while planning to foresee stages of the evolution of the work. But during the tool-building stage—solving the musical problems or creating the musical functions—the results are never completely foreseeable. Things that emerge in the development of those tools can alter the way in which I finally realize the initial ideas—those intentions which I had fairly clearly mapped out

before I started the tool building. Thus, there is a fair amount of interaction.

Boulanger: As I understand it then, your compositional research or "tool development" is an ongoing process, one which might carry over from composition to composition and whose results might alter your preconceptions about the piece. What about the real-time feedback aspect of the medium?

Reynolds: If it were possible to have real-time control over balance, timing, rhythmic and spatial character, dynamic interaction and blending, I would find a very different palette of potential. And I think that instead of finding it more attractive I would find it less attractive. The reason that I would find it less attractive is that I am most interested in that interplay between preplanning or rational conception and the resistance encountered by one's intuitive faculty during the course of the actual manifestation of the plan. I find the friction which exists between the thing which is definite as an idea, and the thing which is definite as an experience, very engaging. Paradoxically then, if real-time systems were developed that totally satisfied my requirements of such systems, they would be less attractive to me because I value that resistance and that rather bizarre form of feedback.

Electronic versus Instrumental Composition

Boulanger: Joji, what effect has working with electronics had on your instrumental writing?

Yuasa: There is a strong interaction between my electronic and instrumental music, but there are definitely differences between them. Yet from the very beginning I felt I should try to unite the two worlds. And while I am deeply aware of the characteristic differences and functions of the two mediums, I do not like to differentiate as far as my compositional attitude is concerned.

Boulanger: Are there any specific instances which illustrate the crossover of ideas or typify your "unified attitude"?

Yuasa: When attempting to create written scores for my early concrète works I was confronted by the fact that the sounds and music that I was making could obviously not be represented on the five-line staff, yet I wanted to provide a written counterpart to the tape. This basic need led me to consider and employ various forms of graphic notation, and I soon realized that it would be possible to create unique formal situations by employing graphic notation for instrumentalists.

But it has not only been the tape medium that has influenced my instrumental writing. Rather, the whole set of changes associated with the technological revolution have had a most significant impact on my compositional views. Technology has objectified our perceptions in a unique way. In a sense, through it we have gained access to "pure experience." For example, in our age it is commonplace for people to observe their world from a "bird's-eye" view. Yet traditionally this perspective would not have been possible without the exertion of a great deal of energy on the part of the individual—to view the panorama one would have to literally climb the mountain. Also, our relative perception of distance and speed and its impact on our sense of time has affected considerable changes. Thus the fundamental revolution is our capacity to alter our perspective with regard to space and time, of which the ability to create, control, and manipulate sound is but one such manifestation, has altered in a most drastic way the type of music I write. Obviously these fundamental changes would have a strong impact on the arts and it is these new sensations that have resulted in a new sense of music.

Computer Transformation of Sound

Boulanger: Roger, in your more recent CARL composition, *Transfigured Wind* for flute, orchestra, and four-channel tape, the source material, limited to solo flute, is subjected to a wide range of computer transformations, or perhaps more appropriately, "transfigurations." Describe, if you would, some of your ideas concerning your concept of "identity" under algorithmic transfiguration.
Reynolds: In 1968 I came upon a story by Samuel Becket called *PING* and decided that I wanted to do a work on it. The story was an extraordinary exercise in permutation: the reconfiguration of meaning

by the reordering of a very slowly evolving set of words. My first thought was song, but I later decided that a more appropriate approach would be to use the voices of old men. So I sent this text to six elderly men that I knew and asked people in the area to record their voices. When I got the tapes back and I started splicing, first sentence by sentence, then phrase by phrase, word by word, and even sections of words, I discovered, somewhat to my surprise, that there was no useful element that was small enough to be free of the meaning that the reader had invested in his reading. In other words, the work itself and the sound of the word being spoken could not be made neutral, no matter how many splices I made. No matter how I interleaved these six different voices, I couldn't make the statement neutral.

When I first heard Harvey Sollberger playing the flute lines I had written for him in *Transfigured Wind*, I realized that, although he was playing all the correct rhythms, dynamics, and pitches, I often wasn't hearing what I had meant the phrases to say.

Of course it wasn't that the line should "say" something literal or be some form of narration, but there was a direction, a character to the phrase, and I would often have to explain to Harvey the sort of thing I had in mind. He would, of course, instantly understand and invest the phrase with this other meaning, this other musicality that was there in some shadowy form. The computer gave me an opportunity to play with and to explore this meaning, this musicality that is not completely specified by a succession of notes and rhythms because it allowed me to alter the recorded flute's horizontal and vertical structure and to distribute these sounds in various simulated spaces.

Horizontal reconfiguration was achieved with a phase-vocoder. This signal processing tool allowed me to examine and resynthesize "slices" of the flute sonority. Via the vocoder, the actual sonority of the instrument—which was previously considered to be impenetrable—becomes available for partial or modified reconstruction and truly marvelous extension.

Vertical reconfiguration of the source material was achieved through the implementation by Mark

Dolson, a staff researcher at CME, of two algorithms that I designed for this purpose. The two algorithms—*spirlz* and *splitz*—"splice" the source material into a user-specified proportion series and then, according to various permutation schemes, reconfigure the fragments into unprecedented structures. Although these algorithms totally alter the contour of the original phrase, in some sense its meaning or identity remains the same.

Use of Metaphor and Randomness

Boulanger: Joji, the title of your composition, *Toward the Midnight Sun*, for piano and four-channel tape, refers to an attitude found in traditional Noh Theatre—the midnight sun represents the unattainable goal of perfection. How does a guiding metaphor of this sort act as a compositional impetus or focus? Does it suggest the sonic vocabulary for the composition? Is this metaphor your *Icon*?

Yuasa: It is rather difficult to describe with my poor English. I am mainly concerned with the basic image of the midnight sun. It is apparent that sunshine at midnight is beyond verbal or literal description. I am trying to make computer sounds that are beyond the world, beyond literal description.

I am most interested in the computer's ability to simulate artificial spaces and to distribute sounds in them. I don't think that, at this stage, the sound of computer music itself has surpassed the achievements of analog and concrète electronic music, but the spatial capabilities far exceed what was possible with the analog technology of the past. I make use of these new distributional possibilities to create the "sense of the beyond."

Boulanger: Charles, could you describe the utilization of randomness and natural modeling in *Bamboula Squared*?

Wuorinen: The tape part is the only aspect of the work that engages itself in the invocation of randomness. It uses a $1/f$ noise process for the selection of both the pitch content and the set of attack times. The intent, in part, is to create an intersection between the world of Western traditional musical values and certain modes and forms of natural

behavior. I believe that this goal has been achieved in some areas of the composition.

Thus, I use the computer not only to produce the sounds but to model certain kinds of behavior that are taken, ultimately, from contemplation of the natural world. These are transformed into musical entities, not in a literal way, but through metaphorical means. Composers have always tended to use musical object as pointers to objects outside the world of music. I believe my application to be in very much the same spirit.

Limiting Synthesis Possibilities

Boulanger: Allow me to play devil's advocate. *Icon* uses a single sound source—white noise. *Transfigured Wind* uses a single sound source—the flute. *Bamboula Squared* uses a single sound source—the plucked string algorithm. Since it is possible to create any type of sound with the computer, especially those that have never been heard before, why use only one? With an instrument of obviously limitless sonic possibilities at your disposal, why limit yourselves to such a degree?

Reynolds: It is simply evident that relationships and transformations can be more easily perceived and can be more effectively dealt with compositionally when they are sufficiently related to a single image. It seems to me that it is simply parsimonious to work that way. Thus, it is not an engineering compromise but an obvious artistic necessity.

Yuasa: The ability to produce a wide variety of sounds does not represent any unique feature of the computer. A good musician (in real time for that matter) can produce an equally wide variety of sounds which "have never been heard before." My main interest is to discover and then utilize those features that are truly unique. One such feature, as I stated previously, is the computer's ability to simulate the movement of sounds through virtual space. The subtle shaping of noise and the equally refined synthesis of various listening environments seem truer to the intrinsic nature of the computer than the ability to emulate or create sounds.

Wuorinen: Freedom is an illusion, and limitations are necessary to art.

Unpredictable Algorithms

Boulanger: In *Toward the Midnight Sun* portions of the solo piano part were determined by probabilistic means. In *Bamboula Squared* the pitches and rhythms of the tape were selected by a $1/f$ algorithm. In *Transfigured Wind* algorithms scramble original flute phrases into totally different ones. What is the role of the composer when some of the outcome is predictable and some is not?

Wuorinen: The role is the same as it always is, namely, to specify as much detail as the plan of the work decrees is essential in order that the realization of the plan results in an object that is identifiable as itself.

I wanted to be in total control of the instrumental writing and so the computer plays no part in it. As for the tape, I make no specific pitch or rhythmic choices, but the algorithm by which the computer makes its choices had been thoroughly tested and modified until it produced results which were of the class and nature that I wanted. There are many instances of music old and new, Eastern and Western, in which choices are made spontaneously by human performers. Here is simply a transference of what some might say is a very modest application of artificial intelligence.

Yuasa: It depends upon what kind of music I write. When I work, I am engaged in an intuitive way of composition and at the same time a systematic way of composition. What this means is that I place myself between control and decontrol. I don't hate intuition—it is quite important. But if we always use the intuitive, we tend to behave stereotypically. So in order to counterbalance stereotypical behavior, I employ strict systematic procedures. What results is an interesting interactive relationship between system and intuition.

Over the past twenty-five years I have devised various methods for controlling randomness and have employed the output of these processes in my instrumental as well as my electronic music. (The values were attained by throwing dice thousands of times.) Obviously, the computer is a very efficient tool for generating a wide variety of weighted random functions, and so at present I am automating a number of my algorithms.

Boulanger: How good a composer is the computer in *Transfigured Wind*?

Reynolds: I've started to employ certain algorithms and am involved in the study of their effect on pre-existing musical material. What interests me is the way that an ordering strategy affects the way I perceive a structure that has already been ordered. I find this interaction, between an initial integrity and an overriding structural procedure, quite fascinating.

In *Transfigured Wind* for the first time, I have applied these algorithmic notions—notions about systematic ways of shuffling parts of a real or an imaginary original—to the generation of the instrumental material as well as the tape sounds. Most of the instrumental textures are derived from the same procedure, but the original in this case is theoretical; it has not been recorded. The original exists only as a musical scheme. What one hears is nothing but that original's transformation through the algorithmic reordering.

I am most intrigued and interested when the resultant order is manifest in such a way that its recognition is slightly out of reach. With my current set of algorithms it is possible to produce a resultant order that points clearly to the process. But it is also possible to "seed" the algorithm in such a way that it is impossible to determine how the resultant order was arrived at, yet this resultant is still clearly recognizable as a member of the same class. This interaction—between a structure that is compelling because it is perceived and one that is more subtle because it is (perhaps just) beyond conscious apprehension—is what interests me the most.

Music and Science

Boulanger: In his 1958 article "Who Cares if You Listen," Milton Babbitt seems to assert that there is such a thing as "musical intelligence" and that music is as refined and complex a discipline as any branch of the sciences. Might not the computer, then, be considered the composer/scientist's laboratory apparatus—a tool for the evaluation of theoretical constructs against perceptual realities? And if so, is it possible at such an early stage to characterize this new breed of "scientartist" and to possibly draw some distinctions between musical and scientific experiment?

Wuorinen: The title of the Babbitt article was added by an editor and it is very unfortunate that Milton has been associated with the sensationalist and illiterate sentiments represented by that title. It has nothing to do with what he was saying.

I do not necessarily enjoy nor subscribe to the notion of a small group of grave eggheads sitting around discoursing on the most rarefied realms of music. Whether or not that is truly Babbitt's ideal, I am not sure. I have enormous affection, respect, and friendship for him and a high regard for his music, and these remarks do not in any way represent a criticism of his attitude.

I think that it is a very unfortunate fact that the word "theory" is used to describe speculation or generalization in music and the other arts, because the notion of theory in the sciences means something that can be falsified by fact or by experiment. There is really no such analogous situation in the case of the arts. If you show me something that you claim is a successful manifestation of your theoretical ideas, and I tell you that I can't stand it, that's the end of the discussion. And even if I do like it, even if we all like it in some sense, it still proves nothing.

Music research might conceivably consist of certain proposals. Some have been made about as-yet-untested resources that composers or other musicians might find interesting. The proof of that pudding, of course, is always in whether they do indeed find them interesting. It's true in the case of the sciences as well that there are areas of fashion, that there are good ideas that are ignored and shouldn't be, and ideas that are held long after the time in which they were useful. Nevertheless, in the case of the arts, it really is what everybody likes in the long run that determines what has validity. And while others may engage themselves with the question of why it is that this or that person or group likes this or that artistic manifestation, I think a practicing composer has enough to do with simply writing his music.

So the Babbittonian vision, if it ever existed (and

in fact it never did), of music turning into an objective discipline in which we could all measure, at least successfully as some of the sciences claim to do, the worth of individual work, seems to me to be a dream. And not a dream that seems to be particularly worth realizing either.

Reynolds: Certainly one thing that may be a parallel between the scientific and the artistic use of machines is that a certain amount of orderliness is called for. One needs to understand how to communicate with the machine. You need to give it your specifications in an acceptable order and have some notion about the difference between the demands which you are making and the possible capacities of the machine. There are, in other words, a lot of planning stages that are still necessary even in the case of a very sophisticated computer music facility.

Another distinction between scientists and artists might have something to do with the circumstances under which compromise seems to be admissible. I have noticed that there are often remarkable and sometimes unbridgeable conflicts between scientifically oriented people and artistically oriented people at points where compromise seems called for on one or another's part. It suggests to me that underneath the procedural surfaces of our different areas or our different ways of approaching knowledge, there are some fairly strong and unspoken sets of assumptions. I don't think that it's just procedure, and I don't think that it's just value. It's at those points where one has to say, "I'll let it go" or "I won't let it go" that we find the fiber of the person.

Commercial Music Technology

Boulanger: I bought my two-year-old son an eight-dollar keyboard which, when you pressed middle C, would play "Yankee Doodle," and when you pressed the D above, would play "London Bridge." With it, I thought he might learn a few simple folk songs. A week later, I was working on something at the piano and he came over, sat beside me, and began repeatedly striking an F-sharp and shouting "happy birthday, Daddy, happy birthday!" The experience shook me somewhat. He had obviously concluded that all keyboards should play your favorite song when you press the correct key. What are your feelings about the popular manifestations of the music technology?

Wuorinen: "Happy Birthday" is still copyrighted. I hope that the manufacturer of that device has paid proper licensing fees to Sonny Burcher.

I have one very brief remark to make about this. Sooner or later there has got to be a reckoning between musicians and designers of commercially available equipment. Some scientists believe that their mere capacity to respond, in some vague way, to art qualifies them to make judgments about it. This attitude is representative of a terrible cultural problem. Their naïve judgments are manifested musically in the sounds and design of commercially available instruments that are just appalling. I shudder to think about the effect on the generation of young listeners who are being exposed to such a low acoustic standard, especially at such high volume levels. I think it's very serious.

Reynolds: I think that we are at an extraordinarily exciting stage. But the difficulty that we will increasingly face relates to something Joji said at the very beginning concerning our ability to view the electronic medium as an instrument. I think that this will definitely become the way it is thought of. Yet, it was the generality and flexibility of the system here at CARL that made it possible for each of us to design special capabilities that had not existed before. We were able to build strong allies (tools) as we went along because we were in no way predisposed by engineering compromise or negligence. It certainly appears inevitable that, when the general-purpose facility gives way to, in the most exalted cases, "work stations," and in the least exalted ones, "glorified organs," the inflexibility that will result will be attended, I fear, by a cessation of imaginative developments, both in terms of the materials of music and in the ways of organizing these materials.

Yuasa: I agree with Roger. It is the essential and intrinsic nature of the artist that as soon as something becomes a convention we cannot stand it.

II

Composition

Curtis Roads

Overview

The practice of composition has been deeply affected by the spread of computer music systems. The computer music tool kit includes, but is not limited to, the following: digital sound synthesis, sampling, sound processing, and editing; algorithmic composition software; music notation editors and printers; performance software; and a battery of musical input devices or controllers (the physical instruments that performers manipulate to make music).

The input device is often, but not always, the starting point for compositional work. In computer music, input devices do not always generate sound by themselves; but they do generate control signals that can be sent to a synthesizer, which in turn produces sound. Some input devices are based on traditional instruments (such as electronically rigged saxophones or keyboards), and some are based on new designs that present radically different musical possibilities. These include the control of entire ensembles of electronic instruments, the control of a synthesizer by a dancer, and interaction with musically intelligent machines. Michel Waisvisz's "Hands"—a pair of electronic gloves outfitted with switches—is a prime example of the kind of innovative input device that is now possible with digital technology (Roads 1986a).

These striking changes in instrumentation and in compositional practice have prompted a new view of the sound materials and structures of music (Roads 1986). The French composer Tristan Murail (1984) has asked: "Why speak anymore of music in terms of notes? . . . Why distinguish the notion of harmony from that of timbre? . . . Why divide the frequency space into octaves, and then each octave into twelve?" Present technology imposes no such constraints; we are bounded only by our cultural prejudices.

Since the middle of the twentieth century there has been an increasing number of composers, and an explosion of compositional methods. The growth of electronic and computer music has accelerated this diversity. No one book could begin to cover all the techniques of composition that now exist. It may be years before a sharper picture emerges

from the diffused energy of late-twentieth-century composition.

The role of the composer has also changed. In the 1960s and the 1970s many institutes were founded to develop high-technology music-making. These were based at universities in the United States and at radio stations and government-sponsored foundations in other countries. The formation of the institutes, and the associated need to raise funds to support them, mandated that the notion of scientific research become enmeshed with that of composition. Many composers took on dual roles as composers and researchers.

During the early years of computer music, composers worked with relatively primitive technology, obtaining mixed results. Some pieces will be appreciated only in historical context. In a few cases (Jean-Claude Risset's 1970 work *Mutations* comes to mind), composers transcended technological limits to create pieces that deserve a more general and enduring status. Fortunately, the technological climate has improved greatly. Thousands of musicians have set up home computer music systems, and much research can be pursued independently.

Today two overlapping categories of computer music systems stand out. One is based on live performance, the other on studio technique. Live-performance computer music has seen a flurry of development prompted by the availability of inexpensive equipment linked by the Musical Instrument Digital Interface (the subject of the articles in part III). Live improvisation using computers and digital synthesizers, which was impossible just a few years ago (see Hiller and Isaacson 1959 and Hiller 1970 for a historical perspective), is now a hotbed of activity. The groundwork for much of the advanced work being done in this area was laid (as George Lewis has noted; see Roads 1985a) by Charlie Parker, John Coltrane, Ornette Coleman, Cecil Taylor, and other jazz musicians in the 1950s. They expanded the musical vocabulary while also redefining the interaction in ensembles. Electronic music ensembles formed in the 1970s and the 1980s also contributed to this process (Bernardini 1986).

Electronic studio technique began in the early

1950s with tape music in the United States, elektronische Musik in Germany, and musique concrète in France, and was refined in many other countries. From these beginnings, studio technique has evolved into powerful computer-based environments for generating, sampling, processing, mixing, and editing sound. At its best, studio technique offers the composer the ultimate in tools for refining individual sounds and organizing complex sound structures. Studio work usually results in a finished composition, recorded on tape or in another medium. This finished composition can be performed on its own in a concert hall, integrated with elaborate multimedia effects, or distributed as a tape or a disk for home playback.

Jean-Claude Risset, a master of studio technique, is one of the most respected composers of computer music. His contribution is a kind of musical autobiography that traces his research and composition efforts from the early 1960s at Bell Telephone Laboratories to the 1980s in Marseille. Although Risset was one of the pioneers in the development of computer-generated sound spectra and rich inharmonic effects (Risset 1968, 1985), his recent work reflects a general trend among composers: an increasing affection for natural sound, recorded and processed with digital techniques. A prime example is Risset's 1986 composition *Sud*, which mixes recorded ocean sounds with synthetic sounds.

The English composer Jonathan Harvey also manipulates natural sounds, such as the sounds of boys' voices or bells in his composition *Mortuous Plango, Vivos Voco (I cry for the dead, I call the living)*. His article describes the methods he used to analyze and resynthesize bell sounds, substituting a synthetic boy's voice for the partials of the bell. This work was completed on a large computer system at IRCAM, the Paris-based computer music institute sponsored by the French government.

Digital sound requires a loudspeaker or headphones to be heard. Naturally, the quality of the speakers used affects the sound heard by the listeners. And, as the composer Dexter Morrill points out in article 10, the placement of the speakers is an important compositional parameter, particularly in works that involve human performers on stage.

A major question is whether to merge or to contrast the sound of the performers with other sounds.

Behind the sound of a composition stands its theory—the set of beliefs and logical concepts that inform compositional decision-making. Formalism—the tendency to base the theory of work on an explicit logical system—is an ever-present impulse in all art forms. Music has an especially rich formalist history, so it is no surprise that issues of compositional structure and process are just as important to many composers as the audible result. In computer music, this is borne out by the widespread use of *algorithmic* or *procedural* composition. In algorithmic composition, the composer uses computer programs to determine fundamental elements of the piece. Algorithms can be used to create form on many levels, from macrostructure (the number and ordering of large-scale events, the phrase structure, and the overall amplitude shape) to microstructure (the shape of the digital waveform, the amplitude curves of individual partials, and microvariations in numerous synthesis parameters, such as vibrato) (Roads 1987).

History records as the first computer-composed piece *Push-Button Bertha*, a light-hearted ode to a robot created in 1956 by programmers Martin Klein and Douglas Bolitho and Hollywood lyricist Jack Kirby (Hiller 1970; Ames 1987). The concept of algorithmic composition by computer was furthered by Lejaren Hiller and Leonard Isaacson in the late 1950s at the University of Illinois (Hiller and Isaacson 1959). Hiller was the first composer to apply algorithmic composition methods to art music. In addition, he is a vigorous experimenter and an articulate spokesman for the methodology. Article 8 is a retrospective by Hiller on his many experiments, including his famous collaboration with John Cage on the multimedia spectacle *HPSCHD*.

More possibilities of algorithmic composition are described in the articles by McNabb, Laske, Englert, Truax, Chadabe, Vaggione, and Arveiller. To be sure, the application of algorithmic techniques varies widely among these composers. For Michael McNabb, a Stanford-based composer whose works are available on several commercial recordings, large-scale form is determined by the composer but software procedures sometimes determine the sound microstructure. For example, McNabb used various automated procedures to precisely control vibrato effects throughout his lushly orchestrated 1978 composition *Dreamsong*. Vibrato plays an important structural role in *Dreamsong* by causing seemingly unrelated tones to fuse into a single sound object. *Dreamsong*'s technical virtuosity makes it a landmark composition in the development of computer sound synthesis.

In contrast to McNabb's romantic compositional tendencies, Otto Laske is a representative of the systematic and rational tradition in composition. Laske was trained under Theodor Adorno as both a philosopher and a composer. (Adorno was an ardent defender of Arnold Schoenberg's twelve-tone method of composition—see Adorno 1973.) Laske traces the systematic tradition back to Guillaume de Machaut's isorhythmic motets and Anton von Webern's concentrated structural methods. His article explicates the logic and the musical implications of two influential composition programs: Project One and Project Two, written by Gottfried Michael Koenig in the early 1970s. (On Koenig, see Roads 1978 and article 32.)

Barry Truax has long used computer software for composition. In the early 1970s, he was one of the first to take advantage of the *frequency modulation* (FM) method of digital synthesis (Chowning 1973). In article 14, his exegesis of *Arras* (1980), Truax describes his application of systematic variations of the FM technique to generate bands of evolving harmonic and inharmonic spectra. (For more information on the theory of *carrier-to-modulator ratios*, see Truax 1977.)

Like Truax, the Paris-based composer Giuseppe Englert writes his own algorithms to determine the musical structure of his works. In article 13 he describes an algorithm he calls the *intersecting sine function polynomial*—a pair of interacting sine functions—which he uses to generate the macrostructure of his onstage performance with a digital synthesizer.

In article 16 another Paris-based composer, Horacio Vaggione, describes the realization of his award-winning piece *Octuor* (1982) at IRCAM. This composition employs a novel approach of creating several sound files using various synthesis techniques, and then applying automated editing and mixing techniques to elaborate this material into an extremely animated work.

Affordable computer music systems have fostered the new genre of *algorithmic music performance*. Sequencer and performance software enable a musician sitting at a keyboard or manipulating an input device to take on the role of conductor of an ensemble of synthetic players reading from a previously entered score. (The synthetic players are actually synthesizer voices.) In addition, some musicians are intrigued with improvising live with an ensemble of synthetic players, which respond to cues, riffs, and stylistic constraints that the musician has entered into the computer. In article 15 Joel Chadabe calls this real-time variation on algorithmic composition *interactive composing*. This is one of the most rapidly expanding areas of computer music. Chadabe's enterprise, Intelligent Music, is one of several companies that distribute software and hardware for interactive composing (Zicarrelli 1987). (Interactive composing involves a musician, an input device, a computer running musical algorithms, and a real-time sound synthesizer controlled by the computer. Since much of the responsibility for creating the music is shifted to the computer, the musical effectiveness of this approach is very much constrained by the software that interprets the performer's gestures and translates them into music.)

With all the technical and musical developments that have taken place in recent years, the teaching of algorithmic composition clearly requires a departure from traditional conservatory training. Music conservatories are struggling, not always successfully, to adapt to the changes in the musical world wrought by electronic instruments and compositional workstations. Pedagogy in computer music composition is the subject of article 18, in which Jacques Arveiller (a former colleague of Giuseppe Englert at the Université de Paris VIII–Vincennes) argues that writing composition programs is a good way to learn about composition. Although there is a danger that the student will get lost in the "recursive" activity of writing programs without "musical side effects," Arveiller points out the benefits of musical programming for both music and computer science students, and describes the challenges that instructors face in teaching students to cross the traditional disciplinary boundaries.

The articles in this part demonstrate the interdependence among musical thinking, musical practice, and technology. As Herbert Brün noted years ago, the tools we use to compose shape our compositions, whether or not we are aware of this influence (Brün 1970). *Computer Music Journal* has always served as both a record of research in music technology and a medium in which composers can describe their theories and techniques. Hence, the articles in this part, together with recent books (e.g. Roads 1985b; Dodge and Jerse 1985; Emmerson 1987) and recordings, constitute an important resource for those interested in the development of contemporary musical thought.

References

Adorno, T. 1973. *Philosophy of Modern Music*. Tr. A. Mitchell and W. Blomster. New York: Seabury.

Ames, C. 1987. "Automated Composition in Retrospect." *Leonardo* 20(2): 169–186.

Bernardini, N. 1986. "Live Electronics." In A. Vidolin and R. Doati, eds., *Nuova Atlantide* (Venice: Biennale di Venezia).

Brün, H. 1970. "From Musical Ideas to Computers and Back." In H. Lincoln, ed., *The Computer and Music* (Ithaca, N.Y.: Cornell University Press).

Chowning, J. 1973. "The Synthesis of Complex Spectra by Means of Frequency Modulation." *Journal of the Audio Engineering Society* 21(7): 526–534. Reprinted in C. Roads and J. Strawn, eds., *Foundations of Computer Music* (Cambridge, Mass.: MIT Press, 1985).

Dodge, C., and T. Jerse. 1985. *Computer Music*. New York: Schirmer.

Emmerson, S. 1987. *The Language of Electroacoustic Music*. New York: Harwood.

Hiller, L. 1970. "Music Composed with Computers—A Historical Survey." In H. Lincoln, ed., *The Computer and Music* (Ithaca, N.Y.: Cornell University Press).

Hiller, L. and L. Isaacson. 1959. *Experimental Music*. New York: McGraw-Hill.

Murail, T. 1984. "Spectres et lutins." In *Algorithmus, Klang, Natur: Abkehr vom Materialdenken* (Mainz: Schott).

Risset, J.-C. 1968. *An Introductory Catalogue of Computer Synthesized Sounds*. Murray Hill, N.J.: Bell Telephone Laboratories.

Risset, J.-C. 1985. "Digital Techniques and Sound Structure in Music." In C. Roads, ed., *Composers and the Computer* (Los Altos, Calif.: Kaufmann).

Roads, C. 1978. "An Interview with Gottfried Michael Koenig." *Computer Music Journal* 2(3): 11–15. Reprinted in C. Roads and J. Strawn, eds., *Foundations of Computer Music* (Cambridge, Mass.: MIT Press, 1985).

Roads, C. 1985a. "Improvisation with George Lewis." In C. Roads, ed., *Composers and the Computer* (Los Altos, Calif.: Kaufmann).

Roads, C., ed. 1985b. *Composers and the Computer*. Los Altos, Calif.: Kaufmann.

Roads, C., ed. 1986. "A Symposium on Composition." *Computer Music Journal* 10(1): 40–63.

Roads, C. 1987. "Esperienze di Composizione Assistata da Calculatore." In S. Tamburini and M. Bagella, eds., *I Profili del Suono* (Rome: Musica Verticale–Galzerano).

Truax, B. 1977. "Organizational Techniques for *c:m* Ratios in Frequency Modulation." *Computer Music Journal* 1(4): 39–45. Reprinted in C. Roads and J. Strawn, eds., *Foundations of Computer Music* (Cambridge, Mass.: MIT Press, 1985).

Zicarrelli, D. 1987. "M and Jam Factory." *Computer Music Journal* 11(4): 13–29.

7

Jean-Claude Risset
Faculté des Sciences de Luminy
et Laboratoire de Mécanique et d'Acoustique
Marseille, France

Computer Music Experiments 1964– . . .

My initial motivation to enter the computer music field was musical rather than technical, although I had a background in both music and science. My scientific training at the Ecole Normale Supérieure in Paris was in mathematics and physics, not in computer science, a field that did not exist in the 1950s. Independently, I studied piano with Robert Trimaille, and this was an essential experience for me. I also studied harmony, counterpoint, and composition with André Jolivet. The late French composer had worked with Varèse in the 1930s; he had a strong temperament and a deep feeling for the idiosyncrasies of instruments. During a composition seminar he held in 1962 in Aix, he had Lejaren Hiller give a presentation of his work. The computer excited little musical interest in France at that time, except among a few individuals like Moles, Barbaud, Philippot, and Xenakis. My first piece for orchestra was played in 1963 at the French Radio: it reinforced my vivid interest in timbre and its capacity to convey specific musical ideas.

I wanted to increase the functional part of timbre in my composing. Yet I resisted turning to electronic music—in Paris, it was mostly Pierre Schaeffer's *musique concrète*. I felt that electronic music yielded dull sounds that could only be made lively through manipulations which, to a large extent, ruined the control the composer could have over them. On the other hand, *musique concrète* did open an infinite world of sounds for music—but the control and manipulation one could exert upon them was rudimentary with respect to the richness of the sounds, which favored an esthetics of collage. Both techniques seemed to me to rely on ready-made objects or processes, which the composer could only warp for his purposes. In 1962, I met

Pierre Barbaud, the French pioneer of computer music composition, but I was not so interested in this direction.

Thanks mainly to Max Mathews, a new branch of electronic music appeared with computer synthesis of sound. I had the privilege to be able to come work with Max in 1964. My science professor, Pierre Grivet, had been impressed by the clear and lucid article Max published in *Science* in 1963: "The Computer as a Musical Instrument." With the help of John Pierce, Grivet arranged for me to get a grant from D.G.R.S.T., a French agency for research, permitting me to work at Bell Laboratories as a research-composer in residence. In this capacity, I succeeded Jim Tenney, who was, I believe, the first composer to make a significant musical use of computer synthesis of sound.

Arrival at Bell Laboratories

My arrival in the States in 1964 was an unforgettable experience. I met Max Mathews, John Pierce, Jim Tenney, Varèse, and many lively scientists and artists. Max had several ideas for research, including computer composition, but I elected to focus on timbre. The palette of computer sound, potentially boundless, was in fact quite restricted, and one did not know how to generate certain sounds.

In particular, brassy sounds resisted synthesis efforts. I had to convince myself that the recipes of respected acoustics treatises (like H. F. Olson's) did not work. As one may judge from tones synthesized from such recipes, they did not (cf. Sound Example 1). So I began a study on the correlates of trumpet tone quality. I recorded trumpet samples, analyzed them with the sound spectrograph and with the computer, displaying the evolution in time of individual harmonics' amplitudes. From this analysis, it was possible to imitate isolated tones with the help of the Music V program, written by Joan Miller and Max. I used a different envelope function for each harmonic, approximating the curves yielded by the analysis in terms of piecewise linear func-

This article is an adaptation of a lecture presented by the author as a guest composer at the 1983 International Computer Music Conference, organized at the Eastman School of Music, Rochester, and directed by Allan Schindler.

Computer Music Journal, Vol. 9, No. 1,
Spring 1985

Fig. 1. Jean-Claude Risset, 1984.

Fig. 2. Line-segment functions that approximate the evolution in time of 13 harmonics of a D4 trumpet tone lasting 0.2 sec. I have used such functions, drawn from analysis of real tones, to control the harmonic amplitudes of synthetic tones (Risset 1965).

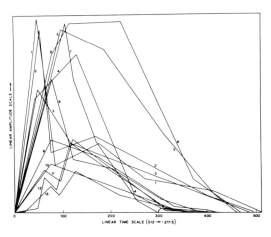

tions (Fig. 2). (Despite the long turnaround time of the computer center, I was lucky to have the converter down the hall, while Jim Randall, Hubert Howe, the late Godfrey Winham, and others had to come from Princeton to use the converters) But the descriptions of the tones were very complex, and varied from one tone to another. I had to try to reduce this information to the essential, that is, to those features that are the most significant to the ear. I checked by synthesis the aural relevance of several aspects, and I found that the most salient characteristic of brass tones was the fact that the spectrum varied with loudness, so as to increase the proportion of high-frequency energy when the loudness increases. Thus the timbre is mainly characterized here by a property, a law of variation, a relationship between physical parameters, rather than by a physical invariant such as a spectrum (Risset 1965; Risset and Mathews 1969; Risset and Wessel 1982). This nonlinear behavior, later studied by James Beauchamp, was operational over a rather wide range to obtain brassy sounds. Robert Moog designed a voltage-controlled filter whose bandwidth increased with the control voltage. It generated brassy sounds by deriving the control voltage from the amplitude envelope of the input. John Chowning (1973) implemented this characteristic in a very ele-

gant fashion using frequency modulation (FM). Dexter Morrill has used this very effectively in his synthesis work. The point of instrumental imitation is not only instrument duplication, of course. In particular, it sheds light on properties that can endow sounds with naturalness, richness, and also give them a characteristic identity.

Despite Varèse's assistance, my efforts to postpone my military service to continue this work were in vain, and I had to come back to France in 1965, so I could not exploit this study and compose pieces at that time. I obtained my "Thèse d'Etat" in Orsay in 1967. My thesis centered on this trumpet study and on previous studies of auditory processes.

I returned in 1967 to Bell Laboratories, where I stayed two years. When I arrived, Vladimir Ussachevsky was working there, and I enjoyed and benefited by interacting with him. At that time, Max Mathews had designed Music V as a more easily portable music compiler, and the program coding was nearly completed thanks to Dick Moore, whom I met then, and Joan Miller (Mathews et al. 1969). I helped complete and debug the program, and I tried a number of sonic structures I had in mind.

Many of the processes I worked on then were intended for *Little Boy*, a play by Pierre Halet (1968). My contribution was more than plain incidental

Fig. 3. Spectral analysis of a chord. Successive harmonics of each tone of the chord appear successively in decreasing order, at different rates for different notes of the chord (cf. Sound Example 3).

Fig. 4. Belllike tones (a) transformed into fluid textures (b). The unequally spaced components of the bellliketones have different durations but the same amplitude envelope: a short attack followed by an exponential decay. (b) is deduced from (a) by changing the envelope to a smooth belllike shape. The various components reach their maximum amplitude at different times. Hence, instead of fusing into a belllike attack, they yield textures in which the components are dispersed like white light through a prism (cf. Sound Example 5).

Frequency

(linear scale)

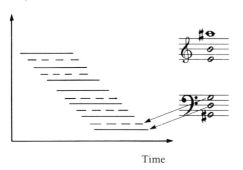

Time

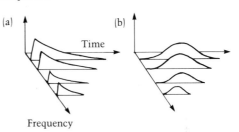

Amplitude

(a)   Time   (b)

Frequency

music. I worked with the playwright while he was writing, before the intervention of any stage director. The theme was the bombing of Hiroshima, revived through the phantasms of the pilot Eatherly—hence the music was to include realistic sound effects, but in close relation to the instrumental part—soprano and chamber ensemble as well as computer-synthesized tape (*Voice of the Computer*, Decca Records DL 710180). So, for example (Sound Example 2), a jazzlike theme, initially played by the instruments, is messed up in the agitated mind of the pilot: the instrumentlike synthetic sounds run wild and turn into gunfire. Also I used harmonic arpeggios, to make textures emanate from a given chord. In Sound Example 3, the harmonics of different notes of a chord appear in succession as shown by Fig. 3, with a gradual attack and decay. The rate of succession is different for different notes of the chord. Only at the end is the underlying harmony clearly revealed. (I called this process *spectral analysis* of a chord.) Then slowly gliding sounds take over in the example, suggesting plane noises but based on the same chord. I used such gliding inharmonic chords—maintaining a fixed frequency difference between the components, as hinted by John Clough—in nested structures. The relationship between the frequencies of the components is reproduced in the relationship between the frequencies of the tones.

If I change some of the harmonic envelopes into percussive ones, I get a new harmonic arpeggio—related but different (Sound Example 4). I am interested in these kinds of intimate transformations that change certain aspects while preserving others. Synthesis makes this easy. To do it from recorded sounds, one has to warp the synthesis parameters after a preliminary analysis, as can be done with linear predictive coding (LPC) or the phase vocoder. Similarly, I took advantage of synthesis to turn belllike sounds into fluid textures. The percussive, synchronous attack biased the listener toward synthetic perception of "bells," while a gradual bell-shaped curve makes amplitude behavior asynchronous for the components that have different durations (Fig. 4). Thus it biases the listener toward a more analytic perception of the sound "content." (This can be heard in Sound Example 5.) I used these transformations in *Little Boy*, *Mutations*, and other pieces, specially *Inharmonique* and *Mirages*. At the beginning of my piece *Mutations*, commissioned by the Groupe de Recherches Musicales and realized at Bell Laboratories in 1969 (INA-GRM recording AM 546 09), an arpeggioed chord is followed by a gonglike sound, composed like a chord, with the same implicit harmony. Here harmony is prolonged to become timbre, and timbre can become harmonically functional (Sound Example 6).

Back to *Little Boy*. The play by Pierre Halet staged the fall of the bomb. This fall was in fact only in the mind of the pilot, who identified himself with "Little Boy," the actual code name of the bomb.

Experiments 1964 – . . .   **69**

Fig. 5. Escher's waterfall in perpetual motion. I have synthesized tones be-having similarly to the flow of water, e.g., going up the scale but getting lower in pitch (cf. Sound Ex-ample 8).

Thus the fall did not reach any bottom, and I en-deavoured to convey this feeling with the music. At Bell Laboratories in 1964, Roger Shepard syn-thesized endlessly ascending successions of chro-matic tones. These tones were made up of octave components, with a bell-shaped spectrum tapering down at both ends. But I wanted gliding tones, not chromatic scales. Roger believed that a gap was needed between tones to achieve the illusion. Joe Kruskal did not succeed in making endless glis-sandi. I generated the effect by dynamically chang-ing frequencies and amplitudes in the Pass III of Music V, by increasing the spectral attenuation at the ends of the spectrum and by keeping a slow enough descent. I also obtained a quasi-spatial effect by delaying one track with respect with the other. Sound Example 7 presents in succession two por-tions of this "fall." In the first one, the tone de-scends in large spirals that are passed by some fast objects. In the second example, the context is a bit more complex, with some Shepardlike chromatic tones but also some gliding choruslike textures.

For the end of the play, I generated inverted *pitch helices*—sounds that go up the scale while getting lower, in a way similar to the flow of water in the drawing by Escher (Fig. 5). This was done by shift-ing down the spectral distribution while all compo-nents go up. Sound Example 8 is actually drawn from *Mutations* (1969). It begins with such an un-usual sound, then followed by tones with spectral scanning taking advantage of Chowning's frequency modulation (FM) technique. I met John Chowning in 1967. He explained his ongoing experiments on illusory moving sound sources and on spectral change through high-speed frequency modulation. He gave me his data together with a tape, so I could use the process right away.

Other Sound Paradoxes

The sound paradoxes I developed following Shepard interested me for *Little Boy*, but also for them-selves, since they are produced by independently controlling cues for two complementary aspects of pitch: tonal pitch, related to Cness, and spectral pitch, related to timbre. I studied the phenomenon,

playing various stimuli with conflicting cues to a number of listeners (including Stokowski, Berio, and others). Evidently various people weigh these at-tributes differently. Musically trained people always attribute a more or less substantial importance to tonal pitch, while a surprisingly large proportion of listeners (including music lovers and hi-fi fans) ap-pear to be tonedeaf (Charbonneau and Risset 1975; Risset 1969a, 1971, 1978; Wessel and Risset 1979). This gives a dizzying feeling about the distance be-tween what the musician intends and what is really perceived.

Sound Example 9 presents two weird sounds; more people hear the first one higher in pitch than the second one, but a few hear the contrary. The physical relation between these sounds may not be obvious: the second sound is obtained from the first one by doubling all its frequencies. Here is a sound that goes down for most listeners when one doubles the speed of the tape recorder! It shows that, especially for inharmonic sounds, pitch is not isomorphous to frequency, and more generally that auditory perception implies complex and specific procedures that should be taken into account.

I further investigated these paradoxes with Gérard Charbonneau in France, through multidimensional scaling and also evaluation of ear differences (Charbonneau and Risset 1975). In 1974, I heard an endlessly speeded pulse generated by Kenneth Knowlton. The year after in Marseille, I separated rhythmic cues just as I had with pitch cues. I produced, for instance, a rotating sound that goes up and down in pitch, but also with a beat that constantly speeds up while gradually getting slower (Sound Example 10). I used this in *Moments Newtoniens* (1977), a programmatic piece purporting to present musical analogs for some of Newton's scientific achievements (INA-GRM AM 546 09).

The Catalog of Computer-synthesized Sounds

In the spring of 1969, Max Mathews went to Stanford University to participate in one of the earliest computer music courses. He asked me for data about various sound structures I had been synthesizing for *Little Boy* and *Mutations*. I hastily assembled a recording of excerpts, with the Music V scores and some words of explanation. I entitled this document "An Introductory Catalog of Computer-synthesized Sounds" (Risset 1969b). My examples, of course, were meant as instances, as points of departure for developing timbres or sonic processes, and by no means as models. I believe such documents can be very useful. I often find it difficult to get started making a sound. Within a certain class of timbres it is easier to tune an instrument to one's specific desires. Throughout the music community, programs had been widely distributed (Music IV, Music 4BF, Music V, Music 360) but not synthesis data. Yet I had been impressed with the efficiency of communication when John Chowning left his data at Bell Laboratories. The input data for programs like Music V give a thorough record of the physical structure of the sounds and of their combination—a genuine score for the control of the sound structure.

I never really updated this catalog as I intended to, although I have been distributing some computer scores. At IRCAM, Denis Lorrain prepared such a catalog of my piece *Inharmonique* (Lorrain 1969) intended for student composers. Such documents are still not widespread enough in my opinion, although more and more have been coming out since my catalog and John Chowning's classic article on frequency modulation (1973), for instance Stanley Haynes's IRCAM reports and the data published in *Computer Music Journal* by Grey, Moorer, Morrill, Schottstaedt and others.

In 1968, Max Mathews and Dick Moore developed the real-time GROOVE system (Mathews and Moore 1970), while I was doing Music V synthesis. Pierre Ruiz and I adapted Music V to a minicomputer—actually a midicomputer, a Honeywell DDP-224, a 24-bit machine. (I realized *Mutations* on the 224 in 1969.)

Return to France

My return to France in 1969 was difficult. I keep good memories of a UNESCO conference on Music and Technology held in Stockholm in 1970. Max Mathews and Pierre Schaeffer were there, as well as Peter Zinovieff, Gustav Ciamaga, Herbert Brün, Murray Schaeffer, Lars Gunnar Bodin, and Jon Appleton (UNESCO 1971). Also the development of FM by John Chowning comforted me in the hope that computer synthesis could become simpler and cheaper, but there was no computer music system available. After one year of fund-raising, I implemented music synthesis in 1970 on a Hewlett-Packard computer in Orsay with the help of Gérard Charbonneau and Pierre Karatchenzeff. I believe this was the first installation in Europe. However, the Electronics Institute where this happened was not congenial to music. I went to Marseille in 1972 as professor in a short-lived music department. There I was helped by the artistically-inclined physicist Daniel Kastler to raise funds for a computer to equip a music research laboratory at the Centre Universitaire de Luminy. (I made the application with Alain Colmeraurer, the author of the Prolog programming language.) Eventually we got a Telemecanique T 1600 in 1974. (I used it until 1983.) With the help of Françoise Nayroles and Pierre Karatchenzeff, we got the first sounds from the T 1600 in 1975. John Chowning was visiting at this time. Despite the slow speed of the T 1600, I have realized several pieces on this machine with the Music V program. Sound Examples 11 and 12 present two excerpts from *Dialogues*, realized in 1975 (INA-GRM AM 546 09), a piece that attempts to closely intertwine instrumental and computer sounds. The computer begins and the instruments sneak in (Sound Example 11). In a later section, one hears a dialogue between piano and celesta—in chromatic scale—and high pitched computer sounds—in a linear scale: the computer plays harmonics of the notes D, F-sharp, G-sharp, A-sharp, C-sharp (Sound Example 12).

At that time, I was keen on a project I discussed with Max Mathews and John Chowning: to "marry" GROOVE and Music V, that is, to extract performance information to control non-real-time synthesis of a possibly different and complex nature. I never had a chance to really implement it, but I am glad to see that this kind of approach is being developed now, as exemplified by several papers presented at the 1983 International Computer Music Conference.

Founding of IRCAM

In 1972, Pierre Boulez had sketched his project for the Institut de Recherche et Coordination Acoustique/Musique (IRCAM), and he asked me to participate. Although I had just settled in Marseille, this was an irresistible call. IRCAM seemed a very unlikely venture, especially in France, but Boulez was in a position to demand its existence. From 1972 on, meetings were held to plan and prepare the Institute. As Pierre Boulez wrote (1973): "The creator's intuition alone is powerless to provide a comprehensive translation of musical invention. It is thus necessary for him to collaborate with the scientific research worker in order to envision the distant future, to imagine less personal, and thus broader, solutions." IRCAM was initially structured in departments. I headed the Computer Department,

which was to be well equipped. The other department heads were Vinko Globokar (instruments and voice), Luciano Berio (electronics), Gerald Bennett ("diagonal"), and Michel Decoust (pedagogy).

I moved to Paris in 1975, and we started to implement music on a DEC PDP-10 and on PDP-11 computers. We got much help from Stanford's Center for Computer Research in Music and Acoustics (CCRMA) and from Max Mathews, who for a few years advised on the project in the capacity of scientific director. With very good people like Jim Lawson, John Gardner, and Brian Harvey—succeeded in 1977 by Jean-Louis Richer, Philippe Prévot, Raymond Bara—we had computer-generated sound in 1976 and we moved into the new IRCAM building in 1977. Peppino DiGiugno had started his work on real-time digital processors in the electronics department, which thus went digital, and David Wessel had joined the diagonal department, followed in 1977 by Andy Moorer, who was to leave in 1979. IRCAM gave many concerts, with the series "Passage du XX° siècle" in 1977, and started to build tools and conduct research. Despite too many distractions, in particular an endless flow of visitors (25,000 persons visit the Centre Pompidou every day—fortunately only a small proportion go through IRCAM), I managed to do a few experiments and pieces (mostly during the quietest periods of the summer). I realized *Inharmonique*, *Moments Newtoniens*, and *Mirages*, from which I abstracted *Songes*. (See the soundsheet in *Computer Music Journal* 7[1], 1983, and also the record *IRCAM: un portrait* distributed by IRCAM.) However, I soon became impatient with the difficulty of working quietly and maintaining my longterm research. In 1978 I decided—to Pierre Boulez's surprise—to resign in 1979. Pierre later changed the structure of IRCAM.

Even though I disagreed with some options at IRCAM—especially the too great subordination of research activity to musical production priorities—I view IRCAM as an exciting institution. A number of computer music pieces have been realized and performed there, mostly with non-real-time programs like Music V or Music 10, but also with DiGiugno's powerful 4C and 4X processors. Important research has been performed and is under way, for example, experiments on reverberation and sound processing (Moorer), vocal synthesis (Sundberg, Chowning, Rodet, Bennett), musical perception (Wessel, McAdams), fast real-time digital processors (DiGiugno, Boulez, Gerszo, Machover), and advanced music languages (Abbott, Rodet and his collaborators of the FORMES project), to give instances of only computer-related research.

Work at Marseille

Meanwhile the T 1600 computer in Marseille did not stay idle. In 1975, Barry Conyngham synthesized sounds that he incorporated into an opera presented in Australia. In 1976, Denis Lorrain synthesized a computer version of his stochastic composition *P-A*, initially for eight voices. And in 1978, Marc Battier realized his piece *Géométrie d'hiver*. Bernard Nayroles, Director of the Laboratoire de Mécanique et d'Acoustique of the C.N.R.S. (Centre National de la Récherche Scientifique) in Marseille, welcomed computer music research in his laboratory, and he was instrumental in getting a research position for Daniel Arfib (in 1977). It is a great pleasure to collaborate with Daniel, an inspired and inspiring person. Daniel has been doing outstanding work, including research on nonlinear distortion or waveshaping (Arfib 1979) as well as computer pieces marked with his own imprint (*Musique numérique*, available from the composer at LMA-CNRS, B.P. 71, 13277 Marseille, Cedex 9, France). I must make it clear that our Marseille group is financed for research, not for making music: hence we can only exceptionally have composers' work on the machine, and we cannot organize concerts. Fortunately, we have a good connection with the Groupe de Musique Expérimentale de Marseille, equipped with a tape studio and a Synclavier (among the members of the Group are Georges Boeuf, Michel Redolfi, Jacques Diennet, and Franck Royon Le Mée).

Since 1979, I have done further experimentation in Marseille on music synthesis, particularly on processes for sonic transformation and development. Some of this research has been embodied in pieces such as *Contours, Profils, Aventure de*

lignes. The latter piece was written for the Electronics Instruments Ensemble of l'Itinéraire, playing together with a computer-generated tape. This tape was partly synthesized in Marseille and partly realized in Dartmouth with Jon Appleton's Synclavier II.

The last Sound Example (13) presents an excerpt of *Passages*, for flute and tape, commissioned by the Laboratorio per l'Informatica Musicale della Biennale di Venezia for the 1982 International Computer Music Conference. In this section, I used a method to evoke voicelike sounds suggested by Mike McNabb and John Chowning. The spectrum is fixed, but the fundamental frequency is gradually modulated, partly periodically and partly randomly. When the modulation becomes similar to that of a singing voice, the spectrum exhibits a suggestive voicelike quality. This transition toward vocal timbres happens in dialogue with the flute player, who occasionally sings while blowing.

A Summary

I shall now try to sum up the reasons for my interest in using computers. The computer makes it possible to work in ways I have been longing for more or less consciously. It provides a refined control over the sound structure, and it helps to extend compositional processes at the level of this sound structure, thus permitting one to compose the sounds themselves and to give some functional role to the timbre. Let me state a few compositional fantasies, some of which no longer appear to me as ever-receding goals:

Creating a flexible sonic world that could diverge from the instrumental world but also merge with it in subtle ways

Experimenting with the design of one's own constraints instead of having to dwell with instrumental and electronic constraints

Assembling a personal palette of lively sounds, endowed with some characteristic of identity, but also very ductile, thus susceptible to intimate transformations that preserve certain characteristics and alter others (for instance, crystallization or melting of a preserved "substance")

Taking advantage of the operational power of the computer to suggest and achieve specific compositional transformations, thus extending the role of structural notation

Evoking a suggestive yet illusory world, free of material constraints, by playing directly, so to speak, upon perceptual mechanisms, thus unveiling perceptual "primitives" and guiding perception toward one mode or another (e.g., synthetic versus analytic)

I shall not be more specific about music here. I think the music should speak for itself. Yet I want to state that I intend to do more work to relate compositional processes to the sound material and its structure, using the computer for this purpose, as I mentioned above (extending the role of structural notation). This requires advanced music input languages, which are beginning to come of age. I would like to make a plea for compatibility and transportability, so that such languages can be used in other places besides a couple of large centers.

The contribution of more and more people is essential in making the computer music field practicable and fertile. Much progress has been made and is being made, and I am confident that the members of the computer music community, and especially the bright young talents that are not in the least intimidated by computers, are leading a genuine mutation for music.

References

Arfib, D. 1979. "Digital Synthesis of Complex Spectra By Means of Nonlinear Distorted Sine Waves." *Journal of the Audio Engineering Society* 27(10):757–768.

Boulez, P. 1973. IRCAM brochure. Paris: IRCAM.

Charbonneau, G., and J.-C. Risset. 1975. "Jugements relatifs de hauteur: schémas linéaires et hélicoïdaux." *C. R. Académie des Sciences, Paris. Série B.* 281: 289–292.

Chowning, J. 1973. "The Synthesis of Complex Audio Spectra By means of Frequency Modulation." *Journal of the Audio Engineering Society* 21(7):526–534. Reprinted in *Foundations of Computer Music*, ed. C. Roads and J. Strawn. 1985. Cambridge, Massachusetts: MIT Press.

Halet, P. 1968. *Little Boy*. Paris: Editions du Seuil.

Lorrain, D. 1979. "Analyse de la bande magnétique d'*Inharmonique*." IRCAM Report 26. Paris: IRCAM.

Mathews, M. et al. 1969. *The Technology of Computer Music*. Cambridge, Massachusetts: MIT Press.

Mathews, M., and F. R. Moore. 1970. "GROOVE—A Program to Compose, Store, and Edit Functions of Time." *Communications of the Association for Computing Machinery* 13(12):715–721.

Risset, J.-C. 1965. "Computer Study of Trumpet Tones." *Journal of the Acoustical Society of America* 38:912 (abstract only).

Risset, J.-C. 1969a. "Pitch Control and Pitch Paradoxes Demonstrated with Computer-synthesized Sounds." *Journal of the Acoustical Society of America* 46:88.

Risset, J.-C. 1969b. "An Introductory Catalog of Computer-synthesized Sounds." Murray Hill, New Jersey: Bell Laboratories.

Risset, J.-C. 1971. "Paradoxes de hauteur." In *Proceedings of the 7th International Congress of Acoustics*, pp. 205–210.

Risset, J.-C. 1978. "Paradoxes de hauteur." IRCAM Report 10. Paris: IRCAM.

Risset, J.-C., and M. Mathews. 1969. "Analysis of Instrumental Tones." *Physics Today* 22(2):23–30.

Risset, J.-C., and D. Wessel. 1982. "Exploration of Timbre by Analysis and Synthesis." In *The Psychology of Music*, ed. D. Deutsch. New York: Academic Press, pp. 25–28.

UNESCO. 1971. *Music and Technology*. Paris: UNESCO and La Revue Musicale.

Wessel, D., and J.-C. Risset. 1979. "Les illusions auditives." In *Encyclopedia Universalia*. Paris: Encyclopedia Universalis, pp. 167–171.

Lejaren Hiller
Department of Music
State University of New York at Buffalo
Buffalo, New York 14214

Composing with Computers: A Progress Report

Computer music has come to have two different meanings that are not competitive but complementary. The first, *computer-composed music*, involves composition, that is, note selection. The second, *computer-realized music*, involves conversion into electronic sound of a score that may or may not have been composed with the aid of a computer. These two operations can be performed in sequence, so that a composer's score can be both composed and realized by means of a computer (Fig. 1). Depending on the computer configuration and the composer's objectives, the boundary between these two processes can be sharply defined or rather fuzzy.

Although computer composition has been going on since 1956, when Leonard Isaacson and I started work on the *Illiac Suite for String Quartet*, more effort has been expended over the years on sound synthesis. This is because there is a pressing need for accurate, reproducible electronic sound and for modern tools for acoustic research. Sound synthesis has applications in music education, and the commercial possibilities of sound synthesis far transcend the concerns of the avant-garde composer. Perhaps the most important reason for greater emphasis on sound synthesis is that computer-assisted composition is inherently a more obscure, difficult, and controversial topic. Computer-assisted composition is difficult to define, difficult to limit, and difficult to systematize. As with any kind of composing, work in this field tends to be highly personalized and hence less accessible to others. Computer composition also requires the attention of a skilled composer who has enough experience to ask the proper questions. Despite all these barriers, substantial progress has been made in computer composition over the last 25 years.

Computer Music Journal, Vol. 5, No. 4, Winter 1981

Some 12 years ago, I prepared an exhaustive review of computer music composition until that time (Hiller 1970b). Among the composers mentioned therein were Pierre Barbaud and Iannis Xenakis of Paris, Gottfried Michael Koenig of Utrecht, Herbert Brün of Urbana-Champaign, Illinois, and James Tenney, now of Toronto. This list could be considerably extended today. In our own group, John Myhill and Charles Ames are particularly active. Reports in this issue of *Computer Music Journal* of other composers' recent work will fill in the present picture.

Writing compositional algorithms forces me to scrutinize composition as process. I have to be aware of how compositional logic really works and how compositional priorities arrange themselves. In working with computers, musical ideas come to me that I probably would not otherwise have imagined. This carries over to composing I now do without computers as well.

I shall review here some of my own work, especially that of recent years about which I have published relatively little so far. (Instead of doing much publishing, I have been slowly but steadily gathering all the documentation into a series of technical reports. The relevant reports are listed in the References.)

The composition list shown in Table 1 provides a framework for the discussion to follow. The list can be split into two parts: (1) earlier compositions produced at the University of Illinois and (2) more recent works written in Buffalo since 1968. This split is a logical one, because if I include *Algorithms I* with the latter group, all of these either point toward or actually make use of the programming package I currently use.

One striking feature of all this work has been its pragmatism. I like to get the music performed. Performance is, without a doubt, the best test of the results. Nowadays, for example, I plan a piece like *Algorithms III* with my basic system, program

Fig. 1. The computer used as a composing machine, with facilities for compositional algorithms, analog-to-digital conversion of natural sounds, sound synthesis algorithms, high-level score language interpreters, and digital-to-analog conversion into sound.

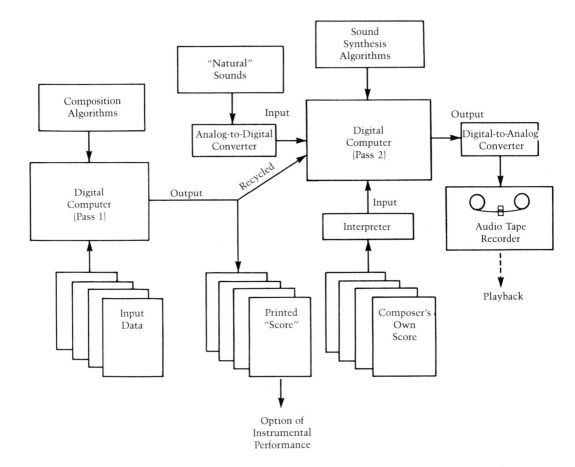

PHRASE, in mind, and during the compositional process I improve program PHRASE by adding new algorithms or improving existing ones.

A second feature of my approach to computer composition has been its emphasis upon probability and statistics. My music tends to proceed from disorder to order. It starts with random generation of musical elements and proceeds with the imposition of more and more constraints on the elements' acceptability. I have done this consistently since the original *Illiac Suite*. To be sure, I was much influenced by readings I had done in information theory.

Not only does this procedure work, but it seems philosophically satisfying. The trap in writing a completely deterministic set of algorithms is that they reduce the whole process to mere data transformation.

Early Compositions

Because the *Illiac Suite* (which I now also call *String Quartet No. 4*) was the first composition written with a digital computer, Leonard Isaacson

Table 1. Lejaren Hiller: computer music compositions

Illiac Suite for String Quartet (1957)
(composed with Leonard Isaacson)
    Duration: 18 min
    Publisher: Theodore Presser
    Recording: Heliodor HS25053

"The Flying Lesson" from Music for "The Birds"
(by Aristophanes) (1958)
    Duration: 2 min
    Publisher: None
    Recording: Private tape

Computer Cantata (1963)
(composed with Robert Baker)
    Duration: 24 min
    Publisher: Theodore Presser
    Recording: Heliodor HS25053, reissued on CRI-SD-310

An Avalanche for Pitchman, Prima Donna, Player Piano,
Percussionist and Prerecorded Playback (1968)
    Text: Frank Parman
    Duration: 9–13 min
    Publisher: Theodore Presser
    Recording: Heliodor 2549006

HPSCHD for 1 to 7 Harpsichords and 1 to 51 Tapes (1968)
(composed with John Cage)
    Duration: 20 min to any length
    Publisher: C. F. Peters
    Recording: Nonesuch H-71224

Algorithms I for 9 Instruments and Tape (Versions I to IV) (1968)
    Duration: 9 min per version
    Publisher: Theodore Presser
    Recording: Version I: DGG2543005
              Version II: Private tape
              Version III: Private tape
              Version IV: DGG2543005

Computer Music for Percussion and Tape (1968)
(composed with G. Allan O'Connor)
    Duration: 7 min
    Publisher: Theodore Presser
    Recording: Heliodor 2549006

Algorithms II for 9 Instruments and Tape
(Versions I to IV) (1972)
(composed with Ravi Kumra)
    Duration: 5 min per version
    Publisher: Theodore Presser
    Recording: Version I: Unperformed
              Version II: Unperformed
              Version III: Private tape
              Version IV: Private tape

Table I. (cont'd)

A Preview of Coming Attractions for Orchestra (1975)
     Duration: 16 min
     Publisher: Theodore Presser
     Recording: Private tape

Electronic Sonata for Four-Channel Tape (1976)
     Duration: 53 min
     Publisher: None
     Recording: Private tape

Midnight Carnival for an Urban Environment (1976)
     Duration: Indeterminate
     Publisher: None
     Recording: Private tape

Persiflage for Flute, Oboe and Percussion (1977)
     Duration: 11 min
     Publisher: Waterloo
     Recording: Commercial release in preparation

Algorithms III for 9 Instruments and Tape (Versions I to IV) (in progress)
     Duration: 9 min
     Publisher: None yet
     Recording: Unperformed (unfinished)

and I had to deal with many elementary questions as to how computer music might be composed.

I had been working since late 1952 as a chemist on a research project sponsored by the United States Government. Although I had had a bit of exposure to analog computers at Du Pont prior to this, it was at the University of Illinois that I first learned how to use digital computers, specifically the Illiac I. This was very much brute force machine language work—no fancy, high-level languages. My research director, Frederick Wall, assigned to me the problem of computing statistically the dimensions of idealized polymer molecules in solution. This work introduced me to the Monte Carlo, or Markov, processes of calculation that became central to my later work.

It occurred to me that, by changing the controlling conditions from geometric to contrapuntal, the same basic program could be adapted to writing some counterpoint exercises. I suggested this idea to Leonard Isaacson, who was also a chemist on the same project. He liked the idea as a programming challenge, even though his knowledge of music was purely that of a listener. So we started with a few small experiments and, little by little, the project grew. Around this time I mentioned the project to Milton Babbitt, my former composition teacher, and he was both intrigued and encouraging, partly because he himself was beginning to think a lot about electronic music.

One evening, when we had some results, I showed them to a composer friend. He said that what we had was all very good but that it wasn't music, and that he would be more impressed were the counterpoint really correct. Isaacson and I thought about going on to more complex strict counterpoint but soon dropped this idea in favor of composing some experiments more related to contemporary music. This resulted in the final two movements of the *Suite*. When we first performed the *Illiac Suite*, or rather three movements of it, a huge amount of publicity was generated (a lot of it rather silly).

The first time I gave a talk on the subject of computer music was in 1956 before an audience of about 2000 computer experts and engineers at a Los Angeles meeting of the Association of Computing Machinery. Attitudes toward this early work ranged from curious to skeptical to overtly hostile. Rather interestingly, computer scientists were more open minded than musicians, and musicians were more open minded than scholars in the humanities, many of whom seemed to regard me as monstrous.

I did not hear a complete performance of the *Illiac Suite* until several years later. I was giving a talk at a conference, and afterward a man introduced himself to me as Max Mathews. He said he had a present for me—a tape recording of the *Illiac Suite* he had gotten the WQXR String Quartet to make. This was around the time he was developing Music IV.

Since the *Computer Cantata* has been rather thoroughly described elsewhere (Hiller 1964; Hiller and Baker 1964), there is little I need say about it here except that in it Robert Baker and I were concentrating again on basic problem solving, this time with an emphasis on statistics, stochastic processes, and rhythmic complexities more profound than those attempted in the *Illiac Suite*.

Both *An Avalanche . . .* and *HPSCHD*, though composed with computer algorithms, are theatrical compositions and hence differ from the earlier didactic works. *An Avalanche . . .* is a satirical piece dealing with the state of the performing arts in the United States, and *HPSCHD* is a gigantic multimedia spectacle. *HPSCHD* involved three sets of computer programs, one for composing the tape parts and realizing them in sound by means of digital-to-analog conversion, the second for composing harpsichord parts derived from Mozart's *Musical Dice Game*, and the third for creating a performance part for the high-fidelity enthusiast sitting at home listening to the collage we prepared for a commercial phonograph recording. Contrary to what many critics thought (Will they never learn?), this was not a chaotic piece. The basic note generator was a subroutine called ICHING that recreated the Oracle of the *Book of Changes*. The results of subroutine ICHING were not haphazard, but were based on a polynomial distribution. Also, much of the programming was concerned with melodic con-

structions that Cage hoped would express his admiration for the melodic writing of Mozart.

Recent Compositions

Both *Electronic Sonata* and *Midnight Carnival* are realized with computer sound synthesis and have nothing to do with computer-assisted composition. *A Preview . . .* and *Persiflage* represent successive stages in the development of the substantial library of compositional programs and subroutines I currently use. The *Algorithms* cycle, consisting of *Algorithms I*, completed in 1968, *Algorithms II*, completed in 1972, and *Algorithms III*, currently being composed, are central to this development. The structural plan of the entire *Algorithms* triptych is shown in Table 2.

As I write this, the second movement of *Algorithms III* is done and the first movement well along toward completion. Debugging, code conversion, and documentation have all been nearly as time-consuming as the writing of the programs.

The *Algorithms* cycle is actually more complex than shown in Table 2 because each movement exists in four versions, any one of which can be chosen for a given performance. There are 28 movements in all. Each version reflects small but important changes of parameters or data. This plan provides a rather neat method of testing the practical effectiveness of various compositional algorithms. Also, varying some components of a system under investigation while keeping others constant is, of course, a standard type of experimental design. First, I specify a compositional system in which a particular composition is but one example from a class of essentially similar compositions. If certain elements are changed in the matrix of elements making up the system, its details will be new but its gross properties will remain essentially the same. It is interesting to speculate how much must be changed to create a new work. We can test the effect of variance of controls in relation to the whole system to gain some insight into this problem. If we use a computer to do this, we retain a precise record of how the variance is produced and what its limits are. Let us take *Algorithms I* as the first example of the application of this idea.

Table 2. The complete set of *Algorithms* compositions

Algorithm	Duration in minutes
Algorithms I	
I. "The Decay of Information"	2
II. "Icosahedron"	3
III. "The Incorporation of Constraints"	4
Algorithms II	
IV. "Campanology"	5
Algorithms III	
V. "Refinements"	4
VI. "Quotations and Phraseology"	3
VII. "Synthesis"	2
Total	23

Algorithms I

The first movement of *Algorithms I*, "The Decay of Information," is a short introductory piece that recapitulates (in very condensed form) the formal structure of *Computer Cantata*. In an evolving plan of stochastic control, transition probabilities are allowed to increase from zero order to sixth order. These transition probabilities are not the same at any time for the different instruments, since some instruments reach the sixth-order level sooner than others. I employed this process to cause the information level of this movement to drop from 100% to approximately 50% from its beginning to its end, hence "The Decay of Information." The four versions of this movement were obtained by varying the rest/play ratio assigned to this movement. "Version 1" is the emptiest and "Version 4" is the fullest.

Because more recent work has superseded most subroutines from this movement, only three are in my current library of subroutines. These have been both translated and updated. One rather simple subroutine provides a distribution according to Zipf's law, which, whether valid or not, is a nice way of emphasizing some choices at the expense of others (Pierce 1961). It states that the probability of selecting an item in a list is inversely proportional to rank order, that is,

$$P_i = P_1/i,$$

where P_i is the probability of choosing item i and P_1 is the probability of the first item in the list. The flow chart of the original subroutine is shown in Fig. 2, and the results of 10,000 trials of the current subroutine IZIPF, with limit $n = 12$, is shown in Fig. 3.

The second movement of *Algorithms I*, "Icosahedron," was my first extended effort at programming a reasonably complex serial composition. The movement consists of 576 notes made up of a 12-tone row, its three permutations, and the 11 transpositions of these four fundamental forms. Thus, each variant of the row occurs just once. The row, the sequence of its variants, the dynamic plan, and all the rhythmic units were chosen by random processes. The whole assembly of note occurrences was compiled into the triangular plan shown in Fig. 4.

Another feature of this movement involved sorting out randomly generated rhythms in such a way that rhythmic simultaneities would be maximal at the center of the movement. This was accomplished by a large subroutine called MATCH (Hiller 1969). I used an instrumentation process for this movement that interchanges instruments, giving the high, wind instruments breathing space. The individual lines can be quite long and taxing otherwise.

The third movement, "The Incorporation of Constraints," is a rondo. Here I added a number of

*Fig. 2. The flow chart for
implementing Zipf's law,
used for the composition
Algorithms I.*

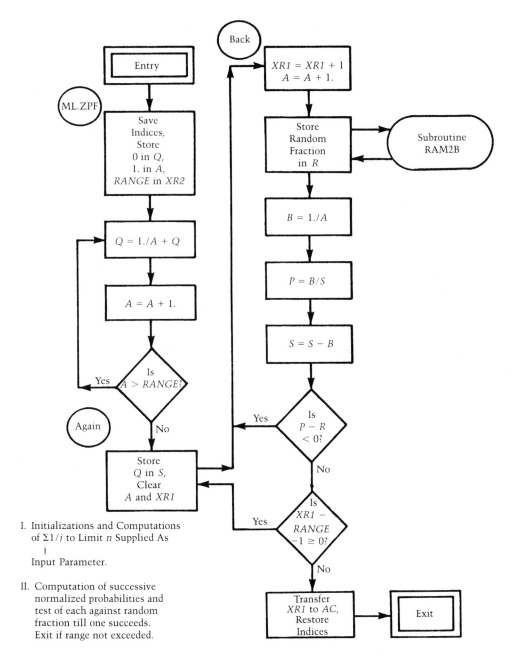

I. Initializations and Computations
   of $\Sigma 1/j$ to Limit n Supplied As
    j
   Input Parameter.

II. Computation of successive
   normalized probabilities and
   test of each against random
   fraction till one succeeds.
   Exit if range not exceeded.

Fig. 3. A graph of a test of
10,000 trials using the procedure outlined in Fig. 2.

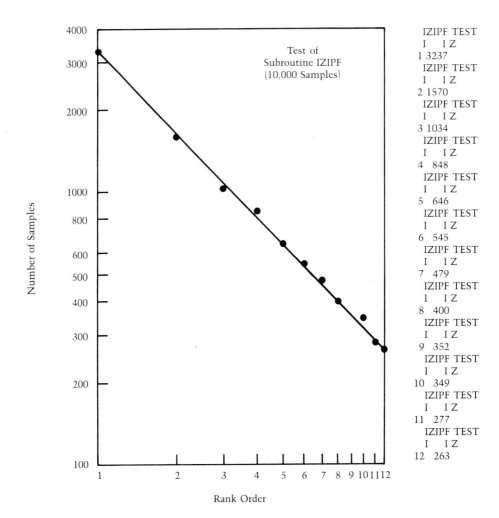

Fig. 4. Structural plan of the second movement of Algorithms I, *called "Icosahedron."*

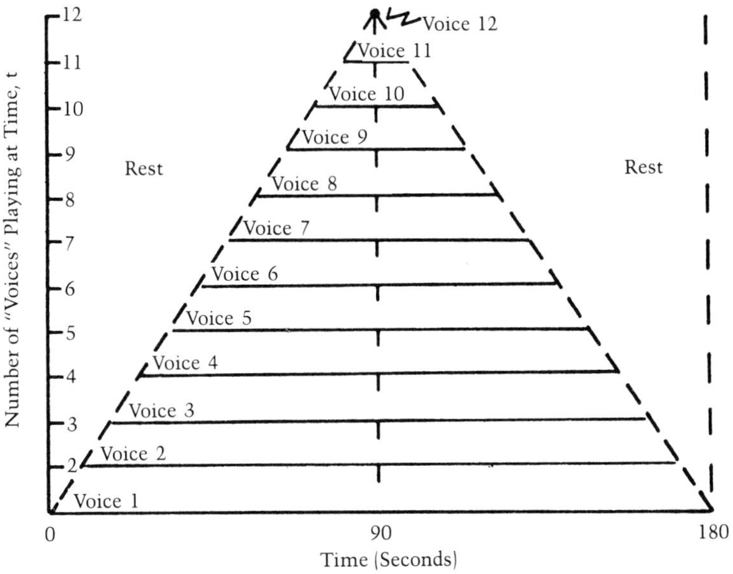

Number of "Voices" Playing at Time, t
12
11
10
9
8
7
6
5
4
3
2
Rest
Rest
Voice 12
Voice 11
Voice 10
Voice 9
Voice 8
Voice 7
Voice 6
Voice 5
Voice 4
Voice 3
Voice 2
Voice 1
0
90
180
Time (Seconds)

modifying processes suggested by more familiar processes of composition to the basic stochastic generators of the first movement. The structure of this movement is shown in Table 3. (This is somewhat different from a similar table published earlier [Hiller 1969], mainly because I replaced phrase generation and imitation with programs for grouping rhythms into choirs.) I was interested in writing compositional subroutines that can be called at will to modify and refine a stochastic matrix. This was when I began to use a kind of programming logic that will be illustrated later. In general, subroutines of this sort provide variety in a composition, primarily dependent on the slow-moving statistical patterns of stochastic music.

Algorithms II

In *Algorithms II*, the point of departure is the application of one central idea, that of *change ringing*. This is a permutational compositional technique that produces nonrepeating melodic sequences and is used in the ringing of church bells in England. It is, in addition, a process that seems to subsume, if there are 12 bells in the set, all the linear operations of 12-tone music (a research topic I should think would be fascinating to 12-tone specialists).

The simplest operation in change ringing involves pair interchanges such as those shown in Table 4. Once the possibility for novel permutations produced by this simple operation is exhausted, recourse is had to somewhat more complex operations called *plain bob, bobs,* and *singles*. Complete *peals* range from 24 for 4 bells to 479,001,600 for 12 bells and, of course, still more for ranks of more than 12 bells.

Each of the four versions of *Algorithms II* is more complex than the one that precedes it, principally because the use of change ringing increases with each version. In "Version 1" change ringing is not used at all; in "Version 2" it controls pitch; in "Version 3" it controls both pitch and rhythm; in "Version 4" it controls pitch in four out of five simultaneously performed polyphonic textures.

To increase the effect of the change-ringing pro-

Table 3. Structural plan of the third movement of *Algorithms I*, "The Incorporation of Constraints"

Section	Content	Duration in Seconds	
1A	Sixth-order stochastic music	8	48
1B	Chord evaluation with regard to a dissonance-consonance index	40	
2A	Combination of the content of section 1B with fifth-order stochastic music	16	48
2B	Three contrapuntal processes	32	
3A	Combination of the content of section 2B with fourth-order stochastic music	24	48
3B	Fixed choirs of rhythms	24	
4A	Combination of the content of section 3B with third- and second-order stochastic music	32	48
4B	Varying choirs of rhythms	16	
5A	Combination of the content of section 4B with first- and zero-order stochastic music	40	48
5B	Process for a statistical tonal cadence	8	
	Total:	240	

Table 4. Basic change-ringing process for even-numbered sets of bells

Row 1 (lead-end)	12345678
Row 2	21436587
Row 3	24163857
Row 4	42618375
Row 5	46281735
Row 6	64827153
Row 7	68472513
Row 8	86745231
Row 9	87654321
Row 10	78563412
Row 11	75836142
Row 12	57381624
Row 13	53718264
Row 14	35172846
Row 15	31527486
Row 16	13254768

Note: Eight bells is a typical number. The lead-end is called *rounds* if this is the very start of ringing.

cess with each version, Ravi Kumra and I wrote a large number of programs and subroutines, the most important of which were RING1, RING2, and RING3, that dealt with various ways permutations could be propagated and brought to full cycle, returning to the original sequence (*rounds*). A flow chart showing how the compositional process was organized is shown in Fig. 5. Subroutine FLIP carries out the operation shown in Table 4.

Program PHRASE

All the more recent computer compositions listed in Table 1 have been produced by means of a large main program called *PHRASE*. The first of these compositions is the orchestral work *A Preview of Coming Attractions*. Program PHRASE is now being combined with an ever growing number of subroutines that place constraints on choices of the five note parameters of pitch, dynamics, timbre, playing style, and rhythm. In contrast to earlier algorithms for music composition, program PHRASE can be used to compose themes, motives, and phrases, and, even more importantly, to imitate and combine these phrases in a number of ways. This system transcends the manipulation of individual musical elements because it can handle substantial groups of elements that can be related to the total score.

The importance of this, it seems to me, is the recognition that hierarchical structure is the fundamental architectural principle that makes a musical work into a coherent whole. In a hierarchical structure, some events in a score are more significant than others in the pattern created when a concept

Fig. 5. The flow chart for
change ringing used in Algorithms II.

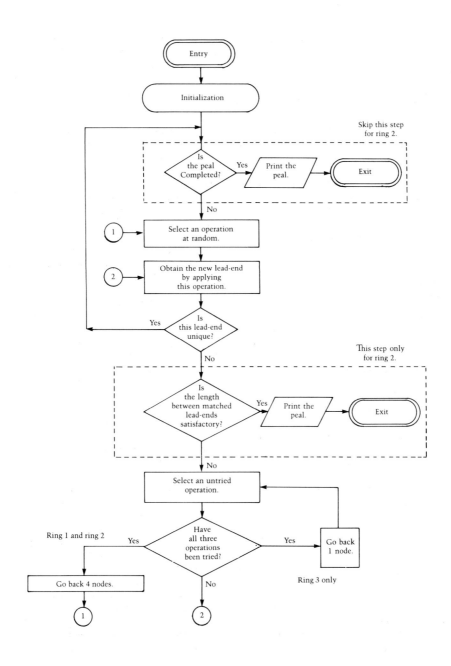

is encoded into music. A message is seldom just a linear string of events like beads on a chain. Rather, the events in a message are tied together by complex network structures that subordinate some events to others.

Notions of this sort are already embodied in more sophisticated analytic systems such as that of Heinrich Schenker (1979). In similar studies of language, the idea of hierarchy forms the basis of the development of generative grammars.

For a variety of reasons, the concept of hierarchy was little used in the early development of computer music algorithms. Because I felt this lack, I set about writing the programs I shall now discuss.

In designing program PHRASE, I defined three processes that might occur during composing. These are

1. Free flow
2. Phrase assembly
3. Imitation

Free flow is used for musical textures that are not phrase oriented. *Phrase assembly* produces the material that is imitated. If codified relationships do not exist among notes, as is the case in free flow, then there is nothing to imitate; thus the need for phrases. *Imitation* is the most complex set of operations in program PHRASE. It is here that we "do something" with the raw material provided by phrase assembly. By *imitation*, I mean the many ways a phrase or group of notes can be imitated, placed into new contexts, transformed, developed, and modified. This applies not just to traditional tonal music but to innovative patterns as well.

To codify these imitation processes into a manageable form, I limited processes of imitation to the following options:

1. Transposition
2. Choice of voice
3. Permutation
4. Strict or free rhythmic imitation
5. Optional phrase-imitation overlap

To summarize, program PHRASE does not in itself define a musical style; rather, it provides three alternative paths for producing and extending a musical texture. These paths are shown in Fig. 6, as are

some of the subroutines that program PHRASE requires to operate properly. For example, subroutine READL is used to read in the stochastic orders to be used in making note parameter choices and the available choices for the five parameters of pitch, dynamics, timbre, playing style, and rhythm. Subroutine BRANCH governs many of the actual choice operations; for example, whether assembly of a phrase should be continued or terminated, whether rest or play should be chosen, or which phrase should be imitated. Subroutine FILL does the actual choosing of note parameters by calling in turn other subroutines. One line of development that demonstrates hierarchy is as follows: program PHRASE is the master program; subroutine FILL is subordinate to it; subroutines such as PITCH and TIMBRE are subordinate to FILL; and still other subroutines, such as MODE and GOAL, are subordinate to PITCH.

Figure 7 is a sketch of subroutine FILL. The boxes with dotted lines indicate subroutines that are incomplete at the time of this writing.

If the diagram of program PHRASE is now recalled (Fig. 6), it is easy to see how a musical structure is set up. Whenever composers wish to obtain a change in texture, they simply set a limit expressed in $\frac{1}{32}$ notes. This is tested at the end of the big loop in program PHRASE each time a note is generated for each voice of the score. When all voices have reached this limit, the large loop returning to the very beginning of the program is entered, and fresh data are read for whatever addition is desired, such as new themes to be quoted, new probabilities to be supplied to subroutine BRANCH, and so on. One type of refinement I add bit by bit in programming is reduction of the amount of such data that must be specified by the composer. My general attitude is that the more such data are internally generated, including long-range variance of such data, the more effective and interesting the entire process becomes.

Persiflage required 20 sets of data. These imposed a gradual change of texture by changing the amount of phrase assembly, amount of imitation, types of rhythms, loudness levels, and so on. Other controls, mainly those concerned with pitch choices, more or less took care of themselves. Further de-

*Fig. 6. An outline of the
program PHRASE, with its
three main subroutines:
FREE FLOW, PHRASE AS-
SEMBLY, and IMITATION.*

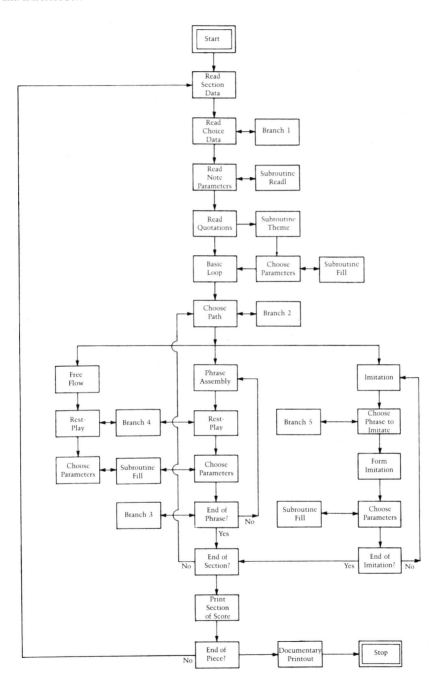

Fig. 7. A simplified block
diagram of the subroutine
FILL called by the program
PHRASE.

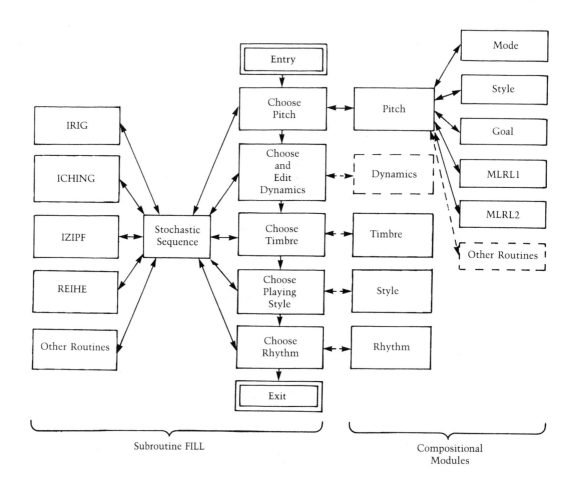

Subroutine FILL

Compositional
Modules

tails concerning *Persiflage* appear elsewhere (Hiller
1978; 1980).

Algorithms III

At present, I am much involved in programming
the first movement of *Algorithms III*. The second
movement is already done. Although quite a bit of
new programming was needed for the second move-

ment, the thorough reorganization and refinement
contemplated for the first movement was not
needed. The title of the first movement, "Refinement," means just that. The final movement will
be a synthesis of just about all the programming
written for the whole cycle.

The second movement, "Quotations and Phrase-
ology," is partitioned into blocks, some of which
are assigned the function of "phrase assembly" or
"theme quotation," depending on the version; some

of which are assigned the production of "free flow" or "imitation"; and some of which are assigned a new process, "double imitation," which is an attempt to imitate whole blocks of material, not just single lines. The parameters controlling all this are now assigned to individual voices, so it is possible to assign different textures to different portions of the performing body at the same point in the score.

A modulating scheme is also imposed. "Version 1" does not modulate, but each voice has its own transposition scheme. "Version 2" is built on a tone row, and its modulation scheme depends on this row. "Version 3" makes use of a cycle of fifths, and "Version 4" incorporates a simple representation of the tonal scheme of a traditional sonata form structure.

The first movement, "Refinements," will be made up of 10 sections, as is the third movement of *Algorithms I*. However, the addition of compositional options makes it vastly more complex. As I program successive sections of this movement, I also steadily tighten up and make more clear and logical all that is going on. This is rather slow going because so many operations interlock and depend on one another that it is very easy when instituting changes to cause the whole system to jam up. Debugging is slow and costly. A typical run now is about 5 min of machine time on the CYBER 173, a very fast computer.

Three sections of the movement are done, and in these I have introduced quite a number of new subroutines involving, for example, a fully realized stochastic choice generator, subroutines for timbre and style controls, and a subroutine (REIHE) containing all current tone row operations. The next step is the introduction—at last—of vertical controls such as harmonic rules.

References

Hiller, L. 1964. "Informationstheorie und Computermusik." In *Darmstädter Beiträge zur Neuen Musik* 8. Mainz: B. Schott's Söhne.

Hiller, L. 1967. "Programming a Computer for Musical Composition." In *Computer Applications in Music*, ed. G. Lefkoff. Morgantown: West Virginia University Library, pp. 65–88.

Hiller, L. 1969. "Some Compositional Techniques Involving the Use of Computers." In *Music by Computers*, ed. H. von Foerster and J. W. Beauchamp. New York: John Wiley, pp. 71–83.

Hiller, L. 1970a. "Programming the I-Ching Oracle," *Computer Studies in the Humanities and Verbal Behavior* 3 : 130–143.

Hiller, L. 1970b. "Music Composed with Computers—A Historical Survey." In *The Computer and Music*, ed. H. B. Lincoln. Ithaca, New York: Cornell University Press, pp. 42–96.

Hiller, L. 1972. "Computer Programs Used to Produce the Composition *HPSCHD*." Technical report 4. Buffalo, New York: SUNY, Department of Music.

Hiller, L. 1978. "Phrase Generation in Computer Music Composition." Technical report 10. Buffalo, New York: SUNY, Department of Music.

Hiller, L. 1979. "Phrase Structure in Computer Music." In *Proceedings of the 1978 International Computer Music Conference*, vol. 1, ed. C. Roads. Evanston, Illinois: Northwestern University Press, pp. 192–213.

Hiller, L. 1980. "Composing the Second Movement of *Algorithms III*." Technical report 12. Buffalo, New York: SUNY, Department of Music.

Hiller, L. 1981. "Computer Programs Used to Produce the Composition *Algorithms I*." Technical report 13. Buffalo, New York: SUNY, Department of Music.

Hiller, L., and R. A. Baker. 1962. "Computer Music." In *Computer Applications in the Behavioral Sciences*, ed. H. Borko. Englewood Cliffs, New Jersey: Prentice-Hall, pp. 424–451.

Hiller, L., and R. A. Baker. 1964. "Computer Cantata: An Investigation of Compositional Procedure." *Perspectives of New Music* 3 : 62–90.

Hiller, L., and J. Cage. 1968. "HPSCHD: An Interview by Larry Austin." *Source* 2(2) : 10–19.

Hiller, L., and L. M. Isaacson. 1959. *Experimental Music*. New York: McGraw-Hill. (Recently reprinted by Greenwood Press, Westport, Connecticut.)

Hiller, L., and R. Kumra. 1979. "Composing *Algorithms II* by Means of Change-Ringing." *Interface* 8 : 129–168.

Kumra, R. 1973. "The Composition of *Algorithms II* with a Digital Computer." Technical report 6. Buffalo, New York: SUNY, Department of Music.

Pierce, J. R. 1961. *Symbols, Signals and Noise*. New York: Harper, pp. 238–249.

Schenker, H. 1979. *Free Composition*, trans. and ed. E. Oster. New York: Longman.

Jonathan Harvey
University of Sussex
Falmer, Brighton
Sussex, England BN1 9QN

Mortuos Plango, Vivos Voco: A Realization at IRCAM

Introduction

Mortuos Plango, Vivos Voco for eight-track tape was commissioned by the Centre George Pompidou in Paris and was realized at the Institut de Recherche et Coordination Acoustique/Musique (IRCAM) with the technical assistance of Stanley Haynes. It is a very personal piece in that the two sound sources are the voice of my son and that of the great tenor bell at Winchester Cathedral, England. I have written much music for the choir there, in which my son was a treble chorister, and have often listened to the choir practicing against a background of the distant tolling of this enormous black bell. The text for the voice is the text written on the bell: *Horas Avolantes Numero, Mortuos Plango: Vivos ad Preces Voco* (I count the fleeing hours, I lament the dead: the living I call to prayer). In the piece the dead voice of the bell is contrasted against the living voice of the boy.

Analysis of the Bell

The spectrum of the bell was analyzed with the fast Fourier transform (FFT) program at IRCAM, part of the interactive sound analysis package S imported from Stanford University. The analysis commenced ½ sec after the initiation of the sound. The spectrum is shown in musical notation in Fig. 1.

This typical moment, when the spectrum was at its fullest, forms the structural basis of *Mortuos Plango, Vivos Voco*. I added to the analyzed spectrum one of the most, to me, supernatural attributes of this extraordinary sound, a clearly audible, slow-decaying partial at 347 Hz with a beating component in it. It is a resultant of the vari-

Computer Music Journal, Vol. 5, No. 4, Winter 1981

ous F harmonic series partials that can be clearly seen in the spectrum (5, [6], 7, 9, 11, 13, 17, etc.) beside the C-related partials. Such "unanalyzable" secondary strike notes are quite common in bells.

The eight sections of the work, with their central pitches, are structured around the partials shown in Fig. 2.

Techniques Using the Bell Sound

The synthesis and mixing work was done with the IRCAM version of Music V (Mathews 1969). This version was greatly expanded by John Gardner (prior to 1977) and Jean-Louis Richer (after 1977). (See Haynes's 1980 article for a description of some of its features.)

I first synthesized the bell spectrum shown in Fig. 1. Then, using Music V (IRCAM) I could give the partials any envelope I chose, for instance I could turn the bell inside out by making the low partials, which normally decay slowly, decay quickly. The normally fast-decaying high partials could be made to decay slowly or even crescendo over varying durations. Modulations from one bell transposition to another were achieved by sine-tone glissandi. To avoid banal parallelism, I chose different slices of the spectrum as beginning and end sounds, and the current central note was the "pivot" of the modulation (Fig. 3).

Thus subsidiary "bell-tonics" are set up in hierarchies analogous to (but distinct from) the traditional western tonal system. Each of the eight sections is announced by and based on a bell transposed to the pitches indicated in Fig. 2, with all its structural implications of secondary pitches. The straight digitized recording of the Winchester bell in various transpositions was read by the computer in different ways.

The sound file reading modules in the IRCAM version of Music V are able to read files forward or

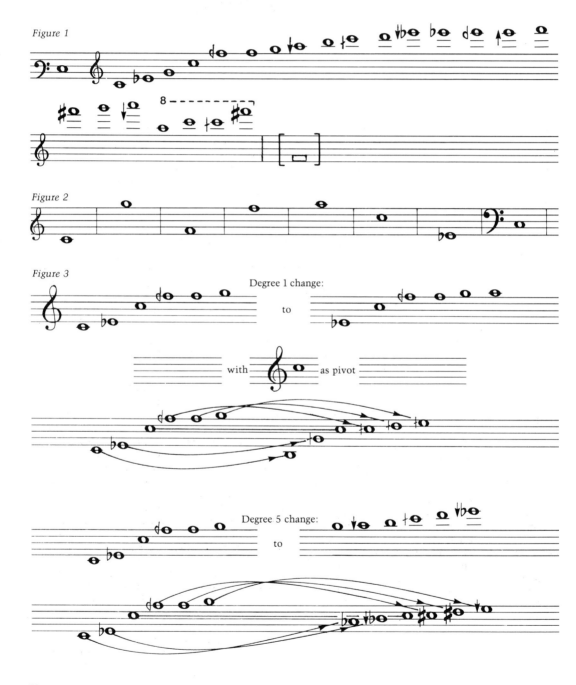

Figure 1

Figure 2

Figure 3

Degree 1 change:

to

with ... as pivot

Degree 5 change:

to

backward, with the option of continuously varying the speed. Often a rapidly oscillating forward/backward reading was made that gave a decrescendo/crescendo of high partials as the attack was left or approached. Rhythmic patterns of great subtlety were easy to devise, sometimes in interplay with programmed spatial movement. Elsewhere the partials of the bell, or selections from them, were individually distributed around the eight speakers, giving the listener the curious sensation of being inside the bell.

Techniques Using the Boy's Voice

Recordings were made of the boy (1) chanting the Latin text on one partial-note, (2) singing all the phonemes of the text separately, and (3) singing a short melody based entirely on the spectrum pitches. I was able also to simulate these sounds using the singing synthesis program CHANT developed by Gerald Bennett and Xavier Rodet, though getting the degree of random fluctuation and rudimentary vibrato right for the pure treble voice was a problem at first. I often disguised the beginning of the synthetic transformations with a "real" voice fragment. In another technique, recordings of vowels sung by the boy were digitized. The digitized files were then read by the sound-input modules, looped, and given pitch and amplitude contours analogous to those applied to the sinusoidal components in the synthetic bell spectra. The boy's synthetic voice sang on the bell partials instead of sine tones, and modulations as described previously were effected. Bell-like envelopes were given to some of these "bell sounds composed of boy's

voice." Transformations were also applied to the spectra of the boy's vowels, which could be made into pitch and amplitude glissandi to the nearest bell equivalents in a bell spectrum. Such a file could again be read backward and forward, giving rapid oscillations of "boyness' with "bellness" in varied rhythms.

Conclusion

The computer's ability to read a recorded concrete file, to analyze it, to isolate the minutest fragment, and then to reproduce it rapidly in all sorts of patterns and multiplications (mixed or unmixed with synthetic material) comprises its most intriguing potential. The technology of programs like Music V (IRCAM) and CHANT at last make possible the precision whose lack made *concrète* work so conceptually problematic in the past.

Acknowledgment

The editor would like to acknowledge the assistance of Stanley Haynes in the preparation of this manuscript for publication.

References

Haynes, S. 1980. "The Musician-machine Interface in Digital Sound Synthesis." *Computer Music Journal* 4(4):23–44.
Mathews, M. 1969. *The Technology of Computer Music.* Cambridge, Massachusetts: MIT Press.

10

Dexter Morrill
Department of Music
Colgate University
Hamilton, New York 13346

Loudspeakers and Performers: Some Problems and Proposals

Perhaps some confusion has resulted in recent years from the continued use of the words *computer music* and *electronic music* to describe the medium in which many of us work. Indeed, Max Mathews's title for his paper "The Computer as a Musical Instrument" (1963) may have seemed appropriate at the time but suggested that our new music should be defined according to the means of signal generation rather than according to the transducer, which has always been the loudspeaker. The term *synthesizer* does not help us much either. In 1981 the differences among devices that generate sources for loudspeakers are growing less obvious and less important. Soon we may realize that we are working in a loudspeaker medium, regardless of how the signals for the loudspeakers are generated. Musicians working in real time and in performance using computers, synthesizers, and circuits might rather think of themselves as loudspeaker performers. During the 1970s we witnessed a revolution in the technology of loudspeaker music. Thousands of pieces have been composed for tape alone and for tape and performers. Those of us who were working 10 years ago have seen an incredible number of musicians and researchers begin to work in the tape medium.

What problems are encountered with use of loudspeakers in musical performance? The problems I will discuss here are nontechnical and are limited to the use of loudspeakers where performers do not control the sound-generating equipment directly. Many of the ideas expressed in this article have

Computer Music Journal, Vol. 5, No. 4, Winter 1981

grown out of my experience in performance over the past five years, first with a purely quad-tape program called *Rotations*, which I began doing in 1975, and later with a performer-tape series of programs called *Singing Circuits*. My awareness of the problems of using loudspeakers in performance began after 1978 when the newness of the "computer music" medium had worn off somewhat and I had repeated the *Singing Circuits* program many times. During the early part of 1975 I decided to spend part of my time performing my own "computer" music and that of some other composers. I felt it was important to see that this music went forward with some care and direction, and I was already very unhappy with the "electronic" music concerts that I had heard. Too often, the equipment for these programs was inadequate or the programs poorly constructed, and both music and composers suffered. I decided to organize my own equipment for concerts and to put together a basic program of music whose organization could begin to compete with more conventional programs. Whenever possible I would travel to a concert with my own equipment even if only one of my pieces was to be performed.

By definition, *loudspeaker composers* take on much of the performer's role because the music is fixed in some important ways. Because at least part of the piece is often stored on tape, the composer must find a way to add what is normally the performer's information. This task can slow down the composing process. The loudspeaker instrument through which the music is realized for an audience remains somewhat passive unless the composer can be actively involved with the equipment during each performance. We need to exert some control over the performance of our tapes, much as performers control the output of their instruments.

The next five years will be critical ones for loud-speaker composers. Few resources and little money are available, our medium is no longer new, and we will need to demonstrate for our colleagues some good results if we hope to have their continued support. While the cost of hardware is declining rapidly, the overall cost of maintaining good studios will never be cheap.

Social Factors and Performance Spaces

Some obvious improvements have been made in loudspeaker design over the past 10–20 years. The commercial music industry has contributed to development of recording techniques, and our understanding of equalization and concert hall acoustics has grown. The proliferation of loudspeaker uses is staggering. It has been used to broadcast antisocial ideas, advertising, social anger and frustration, pleasure, and even social healing. The loudspeaker invades our privacy constantly. It can be hidden, purchased at very low cost, and can have enough acoustic power to kill a human being. The loudspeaker may also represent the end of music that is often described as heroic. All of these facts about loudspeakers relate to the social implications of their use—implications that have a direct bearing on how composers use loudspeakers in performance.

Many musicians in the 1960s looked forward eagerly to the construction of new performance spaces. *New music,* as most widely defined, needed new spaces desperately. This expectation, for the most part, was never met. There are very few good spaces in Europe and the United States for the performance of new music. We may even be stepping backward in this respect; some new university music buildings have worse halls than were formerly available. What is available to musicians using loudspeakers are conventional spaces, usually proscenium stages, meant for frontal and conventional heroic performances. We cannot ignore these spaces if we expect to perform often, even though the loudspeaker is at a disadvantage in them. Problems regarding performance spaces are also faced by musicians performing much of the historical repertoire.

The Question of Balance

I can vividly remember doing a concert of computer music at Colgate several years ago that consisted of some tape pieces and some pieces for performers and tape. The program began with two beautiful tape pieces and was followed by one that called for a performer. The audience reacted quite favorably to the first two pieces, but there was a sudden and noticeable increase in interest when the performer walked onstage. This phenomenon is well understood by most of us. It raises the question of roles and balance. My own guess is that in this mixed-media situation the performer commands about 80% of the audience's attention and the loudspeaker 20%. With supreme effort, the composer might equalize these percentages somewhat, but not much. Is there any reason to disturb this natural imbalance? I am not as interested in the imbalance itself as in the danger that we will end up composing a kind of "music minus one." This danger is rather great when we compose for loudspeakers and performers, and some considerable thought is required to overcome it.

Performers often respond to poor balance by turning up the loudspeakers. At a rehearsal recently, I heard a very nice piece for tape, piano, and saxophone. The performers were frustrated with the balance between themselves and the tape and tried the ineffective solution of turning up the amplifier. Acoustic power is rarely the reason for lack of balance. We can easily identify an instrument played softly against some loud competing noises because, as listeners, we are trained to pick out performance cues. The brief but powerful cues found in the attack portion of many natural instrument tones enable us to find that sound and follow it within a complex acoustic event. This is not unlike the cocktail party effect, where we can easily follow the conversation of a single person. A possible solution to the balance problem is to lessen the acoustic power of the loudspeaker and to limit its musical activity to one voice. If, as composers, we can generate a high level of information in one voice that is a processed signal, we can begin to create on tape enough musical information to balance that supplied by live performers. Henry Brant points to the problem of balance in his writing about space and musical composition (1966). He suggests that loudspeakers have a concentrated and directional projection that is at odds with the diffused sounds made by live performers. Although Brant's reasons for proposing a maximum diffusion of sound are somewhat different from my own, his notion of an expanded spatial effect relates to the problems discussed here.

Perhaps we can achieve balance by measuring the musical activity of the players against that of the loudspeakers. A complex tape's texture and rhythmic activity suggest that the performer is a soloist who plays in a concerto role rather than in a more balanced musical one. We who compose in studios, hearing only the tape portion of a work for tape and performer, are probably going to err on the side of tape complexity if we are somewhat unhappy with the tape-performer balance.

Balance and Timbre

Most tape compositions are constructed with simple timbres. Often listeners are fooled when the sounds contain some unusual elements not heard before. But, too frequently, repeated hearings reveal that there is a low level of timbral information, and the music does not wear well. Although performers are not able to modify greatly many of the parameters that control their timbres, they do produce an enormous wealth of timbre information that may unfold rather slowly. Part of my initial and continuing excitement about using computers to generate acoustic signals is their great power in the area of timbre.

With Risset, Chowning, Grey, Beauchamp, Wessel, and others, I have felt that a natural task for composers of new music using computers is the study and synthesis of natural sounds. Our collective intuition was that we needed experience in simulating natural tones in order to build a solid base for unnatural or synthetic ones that we hoped would contain a high level of musical information. At least two other ideas are related to these interests: (1) the idea of interpolating synthetic timbres and (2) confusion between real and synthetic sound

sources. My *Studies* for trumpet and computer (1975) were directed at timbral confusion and balance with a live trumpet player. In the past five years the progress made in timbre research has been significant, and there has been a high degree of interest in simulating and processing the human voice. Petersen's cross-synthesis techniques and the Bennett-Rodet CHANT voice programs at the Institut de Recherche et Coordination Acoustique/Musique have produced startling results. Compositions that feature timbres similar to those of live performers have a potential for balance that might not otherwise exist, especially if loudspeakers are placed with care. In the case of my *Studies*, I found it important to have the loudspeakers elevated to the height of the trumpet bell and to have both the loudspeakers and the player a good distance from the audience. Jean-Claude Risset's *Inharmonique* is marvelous for its balance of voice and tape, even without synthetic voice timbres in the tape part. The opening is especially interesting and is enhanced if the singer gradually walks toward center stage from a distance.

Recent timbre research has led to the study of larger questions about phrasing and other musical elements that are not contained in the single note. We are not very far along on this path, and the amount of information gained and its management pose significant problems. We know that performers demonstrate a personality or style at the level of the phrase and that this information is communicated well to audiences. If the music emanating from loudspeakers does not also communicate some higher-level information, balance will be hard to achieve. In at least one sense, our apparent need for higher-level information in sound synthesis suggests that timbre may not help much to achieve balance in the mixed, tape-performer medium and that composition may have to do this. We do not attend string quartet concerts and hear complaints that the quartets all sound alike. This is because audiences always focus on variety in compositions, even if the timbre of the four string instruments is only rich in information within well-defined limits. Very little can compensate for poor musical ideas in compositions. As composers, we need to be sure that our musical ideas are sufficient for achieving the tape-performer balance we desire. Even if we are sometimes discouraged about the hall, the placement of speakers, the quality of sound that each speaker imposes on all sounds passing through it, the limited dynamic range available, and a host of other limitations, we can always capture the attention of listeners by musical means. That is, we can shift listeners' focus or attention through composition. Good performers will want to contribute to our desired balance by not always being in the foreground.

Placement of Loudspeakers

The social and performance-space problems discussed earlier convince me that we cannot expect our concerts to be successful if we use a couple of ordinary loudspeakers, even if they are perfectly adequate to fill the room with sound and are of high quality. At least for the next few years, audiences will expect something special and unusual from our concerts, something that they feel they cannot hear in their own living rooms. If we place two speakers on a stage, audiences will form preconceived notions about what they are going to hear. An entire concert heard from speakers in one location can only be dull, and it is not much work to move them. It was established more than 30 years ago that to create a good stereo image the proper angle for two speakers is 30° from center (Wallach, Newman, and Rosenzweig 1949). Musicians still make the mistake of placing two speakers at the extreme right or left sides of a stage, thereby creating an enormous separation. In a large hall it is a good idea to use two or three speakers for each side and set them at different angles to the audience.

Musicians may want to use as many speakers as they can reasonably gather together and to place them in a variety of patterns. This does not mean that all of the speakers need to be used for each piece. If we are traveling with equipment, the limitations can be quite severe. But we might accomplish a good bit with a large number of very small speakers supported by two efficient woofers that can handle the low frequencies. Since low frequencies do not localize well, two woofers may be suffi-

cient. We rarely attempt to raise speakers because this is often difficult. Yet it is often worthwhile. I constructed four 6-ft portable stands from plastic plumbing pipe for my *Rotations* loudspeakers and found that the sounds were enhanced enormously. If we are going to be limited by frontal performance situations and constrained by time and resources, we should make every effort to achieve performance depth and height. Synthesis algorithms can create the feeling of depth through control of amplitude, reverberation parameters, and equalization of high and low frequencies for distance cues.

Composers do not use odd speaker arrangements often enough. Larry Austin has a delightful piece for viola and tape in which he uses one speaker. The limited dynamic range does not seem to be a problem, and I suspect that audiences may appreciate a piece that has a small and well-focused loudspeaker sound. Perhaps we should build sound equipment systems especially to meet our own performance needs. Planning and imagination can make up for the lack of expensive equipment. If we do not have a large power requirement, we should be able to use cheaper speakers and amplifiers chosen to work within a limited frequency range. In most cases, cheaper equipment produces acceptably low distortion if it is not operated at peak levels.

Conclusion

In this century we have expanded performance possibilities with equipment, and we have radically altered performance spaces. The elaborate sound system at Bourges (GMEBaphone) and the one designed by Varèse for the Brussels World Fair are two successful examples. Twentieth-century compositions frequently require large forces, special equipment for sound reproduction, extramusical media, and the like. While we might admire composers for daring to impose these requirements, we might sometimes question their motives for doing so. Does the spectacular requirement reflect spectacular vision or an eye for publicity? At a concert I attended recently in the Centre Georges Pompidou, a few players were surrounded by a stage full of electronic equipment. It struck me that this music will have to go forward with a vast amount of electronic baggage (I might add, the same set of baggage). Perhaps technology will have some dirty tricks to play on the music of our century.

We will continue to find loudspeakers a challenge to use in performance, even if the available equipment is not elaborate. We will also discover a thousand compositional ways to compensate for loudspeaker-performer imbalance. And, if we pay some attention to the performance spaces and loudspeaker placement in them, the good compositions will succeed as always.

References

Brant, H. 1966. "Space as an Essential Aspect of Musical Composition." In *Contemporary Composers on Contemporary Music*, ed. E. Schwarz and B. Childs. New York: Holt, Rinehart, and Winston, pp. 223–242.

Mathews, M. 1963. "The Computer as a Musical Instrument." *Science* 142:553.

Wallach, H., E. B. Newman, and M. R. Rosenzweig. 1949. "The Precedence Effect in Sound Localization." *American Journal of Psychology* 62:315–336.

11

Michael McNabb
Center for Computer Research in
Music and Acoustics
Stanford University
Stanford, California 94305

Dreamsong:
The Composition

General Description

Sound Elements

Dreamsong was composed and realized during 1977 and 1978 at the Center for Computer Research in Music and Acoustics (CCRMA). The basic intent of the piece was to integrate a set of synthesized sounds with a set of digitally recorded natural sounds to such a degree that they would form a continuum of available sound material. The sounds thus range from the easily recognizable to the totally new, or, more poetically, from the real world to the dream realm of the imagination, with all that that implies with regard to transitions, recurring elements, and the unexpected. The essential sound elements in *Dreamsong* can be divided into five categories: simple frequency modulation (FM), complex FM, sung vocal processing and resynthesis, other additive synthesis, and processed crowd sounds and speech.

The sung vocal sounds were originally those of a single soprano, Marilyn Barber. A total of 10 single held notes and one glissando, on different pitches and syllables, were digitally recorded. Most of the soprano sounds in the work are these tones processed in various ways. In certain cases, however, the tones were synthesized using additive synthesis based on a single Fourier transform of the steady state of the original signal. The resynthesized tones were overlapped with the originals when it was necessary to have individual control over each harmonic.

The other main melodic and drone instrument is an additive synthesis instrument that generates its own time-varying formants using a particular kind of random process. The oscillating chords that appear toward the beginning and again near the end

Computer Music Journal, Vol. 5, No. 4, Winter 1981

were produced with simple FM, and all the bell sounds are various types of complex FM.

The ambient crowd sounds were recorded from the catwalks of a large auditorium. Two microphones were suspended about 20 ft below the ceiling, and the sound was recorded on tape and later digitized. The speaking voice at the very end of the piece is that of Dylan Thomas.

Musical Material

Musically, *Dreamsong* presents a relatively simple harmonic and melodic structure so as not to obscure the important textural and timbral transitions. There are two major modes from which most of the melodic and harmonic material is derived (Fig. 1). Mode 1 is essentially B-flat mixolydian, although it is not always centered on B-flat. Mode 2 extends through a two-octave range before repeating and is characterized by chromaticism and a division into two regions, one in whole and half steps, the other in thirds.

The primary theme, which builds up over the course of the piece, is from Mode 1 and is the setting of a line taken from a Zen sutra (Fig. 2, top). The secondary theme, the first three notes of which appear at the outset and ending of the work and the whole of which is heard in the middle, derives generally from Mode 2 (Fig. 2, bottom).

As regards duration in general, most of the slower rhythms and section lengths derive from Fibonacci relationships, not because of their numerologic or mystic implications, but because they present a convenient and effective alternative to traditional rhythmic structures. Of course, a little acknowledgment of the gods of mathematics never hurt any computer musician.

Some rhythmic units are based on a suboctave of a central pitch being used at the time. For example, the primary tone in the first oscillating chord at 102 sec is F, 349.23 Hz. Six octaves below that is

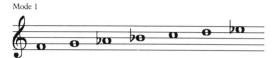

Fig. 1. Two modes from which much of the pitch material in Dreamsong was derived.

Fig. 2. Themes in Dreamsong. The primary theme (top), a setting of a Zen sutra derived from Mode 1. Secondary theme (bottom), derived in part from Mode 2.

Mode 1

Mode 2

From per — fect noth—ing—ness the wond'—rous be—ing ap —pears

(from a Zen sutra)

5.457 Hz, which is a period of 0.183 sec. This is the rate at which the chord oscillates from channel to channel and is four times the rate of the octave bells on B-flat in the background.

Programs, Machines

The primary program used was MUS10, Leland Smith's version of Tovar's MUSCMP (Tovar 1977; Tovar and Smith 1977), which is an extended version of Stanford's original music program (written by David W. Poole). That program was a descendant of Music IV, written by Max W. Mathews. This music compiler features a subset of Algol with special operations directed toward music synthesis. Thus, in addition to the usual unit generator–type functions, one can program one's own initialization-time and run-time functions, which allows a tremendous degree of flexibility in instrument design—yet to be matched by any hardware synthesizer currently operational. This flexibility was critical to the production of Dreamsong.

Sound editing, filtering, and analysis were done using the programs EDSND by Loren Rush (Rush and Mattox, forthcoming) and S by James A. Moorer. In certain cases, note lists were generated with Leland Smith's SCORE program (Smith 1972), although most of the work was generated in small sections to be digitally mixed, so that note lists could usually be typed in directly using the text editor. All computation was carried out on the DEC KL-10 processor of the Stanford Artificial Intelligence Laboratory.

About MUS10

Since much of the discussion in this article will be illustrated with code listings, it will be necessary to digress slightly to give a general introduction to the MUS10 language.

MUS10 code includes a mixture of floating-point variables and arrays, simple Algol statements and functions, and *unit generators*, which are special functions designed to cycle through waveform tables or envelopes or perform other processes such as random-number generation. These unit generators are very similar to the unit generators in Music V (Mathews 1969).

The code for a particular sound or process is grouped into what is known as an *instrument* block, which begins with the declaration "**instrument** ⟨name⟩;" (an example to be discussed later is given in Code Listing 3). The code in an instrument block is evaluated once per sample, with all current instruments being evaluated in order of definition. The output of each instrument for that sample for each channel is then stored, and the process begins again for the next sample.

An instrument declaration may be followed by the declaration of variables local to that block, using the declaration "**variable** ⟨variable 1⟩, ⟨variable 2⟩, . . . ⟨variable n⟩;". If the variables are to change in value during the course of a note (e.g., receive the value of a unit generator), they are known as *run-time variables* and are preceded by a slash in the declaration (the first such example is in the code for RANDF, Code Listing 2). Otherwise they are *initialization-time variables* and will retain the first value that they are assigned. Arrays are declared with "**array** ⟨name1⟩, ⟨name2⟩, . . . ⟨name n |x|⟩;" where the elements of the array are numbered from 0 to $x - 1$. Variables and arrays may also be declared outside of an instrument block, in which case they are global to all subsequent instruments. These are often used for communication between instruments.

Following the instrument and variable declarations may come a block of code that is to be executed only at the onset of a note. This block is prefaced with "**i__only**" (i.e., initialization only). Either run-time or initialization-time variables may be assigned values in this block.

There are a number of predeclared variables. **SRate** contains the sampling rate in Hertz. **Outa**, **outb**, **outc**, and **outd** store the final values of samples going to each of four possible channels. A set of variables P1, P2, P3, . . . P*n* stores the parameters for each instrument call. **Mag** (for *magic number*) stores a value needed in unit generators and elsewhere to compute the increments. **Mag** is normally set to the standard wavetable length divided by the sampling rate. Multiplying this by the desired frequency gives the increment. For example, if the

wavetable is 512 words in length and **sRate** is 25600 Hz, then **mag** is 0.02. If the waveform is to be played at 200 Hz, then the increment becomes **mag** $* 200 = 4$.

The unit generators referred to in this article are only a subset of those available in MUS10.

Oscil (⟨amplitude⟩, ⟨increment⟩, ⟨array⟩) returns a value from the given waveform array, depending on ⟨increment⟩, and scaled by ⟨amplitude⟩.

Zoscil is similar to **oscil**, but interpolates between adjacent array elements for increased accuracy (i.e., less noise).

Expen (or **zexpen**) is like **oscil** (or **zoscil**), but reads through the array only once, holding the final value thereafter.

Zosca is a form of **zoscil** that allows the waveform index to be initialized to **zosca**'s first argument.

Linen(⟨amp⟩, ⟨attack time⟩, ⟨decay time⟩, ⟨duration⟩, ⟨array⟩, ⟨internal variable⟩) allows independent control over the attack and decay portions of an envelope, like the **LINENS** unit generator of Music IVBF (Howe 1975). The ⟨internal variable⟩ must be declared by the calling routine (an example will be given in Code Listing 3).

Randh(⟨amplitude⟩, ⟨increment⟩) returns a value from a stepwise random function.

Value[n](⟨expression⟩) is not a unit generator as such, but simply causes the given expression to be evaluated every *n* samples.

Algol functions may be declared using the construct "**function** (⟨argument 1⟩, ⟨argument 2⟩, . . . ⟨argument *n*⟩)" followed by a block of code that performs operations on the given arguments or global variables or both. These functions may also **return** a result to the instrument or function from which they are called. A number of predeclared functions exists:

Int(R) returns the integer part of a real number *R*.
Rand returns a random number between -1 and 1.
Power(x,y) returns x^y.
Zero(A) sets all elements in array A to 0.
Sqrt(x) returns the square root of *x*.

Two special operators, **seg** and **synth**, are used to set up envelope and waveform tables. **Seg** is used

Code Listing 1. Code for the ZDELAY and SDELAY functions, which are interpolating variable-length delay units.

```
function ZDELAY(Input, Curlen, BufLen, array Buffer, Inptr);
   begin
   variable Samp1, Samp2;
   Buffer[Inptr] ← Input;                              ⟨Read in the new sample
   Samp1 ← Inptr − Curlen;                             ⟨Position readout pointer
   if Samp1 < 0 then Samp1 ← Samp1 + BufLen;           ⟨Might have to wrap around
   Inptr ← Inptr + 1;                                  ⟨Increment input pointer
   if Inptr ≥ BufLen then Inptr ← 0;                   ⟨Wrap around if at end of array
   if Samp1 < BufLen−1 then Samp2 ← Samp1+1
      else Samp2 ← 0;
   return(Buffer[Samp1] + ((Samp1−int(Samp1)) * (Buffer[Samp2]−Buffer[Samp1])));
   end;

function SDELAY(Curlen, BufLen, array Buffer, Inptr);  ⟨Just reads out of same buffer
   begin
   variable Samp1, Samp2;
   Samp1 ← Inptr − Curlen;                             ⟨Position readout pointer
   if Samp1 < 0 then Samp1 ← Samp1 + BufLen;           ⟨Might have to wrap around
   if Samp1 < BufLen−1 then Samp2 ← Samp1+1
      else Samp2 ← 0;                                  ⟨Check for end of array
   return(Buffer[Samp1] + ((Samp1−int(Samp1)) * (Buffer[Samp2]−Buffer[Samp1])));
   end;
```

to fill a table with a line-segment function. If env is declared as an array, then "**seg** (env); y_1 x_1, y_2 x_2, . . . , y_n x_n;" fills the array with a function defined by the given coordinate pairs, where the x_n are between 1 and 100, and the y_n may be any value. The function is normalized in the x domain to fit the bounds of the array. **Synth** is used when a set of harmonic numbers and corresponding amplitudes are to be defined. **Synth** (wave); h_1 a_1, h_2 a_2, . . . , h_n a_n 999;" will fill the array wave with a waveform containing the harmonics humbered h_n at their respective amplitudes a_n. The waveform is normalized to fit within the range $[-1,1]$. The number 999 is used to mark the end of the definition. If desired, two additional numbers may be added to each pair, representing the initial phase in degrees, and the amplitude ("DC") offset. In this case, "99" must immediately precede the definition (Arnold 1978).

Some Key Functions

ZDELAY, SDELAY

The Algol part of MUS10 allowed the creation of several run-time functions that were used throughout *Dreamsong* for many different purposes. These include ZDELAY (an interpolating delay line), SDELAY (which provides an additional output from ZDELAY), and RANDF (a correlated noise generator).

ZDELAY (see Code Listing 1) consists of a buffer array that can be thought of as a ring. Samples are written sequentially into the array, wrapping around when the end of the array is reached. Samples are then read out from a "delayed" location, some real number of samples behind where the new samples are being written. The length of the delay may be dynamically variable, and a linear interpolation is done to provide the fractional part of the delay length. SDELAY simply provides an additional output tap at a different point on the same delay line.

Randf

MUS10 includes three functions that deal with random numbers: **rand**, **randh**, and **randi**. **Rand** (which requires no argument) returns a new random number whenever it is called. **Randh** generates a random stepwise function at a given frequency. **Randi** does likewise, but linearly interpolates between new values, producing a zig-zag function. All values are scaled to $[-1,1]$.

Attempts to use **randi** as a frequency modulator to produce a natural-sounding random vibrato met with little success and led to extensive experimentation with $1/f$ and other types of noise. $1/f$ noise has a power spectral density that decreases proportionally to 1/frequency, as opposed to white noise, whose power spectral density is flat. The essential difference is that white noise is uncorrelated: each new random value is chosen independently of the preceding one. $1/f$ noise, however, is correlated noise: each new value depends to some extent on what the last one was (Gardner 1978). This kind of randomness is frequently found in nature, for example, in profiles of coastlines, mountain ranges, etc., and it is also probably representative of the natural unevenness of human-produced vocal and instrumental tones. After all, in these cases each physical variation is certainly not independent of the adjacent or preceding ones. When used to synthesize a random vibrato, the $1/f$ variety produces a much more natural-sounding result than white noise. A certain smoothness is heard, resulting from the absence of the occasional large skips between values that occur when there is no correlation.

After several complex and computationally expensive $1/f$ noise algorithms (programmed by Julius Smith) were tried, it was observed that for most purposes almost any moderate amount of correlation applied to the random-number sequence would do the job. RANDF in Code Listing 2 does just that in a very simple manner, producing white noise when Factor is 0, and increasingly correlated noise as

Factor approaches 1. The quality of the noise can thus be "tuned." (OldVal keeps track of the previously generated value.) RANDFI produces a linearly interpolating random function at frequency Freq, scaled by amplitude Amp, and correlated according to Factor. Cnt must be initialized to 0, and OldVal and Diff are global variables used to keep track of the preceding value and its difference from the next one. RANDFC is much like RANDFI, but interpolates with the portion of the cosine function taken from 0 to π instead of a straight line. This produces better results in certain applications, such as in controlling the delay time of a ZDELAY unit being used as a choral-effects generator.

Readin

Another special function used frequently is **readin**. This MUS10 function enables input of one or more stored digital sound files into an instrument, where the samples can be modified in any way allowed by the available code. One obvious use of this feature is for processing digitally recorded natural sounds. Another very valuable application is multipass synthesis, in which sounds (phrases, passages) are arrived at gradually in steps. Synthesizing all aspects at once can be very inefficient in a system in which one tiny mistake can cause the recomputation of many minutes of complex sound. For example, one might start by computing a single-voice melody, then process that through a chorus-effect generator, then process that through a panning instrument, and finally add reverberation. Each step of the process may be worked on until it is perfected, without recomputation of the previous steps. For small systems, this method also has the advantage of keeping program core requirements down.

In this fashion, compositions are gradually constructed piecemeal and mixed into larger and larger sections until the work is complete. This is how *Dreamsong* came into being.

Synthesis Techniques

Additive Synthesis: Voice Instrument

As was mentioned earlier, most of the distinctly vocal sounds in *Dreamsong* were produced by pro-

Code Listing 2. Random-number generators used in Dreamsong. RANDF is a random-number function that uses correlated noise. RANDFI, a periodic random-number generator, interpolates linearly between successive values. RANDFC is a periodic random-number generator that interpolates using the portion of the cosine function taken from 0 to π.

```
function RANDF(OldVal, Factor);
  begin
  variable /LowBound, /UprBound, /Range;
  Range ← 2 − 2 * Factor;
  LowBound ← OldVal − Range;
  if LowBound < −1 then LowBound ← −1;
  UprBound ← OldVal + Range;
  if UprBound > 1 then UprBound ← 1;
  return(LowBound + (UprBound−LowBound) * (1+rand)/2);
  end;

function RANDFI(Amp,Freq,Factor,OldVal,Diff,Cnt);
  begin
  variable /Interp;
  Interp ← Cnt/(sRate/Freq);
  if Interp ≥ 1 then Cnt ← Interp ← 0;
  if Cnt = 0 then
    begin
    OldVal ← OldVal + Diff;
    Diff ← RANDF(OldVal, Factor) − OldVal;
    end;
  Cnt ← Cnt + 1;
  return(Amp * (OldVal + Diff * Interp));
  end;
array Curv,CurvDiff(128);                                    ⟨"s" Curve data
variable I,CosLen;
CosLen ← 127;
for I ← 0 step 1 until CosLen do Curv[I] ← (1−COS(PI * (I/CosLen))) *.5;
for I ← 0 step 1 until CosLen−1 do CurvDiff[I] ← Curv[I+1] − Curv[I];

function RANDFC(Amp, Freq, Factor, OldVal, Diff, Cnt);
  begin
  variable Indx, NewVal;
  Indx ← (CosLen/sRate) * Cnt* Freq;
  if Indx ≥ CosLen then Cnt ← Indx ← 0;
  if Cnt = 0 then
    begin
    OldVal ← OldVal + Diff;
    Diff ← RANDF(OldVal, Factor) − OldVal;
    end;
  Cnt ← Cnt + 1;
  return(Amp * (OldVal+Diff * (Curv[Indx]+CurvDiff[Indx] * (Indx−int[Indx]))));
  end;
```

cessing digitally recorded soprano tones. However, if certain kinds of transformations are desired, recorded tones cannot be used. For example, 220 sec into *Dreamsong*, a cluster of bells at random pitches gradually coalesces into a solo singing voice, and soon after that a whole chorus of singers coalesces into a single, low-frequency drone! In these cases, it is necessary to have absolute control over the frequency and amplitude of each harmonic of the voice. If the spectrum is generated by a set of individual sine-wave oscillators, one can easily interpolate from or to other similar sets of data, whether harmonic or inharmonic. The exploitation of *spectral fusion* phenomena (Chowning 1980) becomes relatively simple and is rich with expressive possibilities.

When such control was not needed, it was found that the application of the proper vibrato, overall frequency skew, and overall amplitude envelope to an otherwise steady-state waveform was quite adequate to synthesize a soprano voice convincingly (see Code Listing 3). The spectral information was obtained by doing a Fourier transform of a segment of approximately 200 msec of the original voice. This method of synthesis represents a considerable step in data reduction from complete three-dimensional analysis (time, frequency, amplitude) such as that done by the phase vocoder (Portnoff 1976). All the harmonics remain proportionally the same relative to the fundamental (this would not be the case if an interpolation were taking place). In a complex compositional texture, where the exact reproduction of a specific tone is not needed, this method gives very good results. Essentially, there is only one frequency function and one amplitude function. The frequency function in Code Listing 3 has two parts, vibrato and skew. The *skew* function is a simplified representation of the natural tendency to "home in" on the pitch during the attack of the note. The vibrato is synthesized separately using RANDFI.

Additive Synthesis: Random Formant Instrument

The primary melodic and drone instrument in *Dreamsong*, other than the voice, also uses additive synthesis. It computes its own dynamic spectrum based on a series of randomly generated formant structures. The overall spectral decay shape is supplied as an array of amplitudes or possibly two arrays with a gradual interpolation between them. The formant structure is computed from a random number tree, as shown in Code Listing 4, with the sum of the eight spectral amplitudes normalized to the value N by the GetHarms function. The process is analogous to a binary fractal pattern (Mandelbrot 1977), only each iteration is randomized. The results are quite different from results when eight independent random numbers are selected. For example, with the tree, all eight spectral amplitude values will come out equal only if all the random numbers turn out to be exactly 0.5. This process thus guarantees a much greater variety in the distribution of energy from one function call to the next.

The instrument OMM, given in Code Listing 5, appears many times in *Dreamsong*, in particular between 90 sec and 150 sec, between 265 sec and 415 sec (see Fig. 4), and between 477 sec and 510 sec. At the end of the second low drone (around 400 sec), the controlling spectral shape gradually allows only the 11th and 12th harmonics to be present (in a 12-harmonic version), which become the two pitches around which the following whole section is based, thus effectively blurring the distinction between timbre and normal musical pitch structures in a way possible only with digital synthesis. The instrument as presented here is somewhat simpler than that used in the piece, but all essential elements are present. In addition, envelopes for a sample case are given in the code. Two auxiliary functions are also defined, one that simply copies an array and another that interpolates between two arrays, given the interpolation fraction.

Code Listing 5 contains a sample instrument call that begins generating new formants at 1-sec intervals and gradually speeds up to 0.1-sec intervals. The overall spectral decay shape changes from F1 to F2 (also defined in Code Listing 5) in the first 2.5 sec of the note, which glissandos up from F to G and has 1.2% vibrato at 4.5 Hz.

Frequency Modulation: Two Bells

A complex FM instrument was designed to produce a cathedral-bell-like sound. It uses three carriers,

Code Listing 3. Instrument
SING, used to model a
singing voice with additive
synthesis and RANDFI.

Code Listing 4. Function
GetHarms, which
generates harmonics used
by instrument OMM (Code
Listing 5).

```
array F1,F2,F3(512);
synth(F1);1 1.0000,    2 0.7079,    3 0.0126,    4 0.0050,
            5 0.0316,    6 0.0016,    7 0.0022,    8 0.0014,
            9 0.0018,   10 0.0056,   11 0.0010,   12 0.0010,
           13 0.0010,   14 0.0014,   999;                      ⟨soprano "ah" at D5
seg(F2);  0 1,   1 10,   0.7 25,   0.9 37.5,   0.7 50,   0 75,   0 100;   ⟨Amplitude envelope
seg(F3);−1 1,   0.3 12,   0 25,   0 50,   −.5 75,   −.5 100;   ⟨Frequency skew envelope

instrument SING;                                               ⟨Parameters: Beg, Dur, Freq, Amp
variable /X,/Y,/Cnt,/Va1,/Va2,/Vib,/Env,/Sig,/Skew;            ⟨runtime variables
i__only begin X ← Y ← Cnt ← Va1 ← Va2 ← 0; end;                ⟨Always initialize these to zero
Vib ← 1 + RANDFI(.01, 18, 0.6, X, Y, Cnt);                     ⟨random vibrato generator
Skew ← 1 + linen(.12, 0.2, 0.1, P2, F3, Va1);                  ⟨frequency skew function
Sig ← oscil(P4, (P3 * mag)* Vib * Skew, F1);                   ⟨waveform oscillator
Env ← linen(1, 0.18, 0.15, P2, F2, Va2);                       ⟨envelope generator with attack
outa ← outa + Sig * Env;                                       ⟨   and decay parameters
end;
```

```
function GetHarms(array Harms, array Shape, N);
  begin
  variable I,Sum; array X(9),R(7);
  for I ← 0 step 1 until 6 do R[I] ← abs(rand);                ⟨Choose seven random
                                                               ⟨   numbers (0 ⇔ 1)
  X[1] ←       R[0] *       R[1] *       R[3] ;                ⟨calculate 8 values from tree.
  X[2] ←       R[0] *       R[1] * (1−R[3]);
  X[3] ←       R[0] * (1−R[1]) *       R[4] ;
  X[4] ←       R[0] * (1−R[1]) * (1−R[4]);
  X[5] ← (1−R[0]) *       R[2] *       R[5] ;
  X[6] ← (1−R[0]) *       R[2] * (1−R[5]);
  X[7] ← (1−R[0]) * (1−R[2]) *       R[6] ;
  X[8] ← (1−R[0]) * (1−R[2]) * (1−R[6]);
  Sum ← 0;
  for I ← 1 step 1 until 8 do
    begin
    Harms[I] ← X[I] * Shape[I];                                ⟨Multiply by spectral envelope
    Sum ← Sum + Harms[I];
    end;
  for I ← 1 step 1 until 8 do
    Harms[I] ← Harms[I] * N / Sum;                             ⟨Normalize to N
  end;
```

McNabb

Code Listing 5. Instrument
OMM is an additive syn-
thesis instrument that
generates its own random
series of formants using

GetHarms (Code Listing
4). The sample instrument
call uses typical parameter
values.

```
Parameters:
  P1:  Begin Time
  P2:  Duration
  P3:  Fundamental frequency
  P4:  Peak Amplitude (arbitrary linear scale from 0 to 2047)
  P5:  Amplitude function
  P6:  Formant shift time, function in P8 = 0
  P7:  Formant shift time, function in P8 = 1
  P8:  Formant shift time function
  P9:  Spectral envelope 1
  P10: Spectral envelope 2
  P11: Duration of interpolation from P9 to P10
  P12: Glissando note, function in P13 = 1
  P13: Glissando function
  P14: Percentage of vibrato (0 ⇔ 1) as percentage of P3
  P15: Vibrato rate
  P16: Amplitude envelope attack time (for linen)
  P17: Amplitude envelope decay time
array Env,Ramp1,Ramp2,Gliss,Syn[512];
array F1,F2,CurShape,Shape1,Shape2,Amps,NewAmp,OldAmp[9];

seg(Env); 0 1, 1 5, 0.7 25, 1 37.5, 0.7 50, 0 75, 0 100;        ⟨Amplitude envelope
seg(Ramp1); 0 1, 1 75, 1 100;                                    ⟨Upward ramp
seg(Ramp2); 1 1, 0 100;                                          ⟨Downward ramp
seg(Gliss); 0 1, 0 45, 1 55, 1 100;                              ⟨Upward glissando
synth(Syn); 1 1, 999;                                            ⟨Sine wave
variable I;
for I ← 1 step 1 until 8 do                                      ⟨Two spectral envelopes:
  begin
  F1[I] ← 1 / power(I,2);                                        ⟨A = 1/N²
  F2[I] ← 1 / I;                                                 ⟨A = 1/N
  end;
F2[2] ← F2[4] ← F2[6] ← F2[8] ← 0;                               ⟨F2 gets odd harmonics only

function ArrTran(array X,array Y,I);                             ⟨Copies one array into another
  begin
  for I ← 1 step 1 until 8 do X[I] ← Y[I];
  end;

function FunIntrp
  (array One, array Two, array New, Fraction);                  ⟨Interpolates between two arrays
  begin variable I;
  for I ← 1 step 1 until 8 do
    New[I] ← One[I]+(Two[I]−One[I]) * Fraction;
  end;
  instrument OMM;
  variable /Switch,/Samples,/Amp,/Count,Limit,/Intr,/Vib,Var,
           /AmpScl,/Rate,/Inc,/FormantPeriod,/AttAmp,/Att,/I,/Gliss,
           /H1,/H2,/H3,/H4,/H5,/H6,/H7,/H8;
```

```
i_only begin
  Samples ← Var ← 0;                                    ⟨Initialization code
  Switch ← 1;
  ArrTran(Shape1,P9,I); ArrTran(Shape2,P10,I);          ⟨Get spectral envelopes
  GetHarms(NewAmp, Shape1, Amp ← P4);                   ⟨Initial amplitudes
  FormantPeriod ← sRate * P6;                           ⟨Rate of formant change
  Count ← FormantPeriod + 1;                            ⟨Counter for interpolating
  Limit ← sRate * P11;                                  ⟨How quickly to interpolate
  end;
if Samples ≤ Limit then
  begin
  Samples ← Samples+1;
  Intr ← Samples/Limit;                                 ⟨Interpolate spectral envelopes
  value[16](FunIntrp(Shape1,Shape2,CurShape,Intr));
  end;
if Count > FormantPeriod then
  begin
  Count ← 0;
  ArrTran(OldAmp, NewAmp, I);                           ⟨Save previous formants
  GetHarms(NewAmp, CurShape, Amp);                      ⟨get new formants
  end;
Rate ← P6 + oscil(P7−P6, mag/P2, P8);                  ⟨Get rate of formant change
value[8](FormantPeriod ← int(sRate * Rate));           ⟨Convert to samples
value[4](Switch ← 1);
if Switch = 1 then
  begin                                                 ⟨Calculate current amplitudes
  Intr ← Count / FormantPeriod;
  for I ← 1 step 1 until 8 do
      Amps[I] ← OldAmp[I]+(NewAmp[I]−OldAmp[I]) * Intr;
  Switch ← 0;
  end;
Count ← Count + 1;
AttAmp ← expen(1, mag/.17, Ramp2);                      ⟨Attack noise envelope
if AttAmp > 0 then
  Att ← 1 + RANDH(0.5 * AttAmp, 4000 * mag);           ⟨Attack noise
Gliss ← oscil((P12−P3) * Att * mag, mag/P2, P13);      ⟨glissando factor
Vib  ← oscil((P14*P3) * Att * mag, mag * P15, SYN);    ⟨vibrato factor
Inc ← P3*Att*mag + Gliss + Vib;                        ⟨Calculate frequency increment
H1 ← oscil(Amps[1],    Inc, SYN);                      ⟨generate eight harmonics
H2 ← oscil(Amps[2], 2 * Inc, SYN);
H3 ← oscil(Amps[3], 3 * Inc, SYN);
H4 ← oscil(Amps[4], 4 * Inc, SYN);
H5 ← oscil(Amps[5], 5 * Inc, SYN);
H6 ← oscil(Amps[6], 6 * Inc, SYN);
H7 ← oscil(Amps[7], 7 * Inc, SYN);
H8 ← oscil(Amps[8], 8 * Inc, SYN);
AmpScl ← linen(1, P16, P17, P2, P5, Var);              ⟨Amplitude function
outa ← outa + (H1+H2+H3+H4+H5+H6+H7+H8) * AmpScl;      ⟨Output
end;
play;                                                   ⟨sample instrument call
OMM 0 3 F 2000 Env 1 0.1 Ramp1 F1 F2 2.5 G Gliss 0.012 4.5 0.2 0.2;
finish;
```

Code Listing 6. An oscil-
lator is used to shape
a signal read in by the
readin function; the
shaping envelope name
is passed in P4.

```
instrument SHAPER;                      ⟨Parameters: Beg, Dur, Amp scaler, Envelope
variable /Env;
Env ← zoscil(P3, mag/P2, P4);          ⟨generate envelope
outa ← outa + readin(RD) * Env;        ⟨multiply times input samples
end;
```

each modified by one modulator, one of which contains a complex wave. The second carrier, which produces an inharmonic spectrum, actually contributes relatively little, since its amplitude is kept small. Most of the characteristic sound comes from a combination of one harmonic spectrum, with a second harmonic spectrum having a fundamental a just minor 10th above the first. This instrument is used at the very beginning of *Dreamsong* and again in the middle, at about 350 sec.

A handbell sound was also created, which uses two modulators and two carriers like two simple FM units in parallel. There is no inharmonic ratio in either unit, and again the characteristic sound comes from the combination of one harmonic spectrum with another having a fundamental a just minor 10th above the first.

Processing Techniques

Shaping

Most of the following processing algorithms are constructed around the functions defined in the section entitled "Some Key Functions" and were applied to the digitally recorded sung vocal and crowd sounds and to previously synthesized sounds. They demonstrate in particular the usefulness and versatility of the ZDELAY function.

An introductory example of sound file processing in MUS10, Code Listing 6, is an instrument that reads a sound file, shapes its amplitude by a given function, and writes it out again.

Comb Filtering, Flanging

Perhaps the simplest application of ZDELAY is as a *comb filter*, which results when a delayed signal is added back to itself. Since the peaks thus produced are separated by a constant frequency, they form a harmonic series and can be used to give a pitched effect to an otherwise nonpitched sound. As more feedback is added, the filtering is more severe and the pitched effect is more pronounced. A delay of $sRate/f$ samples (used for curLen in Code Listing 1) will place the first peak at frequency f. If the delay is doubled and the delayed signal subtracted from the original signal instead of added, the peaks form a pattern that corresponds only to odd harmonics, which produces an expectedly "hollow" effect. If feedback is used, the output signal must be renormalized down to a reasonable amplitude.

Modulation of the delay time (curLen in Code Listing 1) with a sine wave results in an effect known as *flanging*. This term originated in the pop music recording industry when somebody got drunk and discovered that an interesting phasing effect could be produced by setting up a very short tape delay and leaning on the flange of the reel to change its speed slightly. Of course, functions other than a sine wave may be used as modulators. The maximum delay time should be around one period of the sound being processed. This produces more than just a nice sound when the function used is not just a sine wave; if the modulating function undergoes discrete changes, a sequence of pitches is heard. This occurs in *Dreamsong* 30 sec into the piece, when the initial crowd noise is processed into playing the opening melodic motif.

Choral Effect

A more useful ability of ZDELAY is to provide a choral-effect generator that can be used on any sound, in particular on digitally recorded sounds and synthesis instruments that are too complex to allow for multiple copies. In Code Listing 7, three delayed

Code Listing 7. Instrument
CHORUS: RANDFC and
ZDELAY functions are used
to generate a choral effect
from any sound.

```
array Buffer[512];
zero(Buffer);

instrument CHORUS;
variable /Sig, /De1,/De2,/De3, /Ds1,/Ds2,/Ds3,
   /Inptr,Len,Dev,Rate,/A1,/A2,/A3,/B1,/B2,/B3,/C1,/C2,/C3;
i_only begin
   Inptr ← A1 ← A2 ← A3 ← B1 ← B2 ← B3 ← C1 ← C2 ← C3 ← 0;
   Len ← length(Buffer);
   Rate ← P3;                                    ⟨4 Hz is typical
   Dev ← P4;                                     ⟨10 msec worth of samples is usually good for this
end;
Sig ← readin(RD);                               ⟨Input the samples
De1 ← Dev + RANDFC(Dev,Rate,.5,A1,A2,A3);       ⟨delays range from 0 to Dev*2;
De2 ← Dev + RANDFC(Dev,1.1*Rate,.5,B1,B2,B3);
De3 ← Dev + RANDFC(Dev,.9*Rate,.5,C1,C2,C3);
Ds1 ← ZDELAY(Sig, De1, Len, Buffer, Inptr);     ⟨three delayed versions of signal
Ds2 ← SDELAY(Sig, De2, Len, Buffer, Inptr);     ⟨SDELAY reads out in a different spot
Ds3 ← SDELAY(Sig, De3, Len, Buffer, Inptr);     ⟨Yet another copy
outa ← outa + (Sig + Ds1 + Ds2 + Ds3) * 0.3;    ⟨combine all with original, rescale
end;
```

copies of the signal are combined with the original. The delay time of each copy is modulated independently by a RANDFC. The frequencies of the three modulators are offset by about 10%.

Panning, Doppler Shift

The instruments discussed in this section make up the spatial movement system used in *Dreamsong*. Since the piece is in only two channels, every effort was made to maximize the effect of depth and movement. To this end, there is a panning instrument used to both simulate Doppler shift and modulate the initial reflection times for reverberation. This instrument is set up to move the input signal in a straight line or in an arc through an imaginary space defined by distances given in meters.

In general, the action may be thought of as taking place on an *x-y* coordinate "stage" (see Fig. 3). The amplitude of the direct (nonreverberated) part of the signal is scaled to be inversely proportional to the "distance" from the listener; maximum amplitude occurs when the sound is positioned at the same distance as the speakers. The delay of the direct signal is made dynamically proportional to the distance by use of a ZDELAY. The first parameter to ZDELAY is the scaled direct signal, and the second parameter is the delay time in samples, which is equal to the distance times the sampling rate divided by the speed of sound. Since only the delayed signal output from the ZDELAY is sent to the output, an accurate Doppler effect results as the distance changes. Computation of a Doppler effect in this manner is efficient, and is equally applicable to synthesized and recorded sounds.

Similar scaling was done on each channel of reverberation as well as in the reverberation instrument. Modulation of the amplitude and reflection times of each channel of the reverberation was proportional to the total distance that the sound would travel—from the apparent source, back to the "wall," then to the listener (who is, of course, assumed to be in the ideal listening position; sigh). Three "sources" of reverberation were calculated this way, one coming from each channel and one

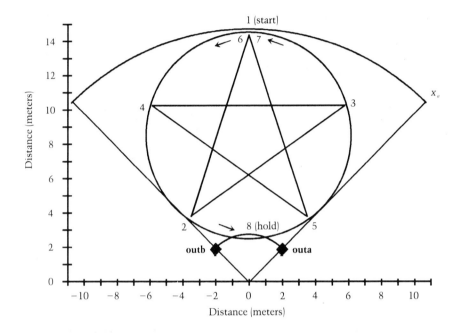

from both channels. Thus, if a sound were positioned on the left, the reverberation from the right channel would be delayed and scaled at a lower amplitude relative to the left channel reverberation. Robert Poor came up with the basic idea for this application of ZDELAY. Figure 3 is an example of how the reverberation instruments can be used to set up an imaginary space 15 m deep, with the speakers positioned 2.8 m from the listener in ideal position.

Amplitude Modulation with Complex Wave

From 70 to 100 sec in *Dreamsong*, a choral texture is gradually transformed into a texture that sounds like strings and brass. This effect was carried out by amplitude modulation (AM) of the digitized vocal tones with a simple FM instrument (see Code Listing 8). The amounts of FM and AM modulation are gradually increased in parallel. For the effect

achieved in *Dreamsong*, the frequencies of the FM oscillators were close to the center frequency of the signal being modulated. Due to the random vibrato in the original signal, the subjective density of the sound is also increased due to phasing and beating effects with the steady FM tone.

Pitch and Envelope Follower

Instrument PITCH (Code Listing 9) reads in a file and puts out its pitch and amplitude contours. It does this by looking for the peaks of the waveform within a window that is dynamically readjusted according to the current amplitude. It remembers the precise time each peak occurs and calculates the frequency every period. After checking to see that a reasonable value results, it sends out the average of the last four values calculated (for smoothness). It is a tricky business, and many of the variables need to be adjusted precisely for each individual file to

Code Listing 8. Instrument AMOD amplitude modulates a signal using an FM-generated waveform.

Code Listing 9. Instrument PITCH puts out an amplitude and pitch contour of the input signal in variables Amp and Freq, which can be read by another instrument (see Code Listing 10). The Squelch removes low-level transients from the more or less silent parts of the input signal.

```
synth(F1);1 1,  999;                              ⟨sine wave
seg(F2);0 0,  1 100;                              ⟨ramp from (0,0) to (100,0)

instrument AMOD;                                  ⟨Beg, Dur, Freq, Deviation
variable /Sig, /FmScl, /Out, /FM, /Am;
Sig ← readin(RD);                                 ⟨input signal
FmScl ← oscil(1, mag/P2, F2);                     ⟨modulation envelope
Fm ← oscil(FmScl*P4*P3*mag, P3*mag, F1);          ⟨FM modulator; P4 is the index
Am ← 1 + zoscil(FmScl, P3*mag+FM, F1);            ⟨FM carrier
Out ← (Sig * Am) / (1+Dev);                       ⟨amplitude modulate and rescale input signal
outa ← outa + Out;                                ⟨  by the FM deviation (see Chowning 1973)
end;
```

```
array Freqs1[16],Freqs2[4],Del1,Del2[2000];
zero(Del1);zero(Del2);

variable /Freq, /Amp, /Samp;                      ⟨Global variables to be read by filter instrument
                                                  ⟨  in Code Listing 10

instrument PITCH;
variable /Max,/Min,/MaxLim,/MinLim,/Peak,/Time1,/Time2,/Avg,/AvDev,/I,
   /S1,/S2,/S3,/S4,/Tmp1,/Tmp2,/Tmp3,/Interp,/Inc,/Cnt,/Cnt1,/Cnt2,/Sum,
   /Ampx,/Amp1,/Amp2,/TmpFreq,/CCR1,CCR2,Inc,Peak__Window,Freq__Window,Squelch;

i__only begin
   for I ← 0 step 1 until 15 do Freqs1[I] ← P3;        ⟨P3 = A guess at the average pitch
   for I ← 0 step 1 until 3 do Freqs2[I] ← P3;
   Avg ← Freq ← P3;
   Time1←Amp2←Max←Min←Peak←Interp←Cnt←Cnt1←Cnt2←S2←0;
   S1 ← S3 ← 1;
   CCR1 ← 2 * sRate/P3;                            ⟨controlled calling rates
   CCR2 ← 960;
   Inc ← 1/CCR2;                                   ⟨increment for amplitude envelope interpolation
   Peak__Window ← 0.12;                            ⟨these variables need to be readjusted for
   Freq__Window ← 0.3;                             ⟨  different kinds of sounds
   Squelch ← 25;                                   ⟨Probably not needed for many sounds
   end;

Samp ← readin(RD);                                 ⟨get next sample of input signal
if Samp > Max then Max ← Samp;                     ⟨Keep track of local maxamp & minamp
if Samp < Min then Min ← Samp;

value[CCR1](S1 ← 1);
```

```
if S1 = 1 then begin                                    ⟨Update limits for finding peaks every CCR1 samples
  Tmp1 ← Max − Min;                                     ⟨Current peak-to-peak amplitude
  Tmp2 ← Tmp1 / 2;                                      ⟨Peak amplitude
  MaxLim ← Max − Tmp1 * Peak__Window;                   ⟨Amplitude window for positive peak
  MinLim ← Min + Tmp1 * Peak__Window;                   ⟨Amplitude window for negative peak
  Max ← Min ← S1 ← 0;                                   ⟨reset variables
  end;

value[CCR2]|(S3 ← 1);
if S3 = 1 then begin                                    ⟨update amplitude for contour every CCR2 samples
  Amp1 ← Amp2;                                          ⟨replace starting amp
  Amp2 ← Tmp2;                                          ⟨goal amp ← current peak from above
  if Amp2 < Squelch then Amp2 ← 0;                      ⟨may not want very low amplitudes
  Tmp3 ← Amp2 − Amp1;                                   ⟨net difference
  S3 ← Interp ← 0;                                      ⟨reset variables
  end;

Amp ← Amp1 + Tmp3 * Interp;                             ⟨Interp from one amp value to the next
Interp ← Interp + Inc;                                  ⟨increment is 1/CCR2

if Samp > MaxLim then                                   ⟨Let's look for the peak now
  if S2 = 0 then
    if Samp > Peak then
      begin
      Peak ← Samp;                                      ⟨update peak value
      Time2 ← Cnt;                                      ⟨note the time (in samples)
      end
    else S2 ← 1;
if Samp < MinLim then                                   ⟨good time to figure out current frequency
  if S2 = 1 then
    begin
    TmpFreq ← sRate / (Time2 − Time1);                  ⟨new frequency value
    Freqs1[Cnt1] ← TmpFreq;
    if TmpFreq > Avg * 2 then Freqs1[Cnt1] ← Avg;
    if TmpFreq < Avg/2 then Freqs1[Cnt1] ← Avg;
    Sum ← 0;
    for I ← 0 step 1 until 15 do Sum ← Sum + Freqs1[I];  ⟨take average
                                                        ⟨  of last 16 frequencies
    Avg ← Sum/16;
    if abs(Freqs1[Cnt1] − Avg) < Freq__Window * Avg then ⟨If new value is not too
      begin                                             ⟨  weird then accept it
      Freqs2[Cnt2] ← Freqs1[Cnt1];                      ⟨Add to 4 most current
      Cnt2 ← Cnt2 + 1; if Cnt2 = 4 then Cnt2 ← 0;       ⟨  acceptable values
      Sum ← 0;
      for I ← 0 step 1 until 3 do Sum ← Sum + Freqs2[I]; ⟨average these for smoothness
      Freq ← Sum/4;
      CCR1 ← 2 * sRate/Freq;
      end;
    Cnt1 ← Cnt1 + 1;                                    ⟨counter for freqs1 array
    if Cnt1 = 16 then Cnt1 ← 0;
    Time1 ← Time 2;                                     ⟨the two peak times
    Peak ← S2 ← 0;
    end;

Cnt ← Cnt + 1;                                          ⟨sample counter
end;
```

Code Listing 10.
Instrument COMB uses
variables Amp and Freq
from the PITCH instrument

(Code Listing 9) to control
amplitude and peak
position of the comb filter
ZDELAY.

```
array BuffA,BuffB[512],BuffC[800];
seg(F1);0,1 0,18 0.6,34 1,50 1,100;
seg(F2);0,1 0,50 0.1,57 0.3,64 0.6,71 1,100;

instrument COMB;
variable /CrowdR, /CrowdL, /DelSigA, /DelSigB,
  /PtrA, /PtrB, /G, /CrowdAmp, /Del, /Voice;
i__only begin
  DelSigA ← DelSigB ← PtrA ← PtrB ← 0;
  zero(BuffA); zero(BuffB);
  Freq ← 200; Amp ← 500;
  end;
CrowdR ← readin(RD);                      ⟨read in crowd sound in stereo
CrowdL ← readin(RD);
VoiceAmp ← oscil(1, mag/P2, F2);          ⟨controls mix of unfiltered voice
AmpMod ← INTRP(1,Amp/500,F1);             ⟨controls modulation of crowd
CrowdAmp ← AmpMod * (1−VoiceAmp);         ⟨   by amplitude of voice

G ← oscil(1, mag/P2, F1);                 ⟨controls gain of filter
Del ← sRate / Freq;                       ⟨Freq comes from PITCH instrument, Code Listing 9
DelSigR ← ZDELAY(CrowdR * G, Del, 512, BuffA,
  PtrA);                                  ⟨stereo dynamic comb filters
DelSigL ← ZDELAY(CrowdL * G, Del, 512, BuffB,
  PtrB);

Voice ← DELAY(Samp, 800, BuffC);          ⟨delay voice to match delayed information
                                          ⟨   from PITCH
outa ← outa + (CrowdR+DelSigR) * CrowdAmp + Voice * VoiceAmp;
outb ← outb + (CrowdL+DelSigL) * CrowdAmp + Voice * VoiceAmp;
end;
```

be read in. In *Dreamsong*, this instrument was used (1) to check the pitch of some of the soprano notes and (2) to follow the pitch and amplitude of Dylan Thomas's voice, which was used to modulate a ZDELAY comb filter on the crowd sound at the very end. The filtering/mixing instrument (COMB) used for that is given in the next section.

Stereo Comb Filters Controlled by Pitch

Instrument COMB, given in Code Listing 10, reads in a stereo signal and filters it with a comb filter that has its first peak at the frequency provided by the PITCH instrument. It also modulates the amplitude of the input signal by the amplitude of the sound being read by PITCH and gradually interpolates between the sound being filtered and the sound doing the modulating. In *Dreamsong*, the modulating sound was Dylan Thomas's voice (taken from a recording) and it was used to filter the crowd sounds that serve as one of the motivic elements. The passage begins with the straight crowd sound, which gradually becomes more and more processed until it takes on the pitch and cadence of Thomas's characteristic speech. At this point it is gradually cross-faded with the unaltered voice.

Fig. 4. Graphic representation of central portion of Dreamsong. The frequency scale is logarithmic, time is in seconds, and the thickness of each line is proportional to amplitude. Instruments OMM, BELL1, and BELL2 are playing here. This plot was produced by the author with the aid of graphics routines by James A. Moorer and the MUSBOX program of D. Gareth Loy.

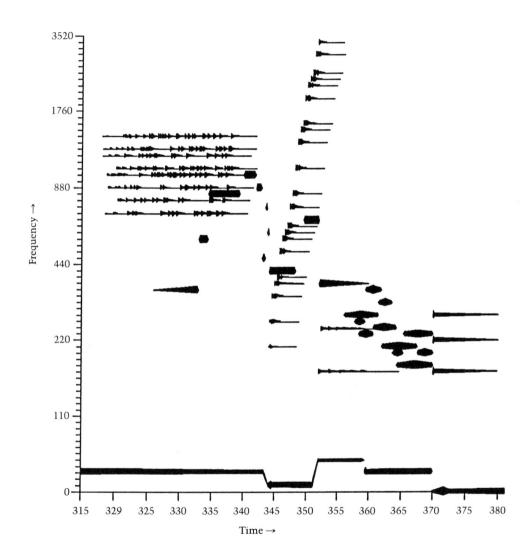

Fig. 4. Graphic representation of central portion of Dreamsong. The frequency scale is logarithmic, time is in seconds, and the thickness of each line is proportional to amplitude. Instruments OMM, BELL1, and BELL2 are playing here. This plot was produced by the author with the aid of graphics routines by James A. Moorer and the MUSBOX program of D. Gareth Loy.

Acknowledgments

The author wishes to thank the many people who wrote and taught him to use effectively the programs used in *Dreamsong*, who helped him over conceptual or mathematical stumbling blocks, and who calmly gave him encouragement when he was mad as hell about some programming bug and wasn't going to take it any more. The many include John Chowning, John Grey, D. Gareth Loy, F. Richard Moore, James A. Moorer, Robert Poor, Loren Rush, Bill Schottstaedt, Ken Shoemake, Julius Orion Smith, Leland Smith, Tovar, and Paul Wieneke.

Thanks also to Stephen Volz, who helped me make that beautiful recording of the crowd, to soprano Marilyn Barber, who provided so much with so few notes, and to John Strawn for his editorial assistance.

References

Arnold, A. 1978. Private communication.

Chowning, J. 1973. "The Synthesis of Complex Audio Spectra by Means of Frequency Modulation." *Journal of the Audio Engineering Society* 21(7):526–534. Reprinted in *Computer Music Journal* 1(2):46–54, 1977.

Chowning, J. 1980. "Computer Synthesis of the Singing Voice." In *Sound Generation in Winds, Strings, Computers*, ed. J. Sundberg. Stockholm: Royal Institute of Technology, pp. 4–13.

Gardner, M. 1978. "Mathematical Games: White and Brown Music, Fractal Curves, and One-over-f Fluctuations." *Scientific American* 238(4):16–31.

Howe, H. S., Jr. 1975. *Electronic Music Synthesis.* New York: Norton.

Mandelbrot, B. 1977. *Fractals: Form, Chance and Dimension.* San Francisco: Freeman.

Mathews, M. 1969. *The Technology of Computer Music.* Cambridge, Massachusetts: MIT Press.

Portnoff, M. R. 1976. "Implementation of the Digital Phase Vocoder Using the Fast Fourier Transform." *IEEE Proceedings on Acoustics, Speech, and Signal Processing* 24:243–248.

Rush, L., and J. Mattox. Forthcoming. "Mama Don't Allow No Tape Machine 'Round Here: The Digital Audio Production Facility." In *Computer Music*, ed. C. Roads and J. Strawn. Cambridge, Massachusetts: MIT Press.

Schroeder, M. R. 1961. "Natural Sounding Artificial Reverberation." *Journal of the Acoustical Society of America* 10(3):219–223.

Smith, L. 1972. "Score: A Musician's Approach to Computer Music." *Journal of the Audio Engineering Society* 20:7–14.

Tovar. 1977. "Music Manual." Unpublished user's manual. Stanford: Center for Computer Research in Music and Acoustics.

Tovar, and L. Smith. 1977. "MUS10 Manual." Unpublished user's manual. Stanford: Center for Computer Research in Music and Acoustics.

12

Otto Laske
Boston, Massachusetts

Composition Theory in Koenig's Project One and Project Two

Introduction

Composition theory is a theory about the process that underlies the design and realization of musical compositions. In particular, composition theory is about processes that are based on the use of explicit rule systems. In this century, the use of such systems has been given a new impetus through the development of computer programs. Programs for composition enable composers to work as musical engineers. This means they can use structured design methods and techniques developed for artificial intelligence (AI) systems such as knowledge-based systems. Composers can define compositional form in a series of steps leading from an overall design of deep structure (set of germinal ideas) to a more and more detailed specification of surface structures appearing in some notation.

In this article, I will discuss problems of composition theory as embodied by two programs written by G. M. Koenig, *Project One* (PR-1) and *Project Two* (PR-2). Both programs were written between 1965 and 1970 and represent a first step toward an AI view of composition. They embody an analysis of the data base and the procedures required in composing. I will deal with the particulars of these programs only so far as is required for my topic, leaving it to the reader to study them in greater depth (Koenig 1970a; 1970b).

General Survey of the Programs

PR-1 and PR-2 are tools for the design of a class of compositions. Each composition consists of sections linked in time and defining a musical form. Members of a class share a common *outside-time*

Computer Music Journal, Vol. 5, No. 4, Winter 1981

structure from which different *in-time* manifestations can be elaborated (see *Formalized Music* [Xenakis 1971] for an explanation of these terms). Within each such manifestation, or composition, the *form sections* themselves are all variants of a pervasive set of germinal ideas. These ideas are embodied by the data base and by the system processes operating on it.

We may view composer-program interaction along a trajectory (Fig. 1) leading from purely manual control to control exercised by some compositional algorithm (composing machine). The zone of greatest interest for composition theory is the middle zone of the trajectory, since it allows for a great flexibility of approach. The powers of intuition and machine computation may be combined. The earlier in the composition process algorithms are used, the greater is the burden on composers as interpreters of the computed results. This does not, of course, alter the fact that each composer is ultimately responsible for the composition's final form.

The Composer's Task

Clearly, the composer using PR-1 is largely a finder of musical sense embodied by computed results. By contrast, the user of PR-2 is a designer who defines both the data base and the procedures brought to bear on it. Once computation is complete, the composer using PR-2 has only the task of redefining the input data should they have failed to produce the intended result.

The internal structure of PR-1 and PR-2 is shown in Figs. 2 and 3. Evidently, PR-1 has a single data base, while PR-2 has two, the second of which is a procedural enlargement of the first. (By *procedural*, I mean produced by PR-2's system processes.) Also, the system processes, which are essentially selection and manipulation operations, are arranged in a different way (Fig. 3). In PR-2 a subset of processes

Fig. 1. Trajectory showing degree of composer control over compositional process. Arrows show alternative approaches to computer-aided composition.

Fig. 2. Control structure of PR-1. C = composer; SP = system process; DB = data base; SC = score; SG = sound generation; SSC = uninterpreted sub- *scores. Figures on the right show an optional extension of score synthesis with subscores. SP1 yields patterns of utmost irregularity, in contrast to SP7.*

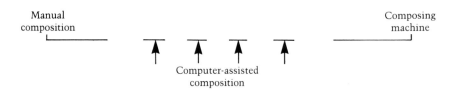

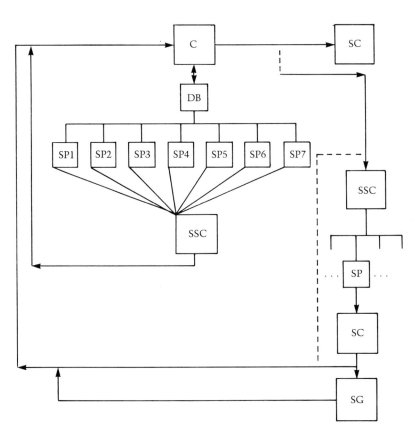

creates the second data base (DB2) and is then reused, together with other processes, in the synthesis of the final score. In PR-2 the hierarchical use of processes, coupled with the fact that the second data base cannot be inspected prior to the output of results, creates a provocative element of uncertainty. The uncertainty is mitigated by the fact that in PR-2 the system processes can be chosen, while in PR-1 they must be used as given. Similarly, the data base in PR-1 is largely predefined (aside from some minimal input data to be specified by the composer). The data base is defined by

Fig. 3. Control structure of PR-2. C = composer; DB = data base; P = parameter; SP = system process; SC = score; SG = sound generation; SP1 = ALEA; SP2 = SERIES; SP3 = SEQUENCE; SP4 = RATIO; SP5 = GROUP; SP6 = TENDENCY.

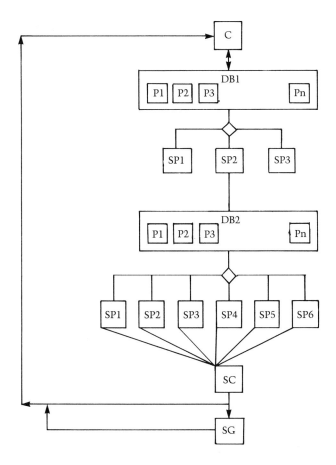

the composer in PR-2. However, results put out by PR-1 can be used for further manipulation by an independent score editor, which leads to an overall outcome similar to that of PR-2 (Laske 1980*b*).

In PR-1 composers encounter a partly program-inherent data base; they have the task of adding to it and readying it to the point when system processes can take over. Consequently, composers encounter their major challenge when the system processes have run their course and they must make musical sense of the computed results. (Perhaps the first to encounter this situation in composition was Arnold Schönberg.) Composers are helped in this task by being permitted to supply three free parameters: octave register, timbre, and duration. While the first two parameters are only nominally specified in the output, the third one, duration, is entirely free. Composers make use of these parameters in the context provided by the computed results; thus, they invent solutions that satisfy a set of tight constraints.

In PR-2 composers are inventors also, but the inventions mainly concern the definition of an initial data base and the selection of system processes for procedural enlargement of the base from which the final score is to be synthesized. Composers can inspect the second data base only ex post facto, but they have to decide what system processes to use in computing the final score. As in PR-1, computation is followed by a manual analysis of the computed results, an activity not supported by the programs themselves. (There are plans for adding analysis modules to both programs, which are now available in interactive versions.)

Whenever the computed results do not satisfy users of PR-2, they can make the program compute another variant of the score, after changing the data base or the system processes, or both, until a satisfactory solution is found. Users thus work with partly unknown data base constellations and with system processes whose outcome is partly opaque. In PR-1 experience teaches users which particular deployment of system processes will yield specific results.

These descriptions of the composer's task in PR-1 and PR-2 are somewhat one-sided for two reasons. First, I have not elucidated the process for designing overall semantic forms in sufficient detail. Second, the unknown, whether embodied by an unseen data base or by system processes that are opaque, is always a challenge to the composer's imagination. There is as much potential for learning in using composing programs as there is for getting lost. A fine line separates challenge from frustration, which sets in whenever the unknown does not contribute to learning.

Data Base and Knowledge Base

A system designer of today might say that the early composition programs are deficient in that they are not built around a knowledge base but merely around a data base. This difference largely amounts to that between *music-syntactic* and *music-semantic* knowledge. (How far this distinction holds up in music is an open question.) A musical knowledge base does more than provide data: it is an agent with authority over data and is the composer's active partner. By contrast, a data base in PR-1 and PR-2 is more of a repository of data: authority over the data remains external.

A *data base* is a conceptual model of a body of

Table 1. Mutual dependencies among individual parameters

Main Parameter	Dependent Parameter
Instrument	P,R,D,A,M
Pitch	I,R
Register	I,P
Entry delay	D,S
Duration	I,E,S
Silence	M
Amplitude	I
Mode of performance	I

Note: In right column, I = instrument; P = pitch/harmony; R = register; E = entry delay; D = duration; S = silence; A = amplitude; M = performance mode.

information. Compositional information can be conceptualized in many different ways, depending on historical conditions and aesthetic intentions. A very common model of compositional information in this century is *parametric data*. In most cases, the parametric model is chosen to allow effective manipulation of relationships among elements in the data base. According to this model, the musical object is conceived as a collection of essentially independent dimensions, each of which is defined by a (different) range of *parametric values*. Some parameters often used in instrumental and vocal composition are pitch class and register (i.e., frequency); entry delay and/or duration; timbre (tone color); intensity (amplitude); and occasionally tempo and mode of performance. (Xenakis also uses global parameters, such as density, which corresponds to Koenig's use of the order/disorder notion in PR-1.)

As Koenig points out in the manual for PR-2 (Koenig 1970b), the complete independence of musical parameters from one another is rather fictitious in music written for acoustic instruments and human voices. Where acoustic instruments are used, there is always a (potential) conflict between timbre and register or even pitch class, since not every instrument can realize tones in every register. As becomes very clear in working with PR-1 and PR-2, much compositional decision making is concerned with resolving parametric conflict that is provoked by the interdependencies of data base elements (Table 1).

Table 2. Score fragment produced by G. M. Koenig's PR-1

Event Number	Instrument	Entry Delay	Pitch/Harmony	Register	Amplitude
1	6	1/1	F,E	3 3	*mf*
2	8	1/4	F,F♯	3 3	*mf*
3	5	1/3	F,F♯	3 3	*mf*
4	2	3/5	F	3	*mf*
5	7	1/8	F,F♯	3 3	*mf*
6	3	3/8	F,F♯,C♯	3 3 3	*pp*
7	4	2/5	F	3	*pp*
8	7	4/5	F,F♯,A,D,D♯	2 2 2 2 2	*pp*
9	5	3/4	F	2	*pp*
10	2	1/2	F	2	*p*
11	9	1/5	F,E,C	2 2 2	*p*
12	1	5/8	F,F♯,A	2 2 2	*p*

Note: Regular patterns in P, R, and A domains.

Only a limited number of pitch classes, octave registers, durations, amplitudes, and modes of performance can be realized with any chosen instrument. Of course, these limitations are altogether removed if the instrument is a computer instrument that can be designed at will. The use of computer music instruments as tools for the reduction of the number of dependencies among parameters has been barely exploited in computer music.

Using Project One

PR-1 challenges the composer to design a musical form on procedural grounds only. By *procedural grounds* I mean that the base material (data base) remains unchanged throughout the composition, and that the music's form is the result of system processes that derive variants of the base material. Users of PR-1 make a limited contribution to the data base by providing the following data:

1. Thirteen entry delays between a unit measure (equaling 1.0) and a smallest time value (grace note, equaling 0.1). (*Entry delay* is the distance, in time, between the onset of sound *n* and sound *n*+1; it is totally independent of duration, with regard to which it can be (1) of equal length, (2) smaller, or (3) larger.

2. The total number of events.
3. Six tempi.
4. A random number seed for starting aleatoric system processes.

In defining these parameters, users have to be aware that the system-inherent data base commits them to (1) 9–15 instruments (or instrument classes); (2) harmony based on four three-note cells from which tone groups and series are elaborated (Koenig 1970*a*, p. 42); (3) subdivisions of a unit measure (equally a whole note) into 12 fractions from ⅘ (0.8) to ⅛ (0.125); (4) four registers that composers are free to interpret (e.g., high, medium-high, medium-low, low); and (5) eight intensity levels (*ppp–fff*). In preparing the entry delay specification, users must also realize that a linkage exists between the index of entry delay elements (listed in array form) and chord size, to the effect that the higher the index, the larger the chord size (which varies from one to six tones per event). Clearly, in using PR-1 composers must be prepared to enter a maze that they must learn in order to interpret the computed result.

As indicated in Fig. 2, composers may decide to postpone score interpretation until after further manipulation of the computed results with a score editor program. They may thus elaborate on the subscores produced by PR-1 to create a definitive score. This way of interpreting PR-1 output enables

Fig. 4. Transcription of entry delay sequence in tables 2 and 3 into metric notation, with the half-note serving as unit measure.

composers to replace traditional instruments with new software or hardware instruments. This is a powerful strategy for resolving parameter conflicts, as I have shown in an essay on my composition *Terpsichore* (Laske 1980*b*).

At the outset, when users of PR-1 are defining the data base, they are largely spared dealing with the problem of dependencies of parameters. They may confront this problem later in interpreting the output. Composers have always established hierarchies to resolve parametric conflict, but they must do so more consciously when using PR-1. In the score fragment in Table 2 we encounter a set of musical events characterized by great diversity (disorder) in the instrument and entry delay parameters associated with a pervading regularity (order) in the pitch class, register, and amplitude domains. Within an ametric context we find a tone center F established by repetition and articulated in two octaves in small dynamic fields (Fig. 4). Conflicting demands of parameters can arise, for example, because instrument 9 cannot play tones in register 2 (as required) and the tone F played in two neighboring registers (perhaps octaves) is unacceptable in the present context; also, instrument 7 may not be able to play a six-tone chord, as required. There are two types of conflict here: conflict between parametric value and context and conflict between parameters themselves. If the composer wishes to maintain the algorithmic integrity of the output, a consistent strategy for resolving such conflicts should be developed. Given the existence of two free parameters, duration and register, and the merely nominal definition of a third, timbre, resolution is not difficult.

By contrast, the case in Table 3 poses far greater interpretive problems. (For the translation of entry delays into the metric scheme, see Fig. 4.) In the fragment in Table 3, irregularity reigns in all parameters except for pitch class. Instrument and register may be irreconcilable, and identical pitch classes occurring in all registers may be unacceptable. Again, the composer may choose to develop a consistent strategy for conflict resolution. In doing so, the composer completes the data base, defining additional constraints (rules) for the free parameters of instrument, register, and duration.

Using Project Two

PR-2 challenges composers to design a musical form on the basis of a mixture of data base definitions and system processes operating on two levels. The main problem is to avoid proliferation of constraints. Since composers design the initial data base in its entirety, they can determine the data base in accordance with their procedural intent, that is, their projected choice of six system processes for score synthesis.

The system processes in PR-2 are ALEA, SERIES, SEQUENCE, RATIO, GROUP, and TENDENCY (SP1–SP6 in Fig. 3 [Koenig 1970*b*, pp. 38–48]). Five of them are aleatoric processes, but with significant differences. They are best viewed with regard to the degree of manual control they afford a composer. First comes SEQUENCE, since it is the algorithmic analog of deterministic (left-to-right) event specification that—outwardly—characterizes manual composition. Aleatoric composition processes vary from group formation (GROUP) and weighted distribution (RATIO) to selection within time-variable limits (TENDENCY); serial sequencing (SERIES, with the classic order constraint removed); and unrestricted aleatoric selection (ALEA). Of these processes, only ALEA, SERIES, and SEQUENCE are

Table 3. Score fragment produced by G. M. Koenig's PR-1

Event Number	Instrument	Entry Delay	Pitch	Register	Amplitude
1	6	1/1	F,E	3 1	*mf*
2	8	1/4	F,F♯	4 2	*ppp*
3	5	1/3	F,F♯	2 3	*ff*
4	2	3/5	F	4	*mp*
5	7	1/8	F,F♯	1 4	*p*
6	3	3/8	F,F♯,C♯	3 1 2	*fff*
7	4	2/5	F	4	*pp*
8	7	4/5	F,F♯,A,D,D♯	4 2 3 1 1	*f*
9	5	3/4	F	2	*mp*
10	2	1/2	F	3	*ppp*
11	9	1/5	F,E,C	4 1 2	*fff*
12	1	5/8	F,F♯,A	3 2 4	*mf*

Note: Regular patterns in the pitch domain (P) only.

available for forming the second data base, whereas all six processes can be used for synthesizing the final score.

Figure 5 can help us to understand the compositional implications of the arrangement of processes in PR-2. As shown, the generation of values for each of the eight parameters dealt with by the program is determined by what might be called a *procedural path*. This path links the process that generates the second data base to the process that ultimately generates the score. Consequently, composers have a large repertory of procedural paths at their disposal, 144 altogether.

The way a composer defines the initial data base ought to correspond with the system processes chosen for synthesizing both the second data base and the final score. What this correspondence entails is not always easy to say, however. Unless SEQUENCE is used as the only system process, there will be some uncertainty in the output, some "unexpected results" along the procedural path. In loosening up the control mechanisms by proceeding from SEQUENCE to SERIES to GROUP to RATIO to TENDENCY to ALEA, the composer can explore the potential unexpected results.

To establish the data base for PR-2, the composer answers questions (65) through which three different sets of data are input to the system processes chosen:

1. A table, or set of element groups drawn from a repertory (list)
2. A stipulated hierarchy of parameters, which determines the order in which parameters are to be calculated and thus the parameter values to be chosen in the case of irreconcilable conflicts between independent calculations
3. Global information concerning such items as total duration, average density of events, combination of groups of parameters, treatment of the second data base as a unit or as a group of self-contained layers (voice combinations), and smallest permitted time value in seconds

Koenig makes a distinction between *schematic parameters* (register, entry delay, duration, silence, amplitude, and mode of performance) and *deviating parameters* (instrument, pitch). This distinction has to do with the complexity of their definitions. Instruments set up a large number of parametric dependencies, and pitch class harmony can occur according to three different principles (ROW, CHORD, and INTERVAL). These complications mean that additional information must be stated for deviating parameters.

A concept of great importance in PR-2 is the *hierarchy of parameters*. This hierarchy ought to be

Fig. 5. Example of a procedural path (linkage of system processes) in PR-2. Path: → ALEA (DB2) → GROUP (SCORE).

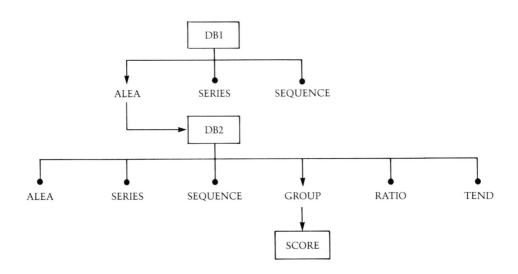

called *hierarchy of system processes*, since it determines, in generating the second data base, how fully the system process associated with a particular parameter will be utilized. Conflict between the results of system processes is automatically resolved by PR-2. It gives precedence to the process of higher order in the hierarchy. For instance, if instrument is a main parameter and its second data base is synthesized via SERIES, then the system processes generating its dependent parameters will take effect only as far as is reconcilable with the output of SERIES.

Designing Musical Form with Project One

The system processes in PR-1 are variations on a common theme, that of selecting from base material to create regular and irregular patterns. (The most irregular patterns, produced by SP1, imply a change of parameter values from event to event.) Patterns (degrees) of order and disorder become the most important design principle. The system processes themselves determine the outside-time structuring of the elements of the data base. The temporal sequencing of their results in a composition and the mapping of system process *x* (determining parameter *a*, say, pitch) onto system process *y* (determining parameter *b*, say, register) determines the in-time structure of the composition. (Both the sequencing and the mapping are based on decisions made by the composer.)

If the most orthodox rule is followed, none of the seven system processes applied to each of the parameters is to be used more than once. Given a composition in seven sections, this means that in each of the sections every parameter exhibits a unique behavior not to be found in another section. A second source of variety is a unique coupling of system processes in each section. Thus, while the data base represents a set of unifying germinal ideas, the system processes implement a radical notion of *Durchkomponieren* (through-composing).

In PR-1, form is designed by the composer in two steps: first, via the definition of a structural formula and second, through the interpretation of materials computed for each form section. The structural formula determines, for each form section, what system process defines each of the parameters needed to compose the section. However, this decision necessitates keeping in mind the total musical form to be created. Consequently, the structural formula directly determines the composition's overall form. It becomes the basis for the interpretation of all computed materials.

Experiences with Project One

In my experience with PR-1 since 1970, I have found the following variables to be important. (See the outline at the end of this section for specific examples.)

1. Completeness or incompleteness of system processes (whether all seven system processes or only a subset is used)
2. Number of form segments (linked to 1)
3. Absence or presence of tendencies (whether developmental trends exist between successive system processes)
4. Absence or presence of symmetries (whether system processes form repeating constellations)
5. Absence or presence of parameter coupling (use of the same system process for a group of parameters)
6. Emphasis on individual segments, emphasis on the whole, or balanced emphasis

The first variable has to do with the original stipulation of PR-1 that each parameter involved is to be associated with one of the seven system processes only once during a composition. Deviations from this orthodox rule lead to interesting results, since syntactic redundancies are introduced.

The second variable is related to but not identical with the first. In my work so far, I have chosen from five to eight segments. We could define fewer than five and more than eight, depending on the overall form we want to achieve.

The third and fourth variables are closely related. If a trio of system processes is used that successively moves from highly constrained parameters to a weighted series to a random succession, the listener will tend to hear these as being part of a trend. Similarly, if two system processes are repeatedly used to follow one another, a certain symmetry may be set up in the listener's mind.

The fifth variable corresponds to the idea of combination in PR-2, the idea of reusing system pro-

cesses for different parameters in order to unify materials.

The sixth variable, emphasis, is easily misunderstood. In my view, the use of tendencies and symmetries of parameter development tends to emphasize the character of the whole over the parts, while their absence provides opportunity for bestowing on each form section an idiosyncratic character. This is to be understood within the limits of the outside-time structural formulas outlined here. In the outline, each structural formula is characterized with lowercase letters for form sections; integers 1–7 for system processes; and uppercase letters E (entry delay), P (pitch), R (register), I (instrument), and A (amplitude) to indicate parameters.

I. Computer-synthesized music

   A. *Terpsichore* for tape and dancers (1980)

	a	b	c	d	e	f	g
E	7	6	5	4	3	2	1
P	7	6	5	4	3	2	1
R	6	4	5	2	1	3	7
I	7	6	5	4	3	2	1
A	7	6	5	4	3	2	1

   Comment: Base score in 7 parts (a–f). Monodirectional tendency (order–disorder) in all parameters except register. All 7 system processes used, each only once. Emphasis on whole over parts.

   B. *Mediations* for tape (1981)

	a	b	c	d	e
E	3	4	5	6	7
P	2	3	1	4	5
R	3	1	7	2	5
I	7	3	4	5	6
A	7	3	4	5	6

   Comment: Base score in 5 parts (a–e). Restriction to five consecutive system processes (1–5 and 3–7) except for register, which uses nonadjacent processes. Clear tendency toward recurrence in the time domain (3→7), similar tendency in the sonic domain but shifted, with parameter coupling. Balance of parts and whole.

C. *Voie lactée* for tape (1984)

	a	b	c	d	e	f	g	h
E	7	7r	3	1r	1	2	4	4r
P	4r	4	6	6r	5	5r	7r	7
R	2r	2	4	4r	5	5r	6r	6
I	5	4r	6	7	7r	6r	4	5r
A	6r	6	4	4r	5	5r	7r	7

Comment: Base score in 8 parts (a–h); "r" means *retrograde*. Process symmetries in the two outer sections, emphasizing high degree of order (recurrence of parameter values). Parameter coupling of time/frequency coordinates and sonic features. In middle part, insistence on recurrence in all parameters but the temporal. Use of retrograde to enable repetition of system processes. Balance of whole and parts.

II. Instrumental/vocal compositions

A. *Perturbations* for seven instruments (1981)

	a	b	c	d	e	f	g
E	2	3	4	1	5	6	7
P	2	3	4	1	5	6	7
R	1	4	7	6	3	2	5
I	7	6	5	1	2	3	4
A	7	6	5	1	2	3	4

Comment: Base score in 7 parts (a–g). Parameter coupling of syntactic (entry delay, pitch) and sonic features (instrument, ampli-

tude) exhibiting clear counter tendencies that are deviated from by register. No system process omitted. Breakdown of all tendencies in the middle part, with restoration toward end of piece. Emphasis on whole over parts.

B. *Nachtstücke* (Night Pieces) for choir a capella (1981)

	a	b	c	d	e	f
E	1	2	4	3	5	6
P	3	5	6	2	1	7
R	4	3	2	1	6	5
I	omitted, replaced by R					
A	4	5	6	6r	5r	7

Comment: Base score in 6 parts (a–f). Counter tendencies in the domains of time and register (equated with four voice categories: soprano, alto, tenor, bass), with insistence on high degrees of dynamic recurrence and harmonic contrast (P: 5,6/2,1) in middle part, in correspondence with the texts used. Tendency toward metricity and complete voice mixture (R, SP1 yielding constant change or register) deviated from near end. Balance of whole and parts.

C. *Reflections* for brass quintet (1983)

	a	b	c	d	e	f	g
E	1	3	5	7	6	4	2
P	4	1	7	3	5	6	2
R	7	6	5	4	3	2	1
I	1	2	3	4	5	6	7
A	1	2	3	4	5	6	7

Comment: Base score in 7 parts (a–g). Clear tendency in register (equated with instrument, with I parameter serving subsidiary articulatory function). Parameter coupling in sonic domain countertendential. Metricity in middle part. Balance of part and whole.

Fig. 6. External scheme of the form realized in G. M. Koenig's Übung für Klavier (1969). The scheme shows the textural symmetries used. T1 = one-dimensional texture covering entire pitch range; T2 = chord successions; T3 = mixture of rapid and slow tone sequences; T4 = mixture of rapid and slow chord sequences; T5 = polyphonic superimposition of layers.

1	2	3	4	5	6	7	8	9	10	11	12
T1	T3	T1	T4	T2	T4	T2	T4	T1	T3	T1	T5

Project Two

While in PR-1 the structural formula is a strictly procedural one that relies entirely on system processes, composition in PR-2 is bound to both data and to system processes. This is because the second data base is itself procedurally determined (being a procedural enlargement of the first one) and is thus a mixed data base. In contrast to PR-1, in which form is designed through the use of system processes alone, design of form with PR-2 can be entirely declarative, entirely procedural, or mixed. If entirely declarative, changes in the data base alone define differences among form segments, the system processes employed being the same throughout. (This strategy most closely approaches manual composition.) If entirely procedural, a close approximation of PR-1 results in that the data base remains unchanged for all variants making up the overall form and the system processes change in a systematic fashion. If design of form is mixed, we enter the uncharted territory of computer composition. In this territory, musical form encompasses adjustments to both data base and system processes. This design corresponds to the "unfamiliar parameter constellations" of PR-1, which result from a combination of system processes we have not encountered before, providing a challenge to the composer's musical identity (also known as *style*).

In designing a form using PR-2, we encounter the same opportunities for parameter coupling (with regard to system processes) and for defining symmetries or tendencies among individual form segments that we did in PR-1. In PR-2, however, the number of sections is entirely free, and each section may have a varying number of subsections. Another difference is that in PR-2 there are not five but eight different parameters (thus not a single free one), and that we can determine global aspects of form such as relation of duration to entry delay, average density, and layered or one-dimensional texture for each variant or subsection. The intuition the composer needs for interpreting PR-1 output must, in PR-2, be channeled into definition of the program input. (It is advisable to master PR-1 before attempting to work with PR-2.)

PR-2 allows the composer to explore new avenues as well as to explicate old paths more succinctly. Take, for example, the notion of texture in music. In PR-2, the perception of textural change is caused by a change in system process brought to bear on an invariant data base, or by a change of both system process and data base. In his *Übung für Klavier* (1969), Koenig uses changes in both system processes and data base to build a sequence of textures embodying the symmetries shown in Fig. 6. Within each section, parameter coupling and parametric tendencies play an important role. The overall form of the piece combines symmetries of a global character with dynamic tendencies at the local level. Other designs of a musical form are, of course, equally possible.

Due to its complexity, I consider PR-2 an excellent candidate for development into a knowledge-based system whose explanation unit assumes some of the burden of providing analytic insights into the results computed. (As it stands now, this burden falls entirely on the composers who use it.) In a further extension, the explanation unit could also warn users of blind alleys, although it might be preferable for composers to find them out the hard way.

Acknowledgments

I want to thank the editor and the referees for their extensive comments on and criticisms of the draft of this article.

References

Banks, J. D. et al. 1979. "SSP (Sound Synthesis Program)." Sonological Report 5. Utrecht: Institute of Sonology.

Berg, P. et al. 1980. "SSP and Sound Description." *Computer Music Journal* 4(1):25–35.

Constantin, L., and E. Yourdon. 1979. *Structured Design*. Englewood Cliffs, New Jersey: Prentice-Hall.

Koenig, G. M. 1979. "Protocol." Sonological Report 4. Utrecht: Institute of Sonology.

Koenig, G. M. 1970a. "Project One." Electronic Music Report 2. Utrecht: Institute of Sonology. (Reprinted 1977. Amsterdam: Swets and Zeitlinger.)

Koenig, G. M. 1970b. "Project Two." Electronic Music Report 3. Utrecht: Institute of Sonology. (Reprinted 1977. Amsterdam: Swets and Zeitlinger.)

Laske, O. E. 1980a. "On Composition Theory as a Theory of Self-Reference." In *Allos*, ed. K. Gaburo. Ramona, California: Lingua Press, pp. 419–436.

Laske, O. E. 1980b. "On Subscore Manipulation as a Tool for Compositional and Sonic Design." In *Proceedings of the 1980 International Computer Music Conference*, ed. H. S. Howe, Jr. San Francisco: Computer Music Association.

Laske, O. E. 1981. *Music and Mind: An Artificial Intelligence Perspective*. Boston: Otto Laske. Collection of published essays 1971–1981.

Roads, C. 1980. "Interview with Marvin Minsky." *Computer Music Journal* 4(3):25–39.

Simon, H. A. 1981. *The Sciences of the Artificial*. 2nd ed. Cambridge, Massachusetts: MIT Press.

Wiederhold, G. 1977. *Data Base Design*. New York: McGraw-Hill.

Winston, P. 1979. *Artificial Intelligence*. Reading, Massachusetts: Addison-Wesley.

Xenakis, I. 1971. *Formalized Music*. Bloomington, Indiana: Indiana University Press.

Yourdan, E. 1975. *Techniques of Program Structure and Design*. Englewood Cliffs, New Jersey: Prentice-Hall.

Zelkovitz, M. V. et al. 1979. *Principles of Software Engineering and Design*. Englewood Cliffs, New Jersey: Prentice-Hall.

13

Giuseppe Englert
86, bis, Boulevard de la Tour-Maubourg
75007 Paris, France

Automated Composition and Composed Automation

Introduction

This article describes work with minicomputers to control sound synthesis systems that function in real time. The particular system utilized for the present research is the Synclavier, made by New England Digital Corporation, Norwich, Vermont. This system comprises a 32-Kword, 16-bit minicomputer with a programmable clock, a 16-channel digital synthesizer with four audio outputs, and a module for up to 16 analog inputs built by Didier Roncin.

The theme of this study is the automation of compositional tasks and the invention of principles for structuring musical form; in particular, principles that can be stated as algorithms. Later, I will introduce the intersecting sine function polynomial (ISFP) as a sound synthesis algorithm capable of economically producing a wide variety of sonic results. I will also attempt to establish principles for the articulation of the time flow of musical discourse, being quite aware that such principles are strongly dependent on the technology used (which, in turn, has its peculiar way of stimulating ideas in its users). The principles of concern here are meant to guarantee the cohesiveness of sound materials and of the musical work based on them.

Definition of Some Important Categories

We consider music not as a succession of sounds but as the development of constantly changing relations among sounds. A *relation* is a quality—or an abstraction of a quality—that listeners are able to discover between two or more elements. For example, relations of pitch are usually called *intervals*, and *rhythm* is the articulation of relations between durations. For example, a sequence of four successive relations (A,B,C,D) of the values 2,1,6,3 represents a series of relations as follows:

1. The values differ from one another.
2. The second pair (C,D) is the augmented form of the first (A,B).
3. The second element of each pair (B,D) is a diminution of the first element.
4. Since $A + B = D$, we observe an evident symmetry around C.
5. A latent symmetry exists because $C = A + B + D$.

By itself, this set of relations is ambiguous and does not establish an order. Only a context—defined by other relations—can establish relations pertinent to the musical discourse. Even though these kinds of relations always consist of quantitative proportions, they are always perceived according to their quality. To be sure, there is music for which such relations are anathema. In his *Wintermusic* and other compositions, John Cage organized aggregates of sound and silence in such a way that it is practically impossible for the listener to establish permanent relations among sounds. The work amounts to an organization of nonrelations. For our purposes, however, we will define *music* as the temporal articulation of relations (and/or nonrelations) among sounds.

When a set of relations is affected in time by the entrance of new elements, *changes* result. Relations can obtain among individual changes. For instance, the evidence of relations may vary with changes. The *complexity* of a composition is therefore qualitative, resulting from the sum of the relations it embodies. Complexity is not perceived as an abso-

Translated from the French by Otto Laske, with C. Roads. This is a revised and updated version of "Musique: Composition Automatique—Automation Composée," in *Informatique et Sciences Humaines* 45, published by the Institut des Sciences Humaines Appliquées, University of Paris–Sorbonne.
© 1981 Giuseppe Englert.

lute value; its impact depends on the variety of means utilized in a composition, that is, in the range of possibilities created. *Economy* is the relation of complexity to the range of possibilities used. Debussy's *Jeux* appears as strongly economical, whereas the opposite can be said of Ravel's *Bolero*. Hence, economy is a measure of the degree to which the composer exploits the available resources. The complexity of a hardware system determines the maximal complexity available to the composer. A compositional system can, of course, temporarily limit the possibilities used; hence, we distinguish *global economy* from *temporary economy*. The latter can be articulated in time.

In composing and programming, we have to face constraints. Some of these are considered positive (i.e., obligations) others as negative, (i.e., limitations). The *positive constraints* are requirements imposed by a particular kind of (desired) complexity. *Negative constraints* are limits imposed by the particular system chosen. A *process* can be defined as a set of rules capable of generating a result or another process. In light of these categories, we can say that a *composition process* relates a particular economy to a particular set of constraints, as in the four-part counterpoint in the compositions of J. S. Bach. Processes can be interconnected in linear configurations, in parallel, in the form of tree structures, and as recursive (cyclic) structures. We are thus really dealing with a *network* of processes (Greussay et al. 1980).

We call a network that is operational and includes hardware a *system*. There are general and specific systems. I am not going to enter into a discussion of their relative merits as regards efficiency. Up to now, I have based my compositions on strong systems of weak generality. In using these, I have assumed that these systems constitute compositions.

In a system that permits real-time functioning, the composer/performer (who is also a musician/programmer) intervenes by referring to *sounding results* perceived in the environment. The scope of the composer/performer's activity and the sounding result depend on the programs used. The composer/performer must also listen for musical

cues. Considered in terms of the system itself, the composer functions as one process among others. A philosopher would say that such composers are objectively encompassed by their own projections (of themselves) onto the external world.

We can, then, describe composition as the realization of a network of interactive processes that engender other, equally interactive processes such that the musician is just a link in the chain of processes. In such systems we must accept sound as a *side effect* of an activated network. Where, then, is the music? The system and its acoustic side effects are the music!

Parameters

For a program to result in music, the composer must control the evolution of numerous parameters: those of sounding events, their links, and the temporal organization of their links. We can distinguish between main and subordinate parameters without establishing a rigid hierarchy. *Subordinate parameters* define sounds produced by the peripheral units of a computer. They refer to the data required by synthesizers, digital-to-analog converters, and programs for sound synthesis. In a given system, the number of subordinate parameters is a fixed one. (The Synclavier has 128.) Also subordinate parameters are the durations of the segments of amplitude envelopes and modulation indexes, that is, data sent to the buffer of the programmable clock (or a register).

Main parameters are introduced into the program by the composer and are the basis from which subordinate parameters are computed. (We could also call these parameters *operational categories*.) Certain parameters can be modified over time by a network of processes. The primary act of composition consists of defining the organization of main parameters.

The temporal evolution of a parameter can be represented by a series of (numerical) values, which form an *envelope*. A composition is therefore a structure made of envelopes in the broadest sense of the term. A single, central envelope-generating process receives data from and emits data to a network of "peripheral" processes.

In Search of the Philosopher's Stone

The last school to have systematically studied the problem of structuring macroforms in music is that of Schönberg and his disciples. Their studies have clearly shown that an excess of correlation and surprise leads to a feeling of boredom (caused by entropy). *Entropy* in musical discourse is a function of the density of information and of the duration of the work in question. A short piece may embody a high degree of density throughout. A longer piece must be structured so that the degree of density varies in unforeseeable ways over the course of time.

A compositional algorithm must therefore satisfy the following postulate: that the dynamic equilibrium between the correlation and contrast of events be guaranteed over large spans of time. Since, with some of my colleagues, I like to play music on our mixed digital synthesis system, I add the following postulate: that an algorithmic interaction between musician and machine be possible in real time. In the next section I will discuss an algorithmic process that satisfies both these postulates.

The Intersecting Sine Function Polynomial

Of all trigonometric functions, the sinusoid is the only one that traverses a limited range without escaping into the infinite along one of its coordinates. In other words, if we consider the x-axis (abscissa), which I will label K, as being the representation of time and the y-axis (ordinate) as representing some musical parameter, then the sine function will always generate a parameter within preestablished boundaries (amplitudes), regardless of the length of time involved:

$$y := \sin(K * L) * A \,;$$

where L is a phase-length constant, and A is an amplitude constant. Musical time (K) can be measured in two different ways: by hardware (such as a clock), or by software (counter of events-envelopes). I prefer the second alternative.

The repetitive and periodic character of the sine function assures the correlation of events but excludes any possibility of contrast and thus of surprise. The polynomial

$$y := \sin(K * L) * A1 + \sin(K * L2) * A2 + \ldots + \sin(K * Ln) * An \,;$$

will provide us with an evolution growing in complexity but always repetitive and periodic. What this function lacks is the presence of breaks, sudden developments, and arbitrary deviations. In order to provide this class of events, I propose the following expressions:

$$v := \sin(K * L1) * A1 \,;$$
$$w := \sin(K * L2) * A2 \,;$$
$$\textbf{if } v > w \textbf{ then } E = v \textbf{ else } E = w \,; \qquad \text{ISF(1)}$$

where E is (an element of) the result.

The variant in which

$$\textbf{if } v < w \textbf{ then } E := v \textbf{ else } E := w \,; \qquad \text{ISF(2)}$$

is of equal interest.

The curve resulting from these functions is still a periodic one, but it incorporates small and enjoyable deviations. Periodicity is here broken and accidents occur that derive from the fact that we deal with a polynomial of intersecting sine functions, namely

$$y := E1 + E2 + E3 + \ldots + En \,; \qquad \text{ISFP}$$

This is the ISFP in which each Ei is computed according to the model ISF(1) or (2) such that all constants of phase length and amplitude are different but without a common denominator.

For an ISFP of four elements, we need eight calls of the sine function for calculating each point of the curve—a complex computational job. Speed is a necessary requirement, especially in live performance. This fact has led me to simplify ISFP so as not to lose its advantages. I obtain the best results with ISF(1) or (2) if v represents a short phase and large amplitude and w represents the opposite values. I can thus substitute a constant (e.g., 0) for w. Thus

$$v := \sin(K * L1) * A1 ;$$
$$\textbf{if } v > 0 \textbf{ then } E := v \textbf{ else } E := 0 ; \qquad \text{ISF(3)}$$

or

$$\textbf{if } v < 0 \textbf{ then } E := v \textbf{ else } E := 0 ; \qquad \text{ISF(4)}$$

If we insert ISF(3) or (4) into the ISFP generator, the number of evaluations of the sine function is reduced by half and the requirements of aesthetics and speed are simultaneously satisfied.

The generator ISFP has only a single argument (K) that represents real time, that is, the event counter (or sequence counter) that has been generated. The value of its increment—which is a second possible argument—is determined either by way of a program or interactively. In playing with the counter and its increment, we can, if we desire, intervene in the evolution of the ISFP. A part of the configuration of four curves generated by ISFP is shown in Fig. 1.

Reflections of a Pragmatic Nature

The considerable complexity of calculations required by ISFP necessitates reflections concerning its use in a program for musical composition, especially if performance in real time is at issue. It would be impossible to generate each of the subordinate parameters with such an algorithm; this would risk computational interruptions to the flow of the musical discourse. In the domain of automated composition for loudspeakers, as in serial music, the composer is above all interested in controlling entire event configurations, not single events. The following main parameters can be controlled in real time by ISFP: the number of events, the nature of attacks, registers, overall intensity, average speed, the number of envelope segments, continuity and discontinuity of envelopes (legato or

staccato), and the relation between modulating and modulated frequency (i.e., timbre), to name only the most important ones. At issue here is the structuring of the overall musical form with regard to such main parameters. For a large-scale work realized with complex means, we can imagine a "mega-form" divided into "mega-sections." For each such section, the increment and the constants in ISFP will be different. They can be replaced by variables whose value is changed by ISFP at the beginning of each section.

Experiences and Applications

I have used this theoretical research in three musical compositions, *Quatuor 'S'* for digital synthesizer (Synclavier), *Les dits d'amenhotep XIX* for digital synthesizer, and *Trinsin funpol* for five instruments ad libitum. I will comment briefly on each of these compositions, especially with regard to their usage of the ISFP.

Quatuor 'S'

Quatuor 'S' was first performed in 1979 as part of the Pro Helvetia concerts in Paris. This composition is based on counterpoint for four independent voices, each of which is articulated in sequences of varying length. The ISFP generator determines the main parameters characterizing the sequences. At the beginning of each sequence, ISFP is called four times, once for each of the voices. This is accomplished by a program written in the XPL programming language of the Synclavier's computer. (For a copy of this listing, send a self-addressed stamped envelope to the editor.)

Les dits d'amenhotep XIX

This composition for digital synthesizer was first performed in 1980 at the Pro Helvetia concerts in Paris. It uses the ISFP in a way similar to *Quatuor 'S'*. The same main parameters are involved, but the constants determining their development are

Fig. 1a

Fig. 1. Graphic representation of the output of four
ISFPs. The top of the figure
represents the maximal al-
lowable value, while the
bottom represents the
minimal value. Each col-
umn of four values repre-

sents a single sound. In
the composition Trinsin
funpol, the oval symbol
represents duration, while
the other three symbols
represent different kinds of
instrumental articulation.

Fig. 1a. The counter increment K to the ISFP is low,
resulting in visible correlations and breakpoints in
the graphs.

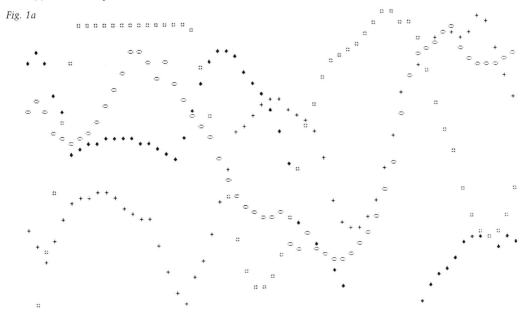

different. Also, while in *Quatuor 'S'* the temporal
development of each voice is independent of that of
the others, in *Les dits d'amenhotep XIX* the four
voices always start a developmental sequence together. Each phrase of the composition is separated
from others by silences, a musical discourse different from that of *Quatuor 'S'*.

Trinsin funpol

This work is written for five instruments ad libitum, and was first performed in Paris in 1980. Its
score is the graphic representation of the evolution
of four ISFP formulas. Figure 1 shows part of this
evolution. Three of the symbols (◆, +, ◦) are interpreted as performance variables of the instruments
chosen. For instance, for trombone they could be

lip pressure, length of the slide, amount of breath.
The fourth symbol (◯) represents the duration of
a sound as linked to length of the breath or bow
movement. The height of the page indicates the
ambitus of parametric values (maximal at the top,
minimal at the bottom).

In *Trinsin funpol*, then, the model elaborated
with the aid of algorithm ISFP is transposed
into the domain of human interpretation and approximation: it becomes the responsibility of
performers.

Some Consequences

I am quite aware that the foregoing deliberations
are based on an unstated musical conviction. The
debate that once engaged Baudelaire (poet of the ar-

Fig. 1b

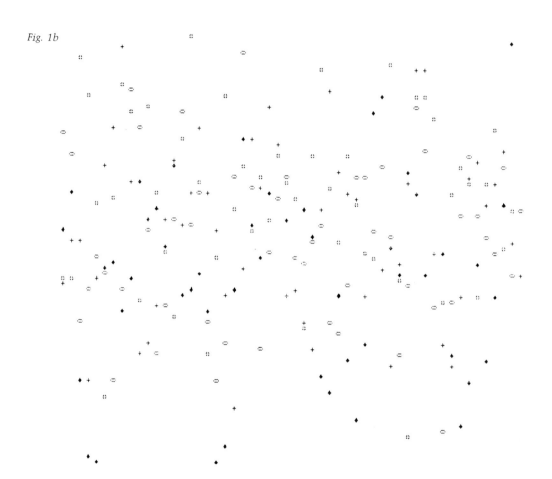

tificial) and the disciples of Rousseau (who yearned to return to nature) is always at issue in the arts and is essentially unresolved. More than that, we ought to realize that in our own time Rousseau's ideals have more supporters than ever, even among musicians touched by the existence of computers. Recent research in acoustics and psychoacoustics has shown that with the aid of computers we can synthesize instrumental sounds and even the human voice. We have learned to imitate nature very effectively.

In the domain of art and especially of music, I continue to agree with Baudelaire. My approach, which is inspired by the new ways of using and augmenting human intelligence, leads me to avoid all that derives from what is called *nature*, my goal being to synthesize something entirely artificial but profoundly coherent.

Reference

Greussay, P. et al. 1980. "Musical Software: Descriptions and Abstractions of Sound Generation and Mixing." *Computer Music Journal* 4(2):40–47.

14

Barry Truax
Department of Communication and
Centre for the Arts
Simon Fraser University
Burnaby, B.C.
Canada V5A 1S6

Timbral Construction in *Arras* as a Stochastic Process

Introduction

My recent work with the POD system (Truax 1977*a*; 1978*a*) has dealt with organizing timbre at a form-determining level. It has been concerned less with timbre as the specific acoustic properties of individual sounds than with large-scale spectral structures that define the entire composition. The relation between spectrum and timbre is complex and not entirely understood, but it is generally conceded that spectrum, particularly its temporal behavior, is a primary determinant of timbre. As discussed by Robert Erickson (1975), there is a considerable "gray" region in which a complex musical event can be heard as a timbre, as a composite sound, or as a chord. Modern psychoacoustics has furthered our understanding of the conditions under which frequencies are heard as individual pitches, heard as components of a spectrum, or not heard at all individually, but rather fused with others as a single percept. In general, we know that it is not only the physical characteristics of the sound that give rise to different perceptions, but also, and perhaps mainly, the context within which the frequencies are heard (McAdams and Bregman 1979). It is the ambiguity among these different modes of perception that fascinates me and that I have explored in *Arras* (1980), a composition for four-channel, computer-synthesized tape.

This paper is a revised version of a longer discussion, "Timbral Construction as a Stochastic Process," published (in Italian) in *Musica e Elaboratore*, Biennale di Venezia, 1980, and presented at the 1980 International Computer Music Conference in New York and the 1981 International Conference on Music and Technology in Melbourne, Australia.

Computer Music Journal, Vol. 6, No. 3, Fall 1982

FM Timbral Construction

The theme of my compositional exploration has been to use acoustic properties as the basis of the structure of the entire composition, that is, to relate sound and structure inextricably. I have been working with frequency modulation (FM) synthesis (Chowning 1973) and the type of acoustic control it allows. I have been using the simple model of sine-wave FM as merely a building block in what I have called *polyphonic timbral construction* (Truax 1978*b*; 1980). In this construction, many simple FM sources are digitally mixed into complex timbres that lack some of the more predictable clichés associated with simple FM.

The basis of the timbral organization I have been using is the distinction between harmonic and inharmonic spectra (i.e., between spectra in which all constituent frequencies are multiples of the fundamental and those in which not all frequencies are such multiples). Since it is the ratio between the carrier and modulating frequencies (the $c:m$ ratio) that determines which partials are in the spectrum, we can speak of *harmonic* and *inharmonic* $c:m$ ratios. The harmonic ratios are

$$1:1 \quad 1:2 \quad 1:3 \quad 1:4 \quad 1:5 \quad 1:6 \quad 1:7 \quad 1:8 \quad 1:9,$$

and the inharmonic ratios are

$$2:9 \quad 2:7 \quad 3:8 \quad 2:5 \quad 3:7 \quad 4:9,$$

where $m \leq 9$. For any given integer n used as a limit for m, the $c:m$ ratios that produce unique spectra are those corresponding to the series of fractions called the *Farey series* of order n (Truax 1977*b*).

For each of the above ratios, the carrier frequency is also the fundamental, since the ratio can be said to be in *normal form*, satisfying the criterion that m is greater than or equal to twice c, with the ex-

Table 1. Partials

Ratio	Spectral Frequencies												
1:2	1.0		3.0		5.0	7.0	9.0		11.0		13.0	15.0	17.0
3:8	1.0	1.67	3.67	4.33	6.33	7.0	9.0	9.67	11.67	12.3	14.3	15.0	17.0

ception of the 1:1 ratio, which produces the complete harmonic spectrum. Each normal-form ratio has a family of ratios associated with it, each of which produces the same set of sidebands and, therefore, the same spectrum. These other family members can be derived from the normal-form ratio $(c:m)$ by applying the operation

$$[c \pm (n \cdot m)] : m, \text{ for } n = 1, 2, 3, \ldots .$$

The entire form of *Arras* is derived from the spectral properties resulting from the duality of harmonic and inharmonic spectra.

The Background Structure of *Arras*

I found a basis for relating harmonic and inharmonic ratios in *Arras* when I observed that inharmonic ratios produce spectra with both harmonic and inharmonic partials. Compare, for instance, the spectra of the ratios 1:2 and 3:8, as given in Table 1, in which partials produced by the harmonic ratio 1:2 are expressed with the fundamental as 1.0. The 1:2 ratio produces all odd harmonics, whereas the inharmonic ratio 3:8 includes harmonics 7, 9, 15, and 17, as well as many inharmonic frequencies. If the spectra of the two ratios overlap when based on the same fundamental, they may fuse as a result of the frequencies they have in common (and which act analogously to a pivotal chord or note in a harmonic modulation).

The basic structure of the piece consists of a 75-sec unit in which a harmonic ratio moves to a related inharmonic ratio and back, for example,

$$1:2 \rightarrow 3:8 \rightarrow 1:2.$$

The overall structure of the work consists of a progression of harmonic ratios, beginning with 1:2

(producing all odd harmonics in a fairly dense spectrum) and proceeding to 1:9 (whose harmonics are widely spaced, e.g., 1, 8, 10, 17, 19, . . .). With the exception of the 1:6 ratio, which does not seem to have an inharmonic equivalent in the sense described, each harmonic ratio is paired with an inharmonic one with which it is expected to fuse. The pattern, therefore, is

$$1:2 \rightarrow 3:8 \rightarrow 1:2 \rightarrow 1:3 \rightarrow 4:9 \rightarrow 1:3 \rightarrow$$
$$1:4 \rightarrow 3:8 \rightarrow 1:4 \rightarrow 1:5 \rightarrow 2:5 \rightarrow 1:5 \rightarrow$$
$$1:6 \rightarrow 1:7 \rightarrow 2:7 \rightarrow 1:7 \rightarrow 1:8 \rightarrow 3:8 \rightarrow$$
$$1:8 \rightarrow 1:9 \rightarrow 2:9 \rightarrow 1:9.$$

In the case of 1:7 and 1:9, there are two choices of inharmonic ratio (2:7 and 3:7; 2:9 and 4:9). In each case, the inharmonic ratio with the more similar spacing of sidebands is chosen. (The Farey series influenced the choice of ratios by specifying which produce unique spectra.)

I aimed at an ordering based on optimum continuity and a consistent progression in spectral density. The overall structure of the work corresponded to the global characteristics of a stochastic process. I assumed that a listener can hear a general pattern in the work, progressing from closely to widely spaced partials, with specific harmonic spectra alternating with related inharmonic spectra. The stochastic decisions guarantee a variety of detail at the level of individual frequency components, the level that corresponds to the unpredictability of the individual events in a stochastic process.

In sine-wave FM, the amplitude of each sideband pair for different modulation indices is determined by the set of Bessel functions. Although these functions are varied enough to simulate the temporal variations of natural spectra, many listeners accustomed to FM note a characteristic spectral development when the modulation index is swept from zero to some value. In earlier research, I discovered

that when two or more events on a common fundamental with $c:m$ ratios belonging to the same family were mixed, spectral predictability disappeared,
even when each event had the same modulation-
index envelope. Moreover, much simpler envelope
shapes and lower maximum-modulation indices
could be used for each component while still producing a rich spectrum. This experience suggested
that if, at the theoretical level, the amplitude of any
given sideband is the sum of several complex functions, then at the perceptual level, the corresponding spectral component appears to behave in an
unpredictable, pseudorandom fashion. Instead of
mixing $c:m$ family members on a common fundamental, however, I used a different technique to
create variety in the background structure of *Arras*.

Event Structure

For each ratio, I created a basic structure comprising 18 overlapping envelopes with total duration of
25 sec and with each event doubled at a slightly different frequency for choral effect. Since 22 different
ratios are used in the piece, 792 separate events are
calculated and mixed together digitally for this
layer of it. The 18 overlapping events in each section are based on just three fundamental frequencies: f_1, f_2, and f_3. Frequency f_1 remains the same
throughout the entire piece, namely 50 Hz. Frequencies f_2 and f_3 were chosen from the harmonics
common to the harmonic and inharmonic ratios
(see Table 2). In some cases, the harmonic frequency f_2 or f_3 is the same between adjacent ratios
and thus provides an additional basis for fusion between overlapping spectra.

The structure of the 18 events comprising the
basic unit for each of the 22 ratios is shown in
Fig. 1. It is an asymmetrical structure with four
long envelopes for f_1 and seven shorter ones each
for f_2 and f_3, the overall effect of which is a more
rapid spectral variation in the upper frequencies
than in the lower ones. The envelopes shown in
Fig. 1 are those for amplitude; the modulation index (or spectral) envelope in each case is a simple
increase from zero to its maximum value and back
again in equal time units. A rule of thumb with FM

**Table 2. The harmonic ratios used in *Arras* paired
with the inharmonic ones with which they share
harmonics**

Harmonic Ratio	Inharmonic Ratio	f_2	f_3	f_4	f_5
1:2	3:8	7	15	9	17
1:3	4:9	8	17	10	19
1:4	3:8	9	17	7	15
1:5	2:5	9	16	6	14
1:6	—	7	13	7	13
1:7	2:7	6	13	8	15
1:8	3:8	7	15	9	17
1:9	2:9	8	17	10	19

Note: f_2 and f_3 are used as fundamentals for additional
components of the background spectrum; f_4 and f_5 are used as
carrier frequencies for additional foreground events.

is that the modulation index corresponds roughly
to the number of sideband pairs present with any
significant strength in the spectrum. Therefore, the
amount of overlap between the spectra based on
each of the three fundamentals is controlled by limiting the index in each layer. For the spectra based
on f_1 and f_2, the index is limited to produce a four-
octave range of frequencies (up to about the 16th
harmonic), and for f_3, it is limited to avoid frequencies over 7250 Hz (i.e., half the sampling rate per
channel). Therefore, the spectrum based on f_1 extends across that based on f_2 up to approximately
the fundamental f_3 and produces a fairly complex
interaction of frequencies between 400 and 800 Hz.

The Foreground Structure of *Arras*

The entire structure described thus far can be
thought of as the background "curtain" against
which other events are superimposed. It creates a
texture of constantly changing frequencies that run
like threads throughout the entire piece. (Hence the
title, *Arras*, which is a tapestry or heavy wall hang-
ing originally from the French town of the same
name.) Pursuing the analogy further, we can imagine patterns superimposed over the background texture but based on the same frequencies, just as
when the colored threads of a tapestry form fore-

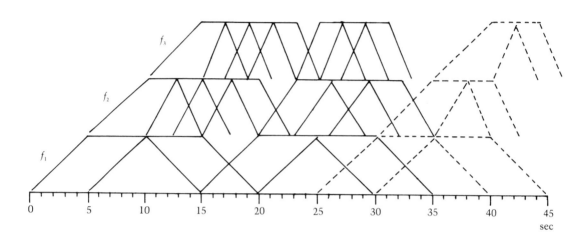

ground patterns while remaining part of the continuous fabric. This interplay of elements creates the
perceptual ambiguity that occurs when we hear a
particular frequency that belongs to the background
texture emerge as part of a foreground event. The
inexhaustible variety of this patterning may be
compared to the constant unpredictability of micro-
level occurrences in a stochastic process.

There are essentially four types of foreground
events mixed with the background, although, as
stated, there is an intentional ambiguity between
what is perceived as foreground or background.
Since the aim of the inclusion of foreground events
is to produce variety, their design includes many arbitrary features and, in several cases, the events are
distributed temporally according to the Poisson
probability function. The four additional elements
may be described briefly as follows:

1. Long, high-frequency, quasi-sine tones
2. Short, quasi-sine-tone events based on frequencies found in the background
3. Three medium-length envelopes with carriers f_1, f_2, or f_3
4. Closely spaced sine tones expanding and
   contracting around two frequency centers,
   f_4 and f_5

Notes on each of these elements follow.

Element 1

The sound texture in *Arras* was designed to maximize the ambiguous perception of any frequency
component as separate or embedded. The auditory
system, however, is limited in its ability to resolve
simultaneous frequencies of similar intensity. This
resolving power is sometimes expressed as the critical bandwidth (Plomp 1964; Scharf 1970). Neighboring frequencies used in the background structure of *Arras* lie within a critical bandwidth above
about 800 Hz and are therefore not likely to be
heard separately. All frequencies above this point
were calculated and used as the frequencies of long,
quasi-sine-tone events with Poisson-calculated entry delays. These high frequencies, which otherwise would be embedded in the texture, emerge as
discrete events.

Element 2

All frequencies in the background texture were calculated and the lowest 16–24 values used as the
frequencies of very short quasi-sine-tone events
with Poisson-distributed entry delays. The event
duration is 0.21 sec, with an average event density
of 4.0 per second.

Fig. 2. Frequency-time
structure of events shown
as horizontal lines lying
with a tendency mask
frame.

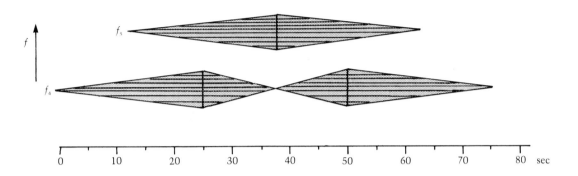

Element 3

Three envelopes with attack, steady-state, and decay times of (2.0, 0.5, 4.0), (0.76, 0.01, 1.24), and (0.01, 0.2, 1.2) sec respectively were designed with various spectral envelopes. The carrier frequency in each case was randomly chosen from f_1, f_2, or f_3, but with a $c:m$ ratio in each case that guarantees a fundamental frequency of f_1 (i.e., 50 Hz). For example, with the $1:2$ ratio, the three carrier frequencies are 50, 350, and 750 Hz for the ratios $1:2$, $7:2$, and $15:2$ respectively. In all three cases the fundamental is 50 Hz, and the sidebands are the same set, namely all the odd harmonics. Since these frequencies are the same in the background texture, these foreground events form a complex relief pattern over the spectral base. The percussive envelope, of course, stands out the most, and the event with the longest attack time blends in the most inconspicuously.

Element 4

In contrast to the other events that rely solely on the set of frequencies found in the background layer, the fourth type of foreground event consists of closely spaced sine waves clustered around two frequencies, f_4 and f_5, as shown in Fig. 2. The choice of f_4 and f_5, given in Table 2, comes from the set of harmonics common to the harmonic and inharmonic $c:m$ ratios, as described earlier. The duration of each structure is 75 sec. The part centered around f_5 enters after 12.5 sec and lasts 50 sec such that it is at its densest point when the lower one is least dense. The effect is that of a constantly expanding and contracting cluster of sine tones with a variable amount of internal beating and roughness. A special program was written to create this effect.

Synthesis

All components of the work were synthesized polyphonically with the POD7 program at a sampling rate of 29 KHz for binaural stereo output. The high-frequency events were calculated and synthesized at half-tape speed and then doubled for greater high-frequency resolution. The stereo output utilized both amplitude and time delays between channels to allow the spectral components to be spread out spatially, both on headphones and loudspeakers. The five layers were mixed onto four channels through conventional studio mixing that kept the left binaural signal on either one or both of the left front and back channels, with the right signal similarly placed.

Conclusion

In this paper I have tried to show how the concept of the stochastic process—in particular its property of global coherence balanced against the unpredictable patterning at the level of detail—can be extended to the timbral domain. More specifically, I have shown how certain acoustic properties of harmonic and inharmonic spectra can give rise to a macro-level structure of precision and complexity and yet allow an interaction at the micro level that is potentially rich in interest. I have described the process elsewhere (Truax 1980) as being based on a respect for "materials"—sound and its behavior. It is also a process that attempts to find its expressiveness within the sounding structure instead of letting the structure arise from a set of expressive gestures. A structure that allows sound to communicate through its own behavior suggests, like an archetype, instances of meaning to each individual listener. When variety is provided within the framework of a coherent whole, the mind seems to have the ability to ascribe pattern and meaning to the perceived relationships. Traditional music in every age and culture has demonstrated how sound can achieve expressiveness through its organizational forms. Modern technology has given us unprecedented powers of control over the design of new sound experiences, but *not*, inherently, over the language with which to ensure communication. A compositional language based on a thorough knowledge of the behavior of sound and on the principle of balance between variety and structural coherence seems to provide a means for realizing the potential of contemporary music.

References

Chowning, John. 1973. "The Synthesis of Complex Audio Spectra by Means of Frequency Modulation." *Journal of the Audio Engineering Society* 21(7):526–534. Reprinted in *Computer Music Journal* 1(2):46–54, 1977.

Erickson, Robert. 1975. *Sound Structure in Music*. Berkeley: University of California Press.

McAdams, S., and A. Bregman. 1979. "Hearing Musical Streams." *Computer Music Journal* 3(4):26–43.

Plomp, R. 1964. "The Ear as Frequency Analyzer." *Journal of the Acoustical Society of America* 36(9): 1628–1636.

Scharf, B. 1970. "Critical Bands." In *Foundations of Modern Auditory Theory*, vol. 1, ed. J. V. Tobias. New York: Academic.

Truax, Barry. 1977a. "The POD System of Interactive Composition Programs." *Computer Music Journal* 1(3):30–39.

———. 1977b. "Organizational Techniques for C:M Ratios in Frequency Modulation." *Computer Music Journal* 1(4):39–45.

———. 1978a. "Computer Music Composition: The Polyphonic POD System." *IEEE Computer* (August):40–50.

———. 1978b. "Polyphonic Timbral Construction in *Androgyny*." In *Proceedings of the 1978 International Computer Music Conference*, vol. 1, ed. C. Roads. Evanston: Northwestern University Press, pp. 355–377.

———. 1978c. *Handbook for Acoustic Ecology*. Vancouver: A.R.C. Publications.

———. 1980. "The Polyphonic POD System and Its Use in Timbral Construction." In *Computer Music*, ed. M. Battier and B. Truax. Ottawa: Canadian Commission for UNESCO, pp. 169–190.

———. 1982. *Androgyne: Electroacoustic and Computer Music by Barry Truax*. Waterloo: Melbourne Records SMLP 4042/43 (includes *Arras* and *Androgyny*).

15

Joel Chadabe
P.O. Box 8748
Albany, New York 12208 USA

Interactive Composing: An Overview

Introduction

Interactive composing is the name I have given to a method for using performable, real-time computer music systems in composing and performing music. The concept of interactive composing has grown in my work since 1967, at which time I proposed the design for a sequencer-programmable analog synthesis system, subsequently built by the R. A. Moog Co. and installed in the Electronic Music Studio at State University of New York at Albany in December 1969. That system's special capability in automating controls made possible the techniques that led to several compositions, in particular *Ideas of Movement at Bolton Landing* (1971) (Chadabe 1972), which involved the control of timbre and rhythm interactively with automated controls generated by sequencers, and *Echoes* (1972) (Chadabe 1975; 1977), in which the sounds performed by an instrumentalist are delayed for a few seconds, then transformed by a sound-processing system, then distributed to various loudspeakers. The transformed sounds appear as distant echoes to which the performer reacts in deciding how to play the next notes.

Echoes is an example of what I referred to at that time as a *design-then-do* procedure for composing, that is, the creation of a system followed by its functioning. That procedure was also the basis of other compositions, such as *Flowers* (1975) (Chadabe 1977) and *Settings for Spirituals* (1976), where the do stage, because of the impossibility of transporting the equipment to a concert hall, was performed in the studio and resulted in tapes. It was the basis also for *Play*, a computer program for control of an analog synthesizer, written by myself and Roger Meyers in the spring and summer of 1977. *Play1*, the first version of the program, was described at the time as "functioning in two stages: (1) a design stage, where the composer designs a specific compositional process, using any of the modules available in the program, and (2) an operation stage, where the composer's process plays back and the composer interacts with the playback according to the design" (Chadabe and Meyers 1977).

In 1977, I began to compose for and perform with a small computer and digital synthesizer system, which I carried and still do carry to concerts. To my knowledge, it was the first instance of a completely digital system used in musical performance. Two compositions have grown out of those performances, *Solo* (1978) and *Rhythms* (1980), which are the first computer music statements of interactive composing (Chadabe 1982).

The computer's function in *Solo* is to compose automatically the notes of a melody, its accompaniment chords, and other aspects of the music, and to interpret the positions of a performer's hands in relation to two proximity-sensitive antennas (Fig. 1). As I perform, I move my right hand in relation to the right antenna, thereby controlling the speed of the melody by increasing or decreasing the duration of each note. As I move my left hand in relation to the left antenna, I control timbre by passing my hand through zones in which different computer-generated instruments, reminiscent of vibraphones, clarinets, and flutes, are playing. I cue two clarinets and two flutes to play slowly, for example, but I cannot foresee what chord they will play. Reacting to what I hear, I decide what to do next.

In *Rhythms*, the computer automatically generates melodies and rhythmic patterns, articulated in sounds reminiscent of Indonesian, Caribbean, and African percussion instruments. I perform by pressing keys at the terminal keyboard, thereby transposing chords, changing pitch relationships within chords, triggering melodic variations, altering rhythmic patterns, overlapping voices, and introducing random notes. But although I trigger each set of changes to begin, I cannot foresee the details of each change. I must react to what I hear in deciding what to do next. It is a distinctive characteristic of interactive composing that a performer, in deciding each successive performance action, reacts to information automatically generated by the system.

143

Another Early Example

Although some of the elements of interactive composing are evident in works by other composers (automated decision making is an essential aspect of
the music of John Cage, Lejaren Hiller, and Iannis
Xenakis, for example, and performance with automated electronic systems plays an important role
in much of the music of Giuseppe Englert, Morton
Subotnick, and many others), Salvatore Martirano's
SalMar Construction, built between 1969 and 1972
at the University of Illinois, exemplifies the primary characteristics of the approach. It consists of
analog sound generators and modifiers controlled
by digital circuits, a console with over 200 touch-
sensitive switches, and 24 loudspeakers arranged
throughout a performance space. The system automatically generates sounds with different timbres,
pitches, and loudnesses, and routes the sounds along
four paths through the arrangement of loudspeakers.
Martirano performs in reaction to what he hears,
manipulating aspects of the music, such as pitch,
rhythm, tempo, pattern, octave, spatial distribution, and cycling.

A Definition of Interactive Composing

Interactive composing is a two-stage process that
consists of (1) creating an interactive composing
system and (2) simultaneously composing and per-

forming by interacting with that system as it functions. Creating the system involves bringing
together a programmable computer, synthesizer,
and at least one performance device, and programming the computer with algorithms that function
automatically and in real time to

> Interpret a performer's actions as partial controls
> for the music
> Generate controls for those aspects of the music
> not controlled by the performer
> Direct the synthesizer in generating sounds

An interactive composing system operates as an
intelligent instrument—intelligent in the sense
that it responds to a performer in a complex, not
entirely predictable way, adding information to
what a performer specifies and providing cues to
the performer for further actions. The performer, in
other words, shares control of the music with information that is automatically generated by the computer, and that information contains unpredictable
elements to which the performer reacts while performing. The computer responds to the performer
and the performer reacts to the computer, and the
music takes its form through that mutually influential, interactive relationship.

Description of the System

The organization of an interactive composing system is indicated by the block diagram in Fig. 2. The
performance interpretation algorithm translates a
performer's motions into specific control information. In *Solo*, the computer "sees" the space around
each antenna as divided into concentric zones and
interprets a performer's hand's distance from an
antenna as being in a certain zone. In *Rhythms*,
pressing a key interrupts one process and initiates
another.

The *composition algorithm* consists of the variables that define the composing processes of the
system. In *Solo*, the most important variables
define the way the melody and accompaniment
chords take form. In *Rhythms*, the important vari-

Chadabe

Fig. 2. Organization of an
interactive composing system, from human per-
former to sound output.

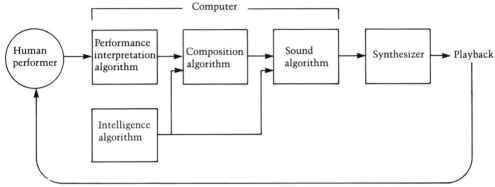

Feedback loop contains information generated by computer in addition
to information specified by performer.

ables define the way the rhythmic and melodic patterns occur.

The *sound algorithm* translates the variables that define the sounds into the format required by the synthesizer. The synthesizer used in *Solo* and in *Rhythms* is the Synclavier I, which is used to generate eight voices of frequency-modulated sounds. Each voice requires specifications for modulator and carrier frequencies, a modulation index, amplitude envelope, and loudness.

The variables of the composition algorithm are the most important determinants of how the system will function. In *Solo*, the melody algorithm, which is the basic component of the composition algorithm, functions as indicated in the flowchart in Fig. 3.

Stated as questions, the melody variables are the following:

Will the next phrase go up or down?
What is the number of notes in that phrase?
What will be the next note, as determined by a jump measured in semitones from the present note?
If the melody exceeds the range of note possibilities, what is the new starting note for a phrase?

The notes of the accompaniment chords are determined by the specification of intervals higher or lower than each melody note.

In *Rhythms*, the important variables derive from two lists, the first a list of randomly placed ones and zeros, the second a list of randomly chosen notes. At the start of each variation, the following two questions are asked for each of eight voices: At what location in the first list shall a cycle begin? How long, from two to nine positions in the list, shall a cycle be?

Rhythms is based on synchronous beats, and the first list is used to determine whether or not a voice will sound on a particular beat. If voice 1, for example, were directed to start at position 23 in the first list and play a cycle of three, and if positions 23, 24, and 25 in the list contained 0, 1, and 0, then voice 1 would not play on the first beat, play on the second, not play on the third, and then begin the cycle again. Six voices repeat their rhythmic patterns on single notes that are chosen at the beginning of each variation. The remaining two voices read a cycle of notes from the note list, also by choosing a starting location and cycle length. Performer-selected routines call into play other sets of variables, such as continually changing notes within patterns, intervals of transposition, and tempo.

Fig. 3. Flowchart of the
melody algorithm for Solo.

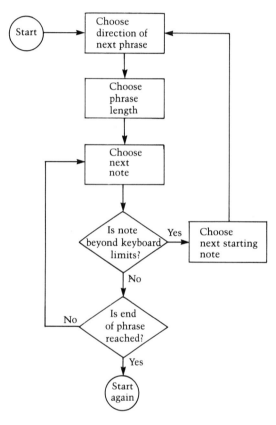

shared control. The performer controls certain of the composition variables and the intelligence algorithm controls others.

In *Solo*, the intelligence algorithm determines the details of the melody and shares control of tempo and timbre with the performer. The primary tempo variable is the period allowed to pass between points in time that mark the beginnings of sounds. In specifying a particular period, the performer, with the intelligence algorithm adding a bit of randomness, sets the envelope segments of each sound to expand or contract to fit within the specified period. The performer exerts a powerful control, determining the ranges within which the durations of the envelope segments will occur, and the intelligence algorithm fills in the details with some unpredictability.

The timbre of the sounds in *Solo* results from the performer's specifications of which instruments are playing, from the nature of the sounds themselves (which is a function of the sound algorithm), and, most important for the performer, from the particular voicing and spacing of the accompaniment chords as controlled by the intelligence algorithm. The performer may specify two flutes and two clarinets, for example, but without knowing the voicing and pitches of the resulting chord, the performer cannot predict precisely the timbre of the total sound. The performer is sufficiently surprised to have to react to the sound in deciding the nature of the next event.

In *Rhythms*, the performer triggers complex patterns of pitches and rhythms to change, but the details of each change are determined by the intelligence algorithm. The successive intervals of a rising melodic pattern, for example, are not predictable, which causes the pattern to be different every time it occurs and propels the performer toward the next decision.

The intelligence algorithm in *Solo* and in *Rhythms* consists of a random-number generator. Like other random-number generators, it is mechanistic and, by itself, does not suggest intelligence. The important quality of random-number generators, however, is what I have come to call complexity. In general, by *complexity*, I mean that the rules which determine a certain succession of events, as, for example, the numbers in the number series 15, 7, 11, 5, 10, 13, 6, 3, 9, 4, 2, 1, 8, . . . , are underlying and

Intelligence in the System

In interactive composing, the system's response to the performer must be interesting and informative; that is, it must contain new, unexpected information. Yet the response must also be recognizably related to the performer's actions, because if the performer did not perceive clearly the effects of his or her actions, the act of performing would cease to have any meaning. The response must be as in a conversation, where the reply to a statement is related to the statement but not a repetition of it.

The seemingly contradictory qualities of newness and recognizability are brought together through

elusive and not evident in the succession of events they generate. Throwing dice, for example, where the numbers that appear are the result of a multitude of underlying and elusive causes, such as the way the dice are held as they are thrown, the strength with which they are thrown, the balance of each die, the relative weight of each die as it strikes another, and so on, may be seen in this light as a method for generating a complex series of numbers. In contrast with *simplicity*, where the rules that determine a succession of events are evident in the events they generate, as in the number series 1, 1, 2, 3, 5, 8, 13, 21, 34, 55, 89, . . . , the events in a complex series seem to occur as if by chance.

The reason for thinking of a random-number generator as complex rather than random is that other complex generators, based on other operating principles, might be devised. A future intelligence algorithm, for example, might embody the artificial intelligence model of the knowledge-based, self-aware, self-organizing system, responding to and evaluating a performer's actions in framing an interesting response.

For the present, however, one might generalize that complexity results in whimsy. It is certainly true that, from the point of view of the performer of an interactive composing system, aspects of the music that are determined by a complex procedure contain whimsical, unpredictable elements. When a complex procedure is used to provide a performer with new yet intelligible information (e.g., in *Solo* and in *Rhythms*), the random-number generator causes the computer to exhibit attributes of intelligent behavior.

The Significance of Interactive Composing

Interactive composing redefines composing and performing. Instead of composing a particular musical structure, as does a composer of traditional music, the creator of an interactive composing system composes a mode of functioning for computer system and performer that, in operation, generates a new particular structure in every performance.

The tasks of interactive composing are substantially different from those of traditional composing.

The problems central to creating a mode of functioning are those of defining a composition algorithm and deciding which of its variables are best controlled by a performer and with what device. This is quite different from writing music for a traditional instrument, where a performer's actions are dictated by the mechanical construction of the instrument and always control the same sound variables. (In playing a piano, for example, depressing a key always controls pitch and loudness.) The creator of an interactive composing system specifies freely a performance action (by specifying an appropriate device) and specifies freely which composition variable or group of variables it will be used to control. The choice of performance device influences the behavior of the system (and the music it produces), because each type of performance action evokes a different musical sensibility. Each type of action, consequently, leads a performer to think and feel in a certain way about the music and about the specific musical variable that is being controlled. For example, proximity-sensitive antennas reinforce the feeling of performing *Solo* as if conducting an instrumental ensemble, because the motions of moving one's hands in the air resemble what a conductor does, and the musical effects of those motions, instruments entering and tempos changing, are typical effects of conducting.

Also different is the nature of a composer's control over the music. When a composer of traditional music creates a particular structure, the whole is known as the parts are made, and the parts can be made to fit. Music produced by an interactive composing system, however, unfolds only as the result of the specific functioning of the system in a particular performance, and the composition as a whole is known only retrospectively, after the parts have been made.

Further, a traditional composition exists apart from any particular performance of it. But in interactive composing, because the music and the performance are inseparable, the quality of the music itself, rather than simply the quality of its execution, is in large part dependent on the ability and talent of the performer. The performer is simultaneously a participant and an overviewer who functions interactively within the system, devising strategies for using the unexpected to advantage, and also functions outside the system by supplying a more global perspective and guiding the progress of the music as a whole.

A Closing Remark

The ultimate significance of interactive composing is that it represents a new way for composers and performers to participate in a musical activity. I offer my nontechnical perception that good things often happen—in work, in romance, and in other aspects of life—as the result of a successful interaction with opportunities presented as if by chance; to that I would add only that it seems to me reasonable that such a perception should also find expression in music.

References

Chadabe, J. 1972. *Ideas of Movement at Bolton Landing.* Greenville, Maine: Opus One Records 17.

Chadabe, J. 1975. *Echoes.* (Jan Williams, percussionist.) New York: Folkways Records FTS 33904.

Chadabe, J. 1977. *Echoes, Flowers.* (Paul Zukofsky, violinist.) New York: CP2 Records 2.

Chadabe, J. 1982. *Rhythms.* (Jan Williams, percussionist.) New York: Lovely Music VR 1301.

Chadabe, J., and R. Meyers. 1977. "An Introduction to the Play Program." *Computer Music Journal* 2(1):12–18. Revised and updated version forthcoming in *Foundations of Computer Music*, ed. C. Roads and J. Strawn. Cambridge, Massachusetts: MIT Press.

16

Horacio Vaggione
22, Quai de Béthune
75004 Paris
France

The Making of *Octuor*

Introduction

Octuor was realized at the Institut de Recherche et de Coordination Acoustique/Musique (IRCAM), Paris, with a Digital Equipment Corporation PDP-10 computer. The main compositional goal was to produce a musical work of considerable timbral complexity out of a limited set of sound source materials. The process began with the generation of five synthesized files, employing additive synthesis and frequency modulation (FM) algorithms written in the Music-10 language. Once this collection of sound files was completed, the next step was to analyze, reshape, multiply, and combine its elements through relatively simple software manipulations, using the program S as the main analytical tool, SHAPE for control of overall amplitude envelopes, MIX as a means for blending sound objects into complex timbral entities, and KEYS for immediate random-access playback.

With the help of these programs, the sound files were segmented into small portions, regrouped into several pattern and timbral families, processed, and mixed into medium and large sound textures. The product of these compositional procedures was stored as a set of new sound-object files. Then, using the KEYS program, these files were organized and finally played automatically in eight-channel polyphony, according to a score that specified the overall form of the piece.

Source Sound Files

The five source sound files were self-contained musical structures, sometimes heard during the piece in their original form.

Computer Music Journal, Vol. 8, No. 2,
Summer 1984

KALF

KALF (kaleidoscopic FM) is a 40-sec sequence made of highly differentiated inharmonic sounds generated with a simple sine wave FM instrument (Chowning 1973). For each event, important parameters, such as the relationship between carrier (c) and modulating (m) sine waves, the modulating index, and the amplitude envelope functions, were set with different values. The whole sequence can be defined as a linear *klangfarben* structure based on inharmonic $c:m$ ratios. The modulating index controls the spectral energy distribution for each one of the $c:m$ ratios, contributing in this way to create a complex time-variant flow. The durations of events were, in general, very short (but never equal). Silences of different lengths were placed between events. The density (or speed of succession) was very high: more than 20 events per second. This rate exceeds the limit of applicability of the Poisson law, which is valid to control sound distributions whose densities are lower than 10–20 events per second (Truax 1977). Beyond 10–20 events per second, one is no longer dealing with sounds as individual entities. However, the goal in building this linear structure by combining high density of sounds with highly contrasted parametric values was to create a texture showing a kind of kaleidoscopic "internal" behavior.

FILS

FILS (FM instrumentlike sounds) was realized with the same sine wave FM instrument, but in this case the $c:m$ ratios were kept constant in order to produce spectra resembling traditional instruments. Depending on these $c:m$ ratios and on the modulating-index power, these spectra approached instrumental models like horns, plucked strings, marimbas, xylophones, and more unidentifiable sounds. The sequential density is much lower than in KALF: between 5 and 10 events per second. The Poisson law applies here, and the note lists were calculated according to this stochastic distribution. (For a description of the implementation of the Poisson law in terms of the Music-10 language, see the article by Lorrain [1980].) In contrast with KALF, this second FM sound file shows slower changes in all parameters, and hence the resulting patterns can be easily recognized when reheard.

PIAL

PIAL (piano algorithm) basically uses Schottstaedt's algorithm for simulation of piano tones using two sinusoidal modulating waves and two separate modulating indices (Schottstaedt 1977). The main features of this algorithm are (1) the frequency-dependent response of the modulating indices, whose values create rich spectra in the low frequency range but simpler ones in the high range; (2) a certain amount of inharmonicity (0.5% of the carrier's frequency) in order to simulate the spectral frequency structure of a piano tone; and (3) the use of the LINEN procedure (McNabb 1981) in the note-to-note articulation, equalizing the envelopes of sounds having different durations.

This double-modulator FM instrument was used to make highly contrasted sequences by controlling the individual duration and the relative octave position of each event. However, the procedure for building these sequences was not related in this case to any stochastic distribution model. Rather, it was specified manually by the composer.

ASBYR

ASBYR (additive synthesis by rule) was built using an additive instrument designed by Stephen McAdams (McAdams and Wessel 1981) in which the spectral frequencies were computed automatically by rule. This rule included an algorithmic deviation from the harmonic series, which offered the possibility of shifting, expanding, or contracting the series by declaring a displacement proportion,

that is, by replacing the octave with another base (McAdams 1982). The amplitudes of the spectral frequencies were also specified by a rule that controlled the spectral envelopes utilizing a GEN function in Music-10. This latter was essentially a table-lookup transfer function. At each sample, the instantaneous frequency of a spectral component was used to address its instantaneous amplitude in the table. With this method of global spectral control, the amplitudes of each partial always contained the desired spectral form. Finally, another feature of this additive synthesis instrument was the possibility of independent control of *roughness*, as well as random or periodic vibrato, all of which are important factors for generating fused or parsed spectral structures.

This instrument was programmed to generate mainly reedlike sounds. The resulting ASBYR sound file was a musical structure divided into three consecutive sequences: (1) strings of tones of equal duration (of 0.3 sec each); (2) isolated short tones; and (3) sustained tones (alternating with some grace notes that punctuate the passage from one sustained tone to another).

CTP

CTP (circular timbral paths) also used an additive instrument designed by McAdams that included the possibility of interpolation between three spectral envelopes. This allowed me to build circular paths of spectral evolution using polar coordinates to control the change of radius and angle of a vector centered at the origin of a circle (see Fig. 1).

With this procedure, I could define the time functions of radius and angle that control movement in the spectral "space." The radius varied between 0 (center) and 1 (circumference); the angle varied between 0 and 2π. Three of these functions controlled the time-varying "weights" or relative amplitudes of three spectral envelopes. These weighted spectral forms were added linearly to determine the final spectral result. For example, if the radius, r, is fixed at a value of 1, and the angle, Θ, varies linearly between 0 and 2π, the point, P, of movement

Fig. 1. Circular spectral
path with polar coordi-
nates (from the McAdams
AD10F additive instru-
ment). Θ = angle; r = ra-
dius; p = the point in
motion inside the circle;
A = first spectral envelope
(0); B = second spectral
envelope (2π/3); C = third
spectral envelope (4π/3).
The point 1/3(A + B + C)
represents the linear average of the three spectra.
The three spectra are
shown with a for ampli-
tude and f for frequency.

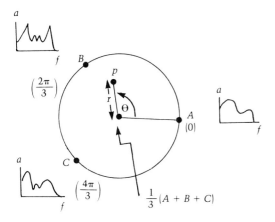

grams, written by J. A. Moorer (Roads 1982). The
methods used in these programs are familiar to
composers working with sound-processing techniques oriented toward digital *musique concrète*,
including the phase vocoder and linear predictive
voice synthesis (Haynes 1982).

The S program allowed me to visualize the spectral structure of a given file. The S program also
permitted me to isolate small file segments and to
write new sound files containing only these specific
segments. These were later processed, multiplied,
and combined in a variety of ways. In order to use
S, one must set the time limits for each segment
(e.g., 1 sec). These limits constitute the window
through which one can see in detail the waveform
of any portion of a given file. Once the size of the
window is defined, one can move it forward or
backward along the whole file, or use a zoom command to increase or decrease the defined size while
retaining the same point at the center of the window.

S is an interactive, micro-level analysis program
useful for dealing with very short segments (its
analytical power goes down to the sample level).
SHAPE, on the other hand, is a nonanalytical,
purely procedural system for manipulating bigger
chunks of material. SHAPE allows one to modulate
any sound file by applying a new amplitude envelope to it. Since this envelope does not need to correspond to the whole duration of the sound file, one
can proceed to reshape any portion of it by specifying the begin and end times. Each run of SHAPE
generates only one overall amplitude envelope
(which can contain any number of breakpoint functions). However, SHAPE is not time-consuming,
and it can be repeated many times to produce a collection of different envelopes modulating the same
sound material. These SHAPE variations can then
be digitally mixed to form complex overlapping and
time-variant structures.

The MIX program, also written by J. A. Moorer,
is a useful means of building *timbral polyphonies*
(Wessel 1979) based on portions of preexisting
sound files. Using output data from the S program,
one can create timbral families, enter them into
MIX, and experiment with their interactions. In
Octuor, such interactions were a main factor in
creating "context." (The Gestalt concept of "be-

makes one complete revolution on the circumference of the circle. For $0 < \Theta < 2\pi/3$, a linear
interpolation between spectra A and B occurs. For
$2\pi/3 < \Theta < 4\pi/3$, an interpolation between B and
C occurs. And for $4\pi/3 < \Theta < 2\pi$, an interpolation
between C and A occurs. If $r = 0$, an exact linear
average of the three spectra results. Figure 2 gives
the Music-10 code of the function.

The CTP structure used in *Octuor* was made of
five circular timbral transitions, each one repeating its path at several uniform or variable rates of
change. The faster transitions were those showing
the sharper onset attacks; they were placed in their
original form at the center of *Octuor's* overall time
span (between 4 and 8 min). Toward the end of the
piece, CTP is heard again, this time as a tapestry
formed by combining several different rates of
change.

Manipulation of the Sound Files

The second step taken in composing *Octuor* was
to analyze in detail the sound structure of the synthesized files and to select segments showing interesting features for further musical elaboration. This
was done mainly through the S and SHAPE pro-

Fig. 2. Function Spec-
Arrays of the AD10F ad-
ditive instrument (Mc-
Adams 1981) traversing
a circular path between

three spectral envelopes.
This function was used for
building the timbral structure of the CTP sound
source file.

```
function specarrays(array speca, array specb, array specc, array anglefun, array radiusfun);
⟨
⟨    This function takes as input two functions—anglefun and radiusfun—which describe the motion of a point
⟨    inside of a circle as the endpoint of a vector. These functions are translated into the time-varying
⟨    "weights" or relative amplitudes of the three different spectral envelopes. In effect, the three spectral
⟨    shapes are added linearly, with the time-varying weighting functions determining the mix.
⟨
begin
     array tangle(512);          ⟨    temporary angle: allows anglefun to be expressed both positively and
                                  ⟨    negatively and the function repeats every multiple of 2π.
   variable twopi, i;            ⟨
     twopi ← 6.283185307;
     for i ← 0 step 1 until 511 do
     begin
         if anglefun(i) ⩾ 0 then
         begin
             tangle(i) ← anglefun(i);
             while tangle(i) > twopi do
                 tangle(i) ← tangle(i) − twopi;
         end
         else begin
             tangle(i) ← (−1)*anglefun(i);
             while tangle(i) > twopi do
                 tangle(i) ← tangle(i) − twopi;
         end;
     end;
     for i ← 0 step 1 until 511 do
     begin
         if tangle(i)<twopi/3. then
         begin
             speca(i) ← − 3./twopi * radiusfun(i) * tangle(i)
                     + (1. + 2. * radius fun(i))/3.;
             specb(i) ← 3./twopi * radiusfun(i) * tangle(i) + (1. − radiusfun(i))/3.;
             specc(i) ← (1. − radiusfun(i))/3.;
         end
         else
             if tangle(i)<2.*twopi/3. then
             begin
                 speca(i) ← (1. − radiusfun(i))/3.;
                 specb(i) ← −3./twopi * radiusfun(i) * (tangle(i)−twopi/3.)
                         + (1. + 2. * radiusfun(i))/3.;
                 specc(i) ← 3./twopi * radiusfun(i) * (tangle(i)−twopi/3.)
                         + (1. − radiusfun(i))/3.;
             end
             else
             begin
                 speca(i) ← 3./twopi * radiusfun(i) * (tangle(i)−2*twopi/3.)
                         + (1. − radiusfun(i))/3.;
                 specb(i) ← (1. − radiusfun(i))/3.;
                 specc(i) ← −3./twopi * radiusfun(i) * (tangle(i)−2*twopi/3.)
                         + (1. + 2. * radiusfun(i))/3.;
             end;
     end;
end;
```

longingness" can be used here to define how a context is established and perceived in musical terms.)

With the help of the S program, which provides both the micro-level data and the materials, one can formalize the mixing procedure by manipulating timbres according to criteria such as the degree of brightness (or spectral energy distribution) and the degree of synchronization of onset attacks (Risset and Wessel 1982). This is the way *Octuor*'s timbral structures were built. Complex sound objects were created by layering and blending of many individual sources.

Finally, the MIX program allows one to multiply the sound segments in order to form long, sustained textures using a single file as an input any number of times. In this way, one can produce heterophonies, overlapping textures, and high polyphonic densities, showing an intense internal activity and at the same time a clear economy of source materials.

The KEYS Program

My primitive collection of five sound files was enlarged with the addition of the new files created by the procedures already mentioned. Now began the third step in *Octuor*'s compositional process, that of high-level musical organization. The main software tool used for handling the whole collection of materials was the KEYS program (Wessel and Smith 1977). KEYS is an interactive, random-access playback program that allows one to play already existing sound files without having to retype their names to the main PDP-10 PLAY program each time. The procedure is as follows. First, users make a list of sound file names, in any order, including all the files they want to play. This list of files is called an MFL file and constitutes the proper input format requested by KEYS. Once an MFL file has been entered into KEYS, the program produces a display where each individual file name of the list is attached to an alphanumeric character. In producing this display, KEYS allows one to play any sound file from the MFL file by merely typing the

corresponding letter on the terminal's keyboard. Furthermore, KEYS offers the possibility of playing automatically any sequence of files by entering a string of letters, corresponding to the files desired, in a specific order.

I used both manual and automated possibilities in *Octuor*. The manual playing of individual files was useful in performing quick perceptual comparisons. It gave me the aural feedback I needed to select materials for building up the macroform of the piece. Classification of files was done in this way according to perceptual criteria, such as those mentioned earlier (brightness and onset attack), plus others like harmonicity and density.

After this perceptual analysis and timbral grouping was completed, I edited the files and organized the general time flow by writing a mixing score in eight parts. Figure 3 shows the mixing score corresponding to the beginning of the piece. Each channel was organized separately, keeping track of the necessary time precision and controlling minutely the synchronization of the eight channels.

Automated Execution

The overall form of the composition is based on a sort of growth principle. This principle is stated as a gradual exposition of materials covering the work's whole time span, from (1) inharmonic to harmonic spectra, (2) random distributions to periodic rhythms, and (3) sparse textures to high-density spatial and temporal configurations. These three dimensions are developed simultaneously, each one contributing to the growth effect, and they arrive together at a point of maximum evolution.

As stated above, the procedure for building this overall time structure was produced by entering strings of files into the KEYS program, according to the specifications of the mixing score. Since the eight sequences were synchronized with a click tone before the starting of the music, it was easy to transfer each sequence to a separate track on an analog tape recorder. The final product was thus achieved in the form of an eight-track analog recording of the automated execution.

Fig. 3. Mixing score for Octuor (first page). Amplitude is shown on the vertical axis, while time (in blocks of 5 sec) is shown on the horizontal axis. Letters are attached to the sound files according to the KEYS program display.

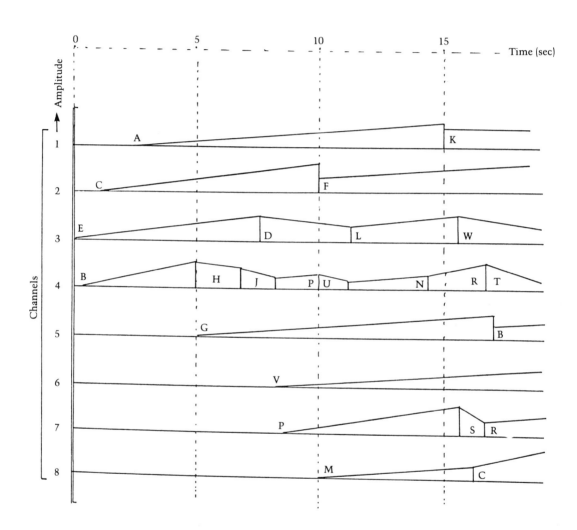

Acknowledgments

Octuor was premiered in June 1982 at the Festival des Musiques Experimentales in Bourges, France. The work won the first prize at the 1983 Newcomp Computer Music Festival in Cambridge, Massachusetts.

I would like to thank the following members of the IRCAM staff: Marc Battier, J. B. Barrière, Stanley Haynes, Thierry Lancino, Stephen McAdams, and especially David Wessel, for his openness and creative thinking.

References

Chowning, J. 1973. "The Synthesis of Complex Audio Spectra by means of Frequency Modulation." *Journal of the Audio Engineering Society* 21(7):526–534. Reprinted in *Computer Music Journal* 1(2):46–54. Also reprinted in C. Roads and J. Strawn, eds. Forthcoming. *Foundations of Computer Music.* Cambridge, Massachusetts: MIT Press.

Haynes, S. 1982. "The Computer as a Sound Processor." *Computer Music Journal* 6(1):7–17.

Lorrain, D. 1980. "A Panoply of Stochastic 'Cannons.'" *Computer Music Journal* 4(1):53–81.

McAdams, S. 1982. "Spectral Fusion and the Creation of Auditory Images." In *Music, Mind, and Brain*, ed. M. Clynes. New York: Plenum, pp. 279–298.

McAdams, S., and D. Wessel. 1981. "A General Synthesis Package based on Principles of Auditory Perception." Paper presented at the 1981 International Computer Music Conference, 5–8 November, Denton, Texas.

McNabb, M. 1981. "Dreamsong: the Composition." *Computer Music Journal* 5(4):36–53.

Risset, J. C., and D. Wessel. 1982. "Exploration of Timbre by Analysis and Synthesis." In *The Psychology of Music*, ed. D. Deutsch. New York: Academic, pp. 26–58.

Roads, C. 1982. "A Conversation with James A. Moorer." *Computer Music Journal* 6(4):10–21.

Schottstaedt, B. 1977. "The Simulation of Natural Instrumental Tones using Frequency Modulation with a Complex Wave." *Computer Music Journal* 1(4):46–50. Reprinted in C. Roads and J. Strawn, eds. Forthcoming. *Foundations of Computer Music.* Cambridge, Massachusetts: MIT Press.

Truax, B. 1977. "The POD System of Interactive Composition Programs." *Computer Music Journal* 1(3):30–39.

Wessel, D. 1979. "Timbre Space as a Musical Control Structure." *Computer Music Journal* 3(2):45–52. Reprinted in C. Roads and J. Strawn, eds. Forthcoming. *Foundations of Computer Music.* Cambridge, Massachusetts: MIT Press.

Wessel, D., and B. Smith. 1977. "Psychoacoustic Aids for the Musician's Exploration of New Material." Paper presented at the 1977 International Computer Music Conference, Center for Music Experiment, University of California at San Diego, La Jolla.

17

Charles Ames
Department of Music
State University of New York at Buffalo
Buffalo, New York 14260

Stylistic Automata in *Gradient*

Introduction

My involvement with automated composition over the past several years has made me increasingly disenchanted with procedures based on random selection. In *Gradient*, for solo piano, I eliminated random selection entirely and based automated decisions directly on stylistic criteria.

The Automated Techniques

Along with *comparative search*, the automated techniques used to compose *Gradient* include two additional approaches: *constrained search* and *sorting*. Comparative search, constrained search, and sorting provide judicious solutions to compositional problems that involve some collection of *entities* (e.g., sections, chords, notes) and that attempt to select an *attribute* (e.g., durations, registers, pitches) for each entity. In describing these techniques, it will be convenient to refer to individual acts of selection as *decisions* and to refer to a collection of decisions, one for each entity, as a *solution* to a problem.

In a comparative search, the computer compares many different solutions in order to discover the solution in greatest accord with a *protocol* (i.e., a ranked collection) of directives established by the composer. This technique derives historically from Claude Shannon's algorithms for playing chess by computer (1950). I have discussed comparative search extensively in my article on *Protocol* (1981).

A constrained search seeks a solution conforming to one or more strict rules, again provided by the composer. Whenever a constrained search encounters some decision in which no option satisfies all of these rules, the search backtracks, revises one or more earlier decisions, and tries again. Constrained searches are much faster than comparative searches,

but only produce acceptable solutions, not optimal ones. They have the disadvantage that since all constraints are absolute, one cannot rank them. The composer can, however, supply heuristics controlling the order in which the computer schedules options for each decision. Since a constrained search accepts the first solution it finds, such heuristics will bias this solution toward tendencies which, though desirable, do not merit absolute status as constraints. Constrained search is a basic technique of artificial intelligence (Nilsson 1971). It was first applied to musical problems by Stanley Gill (1963), but languished until its revival as a theoretic tool by my colleague Kemal Ebcioğlu (1981).

Sorting can be used to solve compositional problems when all of the attributes are drawn from a common *pool* containing one attribute per entity. We assume that attributes are drawn from the pool in either ascending or descending order. The idea here is to set up pointers to each entity and to use one or more already existing characteristics of the entities as *keys* by which to sort these pointers. Sorting algorithms are among the most versatile operations in computer programming (Knuth 1973).

The Music

Table 1 summarizes the stages of production for *Gradient* and indicates the automated technique used at each stage. These stages are divided into three phases corresponding to the global form and two levels of syntax, median and local.

Form

Gradient adheres to a monolithic aesthetic in that it subjects a continuing mass of notes to a sequence of gradual transformations. This process resolves into nodes and segments. Each node presents a *musical state*, defined as a configuration of four attributes: register, dynamics, tempo, and "texture." Segments

Table 1. Stages of production

Phase	Function	Technique
Global	Select gamuts for nodes	Comparative search
	Select numbers of chords for segments	Sorting
	Select pairs of dynamics for nodes	Comparative search
	Select tempi for nodes	Comparative search
	Select textures for nodes	Comparative search
Median	Compose progression of chords	Constrained search
	(Select letter names for each pitch in each chord)	(Constrained search)
	Select durations for chords	Sorting
Local	Assign a priority to each pitch in each chord	Sorting
	Select number of repetitions for each pitch in each chord and durations for each repetition	Sorting
	Determine sequences of long and short durations for each pitch	Comparative search
	Compose arpeggios for each chord and create a mnemonic listing	Constrained search

Note: The global stages produced the profile illustrated in Fig. 1, from which the median stages produced the progression of chords illustrated in Fig. 4. The local stages arpeggiated these chords to create the final product illustrated in Fig. 5.

effect transformations from the state defined at one node to the state defined at its successor. There are 55 nodes and, consequently, 54 segments. The four attributes evolve quasi-independently to determine the global profile illustrated in Fig. 1.

Register

The most salient attribute characterizing a node is its register. The register at each node is manifest as a momentary *gamut*. Equally spaced (vertically) along each gamut are registral loci for six contrapuntal parts; straight lines connecting loci from one node to the next define trajectories for these parts. The six parts, taken together, move as a progression of chords.

The disposition of gamuts determined the number of nodes in the work. Referring again to Fig. 1, one may see that I split the full range of the piano into 12 divisions. Trial and error established 3 divisions (a little under two octaves) as the narrowest practical gamut; even at this constriction, adjacent parts interfered with one another enough to impede the counterpoint. The registral profile illustrated in Fig. 1 exploits all 10 distinct gamuts spanning 3 divisions, all 9 gamuts spanning 4 divisions, all 8 gamuts spanning 5 divisions, and so on for a total of 55 distinct gamuts. Comparative searches produced an arrangement of these gamuts that excluded similar motions and suppressed the most oblique motions.

Number of Chords per Segment

My approach to determining the number of chords in each segment involved first generating 54 numbers of chords as a pool (see the second line of Fig. 1). These numbers ranged from 0 to 20, and emphasized values around 10.

The next step was to make pointers to each of the 54 segments according to three keys: (1) differences in range between terminating nodes, (2) contrariness, and (3) "exoticism" of register. For example, segments 9, 16, 18, 27, 31, and 48 all had differences of six divisions. In such cases, I wanted to slight more oblique segments, for example, segments 18 and 27, while favoring more contrary segments, for example, segment 48. Even at this second level of discrimination, however, there were also multiple segments sharing both the same difference in range and the same contrariness. Here, I wanted the computer to favor the more exotic registers. Segments 9, 16, and 31 are equally contrary, but segment 31 lies in the center of the piano, while segment 9 lies just a little less solidly in the treble than segment 16 lies in the bass. Therefore, segment 16 received one more chord than segments 9 and 31 received.

Dynamics

The treatment of dynamics in *Gradient* is unusual. Two dynamic indications occur in the score at each node, one for the lowest notes sounding and one for the highest. The pianist must graduate dynamics vertically as well as horizontally. A pragmatic constraint suppressed loud dynamics in extremely high registers. Subject to this restriction, my goal was to maximize changes in the vertical distribution of dynamics from one node to the next.

Tempo and Texture

Two aspects of rhythm evolve globally, the tempo and what I call the texture. The rhythmic unit of *Gradient* is the sixteenth note, but the arpeggiated idiom neutralizes any sense of ictus. No rhythms at any broader level of design are periodic, and the rhythms within each contrapuntal part are similarly irregular.

Tempi range from 40 to 124 quarter notes per minute, where the grouping of sixteenths into quarters is solely a convenience for the pianist. The slower tempi occur proportionally less often, since they occupy longer durations.

By *texture*, I refer both to the average number of contrapuntal parts sounding simultaneously and to the average number of attacks per sixteenth note, for a single evolution governs both of these averages. The average number of sounding parts ranges from 1.0 to 3.0. The average number of attacks follows the same contour as the average number of sounding parts, except that it ranges from 1.0 to 1.5.

Median Syntax

The contrapuntal search selected pitches for each part on a chord-by-chord basis. Detailed constraints upon sonorities, contrapuntal interactions, and the rate of tonal flux assured a uniformly dissonant mass of notes, which progressed smoothly from node to node. (I use the word *tonal* throughout this article in its literal sense, to denote concepts relating to tone or to degree, rather than to key.)

Sonorities

Fundamental among the constraints on sonorities was a requirement that all six pitches in a chord be distinct degrees of the chromatic scale; the number six represented a compromise between providing sufficient tonal resources for the moment and allowing tonal variety from chord to chord.

Figure 2 illustrates various additional constraints against consonant triads. These constraints were applied to the following materials:

> Triads of *consecutive* pitches in one part
> Triads of *simultaneous* pitches in adjacent parts
> Triads of simultaneous pitches in nonadjacent, *moving* parts
> Triads of *two* consecutive pitches in one part and *one* pitch occurring alongside these other two pitches in an adjacent part

Rules of Counterpoint

Individual parts could sustain pitches from one chord to the next, provided that no pair of sustained pitches formed a perfect consonance and that no two parts both approached and departed with a pair of sustained pitches in concerted motion (Fig. 3a, b, c). Parts could not explicitly cross, though they could cross virtually (Fig. 3d, e); part crossings did not matter directly to me, but they would have wreaked havoc with other constraints. Parts could not move in parallel, regardless of interval; when pitches changed, sonorities had to change as well (Fig. 3f, g, h).

A tolerance of four semitones to either side of the trajectories illustrated in Fig. 1 restricted individual

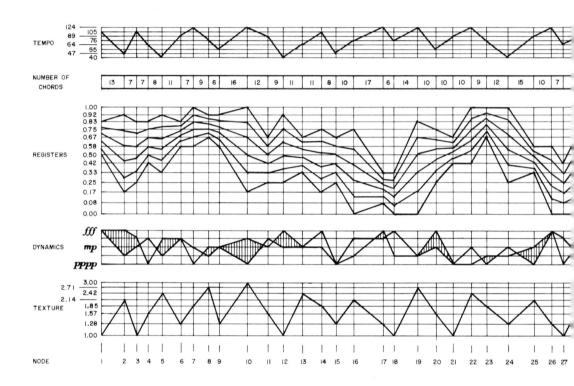

Fig. 1. Profile of Gradient. Tempi indicate quarter notes per minute. Registers range from the lowest extreme of the piano (0.00) to the highest (1.00). The two dynamic contours show dynamics for the lowest and highest contrapuntal parts; shadings indicate where the dynamic for the lowest part exceeds the dynamic for the highest part. Textures indicate the average number of notes sounding simultaneously.

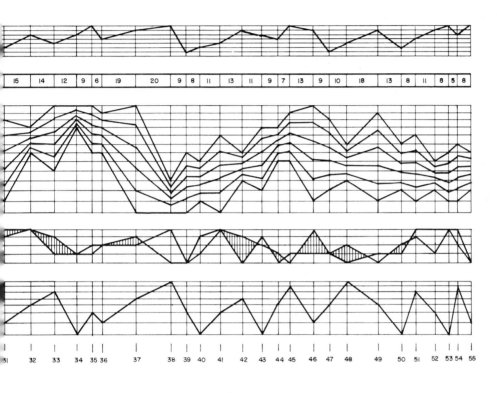

Fig. 2. Tests for consonant triads. Each lattice of pitches represents segment 43 of Gradient. The four groups of lattices illustrate configurations of triads around a single reference, the E5 in the third row and the fifth column.

Group A: No major, minor, diminished, augmented, or quartal triads

```
-D♮6  C#6  F♮6  D♮6  G♮6  D♭6-D♭6  D♮6-D♮6      -D♮6  C#6  F♮6  D♮6  G♮6  D♭6-D♭6  D♮6-D♮6      -D♮6  C#6  F♮6  D♮6  G♮6  D♭6-D♭6  D♮6-D♮6
- E♭5 - E♭5 - E♭5  F#5 - F#5 - G♭5  G♮5  C♮6  G#5  - E♭5 - E♭5 - E♭5  F#5 - F#5 - G♭5  G♮5  C♮6  G#5  - E♭5 - E♭5 - E♭5  F#5 - F#5 - G♭5  G♮5  C♮6  G#5
F♮4 [A♮4  A♭4-A♭4  E♮5] F♮5  B♮4  C#5-C#5 -       F♮4  A♮4 [A♭4-A♭4  E♮5] F♮5  B♮4  C#5-C#5 -       F♮4  A♮4  A♭4-A♭4 [E♮5  F♮5  B♮4] C#5-C#5 -
B♮3 - B♮3  G♮4  F♮4  E♭4  G♮4  F♮4-F♮4  A♮4       B♮3 - B♮3  G♮4  F♮4  E♭4  G♮4  F♮4-F♮4  A♮4       B♮3 - B♮3  G♮4  F♮4  E♭4  G♮4  F♮4-F♮4  A♮4
C♮3  G#3  B♭3  A♮3-A♮3-A♮3-A♮3  E♮4  E♭4          C♮3  G#3  B♭3  A♮3-A♮3-A♮3-A♮3  E♮4  E♭4          C♮3  G#3  B♭3  A♮3-A♮3-A♮3-A♮3  E♮4  E♭4
E♮2  F#2  A♮2  B♮2  D♮3  E♮3  F#3  B♭3  B♮3       E♮2  F#2  A♮2  B♮2  D♮3  E♮3  F#3  B♭3  B♮3       E♮2  F#2  A♮2  B♮2  D♮3  E♮3  F#3  B♭3  B♮3
```

Group B: No major, minor, diminished, augmented, or quartal triads

```
-D♮6  C#6  F♮6  D♮6 [G♮6] D♭6-D♭6  D♮6-D♮6        -D♮6  C#6  F♮6  D♮6  G♮6  D♭6-D♭6  D♮6-D♮6      -D♮6  C#6  F♮6  D♮6  G♮6  D♭6-D♭6  D♮6-D♮6
- E♭5 - E♭5 - E♭5 [F#5 - F#5 - G♭5] G♮5  C♮6  G#5  - E♭5 - E♭5 - E♭5 [F#5 - F#5 - G♭5] G♮5  C♮6  G#5  - E♭5 - E♭5 - E♭5  F#5 - F#5 - G♭5  G♮5  C♮6  G#5
F♮4  A♮4  A♭4-A♭4 [E♮5] F♮5  B♮4  C#5-C#5 -       F♮4  A♮4  A♭4-A♭4  E♮5  F♮5  B♮4  C#5-C#5 -       F♮4  A♮4  A♭4-A♭4 [E♮5] F♮5  B♮4  C#5-C#5 -
B♮3 - B♮3  G♮4  F♮4  E♭4  G♮4  F♮4-F♮4  A♮4       B♮3 - B♮3  G♮4  F♮4 [E♭4] G♮4  F♮4-F♮4  A♮4       B♮3 - B♮3  G♮4  F♮4 [E♭4] G♮4  F♮4-F♮4  A♮4
C♮3  G#3  B♭3  A♮3-A♮3-A♮3-A♮3  E♮4  E♭4          C♮3  G#3  B♭3  A♮3-A♮3-A♮3-A♮3  E♮4  E♭4          C♮3  G#3  B♭3 [A♮3-A♮3-A♮3-A♮3] E♮4  E♭4
E♮2  F#2  A♮2  B♮2  D♮3  E♮3  F#3  B♭3  B♮3       E♮2  F#2  A♮2  B♮2  D♮3  E♮3  F#3  B♭3  B♮3       E♮2  F#2  A♮2  B♮2  D♮3  E♮3  F#3  B♭3  B♮3
```

Group C: No major, minor, or quartal triads

```
-D♮6  C#6  F♮6  D♮6 [G♮6] D♭6-D♭6  D♮6-D♮6        -D♮6  C#6  F♮6  D♮6  G♮6  D♭6-D♭6  D♮6-D♮6
- E♭5 - E♭5 - E♭5  F#5 - F#5 - G♭5  G♮5  C♮6  G#5  - E♭5 - E♭5 - E♭5  F#5 - F#5 - G♭5  G♮5  C♮6  G#5
F♮4  A♮4  A♭4-A♭4 [E♮5] F♮5  B♮4  C#5-C#5 -       F♮4  A♮4  A♭4-A♭4 [E♮5] F♮5  B♮4  C#5-C#5 -
B♮3 - B♮3  G♮4  F♮4 [E♭4] G♮4  F♮4-F♮4  A♮4       B♮3 - B♮3  G♮4  F♮4 [E♭4] G♮4  F♮4-F♮4  A♮4
C♮3  G#3  B♭3  A♮3-A♮3-A♮3-A♮3  E♮4  E♭4          C♮3  G#3  B♭3  A♮3-A♮3-A♮3-A♮3  E♮4  E♭4
E♮2  F#2  A♮2  B♮2  D♮3  E♮3  F#3  B♭3  B♮3       E♮2  F#2  A♮2 [D♮3] E♮3  F#3  B♭3  B♮3
```

Group D: No major or minor triads

```
-D♮6  C#6  F♮6  D♮6  G♮6  D♭6-D♭6  D♮6-D♮6        -D♮6  C#6  F♮6  D♮6  G♮6  D♭6-D♭6  D♮6-D♮6      -D♮6  C#6  F♮6  D♮6  G♮6  D♭6-D♭6  D♮6-D♮6
- E♭5 - E♭5 - E♭5 [F#5 - F#5 - G♭5] G♮5  C♮6  G#5  - E♭5 - E♭5 - E♭5  F#5 - F#5 - G♭5  G♮5  C♮6  G#5  - E♭5 - E♭5 - E♭5  F#5 - F#5 - G♭5  G♮5  C♮6  G#5
F♮4  A♮4 [A♭4-A♭4] E♮5 [F♮5] B♮4  C#5-C#5 -       F♮4  A♮4 [A♭4-A♭4] E♮5  F♮5  B♮4  C#5-C#5 -       F♮4  A♮4  A♭4-A♭4 [E♮5] F♮5  B♮4  C#5-C#5 -
B♮3 - B♮3  G♮4  F♮4  E♭4  G♮4  F♮4-F♮4  A♮4       B♮3 - B♮3 [G♮4  F♮4 [E♭4] G♮4  F♮4-F♮4  A♮4       B♮3 - B♮3  G♮4 [F♮4  E♭4] G♮4  F♮4-F♮4  A♮4
C♮3  G#3  B♭3  A♮3-A♮3-A♮3-A♮3  E♮4  E♭4          C♮3  G#3  B♭3  A♮3-A♮3-A♮3-A♮3  E♮4  E♭4          C♮3  G#3  B♭3 [A♮3-A♮3-A♮3-A♮3] E♮4  E♭4
E♮2  F#2  A♮2  B♮2  D♮3  E♮3  F#3  B♭3  B♮3       E♮2  F#2  A♮2  B♮2  D♮3  E♮3  F#3  B♭3  B♮3       E♮2  F#2  A♮2  B♮2  D♮3  E♮3  F#3  B♭3  B♮3

-D♮6  C#6  F♮6  D♮6  G♮6  D♭6-D♭6  D♮6-D♮6        -D♮6  C#6  F♮6  D♮6  G♮6  D♭6-D♭6  D♮6-D♮6      -D♮6  C#6  F♮6  D♮6  G♮6  D♭6-D♭6  D♮6-D♮6
- E♭5 - E♭5 - E♭5 [F#5 - F#5 - G♭5] G♮5  C♮6  G#5  - E♭5 - E♭5 - E♭5  F#5 - F#5 - G♭5  G♮5  C♮6  G#5  - E♭5 - E♭5 - E♭5  F#5 - F#5 - G♭5  G♮5  C♮6  G#5
F♮4  A♮4  A♭4-A♭4 [E♮5] F♮5  B♮4  C#5-C#5 -       F♮4  A♮4  A♭4-A♭4  E♮5 [F♮5] B♮4  C#5-C#5 -       F♮4  A♮4  A♭4-A♭4 [E♮5  F♮5] B♮4  C#5-C#5 -
B♮3 - B♮3  G♮4  F♮4  E♭4  G♮4  F♮4-F♮4  A♮4       B♮3 - B♮3  G♮4 [F♮4  E♭4] G♮4  F♮4-F♮4  A♮4       B♮3 - B♮3  G♮4 [F♮4] E♭4 [G♮4] F♮4-F♮4  A♮4
C♮3  G#3  B♭3  A♮3-A♮3-A♮3-A♮3  E♮4  E♭4          C♮3  G#3  B♭3  A♮3-A♮3-A♮3-A♮3  E♮4  E♭4          C♮3  G#3  B♭3  A♮3-A♮3-A♮3-A♮3  E♮4  E♭4
E♮2  F#2  A♮2  B♮2  D♮3  E♮3  F#3  B♭3  B♮3       E♮2  F#2  A♮2  B♮2  D♮3  E♮3  F#3  B♭3  B♮3       E♮2  F#2  A♮2  B♮2  D♮3  E♮3  F#3  B♭3  B♮3
```

Fig. 3. Rules of counter-point. Examples (a)–(c) il-lustrate sustained pitches. Examples (d) and (e) illus-trate explicit and virtual

part crossings. Examples (f) and (g) illustrate ex-plicit parallel motion; the "hidden" parallelism in example (h) is allowed as

a change in sonority. Ex-amples (i) and (j) illustrate virtual octaves, while ex-amples (k) and (l) illus-trate transfers of pitch.

Example (m) illustrates a close approach.

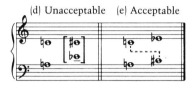
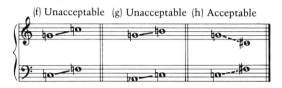

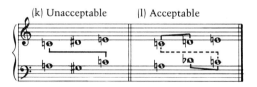

Fig. 4. Contrapuntal solution for segments 40–43.
Lines connecting pitches
show tonal relationships

of various strengths. The
bold lines indicate pitches
sustained between adja-
cent chords, while the me-

dium lines indicate shared
degrees. The thin lines indicate degrees shared be-
tween nonconsecutive

chords. The number be-
neath each pitch indicates
the pitch's priority within
the respective chord.

Segment 40	Segment 41

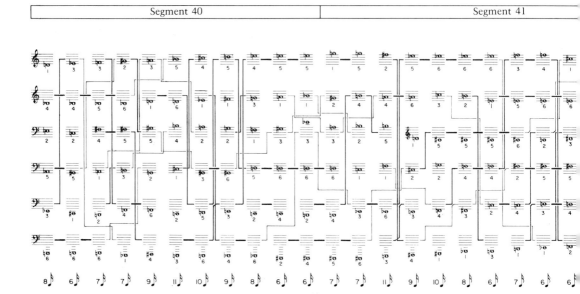

parts to a narrow band of nine pitches around these
trajectories. This tolerance favored motion by melodic steps (major and minor seconds) or by less
frequent, small leaps. Indeed, I required stepwise
motion within parts when strong melodic links
were necessary to offset virtual consonances, such
as consecutive octaves (see Fig. 3i, j) and transfers
of unisons (see Fig. 3k, l). Close approaches (see
Fig. 3m) could happen freely even though the parts
are arpeggiated rather than sustained; it is not important to "hear out" individual parts, per se, in
this music.

Tonal Flux

The term *tonal flux* refers to the rate at which new
pitches enter (and leave) the tonal environment. At
least one part per chord was required to hold its
pitch over from the preceding chord, while forbid-
ding more than three parts to do so. Each chord was
required to contain at least one chromatic degree
not present in the preceding chord.

Durations of Chords

The fewer pitches and/or degrees held over by a
chord from its immediate predecessors, the longer
the chord's duration. Longer chordal durations occur proportionally less often than shorter ones,
though each individual segment received its fair
share of long and short values.

Figure 4 presents the contrapuntal solution for
segments 40–43 of *Gradient* and illustrates how
tonal relationships affect chordal durations.

Local Syntax

The constrained search that arpeggiated *Gradient*'s
chords imposed several constraints. These constraints served two purposes: (1) to make the music
playable and (2) to make it conform to the aesthetic
and stylistic premises already described. Within
this context, there remained considerable latitude
as to which pitches should appear in what order;
this order was derived heuristically on the basis of
tonal *priorities* established for each pitch in a chord.

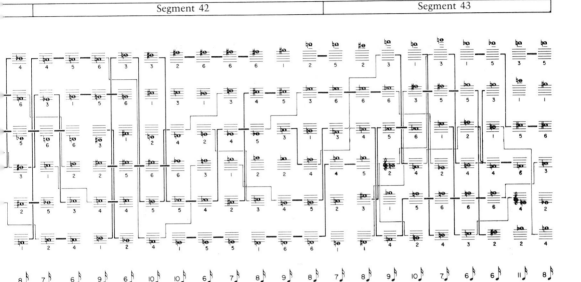

Segment 42 | Segment 43

Constraints

The most important constraint was that the pianist had to reach the notes. Beyond this, arpeggios were to reflect the general dissonance of the counterpoint by avoiding double attacks on perfect consonances and consonant triads. (Remember that the constraints illustrated in Fig. 2 do not exclude triads between nonadjacent parts.) Voice leading that offset virtual consonances (review Fig. 3i–l) was ensured locally by a rule requiring the melodic motion to occur prior to the consonance. *Gradient*'s monolithic character was enforced by requiring that the music be relatively seamless: no gaps larger than an eighth note could occur between consecutive attacks.

Tonal Priorities

Beyond presenting the counterpoint for segments 40–43, Fig. 4 indicates priorities for each pitch and illustrates how tonal relationships affected these priorities. Pitches with higher priorities received the greatest accent within an arpeggio. These pitches normally occurred earlier, were repeated more often when the number of notes permitted, and received longer durations when textures were thick. In the last case, the program evaluated thickness of texture and registral span to determine whenever it became impractical for the pianist to sustain each note independently. If so, it requested the pedal. Figure 5 illustrates the final product for segments 40–43.

Conclusion

Gradient demonstrates that random selection is often not the most effective way to generate musical scores by computer. Indeed, when the objective involves maintaining one or more consistent stylistic qualities (including consistent asymmetry), random selection is inappropriate. Automated techniques can provide detailed stylistic directives expressed either as absolute rules or as ranked pro-

Fig. 5. Charles Ames: Gradient, measures 217–240. This excerpt illustrates the final product for segments 40–43. In the analytic strip beneath each system of music, the solid vertical lines demarcate segments, while the broken vertical lines demarcate chords.

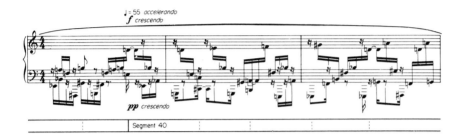

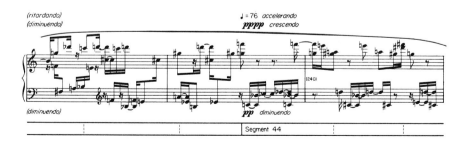

tocols. If one measures the effectiveness of a compositional method (that is, a way of composing, rather than a musical system) by the degree to which the musical details reflect such directives, then these stylistic automata can easily outperform any manual effort.

Acknowledgments

I would like to thank John Myhill and Lejaren Hiller for their encouragement and for their many helpful suggestions for the preparation of this article.

References

Ames. C. 1981. "*Protocol*: Motivation, Design, and Implementation of a Computer-Assisted Composition for Solo Piano." In *Proceedings of the 1981 International Computer Music Conference*. San Francisco: Computer Music Association. (Revised version: "*Protocol*: Motivation, Design, and Production of a Composition for Solo Piano." *Interface* 11(4), 1982:213–238.)

Ebcioğlu, K. 1981. "Computer Counterpoint." In *Proceedings of the 1980 International Computer Music Conference*. San Francisco: Computer Music Association.

Gill, S. 1963. "A Technique for the Composition of Music in a Computer." *The Computer Journal* 6(2):29–31.

Hiller, L., and L. Isaacson. 1959. *Experimental Music*. New York: McGraw-Hill. (Reprinted in 1979. Westport, Connecticut: Greenwood Press.)

Knuth, D. 1973. *The Art of Computer Programming. Vol. 3: Sorting and Searching*. Reading, Massachusetts: Addison-Wesley.

Nilsson, N. 1971. *Problem Solving in Artificial Intelligence*. New York: McGraw-Hill.

Shannon, C. 1950. "Automatic Chess Player." *Scientific American* 182(48). Reprinted in *Computers and Computation*. 1971. Ed. R. Fenichel and J. Weizenbaum. San Francisco: W. H. Freeman, pp. 104–107.

Xenakis, I. 1971. *Formalized Music*. Bloomington, Indiana: Indiana University Press.

18

Jacques Arveiller

Université de Paris VIII—Vincennes
2 rue de la Liberté
93526 Saint Denis Cedex 02
France

Comments on University Instruction in Computer Music Composition

Introduction

In practice, a composer always refers to other composers of the past and present. The very idea of musical composition is inseparable from the question of its pedagogical transfer, with everything this involves on psychological and institutional levels. This is because only a part of compositional expertise can be submitted in writing in the form of a treatise, manual, or primer. When computers come on the scene, though the fundamental issue remains the same, the didactics of composition exhibit certain distinctive features and have specific problems. Since the computer is going to figure increasingly in musical composition, it seems an auspicious moment to give the details of an experiment in effect since 1970 and indicate some solutions we have tried to find for these problems.

Creative Activities of Composition and Programming

First, let us go over some of the particular features of computer music.[1] Two points seem important,

1. In speaking of *computer music composition*, the author is referring specifically to what has been called *algorithmic music composition*, that is, music composed with the aid of a computer and in which the score is generated by the machine—Ed.

These are retrospective comments, since I have given over the teaching of computer music composition at Vincennes to my colleague Giuseppe Englert. My present teaching assignment is the psychology of music—J. A.

Translated by H.-L. Bull, with C. Roads

Computer Music Journal, Vol. 6, No. 2, Summer 1982

since they raise new questions warranting fresh pedagogical solutions.

On one hand, computer music composition presupposes the simultaneous performance of two overlapping creative activities, and there is always the risk that one will take precedence over the other. I consider programming a very complete creative activity that in some cases is sufficient unto itself, artistically speaking.

On the other hand, traditional musical functions are currently merging. Beyond the lack of distinction between composer and performer—in improvisation, for example—computer music perpetuates a blurring of function among composition, performance, and instrument-building. This has decided effects on students.

The University Setting

A second feature of much computer music is related to the university setting. Indeed, computer music can be performed only where there are computers and people prepared to use those computers to make music. Computer-generated music is still often expensive to produce. Therefore, for the beginner the preferred place of learning is still the university.

At the University of Paris VIII—Vincennes, it is mainly students from both the music and computer science departments who take the computer music courses. Since the courses are open to anyone wishing to attend, instructors find considerable diversity in student background and knowledge.

The University of Vincennes was created with interdisciplinary pursuits in mind. As a result, constant collaboration among the different departments (computer science, music, and art), as well as collective work realized by musicians and other artists, have always been encouraged. The computer science department itself was created in 1969 by painters and musicians searching for a new creative tool. The Vincennes approach is therefore a bit special: while all branches of computer science are taught, the predominant thought is that the creation of sound and images is one of the most important functions of a computer and not a useless or vaguely shameful activity. As a result, students are free to use computer equipment to these ends whenever they choose and not only at designated hours.

One other feature of the Vincennes setting that I should mention is the Groupe Art et Informatique de Vincennes (GAIV). It is responsible for the organization of concerts, exhibits, performances, and lectures and unites instructors and students as artists. Its connection with the university is flexible: it is independent on an administrative level, though use of university equipment is permitted.

A university is essentially a place that one passes through. So is the GAIV. It does not draw its coherence from a shared direction or collective project (though this might be advisable) but from common reference to the same technological tool (the microprocessor, for example) and the same methodology (such as the use of artificial intelligence techniques).

While the software is most often shared, the musical design is always personal; we steer clear of esthetic orthodoxy. The computer-generated music at Vincennes is therefore quite varied in style and with respect to points of reference. Since I do not wish to cover Vincennes in all its diversity, the rest of this article will consist of personal thoughts on the way I, among others, view the position of instructor.

Pedagogical Style

Instruction in computer music seems to feature a rather particular pedagogical style. In traditional scientific education, the learning stage can be equated with the research stage on many levels. The two stages use the same avenues and demand the same efforts, except for one point: the student is not asked to discover but to rediscover what others have previously learned. The goal of the scientific researcher is clear: to demonstrate to other researchers an original result, often obtained using perfected laboratory equipment. Student efforts—like those of children—lead to something different. Students show an instructor, through example, that they know how to demonstrate a theorem. But in all this there are no colleagues or equipment involved—and certainly no pleasure. All too often, scientific instruction insists on effort from students before they can enjoy the pleasure of discovery. But this excludes them from the pleasure inherent in the discovery process itself.

Using musical or visual peripherals, we can give (albeit partial) intuitive, prompt, and responsive understanding of abstract concepts customarily communicated in the teaching of mathematics, logic, and physics. The mastery of a new concept, then, is first related to pleasure and then to the teaching method. Because of this pleasure, the student will want to master new concepts.

Communication Between Students

In our evolving pedagogical style, we favor a mode of communication between students similar to the one linking two researchers. As this develops, the student-teacher relationship also seems to change.

In the standard mathematical and logical context, it is normal to think that there are good solutions to a problem and that some solutions are better than others. In a typical programming task, it can be said that, with respect to a predetermined goal, there are programs that perform better than others. The programming of musical composition is entirely different. We can change the predetermined goal during the creative process. Composers do just that. In effect, it is possible to outline an itinerary when the destination is not known in advance. This kind of process leads the student and the teacher to maintain relationships that differ from the standard model. Additional factors affect student-teacher relationships. The computer is a dispassionate judge when it comes to running a program (this allows the instructor to avoid subjective evaluations). Also, the student and the teacher take the same risks when presenting their music before

Fig. 1. Production of music as a side effect.

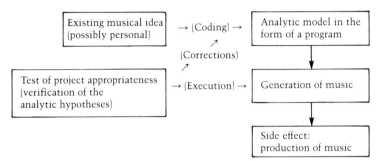

an audience. Finally, composing per se does not imply a university rank, which helps students and instructors to disregard the "identity" processes usually at play in the university.

The pedagogical plan at Vincennes suggests that students integrate whenever possible the act of *doing* with the act of *seeing themselves do*. Computer science has this special characteristic: it allows the immediate reversibility of the analytic models. The analysis of a piece of music in program form—just as approximate and incomplete as the deciphering of compositional processes supposedly underlying it—facilitates the immediate use of this program "in generation" to confirm or invalidate the analytic hypotheses formulated. But in both cases music is produced through *side effects*.[2] The music can be heard with regard to criteria other than those related to analytic activity (Fig. 1).

Is it daring to suppose that there might exist a seesaw effect between Truth and Beauty? Is it daring to claim that successful music can originate in an invalid analysis? An error is never accidental. Is not an error in analysis solely specific to the analyst and the mark of the composer's subjectivity?

Leaving these questions open, we must in any case insist on the idea of completion. A program in composition is never finished; it is nothing but a sequence of steps interspersed with modifications and error corrections, corrections that reveal much about how the composer sees the work in progress and what the composer knows of him- or herself.

2. The term *side effects* is used here in a sense specific to computer science. For example, in a Lisp program, a function may return a single value while altering many other values in the global environment as a side effect.

This brings us to one point I feel students should grasp. Writing compositional programs is certainly one way of learning about music, but it is also one way of learning about ourselves as we make music. I can easily imagine programs for use in composing (but also reading and improvising) music, such as artificial intelligence programs. I am trying to make students work from the perspective that programmed composition partially involves the simulation of ourselves in the process of composing.

Composers and Programmers

We must recognize that there is a difference between the work style of the traditional composer and that of the composer as programmer. The traditional composer can work alone, aiming for a totally original piece. The compositional process is controlled from start to finish by one person alone.

Implicit in computer work is considerable dependence on the computer (consider machine failure, for example) and on a number of other people with specific technical expertise. But more importantly, composers lose control over the process that they themselves have initiated. A program can return unexpected or musically unacceptable results. This is because a program is the delineation of a general process with such potential that we cannot be exhaustive in our exploration of all possible results nor can we represent them a priori. My opinion, which falls short of adopting in principle the position of accepting program output unconditionally, is that this loss of prediction of the musical result causes certain traditionally trained composers to fail in their attempts to make the transition to computer composition.

Relations Among Musicians, Scientists, and Technicians

Relations between musicians and those around them (scientists, i.e., mathematicians and physicists, engineers, and programmers) are sometimes a bit strained. We occasionally witness mute dialogues between the musician and scientist, the latter tending to index an esthetic decision to an argument based on the mathematical triviality of algorithms used in composition. A musician does not take this very well. For the musician, the musical result is all-important.

In some cases, collaboration between musical and technical people tends to take a disturbing turn. The engineer feels responsible for most of the work but does not enjoy public recognition. It appears that the composer merely signs the work to get the applause. Engineers can experience a certain ambivalence: in realizing music-oriented hardware and software never to be used in their own name (since they do not claim to be artists and do not feel qualified to perform in concert), engineers can more-or-less consciously prevent musicians from using the hardware and software. (Their repressed creativity is then embodied in hard or soft modifications made two days before the concert, to the great chagrin of the musician!)

Musicians can be dispossessed of their own works on two levels: conceptually by the scientist and technically by the engineer. This slightly puzzling feeling of being dispossessed is nothing new. It has existed since the beginnings of electronic music, when a change occurred: the instrument-building trade was no longer a small-scale business but a privileged branch of the industry, with all the profit-making and commercial depreciation of new equipment that that entails.

To avoid these obstacles, which I have exaggerated slightly to make a point, I insist that music students need relative independence. This does not mean that they should be omniscient or omnificient, but that, as composers, their computer expertise should be adequate to enable smooth and precise expression of personal compositional directives.

Relations with the Self

Certainly the most difficult human relations are those carried on with the self. From the start, computer-oriented compositional work seems particularly prone to waste. The programs realized are often not shared because we do not have the time to annotate them. There is no time to put our legible comments on a program because we have already started working on a new one. Thus, it is possible that only the person who conceived that impressive software, product of an incredible expenditure of energy, will actually ever use it.

Also, the program with the greatest potential is often used only once by the person who wrote it for a particular piece. In some cases, this touches on real conceptual art—the musical program never produces music. If it runs, that is enough; we move on to another program. At times, we have the impression that the effort expended in writing a program is disproportionate to the parsimonious use (if any) that will be made of it.

In some of us, the risk is even more pronounced. By describing our personal selves in the process of creating music, with all the narcissistic complacency that that involves, we are no longer creating music. The realization of a program leads to the conception of another program, and musical production per se vanishes in favor of writing programs never to be used.

At a university, where the function of communication should take priority, we are not always obliged to use written outlines to justify our work. How, then, can we counter the danger of pursuing a potentially recursive activity that does not provide for termination or musical side effects?

At Vincennes we insist that a musical program, whether written by student or teacher, be communicated and that it approach audible music. This is why I lend so much importance to the arrangement of auditions and concerts and to the availability of documented programs, no matter what the level. To this end, we created a periodical, published irregularly, which is devoted to the computer arts: *Artinfo/Musinfo*.

The Viability of Computer Music at the University

Another difficulty with computer music is related to the university setting. Let me merely cite in passing one question all of us ask. Will the university pay for such an expensive activity when the fruits are apparently so meager? Sometimes a university administration has trouble understanding that a subject considered literary or artistic requires a budget similar to the budgets of the scientific disciplines. We must remember that a university should be able to draw favorable publicity from the concerts it sponsors, just as it does from the scientific papers written and researched under its auspices.

One very positive aspect of university life is that it allows composers to live while concentrating on their personal research. But the teaching profession is not without its obstacles. The instructor must satisfy both those music students just beginning their studies in computer science and nonmusical students (who are uninterested in receiving basic instruction in music, which the university, in any case, is not there to give).

I am trying to circumvent this first obstacle by suggesting as many different roads to computer science as possible. We immediately advise the music student, who is often already engaged in a music project, to begin work on a personal program and to learn programming "on the job" as much as possible, as desired, and *mutatis mutandis*. We also insist upon the analysis of existing programs simply to show the student which types of algorithms composers have used to satisfy specific compositional needs. The music student begins to accumulate a personal storehouse of algorithms, starting with musical ones. With the computer science student, we emphasize listening to tapes and the concrete manipulation of sound. Since these students are already familiar with the elements of computation, they must discover musical peripherals and

learn to *play* them. Using the game approach, they can often circumvent feelings of helplessness.

One more thing: the essential goal of the university is to train both music instructors and computer engineers—but not professional composers. This kind of contradiction, which poses no problems for most students, may perturb those music students for whom musical programming is almost an obsession. We generally advise them to get two degrees, one in music and the other in computer science. This will guarantee them a livelihood as a programmer while allowing them to pursue their favorite obsession with impunity.

Problems Encountered in Learning and Teaching

A third concern common to our field directly involves pedagogy. This concern has three aspects: what the music student must face, what the computer science student must overcome, and the role of the instructor.

Music Students

Music students in general are quick to learn programming. They are accustomed to the manipulation of symbols, and they are familiar with temporal processes. But they often make a serious mistake. They want to move too fast, and consequently they expose themselves to what we call "second-month depression." Equipped with illustrious musical references and elaborate projects, they are disappointed by the extreme poverty that results from their still inarticulate efforts at programming.

In my opinion, preventive medicine for this kind of depression is based on the creation of specialized pedagogical systems that allow students to handle interesting musical material despite their elementary knowledge. In this vein, Vincennes has developed systems—still too few—such as J. Chailloux's KRWTH or P. Greussay's Bisequenceur.

Students risk another danger in thinking that their implicit musical knowledge, which is considerable, will be recognized by the machine. In order to make it clear to the beginner that the computer knows only what it is told, I always insist that musicians formulate in natural language their own knowledge on a particular point before organizing a computer representation.

For some, there is another difficulty manifested in the writing of programs without data: it involves the assumption that a program defines a general process renewable at each performance. The idea of defining the parameters of a piece of music is indeed difficult for some musicians to comprehend.

Finally, we are faced (rarely, it is true) with some students who have a block about computer programming ("I understand, but I cannot do it"). This block seems linked to the apparent impossibility of formalizing and thus reducing a musical problem into its parts. Indeed, how can we preserve the student's personal musical ideals if we start to fragment them and reduce the irreducible into finite automatons?

This kind of block, it seems to me, can be avoided if students are put in contact with the computer from the very first day and run their first programs at the end of the first class. They must have fun with the computer in an undramatic way, not letting a gap develop between theoretical knowledge and practical programming, which could only aggravate the situation. The writing of an initial set of programs, where any exercise, however simple, has a musical pretext, has proved very useful.

As for the risk of self-contemplation through self-simulation, mentioned earlier, it usually crumbles before visual or sound peripherals, which limit self-contemplation through the imposition of physical reality.

Computer Science Students

The computer science student must cope with totally different problems, summed up in the following statements, heard hundreds of times:

I am not an artist.
I know nothing about music.
I am not familiar with solfeggio.
I have no musical ideas for programming.

The instructor must then try to evolve a number of arguments. Sometimes it takes a long time and in some cases requires an incredible persuasive effort. The students must realize that music exists within them and that it is important to communicate this musical knowledge orally. They must conquer problems related to notation; so we, as instructors, must demonstrate that traditional notation is neither exhaustive nor definitive, that musical notation accounts for only a part of the music that will be drawn from it (any notation is incomplete), that elementary notation can generate substantial audible effects, and that it is possible eventually to create musical notation designed for one's own needs. All this can be proved on acoustic instruments, using audible examples. (These difficulties are even greater for the many students at Vincennes who come from the third world countries. We must help them dispense with the postcolonial idea that western music and its notation are universal and absolute.)

It always helps to advise students to work in pairs (a music student and a computer science student) and to advocate the recycling of algorithms. They can often find musical applications for existing nonmusical programs that have been well tested by the computer science student.

Instructors

Finally, I would like to mention some of the difficulties I have encountered as an instructor. First of all, it is difficult to maintain student interest. People are interesting only when they are speaking with enthusiasm, and they are enthusiastic only about what they are currently doing. This sometimes works against traditional pedagogy. But computer music composition is a contemporary field and is rapidly expanding. We cannot provide students with "the basics," the kind of collective knowledge shared by all professionals in this field. Therefore, we can teach only a body of knowledge related to current compositional research, knowing that it cannot be summarized and that our own speculations sometimes stray from our students' fields of interest. This explains the importance of other sources of information: the library, journal subscriptions, and copies of tapes. Even if an instructor is not abreast of current progress, the student must be able to assess what is happening elsewhere that may be relevant to personal needs.

Conclusion

My remaining comments are added in no particular order. In my opinion, two programming languages should be used at the same time: an evolved high-level language (e.g., Lisp) and an assembler. What should courses cover? They should be as varied as possible and include theoretical and practical programming, analysis of programs and works, music listening and the international panorama, and the historical approach that students always appreciate in anecdote form. For example, What place does computer music hold in contemporary music?

What role does the composer we are studying play in computer music?

Finally, I submit two questions to the reader that I intend to leave unanswered. They concern the specific relationship between the music and the computer. Could the analysis of a work composed using a computer amount to the analysis of the program that generated it? Should we teach computer music composition as an independent discipline? In other words, do the traditional techniques of musical composition constitute a necessary basis or are they a useless burden for the composer working on a computer?

Acknowledgments

I wish to thank Patrick Greussay, who gave me one of his teaching assignments. I am indebted to him for some of the ideas expressed in this article.

III

The MIDI Interface

Curtis Roads

Overview

The Musical Instrument Digital Interface (MIDI) specification is a software language and hardware interconnection scheme for communication between computers and computer-controlled devices (such as synthesizers). When MIDI was launched in 1983, few could have predicted the tremendous impact it would have on the music and computer industries and on musicians around the world (Anderton 1986; Moog 1986; Yavelow 1987).

Two reasons for MIDI's success are its simplicity and its low cost. All communication is organized into 10-bit *messages*, which are sent at a fixed rate of 31.25 kilobits per second between instruments, computers, sequencers, and other devices. The hardware required to build a MIDI interface is very inexpensive. Virtually every drum machine, sequencer, synthesizer, or signal processing effects box contains a MIDI interface and a microprocessor for decoding and generating MIDI messages.

Although its designers did not attempt to solve all the control and communications problems of computer music, MIDI is a godsend for performers, on stage and in the recording studio. It is a simple and reliable means of synchronizing synthesizers and other devices and of capturing performance data for later playback. As industry has caught on to the potential of MIDI-based communications, more and more MIDI-controllable devices and applications have been developed, including sound mixers, lighting systems, and even robot arms. With extensions of the original standard, such as the MIDI sample format and MIDI time code (a method of converting between the timing of MIDI events and events synchronized by means of SMPTE time code), MIDI has evolved into a more versatile communications medium.

Despite its widespread acceptance in the musical instrument industry, MIDI has always been a controversial topic in research circles (Buxton 1987; Moore 1988). Although it solves many of the control problems associated with performance in a straightforward way, it ignores other important aspects of music-making with computers. MIDI has poor provisions for microtonal music, timbral control, and digital audio processing. Although the standard response of the devout MIDIphile is that it

wasn't designed for such purposes, the only alternative to MIDI is the Audio Engineering Society/European Broadcast Union standard. The AES/EBU standard was designed for transmission of digital audio samples, and has not been widely used as a control protocol. Thus, MIDI's *de facto* monopoly means that if it does not provide a certain functionality, it is difficult to find that functionality elsewhere. In the research community, there is a sense that someday MIDI must change, or that a more powerful successor should be developed (Buxton 1987; Moore 1988).

Part of the problem inherent in MIDI is its low data rate. In an age in which 10-Mbit/sec communications between digital devices are commonplace, the 31.25-Kbit/sec data rate of MIDI seems anachronistically slow. Another problem is the one-way bias of MIDI communications: all communication with MIDI emanates from a "master" device to a "slave" device, and two-way communication among several devices is awkward to implement (it generally requires repatching of MIDI cables). The proliferation of MIDI "black boxes" for routing, mixing, and modifying MIDI data is symptomatic of the limited bandwidth and the unidirectional bias inherent in the MIDI specification.

MIDI could be extended by integrating it with a *local area network*. LANs are a more complicated and costly communications scheme than MIDI, but they operate many times faster and allow easy *n*-way communication; any device connected to the LAN can talk to any group of devices on the LAN. An evolution from MIDI-based communication to LAN-based communication need not make existing MIDI devices obsolete. In a scheme proposed by William Buxton (1987), a LAN could be used to connect the various devices in a studio or onstage system, and a LAN-to-MIDI converter could be used to communicate with each device that does not have a built-in LAN interface.

But even with its limitations, MIDI has opened up a world of new musical possibilities. MIDI allows a computer music system to be divided into several modular components, including a musical input device or controller, a synthesizer, a sequencer, a signal processor, and a mixer. Each component can be purchased from a different manufacturer. One controller, such as a musical keyboard, can be used to control several different synthesizers. The sounds can be layered simultaneously, or the keyboard can be split into several parts, with each part controlling a different synthesizer. A wind controller—a MIDI input device that is blown and fingered like a saxophone—can play sampled saxophone sounds over a much wider pitch range than is possible with a conventional sax. To be sure, the sampled sound is not exactly the same as the natural saxophone sound (for example, the phrasing is less expressive), but the use of MIDI codes adds new capabilities to the instrument. For example, as the performer plays, the MIDI control information corresponding to the performance can be recorded by an inexpensive MIDI sequencer for later playback and editing, or it can be routed to a computer for response by an automatic improvisation program. MIDI can also be used to inexpensively synchronize synthesizers and other devices with video equipment and multitrack tape recorders, via SMPTE-to-MIDI interfaces and MIDI time code.

MIDI has created a large and diverse software industry, in which giant international conglomerates exist alongside one-person operations. With every MIDI-controllable device that is introduced, a need is created for new computer software. At minimum, each synthesizer requires a *voice* or *patch* editor and a librarian program. Other software replaces the physical front panel of a device with a graphical interface that can be made much more informative and easier to use.

The two articles in part V are outstanding surveys of MIDI and its applications. Gareth Loy's "Musicians Make a Standard: The MIDI Phenomenon" is probably the most widely referenced analysis of MIDI ever published. Christopher Yavelow's informative survey, commissioned especially for this book, points out the wide range of applications that MIDI can support. These articles remind us that the success of MIDI is well established. Millions of MIDI-equipped devices have been purchased throughout the world. MIDI is here now, and every computer musician should be familiar with its capabilities and its limitations.

References

Anderton, C. 1986. *MIDI for Musicians.* New York: Amsco.

Buxton, W. 1987. "Masters and Slaves Versus Democracy: MIDI and Local Area Networks." In J. Strawn, ed., *The Proceedings of the AES 5th International Conference: Music and Digital Technology* (New York: Audio Engineering Society).

Moog, B. 1986. "MIDI: Musical Instrument Digital Interface." *Journal of the Audio Engineering Society* 34(5): 394–404.

Moore, F. R. 1988. "The Dysfunctions of MIDI." *Computer Music Journal* 12(1): 19–28.

Yavelow, C. 1987. "Personal Computers and Music—The State of the Art." *Journal of the Audio Engineering Society* 35(3): 160–193.

19

Gareth Loy
Computer Audio Research Laboratory
Center for Music Experiment
University of California, San Diego
La Jolla, California 92093 USA

Musicians Make a Standard: The MIDI Phenomenon

Introduction

MIDI (Musical Instrument Digital Interface) is a specification of a communications scheme for digital music devices. Like all products of human cunning, it has its good aspects, and bad ones. Its advent is more notable for the effect it has had on the music community than for its prowess as a network. Whether MIDI gets good or bad reviews depends to some extent on whether it represents a step up or down in expressive potential from the system the reviewer is currently using. It makes some happy that a networking standard exists for music instruments; it makes others frustrated that it has so many limitations. The limitations include limited bandwidth between devices, limited frequency and time resolution, limited access to synthesizer parameters for such things as timbre modification during synthesis, and lack of bidirectionality in communications. The conception of music embedded in the standard seems archaic and inflexible, and favors piano-keyboard type synthesizers. However, MIDI has flourished and is now the *de facto* industry standard. In spite of its limitations, it is quite serviceable for a variety of tasks. Its usefulness comes in no small part from its being a standard, whatever its limitations. Its success has sparked interest in the development of other standards for domains such as music databases, editing, and for extensions or replacement of the MIDI standard itself.

This article is something of a survey, tutorial, and review, all mixed together. Under discussion are the following topics:

The reference model for MIDI
The MIDI 1.0 specification
The control paradigm MIDI implements

Computer Music Journal, Vol. 9, No. 4, Winter 1985

The implications of this paradigm for performance capture and synthesizer control
Conclusions regarding its usefulness for the variety of different tasks in which it could find application

Beyond this, we will look at the forces that brought MIDI into being, and consider what the future holds, now that we know that MIDI will be a part of it.

The basic message is that while MIDI has been characterized as rock-n-roll's answer to computer music, this condescension is not warranted. If the number of articles published on the subject of music networking is any indication (Bischoff, Gold, and Horton 1978), the subject has been almost completely ignored. This will change now that there is a common technological base from which to work. For instance, networking is very important to the study of live performance, since the latter can be viewed in terms of the former.

In spite of its limitations, MIDI provides tools that can be helpful to the study of performance practice, computer-assisted performance, and improvisational composition. Simple as it is, it has intrinsic worth for practicing musicians and composers. Grasping the lessons that the MIDI phenomenon has to teach will be revealing no matter what its direct usefulness. It will probably lead more people to more new insights about music performed live with computers than anything since the GROOVE system (Mathews and Moore 1970). To this end, my hope is that the serious study of MIDI will lead to its own betterment.

Motivations for MIDI

MIDI was developed by several commercial synthesizer manufacturers over the last few years. The original motivation was to allow commercial synthesizers to be connected together so that they

Fig. 1. Block diagram of
MIDI transmitter and re-
ceiver circuitry.

might share control information, such as the gestures of a musician. Other benefits sought included hardware extensibility, protection from obsolescence, and interfacing to digital computers. The latter can provide for multitrack recording/playback, sequence editing and composition, score display, and music printing.

It is important at the outset to say that MIDI is designed as an *event-based* network, not a *sample-based* one. What MIDI communicates is not sampled waveforms, but indications about pressed keys and switches, turned knobs and pedals—in other words—human gestural control information.

MIDI Specification

The first order of business is to present the MIDI 1.0 specification, which is given here in an abridged form, suitable for the issues under consideration.[1] While I have tried to keep back my observations until the concluding section, it seems that some blows must be struck while the iron is hot; so where I have been unable to restrain myself from critical observation, I have enclosed these comments in braces {}.

MIDI was loosely adapted from the serial data transmission technology developed for computer terminals. The basic idea involves a two-layer specification: a physical interconnection scheme, and a code to communicate information across the channel so created. Obvious requirements for the physical layer are that it must be rugged, capable of driving signals over medium distances without loss, resistant to electrical and magnetic interference, noninterfering so as not to pollute nearby analog signals, and capable of the requisite transmission bandwidth. The code layer must be as concise as possible while still permitting all the forms of expression required by the communicating devices. It must be extensible, fault tolerant, and yet efficient. Both layers are also constrained to be extremely

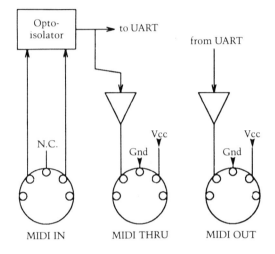

1. Readers interested in obtaining a copy of the complete specification should contact the International MIDI Association, 11857 Hartsook St., North Hollywood, California 91607, telephone (818) 505-8964.

cost-effective, meeting the demands of high volume manufacturing. While we will find that MIDI satisfies these criteria, later we will discuss some other criteria that were overlooked.

The Physical Specification

The physical medium is a simple point-to-point opto-isolated 5 ma current loop utilizing a unique 180 degree 5-pin DIN connector (Fig. 1). Only three of the pins are used. Cannon XLR connectors were originally specified as an alternative suitable connector, but this was subsequently dropped. The cable is made of a shielded twisted pair, the shield being grounded only at the source end. Each twisted pair is a separate run that implements a one-direction transmission line. MIDI devices are to have a MIDI input, and output jack. In addition, devices can have a MIDI THRU (through) jack, which passes a buffered electrical copy of the input signal. (Note: MIDI input is not connected to MIDI output, but to THRU.) Information is transmitted as asynchronous serial data at an aggregate data rate of 31.25 Kbaud (31250 bits per second). {No one seems to know for sure why this particular figure was

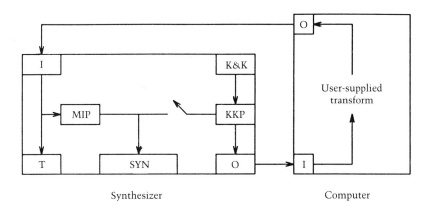

Synthesizer   Computer

chosen, but it is noted that it equals a 1-MHz clock divided by 32.} Serial MIDI data is transmitted as ten-bit code bytes, consisting of a start bit, eight data bits, and a stop bit. This results in a 320-μs-byte transmission time. The outer two framing bits are added by the transmitter for synchronization and are stripped off by the receiver, leaving a conventional eight-bit byte. Typically, a UART (Universal Asynchronous Receiver/Transmitter) or ACIA (Asynchronous Communications Interface Adapter) chip can be used to convert from parallel to serial data formats. Some microprocessor chips contain on-chip serial input/output (I/O) ports and timers suitable for this purpose.

The "reference model" for MIDI only defines the network. However, several aspects of the synthesizer are implied by the specification. The specification says only that a synthesizer shall have a MIDI receiver, a MIDI transmitter, and optionally, a MIDI THRU port. An electrical copy of the signal sent to the MIDI receiver is passed to MIDI THRU. The synthesizer is presumed to have on-board knobs and switches, and some sort of synthesis engine. Ordinarily, the knobs and switches connect both to the synthesis engine and to the MIDI transmitter (Fig. 2). {This standard layout—emulated by most manufacturers—provides no way to decouple the synthesizer's on-board controls from its synthesis engine. This precludes the insertion of an external

computer between the controls and the synthesis engine of a single instrument. Such synthesizers are conceptually similar to half-duplex computer terminals. There is a command in the MIDI specification to break the internal connection between controls and synthesis (described later), but it seems to be rarely implemented.}

Some interconnection schemes for multiple synthesizers are as follows:

Unidirectional—master talks to slave.
Bidirectional—two masters drive each other as slaves.
Ring—an extension of bidirectional connection to three or more devices.
Daisy chain—one master drives several slaves using MIDI THRU.
Star—one master has several unidirectional or bidirectional links.

These interconnection schemes are shown in Fig. 3–6.

In the general case, we see that the IN/OUT/THRU connection scheme forms a triple that joins with other triples to form a binary tree. This is illustrated in Fig. 7. The left branches receive MIDI input only from the root of the tree via MIDI THRU, plus they respond to their own controls. Right branches inherit MIDI input only from their immediate parent, but pass it along to all

Fig. 3. Multiple master/ slave configuration. Each box is a MIDI synthesizer expressed as a triple: T, I, and O are MIDI THRU, IN, and OUT, respectively. Synthesizers are labeled to the left with a capital

letter; the expression to the right indicates the source of control information for each synthesizer.

Fig. 4. Dual master/slave configuration.

Fig. 5. Ring configuration.

Fig. 6. Star configuration. M is a master controller.

Fig. 3

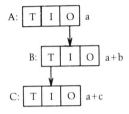

Fig. 5

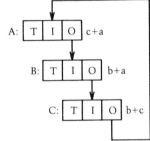

Fig. 4

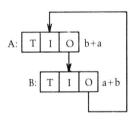

Fig. 6

left-branch children, while passing the result of their own control input only to their right-branch children.

{It is important to emphasize that a single MIDI cable is a unidirectional single-talker/single-listener network. Using a MIDI THRU connection, it can become a multilistener network, but there is always just one fixed transmitter for any subtree. What is more, there is nothing in the specification that even hints at two-way communication. Thus, there are no provisions in the specification for methods of interrogation and response of networked synthesizers. The significance of this limitation is elaborated later.}

The Code Specification

The other half of the specification details the nature of the information that is communicated over the physical medium. The code specification consists of three elements, *modes, channels,* and *commands.*

MIDI Modes and Channels

There are three modes and sixteen channels. The channels provide for multisynthesizer control with a single MIDI network, while the modes establish the relationship between the channels and the voice-assignment method within a synthesizer. The term "channel" is confusing to those who are familiar with the term as used in the recording industry. {Many terms used in the MIDI specification are only abstractly related to their more conventional meaning, as we see shortly.} Here is an explanation of MIDI's notion of channels. Many MIDI commands, collectively known as *channel commands,* have a field for a channel number. Synthesizers can be configured to receive or ignore channel commands depending on the channel number. This can

Fig. 7. The general case of MIDI interconnection forms a binary tree. The left branches receive MIDI input only from the root of the tree via MIDI THRU, and they respond to their own controls. Right *branches inherit MIDI input only from their immediate parent, but pass it along to all left-branch children, while passing the result of their own control input only to their right-branch children. Syn-* *thesizers are labeled with capitals to the left of each box; the sum of their input and local controls is expressed in lowercase to the right of each box. An implicit synthesizer A (not shown) is connected to the* *input of synthesizer B. The polynomial at the bottom of the figure shows the number of synthesizers playing each part.*

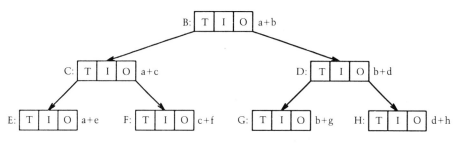

$$3(a+b)+2(c+d)+e+f+g+h$$

be used to restrict which synthesizer(s) will respond to a particular channel command.

The modes are called *omni*, *poly*, and *mono*. *Omni* mode causes a MIDI unit to accept commands on all channels. The synthesizer transmits on only one channel. In *poly* mode, each MIDI unit only receives and transmits commands on one channel. Voices are assigned polyphonically; that is, sequential *note on* commands generate chords. *Mono* mode is not what it sounds like: it is supposed to mean "one voice per channel." A synthesizer capable of *mono* mode operation will be assigned a range of channels (perhaps only one) to which it is to respond. Commands for each channel will control a single voice. *Mono* mode is used to provide for certain portamento effects not obtainable with *poly* mode. Here subsequent *note on* commands could cause a glissando to the new note instead of a chord. Also, for polytimbral synthesizers—that is, ones capable of generating more than one timbre at a time—when *mono* mode is used, the different timbres of the single instrument can be assigned to particular channels.

The modes are grouped into four states. {The MIDI specification refers to these states as "modes" as well, a confusion I have sought to avoid.}

State 1 (*omni on* and *poly*). All commands regardless of channel are recognized by the receiver and assigned to voices polyphonically.

State 2 (*omni on* and *mono*). All commands regardless of channel are recognized by the receiver and assigned to one voice. Only one voice sounds.

State 3 (*omni off* and *poly*). Only channel commands matching that of the receiver are recognized and assigned to voices polyphonically.

State 4 (*omni off* and *mono*). Channel commands that match a range of preselected channels are recognized and are assigned one channel to one voice.

{Dynamic voice allocation in *poly* mode can be problematic. If all voices are in use in a synthesizer and another *note on* command arrives, the synthesizer must decide how to cope with the new demand. While there are numerous solutions, the one most often chosen by manufacturers is to have the synthesizer steal the voice of the oldest sounding note on the presumption that the attention of the listener has been shifted away from it by subsequent notes. This method fails badly when the note being stolen is, for example, a pedal point, in which case its absence becomes quite glaring. This is an example of a problem that requires musicological awareness to solve.}

Where there are modes and channels, there are, or should be, means to change them. {Alas, while there are *mode select* commands, there are no *channel select* commands.} Mode select commands target selected channels, and the synthesizers on those channels are to switch to that mode if they can. {But if they cannot, their failure to do so will never be reported because MIDI is a unidirectional network.}

MIDI provides no method to change channel assignments. They must be changed by physically

The MIDI Phenomenon

Fig. 8. MIDI byte stream
sequence.

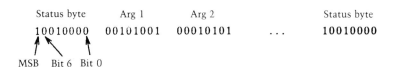

manipulating the synthesizer. Some synthesizers only transmit on MIDI channel 1 but can receive on any channel. Channel 1 is supposed to be the power-up default, but many manufacturers simply remember the last set channel across power cycles. This means there is no way for a MIDI network to be configured under program control; it must be done manually.

MIDI Command Types

A MIDI command is a sequence of one or more bytes of data. There are five categories of MIDI commands: *channel, system common, system realtime, system exclusive,* and *reset.* The *system realtime* category is highest priority, followed by *system exclusive,* with the rest grouped below them. *System exclusive* commands cannot be interrupted by any lower priority command. *Realtime* commands can interrupt any multibyte commands. The salient characteristics of the command types are as follows.

> *Channel* commands communicate event data, such as *note on/off* and status of device controllers.
> *System common* commands deal with sequence selection and location within the sequence. This is mostly for MIDI sequencers, which are devices that can store and regenerate MIDI commands.
> *System realtime* commands are for synchronizing a network of MIDI sequencers to a common clock.
> *Reset* terminates any activity in progress and re-initializes to the power-on condition.
> *System exclusive* is for device-specific data transfer, for sending patches, parameters, etc. The format of *system exclusive* only designates how it starts and where it ends; the content of the transfer is unspecified and is presumed to

refer only to one vendor's equipment. Part of the preamble for *system exclusive* is a byte containing a unique manufacturer's identification number. Synthesizers matching that number know to respond to the command, others ignore it. {*System exclusive* is the great escape hatch of MIDI. There are strong tendencies to solve problems by dumping solutions under this category of command. This both subverts what little standardization MIDI provides and helps guarantee that it will never be improved upon.}

Format of Commands and Data

Figure 8 illustrates the bitwise sequence and layout of a MIDI command, after the start and stop bits have been stripped off. The most significant bit (MSB) is a *sentinel* bit, which signals the beginning of a new command if it is set. If set, the rest of the byte is decoded as a status byte. Bits ⟨6:4⟩ contain a partial command type identification (ID). If they indicate a *channel* command, then bits ⟨3:0⟩ are the channel number of the command, otherwise bits ⟨6:0⟩ are taken as the complete command type identification (Fig. 9).

MIDI specifies the number of trailing data bytes for each command type. Some commands take no data (such as *reset*), some one byte, some two, some any number. A new command is defined to commence whenever the sentinel bit of any byte is set. This restricts data to occupy the low-order 7 bits of each data byte. Table 1 provides a tabulation of the MIDI codes, their meanings, and the number of data bytes and their meanings. The Appendix provides additional descriptions of the commands.

{Note that the *control change* command in Table 2 includes mode changing, *all notes off,* and local/remote controls as well as device controls. It strikes me that this is an unhappy mixture of meta-

Fig. 9. Channel command layout.

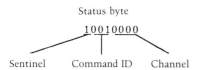

Status byte

10010000

Sentinel   Command ID   Channel

phors. There should have been a separate command dealing with global status and control.}

The specification says that when a subsequent command is identical to the preceding one (same command ID, same channel), the status byte need not be sent. This means that after the first command, only data bytes need be sent until a command with a different status byte must be sent. This can significantly reduce the amount of data transferred, but it depends upon the statistical properties of the command stream how much savings is realized.

Interfacing MIDI to Computers

Insofar as MIDI implements a very similar physical discipline to standard computer terminal interfaces, one approach to interfacing MIDI devices to computers is to modify a standard computer terminal line. The adjustment includes modifying the baud rate to 31.25 Kbaud, and installing an opto-isolator. However, the host computer would be dealing with a large volume of time-critical, continuous programmed I/O to support MIDI. This would place a major load on most microprocessors, reducing their ability to simultaneously address other tasks. It is better to offload the task to a peripheral processor designed to interface to MIDI on one side and to a computer on the other.

I have worked with two such devices, one made by Sound Composition Systems (SCS), the MIDI Performer, the other a Roland MPU-401 MIDI Processing Unit.[2] Both are small boxes containing

2. Note: Sound Composition Systems (Pasadena, California) has apparently gone out of business. A new company called Hinton Instruments (Oxford, England) makes a serial-to-MIDI interface called MIDIC (see *Computer Music Journal* 9[2]:71). The Hinton box may not suffer from the same throughput problems as the SCS box did because the Hinton box will run at 38.4 Kbaud.

microprocessor systems with I/O ports for MIDI and host computer communications. The host computer sets the unit to perform an operation such as record or playback, and the unit then interrupts the host only when MIDI commands or data are available or needed. This frees the host to perform higher level support functions such as compositional algorithms, analysis, display, and so on. The SCS device communicates with the host via a standard RS-232 computer terminal interface while the Roland unit interfaces directly to the bus of the host computer. By using a standard computer terminal interface, the SCS device can be hooked up to just about any computer using whatever driver software exists in the host for talking to terminals. Roland provides bus interfaces for some personal computers (including the IBM PC and Apple II). The interface itself is extremely trivial, and interfaces to other busses are easy to build, but it is not so easily integrated as the SCS, since it also requires that a device driver for the unit be written for the host computer.

The Roland unit, by going straight to the host computer's bus, does not have bandwidth problems as does the SCS unit. The SCS interface problem is a result of the difference between the 31.25 Kbaud MIDI rate and its 9600 baud host computer communication rate. Data overrun from a MIDI source to the SCS unit is quite likely when recording MIDI data, since the SCS unit can only pass along the incoming MIDI data to the host at about a third of the speed of MIDI. While the SCS unit can buffer up to 8 Kbytes of MIDI commands, it will always remain a statistical question as to whether this will be sufficient for any particular MIDI command stream. For this reason, one is usually driven to use the methods SCS provides for filtering out continuous controller information, such as pitch bend and modulation, passing only the lower bandwidth event-oriented commands such as *key on* and *key off*. However, the necessity of doing this limits the unit's generality. The SCS unit could presumably run its host-computer link faster than 9600 baud (e.g., at 38.4 Kbaud). However, the software provided on most computers to interface to standard computer terminals is not designed to handle sustained high transfer rates. Also, UARTs that support

Table 1: Summary of MIDI codes

		CHANNEL COMMANDS	
Status	*Arg 1*	*Arg 2*	*Mnemonic*
80	Key	Velocity	Key off
90	Key	Velocity	Key on
A0	Key	Pressure	Polyphonic key pressure (*after-touch*)
B0	Index	Value	Control change
C0	Index	(None)	Program change
D0	Pressure	(None)	Pressure (*after-touch*)
E0	LSB	MSB	Pitch wheel change

		SYSTEM EXCLUSIVE COMMAND	
F0	Mfg. ID	. . .	System exclusive command

		SYSTEM COMMON COMMANDS	
F2	LSB	MSB	Program position select
F3	Index	(None)	Program select
F6	(None)	(None)	Tune request
F7	(None)	(None)	End of system exclusive

		REALTIME COMMANDS	
F8	(None)	(None)	Timing clock
F9	(None)	(None)	Undefined
FA	(None)	(None)	Start
FB	(None)	(None)	Continue
FC	(None)	(None)	Stop
FD	(None)	(None)	Undefined
FE	(None)	(None)	Active sensing
FF	(None)	(None)	System reset

Note: All values are in hexadecimal notation. See the text for a further description.

rates beyond 19.2 Kbaud are still somewhat rare. One must trade off the simplicity of the SCS hardware interface against these considerations.

Storing MIDI command streams on disk in a host computer necessitates time-stamping the MIDI commands. Both the SCS and the Roland prepend a time stamp to all recorded MIDI commands, and expect a time-tag to precede all MIDI commands played back. The SCS unit provides a 16-bit resolution time-tag, while the Roland provides 8 bits. The tick time is adjustable, with usable values in the range of 1–5 msec. The SCS unit does not provide a clock-continuation command, presumably figuring that 16 bits of clock resolution ought to provide enough distance between any two MIDI commands for their standard clock time. Roland's 8-bit counter resolution only covers about 1.2 sec at their default clock rate, requiring that the number of clock overflows occurring between commands be kept. Roland uses the MIDI *timing clock* command to indicate clock overflows. While both methods seem adequate, I favor Roland's. For a performance of average

Table 2: Control change command indexes

Status	Index	Argument	Meaning
D0	0 ⇔ 1F	Value	MSB of continuous controllers
D0	20 ⇔ 3F	Value	LSB of continuous controllers
D0	40 ⇔ 5F	Value	Switches
D0	60 ⇔ 79	Value	Undefined
D0	7A	(Value)	Local control (7f = on, 0 = off)
D0	7B	(0)	All notes off
D0	7C	(0)	Omni off (All notes off)
D0	7D	(0)	Omni on (All notes off)
D0	7E	(Channels)	Mono on (Poly off) (All notes off)
D0	7F	(None)	Poly on (Mono off) (All notes off)

Note: All values are in hexadecimal.

musical density, it is likely that the Roland format will be more economical in bytes transmitted. Also, there is no limit to the size of the interval between two MIDI commands in the Roland format.

A difficulty with both methods of time tagging is that the time-tag can legally have the MSB set, leading to uncertainty when trying to parse corrupted data. This is no problem for well-formed command streams. However, if a stretch of bad data is encountered, one can't simply look for the next byte with the MSB set in order to resynchronize on a status byte, as this might be just a time-tag. One must also look at the byte following to make sure its MSB is off.

The protocol through which the MPU-401 communicates to the host is rather convoluted. Instead of communicating state information to the host as to its place within the commands being processed, the MPU-401 requires that the host essentially duplicate the internal state of the MPU in order to know what is going on. As a result, a device driver that avails itself of all of its diverse capabilities will be relatively complicated.

Packaged computer/synthesizer/software systems are beginning to appear using these interfaces and others like them. Other vendors include Passport Designs, Musicdata, Hybrid Arts, and Jim Miller, an independent. Without a computer, about all one can do with MIDI is double voices. In order to get any compositional or editorial power, one must have a general-purpose computer (or a MIDI "se-quencer," which is usually a general-purpose computer with a custom user interface and MIDI I/O). Interfaces for computers usually target home computers, such as the IBM-PC, Apple II, Apple Macintosh, Commodore 64, etc. Some microcomputers from Yamaha and Atari are now being manufactured with a MIDI interface as a standard peripheral port. In other cases, a synthesizer is integrated directly into the microcomputer, such as the Yamaha CX5M. [Reviewed in *Computer Music Journal* 9(3)—Ed.] In addition, a multitude of homebrew interfaces are being constructed for everything from mainframes to lap computers. One company, J. L. Cooper, markets MIDI interfaces and converters, including devices that use MIDI to control theater lighting.

Packaged software for these systems provides for basic record/playback functions plus simple editing. Most of the software adopts the metaphor of the multitrack tape recorder to structure the user interface. Thus, editing takes the form of "fast forward/rewind" and "punch in." Event-time correction is usually provided to "discretize" notes to the nearest selected integer ratio of the beat. Some packages provide means to display MIDI data as common practice music notation. Results vary widely with the adequacy of the graphics, user interface, and the grip of the programmer on basic musical issues.

Most packaged systems for MIDI, like MIDI itself, are aimed at the working pop musician. As such, most are closed, proprietary systems. Few, if any, provide a means whereby someone could adapt or extend a system to their own ends. Of course, absolutely none of them were written with the idea of providing a development environment for computer music research.

Misconceptions About MIDI

The foregoing is a relatively complete summary of the MIDI specification. However, there are still things that neither the specification nor my explanations have yet made clear. I will attempt to shed light on these by discussing some common misconceptions. Regardless of what it is, MIDI serves no one if it is perceived for what it is not.

Misconception 1: **MIDI is a bus.** It is not. A bus implies bidirectional communications and the possibility of more than one bus master. MIDI is a unidirectional talker-listener network. The term "network" is even a little broad for MIDI. The MIDI specification does not preclude devices from being connected for interrogate/response communication, but this form of communication would require that the specification be extended to develop a vocabulary of what they could say. Such a capability could be used, for instance, by a master to configure a MIDI network automatically, by invoking responses that would return manufacturer's ID, channel number, and reception mode. Based on this information, the master could then emit change-mode commands, and (if they existed) change-channel commands. This is just for starters; the compositional and performance possibilities for true networking are endless (Bischoff, Gold, and Horton 1978).

Misconception 2: **MIDI does not have sufficient bandwidth to capture human performance.** If we restrict ourselves to keyboard instruments, the experience of musicians I know who have used it is that it does have acceptable bandwidth. Its very success is a kind of proof of this, but let's take a closer look. As we have seen, a byte can be transmitted every 320 μsec over MIDI, and it typically takes 3 bytes per command, which gives us 1 msec per command, worst case. Let us take for example a keyboardist striking ten keys simultaneously. This produces ten *note on* commands, which serialized would be smeared over 10 msec. (This is assuming the unlikely event that all ten fingers managed to strike the keyboard simultaneously. This also does not account for the MIDI command-continuation feature, which would reduce the transmission time to 7 msec.) When compared to an average attack time for percussive instruments of 10 msec, we see that the smearing is not liable to be heard as multiple attacks, even when percussive timbres are being synthesized.

Another way to view this is to realize that sound travels about ⅓ meter per millisecond. A delay of 10 msec represents a distance between musical sound sources of 3 m. Amplified musicians typically do not complain about being this distance from their loudspeakers. Also, this can be compared to the size of a symphony orchestra, which can successfully fuse a musical percept while flung out over more than 30 m.

These are merely analogies, however, and this is not to say that millisecond-level serialization delays have no effect, only that they have no effect for the case of a keyboardist using MIDI. Recently, my colleague F. R. Moore did a simple experiment to observe the effect of such delays on timbre. He generated a waveform consisting of two single periods of a 1000-Hz sine wave which were separated by a 1-msec silent interval. He then synthesized another sine wave pair separated by 2 msec, continuing this until he had pairs separated by all intervals between 1 and 10 msec. The pairs were separated by 1 sec of silence each. What was heard when this was played was a sequence of clicks, where the pitches of the successive clicks described a subharmonic series. He concluded that while serializing commands does not have the effect of producing multiple attacks, it does have an effect on timbre, similar to comb filtering. Issuing MIDI commands that cause two instances of the same exact waveform to be started 1 msec apart is equivalent to applying a one-shot delay of 1 msec to the first one.

Because of the crude nature of time control, MIDI is utterly inadequate for phase-level control of waveforms. This means synthesis of a single-fused timbre cannot be split reliably across MIDI synthesizers. This would also rule out control of stereo or dichotic sound imaging via MIDI. Even though the effect of the serialization delays can occasionally be seen as a plus, as when chorusing effects are desired, however, we must not confuse an inherent artifact of a system with a feature of the system. The important question is not "does it matter?" so such as "when does it matter?"

In addition to event data, MIDI can be used to transmit continuously sampled data. The 7-bit sampling rate is 3125 Hz, while the 14-bit rate is 1562 Hz. While this is very slow for acoustic pressure functions, it is not too bad as a control rate for limited applications. For comparison, we can recall the GROOVE system at Bell Laboratories (Mathews and Moore 1970), where it was experimentally determined that functions of time representing general human performance gestures could usually be adequately represented at a sampling rate of about 200 Hz per function. Assuming this is correct, it shows that, for the worst case, MIDI is capable of transmitting nearly eight 14-bit functions at the rate of 200 samples per second. This means, for instance, it could presumably handle continuous pitch change information for all strings of a violin or guitar. However, this leads us to our next assumption.

Misconception 3: **Existing commercial synthesizers run at full MIDI bandwidth.** Some do, maybe, but not the ones I looked at. I discovered this while researching the question of command smearing for Misconception 2. I attempted to hear the result of ten simultaneous attacks by transmitting first one, then two, and so on up to ten *note on* commands at maximum MIDI bandwidth to a well-known MIDI synthesizer from a host computer. The results were surprising, to put it mildly. The synthesizer required an average of about 2.5 times as long to turn on a voice as to receive a MIDI command. In the worst case this was 20 msec to turn on six voices. Mysteriously, it ran faster turning on 10 voices (taking about 17 msec). I then tried another well-known synthesizer with mixed, but generally poor, results. This experiment was limited and informal, but it points up that performance is not dictated by the MIDI specification.

Misconception 4: **The data rate requirement for performance gesture capture is the same requirement as that for synthesizer control.** MIDI builds this assumption into the specification. In fact the data rate requirement for synthesizer control is usually far greater than for gesture capture. The one instance where the rates are equal is where a straight performance recording is made from a gesture input device to a host computer which then simply regurgitates the performance. However, this is the most trivial use of MIDI. More likely uses include overdubbing and computer-generated scores, both of which would typically involve much greater bandwidth than that generated by a single performer. Indeed, a critical aspect of any such system would be that it does not limit the output to the capabilities of performers!

Another strong temptation will be to use MIDI *system exclusive* commands to modify synthesizer parameters during performance execution to simulate more interesting control functions than are available in the synthesizer's hardware. Thus the host-computer-to-synthesizer direction will tend to be denser than the performance-input-to-host-computer direction. The density will grow with increasingly sophisticated use of MIDI. That MIDI does not address this obvious problem stems from MIDI's apparent origin as a gesture capture mechanism, for which the prevailing low data rate seemed acceptable.

This problem will probably not deter people from trying to squeeze blood from this turnip by using MIDI to control ever larger arrays of more and more capable digital music devices. The results obtained are likely to be sufficient for small networks and initial efforts, but as the idea of music instrument networking takes hold, I expect to see serious attempts to address the bandwidth limitations.

Another concern that falls into this category is the quantity of synthesis resources a single performer is capable of manipulating in real time. In the case of keyboards, the temptation is to apply the "ten finger" rule: "nobody can play more than 10 fingers at once," as a way of justifying low numbers of polyphonic voices. However, standard Romantic keyboard literature (e.g., Chopin) shows that this rule does not hold as soon as the sustain pedal is depressed. On pianos, the sustain pedal lifts the dampers on the strings, causing all notes initiated to be sustained while the pedal is down. It is not clear how many voices are required by such music, but a good guess is no less than 88, the number

of keys on a standard piano. Also, consider conducting: a wave of the hand can result in a mass
of instruments playing. When musicians are given
computer control over synthesizers, the natural
course of things is to require ever more control over
ever more resources.

What, Then, Is MIDI Good for?

MIDI is certainly good for what it was designed to
do and to be. It was designed by manufacturers to
extend the means of control over their synthesizers
in a device-independent and vendor-independent
way. It is standard, simple, inexpensive, and effective at what it does. These positive achievements
cannot be denegrated. Beyond the obvious bugs
in the specification, most of the difficulty with
MIDI comes not from MIDI but from the attempt
by others to make it do that for which it was not
designed.

Like most things, MIDI was not designed with
the full significance of what it could be in mind.
MIDI has opened a Pandora's box of possibilities for
music instrument networking that were either not
forseen by its developers, or were ignored. The problem is that none of these dreams will now fit back
into the box. It seems that we can either ignore
the issue altogether, make do with MIDI, or try to
make a more adequate vehicle for our networking
aspirations.

What Are the Chances that MIDI Can Be
Improved?

All who talk of change to the MIDI specification
must first examine the forces that brought it into
being. There are two ways that standards come into
the world. A formal standard is wrought by a committee working under the auspices of an organization such as the American National Standards
Institute (ANSI). On the other hand, an informal
standard is worked out by a group of practitioners
in need of a common approach. MIDI is clearly in
the latter category. The MIDI specification came
from an informal group of manufacturers working
together. Today it is the province of a group known

as the Manufacturers MIDI Association (MMA),
whose authority comes from their joint share of a
majority of the commercial synthesizer market.
Membership is restricted to commercial interests
such as manufacturers, software houses, and systems integrators. Another major force in this arena
is the Japan MIDI Standards Association, which
works closely with the MMA.

The manufacturers have a considerable stake in
the commercial success of MIDI and have an understandable unwillingness to fiddle with it. They are
unwilling at this time to go beyond ironing out the
remaining ambiguities in the standard, and making
sure that all vendors' synthesizers will work together under MIDI. Even this little should be considered an heroic accomplishment, considering the
distance they have come to get as far as they have.
It was by no means a foregone conclusion that the
"iron curtains" that existed between manufacturers
could be broached by MIDI.

The International MIDI Association (IMA) is the
"users group" for MIDI. Started in 1983, this group
describes itself as

> a non-profit organization dedicated to the evo-
> lution, integrity and continuity of the Musical
> Instrument Digital Interface. IMA maintains a
> non-competitive organization interested in the
> accurate dissemination of information concern-
> ing all aspects of MIDI-related instruments and
> products. The International MIDI Association
> believes in the privacy of its membership and
> the protection of proprietary information (IMA
> 1983).

They publish a newsletter to members called the
IMA Bulletin, which contains product announcements, reviews, short articles, tutorials, and broad-
sides.

What the manufacturer's group refers to as "independents" are the most active constituency of the
IMA. These are individuals and small businesses
who have an interest in utilizing MIDI, either commercially or musically. This is the group that most
actively presses for a more adequate networking
standard, since it is this group that, by working
with MIDI, experiences its limitations most keenly.

Although the IMA has attempted to address issues of standardization and the limitations of MIDI,

they have not received much support from the manufacturer's group, as many expected. For instance, in the spring of 1984 the IMA sponsored a conference called MIDISOFT-84 at the Mark Hopkins Hotel in San Francisco. The population of the conference consisted almost entirely of independents, with a sprinkling of engineers and management from the more enlightened manufacturers. Papers centered on two issues, how to exploit the potential of MIDI, and how to formalize standards. Much rhetoric was spent on lamenting the polarity between manufacturers and independents. This was interspersed with some very insightful comments on the current state of affairs, and on the likely future directions, some of which I am repeating here.

Yet it would be wrong to view the manufacturers as inextricably locked into the current MIDI specification. One must assume that the manufacturers see the limitations of MIDI as a threat to their own well-being in the long run. The worst-case scenario would be if individual manufacturers attempted to undercut the MIDI standard with proprietary networking improvements for their own line of machines. One of the most profound impacts of MIDI on the manufacturers is that it has converted a vertically integrated market into a horizontally integrated one. Before MIDI, each manufacturer produced product lines that were self-contained and often incompatible with the product lines of other manufacturers. Now manufacturers can no longer count so heavily on sales of one item of their product line carrying a package sale. The possibility of both improving MIDI and regaining a vertical market must be sorely tempting. This, however, would be a fatal way to improve MIDI. The fact of the matter is that independents and musicians using MIDI depend for progress on a strong, cohesive manufacturers' MIDI group that can impose change in a uniform way.

What to Improve about MIDI and How

Politics aside, MIDI will certainly change sometime, or be superseded. When that happens, what will we have learned from it?

First let's consider the issue of speed. Clearly, 31.25 Kbaud will become too slow soon if it is not already. But how fast should it be?

One idea is that it could be any speed. Some UARTs are able to detect the speed of transmission and adapt automatically. This way, speed could grow as needed and as the technology was able to keep up. This argument is curiously reminiscent of arguments to the same effect made by the manufacturers of computer terminals in years past. In the beginning, everyone said, "terminal networks do not have to run any faster than a fast typist can type." So the initial baud rates ranged from 11 to 15 characters per second, comfortably beyond this range and comfortably within prevailing technological limits. However, then came word processors. As text editing programs became smarter at getting the computer to do more work with fewer keystrokes, users started wishing they could see the results more quickly too. The baud rates went up. And they are still climbing. Rates of 9600 baud are now common, with much higher rates not far behind. What drove the increase was not faster typing, but the greater bandwidth required by powerful text and graphics editors to drive the display. To my mind this neatly parallels the situation with MIDI: even if we assume that the current rate is sufficient for performance capture (the analog of typing speed), it will certainly not long be sufficient for computer control of synthesizers (the analogy to driving the display) as users become smarter at getting more music from less performance. The real result of this *laissez faire* attitude in the development of computer terminal networking was that it suffered decades of accretions and kludges as it grew, resulting in a kind of anti-standard. Is this what we want for music?

An interesting alternative was proposed spontaneously on the floor of the MIDISOFT-84 conference, alluded to above, by Guruprem Khalsa. He invited the attendees to consider estimating the bandwidth requirements that will be needed at some point in the future, then identifying some technology which would allow us to achieve that bandwidth now. This would resolve the issue of throughput in a way that would satisfy everyone for that period of time, freeing us to focus on the task of using that bandwidth instead of being drained by the subtask of retrofitting as data rates evolved. Gordon Moore, one of the founders and current chief executive officer of Intel Corp., presented a formulation that has since become known as "Moore's law" as a way to estimate growth in the electronics industry. It states that for year y, $C \propto 2^{y-1960}$, that is, complexity will double every year from 1960, which was the year he proposed it. If we were to update the year and apply that to MIDI, we might have $C \propto 3125 \cdot 2^{y-1985}$. In 12 years the bandwidth requirement would be on the order of 12 Mbytes/sec. This is a comfortable rate using current networking technology. It can be objected that the technology to run at these rates will be more expensive and for the current purposes of MIDI would not be warranted. Cost is a powerful argument when considering the economies of large-scale manufacturing. But is it ultimately economical to live with a serious flaw that weakens the standard?

Another attendee at the MIDISOFT-84 convention, Charles Goldfarb, questioned the nature of MIDI coding. To explain his position, we need another lesson from the history of word processing and terminal technology. In the beginning of computer terminal technology, the ASCII code (American Standard Code for Information Exchange) was developed with Teletype technology in mind. Some codes were reserved for control of (then state of the art) Teletype machines, such as line feeds, form feeds, carriage motion, and simple communications protocols. It quickly became apparent that document preparation could be done more easily with a macro language embedded in the text that condensed the complicated control codes required to do anything useful into simple mnemonics. Eventually it was noticed that this approach was not device-independent since the mnemonics themselves still referred to device specific actions. Transferring the document to a different printing system required substantial alteration of the document. It became clear that what was really needed was a way to describe page layout in the terms of the formal structure of the document, rather than in terms of the actual structure of the printer, leaving the job of achieving this structure for any given printer to a document compiler. This resulted in the development of high-level document compiler programs such as troff and T_EX. Standards for representing document formatting, such as SGML, are emerging to consolidate this area. Goldfarb suggests that we can ask the same thing about MIDI: is its collection of codes targeting the wrong thing?

While this analogy between MIDI and terminal technology is suggestive, it is not complete. By design, MIDI codes represent the performed structure of music. This is a higher level than coding for synthesizer parameters, and a lower level than representing the formal structure of the music. MIDI is to a small degree already device-independent, since the encoded performance does not carry with it a specific meaning as to the sound the resulting synthesizer is to make. It is perfectly adequate for MIDI synthesizers to communicate MIDI codes; a higher level representation is not needed here.

However, the picture changes when we consider how we should represent music made on MIDI synthesizers in a computer memory. Here, we will indeed make the same mistake with MIDI that was made for document preparation unless we develop representations which can express the formal structure of music. A good example of a hierarchical data structure for music can be found in the work of William Buxton (1980). To this end, Goldfarb has recently broached the subject of developing a standard for music databases through ANSI. A meeting was held in Palo Alto in May of 1985 to the end of establishing an ANSI study group to consider this problem.

A problem with MIDI is that it resists attempts to abstract it further. Speaking at a panel on MIDI during the 1984 ICMC in Paris, Buxton pointed out the confusion in MIDI between a network and a data structure. For him, basic to fixing MIDI is separating the structure of the information being communicated from the structure of the network. As it stands, they are inextricably linked, which means that the one can't be changed without the other.

What of the Future?

A corollary of Moore's law states that $\$ \simeq \sqrt{C}$, in other words, cost goes up linearly for exponential growth in complexity. F. R. Moore has argued (Moore 1981) that while traditional musical instruments are becoming more and more costly to produce, electronic instruments are becoming both more interesting and cheaper. Four years ago he predicted that there would be a point at which these two functions of time would cross, and that there would soon be a time when interesting electronic instruments would be cheaper than traditional instruments. Were this to happen, he argued, it would mean the wide availability of these new instruments, and the serious utilization of them in the music of our culture. Surveying today's popular music scene, it can be easily argued that this time has already arrived. The impact is also evident in schools of music. Projects to explore these new low-cost technologies in many computer music laboratories are underway.

Those who have access to more powerful tools can often be quite caustic about MIDI, seeing only its (numerous) limitations.

> Sooner or later there has got to be a reckoning between musicians and designers of commercially available equipment. Some scientists believe that their mere capacity to respond, in some vague way, to art qualifies them to make judgments about it. This attitude is representative of a terrible cultural problem. Their naive judgments are manifested musically in the sounds and design of commercially available instruments that are just appalling. I shudder to think about the effect on the generation of young listeners who are being exposed to such a low acoustic standard, especially at such high volume levels. I think it's very serious.— Charles Wuorinen (Boulanger 1984).

Irritating as Wuorinen's comments may be to some, he has a point. Engineers and scientists who want to contribute to the technology of music must have a deep insight into the aesthetics of music, otherwise the systems implemented will be archaic and inflexible. Of course, it works the other way too: without deep insight into the means of production, composers and performers will miss the essential contribution which computer technology can make, and the resulting music will be anachronistic.

There are also complaints about the nature of the human interface provided by typical commercial synthesizers.

> A major problem of synthesizers to date, especially recently, is that they constrain the performer to expressing ideas through a limited set of gestures. (Ironically, some electronic instruments from the 1930s to the 1960s were more flexible in this regard.) This "straitjacket" of most "over-the-counter" systems (for example the piano-type keyboard synthesizer), has meant that in many cases, the medium of expression is totally at odds with the musical idea. To follow on this, then, if gesture and idea are tied, and the device is the instrument for capturing the gesture, then the range of input devices could be as diverse as the range of musical ideas.—William Buxton (Appleton 1984).

There are reasons to be happy about MIDI, in spite of what it is, when we consider that it is helping to stimulate research in performance, improvisation, and interactive composition. Many are enthusiastic about using MIDI to help move beyond the limitations of tape music. Most are willing to put up with temporary gestural and sonic limitations to achieve this. Joel Chadabe's work in interactive composition (Chadabe 1984; Chadabe and Meyers 1978), Buxton's work with human interfaces (Buxton 1980), Appleton's work with the Synclavier, and many other projects as well stem from the motive to reclaim performance gesture as a part of the process.

My enthusiasm for this subject is similarly motivated. Throughout my career in electronic and then computer music, little of substance could be done in live performance. Analog synthesizers offered real-time control, but over pathetically limited resources. Software sound synthesis offered tremendous resources, but none of it in real time. Compositions for tape and live instruments usually required the live instrumentalists to synchronize their performance to the tape (unless one chose to declare that synchronization was unimportant, a limited aesthetic option). This made the live performers slaves to the tape part. Now at last we are in a position to make the performer the independent variable and the synthetic part the dependent variable. A whole continuum of possibilities has opened up. Tape music is at one end, where the electronics ignores the performer. At the opposite end of the continuum are systems that drive synthesizers directly from sensors that extract performance parameters. Here the electronics is slave to the performer. In between are many interesting areas, such as automatic accompaniment (Dannenberg 1984; Vercoe 1984), and numerous other strategies where the electronics and the performer share control. A computer science discipline called control theory (Rouse 1981) is devoted to considering human/machine interaction modalities, static and dynamic systems, and related issues. Suddenly, this seems quite germane to computer music.

Unfortunately, it appears that the needs of the research community will continue to be unaddressed in the marketplace. Most MIDI-based computer systems will continue to be directed at standard applications for nonprogrammers. Many will not even be directed at musicians but will be used for such things as to correct "wrong notes" and provide simple accompaniment for novices.

> It certainly appears inevitable that, when the general-purpose facility gives way to, in the most exalted cases, "work stations," and in the least exalted ones, "glorified organs," the inflexibility that will result will be attended, I fear, by a cessation of imaginative developments, both in terms of the materials of music and in the ways of organizing these materials.— Roger Reynolds (Boulanger 1984).

It is clear that we will continue to have to improvise systems that meet our needs from the best available technology. As a result, the field seems destined to be driven by technological imperatives for at least the near future. This has an interesting implication, which can be exposed with the following syllogism: computer music is to computer technology as the steamboat was to steam engine technology, meaning that computer music is still mostly an applied discipline, like the development of steamboats. We are aligned with the historical position of Fulton, rather than Watt. Furthermore, we are at the point in the development curve prior to where steamboats became capable of reliable navigation. We are still mostly engaged in improv-

ing the technology to yield the benefits we know are there. Just as reliable worldwide navigation had to wait for the steamboat, many of the experimental research fields awaiting us depend on the availability of appropriate tools. To take other examples, the field of microbiology was only possible after the advent of the electron microscope; astronomy was only possible after the perfection of the telescope. (Another analogy to computer music can be borrowed from the history of astronomy: before the telescope, astronomy was called astrology. After the perfection of the musical equivalent of the telescope, will musicology become musiconomy?)

The musical equivalent of the telescope will probably be a system that combines a special-purpose synthesizer with a general-purpose computer to provide extensible musical data abstractions and operations. While the hard part of systems integration would be accomplished this way, every level of the hardware and software of the resulting system would have to be in the public domain, be easy to modify, and be completely documented.

Fortunately, progress is being made along these lines in many places. One example is the computer music workstation development project at the Computer Audio Research Laboratory. We mean by this term a microcomputer system with the capability of running either out of real time for general-purpose signal processing and composition, or running in real time for performance processing and direct synthesis. In the latter case, the system uses special hardware to do performance capture, analysis, and synthesis. The goal is to extend the range of musical research with such a tool to include performance. Our current prototype uses MIDI devices in combination with other sources and sinks of information (Fig. 10), and it is from this work that I have garnered most of the experience related in this article. This development effort is aimed at providing low-cost tools to the research community that attempt to meet the criteria of those whom I have quoted above (among others). This work would not have been possible prior to the advent of sophisticated, standardized, low-cost, open-architecture components.

The relationship between electronic-instrument manufacturers and the computer music community has been rocky in the past. However, I see the ad-

Fig. 10. Performance laboratory at CARL. Oval components are MIDI devices; squares are processors. Components are: Yamaha DX7 synthesizer, Roland MKB-1000 weighted-action piano keyboard, Yamaha TX-816 synthesizer, Roland MPU-401 MIDI controller, Force II MC68000 VME-bus CPU, Sun Microsystems Inc. SUN workstation. The Performance Processor is an in-house real-time performance processing system under development. These facilities are in addition to our regular timesharing computer resources.

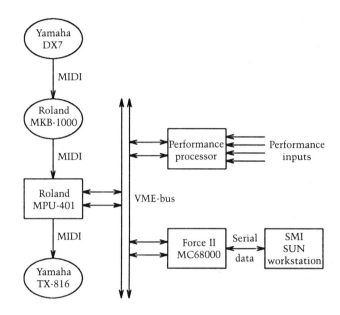

Fig. 10. Performance laboratory at CARL. Oval components are MIDI devices; squares are processors. Components are: Yamaha DX7 synthesizer, Roland MKB-1000 weighted-action piano keyboard, Yamaha TX-816 synthesizer, Roland MPU-401 MIDI controller, Force II MC68000 VME-bus CPU, Sun Microsystems Inc. SUN workstation. The Performance Processor is an in-house real-time performance processing system under development. These facilities are in addition to our regular timesharing computer resources.

vent of MIDI as the first sign that the commercial synthesizer industry is becoming relevant to the computer music community. By providing low cost, standardized performance processors and synthesizers, our field is gaining tools that will have a broad impact on the kinds of subjects we can investigate and on the numbers of researchers who can participate. In a sense, real-time control research is now the province of anybody with a MIDI synthesizer and a desktop computer. Some (McConkey 1984) even see the fading away of "the distinction between synthesizers and computer music"—meaning, presumably, the distinction between those who use commercial synthesizers and those who have access to facilities of computer music research centers. Perhaps so, but there will always be a distinction between making music and doing musical research, even if the latter is in the form of musical compositions that use commercial synthesis systems. The research uses of computer music tools—both scientific and musical—will always lead commercial application. The development of MIDI signals the emergence of several important technologies from the laboratory and into the field. If the intercommunication between the synthesizer industry and the computer music community can grow, as I see happening all around me, it presages better things to come.

References

Appleton, J. 1984. "Live and in Concert: Composer/Performer Views of Real-Time Performance Systems." *Computer Music Journal* 8(1):48–51.

Bischoff, J., R. Gold, and J. Horton. 1978. "Music for an Interactive Network of Microcomputers." *Computer Music Journal* 2(3):24–29. Reprinted in C. Roads and J. Strawn, eds. 1985. *Foundations of Computer Music.* Cambridge, Massachusetts: MIT Press.

Boulanger, R. 1984. "Interview with Roger Reynolds, Joji Yuasa, and Charles Wuorinen." *Computer Music Journal* 8(4):45–54.

Buxton, W. 1980. "A Microcomputer-based Conducting System." *Computer Music Journal* 4(1):8–21.

Chadabe, J. 1984. "Interactive Composing: An Overview." *Computer Music Journal* 8(1):22–27.

Chadabe, J., and R. Meyers. 1978. "An Introduction to the PLAY Program." *Computer Music Journal* 2(1):12–18. Reprinted in C. Roads and J. Strawn, eds. 1985. *Foundations of Computer Music.* Cambridge, Massachusetts: MIT Press.

Dannenberg, R. 1984. "An On-Line Algorithm for Real-Time Accompaniment." In W. Buxton, ed. *Proceedings of the 1984 International Computer Music Conference.* San Francisco: Computer Music Association.

International MIDI Association. 1983. *MIDI Musical Instrument Digital Interface Specification 1.0.* North Hollywood: International MIDI Association.

Mathews, M., and F. R. Moore. 1970. "GROOVE—A Program to Compose, Store, and Edit Functions of Time." *Communications of the Association for Computing Machinery* 13(12):715–721.

McConkey, J. 1984. "Report from the Synthesizer Explosion." *Computer Music Journal* 8(2):59–60.

Moore, F. R. 1981. "The Futures of Music." *Perspectives of New Music* 19(1):212–226.

Rouse, W. B. 1981. "Human-Computer Interaction in the Control of Dynamic Systems." *ACM Computing Surveys* 13(1):78–91.

Vercoe, B. 1984. "The Synthetic Performer in the Context of Live Performance." In W. Buxton, ed. *Proceedings of the 1984 International Computer Music Conference.* San Francisco: Computer Music Association.

Appendix

In the following descriptions, the values in parenthesis indicate arguments to the command.

Channel Commands

key off (*key, velocity*)—turns off one voice playing *key. Velocity* is used to determine the characteristic of decay.

key on (*velocity, key*)—turns on one voice with pitch *key. Velocity* is used to determine the characteristic of attack. In *poly* mode, sequential *key on* commands create chords. In *mono* mode, if a voice was sounding, a new *key on* command will simply shift pitch to the new key, providing the mechanisms for a legato effect. As a special case, a *key on* command with a velocity of 0 is a form of *key off.* Key indices encode equal-tempered semitones. Middle C is key index 60. Five-octave keyboards range from 36 to 96. Eighty-eight-note keyboards range from 21 to 108. Default velocity, in the absence of pressure sensors, is 64.

polyphonic key pressure (*key, pressure*)—encodes key bottom pressure change for the indicated key on the indicated channel. It is sent by keyboards that discriminate individual key bottom pressure; it is recognized by polyphonic synthesizers capable of responding to individual key pressure changes.

control change (*index, value*)—supplies a new value for indexed performance controllers, such as modulation wheels, joysticks, switches, pedals, etc., but not pitch benders. The upper range of indexes are reserved for mode-setting commands. (See Table 2.)

program change (*index*)—selects a timbre or synthesis technique.

channel pressure/after-touch (*pressure*)—pressure change affects all voices responding to that channel.

pitch bend (*LSB, MSB*)—encodes a 14-bit pitch bend quantity from a pitch wheel. The value of 8192 corresponds to the center detent. The actual range of pitch change for any value of pitch bend is defined in the synthesizer.

System Exclusive Command

system exclusive (*manufacturer ID number*)— sends manufacturer-specific synthesizer information, such as patches, parameters, functions, and messages. Manufacturer ID numbers are assigned by the International MIDI Association. Information following the ID number is manufacturer-specific. This command is terminated by the *end of block* command or by starting any other command. System exclusive commands are nonpreemptive.

System Common Commands

These commands are for sequencer control. For "sequencer" one can also read "computer."

20

Christopher Yavelow

Music and Microprocessors: MIDI and the State of the Art

Although the concept of the "personal computer" is relatively old by now, the concept of the "personal computer music studio" is just coming into its own (Yavelow 1986a, 1986b, 1987). In this article I describe the elements of a typical microcomputer-controlled setup, examine the stages of turning sound into music, classify the musical applications of personal computers, and consider in detail some representative commercially available examples of each type of application.

Microcomputers in the Music Studio

The elements of a microcomputer music studio that can be put under software control include synthesizers, digital signal processing effects, audio mixers, hard-disk-based digital recorders, and sequencers that record MIDI information (i.e., performance information rather than acoustic information). Common peripheral devices include MIDI adapters, mergers, and THRU boxes, hard disks, printers, modems, and devices dedicated to synchronization (figure 1).

The Computer

The typical home personal computer music studio centers around a single computer. The processor chip, also known as the *central processing unit* (CPU), is the computational heart of the machine. It interacts with and controls the computer's memory, the data currently being processed, and the

Portions of this article are based on material that originally appeared in the author's article "Personal Computers and Music: The State of the Art" (*Journal of the Audio Engineering Society* 35[3]: 160–193).

sound samples being queued up for the digital-to-analog converter (DAC). The memory is typically organized in bytes (eight-bit quantities). The typical modern microcomputer contains several megabytes (millions of bytes) of internal memory. Such memory is often referred to as *random-access memory* (RAM). The contents of RAM can be changed by writing into it, whereas the contents of *read-only memory* (ROM) cannot be changed. (ROM is used to contain system-specific instructions and routines programmed by the manufacturer.) As memory chips become cheaper, personal computers will contain more and more memory. This is a welcome development; more memory makes it easier to process large soundfiles. (At a sampling rate of 44.1 kilohertz, 4 megabytes could hold only about 44 seconds of monaural 16-bit sound.)

The current personal computers are excellent for music because of their speedy processors (such as the Motorola MC68000 series, of which the MC68020 and the MC68030 are the standards), their high-resolution graphic capabilities, and their portability. Issues of the user interface are becoming paramount in the design of software for microcomputers. This has led to the widespread adoption of a pointing device called a *mouse*, which the user moves on a flat surface next to the terminal. Furthermore, it is becoming increasingly common to view data in "windows" on the display screen. Various windows can provide different representations of data—usually symbolized by graphics or icons (intuitive self-explanatory symbols), which provide for a more immediate understanding of the data than would be possible if it were displayed as a list of numbers. The axiom "a picture is worth a thousand words" has reached fruition in the graphic interface between human and software. The mouse may be used to "pull down," "pop up," "roll off,"

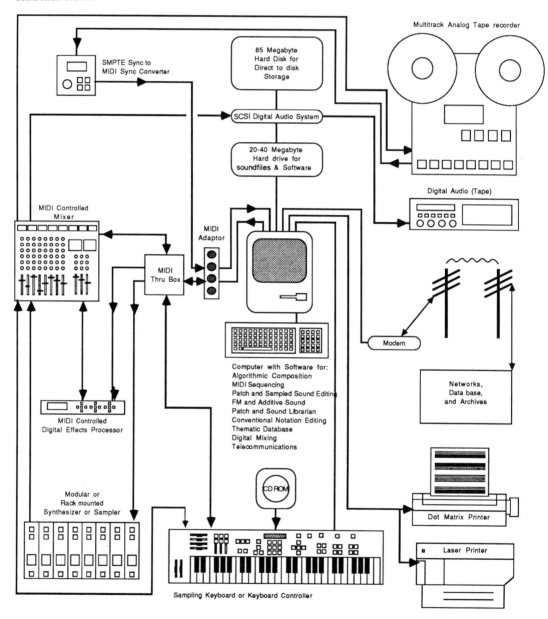

Fig. 1. Elements of a home
computer music studio.
With the exception of the
laser printer and SCSI digital audio system, this
setup is typical of a low-
cost microcomputer-
controlled studio.

or "tear off" menus and palettes of available commands.

Personal computers suitable for handling all the tasks of a home computer music studio include the Apple Macintosh family (including the Mac+, the Mac SE, and the Mac II), the Atari ST family, the IBM PC/PS family and its clones, the Apple II family (including the II+, the IIe, and the IIGS), and the Commodore family (including the 64, the 128, and the Amiga). The Mac II, the Apple IIGS, and the Atari ST all have built-in sound chips; the Apple's is the most powerful. The Mac II and the Apple IIGS incorporate a digital oscillator chip, made by Ensoniq (the manufacturer of the Mirage sampling keyboard), that can (theoretically) play up to 15 simultaneous parts of internally synthesized sound or up to 2.2 seconds of 12-bit sounds sampled at up to 30 KHz using 32 digital oscillators. In deference to musical applications, the Ataris have built-in MIDI interfaces (discussed below) and a dedicated sound chip that provides for up to three parts of harmony.

Software

In order for a single computer to function as the central control device in a home computer music studio, a wide range of software is necessary to manage a variety of musical activities that occur on a day-to-day basis. This includes software for purposes such as MIDI sequencing, sound editing and/or generation, sound and sequence library management, conventional music notation, digital mixing, algorithmic composition, and telecommunications. Users of personal computers for musical applications need not expect to be required to write their own software programs any more than people who use personal computers for word processing or accounting do. Many commercial developers are producing inexpensive software packages that cover even sophisticated applications. Furthermore, most of the commercially available software packages have reached the point where one can accurately use the term "second generation." This implies that the musical community has entered a stage where the responses to and the capabilities of the initial software releases have all been tallied, and the current undertakings endeavor to learn from early mistakes and to address a wide range of responses and requests from users.

The recent advances in object-oriented programming, data-compression, and searching techniques engendered by Apple's Hypercard software-authoring package are changing the face of the industry by putting the power to create extremely sophisticated applications into the hands of people with little or no actual programming knowledge. With Hypercard, the dream of computers writing their own programs based upon near natural (English) language input from the user has been fulfilled. The ramifications of this concept are just beginning to be realized by the music software industry.

MIDI Adapter and THRU Box

After software, the next required item (immediately to the left of the computer in figure 1) is a MIDI adapter. (The Atari STs feature a built-in MIDI adapter with one input and one output, although most serious synchronizing applications require two or more MIDI inputs.) MIDI is the industry's standard set of device-control codes for communication between computers and microprocessor-based musical instruments. With MIDI, data flows over cables with standardized five-pin DIN connectors. The format of the data is determined by the MIDI specification (IMA 1983). The bits are organized into MIDI "codes." Some of these, called *system exclusive codes*, are reserved for special use by each manufacturer.

MIDI cables carry MIDI data in one direction; hence the necessity of having both MIDI IN ports and MIDI OUT ports. A MIDI THRU port for the purpose of immediately passing on information received at a device's MIDI IN port is becoming more and more common. By using a device's MIDI THRU port, information not addressed to the specific device can be passed on to the device intended to respond to the information. In this manner, many devices may be "daisy-chained" together, all responding to a single computer.

Because the chaining of MIDI devices can introduce timing delays into the network as a signal passes from a device's MIDI IN port to its MIDI THRU port, it may be necessary to introduce a MIDI THRU box into the link. A THRU box usually guarantees that MIDI messages are at least received at their designated sources simultaneously; then, the only major delays are produced by the times that it takes various devices to process incoming MIDI data. Other MIDI processing devices often found at this point in the studio network include MIDI matrix switchers (used to route different MIDI inputs to any of a number of different MIDI outputs), MIDI mergers (which use a microprocessor to mix several incoming MIDI data streams into a single MIDI data stream), and a MIDI effects-generating device (which can produce, for example, echoes by delaying and/or retriggering incoming information).

Hard-Disk Storage

Despite the fact that the majority of home computer music studios are being driven by fast microprocessors, music applications normally have such a high computational overhead that most setups include a hard disk of 20 or more megabytes. (The more familiar floppy diskettes usually store less than one megabyte.) Computer programs, with their associated data, usually must reside in the computer's RAM before they can be worked with, and the quicker access time of a hard disk means that programs and data stored on the disk are loaded into the computer's RAM at speeds of 6 to 24 times that of floppy disks. To get a picture of how much data 20 megabytes is, consider the following: 1 kilobyte (1,024 bytes) is often thought of as equivalent to a single double-spaced typewritten page—thus, 20 megabytes provides enough storage capacity for 20,000 pages of text.

Although a hard disk is much faster and more capacious than a floppy disk (but often not much bigger in physical size), the user interacts with a hard disk in much the same way as with a floppy: files can be created, examined, modified, and deleted. The files on a hard disk can contain MIDI sequencing information, synthesizer patches, sounds, programs, and digital audio recordings equal or superior in quality to compact disks (CDs). Soundfiles for commercial sampling keyboards consume memory quickly (each of the four RAM banks of the Kurzweil 250 holds 658 kilobytes of samples). Like the computer memory chips mentioned above, hard disks continue to become less expensive and larger in capacity—80-megabyte and larger hard disks are becoming more and more popular among serious home and studio computer users.

As the capacity of hard disks continues to grow, how to "back up" one's hard disk is becoming a major consideration. "Backing up" is saving a copy of one's data as a precautionary measure against the ever-present possibility of a "crash" (failure) of one's hard disk, which could result in the loss of irreplaceable work. Crashes are relatively common, and the larger the hard disk, the more one stands to lose. Because it is advisable to back up the drive at least once a day (to ensure that only a single day's work might be lost), some people are turning to tape backup systems that can run without human supervision. Others keep two identical drives on line at all times, incrementally backing up the main drive by copying the files that have been modified during the day's computing onto the dedicated backup drive. Because recent advances in backup software include utilities that can transfer 80 megabytes of data between two identically sized disk drives in 3 minutes, many users may turn to the practice of having two identical hard disks.

Some manufacturers of sampling keyboards have developed ways to transfer small sample soundfiles via MIDI, and some have found a way to go into a double MIDI speed mode; however, this is far too slow for the file sizes employed by high-end sampling machines. Some samplers have an interface to soundfiles stored in CD ROM (a high-speed read-only memory on a disk that looks like an audio CD).

Printers

Many people who are making music with personal computers get along fine without a printer. However, if score notation or part extraction is required, a printer of some kind is necessary. Because of the graphic nature of music notation, a dot-matrix printer is the cheapest solution to musical printing requirements. Daisy-wheel and impact printers are designed for letter writing and do not provide the graphic capabilities required by conventional musical notation. The price of some higher-resolution laser printers has dropped below $4,000.

A major factor favoring a laser printer for music is the advent of a versatile device-independent page-description language known as PostScript and the development of a publishing-quality PostScript music font (Sonata). Unlike earlier bit-mapped music fonts, Sonata defines symbols as vectors or Bezier curves. Using Sonata in conjunction with software such as Deluxe Music Construction set, Concert-ware, Professional Composer, HB-Engraver, Finale, High Score, or Nightingale for the Macintosh, one can print a music file for proofing on an Apple ImageWriter (bit-mapped at 160 dots per inch) and then output it to a PostScript printer (such as the Apple LaserWriter, the Qume Laser ScripTEN, the Texas Instruments OmniLaser, or the Laser Connection PS Jet+) or to a Mergenthaler Linotronics phototypesetter for publishing-quality printing (figure 2).

Synthesizers

There are three main types of MIDIable sound-generating devices: digital synthesizers, analog synthesizers, and samplers. (A few hybrids exist.) The main distinction is in the manner in which the devices create sound. Synthesizers create new sounds through the manipulation of digital or analog oscillators. Synthesized sounds can attempt to imitate naturally occurring sounds, but commercially available synthesizers have not evolved to the point where the actual reproduction of complex natural waveforms is possible; their forte is the creation or design of sounds not normally found in nature. On the other hand, samplers have the ability to play back sounds that have been digitally recorded from nature (or from other synthesizers) and to modify this output with much the same flexibility as any non-sampling synthesizer.

The number of separate notes a single device can sound simultaneously is a matter of great concern, because this defines concrete limitations on the musical polyphony available to the user. Whereas a traditional acoustic piano can sound 88 notes together, until very recently most synthesizers and samplers were restricted to 8-to-16-voice polyphony; more devices were required for thicker textures. Newer models are overcoming these limitations. For example, Kurzweil's recent K1000 series, when fully configured, provides 84-voice polyphony.

After considerations of polyphony, another main criterion is whether an instrument is multi-timbral—that is, whether it outputs more than one type of sound at a time. Multitimbral synthesizers and samplers are now standard. In the past, the vast majority of commercially available electronic sound-generating devices were restricted to playing back a single sound at a time. Now, with a multi-timbral synthesizer or sampler, it is possible for a single instrument to respond to specific MIDI channels, each assigned to a separate patch or soundfile; thus, a single device can produce different sounds or timbres, which can be played simultaneously.

Most sound-generating devices are available either with a piano-style keyboard or as a rack-mountable module without keyboard. In the latter case, it is common to control a network of modular synthesizers and samplers with a "dumb" keyboard, generally known as a *MIDI keyboard controller*. Such a controller, with no sound-generating capabilities of its own, is designed for optimal interaction with a large body of existing devices. In another configuration, any nonmodular synthesizer with its own keyboard could be used as the controller.

For people without keyboard ability, many new types of non-keyboard-oriented MIDI controllers have appeared, including guitar controllers, mallet (percussion) controllers, electronic wind or valve instruments, and pitch trackers (which can convert any audio source into appropriate MIDI note codes). Using a pitch tracker, any singer or instrumentalist can control a MIDI device without having to know anything about the traditional piano keyboard. This does not mean that one could play symphonic audio recordings through a pitch tracker and have all the notes transcribed into their appropriate MIDI codes.

Fig. 2. Conventional music notation and PostScript. Adobe Systems' PostScript music font, Sonata, is device-independent. This example was printed on a Linotronics phototypesetter with 1,270 dots per inch resolution. Most second-generation notation packages implement compatibility with this font, and many first-generation programs have been updated to include Sonata.

SONATA II.

J. S. Bach

Grave.

Current pitch-tracking technology is really success-ful only at tracking a single melodic line. Accu-rately tracking multivoiced polyphonic textures is one of the few things left to look toward the fu-ture for.

Michel Waisvisz and other artists are inventing new MIDI controllers that have no resemblance whatsoever to traditional musical instruments. For his own work, Waisvisz uses a pair of glove-like "hands" that have mercury switches to sense their angle relative to the horizon, sonars to sense the proximity of the gloves to one another, and a number of switches under each finger (Roads 1986; Wergo 1987).

The mouse has engendered a wide range of alter-native MIDI controllers. Notable examples are Laurie Spiegel's "Music Mouse" (from OpCode Sys-tems), David Zicarelli's "Jam Factory" (Intelligent Music) and "Ovaltunes" (OpCode Systems), and "Upbeat" and "M" from Intelligent Music.

Telecommunications

We are quick to admit that music is a form of com-munication, but in the computer age music can be a form of telecommunication as well. There are many bulletin-board systems and national net-works devoted to music that a computer owner with a modem can access by telephone.

One usually joins a network by dialing a tele-phone number and typing something like "join," after which a credit-card or a bank-account number is entered for billing purposes. The charge for open-ing an account is between $25 and $200, and the additional online charges range up to $24 an hour during business hours and between $6 and $12 an hour in off-peak times. Such networks allow their users to participate in ongoing discussions (referred to as *forums*), to communicate with other users via electronic mail, or to access databases (which often store synthesizer patches, sampled soundfiles, and utilities for practically every sound-generating de-vice in existence). Thus, if one finds oneself in Timbuktu having forgotten the floppy disk that had the bagpipe samples, it is an easy job to log onto the PAN music group and download the file from its archives.

One significant example of such a telecommuni-cations system is the Performing Arts Network (PAN), which runs on a large mainframe computer with well over a gigabyte (a million megabytes) of storage. Local telephone numbers all over the world provide users with access to many different elec-tronic mail services (including Telex) and to a vari-ety of special-interest groups and subnetworks. There is one of the latter dedicated to practically every facet of the music industry—recording, pub-lishing, touring, booking, promotion, hardware and software development, synthesizer techniques, sampling, MIDI, online equipment shopping, and classified ads for just about any kind of computer or audio equipment.

On PAN there is a very active "synthesizer and MIDI development forum," where people post mes-sages (often of considerable length) and debate fu-ture developments with the programmers and the manufacturers. This forum provides the users with information (often months in advance of the press) and gives software and hardware developers an effective way of monitoring what new features or revisions are required by professional and amateur users of their products. Real-time worldwide con-ferences are regularly scheduled, in which everyone participating can see and respond to what everyone else is typing. Often one of these conferences is centered around a single theme, such as a software package or a hardware device.

There are so many computer networks that keep-ing track of all of them would be a full-time job. For this reason, more and more people are employing the strategy of using *macros* to automatically dial up these mainframe networks in the middle of the night (when the rates are considerably lower). A macro, in this case, is a little computer program that automates a number of keyboard actions into a single command. Usually, these are so simple to create that no knowledge of computer program-ming is required. Most serious telecommunications software packages include similar features. For ex-ample, the popular telecommunications software Red Ryder (by Scot Watson) includes a feature that "observes" and "records" everything the user does while online for future playback. One doesn't have to know any programming to use this feature; all one does is select the menu option "Write a procedure for me" and go through the required actions once (for example, dialing up a network, "logging on" by typing one's name and password, and then reading and saving electronic mail before going on to capture new forum messages on a specified topic). The computer "writes" the macro, and in the future merely calling up this macro is all that is necessary to go through the entire e-mail/forum capture procedure. It is possible to create a macro that automatically logs the computer onto one telecommunications network after another, automatically saving new electronic mail to the hard disk, uploading electronic mail to others, capturing new bulletin-board messages or announcements about MIDI and synthesizer developments, searching databases for updates to directories of sample file libraries, public-domain software, and utilities, and downloading files. It is a simple matter to arrange a macro in such a way that if there is electronic mail in one's e-mail box, it will be saved to a disk file in the personal computer or immediately printed; if one's e-mail box is empty, the macro can be structured to branch to another area of the network to take care of other business. Furthermore, since almost all "host computers" of these systems "remember" the previous session's activity, it is possible to have the macro automatically save a listing limited to new additions to the file directory and databases or new messages posted in the public forums. Many microcomputers are fast enough to run telecommunications macros and print other files (such as music notation) simultaneously.

For the Future: The Home Computer Music Studio as a Local Area Network

The personal computer-music studio I have been describing is, essentially, a local area network (LAN) using a variety of protocols to communicate between its constituent parts: MIDI, SMPTE, SCSI, ASCII, and PostScript (the latter is used as the page-description language for the laser printer).

Other LAN formats for controlling additional media as well as music are being developed at MIT by David Levitt (HookUp!) and at the University of Western Ontario by Kristi Allik, Shane Dunne, and Robert Mulder (AcroNet—see Allik et al. 1986). The integration of such communication systems seems likely to improve.

Some people are adapting ready-made networking software (much of it developed with the business community in mind) to serve musical purposes. The Berklee School of Music in Boston has created a network of digital music workstations, each with a Macintosh Plus, a Kurzweil MIDI keyboard controller, modular synthesizers and samplers (including a fully loaded Kurzweil Expander, a Yamaha RX-11 drum machine, a Yamaha TX-816 modular synthesizer, and an Oberheim Expander), a Kamlet Matrix MIDI switch box, a Yamaha SPX-90 digital effects processor, a D-1500 digital delay, a multichannel mixer, and a multitrack recorder. Using 3Com's EtherMac network, each computer is networked to a central *file server*, which automatically backs itself up to tape every morning at 2 A.M. (A file server is a large hard-disk storage unit that a number of computers can access.) All the workstations' MIDI devices are networked, so that a single workstation can control several others. Finally, the audio output from each workstation can be routed to any other workstation or group of workstations.

From Sound to Music (and Back)

Controlling sound and manipulating musical ideas with personal computers may require a wide range of interactive software during the creative process. The developmental stages of this process encompass three transformations: sound is organized into music, which is then expressed as sound. Before the sound is actually transformed into music, a microcomputer may have been instrumental in its creation, editing, and organization within a sound library. Only when sounds exist can they be organized into music with a MIDI sequencer. Three input methods are possible: *real-time, step-time* (one note at a time) and *algorithmic* (generated by a composition program). In the final transformation,

Fig. 3. From sound to music. The software applications used at various stages of the production of music from sound range from creating or editing the raw sonic material to using a MIDI sequencer for organizing the musical ideas created with the sound and controlling the digital effects processing and final mix.

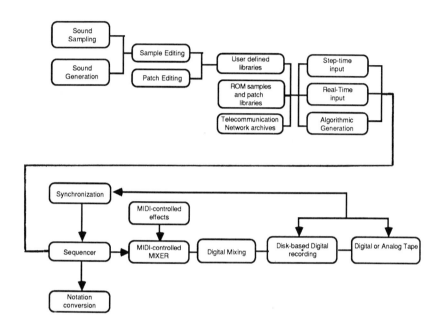

the whole assemblage is turned back into sound as the MIDI sequencer controls the various synthesizers, effects devices, and mixers. If this output is to be recorded into multitrack tape, a synchronization device is necessary to maintain the temporal alignment of the separate tracks when they are recorded in multiple passes (the usual procedure). Conversely, the output can be recorded using the increasingly common (and inexpensive) *direct-to-hard-disk* method. In this case, the user can have another crack at "fixing it in the mix" using state-of-the-art digital mixing software running on microcomputers. Newer direct-to-hard-disk digital audio recorders permit digital audio tracks to be figuratively aligned with MIDI data tracks so that additional MIDI-sequenced parts can be synchronized to real audio information and for the purpose of automating mixers and effects devices which respond to MIDI. Figure 3 illustrates this continuum in detail.

Creating Sound

Music that is played using electronic instruments usually draws its material from one of two domains: sampling and synthesis. The first point at which a personal computer can be introduced into the musical process is in the creation or capturing of sonic material through sound generation or sound sampling. Although software and related analog-to-digital hardware devices exist that allow personal computers to function as veritable digital sampling machines, until very recently microcomputers themselves were not capable of attaining the minimum level of fidelity required by professionals or even most amateurs and hobbyists. Newer 32-bit computers have challenged this limitation. Systems based on an "open architecture" are stimulating third-party developers to produce digital audio cards that, when plugged into one or more of the computer's slots, transform the computer into a complete digital-audio workstation—at a fraction (roughly 1/100) of the expense of such technology prior to this point in technological history.

On the other hand, a personal computer with a 16-bit CPU is perfectly capable of synthesizing high-quality complex sound using popular synthesis techniques, such as additive or frequency-modulation (FM) synthesis. Sounds created in this manner can sometimes be tested using the hardware of the microcomputer generating them, but because of physical limitations they are not often played back for musical purposes by the computer that created them. Ironically, a sort of hybrid process is necessary: the sounds are transformed into a file that is compatible with a digital sampling keyboard's file format. Typically, sound synthesized in this manner is converted into an accurate reproduction of what the resultant sampled soundfile would have been had the sound been sampled from the real world. This permits the sound to be transferred to a sampling keyboard for playback later—in essence, the sampling keyboard is "tricked" into thinking that the file is one that it created.

Editing Sound

Often the first software used by a computer musician is a sound editor. Depending upon whether the musician's sonic material is sampled or synthesized, the editing procedure may include modifying sampled sounds by means of an on-screen graphic waveform editor or it may mean editing the *patches* of a synthesizer in real time via on-screen simulation of the physical controls of the synthesizer. Many devices use a limited number of buttons and controls that may function in a vast variety of ways, depending on the parameter being edited; however, the computer simulation of a device's front panel that appears on screen is not similarly limited— each editing function may have its own simulated control. This often provides a far easier and more efficient interface to the sound-modification potential of the device than the manufacturers have built into the physical hardware.

Editing can be as simple as boosting a sound's gain or creating an ADSR (attack-sustain-decay-

release) envelope or as complex as microscopically examining and altering single sound samples in a file consisting of half a million samples. In the latter case, the edit base—historically defined by the width of the razor blade used to cut and splice analog tape together—can be as small as 1/100,000 of a second. (Many analog recorders transport tape at $7\frac{1}{2}$ inches per second—imagine trying to cut a $7\frac{1}{2}$-inch piece of tape into 1/100,000-inch strips with a razor blade.)

The increase in the speed at which complex editing operations can be accomplished, coupled with the convenience of being able to switch between and edit numerous devices without leaving one's position in front of the computer screen, is a boon to creative work that cannot be overstressed.

Sound Libraries

After creating the sounds that are to be used, through either sampling or synthesis, the next function of the personal computer is to manipulate the sound library. Although most sound-generating devices include factory-supplied patches (referred to as *presets*) or sampled soundfiles in their ROM chips, most of these devices also provide RAM into which user-defined *banks* or *libraries* of user-sampled soundfiles or user-created patches can be loaded as a unit.

Librarian software can serve several purposes. First and foremost is the organization of soundfiles or patches into larger groups or banks that are to be associated together on the basis of musical considerations. This is of primary importance because the amount of available RAM within a given device places physical limitations on the number of patches or soundfiles that can be stored in it. This capacity is invariably exceeded by the number of patches or soundfiles available through one's own sound editing, from public-domain libraries, from users' groups, or from sound designers or software manufacturers.

As RAM becomes cheaper, many devices are providing onboard storage space for more sound objects than MIDI is capable of dealing with. MIDI expects there to be 128 different sound "programs" (numbered 0 to 127), and that is the maximum number that can be addressed. It is becoming increasingly common for a device to have more than 128 sounds online in immediately accessible RAM—but any sound numbered greater than 128 cannot be called up in a MIDI "Program Change" message. To take care of this anomaly, librarian software that maps the 128 MIDI program numbers to a user-specified subset of the sounds available online is needed.

Many synthesizers allow the user to create a library consisting of configurations of the instrument's keyboard mapping. In such cases, the musical keyboard is divided at *split-points* into separate regions, each of which can have different patches or soundfiles associated with it. Musical keys are losing their scale-associated, do-re-mi-fa-sol-la-ti-do orientation and becoming mere triggers. Consider an extreme case, the Kurzweil 250. This sampling keyboard allows each of its 88 keys to be tuned to any frequency (expressed in cents), to trigger any instrument or sound, and to have its own *effects file* (a group of its own unique digital processing effects). As if that were not enough, Kurzweil keyboard setups may include configurations consisting of up to six *layers*, each of which can be divided into 88 regions in the same manner. With 449 configurations online in a fully loaded machine, librarian software is a welcome aid.

At the next plateau beyond libraries dedicated to the organization of sounds, patches, keyboard-mappings, and MIDI assignments, there is librarian software for dealing with melodies, motives, themes, and patterns. Once musical fragments and ideas have been identified as entities within such a database, these tools provide composers and arrangers with a way to assemble and manipulate their material from increasingly higher levels of abstraction. This is far more efficient and effective than addressing each musical note as an individual event, since this methodology is often much closer to the way that a composer conceptualizes a work of music.

The most advanced computer music software permits the creation of a library of *processes* that generate music. Commercial software of this sort has already become general enough to address the needs of composers of many different and philo-

sophically incompatible genres and styles. Research in this area has led many to speculate that the codification of *style templates* is just around the corner. Such templates would allow users to manipulate the stylistic and emotional elements of musical material with a great amount of control. Consider, for example, the processing of musical ideas through a sieve that filters out all influences of Schoenberg, replacing them with modules from a Bartokian style template, introducing a 23% bias towards Debussy's aesthetics of the period 1911–1913, and finally orchestrating the material in the manner of late-nineteenth-century romanticism with an intermingling of 1960s jazz. CDI (Compact Disc Interactive) technology promises to provide such capabilities through controllers similar to the joysticks used in computer games.

MIDI Sequencers

The most common use of MIDI information is to record and store sequences of musical events played on a computer-controlled sound-generating device such as a synthesizer. Hardware devices and software programs that record MIDI data are called *MIDI sequencers*. MIDI data recorded in this way is often compared to piano-roll data; in neither case are sounds actually recorded, only the information that triggers a sound to occur. Thus, each playing of a MIDI sequence results in a reperformance of what was played initially. This carries the implication that there will be no signal degradation from multiple-generation recording.

Besides channel designation (MIDI translates this data over 16 discrete *MIDI channels* simultaneously), MIDI communicates pitch, key on and off velocity, duration, program (patch or soundfile) change, and the status of a variety of front-panel controls. Furthermore, because MIDI data consists entirely of numerical information, any mathematical operation or calculation that can be applied to a number or a sequence of numbers can be applied to MIDI data as well. This permits MIDI data to be edited and manipulated in numerous ways.

Most MIDI sequencer software is organized to operate like a typical multitrack analog tape recorder.

Indeed, many software sequencers emulate the front panel of a tape recorder on the computer screen—complete with familiar play, record, pause, rewind, and fast-forward controls. The main difference between tape recorders and MIDI sequencers is that the latter can have hundreds of tracks upon which the data can be edited very quickly and easily. In both scope and type, the editing operations that one may apply to MIDI data greatly exceed those available on a tape recorder. Furthermore, professional MIDI sequencer software costs much less than a multitrack tape recorder.

Input and Editing Methods

There are three fundamental ways to record musical ideas into a MIDI sequencer: the *real-time* method, the *step-time* method, and *algorithmically*. In this case, the term *real-time* indicates recording in a manner identical to tape recording (except that no sound is recorded, only trigger information—note name, key velocity, and duration). Usually, real-time data emanates from a MIDI synthesizer or keyboard controller, although recent breakthroughs in pitch recognition make it possible for people with no music-keyboard ability to have notes played on any instrument (or sung) accurately converted into MIDI information. Techniques borrowed from tape recording, such as automatic punch-in and punch-out, are available and much more precise with a MIDI sequencer.

Step-time refers to a popular input method that allows music to be recorded step by step in non-real time—the playback rhythmic value of every next note is specified manually upon entry. Often, this method allows the user to choose a note's duration, such as "quarter note," from a menu on the computer screen. Then, until a new rhythmic value is selected from the menu, every note played from that point on will have the designated temporal value, whether it is held for a tenth of a second or for 10 minutes.

The third method for inputting musical material into a MIDI sequencer is by generating a stream of MIDI data algorithmically—that is, from a composition program. This is becoming increasingly popular as computers become more user-friendly and as the user interface to complex compositional algorithms becomes simpler. Indeed, graphic user interfaces permit the precise creation and manipulation of such algorithms without any need to refer to numbers or mathematical operations. Recent software permits the generations of credible music from probabilistic, cyclical, and statistical distributions of user input pitches, rhythms, dynamic (loudness) patterns, and articulations (subtle performance techniques such as accents).

No matter how the information is recorded into a MIDI sequencer, the sequencer's real strength is how it can be edited. Correcting a note is child's play, as are transposition and tempo changes. Even though these simple editing operations require mathematical operations, it should be stressed that such calculations are considered to be "invisible to the end user." A single example will clarify this statement. Consider the act of transposing a piece of music up one key. The internal operation of the MIDI sequencer will look at the note numbers of each note and add "1" to them. However, the user will merely specify the beginning and the end of the edit region and issue a completely musical command such as "transpose up one semitone"— the computer takes care of all the calculations behind the scenes.

Rhythmic correction or *quantization* is a standard operating procedure often required by the tendency of computers to record rhythmic information too precisely. Quantizing a passage automatically "rounds off" performance data to a user-specified rhythmic grid (typically the smallest rhythmic duration in the piece). Various methods of quantization displacement or sensitivity are employed to counteract the inhuman, "machine-like" quality of music played back with perfect rhythmic accuracy. Until very recently, all commercially available sequencing software required that a performer play along with a metronomic "tick" generated by the computer to serve as a reference frame for subsequent quantization. Some sequencers allowed the user to specify a small set of possible rhythmic values in advance of performance in order to speed up the quantization process. Newer strategies do not require performance to a given beat or performance without rubato (a normal, expressive speeding up and slowing down). Instead, these strategies either employ post-determination of beats and measures (by tapping on a specific key, for example) or else they use advanced pattern-recognition processes to build a table of rhythmic relationships and then apply this information to input data for the purpose of deducing intended durational values from tempo-varying human performance.

Editing practices, such as cut, copy, paste, merge, and insert, are powerful MIDI sequencer operations that have analogues in tape recording in the splicing of tape and the bouncing of tracks.

Finally, many sequencers provide for the translation of MIDI data into conventional music notation (CMN), and CMN editing software often includes such features as automatic transposition, instrumental-range proofreading, rhythmic-error detection, and part extraction. In general, when MIDI sequencing is introduced into the studio, fundamental activities such as recording, editing, and effect synchronization are performed with increasing time-efficiency. In the music business, where time is often equated with money, these savings can be significant.

MIDI-Controlled Mixing and Effects

As the sequence of MIDI events is converted back into sound, preprogrammed digital sound processing effects are also often triggered by embedded *system-exclusive* commands (reserved for a particular manufacturer). When the sound-generating device or effect box receives a system-exclusive code identifying a particular manufacturer, if the device or box was made by that manufacturer it will respond to subsequent data in a way that is unique to the particular device. Most digital effects processors include MIDI IN ports through which particular effects (either ROM-based or user-defined) can be assigned to particular synthesizer patches or triggered by particular MIDI codes. In the simplest implementation, a specific synthesizer patch or soundfile can have its own associated effects, such as flanging, chorusing, reverberation, echo, and delay. This patch or soundfile is called up at the same

time the MIDI program change command is sent from the sequencer to the synthesizer. In this fashion, each of the 128 possible program changes can trigger its own associated reverberation or other effect.

Using MIDI data itself to generate effects that mimic those created by digital signal processing is becoming increasingly common. Software-based MIDI effects generators take incoming MIDI data and juggle the numbers before passing them on to the sound-generating device. For example, in such a setup it is a simple matter to delay repetitions while progressively varying velocity (i.e. loudness) to create echo effects, to add constants to incoming MIDI note numbers in order to create chorusing or a harmonizer, or to change the channel numbers for preassigned pitch ranges to effect real-time orchestration via intelligent keyboard splitting. Dr. T's "Echo Plus" software does practically anything one might want to do with MIDI note numbers being sent to it. These effects, such as doubling, harmonizing, MIDI echo, one-finger chords or other chorusing effects, and infinite MIDI loops, are produced entirely from the multiple retriggering of notes rather than through digital audio processing.

Automation, the most desirable feature of astronomically expensive mixing boards, is being brought into the financial range of the typical owner of a microcomputer-controlled music studio. MIDI-controlled mixers are well within the reach of people using personal computers for music applications. Typically, mixes can be stored in battery-backed RAM or on disk files. Software has been developed at IRCAM to control the Akai MIDI-controlled mixing board. This software (called SNOX) takes a "snapshot" of each knob's and each slider's current value and then provides for gradual fading from one setting to another. Mix "patches" can be saved as files and caused to fade from one setting to another over designated periods of time. A single MIDI sequencer track, transmitting over an unused MIDI channel, can store all the information needed to replicate the mixing "score." Digidesign's Q-Sheet software package is more generic in function. The front panels of many MIDIable mixing boards and effects panels can be emulated on the computer's screen. The user simply drags graphic knobs, buttons, and faders into a window and, in a one-step operation, assigns them to the appropriate MIDI codes that the external device expects to receive. When the program is in operation, these sliders, knobs, and buttons animate in real time as they send the appropriate data to the external device.

Less obvious uses of MIDI data include the control of lighting by assigning specific notes, patches, or songs to specific lighting configurations. An Apple Macintosh personal computer is even being used to control the acoustics of the main performance hall at IRCAM. The room's walls and ceilings have 171 motorized three-part panels, each of which can be rotated to exhibit one of three main acoustic properties (reflection, diffusion, absorption) or three mixed properties (reflection-diffusion, reflection-absorption, diffusion-absorption). Theoretically, the room can be "tuned" to enhance the resonance of a specific musical key. The operator uses the mouse to "paint" the desired acoustics on the screen of the Macintosh, which displays a representation of the room as it would look if the walls were flattened out.

Hard-Disk-Based Digital Recording

Perhaps the most impressive personal computer peripheral now available is the inexpensive yet high-quality direct-to-hard-disk digital audio system. These systems record 16-bit samples at 44.1KHz (i.e., CD mastering quality) or 48 KHz. They take advantage of the computer's SCSI (small computer systems interface). SCSI is an interface standard that makes it possible for a variety of manufacturers to produce disk drives of large capacity for a wide variety of computers. One can now purchase an 80-megabyte SCSI hard disk for under $1,000. The disk drives provide for about 10 minutes of direct-to-hard-disk recording using inexpensive (under $3,000) analog-to-digital converters. The maximum recording time of such a system is limited only by the size of the hard-disk storage medium. Some systems require a dedicated hard-disk drive upon which only digital audio sample data will be recorded; others provide for a "partition" of

the hard-disk drive to digital audio, leaving the remainder of the drive free for other uses. The computer is used as an interface to digital mixing of tracks recorded on a hard disk, providing a means for testing and saving "mix scores" rather than the actual soundfiles or digital sample tracks. Several manufacturers of these devices provide the possibility of easily synchronizing digital audio tracks with MIDI sequence tracks for even greater flexibility.

Synchronizing MIDI to Tape

The output of this digital recording process is usually on multitrack analog or digital recording tape. The final link in the personal computer music setup is a synchronization conversion box (indicated by the loop back in figure 3). When it becomes necessary to record separate tape tracks of MIDIed music at different times—usually one at a time—the only way to ensure that the events on each track will line up on the audio track from beginning to end is to use some form of synchronization. One of four popular synchronization protocols is used, depending upon the situation at hand: FSK sync, MIDI sync, SMPTE sync, or MIDI Timecode.

In FSK sync (or tape sync), a "sync track" consisting of evenly spaced pulses is recorded onto audio tape and used as a "master" temporal reference to slaved MIDI sequencers. Other MIDI devices can be synchronized to the original slave device or to one another via a slightly more accurate type of synchronization called MIDI sync. By recording on multiple tracks with multiple passes, it is possible to greatly exceed the number of musical parts dictated by the number of audio channels in the various synthesizers. FSK sync does not provide a device with any way of "knowing" where it is in a sequence. Therefore, when using this method, one must begin each recording pass at the very beginning of the sync track, even if the current track being synchronized doesn't actually produce any sound until a half-hour later. MIDI sync gets around this by including "start," "stop," "continue," and "song position pointer" codes to provide two MIDI devices to "lock up" and function as a single unit with some degree of accuracy. The video industry's standard—SMPTE (Society of Motion Pictures and Television Engineers) time encoding—provides precise ($\frac{1}{30}$ second accuracy) information about the location of any particular point in time with respect to any point on a tape. SMPTE time encoding is being used in conjunction with the above-mentioned MIDI synchronization codes (start, stop, continue, etc.) to effectively lock together MIDI sequencer software with multitrack audio or video tape, thus guaranteeing that, when one device is rewound or fast-forwarded, the other device will "chase" it to the same point in time. The International MIDI Association recently approved MIDI time code (MTC), which adds greater precision to the SMPTE-to-MIDI lockup and opens the doors to applications that use MIDI time code as a way of achieving synchronization precision close to that of SMPTE at much less expense. Unfortunately, MIDI time code requires a large portion of the MIDI bandwidth to send time-location information—about eight times that of MIDI sync. Therefore, the amount of musical information that can be sent during the 3,125 ten-bit bytes that are being transmitted every second is significantly reduced. The JamBox 4, a SMPTE-MIDI interface from Southworth Music Systems, introduced a type of SMPTE synchronization called *direct time lock*, which greatly reduces the amount of data required to send synchronization information, thus freeing the MIDI data path for more musical information.

Applications of Computers to Music

The musical applications of personal computers can be divided into seven classes, as figure 4 shows.

In *sound laboratory* applications, the computer is used as a sound-generating/patch or a soundfile-editing/analyzing device. Computer software often greatly simplifies the user interface to the sound-modification capabilities of an external sound-generating device. This is because many more controls can be simulated on a computer screen than are economically feasible on a hardware device. Also, the capability of manipulating graphic representations of such obtuse concepts as amplitude

envelopes makes it easier to conceptualize correspondingly complex editing procedures.

In *composition* applications, the computer simplifies the process of creating and editing patch libraries, soundfile libraries, sequence libraries, and musical databases, and can generate music algorithmically. It allows experimentation within an immense set of transformations of one's musical material (for example, one can quickly experiment with many alternate juxtapositions of musical material through cut, copy, and paste operations). It also allows for the otherwise impossible control of a great number of musical materials (whether such materials consist of multiple synthesizers, multiple musical themes, or motives). It permits the fine tuning of musical ideas in ways that would be time consuming under normal circumstances (for example, one can test many alternate orchestrations through the simple reassignment of MIDI channels).

As the computer evolves toward a music processor (analogous to a word processor), it becomes useful for the *copying and editing of scores* for eventual printout using manual input from keyboard, mouse, or digitizer or transcription information obtained from a MIDI keyboard or converted from a pitch-tracking device. Analyzing a work in progress through the availability of practically instantaneous visual representations of a performance, either in graphic notation or in CMN, can be quite constructive. The time traditionally wasted in copying out musical scores and extracting parts is completely eliminated.

In *performance* applications, software-based MIDI sequencers can be used to control sound-generating devices, MIDI effects processors, lighting, and video animation. Computers can make extremely complicated decisions in real time, at speeds equaling thousands of decisions in the space between two notes. This, coupled with their ability to keep track of all the necessary musical rules and aesthetic principles (providing the benefits of knowledge equivalent to years of advanced musical training), has engendered a sort of hybrid creative process known as *interactive composition*—a concept with roots in both composition and improvisation (Chadabe and Zicarelli 1986a, 1986b).

Fig. 4. Applications of computers to music. Personal computers are used in five main areas of music production. Non-produc-tion-related music applications include computer-aided instruction and telecommunications.

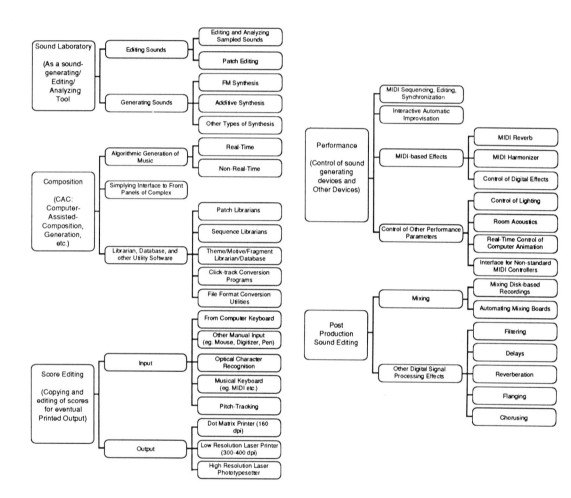

The *digital audio and post-production sound editing* function involves the automation of MIDI-controllable mixing boards by software and the control of other digital signal-processing effects (such as delays, reverberation, flanging, filtering, and chorusing). Professional disk-based digital audio systems, and the digital mixing of material recorded on them, have also moved into the domain of the microcomputer.

Education-related applications include ear train-ing (with automatic pacing), harmony instruction (with automatic correction and feedback), and the teaching of orchestration (with sampling devices used as an orchestral "sketch pad"). The fruits of the applications generators that require no knowl-edge of computer programming (such as Apple's Hypercard) and provide software authoring tools to educators are exponentially expanding. Hypercard has stimulated much development in the musi-cological domain, including sophisticated instructional interfaces to educational video-disks such as those published by the music department of the University of Delaware.

Telecommunications is becoming a standard part of the home microcomputer music studio. It is used to communicate with music networks, bulletin-board systems, and local area networks), for remote MIDI control, and for the archiving of sample files, patches, and utilities for downloading.

In the remainder of this article, I will examine in greater detail representative software packages that typify various musical applications of microcomputers.

Sound Laboratory

Sound Designer: Editing and Analyzing Sampled Sounds

Sound Designer from Digidesign is one of the most powerful waveform-editing software packages currently available on a microcomputer. For around $500, its features rival those of professional digital audio systems in the $100,000 range. Digidesign's approach is to convert soundfiles from different manufacturers into a single 16-bit linear format regardless of whether the original sample resolution is 8, 10, 12, 14, 16, or 18 bits. The soundfiles are reconverted to whatever format the playback instrument requires. Sampling instruments currently supported by Digidesign are Akai's samplers, EMU's Emulator family, Ensoniq's Mirage, Korg's DSS1, Sequential's Prophet samplers, and Kurzweil's 250. One laudable side effect of converting all these manufacturers' file formats into a single standard for editing is that previously incompatible soundfiles can be passed from sampler to sampler via Sound Designer. That is, you convert a file from one manufacturer's format into Sound Designer's format and then translate the resulting Sound Designer file into another manufacturers' format. This has propagated whole libraries (including some CD-ROMs) of files in the generic Digidesign format and of devices that provide playback access to many competing manufacturers' sampled sounds.

Sound Designer displays sampled waveforms in

Fig. 5. Two views of a soundfile being edited with Digidesign's Sound Designer—the normal waveform view (the window entitled "CELINA SD—No Backup" on the bottom of the screen) and an FFT (the window entitled "CELINA SD"). Note the four icons on the left of the screen. Using the mouse to select (by touching the symbol and pressing the mouse button) the little mixer icon brings up a series of question/responses, which start the procedure of mix-

ing two soundfiles together. Likewise, selecting the little pencil icon turns the cursor into a pencil, after which mouse motion is interpreted as drawing the waveform. Selecting the icon consisting of a little note and a musical keyboard sends the current soundfile to the sampling device connected to the computer, and selecting the little speaker icon causes an immediate (low-resolution) preview of the sound through the computer's built-in speaker.

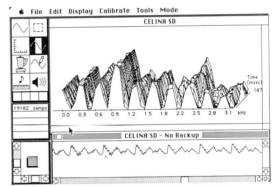

any magnification desired (figure 5). The screen can show an entire soundfile of hundreds of thousands of samples or zoom in to the level of individual samples for the purpose of "drawing" new samples into the file with a mouse-controlled pencil. Besides a five-mode non-real-time digital equalizer, Sound Designer allows easy cutting, pasting, mixing, and merging between parts of soundfiles or between different soundfiles. Gradually changing the sound of a trumpet into that of a violin is no problem with Sound Designer. There are also provisions for sound synthesis from within the program, although the only method that has been implemented is the Karplus-Strong plucked-string algorithm. Display of a three-dimensional spectral frequency analysis or FFT (fast Fourier transform) is also available, although editing the spectrum in a three-dimensional form is not possible. Because transferring the soundfiles to the sampler can take up to a minute, there is a preview function that plays back the sound through the computer at a fixed sample rate. Although playback through the audio capabilities of the computer usually results in lower quality than would be available were the sound actually loaded into the appropriate device for which it is intended, this feature provides a quick and easy way to spot-check sounds that are being developed or undergoing modification.

One important feature of sound sampling that is handled very elegantly by Sound Designer is looping. When used musically, portions of sampled soundfiles are usually looped over and over to allow for the sampled sound to sustain for any desired length (the length being dictated by the duration of the musical key being pressed or by the duration between a note-on MIDI code and a note-off MIDI code). This can be a problem, because a click or a pop will be heard if both the start point and the end point of a loop are not at zero crossings, or if the waveform slope resulting from the loop is not smooth. With Sound Designer, after coarse loop points have been designated, fine tuning of a sound loop is accomplished by displaying the crucial "seam" created at the exact point where the end-point loops back to the beginning part of the loop. This seam can be moved, sample by sample, until a point at which the wave slope coming into the loop complements the slope immediately following the loop point.

Generating Sounds with Softsynth

Softsynth, also from Digidesign, is a powerful software package that allows sounds generated by additive or FM synthesis to be saved as sample files for loading into popular sampling keyboards, such as those by Akai, EMU, Ensoniq, Korg, Sequential, and Kurzweil. Like the companion program, Sound Designer, Softsynth creates 16-bit sample soundfiles that are converted to the 8, 10, 12, 14, or 18-bit format, depending on the sampler being used for playback. The other convention borrowed from Sound Designer is the preview mode for playing back sounds through the computer. This means that one doesn't need to have the sampler present to work on sounds. Because the sounds are generated, as opposed to having originally been sampled, the program also creates very tiny (30 Kbyte) *pa-*

rameter files that contain the only information necessary to regenerate a specific sound rather than the actual sound data (which may require 600 Kbytes or more). These parameter files have the advantage of being small enough to inexpensively circulate through the telecommunication networks.

The additive synthesis portion of the program provides a graphic interface, via 32 mouse-driven "faders" across the bottom of the screen, to 32 oscillators simulated by the software. These represent the up to 32 partials of the sound whose amplitude envelopes are displayed on the main screen in three dimensions. Another screen provides a graphic interface to both the individual partial's up-to-40-segment amplitude envelope and the up-to-15-segment frequency envelope. Here the user can preview the sound of the individual partial, select from one of five waveforms to use for it, and set the particular partial's ratio to the fundamental frequency of the sound. The default ratio corresponds to the natural harmonic series, but this can be easily changed.

When the user chooses the FM synthesis mode, the faders of the main screen are used to control the 32 available FM operators. With the exception of a very small group, most FM sounds possible on the Yamaha FM-based synthesizers can be created, as well as a large number of sounds not possible on traditional FM instruments. Using the program Softsynth together with Sound Designer makes it possible to apply to FM synthesized sounds waveform editing techniques hitherto confined to the domain of sampled sounds, such as various types of looping, merging, reversing, and digital equalizing (figure 6).

Patch Editing using Graphic Interface with DX/TX Editor

Opcode Systems markets patch editors for almost every existing make and model of synthesizer. The main screen of one of these editors typically displays all algorithm and patch parameters simultaneously. Using the mouse pointer to click on any item selects that item for editing. Envelope editing is accomplished entirely by using the mouse to shape graphic representations of the envelope's pa-

Fig. 6. A three-dimensional display of a waveform resembling an FFT. The changing amplitudes (expressed vertically) of the constituent harmonic partials (expressed from front to back) are plotted over time (expressed horizontally in milliseconds). On the bottom portion of the screen are 32 faders that can be adjusted by sliding the mouse arrow over them. These control the overall gain of each separate partial.

Fig. 7. Opcode Systems's DX/TX Patch Editor. This graphic-oriented patch editor illustrates several standard user interface components. The horizontal bar under the words "Fine Frequency" is known as a scroll bar. Touching the arrows at either end with the mouse arrow causes the white box to move in the direction of the arrow, simultaneously updating the value in reverse video in the "Operator 1" window at the left of the screen. Large skips in values can be accomplished by touching the white square box on the scroll bar with the mouse and pulling quickly toward either end. The graphic representation of the "Keyboard Scaling" at the bottom of the screen is similarly manipulated with the mouse, as are the envelopes under each operator at the top of the screen.

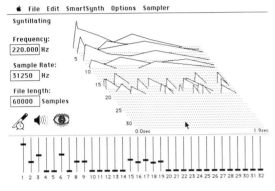

rameters. The computer converts the graphics into the appropriate MIDI data that will generate the envelope. The results of all editing operations are heard immediately if the synthesizer is connected to the computer via MIDI. Similarly, any voice and function settings created on the synthesizer can be transferred to the computer for fine tuning, and these may be transferred to the synthesizer singly or in banks. A simple built-in sequencer allows a recorded sequence to be played back automatically every time a patch is changed. In addition, it is possible to copy and paste envelopes, operators, and other parameters within or between patches (figure 7).

Newer Approaches to Patch Editing

IRCAM (Institut de Recherche Acoustique/Musique) has worked on FM patching from a unique standpoint. In their prototype, the onscreen display is a bar-graph FFT, and the relative values of individual frequency spectra are transformed to initiate the corresponding FM operator changes needed to produce the FFT. While equally valid, this is essentially the opposite approach to most patch editors, which require the entire patch to be created before an FFT can be calculated. Other researchers working on tangential lines to the IRCAM approach are developing patch editors that convert natural-language descriptions of desired sounds into the MIDI codes necessary to realize the sound de-

scribed. These systems endeavor to convert into usable MIDI data such subjective and ambiguous depictions of sound as "mellow," "sweet," "biting," and "raspy."

The newer patch editors allow the user to generate patches that result in usable sounds with little human intervention. The TX81Z Editor Librarian from Beaverton Digital Systems include a patch-generation module (Genesis—see figure 8) that lets users program custom voice-randomizing algorithms to generate new patches. Hybrid Arts claims that its DX-Android and CX-Android packages use artificial intelligence techniques to create instantaneous new patches or distorted variations of existing patches. All Opcode Systems patch editors and librarians now include Patch Factory, a utility supporting random patch generation using any of several supplied algorithms. The Synthworks series of patch editor/librarian software includes "intelligent sound creation" facilities for "mix creation" from existing patches, completely new patches ("patch creation"), or "slight" or "medium" variations on user-supplied patches.

Fig. 8. Beaverton Digital Systems' TX81Z Editor Librarian. The "Genesis" option in this editor permits users to program custom voice-randomizing al-gorithms that generate new (and often quite usable) patches.

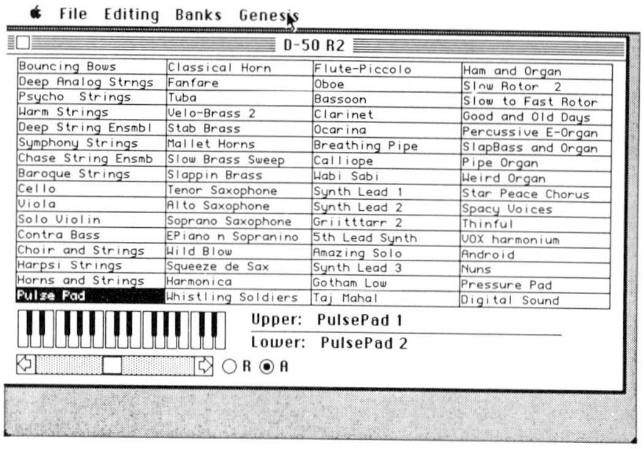

for whatever purpose they desire), it is a simple task to provide for on-screen real-time emulation of the synthesizer's controls. These controls can be manipulated with a mouse or with the computer keyboard. Digidesign provides this for most of the devices that are compatible with its Sound De-signer package. Editing efficiency increases because much more information is available on a computer screen than in a 24-character LCD, and navigation through a synthesizer's menu tree can be more visible to the user. Graphic interfaces for the ma-nipulation of certain parameters that lend them-selves to a graphically expressed model increases the "conceptual contact" with the sound data. Look at Opcode's TX/DX editor in figure 7: Using the mouse to drag on the "handles" of the line repre-senting the envelope on the graph sends the value changes over MIDI and updates the parameter value indicators on the screen. Such a graph is more con-sistent with our conceptual model of the envelope than typing a series of numbers. Kurzweil has a non-real-time interface to the K250's Instrument Editor that places the combined options of several entire branches of their effects-editing menu tree on the screen simultaneously.

Composition

Front-panel emulation for complex devices: Digidesign, Kurzweil, Opcode

Although nearly all of the software applications discussed above can be thought of as relating to the act of composition, some are more concerned with the manipulation of ideas than with the manipula-tion of sound properties. In this category one finds a wide range of utility software aimed at facilitating the composer's task.

The simplest application is the emulation of MIDI-addressable front-panel controls in syn-thesizers and samplers. The user interface of these instruments is usually little more than a 24-to-48-character liquid-crystal display (LCD) used in con-junction with a number of buttons that assume dif-ferent functions depending on what mode the user is in. Often, cursor keys are used to scroll within a menu of selections, which may have as many as 500 options, any number of which might need to have a value set or be confirmed with a "yes" or "no" button. To grasp the difficulty of dealing with such a system, imagine a typewriter that could only display 24 characters at a time and whose keys functioned in 20 modes rather than the traditional two (upper and lower case).

With many front panels addressable via the use of MIDI system-exclusive commands (unassigned commands that individual manufacturers can use

Librarian, Database, and Other Utility Software

Musical data that can't be readily retrieved is prac-tically useless. This consideration leads one to seek out so-called librarian software for the organization of such ephemeral items as patch banks, sequences, musical phrases, and even the processes used to create music.

Patch Librarians: MIDIMac Librarian Series

By far the most popular librarian software is that produced by Opcode Music Systems. One reason for this popularity is that this software covers al-most every widely used commercial synthesizer (including the most popular Yamaha, Casio, Ober-heim, Roland, Korg, and Fender synthesizers, and the late Linn Drum). Moving patches from the mas-ter library in the personal computer to a patch bank in the synthesizer is as simple as pointing to the

Fig. 9. Opcode Systems Patch Librarian. Moving patches from the library to a specific bank is as simple as pointing at the name of the patch in the library and, while holding the mouse key down, drag-
ging the name into the desired bank. Loading patches into the synthesizer is accomplished nearly instantaneously when a patch in a bank is touched with the mouse.

Fig. 10. TX81Z Pro from Digital Music Services. The bar at the left of the screen is called a palette. *Different modes of the program are entered by click-* *ing the mouse on the various choices of the palette.*

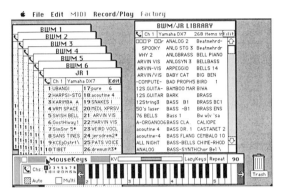

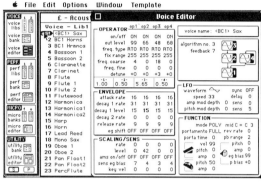

patch name with the mouse and dragging the item into the list designating the individual patch banks. Single patches can be auditioned on the receiving synthesizer, and whole banks can be loaded from within the library. With the more popular Casio and Yamaha synthesizers, the patch editor and the librarian are integrated into a single package, further simplifying things for the user (figure 9). Digital Music Services markets a similar package (figure 10).

As musicians accumulate more and more synthesizers, the need for a single librarian package to be able to deal with patches in various manufacturers' formats has led to the creation of powerful all-in-one librarian packages. Opcode Systems was one of the first to release librarian software for the Macintosh that permits the combination of separate libraries from various devices into a single program. Hybrid Arts markets a generic patch utility, GenPatch ST, which is configurable to work with any instrument that does MIDI data transfers (this includes some samplers, such as those from Ensoniq and Sequential).

Phrase Databases: Studio Session

Bogas Software's Studio Session for the Apple Macintosh includes a music editor that takes a hierarchical approach to music composition. With Studio Session it is possible to play back pitched music

in eight parts through the Macintosh's internal speaker or through an external sound system connected to the Macintosh's audio output. The program (which does not handle MIDI) uses sound that has been sampled and looped via an inexpensive 8-bit converter (such as the MacNifty Audio Digitizer) that records sound into the microcomputer in a manner similar to that employed by dedicated sampling keyboards. The software uses linear interpolation of the sound samples to recompute the sampled soundfiles for playback at various pitches for the creation of melodies.

Regions of tracks (essentially melodic fragments) can be looped for up to 999 repetitions, and loops of varying length can occur at different places on separate tracks simultaneously. Loops, which are represented by musical repeat signs, can be nested to ten levels. Any selected region can be saved as a "phrase" for database-like access within a phrase library. Phrase categories are labeled with one of 15 user-defined descriptive names. The phrase library holds up to 16,384 phrases. Sorting and searching are available by specifying type, and/or meter, and/or phrase length. The ability to define musical ideas as objects that can be dealt with individually permits extensive experimentation by allowing users to view musical ideas on a more global level. MIDI software developers such as Steinberg (Pro 24 sequencer) are following Bogas' example to a certain extent (figure 11).

Fig. 11. Bogas Software's
Studio Session with phrase
database. Studio Session
includes a library of
sampled sounds (see win-
dow at lower right) as well
as a phrase library. Musical material can be stored
in the phrase library
within 15 user-defined categories, with associated
length and metrical in-
formation. Later, the li-
brary can be searched for
phrases fulfilling search
criteria based on category
and/or meter and/or
length. Once located,
phrases can be inserted
into the current point in
the score by clicking on
their names.

Fig. 12. UpBeat from In-
telligent Music. Besides
giving the user complete
control over randomizing
algorithms for the purpose
of defeating the "machine-
like" accuracy of the computer, UpBeat includes a
device library, a library
of patterns, and a song
library.

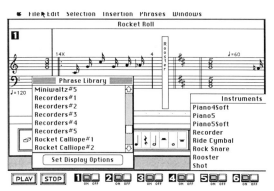

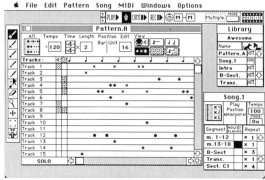

Process Databases: UpBeat

UpBeat and M (from Intelligent Music) can function as *process databases*. UpBeat provides the capability of building a library of fixed phrases inter-
mingled with processes that generate phrases by
applying user-specified amounts of randomness or
probabilities to particular information. The device
is actually a rhythm programmer intended to be
used in conjunction with a drum machine, although it is flexible enough to deal with pitch information supplied by synthesizers. The developer's
intent was to provide a means of introducing enough
randomness and variation so that playback would
more accurately simulate human performance. In
creating the software, they succeeded in removing the dreaded mechanical sound of computer-
controlled music well beyond most expectations.
The library contains two main classes of objects:
patterns and songs. Patterns can be named and
linked in any combination to form songs. Songs and
patterns can be freely grouped to form songs of a
higher level, and this nested hierarchy may include
as many levels as desired (figure 12).

File Format Conversion Utilities

One of the problems facing computer music studios
is that most developers have unique and often proprietary data formats for saving information into
files. Naturally, a wide variety of data formats paves
the way for utilities that can convert data, MIDI or
otherwise, from one application's format to that of
another. Rather early in the scheme of things, one
company—Musicworks, Inc.—released a software
package called MIDIWorks that converted sequencer data to and from most of the then popular
data formats. Unfortunately, the company was unable to keep up with the ever-changing data formats
(which, as the microcomputer music applications
industry grew, became increasingly more protected
trade secrets).

One approach to file incompatibility is the possibility of using one program as a "gateway" to other
programs. Digidesign's Sound Designer and Softsynth software packages function in this manner by
converting all the various sample formats to a 16-
bit linear format for editing. Reconversion into the
separated manufacturers' file formats is done after
editing.

Another approach to this issue is an alternative
standardized MIDI file format being championed by
Dave Oppenheim of Opcode Systems. MIDI products from Opcode Systems, Intelligent Music, Electronic Arts, Southworth Systems, Passport Designs,
and some other companies, while retaining the option to save files in their own proprietary data format, also provide the opportunity to save a copy of
the data in the generic MIDI File proposed by Oppenheim. This feature allows these programs to
share data with one another. This is facilitated by

the fact that these companies are generally concentrating on areas of software that do not compete with one another: sequencing, algorithmic or interactive composition, and notation. Opcode's MIDI-Mac Sequencer offers the additional capability of saving files in the SMUS, Deluxe Music Construction Set, and Professional Composer formats, thereby serving as a much needed gateway to the popular Mark of the Unicorn products. This is fortunate, because Mark of the Unicorn, the developers of Professional Composer, have expressed little interest in making their software compatible with any standardized file format.

Standardization of MIDI upload data has been a hot topic on the Performing Artists Network. Up until now, the archived sound sample files, the MIDI sequence, and the patch files available in the storage areas of PAN have been valuable only to owners of identical synthesizers. With MIDI sequence data as well as MIDI-communicated sample data and now Softsynth parameter files, there seems to be the possibility of establishing a standard upload format, which could then be converted after download for use by any company's software or hardware.

Algorithmically Generated Music: M

For composers and performers who may have shied away from algorithmic composition because of a lack of programming knowledge, M from Intelligent Music provides sophisticated tools that are easily adaptable to a wide range of applications. The intuitive user interface offers a generic variety of manipulative control and real-time interaction that many find to be perfectly consistent with their normal compositional process and thus capable of being molded to express an individual's unique personal musical voice. Because many of the more tedious aspects of composition and experimentation are controlled from higher levels of abstraction, the user is free to work with processes and transformations rather than notes. Best of all, while this program includes features that will satisfy even the most demanding composers, it offers an excellent entrée for the novice as well.

The operation of M entails a setup stage and a

Fig. 13. Intelligent Music's M. The main screen of M uses icons from many purposes. Clicking on any element with the mouse brings up additional windows for further customization. In the center of the screen is a little mouse waiter "taking an order," and this is exactly what that portion of the screen controls: note order. Exclamation points indicate that notes are to be played back in exactly the order that they came in, and question marks show various degrees of randomness. The footprints indicate that that particular pitch material was recorded in step time, and the reel-to-reel tape recorder indicates that that pitch collection was recorded in real time.

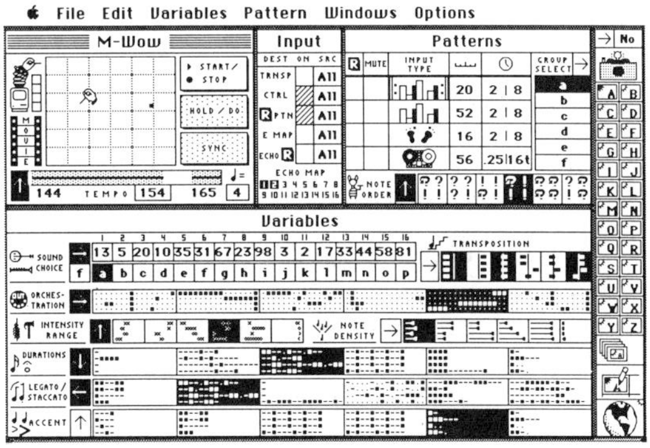

performance stage. During the setup stage, the user determines the basic musical material for four separate parts—e.g., melodic patterns and/or pitch distribution (input can be in step or real time, monophonic or polyphonic), rhythmic patterns, accent patterns, articulation patterns, intensity ranges, orchestration (program numbers as well as MIDI channel assignments), transposition configurations, proportions of pattern-variation methods (original order / permutation / random), and tempo range. In most cases the user can define at least six alternative settings for the various parameters. Why six? This is due to an innovative aspect of the software: A grid of six by six squares in the upper left corner of the screen displays a parameter (figure 13), which can be assigned to cycle to the next variation when the conducting baton is moved up, down, right, or left in the grid. The little arrows immediately to the left of each parameter setting show the associated conducting direction, and the reverse video selection is always the currently active variation. As was mentioned above, the program's output can be captured in a file and subsequently read by Opcode's MIDIMAC Sequencer and thence converted into notation using Electronic Arts' Deluxe Music Construction Set or Mark of the Unicorn's Professional Composer. Operating the program is like conducting an orchestra of ideas and transformational processes rather than one of musicians and instruments.

Interactive Composition: Jam Factory

Whereas M can be considered an algorithmic composition generator, an "intelligent instrument," or an interactive composition environment, Jam Factory (also from Intelligent Music) leans closer to the interactive composition/improvisation camp. Jam Factory (figure 14) provides features that simulate a situation that might be compared to improvising with a group of clones of oneself. The software consists of four polyphonic sequencer modules, or *players*, which the user "teaches" by playing MIDI data into them. All four players can be taught by a single user, or by four separate users all interacting with Jam Factory in real time. The data is placed in a Markov chain—a structure that records all the transitions between notes so that, upon playback, the player can pick from among all the transitions it has "learned." Intelligent or likely variations of the input musical material are created.

Markov processes require that the relative likelihood of each option be conditioned by one or more immediately preceding choice(s). What this means for all but first-order Markov chains is that the music is constantly looking back to see where it has come from. (First-order Markov chains are merely random reorderings of input material that maintain the overall probability distribution or weighting of the original events—that is, choices are based solely on the probability that an event will occur.) A second-order Markov chain uses an entirely different set of probabilities (called a *transition table*) depending on what the immediately preceding event (i.e. note) is, third-order Markov chains base their transition tables on probabilities dependent upon the previous two notes, fourth-order Markov chains "look back" three notes, and so on. The spelling rule "I before E except after C" is a good analogy for a Markov process. The user manipulates graphic sliders on the screen to determine the mixing of first-, second-, third-, and fourth-order Markov chains generating the output.

Fig. 14. Jam Factory. The upper right corner of each module shows four boxes labeled (horizontally) 1 to 4 and (vertically) 0% to 100%. Each box has two columns in it, one representing pitch and the other duration. The horizontal numbers 1 through 4 represent first- through fourth- order Markov chains, which are applied in the percentages indicated by the vertical bars. Clicking the mouse button while the arrow is in one of the boxes raises that box's percentage and causes the other boxes' percentages to be unweighted correspondingly.

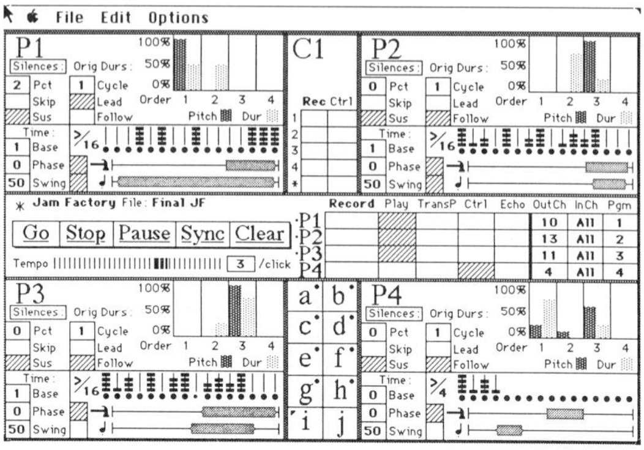

Separate sliders are provided for pitch and rhythm because, when this information is viewed independently, entirely different transition tables result. Velocity ranges and durational ranges are also user-defined, as are cyclical accent patterns. Jam Factory and Intelligent Music's other packages, M and Up-Beat, are opening doors to new dimensions of artistic creation.

The Mouse as Musical Instrument: Music Mouse and Ovaltunes

Research and development in the field of interactive composition is taking place in two main areas: the *controller* or *input device* (i.e., how information is communicated to the computer) and the *processor* (what the computer does with the information once it gets it, before it is passed on to an output device). This process is analogous to the action-reaction paradigm (action/controller–reaction/processor). Because many popular microcomputers use a pointing device called a *mouse*, the mouse itself is being used as the controller for communicating information to the computer for processing into music.

Music Mouse was one of the first commercially available "intelligent instruments" combining the functions of controller and processor. The software, developed by Laurie Spiegel and now marketed by

Fig. 15. Music Mouse con-
verts the user's motion of
the computer's mouse di-
rectly into an analogous
position within the mu-
sical grid displayed on
screen. Four lines are thus
controlled, and these map
onto the piano-style key-
board to output the corresponding MIDI notes to a
MIDI-controlled sound-
generating device. The
menus provide options for
changing the scale type,
adding computer-gener-
ated melodic embellish-
ments, or extending this
control to other syn-
thesizer parameters (such
as volume or patch
number)

Fig. 16. Ovaltunes creates
a synergistic relationship
between music and graph-
ics. The screen graphics
are generated in real time
by moving the mouse. Each
mouse gesture generates a
corresponding musical
event. The setup window
(top left) assigns program
number, MIDI channel,
musical algorithm (mel-
ody, accompaniment, or
drum), melody number,
number of pitches, rhyth-
mic pattern, and velocity
range.

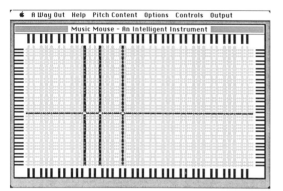

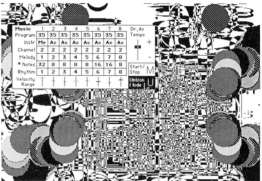

Opcode Systems, uses the mouse and the keyboard
as the only input devices. The program also takes
care of processing the user's input to provide a
pleasing continuum of interesting music. Output
can be directed either to a MIDI synthesizer, to the
computer's built-in speaker, or to a sound system
attached to the computer's audio output jack.

The flow of music is directed by moving the
computer's mouse. The user's motion of the computer's mouse is converted into analogous motion
within a two-dimensional grid on the computer
screen, the axes of which correspond to two musical keyboards (figure 15). The user can specify that
the displayed keyboards are quantized as chromatic,
diatonic, pentatonic, quartal, or Middle Eastern
scales. Different configurations of four voices
grouped as three plus one or two plus two, in contrary or similar motion, are available. Completely
vertical motion means that the part or parts assigned to the vertical axis move within the selected
pitch collection while the other parts sustain. Conversely, horizontal motion moves those parts assigned to the horizontal axis while the remaining
"melody" or "melodies" sustain. Diagonal motion
allows all parts to move simultaneously. Discontinuous motion is also available. The keyboard is
used simultaneously to access other modification
features of the program.

Because the computer's mouse can indicate only

a single x,y coordinate at a time, the program is required to make choices for the remaining three
notes of the musical texture. These automatic decisions are based upon rules that are hard-coded into
the program. Thus, Music Mouse fulfills the primary criterion of an expert system: it enables non-
experts to function as though they were experts (in
this case, composers). It may seem like an anomaly
to advertise a musical instrument with the words
"No music notation or keyboard skills needed";
however, in the case of Music Mouse this is entirely appropriate, and it is probably the way that
most expert systems will be marketed as they become more popular.

Ovaltunes is similar to Music Mouse in that it
uses the computer's mouse and keyboard as the primary input device. Pitches, however, are normally
entered from a MIDI keyboard. A significant difference between the two programs is that Ovaltunes
allows the user to configure the entire system,
rather than depending upon hard-coded routines.
Because of this, effective use of the program requires a setup stage, during which melodic, rhythmic, and timbral elements are delineated. Furthermore, while Ovaltunes creates music from the
motion of the computer's mouse, it also creates
graphic images in response to the same movement
(figure 16).

Up to eight melodies can be taught to Ovaltunes,
and these can be modified interactively while the
software is running. Eight rhythmic patterns of dif-

fering lengths can be entered, and each can be associated with a probability cycle (which is also user-defined). Because neither the pitch patterns, nor the probability cycles, nor the rhythmic patterns are obliged to be of the same length, the resulting cyclical combination can be extremely lengthy before it repeats itself. All these elements can be grouped together in nine "presets" for quick recall from the computer keyboard. Presets also store such information as velocity range and melodic algorithm. A pattern can be fed through a melody, accompaniment, or drum algorithm). In addition, presets store graphic parameters such as drawing mode, shape, pattern, or color. (If a color monitor is being used, the "Strawberry" version of the program is required.) Although most musical and graphic parameters can be changed "on the fly" from the computer keyboard, the operation of the program often establishes a strong identity between certain musical textures and their associated graphic images. As a result, the audience is able to effectively experience a synergistic relationship between the music and visual images.

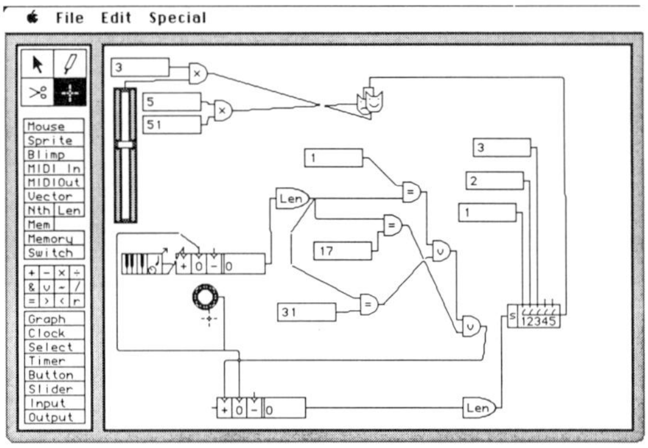

Languages and Programming Environments: Hookup!, MIDI-Lisp, and HMSL

Visual (icon-based)programming languages have now appeared on microcomputers, and some of them are optimized for the control of MIDI data and/or digital signal processing.

HookUp!, developed by David Levitt and his students at MIT, supports MIDI data processing. The user connects icons, representing input (currently a MIDI keyboard, a computer keyboard, or a mouse), output devices (MIDI synthesizer, Macintosh screen radio-controlled blimp, etc.), timing clocks data structures (memory cells and vectors), as well as arithmetic, logical, and comparative operators (figure 17). Many icons can be "opened up" by clicking on them with the mouse to reveal their own control panels or operating "circuitry." Icons can also be picked up, dragged around the screen, and interconnected (using a "wiring tool") to create functional algorithms for real-time control of and/or interaction with data from external devices (typically, MIDI-addressable synthesizers). Even-

Fig. 17. HookUp! screen. The left side of the screen displays a menu of options, which turn into icons when they are pulled out into the program area with the mouse. In the upper left corner is a "wiring" tool, which is used to "wire" the various elements together. In the program shown, we can see slider icons (which function like physical slides for changing values from 0 to 100), a MIDI input icon (like a little piano key), and a length operator, which passes on the number of notes played to an equals operator to check to *see if the number of notes played is equal to 1, 17, or 31. When it senses that this many notes have been played, it sends a pulse to the selector switch (far right), which increments to frames 1, 2, or 3 of an associated screen animation sprite (upper center). In this case the animation frames are actually pictures of pages of music— thus, the program listens to MIDI input and "turns" the pages of music at the appropriate time for someone who is reading the music off the computer screen.*

tually, complex algorithms so created will be accessible from progressively higher levels of abstraction—that is, within larger systems of interactive modules or modules within modules.

LISP is a computer language as old as the well-known Fortran. Some things are easy to do in Lisp that are more difficult in other computer languages. For example, a melody can be treated as a list of notes and durations. Lisp provides a rich collection of functions for manipulating lists. A company called ACT Informatique in Paris has developed a dialect called Le_Lisp. IRCAM has joined this dialect with MIDI to create a programming environment called MIDI-Lisp. Within this environment they have also developed PREFORM, an object-oriented graphic programming toolkit with which the user can select and arrange the constituent parts of MIDI programs as visual building blocks. MIDI-Lisp is being used to teach the principles of programming to music students at the Paris Conservatory.

Frog Peak Music is distributing the Hierarchical Music Specification Language (HMSL), developed at the Mills College Center for Contemporary Music by Phil Burk, Larry Polansky, and David Rosenboom. HMSL is an interactive object-oriented extension of Mach-2 Forth for experimental composition, catering to the avant-garde and to people who are experimenting with artificial intelligence and with *process-oriented* music as opposed to *data-oriented* music. For example, *shape* is an object in HMSL consisting of a set of points in an *n*-dimensional space (the number of dimensions and their functional characteristics are up to the composer). Another *translator* object can read the shape and perform a variety of operations upon it, such as translating the shape into musical parameters. These shapes and interpreters can be arranged in a hierarchy of user-defined sequential or parallel processes. Like Jam Factory and M, HMSL possesses the ability to interpret incoming MIDI data (using an intelligent MIDI parser) for the purpose of extracting events that have been predefined to control other processes.

The Future: Musical Databases and Hierarchical Interfaces

Bogas Software, Southworth Music Systems, Intelligent Music, and other developers point to increased concern with the possibility of defining musical fragments as objects within a library. The definition of such objects or modules is moving toward encompassing not only fixed event lists but also processes. Free interaction between lists and processes is expected. Such libraries often include searching, sorting, generation of reports (statistics), and group edit operations. Composition with objects or modules may yield new modules of greater complexity, nestable to any degree of abstraction. Conversely, *decomposition* should permit a return to the note or instruction level. The ability to work with entire musical ideas as single units or objects from the database that can be manipulated from different levels of abstraction is beginning to have a major impact upon the musical community.

Score Editing

People often speak of music processing and word processing in the same breath. In actuality, they have less in common than one might expect. Of course there are the obvious similarities: musicians record the sounds of their instruments using a tape recorder, and people record their own words the same way. Everyone can understand how a typewriter works, and there are cumbersome music typewriters as well. What we call word processors are really computerized typewriters. People believe that so-called music processors should allow one to play music on a keyboard and have that music printed out perfectly, although few people expect to be able to talk to a typewriter and have it print out the words.

"First-generation" microcomputer-driven professional notation software has been available for several years on the IBM PC (Jim Miller's Personal Composer) and the Apple Macintosh (Mark of the Unicorn's Professional Composer, Electronic Arts' Deluxe Music Construction Set, and Great Wave's Concertware). It has recently appeared on the Atari ST (Dr. T.'s Copyist, Sonus' Superscore, and Hybrid Arts' EZ-Score Plus) as well. Passport Designs, Inc., is now marketing one of the most famous score-editing programs: SCORE, which was written over 15 years by Leland Smith for the mainframe computer at Stanford University.

Things have been moving fast ever since Adobe Systems' device-independent PostScript music font was introduced in 1986. A font is a collection of typological characters all of one style (the term is most often associated with alphabets). As remarkable as it may sound, until the release of the Adobe music font, there was no standardized musical symbol set, much less one that was not inherently tied to a single manufacturer's printing device. The vast majority of printed music was hand-produced. Many of the producers of first-generation notation packages are rushing to include PostScript compatibility in their products as software upgrades.

In 1987, "second-generation" microcomputer music-notation programs appeared: HB-Imaging's HB-Engraver, Coda's FINALE, Notation Research's High Score, and Advanced Music Notation Sys-

Fig. 18. Deluxe Music Construction Set accepts note input from a MIDI keyboard (in step time) or by using the mouse to click on the piano keyboard at the bottom of the screen. Symbols are selected from the menu at the left. Any

tems' Nightingale. These products all had as a prerequisite PostScript compatibility, and most of them showed improvements over the first-generation packages. The knowledge that Adobe Systems' music font had provided the cornerstone upon which to build programs that could truly equal the high standards of professional engraving has opened up the entire music-publishing industry to computer automation. Music publishers normally invest a five-figure sum in the engraving, printing, and distribution of each composition they publish. In one fell swoop, the PostScript music font has eliminated these expenses. Publishers no longer have to weigh the odds pertaining to whether or not they will recover their investment in a publication; now all works can be stored on a disk and printed as orders arise. Furthermore, it is becoming increasingly common for composers to supply their music already on disk—a practice that represents further savings for the publishers. As more and more musical works are being routed to distribution centers via telecommunications in the form of notation files, the long-awaited concept of "publication on demand" is rapidly becoming a reality.

Deluxe Music Construction Set

Deluxe Music Construction Set (DMCS), the first commercial package offering PostScript compatibility, takes a graphic-based approach to notation (figure 18). After the program's built-in rules have made their best guess about the way a passage should be notated, the user can still drag any symbol to change its location, angle (in the case of beams), or size. It is possible to produce near-engraving-quality music notation using DMCS in conjunction with the Adobe music font and a PostScript printer of high enough resolution, although the software has an eight-stave limitation and thus, few automatic features for dealing with instrumental parts.

Professional Composer

Mark of the Unicorn's Professional Composer was one of the first products to offer the minimum amount of features required by professional musi-

Fig. 18. Deluxe Music Construction Set accepts note input from a MIDI keyboard (in step time) or by using the mouse to click on the piano keyboard at the bottom of the screen. Symbols are selected from the menu at the left. Any notation graphic can be repositioned by moving it with the mouse. In this way, beam angles and measure lines can also be modified to permit formatting of each page when it is printed.

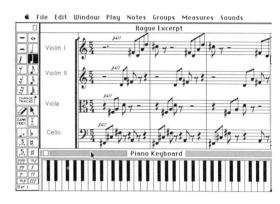

cians. When the Adobe Systems' music font appeared, they were also among the first to "retrofit" their software with PostScript compatibility. The capabilities of Professional Composer include the ability to handle orchestral scores of 40 staves, automatic part transposition, automatic part extraction with rest concatenation, automatic instrumental range checking, automatic rhythm checking, n-tuplets, automatic text reformatting (when the music is reformatted), a usable set of symbols, a rudimentary form of rhythmic polyphony, and the ability to merge staves for the purpose of creating functional piano reductions of larger works (figure 19). Notes and symbols can be entered by means of the symbol menu and the mouse, the computer keyboard and the mouse, or (in real time or step time) the companion MIDI Sequencer software, Performer (discussed below). The many automatic features of Professional Composer demonstrate that it is primarily a rule-based system that does not often permit manual intervention to correct cases where the built-in rules are insufficient to solve notational problems (such as symbol collisions).

Concertware+MIDI

Great Wave's Concertware+MIDI provides the closest emulation of word processing in a music-processing package. Music played on any MIDI keyboard in real time or step time may be auditioned, rerecorded if necessary, or inserted directly into the

Fig. 19. *Professional Composer shows a number of symbol menus at the left of the screen (about half of the available menus are showing). The software offers such features as part extraction, rhythm and range checking, and PostScript compatibility. Music is entered by select-* *ing a symbol from the menu and then clicking at the desired location on the screen. Alternatively, Mark of the Unicorn's MIDI sequencing package Performer can be used to capture MIDI performance data for conversion into notation with Professional Composer.*

Fig. 20. *Concertware+ MIDI Version 4. Great Wave's notation package accepts note input using the symbol menu and mouse or directly from a MIDI keyboard. In the later case, an innovative implementation of quantization allows the user to specify a small set of* *rhythmic values that the program will use to assign to incoming data. This approach speeds up the conversion of MIDI performance data into notation and contributes to the user's perception of the program as a music-processor analogous to a word-processor.*

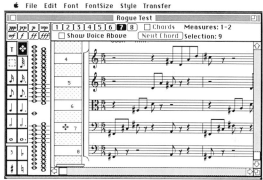

score. Alternatively, notes can be input with the mouse or played in real time on the Macintosh keyboard. Cut, copy, paste, search, and other standard commands are available. The speed with which Concertware+MIDI converts MIDI data into conventional music notation is unparalleled. Much of this speed comes from Concertware+MIDI's new type of quantization, which allows the user to preselect a set of rhythmic values to which the software will round off MIDI-supplied performance rhythms. With Version 4 of Concertware+MIDI, Great Wave introduced user control over the spacing between staves and systems, page, measure, and line breaks, brackets, braces, and clefs (figure 20). Nonetheless, the program's limitations on the number of staves (eight) and the number of vertical notes per part (eight), coupled with an incomplete symbol complement and the absence of part-extraction capabilities, place great restrictions upon its professional applications.

HB-Engraver

HB-Engraver, from HB-Imaging, includes many utilities distinctly aimed at the professional music-publishing industry. These features include utilities for bookkeeping, time-logging of editing prepara-

tion, and a "Tool Box" for configuring the default preferences of the printing routines to permit the hard-copy output to retain the individual "look and feel" of the engraving style associated with a particular publisher. As a second-generation product, besides stretching the specifications to fifty staves, with eight parts per staff and thirty notes per part, many new capabilities not found in other notation packages have been implemented (figure 21). These include merging of a text file with a music file for adding self-adjusting lyrics; complete independence of staff, note, and symbol size; complete support of "cautionary" symbols; support for gray-scale printing; fitting a piece of music into a given number of pages; numerous levels of front and back staff indentation; automatic system rebalance; absolute control over slurring, beaming, and stemming; creation of nonstandard symbols; and dropping of staves that do not contain music in a given system. One major innovation is a smart MIDI input interpreter that does not require performance to a computer-generated metronomic tick but, rather, applies post-determination of metrical data using pattern-recognition techniques to build a table of quantization values. This approach permits input MIDI performance data to include rubati, accelerandi, and ritardandi.

Fig. 21. HB Engraver. This is the system setup window for HB-Imaging's second-generation PostScript notation package. Here, one assigns voices to staves and determines the output size and gray-scale. Beneath this window, the note entry window is visible. While entering notes,

the user can view only a single staff at a time, and the noteheads are 20 pixels high. The advantage to this system is that mouse clicking doesn't have to be very accurate to get within the range of a desired 20-pixel area. Thus, mouse input speed is greatly increased.

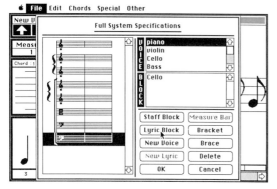

FINALE

Coda's FINALE is actually a front-end user interface to their ENIGMA engine (Environment for Notation utilizing Intuitive Graphic Music Algorithms). The ENIGMA kernel, which "understands" anything about music notation from the nineteenth century onward, offers portability to many makes and models of computers and can serve as a base technology for building a number of other programs. As a second-generation product, FINALE offers many of the features implemented in the other second-generation products but also permits an unlimited number of staves, the use of any complex or compound meter at any time, the defining of linear and nonlinear scale relationships, the use of MIDI-executable nonstandard shapes and symbols, automatic hyphenation placement for lyrics, the automatic calculation of chord symbols, and the intelligent assignment of sharps and flats.

Several innovations should be noted. In addition to the standard cut, copy, and paste editing operations, *hocketing* is included. Hocketing is a type of copying of a musical material that retains links to the fragment from which the copy was made, thus ensuring that changes in the source material are reflected in all the copies. While also utilizing post-determination of rhythms and durations as opposed to metronomic quantization, FINALE includes an *active keyboard split* facility that tracks individual musical parts as they are performed simultaneously on a MIDI keyboard, continually moving the bass-treble staff split point or adjusting the stemming and beaming to accurately correspond to the actual progress of each melodic line.

High Score

High Score by Notation Research is a MIDI post-processor for the conversion of MIDI data into publication-quality output using the Adobe Systems laser music font. Extensive graphic editing allows the placement of any PostScript character from any font at any place on the score. The program is designed to work in conjunction with Southworth Systems' MIDI sequencer package, MIDIPaint, which also includes a separate utility intended to convert all known MIDI file formats to the Southworth format needed by High Score. Because MIDI-Paint is compatible with the standard MIDI File format, the program can already function as a gateway to other popular packages that support MIDI Files. Conversion of MIDI data into High Score PostScript notation is a one-way process—there is no conversion back into MIDI data. (Kim Stickney, the creator of High Score, believes that there are so many important differences between the physical and logical representations of music that it is unrealistic to try to go back and forth between the two in a one-to-one correspondence.) The program works in three linked windows simultaneously, each displaying the data from a different viewpoint. The logical window displays an endless scroll of the notation. The physical window displays a bar graph of input MIDI data à la piano-roll notation. The graphical window is concerned with three types of formatting: score, parts, and transposed score. While other packages use three points in the determination of slur curves, High Score uses four "dragable" points for greater placement accuracy. Other features include arbitrary voice assigned to arbitrary staves and the ability to zoom (as if with a magnifying glass), with full editing capabilities at any of the zoom levels.

Nightingale

Advanced Music Notation systems Nightingale is a second-generation package developed by Donald Byrd, whom many consider to be the foremost authority on computer applications to music notation. Because it was the developer's intent to eventually accommodate all possible users and uses, the software is requiring a long development period. Like the other three second-generation products, Nightingale saves files in a number of different file formats for exporting to other software packages. Perhaps the most significant of these formats is the standard EPS (Encapsulated PostScript) format, which the laser printing service can print on the corner (regardless of whether the service owns the Nightingale software). EPS can be imported into any of the current PostScript graphics software packages for further fine tuning of the symbols.

For the Future: Instant "Intelligent" Notation Conversion

The above-described conversion of MIDI data into professional publishing-quality conventional music notation has been a two-stage process for the most part. MIDI data files are subsequently converted into a file, which may be read and modified by a notation editor. It is everyone's dream to create a system that will display music played on a MIDI keyboard instantly converted to notation on the computer screen, and there is serious development moving in that direction. As was mentioned above, Concertware+MIDI comes closest to the realization of this dream, but unfortunately at the sacrifice of other crucial features. Because all music data is contextual, it is likely that even near-instantaneous conversions of performance data into conventional music notation will require that barlines be reached before each next measure is displayed upon the screen.

Performance

After computers and synthesizers, MIDI sequencers are the most important element in a personal computer music setup. When MIDI first appeared, dedi-

cated hardware sequencers were common. Now it is more common to fulfill this function with sequencing software, which offers more power and flexibility, a better user interface, and easier updating than its hardware counterpart. Instead of sending a hardware sequencer back to the factory for the installation of new ROM chips, software-based sequence developers need merely send out an inexpensive diskette with the upgraded program on it.

Today, software sequencers are used not only to capture performance data or to assume the role of the master synchronizer with respect to a variety of sound-generating devices, but also to synchronize all other sorts of performance effects and to provide for the conversion of MIDI data into conventional music notation (either as an integrated module of the sequencing program or through built-in provisions for passing files between the specific sequencer and popular notation software).

MIDI Sequencing Editing and Synchronization: Performer

Mark of the Unicorn's Performer package is one of the most powerful software-based sequencers available. It includes a graphic emulation of a standard tape recorder, so its operation is intuitive (figure 22). It is possible to record over 300 polyphonic tracks, each of which can be displayed as a MIDI data stream in alphanumeric format showing measure number, beat number, fraction of the beat (or, alternatively, real time in minutes, seconds, and fractions of a second, or frame location—the latter designed for film music applications), event type and specific value, and (if the event is a note) the note name, note register, keystrike on-velocity, keystrike off-velocity, and duration (once again in measures, beats, and fractions). Any data can be edited at the level of a single event, or as a region of temporally contiguous events on a single track or group of n tracks. With Version 2, edit operations can be applied to temporally discontiguous events on a single track. Regions selected for editing may include constraints that define exactly which data subsequent edit operations will affect—for example, only notes within a specific on- or off-velocity ranges, notes within a given pitch range,

Fig. 22. Performer is a MIDI-software-based MIDI sequencer. At the top right of the screen, typical controls of a normal analog tape recorder are emulated. "Punch In" and "Memory Rewind" regions are indicated at the bottom of the controls. Additional interactive windows provide meter and tempo information, markers, and location in measures (with beat number and tick), real-time, and SMPTE frames. The "Tracks" window shows all current tracks. In this screen shot, the track "Upper Source" has been selected for editing. The center left window shows all events occurring on the track, their location, type of event, event parameters, and duration.

Fig. 23. MIDIPaint displays music in an endless scroll of "piano-roll" notation. Because the editing interface is similar to that of MacPaint and other popular graphics programs, the learning curve is greatly enhanced. The menu at the left of the screen provides tools for painting notes, erasing notes, zooming in and out to greater degrees of resolution, and editing any parameter to a given note. The software has been optimized to work with Southworth's own MIDI/ SMPTE interface, JamBox. In addition, the second-generation PostScript notation package High Score (also published by Southworth) is designed to take full advantage of MIDI-Paint and Jam Box.

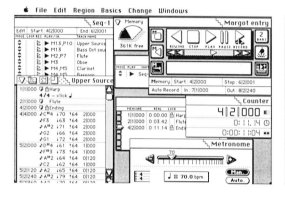

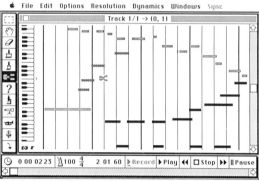

notes within a given durational range, or a specified number of part layers. Some Boolean operators (AND, NOT, OR, etc.) can be applied to these selection criteria to allow for the further zeroing in on specific data to be modified. Edit operations such as cut, copy, paste, transpose, invert, retrograde, or scale by ratio are common to many sequencers, but Performer provides such necessary editing operations as repeat (which repeats the selected region a user-specified number of times), snip (which slides data to close up a gap left by a cut operation), and splice (which slides data to open up a gap for a paste operation). It also offers the ability to set any MIDI data to a constant, to add or subtract a constant to any values, to multiply any data by a constant, to set minimum and maximum value limits, and to interpolate linearly or logorithmically between two values or two percentages over a time span. (This last effect, when applied to key on-velocity, produces the musical effect of crescendo or descrescendo while retaining the metrical accents of the prevailing meter—a smooth gradual increase or decrease in volume.) Regions of tracks can be looped, and loops can be nested within other loops to any depth. Performer's approach to quantization is metronome oriented, but it includes

many options for "humanizing" the playback to avoid the machine-like accuracy many people bemoan in MIDI sequencers. Abrupt and gradual tempo changes are easily stored with the performance data, and are accessible for editing. Finally, Performer provides the capability for converting its sequence files to the format used by Mark of the Unicorn's companion program, Professional Composer. This makes easy work of the conversion of MIDI data into conventional music notation. Changing meters, a major problem for many sequencers, is fully transportable back and forth between notation files and sequence files.

Many other excellent sequencers are available for the Apple Macintosh. All provide a high degree of interactive editing capabilities. Southworth's Total Music went so far as to provide a table-replacement editing function, which can be used to replace a selection of values relating to any musical parameter with those of a user-defined table. One might use such a table to create crescendi, descrescendi, changes of key or mode, or patterns of rhythmic accent. Southworth's newer MIDIPaint takes a graphic approach to editing (figure 23). Opcode's MIDIMAC Sequencer (figure 24) provides for the nesting of subsequences to n levels in a fashion analogous to

Fig. 24. MIDIMac Se-
quencer allows 26 se-
quences to be active at
once. These can be any
combination of sequences
recorded in real time or in
step time or generated.
The main list of sequences
is displayed in the upper
left corner of the screen.

Several of the individual
tracks' windows are open
on the left, including one
that has nested subse-
quences and one of the
generated variety. The controls at the bottom left of
the screen are set up to begin step-time recording.

Fig. 25. Master Tracks Pro
provides many of the fea-
tures of other packages
while adding an overview
that displays each mea-
sure of each track as a

little bar (a sort of "zoom-
out" effect, which greatly
increases editing speed),
and graphic editing on the
track level.

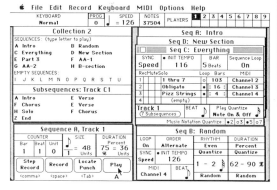

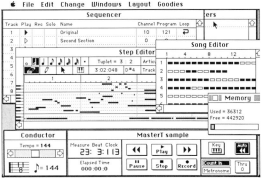

subroutines in a computer program. In deference to
the repetitive nature of music, the Steinberg Pro-24
sequencer software for the Atari computers implements a special type of copy command that keeps
the original data and the copies linked in such a
way that any changes to the original data are reflected in all the copies (this may be disabled). Passport Designs' Master Tracks Pro (figure 25) MIDI
sequencer provides many of the features of Mark of
the Unicorn's Performer and also includes an "overview," which displays each measure of each track
as a little bar (a sort of "zoom out" effect) and allows certain types of normally time-consuming editing operations to be accomplished at this level.

Direct-to-Hard-Disk, Digital Audio

The Dyaxis direct-to-hard-disk digital audio system
from Integrated Music Systems features 16-bit
stereo sampling at 258 sampling rates (256 different
rates derived by the computer and two others, 44.1
KHz and 48 KHz, which are crystal-derived). A 48-
KHz sampling rate provides 20-KHz frequency response in both channels with less than 0.01% distortion. This is equivalent to digital mastering
machines found at most professional recording studios, although the Dyaxis costs much less. Both the
44.1-KHz and the 48-KHz rate offer linear phase fil-

ters. The disk used is a SCSI hard disk (85 to 768
Mbytes) daisy-chained to a Macintosh microcomputer. The system can be set to have n tracks—
stereo playback and recording are directly supported, but once the data is inside the disk it may
be partitioned into as many channels as are needed.

Southworth Music Systems has released a similar
direct-to-hard-disk device at the same price. While
Dyaxis is a peripheral hardware device connected to
the computer via a SCSI link, Southworth's product
is an internal add-on board that connects to the internal NuBus of the Mac II. It uses four custom
chips plus a Motorola MC 56000 digital signal-
processing (DSP) chip running at 50 MHz (20 million instructions per second) with parallel processing to effectively increase processing time to 40
times faster than the Mac II. Other notable distinctions include a higher sampling rate and higher
resolution (20-bit stereo samples at 192 KHz for a
120-db signal-to-noise ratio), a 200-tap real-time filter with 200 associated graphical digital sliders, digital audio tape format in and out at 20-bit or 16-bit
resolution, and the fact that a dedicated hard disk is
not necessary. The user can create a partition on a
hard disk devoted to digital audio while still retaining the remainder of the hard disk for other applications. Finally, the Southworth product introduces
features that permit MIDI sequence tracks to be
synchronized to digital audio tracks and permit the
two media to be manipulated simultaneously.
Third-party developers are using the Southworth

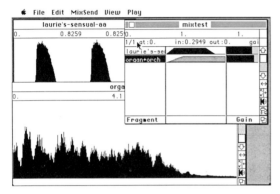

Board to create applications in sampling, harmonizing, Doppler shift, scientific research, pitch tracking, digital mixing, and digital effects processing.

Mixing Disk-Based Recordings: MacMix

Adrian Freed has created MacMix, a program for mixing soundfiles and tracks on the Dyaxis direct-to-hard-disk digital recorder. The object is to provide a graphic interface to mixing digital soundfiles that is powerful enough to fulfill or surpass the functions expected of a traditional analog mixing board (figure 26). Soundfiles (often equivalent to disk-based tracks) can be examined in a view window, with magnification ranging from the overall amplitude envelope lasting several seconds to individual samples. The view window provides timing information in seconds, samples, percents, or SMPTE time code. It also allows one to preview any sound. Besides *peak cue* indications of the largest sample in the window, *events of interest* can be marked with vertical tick marks and the linear breakpoint envelope superimposed upon the fragment. Mix windows are graphical cue sheet editors that display a graphic representation of the soundfiles or tracks. The temporal location of a soundfile can be changed by dragging the represen-

tative graphic with the mouse (the fade-in and fade-out points can also be mouse-adjusted). A gain control (amplitude) is provided for each soundfile. Cut, copy, and paste are fully implemented. Mixes, which may last from a few samples to several hours, can be auditioned along the way. Dan Timis of the University of California at Santa Barbara (and formerly of IRCAM) has ported a complete reimplementation of MacMix to the Sun Workstation. A graphic interface to add reverberation and time dilation within MacMix is being developed.

Other hard-disk-based recording systems include the Ariel and Waveframe systems (for IBM computers) and the Composer's Desktop Project and Audio + Design SoundMaestro for Atari computers.

Conclusions

"Meta-Composition"—"Hyper-Composition"

Macros were discussed in the section about telecommunications. More generic macro-creating utilities can be used to construct a music-creation environment that corresponds to one's personal methodology and increases efficiency and output. I use a macro generator called Tempo (there are no musical connotations implied by the program's name) to automate the more time-consuming activities associated with computer music. Tempo facilitates the creation of macros within the context of any software package, permitting numerous actions and decisions to be made by a single keystroke or by the mere result of another operation. Tempo's ability to conditionally branch from one macro to another based upon the state of specified conditions or to repeat a macro while certain conditions are met creates a powerful automation tool for anyone using a microcomputer.

My macro, Music Slave, is really seven modular Tempo macros, each consisting of dozens of tiny condition-dependent, repeating, and branching macros. After a day's work, when numerous MIDI sequences have been created and saved to the hard disk, a single keystroke initiates Music Slave, which then goes on to process the MIDI sequences through the night. First, all the day's sequences in their current state are copied and archived to a separate partition of the hard disk. Next, the files are opened one after another. While the files are open, each track of each file is quantized to the appropriate durational value. The files are all converted to notation and then reopened with the notation software. The scores are examined for clef discrepancies, and if such discrepancies are discovered the appropriate clefs are substituted. Systems are bracketed at this point, and the number of staves per system is used by the macro to determine the appropriate printing reduction for maximum page coverage. Then, one by one, the notated scores are printed by the laser printer. Parts are extracted as well if certain flags are set. If the macro finishes its work before 4:30 A.M. (when certain online charges go to the full rates), it dials my electronic mail service and downloads any mail it finds on the network. This mail is also automatically printed by the laser printer (a disk copy is maintained). Any files that the macro finds in an area of the hard disk labeled "to upload," it sends to the specified electronic mail address. Last but not least, the macro opens my computer-based "appointment diary" and prints out my appointment list for the day. All this activity occurs while I am asleep. When I awake, I find in my laser printer's tray printed scores of all the previous day's MIDI sequences, any electronic mail I received during the night, and on top of the whole stack of printout a sheet listing the times and natures of the current day's appointments.

The Future is Now

The convergence of major breakthroughs in four areas of the microcomputer music scene is affecting the music industry in ways that are comparable to the effects of the invention of the printing press. These four factors are second-generation notation software, second-generation sound-generating devices with polyphonic capabilities, inexpensive direct-to-hard-disk digital audio recording, and object-oriented programming.

With the arrival of second-generation score editing, any home studio can expect to produce publishing-quality manuscripts. With the development of inexpensive professional modular samplers, one can easily assemble a personal "orchestra in a box" consisting of 84 or more players. With the introduction of direct-to-hard-disk digital audio and the digital audio tape (DAT) format, the average composer/musician can count on CD-quality recording of every note and sound. Finally, with the commercial release of such object-oriented programming environments as Apple's Hypercard, anyone, regardless of how computer-literate he might be, can construct sophisticated programs tailored to his own unique applications and needs (Yavelow 1986c).

Microcomputers communicating with sound-generating devices via MIDI and other protocols are affecting music-making in a great number of ways, many of which have been discussed above. For composers, the most important feature offered by these tools may be the immediate opportunity to hear, in real time, a rendition of a complex work—a rendition that, because of tempo, rhythmic complexity, or the sheer number of simultaneous interdependent parts, would otherwise be possible only in an actual performance. The capability of having a score of one's work printed automatically at almost no cost with quality equalling that of history's greatest engravers, coupled with the capability of using the same computer-produced score to control a personal orchestra of sound-generating devices and capturing the entire performance on tape or hard disk at CD quality, completes the musical communication circle: that of making one's music accessible to others. We are certainly at the beginning of what is proving to be one of the most interesting and creative periods in the history of music-making.

References

Allik, Kristi, Shane Dunne, and Robert Mulder. 1986. "Arconet: A Proposal for a Standard Network for Communications and Control in Real-Time Performance." In P. Berg, ed. *Proceedings of the 1986 International Computer Music Conference* (San Francisco: Computer Music Association).

Ames, C. 1987. "Automated Composition in Retrospect: 1956–1986." *Leonardo* 20(2): 169–186.

Byrd, Donald, and Christopher Yavelow. 1986. "The Kurzweil 250 Digital Synthesizer." *Computer Music Journal* 10(1): 64–86.

Chadabe, J., and D. Zicarelli. 1986a. *JAM Factory—The Improvisation and Live Performance Processor.* Albany: Intelligent Computer Music Systems.

Chadabe, J., and D. Zicarelli. 1986b. *M—The Interactive Composing and Performing System.* Albany: Intelligent Computer Music Systems.

Hofstadter, D. 1979. *Gödel, Escher, Bach: An Eternal Golden Braid.* New York: Basic Books.

IMA. 1983. "The MIDI Manufacturers Association Technical Standards Board. MIDI 1.0 Detailed Specification." North Hollywood: International MIDI Association.

Kurzweil, Ray. 1987. *The Age of Intelligent Machines.* Cambridge, Mass.: MIT Press.

Levitt, David. 1985. "A Representation of Musical Dialects." Sc.D. dissertation, Department of Electrical Engineering and Computer Science, MIT.

Moog, Robert A. 1986. "MIDI: Musical Digital Interface." *Journal of the Audio Engineering Society* 34(5): 394–404.

Pope, Stephen T. 1986. "The Development of an Intelligent Composer's Assistant—Interactive Graphic Tools and Knowledge Representation for Music (or: Thoughts about Music Input Languages: Several Generations of MILs and Orchestra/Score Editors)." In P. Berg, ed., *Proceedings of the 1986 International Computer Music Conference* (San Francisco: Computer Music Association).

Roads, C. 1986. "The Second STEIM Symposium on Interactive Composition in Live Electronic Music." *Computer Music Journal* 10(2): 44–50.

Spiegel, L. 1986. *Music Mouse—An Intelligent Instrument.* New York: Laurie Spiegel.

Wergo. 1987. *New Computer Music.* Compact disk WER 2010-50. Mainz: Wergo Schallplatten.

Yavelow, Christopher. 1986a. "From Keyboard to Score." *Macworld* 3(12): 108–117.

Yavelow, Christopher. 1986b. "MIDI and the Apple Macintosh." *Computer Music Journal* 10(3): 11–47.

Yavelow, Christopher. 1986c. "The Impact of MIDI Upon Compositional Methodology." In P. Berg, ed., *Proceedings of the 1986 International Computer Music Conference* (San Francisco: Computer Music Association).

Yavelow, Christopher. 1987. "Personal Computers and Music—The State of the Art." *Journal of the Audio Engineering Society* 35(3): 160–193.

IV

Music Software

Curtis Roads

Overview

The first-generation computer music systems were oriented around *batch* technology. Batch-oriented computers ran just one program (one batch) at a time. The program was typed on punched cards or paper tape, and then fed into the computer by a computer operator. Most early computer music software ran overnight, and the programmer picked up the result the next day.

The 1970s saw a shift to *timesharing* systems. A timesharing system works on many programs at a time by doing a little bit on each and switching between them rapidly. Such systems, exemplified by the Unix operating system introduced in the mid-1970s, permitted interactive program development and the first *real-time* music applications. (A real-time system responds with little or no delay.) Many early experiments in automated music printing were also based on large timesharing computer systems—for example, Leland Smith's MSS system at Stanford University and Donald Byrd's SMUT (System for Music Translation) program, originally developed at the University of Indiana (Byrd 1977, 1984).

By the mid-1980s personal computing had taken over, and today music editing and scoring programs abound. While the print quality and the layout do not always match those produced by a skilled traditional music engraver, the convenience of editing, automatic part extraction, and autocorrection built into these programs often outweighs such concerns. The linkage of computers to synthesizers via the Musical Instrumental Digital Interface (MIDI) means that real-time synthesis can be built into virtually any music application software.

This part of the book covers the six main areas of music software applications: score editing, music printing, timbre editing, computer-assisted composition, control of real-time synthesizers, and digital audio editing.

Score editing is a practical application that has received a great deal of attention in recent years. In article 21, Roads summarizes the results achieved in the landmark Mockingbird system developed at the Xerox Palo Alto Research Center by Ornstein and Maxwell, and cites other research. In article 22, Jim Miller details the features of his popular IBM

Personal Composer system for editing, sequencing, and music printing.

In article 23, William Buxton and his colleagues at the University of Toronto point out the difficult problems of specifying the scope of a score editing operation such as "delete." Consider the command "Delete all non-flute notes that have a duration less than a quarter note." A human assistant would have no trouble understanding such a directive, but how do we convey it to a computer? Buxton's group proposes the use of database-type command strings as a partial solution to the problem. An earlier paper by the same group (Buxton et al. 1979) attacked the problem from a graphical angle—the user draws a circle around the notes or "taps" them with the cursor to specify scope. This is a useful method as long as the intended scope does not extend beyond what can be displayed on a single screenful.

Several of the articles in this part deal with the software that links computers with special-purpose synthesis hardware. The software described by Abbott (article 28), Loy (article 29), and Schottstaedt (article 26) was essentially completed by the time the MIDI standard was introduced. However, the lessons learned in these projects provide a foundation for today's interfaces. The scheduling and system-programming issues described by Abbott and Loy, for example, are dealt with today by microprocessors embedded in commercial digital synthesizers. In effect, MIDI messages sent into a synthesizer constitute a higher-level protocol grafted onto the low-level processing described by Abbott and Loy.

It is also important to realize that the synthesis engines programmed by Abbott and Loy were relatively general digital signal processors (DSPs), in contrast to the limited-function synthesis engines embedded in some of today's commercial synthesizers. For example, many *frequency modulation* (FM) synthesizers, such as the Yamaha DX series, can do only FM, because the circuitry was designed expressly for that method. A music system based on a general-purpose DSP chip is capable of many different synthesis methods. However, the challenge of flexibly controlling DSP engines is greater than that posed by the control of a limited-function synthesizer. With the availability of powerful DSP chips, the question of flexible software control returns to the top of the programming agenda.

Addressing these issues, Schottstaedt (article 26) and Rodet and Cointe (article 33) describe languages for the specification of complex musical processes. In Schottstaedt's Pla system, a composition is created out of the activity of several interacting *voice objects*. A voice object is a software construct that encapsulates an instrument and its parameter settings. Computation occurs as a result of sending *messages* to objects, such as a "start playing" message to a voice object (Krasner 1980; Lieberman 1982). In the FORMES system (article 33), the basic unit is a *phrase object* representing a group of events (notes) and a set of related envelopes that shape the phrase.

A major benefit of an *object-oriented* system is that it is highly modular, so that programming complexity is reduced. Both Pla and FORMES provide mechanisms for "high-level" music specification; that is, the user does not have to specify every detail of compositional architecture, since automatic routines "fill in" the outlines specified by the composer. In Pla and FORMES these routines are largely deterministic, but many composers are also interested in *stochastic* systems that incorporate randomness. Lorrain's article (30) is a catalog of stochastic algorithms that can be built into music systems. Jones's article (31) combines stochastic procedures with the notion of a *formal grammar*— a set of rules for expanding a shorthand specification of musical structure into a large-scale form (Roads 1985a).

Perhaps the ultimate formalism for musical specification is a full-fledged programming language, such as Lisp, C, Smalltalk, or Forth, all of which have been used to this end. A current trend is to create an *environment* or *microworld*, consisting of a collection of musical procedures and data structures, that lets musicians "roll their own" musical processes through interactive programming (see article 27, Boynton et al. 1986, Polansky et al. 1987, and Dannenberg 1986). In such environments,

invoking a procedure causes a musical "side effect"—sound is generated or another musical action is performed, so programming is composing. As John Chowning has noted, inspiration can derive much from the interaction among composer, language, and computer (Roads 1985b).

References

Boynton, L., P. Lavoie, Y. Orlarey, C. Rueda, and D. Wessel. 1986. "MIDI-Lisp, A Lisp-based Music Programming Environment for the Macintosh." In P. Berg, ed., *Proceedings of the 1986 International Computer Music Conference* (San Francisco: Computer Music Association).

Buxton, W., S. Sniderman, W. Reeves, S. Patel, and R. Baecker. 1979. "The Evolution of the SSSP Score-editing Tools." *Computer Music Journal* 3(4): 14–25. Reprinted in C. Roads and J. Strawn, eds., *Foundations of Computer Music* (Cambridge, Mass.: MIT Press, 1985).

Byrd, D. 1977. "An integrated computer music software system." *Computer Musical Journal* 1(2): 55–60.

Byrd, D. 1984. "Music Notation by Computer." Ph.D. dissertation, Department of Computer Science, Indiana University, Bloomington.

Dannenberg, R. 1986. "The CMU MIDI Toolkit." In P. Berg, ed., *Proceedings of the 1986 International Computer Music Conference* (San Francisco: Computer Music Association).

Krasner, G. 1980. "Machine Tongues VIII: The Design of a Smalltalk Music System." *Computer Music Journal* 4(4): 4–14.

Lieberman, H. 1982. "Machine Tongues IX: Object-oriented Programming." *Computer Music Journal* 6(3): 8–21.

Polansky, L., D. Rosenboom, and P. Burk. 1987. "HMSL: Overview (Version 3.1) and Notes on Intelligent Instrument Design." In J. Beauchamp, ed., *Proceedings of the 1987 International Computer Music Conference* (San Francisco: Computer Music Association).

Roads, C. 1985a. "Grammars as Representations for Music." In C. Roads and J. Strawn, eds., *Foundations of Computer Music* (Cambridge, Mass.: MIT Press).

Roads, C. 1985b. "John Chowning on Composition." In C. Roads, ed., *Composers and the Computer* (Los Altos: Kaufmann).

21

C. Roads

A Note on Music Printing by Computer

Music printing by computer began with the control of a limited music typewriter (Hiller 1965; Dal Molin 1975) and has evolved by means of a variety of output devices. These include digitally controlled *x-y* plotters (Smith 1973; *Computer Music Journal* 1979), photographic devices and, recently, laser-scanned photocopier-type machines. Readers of *Computer Music Journal* have seen the excellent-quality automated music printing made available to us by Professor Leland Smith at Stanford University. (See, for example, the music on pages 49, 50, 51, and 56 of *Computer Music Journal* 5[2].) This system is highly regarded for its notational flexibility. The covers of issues 4(2) and 4(3) of *Computer Music Journal* displayed examples from another system, MUZACS. The examples demonstrate the first phase of development of this music editor, developed by William Kornfeld at the Massachusetts Institute of Technology (M.I.T.) Artificial Intelligence Laboratory. In MUZACS, images can be displayed on a Lisp Machine screen or printed out on a Xerox Graphics Printer.

Another current sample of computerized music printing has come to our attention (Fig. 1). This image is a product of the Mockingbird music-editing system designed and built at the Xerox Palo Alto Research Centers (PARC) by Severo Ornstein and his associates. The Mockingbird system runs on a Dorado computer, a powerful personal system based on high-resolution graphics and an Ethernet connection to other machines. The Dorado was also developed at Xerox PARC. The purpose of the Mockingbird music system is, according to Mr. Ornstein, "to investigate interactive tools applied to the problem of composing music" (Ornstein 1981). Music can be entered into the system directly by playing on a Yamaha synthesizer keyboard attached to the Dorado. Alternatively, powerful interactive graphics-input tools are available. As the score is built up, its current image appears on the Dorado's screen, where it can be scrolled, cut and pasted, and amended. The score can also be played back or printed. The Mockingbird editor recognizes and interprets such things as ties, embellishments, transpositions, clef switches, and octava notation, so that the music will be properly displayed and auditioned. Various music staff arrangements are available, and separate parts can be printed.

Mr. Ornstein says, "The main interest of the system is in the powerful graphical tools which give the feeling of easy control over the score" (Ornstein 1981). As Mockingbird was designed to be primarily a music editor, Mr. Ornstein points out that, "The fact that scores produced by the system are 'pretty' is not the main purpose of the work. Nonetheless, all horizontal positioning of every item in the score is automatically done—there is no 'hand' adjustment. The user can designate a desired level of horizontal 'density,' but with that as a guideline, justification of measures to lines, positioning of accidentals and notes, etc. is all done automatically in just a second or two for the entire piece" (Ornstein 1981). So far, Mockingbird has produced only common music-notation examples, and it is not clear that it will be extended beyond this level. The complexities of computer music notation and editing tackled by such researchers as Wallraff (1978) and Buxton and his associates (1979) are ignored in Mockingbird. But in case you are wondering just what Fig. 1 represents, Mr. Ornstein says, "That music, by the way, is the opening of a piano sonata of my father's [Leo Ornstein]—and of course it has a mistake in it" (Ornstein 1981).

We are sure it can be easily corrected.

Computer Music Journal, Vol. 5, No. 3, Fall 1981

Fig. 1. Image produced by the Mockingbird music editor.

References

Buxton, W. et al. 1979. "The Evolution of the SSSP Score Editing Tools." *Computer Music Journal* 3(4) : 14–25.

Computer Music Journal. 1979. "Music Printing: Dataland's Scan-note System." *Computer Music Journal* 3(1) : 60–61.

Dal Molin, A. 1975. "The X-Y Typewriters and Their Application as Input Terminals for the Computer." In *Proceedings of the Second Annual Music Computation Conference*, part 4, ed. J. Beauchamp and J. Melby. Urbana, Illinois: University of Illinois Office of Continuing Education, pp. 28–53.

Hiller, L. 1965. "Automated Music Printing." *Journal of Music Theory* 9 : 129–150.

Ornstein, S. 1981. Personal communication.

Smith, L. 1973. "Editing and Printing Music by Computer." *Journal of Music Theory* 17 : 292–309.

Wallraff, D. 1978. "NEDIT—A Graphical Editor for Musical Scores." In *Proceedings of the 1978 International Computer Music Conference*, vol. 2, ed. C. Roads. Evanston, Illinois: Northwestern University Press, pp. 410–429.

22

Jim Miller

14080 Edgewater Lane NE
Seattle, Washington 98125 USA

Personal Composer

Introduction

Personal Composer is an IBM-PC-based integrated
software package for music processing. The package
provides a complete set of MIDI (Musical Instrument Digital Interface) (IMA 1983) tools, including
(1) a high-resolution music manuscript editor, (2) a
32-track MIDI multifunction recorder, and (3) a librarian and frequency-modulation (FM) synthesizer
(Chowning 1973) voice editor.

These tools are used to automate or aid in working through the many time-consuming details in
the compositional process. The musician has more
time for creativity and can experiment quickly
using the sonic feedback from the MIDI equipment
connected to the computer.

The composer can capture real-time recordings
from a synthesizer or produce sequences using the
graphically oriented notation editor. Sequences can
be played, overdubbed, or converted back into music manuscript. Manuscript can include lyrics and
can be printed in sheet music form.

Personal Composer also supports archiving of any
MIDI synthesizer voices (patches) and Yamaha DX
and TX synthesizer voicing. midiGraphics™ allows
the musician to design custom symbols and associate them with a MIDI sequence for playback control of any MIDI parameter.

Hardware Supported by Personal Composer

Personal Composer runs on the IBM-PC, IBM-XT,
and IBM-AT personal computers and strict IBM
compatibles. It requires 320-640 Kbytes of random-
access-memory (RAM) and one or more floppy or
hard disk drives. The graphics resolution of the music manuscript editor is 720 by 348 pixels with the
Hercules monochrome graphics adapter, and 640 by
350 by 16 colors when using the IBM Enhanced
Graphics Adapter (EGA). An Epson FX-80 dot-

matrix printer is used for music printing. A Roland
MPU-401 provides the MIDI interface, the metronome, and the synchronization pulse (sync) to tape.
A MicroSoft Mouse is useful for menu-driven manuscript editing, although the IBM keyboard suffices
for mnemonic command input.

A studio setup can become quite sophisticated
with the addition of other hardware. The sync-to-
tape will interface to any multitrack analog or
digital tape recorder. Through MIDI the Roland
SBX-80 allows Society of Motion Picture and Television Engineers (SMPTE) standard time code synchronization for capstan control of tape recorders.
Tape is useful for recording acoustic instruments
and vocals which, upon playback, can slave Personal
Composer for synchronization with the MIDI-
driven synthesizers.

Any number of MIDI synthesizers can be controlled by Personal Composer, with up to 16 discrete MIDI channels per MPU-401. The many synthesizers available provide analog synthesis, FM,
and digitally recorded voices. Also, many MIDI
effects devices are available such as digital delays
and reverberators, all of which can be controlled
during the score playback.

Personal Composer Modes

With Personal Composer, music is composed in
two ways: graphically using common music notation, and in real time by playing a clavier and using
the 32-track sequencer. These are two of five modes
(subsystems) within Personal Composer (EDIT mode
and RECORDER mode respectively). Each of the
five modes has its own user interface and internal
database. The three remaining modes are LIBRAR-
IAN mode, CHANNEL NAME mode, and MIDI-
GRAPHICS mode.

EDIT Mode

Using a mouse or the IBM keyboard, composers
score music in EDIT mode as if they were using a
pencil. Scoring for vocal, orchestral, piano, and per-

cussion is supported with up to 64 staves in parallel. Music notation symbols all affect the MIDI sequence appropriately upon playback. Figure 1 illustrates many of these symbols.

When using a MicroSoft Mouse, the right mouse button invokes a pop-up menu. The cursor is moved to the appropriate icon, and a second press of the mouse button selects the icon and hides the menu. The left mouse button is then used to place the icon (a note, rest, etc.) into the score.

A mouse is not necessary for manuscript editing. The IBM keyboard can be used just as efficiently for manuscript editing if the user is a touch typist. All EDIT mode commands are two-character mnemonics and are listed in Table 1. Possible second-keystroke responses are given on the bottom menu-line. The menu-line format is:

⟨filename⟩ p:⟨page#⟩ s:⟨scroll#⟩ ⟨prompt and menu area⟩.

On the menu-line, *page#* refers to one of 99 monitor screens, left to right. *scroll#* refers to one of 99 vertical monitor half-screens. This provides a large virtual "sheet of paper" for the manuscript.

EDIT mode commands are toggle commands. That is, if a command is given such as "no" for note, and a note is already underneath the cursor, the note will delete instead of appear. Also, commands such as "oc" (octave) and "tr" (triplet) generally affect flags-up or flags-down depending upon their placement above or below a staff respectively. The entire system is case-sensitive.

Figure 2 depicts part of Bach's *Mass in B minor No. 16*, "Crucifixus," where the vocal parts have been merged and replaced for playback by a string part.

Figure 3 demonstrates a larger orchestral score page using percussion and a digital delay (intended to automatically set up delay effects for an electronic guitar).

MIDIGRAPHICS Mode

Icons not defined within EDIT mode can be user-designed using another subsystem: midiGraphics. This mode is entered using the "mg" command from the EDIT mode. A two-letter mnemonic is required to identify the icon. This extends the EDIT mode command language, allowing placement of midiGraphs on staves when the mnemonic is entered.

Figure 4 shows the midiGraphics user interface for icon design. Grid squares are toggled by typing an "x" with the cursor in the desired square. This toggles a pixel in the midiGraph. In this example, an arrow has been designed. Notice it is shown to scale to the right of the grid. It has been named "ar," which becomes an extension of the 'a'-commands available in EDIT mode.

The ZAP command reinitializes (zaps) the entire state of midiGraphics to start anew. ERASE is used to erase any part or all of the current midiGraph. The NAME command can be used to rename the current midiGraph or change to another midiGraph.

Fig. 2. Excerpt from J. S.
Bach's Mass in B Minor,
scored for synthesizer
voices and printed with
Personal Composer.

TEXT can be used to associate text with or completely replace the graphical font.

The MACRO command is used to assign any MIDI sequence to the midiGraph. This constitutes an action-oriented, graphically-based MIDI programming language capable of note sequences (motifs, drum patterns, etc.) or any other sequence, including *system-exclusive* MIDI data (IMA 1983; Droman 1984; Loy 1985).

EXIT quits midiGraphic mode and returns the user to EDIT mode.

RECORDER Mode

The 32-track sequence recorder is entered using the "rc" EDIT mode command. RECORDER mode is used to make multitrack sequencer recordings

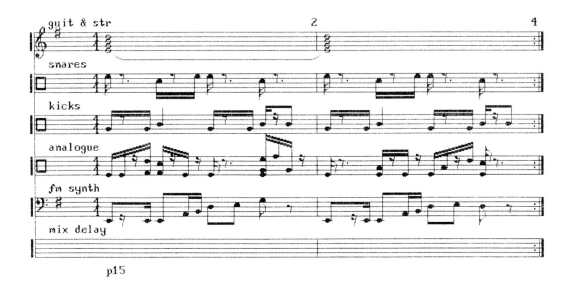

Fig. 3. Orchestral-type score page excerpt scored for synthesizer voices with stave for digital delay.

of any MIDI device capable of sending MIDI data while being played. MIDI keyboard synthesizers, MIDI guitars, MIDI drums, MIDI voice, and wind instrument transducers are all available for this purpose.

Figure 5 shows the 32-track MIDI RECORDER interface. The 32 tracks are separated into 2 groups of 16 to fit on the screen. Notice that tracks 1–3 are shown in reverse video, indicating that these tracks have been recorded. Tracks can be overdubbed any number of times with any combination of MIDI channels.

Under each track there are five control fields. The top three are used to control playback quantization (rhythmic autocorrection). Q FACTOR is the quantization note value ranging from 4 (quarter-note) and 4T (quarter-note triplet) to 32 (32nd-note), or OFF. Q DOMAIN selects the domain of the quantization; "O/x" quantizes only note-on events, and "O/o" quantizes both note-on and note-off events. Q TOLERANCE positions the boundary between the Q FACTOR quantum unit, where 50% is dead center. In Fig. 5 only track 1 is being quantized, using a 16th-note quantum unit, quantizing both

note-on and note-off events, with the quantum boundary moved forward in time by 25% of a 16th note (the current Q FACTOR).

The remaining three fields control playback level and channel. FADER provides an overall volume scaling, useful for MIDI mixing. A FADER value of 0 is the same as mute. PORT forces output through a specific MPU-401 (1 of 4, when supported by Roland). CHANNEL forces output to a specific MIDI channel, regardless of the original event channels. In Fig. 5 track 2 is set below half-volume and is being forced out channel 1. All other tracks play on the MIDI channels on which they were recorded.

Figure 5 also shows command fields below the 32-track fields. The far left command column is used to control the recording process, the middle column controls playback, and the far right column controls timing, synchronization, and miscellaneous, with memory and measure quantity status below.

PLAY starts playback if recorded tracks exist. It records if RECORD is ON, beginning with a measure lead-in from the 1ST MEAS value until the LAST MEAS value. If LOOPING is ON, playback

Fig. 4. midiGraphics design example.

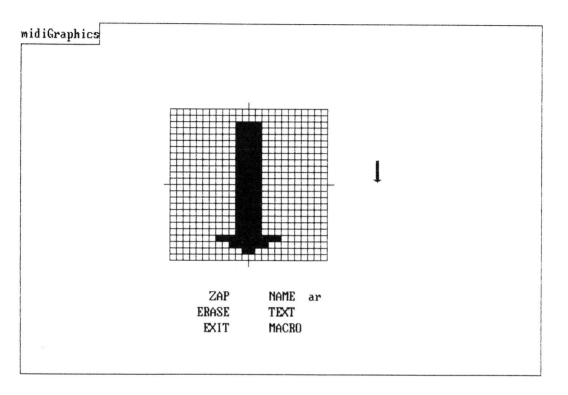

cycles continually between these limits until a key is struck on the IBM keyboard. Figure 5 shows that eight measures (see lower status area) will loop from start to finish, since 1ST MEAS = 1 and LAST MEAS is OFF. During playback the METRONOME will beat in 4/4 time with a tempo of 100 as indicated in the far right column. CONTINUE is the same as PLAY but resumes where playback was last interrupted.

When RECORD is ON during the playback process, synthesizer input is recorded. Recording parameters are controlled by the lowercase commands available below the RECORD command. Figure 5 shows that track# 4 is ready to record. Recorded MIDI data will be assigned to port# 1, channel# 4. Only NOTE-on/off and PROGRAM change (patch) information will be recorded. CONTROL, PRESSURE, and PITCHBEND information will be filtered. If, however, CONTROL were ON, only the MIDI controllers enabled by the CONTROLLER page shown in Fig. 6 would record. The only controller enabled in Fig. 6 is 64, corresponding to the sustain pedal for the particular synthesizer being used. Specific control of each controller is necessary due to their nonstandardization across different synthesizer lines.

The remaining commands in the middle command column of Fig. 5 are BOUNCE, ERASE, and GRAPHICS. These commands, like PLAY, use the 1ST and LAST MEAS limits for their actions. BOUNCE allows copying of any track to any other track with a possible channel change en route. ERASE is also track specific.

GRAPHICS produces a graphical representation of the recorder tracks in EDIT mode. After conversion to graphics, 32nd-notes, triplets, pentuplets,

Fig. 5. RECORDER mode
screen image.

```
RECORDER
              1     2     3     4     5     6     7     8     9    10    11    12    13    14    15    16
 Q FACTOR    16   OFF   OFF   OFF   OFF   OFF   OFF   OFF   OFF   OFF   OFF   OFF   OFF   OFF   OFF   OFF
   DOMAIN   0/o   0/x   0/x   0/x   0/x   0/x   0/x   0/x   0/x   0/x   0/x   0/x   0/x   0/x   0/x   0/x
TOLERANCE  25%   50%   50%   50%   50%   50%   50%   50%   50%   50%   50%   50%   50%   50%   50%   50%
    FADER     6     4     9    10    10    10    10    10    10    10    10    10    10    10    10    10
     PORT           1
  CHANNEL           1

             17    18    19    20    21    22    23    24    25    26    27    28    29    30    31    32
 Q FACTOR   OFF   OFF   OFF   OFF   OFF   OFF   OFF   OFF   OFF   OFF   OFF   OFF   OFF   OFF   OFF   OFF
   DOMAIN   0/x   0/x   0/x   0/x   0/x   0/x   0/x   0/x   0/x   0/x   0/x   0/x   0/x   0/x   0/x   0/x
TOLERANCE  50%   50%   50%   50%   50%   50%   50%   50%   50%   50%   50%   50%   50%   50%   50%   50%
    FADER    10    10    10    10    10    10    10    10    10    10    10    10    10    10    10    10
     PORT
  CHANNEL

  RECORD  ON          PLAY              TIME SIG 4/4
   track# 4           CONTINUE          TEMPO 100
 channel# 4           METRONOME ON   MIDI THRU ON
    port# 1           1ST MEAS 1         SYNC INTERNAL
    notes ON          LAST MEAS OFF      EXIT
  control OFF         LOOPING ON         ZAP
  program ON          BOUNCE
 pressure OFF         ERASE          232 bytes (2%) used
pitchbend OFF         GRAPHICS       8 measures
```

and other icons are edited. Graphical staves can be merged back into the recorder or can replace the recorded tracks.

Finally, MIDI THRU, if ON, passes keyboard input directly to the output, allowing use of a keyboard controller driving another synthesizer via the MPU-401, which can tap the input during recording. SYNC allows INTERNAL, TAPE, MIDI CLOCK, or SMPTE (via the Roland SBX-80) synchronization. ZAP reinitializes the recorder, and EXIT quits RECORDER mode and returns to EDIT mode.

CHANNEL NAMES Mode

This mode is entered using the "cn" command from the EDIT mode. It is used to convert recorded tracks to manuscript and vice versa. CHANNEL

MODE features give some flexibility in determining how tracks are assigned to staves when converting recorded tracks into a score. It also determines how staves of the score are assigned to MIDI channels on tracks of the recorder when merging the score back into the recorded tracks.

Up to 32 tracks are available in the recorder, and up to 16 channels are available over MIDI. Up to 64 staves can appear in the score. A recorder track can have up to 16 MIDI channels of information on it. An EDIT mode staff can represent up to two MIDI channels (one channel for stems-up, and one for stems-down). To minimize confusion and still retain flexibility, the CHANNEL NAMES mode is used to establish a correspondence between these musical representations.

Figure 7 shows the CHANNEL NAMES interface. The 16 MIDI channels are listed vertically at the far left. For each channel there are eight fields. NAME

Fig. 6. CONTROLLER page
screen image.

```
CONTROLLER

 EXIT    0  OFF  16  OFF  32  OFF  48  OFF  64  ON   80  OFF  96  OFF  112 OFF
         1  OFF  17  OFF  33  OFF  49  OFF  65  OFF  81  OFF  97  OFF  113 OFF
         2  OFF  18  OFF  34  OFF  50  OFF  66  OFF  82  OFF  98  OFF  114 OFF
         3  OFF  19  OFF  35  OFF  51  OFF  67  OFF  83  OFF  99  OFF  115 OFF
         4  OFF  20  OFF  36  OFF  52  OFF  68  OFF  84  OFF  100 OFF  116 OFF
         5  OFF  21  OFF  37  OFF  53  OFF  69  OFF  85  OFF  101 OFF  117 OFF
         6  OFF  22  OFF  38  OFF  54  OFF  70  OFF  86  OFF  102 OFF  118 OFF
         7  OFF  23  OFF  39  OFF  55  OFF  71  OFF  87  OFF  103 OFF  119 OFF
         8  OFF  24  OFF  40  OFF  56  OFF  72  OFF  88  OFF  104 OFF  120 OFF
         9  OFF  25  OFF  41  OFF  57  OFF  73  OFF  89  OFF  105 OFF  121 OFF
        10  OFF  26  OFF  42  OFF  58  OFF  74  OFF  90  OFF  106 OFF  122 OFF
        11  OFF  27  OFF  43  OFF  59  OFF  75  OFF  91  OFF  107 OFF  123 OFF
        12  OFF  28  OFF  44  OFF  60  OFF  76  OFF  92  OFF  108 OFF  124 OFF
        13  OFF  29  OFF  45  OFF  61  OFF  77  OFF  93  OFF  109 OFF  125 OFF
        14  OFF  30  OFF  46  OFF  62  OFF  78  OFF  94  OFF  110 OFF  126 OFF
        15  OFF  31  OFF  47  OFF  63  OFF  79  OFF  95  OFF  111 OFF  127 OFF
```

is a label that automatically appears at the top left of each staff assigned to the MIDI channel. In Fig. 7, MIDI channel 16 is labelled "SDS5," a Simmons Drum Synthesizer mnemonic. As long as the NAME's command at the right of the CHANNEL NAMES pages is turned ON, all staves on MIDI channel 16 appearing in EDIT mode will be labelled "SDS5."

The next field is XPS allowing a playback transposition factor for the MIDI channel. Figure 7 shows MIDI channel 16 being transposed down 28 semitones.

The next two fields assign MIDI controller values to the volume controller (VOL) and sustain pedal (PED) respectively. In Fig. 7, channels 1–3 are all assigned according to the Yamaha DX/TX series conventions. If a volume controller value is 0, all volume markings (ppp–fff, cresc., dim.) affect note key velocity instead of issuing volume controller

markings. If a sustain pedal value is 0, pedal markings on staves are ignored during playback.

The TRK field shown in Fig. 7 controls the target track number in the 32-track recorder to which graphical staves are compiled. Here channels 17–32 are being used to receive the note list compiled from the graphical staves on channels 1–16 respectively. It may be convenient to reserve tracks 1–16 for recordings, and tracks 17–32 for merging from graphics as was done in this example.

The last three fields affect the conversion to graphics process initiated in RECORDER mode. CLF determines the clef type of the staff to which the MIDI channel will convert (a=alto, b=bass, t=treble, T=tenor, p=piano). DIS gives the distance to the next channel's staff in pixels. SPL is used to give a split point between the treble and bass staves if a piano staff is used. If the SPL value is 0 when using a piano staff, an automatic splitting algo-

Fig. 7. CHANNEL NAMES
screen image.

CHAN NAMES	NAME	XPS	VOL	PED	TRK	CLF	DIS	SPL		
1	DX7	0	7	64	17	b	45	0	MEASURE#s	ON
2	TX216/1	0	7	64	18	t	45	0	PROGRAM's	OFF
3	TX216/2	0	7	64	19	t	45	0	NAME's	ON
4	JX8P/1	0	0	0	20	b	45	0	EXIT	
5	JX8P/2	0	0	0	21	p	45	60		
6	OB8	0	0	0	22	p	45	58		
7	EMu2	0	0	0	23	p	45	0		
8		0	0	0	24	p	45	0		
9		0	0	0	25	p	45	0		
10	MIX DELAY	0	0	0	26	t	45	0		
11	GUIT DELAY	0	0	0	27	t	45	0		
12		0	0	0	28	p	45	0		
13		0	0	0	29	p	45	0		
14		0	0	0	30	p	45	0		
15	JLC LITES	0	0	0	31	t	45	0		
16	SDS5	-28	0	0	32	t	45	0		

rithm is activated that looks for the largest gap. Figure 7 shows MIDI channel 5 will be graphically represented on a piano staff with a split point at middle C (middle C = 60 with an ascending scale as semitones ascend).

To the right of the channel fields as shown in Fig. 7 are four commands. MEASURE#s is used to toggle automatic measure numbering on graphical staves. PROGRAM's is used in the same manner for hiding or displaying program changes on staves. NAME's toggles the automatic staff labelling on and off. EXIT quits to EDIT mode.

LIBRARIAN Mode

This mode is entered using the "li" command from the EDIT mode. The LIBRARIAN can be used for uploading/downloading synthesizer voices and for manipulating them in order to derive synthesizer keyboard setups specific to a desired musical context.

Additionally, the LIBRARIAN mode has graphical facilities for Yamaha DX/TX (FM) synthesizer voicing. All operator parameter data is displayed, and all envelope generators and keyboard breakpoints are presented and can be changed in line-graph format. A set of piano staves is also provided for a short motif useful for testing the synthesizer voice at any point in its development.

Figure 8 shows the user interface to the librarian. The bottom status line is interpreted as follows:

string 1 —the name of the current library item.

Fig. 8. LIBRARIAN mode screen image.

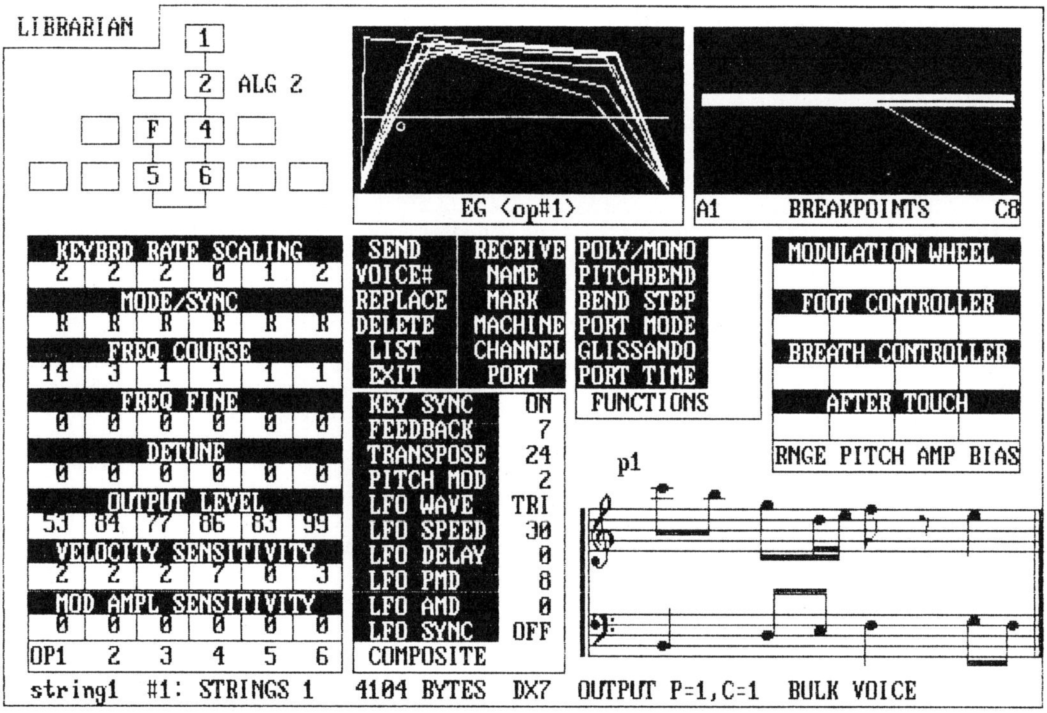
LIBRARIAN
1
2
ALG 2
F
4
5
6
EG <op#1>
A1 BREAKPOINTS C8
KEYBRD RATE SCALING
2 2 2 0 1 2
MODE/SYNC
R R R R R R
FREQ COURSE
14 3 1 1 1 1
FREQ FINE
0 0 0 0 0 0
DETUNE
0 0 0 0 0 0
OUTPUT LEVEL
53 84 77 86 83 99
VELOCITY SENSITIVITY
2 2 2 7 0 3
MOD AMPL SENSITIVITY
0 0 0 0 0 0
OP1 2 3 4 5 6
SEND RECEIVE
VOICE# NAME
REPLACE MARK
DELETE MACHINE
LIST CHANNEL
EXIT PORT
KEY SYNC ON
FEEDBACK 7
TRANSPOSE 24
PITCH MOD 2
LFO WAVE TRI
LFO SPEED 30
LFO DELAY 0
LFO PMD 8
LFO AMD 0
LFO SYNC OFF
COMPOSITE
POLY/MONO
PITCHBEND
BEND STEP
PORT MODE
GLISSANDO
PORT TIME
FUNCTIONS
MODULATION WHEEL
FOOT CONTROLLER
BREATH CONTROLLER
AFTER TOUCH
RNGE PITCH AMP BIAS
p1
string1 #1: STRINGS 1 4104 BYTES DX7 OUTPUT P=1,C=1 BULK VOICE

#1: STRINGS 1	—voice #1 (out of 32), subnamed "STRINGS 1."
4104 BYTES	—size of the current library item.
DX7	—current library item machine type.
OUTPUT P=1,C=1	—output port and channel of target synthesizer
BULK VOICE	—data type of current library item.

The staves shown in Fig. 8 contain a motif edited in the same manner as in EDIT mode. The "pl" (play) command can be used any time to play the motif. The "p1" shown over the staves is a program change command that corresponds to the number of the voice given on the bottom prompt line (#1).

Central in the LIBRARIAN interface of Fig. 8 is the command menu headed by the commands SEND and RECEIVE. These are used to send and receive any type of MIDI system exclusive data (such as voice data or performance parameter information). If the type of data being communicated is for Yamaha DX/TX series machines, the other blocks shown can be used to display and edit the data.

DX voicing starts with a bulk dump from the DX by executing the RECEIVE command, using the CHANNEL (and PORT) command to communicate with the relevant synthesizer. The musician chooses the specific voice within the bulk voice using the VOICE# command. The name of the bulk voice can be changed or another bulk voice can be activated using the NAME command. Individual voices can be moved anywhere within any bulk voice of the same MACHINE type by MARKing the desired individual voice and REPLACEing over the target voice number. Individual voices within a bulk voice can be LISTed for quick reference.

Once an individual voice has been chosen for editing, the cursor can be moved to the screen location where a change is desired. The algorithm is changed by moving the cursor within the algorithm area and striking Enter. EGs (envelope generators) and BREAKPTS may be modified by moving the cursor into the window, and hitting Enter at a waveform node. Then cursor movements move the node until the next Enter is struck. If Enter is hit away from any nodes, the current operator cycles to the next operator, and its waveforms are displayed for editing. Other values can be changed by moving the cursor to the value, hitting Enter, and responding to the given prompt.

In Fig. 8 operators (the Yamaha term for oscillator) are shown numbered with an F representing the feedback operator (top left). All boxes shown containing data are operator specific except for the COMPOSITE box. The current operator is listed in the EG box. COMPOSITE values affect the composite voice resulting from the modulation of carriers given in the algorithm.

The FUNCTIONS box and the box to its right have no data displayed. These are used for DX function parameter and TX performance parameter data types.

Conclusion

The music industry's adoption of the MIDI 1.0 specification has standardized synthesizer interfacing. Complete studio and performance setups even down to the lighting equipment and digital delays can be controlled from a single microcomputer using MIDI messages. To control all facets of synthesizer-based music processing, however, requires software that integrates the necessary interfaces for recording, playback, composition, printing, archiving, and voicing. This requirement has been the goal in the evolution of Personal Composer.

Acknowledgments

I am deeply indebted to many people for their help and inspiration over the past several years. Professor James Angell at Stanford University has been my advisor on the project throughout its development. Peter Redford provided the motivating force that started me on the project in the first place. Ed Simeone lent financial support during the critical start-up phase and continually advises on the program's application in the studio environment. Rick Reed and David Moore have given of their musical talents, consulting on percussionist and keyboardist requirements. David Burling is chiefly responsible for the continuity of the business that in turn supports Personal Composer's evolution. Hundreds of Personal Composer licensees have sent volumes of excellent criticism. And thanks also to many others, corporate and personal, especially my family.

References

Chowning, J. 1973. "The Synthesis of Complex Audio Spectra By Means of Frequency Modulation." *Journal of the Audio Engineering Society* 21(7):526–534. Reprinted in C. Roads and J. Strawn, eds. 1985. *Foundations of Computer Music.* Cambridge, Massachusetts: MIT Press.

Droman, D. 1984. "Exploring MIDI—The Musical Instrument Digital Interface." North Hollywood: IMA Publications.

IMA. 1983. "MIDI—Musical Instrument Digital Interface Specification 1.0." North Hollywood: International MIDI Association.

Loy, G. 1985. "Musicians Make a Standard: The MIDI Phenomenon." *Computer Music Journal* 9(4):8–26.

Table 1. EDIT Mode Commands

/n —search for next note (cursor moves to next note on staff)

/s —search for next staff (prompts for channel #)

ac —accelerando (target tempo on same staff after accelerando)

ba —barline

br —bracket: full or line

ch —channel and port assignments for a staff
Flags-up and Flags-down can be assigned different MIDI channels

cl —clef: treble, bass, alto, tenor, or percussion

cn —CHANNEL mode for assigning name and synthesizer parameters

co —copy notes (with or without transpose), staves and/or text. "co" and "mo" commands allow bounding of an area

cr —crescendo

dd —double dot for note or rest
Cursor is placed directly on note or rest to be double-dotted (same for dot below).

di —diminuendo

dp —delete page

ds —double sharp

dt —single dot note or rest

en —end bar for end of score

er —ending for repetition

ex —exit, either saving or discarding session

fe —fermata

fi —access another disk file (up to eight simultaneously).
This is the means of accessing disk-based databases. Material can be copied from one file to another using the move "mo" and copy "co" commands.

fl —flat

fn —flip note stem direction

gc —go to/from coda—goto using forward reference

gs —go to/from segno—goto using reverse reference

ip —insert page before current page

jo —join specified notes into same group

kb —double barline with optional secondary key signature

ke —key signature.
Prompts for the key where upper case indicates major keys and lower case minor keys. Also, an "s" can be appended for sharp and an "f" for flat.

ks —key stroke assignment ("Esc" key ends keystroking).
This is a macro facility. For example, a keystroke macro could be named "ls" and could consist of drawing and bracketing three staves in lead-sheet

format. This command would then work in EDIT mode. Single-stroke function keys (the Fn-keys and the Alt-keys) can also be assigned, making the command syntax completely programmable.

kv —key velocity

li —LIBRARIAN mode for synthesizer patch archival and FM voicing

me —merge graphical score in with RECORDER tracks

mg —MIDIGRAPHIC mode for custom graphic font/MIDI action definitions

mo —move notes (with or without transpose), staves and/or text

na —natural

nf —next file (cycle between currently opened files)

no —note. Prompts for note type, flag direction, and grouping, if any

n2 —superimpose stem-up note on top of stem-down note or vice versa

oc —octave up or down

pa —page horizontally

pc —program (synthesizer patch) change

pe —pedal (sustain on/off)

pl —play score from top of page to endbar or end of score

pr —print from cursor

qu —quintuplet

rc —32-track RECORDER mode

rd —redraw screen

ri —ritardando

rm —rest for n measures

rp —begin/end repeat line (up to 127 repetitions)

rs —rest

sa —save graphic and/or recorded tracks to file(s)

sc —scroll vertically

sh —sharp

sp —split group of notes

st —staff

ti —tie

tm —tempo

tr —triplet

ts —time signature

tx —text, for lyrics, titles, and comments

ve —verify rhythmic timing for a staff

vo —volume marks (*ppp–fff*)

wh—wait for PC keyboard hit

wt —wait 10 seconds

xp —transpose staff up or down

zk —zap (erase) keystroke database

zr —zap (erase) recorder tracks

zs —zap (erase) score, including staves and text

23

W. Buxton, S. Patel, W. Reeves, and R. Baecker

Structured Sound Synthesis Project
Computer Systems Research Group
University of Toronto
Toronto, Ontario, Canada M5S 1A1

Scope in Interactive Score Editors

Introduction

In conversation, we typically constrain our comments to fall within the scope of the topic at hand. *Scope* can be used to define the sphere of action of any activity. When conductors request that players "play a little more staccato in the lower brass," they are imposing a certain scope (lower brass) on a specific action (play). Scope is an important concept in many contexts in which we desire to specify the precise range of some command. In this article we will consider the expression of scope in interactive score editors (Buxton et al. 1979).

Most existing score editors restrict the degree to which they permit users to impose scope upon operators, or commands (Smith 1972; Reeves et al. 1978; Wallraff 1978). For the most part, operators (such as "play" or "delete") can only be directed toward single notes or entire scores. This is unsatisfactory because ideally any operator should be able to be directed to any arbitrary grouping of notes the composer thinks of in the mind's ear. There are, however, considerable problems in implementing such a facility, most notably developing the semantics and syntax appropriate for such specification in a musical context. Addressing these issues is a current topic of research with the Structured Synthesis Sound Project (SSSP). Although this research is still in progress, we believe that the interim results presented here help to give some structure to the problem and will be of use to those currently writing or designing score-editing software.

S. Patel is currently with Human Computing Resources, Toronto, Canada. W. Reeves is now with Lucasfilm Corp., Novato, California. R. Baecker is with both the University of Toronto and Human Computing Resources.

Computer Music Journal, Vol. 5, No. 3, Fall 1981

The Semantics of Scope

The objective in scope specification is to identify without ambiguity the notes that serve as the operand of a command. If this is to be done fluently, the grouping criteria must match the way that the notes may be grouped in the composer's mind. Such criteria form the basis for an unambiguous description of the notes. A first step in our research was to attempt to gain some understanding of these criteria through techniques of observation and interrogation. As a result, we have come to view grouping criteria as falling into five basic categories:

Simple grouping criterion — scope is either the whole score or a single note (e.g., "play the third note").

Block-of-time grouping criterion — scope is a set of notes contained in a particular time interval (e.g., "delete the notes of the third bar").

Local-attributes grouping criterion — notes are encompassed in the scope on the basis of self-contained attributes such as pitch or duration (e.g., "raise the volume of all notes below C3").

Contextual-attributes grouping criterion — a note's context (relationship to other notes and their attributes) determines whether the note is included in the scope of an operator (e.g., specifications such as "all notes followed by a leap of an octave upwards" or "sounding simultaneously with three or more other notes").

Named-structural-entities grouping criterion — scope is specified by naming the musical structure to be affected (e.g., "motif A").

We see each successive category as growing in semantic power. Together, these categories form a foundation for the semantics of scope specification.

Simple Scope

When scope can only be expressed as a single note or an entire score, we refer to it as *simple scope.* If a program allows both single-note and whole-score scope to be expressed, the minimum basis for a score editor is provided. With regard to the underlying representation of the score data, simple scope presents no real problems since the operand of a command is either the entire data set or a single record. At this level, scope lends itself well to either a graphics or alphanumeric mode of specification. In graphics mode, for example, the entire score can be encompassed by activating the light-button corresponding to the desired operator. An operator can modify a single note by pointing at the desired note. (See the article by Buxton et al. [1979] for more details on such graphic techniques.) Alphanumeric-based interaction, on the other hand, can be modeled on line-oriented text editors. In such cases, scope can be specified as the line currently being edited or as the entire score file.

Scope by Block of Time

While simple scope can provide the basis for an elementary score editor, many compositionally important concepts are commonly encountered that cannot be handled by such an editor. For example, we might want to audition the last section of a long score or a sequence of notes in the middle, or we might want to transpose a particular chord. In each case, we want to address the set of notes falling within a particular *block of time.* The situation is commonplace in which such blocks are expressed with regard to note position by number (as in our first example), bars, rehearsal marks, seconds, or beats. If such concepts can be expressed in a congenial way, the editor's power is substantially increased, as is its usefulness to the composer. For example, notes of isolated "chunks" of the score can be heard in context, chords can be treated as single entities, and entire sections can be saved or copied in a single gesture for the purpose of repeats.

In making scope specification available by block

of time, the designer must pay close attention to delimiters and their effect on the underlying data structures. Bar lines or rehearsal marks cannot be used unless these concepts are kept in the data base. If time is represented by fractions of a beat with respect to a metronome marking (as in the SSSP system described by Buxton et al. [1978]), specification by units of real time (such as seconds) may be awkward to implement.

The mode of interaction also has an effect on the techniques of delimitation available in a system. Graphics-based systems that permit scrolling through and zooming in and out of the score lend themselves well to use of the current viewport as the scope delimiter. The specification of blocks of time by the use of markers on a time line is another technique better suited to a graphics-based approach. Alphanumeric systems are often more appropriate when numerical values are used as delimiters, such as when precise timings in seconds are required.

An ideal environment would provide a number of alternative methods for delimiting scope. For the purposes of the current discussion, however, we will present only one sample approach taken from the SSSP alphanumeric score editor *sced* (Buxton 1981a). *sced* is modeled on the line-oriented text editor *ed* (Kernighan 1974). *ed* is the most commonly used text editor at our facility. While from a purely musical perspective it is not the best model to use, *sced* was based on *ed* to permit text-editing skills to be applied to music and vice versa. However, we chose not to edit scores as text files. Rather, SSSP music editors operate directly on the musical data structures. This has several advantages: (1) scores need not be compiled into a lower-level representation to be performed, which results in fewer files and operations and permits real-time synthesis for purposes of verification; (2) the editor can be interpretative because it has knowledge about the various operations and can therefore provide error checking and other forms of help; (3) scores are edited in the common language of the SSSP system and therefore any score can be edited by any score editor whether or not it is graphics-based.

In *sced* note numbers rather than line numbers are the basis for navigating through the score. Thus note number is the basis for scope delimitation.

The following examples illustrate sample implementation of scope by block of time. First, the specification of scope at this semantic level encompasses the previous level, simple scope. The first example,

3d

means "delete the third note," while

*p

means "print the entire score" (by convention, * means "all notes"). Double delimiters are used to expand upon simple scope. The example

3,8l

means "let me listen (l) to notes three through eight," while the statement

10,$w fred

means "write (w) or save notes ten through to the end (specified by the special symbol $) as a new score called fred."

The specification of scope at this level has met with a very positive response from composers. Certain frustrations have arisen, however, which demonstrate that extraction of a block of time cannot enable us to handle all cases encountered in the editing of scores. Therefore the technique is insufficient, regardless of the units used for boundary delimitation.

Scope by Local Attributes

The problem with specifying scope using the techniques discussed thus far is that all notes in the indicated block of time are encompassed. Thus concepts such as "all quarter notes in the third bar" or "all brass playing *mf* below middle C in this sec-

tion" cannot be accommodated. While time-block specification helps the composer focus in on one whole area of the score, it does not permit the identification of the specific notes in question. Such identification can be made if a note has some user-specified characteristic included in the scope. For the purposes of this discussion, let us say that the "legal" characteristics are the *local attributes* of the notes themselves. Besides block of time, we should be able to take a note's pitch, duration, loudness, instrument, and other properties into consideration before we include it in the scope.

The power of scope specification at this level depends on the composer's ability to express arbitrarily complex relations among these attributes. This implies that logical relations (e.g., equivalence, greater than, not equal to, etc.) and conjunctions (e.g., and, or, and exclusive or) must be expressible.

With implemented score-editing systems, the crucial limitation is that only attribute fields that form part of the data base can be considered as criteria for inclusion in the current scope. It is not possible to specify "all notes played by trumpets," for example, if no record is kept of orchestration. (The only exceptions to this are attributes that are implicit, such as note number or time. With this provision, it becomes clear that simple and block-of-time levels of scope specification are encompassed by the local-attributes level.) While it is easy for a musician to group notes mentally according to some relationship, it becomes more difficult when notes must be unambiguously identified to a computer. To get a feeling for some of the problems involved, let us look at some specific examples. Again, these are taken from the alphanumeric score editor *sced*.

{freq < C4}p

means "print all notes having a frequency less than C4." (In *sced*, the relational expression appears between braces and before the operator. In this and other examples, key words such as "frequency" indicate particular note attributes. All key words can be abbreviated in order to reduce typing.)

{freq = C4, G3}orch flute

will cause all notes having a pitch of C4 or G3 to be orchestrated with the "flute." An example of a more complex relation would be

{dur <= ¼ & obj != flute}d

which would delete all notes not orchestrated by "flute" that had a duration less than or equal to a quarter note.

{# >= 3 & # <= 12 & vol <100}setvol +20

can also be written as

3,12{vol < 100}sv +20,

which means "increment by 20 units the volume of all notes from the 3rd through the 12th whose volume is less than 100."

There are several points worth noting about these examples. First, it would be difficult to express such logical relations using graphical techniques. Although the concepts can be expressed easily in natural language, the only way to express them to a computer is with typed alphanumerics. The syntax used to express the relational concepts in the examples is rather arcane. From a human-factors point of view, some trade-off must be made between similarity to natural language and succinctness. (Some feeling for this conflict can be seen in the last example—compare the natural-language interpretation with the second version in *sced* notation.) Clearly, much research remains to be done. We hope that work such as that of Card, Moran, and Newell (1980) and Ledgard and coworkers (1980) will help pave the way. These researchers raise issues that must be dealt with in future score editors. The paper by Card, Moran, and Newell is a study quantifying the relationship between the verbosity of a message and the efficiency of the human-computer dialogue. The paper by the second group investigates the influence of natural-language-based constructs on the efficiency of text-editing tasks.

Second, while the simple and block-of-time levels of scope could be carried out using general-purpose text editors (if the score is represented as a text file), this is not the case with the local-attributes level. Here it is clear that the application-specific nature of the attributes (and the operators, e.g., "orch," or "orchestrate a note by attaching an instrument to it") makes the expression of complex logical relations impractical. We are no longer dealing with concepts that can be expressed simply as typographical operators. To enable scope specification at this level, it appears that a special-purpose editor that understands musical attributes must be provided.

Scope by Contextual Attributes

The previous section showed how a score editor's power can be increased by having a note's inclusion in the scope depend on the note's conformation to certain composer-defined characteristics. Often, however, more complex relations than those seen thus far are required. Simple relations based on pitch or duration are not enough. Rather, scope inclusion is sometimes best specified in terms of the notes' *contextual attributes*, or of the relationships among different notes and their attributes. We might want to specify, for example, a type of chord: "all notes that sound in combination with three or more others," or a motif: "all notes orchestrated with brass playing a dotted eighth, followed by a sixteenth," or an intervallic sequence: "all notes preceded by a step downward of a minor second and followed by an upward leap greater than a perfect fifth."

The ability to express such constraints is clearly of musical value, and musicians have no difficulty in grouping notes according to such criteria verbally or mentally. When it comes to identifying (unambiguously) such groups to a computer, however, problems arise. In contrast to the situation in which scope is defined by local attributes, the number of criteria for grouping in context is infinite. To understand context, the editor must have a far higher level of musical "knowledge" (1) to understand the various criteria and (2) to perform the consequent pattern recognition on the data base that will isolate the notes in question. Even if the appropriate concepts could be understood by the editor, the specification language used by the com-

Buxton et al.

poser would probably be too cumbersome to be useful. We have seen, for example, how specification of local attributes can approach the threshold of practical complexity.

As formulated, specification of scope at the contextual level would seem impractical without a great deal of research. We can either undertake this research or reformulate the problem. For the purposes at hand, we have chosen to reformulate the problem.

Musicians have no problems dealing with the concepts under consideration. An alternative approach, therefore, would be to make best use of the requisite knowledge of the composer. The task is then to provide an environment in which the composer can use this knowledge to identify manually the desired notes in an efficient way. The original problem involved the computer collecting the notes that fit a description supplied by the composer. We are now sidestepping the description problem and having the composer identify the notes. A descriptive approach is being replaced by a demonstrative one.

The success of this demonstrative approach depends on two conditions. First, the notation must highlight the relevant features of the musical data. Second, a straightforward means of interaction must be provided. As a result of both of these conditions, we have chosen to take a graphics-based approach in our experiments at the contextual level. With graphics, we have the notational flexibility to highlight most of the different features and relationships involved. We also have a far greater range of options as means of interaction (alphanumerics is one such option).

We have implemented this technique in the program *scriva* (Buxton 1981b). In *scriva*, an intuitive gesture—circling—can be combined with spatially distributed data as a means of isolating desired groups. More than one circle can be drawn on the screen (Buxton et al. 1979). Doughnutlike circles within a circle can be drawn, with the effect that all notes within the larger circle, except those contained in the inner one, are included in the current scope. There can be as many "holes in the doughnut" as desired and a circle within the hole is again a circle of inclusion.

Often the notes we want to group into the contextual-attributes level of scope are distributed throughout the score, making circling impractical. In such cases, the desired notes can be "collected" if we point at them one by one with the graphics cursor (Buxton et al. 1979).

With the techniques seen in the examples we can make some headway in the specification of scope according to context. The techniques are still rather primitive, however, and much work remains to be done.

Scope by Named Structural Entities

At the contextual-attributes level of scope, we encountered problems owing to our inability to describe adequately the notes constituting the scope of an operator. As a result, we resorted to a demonstrative approach. Another alternative is to identify the notes in question by name. In cases where these notes constitute a musically significant structure in the score, this is common practice among musicians. Simple examples would be "motif A," "the second theme of the first movement," or "the ostinato in the second section." Names such as "the second theme" are too vague for automatic isolation of the intended notes by a computer program. This problem can often be circumvented if (1) we are more rigorous as to what constitutes a name and (2) if, when composed, musically significant structures are named by the composer.

What does this mean musically? Our approach to scope at the *named-structural-entity* level is based on the assumption that the score is more than a collection of notes. It is assumed that the score is made up of sections, motifs, and parts, each of which has an explicit name. Our approach is also based on the assumption that the composer has assembled the score so that there are relationships among these structures. Finally, our approach assumes that the internal representation reflects this structural "recipe." If these three conditions are met, there is no reason why any of these structural entities cannot be identified directly by name. At the contextual-attributes level, we failed to perform

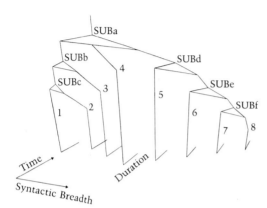

Fig. 1. Snapshot of an image generated by a three-dimensional score display and editor developed at the SSSP.

Fig. 1. Snapshot of an image generated by a three-dimensional score display and editor developed at the SSSP.

nique. Smaller structures that are not well suited to the naming technique are generally easily handled by the demonstrative approach.

Our first experiments with structuring data by named entities had to do with notational techniques. How could the external representation of the data reflect the underlying structure so as to aid the composer in exploiting the information? The example shown in Fig. 1 is an illustration of this work. Illustrated is an example score called SUBa taken from the program *treed* (Kwan 1978) (contrived for the purposes of demonstrating the system). The feet at the bottom of the display represent note events whose durations are proportional to the length of the line that is the foot, along the time axis. The triangles labeled SUBb, SUBc, and so on represent large syntactic categories, that is, subscores. These subscores encapsulate two or more notes. Thus SUBa is the root of the tree, and SUBf is the lowest nonterminal. The numbers 1, 2, . . . 8 next to the terminal branches of the tree are labels used in editing. Since this is a snapshot of a dynamic program display that can be rotated in various ways, certain features that emerge in movement cannot easily be seen in this static image. For example, frequency information is embedded in this representation that comes out more clearly in the dynamic image. A clear structure is provided (in this example, at least) that facilitates the expression of concepts such as "play SUBb," or "transpose SUBd."

We do not yet have usable score editors that work on scores structured in this way. The number of problems encountered make progress very slow. One key challenge has been to use this complex level of internal representation while retaining our ability to play the scores in real time without any compilation or preprocessing. Our recent efforts to meet this challenge have focused on the performance of such structures. These efforts resulted in the *conduct* system (Buxton et al. 1980). One of the key concepts reflected in the *conduct* system is the ability to address and transform named structural entities in real time. *conduct* is a convincing example of the power and practicality of scope specification at this level. We are now trying to bring this power into the domain of our score-editing tools.

the analysis that would extract the referenced part of the score. At the named-structural-entities level, the equivalent to such an analysis is given: it is the explicit structure as pieced together by the composer. This structure is reflected in the data structures.

Rendering such an approach practical has one other property. Whereas up to this point scope has been based on purely physical or acoustical properties of the data (time, pitch, timbre, etc.), we now have a means of scope specification with a compositional foundation!

There are, however, practical limitations to the named-entity approach. Fundamental among these is the need for an appropriate model for the underlying structure of scores. A list structure is too simple musically and a general relational network too complex to handle (due to space/time trade-offs that would result in poor performance). We have chosen a hierarchical "tree" structure (Buxton et al. 1978). While this clearly has musical limitations, it is the most general structure we feel to be manageable at this moment.

The technique is impractical except for larger-scale structures. It would not be reasonable to expect the composer to name every single entity. Yet it is exactly these larger structures that are the most poorly handled by the demonstrative tech-

Conclusion

In this article we have described how the notion of scope can be developed within the context of interactive score editors. Our objective is to extend the means by which composers can express scope according to musically relevant constraints. There are three different syntactic approaches to scope definition: the descriptive approach, the demonstrative approach, and the naming approach. Differing combinations of syntactic approach and semantic level sometimes make conflicting demands on both the underlying internal representation and the mode of the musician-machine dialogue. With the descriptive approach, greater semantic power can be achieved by use of alphanumerics than by use of graphics-based techniques. On the other hand, graphics appear to be the most appropriate technique for the demonstrative approach. Both graphics and alphanumerics can be used in addressing named syntactic entities.

Acknowledgments

The work reported in this paper has benefited from discussions, comments, and other types of input from many people associated with the SSSP. In particular, we would like to acknowledge the contributions of James Montgomery, Martin Lamb, Wesley Lowe, William Matthews, Otto Laske, Leslie Gondor, K. C. Smith, Susan Frykberg, and Curtis Roads. The research has been funded by the Social Sciences and Humanities Research Council of Canada, whose support we gratefully acknowledge.

References

Buxton, W. 1981a. "A Tutorial Introduction to *sced.*" In *Music Software User's Manual*, 2nd ed., ed. W. Buxton. Toronto: Computer Systems Research Group, University of Toronto.

Buxton, W. 1981b. "Tutorial Introduction to *scriva.*" In *Music Software User's Manual*, 2nd ed., ed. W. Buxton. Toronto: Computer Systems Research Group, University of Toronto.

Buxton, W. et al. 1978. "The Use of Hierarchy and Instance in a Data Structure for Computer Music." *Computer Music Journal* 2(4): 10–20.

Buxton, W. et al. 1980. "A Microcomputer-Based Conducting System." *Computer Music Journal* 4(1): 8–21.

Buxton, W. et al. 1979. "The Evolution of the SSSP Score Editing Tools." *Computer Music Journal* 3(4): 14–26.

Card, S. K., T. P. Moran, and A. Newell. 1980. "The Keystroke-Level Model for User Performance Time with Interactive Systems." *Communications of the Association for Computing Machinery* 23(7): 396–410.

Kernighan, B. W. 1974. "A Tutorial Introduction to the UNIX Text Editor." Murray Hill, New Jersey: Bell Laboratories *Technical Memorandum 74-1273-17.*

Kwan, A. 1978. "Treed Project Report." Unpublished manuscript. Toronto: C.S.R.G., University of Toronto.

Ledgard, H. et al. 1980. "The Natural Language of Interactive Systems." *Communications of the Association for Computing Machinery* 23(10): 556–563.

Reeves, W. et al. 1978. "Ludwig: An Example of Interactive Computer Graphics in a Score Editor." In *Proceedings of the 1978 International Computer Music Conference*, vol. 2, ed. C. Roads. Evanston, Illinois: Northwestern University Press, pp. 392–409.

Smith, L. 1972. "SCORE—A Musician's Approach to Computer Music." *Journal of the Audio Engineering Society* 20(1): 7–14.

Walraff, D. 1978. "Nedit—A Graphical Editor for Musical Scores." In *Proceedings of the 1978 International Computer Music Conference*, vol. 2, ed. C. Roads. Evanston, Illinois: Northwestern University Press, pp. 410–450.

24

W. Buxton, S. Patel, W. Reeves, and R. Baecker

Structured Sound Synthesis Project (SSSP)
Computer Systems Research Group
University of Toronto
Toronto, Ontario, Canada M5S 1A1

Objed and the Design of Timbral Resources

Introduction

One of the main attractions of electroacoustic music is the potential for composers to design and control their own palette of timbral resources. A key frustration, however, results from the difficulty in actually doing so. Consequently, in spite of technological advances, systems appearing on the market are reminiscent of organs and conventional instruments in their reliance on preset timbres. Very little progress seems to have been made in the development of tools to aid composers in "rolling their own" timbres.

With analog equipment, the musician could use a "hands-on" approach to exploring the timbral potential of various configurations. The adoption of digital technology provided greater precision, sophistication, and potential, but initially made timbral exploration more remote. With the current trend toward highly interactive real-time digital systems, the composer should now have the best of both worlds. It is toward such an end that this paper is directed.

Ideally, timbre should be controlled according to perceptual rather than acoustic attributes. However, our limited understanding of perception, cognition, and acoustics makes this difficult at present, although work by Grey (1975; 1977) and Wessel (1979) is making considerable headway in this direction. If we must deal with timbral specification in mainly acoustic terms, it is important to provide an environment for doing so that minimizes the

Patel is currently with Human Computing Resources, Toronto, Canada. Reeves is now with Lucasfilm Ltd., San Rafael, California. Baecker is with both University of Toronto and Human Computing Resources.

Computer Music Journal, Vol. 6, No. 2, Summer 1982

nonmusical problems of the task and that permits the composer to develop an ability to understand and predict the perceptual consequences of changing acoustic parameters. The realization of such a timbre editing environment requires that:

1. The data being edited is clearly represented.
2. There is a good correspondence between the things that the composer wants to do and the operators that the editing environment provides.
3. The bookkeeping and administrative tasks of the user are minimal.
4. The syntax for all transactions is succinct, intuitive, and consistent.
5. The system have a high tolerance for user error, and that it encourage exploration and experimentation (i.e., learning).

We will examine one program that attempts to fulfill these requirements. The intention is to provide a case study that will serve as the basis for discussion of the issues involved. It is hoped that as much will be learned from the program's deficiencies as from its strengths.

Objed and Objects

Objed is a program that permits named sets of timbral characteristics (called *objects*) to be defined, auditioned, and modified. Objects have three properties:

1. Each is contained in a separate, uniquely named file.
2. Each defines a set of timbral characteristics (including time-varying functions) that can be used to orchestrate one or more notes.
3. The parameters determining pitch, maximum amplitude, and duration of each instance of an object are determined by the

orchestrated note rather than the object itself.

Objects can be compared to Music V instruments (Mathews 1969), and *patches* on analog synthesizers. The usage described derives directly from Truax's POD system (1976). The concept is general, but the current SSSP implementation restricts the composer to working with the following limited set of object types (type is determined by the method of sound synthesis employed): *fixed waveform, frequency modulation* (FM) (Chowning 1973), *additive synthesis* (Moorer 1977), *Vosim* (Kaegi and Tempelaars 1978), and *waveshaping* (Arfib 1979; Le Brun 1979). Each object type is like a Smalltalk "class" (Krasner 1980), although the two were developed independently.

The composer's task in object editing is one of plugging values into the fixed template defined for the object type being used. As a result, the composer works at a level halfway between the two extremes of instrument definition at the unit-generator level (as in Music V-type programs) and the use of presets. (*Unit generators* are signal processing elements, which are the lowest-level modules used in defining Music V instruments.) In this approach, the composer is restricted by the object types available as to the range of timbres that can be generated. However, if the available object types are well chosen, a musically rich palette of timbres is possible. Furthermore, the number of object types or the synthesis techniques used are not restricted by the object concept. New methods can and have been introduced. (In fact, the concept of a meta-object editor would be worth developing, so as to facilitate the specification of new object types, using the unit-generator concept, for example.)

Our rationale for taking the somewhat restrictive template approach of the object formalism is based on the resulting ability to build a powerful user interface for timbre specification. Since each object has a system-defined template, the program can provide an "intelligent" editing environment that "understands" what the user is trying to do. Errors are detected more easily, diagnostic messages are clearer, and the assignment of default values is simplified. While the timbre space offered by this approach is limited when compared to the *potential*

of the Music V instrument paradigm, in many cases the tools offered by Objed, for example, give the composer control over a broader timbral range. Potential is only meaningful to composers if it falls within their "threshold of patience." The approach exemplified by Objed is intended to extend this threshold as far as possible.

The use of objects, as described, is not incompatible with either Music V-type instruments or presets. Objed provides a middle ground between the two. As has already been pointed out, the unit-generator approach could be used to define the template of new object types. On the other hand, objects whose parameters have been previously defined can be used as presets. In this case, the composer can select the preset closest to the timbre desired and use Objed to "clone" a new object that is a variation of this existing one.

Objed in Perspective

Before progressing, it is important to put the task of editing objects in perspective with respect to the overall task of composing using the SSSP system. The description given below is brief. Those readers wishing detailed information on the software available in the SSSP system are referred to *Music Software User's Manual* (Buxton 1981).

We view the SSSP software as providing suitable environments for performing three basic tasks:

1. Defining and editing a palette of timbres to be used in a composition. This is referred to as *object definition*.
2. Defining and editing musical scores, including the task of orchestrating the notes of these scores, using the lexicon of objects defined by the composer.
3. Defining the performance information affecting a composition, usually by real-time interpretation, or conducting, of the material.

Each computer program is designed to assist the composer in the performance of one of these three tasks. Objed, for example, is the primary environment for performing the first task. Usually, however, there are alternative ways of performing a particular task. The most appropriate environment for expressing one musical idea during score definition, for example, may not be the best for expressing some other (equally valid) idea. Hence, the two different programs Sced and Scriva (Buxton et al. 1979), support alternative approaches to performing the second task of score editing. For carrying out the third task (performance), the Conduct program (Buxton et al. 1980) is the environment available.

There are two benefits gained from viewing the software in terms of different task environments. First, composers are provided a simple mental model with which to view what they are doing; that is, in terms of one of these three tasks. As the number of alternative ways of performing a task increases, having this mental model available becomes more and more helpful to the composer. Second, this approach allows the software to be structured in such a way that no order of performing these three tasks is forced upon the composer. In fact, the composer can ignore tasks that are not of immediate interest. For example, if the composer just wants to deal with scores, the material can be auditioned with automatically assumed default timbres from within the score-editing environments. Similarly, as we shall see in more detail, the composer who wants to work on timbres without having to think about scores may do so, by using Objed. The point is that the system can be introduced and compositions built up incrementally. The composer need not be confronted with detail until it is needed.

In practice, the expert composer usually jumps from environment to environment. As stated earlier, the system is designed to facilitate this type of action as well. For example, one can jump into a score-editing environment from within Objed. This is often useful if one suddenly wants to specify a special score to test the object being designed. Similarly, one can temporarily jump into Conduct or Objed from any of the score editors, without ever having to suspend explicitly or save the material being worked upon. It would be fruitless to try to design one environment that fulfills all musical needs. Our philosophy is to make a number of strong, specifically oriented, software packages and obtain completeness by allowing the composer to access one environment from within another.

On Entering Objed

On initial entry, the Objed display is as shown in Fig. 1. The display is divided into five regions, each with a different function. The main region, which occupies the upper two-thirds of the screen, is where the actual data being edited is displayed. In the example, a simple, fixed-waveform object is being edited. Its components, all of which are graphically displayed, are a waveform; a time-varying function, controlling pitch; and an envelope, controlling the contour of the note's volume.

To the left, below the main region, is an area containing data pertaining to the pitch, volume, and duration at which the object being edited can be auditioned. These values are not part of the object: they are simply conveniences for exploring its behavior at different pitches, durations, and volumes.

The central panel in the lower part of the screen contains various options that allow the user to change the state of the editing environment. The user can change the type of object being edited and change the way in which the edited object can be auditioned.

The panel to the lower right is dedicated to the saving and retrieving of objects with a minimum of effort. The elongated region along the bottom left edge is a *window* that permits the composer to access the "outside world" without leaving Objed.

Objed is designed to minimize the amount of rote learning that must be undertaken by the user. Rather than memorize a large number of commands, the user need only remember a simple strategy that forms the basis for all interactions: when one wants to change something, one just points at the diagram or word that represents it on the display and depresses the selection (Z) button on the tablet's cursor. Any consequent options will then be presented, and the same method of interaction is applied to them.

*Fig. 1. Screen image gener-
ated by Objed upon entry
to the program.*

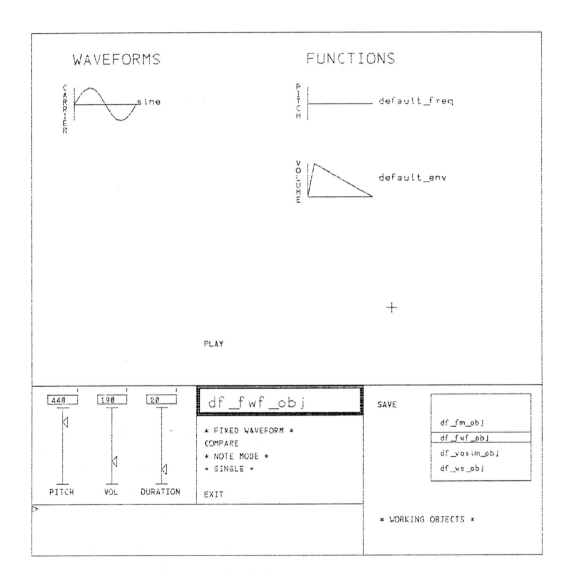

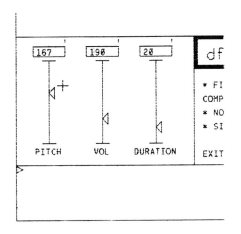

*Fig. 2. Graphic poten-
tiometers, used to control
parameters of the sound.*

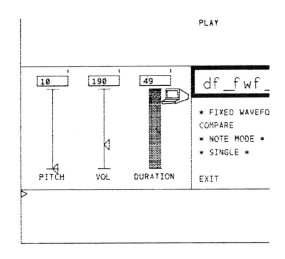

*Fig. 3. Setting a level on a
graphic potentiometer by
typing. The tracking sym-
bol has changed into the
icon of a terminal.*

Hearing an Object

It is often useful to begin by listening to the displayed object. This establishes a frame of reference
for future changes. The object is played when the
user activates the word (or light button) PLAY, seen
in the lower part of the work area. The sound is
immediately heard. The object itself has no specific
pitch, duration, or amplitude associated with it.
These must be provided externally for the object to
be heard. Assume that when PLAY was activated,
the sound had a pitch of A4, dynamics of about
mezzo-forte, and a duration of one-fourth note at
M.M. = 60. Obviously, it is desirable to be able to
change these values so as to learn more about the
object's behavior in different contexts. This is the
function of the lower-left subpanel seen in Fig. 2,
where there are three *graphic potentiometers,* or
pots, one for each performance parameter. The
value for each parameter is displayed numerically
in one of the boxes above, and its relative value is
seen by the position of the potentiometer's *handle*
(the triangular pointer). The user can change the
value of any graphic potentiometer by "dragging"
its handle up or down, using the cursor. Alternatively, the user may point at the box above the
graphic potentiometer, activate the Z button, and
type in a numerical value. In this case, the tracking

symbol becomes an icon of a terminal (as seen in
Fig. 3), which acts as a *prompt,* signaling to the
user that something must be typed.

What has been seen thus far? First, *nothing* has
been defined from scratch. New objects are always
created by modifying existing ones. On entering the
program, the user can immediately audition a reference sound and begin working from there. A basis
for learning is provided, even for the user who does
not know what a sine wave is. Second, parameters
such as pitch and volume are changed using a technique that has an analogy in most users' previous
experience. Third, iconic prompts appear where the
user's attention is already focused, as was seen in
Fig. 3.

Waveform Selection

We will now consider changing one of the attributes of the object itself. As an example, let us alter
the waveform associated with the object. Pointing
at the picture of the current waveform and depressing the Z button will cause the panel seen in Fig. 4
to appear. A menu consisting of the eight waveforms currently loaded in the synthesizer appears
down the right margin of this panel. Selecting one

Objed and the Design of Timbral Resources   **267**

Fig. 4. Window for wave-
form selection.

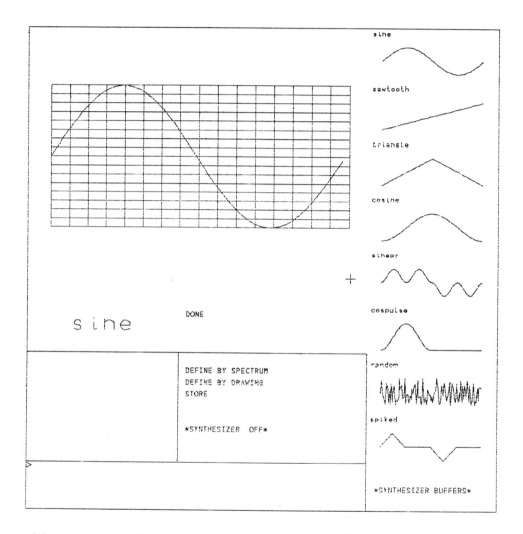

of these waveforms with the cursor and then activating the light button DONE restores the original panel of Fig. 1, with the one difference that a
drawing of the selected waveform has replaced that
of the sinusoid. This brings up an important point:
the current state of the object being edited is always clearly displayed, thereby eliminating the
mental task of remembering its current attributes.

Creating New Waveforms by Spectrum

In the previous example (Fig. 4), if we had wanted
to define a new waveform rather than use one of
those in the synthesizer, we could have done so. By
activating the light button DEFINE BY SPECTRUM
in Fig. 4, we cause the panel shown in Fig. 5 to appear. What is seen in the work area is a bar graph in

Fig. 5. Defining a wave-
form by spectral content.
Each bar represents a harmonic; its height is the
amplitude of the harmonic
relative to the others.

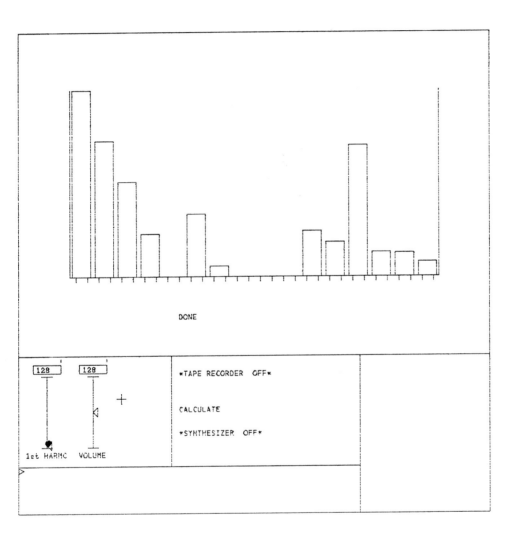

Fig. 5. Defining a wave-
form by spectral content.
Each bar represents a harmonic; its height is the
amplitude of the harmonic
relative to the others.

which the height of the bars represents the relative amplitude of the harmonics of a sound. Harmonics 1–16 appear from left to right. Any bar will jump to the height of the cursor when the cursor passes over the bar while the Z button is depressed. Thus, a simple hand gesture can sketch the spectral envelope of a waveform. More importantly, the waveform is being synthesized all the while, and we can use the graphic potentiometers in the lower left-hand panel to adjust the overall amplitude and the frequency of the fundamental. (Placement and use of the latter are consistent with the main panel, thereby simplifying learning of the control structure.) Throughout, the spectral content of the sound and the graphics display are updated in real time. The result is that musicians can quickly de-

Fig. 6. Example of a waveform defined by spectral
content.

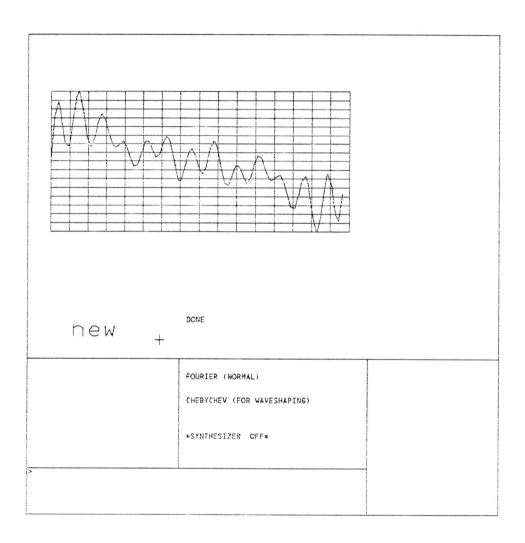

velop a sense of the perceptual effect of spectral content on steady-state tones.

Once the desired spectrum is defined, the composer activates the CALCULATE light button, and the new waveform is calculated and displayed (in the time domain), as seen in Fig. 6. Activating CALCULATE presents the user with the option of having the waveform calculated according to the weighed sum of the Fourier series or the Chebychev polynomials. In each case, the bar heights represent the relative weights of the different-order functions. The Chebychev polynomials are used to generate transfer functions to be employed in waveshaping synthesis.

The waveform is then loaded into the synthesizer, and the user returns to the main panel by

Fig. 7. Editing environ-
ment control subpanel.

activating the command DONE. The new version
of the object can then be auditioned, and other
changes can be made. For example, the envelope
associated with the object can be redefined using
techniques comparable to those seen with the
waveform.

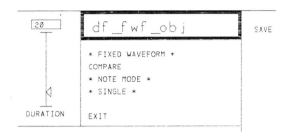

Other Object Modes

Thus far, the object being edited has been of the
fixed-waveform type. We can experiment with another mode by activating the light button FIXED
WAVEFORM seen in the lower central panel of
Fig. 7. As a result, the panel will switch to present
the set of object-type options. If we select "Frequency Modulation" (FM), the display will appear
as seen in Fig. 8. The panel is the same as that seen
in Fig. 1, except that there are five additional elements in the work area. There is now a waveform
displayed for both the carrier and modulating waves.
In addition, graphic potentiometers are provided to
set both the maximum index of modulation and the
carrier-to-modulator (c : m) ratio. Finally, there is a
third time-varying function, which controls the
evolution of the index of modulation.

Figure 8 illustrates two points. First, the environment is the same regardless of object type. Second,
the work panel previously seen is a subset of the
current one. The benefit resulting from this consistency is that skills learned at a simple level can be
applied to more complex tasks. Thus, the basis for
good pedagogical practice is provided.

More on Auditioning Objects

During an editing session, it is often desirable to be
able to audition the object repeatedly. One way to
do this is to activate the SINGLE button at the bottom of the environment control panel (Fig. 7). The
button will be renamed CYCLE, indicating that
when PLAY is activated the sound will play repeatedly until stopped by the user.

One problem that still exists, however, is that all
of our interactions with the object's data take the
two-part form: (1) change a value, (2) listen to the

effect. It would often be more useful, when setting
the index of maximum modulation, for example, to
emulate the operation of an analog synthesizer.
That is, it would be useful to turn the sound on in
its steady state and hear the effect of adjusting parameters while they are being changed. (Sound is
heard when we define waveforms by spectrum.)
This can be accomplished by activating the CYCLE
button, which then switches to STEADY. Activating PLAY causes the object to sound, and the effect
of adjusting any of the graphic potentiometers (including those affecting pitch and volume) is heard
immediately. When desired, we can return to the
original SINGLE mode by activating the button
STEADY. Thus, we have not only seen some new
modes of auditioning objects, but we have also introduced a new concept: that of the *rotary switch*.
By convention, any light button enclosed by "*"
characters functions as a rotary switch. Activating
the button will cause it to change to a new label.
Repeated activation will cause it to rotate through
its "cycle" and return to its original value. Each
such button, then, provides a means of selecting
from a set of options for a particular function. The
mode currently in effect is that displayed. A means
is provided, therefore, of accessing significant complexity that can be "hidden" until the user is ready
for it.

The effect of hearing an object in isolation is
often (usually?) very different from that of hearing
it in some musical context. So far, we have only
been able to hear an object as a single note. This
can be altered by activating the NOTE MODE button (Fig. 7). Once activated, the button is renamed
SCORE – UNIFORM ORCHESTRATION, and the

Fig. 8. Work panel for editing an FM object.

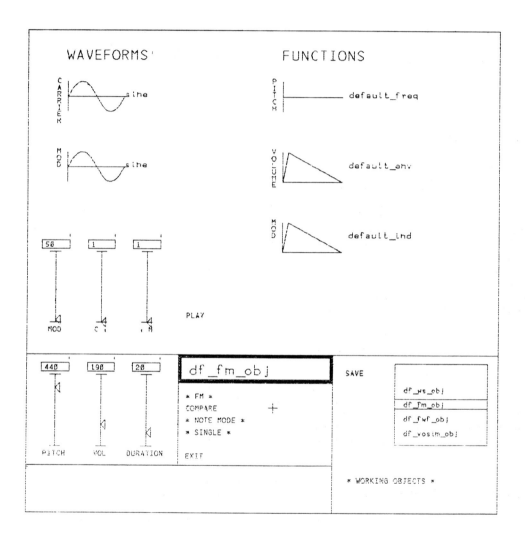

subpanel controlling note parameters is switched, as seen in Fig. 9. The box that appears can be thought of as a window that looks out on all of the scores the composer has created. The name of each score is listed in this directory window, and if there are more names than will fit, a means of scrolling through them is provided. When the PLAY button is activated, the score whose name appears between the horizontal lines of the window is heard. More importantly for our purposes, the score is temporarily orchestrated with the object currently being edited! Furthermore, the metronome marking controlling the tempo of the performance can be changed by adjusting the graphic potentiometer be-

Fig. 9. Control panel for
auditioning objects in the
context of user-defined
scores.

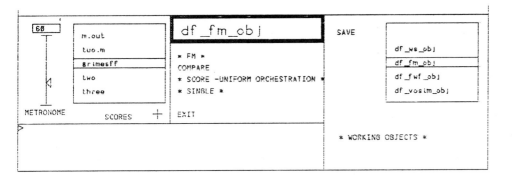

side the window. Pointing at any other name in the window will cause it to move between the horizontal lines so that it, too, can be played.

In the above way, the material being edited can be heard in a variety of musically useful contexts, allowing the composer to discover important musical properties of the material being designed.

Naming, Saving, and Retrieving Objects

Before an object can be used outside the context of the editing environment, it must be named and then saved. An object's current name appears in the heavily outlined box at the top of the environment-control subpanel (Fig. 7). A name can be changed in the same way as anything else: the user points at it, activates the Z button, and types in the new name in response to the appearance of the terminal prompt (icon). Saving an object for future use is equally straightforward: the light button SAVE seen in the bottom right-hand subpanel is activated. This same subpanel also provides the mechanism for retrieving previously defined objects. The technique is, again, use of the directory window. In this case, instead of previously defined scores, the window provides selective vision of objects. The name between horizontal lines is always the same as that of the object being edited. Selecting a different name causes that object to be displayed in the work area for purposes of editing or audition. One interesting

option is that the window provides views of objects that have been defined and stored on disk (* SAVED OBJECTS *) or objects that are in primary memory, having been worked on in the current session (* WORKING OBJECTS *). Thus, while only one object can be edited at a time, several *working objects* can be kept in primary memory during a work session. Nothing need be saved unless it is desired for a future session.

Buffering Working Objects

In the preceding discussion, it was seen that all objects that have been accessed during a particular work session are kept in primary memory. Although Objed only allows one object to be edited at a time, the design of one object may depend on that of another. This is the case in certain chords, for example. In such cases, there are two requirements. First, we want to be able to switch rapidly among the objects concerned in order to make adjustments, without having to save any of them until they are in an acceptable state. Second, we want to be able to audition the chord with the current version of these objects.

Objed supports both of these features. The first is accomplished using the WORKING OBJECTS window and the buffering mechanism already described. The second feature is achieved by activating the * SCORE – UNIFORM ORCHESTRA-

TION * button seen in the central panel of Fig. 9. The result of doing so is that the button will read * SCORE – NORMAL ORCHESTRATION *. On activation of the PLAY button in this mode, the score played will be performed using the objects specified by its orchestration, rather than by the object currently being edited. The special benefit of this is that the performance *uses the versions of the specified objects that are buffered in primary memory by Objed.* (Of course, if there is not a version in primary memory, the disk copy is used.) Thus, buffering the working objects of a session allows faster interaction and enables a valuable feature to be added to the editor.

Comparing Objects

Another benefit of providing easy access to a set of working objects can be seen in our next example. One function that we feel is important is the ability to compare objects in rapid succession. To do so, the data for each object to be auditioned must already be in primary memory. Even then, if we have to point to the object name, wait for its data to be displayed, and then move the cursor to activate the PLAY button, we have lost the instantaneous response we desire. As a result, another light button, COMPARE, is provided in the environment control area. Activating this button causes almost everything except the object window to disappear from the display. In this mode, an object is played immediately upon having its name selected with the cursor. Since the objects are already in primary memory and hand movement is minimized, rapid comparisons are possible.

The directory windows seen in the previous examples are the most important feature of the system with respect to one of our initial demands: that the cognitive effort required for administration and bookkeeping be minimized. In computer science terms, this represents file input and ouput. The windows allow files to be input without the user having to type names, remember spelling, or extract the score or object files from among the text files and other items in the directory.

Conclusions

We have examined a particular program as a means of improving our understanding of how to provide composers with better control over timbral resources. The examination has concentrated more on the overall means than the specific content of the editing process. Some of the guiding principles of value in the design process are consistency among interactions, flexibility in modes of operation (such as in audition), clarity of presentation of data and operators, and the use of defaults.

While our experience with Objed has been positive, there are still some fundamental problems. Musically, the most important is this: designing a system around a score editor on the one hand, and an object editor on the other hand, implies that composition can be partitioned between the sonological and deep-structural levels. This is a large assumption; one that is clearly not justified in some music. A more specific but related problem concerns the program's weakness in dealing with timbres that are aggregates of two or more objects functioning together. Finally, defining objects in terms of data plugged into a template leaves very little room for the specification of how the object adapts its behavior in particular contexts. How can the specification of adaptive information (such as volume varying with pitch) be combined with the environment described?

Clearly, the issue of timbral specification and control is one that still requires a great deal of research. It is hoped that the work presented here will help in bringing such control to the composer.

Acknowledgments

The results reported in this paper have benefited from the input of numerous composers who have worked on the SSSP system, especially James Montgomery and Philippe Menard. Several conversations with David Wessel have also strongly influenced our approach. Finally, Bob Pritchard and M. R. Lamb have made many helpful comments during the preparation of this manuscript.

The research reported in this paper has been undertaken as part of the SSSP of the University of Toronto. This research is supported by the Social Sciences and Humanities Research Council of Canada. This support is gratefully acknowledged.

References

Arfib, D. 1979. "Digital Synthesis of Complex Spectra by Means of Multiplication of Non-linear Distorted Sine Waves." *Journal of the Audio Engineering Society* 27(10): 757–768.

Buxton, W. 1981. "Music Software User's Manual." Tech. Note No. 22. Toronto: University of Toronto Computer Systems Research Group.

Buxton, W. et al. 1979. "The Evolution of the SSSP Score Editing Tools." *Computer Music Journal* 3(4): 14–25.

Buxton, W. et al. 1980. "A Microcomputer-based Conducting System." *Computer Music Journal* 4(1): 8–21.

Chowning, J. 1973. "The Synthesis of Complex Audio Spectra by Means of Frequency Modulation." *Journal of the Audio Engineering Society* 21: 526–534. Reprinted in *Computer Music Journal* 1(2): 46–54.

Grey, J. 1975. "Exploration of Musical Timbre." Tech. Rep. STAN-M-2. Stanford, California: Stanford University Department of Music.

Grey, J. 1977. "Multidimensional Perceptual Scaling of Musical Timbre." *Journal of the Acoustical Society of America* 61: 1270–1277.

Kaegi, W., and S. Tempelaars. 1978. "VOSIM—A New Sound Synthesis System." *Journal of the Audio Engineering Society* 26: 418–424.

Krasner, G. 1980. "The Design of a Smalltalk Music System." *Computer Music Journal* 4(4): 4–14.

Le Brun, M. 1979. "Digital Waveshaping Synthesis." *Journal of the Audio Engineering Society* 27: 250–266.

Mathews, M. V. 1969. *The Technology of Computer Music.* Cambridge, Massachusetts: MIT Press.

Moorer, J. A. 1977. "Signal Processing Aspects of Computer Music—A Survey." *Proceedings of the IEEE* 65: 1108–1137. Reprinted in *Computer Music Journal* 1(1): 4–37.

Truax, B. 1976. "A Communicational Approach to Computer Sound Programs." *Journal of Music Theory* 20(2): 227–300.

Wessel, D. 1979. "Timbre Space as a Musical Control Structure." *Computer Music Journal* 3(2): 45–52.

25

Colin Banger and Bruce Pennycook
Department of Computing and Information
Science and Department of Music
Queen's University
Kingston, Ontario, Canada

Gcomp: Graphic Control of Mixing and Processing

Introduction

The Queen's University Computer Music Facility has focused on the development of computer tools for digital *musique concrète* composition. Over the past few years, we have been working on a set of programs and sound file management utilities to assist users in the manipulation of digital sound files generated by Cmusic (Moore 1982) on a VAX 11/750 or digitally recorded and stored on a 300-Mbyte disk. The central programs are Waves and Gcomp (Pennycook 1981).

Waves is an interactive sound file editor that essentially duplicates the features of other sound file editors, such as S by James A. Moorer, Edsnd (Chafe, Mont-Raynaud, and Rush 1982), and the system at the New York Institute of Technology (Kowalski and Glassner 1982). Waves has one unique feature, however, which will be described in the section on other features. Waves operates much like a screen editor in that commands typed in at the display terminal result in corresponding changes in the contents of the display. In fact, Waves behaves much like Vi, the Unix screen editor (Joy 1980).

Gcomp is an interactive graphics program that permits the user to define and edit time-varying control functions for processing individual sound files and mixing together several sound files stored on disk. In contrast to the "what you see is what you get" screen editing operations of Waves, Gcomp can be compared to a text formatter such as Nroff, the Unix document formatting program. In this type of program, formatting commands and source data (text) are merged and submitted to a program. The output, in our case a stream of digital sound samples, is written on disk for audition through the audio conversion system.

Although this approach has some obvious limitations compared to systems like that developed at Lucasfilm (Snell 1982) or more modest machines

Computer Music Journal, Volume 7, No. 4,
Winter 1983

like that developed a few years ago for the B.B.C. (McNally 1979), Gcomp is a readily learned, flexible visual aid to sound file processing and mixing within a software-based computer music environment.

The Analog Mixing Console Model

Gcomp has been modeled on a set of sound-processing and mixing functions found on most audio consoles. It also models the order in which these functions are most commonly used during the mixing session. Figure 1 is a schematic diagram of five electronic components joined into an audio input "strip." It includes controls for modifying the signal input level, four bands of parametric equalization (variable filters), reverberation send/return mix, location of the output over two channels, and control of the overall output level. Several of these input strips, typically 4, 8, 16, 24, and so on, are linked through output buses providing one, two, four, or more output channels. The output levels are controlled by a separate set of amplitude faders that on most mixing consoles are situated to the right of the input strips. Of course, a large studio console includes several other essential functions, such as track assignment controls for routing audio to and from the tape machines, signal level metering, and numerous switches for monitoring selected tracks. The five basic functions we have chosen serve as a practical, working model, however.

In a "typical" mixing session, the engineer first sets the controls (such as those in Fig. 1) for each individual channel of sound. Once the sound quality, reverberation, and stereo location are established, several or all of the channels are played simultaneously to determine the relative output levels for the mix. As anyone who has ever mixed audio in this fashion will readily testify, the mixing process is one of continuous audition, adjustment, and re-adjustment until all of the sounds are properly located in the stereo (or quadraphonic) image and are

Fig. 1. Analog recording
console components.

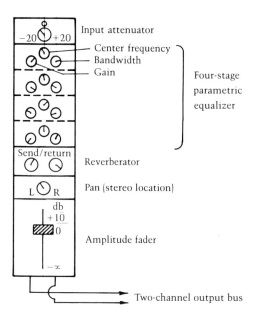

be defined in terms of graphic display, we considered at length the correlation between the physical action of turning a knob or sliding a fader and the image presented to the user on the vector display terminal. In most cases, we chose straight-line segments or curves varying with respect to time above or around an appropriately labeled x-axis. This approach, rather than graphic simulations of moving meters or knobs, provided the least confusing representation. Only the filter parameter required a different graphic approach, as will be shown later.

Other design considerations included the following:

1. Portability. Gcomp is written entirely in C (Kernighan and Ritchie 1978). The graphic display drivers have been isolated into separate program modules to reduce implementation time on different graphic systems. (At Queen's, Gcomp runs on a Norpak IGP Vector Graphics System.)

2. Independence from the processing software. The first versions of Gcomp automatically produced Music 11 (Vercoe 1980) instrument code and note lists. The current version produces a set of time-ordered functions and pointers to the sound file names. This output can be readily interfaced to any software synthesis system, to specially constructed processing routines, or to a real-time sound processor.

3. Independence from the processing algorithms. The control functions generated by Gcomp are loosely associated with the actual signal processing routines. The three parameters, location, distance, and reverberation delay time, can be interpreted in many ways. The user is not necessarily responsible for the implementation of these algorithms, yet retains direct control over the stereo image through three simple parameters.

at each moment in time at the desired relative volumes. Without real-time sound-processing capabilities, this aspect of sound mixing could not be implemented with our model.

Gcomp Design

Although we could not experiment with a real-time system, we recognized the need for continuous time-varying adjustment of each and every controllable operation in the mixing process. The central operation in Gcomp, therefore, is the construction and editing of time-varying functions. A set of graphic function-editing tools form the basis of the user interface. In order to avoid excessive screen clutter, the processing and mixing operations were separated into two modes. A third mode was added to provide a generalized function editor for use within Gcomp or to build functions for use in other programs, such as Cmusic (Moore 1982a).

As the entire processing and mixing task was to

Modes of Operation

The three modes of operation are *function-definition mode*, *process mode*, and *mix mode*.

Fig. 2. Function-definition mode: facsimile of a graphic display showing a damped sine wave. Note that the label amplitude *below the x-axes refers to the parameter last used in process mode before function-definition mode was invoked.*

Fig. 3. Process mode: facsimile of a graphic display showing the five parameters of amplitude, location, distance, reverb delay time, and equalization. In this case, only two of the equalization stages have been assigned control functions. Note that the damped sine wave of Fig. 1 appears in the first 30 sec of the amplitude parameter.

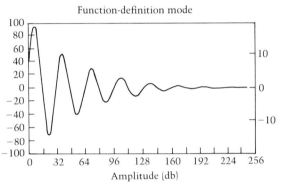

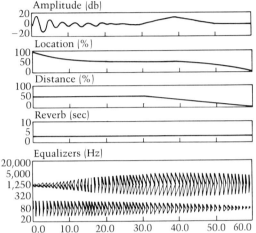

Each mode can be accessed by a single uppercase key at any time during the Gcomp session. All pertinent information in the current mode is retained and, when applicable, passed to the next mode automatically. For example, the user may wish to leave the process mode in order to build a new function in function-definition mode. The axes of the function editor will automatically be labeled according to the operation last invoked in process mode. Upon returning to process mode, the program maintains the previous state. In all modes, only the first one or two letters of the commands need be typed. The remainder of the command is instantaneously filled in and followed by a half-intensity prompt to remind the user what type of response is appropriate. Illegal entries are ignored. The program simply waits for a legal entry or for a new command. All data generated within Gcomp are stored in compact binary form for maximum efficiency, yet the user can request alphanumeric listings of the data within each mode if desired.

Function-Definition Mode

Function-definition mode provides a wide variety of function-building tools. Figure 2 is a drawing of the screen showing a damped sine function. In addition to the stored trigonometric functions and arithmetic operators, there is a drawing mode that engages the cursor controls on the graphic terminal. A feature not present in most function editors is the tag command, which marks and saves any number of x-axis positions. This permits function-editing commands to affect subranges between pairs of tag markers. All types of commands may be freely mixed, permitting the user to build a wide range of functions. A smooth command reiteratively rounds discontinuities or line-segment junctions to produce continuous curves if desired. As previously mentioned, functions can be named and stored on disk for use outside of Gcomp.

Process Mode

Figure 3 is a drawing of the vector screen showing the five parameters of this mode: amplitude, location, distance, reverb delay time, and four equalizers. The function in the amplitude box has been assembled from the damped sine wave constructed in function mode (Fig. 2), which occupies the first 30 sec of the 60-sec window, and from three line segments constructed directly in process mode.

The location parameter in Fig. 3 has been made from an exponential curve constructed in function mode, which is followed by a constant, which is followed by another instance of the exponential curve. The distance and reverb delay parameters both contain line segments drawn directly in process mode.

Fig. 4. Process mode, al-
phanumeric terminal.
Data are entered at the alphanumeric terminal. In
this case, the program is

waiting for a duration of
an equalizer function. The
prompt "float" is displayed
at half intensity as a reminder to type in data.

```
Soundfile: foo.snd                                    Channels: 1
Sample Rate: 22500          Samples: 45000            Duration: 2.000
------------------------------------------------------------------------
Parameter: Equaliser 1      Total Time: 2.000         Total Segments: 4
------------------------------------------------------------------------
Control File: tex5          Duration: 30.000
------------------------------------------------------------------------

Command: Insert Insert Equaliser
Centre Frequency: Linetype = Line Segment
                  Initial frequency (20..20000): 1004.00
                  Final frequency: (20..20000): 2034.24
Bandwidth:        Linetype = Constant
                  Constant # of octaves (0..5): 2.5 8ve
Gain:             Linetype = Function
                  Function: exp
                  Duration: _float>
```

The display image for the four-band filter parameter in Fig. 3 is slightly more complex. The filter
bandwidth is defined by the vertical boundaries of
the set of arrows, the center frequency by the midpoint between these, and the amount of attenuation
or increase by the angle of the two lines forming
the arrows. A backward arrow represents attenuation, a forward arrow increase. This provides an immediately recognizable correlate for the turning of
the filter gain knob in either direction from straight
up, which on most consoles produces no attenuation or increase. The upper or lower line segments
of the arrows are shaded when gain is increased or
decreased respectively to intensify the implied
knob direction.

The data for the five process mode parameters
can be entered quickly from the terminal. Each request for data is accompanied by a half-intensity
prompt that eliminates the need for printed manuals and time-consuming calls to the on-line help
file. Figure 4 shows the alphanumeric terminal display in process mode. The program is waiting for
the equalizer duration and has prompted the user
with "float" as an input-data-type reminder.

A complete list of the process mode commands is
shown in Fig. 5. Most commands require only the
first two characters to be typed (in uppercase).

Mix Mode

We decided that the most important aspect of the
mixing operation was the alignment of the entry
timings of each sound file. To minimize screen
clutter in this mode, only the amplitude and location curves are shown for each of up to 6 displayed
channels of sound files. A total of 40 channels of
sound files can be mixed together, assigning one of
6 channels to any of the boxes at any one time.

Figure 6 is a drawing of the vector screen in mix
mode. In this diagram, sound file channels have
been assigned to boxes one, three, four, five, and
six. The functions displayed have been constructed
in process mode. The user declares a sound file
name and a starting time. The amplitude and location functions are automatically inserted. As in process mode, the window size (in seconds) and the
starting times are fully adjustable.

Other Features

Most large professional mixing consoles include the
machinery for partially or fully automating the
mixing task. *Automated mixdown* alleviates the
often impractical process of manually controlling
many amplitude faders at once. Automated mix-

Banger and Pennycook

Fig. 5. Process mode, command summary. The uppercase characters denote that only those characters need be typed. The program fills in the remainder of the command. The commands for function-definition mode and mix mode have a similar format.

Fig. 6. Mix mode, facsimile of graphic display. The six boxes in this window contain amplitude and location functions constructed and transferred from process mode (or function-definition mode). Note that the functions in box six are identical to those in the corresponding parameters shown in Fig. 3 for process mode.

CLear: clear IGP screen
ERase: erase current display segment
INsert ⟨linetype⟩⟨values⟩⟨duration⟩:   insert segment
LIst ⟨parameter⟩:   print parameter data on terminal
MArk ⟨name⟩⟨time⟩:   mark a time on a trigger track
NAme ⟨name⟩:   give name to current segment
OVerwrite ⟨filename⟩:   write data to existing file
PArameter ⟨parameter id⟩:   select a parameter
REad List ⟨filename⟩:   read data from disc
REad Trigger ⟨filename⟩:   read trigger track from disc
SEt up ⟨control data⟩:   alter control data parameters
SCore ⟨filename⟩:   produce output file
TIme ⟨integer⟩:   set start time of window
WIndow ⟨op⟩ ⟨integer⟩:   set window size of display
WRite List: save current data on disc
WRite Trigger: write trigger track on disc

⟨ctrl⟩ 0:   return to UNIX
⟨ctrl⟩ S: reverse scroll mode (window moves
             backward with respect to time)

cursor left: move current segment one place to left
cursor right: move current segment one place to right

M: go to Mix Mode
F: go to Function Definition Mode
q: exit program

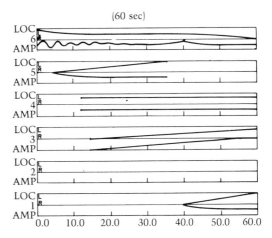

down is accomplished by a device that samples the motion of the faders and stores the samples as a sequence of control voltages on magnetic tape or as binary data in a computer memory. Engineers can then prepare and store their actions on as many channels of sound as can be effectively operated at once.

Gcomp accomplishes essentially the same results by controlling the mix parameters with sets of time-varying control functions. Unlike the analog console, however, each and every parameter in Gcomp can be controlled by a time-varying curve.

The Trigger Track

Gcomp includes an important extension to the automation of sound mixing. A feature called the trigger track enables the composer or engineer to mark and label important moments in any sound file. The *trigger track* is a file that stores these marked times for use in any of the three Gcomp modes. Furthermore, the trigger track can be constructed within Waves, the sound file editor. This feature is used for synchronizing events in any sound file with events in other sound files. Thus, automatic interchannel timing coordination can be achieved. For example, the nth note of a digitally recorded passage can be located (using the note-boundary detector in Waves) and marked with a logical name. This name and others can be stored in the trigger-track file and recalled during mix mode to indicate an entry time for other sound files. This greatly simplifies the often tedious task of keeping track of absolute entry times among the many sound files that may go into a mix.

Gcomp contains several other user-interaction conveniences. These include a *verbose mode*, which displays a running history of the terminal operations, complete on-line documentation, commands for escaping to the Unix Operating System or Waves, and on-line access to alphanumeric representations of the binary files containing the function and timing data. A status line at the top of the screen displays information about the sound file currently being processed (name, sampling rate, total duration, number of samples) and the position and duration in seconds of the current display window. These features have been included in an attempt to reduce the need for external information sources (other files, scraps of paper, etc.) and to make the integration of Waves and Gcomp as transparent as possible.

Gcomp Output

The output from this software is a file of linked lists containing the functions and pointers to the sound files declared during a Gcomp session. As this program is intended to produce functions that change the value of control-rate rather than signal-rate parameters, the time increment is set at $\frac{1}{10}$ sec. (This is the default value based on a sampling rate of 45,000 samples per second per channel.) Each function point is stored as an 8-bit byte.

SPAM

A stand-alone set of C routines that take in the Gcomp output files and produce a stereo sound file as output were written by Greg Hermanovic of Human Computing Resources, Toronto, while under contract to the Defense and Civil Institute for Environmental Medicine, Downsview, Canada. Under this contract Gcomp, Waves, the CARL software (Moore 1982a), Objed (Buxton and Fedorkow 1978), and several other music and sound-processing programs were installed for use by the audio research group under Dr. Martin Taylor, Chief Scientist. Hermanovic's program, Signal Processing and Mixing (SPAM), contains all of the processing and mixing algorithms designated by Gcomp. Most were based on routines in Cmusic. The extremely large number of control functions that can be generated in Gcomp were difficult to fit into the limited address space of the Digital Equipment Corporation (DEC) PDP-11/34, necessitating a scheme that relied heavily on the Unix pipe mechanism. This mechanism unfortunately adds considerable overhead to the already time-consuming signal processing and mixing procedures (Moore 1982a).

At Queen's, we have been developing a more efficient, DEC VAX version of SPAM, again based on

routines borrowed and modified from Cmusic and the CARL library. It is also possible to use the sound file reading and external table-lookup features of Cmusic directly.

The Future

We hope to purchase or construct a real-time signal processing machine in the near future. The design criteria for this machine include the capacity to process at least eight channels of input and two channels of output, realizing the processing and mixing requirements of Gcomp. A preliminary design for such a machine has been completed at Queen's University (Kulick, Dove, and Pennycook 1983).

Conclusion

Gcomp and its companion program Waves constitute the main programs for editing, processing, and mixing sound files on the VAX-11/750 at Queen's. We have proved that the software is robust and portable and that most of the operations required for constructing compositions from digital sound files have been supported. We recognize the severe limitation that the software environment poses compared to real-time systems. We have, however, learned a great deal about the problems of graphic representation of editing, processing, and mixing, and feel that Gcomp offers the composer a useful, readily learned aid for digital *musique concrète* composition.

References

Buxton, W., and G. Fedorkow. 1978. "The Structured Sound Synthesis Project (SSSP)—An Introduction." Report CSRG-82. Toronto: University of Toronto Computer Systems Research Group.

Chafe, C., B. Mont-Raynaud, and L. Rush. 1982. "Toward an Intelligent Editor of Digital Audio: Recognition of Musical Constructs." *Computer Music Journal* 6(1):30–41.

Joy, W. 1980. "Vi." *UNIX Programmer's Manual, Volume*

2c—*Supplementary Documents. Seventh Edition, Virtual VAX-11 Version.* Murray Hill, New Jersey: Bell Laboratories.

Kernighan, B., and D. Ritchie. 1978. *The C Programming Language.* Englewood Cliffs, New Jersey: Prentice-Hall.

Kowalski, M. J., and A. Glassner. 1982. "The N.Y.I.T. Digital Sound Editor." *Computer Music Journal* 6(1):66–73.

Kulick, J., D. Dove, and B. Pennycook. 1983. "A Multibus Compatible Audio Signal Processor." Unpublished paper.

McNally, D. 1979. "Microprocessor Mixing and Processing of Digital Audio Signals." *Journal of the Audio Engineering Society* 27(10):793–803.

Moore, F. R. 1982*a*. "The Computer Audio Research Laboratory at UCSD." *Computer Music Journal* 6(1):18–29.

Moore, F. R. 1982*b*. "Musical Signal Processing in a UNIX Environment." In *The CARL Startup Kit.* La Jolla: Computer Audio Research Laboratory, University of California at San Diego, pp. 121–122.

Pennycook, B. 1981. "Computer Music at Queen's." In *Proceedings of the 1981 International Computer Music Conference.* San Francisco: Computer Music Association, pp. 75–93.

Snell, J. 1982. "The Lucasfilm Real-Time Console for Recording Studios and Performance of Computer Music." *Computer Music Journal* 6(3):33–45.

Vercoe, B. 1980. *Music-11 Reference Manual.* Cambridge, Massachusetts: M.I.T. Experimental Music Studio.

26

Bill Schottstaedt
Center for Computer Research
in Music and Acoustics
Stanford University
Stanford, California 94305

Pla: A Composer's Idea of a Language

Introduction

Composers have often found the computer to be a difficult instrument. It can take weeks of effort just to produce a few disappointing tones, and pity the poor composer who wants to use the computer as a compositional aid! That, however, is the state I found myself in several years ago, and the resulting level of frustration was rather high. This article describes an attempt to develop a compositional system that reduces that level of frustration.

Most existing high-level languages do not explicitly support the special needs of composers. Several simple programs exist that seem to be oriented toward providing a shorthand for the entry of piano music; examples include Score (Smith 1972) and Scot (Gold, Stautner, and Haflich 1980). What we really want, so we are told, is a musical data-entry system where composers need know nothing of the machine. But composers are expected to learn the rudiments of other instruments; why should the computer be different? None of the composers I have discussed this with has groused about the need for a little programming, and many have pointed out that most compositional devices are actually little programs that happen to be expressed in an obscure notation (common music notation). Why not write these algorithms in a much more explicit programming language? But before I go on to that topic, it might be useful to examine one of the existing programs.

Score and Its Ilk

Score is a well-known musical data-entry program. It has no provisions for variables, expressions, or subroutines. Its only statements are assignment

Computer Music Journal, Vol. 7, No. 1,
Spring 1983

statements. Our trusting composers find themselves immersed in a world of random deviations, invisible instruments, and duty factors, surrounded with flourishes of asterisks, arrows, and frightening error messages (an example of Score input and output is given in Code Listing 1). If composers want to develop their own unintelligible shorthand, the underlying language should certainly not get in their way, but it is inexcusable to base the language itself on a mass of arcane abbreviations and weird characters.

Score at least can "escape" to Fortran IV when its features are exhausted, but the interface between Score and Fortran IV is not very flexible. Perhaps the worst aspect of Score-like programs is that they represent a restricted notion of what a composer does. It is hard to avoid the conclusion that the writers of this type of data-entry program view computer music composition as primarily the laborious specification of the parameters of one note after another. In their view, apparently, the best that can be offered is a program that reduces the number of keystrokes required to enter the data. My impression, on the other hand, is that composers are less concerned with the mechanics of typing and are more concerned with the clarity, readability, and flexibility of what they are typing.

It is also not inconceivable that composers might want to interact with their musical material in a more friendly, fluid environment where more aspects of the music composition system can be extended and modified. During the last four years at the Center for Computer Research in Music and Acoustics (CCRMA), I have been developing a language I call *Pla* to give composers just such a system.

The general syntax of Pla is borrowed from Sail (Reiser 1976), a baroque Algol dialect. The music-oriented features, however, directly fill the specific compositional needs of the composers. Although this method of language development may seem ad hoc, the resulting language need not be an ugly

Code Listing 1. Use of the Score language. Fragment of music in Score language (a); result of Score language output (b); and score error messages (c).

```
              BUZZ;
              P2 RHY/4/2/8/ /REP 3,2/ /;
              DF 1000.2;
              P3 NOTES/P C4/B/C/O B3/C/FINE;
              P4 LIT/P3%2/!−52;
    (a)       P5 .2 10,100 .4 200,210 .2 1,1;
              P6 −9999.5;
              P7 1000; CO "∗"; CO MOVX/10 1 3;
              P8 FU/1/2/ /;
              END;
              RUN;

              < BUZZ .SCR − RANDOM NUMBER = 1
              PLAY;
              BUZZ      0.000      1.200 C   P3/2   1.000   0.000   1000.0 ∗   1.000 F1
              ;PRINT P1;< BUZZ       1
              BUZZ      1.000      2.200 B/2 ,−52   1.000   0.000   1000.0 ∗   1.116 F2
              ;PRINT P1;< BUZZ       2
    (b)       BUZZ      3.000      0.700 C   P3/2 202.690   0.000   1000.0 ∗   1.390
              ;PRINT P1;< BUZZ       3
              BUZZ      3.500      0.700 B/2 ,−52   1.000   0.000   1000.0 ∗   1.469
              ;PRINT P1;< BUZZ       4
              BUZZ      4.000      2.200 C/2 P3/2   1.000   0.000   1000.0 ∗   1.552 F1
              ;PRINT P1;< BUZZ       5
              FINISH;   < BUZZ .SCR

    (c)  ↑ ↑ ↑ ↑ ↑ ↑ REMEMBER ↑ ↑ ↑ ↑ ↑ PARAMETER OFFSET= 1
         ↑ ↑ ↑ ↑ ↑ ↑ REMEMBER ↑ ↑ ↑ ↑ ↑ PARAMETER OFFSET= 2
```

mess. At least we know that what we have, we need.

Where Do We Start?

What constructs can be added to a normal programming language that will be of most use to composers? We assume that the language has the standard control structures, data types, input/output capabilities, and error handlers. We start with a general-purpose programming language (the Algol part of Sail), thereby incorporating a vast body of practical knowledge that computer programmers have built into their languages. With this base we ensure that future needs and new ideas can be incorporated without undue pain, and we ensure that our composing environment is, at some level, "customiz-able." We do not assume that we have already imagined every possible compositional method. To maximize the flexibility and friendliness of the Pla environment, we decided to make Pla an interactive interpreter, rather than a compiler. Because it was originally feared that some complex programming problem would appear that Pla syntax could not handle, an extensive interface to Sail was provided to ensure that we could handle anything. As it happens, the Sail escape hatch has been used very little. If desired, however, Pla can be used either as a Sail interpreter or as nothing more than a collection of handy Sail routines driven by some other program.

Given that base, our language design is driven by the needs of the users. Some of these needs are determined by the structure of the rest of the music software at CCRMA. Pla works in conjunction with the music compilers, MUS10 (Tovar 1977) and MUSBOX (Loy 1981). Both of these compilers read Music V note lists and crank out either the sound samples themselves (MUS10), or a code stream for the synthesizer (MUSBOX).

Music V Syntax

The Music V-style note-list syntax (Mathews 1969; Loy 1981) that Pla generates can be looked upon as a series of process calls ordered in time. The syntax is extremely limited; the only legal statements are comments, process calls, and assignments. In Pla, as in Score, composers normally ignore the note list altogether, treating it merely as a communication channel between Pla and the music compiler. The note list is a score of the piece, however, so its usefulness extends beyond debugging. The format and contents of the note list should, therefore, be left up to the composer as much as possible. The limitations of the note-list syntax become much less painful if the note-list generator provides all the control and flexibility the composer needs. At CCRMA, whether the composer is using Pla, Score, or the text editor, a compositional work session involves repeated editing passes over a large group of note lists. Each note list contains the current state of a phrase or section of the piece. The composition is usually broken up into phrases in this manner because testing and polishing each phrase can go faster if we do not have to recompute the entire composition each time we want to hear a new version of a phrase. Clearly, our language should also be able to help with the chore of editing and mixing these lists.

Try to read a Music V note list (Code Listing 1b, for example). The first thing that strikes most composers is the bewildering morass of numbers, interspersed with just enough envelope names so as to be completely meaningless.

The note list, despite its drawbacks, is the definition of the composition from the music compiler's point of view. To create and edit note lists, we obviously need a general parameter-naming facility. In Pla, the parameters can be referred to by their Score-like "P" names (P1 is the first parameter).

Macros can be defined to give these P numbers more mnemonic names. There is also a predeclared array P that can be used to refer to the parameters. But the solution that has been most widely used here is the PARS statement.

PARS Name Onset Duration Frequency Amplitude;

This tells Pla that the voice's parameters are Name (P0), Onset (P1), and so on. A similar naming facility exists in the Sail software used to write instruments for MUSBOX, so composers need only copy the PARS statement to ensure that their note-list parameters match those of their instruments.

Message Passing in Note Lists

In complex cases where we want to pass an instrument many parameters, even this naming facility becomes cumbersome. It is no mean feat to keep track of all the various parameter interrelationships that go into producing a convincing legato, for example, and the set of relationships is different from one instrument to the next. We have implemented a form of *message passing* (Krasner 1980; Weinreb and Moon 1981) to deal with this explosion of interconnections. Each instrument has a default value it assigns to each parameter. When invoked, the instrument scans its parameter list. If a normal parameter is found, its value replaces the default. If, however, a message name is encountered, the default value is kept, and the code associated with the message is executed. Messages can have modifiers (also a form of message) and arguments. The idea is to keep all the performance-practice related information hidden in the instrument. The message Legato can then be passed to either a violinlike or a pianolike instrument, and each does whatever is needed to produce a correct legato. The note list is kept as uncluttered and as readable as possible. As an example, consider a typical violinlike instrument. In the normal case, we must keep track of hundreds of instrument calls of the form

Violin .000, 1.210, A/2, .005, Amp, .000, .000, .065, Ind, .000,
    .000, 2.501, F23, .000, .000, 5.000, .015, Amp, 70.135,
    1.000, .100;

where P17 is the vibrato amplitude (try to find P17!). With the message system, the same call can become

> Violin .000 1.210 A/2 Soft Pizzicato Locate: 70.125 1 Molto Vibrato.

The exact order of the messages is unimportant. The Locate message used in this example takes two arguments that determine the spatial location at which we want to place the sound. A note list made up of these messages is far more readable and far more flexible than its predecessor. Of course, our note-list editing facilities have to be slightly smarter. To change the amplitude parameter, for example, Pla now has to be able to find either the amplitude parameter (P4 in this case), or the message that sets the amplitude (Soft).

Messages make compositional gestures explicit. There is no necessity to use Italian musical directions, although there are good reasons why they exist (they are useful macros even in computer music). If all instruments are able to recognize a core of messages, reorchestration of a score becomes easy, even when the parameters of the various instruments do not fall in the same order.

Some Basic Needs

Most composers are familiar with a number of "musical macros." These include the pitch names (A for 440 Hz), rhythmic values (eighth note), motives, transpositions, tempo indications, and so on. Most of these have a direct counterpart in Pla.

The pitch names are predeclared and preinitialized variables. The Score constructs of NOTE and RHYTHM have been borrowed, along with its motive declaration and transposition syntax. These enable composers to enter lists of data when they actually want to do that. A more general cyclic list has also been implemented, allowing streams of expressions to be included anywhere a variable of the same type is allowed. For example, we can pass a cycle of the pitches G,A,B as an argument to a procedure.

> Frequency ← FreqProc([g,a,b]);

The square brackets indicate that the contents constitute the definition of a cycling stream of expressions.

Another basic feature is a random-number generator. Although there are strong reasons to avoid random numbers whenever possible, there are cases where they can be used without completely trivializing our music. Pla provides both a white-noise random-number generator (RAN) and a procedure written by Michael McNabb that turns out a sequence of numbers that approximates almost any desired power spectral density. (The original impetus for this was interest in the uses of $1/f$ noise, but few composers at CCRMA have used it much.)

The overall tempo of the composition can be set according to any expression by using the TEMPO statement. There are a variety of subtle problems involved with changing tempos, not the least of which is the fact that the ear is very sensitive to the nature of the tempo change. Tempo changes constructed of line segments do not sound natural, so much ingenuity has been exercised to find alternative ways to make them work. Because line-segment envelopes are sufficient in other realms, such as the amplitude envelopes of individual notes (Grey 1975), we might have thought that larger scale changes like crescendos and accelerandos could also be done with line segments. Had this otherwise reasonable assumption been built into our language, we would have ended up with garbage. This small surprise demonstrates a fact we have encountered repeatedly while working on Pla: flexibility and programmability are necessities, not luxuries.

In Pla, envelopes can be applied at any level of the structure. They can serve as constraints upon random fluctuations, for example, or they can act as filters. Pla's other basic data types are reals, integers, and strings. These are handled exactly as Sail handles them. Lists and contexts have also been borrowed from Sail. A *list* is an ordered sequence of atoms that indicates where the atoms can be real, integer, or string constants. A *context* is a list of name-value pairs defining the state of some arbitrary group of variables at a given time in a compilation. For user-defined types, Pla provides the flavor mechanism of Lisp Machine Lisp cast in

Code Listing 2. In its simplest form, Pla code can resemble Score input. In keeping with Score conventions, c4 is middle C, c5 is an octave above middle C, and so on. The func- tion Ramp is defined directly in Pla code. AmpFunc and FreqFunc specify function names, with the functions stored in an external file. Code Listing 3. Output produced by Pla from Code Listing 1. In this format, C is middle C, C*2 is an octave above middle C, and so on, as required by the music compiler.

```
SEG(Ramp); 0 0 1 100;              COMMENT define a line-segment envelope ("FUNCTION") to ramp
                                           from (0,0) to (100,1);
PARS VoiceName Onset Duration Frequency Amplitude
AmpFunc FreqFunc;
                                   COMMENT declare voice parameter names;

VOICE Simp;                        COMMENT define a process named Simp;
BEGIN
   Duration ← RHYTHM:q;            COMMENT duration is always 1 quarter note. If Onset time is not
                                           set explicitly, Pla automatically increments it by P2;
   Frequency ← NOTE:c4,e,g,c5,END; COMMENT after the fourth note, terminate Simp;
   Amplitude ← Ramp[(OnSet+1)*25]; COMMENT ramp the amplitude from 0 to 1 across all notes;
   AmpFunc ← "amp";               COMMENT The amplitude envelope name is the string "amp";
   FreqFunc ← "Gliss_Down";       COMMENT The frequency envelope name. Both the frequency and
                                           amplitude envelopes will be handled by the music
                                           compiler;

END;
```

Code Listing 3

```
                   PLAY ;
                   Simp, .000, 1.000, C, .250, Amp, Gliss_down;
                   Simp 1.000, 1.000, E, .500, Amp, Gliss_down;
                   Simp, 2.000, 1.000, G, .750, Amp, Gliss_down;
                   Simp, 3.000, 1.000, C*2, 1.000, Amp, Gliss_down;
                   FINISH;
```

an Algol-like syntax. A *flavor* is a definition of an abstract object that responds to various message-passing protocols. Arrays of any of these types can be declared.

Voices

Higher levels of musical control are implemented as *voices* and *sections*. In Pla, notes that somehow belong together are grouped under the rubric of a voice. The notion of a computer-language-based voice is not exactly revolutionary; Score has a similar facility. In Pla, voices have additional capabilities. They can

   Occur within expressions
   Be passed parameters
   Create other voices

Read and edit existing note lists
Serve as background processes, handling multi-voice phrasing details or scheduling

The need for the last capability, a flexible, concurrent process system for music, was a major motivation for inventing Pla.

Voices can operate with a large number of defaults, making Pla easy to use. As a simple example, in Code Listing 2 we create a mundane little voice that turns out a C-major arpeggio. Because this voice statement is at the top level of the interpreter, it is executed once, thereby creating one instance of the voice (Code Listing 3). Voice statements can occur in many far more interesting places. As another simple example, we create a well-known canon in Code Listing 4. We have also chosen here to override a few of the voice's default actions.

Code Listing 4. Two
streams can be used to
generate the frequencies
and durations for a well-
known round.

```
INTEGER i;
DEFINE   Duration=p2,
         Frequency=p3;                COMMENT text macros;

FOR i←0  STEP 1 UNTIL 3 DO
   VOICE ["Bass","Tenor","Alto","Soprano"];
      BEGIN                           COMMENT first voice is called BASS, next TENOR, etc;
      REAL MyRange;
      I_ONLY:
         BEGIN                        COMMENT I_Only=initialization block;
            MYBEGIN ← i*4;            COMMENT when voice becomes active;
            MYEND ← MYBEGIN+16;   COMMENT when voice is terminated;
            MyRange ← 2 ↑ (i−2);      COMMENT octave in which notes occur;
         END;
      duration ← .5*(RHYTHM: q×4, q×4, q×2,h, q×2,h, e×4,q×2, e×4,q×2, q×2,h, q×2,h);
      Frequency ← MyRange*(c,d,e,c, c,d,e,c, e,f,g, e,f,g, g,a,g,f,e,c, g,a,g,f,e,c, c,g/2,c, c,g/2,c);
      END;
```

Voice Communication

Just as chamber musicians follow one another's activities and an orchestra follows the directions of its conductor, voices often need to communicate with each other. For example, we often want several independent voices to synchronize some portion of their activities. The voices might all crescendo together or might suddenly decide to march together for a measure.

In Pla, the easiest way to synchronize voices is to have a mute voice (one that is not turning out any notes) running in the background, keeping track of, for example, the current status of an amplitude or tempo envelope. All the voices that wish to follow that envelope send messages to the mute asking for the current envelope value. The mute voice encapsulates all the knowledge about the envelope, rather than having it spread out among many voices, so the code is simpler and the musical directions become more obvious.

When a voice is deeply nested within some structure, it is not always easy to see how to make small changes in the behavior of that voice from outside the structure. But without that access, the communication paths between the program levels become a nightmare.

The access method most commonly used involves a group of predeclared messages to which all voices can respond. If a voice Simp exists, any other voice can get access to Simp's parameters with the construct Simp:P[i] or Simp:P2 (if we know we want P2). In addition, all the internal state variables are accessible through predefined names such as Simp: MyBegin (for the time at which Simp came to life), or Simp:MyStatus (for the scheduling status of the voice). A simple example is given in Code Listing 5.

Additional messages can be defined for each voice. The messages can have any number of arguments and can return any Pla data type to the calling voice. When passed the message (using the colon syntax shown previously), the voice executes the method (procedure body) associated with that message using its own process context.

Voices can also explicitly affect the scheduling of other voices. A common example is the use of a mute voice as a conductor. As it meanders through the "score," it directs some voices to begin execution, tells others to stop for a while, and terminates some voices altogether. The scheduler's queue is directly accessible, so voices can see what other voices are active and what they are doing.

It is possible to build a rich system of process intercommunication using these constructs. Voices can watch and talk to each other and base their actions on the state of the rest of the world. David Jaffe used Pla's voice communication extensively in his pieces, *May All Your Children Be Acrobats*

Code Listing 5. Voice communication using messages. The voice Accent *watches the voice* Main. *Whenever* Main *produces a note whose* Frq *is 220*

and whose Amp *is .2,* Accent *produces a note whose* Frq *is 660. Otherwise,* Accent *plays a slow trill.*

```
PARS Name Beg Dur Frq Amp;

VOICE Main;
  BEGIN
    Dur←1;
    Frq←[220,330,110];
    Amp←[.1,.2];
  END;

VOICE Accent;
  BEGIN
    Dur←1;
    Amp←.1;
    IF Main:Frq=220 AND Main:Amp=.2
      THEN Frq←660
      ELSE Frq←[45,55];
  END;
```

(1981) and *Silicon Valley Breakdown* (1982). In these compositions, groups of voices play independently a while, synchronize all their actions for a few measures, and then go their separate ways.

What Is a Voice?

Over the last four years of working on Pla, I've done a lot of thrashing about trying to find the "right" way to define a voice's behavior. The problem first arises when we leave the land where each voice parameter is defined by a long list of individual values and enter the great swamp where voices are the algorithms they execute. These voices often want to share or slightly modify the behavior of other voices, and it quickly becomes tiresome to rewrite the same code over and over.

Consider a composition program that creates short phrases consisting of independent but synchronized voices. Each voice in the phrase has its own melody, rhythmic pattern, and timbre, but shares with the other voices in the phrase such attributes as accent pattern, tempo fluctuation, and perhaps spatial location. In addition, certain voices add a glissando to certain notes. If we had unlimited time, space, and patience, we could conceivably write out every possible voice in advance,

then choose among them at execution time. In most cases, this is not feasible.

The first solution that comes to mind is to write a procedure that creates a voice. We pass it parameters that specify the mix of behavior that voice should display. It may be evident upon a little reflection (it is certainly evident after a little coding!) that this voice-creating procedure requires a large number of parameters. To add a new kind of behavior (an overall amplitude envelope, for example) requires rewriting the procedure and rewriting every call on that procedure. The procedure calls quickly threaten to become as unwieldy as the note lists.

We can get around the plethora of parameters by passing the procedure a context containing the values the parameters would otherwise have affected. The voice can then use defaults for any variables not specified in the context. We still have to rewrite code in several places if we want to add another kind of action. And by using contexts we have made it even harder to figure out why a given voice is behaving as it is. It is often not easy to look at the code and tell what the context is going to contain at any given time. Procedure parameters become unwieldy; contexts become opaque. Neither directly addresses the problem.

We really want to be able to create a voice by combining in arbitrary ways the parse trees that define the voice's behavior; we want to be able to ignore the inner details of how that behavior is defined; we want to define each separate action only once; and finally, we want the code to give us a clue as to what the mixture is in a given case.

My own efforts to design a language extension that would provide this facility got completely bogged down. Luckily, at this moment of befuddlement, Marc LeBrun pointed out that the people building Lisp Machine Lisp had already dealt with the problem by inventing the Flavor system. [The Flavor system was designed and implemented by Howard Cannon.—Ed.] Because Pla syntax is borrowed from Algol, its form of the Flavor system looks somewhat different from that of Lisp Machine Lisp, but it provides the same facilities.

Using flavors, we define messages that help the voice determine an appropriate action. For each voice, we then mix together the various flavors we want, and give this new flavor object to the voice when it is instantiated. Although I have not yet had enough experience writing "flavorful" code to make any grand pronouncements, I would probably base the entire language on something like flavors if I were to start again from scratch.

Sections

Some music can be thought of in terms of ever-larger groupings of events. A phrase might be used over and over with slight variations, a section might return with a new orchestration, a repeated melody might be clothed in elaborate ornamentations. In Pla, there are several ways to organize and control events of this nature. Arbitrarily large groups of voices can be organized into a *section*, which then becomes nearly equivalent to a voice. A section can be recalled, reprocessed, and transformed in a variety of ways.

Another kind of grouping is based on voices. In Pla, voices can create other voices to any level of nesting. This is commonly used when we want to double a melody at an octave or create a flurry of notes for each basic note of the parent voice. Finally, Pla can read and edit its own output (note lists).

Graphics

Many composers find it useful to deal with their compositions graphically. Besides its obvious mnemonic value, a graph of a piece can serve to clarify its structure. Pla can produce many graphic representations of a piece. Figure 1 shows the output of Pla code, which accepts a note list created by Pla and produces a graphic representation of that note list. In this case the height of a line is based on the frequency (taking glissandi into account), and the width of the line is proportional to the note's amplitude.

To make the graphics more useful, we added a graphics-oriented note-list editor to Pla. It has a Lisp-like Read-Eval-Show loop, which allows the composer to place the graphic representation, text representation, and/or common music notational representation of a score into an editor buffer, then operate upon the buffer using various windows and cursors. Because the editor uses virtual paging, it can accommodate any size composition. The editor executes any arbitrary Pla code as an extended command and gives Pla enough hooks into its data structures that it can be customized to whatever extent the composer desires. Nearly all the commands available in the E text editor used at CCRMA are available in the note-list editor as well. From within the Pla editor the composer can, for example, compile and play the portion of the music in the window or the entire current state of the editor buffer. The composer can extract voices, mix in other note lists, or compile Pla code while working within the editor. The purpose of the editor is to enable composers to act upon musical ideas using almost any desired visual representations, compiling and listening to the results without having to leave the composer's customized environment.

The graphics editor was the first heavily interactive use of Pla. It quickly became apparent that two more capabilities were needed to support fully this style of work: *Save/Continue* and the ability to call and control other programs while remaining in Pla. In interactive systems it is not feasible to repeat all the keystrokes that got us to a certain state every time we want to pick up where we left off. The

Fig. 1. Graphic output from the Pla program. In this representation, frequency is shown on the vertical axis, while time is shown on the horizontal axis.

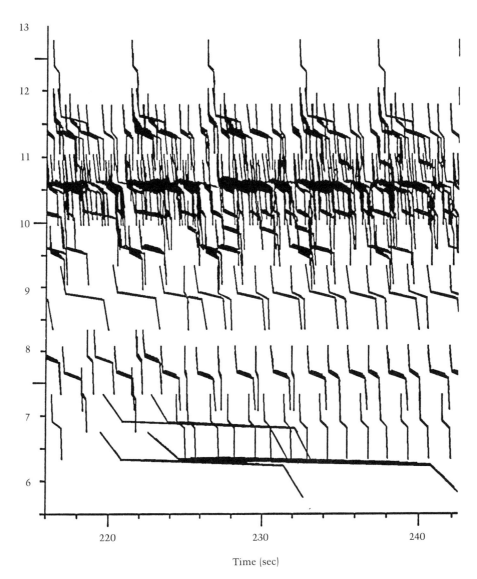

Frequency (octaves)

Time (sec)

Save/Continue feature saves the complete state of Pla in a special executable file. When executed, this file restores exactly the state of Pla that was saved. Long interactive sessions or extremely long compilations can be broken into as many short pieces as necessary without any loss of information. It is also convenient to have a backup version if we find ourselves stuck somehow.

Similarly, composers often need to try out short sections, but in an interactive environment it is bothersome to have to save everything, run a separate program or two (two at CCRMA), then re-establish the original context. With the ability to run other programs, Pla gives the composer a far more fluid working situation. Not only are Pla, the editor, the music compiler, and the synthesizer at the composer's fingertips, but any other program that happens to be useful is also available.

Problems with Pla

I do not consider Pla to be the last word in composition systems. In one sense I would say it has failed, because Pla code is, in general, not much easier to read or write than Sail or Lisp. The path from the code to the music is not always very obvious, especially in cases where complex synchronizations occur between voices. Pla's advantages are that it does not restrict composers to plunking down every detail in interminable lists, nor does it restrict them to a predetermined palette of supposedly useful gestures. There is a wide variety of nontrivial cases in which Pla provides a reasonably flexible and readable notation for composers. My hope is that it will continue to grow in usefulness as we gain more experience in computer composition and as composers become more demanding.

Conclusions

About 50 composers and several psychoacousticians have used Pla during the last four years. In general, their reactions have been favorable. Pla is fast, at least compared to the music compiler, so little of the composer's time is wasted watching it compute. It is flexible enough to handle most of the compositional needs that have arisen so far. It is implemented in Sail, so it is not very portable, but portability was not a design consideration. If I were to start over I would build it in a more robust programming environment than that provided by Stanford's Waits (Harvey 1976) and Sail—probably in Lisp Machine Lisp (Weinreb and Moon 1981). In any case, I think our experience demonstrates that composers find a programming language far more congenial than a data-entry system when trying to write computer music.

Acknowledgments

Pla grew initially out of many conversations with a number of people. Especially valuable were the criticisms and suggestions of Chris Chafe, David Jaffe, Marc LeBrun, Gareth Loy, and Ken Shoemake.

References

Gold, M., J. Stautner, and S. Haflich. 1980. "An Introduction to SCOT." Cambridge, Massachusetts: M.I.T. Experimental Music Studio.

Grey, John. 1975. "An Exploration of Musical Timbre." Department of Music Report STAN-M-2. Stanford: Stanford University.

Harvey, Brian. 1976. "Monitor Command Manual." Stanford Artificial Intelligence Laboratory Operating Note 54.5. Stanford: Stanford University.

Krasner, G. 1980. "Machine Tongues VIII: Design of Smalltalk Music System." *Computer Music Journal* 4(4):4–14.

Loy, D. Gareth. 1981. "Notes on the Implementation of MUSBOX: A Compiler for the Systems Concepts Digital Synthesizer." *Computer Music Journal* 5(1):34–50.

Mathews, M. 1969. *The Technology of Computer Music.* Cambridge, Massachusetts: MIT Press.

Reiser, J., ed. 1976. "SAIL." Report STAN-CS-574. Stanford: Stanford University Artificial Intelligence Laboratory.

Smith, Leland. 1972. "SCORE—A Musician's Approach to Computer Music." *Journal of the Audio Engineering Society* 20(1):7–14.

Tovar. 1977. "Music Manual." Stanford: CCRMA, Stanford University.

Weinreb, D., and D. Moon. 1981. "Lisp Machine Manual." Cambridge, Massachusetts: M.I.T. Artificial Intelligence Laboratory.

27

C. Fry
Cambridge, Massachusetts, USA

Flavors Band: A Language for Specifying Musical Style

The Problem

One of the tasks of music composition is the precise expression of a tremendous number of sonic events. Traditional notation does not permit composers to communicate precise sonic details to the performers of their works. The composer uses the performers to interpret the unwritten details of the score. Composers who use computers must somehow teach the computer-performer exactly what to play. For a large score this is a burden.

Many operations on scores are conceptually simple yet difficult to realize using conventional music media. Transposing of whole sections, global articulation modifications, insertion of several bars in all parts, and filling in harmonies are all examples of processes that are easy to specify, yet hard to implement using pen and paper or even scores typed into a word-processor-like musical interface. More difficult to specify but still imaginable are operations that generate original melodies and harmonies, and produce variations on themes.

The Goal

Precision of specificity is a term I use to describe the degree of detail in the plan for a final product (which could be a musical score, a building, or anything). The composer should be able to choose the precision of specificity for each piece. Some pieces may require every nuance of every sonic event to be described exactly from the beginning. Alternatively, the composer might want to start with a very sketchy description by specifying a composition whose only important qualities are a duration of five minutes and a common time signature. Values for tempo and amplitude, as well as note durations and pitches could come from default values. (De-

faults are preset values that are used in the absence of a composer's explicit specification.) Incremental modifications could be made to the entire score, refining it from the top down, rather than making hundreds of separate, local changes to achieve the same end.

Typically the composer would want to specify certain sections very carefully, while other sections need not have the same accuracy. The precision of specificity would vary throughout the piece as well as from part to part.

Features of Languages

Completely general composition programs are impossible to design because the problem space of composition is unbounded. The programmer can't know in advance what algorithms a composer would like to use, even if the programmer is the composer (as in my case). However, for certain styles of music, the programmer can guess the functionality of some likely to be desired compositional algorithms. These algorithms should be configurable in a wide variety of juxtapositions. The program should also allow hooks to a general-purpose programming language to aid the construction of new algorithms.

Flavors Band: A Solution

Flavors Band is a language for specifying jazz and popular musical styles procedurally. The procedural representation allows the generation of a large number of scores in a specified style by making only minor changes to a score specification. A style can be specified very narrowly such that all tunes generated by a style sound similar (Levitt 1981, 1984). A broader specification allows more diverse compositions to come from the same specification. Since the precision of specificity is easily controlled in Flavors Band, styles often have some tightly con-

Fig. 1. Hardware block
diagram.

Fig. 2. Flavors Band Score
topology. (PP = Phrase
Processor)

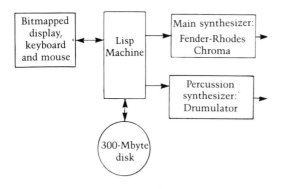

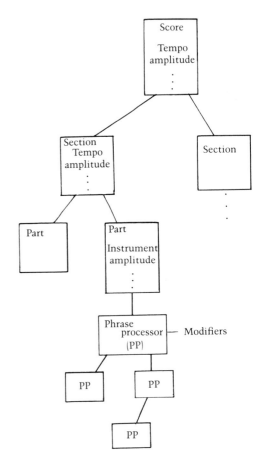

trolled aspects and some loosely described aspects
that can provide musical scores with a predetermined amount of self-similarity. (For a fascinating
discussion of musical styles and their relationship
to natural language, see Moorer 1972.)

Flavors Band is embedded in Lisp. The languages
are entwined such that each may call the other in
a structured but flexible way. A Flavors Band construct can explicitly evaluate a composer-specified
Lisp expression that itself uses a second Flavors
Band construct, and so on.

System Overview

The essential hardware of Flavors Band consists of
a Lisp Machine with a bitmapped display, alphanumeric keyboard and mouse, and a sound synthesizer for realizing scores. I also use a drum
synthesizer in addition to the main synthesizer
(Fig. 1).

Inside the Lisp Machine, Flavors Band organizes
musical structure into a tree topology (Fig. 2). Modifiers of musical structure can be applied to each
level of a Flavors Band score, from the entire score,
to its sections, parts, and phrase processors.

A musical style is represented as a *phrase-
processing network*. Each phrase processor exhibits
a particular low-level musical behavior. By interconnecting phrase processors in various ways, different higher-level musical behaviors are specified.
Currently about 60 kinds of phrase processors are

implemented in Flavors Band. Since all phrase processors conform to the same input/output (I/O)
conventions, a new phrase processor can be added
to Flavors Band and used in conjunction with the
existing phrase processors without modification.

Pitch-time Events

Phrase processors manipulate *event streams*. In Flavors Band, a note is specified by two events, an "on"
event and an "off" event. Each event has a time (in

Fig. 3. Phrase processor
input types. (a) Single
event stream input. The
normal case. (b) Multiple

event stream input. (c) No
event stream input. An
event generator.

Fig. 4. Phrase processing
networks.

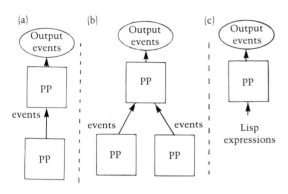

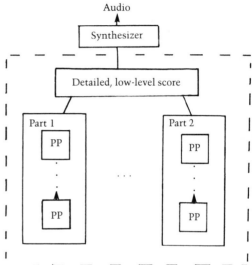

beats), a flag indicating whether the event is an
"on" event or an "off" event, a pitch-class (0–11),
an octave (0–10), another flag indicating whether it
is a rest or not, and a note identification number
(ID). The two events of a note travel independently
through a phrase processing network. The only way
a phrase processor can tell whether two events are
for the same note is to check if they have the same
ID. IDs are manufactured in such a way as to guarantee that each note's ID is unique.

An optional characteristic of an event is a property list that can hold any number of additional
properties. (Read any text on Lisp for an explanation of property lists.) Properties may be added, deleted, and read by phrase processors as an event
progresses through a network.

Flavors Band deals primarily with the pitch-time
structure of a score. The property list could be used
to hold timbre modifications, but the synthesizers
in the current system support few such modifications. Frequently the property list is used to hold
amplitude, and sometimes scales, or voicings of
chords. Two languages that go beyond Flavors
Band from the standpoint of timbre modifications
are FORMES (Rodet and Cointe 1984), and Pla
(Schottstaedt 1983).

The Anatomy of a Phrase Processor

Each phrase processor produces an event stream
that becomes the input to another phrase processor.
Most phrase processors have one input event stream

and act like a black box whose behavior depends on
the kind of phrase processor used, and the parameter values used to refine the behavior of the phrase
processor. Some phrase processors have more than
one input event stream, where the output events
are some combination of the input events. Other
phrase processors have no event streams as inputs.
This kind of phrase processor acts more like a generator than a filter (Fig. 3).

Phrase Processing Networks

A connected set of phrase processors forms a network. Scores are specified in terms of such networks.
When a score specified by a network is computed,
an array of events suitable for performance by a synthesizer is created (Fig. 4). These events are stored
in the *events* slot of the part that made them. Thus
the output of Flavors Band is stored in the same
data framework used for input and computation.
This insures the association between a score specification and the computed score, as well as facilitating inheritance (described later).

The input and output behavior of a phrase-processing network is no different in syntax from that of a single phrase processor. A sophisticated user can build a small network containing several phrase processors that can then become a construct in the language. This new construct performs semantically just as the subnetwork it was constructed from and syntactically just like other single phrase processors (Fig. 5).

Kinds of Phrase Processors

Phrase processors fall logically into three categories: *note modifiers, control flow modifiers,* and *accessors* to precomputed event arrays. Phrase processors typically have several arguments, one of which is a phrase processor from which to get the input event stream, and the rest of which are Lisp expressions that customize the phrase processor for each particular use. Any number of a particular kind of phrase processor can be used in a network, as can any mix of phrase processor types. In the rest of this section, I describe some of the more interesting phrase processors.

Note-Modifier Phrase Processors

notes is a phrase processor that allows the specification of the begin-end pairs of events that make up a note. Each of the *characteristics* of a note (duration, pitch, octave, and rest) has a Lisp expression associated with it that is evaluated to yield the value for the characteristic. For example, the value for pitch must be a number, typically between 0 and 11. The specification for pitch could be any of the following:

3	The pitch E-flat
e-	A Flavors Band global variable representing the pitch E-flat
my-favorite-pitch	A user-declared global variable
(+ 1 my-favorite-pitch)	One greater than the above

The important point here is that all of the expres-

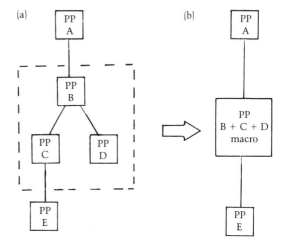

sive power of Lisp can be used with little effort on the part of Flavors Band. **notes** allows the specification of the start time as either an absolute time (in beats) or as the ending time of the previous note. The ending time of a note may be specified either as a duration from the starting time, or as an absolute time. **notes** is an event generator rather than a filter since it has no event stream as input. It creates events as they are requested from the phrase processor controlling **notes**.

Several phrase processors use pitch modes and scales (Coker 1964; Russell 1959). Modes are formal objects in Flavors Band. Each mode contains a set of intervals in semitones specified by integers between 0 and 11 inclusive. Certain mode objects include just the chord tones of seventh chords while others include more than seven intervals that represent altered jazz modes (Fig. 6). Additional modes are easily specified by the user.

A scale in Flavors Band is a mode with an associated pitch class that is designated as the root of the scale. Scales with any defined mode containing any root are easy to specify.

transpose has the arguments of *interval, scale,* and an *input phrase processor*. It requests events from its *input phrase processor* and adds *interval* to the pitch of the incoming events before returning them. The interpretation of *interval* depends on

Fig. 6. The Flavors Band
modes menu. From this
menu, you can modify the
current root; then see,
hear, or edit the intervals
in any mode.

```
 FLAVORS BAND Defined MODES
        Current Root = C
CHROMATIC
DIMINISHED            (DIM)
DIM-HALF-STEP-1ST
LYDIAN               (LYD)
IONIAN               (ION MAJOR)
MIXOLYDIAN           (MIX)
DORIAN               (DOR)
AEOLIAN              (AEO MINOR)
PHRYGIAN             (PHR)
LOCRIAN              (LOC)
MELODIC-MINOR
HARMONIC-MINOR
HUNGARIAN
LYD-AUG
LYD-DIM
LYD-NO-4TH
DORIAN-NO-6TH
WHOLE-TONE
PENTATONIC           (PENT)
PENT-NO-3RD
PENT-MINOR
BLUES-9              ×
BLUES-7
BLUES-6
MAJOR-7-CHORD
DOM-7-CHORD
MINOR-7-CHORD
4THS
1-SCALE-DEGREE
              EXIT
```

an *input phrase processor*. If the pitches of the input events are not in the *scale*, they are modified by the smallest amount to make them be in the *scale*. This phrase processor can correct the output of a previous phrase processor that plays "out of key."

shift-time adds one number to the time of an ending event and the time of the next starting event. The number may be negative and expressed as a floating point number or as a rational (−0.5 and 1/3 are legal values). Shifting the onset times of a melody by varying amounts can cause it to lag behind the original, then get ahead of the original, a technique used frequently in jazz performance.

swing represents a more specialized functionality. It adds the value of its *time-increment* argument to the times of events that occur halfway between beats. For example, with a time-increment of 1/6, an event at beat 2 1/2 will be shifted to 2 2/3. Events on the beat (such as events at time 2 or 3) will be unmodified.

phrase-gap makes it easy to insert rests periodically in a long phrase. One motivation for this phrase processor is to give the effect of a horn player taking a breath.

context-mapper is a very general phrase processor. It takes as its arguments a *Lisp expression* and an *input phrase processor*. The *Lisp expression* is evaluated during the processing of each input event. Before evaluation of the *Lisp expression*, certain variables are bound to the characteristics of the current event as well as the two previous and two next events (the event's context). The *Lisp expression* can read and/or modify these variables. In computing the characteristics for the current event, **context-mapper**'s ability to read the values of the surrounding events' characteristics gives it a limited context within which it can operate.

For example, **context-mapper** could be used to limit melodic leaps in the input event stream by coercing the pitch of the current event to be no more than a certain interval from the previous event. A smarter use of **context-mapper** might choose to smooth out leaps by placing the current pitch between the previous pitch and the next pitch. The *Lisp expression* can access both the previous events from its input stream and the previous events in its

scale. If the interval is 1, the scale is C Chromatic, and the input pitch is D, the output pitch will be D-sharp. However, if the scale is C Ionian, the output pitch will be E. Since *interval* is evaluated for each event, the transposition need not be by a constant value throughout the life of an instance of the **transpose** phrase processor.

harmonize is similar to **transpose** except that it takes a list of intervals rather than just one interval as an argument. For each input event, **harmonize** puts out an event for each of the intervals in the list transposed by that interval from the original input event. Thus with the intervals of (0 2 4 6) and the scale D Lydian, **harmonize** will output a major seventh chord for each input event. The root of the chord will be the same pitch as the incoming event (transposed by the 0 interval), and the rest of the pitches will be above that root using every other scale degree in D Lydian.

coerce-into-scale takes as arguments a *scale* and

output stream. The **context-mapper** can generate precisely one output event for each input event.

embellish initializes and runs an entire subnetwork of phrase processors for each input event. The phrase processors in the subnetwork can read the values of characteristics in the input event as well as a limited context surrounding it. When the subnetwork is done, a new input event is acquired and the subnetwork is computed all over again. One of my uses for **embellish** is to add off-beat eighth notes to a walking bass line that originally contained only quarter notes.

Control Flow Phrase Processors

concat is used to put together serially two or more event streams. This permits phrase processors to generate events with a time base of zero, and yet still have their output appended onto that of another phrase processor rather than played concurrently with it.

repeat allows its argument *phrase processor* to be reinitialized and run a specified number of times. (Without **repeat**, most phrase processors finish when their input stream is used up.) If **repeat** is given an argument of *forever* instead of a number, it will continue reinitializing and running its input phrase processor until either the machine's memory is full, the user kills the process, or a controlling phrase processor somewhere up the network kills the **repeat**.

coerce-time passes events from its *input phrase processor* until an event more than a *specified time* is produced. **coerce-time** then kills its input phrase processor and returns an event equal to the *specified time*. **coerce-time** can also be used to pad short phrases with rests, should the input processor die a natural death before it reaches the specified time.

repeat *forever* phrase processors are often limited by a **coerce-time** processor. For example, the user could have an ostinato bass figure that he or she wanted to repeat many times. If the user didn't know the number of times to repeat, but did know how long the entire bass line must be, a **repeat** *forever* controlled with a **coerce-time** phrase processor is called for. This does more than simply save the

user from doing some arithmetic. If the duration of the ostinato figure is not a whole number multiple of the entire bass line duration, or the user simply can't figure out the duration of the ostinato figure before the score is computed, the functionality of **coerce-time** is needed.

gate behaves like a transistor. It takes two arguments, both of which are phrase processors. The event stream from one phrase processor (the *control stream*) allows the events from the other phrase processor (the *main stream*) to pass through the gate only when there is an ongoing note in the control stream that is not a rest. The control stream can be modified just like any other event stream. The **invert** phrase processor was initially designed to invert the control stream to a **gate** phrase processor, allowing events from the main stream to pass when there are no ongoing notes in the control stream. These phrase processors used in conjunction with **filter** (which conditionally removes events based on a Lisp expression) and **merge** (which combines two event streams into one) allow a user to construct phrase processing networks analogous to the networks that synthesizers use for generating sound.

Event Array Accessors

Event array accessors are designed to store intermediate event streams to be used and modified in numerous other places.

set-events passes its input unmodified, but has the side-effect of storing copies of the events that go through it into an array. These events may be accessed with the **use-events** phrase processor from anywhere in the network after the **set-events**, or by the phrase processing network of another part.

As an example of the use of event array accessors, a bass part might generate roots of chords in its early processing. These roots could be saved, and the bass part could go on to transpose its events such that it played only the thirds and fifths of the roots. Meanwhile a melody part could extract the roots from the saved array and embellish them to form a melody. Both parts used a musical skeleton that was never explicitly output by any part. For accessing the final score of a part, **use-events** can be applied since the data format for storing a part's completed score is an array of events.

Lisp Functions

Most of the arguments to most of the phrase processors can be passed by arbitrary Lisp expressions. Some of the more commonly used expressions have been coded into Lisp functions and made available for use in constructing a network. Currently there are about 30 of these functions. Like phrase processors, these functions can be added to Flavors Band with no modification to the rest of the language. Calls to these functions can occur everywhere that Flavors Band calls the Lisp evaluator, which is just about anywhere within a network. Here are descriptions of two particularly interesting user functions.

make-line-envelope makes line-segment envelopes from specified points. It is used by sending it a value (the *address* or *x* value). It returns a value (the *y* or *data* value). The address can come from anywhere, but usually comes from the time of an event. A melody with a particular pitch contour can be generated by making an envelope of the desired contour, generating an event stream, using the events' times as addresses into the envelope, and assigning the events' pitches to the output of the envelope. Only the rhythm of the input event stream is important, which can come from anywhere, for instance from another part. Inputs and outputs of the envelope generator can be scaled and offset with common Lisp functions.

sequencer is used because sometimes an application calls for a series of numbers that are not easily specified as an envelope, or may require a series of objects which are not numbers. **sequencer** can contain a list of any number of objects to sequence through. Each object has a *count* and a *value specification*. Each time the sequencer is asked for a value, the *count* of the current object is decremented, and its *value specification* is evaluated and returned. When the current object's *count* reaches 0, the next object is made the current object. The evaluation of an object's *value specification* can

modify the *count* of the object. Thus the sequencer can modify itself as it is run. **sequencer** is an experiment in sequencer autonomy.

Use of Indeterminacy

The user can allow Flavors Band to choose from among a constrained set of values to generate arguments to phrase processors or other Lisp functions. This makes it possible to construct a network that has bounded indeterminacy, permitting the specification of a potentially wide range of musical styles with a comparatively short and simple syntax.

fb-random, the Flavors Band random number generator, takes as its arguments a *minimum output value*, a *maximum output value*, a *granularity*, and a *seed*. If this were used for note duration, a composer could say, "I want the duration of each note to be between 1/4 and 1 with a granularity of 1/8." The possible values would all be multiples of 1/8. Changing the seed would change the sequence of numbers, but not their other specified characteristics.

Another Flavors Band generator allows the user to specify the probability that a particular value will be returned. In the previous example on duration, the user might wish to specify that half of the durations be 1/4, and assign correspondingly smaller probabilities to the remaining possible durations. The value returned from this probability generator could be any Lisp object, not simply a number. The value could even be a phrase-processing subnetwork, effectively allowing Flavors Band to choose a composition strategy based on user-supplied probabilities. An extension to this probability generator allows the user to specify the number of times a particular value is returned once it is selected. This lends consistency to the output values.

random-segment allows the network to determine which one of a number of subnetworks is to be used, based on user-supplied probabilities. A **repeat** wrapped around a **random-segment** phrase processor allows the generation of event streams that are composed using the variety of techniques specified by the phrase processors selected by **random-segment**.

Fig. 7. Deriving pitch from envelope. (a) Block diagram of the network. (b) Network specification in the Flavors Band language. (c) A random melody generated by the network in (a) and (b). (d) The random melody modified by a pitch envelope.

A

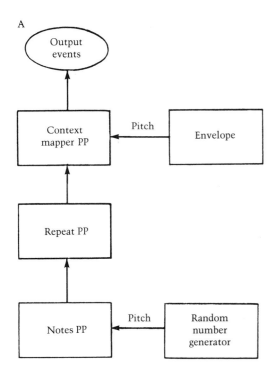

B

```
(part :init-expression
      '(setq envl (make-line-envelope
                     'error
                     '((0 0) (8 8) (16 0) (24 4))
                     'wrap-around))
      :segment-source
      '(context-mapper
            '(setq pitch (+ pitch
                (get-envelope-value
                  envl time)))
            (repeat
              72
              (notes (n (d 1)
                     (p (fb-random 0 3 1))
                     )))))
```

C

D

Phrase Network Architectures

An instance of a phrase processor with its arguments could be thought of as a sentence in the Flavors Band language. Most sentences can be placed adjacent to most other sentences permitting an unlimited variety of paragraphs. However, as in natural languages, only a small subset of such paragraphs are likely to be coherent and/or interesting. This section examines how meaningful paragraphs are constructed in the Flavors Band language.

Example 1: Deriving Pitch from Envelope

An interesting pitch generation technique is to get a value from an envelope and add a slight amount of deviation to it. If the deviation comes from a random number generator, then each pass through the envelope will produce a phrase with a similar pitch contour as the previous pass, but not exactly the same (Fig. 7). Figure 7a is a block diagram of such a network; 7b gives the actual code; 7c is an unmodified random melody; 7d is a random melody modified by a pitch envelope.

In Fig. 7b a random number between 0 and 3 (with a granularity of 1) is generated with **fb-random** and assigned to pitch in the **notes** phrase processor. Seventy-two of such notes are made by the **repeat** phrase processor. In **context-mapper**, the starting time of each note is used as an index into the envelope generator specified in the **init-expression** of this part. The output of the envelope generator is added to the pitch that was assigned in **notes**. Since the envelope is just 24 beats long, and the last note will end on beat 72, three groups of notes will have the general pitch contour specified by the envelope. Each of the three groups will be slightly different due to the deviation from the **fb-random** function.

Fig. 8. Phrase library
example.

```
(shift-time 1/8 ;minimum-duration
            (random-alist '((.8 0) (.9 -1/4) (1 1/4)))
            (REPEAT 32 ;number of repetitions
                    (random-segment
                     13 ;seed
                     ;phrase library with probabilities
                     '((.3 (NOTES (N (S 0.))
                                  (N (S 0.5))
                                  (N (S 1.) (E 2.))))
                       (.6 (NOTES (N (S 0.))
                                  (N (S 0.5))
                                  (N (S 1.))
                                  (N (S 1.5) (E 2.))))
                       (1. (NOTES (N (S 0.))
                                  (N (S 1.) (E 2.)))))))))
```

Example 2: Phrase Libraries

Long phrases can be constructed out of short phrases whose notes are specified directly. The particular combination of the short phrases to form longer phrases can be determined by a Flavors Band network. I call a group of fully specified phrases a *phrase library* from which a network may borrow. There can be any number of phrase libraries in Flavors Band, each of which can contain any number of phrases. In my use of this technique, each library rarely contains over 20 phrases. Phrase libraries allow a user to precisely specify the details while imprecisely specifying the higher-level structure of the phrase being constructed (Fig. 8).

The phrase library contains three phrase processing subnetworks each made from **notes** phrase processors. (Syntactically, any one of these could be replaced by an arbitrary network.) Each of the three **notes** phrase processors has about an equal probability of occurring. (Actually the probability for the third is 1.0 − 0.6 = 0.4.) Thirty-two times during this score, **random-segment** selects one of the three subnetworks and returns the events generated by it. The times of these events are subject to possible modification by **shift-time**. Eight percent of the events' times go unmodified, while 10% are retarded by 1/4 and 10% are advanced by 1/4. Since this net doesn't vary pitch at all, it would most likely be used as a drum part or the rhythm generator in a larger net.

Nonstandard Communication

Typically, the topology of a phrase-processing network is a tree where the highest processor on the tree is the processor between the rest of the network and the output event stream of the network (Fig. 9). The flow of control is from the later, higher phrase processors to the earlier processors near or at the leaves of the tree.

Events move opposite to the direction of control; from the earlier processors (at the bottom of the tree) through the later processors. A surprising variety of composition algorithms can be supported with this architecture, but not all. For example, many levels of nested repeats work well in the Flavors Band treelike topology. However, some kinds of networks whose control-flow branches dynamically are difficult to implement as a treelike topology. Such an architecture might occur if you wanted to design a network containing subnetworks that are not yet fully specified at the time of initialization of the whole network. Branching based on events to be computed is also a difficult architecture. You might want to do this if the technique to be used next depends on the last note of the previous technique.

For miscellaneous communication between processors, Lisp global variables can be used. A processor can set a flag during the course of computation of an event. That flag can be read by any other processors that choose to at any time after the flag is set. Sometimes I pass starting times or indicate the

Fig. 9. Control flow.

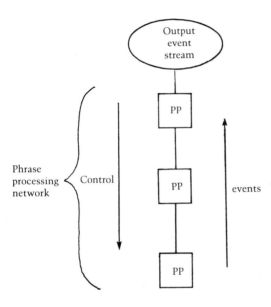

current pitch mode (e.g., Ionian or Dorian) via a global variable. A variable can contain a subnetwork.

As previously mentioned, *Event Array Accessors* can conveniently store and retrieve event arrays. The reading phrase processor can be placed anywhere in the network (before as well as after the writer) or in the network of a different part. Thus event streams, as well as control information may move nonhierarchically within a score's phrase processing networks.

Event arrays can be used to store themes to be read by another phrase processor in order to generate a variation. A subnetwork whose output is fed back into its input constitutes a *phrase-locked loop*. A predecessor to Flavors Band, the program called Computer Improvisation (Fry 1980), could create original phrases but didn't have the ability to make variations on them.

Within a section, parts are computed in parallel such that no part computes far ahead or behind the other parts. This permits parts to share recently computed events among themselves.

Defaults and Inheritance

Scores, sections, and parts have ten to fifteen characteristics each. For a score of several sections with several parts each, a large number of parameters must be specified. To automate this task, all parameters have default values. A human composer can start with a procedural outline of a score and then fill in particular characteristics as desired, some of which are available via menus.

There is still a complexity problem with default values that must be explicitly overridden. Frequently a new score will have characteristics in common with previously computed scores. Flavors Band takes advantage of this by permitting inheritance of characteristics between scores.

The entire score, individual sections, or whole parts can be inherited from a previously computed score. The user can specify that only particular characteristics are inherited. Most importantly, the set of defaults can come from other scores, sections, or parts. This permits easy construction of a new score that behaves just like a previous score except for certain characteristics. Being able to use pieces of existing scores facilitates the specification of a new musical style that has similarities to a previously-coded style.

The entire description of a phrase-processing network can be inherited from one part to another. But if the new part is really supposed to behave exactly as its parent did, it can inherit the output events of that part as well. This saves redundant computation and facilitates building very large scores by combining smaller, previously debugged, and computed scores.

User Interface

Flavors Band uses a careful interaction between custom menus (Symbolics 1984a) and a text editor (Symbolics 1984b) as its user interface. A user remains continually in the text editor while constructing and performing Flavors Band scores. Over 20 menus are used in Flavors Band (Fig. 10). All of them are accessible through the Flavors Band Command Menu, which pops up on the screen via a key-

Fig. 10. Some of the menus in the Flavors Band user interface. (a) Flavors Band Command Menu. (b) Phrase processors sub- *menu. [See (d).] (c) Instrument menus for the parts of a section. (d) Phrase processors menu.*

A

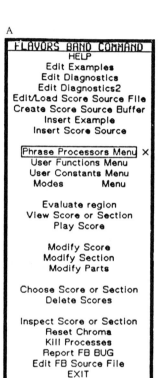

```
FLAVORS BAND COMMAND
         HELP
     Edit Examples
    Edit Diagnostics
    Edit Diagnostics2
Edit/Load Score Source File
Create Score Source Buffer
     Insert Example
    Insert Score Source

 Phrase Processors Menu  ×
   User Functions Menu
   User Constants Menu
   Modes         Menu

    Evaluate region
  View Score or Section
       Play Score

     Modify Score
     Modify Section
      Modify Parts

 Choose Score or Section
     Delete Scores

Inspect Score or Section
     Reset Chroma
     Kill Processes
     Report FB BUG
   Edit FB Source File
        EXIT
```

B

```
FLAVORS BAND Operation on segment: GATE
              Arglist
           Documentation
         Insert into buffer
          Edit Definition      ×
```

C

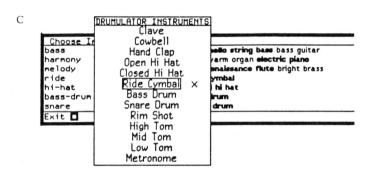

```
DRUMULATOR INSTRUMENTS
        Clave
       Cowbell
      Hand Clap
      Open Hi Hat
     Closed Hi Hat
     Ride Cymbal   ×
      Bass Drum
      Snare Drum
       Rim Shot
       High Tom
       Mid Tom
       Low Tom
      Metronome
```

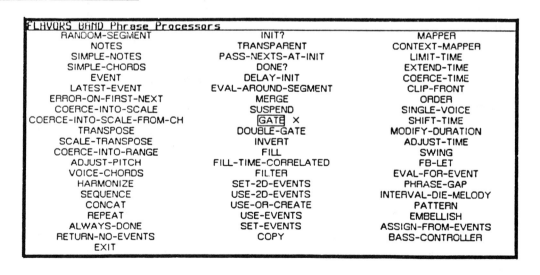

FLAVORS BAND Phrase Processors		
RANDOM-SEGMENT	INIT?	MAPPER
NOTES	TRANSPARENT	CONTEXT-MAPPER
SIMPLE-NOTES	PASS-NEXTS-AT-INIT	LIMIT-TIME
SIMPLE-CHORDS	DONE?	EXTEND-TIME
EVENT	DELAY-INIT	COERCE-TIME
LATEST-EVENT	EVAL-AROUND-SEGMENT	CLIP-FRONT
ERROR-ON-FIRST-NEXT	MERGE	ORDER
COERCE-INTO-SCALE	SUSPEND	SINGLE-VOICE
COERCE-INTO-SCALE-FROM-CH	GATE ×	SHIFT-TIME
TRANSPOSE	DOUBLE-GATE	MODIFY-DURATION
SCALE-TRANSPOSE	INVERT	ADJUST-TIME
COERCE-INTO-RANGE	FILL	SWING
ADJUST-PITCH	FILL-TIME-CORRELATED	FB-LET
VOICE-CHORDS	FILTER	EVAL-FOR-EVENT
HARMONIZE	SET-2D-EVENTS	PHRASE-GAP
SEQUENCE	USE-2D-EVENTS	INTERVAL-DIE-MELODY
CONCAT	USE-OR-CREATE	PATTERN
REPEAT	USE-EVENTS	EMBELLISH
ALWAYS-DONE	SET-EVENTS	ASSIGN-FROM-EVENTS
RETURN-NO-EVENTS	COPY	BASS-CONTROLLER
EXIT		

stroke. The Flavors Band Command Menu allows access to the following:

Documentation (including this article on-line)
Examples of score descriptions
Menus of phrase processors and user functions
Evaluation of the current score description
Performance of computed scores
Modifications to computed scores
Debugging aids

For each phrase processor type and user function, the user can get via menu: documentation, the argument list, the source code, or insert the name of the processor or function into the current text buffer. Examples of the use of every phrase processor can be found in the examples file that is accessible via menu. For beginning users, two simple examples can be inserted directly into the current buffer via menu.

Once a score has been computed, it can be played as many times as desired via menu. Certain parts of the score can be modified without complete recomputation. Instruments can be assigned to parts via menu; approximately a hundred instruments are available. The amplitude of each part can be modified via a simple "mixing console" menu. Each part can also have its octave offset modified via menu without recomputation of the whole part.

A history list of the previously computed scores during the current terminal session is maintained. Any previously-computed score can be selected via menu as the current score and have all of the aforementioned operations performed on it.

Implementation

I started coding Flavors Band in the fall of 1982. The core of the program is fairly stable, although extensions occur regularly. Currently about 35 source code and peripheral files contain over 10,000 lines of code. I'm the sole programmer up to now. Flavors Band is written entirely in Lisp Machine Lisp (Symbolics 1984c; Symbolics 1984d). It runs on both the Symbolics LM-2 and 3600 systems.

A Fender-Rhodes Chroma synthesizer is connected to the Lisp Machine for sound output. The

Chroma is a digitally-controlled analog synthesizer. It can produce eight voices (with eight different instruments) in real time, with each voice consisting of several oscillators, filters, and envelopes (Fender-Rhodes 1982). An E-mu Drumulator synthesizer (E-mu 1983) provides realistic percussion sounds.

The Flavors Band software takes advantage of numerous Lisp Machine system features making the code both powerful and unportable. Flavors, the Lisp Machine mechanism for object-oriented programming, is used extensively (Cannon 1982). (The "Band" part of "Flavors Band" is a pun on the term *band* used to refer to a disk partition on the Lisp Machine.) Each phrase processor is implemented as a flavor. Most communication between phrase processors occurs via message-passing.

Each musical part is implemented as a process with its own stack. The scheduling of these processes is determined by a combination of the Lisp Machine scheduler and a special scheduler inside the Flavors Band interpreter.

Musical Applications

I am still at an early stage of musical application. So far, most of the scores made with Flavors Band have been developed for experimentation with compositional algorithms and for diagnostic purposes. A few short works have been produced and are described in this section.

My Favorite Things

In the Flavors Band arrangement of *My Favorite Things* (written by Richard Rodgers and adapted from John Coltrane's arrangement) the melody and chords were coded directly. One verse of the melody was constructed by merging the rhythms from a phrase library with the pitches from the original melody. Another verse used **shift-time** on the original rhythms with sporadic applications of **transpose** to pitches. The piano part used **harmonize** on the supplied chords with nonmetrical starting times for the chords. The bass player arpeggiated the chords with a certain amount of deviation rhythmically and harmonically. For drums I used only a brushlike sound. The drummer played a traditional ride cymbal figure by attacking on every beat and playing a high percentage of the swing eighth notes between beats.

Norwegian Wood

As an experiment, I decided to reuse the score description of *My Favorite Things* to arrange *Norwegian Wood* (written by John Lennon and Paul McCartney). I changed only the input melody and chords. Both pieces are in related meters (*My Favorite Things* in 3/4 time and *Norwegian Wood* in 12/8) and have a two-part structure (A and B sections). The similarities between the two pieces end there. The chord structures and melodies are very different. Recorded versions of the compositions also have very different arrangements and instrumentation.

What I had really done in arranging *My Favorite Things* in Flavors Band was to specify a style in machine-readable form. One way to observe the essential characteristics of that style was to listen to more than one piece in the style. I do not consider the Flavors Band version of *Norwegian Wood* as played in the style of the Flavors Band version of *My Favorite Things* to be a musical success. *My Favorite Things* sounds better. Perhaps this is primarily due to the fact that I developed this style with *My Favorite Things* in mind.

Regardless of this result, the technique of using a style adapted from one piece to realize another piece is still a fascinating concept. For once, the phrase "as played in the style of" is not ambiguous. Moreover, the building of libraries of networks, each of which concretely describes a style, is both technically feasible and conceptually powerful as a composition technique.

Light My Fire

The longest piece I have produced with Flavors Band is an attempt to capture the style of the guitar solo section of the long version of *Light My Fire*

(written by The Doors). The bass plays an embarrassingly consistent one-measure line throughout on the record, so I simply used **repeat** on those notes. The organ part uses numerous two-measure licks selected from a phrase library. The drummer plays both a bass drum and a snare drum. The snare drum part is minimally conscious of phrasing: a short fill is played every four measures, and a longer fill is played every sixteen measures.

The lead guitarist knows eight one-measure licks. They are coded in scale degree rather than chromatic notation. As a lick is selected, it is transposed based on previous transpositions and the location of the current measure in the current four-measure phrase. Quite a bit of the code is devoted to making certain that phrasing over four-measure periods is consistent with the style being imitated.

Giant Steps

The most advanced use of Flavors Band is an arrangement of *Giant Steps* (by John Coltrane). *Giant Steps* is a classic, fast (285 beats per minute) jazz composition with many II-V-I chord progressions. The most interesting parts of the Flavors Band arrangement are the bass line and the improvised solo, played on the Chroma synthesizer.

To create a walking bass line, I use a special phrase processor called the **bass-controller**. The **bass-controller** sets up a context in which a bass style computes. The **bass-controller** provides its bass style with the current chord, the next chord, the pitch of the expected first bass note to be played during the chord, and the pitch of the expected first bass note for the next chord.

It is the responsibility of each bass style to choose the notes to be played during the chord. For walking bass, Flavors Band uses a bass style that makes a trajectory of pitches aiming toward the expected first note of the next chord. The pitches are usually constrained to be within the scale indicated by the current chord. Constraining the legal scale degrees to the root, the third, the fifth, and the seventh produces a more conventional-sounding bass line.

Although the improvised solo does not occur in

the bass register it uses the **bass-controller** and a bass style that is similar to the one mentioned in the previous paragraph. The main difference is that the expected first pitch of each chord is not the root of the chord as it is in the bass part. It is rather a pitch that is a small interval from the last pitch of the previous chord. This causes the solo to wander more freely through the chord changes than the bass part.

Not surprisingly, the resulting score did not sound as good as the John Coltrane Quartet. However, except for the unnatural sound of the Chroma synthesizer, it is conceivable that the piece could have been performed by a human jazz band.

Original Compositions

Flavors Band has also been used to produce original pieces. Chord progressions, melodies, and rhythms can be made via complex use of phrase libraries, envelopes, sequencers, probability functions, and other phrase processors.

Conclusions

The core of Flavors Band is a framework upon which many kinds of phrase processors can be hung in a wide variety of configurations. The architecture has proven successful with respect to extensibility.

Flexibility is more difficult to measure. When constructing compositional algorithms, it is much easier to build them from the bottom up based on the tools immediately available. If you attempt to build them to conform to an existing style, as I chose to in the aforementioned compositions, the task is considerably more difficult. Deficiencies in the toolkit become apparent and suggest the need for new constructs in the language.

For each of the pieces described previously, I built new phrase processors or adopted new styles of using the language. Flavors Band was able to accommodate concepts I had not considered before completing the majority of the code. Given the impossibility of predicting future uses, this is a necessary characteristic of any flexible language.

Throughout the implementation of Flavors Band, flexibility had a higher priority than ease of use. Consequently, despite my efforts at user interface, Flavors Band is not simple to use. Maintaining the ability to have a widely variable precision of specificity means that when a high level construct is built, all of the obvious levels below that high level must be accessible. This increases generality at the expense of complexity and size of the language. No doubt simplifications could be made to Flavors Band that would both increase flexibility and reduce complexity to the user. Such elegant solutions are difficult to discover. If they are not found, Flavors Band will continue to have the trait of complexity in common with the domain it attempts to describe.

Acknowledgments

Tom Trobaugh is to be credited with random theoretical insights. Jim Davis developed key parts of the Flavors-Band-to-synthesizer software interface. Curtis Roads, Jim Davis, and Gareth Loy made comments on drafts of this paper. John Coltrane and The Doors provided musical inspiration. David Clark and John Voigt gave me insights into jazz bass theory. Most importantly, my thanks to David Levitt and Bill Kornfeld for Lisp Machine tutorials over the last three years along with essential friendship.

References

Cannon, H. 1982. "Flavors: A Nonhierarchical Approach to Object-oriented Programming." Cambridge, Massachusetts: Symbolics.

Coker, J. 1964. *Improvising Jazz*. Englewood Cliffs, New Jersey: Prentice-Hall.

E-mu. 1983. *Drumulator Service Manual*. Santa Cruz, California: E-mu Systems Inc.

Fender-Rhodes. 1982. *Chroma Programming Manual*. Fullerton, California: Fender-Rhodes.

Fry, C. 1980. "Computer Improvisation." *Computer Music Journal* 4(3): 48–58.

Jackson, C. P. 1980. *How to Play Jazz Basslines*. Boston, Massachusetts: Hornpipe Music Publishing.

Levitt, D. 1981. "A Melody Description System for Jazz

Improvisation." M. S. Thesis, Cambridge, Massachusetts: Massachusetts Institute of Technology.

Levitt, D. 1984. "Machine Tongues X: Constraint Languages." *Computer Music Journal* 8(1):9–21.

Moorer, J. A. 1972. "Music and Computer Composition." *Communications of the Association for Computing Machinery* 15(2):104–113.

Rodet, X., and P. Cointe. 1984. "Formes: Composition and Scheduling of Processes." *Computer Music Journal* 8(3):32–50.

Russell, G. 1959. *The Lydian Chromatic Concept of Tonal Organization*. New York, New York: Concept Publishing.

Schottstaedt, B. 1983. "Pla: A Composer's Idea of a Language." *Computer Music Journal* 7(1):11–20.

Symbolics. 1984a. "User Interface Support." *Symbolics 3600 Documentation, Release 5.0 version*. Cambridge, Massachusetts: Symbolics.

Symbolics. 1984b. "Program Development Tools." *Symbolics 3600 Documentation, Release 5.0 version*. Cambridge, Massachusetts: Symbolics.

Symbolics. 1984c. "Lisp Language." *Symbolics 3600 Documentation, Release 5.0 version*. Cambridge, Massachusetts: Symbolics.

Symbolics. 1984d. *Symbolics 3600 Technical Summary*. Cambridge, Massachusetts: Symbolics.

28

Curtis Abbott
IRCAM
31, rue S. Merri
75004 Paris
France

The 4CED Program

Overview

This article reports my work on real-time software for di Giugno's 4C digital synthesizer at IRCAM, in particular a program called 4CED. This program (which exists in various versions) is based on certain design principles that appear valid in a variety of contexts. The article gives special emphasis to these.

4CED attempts to put "under one roof" most of the operations that might be desirable for a musician developing a piece of music in a studio environment using real-time equipment. It also attempts to present this real-time equipment quite abstractly to allow a musician to be insulated from the internal workings of the machine while retaining access to the machine's possibilities. This prevents the program from being a toy that is quickly outgrown.

4CED and the 4C synthesizer itself are not only practical tools for music-making, but also steps in the development of knowledge about how to realize the potential of digital synthesis. Therefore it is within the proper domain of this paper to discuss inadequacies and compromises of 4CED and the improvements these suggest.

Introduction

The components of the system upon which 4CED is built are a PDP-11/34 computer, a 4C digital synthesizer, a computer terminal, a bank of 16 digital potentiometers interfaced to the PDP-11/34, four channels of digital-to-analog converter (DAC) sound output, and an analog studio (mixing board, tape recorders, etc.).

The 4C itself has been described elsewhere (Moorer et al. 1979) and only a brief resumé will be given here. It is a sample-locked processor that op-

Computer Music Journal, Vol. 5, No. 1, Spring 1981

erates at a basic sampling rate of 16 kHz. During a sample period, it executes a certain program 32 times. This program realizes a fixed set of *unit generators*, which can be interconnected in arbitrary ways. The unit generators are two unscaled frequency modulation (FM) oscillators (essentially a lookup and a three-input adder), two multiply/adds (a multiply followed by an addition), one envelope generator (a linear ramp generator that can "stick" at a final value and that also incorporates another multiply/add unit generator useful for applying the ramp to a signal), an output (sending a signal to a DAC channel), and a timer (each timer is decremented every msec, and may cause an interrupt to the PDP-11 when its value goes below 0).

All of these unit generators read and write their data out of a scratchpad called *data memory*. Another memory, called *address memory*, determines exactly which scratchpad registers are associated with each of the operands for each particular unit generator. Thus it is through this address memory that unit generator interconnection is done. Numbers in the 4C are fixed-point and generally have 24 bits of precision. The numbers that result from wavetable lookups, however, have 16 bits of precision, and multiplications are done on 16-bit portions of numbers, returning a 24-bit result. Also, all numbers are considered fractional for the purposes of multiplication—this means essentially that multiplication can only make numbers smaller. These and other aspects of the 4C hardware definition affect the way users must present their ideas to the 4C (subtraction is a tricky affair, for example), and this is necessarily reflected to a certain extent in 4CED.

Besides the data and address memories, there is a single 16K *wavetable memory* which can be divided up logically into any combination of 1K, 2K, 4K, 8K, and 16K wavetables (as long as the memory requirements of all the wavetables do not exceed 16K). In this article and in 4CED these are referred to by size and number: 8K1 and 8K2 represent the first and second 8K wavetables. 2K5 is the fifth 2K table, but 4K5 is an error since there are only four 4K tables.

In summary, the 4C realizes five kinds of unit generators, called oscillator, multiply/add, envelope generator, output, and timer, all of which can be interconnected via a set of registers. There are 64 oscillators, 64 multiply/adds, 32 envelope generators, 32 outputs (into four channels) and 32 timers. Oscillators and envelope generators can also be used to realize adders, waveshapers, and a variety of nonlinear functions.

Program Design Considerations

4CED is designed to cater to users with different levels of sophistication. Just as the 4C Machine is a versatile digital synthesizer, 4CED should be a versatile program, both in the way it allows users to address the 4C itself, and in the way it allows users to work with it in creating and modifying a piece of music.

Within the limits of this constraint, we would like to identify ways of using the machine that are the most common and make these as easy as possible to realize. To the extent possible, users themselves should be able to identify and package common ways of using the 4C.

It is hoped that 4C will be presented in such a way that users who are familiar with software synthesis programs like Music V, Music 10, and Music 11 can benefit from their experience. This goal is furthered by the unit generator design of the 4C itself, as discussed previously.

4CED provides the possibility of creating text files in advance that define synthesis algorithms, scores, and envelopes in a fairly abstract way, one that will not be totally unfamiliar to users of conventional computer music languages run in a non-real-time setting. It provides means for interrogating the state of things and for modifying any aspect of this state in a controlled way, including modification of text with a simple text editor that exists within the program. It allows users to use symbolic (and therefore mnemonic) names for most entities that the program manipulates. It allows users to control the usage of memory (a scarce resource in the PDP-11) by the program.

It is worth mentioning that 4CED is written almost entirely in the C programming language, which improves considerably its tractability for debugging and modifications as well as its portability across machines. Naturally, it is modular where possible; for example, program changes required by different hardware for the potentiometers could normally be accomplished in a matter of minutes.

In the following four sections we will discuss the major software structures of 4CED as seen by a user: the patching language, the envelope language, the score language, and the command language.

The Patching Language

There are a variety of approaches to expressing synthesis algorithms: Music V does it by interconnecting unit generators, Music 10 and Music 11 do it by a combination of unit generators and arithmetic expressions. The structure of the 4C Machine dictates the choice of the unit generator approach for 4CED—compiling arithmetic expressions into code for the 4C is simply impracticable.

When we talk about unit generators in this section, we will generally mean those of 4CED rather than those of the 4C Machine, with the understanding that there is a simple mapping between the two. 4CED's unit generators take arguments that normally represent 4C registers. There are exceptions for output (which requires a DAC channel number) and for oscillator and waveshaper (which require an argument specifying which of several possible wavetables to use). The unit generators and their arguments are presented in a compact form in Table 1. They are designed to allow users to do essentially anything of which the 4C hardware is capable, but at the same time to minimize the number of annoying extras needed when using the hardware in conventional ways. For example, consider OSC and PHO: for an OSC (the usual case), 4CED will find a register to be used for phase accumulation, while for a PHO, the user names an explicit register for the purpose. PHO is available for the rare cases where this is necessary.

Table 1. Opcodes and arguments for the 4CED patching language. Optional arguments are enclosed in {...}. When optional arguments are left out, 4CED does something predictable. The optional WT argument to OSC, PHO, and MOD represents a wavetable, not a 4C register. The CHAN argument to OUT represents a DAC channel number. The EGRP argument to ENV and RMP is a special kind of 4C register used to control the linear ramp generated by the hardware, and in the explanation of these unit generators ramp is not a register but the operation of generating the next value in this linear ramp. The DCN unit generator is for experts only—it is used to configure the hardware to realize nonlinear functions such as rectification, zero-crossing detection, and so on.

Opcode	Argument	Function
OSC	{WT} F1 {F2} OUT	Oscillator: OUT → WT[phase]; phase += F1 + F2;
PHO	{WT} PHZ F1 {F2} OUT	Oscillator: OUT →WT[PHZ]; PHZ += F1 + F2;
MOD	{WT} IN OUT	Waveshaper: OUT → WT[IN];
ADD	A {B} {C} OUT	Adder: OUT → A + B + C;
MUL	A B {C} OUT	Mul/add: OUT → A * B + C;
ENV	EGRP {SCL} {ADD} OUT	Envelope: OUT → Ramp * SCL + ADD;
RMP	EGRP {ADD} OUT	Ramp: OUT → Ramp + ADD;
DCN	C I F SCL ADD OUTR OUT	Decision: OUTR → C + I ? F; OUT — OUTR * SCL + ADD;
OUT	CHAN SOURCE	Output: DAC[CHAN] → SOURCE:

Naming 4C Registers

We have seen how symbolic names are given to various configurations of the 4C's hardware unit generators—this is one step in the process of presenting the 4C more abstractly. Naturally, we would like to apply the same kinds of ideas to naming the 4C registers that are arguments to the unit generators. It turns out that we would like considerably more flexibility in the ways we can give names to 4C registers than is the case for unit generators.

The reason for this can be illustrated by an analogy to computer programming languages in which the names for operators (like + and *) are fixed in the definition of the language, while the names of variables are freely chosen by the programmer. Furthermore, variable names typically can be used in a variety of contexts, for example, as local or global to a procedure, as parameters, and so on.

This situation is mimicked in 4CED—it is possible to think of patches as procedures in a programming language that can be called with parameters (which will typically be register names). It is possible to declare certain register names as being globally known. For example, if we declare BASEFREQ as a *global* register name, then any number of patches that refer to BASEFREQ will in fact refer to the same 4C register. This facilitates sharing of signals between patches. For example, communication between a set of signal-producing patches and a standardized mixing module can be accomplished by making the output signals from each patch global and using these global names as *parameters* to the mixer.

Similarly, it is necessary to declare, in each patch, which register names correspond to parameters. When the patch is called (or, more exactly, loaded into the 4C), register names must be given with the call, and the meanings of these register names are then associated with those names within the patch that are declared as parameters.

Normally, a register is *local* to a patch—there is no need for anything outside to know about it. For example, if we define a patch that realizes a two-pole filter, it needs local registers for its delays. Typically, we would want to give these registers suggestive names, perhaps DELAY1 and DELAY2.

Fig. 1. Graphic structure of a patch.

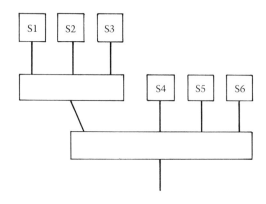

It is important that each time we call (that is, load) this filtering patch, different 4C registers be used for DELAY1 and DELAY2—otherwise, the different filters will interfere with each other in extraordinary ways!

Besides these varieties of symbolic register names, it is possible to specify registers in patches explicitly by number or to assign a global register name to a specific register. There are two predefined global 4C registers: Z (a register whose value is zero), and ONE (a register whose value is one).

Describing Parallelism in Synthesis Algorithms

Consider the schematic synthesis algorithm in Fig. 1. Here, each box represents a unit generator of arbitrary complexity, and the arrows between boxes represent the relationships between them in the sense that if an arrow goes from box S1 to box S2, the calculation in box S1 must be done before that in S2.

In 4CED it is possible to express these relationships textually in patch definitions, using semicolons as special symbols to denote sequential execution and vertical bars to denote parallel execution. For example, given the labeling of boxes in Fig. 1, we would express the same relations textually in 4CED by writing ((S1 | S2 | S3); S4 | S5 | S6). Since the 4C hardware is capable of executing a few operations in parallel, there are cases where it is useful to express potential parallelism in synthesis algorithms (this can also aid in clarifying the logical structure of an algorithm). From a practical point of view, however, it is seldom really necessary in the 4C, which in any case is largely sequential.

An Example

Suppose we wish to generate a signal and then pass it through two bandpass filters, one after the other. The center frequency, bandwidth, and gain of each filter can be changed dynamically, and we assume that these parameters will be global registers named CF1, BW1 and GAIN1 for the first filter, and CF2, BW2 and GAIN2 for the second. Rather than defining each filter separately, we prefer to package the idea of a bandpass filter in a separate patch definition and load two copies of it in creating our desired patch. This patch definition will create a higher-level unit generator that takes five arguments: center frequency, bandwidth, gain, input signal, and output signal. Here is the definition as it appears in 4CED.

```
BPASS: PATCH
PARAM CENTER, BW, GAIN, IN, OUT;
MUL BW IN DELAY1 ZHP
MUL ZHP CENTER BPSIG BPSIG
MUL BPSIG CENTER ZLP ZLP
MUL BPSIG BW ZLP DELAY2
MUL DELAY2 MINUS1 DELAY1
MUL GAIN BPSIG OUT
END
```

Now suppose we generate a signal very simply, using an oscillator on the third 4K wavetable. Then our example patch can be written as follows.

```
EXAMPLE: PATCH
OSC 4K3 FREQ SIG
AP BPASS CF1 BW1 GAIN1 SIG SIG
AP BPASS CF2 BW2 GAIN2 SIG SIG
OUT 1 SIG                 ! listen on channel one
END
```

Here the AP keyword indicates that a user-defined unit generator is to be loaded. The exclamation point starts a comment to the end of the line. Notice that in the arguments to BPASS, SIG is used as both input and output. This is perfectly legal and causes no problems. Furthermore, it helps clarify the fact that there is logically only one signal in this synthesis algorithm, a signal that is passed through successive operators.

The EXAMPLE patch assumes that certain global register names will be declared before it is loaded, otherwise CF1, CF2, and so on will be treated as local names and it will be impossible to refer to them symbolically after the patch is loaded. Making register names global is, however, only one way of obtaining access to them from other parts of 4CED. In the next section we will discuss another way.

Connecting Patches to Scores

Suppose we wish to play a sequence of pitches on the patch defined previously, and program the pitches and rhythm in a score while modifying the filter parameters (by hand) as the score is being played. In this case, the filter parameters should be global, as was the case previously. But the score needs to change the value of the local register called FREQ in order to change the pitch. In general, any patch will define some registers that are to be controlled by one or several scores. These registers are declared with a CONNECT statement. Whether a register is local, global, or a parameter, it may appear in a CONNECT statement. The result is simply to record the register designated by the symbolic name so that it can be made available to a score. Other details of how this works will be given later.

Since envelopes are somewhat special, there is an EGRP statement that functions as a CONNECT statement for envelope definitions. This will be more carefully explained in the next section.

Patches and Patch Images

Declarations such as those just discussed are useful when the intended use of a patch definition is to create a musical voice (or instrument). As was stated, the registers given in CONNECT and EGRP statements must be remembered somehow for later connection to a score or envelope definition. Furthermore, it is sometimes desirable to be able to remove a patch from the 4C and reclaim the resources it used. In order to do this, we must remember exactly which resources are used by each patch. All of these things are remembered in a *patch image*. The name is intended to suggest the fact that if a single patch definition is loaded twice or more the resulting patch images will all be different, since distinct parts of the 4C are used each time. In order to refer to different copies of a single patch definition, it is possible to name patch images explicitly when they are created by loading. Ordinarily this is not necessary—the default name for a patch image is the same as the name of the patch definition itself. In this way, users are not burdened with concepts (like patch image) needlessly.

There is a certain amount of room for improvement in 4CED here, as patch images are created exactly when a patch definition is loaded by a user command. This means that subpatches called inside a patch definition using the AP keyword will not create patch images, and therefore that they must not contain CONNECT statements, and so on. In general, this means that a particular patch definition must be designed to act either as a higher-level unit generator or as a musical voice, but not both. This is not the height of elegance, but a better solution is not obvious.

Debugging Patches

Sad to say, a patch definition does not always work the first time as the user has imagined it will. 4CED provides a number of facilities to help out when this happens. It is possible to obtain a detailed listing of the complete 4C program or of an individual patch. This listing is created by reading the contents of the 4C's address memory directly and formatting it into a readable printout, so it is unusually trustworthy. An example of this formatted output is listed to the right of its corresponding patch definition in code listing 1.

```
OSC FREQ1 OUT1
        0 OSCA 4 = 4K1[5]; 5 += 3 + 1
MUL OUT1 SCALE1 OUT1
        0 MULB 4 = 4 * 6 + 1
OSC 2K7 FREQ2 OUT2
        1 OSCA 7 = 2K7[8]; 8 += 6 + 1
MUL OUT2 SCALE2 OUT1 OUT2
        1 MULB 7 = 7 * 8 + 4
OUT1 OUT2
        2 OUT 7 → chan 1
```

Another facility provided by 4CED is the *immediate mode* patch that will be described in the section on the command language. This allows us to "poke around" in a patch, sending various internal signals to DAC channels to pinpoint the problem.

The Envelope Language

In computer music, *envelope* has come to signify a signal that changes slowly compared to an audio waveform but not so slowly that each discrete or continuous change in its value becomes a distinct perceptual event. Normally, envelope signals are imagined to change in a nondiscrete fashion, but this criterion is vague—for example, the amplitude envelope of a struck xylophone bar is nearly discrete at its beginning.

This definition is given purely to point out that the notion is imprecise. If we wish to sound more precise, we might say that an envelope is a low bandwidth signal, thus concentrating the impreciseness in the word *low*. Since the notion is imprecise, it is relatively certain that no precise definition will capture it completely. This is indeed the case in 4CED.

The 4C's envelope generator is capable of generating a linear ramp at a given slope and preventing its value from going past a given final value. This hardware facilitates a realization of envelopes commonly called *breakpoint envelopes*.

Since a breakpoint envelope is defined by a sequence of linear ramps while the 4C hardware can only realize a single linear ramp, the realization of

4CED's envelopes is necessarily broken down into a hardware component and a software component. This section is about the software component. It is assumed that an envelope definition (to be described) will be connected via an EGRP statement to a patch definition. In this way, the hardware and software components are linked together to complete the realization of breakpoint envelopes.

Logically Related Groups of Envelopes

Many synthesis algorithms require several envelopes; in additive synthesis, for example, each partial has a separate amplitude envelope (and sometimes a separate frequency contour as well). In 4CED, this situation is eased by the notion of *envelope families*. An envelope definition is always implicitly an envelope family and the limiting case is a family consisting of a single envelope. All the logical envelopes in a family are always triggered at once—they are independent in terms of their shapes, but cannot be triggered independently of one another.

Envelope Families

An envelope family is defined by declaring how many logical envelopes it contains and by naming each one using an EGRP statement. The EGRP statement allows it to be connected to a patch that contains a corresponding EGRP statement and uses a set of hardware envelope unit generators. Each logical envelope defines a sequence of linear ramps that are realized by the 4C hardware in combination with special software contained in the real-time part of 4CED.

Since each logical envelope defines a sequence of linear ramps, the only remaining question is how these are to be notated. There are a variety of possibilities. In 4CED, each linear ramp is defined by a line of the form *value @ time*. The intended meaning is that after the end of the duration given by *time* the envelope will have the value given by *value*. This value is given in any of the usual ways—as an amplitude, frequency, note name, or uninterpreted value (a more detailed discussion of

Fig. 2. An envelope and its corresponding definition.

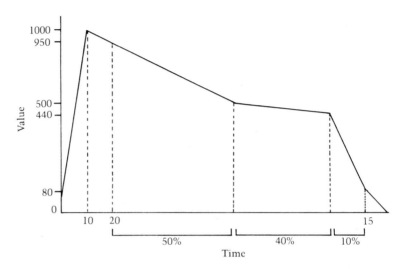

```
1000 @ 10
950  @ 10
500  @ 50%
440  @ 40%
80   @ 10%
0    @ 15
```

these ways of specifying values is given later on). The time is given as a number of milliseconds or as a percentage of the note duration. In the latter case, the envelope will adapt itself to notes of differing lengths. Fig. 2 shows a schematic envelope diagram and the way it would be defined in 4CED.

It is important to note that there is no a priori division of envelopes into attack, steady-state, and decay portions. Percentage-type durations can be used in any part of an envelope. An example of one use of this flexibility is in the following definition.

```
1000 @ 20
900  @ 40%
200  @ 10%
0    @ 20
0    @ 50%
```

This is a classic amplitude envelope such as might be associated with a wind instrument. The last 50% of the envelope is silence (a ramp from 0 to 0), however, so that the effect will be staccato.

Envelope Extensions

The facilities already discussed allow for definition of classic amplitude envelopes, but we have not yet covered some special situations. One of these is when we want an envelope to start from a nonzero value. This is accomplished by giving an explicit initializing value after the name of the envelope. As an example, suppose we wish to define an envelope that will be multiplied by a maximum deviation value and the result added to a base frequency to give a kind of "wobble" or vibrato whose frequency depends on the duration of the note, and which can be made quite irregular. We can define such an envelope as follows.

```
ENV WOBBLE = −1000
800   @ 10%
−600  @ 10%
500   @ 10%
−400  @ 15%
200   @ 15%
−80   @ 20%
0     @ 20%
FIN
```

(It is necessary to realize here that since the envelope value will be multiplied by something, and since multiplication is fractional in the 4C, −1000 corresponds to −1, 500 corresponds to ½, etc.)

There are cases where we don't want an envelope's value to be initialized at all. For example, suppose we have a synthesis model that simulates a piano. One long decay envelope simulates the normal string decay, and another simulates the damper felt that comes down on the string when the key is released. The damper envelope is to be activated when a key-release trigger is received from a score (or conceivably from an actual keyboard), and its function is simply to apply a large negative slope to the string amplitude so that it will die away quickly. This situation is notated in 4CED by a special kind of initialization, a * before the initial value. The value is still needed, since 4CED represents linear ramps internally by their slopes, so it must have some idea of where the envelope starts. For a damper envelope then, we might write the following.

ENV DAMPER = * 100
0 @ 50

Certain kinds of more general extensions are possible in 4CED envelope definitions. Suppose, for example, that we wish to vary the attack time of an envelope from a score or potentiometer so that we can simulate the sense of harshness or stress that results from a shorter attack time. This is done by replacing the time field of the appropriate linear ramp with an instruction to read the value in some 4C register and use that value as the duration of the ramp. The form of this instruction is V# (value of register #), where # is replaced by the number of any 4C register. (Symbolic names cannot be used here—this is one of the compromises in 4CED caused by the need to support precompilation of scores and envelopes for the common situation in which lack of memory becomes a problem.) Thus we might define a variable attack time envelope as follows.

1000 @ V3
500 @ 15%
220 @ 40%
0   @ 40%
0   @ 5%

This definition assumes that the user will reserve

register 3 and arrange that it contains a meaningful attack time when the envelope is triggered.

Using a 4C register value as the value field of an envelope definition can also be a reasonable thing: in the following example the "peakedess" of the envelope is determined by the value in register 3.

V3 @ 20
500 @ 15%
220 @ 40%
0   @ 40%
0   @ 5%

It is also possible to use a V# instruction for the initial value of an envelope. All these ways of using the V# instruction can be combined so that it is possible to define a whole envelope completely in terms of 4C register values, changing its configuration in arbitrary ways even as it unfolds. Naturally, there are numerous practical limits on this, the most serious of which is probably the burden it imposes on the host computer, which must do much more calculation in real time than for well-defined envelopes. 4CED's envelope compiler arranges envelope definitions internally so as to minimize this time-critical calculation.

The Score Language

Imagine a table with 32 music boxes on it, each one with a button. When we push the button of any particular music box, it plays something. The situation in 4CED is a bit like this. A score is the music box. In general it will always play the same thing, but there are ways of influencing from the outside how or what it plays.

In 4CED it is possible to have 32 scores acting independently and simultaneously. In computer science terminology, we would say that up to 32 parallel processes are possible. When such a situation obtains, we need a way to name each of the processes. In 4CED, these processes are called *attach points*, and each one is potentially active at all times. Whenever we trigger an attach point, it is like pushing the button on the music box—whatever is attached to the attach point plays its thing.

If nothing is attached, the bell on the computer terminal is sounded as a complaint.

There are several ways of pushing these buttons. One score can push the button for another score. This feature allows hierarchical structuring of score activations. The first 26 attach points are named A through Z. When one of these keys on the computer terminal is touched in lowercase mode (normally a, b, etc.) 4CED immediately triggers the corresponding attach point. This feature allows interactive and intuitive activation of scores. Finally, there is a special command that triggers several scores together. This turns out to be useful too.

Before continuing, it is necessary to correct one simplification. Actually, each of the 32 parallel processes in 4CED represents either a score or a family of envelopes. Envelope families are not contained within scores, just as they are not contained within patches. They are independent and need an attach point to call home. This organization is not the most obvious possible—in particular, it is not obvious to new users of 4CED why envelopes require so much special attention. The generality of this scheme increases the flexibility of 4CED, however, and provides other advantages of a more technical nature (for example, synchronization of independent voices is facilitated by the separation of envelopes from scores).

Score Language Design Considerations

Traditionally, software synthesis languages in the Music V family have represented scores as lists of data, each list (or column) being associated with some parameter (*pfield*). This is a perfectly sensible decision, since it creates a logical interface between a score representation at the program's level and another at a more user-oriented level (supported by special features like PLF in Music V and I-only code in Music 10). In a performance situation, however, it becomes impossible to separate these levels in time—if a score is to respond in sophisticated ways to performance inputs, it must be possible to express these sophisticated responses directly in the score—no intervening level of processing is possible.

This article will describe two score languages used in different versions of 4CED: one of these is essentially lists of data, while in the second a score can execute arithmetic and control expressions that vastly increase its flexibility for complex and interesting performance situations. Both of these are reported on because I believe that each one represents a reasonable response to a certain set of perceived needs. (Naturally, there exist situations to which neither one represents a good response, but extended speculation on score language design warrants another article.)

The Original Score Language

In the original score language a score is a list of events. An event is a list of actions followed by a description of how the next event is to be caused. The program that interprets scores simply carries out each action associated with the current event, then follows the instructions that tell it how to cause the next event. It then "disappears" until the next event takes place. Each of these events is imagined to be instantaneous. (Durations will be discussed later.)

The most common action in an event is assignment of a value to a 4C register. Generally, this is done with the form *register = value*. This form allows complete generality—a score can refer to any register, either by name (typically for CONNECTed registers) or by number. This organization is more general than the pfield notation used by Music V and friends, but this generality is often unneeded and so a pfield construct is available. For columns of data declared as pfields, the *register =* part is implicit. Declaration of pfields will be shown in an example to come.

The assignment action is important because it is the only way in which a score can directly influence the sound. Other actions correspond to indirect influences, for example: triggering an envelope, triggering another score, stopping the execution of any score or envelope, or invoking a sequence of commands as if they had been typed directly at the terminal. This last kind of action allows scores to have very generalized control functions.

Specifying how the next event is caused usually corresponds to giving a number that represents the duration of the note started by the current event. However, these "durations" are ordinarily uninterpreted—there is no requirement that each event correspond to a single note. Indeed, it can be useful to break up a single note into a sequence of events, each of which does a different kind of thing. The general form of the assignment statement supports this.

When an event triggers an envelope, a duration is passed to the envelope. Typically, this is the duration of the triggering event itself, although this can be explicitly overridden. It is also possible to cause the duration of an event (that is, the amount of time until the next event) to be read from a 4C register. This is notated by the V# form, just as for envelope definitions. In this case, it is also possible to give a number by which the value read from the 4C is multiplied. This feature allows for simple rhythmic structures in the framework of a tempo that can be varied in real time. A more general way of doing this will be shown further on.

Finally, writing T as the instruction for the next event causes the score interpreter to wait for an explicit trigger, either from another score or from the computer terminal. This feature is essential for situations in which rhythm is not prespecified—it effectively allows the duration to be decided by any outside agent.

Let us now consider the notation of the original score language in more detail, by an example. The following score plays a C major scale in two tetrachords. The idea is to trigger the score that then plays the first tetrachord, then trigger it again to get the second tetrachord.

CONNECT FREQ;		!connect statement
(FREQ:N)		!pfield declaration
C4	TE Z @ 1000	!first note one second long
D4	TE Z @ 1000	
E4	TE Z @ 1000	
F4	TE Z = 1000 @ T	!end of first tetrachord
G4	TE Z @ V3	
A4	TE Z @ V3	
B4	TE Z @ V3	
C5	TE Z @ V3	

This example is certainly contrived, but it demonstrates almost all the features of the notation! The first line declares a symbolic register name FREQ that is to be linked up with a corresponding one found in a patch definition. The second line declares that the first column of data in the score should go to the register FREQ and that the data will be written in the note-name format (this is what :N means). This first column of data should then be easy to understand—the notes of a C scale. The second column is a line of TE Z, which stands for trigger envelope at attach point Z. Continuing to the right we find @, which indicates that the next event instruction follows (and that data for the current event are all given). In the next event field, we find a variety of things. For the first three events we see 1000, which is a duration in milliseconds. This duration is automatically passed to the envelope on attach point Z. In the fourth event we see a T, which causes a wait for an explicit trigger, as has been explained. Since the duration of a T is completely unknown, it is necessary for this event to program explicitly the duration of the triggered envelope by writing TE Z = 1000 before @. The last four events use a V3 for the next event instruction, meaning that we expect to find a tempo for the second tetrachord in 4C register number 3. Naturally, this tempo can change while the tetrachord is playing. The correct duration is always passed to the envelope on Z.

In the original score language, the pfield concept is not generalized to allow, for example, the name of an envelope function to be a parameter, nor is it possible to specify (except explicitly) the common situation that a particular envelope is triggered on each and every event. These problems are not only problems of convenience; they represent a lost opportunity to reduce the memory requirement of a score in the computer. They are difficult to solve within the framework of the original score language, however. Consider the problem represented by the fourth event in the preceding example, where we had to write TE Z = 1000.

In general, the original score language is easy to learn and works very well for applications in which it is appropriate. We now turn to the second score language, which attempts to address some of the situations for which the original is not appropriate.

The Second Score Language

The basic idea of the second score language is that a list of expressions is executed on each event. These expressions consist of arithmetic, relational, and special *operators*, which act on 4C registers, user-defined variables, user-defined arrays, attach points, and so on. Special provisions are made for lists of data with a window onto the data that can be moved explicitly by an operator called GOTO. Further generality is provided by allowing each event to have its own expressions and the opportunity to turn on or off some of the expressions normally executed on each event.

Clearly, the conceptual complexity in the second score language is much greater than that in the original. It is probably for this reason that the notation seems more systematic. Through a discussion of notation we will explore what can be done with the second score language.

First, let us consider something similar to but simpler than the example for the original score language.

```
CONNECT FREQ;
COL 1:N;                !declare one column of data
                        !written as note-names
(HDR                    !create a list of expressions
                        !to execute on each event
    (= FREQ F1)         !first expression
    (TRIG Z 1000)
    (WAIT 1000)
)                       !end of expressions
C4; D4; E4; F4;
G4; A4; B4; C5;         !data
```

This score will play the C major scale, each note 1 sec long. Although the appearance of this score is considerably different from that of the one that preceded it, a number of things have changed very little. The COL statement replaces the pfield declaration. The expression (TRIG Z 1000) replaces TE Z = 1000, and (WAIT 1000) replaces @ 1000. The assignment statement is explicit because it normally must be written only once. The fact that it is written (= FREQ F1) rather than FREQ = F1 is characteristic of this score language: the convention for writing expressions is called "Cambridge Polish" or, more commonly, *Lisp notation*, since it is the style used in the programming language Lisp. This style was chosen largely for implementation reasons, and we have no desire to discuss its aesthetic strengths and weaknesses. The important thing is that it provides the necessary expressive power to develop fairly complex performance-oriented scores.

All three expressions are collected between an opening marker, (HDR, and a closing parenthesis. These are called *header expressions* and are normally executed for each event. A special convention allows these expressions access to the data currently in the window: this form is F# (field number #). This construct is used in the first expression (= FREQ F1) that therefore assigns the frequency value of the current note to the 4C register FREQ.

The line of data shows off the free formatting rules—the data for each event is terminated by a semicolon. In this score language the number of items of data must be the same for each event, but each event's data can be decorated in a number of ways (all optional). These are

1. Labels. Labeled events can be the targets of GOTO expressions.
2. SKIP statements. These turn off (or on) some of the normally executed header expressions.
3. Extra expressions. Any number of expressions can be written between the data for an event and the semicolon that terminates it. These are evaluated just before the header expressions when the event is encountered.

It is convenient to think of HDR as the name of an operator in prefix form (like all operators in this language), which takes a variable number of expressions as arguments and evaluates them on each event. The header expression therefore represents the set of things we normally want to do on each event. For exceptional cases the SKIP statement is used. For example, to add a rest between the first and second tetrachords in the last example, we would add an event that executes only the WAIT operation by decorating it with SKIP(1,2).

A detailed and complete description of all available operators and conventions is beyond the scope of this article, but the following paragraphs will outline the important features.

Most of the operators are straightforward—there are the classic arithmetic, relational, and logical operators as in typical programming languages, and there are specialized operators like TRIG and WAIT, which have easily understood functions. Certain other specialized operators are somewhat trickier. Two of these are SETSKIP and CLRSKIP, which function like the SKIP statement mentioned previously, but do so in a data-dependent way. These are analogous to the *if statement* of classic programming languages. To understand the reason for CLRSKIP, we must know that we can define certain header expressions to be skipped ordinarily; CLRSKIP can then enable their execution selectively.

Another slightly tricky operator is the GOTO statement, which allows explicit control over the movement of the window on the data. Recall that there is a window on the data for each event, which normally is moved forward by one step after each event. A GOTO statement allows this movement to be, instead, to any labeled event. This statement is always conditional. The GOTO statement allows realization of performance instructions such as "Play phrase A three times or until I move potentiometer two, then play phrase B." Labels also serve to indicate rehearsal marks, and a command is provided to preset a score at a certain label so that when the score is triggered it starts there.

Having considered at some length the operators available in scores, we now turn to the various kinds of data. Each instance of a score has a local variable called LCL that is protected from outside interference. This is typically used to store intermediate results of calculations or to save a state between events. Normally, scores communicate with one another (and the outside world) using variables and 4C registers. There are 30 *variables*, referred to in scores as X1 through X30. A number of user commands is added to 4CED to allow for direct intervention and readout of the values of these variables.

Another feature added to 4CED to increase the power and flexibility of the second score language is the *lookup table*. Users can define lookup tables of arbitrary length, and scores can access them as arrays. They are intended to facilitate complex relationships between parameter values and their meanings. For example, they can store internal frequency representations corresponding to degrees of arbitrary scales, making it possible to write scores that use different scales at different moments, and in which the choice of scale can be a performance variable.

Example: Complex Rhythms

This example shows one way arithmetic expressions in scores can be useful. Suppose we want to define the tempo of a melodic line with a 4C register, but also wish to impose a rhythm. Imagine that the value in the 4C register defines the duration of a quarter note, and that our desired rhythm is quarter note, three triplets, three eighth notes, and a dotted quarter note.

The plan is to represent rhythms as rational fractions. Assume that a global 4C register called TEMPO gives the duration of a quarter note. Other durations are derived by multiplication and division; for example, TEMPO/3 is the duration of a triplet. Assume we wish to play a C major scale in the tempo. We will calculate the duration and store it in LCL, then use it as a duration for the triggered envelope and for the event duration. All this is summed up in the following score.

```
CONNECT FREQ;
COL 1:N, 2:U, 3:U;
(HDR
   (= FREQ F1)
   (= LCL (DIV (* (RD4C 3) F2) F3))
   (TRIG Z LCL)
   (WAIT LCL)
)
!freq   numer   denom
C4      1       1;
D4      1       3;
E4      1       3;
F4      1       3;
```

G4	1	2;
A4	1	2;
B4	1	2;
C5	3	2;

In this score, the COL statement specifies a U for the second and third columns. This means *unscaled* data and is used when we do not wish a value to be interpreted as a note name, frequency, or amplitude. It is a general rule in 4CED that *values* can always be specified in a number of ways by using a letter prefix: N (notes), H (Hertz), U (unscaled), or A (amplitude). Normally A is default.

Clearly, we can incorporate more complex rhythms within this framework. It is important to be aware of limitations on the technique though: durations are not of infinite precision, and arithmetic errors can accumulate. It is possible to introduce more complicated schemes, still within the framework of the score language, which correct accumulating errors of synchronization. (Naturally, these introduce more overhead as well.)

Example: Overlapped Notes

In some traditional instruments like the piano, several notes can sound at once. This is often true even in completely melodic passages on these instruments, and it is important to model this in synthetic imitations of such instruments. Although 4CED has no built-in features for this, it can be implemented directly.

In the 4C, any patch can only do one thing at a time. This precludes the neat trick found in software synthesis languages such as Music V and Music 11, in which sufficient "copies" of a patch are automatically allocated to cover all the notes playing it at any given moment. This removes the need to think about allocation of instrument resources when we write a score. This works because of the non-real-time nature of these programs. In the 4C, the digital instruments are more like physical instruments—if we want 15 violins in a piece of traditional music, we must go out and find 15 violinists.

Since playing overlapped notes requires two or more copies of the same patch definition, we will have several patch images derived from a single patch definition. A score can be connected to only a single patch image. For this reason, the standard technique for overlapping in 4CED is to use a single master score that triggers two or more slave scores alternately. The master score puts all the information needed to play a note in some "public" place (for example, in variables or 4C registers not used for other purposes), and the selected slave score then has the job of using this information to trigger a note in the appropriate patch image. The implementation of this idea in 4CED will be more fully developed in the detailed example given later.

The Command Language

The preceding sections have covered three major sublanguages of 4CED in some detail. The command language constitutes the direct user interface of 4CED. The name *4CED* is derived from the structure of the command language which, like a good text-editor command language, imposes few constraints on the order of doing things and provides plenty of feedback to the user about the state of the system.

In general, commands to 4CED consist of two letters followed by zero or more arguments that depend on the specific command. Wherever possible, these two-letter commands consist of a first letter that acts like a verb, and a second that acts like a noun. Thus the AP command can be conceptualized as meaning apply patch. As will be seen this convention sometimes leads to unhappy results, but it seems to be a good compromise since verbosity is generally unwelcome in an interactive environment.

Command Lists

Although the command language is designed for interactive use, often a long sequence of commands is used to set up a certain situation. Command lists provide a way of doing this conveniently. Command lists may be defined in disk files, just like patches, scores, and envelopes. Using command lists, we can plan our use of the command language, thereby further reducing the amount of typing necessary in actual interaction.

Input/Output Commands

Since it is possible to prepare disk files of patch, score, and envelope definitions and modify them with a text editor, there must be a way of getting access to the definitions in these files. These considerations have led to the IT (input text) and OT (output text) commands. There is also an FT (find text) command, which searches a library file for definitions with certain names. There is an internal *compiled form* for scores and envelopes that 4CED creates automatically when things are attached to attach points. When long scores are used and it is important to minimize space, the compiled forms can be created beforehand and read in directly. The compiled file of definitions is created by another program called ISQ and read in with the IS (input sequence) command. There is an OS command as well, for saving definitions compiled during a program run. Each input command reports the name and type of all definitions found. In addition, FT reports on any requested definitions that were not found.

Activation Commands

There is a class of commands for activating or applying definitions. These are as follows.

AP — Apply patch (load into 4C)
AC — Apply command list (execute all commands in list)
AW — Apply wavetable
AG — Apply connection between pot and 4C register
AS — Attach score (or envelope) to attach point
AA — Trigger attach point(s)

The letter G for pot/register connections is one un-

happy result of the limited, two-letter command structure. The G is used consistently in related commands, however. The AW command serves to define the function associated with one of a fixed set of wavetables by loading the function from a disk file. 4CED is not capable of dealing with definition or modification of these functions—instead, an auxiliary, graphic program is used.

Definition Commands

Certain kinds of program entities are best defined directly; for example, the lower- and upper-limit values for a pot/register connection, the lengths and values of user-provided arrays (lookup tables), the values of user variables, and the names of globally known 4C registers. This leads to a set of commands shown here.

range	DR *name* (*lower-bound, upper-bound*)
lookup table	DL *number* (*value1, value2, . . . , valueN*)
variable	DX *variable-number value*
4C register	DZ *name1, name2, . . . , nameN*

Feedback Commands

When working in a preplanned, off-line fashion, it is always possible to walk through a set of instructions, figuring out in the process what the state of things will be when they have been executed. In an interactive situation it is important to have access to detailed information about the state of everything in the system, which can be selectively requested. A large number of commands are devoted to this. Most of these commands begin with S (show) or L (list). For example, S by itself prints out the content of named definitions (patches, scores, etc.); SR prints out values of 4C registers; SX prints values of user variables; SL prints the definition of selected lookup tables; and SI prints part or all of the 4C image, as discussed in the section on patch definition.

Similarly, LT (list text) prints the names and types of all definitions; LS prints the names of all compiled scores and envelopes; LA tells which attach points are in use, and by what; LG tells which potentiometers are connected to which 4C registers; LZ prints the name and number of each global 4C register; and so on.

The verb R (remove) also applies to many of these, serving to remove definitions selectively. For example, RP removes the patch images whose names are given as arguments and reclaims the 4C resources thus released. A number of these commands are little used, but are included for completeness.

The verb M (modify) applies to range definitions, allowing simple adjustment of the way potentiometer values are scaled; and to text definitions, allowing the internal text editor to be applied. This editor is too simple to be useful for extensive changes to a definition, but it can be used without leaving the program (and, therefore, the accumulated state). This is sometimes appreciated. The editor can also be used to create new definitions.

Miscellaneous Commands

One command that doesn't fit in elsewhere is a command to print out a text string given as argument. This is normally used inside command lists to make them seem friendlier. A more important example is the "immediate mode" patch line, which is useful for directly changing 4C register values and for detailed debugging of patches. Any command line preceded by a solidus is treated this way. (An example is found in Fig. 6.)

A Detailed Example

Before concluding, we will attempt to bring together the numerous individual aspects of 4CED already discussed by developing a detailed example that incorporates overlapped 4C patches and some of the control structures mentioned previously in the section on scores.

Review

Understanding of the fabric of relationships among scores, envelopes, patches, and attach points is probably the most troublesome aspect of learning to use 4CED, so it is reviewed first.

The attach point serves two main functions. First, it is the unit of independent execution for scores and envelope families. This means that a score or a family of envelopes must be attached to an attach point before it can be triggered. Second, an attach point is the binding unit between scores or envelope families, and patches. This means that when we make a connection via a CONNECT (for scores) or EGRP (for envelopes) statement, the actual abstract-to-concrete binding takes place when the score or envelope family is attached to an attach point. Furthermore, any score that needs to trigger events in several different patch images must do so through the intermediary of slave scores bound to different patch images. (Actually, another strategy is possible that is appropriate for situations where a score is automatically generated by a user-written program, but it will not be considered here.)

A clear understanding of the difference between internal and external forms of definitions is important. For example, if P is the name of a patch, then the textual definition named by P can be loaded into the 4C by writing AP P. This command also creates an internal form of the definition of P called a patch image, which is normally called P as well. When we attach a score to an attach point and wish to bind the CONNECTed registers of the score to some corresponding registers in a patch, we give the name of a patch image. (One implication of this is that patches must be loaded before the scores that use them can be attached.) If we wish to load two instances of the patch P, we must explicitly give them different names. For example, we might write the following.

    AP P = IMG1
    AP P = IMG2

It was stated that to realize the effect of overlapped

*Fig. 3. Patch definition
for a piano synthesis
instrument.*

```
PNO: PATCH
PARAM OUTP;                    !output register passed for later mixing
CONNECT PHASE1, PHASE2, FREQ;
EGRP EG1, EG2;

STRETCH = 5        !used as a multiplier, this acts like 0.005

{ PHO 4K3 PHASE1 FREQ SIG1;       !wavetable 4K3 has a piano waveform
  ENV EG1 SIG1 SIG1               !note that the two "strings" are computed
| MUL STRETCH FREQ FREQ SFREQ;    !in parallel
  PHO 4K3 PHASE2 SFREQ SIG2;
  ENV EG2 SIG2 SIG2
}
ADD SIG1 SIG2 OUTP
END
```

notes requires that two (or more) slave scores medi-
ate between the master score that triggers notes
and the patch images that actually make the
sounds. Thus if we have two such scores called
SLAVE1 and SLAVE2, we bind them to different
patch images by writing something like this.

    AS A SLAVE1 IMG1
    AS B SLAVE2 IMG2

Let us suppose that our patch P uses an envelope
family whose definition is called ENV. Then we
need two independently executing copies of this
definition, one for use by SLAVE1 and the other for
SLAVE2. (Typically, the only difference between
such slave scores is that they refer to different copies of a single envelope definition.) We can get this
effect by writing the following.

    AS C ENV IMG1
    AS D ENV IMG2

Notice that attachment of ENV to two different attach points automatically creates two independent
instances (internally, these are treated like parallel
processes that share their program but have distinct data for execution).

A Synthetic Piano Playing Arpeggios

The example to be developed is that of a synthetic
piano playing arpeggios from a scale chosen by the
user. The synthetic piano is set up to allow a note
to start while its predecessor is still finishing. This
makes the simulation vastly more realistic. We will
discuss in turn the patch definition, envelope definitions, score definition and, finally, a command
list definition that sets up the whole thing.

The piano synthesis instrument is very simple. It
consists of two oscillators playing at slightly different frequencies from the same wavetable with
two slightly different envelopes. The wavetable is a
complex one derived from the analysis of an actual
piano sound. The envelope applied to each oscillator shapes its amplitude in a manner that approximates the decay of a string struck by a piano
hammer. At some point along the course of this envelope, a different envelope may be interposed that
simulates the application of the damper felt when
the key is released. Otherwise, the note decays naturally. This synthesis technique was first developed
by Andy Moorer and David Wessel. It was first applied to the 4C by Jean Kott, Pepino di Giugno and
Tod Machover.

Figure 3 shows how this algorithm might be de-

Fig. 4. Envelope defini-
tions. Historical accident
dictates that envelopes
and scores both be called
sequences. They differ in
the first words of their definitions: SEQ means
scores and MLSEQ means
envelope families.

```
SDCY: SEQUENCE
MLSEQ
NENV=2
EGRP STRG1, STRG2;

ENV STRG1
500 @ 3
400 @ 4
350 @ 25
320 @ 40
300 @ 60
280 @ 80
260 @ 100
240 @ 120
220 @ 150
200 @ 200
. . .
40  @ 1000
20  @ 1200
0   @ 1450
FIN

ENV STRG2
0   @ 2
500 @ 3
400 @ 5
350 @ 25
. . . (as for STRG1)
FIN
END

DAMPER: SEQUENCE
MLSEQ
NENV=2
EGRP STRG1, STRG2
ENV STRG1 = * 100     !Do not initialize envelope value when triggered.
0 @ 120               !Imagine that it starts at 100 and goes to 0 in 120 msec.
FIN
ENV STRG2 = * 100
0 @ 130
FIN
END
```

fined in a patch. We use the special PHO form of
oscillator because we wish to initialize the phase of
each oscillator to 0 at the beginning of a note. To
do this we also connect the phase registers to the
score. Naturally, the frequency is also connected.
The EGRP statement says that we will have an envelope family consisting of two envelopes feeding
information to the 4C linear ramp generators.

The 4CED Program **327**

Fig. 5. Score for the simulated piano example (see
Fig. 4).

```
ARPEG: SEQUENCE
SEQ
COL 1:U, 2:U, 3:U;
LABEL NXTARP;
(HDR
    (= LCL (+ F1 X3))
    (= X5 (RSH ( * (LKP 1 (+ (DIV LCL 7) 1)) (LKP X1 (+ (MOD LCL 7) 1))) −6))
    (= X4 (− F2 (RD4C OVERLP)))
    (TRIG F3 0)
    (WAIT F2)
)
!special first event:
SKIP(1,2,3,4,5)
            *        *       *      !dummy data
(= X3 0) (WAIT 1);                  !this is what we really want to do
!data: scale degree, duration, attach point number
NXTARP:
                0      450      1
                2      450      2;
                4      450      1;
SKIP(5)         7      1350     2 (WAIT 20); !wait 20 instead of 1350 msec
!looping logic in this event
SKIP(1,2,3,4,5)
            *        *       *      !dummy data
(= X3 (+ X3 1))                     !increment counter
(GOTO (LE X3 X2) NXTARP)            !test for exit
(WAIT 1330);                        !wait till end of current note
END


SLAVE1: SEQUENCE
!Attached to B. SLAVE2 (not shown) is attached to C.
SEQ
CONNECT PHZ1, PHZ2, FREQ;
LABEL TOP;
(HDR)       !no default expressions
TOP:

!event 1: trigger string envelope
(= PHZ1 0), (= PHZ2 0), (= FREQ X5), (TRIG D 0), (WAIT X4);
!event 2: stop string, trigger damper
(STOPAP D), (TRIG F 0), (GOTO 1 TOP);
END
```

Fig. 6. Command list for
the simulated piano exam-
ple. In practice, this command list would be in-
voked to set up the necessary context for the
example.

```
SETUP: COMMAND LIST
DZ OVERLP, VOX1, VOX2
AP PNO = IMG1 VOX1                    !two copies of patch for overlapping
AP PNO = IMG2 VOX2
!next line mixes and outputs the two voices
/H=500 MUL H VOX1 VOX1; MUL H VOX2 VOX1 VOX1; OUT 1 VOX1
AS A ARPEG                           !main score on A
AS B SLAVE1 IMG1                     !two slaves for overlapping
AS C SLAVE2 IMG2
AS D SDCY IMG1                       !envelopes for each copy
AS E SDCY IMG2
AS F DAMPER IMG1
AS G DAMPER IMG2
DR OVRNG (U−200, U200)              !−200 to 200 milliseconds
AG OVERLP 1 OVRNG                    !connect pot 1 scaled by OVRNG to OVERLP register
DL 1 (1,2,4,8,16,32)                 !used for octave to frequency conversion
DL 2 (...)                           !define 7 numbers for equal tempered diatonic scale
DL 3 (...)                           !define 7 numbers for mean-tone diatonic scale
DL 4 (...)                           !try a little just intonation?
SX 1 U2                              !start off with equal tempered scale
P "'A' for Arpeggios"
END
```

These envelopes describe the instantaneous amplitude of the simulated piano strings.

Next, we consider the envelope definitions.
There will be two different envelopes for the instrument that we call SDCY (string decay) and
DAMPER. Each of the envelopes in SDCY consists
of a series of breakpoints that roughly simulate the
approximately exponential decay of a piano string
(the definitions given here are not derived from the
analysis of piano sounds, although this is certainly
possible). These definitions are shown in Fig. 4.

To get the effect of overlapping, we need two copies of everything, as previously stated. Each slave
score consists of two events. The first sets phases
to zero, sets the frequency correctly, and triggers
the SDCY envelope bound to its patch. The second
stops the SDCY envelope and triggers the decay envelope. The master score must provide a frequency
and the amount of time between these two events.
The definition of a slave score is shown at the bottom of Fig. 5. The placement of scores on attach
points, and their bindings to patch images, is
shown as part of Fig. 6.

With this done, we turn to the definition of the
master score that plays the arpeggios. First, we will
let a potentiometer define the amount of overlapping between notes. This is implemented by
defining a global 4C register to contain the value
read from the potentiometer. Then this value is
subtracted from the note duration to determine the
amount of time between the slave score's first and
second events; that is, between the onset of the
note and the beginning of damped decay.

We encode the idea of an arpeggio by giving the
scale degree of each note relative to the current
base note. This is shown in the first column of data
in Fig. 5. The second column of data gives the duration in milliseconds, and the third names the
attach point to be triggered for each note. This
third column defines the pattern of overlapping.
For the moment, the program will not automatically convert attach point names to their underlying numeric representations in these situations.

Two things are especially important in this score
definition: the means by which scale degrees are
turned into frequencies, and the overall control

structure of the score. These will be considered in turn.

Each scale is defined by a lookup table that contains a frequency value for each scale degree, 1–7. A single octave is fully defined by this lookup table. Other octaves are derived by multiplying the frequency in the base octave by $2 ** x$, where x is the octave number. Given a scale degree, the actual frequency is calculated by this means in the first and second header expressions of the score in Fig. 5. The RSH (right shift) operator is there because of some funny things about integer arithmetic, which will not be discussed in detail. The LKP X1 . . . means that the lookup table whose number is in X1 will be used (remember that X1 means user variable number 1). This enables us to change the scale definition by changing the value of X1. A lookup table is used to implement $2 ** x$.

The other header expressions are concerned with defining the time from trigger to decay, triggering the correct slave, and waiting until the next event. Notice that the two values needed by slave scores are passed in X4 and X5. Perhaps the inelegance of this points the way to future extensions of 4CED in which parameter-passing between scores will be more automatic.

We turn next to the control structure of the ARPEG score. There are six events in all, and the middle four are normal events that produce the four notes of an arpeggio. The first event is executed only when the score is first triggered—its purpose is to initialize X3, which serves as a counter. The last event increments X3, compares it to X2 (which is a user-defined limit), and conditionally loops back for another arpeggio. Since X3 is also used as the base scale degree for the arpeggios, the result is several successive arpeggios, each starting one scale degree above the last. Since it is desirable to do this decision making while the last note is going on, the last regular (sound-producing) event waits only 20 msec, and the rest of the note duration comes after the last control event.

To summarize, then, the user's control over this score is in the value of X1, which defines a scale, X2, which defines the number of successive arpeggios to play, and potentiometer 1, which controls the degree of overlap.

Conclusions

4CED is a working program for the 4C digital synthesizer and friends. It is being used in applying interesting synthesis algorithms to the 4C, in using the 4C to make tape music, and in developing the potential of the 4C as a performance instrument capable of interacting with performers in interesting ways. 4CED is based on my strong belief that the most viable paradigm for real-time digital synthesis software is that of computer programming languages. By abstracting the features of any particular synthesizer and the fundamental ideas used by any composer in making music, and by providing means of packaging these ideas in ways imagined by the composer, a powerful conceptual basis is obtained for current and future developments in this area. In this section, some of the implications of this idea will be discussed, then some strengths and weaknesses of 4CED will be described in terms of the perspective provided by this paradigm.

This paradigm applies best in an environment in which a highly programmable digital synthesizer is being used. The 4C is a step in this direction that relates to much other work in digital synthesizer design, and more recent work by its designer continues in this vein (Asta et al. 1980).

The programming language paradigm suggests that design of real-time digital synthesizer software has much to gain from a careful look at programming languages intended for real-time applications. The possible role of *monitors*, *critical sections*, and *explicit parallel processes* are examples. The possibility of a compiler-based design is important too. In such a design, each musical application would involve writing a program that, when compiled, would take over the role of 4CED itself. In this way, different implementations could be chosen for different compositional situations, resulting in a more optimal use of machine resources.

In our striving for generality, certain factors must not be overlooked. The usefulness of graphic interaction has been amply demonstrated (Buxton et al. 1979), and it should be integrated into an ideal real-time program as gracefully as possible. Furthermore, since the majority of composers don't really want to become computer programmers, even given a high-level, specialized language, it makes sense to develop models that are of intermediate generality but easy to use.

From a practical point of view, certain factors will continue to restrict the extent to which real-time software like 4CED can be made more general. Among these are the limits on the underlying synthesizer hardware, the speed limitations of current machines for control functions, and the fact that useful software must be finished in a finite amount of time.

From my point of view, 4CED represents a viable step in the right direction. The patching language provides a good match for the underlying hardware, as does the envelope definition language. The symbolic treatment of 4C registers is quite sophisticated and provides considerable abstractive power to the user. The two score languages each address different needs quite effectively. The command language works quite well interactively without being completely incomprehensible in command lists. Most of the internal structures used by the program (such as patch images and the compiled form of scores and envelopes) are kept out of the user's way whenever possible.

Certain things are missing from 4CED. One of these is any form of graphic interaction. It would be interesting to find out how the development of graphics might change its external appearance. Also, although 4CED provides all the primitives necessary to allow a user to experiment with a digital instrument, searching for parameter values (and perhaps slowly changing gestural values), it would be better if these primitives were packaged so that users could conveniently play, modify, and incorporate gestures into scores. Another kind of packaging needed in performance situations is an allocator, which would allow overlapping of notes to be done as a score unfolds, or in response to real-time inputs (such as keyboard playing).

Everyone involved in digital music is aware that the technology continues to develop, and practical limits change as a result. There is no doubt that minicomputers with larger address spaces, cheaper graphics devices, and developments in signal processing technology will make it possible to develop systems more elegant and powerful than the one described here. It is hoped that 4CED will have some influence on the way these future systems will be presented to their users.

References

Asta, V., et al. 1980. "Il Systema di Sintesi Digitale in Tempo Reale 4X." *Automazione e Strumentazione* 28(2): 119–133.

Buxton, W., et al. 1979. "The Evolution of the SSSP Score Editing Tools." *Computer Music Journal* 3(4): 14–25.

Moorer, J., et al. 1979. "The 4C Machine." *Computer Music Journal* 3(3): 16–24.

29

D. Gareth Loy

Computer Audio Research Laboratory
Center for Music Experiment
University of California, San Diego
La Jolla, California 92093

Notes on the Implementation of MUSBOX: a Compiler for the Systems Concepts Digital Synthesizer

Introduction to the Systems Concepts Digital Synthesizer

In 1978 the Center for Computer Research in Music and Acoustics (CCRMA) at Stanford University acquired a remarkable musical instrument: the prototype of the Systems Concepts Digital Synthesizer (SCS) designed and built by Peter Samson of Systems Concepts, San Francisco, to the specifications of CCRMA.

The principal purpose of the synthesizer design was to address the high computational bandwidth required for real-time high-quality digital audio signal processing. It is well known that digital synthesis techniques have been limited by the sheer speed, precision, and consequent volume of computation required for useful and interesting results. It was hoped that a special-purpose digital computer that directly addressed the nature of the data to be manipulated would be sufficiently fast to do useful amounts of signal computation in real time.

The resulting design is described elsewhere in the literature (Loy 1980; Samson 1980; Samson forthcoming), but a brief review is not out of place here. The synthesizer uses standard TTL logic, relying extensively on time-division multiplexing and pipelining techniques to implement a fixed set of processing capabilities. The synthesizer is divided into modules, called *processing elements*, which can be configured to perform specific signal

processing functions. There are four classes of processing elements, each class being uniquely suited to one kind of processing (Fig. 1). They are *generators*, which produce a variety of periodic fixed-waveform signals; *modifiers*, which modify signals; *sum memory*, which provides a means of intercommunication between the individual generators and modifiers; and *delay units*, which interface the modifiers to a large memory bank (up to 64K 20-bit words) for reverberation and table storage. There are 256 generators, 128 modifiers, 256 sum memory locations, and 32 delay units; not all sum memory locations can be written by all processing elements, however. All of these processing elements can run simultaneously.

Each generator is divided functionally into an oscillator part and an envelope part. The oscillator part produces normalized square, sawtooth, pulse train, $\sin(x)$, $\sin(x+FM)$, and sum-of-cosines waveforms. The oscillator parameters that can be controlled include frequency (28 bits), frequency sweep (20), phase angle (20), number of cosines to be summed (if any), and a sum memory address from which frequency modulation (FM) data are taken. The envelope part can produce a constant (12), plus either a linear ramp (24) or a positive or negative exponential function to control the amplitude of the oscillator, with an overall precision of 20 bits. A final 12-by-13-bit two-quadrant multiply scales the oscillator product by the amplitude product, and the result is written to a specified 20-bit-wide sum memory location. In addition, the generators have degenerate modes in which they perform other nec-

Fig. 1. Block diagram of
the SCS showing the DMA
channels from the CPU to
the processing elements.
The elements are fed data
through their control
memories (labeled C.M. in
the figure), which can be
set by the CPU through a
separate I/O path (not
shown). The generators
can also be data channels
that can transfer samples
or other data to or from
the CPU and to the DACs.
The SUM MEMORY serves
as an interconnection ma-
trix for the processing
elements.

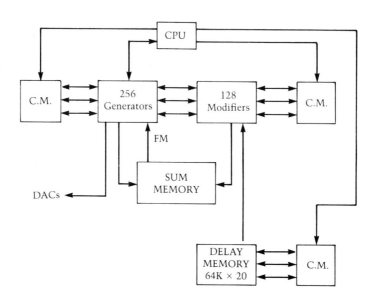

essary functions, such as transferring samples from sum memory to the digital-to-analog converters (DACs) and reading or writing samples between sum memory and the external central processing unit (CPU) via direct memory access (DMA).

Modifiers are functionally simpler but perform a broader range of tasks. Each modifier can read two sum memory locations, perform two 20-by-20-bit multiplies and various additions and tests, and write one datum back to sum memory. The tasks include uniform noise (linear congruential method); filtering (one or two poles or zeros, fixed or variable coefficients); signal adding; scaling and multiplying (including amplitude modulation (AM), ring modulation, and mixing); signal testing (including threshold, maximum, minimum, sign test and zero-crossing test); and others. Modifiers are also used with delay units to form a path between delay memory and sum memory. This combination implements comb, all-pass, simple delay, and table lookup functions.

The speed of processing, sometimes called the *sampling rate*, is determined by how many processing elements must be active to generate the desired sound. In general, the more complex the

sound, the more processing elements must run to produce it. The basic unit of time in the synthesizer is called the *tick*, which lasts 195 nsec. Each generator takes one tick time to process one sample, and each modifier takes two tick times. This covers the time needed for generators and modifiers to perform their calculations and read and write their sample values to and from sum memory, and for modifiers to read and write delay memory via the delay units. The user may choose how many processing elements will be running during the processing of the sound samples. Thus the sampling rate is a function of the number of processing elements active per pass, that is, how many ticks are needed to generate one sample (or one set of samples). For example, with all 256 generators and 128 modifiers running, the sampling rate would be just under 19.5 kHz (there is a pipelining overhead of eight ticks per sample). Using half of the available resources doubles the sampling rate.

Tick time can be spent not only running processing elements, but also updating parameters in those processing elements. It takes one tick to update one parameter in one processing element. This task must run sequentially with sample processing, so the number of ticks that will be required per sample period must include all the processing ticks plus the update ticks. This lowers the sampling rate somewhat. In practice, 96 processing ticks and 32 update ticks proved adequate for most routine needs, yielding a sampling rate of 37707.39 Hz.

Hardware Sound Synthesis

It became possible with such a device to consider new approaches to the synthesis of music at Stanford. Previously, sound synthesis had been done on a large, general-purpose time-sharing computer operated by the Stanford Artificial Intelligence Laboratory. The disadvantage of this method was primarily the amount of time required to generate any reasonable quantity of sound. Compute ratios of 100 times real time were not uncommon. It was a rare person who could maintain a feeling of continuity while writing music or doing research under such circumstances. Since computed waveforms had to be output onto large disks for later use, there were sharp limitations on how much sound could be played at once, not to mention the problems of storage.

While this had proved to be a good environment for the development of software tools for music analysis and synthesis, it was an unmitigatedly bad one for the generation of even medium-scale musical works or for conducting acoustic experiments. A more interactive environment was needed, which in turn required the ability to generate sound in real time.

There were two possible approaches to the usage of this new real-time sound synthesis capability. The first could be categorized as *sequential interaction*, in which the specification for a sound is generated in advance and then played. Modifications to the specification may not take place during audition. The real-time component is merely the calculation and conversion of sound samples in real time. The sequence of commands sent to the synthesizer that specify the sounds to be generated is precompiled (not in real time) and stored on disk. The only improvement this represents over the old software synthesis methods is that the sound sam-

ples are generated in real time. Since a list of commands that specify a sound is much shorter than the equivalent number of samples, however, it still represents significant savings in time and space. Computation ratios of less than 10 times real time are typical for compiling all but the densest of scores using this approach. For test purposes, the turnaround time is short enough to be nearly immediate.

The second approach to using the synthesizer could be categorized as *concurrent interaction*, in which the sound specification is also generated in real time. Thus all phases of the realization of a sound specification are accomplished in real time. The source for the specification can change as the sound changes, introducing the obvious advantage of instantaneous feedback into the sound synthesis chain via a performer who can invent and change the specification of a sound event as it unfolds.

The second approach, concurrent interaction, would clearly have been the more attractive of the two, in my opinion, but it turned out to have requirements that CCRMA could not easily meet at that time. It was an important consideration that sequential interaction was closely akin to the old tried and true software synthesis methods developed previously. Use of the synthesizer along these lines would allow immediate backward compatibility to known techniques and tools.

Another important consideration was that we wanted the system to operate under time-sharing as much as possible. We did not want to lock ourselves into a one-user system such as is employed by many electronic music studios. While we did not try to time-share the SCS, it was felt that the ratio of time spent developing sounds to the time required to play them was sufficiently high to virtually eliminate contention for the SCS. This did turn out to be the case for much of the time.

The final argument for configuring a sequentially interactive system first was the fact that we would only have to write software to run on the general time-sharing system. Concurrent interaction would require a rather long-term hardware development effort to construct an integrated system for collecting real-time user input and generating sound specifications from this in real time. It would also require a host of support programs that could take even longer to implement. As I will discuss later, there are some serious unresolved questions even now as to how to proceed with such a system.

Eventually, we decided to start by developing a sequentially interactive system as a first approximation of the desired goal of a truly concurrent real-time sound synthesis system. The development effort to expand this into a concurrent system would go on at the same time.

Here, then, is what the resulting system looked like: the hardware configuration consisted of the SCS, connected to a general-purpose computer (a Digital Equipment Corporation PDP-6) that was dedicated to the care and feeding of the SCS as well as other real-time hardware at CCRMA, such as stand-alone analog-to-digital converters (ADCs) and DACs, and the synthesizer built by F. Richard Moore (Moore 1977; Moore forthcoming). This dedicated computer (the CPU of Fig. 1) was, in turn, a sort of "wholly owned subsidiary" of the Artificial Intelligence Laboratory's PDP-10, which ran the Laboratory's time-sharing system. A set of six 200-Mbyte mass-storage disk systems was connected to both the PDP-6 and the PDP-10. One of them was available for users' own disk packs, and was used heavily by the music project for sound sample storage. In addition, a special input/output (I/O) bus connecting the PDP-6 and PDP-10 carried messages between programs running on the time-sharing system and the real-time system. Users worked on the time-sharing system, using any of the terminals available in the Artificial Intelligence Laboratory. There were sound studios available for critical listening.

To realize a piece of music, users would first generate a score in a standard notation closely resembling Music V note lists (discussed in detail later). This score would then be fed into my command compiler, MUSBOX, which would convert the score into the appropriate commands to drive the synthesizer. The compiled command list was written out to the disk. Finally, the user would run a special program on the time-sharing computer, which would interact with the real-time operating system to pass the commands to the synthesizer under real-time constraints.

What Does the Compiler Do?

With this perspective on the system, it is possible to begin scrutinizing the position occupied by MUSBOX and to describe the design that developed as a result. As mentioned, it was to serve as a system to convert conventional note lists (also called *play lists*) into a stream of commands to the synthesizer. Let us examine these two ends of the problem one at a time, starting with a finer description of the nature of the input.

Standard Score Format

The standard CCRMA note list resembles the standard Music V note list (Mathews 1969) in that it consists mostly of a sequence of time-ordered statements. By convention, each such statement specifies one complete sound event, with the name of an *instrument* followed by the onset time and duration of the event that the instrument is to perform, followed in turn by a series of fields containing parametric information specifying the details of the event. These statements are also referred to as *instrument calls*, analogous to subroutine calls in regular programming languages. Here is a brief example of such an event list or, if you will, score.

```
PLAY;
SIMP 0 1 A 1 F1 OUTA;
TOOT, 0, .7, C, 1, F2, OUTB;
BLAT 3 .1, E .4, F0 OUTA;
FINISH;
```

The words PLAY and FINISH delimit the list. SIMP, TOOT, and BLAT are names of instruments. The two numbers following each instrument name are the begin time and duration, respectively, of each event. Thus SIMP and TOOT play simultaneously at the beginning of the piece, SIMP for 1 sec, TOOT for 0.7 sec. BLAT enters at 3 sec into the piece and plays for a brief 0.1 sec. The rest of the information on each line specifies the different parameters of each event to the instrument; only the first three fields have a fixed interpretation. Note that either blanks or commas may separate the

Loy

fields (also called pfields). The statements are individually delimited by semicolons. Because the meaning of the quantities beyond the third field is necessarily subject to the interpretation placed on them by the individual instrument, no further generalizations can be made about the sound events without knowledge of the details of the instrument's function. Common usage suggests, however, that the fourth and fifth fields should specify frequency and amplitude where appropriate.

There are some extensions to the standard Music V note list that were added at CCRMA, such as the capability of specifying the parametric fields as arithmetic expressions. These expressions may also contain calls on a library of standard arithmetic functions such as trigonometric and numerical conversion functions. There are also provisions for comment statements, the declaration of variables, and variable assignment statements. Finally, MUSBOX added quoted strings as a datum that can appear in an instrument call. One unannotated example will suffice.

```
PLAY;
VARIABLE I, J, AMP, PI;
I := 0;
J := 1.1;
PI := 3.14159265;
AMP := −20.3;
SIMP I J INT(A*PI) dB(AMP) F1 OUTA;
READ I, "MYSOUND", OUTB;
ADD I J .5 OUTA .1 OUTB OUTC;
FINISH;
```

The intention of this score is to play instrument SIMP through output channel OUTA; simultaneously read a sound waveform file called MYSOUND and put its output on OUTB; and sum the results, weighted 0.5 and 0.1 respectively, into output channel OUTC.

One final interesting feature of this score language is that the program parsing the score is required to determine the true bounds of arithmetic expressions occurring within it. For instance, in the instrument call

```
SIMP 0 1 A * 4 AMP − .5, −5;
```

the program is expected to group this as indicated in the following by commas.

```
SIMP, 0, 1, A*4, AMP−.5, −5;
```

Notice that the comma before the −5 at the end of the instrument call is required if it is to form a separate field; otherwise the line would be parsed as

```
SIMP, 0, 1, A*4, AMP−.5−5, ?;
```

and the value for the last field would be undefined in this case. A fuller presentation of the input syntax available for MUSBOX as well as an example score is given in "Nekyia" (Loy 1979).

The Compiler Output

Before we describe the action of the compiler on a score, let us discuss its output. In order to do that we must describe how the SCS receives data and commands.

The SCS has essentially four data and control I/O ports through which it communicates to its host computer. One is a bidirectional bus for general synthesizer control, such as for queuing buffers, starting and stopping processing, and handling errors. The other three are DMA ports, which allow high-speed access by the synthesizer into the address space of the host computer. Of the DMAs, two are used to pass sample data to and from the synthesizer for reading and writing sound samples from a mass storage system.

The last DMA, which is the one of interest here, is called the *command path*. It is through this path that the host computer sends commands to configure the individual processing elements within the synthesizer. There is a vocabulary of commands that can be issued to the individual processing elements through this command path to cause them to start and stop, change function, reassign their input and output registers, and load values into their various working registers. One command per tick can be read in through the DMA command port from the host. (Recall that ticks used to process commands cannot be used to run processing elements.)

Each command is a triple: the fields of the triple specify which processing element is being referenced, which register in the processing element is being addressed, and the datum to be deposited there. Besides commands to individual processing elements, there are miscellaneous commands that do such things as set the number of ticks per pass and select filters for the DACs.

One important command, called *linger*, is not an instruction to a processing element. Rather it is an instruction to the synthesizer's command processor that tells it to stop receiving new commands for the number of passes specified by the linger command. Ordinarily, the SCS expects to see a constant stream of commands. The linger suspends this flow. The pattern typically found in command streams consists of a series of commands to configure some sound event, followed by a linger command to allow the resulting configuration of the synthesizer to run its course.

It is a problematic feature of the command path that it is a serial stream attempting to control processing elements all running in parallel (Moorer 1981). This turned out to be one of the design conundrums of MUSBOX: the compiler should model the parallel nature of the synthesizer, but the only means of communication with it was through a serial, time-ordered command stream.

Compiler Design Strategies

The design of the compiler must thus accept CCRMA's version of note lists as input and generate as output a time-ordered, sequential command stream, which in turn must control all the processing elements operating in parallel. While many strategies suggested themselves, we were ultimately guided by a combination of prior experience with the design of software synthesis programs such as Music V, and the appropriate features of the programming language in which the compiler would be written: SAIL. From Music V, we adopted the paradigm of the instrument, but we implemented it using SAIL's powerful execution-time parallel processing facilities, which allowed us to model in the compiler the actions taking place in the synthesizer.

SAIL (Reiser 1976) is named after the institution where it was written, the Stanford Artificial Intelligence Laboratory. It can best be described as extended Algol, but it is much more than just that. Besides the core of Algol language features, it has provisions for record structures, routines for associative memory store, a very powerful macro facility, backtracking and context switching as well as an execution-time parallel processing facility, and interrupt and event mechanisms. Of these capabilities, the parallel processing facility seemed to offer a very clean approach to the design of the compiler.

The parallel processing facility essentially allows the programmer to treat a procedure or function as a template for possibly multiple and "concurrent" copies of the procedure or function. The word "concurrent" is used in quotation marks because these multiple copies do not really all run simultaneously, since the computer running them is general-purpose and has only one CPU. There can be a template procedure for a "violin" which can be automatically copied to produce as many violins as we like.

Having multiple copies of a procedure "alive" at any one moment is somewhat akin to a recursive procedure, but with a major difference. A recursive procedure declaration is considered to be a template for possibly multiple copies of the procedure. But multiple copies will exist only if the procedure calls itself at some point in its own code or if the procedure calls another procedure, which then calls the original procedure again. Each time a recursive procedure is called, a new copy (the *child* copy) is cloned from the procedure's template. All *parent* levels of recursion are suspended until all the child levels they have invoked have run their course; then the whole thing unwinds. When each level has finished its job, it disappears back into the bit bucket, and execution picks up where it left off in the parent. At no point can the main program (or any other branch of the program not dependent on the recursive chain in progress) run again until all levels of this recursion have ended.

The parallel processing mechanism uses somewhat the same framework but liberalizes the rules governing copies of a procedure. One or more copies of the procedure can be created from the procedure's template at any time, from any point in the program, and not just recursively (although pure recursion is not ruled out either). Each *instantiation* of the procedure, as we will call these copies, is a separate, fully executable version of the procedure template. In fact, the instantiations of the template are not even called *procedures*, they are called *processes*. A unique process identifier is assigned to each instantiated process (that is, each clone of the original procedure description), so that it can be differentiated from its otherwise identical kin. Each process can be individually executed, either when it is instantiated or at any later time. A process can also be suspended without losing track of what it was doing. Later it can be resumed and will pick up where it left off.

The last feature relevant to our discussion is the fact that a process can clone another process that is either identical to itself or derived from any other process template. To create new processes, a process merely needs to call the SAIL construct SPROUT, which takes as its arguments the procedure template of the process to instantiate, a process identifier by which to refer to the new process, and a list of the parameters to be handed to the new process as its arguments.

How Does This Make a Compiler?

Let us say we have an orchestra of instruments. Each instrument is really just a template. If the score to be played by the orchestra calls for 100 violins, we just SPROUT 100 copies of this template and hand them their individual parts. This is essentially how Music V operates. In SAIL, this clearly translates to making the instruments templates for processes that can run in parallel.

The system that finally evolved was just an elaboration of this model. In general, when the score calls for an instrument to play, a process is SPROUTed from the instrument's template. The process is then handed its parameters from the score. The first step in executing the sound event is for the instrument to claim the processing resources in the synthesizer that allow it to make its particular kind of noise. It does this by calling a set of resource-management routines that keep track

from moment to moment of what processing elements are in use. It then issues commands to the processing elements it was allotted by calling routines that assemble commands to the synthesizer according to values supplied by the instrument. These same output routines write out the resulting commands to a disk file.

The only remaining problem to address is scheduling: How do these potentially simultaneously executing processes interact with one another so as to produce one time-ordered output stream of commands?

Scheduling among Processes

We have already mentioned that processes can be suspended and resumed without losing track of what they were doing. We took advantage of this to provide a way to schedule the running of processes. The central ingredient in this scheme is a procedure called WaitUntil, which causes the process calling WaitUntil to be "put to sleep" until a specified time. The time is specified as an argument to WaitUntil and measured in numbers of passes.

For instance, if the sampling rate were 40,000 passes per second, the procedure call WaitUntil(40000) would cause the calling process to sleep until the current time equaled 1 sec. There is a global variable simply called *pass*, which stores the current time. Therefore, saying WaitUntil(pass +40000) would cause the process to wait until 1 sec into the future from whatever the present moment recorded in pass might be. This gives processes absolute and relative time addressing.

When WaitUntil is called it records the time specified by its argument and the process identifier for the process making the call into a time-ordered queue. This queue is managed such that the element at the top of the queue is always the time in the future nearest to the current moment. New entries are inserted into the queue such that the queue is monotonically ordered in time. The entry on top is always picked to be the next process to run. When a process that has placed itself in the queue finally rises to the top, it is reawakened and resumes execution at the statement in its code immediately after the call to WaitUntil. This simple method thus sorts events according to time by granulating the flow of time into a monotonically increasing series.

Here is the scheduling strategy in detail. When a process wants to issue a command to the synthesizer at a certain time in the future it calls WaitUntil first, which causes the process to sleep until that time arrives. Conflicts between processes awakening at exactly the same time are resolved in favor of the process that has called WaitUntil first. Just before a process is reawakened, the compiler inserts a linger command into the command stream. WaitUntil thus performs exactly the same function for processes generating commands that the linger command performs for the SCS.

Two final comments about the nature of processes are needed before we can go on to describe the general operation of the compiler when it is running. Even the main program can be treated as a process to be suspended and resumed. In fact, in the parlance of this kind of programming, there is no main program, just a main process. (In this application, the MUSBOX scanner-parser is the main process.) The only thing that distinguishes the main process from any other process is that it is always started first when the program is run and it has a special global process identifier.

The second point is that a priority can be assigned to any process. When a situation arises in which all processes are suspended, the SAIL process runtime scheduler will pick the one with the highest priority and force it to be resumed.

Since we need to schedule the running of instrument processes in a time-ordered way, it would seem obvious that we could simply give each process a priority according to the time when it must run. But SAIL only allows for 16 levels of priority, and literally hundreds of concurrent processes may be needed for some applications.

There is a way to bypass the SAIL scheduler, however. Any running process can pick whichever process it wants to run next. The SAIL process runtime scheduler is only invoked to choose the next process to be run when there are no processes already running. This means we can arrange our own scheme for time-ordering processes. The scheme to

be described incorporates the SAIL priority scheduler as part of a specially designed time-ordering scheduler.

There is one crucial point about what is really happening in the simulated parallel processing being described here. Because we are working with a general-purpose computer that has but one CPU, we can really execute only one process at a time. The other processes that could be running reside in program memory but are in a state of suspension awaiting their turns. (The SAIL process mechanism is actually more general than this, but its additional capabilities are not germane to our discussion.) Since the currently running process has exclusive access to the CPU, its ability to pick which process shall run next effectively determines the flow of program control from that point. Keep this in mind during the following discussion.

The compiler operates as follows. As the compiler's score scanner reads instrument calls from the score, it instantiates processes for each of the named instruments and hands each its list of parameters from the score. As soon as each instrument is instantiated, the instrument examines its parameters, determines its begin time, and immediately calls WaitUntil to put it to sleep until that time has arrived. Meanwhile, the score scanner continues to read new instrument calls and instantiate new processes for them until it notices that the instrument specified in the score has a begin time greater than any of the notes previously started. At this point the scanner does not instantiate a new process for this instrument. Instead, it calls WaitUntil to be put to sleep itself until time equals the start time of the new instrument. Even though it is the main process, it can be suspended like every other process. At this point in the operation every process is sleeping, including the main process (i.e., the instrument call parser), with process wake-up times sorted in increasing order in the time queue.

Since all the processes are now asleep, we need some way to get one of them started again. We do this by having a background process with a very low priority waiting around ready to run. We'll call it the *Troll* process. It is ordinarily kept from running because lower-priority processes such as the main process and the instruments will continue to run as long as they suspend and resume each other. But when all of these processes are asleep, the SAIL runtime scheduler picks the Troll process and resumes it. The Troll examines the time-ordered queue and selects the process that has the smallest sleep time (the one on top of the queue). It then fetches the time value entered for that process and sets the pass counter equal to it. In addition, it puts a linger command into the output command stream with a time duration equal to the difference in time between when the Troll was awakened and the time entered for the process it is about to awaken. Then the Troll causes the new process to be awakened and is in turn put back into its waiting state. In this fashion, one process is able to determine which process will run next.

The instrument selected from the time queue is resumed at the statement immediately after its call to WaitUntil. It generates its commands to the synthesizer and places them in the output command stream. It then determines the time at which the score indicated that it should stop playing, and calls WaitUntil again with that time as its argument. All the processes are now asleep again. The SAIL runtime scheduler causes the Troll to emerge from under its rock. It in turn awakens the next process in the time queue and things are rolling again. Eventually, the score parser will be at the top of the time queue. When it is resumed, it reads some more of the score, instantiates a few more instrument processes, goes back to sleep, and the loop starts all over again.

This proceeds until the scanner reads the end of the score. It then calls WaitUntil with an argument of infinite time, meaning the scanner is guaranteed to be placed at the bottom of the time queue. This forces any remaining processes to run and, when the scanner reawakens, it knows it can go about closing up shop.

Dynamic Events

The model of scheduling and execution presented in the last section described the essentials of the method accurately but left out some important de-

tails. The model for instruments was limited to the case in which an instrument waited until its begin time, then claimed processing elements from the pool of free elements and issued commands into the command stream. After waiting until its end time, it would presumably issue more commands to shut off the event and return the processing elements it had claimed to the free pool.

This would be fine for static events, a sort of set-it-and-forget-it kind of patch in the synthesizer such as reverberation instruments and the like, but provision must be made for dynamically changing events as well. The most characteristic event is an instrument involving changes according to a function of time that might be used to control amplitude or frequency. Again, the process structure comes to the rescue with an easy solution. Another facet of the personality of SAIL processes must be revealed to see how this is done. Processes have the capability to suspend themselves until certain conditions are met. For instance, a process may tell the SAIL process runtime scheduler to suspend it until a set of existing processes that it names has terminated. A process can terminate gracefully by "falling off the end" of its code. A process can also "commit suicide," and can even turn vengeful "killer" and destroy other processes.

There is another SAIL construct called JOIN, which takes as its arguments a set of processes. The action performed is to suspend the process calling JOIN until all the named processes are terminated. The process that called JOIN is then resumed at the point immediately after the JOIN statement.

JOIN and SPROUT are thus used as follows. A different set of templates, not instrument templates any longer, is created that takes as argument a time-domain function that is to control some aspect of a sound in the synthesizer. Different templates are constructed for interpreting these functions, depending on what is to be controlled. For instance, the process template for controlling amplitude and frequency of the synthesizer's generators is coded in such a way as to take advantage of the built-in hardware-ramping capacity of the generators. Functions that control processing-element parameters that have no dynamic capability adopt a different strategy. They must issue many single, evenly spaced commands, which creates a stepwise approximation of the function through time. The approximation can be arbitrarily accurate down to the individual pass, but this of course makes a very dense command stream.

In all cases, the fundamental mechanism is the same as that used by instruments; that is, call WaitUntil, issue commands setting the processing element parameters to the value of the function, then call WaitUntil again to wait until the time when the next significant point on the function occurs, and repeat the steps until the function is finished.

An instrument that is to have dynamic amplitude control of a generator, for example, will have as part of its code a call to SPROUT to instantiate one of these function-handling processes. Once instantiated, the instrument then issues a JOIN command naming any process it may have instantiated. This suspends the instrument until these function handlers have run their course, then resumes the instrument. Thus the instrument process brackets the function processes it invokes. There can be a hierarchy of processes such that the instrument process can create and be responsible for all its child processes. The responsibility of claiming and releasing processing elements is given to the instrument, since we can guarantee by use of the JOIN construct that the parent process will remain to clean up after any processes it starts. Why not let the instrument just call WaitUntil for a time greater than the end of the last function handler it SPROUTed as a way of outliving them? The point is that the function handlers are (and should be) perfectly capable of evaluating and perhaps even reevaluating how long they should run. JOIN is a time-independent way of waiting for them to be done, no matter when that is.

Levels of the Compiler

The compiler is organized in hierarchical strata. At the bottom of the pile are the routines that actually assemble machine instructions to the synthesizer and take care of the details of command I/O; pro-

cessing element allocation and deallocation, basic timing functions, and other functions relating to the care and feeding of the synthesizer. This code is the most heavily used and thus is written in FAIL, which is the SAIL dialect of assembly language for the PDP-10 computer. These low-level routines do the dirty work of controlling the synthesizer, and it is a difficult and basically unrewarding task for composers and researchers to work directly with these low-level routines in the generation of complex sounds.

The next higher level consists of the intermediate-level routines. Routines in this level combine a number of calls to the low-level routines into one procedure to accomplish some basic task such as the implementation of a simple oscillator, a mixer, or a reverberator. WaitUntil lives here, for instance. Code at this and all higher levels is written in SAIL and can partake of the parallel processing design strategy outlined in previous sections.

These intermediate routines have expanded from a core of perhaps a dozen basic routines when the system was first put together, to more than 50 or 60 in the last two years. Some of the later additions to the intermediate-level procedure library have been used to implement, for example, reverberators, complex FM, AM, additive synthesis, waveshaping, filtering, sound-location modulation, sound-sample reading and writing, and more sophisticated procedures for manipulating functions of time.

It is at the intermediate level that most of the experimentation with the hardware capabilities of the synthesizer takes place, since both hardware capabilities and limitations are addressed at this intermediate level. Thus it is not uncommon to see two or three routines in the intermediate-level procedure library that have essentially the same function but a slightly different mode of operation to optimize for some aspect of the hardware or the task they address.

The most basic category of intermediate-level routines includes those that simply implement one or another of the built-in functions of the individual processing elements. Routines for a simple fixed-waveform oscillator, for instance, or for a simple mixer merely use a native capability of a single processing element. A more complex category includes routines requiring more than one processing element, such as filters that require amplitude prescaling before the filtering itself.

A third category includes the function-handling routines, which take a two-dimensional line segment function of time, rescale the x and y coordinates, and add in a constant y offset per point. They interact with WaitUntil as described previously and have code to convert the argument function to a corresponding set of commands appropriate for a particular processing mode in the synthesizer. Some have the capability of applying different scaling parameters to different sections of a function in order to implement various kinds of attack and decay strategies. Some of the more advanced designs for function handling include arithmetic manipulation of the values of the function. Some will do all this and apply the function to numerous (similar types of) processing elements.

A final category of intermediate-level routines includes those such as WaitUntil and the time queue. Procedures that control general operating functions of the synthesizer such as setting up DACs, processing element initialization, and other housekeeping operations would also be included here.

Above the intermediate level are the instruments, which make calls to the intermediate-level routines and very occasionally to the low-level routines to implement complete sound events. Instruments are usually created to perform some form of synthesis such as complex FM, waveshaping, reverberation, mixing, and so on, so they are closely related to their corresponding intermediate-level routines. The chief difference between the instruments and the intermediate-level routines is that the instruments are controlled directly from a score and must be able to receive and interpret parameters from it.

Because the instruments are written in SAIL, all the features of SAIL are at their disposal, and SAIL in turn allows easy access to the general operating system of the host computer. MUSBOX itself is written so that an instrument can get into its inner workings rather easily and, for example, examine various symbol tables or investigate what other instruments might be running concurrently and what their parameters happen to be. Thus it is very easy for instruments to examine their environment for cues as to how to proceed or to collect information about what is happening around them. An instrument can interrogate the person running the compiler for input or obtain input and write output of any kind separately from the command stream and score. It is this flexibility that makes this compiler a valuable tool for the kind of experimental research envisioned in the acquisition of the SCS.

One very interesting project of mine involved the use of SAIL's EVENT mechanisms among instruments. Briefly, this is a means whereby processes can communicate either directly or indirectly through *message boards* or *broadcast channels* with each other. A process can INTERROGATE one or more other processes, optionally waiting until there is a respondent. Processes can also CAUSE messages to be placed into one or more event lists or sent to individual processes. The nature of the information that can be communicated is determined by the programmer. Thus it would be easy to begin exploring some artificial intelligence (AI) issues relating to process intercommunication, self-reference, and feedback, and to make models of the actual circumstances in which a performing musician actually works to study improvisation and other such topics.

At the top of the heap of code just described is the MUSBOX main process. It contains the scanner and expression parser, symbol tables, file management, time-base management, time-domain function handling, command stream initialization and cleanup, error handling, and a variety of other bells and whistles. It has the optional capability (depending on which version of MUSBOX is used) to send a compiled score to the synthesizer automatically as soon as it is finished. Another optional feature is a function-editor package that allows interactive editing of time-domain functions.

Second Thoughts: Software

No system is completely perfect, and this one certainly has its problems. In this section we will discuss a few of the outstanding ones that come to mind. As we have seen, this music compiler uses some of SAIL's more arcane features in its basic implementation. It is no trivial task for the naive user, no matter of what background (including computer science), to grasp the minute details of the synthesizer's behavior, the complexities of SAIL, and the implementation of the compiler, and to start writing new instruments. (Using instruments written by others is another thing altogether, and is quite simple by comparison.)

In response to this a cadre of wizards has developed that spends a great deal of time writing intermediate-level code and instruments. Then there is the cadre of users who are stuck with the canned products of the former group for better or for worse. While it will always be true that certain obscure aspects of any problem will be reserved for those few who take the time and make the effort to understand them, it is regrettable if any generally interesting problems are obscured by unnecessary complexity.

It should be pointed out that the canned products of the wizards have been sufficiently general and useful to support all the work of three years of summer students in the computer music seminars at CCRMA. But in principle their use is entirely application- and education-oriented. When it comes to addressing the needs of research, there is no alternative in this system to burying oneself in code up to the neck. In the long run I think the problem of simplifying instrument design, such as taking care of the implementation details for the user wherever possible, will become very important. To this end, special languages may need to be developed for just this task. It is possible that some existing extensible languages could be adapted. Some work on this is now taking place at Stanford.

Another problem with this system is that MUS-BOX is limited to sequentially interactive applications. Of course (as explained) it was never intended to support real-time score generation. Nonetheless, the reasons why this support is ruled out are worth exploring. It turns out that the problems of generating a command stream for a piece of music of even medium complexity can be so time-consuming as to be impossible to implement in

real time even on very fast general-purpose computers. The reasons for this are studied in the general field of scheduling theory (Coffman 1976), but we will take a more intuitive approach here. First of all, there is a lot of computation that must go into scanning and parsing the score.

More fundamental, however, is the unsettling realization that there is no way to predict the amount of interpretation that might be required to generate some arbitrary sound from a high-level score. By high-level I mean Music V notation, which is rather basic in comparison to a real musical score! The reasons behind the problem are twofold. First, when compiling a score one encounters many of the high-bandwidth problems of signal production. On a small scale, there is the fact that interesting sounds must have a fluidity and changeability that allows them to remain fresh to the ear. In computer music, this subtle ingredient is bought at a high computational cost, both in terms of the number of items requiring detail in a score and in the amount of interpretive work the instruments must produce to realize this detail in sound. On a larger scale, there is the necessity for complex interactions between the various levels in the realization of a large musical structure. One of the principal justifications of computer music lies in the fact that it is capable of handling this detail, but at this point it is still largely a promise.

Second, consider the open-ended nature of the material that can be expressed in terms of the available syntaxes for computer representation of music. This causes horrible scheduling problems. Essentially, there is an inverse relationship between the intelligence of the score scanner and the instruments and the likelihood that the interpretation of any one note will have an execution time that can be supported in real time under any circumstances. In short, the more a system can allow us to express ourselves musically, the less likely it will be able to do so in real time.

There are strong reasons for overcoming these problems, however. For instance, execution in real time would allow a work to be edited while being performed live from the original score.

The most obvious approach is to decide that real-time score compilation is more important than score and instrument complexity and to write simpler music. We might laugh, but there are people doing just this! It is a reasonable if confining prospect. A variation on simplification would be to develop pieces using simplified instruments and scores that can run in real time and to flesh them out after the essential structure is in place.

A more interesting possibility would be to precompile a complex score, not in real time, into intermediate code of some kind. The preliminary compilation would have two effects. First, the score would be condensed from text into code. Second, this code could be programmatically optimized to further reduce the complexity of statements and expressions. The code stream might be bifurcated, with the intermediate code instructions going to a real-time interpreter in the CPU that controls the synthesizer. The interpreter would in turn use these intermediate instructions to control a separate stream of commands to the synthesizer. The interpreter would be designed to interface to a real-time console and would have two essential tasks: to scale the values of parameters (e.g., amplitude and frequency) and to start and stop events. It could do either of these tasks from an instruction repertoire including basic conditional tests and arithmetic operations.

Such a scheme would be useful for the full range of user-control schemes such as acting as a performance instrument, playing in a "music-minus-one" mode, conducting and editing, and playing canned pieces (a trivial application by comparison). The real-time interpreter could either run on a general-purpose computer dedicated to this task or it, too, could be a specialized computer optimized around its special task. One drawback of this scheme is that it would be difficult to cause editorial changes at the intermediate level to be reflected back in the original score, although even this might be overcome with appropriate application.

All of this notwithstanding, it turns out that sequential interaction is not a hopeless approach after all, judging from our experience. As long as a big piece can be broken down into subsections it is manageable, since the time required to compile a stream of synthesizer commands is usually much less than the playing time. The only obvious example in which this method becomes tedious occurs when the composer is working on the end of a long piece after its sections have been assembled. The entire piece must be recompiled for each change, and there is no way around this. But during the time we have been using this approach, we have always ended up yearning to get our hands on dynamic controls to add that last touch of perfection to a work. It is amazing how much difference it can make aesthetically on the final result. Maybe it isn't so amazing after all.

Designing Hardware for the Unknown

The design of the SCS took place in the midst of a variety of new developments in signal processing theory and synthesis techniques. Inevitably, as with nearly everything digital these days, there were theoretical developments that could not be foreseen at the time it was built. This was expected, and the designers attempted to compensate for this so that the SCS would not immediately become obsolete.

The strategy used was to design as general a signal processing capability as possible without sacrificing bandwidth. This meant three things: (1) the inclusion of many low-level processing capabilities in the modifiers such as sign testing and maximum and minimum functions, (2) a flexible module interconnection scheme (sum memory) that allows users to build up complex processing networks that were not included in the intrinsic hardware design, and (3) the provision that if the basic processing bandwidth of the SCS is exceeded partial data can be written out to disk and read back in to separate the amount of computation required into layers. These three measures were felt to guarantee against both qualitative and quantitative obsolescence.

Users must still work within the repertoire of the algorithms implemented, however. Adding any new synthesis technique to the hardware would mean drastic redesign. This design strategy is just one of many that could have been adopted, but it was the most natural, given the priority bandwidth had over changeability in the design. The point is that the more something is hard-wired, the more it can be optimized and the faster it will run but the harder it becomes to modify.

To see how this design strategy succeeded, we can take some examples from the history of its use, since inevitably there were new techniques invented after the SCS was built.

First came waveshaping (LeBrun 1979; Roads 1979). Up to that point, the popular table-driven synthesis techniques were based on use of a linear index to address simple functions: sine, square, sawtooth. These functions were then coupled together through FM, AM, and additive synthesis to produce complex spectra. In principle this is also how the SCS was built. Basic waveshaping, in contrast, uses a nonlinear (sinusoidal) index to address a table containing a function that is a sum of Chebychev polynomials. One possible implementation of this on the SCS involved a sine oscillator to generate the index and a table in delay memory to store the function. The table was accessed via a delay unit. But this restricted the number of waveshaping voices that could be played simultaneously to the 32 available delay units. This also meant that waveshaping voices were in conflict with reverberation, since they both required delay units.

Is there a moral to this? In one sense the design strategy succeeded in that it supported waveshaping even though it was an unknown technique when the SCS was built. Of course, it has nowhere near the bandwidth for waveshaping that it has for its intrinsic synthesis techniques, and it was not feasible to redesign the SCS to include waveshaping as an intrinsic algorithm. Its usefulness diminishes, but does not vanish. What about writing partial results onto the disk and building up a piece in layers? Two problems are associated with this. First, depending on the application, it can be a programmer's nightmare to take software designed to run in one pass and split it across two. Second, the number of samples that can be passed in real time between the SCS and main memory becomes the limiting factor, and it is surprisingly severe for the configuration at Stanford. Four channels of sound at 25 kHz approaches the maximum that has ever been supported in real time on the Stanford system. While this figure might be better on some other ideal system, it is not likely to come close to

the single-pass inner processing bandwidth of the SCS. So, as I have said, its usefulness diminishes but does not vanish.

Another new development after the SCS was built was a new reverberation technique (Moorer 1979). This inserts a lowpass filter in the feedback path of the reverberator to simulate the lowpass effect of air absorption over time and distance. The intrinsic reverberation algorithms implemented in the delay units of the SCS include comb, all-pass, and one-shot delay. A delay unit set up for one-shot delay could feed its output to a modifier acting as a lowpass filter, and the result summed with the input signal and fed back to the one-shot delay. Each such tap would require three modifiers and three sum memory locations, and 19 such taps would be considered optimal. This uses up a fair portion of the modifiers and delay units to implement one reverberator.

The moral? Again, we can implement a new technique, but anything that is not an intrinsic algorithm is expensive. For basic research, not much is wrong with that; but I doubt that much basic signal processing research really takes place on hardware synthesizers anyway. Both of the instances cited and many more that could be cited were originally developed in software and only much later given solutions on the SCS. The reason is self-evident: software synthesis is more flexible and accessible for experimentation. Typically, new algorithms are not coded for synthesis with special-purpose hardware until the amount of time needed to generate examples in software on a general-purpose system begins to exceed the hardware-implementation overhead time.

The true users of the SCS are people doing production work with it, either for music or for psychoacoustics research. These users typically require both high bandwidth and the ability to implement and use the results of new signal processing techniques such as waveshaping. Bandwidth should not be made to suffer because new techniques are used.

Now we can draw a moral: for the heavy users of real-time synthesis, hardware flexibility is just as important as bandwidth. It is very important to be able to expand the repertoire of signal processing hardware in a way that does not degrade bandwidth. Fixed-architecture designs such as the SCS suffer in this respect, even though they may be more cost-effective for the intrinsic algorithms they implement. For a discussion of some alternatives to this architecture, see *Multiprocessors and Parallel Processing* (Enslow 1974) and "Signal Processing Aspects of Computer Music" (Moorer 1977).

Second Thoughts: Hardware

On a less philosophical level, there are a few "misfeatures" or nonfeatures in the SCS. First, the SCS was delivered with 14-bit DACs. They are good, clean DACs, but 14 bits is limiting for many musical applications. Quantization becomes very noticeable at very low amplitudes as squarewave distortion. Presumably the reasons for supplying 14-bit converters are historical and any new version will use 16 bits.

No provision was made to include ADCs in the hardware, although it appears that the updated design of the SCS now has that as an option (Samson 1980). The SCS also had no timing references to synchronize with external processors. This was added at Stanford to enable synchronous operation of the SCS with external ADCs.

It proved difficult to generate very small-amplitude sine waves from generators. A typical usage of such signals is to supply low-frequency signals for vibrato to another generator. The problem was that the vibrato generator's amplitude registers lacked the precision needed to represent amplitudes small enough to produce the correct depth of modulation. The higher the sampling rate the worse the problem. The need for smaller amplitudes necessitated routing the signal through a modifier to scale it down, thus wasting a modifier and its sum memory for each vibrato element of an instrument. Fortunately, a more economical method (a *kluge*) was discovered to allow a single generator to produce these low-amplitude waveforms, but this involved using an unrelated generator register for other than its intended purpose, and the results were not completely satisfactory. The final solution involved implementing vibrato in software.

Running throughout this discussion is the idea of the need to conserve processing resources. What were the resources exhausted most quickly in the typical usage of the SCS? The first thing to disappear, typically, was sum memory. This memory is divided so that there are only 64 locations for the outputs of all generators and another 64 locations for all modifiers. This proved to be a stubborn limit on the number of separate tasks that could run simultaneously. Ideally, there should have been as many sum memory locations as generators and modifiers. The next thing to be depleted was delay units during waveshaping. There were enough delay units for most other purposes. Next came modifiers. Comparatively few people ever ran out of generators.

Another resource that occasionally ran out was arithmetic precision, as already mentioned in the case of vibrato. This also happened in IIR filtering. The SCS uses 20-bit fixed-point multiplies with rounding-in modifiers, but even this is not enough to guarantee that IIR filters will not "blow up" on certain signals. In this regard I would like to recount the tale of one researcher, who will remain nameless, who was experimenting with IIR filters. He was sweeping a very sharp, low-amplitude bandpass filter across a white noise spectrum when another researcher entered the room with a cup of coffee. At that moment, a scaling multiply overflowed from the white noise signal and made the filter unstable, producing a viscerally frightening blast of white noise into the room at about 110 db. The coffee went in every direction while other researchers dove by instinct (or was it long training?) for cover. When the SCS was finally stopped, the flabbergasted experimenter turned to the others and said by way of explanation, "But I was dividing by 2 to the 20th!" The moral is to be very careful with integer arithmetic implementation of IIR filtering.

The next resource often in scarce supply was update ticks. The design of the synthesizer allows all important processing-element registers to be set by command during update ticks. Only a small subset of these registers can be set by other processing elements, however. For example, in generators, only the modulating frequency can be set by other elements. Modifiers do have two inputs that can read the outputs of other elements, but (with the exception of variable-coefficient filtering) their control registers can only be changed by commands. This means the command stream must be used for almost all controls.

When large events are to be started or stopped at once, the command stream quickly becomes bottlenecked because of all the commands that must be issued to initialize the processing elements. The main problem involves sending all those commands in real time to the synthesizer from the controlling computer's memory, which is inevitably much slower. The best that can be done is to preprocess the command stream to push non-time-critical commands into less dense places in the stream. This still doesn't work in instances where large numbers of processing elements must all be started in phase during a single pass, such as for additive synthesis involving many partials. In fact, additive synthesis of even one trumpet instrument, specified to the full level of detail shown in John Grey's thesis (Grey 1975; Moorer, Grey, and Strawn 1978), runs out of command stream bandwidth. The SCS has no trouble keeping up with the number of commands; the bottleneck is the slowness of the memory from which the SCS must receive its commands and the length of the FIFO in which the commands are queued.

The command stream also gets filled up because it is often used to increase the apparent processing capacity of the SCS. For instance, instead of using a hardware patch to create random vibrato (which uses two modifiers and one sum memory location per random function for scaled noise), we could use software (at the expense of cluttering up the command stream with minute frequency corrections). Still, software emulation of this kind became very useful where it was desired to have as many processing elements as possible producing audible results rather than generating control functions.

Nonetheless, software solutions only return us to the problem the hardware was originally designed to cure. Generating command-intensive scores takes time and must be done on general-purpose computers, which means that we start spending significant amounts of time waiting for the command stream to compile. This even ignores the storage requirements on disk for these big command streams. Again, the only solution to this, in my opinion, is to have a hardware design flexible enough to allow for expansion in any direction whatsoever; not just to make it easy to implement a new synthesis algorithm, but to be able to beef up the control structure as well.

Another problem is the linger command, which is discussed in detail in Moorer's article (1981). Had the linger command been interruptable, there would have been fewer problems. An additional aid to solving this problem would have been to allow a processing element to interrupt the CPU of the controlling computer. This would have allowed a process running in the SCS to signal the completion of an interval it was timing or an event it was watching, eliminating the potential problems caused by having two clocks time the same event.

Summary

When the SCS was delivered to Stanford in late 1978 it was greeted as both a challenge and a promise. The promise was the ability to generate complex sounds in real time. The challenge was to develop a compiler and an operating environment for it that would fully implement its many features. Since it was in the vanguard of special-purpose digital signal processor design many things, often contradictory, were expected of it. From present perspective it can be seen that the effort had a much better than average success rate in meeting its original goals. The synthesizer did not turn out to be a panacea; neither did the compiler and operating system built for it, for reasons that were often mutually dependent. In the last analysis, however, many hours of music and many major experiments have been run on this system, and both the compiler and the synthesizer are still in heavy use at CCRMA for research and composition several years later. While better tools are surely under development there and elsewhere, they will be better for absorbing the lessons we learned from this experience.

Acknowledgments

The existence of the real-time sound synthesis system at Stanford is due to the contributions of many individuals covering a variety of fronts in its development. First credit must be given to Pete Samson, for the design and construction of the SCS. Additional credit goes to everyone who was involved in coding the low- and intermediate-level software as well as the rest of the real-time operating system discussed here. Those involved include James A. Moorer, Mark Kahrs, Ken Shoemake, Bill Schottstaedt, Mike McNabb, Peter Nye, Tovar, Rob Poor, John Gordon, Julius Smith, John Chowning, John Grey, and Loren Rush. Finally, thanks are due to those who have used the synthesizer; those whose use of the facility, comments, and suggestions form the only known cure for bugs.

References

Coffman, E., ed. 1976. *Computer and Job/Shop Scheduling Theory.* New York: John Wiley and Sons.

Enslow, P., ed. 1974. *Multiprocessors and Parallel Processing.* New York: John Wiley and Sons.

Grey, J. 1975. "An Exploration of Musical Timbre." Report STAN-M-2. Stanford: Stanford University Department of Music.

LeBrun, M. 1979. "Digital Waveshaping Synthesis." *Journal of the Audio Engineering Society* 27(4):250–266.

Loy, D. G. 1979. "Nekyia." Ph.D. thesis, Stanford University Department of Music. Available from University Microfilms, Ann Arbor, Michigan.

Loy, D. G. 1980. "Systems Concepts Digital Synthesizer Operations Manual and Tutorial." Report STAN-M-6. Stanford: Stanford University Center for Computer Research in Music and Acoustics.

Mathews, M. 1969. *The Technology of Computer Music.* Cambridge, Massachusetts: The MIT Press.

Moore, F. R. 1977. "Real Time Interactive Computer Music Synthesis." Ph.D. thesis, Stanford University Department of Electrical Engineering.

Moore, F. R. Forthcoming. "The FRMbox—A Modular Digital Music Synthesizer." In *Computer Music*, ed. C. Roads, J. Snell, and J. Strawn. Cambridge, Massachusetts: The MIT Press.

Moorer, J. A. 1977. "Signal Processing Aspects of Computer Music—A Survey." *Proceedings of the IEEE* 65(8):1108–1137. Reprinted in *Computer Music Journal* 1(1):4–37.

Moorer, J. A. 1979. "About This Reverberation Business." *Computer Music Journal* 3(2):13–28.

Moorer, J. A. 1981. "Synthesizers I Have Known and Loved." *Computer Music Journal* 5(1):4–12.

Moorer, J. A.; Grey, J.; and Strawn, J. 1978. "Lexicon of Analyzed Tones." *Computer Music Journal* 2(2):23–31.

Reiser, J., ed. 1976. "SAIL." Report STAN-CS-574. Stanford: Stanford University Artificial Intelligence Laboratory.

Roads, C. 1979. "A Tutorial on Non-linear Distortion or Waveshaping." *Computer Music Journal* 3(2):29–34.

Samson, P. 1980. "A General-purpose Digital Synthesizer." *Journal of the Audio Engineering Society* 28(3):106–113.

Samson, P. Forthcoming. "Architectural Issues in the Design of the Systems Concepts Digital Synthesizer." In *Computer Music*, ed. C. Roads, J. Snell, and J. Strawn. Cambridge, Massachusetts: The MIT Press.

30

Denis Lorrain
Centre d'Applications Musicales
de l'Informatique (CAMI)
Faculté de Musique
Université de Montréal
C. P. 6128
Montréal, Québec
Canada

A Panoply of Stochastic 'Cannons'

1.0 Introduction

The term *stochastic* was introduced in music by Xenakis (1963). It is a synonym of *random*, but it has been preferred as a more scientific, less commonplace term, used by Xenakis to qualify his use of probability theory. Earlier, this use set it apart from the then frequent use of "random" sections in contemporary music, which are in fact improvised sections—random only from the composer's point of view! *Cannon* is a term Xenakis coined to name algorithms "shooting" random values according to a specific probability distribution. (In French we say *tirer au hasard* for "choose at random." literally "shoot at random.")

In 1954, Xenakis set forth two criticisms of serial composition, which was then undeniably the most widely used technique among avant-garde composers: "The serial system is brought back into question in its two foundations which bear the seed of their own destruction and transcendence" (1971a, p. 120).

His first criticism is general. To begin with, Xenakis stated, serial manipulations are nothing but particular cases in the vast domain of combinatorial analysis. Moreover, he claimed, serialism remains encrusted in its historical inheritance while, especially through electroacoustics, new areas are open: "Why twelve and not thirteen or *n* sounds? Why not the continuity of the frequency spectrum? Of the timbre spectrum? Of the intensity spectrum and of durations?" (1971a, p. 120).

Xenakis's second criticism concerns a contradiction of serial processes with regard to their sound result: "Upon audition, the enormous complexity prevents one from following the tangle of lines, and has as macroscopic effect an unreasoned and fortuitous dispersion of sounds in the whole sound spectrum" (1971a, p. 120).

He concluded: "The macroscopic effect could thus be controlled by the mean of the motions of the *n*

objects chosen by us. Hence follows the introduction of the idea of probability, which again implies combinatorial analysis in this precise case" (1971a, p. 120). This introduces the concept of overall control of complex sound events rather than their analytic and mechanistic elaboration, exactly as in science, where statistical methods are a tool for the overall prehension of exceedingly complex phenomena; this conforms to our intuitive idea of randomness. But it must be added that Xenakis had, on the other hand, a certain musical intuition about sound masses, probably anterior to their rational justification (Xenakis 1963, pp. 19–20).

In the course of a long practice of serial techniques, Gottfried Michael Koenig comes to the same conclusion: "The greater the extent to which parameters adhere to certain arrangements and the greater the extent to which musical meaning is to depend on the perception of these arrangements, the more unpredictable, 'random,' are the effects of one parameter on the other: the various characteristics coalesce into 'sounds' whose order is unequivocally defined neither by the course of an individual parameter nor by the polyphony of all of them" (1971, p. 22). The ambition of systematic composition, "A formalism completely describing in two directions [past and future events] each instant of the work" (Koenig 1971, p. 9), upsets itself. Besides, technically, complex determinisms generate an excess of possibilities, a maze of ambiguities. Hence, for instance, Koenig's concept of *potential* and *actual form:* a piece does not necessarily realize all possibilities in a domain, but they are available: the composer chooses (Koenig 1971, pp. 65–66).

When the composer does not wish to choose throughout, he or she arrives at what serialists have called *randomness*, negotiating a compromise between their conception of musical composition and Cage's ideas. In certain sections of a piece, the composer may supply basic material, on which an ad hoc solution must be "improvised." Or, at the macro-structural level, the composer may make available choices among prefabricated musical modules. In any case, the fundamental question of choice is only postponed; but the work gains generality—attractive combinations of varied perspectives on the soundscape (Murray Schafer) accessible to the piece.

But compositional use of randomness is not the same as randomness as a metaphysical principle; as an impersonal technique intended to let sounds and silence be, simply, which Cage practiced beforehand (Charles 1978). In a sense, Cage wishes to liberate the sounds from music and musicians, whereas Xenakis "is voluntarily in keeping, not with the tradition, but with the history of his art" (Revault d'Allonnes 1973, p. 235).

Stochastic music is more than a technical solution; it is the fruit of a long tradition of rational thought. Indeed, probability theory is a formal structure based on the fundamental question, What can happen in our world, in such and such a given situation? Granted a basic hypothesis (homogeneity or not, varied concepts of mean, etc.), probability theory provides choosing tools, adapted to the hypothesis—even *inferred* from it, and we find our conception of artistic creation in choice.

The stochastic cannons or automata presented here might be used to control various dimensions of a compositional process, such as the elements of pitch, register, duration, amplitude, and so forth. Or they might be employed in the composition of sound microstructure, in particular in the synthesis of sound-wave forms.

I am deeply indebted to Xenakis: my understanding of probability theory has come through him—the case of a nonmathematician introducing to another some mathematical knowledge. In the following pages you will find methods for generating random variables which are not new, original, or exclusive in themselves. For instance, you may read others (Knuth; Maurin 1975) that refer to a large literature. This paper, however, has been written by a musician with the intention of gathering a panoply for musical purposes. My aim is to give musicians with even less mathematical knowledge than I useful tools. A particular aim is to bring many computer applica-

tions in musical composition out of the eternal and poor use of random values directly from the computer's omnipotent black box: the uniform distribution pseudo-random generator.

2.0 Preliminary Definitions

2.1 Probability

A probability is a fraction of a *sample space:* the set of all possible outcomes in a given situation. Outcomes could be card configurations in a card game, the states of a machine, the colors of cars passing on the street, or the 88 keys of a piano. The probability of one specific event amongst the whole sample space (an event is a subset of the sample space) is

$$\frac{\text{number of ways the event can happen}}{\text{number of outcomes in the sample space}}$$

Clearly, the value of this fraction must be between 0 and 1, for

$$0 = \frac{\substack{\text{number of ways an event } absent \\ \text{from the sample space can happen}}}{\text{number of outcomes in the sample space}}, \quad (1)$$

$$\text{and } 1 = \frac{\text{number of outcomes in the sample space}}{\text{number of outcomes in the sample space}}.$$

A probability is thus a ratio comparing two sets of events: the sample space and a subset of the latter—an event, measuring the proportion of a specific event included in the sample space. The larger the probability of an event, the more likely it is to happen, provided that something happens.

In simple cases, probabilities are quite straightforward. For instance, the probability of obtaining an odd result when throwing a die is 3/6 (the event is three outcomes out of six). But if two dice are thrown, some thinking is necessary. Here is a famous problem, "Banach's Match Boxes" (Feller 1966a, p. 166). A smoker has two match boxes of n matches each; when he needs a match he selects a box at random; when he takes the last match in a box, what is the probability that the other still contains x matches? Complex combinatorial calcula-

Lorrain

tions often must be performed merely to determine how many ways can the event happen and how many events are there in the sample space.

This intuitive approach to probability can suffice for our purpose, and will be completed as needed. Except as concrete examples for some basic notions, we will not deal here with real situations or mechanisms; we shall rather describe algorithms—imaginary machines—conforming to some classical schemes of probability theory. For thorough and formal definitions of probability and elements of combinatorial analysis, see Calot (1967, chapters 1 and 2), or Feller (1966a, chapters 1 and 2). Simple introductions to probability theory can be found in college mathematical textbooks; Jacquard (1976) is clear and quite complete, as is Lipschutz (1965).

2.2 Random Variables

A *random variable* (denoted X hereafter) is a variable that assumes specific values randomly (denoted x_s hereafter) corresponding to specific events out of the sample space. Thus if the sample space is an urn containing 12 colored balls: 3 red, 5 blue and 4 white, the random variable X is the color of a ball picked at random: it can assume three values {red, blue, white} which can be *abstracted* and *ordered* as {x_1, x_2, x_3}. Moreover, we know the probabilities P of these values:

$$P\{X = x_1\} = \frac{3}{12},$$

$$P\{X = x_2\} = \frac{5}{12}, \text{ and}$$

$$P\{X = x_3\} = \frac{4}{12}, \tag{1}$$

which are read: "the probability that X is x_1 equals" and so forth.

From the definitions of probabilities and random variables, it follows that the sum of the probabilities of all eventual values of a random variable X equals 1 for s covering the range of values of x,

$$\sum P\{X = x_s\} = 1 = P\{\text{any event in the sample space}\}. \tag{2}$$

In the above example:

$$\sum_{s=1}^{3} P\{X = x_s\} = \frac{3}{12} + \frac{5}{12} + \frac{4}{12} = 1.$$

2.3 Probability Distributions

The concept of random variable leads to that of probability distribution as a function of x: for s covering the range of values of x, the function

$$f(x_s) = P\{X = x_s\}$$

is called the *probability distribution* of the random variable X. We have now only stated that $P\{X = x_s\}$ is a function of x_s. The usefulness of this statement is perhaps not apparent for the time being, but it will prove to be of extreme importance later on, when we shall make use of authentic functions of x to describe probability distributions, particularly for continuous random variables (Section 2.6). We can at least use this terminology in statements such as

$$0 \leq f(x_s) \leq 1,$$

equivalent to Eq. (1), and

$$\sum f(x_s) = 1, \tag{3}$$

equivalent to Eq. (2).

Probability distribution can be visualized in a two-dimensional graph as any function of x; a graph of probability distribution is called a *histogram*. Fig. 1 shows the histogram of the urn example in Section 2.2; each vertical bar has its height scaled to the probability it illustrates.

2.4 Distribution Functions

The above probability distribution $f(x)$ must be distinguished from the *distribution function* $F(x)$ of X, defined as

$$F(x_s) = \sum_{r \leq s} f(x_r) = P\{X \leq x_s\} \tag{4}$$

Fig. 1. Histogram of urn
example in Section 2.2.

Fig. 2. Distribution function of urn example in Section 2.2.

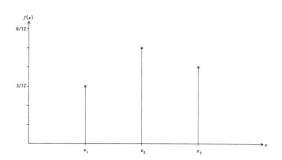

Fig. 1. Histogram of urn
example in Section 2.2.

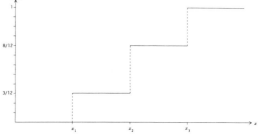

Fig. 2. Distribution function of urn example in Section 2.2.

or, the sum of the probabilities of events not exceeding x_s in order. Stated otherwise: $F(x_s)$ is the probability of X assuming one of the values

$$\{x_1, \, x_2, \, \ldots \, , \, x_s\},$$

forming a subset of the sample space. Equation (3) in Section 2.3 represented the particular case when $F(x_s) = 1$ because s covers the entire sample space. In our urn example,

$$F(x_2) \; = \; \sum_{r=1}^{2} f(x_r) \; = \; \frac{3}{12} + \frac{5}{12} \; = \; \frac{2}{3} \, ,$$

two times out of three X will be x_1 or x_2 (the ball will not be white).

This concept of distribution function may seem pointless now but it will prove fundamental to our discussion of algorithms. A distribution function can be graphed: for our urn example, Fig. 2 shows clearly the cumulative definition of $F(x)$.

2.5 Discrete Variables

A random variable X is said to be discrete if it can take values from an ordered set of a finite number of events. We have only dealt with discrete variables so far in order to establish a solid foundation for the next paragraph concerning continuous variables. Concretely, discrete variables are those which can assume only absolutely distinguishable values, such as x_1, x_2, or x_3, with no alternative in between. This is visible in their histogram made of different vertical bars in Fig. 1 and their stepwise distribution function in Fig. 2.

For a complete theory of discrete variables, see Feller (1966a) or appropriate chapters in Calot (1967). Gnedenko and Khintchine (1969) provide a very good introduction to discrete probability theory that is easy to read. College textbooks are often limited to discrete variables.

2.6 Continuous Variables

A random variable X is continuous when its distribution function $F(x)$ is continuous. This implies that its probability distribution $f(x)$—although it may include some discontinuities—is not, as for a discrete variable, a collection of discrete values $[f(x_1), f(x_2), \ldots , f(x_n)]$. Rather, its distribution is an $f(x)$ defined over a range of real numbers which can be assumed by X. Figure 3 shows the histogram of a continuous distribution (the normal distribution); this random variable can assume an infinity of values—any real number.

In the case of discrete variables, Eq. (3) in Section 2.3 stated that the sum of the probabilities of all events in a sample space must equal one. Graphically, this means that the sum of the histogram's vertical bars must be scaled to one (Fig. 1). In the case of continuous variables, it is the area bounded by the probability distribution and the horizontal axis which equals one. This can be intuitively understood by imagining this area as being filled with an infinity of vertical bars corresponding to the infinity of real values assumable by the random variable, as in the shaded area of Fig. 4. Thus when passing from discrete to continuous variables,

Fig. 3. Histogram of a continuous distribution (normal distribution).

Fig. 4. Distribution function as the area under the probability distribution: the shaded area is $F(x_s) = P\{X \le x_s\}$.

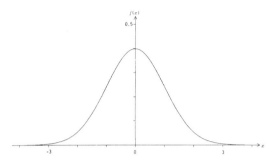

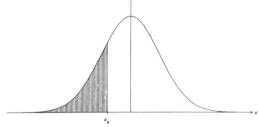

we substitute the integration of Eq. (5) for the summation of Eq. (3):

$$\int_{-\infty}^{\infty} f(x)dx = 1 \qquad (5)$$

In the same manner, the definition of a *continuous distribution function* is

$$F(x_s) = \int_{-\infty}^{x_s} f(x)dx = P\{X \le x_s\}, \qquad (6)$$

instead of Eq. (4) (Section 2.4). This is illustrated in Fig. 4.

In the case of discrete variables, probabilities of events correspond to vertical bars of scaled height in the histogram (Fig. 1). For continuous variables, because of the infinity of possible values, one must abandon the idea of a probability associated with one specific event; indeed, this probability is zero:

$$\frac{\text{one specific event}}{\text{an infinity of outcomes in the sample space}} = \frac{1}{\infty} = 0.$$

Thus the "height" of $f(x_s)$ is not directly the probability of x_s. We must be satisfied with knowing the probability of X assuming a value in a certain interval called *differential* (dx), which can be as "thin" as we wish, but not null. Thus the probability distribution of a continuous variable X is $f(x)$, but the probability of a specific x_s is zero:

$$P\{X = x_s\} = \frac{1}{\infty} = 0.$$

We must introduce the differential in order to handle a "tangible" probability:

$P\{X = \text{ in the interval } dx \text{ around } x_s\} = f(x_s)dx.$

This is illustrated in Fig. 5: the area under $f(x_s)$ is null (the mathematical point $f(x_s)$ has no "width") and we must approximate $P\{X \approx x_s\}$ with a small differential rectangle of width dx. With this mathematical provision, a continuous histogram can be read directly: the higher $f(x_s)$, the more probable is $\{X \approx x_s \text{ in } dx\}$.

For an introduction to differential and integral calculus, and an understanding of these transitions from discontinuities to continuity, one can study Calot (1967) with profit or Guénon (1946) for an historical and philosophical point of view. Feller (1966*b*) and Calot contain complete theories of continuous variables.

2.6.1 Continuous Uniform Variables

The *continuous uniform* variable, for which we will henceforth use the special symbol U, is one that can take any real value u between zero and one. It is defined as follows:

$$f(u) = 0 \text{ if } u < 0$$
$$f(u) = 1 \text{ if } 0 < u < 1$$
$$f(u) = 0 \text{ if } u > 1.$$

Figure 6 shows its histogram. The rectangular area between $f(u)$ and the U axis measures one by one: the total area is thus one, in accordance with Eq. (5) in Section 2.6. Figure 7 shows the continuous uniform distribution function: notice how $F(u)$ is indeed continuous (although $f(u)$ contains two discontinuities), and how it increases from zero to one as u also

Fig. 5. The area of the
rectangle measuring $f(x_s)$ by
dx is the probability of X
assuming a value in the
interval dx around x_s.

Fig. 6. Histogram of the continuous uniform distribu-
tion U.

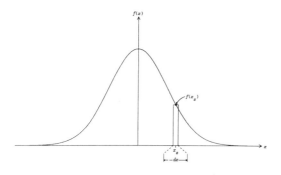

increases in the same interval: in this case, the distribution function is simply equal to the variable, that is

$$F(u_s) = \int_{-\infty}^{u_s} f(u)du = u_s = P\{U \leq u_s\}. \quad (7)$$

We shall make a constant use of this fact in our cannons, since the continuous uniform variable U (see Section 4.0, for more details) is the standard "pseudorandom number generator" available in computers as library function, under names such as **ran, ranf, rand,** and so forth, and all our algorithms will rely on it.

2.7 The Continuous Structure of Musical Parameters

In order to establish the continuous structure of the musical parameters we intend to work with, we will start with a consideration of pitch, and we shall assume the mere capability of perceiving distinct pitches. From a collection of discrete pitches comes forth some terms for qualifying different sensations (the usual "low" and "high"). Then follows the notion of pitch differences—distances between pitch pairs—together with the ability to compare these in terms of size. In comparing, we perform mental operations such as abstracting pitch differences from chronological pitch successions, transferring differences between various higher or lower pitch pairs, inverting the direction of differences, from "toward high" to "toward low" or vice versa, perhaps using

reiterations of a small unit difference (e.g., semitone) to measure larger ones, and so forth.

By these operations we could intuitively arrive at a *total ordering* of pitch sensations, since we could evaluate the relative size and direction of differences between any two pitches. Moreover, we could axiomatically define tempered pitch scales with merely a reference pitch and one arbitrary unit difference, as Xenakis has shown following Peano's axiomatization of numbers (Xenakis 1971a, p. 61).

Of course, musicians take for granted this totally ordered structure of pitches, and have long since gained a great ease in the manipulation of pitch intervals. If we define addition ($\oplus$) of two intervals as making the arrival point of the first and the starting point of the second interval correspond to the same pitch, and consider the result of the operation as the interval from the starting point of the first to the arrival point of the second operand, it can be shown that in such usual musical operations, pitch intervals have the mathematical structure of a *commutative group*. (See Grossman and Magnus, Chapters 1 and 2 for group definitions)

(a) stability: addition of any two intervals yields another interval;

(b) associativity: for any three intervals, $(d_1 \oplus d_2) \oplus d_3 = d_1 \oplus (d_2 \oplus d_3)$;

(c) there exists an identity element I (prime interval, or unison) such that $d \oplus I = I \oplus d = d$;

(d) any interval d has its inverse d^{-1} (the same

Fig. 7. Distribution function of the continuous uniform distribution U.

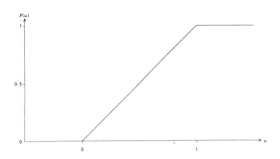

size of interval, but inverted in direction)
such that

$$d \oplus d^{-1} = d^{-1} \oplus d = I;$$

(e) commutativity comes to boot:

$$d_1 \oplus d_2 = d_2 \oplus d_1.$$

Usually this group of intervals of pitch sensations
has the same structure (i.e., is isomorphic to that
of rational numbers under arithmetical addition).
Ancient and traditional music was based on varied
scales and thus handled rational numbers; and we
can only gain in theoretical generality if we extend
this domain to the whole set of real numbers, of
which the rationals are a subset, to all possible pitch
intervals. If the starting situation were tempered
scales, such as twelve-tone equal-temperament, the
connection would be similar: we can label the intervals with the number of unit intervals they represent in size and direction, in which case we form a
group isomorphic to that of integers under
arithmetical addition (a subgroup of the preceding).
We can expand this situation to cover rational, irrational, and real numbers as well.

If we leave the domain of perception for that of
physical phenomena, and speak in terms of frequency, the extension to real numbers is as feasible.
Nontempered scales are built from a group of rational ratios under arithmetical multiplication and
tempered intervals can be considered as irrational
ratios (for instance, involving roots of two if they
possess an octave modulo); from here also the extension to real numbers follows naturally.

In such ways, we gradually fill up the gaps between integers and rationals, tending toward continuity. Leibnitz stated, "It follows, from the actual
division, that in a part of matter, however small it
may be, there exists a sort of world consisting of
innumerable creatures" (Guénon 1946, p. 55). We
arrive at intervals smaller than our perceptual difference threshold, vanishing into continuity, through
speculative subdivision. But perhaps, conversely, we
could consider continuity as given, and look at historical scales as landmark systems arbitrarily extracted from it to satisfy our need for ease of manipulation, hierarchy, order, and comparative norms: "A
continuous set is not the result of the parts into
which it is divisible, but, on the contrary, is independent of them, and consequently, that it is given
to us as a whole by no means implies the actual
existence of these parts" (Guénon 1946, p. 60).

In any case we can claim that the intervals, and
pitches themselves as embodiments of intervals, are
isomorphous to real numbers, and to a straight line
isomorphous to the latter: this musical parameter is
continuous and totally ordered. Some other parameters possess the same structure (e.g., amplitude), except those based on qualitative definitions such as
timbre. Time itself, metrical time, in the mental
operations we can perform on it, exhibits the same
structure deeply rooted in our psychology, as shown
by Piaget (1973, pp. 74–83), where the notion of logical "grouping" is developed. Leonardo da Vinci understood much of this, which is evident from a small
text from around 1500 that I quote with pleasure: "If
one applies to the point the terms reserved for time,
it must be compared to the instant, and the line to
the length of a great duration of time. And as the
points constitute the beginning and end of the said
line, so the instants form the origin and the term of a
certain portion of given time. And if a line is divisible to infinity, it is not impossible that a portion of
time is also. And if the divided parts of the line can
offer a certain proportion between them, it is the
same for the parts of time" (da Vinci 1942, p. 76).

This justification may seem unnecessary to the
reader, but it has not been in our musical tradition
very long. Consider for instance, in 1916, the very
laborious explanations of Russolo about his noise
instruments (*intonarumori*) capable of "a complete
enharmonic system where each tone possesses all

possible mutations by subdividing in an indefinite number of fractions" (Russolo 1975, p. 83). Russolo finally introduces, in the context of a discussion on notation problems, a rather vague notion of "dynamic continuity" (Russolo 1975, p. 87) meaning pitch continuity. It is only quite recently that such notions have been accepted in musical practice. Perhaps now they are taken for granted.

In the following pages, we will stand on the musically rather abstract ground of the group of real numbers, under addition, since we will have no reason to venture out of the perceptual domain. But since we have established the correspondence of real values to musical parameters or characteristics, music will always be "virtually" present, and actual applications will be preferably left to the reader's own imagination.

2.8 Cannons

"In the final analysis, randomness, like beauty, is in the eye of the beholder."—R. W. Hamming (1973)

Probability theory normally finds its practical use in statistics. We can analyze the results of tests and see if they conform to some distribution, if abnormal configurations imply faults in the testing environment. Probability distributions are studied as mathematical models of populations—"natural" events or series of events happening in everyday life as well as in complex scientific experiments. But our purpose is the opposite: we wish to synthesize populations conforming to probability distributions. For this we shall need to transform the formulas of probability theory in such a way that we make the random variable a function of its distribution function; this will be clarified later. We are interested in starting from a definition of a population, a histogram, chosen because of formal, aesthetic, or other musical reasons, in order to give shape to a certain musical characteristic. Then we want to synthesize values fitting it, eventually combining these values into sound events.

Nothing guarantees that our synthetic population, which will be composed of a limited number of random values, will conform with precision and ele-

gance to the intended histogram and embody it in an ideal manner. Random values are random, nevertheless, and do not necessarily follow our imagination and intentions. Conformity of a population to a given probability distribution can only be achieved for a very large number of sample values. This is known as the *weak law of large numbers:* "If, in a trial, the probability of an event is p, and if we repeat the trial a large number of times, the ratio between the number of times the event happens and the total number of trials—that is, the frequency f of the event—tends more and more towards p. . . . if the number of trials is large enough, it becomes highly improbable that the difference between f and p will be greater than a given value, as small as it may be" (Vessereau 1953, p. 31).

Thus we must be ready to accept some "strange" random values, or successions of values, or perhaps choose among some populations the one best embodying our platonistic Idea of the distribution. "This brings up a philosophical point. Do we really want genuine random numbers, or do we want a set of homogenized, guaranteed, and certified numbers whose effect is random but at the same time we do not run the risk of the fluctuations of a truly random source? . . . we usually find that we want to get the security of a large [number of samples] by taking [as few] as we can" (Hamming 1973, p. 143).

2.9 Notation Conventions

In the following pages we shall apply all the preceding notions and continue using the same symbols, reviewed here:

X is a random variable
x represents values of X
x_s is one specific value of X
U is the continuous uniform variable (random real number in the range [0, 1])
u represents values of U
u_s is one specific value of U, standing for a call to the U cannon in statements such as "u_s: = ran(0)"
$f(x)$ is the probability distribution of X
$P\{X = x_s\} = f(x_s)$

Fig. 8. Histogram of the discrete uniform distribution.

in discrete cases the probability of X takes the value x_s

$$= f(x_s)dx$$

in continuous cases the probability of X takes a value within the interval dx around x_s
$F(x)$ is the distribution function of X

$$F(x_s) = \overset{i \le s}{\Sigma} x_i = P\{X \le x_s\}$$ is the probability of X taking a value smaller or equal to x_s in discrete cases and

$$= \int_{-\infty}^{x_s} f(x)d_x = P\{X \le x_s\}$$

in continuous cases

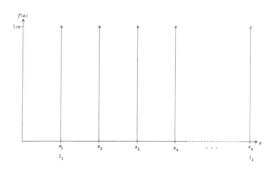

Where a cannon consists in the application of a single formula, this formula only will be given. When complete algorithms are implied, they will be given in Pascal, a common and easily translatable procedural language.[1]

We will examine a number of different techniques for generating stochastic data according to specific formulas. First, discrete distributions will be discussed, including the discrete uniform distribution. In addition, binomial, Poisson, and permutational algorithms will be detailed. Then continuous distributions will be covered, including the uniform distribution; and a number of weighted functions, including: linear, exponential, gamma, bilateral exponential (or First Law of Laplace), Cauchy, hyperbolic cosine, logistic, arc sine, Gauss-Laplace, and beta distributions.

3.0 Types of Discrete Distributions

3.1 The Discrete Uniform Distribution

This distribution concerns n equiprobable events. It is equivalent to the random choice of one of n inte-

---

1. In the original manuscript, the author supplied algorithms written in Fortran. This code has been converted to Pascal by the editor in the interest of readability. The code is Standard Pascal with the addition of the exponentiation operator "**", and a **ran( )** function. Any errors in the code are the responsibility of the editor.

gers between (and including) two limits ℓ_1 and ℓ_2 ($\ell_1 < \ell_2$). The probability distribution is constant for all possible outcomes:

$$f(x) = \frac{1}{n},$$

where $n = (\ell_2 - \ell_1) + 1$, the number of possible integers in the sample set. A histogram is shown in Fig. 8. To choose an item, we could use the general method described for other discrete variables, but since all probabilities are equal the case is simple and we can directly make X a linear function of U:

$$X = nU + \ell_1,$$

and rely on the computer's integer arithmetic to truncate this real X to integers. The preceding equation could be paraphrased as: given a real u in the interval $[0, 1]$, we "stretch" this interval to $[0, n]$, and then transfer it to $[\ell_1, n + \ell_1]$. When truncated, the result will be an integer in $[\ell_1, \ell_2]$. Algorithm (1) performs the task:

```
function inrect (l1,l2: integer): integer;
var n: integer; u: real;
begin
    n: = (l2 − l1) + 1;
    u: = ran(0);
    inrect: = trunc(n*u) + l1
end; {inrect}
```

Algorithm (1)

Fig. 9. $P\{X = \mathbf{x}\}$ as segments on $[0,1]$.

Fig. 9. $P\{X = \mathbf{x}\}$ as segments on $[0,1]$.

3.2 A General Method for Obtaining other Distributions

When the probabilities assigned to n discrete events are not equal, it is necessary to use a *cumulative table* of probabilities. Such a table contains the n following values:

(1) $P\{X = x_1\}$
(2) $P\{X = x_1\} + P\{X = x_2\}$
$\vdots$
(n) $P\{X = x_1\} + P\{X = x_2\}$
$\quad + \ldots + P\{X = x_n\}$,

which are equivalent to

(1) $F(x_1)$
(2) $F(x_2)$
. . . .
(n) $F(x_n)$.

Since $F(x_1) > 0$ and $F(x_n) = 1$, all these values can be assimilated to points dividing a real segment $[0, 1]$ into smaller segments equal to the different probabilities involved (Fig. 9). After obtaining a u_s from our U cannon, we need only look into which segment it falls in order to point at the chosen x_s:

$X = x_1$ if $0 \leq u_s < F(x_1)$
$X = x_2$ if $F(x_1) \leq u_s < F(x_2)$
$\vdots$
$X = x_n$ if $F(x_{n-1}) \leq u_s < 1$.

In the following cannons, this simple method will be used: scanning $F(x)$ from $F(x_1)$ to $F(x_n)$ until the proper x_s is found. Knuth (pp. 101–102) can be consulted for other algorithms.

3.3 Other Discrete Variables

3.3.1 A Choice Between Two Alternatives

The following algorithm makes a choice between two alternatives of given (most likely different) probabilities. Only $P\{X = x_1\}$ need be specified, since $P\{X = x_2\} = 1 - P\{X = x_1\}$. The following parameters are transmitted from the calling program:

x1: the alternative x_1
x2: the second alternative x_2, and
p1: $P\{X = x_1\}$.

```
function alter2(x1,x2,px1: real): real;
begin {alter2}
  u: = ran(0);
  if u < px1 then
    alter2: = x1
  else
    alter2: = x2
end; {alter2}
```

Algorithm (2)

A particular version of the preceding cannon may be useful for choosing between $+1$ and -1 as equiprobable signs in equations involving a $+$ or $-$ alternative. Such cases are frequent (Xenakis 1963, chapter 4) in formulas of the type

$$z_i = z_{i-1} \pm x$$

where x is a random interval obtained from an always-positive random distribution. The preceding equation could be programmed:

z(i):= z(i − 1) + (xsigne(0)*call to a cannon)

with the following:

Fig. 10. Histogram of the
binomial distribution
B(50,0.05).

```
function xsigne(ibidon: real): real;
begin {xsigne}
    u: = ran(0);
    if u < .5 then xsigne: = 1.0
    else
    xsigne: = −1.0
end; {xsigne}
```

Algorithm (3)

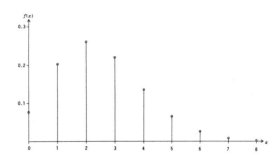

3.3.2 The Binomial Distribution

The choices between two alternatives described in Section 3.3.1 are called *Bernouilli trials*. A succession of n Bernouilli trials synthesizes a population conforming to the binomial distribution:

$$B(n,p)$$

where p is the probability of one of the alternatives, labeled *success*. This distribution looks at a succession of Bernouilli trials, and has as variable the number of successes obtained in n trials:

$$P\{B(n,p) = x\} = \binom{n}{x} p^x (1 − p)^{n − x}$$

$$\text{for } x = 0, 1, 2, \ldots, n$$

where

$$\binom{n}{x} = \frac{n!}{x!(n − x)!}$$

It is thus an analytic view of choices between two alternatives.

It is perhaps not necessary to devise a binomial cannon, since we can seize the problem by straightforward choices rather than by resorting to analytic distribution. But if such an algorithm were needed, it should be similar to that of the Poisson distribution (Section 3.3.3). First, a cumulative table $F(x)$ is prepared:

$$F(0) = P\{B(n,p) = 0\}$$
$$F(1) = P\{B(n,p) = 0\} + P\{B(n,p) = 1\}$$
$$\vdots$$
$$F(n) = P\{B(n,p) = 0\} + P\{B(n,p) = 1\}$$
$$+ \ldots + P\{B(n,p) = n\} = 1$$

Then u_s is used to point at the resulting x_s. We then decide that among the next n events there should be x_s successes, and of course $n − x_s$ occurrences of the other alternative. Another solution would be to use the Poisson cannon directly, since Poisson distributions are approximations to binomial distributions. A histogram of $B(50, 0.50)$ is shown in Fig. 10.

It can be shown (Calot 1967, pp. 310–316; Feller 1966a, Chapter 7) that when n becomes large and p is not small, for example, when np and $n(1 − p)$ are somewhat greater than 15 or 20, with better approximations when p is near ½, the binomial distribution $B(n,p)$ is quite equivalent to a Gauss-Laplace distribution of mean np and standard deviation $\sqrt{np(1 − p)}$. In such cases we could more easily use the Gauss-Laplace cannon (Section 4) and round the result to the nearest integer. Calot (1967, pp. 445–449) shows interesting graphical comparisons between binomial and Gauss-Laplace histograms, while Vessereau (1953, chapter 3) presents a good introduction to the family of binomial, Gauss-Laplace and Poisson distributions. Gnedenko and Khintchine (1969), treating exclusively discrete variables, also approach the Gauss-Laplace distribution through the binomial.

3.3.3 The Poisson Distribution

On the other hand, if n becomes large and p small, it can be shown (Calot 1967, pp. 307–309; Feller 1966a, p. 153) that the binomial distribution can be approximated by the Poisson distribution, which has the advantage of discarding n from the calculations. This approximation is good for values of

A Panoply of Stochastic 'Cannons'   **361**

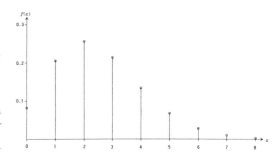

Fig. 11. Histogram of the Poisson distribution for δ = 2.5, quite similar to the binomial B(50,0.05) of Fig. 10.

$n > 50$ and
$p < 0.1,$

such that the product $np = \delta$ is in the order of a few units. This parameter δ is called the average density of the Poisson distribution. This relation between Poisson and binomial distributions implies that, for a large δ (somewhat greater than 20), Poisson also approximates a Gauss-Laplace distribution of mean δ and standard deviation $\sqrt{\delta}$ (Calot 1967, pp. 330–331; Feller 1966a, p. 190). A Poisson algorithm could, under such conditions, be used as an integer Gauss-Laplace cannon. However, the Poisson distribution is quite cumbersome to program, so this is not very advantageous.

The Poisson distribution is thus, as the binomial, an analytic point of view on a series of Bernouilli trials: it gives the probability of obtaining x successes in a large number of trials, when the average density of successes is δ:

$$P\{X = x\} = \frac{e^{-\delta}\delta^x}{x!}, \quad \text{for } x = 0, 1, 2, \dots.$$

Note that n, the number of trials, is not present in the formula. A histogram of a Poisson distribution of density 2.5 is shown in Fig. 11.

We are giving an algorithm for this distribution because it has attained some popularity through its use by Xenakis (1963, p. 35) as an analytic approach to phenomena appearing in the time dimension (*cf.* also Truax, in *Computer Music Journal*, Vol. 1, No 3 (1977) pp. 30–39). In such cases, the Poisson distribution concerns the probability of finding x points per time unit on a time axis, when the average density of points per time unit is δ (small enough) and the distribution of points conforms to a homogeneous exponential distribution (Section 4.3.2). It is as if, from a binomial point of view, we regarded time as a succession of a very large number of small intervals; a success would then be the presence of a point occupying an interval. Our binomial-Gauss-Laplace-Poisson family, which includes in addition a negative-binomial distribution (Calot 1967, p. 321; Feller 1966a, p. 164) that we do not study here, is thus also related to gamma distributions, of which the exponential is a member (Calot 1967, pp. 332–337, 354–356; Feller 1966b, pp. 11–12). ". . . the

remarkable fact that there exists a few distributions of great universality which occur in a surprisingly great variety of problems. The three principal distributions, with ramifications throughout probability theory, are the binomial, the [Gauss-Laplace] . . . , and the Poisson distribution" (Feller 1966a, p. 156).

The following algorithm is devised to handle several Poisson distributions of independent parameters:

```
procedure poissoninit (var i, j, n, itot, nmax: integer;
                        val, d: real);

type
    realarray = array [1..itot,1..nmax] of real;
var
    xfac: real; xk: integer; tab: realarray;
begin {poissoninit}
    xfac:=1;
    for j:=1 to n-1 do
    begin {loop}
        xk:=j-1;
        if xk<=1 then
            val:=((d**xk)/xfac)*exp(-d)
        else
            begin
            xfac:=xfac*xk; val:=((d**xk)/xfac)*exp(-d)
            end
        if xk = 0 then
            tab[i,1]:=val
        else
            tab[i,j]:=tab[i,(j-1)+val]
    end; {loop}
```

```
  tab[i,n]:=1.0;
end; {poissoninit}
```

Algorithm (4)

```
procedure poisson(var i,n,nbr,itot,nmax: integer);
var u: real;
begin {poisson}
  u:=ran(0);
  for j:=1 to n do
  begin {loop}
    if u<=tab[i,j] then
    begin
      nbr:=j−1;        {transmit value}
      j:=n+1           {terminate loop}
    end
  end {loop}
end; {poisson}
```

Algorithm (5)

The statement "poissoninit" begins a section of initialization of the tab tables of the different $F(x)$ required. Tab has two dimensions (itot,nmax) and is considered as itot vectors, each containing the $F(x)$ of the i-th Poisson distribution of a given δ_i:

$$tab(i,n) = \sum_{x=0}^{n-1} \frac{e^{-\delta_i} \delta_i^x}{x!}$$

Such vectors need more or less length, according to the density δ_i. One must figure nmax such that, for δ_{max}, the greatest density used,

$$P\{X = nmax\} = \frac{e^{-\delta_{max}} \delta_{max}^{nmax}}{nmax!}$$

is very small and can be neglected: indeed, the algorithm can never output a result greater than nmax − 1.

A call to poissoninit includes the following parameters:

i:the reference number for the distribution with density δ_i

n($\leq$nmax):the effectively used length of the tab vector for the i-th density, such that $P\{X = N\}$ can be neglected

d:the average density δ_i

tab:the name of the array declared in the main program

itot:the total number of different densities used

nmax:the length of the longest tab vector

The calling program must call "poissoninit" with the proper parameters in order to initialize all tables. After this preparation, the calls are made to proceed with "poisson." There we get a u_s from **ran**(0) and use it to point at an x_s. A new parameter is included in the call:

nbr transmits x_s, the result, to the calling program: there should be nbr events.

All other parameters are as above.

3.3.4 A Choice Between Several Alternatives

If the sample space contains more than two events of given different probabilities, the following algorithm is needed. It simply scans the cumulative table of the probabilities in order to designate a resulting x_s by a u_s.

```
type
  realarray = array[1 . . n] of real;
  :
function altern(var boul, prob: realarray):real
var u, som:real;
begin{altern}
  som:=0; u:=ran(0); i:=1;
  while i <=n do
  begin {loop}
    som:=som + prob[i];
    if u >= som then
    begin {assign values and exit}
      altern := boul[i];
      i:=n {exit loop}
    end; {assign}
  i:=i+1
  end{loop}
  {not yet successful, assign last value}
  altern:=boul[n]
end;{altern}
```

Algorithm (6)

The parameters of the call are

> boul: the name of the calling program's vector containing the list of different alternatives:
>
> $$\text{boul}(i) = x_i$$
>
> prob: the name of the calling program's vector containing the list of different probabilities, such as
> $\text{prob}(i) = P\{X = x_i\}$ and
>
> $$\sum_{i=1}^{n} \text{prob}(i) = 1$$
>
> n: the dimension of boul and prob.

altern returns the chosen $\text{boul}(i) = x_s$.

The preceding algorithms were particular cases of altern: inrect when all probabilities are equal, and alter2 when only two alternatives are valid.

The multinomial distribution is the analytic approach of this problem (Calot 1967, p. 337; Feller 1966a, p. 167). An algorithm using the multinomial distribution would be very cumbersome, since it should handle whole vectors of events: in n events there should be x_{s1} events x_1, x_{s2} events x_2, and so on. It would prove quite impractical in face of the simplicity of the direct synthesis of the events.

3.3.5 Exhaustive Trials, Permutations

A typically serial procedure would be to choose events from a sample space without repetition of any event before exhaustion of the sample space (Koenig 1971, pp. 15–17, 32–33), thus achieving a permutation of the events of the sample space. This idea is of course valid even if some of the available events are identical—twelve-tone rows are but a particular case: the classical analogy is that of picking balls of different colors from an urn without putting them back. The initial configuration is of N balls, n_1 of color x_1, n_2 of color x_2, and so on, so that for the first pick

$$P\{X = x_s\} = \frac{n_s}{N}.$$

Of course, after the first ball, of color x_s, is out of the urn,

$$P\{X = x_s\} \text{ becomes } \frac{n_s - 1}{N - 1},$$

and so forth (Gnedenko and Khintchine 1969, pp. 103–114).

There is an analytic approach to this problem: the *hypergeometric* distribution (Calot 1967, p. 316; Feller 1966a, pp. 43–47), which would be of little use here. A synthetic approach would be to modify the above altern algorithm in order for it to adjust the prob list of probabilities after the result of each successive choice, or to have the main program handle these modifications. But since most likely the sample space will be of a rather small number of events, it is more practical to use the permutation algorithm, Algorithm 7 (Koenig, pp. 70–73) and to read the permuted array one item at a time as the result of an exhaustive series of trials.

```
type
  integerarray=array[1 . . n] of integer;
  integer2array=array[1 . . 2, . . n] of integer;
  ⋮

procedure permut(varlensmb:integerarray; itrav:
                          integer2array;n,iopt:integer);
var
  ic, i, ix, ir:integer;
begin {permut}
  ic:=n;
  for i:=1 to n do
  itrav[1,i]:=i;
  repeat
    ix:=inrect(1,ic); {call to function inrect (cf.3.1)}
    ir:=itrav[1,ix];
    itrav[2,ic]:=lensmb[ir];
    itrav[1,ix]:=itrav[1,ic];
    ic:=ic−1;
  until ic=0;
  if iopt=1 then
  begin
    for i:=1 to n do
    lensmb[i]:=itrav[2,i]
  end
end;
```

Algorithm (7)

The calling program should have declared the two arrays lensmb [0 . . n] and itrav[0 . . 2, 0 . . n]. In the calling sequence, lensmb is the name of the set of events (array) to be permuted

itrav is a working array

n is the dimension of lensmb and the second dimension of itrav

iopt is a switch:

iopt = 1 ⇒ the permutation is returned in lensmb; that is, lensmb is modified

iopt ≠ 1 ⇒ lensmb is not modified, and the calling program finds the permuted events only in itrav[2,j].

In the algorithm, ic is a counter, itrav[1,j] is used to prevent repetitions of the same event, and itrav[2,j] stores the permutation while it is prepared. Permut uses the inrect cannon (Section 3.1). A calling program may well use several lensmb sets, but only one work array itrav[2,n_{max}] is necessary, where n_{max} is the dimension of the largest lensmb.

4.0 Types of Continuous Distributions

4.1 Uniform Distributions

Sol per te le mie ore son generate.
—Leonardo da Vinci

As we have seen, the continuous uniform distribution in the range [0,1] is the basis of all our algorithms, source of all randomness. Of course, continuity must be understood as limited to the precision of the computer words; but current precisions of eight or more decimal digits are quite sufficient for our purposes.

It is taken for granted that a typical U cannon (or pseudo-random number generator) is available; otherwise, one can be programmed with some knowledge or found in the literature. U cannon algorithms are discussed from a general point of view by Hamming (1973, pp. 136–142), Knuth (pp. 1–100), and Maurin (1975, chapter 2). Practical examples can be found in IBM's Scientific Subroutine Package (p. 77) (for 32-bit words), and in Koenig's *Computer Composition* (p. 69) (similar, but for 27(!)-bit words). A complete Fortran algorithm that is not machine-dependent can be found in Schrage's article. We must be aware of the fact that, being the

deus ex machina of all stochastic applications, the U cannon deserves the utmost care. Particularly in cases making use of large quantities of source random numbers, only reliable and tested algorithms should be used for the endeavor to be of some consistency.

It is remarkable that, in accordance with the very concept of algorithm, these random generators are rigorously deterministic in generating each random value through some manipulations of the preceding random value:

$$u_s \rightarrow \quad \text{black box} \quad \rightarrow u_{s+1}.$$

They embody exactly the old epicurian concept of randomness as a subjective point of view on a complex combination of deterministic causalities standing out of our comprehension: "Randomness is an uncertain cause with regard to persons, times and places" (Aetius 1976, p. 72).

In order to obtain a continuous distribution in another range than [0,1], we use a linear function of U, exactly as for the inrect algorithm (Section 3.1), but without truncation:

$$x_s = (r_2 - r_1)u_s + r_1,$$

where r_1 and r_2 are two real limits ($r_1 < r_2$), generates a *rectangular continuous* distribution in [r_1, r_2].

4.2 A General Method for Obtaining Other Distributions

In order to generate a continuous variable X from the uniform variable U, the general method is the following. We can equate the distribution function of U (Eq. 7, Section 2.6)

$$F(u_s) = u_s,$$

to the $F(x)$ of the desired distribution:

$$u_s = F(x_s).$$

We then have u_s as a function of x_s, and this can be algebraically inverted into x_s as a function of u_s. Thus u_s is transformed into an x_s conforming to the desired distribution:

$$x_s = F^{-1}(u_s)$$

(Knuth, pp. 102–103; Maurin 1975, chapter 3;

Fig. 12. Histogram of the
linear distribution of parameter g.

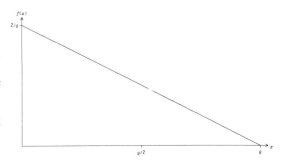

Hamming 1973, pp. 142–143; Calot 1967, chapter 15). This can be intuitively understood as using the u_s in [0,1] to designate a fraction of the area under the desired probability distribution, and looking at the corresponding x_s (see Figure 4). This is simply a more general, continuous application of the discrete method described in Section 3.2.

However, some probability distributions have distribution functions $F(x)$ which cannot be integrated in order to be handled in this manner. Such cases need special algorithms; two (the Gauss-Laplace and beta distributions) will be studied in Section 4.4.

4.3 Directly Obtainable Continuous Distributions

4.3.1 The Linear Distribution

This distribution is described by Xenakis for generating intervals of pitch, time, *etc.* (1963, p. 27, 219) as the probability of picking a segment of length x from a line of length g when the two points delimiting the chosen segment are randomly designated (with rectangular distribution) on the line [0,g]:

$$P\{X = x\} = \frac{2}{g}\left(1 - \frac{x}{g}\right)dx \quad (0 \leq x \leq g).$$

Its histogram is shown in Fig. 12. This distribution is equivalent to the right half of the triangular distribution described by Feller (1966b, p. 50).

The cannon is prepared thus:

$$F(x_s) = \int_0^{x_s} \frac{2}{g}\left(1 - \frac{x}{g}\right)dx$$

$$= \frac{2x_s}{g} - \frac{x_s^2}{g^2}$$

By equalizing with $F(u_s) = u_s$ we arrive at the quadratic equation

$$\frac{x_s^2}{g^2} - \frac{2x_s}{g} + u_s = 0,$$

which has two roots:

$$x_s = g(1 \pm \sqrt{1 - u_s}),$$

of which only

$$x_s = g(1 - \sqrt{1 - u_s})$$

is useful here, since the other would always make $x_s > g$, and we must stay in the interval $0 \leq x_s \leq g$. The term $(1 - u_s)$ being merely a uniform random number in [0,1], symmetric to u_s, we can simplify finally to

$$x_s = g(1 - \sqrt{u_s}).$$

As visible on the histogram (Fig. 12), small values are favored, and this because of the relation

$$\sqrt{u_s} > u_s,$$

which tends to make $1 - \sqrt{u_s}$ always nearer zero.

4.3.2 The Exponential Distribution

As mentioned in Section 3.3.3. about the Poisson distribution, the exponential distribution has been used by Xenakis (1963, pp. 26, 169, 171, 215) to synthesize stochastic time intervals. Its theoretical basis makes it suitable for homogeneous situations (Feller 1966b, p. 8). From a musical point of view, the exponential distribution is particularly suited for time intervals, being at once homogeneous and sufficiently varied. But of course others can be used to introduce variations or radically different configurations (Section 5).

The exponential distribution of average density $\delta > 0$ (average interval $= 1/\delta$) is

$$P\{X = x\} = \delta e^{-\delta x}dx \ (x \geq 0).$$

Fig. 13. Histograms of exponential distributions for different values of δ.

Fig. 14. Histograms of gamma distributions for different values of ν.

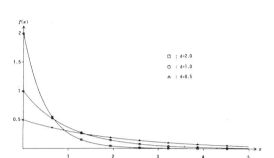

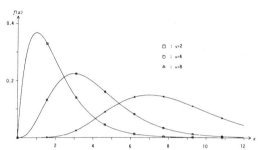

The distribution function is

$$F(x_s) = \int_0^{x_s} \delta e^{-\delta x} dx = 1 - e^{-\delta x_s}.$$

Through equalization with $F(u_s)$, we have

$$u_s = 1 - e^{-\delta x_s},$$

inversed into

$$x_s = \frac{-\ln(1 - u_s)}{\delta},$$

and finally

$$x_s = \frac{-\ln(u_s)}{\delta}.$$

Histograms of exponential distributions for three different densities are shown in Fig. 13.

4.3.3 Gamma Distributions

The gamma distribution γ_ν, of parameter $\nu > 0$, is

$$P\{X = x\} = \frac{1}{\Gamma(\nu)} e^{-x} x^{\nu-1} dx \ (x \geq 0),$$

where $\Gamma(\nu)$ is the Eulerian *gamma function*

$$\Gamma(\nu) = \int_0^\infty e^{-x} x^{\nu-1} dx.$$

The exponential distribution of density 1 is a particular case of the gamma distribution for $v = 1$. Histograms of gamma distributions for three different ν are shown in Fig. 14. They indicate the particular interest of the distribution, its asymmetry. The highest probabilities (*mode*, in statistical terminol-

ogy) are for values near $\nu - 1$, whereas the mean is ν (Calot 1967, p. 350). In rhythmical applications, it can produce a sort of *easing* or *rubato* compared to the exponential (see Section 5). It is quite meaningless to use values of ν much greater than 10: as ν increases, the gamma distribution tends toward a Gauss-Laplace distribution (Calot 1967, pp. 353–354).

A gamma cannon formula allowing any real value for ν cannot be arrived at directly. If necessary, an algorithm for any real ν can be found in Jöhnk's article (pp. 13–15), but it is not so simple. It requires the gamma cannon for integer ν parameters described here, plus a beta cannon (see Section 4.4.2). Otherwise, an algorithm analogous to the first beta cannon described here and in Section 4.4.2 would be necessary. But it can be shown (Calot 1967, pp. 200–201) that for gamma variables of parameters ν and ω, the following equality holds:

$$\gamma_v + \gamma_w = \gamma_{v+w}.$$

Provided we are satisfied with integer valued ν parameters, we can thus synthesize values of γ_ν by summation of ν independent γ_1 variables:

$$\gamma_\nu = \sum_{i=1}^\nu \gamma_1.$$

This restriction is not drastic, since we can always afterward multiply the γ_ν variable obtained by some factor τ in order to set the mode at $\tau(\nu - 1)$ and the mean at $\tau\nu$, or even devise a linear function $\tau\gamma_\nu + \mu$ (Calot 1967, p. 352).

The cannon formula for γ_1 (exponential with $\delta = 1$) being

A Panoply of Stochastic 'Cannons' **367**

Fig. 15. Histogram of the
First Law of Laplace (with
our parameters $\tau = 1$ and
$\mu = 0$).

$$x_s = -\ln(u_s),$$

we need only add successive x_s's ν times in a loop. Since the following equality holds:

$$\ln a + \ln b = \ln(ab),$$

the algorithm can avoid calling the **alog** function ν times:

```
function gamma(nu:real):real;
var sum:real;
begin {gamma}
  sum:=1.0;
  for i:=1 to nu do
    sum:=sum*ran(0);
  gamma:=-alog(sum);
end;{gamma}
```

Algorithm (8)

This method is described by Knuth (p. 115) for the chi-square distribution, closely related to the gamma, and by Jöhnk (pp. 11–12).

4.3.4 First Law of Laplace

The *bilateral exponential* distribution (Feller 1966b, p. 49) is described by Calot (1967, pp. 356–357) as the First Law of Laplace (I adopt Calot's less technical term out of personal admiration for this mathematician). The First Law of Laplace is defined as

$$P\{X = x\} = \frac{e^{-|x|}}{2} dx \quad -\infty < x < \infty.$$

A histogram of this distribution is shown in Fig. 15. It is a symmetrical distribution around a mean, but of quite a different shape than the more common normal distribution (Section 4.4.1).

The distribution function is as follows:

$$F(x_s) = \begin{cases} \dfrac{e^{x_s}}{2} & \text{for } x \leq 0 \\[2ex] 1 - \dfrac{e^{-x_s}}{2} & \text{for } x \geq 0. \end{cases}$$

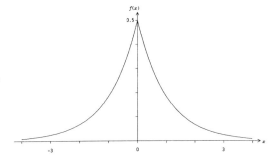

By equalizing with u_s and splitting the outcomes as

$$x_s < 0 \quad \text{if} \quad u_s < 0.5 \text{ and}$$
$$x_s > 0 \quad \text{if} \quad u_s > 0.5,$$

the two following formulas perform the distribution:

$$u_s < 0.5 \Rightarrow x_s = \ln(2u_s)$$
$$u_s > 0.5 \Rightarrow x_s = -\ln(2 - 2u_s).$$

In the following algorithm, we have introduced two parameters in order to make it directly generate a linear function of X:

$$\text{plapla(xmu,tau)} = \tau X + \mu.$$

μ can be a mean other than zero, and τ is a parameter controlling the dispersion (range, or "horizontal spread") of the distribution. Thus our algorithm generates the following random variable:

$$P\{X = \mu + x\} = \frac{1}{2\tau} e^{\frac{-|x|}{\tau}} dx, \text{ for any } x.$$

```
function plapla(var xmu,tau: real):real;
var
  u: real
begin {plapla}
  u: =ran(0)*2.0;
  if u > 1.0 then
    begin
      u:=2.0-u;
      plapla:=(-tau*alog(u))+xmu
    end
  else
```

Lorrain

Fig. 16. Histogram of the
Cauchy distribution
($\tau = 1$, IOPT $\neq$ 1).

```
    plapla:=(tau*alog(u))+xmu
end;{plapla}
```

Algorithm (9)

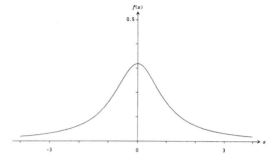

4.3.5 Cauchy Distribution

The Cauchy distribution is another symmetrical distribution centered around zero, but it has the particularity of having no mean and generating very heterogeneous values. The histogram of the Cauchy distribution (Fig. 16) is similar to that of the Gauss-Laplace distribution, but it approaches the horizontal axis so slowly that values of X extremely distant from the mode are quite probable. No finite mean can be computed; this may be difficult to accept intuitively, but the mathematical definition of the mean, or expectation, of a distribution can make it clear (Calot 1967, pp. 213; Feller 1966b pp. 117–118).

With a parameter $\tau > 0$ scaling the dispersion of the variable, the Cauchy distribution is

$$P\{X = x\} = \frac{\tau}{\pi(\tau^2 + x^2)} \, dx \quad \text{for any } x.$$

The distribution function is

$$F(x_s) = \int_{-\infty}^{x_s} \frac{\tau}{\pi(\tau^2 + x^2)} \, dx = \frac{1}{2} + \frac{1}{\pi}\tan^{-1}\frac{x_s}{\tau},$$

from which we obtain the cannon formula:

$$x_s = \tau\left\{\tan\left[\pi\left(u_s - \frac{1}{2}\right)\right]\right\}.$$

The cannon works by taking the tangent of an angle between $-\pi/2$ and $\pi/2$. In order to optimize our algorithm, we may as well take the tangent of an angle between 0 and π, thus implementing this final formula (for a call with iopt $\neq$ 1):

$$x_s = \tau[\tan(\pi u_s)].$$

This formula makes intuitively tangible the absence of mean of the Cauchy distribution: we know that the tangent of an angle near $\pi/2$ is extremely large; since πu_s can designate such an angle with as much probability as any other, very large values of X are quite probable, and can bring out of balance the distribution's eventual tendency toward a mean.

A modified version of the Cauchy distribution is generated when the call parameter iopt is equal to 1: only positive values are generated, producing, in fact, the following distribution:

$$P\{X = x\} = \frac{2\tau}{\pi(\tau^2 + x^2)} \, dx \text{ for } x \geq 0.$$

This version has at least a definite rhythmic interest: it can generate very dense but irregular aggregates of time points, separated by relatively enormous intervals (see Section 5). For the composer, it may involve the risk of losing some listeners because of a gap of a few days between two successive sounds, but it can very well be used with some poetic precautions! Nevertheless, the symmetrical version has been used by Xenakis (1971b, chapter 9) as a source of radical dissymmetries in microcomposition applications (stochastic sound wave forms).

```
function cauchy(var tau,:real; iopt: integer):real;
constant
  pi=3.1415927;
var
  u:real;
begin {cauchy}
  u:=ran(0);
  if iopt=1 then
    u:=u/2.0;
  u:=pi*u;
  cauchy:=tau*(sin(u)/cos(u))
end;{cauchy}
```

Algorithm (10)

Fig. 17. Histogram of the
hyperbolic cosine distribution.

Fig. 18. Histogram of the
logistic distribution for
$\beta = 0$ (mean 0) and $\alpha = 1$.

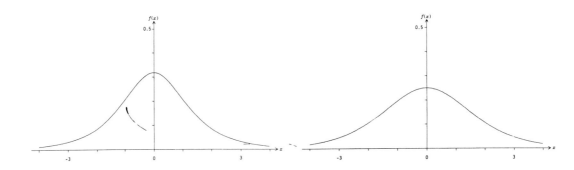

4.3.6 The Hyperbolic Cosine Distribution

This is another symmetrical distribution which can be of some use. Figure 17 shows its histogram. As with the Cauchy distribution, although it is centered on zero, this distribution has no mean. It is defined as

$$P\{X = x\} = \frac{1}{\pi \cosh x} \, dx \text{ for any } x,$$

$$\text{where } \cosh = \frac{e^x + e^{-x}}{2}.$$

The distribution function is

$$F(x_s) = \frac{1}{\pi} \int_{-\infty}^{x_s} \frac{1}{\cosh x} \, dx$$

$$= \frac{2}{\pi} \tan^{-1}(e^{x_s}),$$

we can easily devise a cannon using the formula

$$x_s = \ln\left[\tan\left(\frac{\pi u_s}{2}\right)\right].$$

4.3.7 The Logistic Distribution

With two parameters α and β, the logistic distribution is defined as

$$P\{X = x\} = \frac{\alpha e^{(-\alpha x - \beta)}}{(1 + e^{(-\alpha x - \beta)})^2} \, dx \text{ for any } x \text{ or } \beta, \text{ and } \alpha > 0.$$

Figure 18 shows its histogram: still another symmetrical distribution, of mean $-\beta/\alpha$ and mode:

$$f(-\beta/\alpha) = \alpha/4.$$

The two parameters α and β thus control the mean and dispersion of the distribution (dispersion is inversely proportional to α). The distribution function (Feller 1966b, p. 52) is

$$F(x_s) = \frac{1}{1 + e^{(-\alpha x_s - \beta)}},$$

which can be inverted into the cannon formula

$$x_s = \frac{-\beta - \ln(1/u_s - 1)}{\alpha}.$$

Both the hyperbolic cosine and the logistic distributions have been used by Xenakis in microcomposition (sound synthesis) (1971b, chapter 9).

4.3.8 The Arc Sine Distribution

This distribution is the same as the $\beta(0.5, 0.5)$ distribution (see Section 4.4.2), but it is still useful since it involves a simpler cannon. The histogram is shown in Fig. 19. The arc sine distribution is defined for $0 < X < 1$: the generated values will be in the interval [0,1], with stronger probabilities for values near 0 and 1. As well as for the uniform variable, a random variable can be made a linear function of the arc sine distribution A:

$$X = (r_2 - r_1)A + r_1$$

in order to cover an interval $[r_1, r_2]$. The distribution is

Fig. 19. Histogram of the arc
sine distribution.

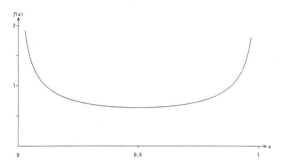

$$P\{X = x\} = \frac{1}{\pi\sqrt{x(1 - x)}}\,dx \text{ for } 0 < x < 1.$$

The distribution function is

$$F(x_s) = \int_0^{x_s} \frac{1}{\pi\sqrt{x(1 - x)}}\,dx$$

$$= \frac{1}{2} - \frac{1}{\pi}\sin^{-1}(1 - 2x_s),$$

which gives the following cannon:

$$x_s = \frac{1 - \sin[\pi(u_s - \frac{1}{2})]}{2}. \tag{8}$$

Jacquard (1976, p. 50), gives us another formula:

$$F(x_s) = \frac{2}{\pi}\sin^{-1}\sqrt{x_s},$$

which amounts to the same thing. This second formula yields the cannon

$$x_s = \left[\sin\left(\frac{\pi u_s}{2}\right)\right]^2. \tag{9}$$

An algorithm using Eq. (9) would involve three multiplications, against which Eq. (8), with two multiplications and two subtractions, can save a few microseconds—life is so short!

4.4 Two Further Distributions

In the following cases, the distributions do not yield a simple cannon formula, and we must rely on approximation algorithms or indirect methods.

4.4.1 Gauss-Laplace Distribution

Strictly speaking, Calot (1967, p. 362) restricts the denomination *normal distribution* to the function of mean 0 and standard deviation 1, defined as

$$P\{X = x\} = \frac{1}{\sqrt{2\pi}}\,e^{-x^2/2}dx \text{ for any } x,$$

and names *Gauss-Laplace* the concrete applications of the normal distribution with any mean μ and standard deviation σ, which can be seen either as a linear function of a normal variable:

$$Gauss\text{-}Laplace = \sigma(normal) + \mu,$$

or as the complete distribution

$$P\{X = x\} = \frac{1}{\sigma\sqrt{2\pi}}\,e^{-(x - \mu)^2/2\sigma^2}dx \text{ for any } x.$$

I have adopted this terminology in the present discussion.

The theoretical importance of the normal distribution has been mentioned (Section 3.3.3). It is the classical bell-shaped distribution shown in Figure 3. Statistically, it accounts for a great number of phenomena because of its very fundamental theoretical basis and role, which explain its "natural look": relatively strong probabilities for the mean and near the mean, rounded mode, smooth vanishing of the probabilities for far fetched values, and so forth. Figure 20 analyzes some characteristics of this important distribution. Note for instance that the probability of values outside the range $[-2\sigma,2\sigma]$ is ≈ 0.04, and outside of $[-3\sigma,3\sigma]$ it is less than 0.003. Tables of values for $f(x)$ and $F(x)$ can be found in any book on probabilities.

In spite of its nobility, we may use the Gauss-Laplace distribution freely. For instance, Xenakis has used it for durations (1963 p. 174) and for his well-known glissandi textures (*Pithoprakta* (1955–56), in particular (1963, p. 27)), through an analogy with the Maxwell-Boltzmann distribution for three-dimensional velocities of molecules in a gas (see also Feller, 1966b, pp. 29–32).

Because of mathematical properties (it is not possible to get the integral out of $F(x)$, so to speak), no simple cannon formula can be programmed. The Gauss-Laplace distribution function has to be approximated. The algorithm described here is

Fig. 20. Histogram of the
normal distribution
($\mu = 0$, $\sigma = 1$). Some important characteristics are

shown. Indicated percent-
ages are of the area under
$f(x)$ (Feller 1966a, p. 178).

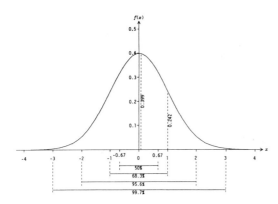

sketched in Hamming's book (1973, p. 143), and developed in IBM's Scientific Subroutine Package
(p. 77). It is based on the following formula (from the
central limit theorem; see *Les Probabilitiés* [Jac-
quard 1976, pp. 91–92], for instance, where it is expressed in a form similar to the following):

$$X = \frac{\sum_{i=1}^{k} u_i - \frac{k}{2}}{\sqrt{k/12}}$$

where the u_i are, as usual, uniform values in [0,1]
and X approaches a truly normal distribution as k
approaches infinity. A compromise is to use
$k = 12$: the algorithm then simplifies into

$$X = \sum_{i=1}^{12} u_i - 6.$$

Adjustment to the required μ and σ are done as

$$\text{gauss} = \sigma X + \mu.$$

```
function gauss(var xmu, sigma:real):real;
var
  s:real;
  i:integer;
begin {gauss}
s:=0.0;
  for i:=1 to 12 do
    s:=s+ran(0);
```

```
gauss:=(sigma*(s−6.0))+xmu;
end;{gauss}
```

Algorithm (11)

The efficiency of this algorithm is poor: twelve calls
to the U cannon are required for each generation;
but its simplicity is quite appealing. In cases where
execution speed is critical, it may be preferable to
use tables of the distribution function $F(x)$, in a procedure similar to the first algorithm described in
Section 4.4.2 for beta distributions. Such tables can
be computed in the algorithm, of course, or given as
data from manuals (Calot 1967, p. 455; Feller 1966a,
p. 176). Methods more effective than straightforward
scanning of these tables can be devised; we can rely
more on linear interpolation in order to reduce the
size of the table and searching time.

4.4.2 Beta Distributions

The beta distribution is defined with two positive
parameters a and b, for a random variable in [0,1]:

$$P\{X = x\} = \frac{1}{B(a,b)} x^{a-1}(1 - x)^{b-1}dx$$

for $0 < x < 1$
and $a > 0$, $b > 0$,
where $B(a,b)$ is the Eulerian beta function:

$$B(a,b) = \int_0^1 x^{a-1}(1 - x)^{b-1}dx.$$

These distributions are closely related to the gamma
distribution. For different parameter values, histograms of the beta distribution can take different
shapes: more or less symmetrical bell shapes, exponential from left to right or from right to left (see
Calot 1967, p. 358; Jacquard 1976, p. 97 for graphs).
However, we will limit ourselves to cases where
$a < 1$ and $b < 1$, because of the very interesting
distributions they imply: more or less symmetrical
"U"-shaped histograms. Figure 21 shows some
cases: the "depth" of the distribution is inversely
proportional to a near 1, and to b near 0. For
$a = b = 1$, we have the *continuous uniform* distribution as a special case. For $a = b = 0.5$, we
have the *arc sine* distribution (Section 4.3.8).

Lorrain

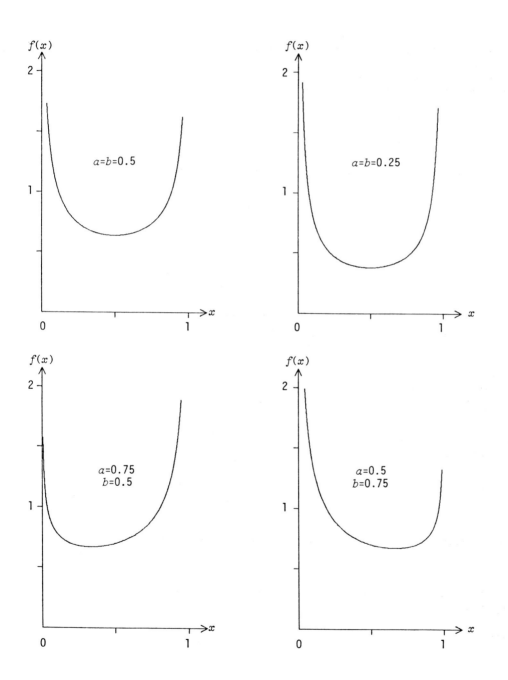

*Fig. 21. Beta distributions for four different (*a,b*) parameter pairs.*

In order to devise a cannon, we can use tables of $F(x)$. The following algorithm can handle several beta distributions of different parameter pairs (a,b); for the i-th pair $(a,b)_i$, it prepares an approximation table of $F(x)$, for x incremented by steps of 0.05 from 0 to 1:

$$tabl(i,n) \approx F(0.05 \cdot [n - 1])$$

$$\approx \frac{1}{B(a,b)} \int_0^{0.05(n-1)} x^{a-1}(1 - x)^{b-1}dx \quad \text{for } (a,b)_i. \quad (10)$$

In order to compute the factor $1/B(a,b)$ we use the property:

$$B(a,b) = \frac{\Gamma(a)\Gamma(b)}{\Gamma(a + b)}$$

(see Section 4.3.3 for a definition of $\Gamma(a)$). We can thus use the fgamma function following to compute this constant, and then approximate $F(x)$ step by step:

$$F(x_s) \approx \sum_{i=1}^{x_s/dx} f(idx)dx$$

We use a microincrement $dx = 0.000125$, entering in table(i,n) only the values for an increment of 0.05, as in Eq. (10). This initialization is done in the first part of the program (procedure beinit), and is of course quite time-consuming, but the resulting tables can be stored for quick reference in actual use.

An actual call for a random value uses the procedure beta. As in discrete cases, we there use a u_s to point between two successive entries of the $F(x)$ table. A linear interpolation is used to simulate continuity.

```
program betauser(input,output);
constant
   ntot=10; {ten a,b pairs}
type
   real2array=array[0 . . ntot,o . . 21] of real;
   .
   .

   .
procedure beinit(var nordr,ntot:integer;
   xa,xb:real; tabl:real2array);
constant
   dx=.000125;
var
```

```
   ab,sbeta,som,x,a,b,px:real;
begin {beinit}
   ab:=xa+xb;
   sbeta:=fgamma(ab)/(fgamma(xa)*fgamma(xb));
      {see fgamma code below}
   tabl[nordr,1]:=0.0;
   som:=0.0;
   x:=-.0000625;
   a:=xa-1.0;
   b:=xb-1.0;
   for i:=2 to 20 do
   begin {outerloop}
      for j:=1 to 400 do
      begin {inner loop}
         x:=x+dx;
         px:=(x**a)*((1.0-x)**b)*sbeta;
         som:=som+(px*dx)
      end; {innerloop}
      tabl[nordr,i]:=som
   end; {outerloop}
   tabl[nordr,21]:=1.0
end {beinit}
end. {betauser}
```

Algorithm (12)

```
procedure beta(var nordr,ntot:integer;
   xx:real; tabl:real2array);
var
   u,z,ds,db:real;
   k:integer;
begin {beta}
   u:=ran(0);
   for k:=2 to 21 do
   begin {loop}
      if u < tabl[nordr,k] then
      begin {innerblock}
         z:=tabl[nordr,k-1]:
         ds:=u-z;
         db:=tabl[nordr,k]-z;
         xx:=0.05*((ds/db)+(k-2))
      end {innerblock}
   end {loop}
end; {beta}
```

Algorithm (13)

The "beinit" call parameters are:

nordr the reference number for the i-th distribution with parameter pair $(a,b)_i$

xa,xb the given parameter pair

tabl the name of the array [ntot,21] declared in the calling program

ntot the number of different parameter pairs used in the calling program(s).

When using the procedure "beta":

nordr, tabl, ntot: as for "beinit"

xx returns the generated random value x_s.

The following function: "fgamma" is called by "beinit." It is an approximation for computing $\Gamma(z)$, (Hastings 1955, p. 157) in a configuration intended for

$$\Gamma(1 + z), \text{ where } 0 \leq z \leq 1.$$

But by the property

$$\Gamma(z) = \frac{\Gamma(1 + z)}{z}$$

we can use it for $0 \leq z \leq 2$:

```
type
  realarray7=array[1 . . 7] of real;
.
.
.
function fgamma(var z:real):real;
type
  flag=(on,off);
var
  x,r:real;      i:integer;     f:flag;
  c:realarray7;
begin {fgamma}
  c[1]:=−.57710166;   c[2]:=.98585399;
  c[3]:=−.87642182;   c[4]:=.8328212;
  c[5]:=−.5684729;    c[6]:=.25482049;
  c[7]:=−.514993;
  x:=z;
  f:=off;
  if x >=1.0 then
  begin {large x}
    x:=x−1.0;
    f:=on;
```

```
  end; {large x}
  r:=1.0;
  for i:=1 to 7 do
  r:=r+(c[i]*(x**i));
  if f=off then
  fgamma:=r/x
  else
  fgamma:=r
end; {fgamma}
```

Algorithm (14)

Once the $F(x)$ tables are computed, Algorithm (14) is quite efficient: it requires one call to the U cannon, a search in the table, and linear interpolation. However, it certainly lacks elegance, and has been described mainly as an example procedure for cases where the computing of tables and linear interpolation would be unavoidable or more efficient, for example, in extensive use of Gauss-Laplace (Section 4.4.1). A very astute beta cannon has been devised by Jöhnk (pp. 9–10), valid for any positive real parameters a and b, and without the theoretical shortcoming of approximation:

```
function beta(var a,b:real):real;
var
  ea,eb,y1,y2,s:real;
begin {beta}
  ea:=1.0/a;
  eb:=1.0/b;
  repeat
    y1:=ran(0)**ea;
    y2:=ran(0)**eb;
    s:=y1+y2
  until s <=1.0;
  beta:=y1/s
end; {beta}
```

Algorithm (15)

The efficiency of Algorithm (15) is interesting, at least for the parameter values in which we are interested ($a < 1$ and $b < 1$). In such cases, "s:=y1+y2;" has a fair chance of not being greater than 1, since the exponents ea and eb are greater

Fig. 22. Right halves of the
histograms of four distributions, all scaled so that
F(3) = 0.99865.

than 1. Thus y1 and y2 are even smaller than the u variables generating them. For $a = b = 0.75$, 3.15 calls to ran are necessary on average; for $a = b = 0.5$, 2.55 calls are required.

5.0 Some Comparisons and Applications

L'action n'est possible que dans une certaine insouciance et la vie n'est qu'un acte de confiance en nous-mêmes et dans la bienveillance des hasards. —Rémy de Gourmont

In order to compare the five symmetrical distributions with one central mode that we have described (of Laplace, Cauchy, hyperbolic cosine, logistic, and Gauss-Laplace) we can adjust them to a common characteristic. For instance, we can scale their dispersions by means of multiplying factors. Let us take as starting point

$$y = F(3) = 0.99865$$

of the normal distribution ($\mu = 0$, $\sigma = 1$): the probability of values greater than 3 is $1 - y = 0.00135$. We can center the other distributions on zero as well, and scale them to conform to this condition. This can be done easily by replacing x_s by 3, and u_s by $y(=0.99865)$ in the cannon formulas, and solving for the scaling factor.

This gives, for the first law of Laplace:

$$-\tau \ln(2 - 2y) = 3 \rightarrow \tau = 0.50723$$

for the Cauchy distribution:

$$\tau \tan[\pi(y - \tfrac{1}{2})] = 3 \rightarrow \tau = 0.01272$$

for the hyperbolic cosine:

$$\tau \ln[\tan(\frac{\pi y}{2})] = 3 \rightarrow \tau = 0.48732$$

logistic (with $\beta = 0$, in order to have the mean at 0):

$$\frac{-\ln(\frac{1}{y} - 1)}{\alpha} = 3 \rightarrow \alpha = 2.2021.$$

Figure 22 shows the right halves of the histograms, with the proper factors. The Cauchy distribution is not shown because its representation is impossible

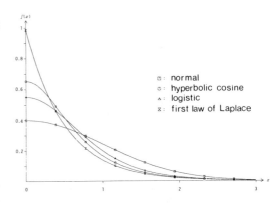

on the same scale as the others: with the above τ, it gives

$$f(0) = 25.02436,$$
$$f(1) = 0.00405, \text{ etc.:}$$

a vertiginously abrupt mode! Otherwise, the figure speaks for itself: each distribution has a certain "personality," a certain demeanor. Their differences can, for instance, be considered in modulating various behaviors of pitch clouds, more or less centered on their mean. Of course, large numbers of random values are necessary for this kind of process to have any significant overall relation to the histograms.

5.1 Application of the Gamma Distribution

Random variables generated by the gamma, exponential, and linear distributions can be applied, for instance, to time intervals. Each distribution again has a personality. In order to make the comparison clear, all sequences of random intervals should be set to the same average density: we choose $e = 2.71828 \ldots$ points per second. The mean of the linear distribution of parameter g is $g/3$. Setting $g = 3/e$ will generate the average value $1/e$ as interval between points, that is: e points per second. The exponential cannon can be called directly with $\delta = e$. For the gamma distributions, we know that the mean of γ_ν is ν; in order to set this mean to $1/e$,

Fig. 23. *The same average density generated by different distributions: (a) linear, (b) γ_1 (exponential), (c) γ_2, (d) γ_4, (e) γ_8, (f) γ_{16}, (g) scaled Cauchy (see text). An "x" represents a* "point"; *rotations of this symbol are used to render somewhat visible clusters of two or more neighboring points, superimposed because of the figure's exi* guity. *There are three lines of points per rectangle,. representing a total of 40 units.*

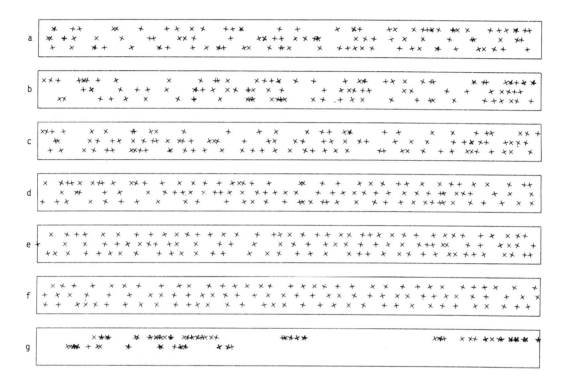

we must set

$$X = \frac{\gamma_\nu}{\nu e}.$$

We have chosen to test these distributions (including the exponential as γ_1) with $\nu = 1, 2, 4, 8, 16$. This exponential scaling of ν amounts to a rather linear rhythmical regularization from the perceptual point of view, obviously due to the fact that the gamma distribution loses its asymmetry for large ν's. Figure 23, from (b) to (f), shows results of this comparison. Each rectangle represents 40 units, and the average density per unit is each time near e (less than 2% difference). From γ_1(b) to γ_{16}(f), the increase of symmetry is clear. The linear distribution (a) stands somewhere between the γ_1 and the γ_2. For the sake of comparison, (g) shows a Cauchy distribution

of intervals (obtained with iopt = 1 in the algorithm in Section 4.3.5) which has been scaled *a posteriori* to give the same density of e points per unit. This distribution's irregularity seems truly unpredictable, and no romantic effort to control it by its parameter τ can overcome the mathematical fact that it has no predictable mean. The example shown has been chosen as an illustration of a sort of maximum acceptable asymmetry; more would be difficult to use in such a context.

5.2 Application of the Beta Distribution

In rhythmic applications also, the beta distributions, including the continuous uniform as the special case $\beta(1,1)$, show an interesting progression. The mean of

Fig. 24. The same average
density generated by different beta distributions: (a)
β(0.125,0.125), (b)
β(0.25,0.25), (c) β(0.5,0.5),
(d) β(0.75,0.75), (e) β(1,1),
equivalent to the continuous uniform. An "x" represents a "point"; rotations of
this symbol are used to render somewhat visible clusters of two or more neighboring points,
superimposed because of
the figure's exiguity. There
are three lines of points per
rectangle, representing a
total of 40 units.

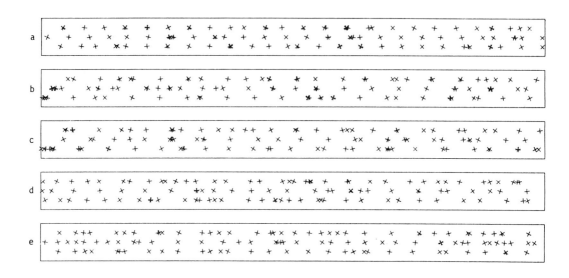

a β(a,b) distribution is

$$a/(a + b)$$

Since here also we would like to compare the different distributions with a common average density of
e points per unit, a multiplying factor must be
applied to the random values generated in [0,1] by
the cannons, in order to bring the mean interval to
1/e:

$$X = \beta(a,b) \left\lfloor \frac{a + b}{ae} \right\rfloor.$$

We then have cases (Figure 24) of time intervals in
the finite range [0,(a + b)/ae].

In our examples, since we have always set a = b,
the actual range is [0,2/e]. As compared with asymmetrical cases of Fig. 23, a greater homogeneity is
achieved even for (a), due to the fact that a sort of
basic pulsation is present, equal to the longest interval, 2/e, and the random values can be perceived as
subdivisions of this quasi-tempo. In (a), since
β(0.125, 0.125) greatly favors values near 0 and 1, we
have many configurations of this type:

with different numbers of short notes. From (a) to (e)
this characteristic becomes less important, since
mean values become more and more probable, until
reaching equiprobability in (e).

6.0 Conclusion

The preceding comparisons and examples are merely
suggested as starting points for composition. Even
with these stochastic generators specified, a central
problem in compositional design remains in applying these automata to some music processes. There
is no limit to the use of stochastic variables in
music. For instance, the points of Fig. 23 could be
read as lists of selected pitches on a frequency axis,
and they could then be used as material for further
development. The durations of sounds could be controlled by some symmetrically centered distribu-

tion, or by some time interval distribution—perhaps different from the ones controlling attack times.

Going beyond these direct applications of static stochastic processes, one may devise stochastic transitions between different distributions. One distribution may be used to control the parameters of another distribution, creating a hierarchical stochastic system.

If probability is an answer to certain problems of compositional choice and selection, there still remains a lot to choose—the music is still left to be made!

7.0 Acknowledgments

I must once again express my deep gratitude to Iannis Xenakis for reading this manuscript and suggesting some modifications. I would also like to thank Michel Decoust and Jean-Claude Risset for providing the occasion of putting nearly all the content of this paper into practice in my tape piece, *Les portes du sombre Dis* (IRCAM, Paris, 1979).

References

1. Aetius. 1976. From *Epicure et les épicuriens*. Paris: P.U.F.
2. Calot, G. 1976. *Cours de calcul des probabilités*. Paris: Dunod.
3. Charles, Daniel. 1978. *Gloses sur John Cage*, coll. 10/18 no. 1212. Paris: U.G.E.
4. Da Vinci, Leonardo. 1942. Translated from *Carnets*, vol. 1. Paris: Gallimard.
5. Feller, William. 1966a. *An introduction to probability theory and its applications*, vol. I. New York: John Wiley.
6. Feller, William. 1966b. *An introduction to probability theory and its applications*, vol. II. New York: John Wiley.
7. Gnedenko, B. V., and Khintchine, A. La. 1969. *Introduction à la théorie des probabilités*, coll. Science-poche no. 9. Paris: Dunod.
8. Grossman, Israël, and Magnus, Wilhelm. *Groups and their graphs*, New Mathematical Library, no. 14. New York: Random House.
9. Guénon, René. 1946. *Les principes du calcul infinitésimal*, Paris: Gallimard.
10. Hamming, R. W. 1973. *Numerical methods for scientists and engineers*. New York: McGraw-Hill.
11. Hastings, C. Jr. 1955. *Approximations for digital computers*. Princeton: Princeton University Press.
12. Jacquard, A. 1976. *Les probabilités*, coll. Que Sais-Je, no. 1571. Paris: P.U.F.
13. Jöhnk, M. D. Erzeugung von betaverteilten und gammaverteilten Zufallzahlen. *Metrika* 8(1):5–15.
14. Kaegi, Werner. 1971. Musique et technologie dans l'Europe de 1970. *Musique et Technologie, La Revue Musicale* no. 268–269. Paris: Richard-Masse.
15. Kleppner, Daniel, and Ramsey, Norman. 1965. *Quick calculus*, New York: John Wiley.
16. Knuth, D. E. *The art of computer programming*, vol. II. Reading, Massachusetts: Addison-Wesley.
17. Koenig, G. M. 1971. *Observations on compositional theory*. Utrecht, The Netherlands: Instituut voor Sonologie.
18. Koenig, G. M. *Computer composition*. Utrecht, The Netherlands: Instituut voor Sonologie.
19. Lipschutz, S. 1965. *Probability*. Schaum's Outline Series. New York: McGraw-Hill.
20. Maurin, J. 1975. *Simulation déterministe du hasard*, Paris: Masson.
21. Piaget, Jean. 1973. *Le développement de la notion de temps chez l'enfant*. Paris: P.U.F.
22. Revault d'Allonnes, Olivier. 1973. *La création artistique et les promesses de liberté*. Paris: Klincksiek.
23. Russolo, Luigi. 1975. *L'art des bruits*, coll. Avant-gardes. Lausanne: L'Age d'Homme.
24. Schrage, Linus. A more portable Fortran random number generator. *ACM Transactions on Mathematical Software* 5(2):132.
25. *Scientific subroutine package*. IBM Corporation.
26. Vessereau, A. 1953. *La statistique*, coll. Que Sais-Je, no. 281. Paris: P.U.F.
27. Xenakis, Iannis. 1963. *Musiques formelles*, La Revue Musicale, no. 253–254. Paris: Richard-Masse.
28. Xenakis, Iannis. 1971a. *Musique architecture*, coll. Mutations-orientations no. 11, Casterman.
29. Xenakis, Iannis. 1971b. *Formalized music*. Bloomington, Indiana: Indiana University Press.

31

Kevin Jones
The Music Department
The City University
London
England

Compositional Applications of Stochastic Processes

Stochastic Processes

A *stochastic process* is a collection of random-variable quantities distributed in space or time. When a statistician makes use of a stochastic process, the object is to find basic patterns in a set of observed data that will provide more coherent information about that data. In practice, a situation of complete randomness, where there is no order, is unlikely to occur. Indeed, the concept of absolute randomness turns out to be extremely difficult to define mathematically (Chaitin 1975). Mathematicians have classified various types of *stochastic structures* as a basic framework for analysis of stochastic processes. When composers make use of stochastic structuring techniques in musical composition, they are usually approaching the problem from the other direction. The main interest is in a synthesis of a sequence of sound data within a structural framework. A *stochastic generative scheme* is a means of setting up and manipulating stochastic control structures. Although a composer has a different objective, mathematical techniques developed for analysis can be of great practical use in the formal, structured environment of computer music systems.

Previous Work

The pioneering algorithmic composition experiments of Hiller (1958) and of Xenakis (1971) are well known. Their programs have made use of simple stochastic constraints to generate output that can be transcribed into traditional notation and played by conventional instruments. At Utrecht, Koenig (1971a) has developed stochastic composing

Computer Music Journal, Vol. 5, No. 2, Summer 1981

routines that permit the user to specify parametric boundaries within a choice of differing degrees of control. Truax (1973) has incorporated structures similar to Koenig's *tendency masks* in his POD systems, which offer possibilities for limited random variation. For digital microsound synthesis, Roads (1978) used a unit called an *event*, similar to a tendency mask, to encapsulate thousands of short-duration *grains* of sound. In spite of these activities, some skepticism has remained over the "controllability" of stochastic techniques in composition. This is a needless concern, since stochastic generative schemes may produce results that sound far more ordered than what might be produced by a supposedly deterministic system.

Uses and Justifications for Stochastic Techniques

Stochastic techniques offer, first of all, a useful means of data reduction. Computer music systems require accurate specification of all parameters concerned in defining a sound. This may be several times as much information as a common instrumental score would supply; a complex sound may require vast amounts of input data and instructions.

By defining sets of parameter limits within which actual values may be generated stochastically, one can reduce significantly the amount of labor required. This is no abdication of composer responsibilities. In the past, composers have always relied on performers' interpretations or on random environmental influences for fine control of such parameters as intonation, precise duration, timbre, and intensity. As always, the choice of which parameters will be specified manually and which will be specified procedurally is up to the composer.

Stochastic techniques may also produce unanticipated possibilities, where the bonds of a restrictive and inaccurate acoustic theory and of a limited aural imagination may be broken. Such an approach only suits some composers, but the author has been delighted by stochastic serendipity on many occasions. In addition, it is possible to use stochastic techniques for overall structural control. For example, one can stochastically control the progressive modulation from one structural type to another by a gradual separation process plotted through a regulated sequence of steps. In this way, a composer is following a precedent formed by centuries of tradition, since many composers in the past have made use of formal calculations to structure their work. Finally, electronic and computer music is frequently criticized for sounding too fastidiously sterile, too regular, and hence too artificial. Stochastic techniques may be used to produce *fuzzy edges* and to "humanize" computer-generated sounds.

Probability Assignment over an Event Space

When a stochastic structure is applied in musical composition, it is necessary to define an *event space* over which it operates. An event space is an ordered set of events that may consist of a natural sequence of common musical material such as the notes in the major scale of C, individually defined sound complexes, selected natural sounds, or whatever basic compositional elements a composer may require. The order of an event space is the number of events it contains.

The most basic type of stochastic structure is a simple probability distribution over an event space. This is represented in software as an array that specifies a set of probabilities corresponding to the elements of the event space. The size of the array must equal the order of the event space, and the sum of the probabilities should be 1. If the probabilities in the assignment are equal, then what can be called an *aleatoric process* will ensue, with all events equally likely to occur. Over time, there will be no evident pattern in any resulting generated sequence. Short sequences containing a very small number of events might, however, appear to have some sort of predetermined quality, as is apparent at the beginning of the author's 1977 tape composition *Macricisum*. Lorrain (1980) describes in detail

how to program and test various probability distributions, so there is no need to enter into those mechanics here. However, one definition should be reviewed. In a program, an efficient way to use a probability distribution is to stepwise-sum it, comparing a random number to the accumulated value in an array. This array holds what Lorrain calls the *cumulative function* (a stepwise-summed probability distribution).

The Random Decaying Function

The author has made use of a probability distribution defined by a *random decaying function* in composing the 1979 orchestral movement *Firelake*, where a random-integer generator was made to call itself recursively. The function RND(N) will produce an integer between 1 and N. The function RND(RND(N)) will therefore produce integers weighted toward 1. So when used over an event space of order n, event e_1 will occur most of all, event e_2 not quite so often, and so on, with event e_n hardly occurring at all. The assignment was applied over a number of different musical event spaces. For example, pitches were derived from an event space defined as the chromatic scale built upon the note G, which served as a quasi-tonal center. The lengths of multiple events, the durations of pauses, and certain rhythmic patterns were all derived from the same function.

Markov Chains

In the systems so far described, the probabilities remain constant over a period of time. More sophisticated control mechanisms may be constructed by using a *Markov chain* that takes into account the context of an event in a sequence making the probability of its occurrence depend on the event that preceded it. In this way a *matrix* of probabilities over an event space may be built up. The row of probabilities corresponding to the first event is used to derive the next event (Lorrain 1980). The row corresponding to the new event is used to derive the next event, and so on for the required sequence length; hence the chain aspect of this kind of stochastic algorithm.

When one defines a Markov chain for a specific musical task, a number of properties of events can be very useful for describing relationships and classifications. These properties are examined in greater detail elsewhere by the author, and brief intuitive proofs of some of the results are given (Jones 1980b). A more detailed mathematical treatment may be found in the literature (Arthurs 1965; Lakacs 1966; Romanovsky 1970; Bhat 1972). A summary of some of these properties follows.

Properties of Markov Chain Events

If an event e_i can be followed by event e_j, then e_j is said to be *accessible* from e_i. If events e_i and e_j are both accessible from each other, then they are said to *communicate*. The communication relation has the three properties associated with an *equivalence relation*. It is *reflexive*: event e_i communicates with itself. It is *symmetric*: if event e_i communicates with event e_j, then event e_j communicates with event e_i. It is *transitive*: if event e_i communicates with event e_j and event e_j communicates with event e_k, then event e_i communicates with event e_k. Thus groups of communicating events can be split into *equivalence classes* of events. The events in one equivalence class will not communicate with any event in another equivalence class, but an event in one equivalence class may be accessible from an event in a different equivalence class. In musical composition, separation into equivalence classes of communicating events provides a convenient way of grouping events into a temporal or sequential hierarchy. This is clarified in the example explained later.

If after an event e_i has occurred it is at some stage certain to occur again, then it is said to be *recurrent*. If there is a possibility that an event will not recur, it is said to be *transient*. It can be shown that if an event e_i is recurrent, then all events with which it communicates are also recurrent. Similarly if an event e_i is transient, all events with

which it communicates will also be transient. Thus recurrence and transience are both class properties, and any Markov chain can be divided into groups of recurrent and transient classes of events.

Some important results follow from this classification that are of great value in analyzing and constructing Markov chains for musical composition. Once a process has left a transient class of events it cannot return to it. On the other hand, once a process has entered a recurrent class, it cannot move out of it. It forms a *closed set*. Thus if a recurrent class consists of just one event, it is called an *absorbing event*. A Markov chain must contain at least one recurrent class. It cannot contain transient classes only. A Markov chain consisting only of one recurrent class (and no transient classes) is irreducible. A Markov chain containing exactly one recurrent class (and possibly some transient classes) is known as an *ergodic* Markov chain. It is possible to make useful predictions about its behavior and eventual outcome. (It is also necessary that the Markov chain should not contain *periodic classes*. For a further discussion and development of periodicity in Markov chains see writings by Jones [1980b] and Romanovsky [1970].) Whether a chain is ergodic or nonergodic makes a significant difference for the type of musical task to which it may be applied.

A Musical Example of Markov Chains

A Markov chain of order eight is defined by the stochastic matrix in Fig. 1. Next to the matrix is a corresponding event-relation diagram that helps one to visualize the structure. (This Markov chain is derived from an example in Kaufman's book [1968].) The events are grouped into equivalence classes $C_1 - C_4$. Classes C_1, C_3, and C_4 consist of transient events. C_2 is the only recurrent class, so this is an ergodic Markov chain. It can be seen that the process will always settle to the events in the equivalence class C_2, when event e_2 will tend to occur twice as often as event e_1. Five possible event sequences that might be generated

Fig. 1. A Markov chain of
order eight (a) and its corresponding event-relation
diagram (b).

(a)

		1	2	3	4	5	6	7	8
					Next Events				
Current Events	1	0	1	0	0	0	0	0	0
$P =$	2	.5	.5	0	0	0	0	0	0
	3	.1	.1	.4	.4	0	0	0	0
	4	0	.2	0	0	.8	0	0	0
	5	0	0	.5	.5	0	0	0	0
	6	.1	0	.1	0	.1	.7	0	0
	7	0	0	0	0	.4	0	.3	.3
	8	0	.2	0	.2	0	0	.6	0

(b)

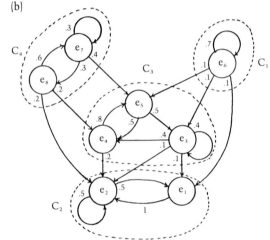

from this matrix are as follows:

$S_1 = e_6\, e_6\, e_3\, e_3\, e_4\, e_5\, e_5\, e_4\, e_2\, e_2\, e_1\, e_2\, e_1\, e_2\, e_1\, e_2\, e_2$
$\quad\; e_2$

$S_2 = e_6\, e_6\, e_6\, e_6\, e_1\, e_2\, e_1\, e_2\, e_1\, e_2\, e_2\, e_1\, e_1\, e_2\, e_1\, e_2\, e_1$
$\quad\; e_2\, e_2$

$S_3 = e_8\, e_4\, e_2\, e_2\, e_1\, e_2\, e_1\, e_2\, e_2\, e_2\, e_2\, e_1\, e_2\, e_2\, e_1\, e_2\, e_1$
$\quad\; e_2$

$S_4 = e_7\, e_8\, e_7\, e_8\, e_4\, e_5\, e_4\, e_2\, e_2\, e_2\, e_2\, e_1\, e_2\, e_2\, e_2\, e_2\, e_1$
$\quad\; e_2\, e_1\, e_2\, e_1\, e_2$

$S_5 = e_8\, e_7\, e_8\, e_4\, e_5\, e_4\, e_5\, e_4\, e_5\, e_3\, e_2\, e_2\, e_1\, e_2\, e_1\, e_2\, e_2$
$\quad\; e_1\, e_2\, e_2\, e_2$

With the event space defined in Fig. 2, these five
sequences will transcribe as shown in Fig. 3. A
comparison of these sequences with the event-relation diagram of the original Markov chain (Fig. 1)
helps to show the musical significance of the different equivalence classes of events.

A Special Case

A special type of Markov chain is the *random-walk*
process. Such a process can only move from an
event e_i to an adjacent event e_{i+1} or e_{i-1}. The matrix
representation of this process has nonzero entries
immediately on either side of the main diagonal
and zeros elsewhere. The random-walk process was
used to control very small incremental changes in
sonic structure, a form of *adjunctive synthesis*

(Jones 1980*a*), in the second study, "Laitrapartial,"
of the author's composition *Macricisum*. The event
space consisted of the harmonics on a given fundamental. The process changed in steps of 1/20 sec.
Twenty such processes were made to operate simultaneously. For some generations a bias was introduced into the process, encouraging upward
movement through the higher harmonics or, alternatively, downward movement toward the fundamental. The aural result was to produce crystalline
shimmering sheets of sound full of complex intermingling harmonics.

The simple probability assignments considered
initially are also a special case of a Markov chain in
which all the rows are equal; the probability of
each event's occurrence will remain the same no
matter which event has preceded it.

Extensions of Markov Chains

The Markov chain structure itself may be extended
in a number of useful ways. These include increasing the order of the Markov system, turning events
from scalar values to vectors, and introducing the
notion of a finite-state grammar.

Fig. 2. An event space for a
simple clarinet piece. (Music printing by Leland
Smith.)

Nth-Order Markov Chains

A three-dimensional Markov chain may be used where the occurrence probability of an event depends on the two preceding events. The probabilities are represented by a three-dimensional stochastic matrix. With greater dependence between events a tighter, more regular pattern structure will be defined. Three-dimensional Markov chains were used to generate rhythms in the third study, "Skirtriks," of *Macricisum*. A two-event space consisting simply of "long" and "short" notes was used. Regular rhythmic patterns were produced in this way that occasionally shift or move out of step, creating a fallible, spontaneous-sounding result. Three-dimensional Markov chains may be further generalized to *n*-dimensions, also called Markov chains of the *n*th order, where the occurrence probability of an event depends on the preceding *n*−1 events. Taken too far, however, such

structures can become unwieldy and almost impossible to use.

Markov Chains with Event Vectors

A different extension is to use Markov chains with *event vectors*. Each event, instead of being considered as a single entity, is described by an event vector that contains the values of a number of controlling parameters, themselves defined by a set of event-parameter spaces. A different Markov chain may be used to control each parameter, or a Markov chain may control more than one parameter. Markov chains with event vectors were used throughout the composition *Macricisum*, but their application is clearest in the first study of that piece, "Sonatanos." Here, each event vector defined a block of clustered points of sound in terms of the following parameters: pitch range, overall pitch,

Fig. 3. Five possible event sequences formed by the application of the Markov chain of Fig. 1 over the event space of Fig. 2. (Music printing by Leland Smith.)

Fig. 3 (Cont'd)

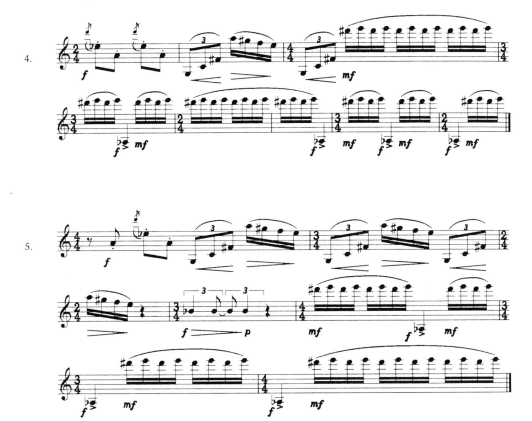

block length, density, intensity, following silence, envelope of elements, harmonic spectrum of elements, and spatial position. Each of these parameters could assume just two values, 1 or 2, which specified a higher or lower range or a choice between two alternatives. Where a range was specified, the individual elements that went toward making up the sound block were chosen stochastically within the specified limits. A set of nine Markov chains, each of order two, were used to control the nine parameters.

Finite-State Grammars

By far the most powerful and potentially exciting extension of Markov chains comes about when use is made of structures from formal linguistics. Formal grammars have been suggested as a powerful means of specifying data in computer music systems (Buxton 1978; Roads 1979; Holtzman 1979). A formal grammar consists of a set of symbols; a set of terminals or events that correspond to the event space in the schemes described previously; a set of production rules, which specify ways in which symbols may be rewritten by combinations of symbols and terminals; and a starting symbol, which is used to begin the generative process. The basic relationships in a Markov chain may be represented by a type of grammar known as a *finite-state grammar* or *Chomsky Type-3 grammar* (Chomsky 1963). In such grammars, each production rule specifies that a symbol may be replaced only by an event followed by one other symbol or by a single event that terminates the process. In this way a linear structure is built up.

Stochastic Grammars

More general context-free grammars, without the linear, one-token-at-a-time restriction on production rules, can produce whole strings of symbols in a single operation. For the types of musical application with which this article is concerned, a stochastic grammar may be used. A stochastic grammar includes a probability assignment over the ordered set of production rules. It is thereby possible to set up a generative structure associating probabilities with each choice of generation possibilities. The definition of a working stochastic grammar is rather difficult. Owing to the complex embedded structures that result, it is possible that a set of productions may never terminate unless provisions for termination are provided. As fast as one branch terminates, another may split into a further set of generations. It is necessary to apply a test for consistency. This is done by setting up a first-moment matrix M similar to a stochastic matrix, with rows and columns corresponding to the ordered set of symbols. Each entry m_{ij} in the matrix is calculated by adding the probabilities associated with each production rule in which symbol V_i is replaced by a sequence including V_j. The stochastic grammar is consistent if the modulus of the largest *eigenvalue*[1] of M is less than 1, in which case any set of generations can be guaranteed to terminate (Gonzales and

Thomason 1978, p. 189). If the grammar is inconsistent, it is likely to generate ad infinitum, and is therefore of no practical use.

Space Grammars

What is called here a *space grammar* can operate across many dimensions. Thus when such a grammar is applied in a musical context, the parameters specifying simultaneously occurring events are intrinsically related to one another as well as to their temporal neighbors. All musical grammatical events are computed in a logical rather than time-sequential order.

One-Dimensional Space Grammars

A simple stochastic grammar is defined as consisting only of a single variable A and a single terminal a. A set R consisting of the following two production rules is defined.

$$A \to AA \qquad (1)$$
$$A \to a \qquad (2)$$

A probability array $P = (p_1, p_2)$ is applied over the set R to determine which production rules should be applied. The sum of p_1 and p_2 will be 1, and p_2 must be greater than p_1 to guarantee termination of a sequence of generations. Obviously, a string of a's per se makes little structural sense. However, the syntactic structure responsible for generating the string may be preserved if the grammar is applied to divide up the space, in this case a one-dimensional straight line, such that whenever rule (1) is applied, the space is split at the center, leaving two halves to be subdivided by further applications of the grammar, and whenever rule (2) is applied, the splitting process will cease. A possible derivation tree of a sequence generated by this simple grammar is shown in Fig. 4. This can be interpreted musically as a means of dividing up the *time-space* that will generate the rhythmic structure transcribed at the bottom of the figure.

An increase in the value of p_1 will cause generations to split to a greater depth, resulting in a fast

1. The eigenvalues of a matrix M are the set of solutions λ to the equation $|M - \lambda I| = 0$, where λ is a scalar variable and I is the identity matrix.

Jones

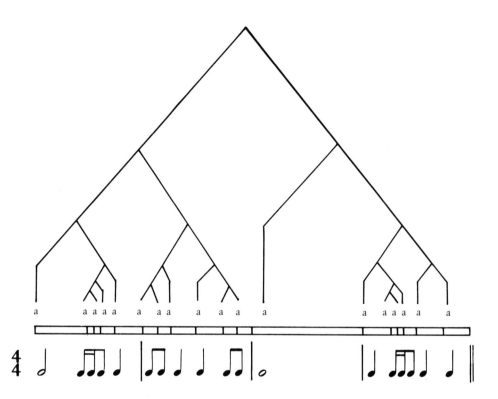

Fig. 4. A spatial and rhythmic interpretation of the derivation tree.

rhythm with many notes of short duration. An increase in the value of p_2 will produce the reverse effect, resulting in more long notes.

Two-Dimensional Space Grammars

The grammar can be extended into two dimensions if one introduces an additional production rule. The symbol $/_n$ will be introduced, indicating a split in the nth dimension. Thus the three production rules are now:

$$A \rightarrow A /_1 A \qquad (1)$$
$$A \rightarrow A /_2 A \qquad (2)$$
$$A \rightarrow a \qquad (3)$$

If applied over the two-dimensional plane, produc-

tion rule (1) will divide the plane vertically and production rule (2) will divide the plane horizontally. It is necessary also to redefine the probability array

$$P = (\, p_1 \, , p_2 \, , p_3 \,).$$

It is not convenient to construct a tree diagram when operating such a grammar in two dimensions, but Fig. 5 demonstrates a method of representing a possible application of the grammar.

When used to divide up the plane, this sequence of productions will produce the result shown in Fig. 6. If the probabilities in P are adjusted to increase p_1 and favor vertical divisions, structures such as those in Fig. 7 will result. When interpreted musically with time moving horizontally and pitches on the vertical axis, an increase in p_1 will favor sequential activity; notes will generally be

Fig. 5. Application of a
two-dimensional space
grammar.

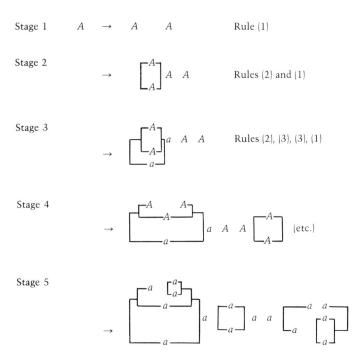

Stage 1 $A \rightarrow A \quad A$ Rule (1)

Stage 2   Rules (2) and (1)

Stage 3   Rules (2), (3), (3), (1)

Stage 4   (etc.)

Stage 5

Fig. 5. Application of a two-dimensional space grammar.

shorter and change more frequently. An increase in p_2 will favor simultaneous activity; generally longer notes will sound in continuously shifting chordal groupings. When a scale of pitches is mapped along the vertical axis and time is mapped along the horizontal axis, Fig. 7(b) is transcribed into the form of the short piano fragment of Fig. 8.

Adding the Null Production

The grammar can be made more powerful by adding a *null production*, $A \rightarrow \phi$, which will reserve an empty space in the structure without actually filling it. Adjusting the probability associated with the null production with respect to the probability of the terminal production (rule [3] described previously) will vary the overall event density of the resulting structure.

Such a grammar was used to generate note data used as input to the Music V sound synthesis program. The grammar adapts conveniently into the recursive procedure definition given in Code Listing 1.

The procedure "note" merely writes the appropriate Music V data statement to "play" a note with values of start, finish, and intensity applying when it is called. By repeatedly calling itself, this short "compose" procedure will generate an entire compositional structure. A considerable variety of output can be achieved by changing the probabilities to vary the horizontal/vertical ratio, the overall sound density, and the depth of detail. In the version of the procedure in Code Listing 1, all the probabilities are equal. Figure 9 is a graphic score representing a sound structure generated by this procedure with the initial call

    compose (1,10,1500);

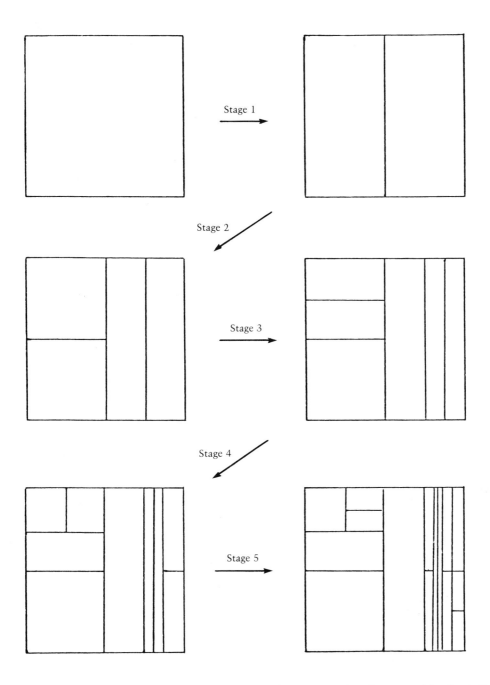

Fig. 6. Stages in a sequence of derivations in application of a two-dimensional space grammar.

Stage 1

Stage 2

Stage 3

Stage 4

Stage 5

Fig. 7. The plane divided
by a two-dimensional
space grammar with a
slight bias toward vertical
divisions.

Fig. 8. A transcription of
Fig. 7(b) into common mu-
sical notation. (Music
printing by Leland Smith.)

(a)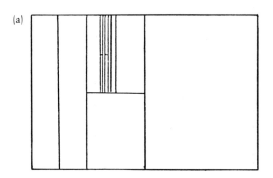

(b)

Fig. 8

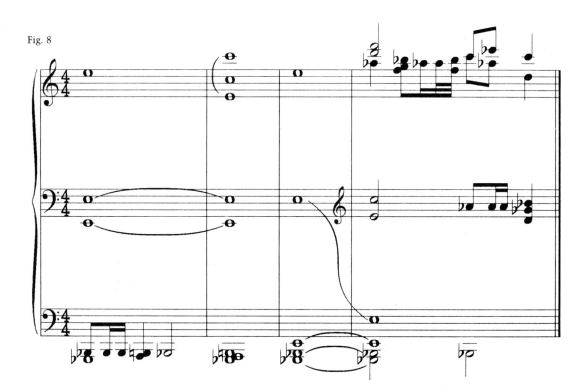

Code Listing 1. Procedure
compose.

Fig. 9. A pitch/time score
of sound data generated
by a two-dimensional
space grammar.

```
procedure compose (var start, finish, intensity: real);
type
  branch = (vertical, horizontal, sound, silence);
var
  production: branch;
begin {work}
  {choose_branch is a procedure, which selects one element of the branch type each time it is called}
  production: = choose_branch;
  case production of
    vertical:    begin {v}
                   mid: = start + (finish − start)/2;
                   compose (start, mid, intensity);
                   compose (mid, finish, intensity)
                 end {v}
    horizontal: begin {h}
                   compose (start, finish, intensity/2);
                   compose (start, finish, intensity/2)
                 end {h}
    sound:       note (start, finish, intensity); {writes a note}
    silence:
  end {case}
end {work}
```

Fig. 9

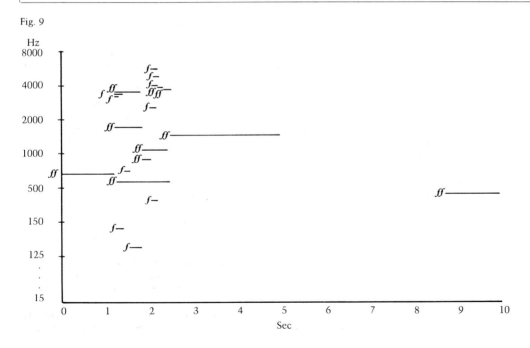

*Fig. 10. Dividing a block
using a three-dimensional
space grammar.*

(a) (b)

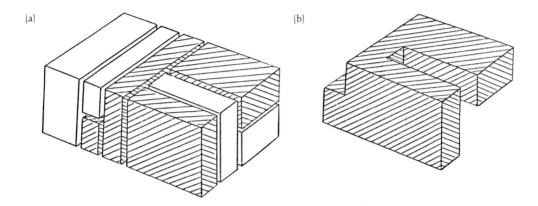

Three-Dimensional Space Grammars

The addition of a third production rule will give a total of five alternatives:

$$A \rightarrow A/_1 A \qquad (1)$$
$$A \rightarrow A/_2 A \qquad (2)$$
$$A \rightarrow A/_3 A \qquad (3)$$
$$A \rightarrow a \qquad (4)$$
$$A \rightarrow \phi \qquad (5)$$

A typical string generated with these production rules could be the following:

$$(\phi/_3 ((\phi/_2 \, a))/_3 ((a/_1 \phi)/_1 \, (a/_2 \, \phi))$$

By extending the previous operations, one may use this to divide up a three-dimensional block by slicing it in half across the width when rule (1) is applied, vertically when rule (2) is applied, and lengthwise when rule (3) is applied. Thus the preceding string is equivalent to the block in Fig. 10(a). Chunks terminated by rule (4) are shaded; chunks generated by rule (5), the null production, are not. These empty chunks have been removed in Fig. 10(b), leaving only the block that has been generated by the grammar. Two additional blocks generated by this same grammar are given in Fig. 11. Each block in this figure is the inverse of the other; a's have been replaced by ϕ's, and vice versa.

If one varies the relation between the p_4 and p_5 probabilities, the solid density of the structure pro-

duced varies. If p_5 is very small, a swiss-cheese-like structure that contains a few holes will result. If p_4 is roughly equal to p_5, a structure with a spongelike quality will result. If p_5 is large, then a few blocks will be left suspended in a largely empty space.

The structures may be mapped into a musical form in the same way as was done for a two-dimensional grammar. The block in Fig. 11(a), for example, may be separated into a series of slices across its width along an arbitrary "timbral plane" to produce the proto-score of Fig. 12.

The examples here have been kept simple for expository reasons and for clarity, but there is no reason why generations should not be continued to a very detailed level and the parameter scales expanded to produce very large and complex structures.

Multi-Dimensional Space Grammars

The basic concept of a space grammar can be extended to an arbitrary number of dimensions with productions of the form $A \rightarrow A /_n A$. This is ideal and even necessary for sophisticated compositional applications. Many dimensions can be useful: three dimensions to specify spatial location; dimensions for pitch, intensity, duration; and more dimensions for representing various timbral indices. Code Listing 2 gives a general form for a multidimensional

Fig. 11. A block (a) and its
inverse (b) both generated
by a three-dimensional
space grammar.

Fig. 12. A partial musical
transcription of the block
of Fig. 11(a).

(a)

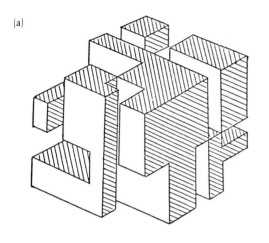

(b)

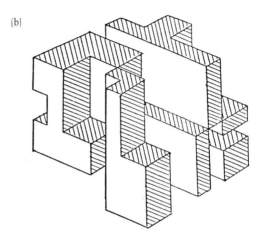

Fig. 12

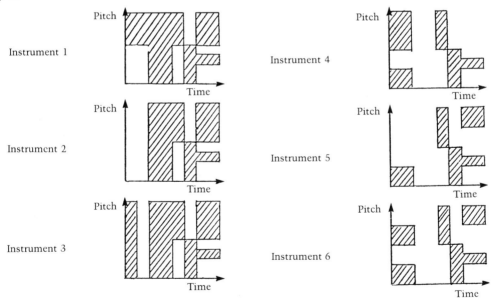

Code Listing 2. Procedure
compose_n

```
procedure compose_n (var L_1, U_1, L_2, U_2, ... L_n, U_n: real);
type branch = (d1, d2, ... dn, sound, silence);
var production: branch;
begin {compose_n}
    {choose_branch a dimension (d variables) to split or a note or silent event}
    production: = choose_branch;
    case production of
        d1:     begin {1}
                    mid: = (L_1 + (L_1 + U_1)/2;
                    compose (L_1, mid, L_2, U_2, ... L_n, U_n);
                    compose (mid, U_1, L_2, U_2, ... L_n, U_n);
                end {1}
        d2:     begin {2}
                    mid: = L_2 + (L_n + U_n)/2;
                    compose (L_1, U_1, L_2, mid, ... L_n, U_n);
                    compose (L_1, U_1, mid, U_2, ... L_n, U_n);
                end
        :
        dn:     begin {n}
                    mid: = L_n + (L_n + U_n)/2;
                    composer (L_1, U_1, ... L_n, mid);
                    compose (L_1, U_1, ... mid, U_n);
                end
        sound: note (L_1, U_1, L_2, U_2, ... L_n, U_n);
        silence:
    end {case}
end {compose_n}
```

space-grammar procedure. In this algorithm, the variable L_i is the lower value limit for the dimension i, while U_i is the upper limit for i.

An additional procedural parameter may be incorporated to monitor the depth of generations. The "choose_branch" procedure selects the appropriate production, making use of a probability array. By changing simple control probabilities, large amounts of material with a great variety of character may be generated. Macro and micro structures may be generated by one procedure that can operate to as great a depth of detail as is desirable or practical. Further extensions of this skeleton space grammar would be possible if one defined a larger set of variables and alternative terminal functions, and made structural divisions at other than equal ratios, for example, at the Golden Section. This article has

merely scratched the surface of what is an extensive and largely unmapped area of compositional exploration.

"So vast is the scope that lies open to things far and wide without limit in any dimension."

Lucretius, Book One

Conclusion

This article has described a number of different types and applications of stochastic processes. Many of these have shown themselves to have practical potential, and a great deal of research remains to be done in their exploration and development. Stochastic approaches can be applied in music analysis, sound synthesis, and composition. There is also much useful research to be done in the psychoacoustic perception of stochastic music structures.

References

Arthurs, A. M. 1965. *Probability Theory*. London: Routledge and Kegan Paul.

Bhat, U. N. 1972. *Elements of Applied Stochastic Processes*. New York: Wiley.

Buxton, W. et al. 1978. "The Use of Hierarchy and Instance in a Data Structure for Computer Music." *Computer Music Journal* 2(4): 10–20.

Chaitin, G. 1975. "Randomness and Mathematical Proof." *Scientific American* 232(5): 47–54.

Chomsky, N. 1963. "Formal Properties of Grammars." In *Handbook of Mathematical Psychology Volume II*, ed. R. Luce, R. Bush, and E. Galanter. New York: Wiley.

Gonzales, R. C., and M. G. Thomason. 1978. *Syntactic Pattern Recognition, An Introduction*. Reading, Massachusetts: Addison-Wesley.

Hiller, L., and L. Isaacson. 1958. *Experimental Music*. New York: McGraw-Hill.

Holtzman, S. R. 1979. *Generative Grammar Definitional Language*. Edinburgh: Edinburgh University Department of Computer Science.

Jones, K. J. 1980a. "Sound Generating Techniques on the ITT 2020 and Apple II Computers." In *Proceedings of the Conference on Computer Music in Britain*. London: Electro-acoustic Music Association of Great Britain.

Jones, K. J. 1980b. "Computer Assisted Application of Stochastic Structuring Techniques in Musical Composition and Control of Digital Sound Synthesis Systems." Ph.D. thesis, The City University, London.

Kaufman, A. A. 1968. *Des points et des fleches: la théorie des graphes*. Paris: Dunod.

Koenig, G. M. 1971a. *Project One*. Utrecht: Institute of Sonology.

Koenig, G. M. 1971b. "The Use of Computer Programs in Creating Music." In *Music and Technology*. Paris: UNESCO/La Revue Musicale.

Lakacs, L. 1966. *Stochastic Processes*. London: Methuen.

Lorrain, D. 1980. "A Panoply of Stochastic 'Cannons.'" *Computer Music Journal* 4(1): 53–81.

Roads, C. 1978. "Automated Granular Synthesis of Sound." *Computer Music Journal* 2(2): 62–63.

Roads, C. 1979. "Grammars as Representations for Music." *Computer Music Journal* 3(1): 48–55.

Romanovsky, V. I. 1970. *Discrete Markov Chains*. Groningen: Woltzer-Noordhoff.

Truax, B. D. 1973. "The Computer Composition—Sound Synthesis Programs POD4, POD5 and POD6." Sonological Report 2. Utrecht: Institute of Sonology.

Xenakis, I. 1971. *Formalized Music*. Bloomington: Indiana University Press.

32

Gottfried Michael Koenig
Institute of Sonology
Plompetorengracht 14-16
3512 CD Utrecht, The Netherlands

Aesthetic Integration of Computer-Composed Scores

Introduction

I have been involved with the algorithmic description of composition processes for about 30 years. My interest started with the analysis of music composed in a strict style (like Bach's or Webern's), and compositions of my own in which the material was to be organized according to a plan. Instrumental music in this category consisted of several pieces for chamber ensemble and orchestra (1952–1955), piano pieces (1957), a woodwind quintet (1958–1959), and a string quartet (1959).

My interest in algorithmic description was reinforced by my involvement with electronic music, which, owing to new kinds of production techniques using electroacoustic devices, required more intensive planning. This period is documented by my *Klangfiguren I* and *II* (1955–1956), *Essay* (1957–1958), and *Terminus I* (1962).

Eventually my attention focused on algorithmic description itself when, instead of obeying compositional rules, I started using a computer to carry them out. This led to my computer programs Project 1 (first version 1964–1966), Project 2 (first version 1965–1969), and my sound synthesis program SSP (1972–1979).

I was able to make certain observations, which I should like to mention in this outline, from the following computer-aided compositions: *Version 1* for 14 instruments (1965–1966), *Version 3* for 9 instruments (1967), *Segments 1–7* for piano (1982), *Segments 99–105* for violin and piano (1982), and *3 ASKO Pieces* for chamber orchestra (1982). I composed all these pieces with Project 1.

At present I am working, albeit sporadically, on

This essay is dedicated to Otto Laske.

Computer Music Journal, Volume 7, No. 4,
Winter 1983

another program (Project 3), which I call a *mentor system*. With it, I will carry on the work started with Project 1 and Project 2.

Modes of Production, Division of Labor

While I was occupied with the algorithmic description of compositional processes, I became increasingly aware of how much the planning and execution of a compositional idea depend on, or are influenced by, the mode of production (solo instrument, ensemble, improvisation, score, tape, synthesizer). By *mode of production*, I mean the technology and social circumstances of sound production. Social circumstances include the function of music (e.g., mythical and ritual, to the glory of God, court splendor, bourgeois status symbol, social contacts, amusement, the reinforcement of the communal spirit, education, mood setting, background, documentation of individuality by musical means), but they also include the social division of labor (solo performance, group performance, ensemble, large orchestra, music making in the home, such automata as music boxes and street organs, electronic sound production, loudspeaker performance). Production modes also include technique in a stricter sense, in the form of the technique of playing instruments, improvised or "from the score"; the extension of the body by complicated tools, such as the piano or organ; the use of electric current (electric and electronic music) and digital circuitry (computer processes). Increasing change, both in technology and in the social division of labor for purposes of musical sound production, gives rise to the question of how a composer reacts to the different variants of the production mode. I have not done any sociological or psychological research on this subject, but as a composer I have felt a need to react "functionally." This means that players should not be treated like generators, nor generators like players; to react functionally means not only to refrain from stylistic imitation, but also to refrain from imitation of a particular production mode in another medium.

Let us, for the sake of illustration, take a look at the relationship between instrumental and electronic music.

> *Instrumental music* involves a division of labor during performance of ensemble music and requires formalization (common tonal system, common metric time basis), yet it allows individual freedom: melody against a harmonic background, expressive rubato, counterpoint in independent parts. (Note that constant spectra are necessary in order to distinguish the parts.) Composition of instrumental music involves central planning.
>
> *Electronic music* involves no performance, hence no division of labor, hence no need for common tonal or metric systems. Melody, harmony, and counterpoint therefore lose their meaning, becoming historically and in a functional sense wrong. Division of labor is limited to the production process in the studio, which causes the composer's planning to acquire engineering dimensions.

If we stress the similarity between instrumental and electronic music instead of the difference, we can attempt a comparison with computer music. By computer music I mean the production of music as a languagelike process, not just the process of making sounds.

> *Instrumental and electronic music* together involve a division of labor between planning (composition) and execution (performance). Execution requires a division of labor between players in the orchestra and working processes in the electronic studio. This type of music embodies composition by a person, who is constantly exposed to psychological influences (memories, perceptions, associations) but who can, at will, write something down and correct it. This is a dynamic process.
>
> *Computer music* involves a division of labor that can be modified by additional formalization of

the composition process. In execution, the division of labor is extended to include transcription and interpretation of the computer printout. Music can be composed by a machine (which can receive no psychological feedback), meaning that time is suspended for the duration of the composing process. This process is static.

In computer music, the computer is introduced in the planning phase, thus splitting the unity inherent in the planning phase of instrumental and electronic music. This occasions a third comparison: that between electronic and computer music. We can forget instrumental music for the moment, because as far as the dynamic compositional act is concerned, it is no different from that in electronic music. Electronic music is a step in the development of computer music from instrumental music. Synthesizer circuits that produce music automatically, that is, algorithmically, belong by analogy to computer music.

> *Electronic music* involves redefinition of the dimensions freed from the production mode of instrumental music (free choice of tonal systems, rhythms, densities, spectra). The result of technical realization is put on tape directly, without any further intervention.
>
> *Computer music* involves a strategy which, freed from the psyche of the human composer, can be taken over by an algorithm. In the algorithm, the elements and methods (selection, permutation, conditional branching in the working schedule) are redefined. The result of algorithmic composition can be converted into performance categories that are foreign to it: voice leading, phrasing, and playing technique—in other words, into a voice model.

Time-Parameter Graphs

For algorithmic composition of instrumental (as well as digital) music, I have designed a *time-parameter graph* with an X (or T) axis for time and a Y (or P) axis for each musical parameter. Each parameter (frequency, degree of vibrato, etc.) has its

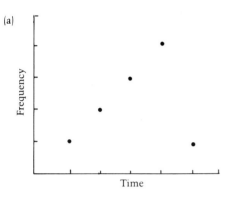

(a)

Frequency

Time

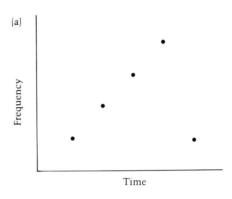

(a)

Frequency

Time

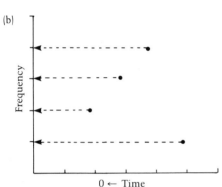

(b)

Frequency

0 ← Time

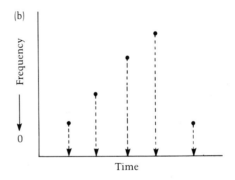

(b)

Frequency

0

Time

own P axis; but all the parameters have a common T axis. (This last condition can be omitted in electronic music and digital sound production.)

The time-parameter graph is meant to illustrate the transition from the composer to the algorithmic system. Imagine a given piece of music reduced to a duration of zero: all parameter data are then imprinted, so to speak, onto the P axes (Fig. 1). Similarly, we can reduce the same piece of music to a parameterless representation: this causes the parameters on the T axis to be imprinted where changes occur in them (Fig. 2). If we go on to imagine that the imprint on the axes becomes stronger as more data coincide at one point, we obtain the multiple histogram of that given piece of music with regard to the time and parameter values (Fig. 3). The histo-

gram cannot enable us to reconstruct the original piece of music, but it does contain characteristic features: rhythms and distributions of all parameter data with regard to the frequency of their occurrence. It resembles the preparations that composers accustomed to working constructively make before they start writing their scores.

A histogram is converted back into one of the many variants of the score by connecting all the imprints on the time axis with all the imprints on the parameter axes. Every time two pieces of data are connected, the imprints become shallower, until they disappear (Fig. 4). In terms of the histogram, the columns decrease by a uniform value with each connection, and all the columns must be used up entirely.

Aesthetic Integration of Scores   **401**

Fig. 3. Histogram for a parameter P_i (a) and for the
sequence of events in time
T in which several param-
eters are involved (b). In
(a), the length of a bar in-

dicates how often a pa-
rameter value was used; in
(b), the height of a bar indicates how many param-
eters were given a new
value at a particular time.

Fig. 4. Generating a variant of a composition.
Here, the parameter values
are redistributed in time.
The composer sets up the
parameter lists and also
influences data selection
by activating selection
algorithms. These algo-
rithms include random de-
cisions, so that when lists
and algorithms are identical, but random sequences
differ, different compositions can result. The problem for the composer is
to choose lists and algo-
rithms (including ones for

time values that affect the
rhythm) in such a way
that under restricted (but
unpredictable) random
conditions, a "meaning-
ful" composition will re-
sult. The graphs are
supposed to show that the
composer's musical idea—
the continuous data
flow—can be divided into
several operational terms
(parameters, selection criteria) that in their turn
can only be experienced
aesthetically in the time
medium after being
combined.

(a)

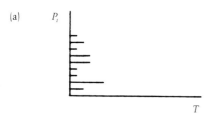

(b)

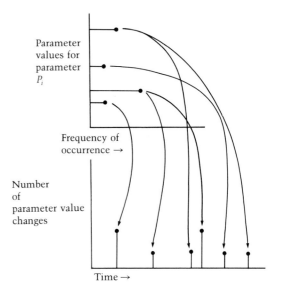

This model lends itself to algorithmic representation if the composer supplies the histograms
and the computer program takes care of the data
connections. Neither the histograms nor the connection algorithm contains any hints about the
envisaged, "unfolded" score, which consists of instructions for dividing the labor of the production
mode, that is, the division into performance parts.
The histogram, unfolded to reveal the individual
time and parameter values, has to be split up into
voices. The trivial condition is that they are "contained" in the histogram (and the connection algorithm); the nontrivial condition is that the parts
also fit into the historical situation (formed and at
the same time urged on by tradition).

Transcribing Scores

The algorithms combined in Project 1 are based on
ways of structuring musical time, as defined in the
techniques of serial and electronic music. The algorithms produce cycles of differing frequency (and
also of differing irregularity of movement), so that
constantly changing overlappings occur. This principle—a circular one—is not goal oriented; the result is static and consequently, I think, suited to

being split up into voices. This is because nothing
urges the music toward particular developments,
not even toward developments with an influence
on the instrumentation. The balanced distribution
of the material permits different interpretations.

Before embarking on transcription, it is advisable
to compare several printouts. To aid such comparison, Project 1 is linked with a sound system
(VOSIM Composite) that plays the composer a kind
of piano reduction. VOSIM produces pitches, entry
delays, and dynamics. It can also produce various
spectra and modify the durations, resulting in staccato tones or superpositions. In this fashion, instrumentation variants for the same score can be

Koenig

simulated. The general decision as to whether a printout is suitable for transcription is only made easier with regard to rhythm, tempo, harmony, and dynamic gradation. The sound system does not impart any information about the possible construction of a voice model, since the score is still presented as a sequence of chords.

Aesthetic Integration

By *aesthetic integration*, I mean the process by which the data of the computer printout are transformed into the "aesthetic object" we hear as a performed piece of music. It appears quite legitimate to substitute for performance a score for different performances of the same piece. This process is comparable to composing itself, because individual data that refer abstractly to one another but are not concretely fixed in time are given their final positions. The process might be compared to the path between an idea and its execution. The length of the path depends on the extent to which the computer program has been able to represent the abstract relationships as concrete time relations. The path depends also on how important this distinction is to the composer. I think that it would be very hard to find an algorithmic solution to this conflict between the idea and its representation in time, because the relation of the composition process (and thus of the aesthetic shape of the finished work) to the mode of performance (or execution) is of prime importance. Performance on traditional instruments requires that instructions be distributed over the parts and that each individual part be granted its historical rights. Algorithmic composing by division of labor introduces a new element while preserving what was given. The algorithms are incorporated into the general idea of a piece, whereas the musical data only sustain abstract relationships and the writing of the score, which gives these relationships a concrete form. The composing algorithm formalizes a critical instance that syntactically groups data that the composer has only roughly presorted, presenting the material in such a way that the composer—the first interpreter of the material—is given distinct information as to the mode of performance (i.e., as to playing technique in passing time).

Summary

Although the composition of music with or without computers depends to a great extent on subjectively experienced criteria, the algorithmic description of the production process adds an objective feature. Because of it, "form" is no longer the personal manner in which the musical material is presented or the listener's perception is guided; rather, it is the rationally discernible, reproducible effect, detached from the composer, of an organized system imposed on arbitrary material.

Composing programs may differ as to the variability of the input data or even to the extent to which the rules can be modified. In any case, composers must settle the conflict between the "objectified" grammar and their subjective awareness of form. Simple programs that leave the material in a relatively "natural" state force the composer to perform radical modifications on the result in a way that resembles "free" composition without a computer. This renders the use of a computer superfluous. More exacting programs mold the material down to the last detail, fending off any subsequent intervention. Composers have to accept the form resulting from the treatment of the material if they wish to avoid conflict with their own conception of form.

Form, here, is not merely a vessel, but a process that starts with the composer's inspiration and proceeds by way of design, execution, correction, and performance to the listener's ear and judgment. The conflict, then, is not due to any difference between the ideas of the writer of the program and the composer, but rather is due to the elimination of the composer during an important phase of the process. Even composers who like to experiment will want to bear responsibility for the aesthetic result, and will therefore try to come to terms with their own form criteria. In doing so, they enter territory that is at least as close to interpretation as to composing. The conflict can be described as long as it is concerned with the algorithm on the one hand and the composer's strategies on the other. Since, however, form is a process (or at any rate the result of processes that leave their traces), it is difficult to describe the conflict, which can only be resolved by making corrections, a process that, like the others, determines the form.

A practical example of the integration conflict is provided, say, by the task of scoring event "points" in the score as parts or lines. Such points (in time) are the result of entry delays[1] being distributed along the time axis; each point can also be given a vertical density value (chord size). In this fashion, a varying temporal density (speed) can be realized, possibly together with a vertical density curve. Lines (tone sequences) can result from an ensemble that does not allow any mass effects, such as a group of solo instruments. In such a case, scoring should satisfy the demand for every voice to have a "meaning"—to conform with the principles governing the harmony. (We are assuming the form pro-

cess to develop in the interaction of horizontal and vertical relationships of a harmonic, rhythmic, and spectral nature.)

Perhaps the integration conflict cannot be resolved because it is caused by peculiarities of the creative act that cannot be formalized or can be formalized only in special cases. The thing to do in such a case is to arrange the compositional algorithm so as to keep the conflict as small as possible or to have the result exhibit some tolerance for the composer's attempts at solution.

A possible aid is a sound-generating system that provides composers with an acoustic rendering of the result (or at least of the most important parameters, rather like a piano score), allowing them to make corrections before transcribing the printout. However useful such a method may be in investigating the conflict described here, it cannot do away with the conflict itself. It would be better to be able to influence the compositional algorithm continuously in order to obtain more insight into these matters. I am currently working on plans for such a system with the provisional title of Project 3.

1. In Project 1 and Project 2, the starting time of a note and its duration are independent. Entry delay is the temporal distance between two successive starting points.

33

Xavier Rodet and Pierre Cointe
IRCAM
31, rue Saint-Merri
F-75004 Paris, France

FORMES: Composition and Scheduling of Processes

Introduction

> Trouver une forme qui accomode le gachis,
> telle est actuellement la tâche de l'artiste—
> Samuel Beckett

For some time, it has been recognized that the development and use of complex systems has been stifled by the inadequacy of ordinary programming languages (Winograd 1979). Music composition and synthesis (MCS) by computer offers a particularly clear example of this "complexity barrier." In the 1970s, a new generation of interactive languages appeared (Cointe 1983), establishing the concepts of *active objects* and *message passing* as a control structure for computation. It is significant that object-oriented programming matches most of the requirements of MCS.

Toward a solution to problems of complexity in computer music, an object-oriented programming environment called FORMES has been developed and implemented at IRCAM. It supports a new language with original features for composition and scheduling of objects. FORMES "processes" are obviously not in exact correspondence with musical processes as perceived by the listener.

FORMES is an interactive system first intended for MCS. However, by virtue of its unique architecture, its flexibility, and its ease of use, it should find applications in a large number of domains such as graphics animation and speech synthesis. Composers use FORMES for score development and sound synthesis. As an example, *Chreode*, a piece composed with FORMES by Jean-Baptiste Barrière, won

the International Bourges Festival award in 1983 (Barrière 1983).

Why is MCS one of the most interesting fields for testing advanced technology for computing? In MCS, perhaps even more than in artificial intelligence, programs have to be tested, modified, and rewritten very often. This modification must be effected quickly and easily; otherwise, the continuity between musical ideas and results gets lost. The complexity usually involved in human composing activity is far beyond what we are nowadays able to code in a few weeks or months. At the same time, scientists and musicians cannot be hampered by esoteric or "hairy" programs in the course of sophisticated musical research. Thus, "friendly" interaction is not a wish but a necessity. Finally, the system must be interactive and fast enough to control a real-time synthesizer.

Requirements of MCS

We developed FORMES after several years of experience in MCS research and production, including our CHANT system (Bennett 1981; Rodet and Bennett 1980; Rodet, Potard, and Barrière 1984). In MCS, the aim of a musician is to capture a certain musical image. An MCS program is an attempt to find and realize this image—using models that implement our knowledge about sound production and perception—within a particular compositional context. Consequently FORMES provides a framework to manipulate and integrate these models as basic building blocks or objects. These models are characterized by their contribution to synthesis and by their (temporal) behavior irrespective of implementation details.

Desirable properties of MCS models include the following, all of which are goals of the FORMES system:

1. Generality: Apart from a specific application a model should not be a portrait of a

particular sound or note but should be as general a representation of a process as possible (e.g., a model of a crescendo or an attack pattern should apply to as many different sounds as possible).

2. Universality: A model should try to be independent of a particular synthesis technique and should refer to universal concepts as found in acoustics and psychoacoustics.

3. Compatibility: Models should be applicable in any context in which they are placed. In any combination they should gracefully cooperate and interact in the universe created by the composer.

4. Simplicity of program text: Models will be much simpler if they follow common human communication conventions and presuppositions (e.g., default values everywhere).

5. Ease of use: For certain interactions, (close to) natural language communication constructs facilitate the apprenticeship and use of that system. Otherwise simple and clear symbolism should be used. Invocation, modification, and integration of models should be direct and easy.

6. Modularity and hierarchical construction: The complexity of models necessitates that they be built from submodels. By such a construction, it is also possible to integrate different specific behaviors into a new and more general one.

Objects and Message Passing

The concepts of objects (actors) and message passing were introduced in computer science by O. Dahl, A. Kay, and C. Hewitt, and first developed by the languages Simula, Smalltalk, and Plasma (Birtwistle and Dahl 1973; Kay 1969; Hewitt 1976). These concepts constitute a very apt response to MCS demands.

Simula introduced the concept of a hierarchical organization of *classes*: a class describes the set of functions that operate on its instances. This is adequate for properties 1, 3, and 6, mentioned above.

Simulation by the management of several processes also appears in Simula.

Plasma (Planner) introduced the concept of *actor*. Each entity of the language is an actor communicating with other actors by a message-sending mechanism using a selective reception of messages by pattern matching (Hewitt and Smith 1975; Hewitt 1976, Pomian 1980; Durieux 1981). An offspring of Plasma called Act 1 perfected message sending by allowing inheritance properties with *delegation*: instead of refusing a message an actor can delegate it to another actor (Lieberman 1981). Plasma and Act 1 made possible the definition of complex control-structures such as backtracking, coroutining, and simultaneous activation of the same actor (Durieux 1981). This is a great help in managing complex musical structures and tasks (Lieberman 1982).

The development of Smalltalk systems (Kay and Goldberg 1976; Ingalls 1978; Goldberg and Robson 1983) and office machines such as the Xerox Star system (Smith 1983) with a bitmapped screen and mouse pointer has motivated the development of interactive software tools using graphic devices (Cointe 1982a, 1982b). With its syntax and structure, Smalltalk is particularly adapted to properties 4–6.

Implementation of multiple windows, graphics editing, and menu systems is greatly facilitated by the use of objects, classes, and inheritance. Several newer-generation Lisp dialects include the concept of objects. A prime example is the Lisp Machine Flavor system (Moon and Weinreb 1980; Cointe 1981, 1982a, 1982b; Novak 1982; Rees 1982; Steels 1983).

Object-oriented Programming and MCS

The power of object-oriented programming is now well known (Lieberman 1982), but let us underline how its properties match MCS requirements. From a user point of view, object-oriented languages have the following properties:

Extensibility: It is always possible to increase the language domain in developing new control

Rodet and Cointe

structures. This property complements requirements 1–3, mentioned above.

Interactivity: Dialogue with the machine is essential for ease of use and for research purposes.

Modularity: The inheritance concept allows one to describe a situation in terms of elementary subsituations (property 6).

Suitability for multiple representations: The object notion allows for multiple implementations and representations of a particular concept (properties 1–3). This is important since our understanding of a phenomenon depends upon the way it is presented to us. Multiple representations favor properties 4–6.

FORMES Guidelines

Keeping MCS requirements in mind, the guidelines for the development of the FORMES system follow.

Accessibility

Our experience in teaching and using FORMES shows that users wish to have access to each component of the system, in order to study, understand, and modify every piece of the global architecture. This wish is satisfied by two features. First, FORMES is an interactive environment, and second, each entity of the FORMES universe is actually an object.

Message-Passing Operation

Each object is a potential receiver of messages linked with functions (methods). Each method embodies the behavior corresponding to a particular message. The set of methods can be read, written, expanded, or contracted by the user. Users can dynamically observe modifications in a family of objects, and they have the choice of keeping or modifying the default behaviors. In this way, we have at our disposal an incremental and self-documented system, the present state of which is always accessible.

Processes

In order to represent the complexity of musical models, we have to deal with time-dependent objects that we call *processes*, built from subobjects called *offspring*.

Implementation

FORMES was developed in Vlisp, first on a DEC PDP-10 then on a DEC VAX-11/780. It is presently available in Vlisp (Greussay 1982) and Le_Lisp (Chailloux 1984). Lisp allows a great flexibility in the development of such a complex prototype system. However, production versions of the FORMES system for other machines could be developed in other languages.

Main Features

Processes

A FORMES process is a named entity that groups together *rules* (procedure bodies), a *monitor* (a kind of scheduler), an *environment* (local variables or fields), and *offspring* (or *children*). A FORMES process has typical process capabilities (like a *script* in Plasma), such as the ability to "sleep," "wakeup," "wait," and "synchronize" when asked. In general, a FORMES process behaves according to the messages passed to it.

The role of each process is to ensure the calculation of a particular musical characteristic, such as an aspect of phrasing, vibrato, loudness control, or timbre. This calculation takes place during a precise duration (called a *span*), that extends from a begin time (*btime*) to an end time (*etime*). (These times are not necessarily explicitly specified.)

In FORMES, computation is accomplished through rules (as in *synthesis by rule* [Rodet 1977; Sundberg, Askenfelt, and Fryden 1983]). It is performed in the specific environment of the process. The environment consists of static *local variables* that keep their value unless they are explicitly changed. A process starts to execute its rules when

Fig. 1. The span of a
CHILD process is included
in the span of a PARENT
process.

it is activated. Thus, the span of a process is the time segment during which it is *active*.

In synthesis, several processes are activated. The role of the monitor is to maintain the *activity* of the process (execution of the rules) during the span, and to maintain the correct sequencing and collaboration of different processes (e.g., the calculation of a general loudness contour, then calculation of the local loudness of a motive, then calculation of the amplitude envelope of a note). Monitors are explained in more detail later.

From a synthesis point of view, the calculation periodically feeds the inputs or controls of a synthesizer with a set of new values or commands. Thus, running a process should start a sound output, and the value of the variable **time** in FORMES (a logical clock) stays close to physical time. However, running a process can result in other effects like screen display, and patch loading.

Process Definition

A process is defined by instantiation of an original generator called **process**. The definition should not be confused with the activation of the process that takes place at its begin time. The definition or creation of a process as an instance of a generator can occur at any time before its begin time. For example, instantiation of process **foo** from a generator can be accomplished by the construct:

(process new 'foo)

This expression passes a message **new** to **process** with the argument **foo**. It is interesting to notice that new processes can be defined from **foo**, or more precisely, derived from **foo** through some changes. For example,

(foo new 'bar
   env: '(partial1 440.0))

defines a new process named **bar** which is the same as **foo** except for the value of the variable **partial1** in its environment.

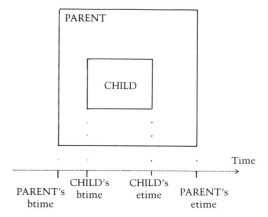

Sequential, Parallel, and Hierarchical Structure

As with any complex system, a computer music system should be modular. To this end, processes can be organized in a structure that reflects some aspects of the desired musical structure, by combination in sequence, in parallel, and hierarchically. A process may be built from subparts, themselves built from subparts, and so on. Thus, a process may have children and a *parent*. The hierarchical relationship "**Process-PARENT** is the parent of **Process-CHILD**" encompasses several aspects. These include the span of **Process-CHILD**, which is included in that of **Process-PARENT** (Fig. 1).

It also includes the respective sequencing of **Process-PARENT** and **Process-CHILD** rules at a precise instant *t*. The "pre-rules" (denoted by the identifier **each-time:**) of **Process-PARENT** are executed before the pre-rules of **Process-CHILD**, and the "post-rules" (denoted by the identifier **each time*:**) of **Process-PARENT** are executed after the post-rules of **Process-CHILD** (Fig. 2).

Let us take a simple example of a hierarchical structure. Suppose that the process **PARENT** has three children named **CHILD1**, **CHILD2**, and **CHILD3**. This lineage will be indicated within the process **PARENT** definition by the list definition construct:

children: (CHILD1 CHILD2 CHILD3)

Rodet and Cointe

Fig. 2. Sequence of rule execution for a PARENT pro-
cess and its CHILD.

Fig. 3. Sequential children.

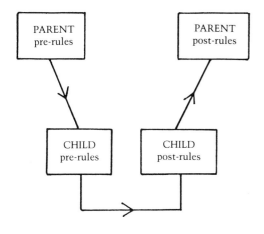

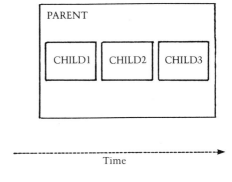

Time

From there, the scheduling of the children is defined by the **PARENT**'s monitor. Let us briefly describe two cases of monitors. With the monitor
called **sequential-node** denoted in **PARENT** by the
construct

monitor: sequential-node

the three children are simply juxtaposed in time,
the first starting its activity at **PARENT**'s btime,
and the others starting when the preceding one is
finished (Fig. 3).

With the monitor called **parallel-node**, denoted in
PARENT by the construct

monitor: parallel-node

the three children start together at **PARENT**'s
btime (Fig. 4).

However, with the parallel monitor, a list of lists
of sequential children are started, so that we have
to add extra parentheses:

children: ((CHILD1) (CHILD2) (CHILD3))

The second monitor shows how some processes
(and eventually their descendents) may not be hierarchically related, from the standpoint of temporal

span. This is what we call *parallelism*, and it is essential for representing many aspects of musical
structure, for instance when different voices are
"not necessarily synchronized," but processes from
different voices can communicate and interact with
each other.

The Calculation Tree

The structure in which processes are organized can
be represented as a (genealogical) *tree*. The root of
this tree is a process, the span of which covers all
its offspring. But at a precise instant t, the only active processes are those that include time t in their
span. These represent a cross-section in the tree
that we call the *calculation tree* (Fig. 5). At a specific time, only the rules of active processes are
executed, in the order determined by the cross-
section corresponding to that time.

At present, the calculation tree is a list of the
rules of active processes in the proper order. The
reason for calling it "tree," however, is that, in a
forthcoming implementation, it will really be organized as a tree.

Communication with Processes

Users converse with processes by passing or sending messages. They send a message when they want
to query a process on its "nature," "state," or "capabilities," and when they want it to do something

Fig. 4. Parallel children.

Fig. 5. A calculation tree.

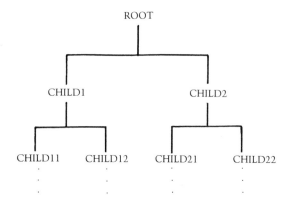

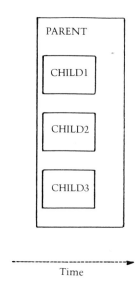

Fig. 4. Parallel children.

Time

For example, the expression **(Process help)** asks the process to display documentation about itself. **(Process selectors)** asks the process to display the list of all messages it knows about.

Portability of Rules

As underlined in the introduction, generality, compatibility, and modularity are essential. In FORMES, it is nearly always the case that a rule refers to the process in which it is placed, for example to access its environment. To fulfill these requirements, rules have to be independent of the name of the process in which they are embedded, so that they can be copied and transferred without modification from a library into any process.

Thus an important construct is the one that refers to the actual active process that calls the rule, without explicitly naming that process. This is the role of the construct **fself**, which refers to the process whose rules are being evaluated. Thus, referring to the process **bar** defined above which has a variable **partial1** of value 440, in its environment, the construct **(fself ? 'partial1)** appearing within **bar** returns 440. The question mark **(?)** is the selector of a message passed to the process **fself** (**bar** in that context), and asks for the value of the variable **partial1** in its environment. Similarly, **(fself ?← 'partial1 'A4)** asks process **bar** to change the value of its **partial1** to A4. In the same vein **(fself ? 'PARENT)** returns the **PARENT** of the designated process. For

like activate a process or display a graph on the screen. In order to pass a message to a process, the user types: **(Process ⟨message⟩)** where ⟨**message**⟩ consists of a message name (the selector) optionally followed by some arguments, as shown in the Backus-Naur Form (BNF) notation below. In BNF, the left side of an expression is replaced by one of the phrases on the right side of the expression.

⟨message⟩   ::= ⟨selector⟩ [⟨argument_list⟩]

⟨argument_list⟩ ::= ⟨arg⟩
                ::= ⟨arg⟩ ⟨argument_list⟩

⟨selector⟩   ::= help
                ::= selectors
                ::= play
                ::= understands
                ::= name
                ::= kill
                ::= sleep
                ::= wake-up
                .
                .
                .

Rodet and Cointe

a certain class of processes called *transition processes*, discussed later, the expressions

(fself ? 'left-sibling)
(fself ? 'right-sibling)

return the **left-sibling** and the **right-sibling** of **fself** in their common parent's list of children. For example, the construct (**fself ? 'left-sibling**) appearing in a rule within process **CHILD2** (as defined above) would designate **CHILD1**. Finally, in **PARENT**, the expression (**fself ? 'active-children**) gives the rest of the list of successive children beginning at the first presently active.

Execution of FORMES Programs

FORMES programs and commands may be prepared in files and then loaded into the system, or typed on-line. A FORMES program is a *structure of processes*. The execution of such a structure involves the repetition at successive times of the following two steps, called the *FORMES System Loop*: (1) update the list of rules that constitute the calculation tree and (2) execute (evaluate) the rules of the calculation tree. The execution of the program (structure) is started by sending the message **play** to the process at the root of the structure (let's call it **Root-Process**):

(Root-Process play)

Note that any process can be considered as the root of a substructure. (If it has no child, the substructure reduces to the process alone.) Execution ends when the root process finds a condition that was given by the user as an exit condition, like a duration elapsed.

The "current time" is found in a variable called **time**, incremented by the message **next-tick**. The expression

(while (Root-Process end?)
    (tree evaluate))

means the following. Repetitively, message **end?** is

passed to **Root-Process**. According to its monitor and some other conditions, **Root-Process** updates the calculation tree and returns "false" if it has not yet finished or "true" if it has. Thus we see that the **while** loop is repeated until **Root-Process** decides the end has occurred.

The evaluation of the calculation tree caused by the message **evaluate** passed to **tree** is also repeated. The last rule that appears in the tree is (**clock next-tick**), where the message **next-tick** passed to **clock** causes **time** to be incremented (**time = time + quantum**). By default, **time** is incremented by the default value of **quantum**, which is 0.01 sec.

Hence the FORMES System Loop can be sketched in an Algol-like form:

WHILE (Root_Process_not_ended)
  DO BEGIN
      Update_the_tree;
      Evaluate_the_tree;
  END

Programming (Composing) in FORMES

FORMES involves the composer in playing (running), and listening to processes and modifying their environment. This can be a simple but very fruitful activity. This is especially the case for beginners who can learn by literally "playing" with the already defined objects (processes and rules of the library) like in an Adventure game, without having to first succeed at building a "hairy" error-free patch. This is also true for expert programmers who sometimes prefer to modify an old program rather than writing a brand new one. Ultimately, this mode of working fulfills our requirements that FORMES be an environment in perpetual evolution, where abstraction and the power of objects grows with the benefit of past experience.

Users can also create rules. Creating processes that incorporate new rules is a second stage of interaction with FORMES, slightly less simple but still accessible to people who are not computer experts.

Creating new monitors is a rarer mode of interaction, since it can sometimes require knowledge of the details of the system.

Fig. 6. FORMES code to
build an envelope for
notes and phrases.

```
; Processes:
                (process new 'CHILD1
                  each-time: '((envelope))
                  env: '(duration 0.2))

                (CHILD1 new 'CHILD2 env: '(duration 0.3))

                (process new 'PARENT
                  each-time: '((envelope))
                  children:      '(CHILD1 CHILD2 CHILD1))

; Rules:
                (de envelope ()
                  (*= amplitude (envelop.fun (tnorm))))

; Initialization:
                (setqq each-quantum (amplitude 1.))

; Load breakpoint functions:
                (bitpad envelop.fun)
```

Elementary Example of Working with FORMES

This example treats a well-known problem: de-scribing the amplitude envelope for a note model, and using this model to build the amplitude enve-lope for a monophonic phrase. The code is shown in Fig. 6. (Comments start with a semicolon.)

As can be seen in Fig. 6, the rule **envelope** ap-pears without modification after the identifier **each-time:** in **PARENT** and in the children (this demon-strates the portability of the rules). The envelope rule is a Lisp function defined by the **(de envelope ( ) . . .)** construct. Using the prefixed Lisp notation, this function sets the global variable **amplitude** to its previous value multiplied by that of the function **envelop.fun** with argument **tnorm**. This last expres-sion stands for "time normalized," which means that its value is proportional to **time** but goes from 0 to 1 during the span of the process using it. In other words,

$$\text{tnorm} = \frac{\text{time} - \text{btime}}{\text{duration}}$$

or more precisely, **tnorm** is defined in FORMES as follows:

```
(setq tnorm '(div (sub time (fself ? 'btime))
  (fself ? 'duration)))
```

The construct **(envelop.fun (tnorm))** is like an enve-lope generator, with the time of the envelope scaled to the process span, and with the **quantum** as the sampling period. The actual envelope definition is obtained by the construct **(bitpad envelop.fun)**, where the argument **envelop.fun** is the name of a file that contains the description of a breakpoint function entered by typing or by drawing a curve on a bitpad tablet, for example:

Value	Time
0	0
1	1
6	2
4	7
0	10

Values and times are normalized to the interval [0, 1].

Fig. 7. Amplitude envelope
created by the envelope
rule.

The way rule **envelope** is written (using $*=$) necessitates that **amplitude** be initialized at each step of the loop and before **PARENT**'s rule. The reason for this apparent complication is to ensure rule portability. A global variable like **amplitude** carries information from one process to the other at low cost. Furthermore, rules may be written with explicit reference to global variables like fundamental-frequency, vibrato-excursion, or tempo. This allows processes to be easily inserted into or deleted from the larger structure, since the global variables are common to most structures.

In defining amplitude at each quantum, we use the following command:

(setq each-quantum '(amplitude 1.))

which has the effect of setting **amplitude** to the value 1 at the beginning of each tree evaluation.

At this point, one can play with the system. First, we send the message **play** to **CHILD1**:

(CHILD1 play)

This starts the FORMES System Loop on the root process **CHILD1**. Its rules ((**envelope**) after the identifier **each-time:**) are executed repetitively at times 0, 0 + **quantum**, 0 + (2 * **quantum**), and so on, (0, 0.01, 0.02 . . .) up to the **CHILD1** end (0.2, which is its duration). Thus the variable **amplitude** samples values of the previously mentioned envelope, and can be sent to a synthesizer amplitude control input.

The result can be checked with the command (**amplitude screen**), which displays successive amplitude values on the screen in the form of a graph that plots amplitude versus time (Fig. 7).

(Actually, this picture was generated by the command (**amplitude plot**), which draws it on a plotter.) Now, we send the message **play** to **PARENT**:

(PARENT play)

PARENT is set "active" from time 0 to time 0.8 (the sum of the durations of its three children). Within the time interval [0, 0.2] only **CHILD1** is also active, and in the calculation tree the rule of **PARENT** is followed by the rule of **CHILD1**. PAR-

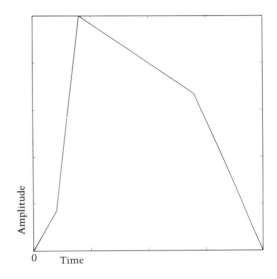

ENT's rule sets amplitude to values corresponding to Fig. 7 scaled on a [0, 0.8] interval. But then the **CHILD1** rule multiplies the amplitude by the same form scaled on [0, 0.2]. Similarly, during the time interval [0.2, 0.5] only **PARENT** and **CHILD2** are active, and the amplitude is the product of the corresponding portion of **PARENT**'s amplitude setting by a [0.2, 0.5] **CHILD2** setting, and similarly for [0.5, 0.8] with **CHILD3**. Finally, the message (**amplitude screen**) results in curve shown in Fig. 8.

Through this elementary example, we have demonstrated several points. Modularity allows one to extend the musical environment by increasing the domain of existing objects, and to test elementary objects independently of each other before grouping them in higher-level objects. The rule we used would be found in a generally accessible library of rules. It is usable in other objects, so that it can be exploited in different contexts by different musicians and researchers.

Notice that a new object, just created, can be tested immediately by sending **play** and listening to the corresponding sound. The value of a process parameter (like duration) is held in the process itself. The user may see it in the process definition code,

Fig. 8. *Interaction between PARENT process and CHILD processes modifies the original envelope.*

Fig. 9. *GRAND-PARENT envelope.*

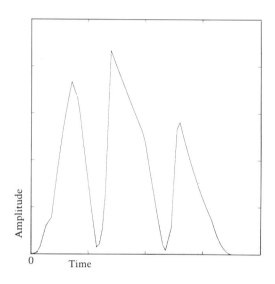

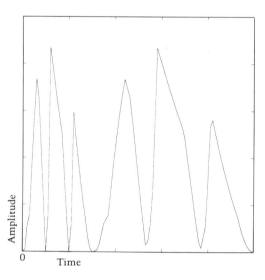

not in a separate list. It is not referenced by its position but is pointed at by a mnemonic identifier, insuring that you can consult or change it easily.

The correctness of a program is quickly checked on a graphic display; we have often recognized that a picture of parameter values could immediately indicate not only the presence of a bug but exactly where and how it occurred within a complex program! Since any process can be played (if it makes sense) in the course of building and experimenting with a structure, one can follow a bottom-up procedure as we have done here. That is, build a *leaf process* (e.g., describing details of the sound), and when you are satisfied with it, embed it in a **PARENT**, then tune the structure **PARENT-child**, and so on.

One can also follow a top-down approach, that is, build the highest level element of the structure, and then fill it in with more and more detailed refinements. Naturally one can start from any intermediate level of structuring, for instance by appropriating it from another structure stored in the library.

The flexibility and adaptability afforded by this scheme are especially favorable to artistic creativity. Furthermore, even this simple example would not be easy to write in other languages.

Further Extensions of the Example

We could benefit from the hierarchy within FORMES and type the following commands:

```
(PARENT new 'UNCLE 'duration 0.3)
(process new 'GRAND-PARENT
    children: (PARENT UNCLE))
```

Then the expression **(GRAND-PARENT play)** would result in the amplitude evolution shown in Fig. 9.

In working with an envelope, you might want to change its basic curve. FORMES gives you the power to effect major changes through simple instructions. For example, we can shift to a much more flexible form by giving the following command that redefines the function **envelope**:

```
(de envelope ()
  (*= amplitude
      (* (power (tnorm) gamma)
         (power (- 1. (tnorm)) (- 1. gamma))))))
```

Fig. 10. Result of adjusting gamma to redefine the envelope.

Fig. 11. Insertion of a part of GRAND-PARENT into an existing envelope.

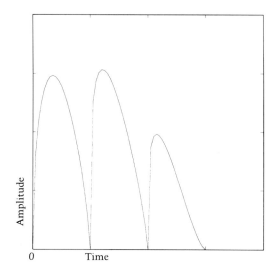

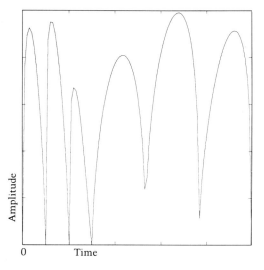

This means that the previous value of the amplitude is multiplied by

$$\text{tnorm}^{gamma} * (1 - tnorm)^{1 - gamma}$$

Now if you set **gamma** to the value, 0.25 and play **PARENT**, the amplitude evolution will look like Fig. 10.

Finally, suppose we want to modify the value of the parameter **gamma** during the span of **GRAND-PARENT**. To simplify the explanation, we chose a ramp from 0.2 to 0.8 during **GRAND-PARENT**'s span. Then we can insert this rule between those already linked with its **each-time:**

    (GRAND-PARENT insert 'each-time: '(set-rampq
    'gamma 0.2 0.8))

After **GRAND-PARENT** is run, the amplitude evolution looks like Fig. 11.

We hope this shows how a relatively simple user program can result in rather complex and powerful results such as amplitude envelopes controlling a synthesizer. The example also shows how rules can be easily modified, and how message passing and the modify-and-test procedure can make the devel-

opment of a composition faster and more intuitive than previous languages have allowed.

The Role of Monitors

A monitor defines a temporal control structure. The monitor of a process is the scheduler of its children. It has three tasks:

Determine the start time (btime) for each child and activate it.

Update the calculation tree when the state of a process is modified.

If possible, determine the duration of the root process (the difference between etime and btime). Different duration algorithms are available. For example, the duration of a sequential process can be defined as the sum of its children's durations, or on the contrary, it can be defined by scaling its children so that their sum equals its explicit duration.

For each monitor those tasks are implemented by three generic Lisp functions called respectively: **init**, **end?**, and **duration**.

In order to define a new monitor the user can

Fig. 12. Example of FOR-
MES used to generate
high-level musical process.

```
; Some function definitions appear in Appendix 1

; PROCESSES:

(process new 'PARENT
    monitor: 'parallel_node
    children:    '((VOICE1) (VOICE2)))

(process new 'VOICE1
    monitor:     'seq-node
    first-time: '((fself change 'children:
                    (derive '<following>
                            '(short short s_asc Ef4)(fself ? 'phrase_number)))
                  (transition?))
    each-time: '((rest? in_n_notes))
    children:      '(???))
    env:         '(phrase_number 14))

(process new 'VOICE2
    monitor:     'seq-node
    each-time: '((rest? in_n_notes))
    children:    (bass))

(process new 'Ef4
    first-time: '((tempo))
    each-time: '((envelope) (warp) (my-pitch)))

(Ef4 new 'Ff4)

(Ef1 new 'Gf1)

;          .
;          .
;          .

; DECLARATIONS:
(synthesizer f0 coefamp freq1 freq2 freq3 freq4 freq5)

(setq each-quantum '(coefamp 1.))
```

choose between redefining it completely (by sending the message **new** to the meta-generator monitor), or by redefining only some methods (generic
Lisp functions associated with the monitor). In this
latter case, the message **new** is also sent but to an
existing monitor.

Utilities in the FORMES Environment

The FORMES environment provides a number of
tools that aid the user in developing programs and
compositions. During execution of a FORMES program, the current value of **time** and the calculation
tree are always displayed on the screen.

The messages **print** and **print:** respectively display the internal (Lisp) and external (as given by the
user) representations of objects.

On-line documentation is provided by the message **help** passed to objects. Furthermore a help program (called Aid, written by Patrick Greussay) may

be called at any time. Another program, written by
Harald Wertz, keeps track of all mail and news concerning FORMES from implementers as well as
users.

A file address is linked with each function in the
system, allowing access to the file that defines the
function if needed. Objects and functions created or
modified by the user can also be interactively saved
in a file. Finally, users can ask for a *trace* of parts of
the FORMES System Loop.

Another Example

In this example (Fig. 12) we describe a FORMES solution to a musical problem. One of the purposes of
the example is to study a "real-life" synthesis problem. Another is to demonstrate FORMES ability to
include the "high-level" or compositional aspects of
the synthesis process. We think there is much to gain
if the "high-level" and the "pure synthesis level"
are developed with the same formalism in the same
program (Rodet, Potard, and Barrière 1984).

Before looking at the synthesis procedure itself
and at the compositional aspects (even though the
separation into "high" and "low" levels is misleading), let us explain some additional FORMES constructs that we use in the example.

Additional FORMES Constructs

In order to produce simultaneously two "unsyn-
chronized" voices, we use in **PARENT** the monitor
parallel_node described earlier. Here, the children
are **VOICE1** and **VOICE2**, each one representing an
independent voice. Thus, both sequences of the
children of **VOICE1** and **VOICE2** will be executed
in parallel.

We also use the function **trelative**, which is a
time relative to the beginning of the current process. The definition of **trelative** is as follows:

```
(de trelative ()
    (sub time (fself ? 'btime)))
```

In the preceding example, the rules of a process appeared after the identifier **each-time:**, and they were executed at each quantum during the process activity, that is, "each-time" the process was executed. Obviously, it is desirable to benefit from rules that are executed once only, at activation of the process (identified by **first-time:**) or at end of the process (identified by **last-time:**).

Finally, the construct

(fself change 'children: '(CHILD1 CHILD2
    CHILD3))

changes the list of children of the process presently pointed at by **fself**, into the list (**CHILD1 CHILD2 CHILD3**). In the code below, it appears in the form:

first-time: ((fself change 'children:
               (derive '(following)
                       '(short short s_asc Ef2)
                       (fself ? phrase number))))

which means that at the initialization of the process (**VOICE1**), its list of children is changed to the result of the evaluation of the form **derive**, explained later.

A FORMES Program

The children of **VOICE2** are in a list named **bass** that we do not explain in detail. For each note process in Fig. 12 (**Ef1**, etc.), we apply an envelope to the parameter **coefamp**, which is a loudness input of the CHANT synthesizer (more precisely, the spectrum slope, and hence the sound richness, varies also with the value of **coefamp**). Also for each note we use the same envelope as in the preceding example.

Here, the function **warp** (in the **each-time:** section of **Ef4**) is in charge of timbre variations. It warps the envelope spectrum by modifying the formant frequencies (Rodet, Potard, and Barrière 1984). (Note that formant frequencies can be used to set a formant filter or to control another synthesis technique. The point is that this rule is relatively independent of the synthesis technique used.)

The fundamental frequency of each note process

is calculated by the function **my_pitch** according to the name of the process.

The note list is *self-generated* in **VOICE1**, and is substituted for the **???** that appears after the identifier **children:**.

The other important point to observe is the interaction between the two voices. Due to slightly varying tempos (function (**tempo**) in **Ef1**, **Ff1**, and so on) the two voices are not synchronous. But, at any instant, one of them is in *master mode* and looks ahead in its children list. Specifically, it tests if a rest is coming in **in_n_notes** notes. This is done by the function called (**rest?**) in the **each-time:** section of **VOICE1** and **VOICE2**. If a rest is coming, the master voice modifies the duration of the forthcoming processes in the other voice in order that both are synchronized with the note following the rest. Furthermore, when such a resynchronization occurs, the master voice may decide to reverse the roles so that the other voice becomes the master. This kind of easy communication between two or more voices is generally very difficult to achieve in most other music languages.

The last important point is that we want to allow a legato articulation between two notes, in the form of a continuous pitch contour from one note to the following note, in place of the two fixed pitches of the note. For this, we use a kind of process called a transition process, whose span covers a time segment before and after the transition between two processes.

The role of the transition is to take information simultaneously from both processes in order to generate a new pattern by combining them with a *transition rule*. Transitions are also a very important class of processes in musical applications, including attacks of successive notes, legatos, and the articulation of successive phrases. Transition processes implement the concept of *anticipation* since they can take information concerning the "future state" of the second process and use it in order to behave in a way that was not originally implemented in the "non-transitional" processes. Note that it is not very easy to deal with such transition effects in music languages that separate the world into patches and note lists.

In our example (Fig. 12), the transition processes

are introduced dynamically in the list of children by the function call (**transition?**) in the **first-time:** section of **VOICE1**.

Generation of the List of Children

We now explain the function call used in **VOICE1** to generate its list of children. The idea of this musical sketch is to use a very simplified and modified version of rules found in the study of jazz improvisation. (We thank Andre Hodeir and Philippe Gautron for communicating these rules.) We have formalized them in terms of rewriting rules. A classical rewriting rule in BNF form is as follows:

⟨identifier i⟩ ::= ⟨list_of_identifiers_1⟩
            ::= ⟨list_of_identifiers_2⟩
               .
               .
               .
            ::= ⟨list_of_identifiers_n⟩

Such a rule means that ⟨**identifier_i**⟩ is rewritten as the list of identifiers ⟨**list_of_identifiers_1**⟩ or as ⟨**list_of_identifiers_2**⟩, and so on. But when using such rules for production of a phrase, it is necessary to specify which of the alternatives is chosen for any derivation. Therefore, each alternative or derivation is accompanied by a condition of application of the derivation:

⟨identifier i⟩ ::= condition_of_application_1 ⟨list_of_identifiers_1⟩
         ::= condition_of_application_2 ⟨list_of_identifiers_2⟩
               .
               .
         ::= condition_of_application_n ⟨list_of_identifiers_n⟩

Let **expression_i** be an expression which, when evaluated, returns the same alternative that would be chosen according to the conditions. Then, the above rule can be simply expressed as follows:

⟨identifier_i⟩ ::= expression_i

This means that when the identifier **i** is found, it is rewritten into the list of identifiers returned by the evaluation of the expression **i** (a function call), the role of which is to choose among the different possibilities and to return one of them explicitly.

Rewriting Rules

In this example, without any loss in generality, a very short set of rules has been chosen:

⟨following⟩ ::= derive_following
  ⟨rest⟩   ::= derive_rest

In rule 1, **derive_following** is the function called to rewrite ⟨**following**⟩ into:

⟨rest⟩ ⟨list_of_notes⟩ [⟨following⟩]

where the brackets [ ] mean that ⟨**following**⟩ is optional. The **list_of_notes** is chosen among several possibilities, according to the previous phrase's features. The previous phrase's features constitute a quadruple:

{**start_beat end_beat class pivot**},

where **start_beat** is the beat (long or short) on which the phrase starts, **end_beat** is the beat on which the phrase ends, **pivot** is the last note of the phrase, **class** corresponds to the pitch contour constituted by the three last notes of the phrase—one of the following forms: descending and ascending is called *ascendant* or *asc*, ascending and ascending is called *super-ascendant* or *s_asc*, ascending and descending is called descendant or *desc*, descending and descending is called *super-descendant* or *s_desc*. These features are used by the function **derive_following** to choose the next phrase in the class of the previous one according to the pivot note.

The function **rest** rewrites ⟨**rest**⟩ into **long_rest**, **short_rest** or nothing, in order to ensure that beat alternation (long, short) is respected, and that the next phrase starts on a beat of the same type as its **start_beat**.

The code for deriving the rules and the code of these functions is given in Appendix 1. For phrases and classes, they use the following structure of data (a portion of real data appears also in Appendix 1):

⟨class⟩ ::=
   ((pivot_1 ⟨phrase_1_data⟩ . . . ⟨phrase_i_data⟩)
   (pivot_2 ⟨phrase_1_data⟩ . . . ⟨phrase_j_data⟩)

            .
            .

   (pivot_h ⟨phrase_1_data⟩ . . . ⟨phrase_m_data⟩))
⟨phrase_x_data⟩ ::=
   ((⟨start_beat⟩⟨end_beat⟩⟨class⟩)
    (note_1 note_2 . . . note_p))

As an example, suppose that we choose (**short short asc Ef4**) as our initial "previous phrase's features" and that we want the derivation to stop after four phrases are produced. Then the evaluation of the expression

(derive '⟨following⟩ '(short short asc Ef4) 4)

returns the following:

(Gf4 G4 Bf4 C5 Ef5 C5
 long_rest Gf5 Bf4 A4 Ef5
 short_rest Gf5
 short_rest F5 Ef5 C5)

In this example, we have shown that complex procedures can be embedded in FORMES to realize a compositional task. The main benefit is that high-level procedures may interact easily with the details of the synthesis procedures since they are implemented not only in the same environment but even in the same program.

Interconnection with Synthesizers

One of the fundamental aims in the FORMES project is to build a library of "models of the processes brought into action in musical production" (Rodet, Potard, and Barrière 1984). As mentioned previously, we try to design these models to be independent of a particular synthesis technique.

FORMES is used to represent both discrete and continuous (i.e., sampled at a high rate) events and control parameters, which describe acoustic, physical, and musical characteristics. In its structure, it makes no assumption about the device that will calculate a signal corresponding (as closely as possible) to those characteristics. As a consequence, FORMES is interfaced to different types of synthesizers. Suppose **PARENT** is the root process of a structure described in Fig. 12. The command (**PARENT chant**) asks process **PARENT** to format the program outputs for the CHANT sound synthesis system. Similarly (**PARENT 4X**) lets this same FORMES program (without any modification) drive a given patch of the 4X synthesizer (built at IRCAM by G. DiGiugno). Any other device can be controlled in the same way, for example (**PARENT ap**) sends the parameters of the program to our Floating Point Systems array processor, and (**PARENT symbol**) draws a symbolic representation (e.g., a score) of the piece.

This kind of versatility guarantees a more uniform access to different devices. It allows use of one device in place of another when the first device is not available or when it is not adequate for musical or technical reasons. (For example, some synthesis devices have a greater number of voices or more precision in the calculations or better control facilities than some others.) Finally, and most importantly, it opens the way to a standard representation or formalization of musical structures and processes, which would be of great use to the computer music community.

The FORMES Environment and Workstation

The environment we want to build for FORMES should have the capability to execute FORMES programs in real time. This requires a fast host computer with floating-point arithmetic in hardware and about 1 Mbyte of main memory—nothing more than current workstations provide. A high-resolution, bitmapped display is indispensible, as are control devices like a mouse, a joystick, and potentiometers.

The host computer should be connected to a floating-point synthesizer (this is presently the rarest component). The synthesizer should embody as few restrictions as possible in terms of its internal control structure. For example, it should be able to handle subroutines and coroutines, as well as the buffering of any input, output, or internal data flow. The synthesizer should also possess a large input/output capacity between FORMES programs and signal-processing programs, in order to ensure rapid updates from the host computer.

The workstation environment should also include a variety of signal and data analysis programs, including sophisticated signal-processing techniques such as multiple pulse analysis and synthesis, algorithms for psychoacoustic data extraction, and good graphic displays (three-dimensional displays, and color displays of symbolic representations).

But the most essential part that we want to build is a library or database of models implemented in predefined processes and rules, which can be accessed through perceptual ("richer," more "grain") and musical terms, as well as through terms concerning physical models of sound production (e.g., G. Weinreich's models of piano and violin [1983]). A fundamental point is that this library should constantly grow richer in processes and rules due to the contributions of composers and scientists working on the station.

Acknowledgments

We thank Yves Potard for his essential contribution to the conception of FORMES, Bernard Serpette and Jean-Pierre Briot for participating in the implementation of the FORMES system, and Jean-Baptiste Barrière for suggestions and musical tests of the FORMES environment. We also thank Patrick Greussay, Jerome Chailloux, Jean-François Perrot, Harald Wertz, Eugen Neidl, Christian Queinnec, and Daniel Goossens for providing the Lisp environment. Finally, we thank Pierre Boulez, Tod Machover, Philippe Manoury, Marco Stroppa, and everyone at IRCAM for their encouragement and comments on the musical aspects of the FORMES system.

References

Barrière, J.-B. Chreode. 1983.

Bennett, G. 1981. "Singing Synthesis in Electronic Music." In Research Aspects of Singing, ed. J. Sundberg. Report 33. Stockholm: Royal Swedish Academy of Music, pp. 34–50.

Birtwistle, G., and O.-J. Dahl. 1973. SIMULA BEGIN. New York: Petrocelli/Charter.

Chailloux, J. 1984. Manuel Le_Lisp. Second edition. Paris: Institut National de Recherche en Informatique et Automatique.

Cointe, P. 1981. "Fermetures dans les λ Interprètes: Application aux Langages LISP, PLASMA, et Smalltalk." Thèse de troisième cycle. Laboratoire d'Informatique Théorique et Pratique. Paris: Université de Paris 6.

Cointe, P. 1982a. "Vlisp: un langage objet?" In Actes de l'Ecole de Printemps d'Informatique Théorique. Paris: Laboratoire d'Informatique Théorique at Pratique, pp. 143–164.

Cointe, P. 1982b. "Une réalisation de Smalltalk en Vlisp." Techniques et Sciences de l'Informatique 1(4):325–340.

Cointe, P. 1983. "Evaluation of Object-oriented Programming from Simula to Smalltalk." In Proceedings of the Eleventh Simula User's Conference. Paris: Simula Information, pp. 17–24.

Cointe, P., and X. Rodet. 1984. "FORMES: An Object and Time Oriented System for Music Composition and Synthesis." To appear in the conference record of the 1984 ACM Symposium on LISP and Functional Programming, Austin, Texas, 5–8 August 1984.

Durieux, J. L. 1981. "Sémantique des liasons nom-valeur: application à l'implémentation des λ langages." Thèse d'Etat. Toulouse: Université Paul Sabatier.

Goldberg, A., and D. Robson. 1983. Smalltalk-80: The Language and Its Implementation. Reading, Massachusetts: Addison-Wesley.

Greussay, P. 1982. "Le Système Vlisp-Unix." Département Informatique. Paris: Université Paris 8, Vincennes.

Hewitt, C. 1976. "Viewing Control Structures as Patterns of Message Passing." A.I. Memo 410. Cambridge, Massachusetts: M.I.T. Artificial Intelligence Laboratory

Hewitt, C., and B. Smith. 1975. "A Plasma Primer." Draft. Cambridge, Massachusetts: M.I.T. Artificial Intelligence Laboratory.

Ingalls, D. H. 1978. "The Smalltalk-76 Programming System Design and Implementation." Presented at the Fifth Annual ACM Symposium on Principles of Programming Languages, Tucson, Arizona.

Kay, A. 1969. "The Reactive Engine." Ph.D. diss. Salt

Lake City: Department of Computer Science, University of Utah.

Kay, A., and A. Goldberg. 1976. "Smalltalk-72 Instruction Manual." SSL-76-6. Palo Alto: Xerox Palo Alto Research Center.

Lieberman, H. 1981. "A Preview of Act 1." A.I. Memo 625. Cambridge, Massachusetts: M.I.T. Artificial Intelligence Laboratory.

Lieberman, H. 1982. "Machine Tongues IX: Object-oriented Programming." *Computer Music Journal* 6(3):8–21.

Moon, D., and D. Weinreb. 1980. "Flavors: Message Passing in the Lisp Machine." A.I. Memo 602. Cambridge, Massachusetts: M.I.T. Artificial Intelligence Laboratory.

Novak, G. S., Jr. 1983. "GLISP: A Lisp-based Programming System with Data Abstraction." *AI Magazine* 4(3):37–47, 53.

Pomian, C. 1980. "Contribution à la definition et à l'implémentation d'un interprète PLASMA." Thèse de troisième cycle. Toulouse: Université Paul Sabatier.

Rees, J., and I. Adams. 1982. "T: A Dialect of Lisp, or Lambda: The Ultimate Software Tool." In *Proceedings of the 1982 Symposium on Lisp and Functional Programming.* New York: Association for Computing Machinery, pp. 114–122.

Rodet, X. 1977. "Analyse du signal vocale dans sa representation amplitude-temps. Synthèse de la parole par regles." L.I.F. Thèse d'Etat. Paris: Université Paris 6.

Rodet, X., and G. Bennett. 1980. "Research in Musical Synthesis Using a Model of Vocal Production." Presented at the 1980 International Computer Music Conference, Queens College, New York.

Rodet, X., Y. Potard, and J.-B. Barrière. 1984. "The CHANT Project: From the Synthesis of the Singing Voice to Synthesis in General." *Computer Music Journal* 8(3):15–31.

Smith, D. C. et al. 1983. "Designing the Star User Interface." In *Integrated Interactive Computing Systems,* ed. P. Degano and E. Sandewall. Amsterdam: North-Holland, pp. 297–313.

Steels, L. 1983. "ORBIT: An Applicative View of Object-oriented Programming." In *Integrated Interactive Computing Systems,* ed. P. Degano and E. Sandewall. Amsterdam: North-Holland, pp. 193–206.

Sundberg, J., A. Askenfelt, and L. Fryden. 1983. "Musical Performance: A Synthesis-by-Rule Approach." *Computer Music Journal* 7(1):37–43.

Weinreich, G. 1983. "Violin Sound Synthesis from First Principles." Presented at the 106th Meeting of the Acoustical Society of America.

Winograd, T. 1979. "Beyond Programming Languages." *Communications of the Association for Computing Machinery* 22(7):391–401.

Appendix 1

```
(de derive (ident S ns)
   (let-named self ((rules rew_rules) (rule* ()))
      (cond
            ((null rules) indent)
            ((setq rule* (apply_rule ident (next1 rules) S ns))
               (if (eq rule* 'no_rest) '* rule*))
            (t (self rules ni1)))))

(de apply_rule (ident (ident1 ::= frule) . args)
   (when (eq ident ident1) (apply frule args)))

(de vcons (elt list) (⟨cf elt (cons elt list) list))

(de following (S ns)
   (lets ((next_data (next_phrase_data S ns))
          (rest (derive '⟨rest⟩ S ns)))
```

```
    (append
       (vcons rest (cadr next_data))
       (when () ns 0) (derive '⟨following⟩ (car next_data) (1 − ns)))))))
(de rest (S ns)
   (letvq (? cb . r) S
      (cond
         ((neq cb (caar next_data)) 'no_rest)
         ((eq cb 'short) 'long_rest)
         (t 'short_rest)))))
(de next_phrase_data ((? ? class pivot) n)
   (car (find (cval class) pivot))))
(de find (1 pivot)
   (when 1
      (letvq ((p . phrases) . r) 1
         (if (eq p pivot) phrases (find r pivot)))))
; REWRITING RULES
(setq
   rew_rules '(
               (⟨following⟩ ::= following)
               (⟨rest⟩       ::= rest)
               )
; DATA
(setq
   s_asc
      '(
      (Ef4
         ((short long asc Bf4)
          (Ef4 Gf4 G4 F4 A4 Bf4 r))
         ((long long s_asc Bf4)
          (Ef4 Gf4 long_rest G4 long_rest Ef long_rest A4 Bf4))
         ((long short asc Ef4)
          (Ef4 Gf4 G4 Gf4 G4 Ef long_rest Ef A4 Bf4 A4 Bf4 Ef4 short_rest))
         )
      (Gf4
         ((long short asc Gf4)
          (Gf4 Ef4 Gf4 G4 Bf4 C5 Gf4 short_rest))
         ((long short asc Gf4)
          (Ef4 Gf4 Ef G4 Ef Bf4 Ef C5 Ef C5 Gf4 short_rest))

                  .
                  .

         )
      )
   asc
      (
```

```
(Ef4
   ((long short desc C5)
    (Gf4 G4 Bf4 C5 Ef5 C5))
   ((long long desc Bf4)
    (Ef4 Af4 Gf4 A4 Ef5))
   .
   .
   .
```

Appendix 2

```
(de rest? (in_n_notes)
   (when (eq master (fself name))
      (let ((notes (fself ? 'active-children)) (t_sum 0))
         (let ((a_note (nthcdr in_n_notes notes)))
            (when (memq a_note '(short_rest 'long_rest))
               (repeat in_n_notes (+= t_sum ((next1 notes) ? 'duration)))
               (ajuste (alter master) in_n_notes (plus time t_sum))
               (whcn (gt (random 0 6) 3)
                  (setq master (alter master)))))))))

(de alter (voice)
   (if (eq voice 'VOICE1) 'VOICE2 'VOICE1))

(de ajuste (voice in_n_notes the-time)
   (let ((reste ((car (voice ? 'active-children)) ? etime))
         (tsum ()) (list-t ()) (list-o ())
         (r-s (cdr (voice ? 'active-children))))
      (setq tsum reste)
      (let ((r-s r-s))
         (when (and (1t tsum the-time) r-s)
            (setq tsum (plus tsum (new1 list-t
               (apply (get new1 list-o (next1 r-s)) 'duration:)))))
            (self r-s)))
      (if (setq aux (sub tsum reste))
      (setq fact (div (sub the-time reste) (- tsum reste))))
      (mapc list-o (lambda (o) (put o 'duration: (lambda ()
                                    (mul fact (next1 list-t))))))
)))
```

V

Synthesis and Signal Processing

Curtis Roads

Overview

Digital sound synthesis and signal processing are central to computer music. Many commercial synthesizers rely on one or two synthesis techniques, but the number of different synthesis methods that have been developed is large and continues to grow. Article 34, by Giovanni DePoli, is a good overview of the various synthesis methods in use today.

Several of the synthesis methods discussed in De Poli's survey have not yet found their way into commercial digital synthesizers. CHANT, developed by Xavier Rodet and his associates at the French music research institute IRCAM and discussed in article 35, is one such technique. CHANT is a flexible and efficient method of synthesizing *formants* (peaks of acoustic energy in specific frequency bands). Since vocal sounds and the timbres of many traditional instruments exhibit characteristic formant regions in their spectra, CHANT has been used to make convincing imitations of vocal and instrumental sounds.

Creating a realistic imitation of a vocal or instrumental sound stands as a kind of "acid test" of a synthesis method. But the potential of creating a new sound universe with electronic synthesis—a vision articulated so well by Edgard Varèse (1966)—offers another standard by which to judge a synthesis method. Techniques such as CHANT, the Karplus-Strong plucked string algorithm (articles 36 and 37), warped linear prediction (article 41), and synthesis-by-rule (article 38) can also be used to create otherworldly extensions of natural sounds or purely synthetic sound objects, and granular synthesis (discussed briefly in article 34) can be used to create *sound clouds* made up of thousands of tiny sound particles (Roads 1978; Jones and Parks 1988; Truax 1988).

Certain sound-generation techniques, such as frequency modulation (FM) synthesis (Chowning 1973), are intrinsically efficient from a computational standpoint. Other techniques, such as additive synthesis, usually require large amounts of computer time or special hardware for real-time work. Additive synthesis can be incorporated into an *analysis/synthesis system*, a package of hardware and software with which it is possible to record sounds, analyze them, and then resynthesize

them using the analysis data to drive the synthesis. More interesting from a musical standpoint, once one has analyzed sounds one can modify the analysis data to create variations of them.

The main problem with this approach is that analysis can result in a tremendous amount of data. *Data reduction* techniques can trim the analysis data into a more usable and storage-efficient form. In article 40, Gérard Charbonneau discusses the task of data reduction and compares three techniques. (In article 53, John Strawn discusses another approach, involving pattern recognition.)

In synthesis-by-rule techniques, such as those described by Claude Cadoz and his colleagues in article 38, the goal is to produce sound by modeling the physics of instrumental sound generation. Although the principles behind synthesis by rule are not new (Hiller and Beauchamp 1967; Ferretti 1975; Hiller and Ruiz 1971), this is currently a very active area of research (Adrien et al. 1987; Smith 1986).

Article 38 is really about two subjects. One is synthesis by rule; but the other is *responsive input devices*—that is, keys and joysticks attached to motors under computer control. The "feel" or "action" of a responsive input device can be programmed so that a piano-type key might feel stiff, mushy, wildly springy, or stepped depending on the musical application. These devices are, for the most part, still in the experimental stage. Their effective deployment depends on their linkage to equally flexible signal-processing methods, so that gestures can be translated smoothly into sounds.

Digital signal processing can be applied to two different representations of signals. One is the *time domain* (that is, operating on sound waveforms as the continuously varying curve seen on an oscilloscope). The other representation is the *frequency domain* (that is, operating on the frequencies, amplitudes, and phases of elementary sound partials). When the partials are added together over time they constitute the *dynamic spectrum* (Strawn 1985). Julius O. Smith's article is an introduction to the mathematics of digital filter theory, which is at the heart of digital signal processing (DSP) methods.

Several manufacturers now market digital audio workstations for recording, editing, and processing sound. It would be useful to have a digital sound editor that could recognize musical structure in a sound signal and respond to musical directives such as "Delete the G played by the trumpet after the percussion enters." A musician can easily understand such an instruction; what does a computer need to know about sound and music in order to carry out such an order? This question is answered in articles 42 and 43, where the investigation is split into two parts: low-level acoustic signal processing and recognition of musical structures.

The last two articles in Part V deal with *sound spatialization*—techniques for simulating the movement of sounds in space using several loudspeakers. Two types of movement are addressed: lateral (angular) movements from loudspeaker to loudspeaker (particularly in a quadraphonic setup), and movements back from the loudspeaker into deep reverberant spaces simulated by computer.

With the palette of possible sounds expanding, technological advances such as increasingly powerful DSP chips bode well for the future of sound synthesis and signal processing. It is now feasible to implement a new generation of sophisticated synthesis and signal-processing methods using inexpensive hardware. This should put formerly rare and costly methods into the hands of more musicians. If these new chips are used imaginatively, then monochromal synthesizers, which generate a single recognizable class of sounds, should disappear in favor of more polychromal instruments, even in low-cost systems.

References

Adrien, J.-M., R. Causse, and X. Rodet. 1987. "Sound Synthesis by Physical Models—Application to Strings." In J. Beauchamp, ed., *Proceedings of the 1987 International Computer Music Conference* (San Francisco: Computer Music Association).

Chowning, J. 1973. "The Synthesis of Complex Audio Spectra by Means of Frequency Modulation." *Journal of the Audio Engineering Society* 21(7): 526–534. Reprinted in C. Roads and J. Strawn, eds., *Foundations of Computer Music* (Cambridge, Mass.: MIT Press, 1985).

Ferretti, E. 1975. "Sound Synthesis by Rule." In J. Beauchamp and J. Melby, eds., *Proceedings of the Second Annual Music Computation Conference* (Urbana: University of Illinois).

Hiller, L., and J. Beauchamp, 1967. "Review of Completed and Proposed Research on Analysis and Synthesis of Musical Sounds by Analog and Digital Techniques." Technical Report No. 19, University of Illinois Experimental Music Studio, Urbana.

Hiller, J., and P. Ruiz. 1971. "Synthesizing Musical Sounds by Solving the Wave Equation for Vibrating Objects: Parts 1 and 2." *Journal of the Audio Engineering Society* 19(1): 462–470 and 19(7): 542–551.

Jones, D., and T. Parks, 1988. "On the Generation and Combination of Grains for Music Synthesis." *Computer Music Journal* 12(2): 27–34.

Roads, C. 1978. "Automated Granular Synthesis of Sound." *Computer Music Journal* 2(2): 61–62. Revised and updated version in C. Roads and J. Strawn, eds., *Foundations of Computer Music* (Cambridge, Mass.: MIT Press, 1985).

Smith, J. 1986. "Efficient Simulation of the Reed-Bore and Bow-String Mechanisms." In P. Berg, ed., *Proceedings of the 1986 International Computer Music Conference* (San Francisco: Computer Music Association).

Strawn, J. 1985. *Digital Audio Signal Processing: An Anthology.* Los Altos, Calif.: Kaufmann.

Truax, B. 1988. "Real-Time Granular Synthesis with a Digital Signal Processor." *Computer Music Journal* 12(2): 14–26.

Varèse, Edgard. 1966. "The Liberation of Sound." In B. Boretz and E. Cone, eds., *Perspective on American Composers* (New York: Norton, 1971).

34

Giovanni De Poli
Centro di Sonologia Computazionale
Istituto di Elettrotecnica ed Elettronica
Università di Padova, Italy

A Tutorial on Digital Sound Synthesis Techniques

Introduction

Progress in electronics and computer technology has led to an ever-increasing utilization of digital techniques for musical sound production. Some of these are the digital equivalents of techniques employed in analog synthesizers and in other fields of electrical engineering. Other techniques have been specifically developed for digital music devices and are peculiar to these.

This paper introduces the fundamentals of the main digital synthesis techniques. Mathematical developments have been restricted in the exposition and can be found in the papers listed in the references. To simplify the discussion, whenever possible, the techniques are presented with reference to continuous signals.

Sound synthesis is a procedure used to produce a sound without the help of acoustic instruments. In digital synthesis, a sound is represented by a sequence of numbers (samples). Hence, a digital synthesis technique consists of a computing procedure or mathematical formula, which computes each sample value.

Normally, the synthesis formula depends on some values, that is, *parameters*. Frequency and amplitude are examples of such parameters. Parameters can be constant or slowly time variant during the sound. Time-variant parameters are also called control functions.

Synthesis techniques can be classified as (1) *generation techniques* (Fig. 1a), which directly produce the signal from given data, and (2) *transformation techniques* (Fig. 1b), which can be divided into two stages, the generation of one or more simple signals and their modification. Often, more or less elaborate combinations of these techniques are employed.

Computer Music Journal, Volume 7, No. 4,
Winter, 1983

Fixed-Waveform Synthesis

In many musical sounds, pitch is a characteristic to which we are quite sensitive. In examining the temporal shape of pitched sounds, we see a periodic repetition of the waveform without great variations. The simplest synthesis method attempts to reproduce this characteristic, generating a periodic signal through continuous repetition of the waveform. This method is called *fixed-waveform synthesis.*

The technique is carried out by a module called an *oscillator* (Fig. 2), which repeats the waveform with a specified amplitude and frequency. In certain cases, the waveform is characteristic of the oscillator and cannot be changed. But often it can be chosen in a predetermined set of options or given explicitly when required.

Usually, in digital synthesis the waveform value at a particular instant is not computed anew for each sample. Rather, a table, containing the period values computed in equally spaced points, is built beforehand. Obviously, the more numerous the points in the table, the better the approximation will be. To produce a sample, the oscillator requires the waveform value at that precise instant. It cyclically searches the table to get the point nearest to the required one. Sometimes a finer precision is achieved by interpolation between two adjacent points.

The distance in the table between two samples read at subsequent instants is called the *sampling_increment*. The sampling_increment is proportional to the frequency f of the generated signal according to the following formula (Mathews 1969):

$$sampling\_increment = \frac{N}{SR} f,$$

where N is the table length and SR the sampling rate.

In the oscillator, the frequency is usually speci-

Fig. 1. *Classification of synthesis techniques. Generation techniques (a) and transformation techniques (b).*

Fig. 2. *Fixed-waveform synthesis oscillator.*

(a)

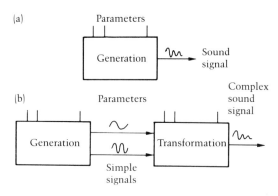

(b)

fied as a sampling-increment and the algorithm that realizes it is as follows:

$$signal\,[t] := amplitude * table\,[phase],$$
$$(Relation\ 1)$$

and

$$phase := mod(n,\ phase + sampling\_increment),$$
$$(Relation\ 2)$$

where

Table contains one period of the waveform;
Phase is the theoretical position in the table of the sample to be extracted at the instant; and
Amplitude is the signal amplitude.

Relation 2 computes the phase value in the subsequent instant, approximating the frequency integration by a summation. The modulus operation keeps the phase inside the table length n.

It is noteworthy that the signal generated in this way is an approximation of the desired one (Mailliard 1976). The approximation depends on the table length, the interpolation method, and the signal frequency. For a sufficiently long table, it is fully satisfactory.

The results of fixed-waveform synthesis are of poor musical quality, as the sound does not present any variation along its duration. This technique can be changed by allowing the amplitude to vary in time. In real sounds, the amplitude is rarely constant: it starts from zero, reaches a maximum after a certain time (attack), remains nearly constant

(steady state) and, after a certain evolution, it returns to zero (decay). This sequence of amplitude behavior is called the *envelope*. Thus, when the amplitude varies according to a control function, we have fixed-waveform synthesis with an amplitude envelope.

The envelope can be generated in many ways. In software-based synthesis, the most frequent method uses an oscillator module, seen previously, using a very low frequency equal to the inverse of the duration. In this case, it performs a single cycle and its waveform corresponds to the amplitude envelope.

By carefully analyzing natural periodic sounds, it has been shown that even the most stable ones contain small frequency fluctuations. These improve the sound quality and avoid unpleasant beatings when more sounds are present at the same time.

The fixed-waveform technique can also be modified so that the oscillator frequency can slowly vary around a value. This enables the production of a tremolo and, with wider variations, of a glissando or melodies.

The combination of these two variations constitutes fixed-waveform synthesis with time-varying amplitude and frequency. The waveform is fixed, while the amplitude and frequency vary. The partials are exact multiples of the fundamental, and they all behave the same.

Fixed-waveform synthesis is realized rather simply. Hence, it is often employed when good sound quality is not required. The constant waveform gives the sound a mechanical, dull, and unnatural character, which soon annoys the audience. Thus, in musical applications, fixed-waveform synthesis is not very effective when used alone. It is employed for its simplicity when timbral variety is not required, for example, for real-time synthesis on very limited hardware.

For economy, other methods of generating waveforms that do not use tables or multiplications have been devised. The simplest generates a square or (more generally) a rectangular wave, alternating sequences of positive and negative samples of the same value. The frequencies that can be obtained are submultiples of the sampling rate.

A sawtooth signal can also be generated by an accumulator to which a constant value is continuously added. The output increases linearly until it overflows and starts from the beginning. The signal frequency is proportional to the constant value. This method is used to produce linearly variable control signals. Every time the additive constant changes, the slope changes. Hence, functions composed of straight segments, such as envelopes, can be obtained.

This technique has been generalized recently by Mitsuhashi (1982a). A polynomial of degree N can be generated by putting N accumulators in cascade. The accumulators are initialized by the value of the forward differences, in decreasing order, of the polynomial to be generated (Cerruti and Rodeghiero 1983). The waveforms obtained exhibit great variety and, in certain conditions, they are periodic.

Granular Synthesis

The technique of fixed-waveform synthesis produces rather static sounds in time. Yet a fundamental characteristic of musical sound is its timbral evolution in time. A sound can be thought of as a sequence of elementary sounds of constant duration, analogous to a film, in which a moving image is produced by a sequence of images.

In computer music, the elementary sounds are called *grains*, and the technique of exploiting this facility is *granular synthesis* (Roads 1978). The grains can be produced by a simple oscillator or by other methods. The duration of each grain is very short, on the order of 5–20 msec.

There are two ways to implement granular synthesis. The first is to organize the grains into *frames*, like the frames of a film. At each frame, the parameters of all the grains are updated. This is the approach sketched by Xenakis (1971). The second way involves scattering the grains within a *mask*, which bounds a particular frequency/amplitude/time region. The density of the grains may vary within the mask. This is the method implemented by Roads (1978).

A problem with granular synthesis is the large amount of parameter data to be specified. In some other types of synthesis (additive and subtractive, to be discussed shortly), these data can be obtained by analyzing natural sounds. However, no analysis system for granular synthesis has been developed. Another possibility is to obtain the parameter data from an interactive composition system, which allows the composer to work with high-level musical concepts while automatically generating the thousands of grain parameters needed.

Additive Synthesis

In *additive synthesis*, complex sounds are produced by the superimposition of elementary sounds. In certain conditions, the constituent sounds fuse together and the result is perceived as a unique sound. This procedure is used in some traditional instruments, too. In an organ, the pipes generally produce relatively simple sounds; to obtain a richer spectrum in some registers, notes are created by using more pipes sounding at different pitches at the same time. The piano uses a different procedure. Many notes are obtained by the simultaneous percussion of two or three strings, each oscillating at a slightly different frequency. This improves the sound intensity and enriches it with beatings.

In order to choose the elementary sounds of additive synthesis, we first note that the Fourier analysis model enables us to analyze sounds in a way similar to the human ear and so to extract parameters that are perceptually significant. When we analyze a real, almost-periodic sound, we immediately notice that each partial amplitude is not proportionally constant, but that it varies in time

Fig. 3. Additive synthesis.

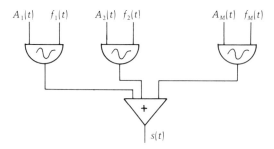

according to different laws. In the attack portion of a note, some partials, which in the steady state are negligible, are often significant.

Any almost-periodic sound can be approximated as a sum of sinusoids. Each sinusoid's frequency is nearly multiple that of the fundamental, and each sinusoid evolves in time. For higher precision, the frequency of each component can be considered as slowly varying. Thus, additive synthesis consists of the addition of some sinusoidal oscillators, whose amplitude, and at times frequency, is time varying (Fig. 3).

The additive-synthesis technique also provides good reproduction of nonperiodic sounds, presenting in the spectrum the energy concentrated in some spectral lines. For example, Risset (1969) imitated a bell sound by summing sinusoidal components of harmonically unrelated frequencies, some of which were beating. In Risset's example, the exponential envelope was longer for the lower partials.

Additive synthesis provides great generality. But a problem arises because of the large amount of data to be specified for each note. Two control functions for each component have to be specified, and normally they are different for each sound, depending on its duration, intensity, and frequency. The possibility of data reduction has been investigated. At Stanford University, a first result has been obtained by representing the control functions of the amplitude and the frequency of each component by line segments, without affecting "naturalness" of the sound (Grey and Moorer 1977).

The next step has been to investigate the relations between these functions (Risset and Mathews 1969; Beauchamp 1975) or their relation to others of more general character (Charbonneau 1981). Additive synthesis is most practically used either in synthesis based on analysis (analysis/synthesis), often transforming the extracted parameters, or when a sound of a precise and well-determined characteristic is required, as in psychoacoustic experiments. In any case, in order to familiarize musicians with sound characteristics and frequency representations, the technique is also useful from a pedagogical point of view.

Additive synthesis can be generalized by using waveform components of other shapes besides sinusoids. To allow the reproduction of any sound, these waveforms have to satisfy specific mathematical properties. Walsh functions are an example of this kind of function; they are used for their simple hardware realization (Rozenberg 1979).

VOSIM

In the synthesis techniques already discussed, oscillators that periodically reproduce a given waveform are employed. Other synthesis techniques, instead of continuously repeating a given waveform, calculate it anew each period, with minor variations. The control of this calculation process allows continuous spectral variations. A common method of this type is the voice simulation (VOSIM) technique. A VOSIM oscillator has been devised in a project at the Institute of Sonology in Utrecht (Kaegi 1973, 1974; Kaegi and Tempelaars 1978).

The VOSIM waveform (Fig. 4) consists of a sequence of N pulses of shape $\sin^2$, of the same duration T, and of decreasing amplitude. The sequence is followed by a pause M. Each pulse's amplitude is smaller than the preceding one, by a constant factor b.

The VOSIM spectrum (Fig. 5a) is described as the product of two terms (Tempelaars 1976; De Poli and De Poli 1979). The first term S_1 (Fig. 5b) depends only on the pulse shape and limits the signal bandwidth to $2F$ (being $F = 1/T$). The second term S_2 (Fig. 5c) depends on the relationship between the individual pulse amplitudes. S_2 is periodic in the frequency domain with a period F, and it is sym-

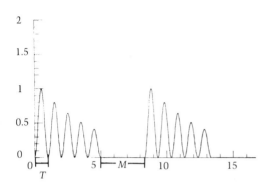

Fig. 4. VOSIM oscillator: T is the duration of single pulse, M the rest between two sequences of pulses.

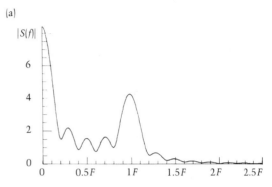

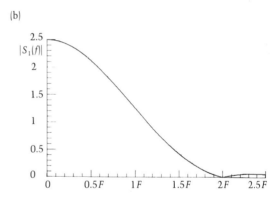

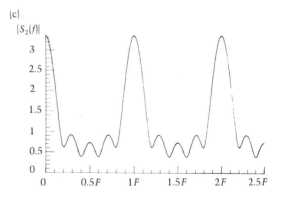

Fig. 5. Spectral envelope of a VOSIM oscillator ($N = 5$, $b = 0$, 8) (a). The envelope is the product of the terms S_1 (b) and S_2 (c).

metric with respect to $F/2$. When $b \approx 1$, its amplitude will be greater around the extremes of the period 0 and F. When $b \approx -1$, its amplitude will be greater in the central position around $F/2$. Thus, a characteristic formant in F or $F/2$ will result. The number of pulses N produces N oscillations in the S_2 term between 0 and F, with strong signals for b near $\pm F$.

This constitutes the spectral envelope of the repeated waveform. Taking α as the ratio between the signal period and a single pulse duration, the number of the harmonic corresponding to the formant is α if b is positive, and $\alpha/2$ if b is negative. Thus, by varying α, the formant shifts, and the relative amplitude of all the harmonics vary continuously but not homogeneously, following the spectral envelope. The signal and the formant frequencies can be separately controlled.

More kinds of sounds can be obtained by modulating (sinusoidally or randomly) the value of the time interval M between two consecutive pulse sequences. This means that α varies independently from T. In this case, the formant frequency remains constant while the harmonic amplitudes vary. Then the ear can easily perceive the spectral envelope and fuse the components together. This property makes the VOSIM oscillator effective in musical applications.

If α variation is strong, practically aperiodic sounds or colored noises are obtained. Adding several VOSIM oscillators allows one to control the position of the formants. This results in an additive synthesis of already complex sounds rather than of sinuosidal components. Instead of the frequency of partials, the position of the formants is controlled. This is a more relevant parameter, from an acoustic standpoint.

The *formant-wave-function synthesis* of Rodet (1980) is analogous to VOSIM, but it allows overlapping of single waveforms. This provides better control and generally richer sounds. Mitsuhashi (1982a) and Bass and Goeddel (1981) generalized the VOSIM model by including the case of pulses of any amplitude and using different elementary waveforms.

Synthesis by Random Signals

Up to now, we have considered signals whose behavior at any instant is supposed to be perfectly knowable. These signals are called *deterministic signals*. Besides these signals, *random signals*, of unknown or only partly known behavior, may be considered. For random signals, only some general characteristics, called statistical properties, are known or are of interest. The statistical properties are characteristic of an entire signal class rather than of a single signal. A set of random signals is represented by a *random process*. Particular numerical procedures simulate random processes, producing sequences of random (or more precisely, pseudorandom) numbers. The linear congruential method is commonly used to produce uniformly distributed numbers. From a starting value X_0, a sequence of random integers $X_0, X_1, \ldots, X_K \ldots$ is generated according to the relation

$$X_{K+1} = (a \cdot X_K + c)_{\mathrm{mod}\, m,}$$

where m is the modulus and the maximum sequence period, and a and c are two specific integer constants.

The modulus operation can be avoided by choosing m as the maximum number representable in the computer, that is, $m = 2^b$, where b is the word length (bit number in a binary computer). So the numbers are automatically truncated. The choice of X_0, a, and c greatly affects the statistical characteristics of the generated sequence, and its accept-

ability has to be accurately verified by statistical tests. A general discussion of various distributions and the methods used to generate them can be found in Lorrain's paper (1980).

Random sequences can be used both as *signals* (i.e., to produce white or colored noise used as input to a filter) and as *control functions* to provide a variety in the synthesis parameters most perceptible by the listener.

In the analysis of natural sounds, some characteristics vary in an unpredictable way; their mean statistical properties are perceptibly more significant than their exact behavior. Hence, the addition of a random component to the deterministic functions controlling the synthesis parameters is often desirable.

In general, a combination of random processes is used because the temporal organization of the musical parameters often has a hierarchical aspect. It cannot be well described by a single random process, but rather by a combination of random processes evolving at different rates.

Linear Transformations

Let us now examine techniques for signal modification. A *transformation* is a set of rules and procedures transforming a signal called input to another signal called output. A transformation is linear if the superimposition principle is valid, that is, if the effect of the transformation caused by a two-signal addition is equal to the addition of the individual signal transformations applied separately. In particular, in a linear transformation a signal can be multiplied by a constant but not by another signal.

Digital filters are linear transformations that can be described by the following difference equation:

$$\sum_{K=0}^{N} a_K\, y(n - K) = \sum_{i=0}^{M} b_i\, x(n - i),$$

where a_K and b_i are the filter coefficients and $x(j)$ and $y(j)$ are the jth sample of the input and output signal. The value of the output sample is thus a linear combination of current instantaneous input with the preceding instant's input and output. When

Fig. 6. Finite-impulse-
response (FIR) filter with
two zeros described by the
equation y(n) = x(n) +
α₁x(n − 1) + α₂x(n − 2)
(a). Infinite-impulse-
response (IIR) filter with
two poles described by the
equation y(n) = x(n) +
β₁y(n − 1) + β₂y(n − 2)
(b).

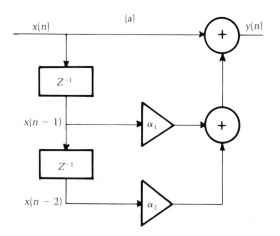

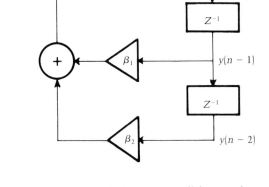

the input is sinusoidal, the steady-state output is sinusoidal with the same frequency. The amplitude and phase of the frequencies are determined by the system. That is why this transformation is called a filter.

Subtractive Synthesis

Sound produced by filtering a complex waveform is called, sometimes inappropriately, *subtractive syn-thesis*. First, a periodic or aleatoric signal rich in harmonics is generated by the previously examined techniques or others. This signal must contain energy in all frequencies required in the output sound. Second, one or more filters are used to alter selectively the specific frequency components. The undesired components are attenuated (subtracted) and others are eventually amplified. When the filter coefficients change, the frequency response changes, too. Thus, it is possible to vary characteristics of the output sound.

In modular diagrams, filters are usually repre-sented by rectangles and the difference equation or the transfer function is given as a label near the rectangle. Two examples of simple digital filters, showing their internal structure, are shown in Fig. 6. The first filter (Fig. 6a) has a finite-impulse response (FIR). This structure is useful to produce

transmission zeros: that is, it can nullify some fre-quencies that depend on α_1, α_2 values and on the sampling rate. The second filter (Fig. 6b) is recur-sive, or has an infinite-impulse response (IIR). Feed-back in the structure amplifies certain frequencies, that is, produces transmission poles. When used as bandpass filter, in general terms, the coefficient β_1 controls the center frequency and the coefficient β_2 the bandwidth.

One of the most attractive aspects of digital filter-ing is that it is analogous to the functioning of many acoustic musical instruments. Indeed, instru-ment physics can be used as a model for synthesis. For example, in the brasses and woodwind instru-ments, the lips or vibrating reed generate a periodic signal rich in harmonics. The various cavities and the shape of the instrument act as resonators, en-hancing some spectral components and attenuating others. In the human voice, the excitation signals are periodic pulses of the glottis (in the case of voiced sounds) or white noise (in the case of un-voiced sounds—for example, the consonants s and z). The throat, the mouth, and the nose are the fil-tering cavities, and their dimensions vary in time. Their great variability makes the human voice the most rich and interesting musical instrument.

Today, subtractive synthesis is the standard means of speech synthesis. An analysis procedure, called linear predictive coding (LPC), allows us to obtain

Fig. 7. Elementary filters
used in reverberators.
Comb filters (a). All-pass
filter (b).

the pitch and the coefficients of a recursive (poles only) filter (see Cann's [1979–1980] tutorial and Moorer's paper [1979a]). These data can be utilized to synthesize the sound directly or following modification. For example, speech can be accelerated or slowed down, and pitch can be varied. An instrument or orchestral sound can be used as input to the filter, producing the effect of a "talking orchestra."

Interesting possibilities for *musique concrète* sound processing arise. Not only simple filtering of sounds is possible, but the modification of their most intrinsic characteristics is also made possible by varying the parameters of the deduced sound-production model.

Generally, LPC is relatively difficult to use. Intuitively, the filter characteristics depend on the position of the zeros and the poles in the transfer function. These characteristics are affected in a complex and nonintuitive way by the filter coefficients. In some simple cases, approximate formulas give the coefficients as functions of significant parameters, that is, center frequency and bandwidth, or cutoff frequency and slope. The filters can be used in series or in parallel. In the most complex cases, a precise analysis is obtained by using specific programs for digital filter design and analysis. Such digital filters can be very stable and precise, but only at the cost of a large amount of calculation. Simple linear digital networks can also be used as oscillators (Tempelaars 1982) by applying a pulse sequence to the input and choosing an impulse response equal to the signal function to be generated.

Reverberation

One application of digital filters is sound reverberation. An acoustic environment can be simulated by distributing sound among different loudspeakers and by adjusting the ratio between direct and reverberated sound (Chowning 1971). Most of the studio reverberators sold today use digital technology.

The two elementary filters used in reverberation are shown in Fig. 7. The first filter is called a *comb filter*; in it, the signal is delayed a certain number of samples, attenuated, and added to the input. An ex-

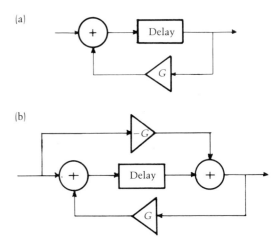

(a)

(b)

ponentially decaying, repeated echo is so obtained. The frequency response is characterized by equispaced peaks—hence this filter's name. The peaks' amplitude increases as G approaches 1.

The second filter is called an *all-pass filter*, since the frequency response is flat and there is only a phase shift. The input signal is attenuated and subtracted from the delayed signal so that the feedback effect is compensated and the echoes are maintained. The all-pass property is valid only in the steady state with stationary sounds, not in transient states. Thus, it has a well-defined sound quality that a skilled listener can easily distinguish.

Reverberators are built combining some of these filters (Moorer 1979b). Distinguishable signal repetitions should not occur in them, since the reverberated result should consist of a diffused sound. The delay time of each elementary filter has to be chosen very carefully. Sometimes a nonrecursive echo generator is added to produce the first aperiodic echoes, which are the main perceptual determinants of the characteristics of the room.

Nonlinear Techniques

In addition to linear transformations, which are used in other fields and have a rather developed theory, nonlinear transformations are used more and

De Poli

Fig. 8. Waveshaping.

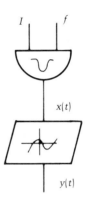

more commonly in musical applications. They derive mainly from electrical communication theory, and they have proved to be promising and effective. One use of nonlinear synthesis is in the large amount of computer music generated by frequency modulation (FM) synthesis (Chowning 1973).

In the classic case, nonlinear techniques use simple sinusoids as input signals. The output is composed of many sinusoids, whose frequency and amplitude depend mostly on the input ones.

Two main types of nonlinear techniques can be distinguished, waveshaping and modulation. In *waveshaping*, one input is shaped by a function depending only on the input value in that instant. In *modulation* (with two or more inputs), a simple parameter of one signal, called the carrier, is varied according to the behavior of another signal, called the modulator. In electrical communications (e.g., radio) the spectra of the signals are clearly distinguished and therefore easily separable. The originality in computer music application is the utilization of signals in the same frequency range. Thus, the two signals interact in a complex way, and simple input variation affects all the resultant components.

Often, the input amplitudes are varied by multiplying them by a constant or time-dependent parameter I, called the modulation index. Thus, acting only on one parameter, the sound characteristics are substantially varied. Dynamic and variable spectra are easily obtainable. In additive synthesis, similar variations require a much larger amount of data.

Waveshaping

A linear filter can change the amplitude and phase of a sinusoid, but not its waveform, whereas the aim of waveshaping is to change the waveform. The distortion of a signal heard from a nonlinear amplifier is common. The output from a nonlinear amplifier of a sinusoidal signal is a signal with the same period, but with a different waveform. The various harmonics are present, and their amplitude depends on the input and on the distortion. In stereo systems, these distortions are usually avoided,

while waveshaping (Arfib 1979; Le Brun 1979; Roads 1979) exploits them to generate periodic sounds, rich in harmonics, from a simple sinusoid.

The function $F(x)$, describing distortion, is called the shaping function, and it associates with each input value the corresponding output value independent of time. If the input is $x(t) = \cos(2\pi ft)$, the output is

$$s(t) = F(x(t)) = F(\cos[2\pi ft]).$$

In analog synthesis, it is difficult to have an amplifier with a precise and variable distortion characteristic. In digital synthesis, this technique is extremely easy to implement (Fig. 8). As in the case of the oscillator, the shaping function can be previously computed and stored in a table. All that is necessary is to look up the proper value from the table.

Generally, if $F(x) = F_1(x) + F_2(x)$, the distortion produced by F is equal to the sum of those produced by F_1 and F_2 separately. Usually, the shaping produces infinite harmonics. But when a polynomial of degree N is chosen as shaping function, only the first N harmonics are present. Thus, foldover is easily avoided. Arfib and Le Brun deal extensively with the mathematical relations among the coefficients d_i of the shaping polynomial and the amplitudes h_i of harmonics generated when the amplitude I of the cosinusoidal input varies.

The shaping function, producing the jth harmonic, is the Chebychev polynomial $T_j(x)$ of degree j (Fig. 9). Thus, to obtain the various harmonics of

Fig. 9. Chebychev poly-
nomial of degree K used as
shaping function produces
only the Kth harmonic. In
the figure, K = 3.

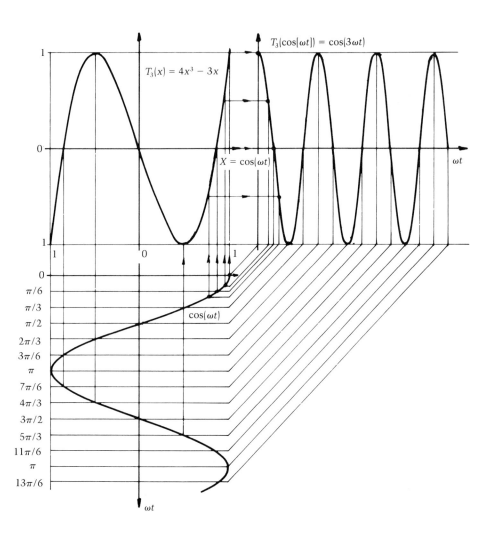

amplitude h_i, it is sufficient to add the correspondent Chebychev polynomials, each multiplied by h_i:

$$F(x) = \sum_{i=0}^{N} h_i T_i(x) = \sum_{i=0}^{N} d_i x^i.$$

From these relations, it follows that the even harmonics are completely separate from odd ones. An even polynomial coefficient affects only the even harmonics. In the same way, odd coefficients affect only the odd harmonics. For example, the coefficient of x^7 affects only the first, third, fifth and seventh harmonics. Moreover, an even (or odd) harmonic of order n is affected only by the even (or odd) coefficients of order n and greater than n. For example, the seventh harmonic is affected by the odd coefficients from the seventh up to the degree of the polynomial.

When the input amplitude I varies, the distortion and the output spectrum vary. This is similar to an expansion or contraction of the function, since greater or smaller range of the function is employed. From a mathematical point of view, the amplitude variation corresponds to the multiplication of each polynomial coefficient d_i by I^i. The amplitudes of the even or odd harmonics depend on I according to the even (or odd) polynomials, which contain the terms from the harmonic order up to the polynomial degree.

If the spectrum is rather smooth, the number of significant harmonics increases with the index. Thus, a typical characteristic of real instruments is reproduced, in that amplitude and spectrum are correlated. The amplitude and loudness of the output vary with the input amplitude. In simple cases, this effect can be compensated for by multiplying the output by a suitable normalization function. But in musical applications, the amplitude of the signal is rarely constant, and it is multiplied by an envelope. Normalization can be avoided by combining it with the amplitude envelope in experimental or intuitive ways after considering the normalization function.

It is also advisable to choose the even (or odd) polynomial coefficients with alternating signs, that is, according to the following model: $+ + - -$ $+ + - -$. It is also advisable that the h_i amplitude not decrease abruptly, sharply limiting the band. Otherwise, a spectrum would result that varied very irregularly with I.

Dynamic spectral behavior cannot be easily anticipated from the coefficients or from the static spectrum. Moreover, the same (absolute-value) spectrum can be produced by many polynomials with different dynamic behaviors (Forin 1982). With waveshaping, listening and graphic considerations have more relevance than purely mathematical formulations.

Another dynamic variation of waveshaping that is easy to implement occurs when a constant is added to the input; the shaping function shifts horizontally. Even in this case, the spectrum varies.

The signal is periodic, with the same number of harmonics. But in this case, the harmonic behavior depends on both the even and the odd coefficients.

Generalizations of waveshaping technique are possible. Reinhard (1981) studied the relations that produce the partials generated by the polynomial distortion of two cosine waves of frequency f_1 and f_2. All the components of frequency $|K f_1 \pm j f_2|$ with $|K + j| \leq N$, where N is the polynomial degree, are present.

Shaping functions that are not polynomial can be used if the spectra produced by them are almost band limited. Of particular interest is the use of trigonometric and exponential functions (Moorer 1977) and of those where the input also appears in the denominator (Winham and Steiglitz 1970; Moorer 1976; Lehmann and Brown 1976; De Poli 1981).

Due to the wide spectral variation induced by only one parameter (amplitude or shift), waveshaping is particularly convenient in musical applications, especially in combination with multiplicative synthesis. Moreover, it is suitable for modeling the sound production of some acoustic instruments (Beauchamp 1979, 1982). There is a large and not intuitive problem in choosing the coefficients, however, and further research is required.

Multiplicative Synthesis (Ring Modulation)

The simplest nonlinear transformation consists of the multiplication of two signals. In analog synthesizers, it is called ring modulation (RM). Sometimes it is also called amplitude modulation (AM), but the two differ, especially in their realization.

With two inputs $x_1(t)$ and $x_2(t)$, the output is $s(t) = x_1(t) \cdot x_2(t)$. Obviously, when the inputs interchange, the result does not vary. The resulting spectrum is obtained from the convolution of the two signals' spectra. Usually, one of the two signals, called the carrier, is sinusoidal; the result is not too complex and noisy.

When x_1 is the sinusoidal carrier of frequency f_1, and x_2 (modulator) is sinusoidal with frequency f_2, from $\cos(\alpha) \cdot \cos(\beta) = \frac{1}{2}|\cos(\alpha + \beta) + \cos(\alpha - \beta)|$, the output consists of two sinusoidal partials of frequency $f_1 + f_2$ and $f_1 - f_2$. The phases of the output are also the sum and the difference of the phases of the two inputs. For example, if x_1 and x_2 frequencies are 400 Hz and 100 Hz, the output has two partials of frequency 500 Hz and 300 Hz.

Negative frequencies may occur, for example, when $f_1 = 100$ Hz and $f_2 = 400$ Hz. This often happens in modulations (foldunder) and can be explained by the trigonometric relation $\cos(\alpha) = \cos(-\alpha)$, from which $\cos(2\pi\, ft + \phi) = \cos(\pi[-f]t - \phi)$. The alteration of the frequency sign only changes the sign of the phase with respect to the cosine. In particular, a cosine signal is unaffected, while a sine wave changes its sign. In the interpretation of the results, only absolute frequency values have to be considered. Usually, the phase is not significant, as the ear is not terribly sensitive to it. But the phase has to be taken into account while summing the amplitude of components of identical frequencies.

In multiplicative synthesis, usually x_2 is periodic with frequency f_2. The multiplication causes every harmonic spectral line of frequency $K \cdot f_2$ in the original signal to be replaced by two spectral lines (called sidebands) of frequency $f_1 + K\, f_2$ and $f_1 - K\, f_2$. The resulting spectrum has components of frequency $|f_1 \pm K\, f_2|$, where K is equal to the order of the different harmonics in x_2 (Fig. 10).

Thus two sidebands, symmetric with respect to the carrier, occur. When f_1 is less than the greatest frequency in x_2, then the negative frequencies fold around zero, as discussed above.

The possibility of shifting the spectrum is very intriguing in musical applications. From simple components, harmonic and inharmonic sounds can be created, and various harmonic relations among the partials can be established. If x_2 is a signal with spectrum X_2, the signal obtained from its multiplication with a sinusoid of frequency f_1 has two sidebands symmetric with respect to f_1 and shaped like X_2.

A periodic signal x_1 can be expanded in Fourier series. Each x_1 partial will have sidebands of amplitude proportional to its own. If f_1 is less than the bandwidth of x_2, then the sidebands overlap with

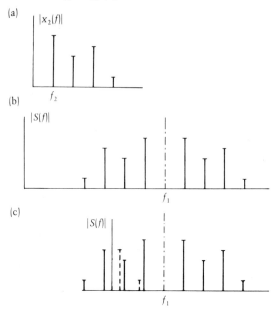

Fig. 10. Multiplicative synthesis. Spectrum of a periodic signal X_2 with four harmonics (a). Resulting spectrum when d_2 is multiplied by a sinusoid of frequency f_1 greater than its bandwidth $(f_1 = 7f_2)$ (b). Resulting spectrum when x_2 is multiplied by a sinusoid of frequency inferior to its bandwidth $(f_1 = 26f_2)$ (c). The components deriving from the folding of negative frequencies are shown as dashed lines.

(a) $|x_2(f)|$
f_2

(b) $|S(f)|$
f_1

(c) $|S(f)|$
f_1

eventual component superimposition. In this case, the phases have to be taken in account while summing. Dashow (1978, 1980) describes some generalization of this technique and employs the generated spectra for particular "harmonizations" of pitches specified by the composer.

Amplitude Modulation

In RM, the carrier does not appear in the spectrum created by the product of a sinusoidal carrier with another signal, except when the modulator has a direct current (dc) component. In carrying out the modulation in AM (Fig. 11), the carrier is present in the output, with an amplitude independent of the sidebands. The formula for AM is as follows:

$$s(t) = x_1(t) \cdot (K + x_2(t)).$$

The result is RM with carrier added. When the carrier is sinusoidal and the modulator is periodic, the spectrum is composed of partials of frequency $|f_1 \pm K\, f_2|$, with $K = 0, 1, \ldots$. It is useful to distin-

De Poli

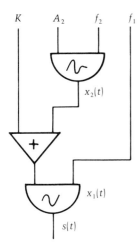

Fig. 11. Amplitude modulation.

guish between the two modulations because they have different realization schemes.

Spectra of Type $|f_1 \pm K f_2|$

The following considerations are valid for all spectra whose components are of type $|f_1 \pm K f_2|$, with $K = 0, 1, \ldots$. The spectrum is characterized by the ratio f_1/f_2. (This is often referred to as the carrier-to-modulator [c:m] ratio.) When this ratio is rational, it can be expressed as an irreducible fraction $f_1/f_2 = N_1/N_2$, with N_1 and N_2 as integers that are prime between themselves. In this case, the resulting sound is harmonic, since the various components are a multiple of a fundamental according to integer factors. The fundamental frequency is

$$f_0 = \frac{f_1}{N_1} = \frac{f_2}{N_2},$$

and the carrier coincides with the N_1th harmonic.

If $N_2 = 1$, all the harmonics are present and the sideband components coincide. If $N_2 = 2$, only odd harmonics are present and the sidebands superimpose. If $N_2 = 3$, the harmonics that are multiples of 3 are missing. The c:m ratio is also an index of the

harmonicity of the spectrum. The sound is more "harmonious" intuitively when the N_1/N_2 ratio is simple and formally when the $N_1 \cdot N_2$ product is smaller.

The ratios can be grouped in families (Truax 1977). All ratios of the type $|f_1 \pm K f_2|/f_2$ can produce the same components that f_1/f_2 produces. Only the partial coinciding with the carrier (f_1) changes. For example, the ratios 2/3, 5/3, 1/3, 4/3, 7/3 and so on all belong to the same family. Only the harmonics that are multiples of 3 are missing (see $N_2 = 3$), and the carrier is respectively the second, fifth, first, fourth, seventh, and so on harmonic.

The ratio that distinguishes a family is defined in normal form when it is $\leq 1/2$. In the previous example, it is 1/3. Each family is characterized by a ratio in normal form. Similar spectra can be produced using ratios from the same family. Different spectra are obtained by sounds of different families.

When the f_1/f_2 ratio is irrational, the resulting sound is aperiodic and hence, inharmonic. Of particular interest is the case of an f_1/f_2 ratio approximating a simple value, that is,

$$f_1/f_2 = N_1/N_2 + \varepsilon.$$

Here the sound is no longer rigorously periodic. The fundamental frequency f_0 is still f_2/N_2, and the harmonics are shifted from their exact values by $\pm \varepsilon \cdot f_2$. When N_2 is equal to 1 or 2, the positive and negative components are not superimposed but beat with a frequency of $2\varepsilon \cdot f_2$. Hence, a small shift of the carrier does not change the pitch, even if it slightly spreads the partials and makes the sound more lively. But the same shift of the modulating frequency f_2 changes the sound's pitch.

Frequency and Phase Modulation

Another type of modulation, suggested by Chowning (1973), has become one of the most widely used synthesis techniques. In general, it consists of *angle modulation* and it can be realized both as phase modulation (ϕM) or as FM. This technique does not derive from models of production of physical sounds, but only from the mathematical properties of a formula. It has some of the advantages of waveshaping and RM, and it avoids some of their drawbacks.

The technique consists of the modulation of the instantaneous phase or frequency of a sinusoidal carrier according to the behavior of another signal (modulator), which is usually sinusoidal. It can be expressed as follows:

$$s(t) = \sin(2\pi \, f_c t + I \sin(2\pi \, f_m t)) = \quad (1)$$
$$= \sum_{-\infty}^{+\infty} {}_K J_K (I)\sin|2\pi(f_c + K f_m)t|.$$

The resulting spectrum is of the type $|f_c \pm K f_m|$. All the spectral considerations discussed previously are applicable, particularly those regarding negative frequency, foldunder, f_c/f_m ratios, and harmonic and inharmonic sounds.

The amplitude of each Kth side component of the FM technique is given by the Bessel function of Kth order computed in I. To plot the spectrum, a table of Bessel functions has to be referenced to obtain the amplitudes of the carrier and of the side frequencies in the upper sideband. The odd-order side frequencies in the lower sideband have signs opposite to those in the upper one, and the even-order side frequencies have the same sign. The negative frequencies, being sine waves, are folded, changing the sign. When superimposition occurs, the amplitudes are added algebraically.

When I (called the modulation index) varies, the amplitude of each component varies as well. Thus, dynamic spectra can be obtained simply by varying this index. Each component varies its amplitude by following the corresponding Bessel function. A Bessel function can be asymptotically approximated by a damped sinusoid. So when the index varies, some components increase and others decrease, all without sharp variations.

In Eq. (1), the sum includes infinite terms, so theoretically the signal bandwidth is not limited. But, practically, it is limited. In the Bessel function's behavior, only a few low-order functions are significant for small index values. When the index increases, the number and the order of the significant functions increase. For a given index, the side amplitudes oscillate with gradually increasing amplitude and slowly increasing period all the way from

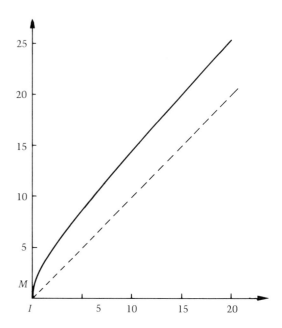

Fig. 12. The number of significant sidebands in FM.

the origin to a maximum, and then decrease rapidly toward zero. The maximum is reached for a value slightly below the modulation index.

Usually, in the bandwidth definition of the FM signal, all side frequencies of amplitude greater than $1/100$ of the nonmodulated signal are considered. The number M of the significant sidebands is

$$M = I + 2.4 \cdot I^{0.27}.$$

(See Fig. 12.) Often, as a rule of thumb, it is roughly considered as

$$M = I + 1.$$

In Eq. (1), the sum can be performed for K from $-M$ to $+M$. For a harmonic sound, that is, when the ratio $f_c/f_m = N_1/N_2$ is simple, the maximum order of significant harmonics is $N_1 + M \cdot N_2$.

For wide index variations, the sounds produced are characteristic of the FM technique. A typical timbre of FM sound is easily recognizable and thus well defined. This does not happen for small index variations or for compound carriers or modulators. Frequency modulation synthesis has another prop-

De Poli

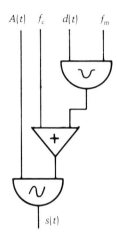

Fig. 13. Frequency
modulation.

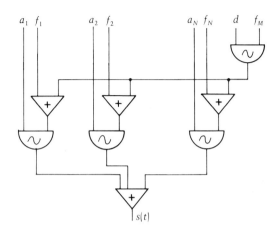

Fig. 14. Frequency modu-
lation with N carriers
modulated by the same
oscillator.

erty that is very important in musical applications:
the maximum amplitude and the signal power do
not vary with the index I. Unlike the situation in
waveshaping, normalization of the output is not
necessary.

Let us now examine the difference between ϕM
and FM. Phase modulation is defined as follows:

$$s(t) = \sin(2M f_c t + \phi[t]),$$

and it corresponds to Eq. (1) if the modulating signal is $\phi(t) = I \sin(2\pi f_m t)$.

Frequency modulation occurs when the instantaneous frequency varies around the carrier value according to the behavior of the modulating wave. For
a signal $s(t) = \sin(\psi[t])$, the instantaneous frequency
is $f_i = (1/2\pi)(d\psi[t]/dt)$. Thus, the instantaneous
frequency of the signal in Eq. (1) is as follows:

$$f_i = f_c + I f_m \cos(2\pi f_m t).$$

The frequency varies around f_c with a maximum
deviation $d = I \cdot f_m$. Thus, with a modulating wave
$I \cdot f_m \cos(2\pi f_m t)$, an FM equivalent to ϕM is obtained. Both phase and frequency modulations are
special cases of angle modulation.

In sound synthesis programs, frequency-driven
oscillators are provided. The integration involved in
calculating the instantaneous phase is therefore

computed automatically. Frequency modulation is
normally implemented as in Fig. 13. A change of
the phase between the carrier and the modulating
wave in Eq. (1) only changes the reciprocal phase of
the partials. If components superimpose, their total
amplitude changes, and a direct-current component
may appear. The next sections examine some useful extensions of the basic algorithm.

Nonsinusoidal Carrier

Here we consider a periodic nonsinusoidal carrier.
The result of its modulation is the modulation of
each of its harmonics by the same wave. Sidebands
of amplitude proportional to each harmonic will be
present around the carrier. The result is a spectrum
with components of frequency $|n \cdot f_c \pm K \cdot f_m|$, with
$K = 0, \ldots, M$ and $n = 1, \ldots, N$, when N is the
number of significant harmonics. The maximum
frequency present is $N \cdot f_c + M \cdot f_m$. In general, there
may be various independent carriers modulated by
the same wave (Fig. 14) or by different modulating
signals. This is like additive synthesis, only instead
of sinusoidal addends, more complex addends are
used. For example, harmonic sounds can be generated by controlling the various spectral ranges with a
few significant and independent parameters. Sounds
of the same "family" are possible.

The frequency of each carrier determines the

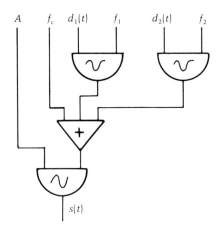

Fig. 15. Frequency modulation with two modulators.

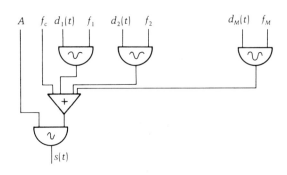

Fig. 16. Frequency modulation with N modulators.

location of the formant position, the amplitude determines its energy, and the modulation index specifies its bandwidth. Chowning (1981) demonstrated these facilities in synthesis of the singing voice of a soprano.

Compound Modulation

Let us examine the case of a modulation composed of two sinusoids (Fig. 15), each with its own modulation index, applied to a sinusoidal carrier. The formula for two-sine-wave ϕM (Le Brun 1977) is as follows:

$$s(t) = \sin(|2\pi f_c t + I_1 \sin[2\pi f_1 t] + I_2 \sin[2\pi f_2 t]|)$$

$$= \Sigma_K \, \Sigma_n \, J_K(I_1) \cdot J_n(I_2) \cdot \sin(|2\pi[f_c + K f_1 + n f_2]t|).$$

The same result can be obtained with FM using as modulating signal the following expression:

$$I_1 f_1 \cos(2\pi f_1 t) + I_2 f_2 \cos(2\pi f_2 t).$$

The resulting spectrum is much more complex than in the one-modulator case. All the components of frequency $|f_c \pm K f_1 \pm n f_2|$ are present, and their amplitude is $J_K(I_1) \cdot J_n(I_2)$.

To interpret the effect, let us consider $f_1 > f_2$. If only f_1 were present, the resulting spectrum would have a certain number of components of amplitude $J_K(I_1)$ and frequency $f_c \pm K f_1$. When the modulator

f_2 is applied, these components become carriers, with sidebands produced by f_2. The resulting bandwidth is approximately equal to the sum of the two bandwidths.

If the frequencies have simple ratios, the spectrum is of the type $|f_c \pm K f_m|$, where now f_m is the greatest common divisor of f_1 and f_2. For example, with $f_c = 700$ Hz, $f_1 = 300$ Hz, and $f_2 = 200$ Hz, the components are $|700 \pm K \cdot 100|$. Thus, by choosing f_1 and f_2 multiples of f_m, sounds belonging to the same family as a simple modulation, but with a more complex spectral structure, can be generated. In general, if the modulating signal is composed of N sinusoids (Fig. 16), the following relations hold:

$$s(t) = \sin\left(\left|2\pi f_c t + \sum_1^N I \sin[2\pi f_s t]\right|\right)$$

$$= \Sigma_{K_s} \prod_{s=1}^N J_{K_s}(I_s) \cdot \sin|2\pi(f_c t + \Sigma K_s f_s)t|.$$

Thus, all the components of frequency $|f_c \pm K_1 f_1 \pm \ldots \pm K_N f_N|$, with amplitudes given by the product of N Bessel functions, are obtained. A very complex spectrum results. If the relations among the frequencies f_s are simple, that is, if the modulating wave is periodic, then the spectrum is of the type $|f_c \pm K f_m|$, where f_m is the greatest common divisor among the modulating components. Otherwise, the sonorities are definitely inharmonic and particularly noisy for high indexes.

Fig. 17. Nested FM.

Nested or Complex Modulation

Let us examine the case of a sinusoidal modulator that is phase modulated by another sinusoid. The signal is defined as follows:

$$s(t) = \sin(|2\pi\, f_c t + I \sin[2\pi\, f_1 t + I_2 \sin\{2\pi\, f_2 t\}]|)$$

$$= \Sigma_K J_K(I_1)\sin(|2\pi[f_c + K\, f_1]t + K\, I_2 \sin[2\pi\, f_2 t]|)$$

$$= \Sigma_K J_K(I_1) \cdot J_n(KI_2)\sin(2\pi[f_c + K_1 f_1 + n\, f_2]t).$$

The result can be interpreted as if each partial produced by the modulator f_1 were modulated in its turn by f_2 with modulation index $K\, I_2$. Thus, all the partials of frequency $|f_c \pm K\, f_1 \pm n\, f_2|$, with approximately $0 \le K \le I_1$, $0 \le n \le I_1 \cdot I_2$, are present. The maximum frequency is $f_c + I_1(f_1 + I_2 f_2)$.

The structure of the spectrum is similar to that produced by the two-sinusoid modulation, but with a larger bandwidth. Even where f_m is the greatest common divisor between f_1 and f_2, the spectrum is of the type $|f_c \pm K\, f_m|$.

In the equivalent realization by FM (Fig. 17), the spectrum is of the same type, but with slightly different amplitudes. A direct-current component in the resulting modulating wave added to the carrier is avoided by choosing a sine wave modulated by a cosine wave.

This technique is made more interesting by an algorithm suggested by Justice (1979), which enables an analysis of a sound according to this model, with the frequency and the index behavior of two or more nested modulators being deducible.

Other Two-Input, Nonlinear Transformations

Mitsuhashi (1980) proposed a more complex two-input, nonlinear transformation, in which the instantaneous phase and amplitude of an approximately sinusoidal signal are simultaneously varied. In another paper, Mitsuhashi (1982c) generalized this technique while discussing some criteria in choosing the two-input, nonlinear function and suggesting two examples. The function is time independent, bidimensional, and considered periodic outside the definition field. Thus, it can be implemented with a two-dimensional table, with analogy to an oscillator. This technique appears very interesting, even if it seems to be difficult to find a simple expression that bounds significant parameters of the resulting spectrum to the input and function characteristics. Another promising modulation technique is linear sweep synthesis, recently suggested by Rozenberg (1982).

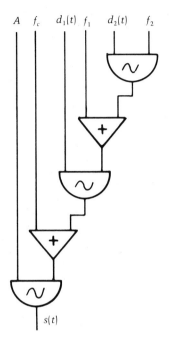

Conclusion

As a consequence of progress in digital hardware and software, the initial antithesis between computing efficiency and timbral richness is lessening. Digital sound quality largely depends on the amount of introduced or controlled detail; excessive simplifications lead often to trivial results. It follows that increased computing power can generate more sophisticated results.

A musically interesting sound can be obtained in two ways. The first consists of the utilization of more complex techniques or of the combination of many of the techniques described here. Many linear and nonlinear transformations are possible. Most of the parameters do not have to be constant and can be varied by control functions and random signals.

The other synthesis approach consists of the superimposition of many simple sounds produced by basic techniques. The evolution of the individual sounds is not complex, and the richness of the result essentially depends on their combination. In this approach, the parameters of many elementary sounds have to be given. Specific programs are often used to define these parameters.

Sound evolution can be regulated either by control functions in the synthesis or by programs computing the parameters for the synthesis. In any case, many details of the sound have to be accurately controlled. Their coherence both within the sound and in the context of adjacent and simultaneous notes has to be guaranteed. The relations among sounds can be more easily highlighted when they are reflected not only in macroscopic parameter variations but also in internal structure.

The extensive utilization of a single technique reveals its peculiar characteristics. This derives from the finite repertoire of obtainable sounds and, more specifically, from the more easily producible dynamic variations associated with it. Thus, it is wise to use different techniques, the better to exploit their different potential. Moreover, the musician must study and experiment with a technique. This is essential in order to determine all its characteristics and to acquire a feeling for the parameter choices necessary for nontrivial use. In any case, a synthesis technique is simply a tool to produce sound, and sound is not yet music.

References

Arfib, D. 1979. "Digital Synthesis of Complex Spectra by Means of Multiplication of Nonlinear Distorted Sine Waves." *Journal of the Audio Engineering Society* 27(10):757–768.

Bass, S. C., and T. W. Goeddel. 1981. "The Efficient Digital Implementation of Subtractive Music Synthesis." *IEEE Micro* 1(3):24–37.

Beauchamp, J. W. 1975. "Analysis and Synthesis of Cornet Tones Using Non Linear Interharmonic Relationships." *Journal of the Audio Engineering Society* 23(10):778–795.

Beauchamp, J. W. 1979. "Brass Tone Synthesis by Spectrum Evolution Matching with Nonlinear Functions." *Computer Music Journal* 3(2):35–43.

Beauchamp, J. W. 1982. "Synthesis by Spectral Amplitude and 'Brightness' Matching of Analyzed Musical Instrumental Tones." *Journal of the Audio Engineering Society* 30(6):396–406.

Cann, R. 1979–1980. "An Analysis Synthesis Tutorial." Part 1, *Computer Music Journal* 3(3):6–11; Part 2, *Computer Music Journal* 3(4):9–13; Part 3, *Computer Music Journal* 4(1):36–42.

Cerruti, R., and G. Rodeghiero. 1983. "Comments on 'Musical' Sound Synthesis by Forward Differences." *Journal of the Audio Engineering Society* 31(6).

Charbonneau, G. 1981. "Three Types of Data Reduction." *Computer Music Journal* 5(2):10–19.

Chowning, J. M. 1971. "The Simulation of Moving Sound Sources." *Journal of the Audio Engineering Society* 19(1):2–6. (Reprinted in *Computer Music Journal* 1(3):48–52, 1977.)

Chowning, J. M. 1973. "The Synthesis of Complex Audio Spectra by Means of Frequency Modulation." *Journal of the Audio Engineering Society* 21(7):526–534. (Reprinted in *Computer Music Journal* 1(2):46–54, 1977.)

Chowning, J. M. 1981. "Computer Synthesis of the Singing Voice." In *Sound Generation in Winds Strings Computers*. Stockholm: *KTH Skriftserie* 29, pp. 4–13.

Dashow, J. 1978. "Three Methods for the Digital Synthesis of Chordal Structure with Non-Harmonic Partials." *Interface* 7(2/3):69–94.

Dashow, J. 1980. "Spectra as Chords." *Computer Music Journal* 4(1):43–52.

De Poli, G. 1981. "Sintesi di suoni mediante funzione distorcente con poli complessi coniugati." *Atti del IV Colloquio di Informatica Musicale* 1, Pisa, pp. 103–130.

De Poli, E., and G. De Poli. 1979. "Identificazione di parametri di un oscillatore VOSIM a partire da una descrizione spettrale." *Atti del III Colloquio di Informatica Musicale*, Pisa, pp. 161–177.

Forin, A. 1982. "Spettri dinamici prodotti mediante distorsione con polinomi equivalenti in un punto." *Bollettino LIMB* 2:62–76.

Grey, J. M., and J. A. Moorer. 1977. "Perceptual Evaluation of Synthesized Musical Instrument Tones." *Journal of the Acoustical Society of America* 62:434–462.

Justice, J. M. 1979. "Analytic Signal Processing in Music Computation." *IEEE Transactions on Acoustics, Speech and Signal Processing* (ASSP) 27(6):670–684.

Kaegi, W. 1973. "A Minimum Description of the Linguistic Sign Repertoire (part 1)." *Interface* 2:141–156.

Kaegi, W. 1974. "A Minimum Description of the Linguistic Sign Repertoire (part 2)." *Interface* 3:132–158.

Kaegi, W., and S. Tempelaars. 1978. "VOSIM—A New Sound Synthesis System." *Journal of the Audio Engineering Society* 26(6):418–424.

Le Brun, M. 1977. "A Derivation of the Spectrum of FM with Complex Modulating Wave." *Computer Music Journal* 1(4):51–52.

Le Brun, M. 1979. "Digital Waveshaping Synthesis." *Journal of the Audio Engineering Society* 27(4):250–265.

Lehmann, R., and F. Brown. 1976. "Synthèse rapide des sons musicaux." *Revue d'Acoustique* 38:211–215.

Lorrain, D. 1980. "A Panoply of Stochastic 'Cannons.'" *Computer Music Journal* 4(1):53–81.

Mailliard, R. 1976. "Les distorsions de Music V." *Cahiers récherche/musique* 3:207–246.

Mathews, M. V. 1969. *The Technology of Computer Music.* Cambridge, Massachusetts: MIT Press.

Mitsuhashi, Y. 1980. "Waveshape Parameter Modulation in Producing Complex Audio Spectra." *Journal of the Audio Engineering Society* 28(12):879–895.

Mitsuhashi, Y. 1982*a*. "Musical Sound Synthesis by Forward Differences." *Journal of the Audio Engineering Society* 30(1/2):2–9.

Mitsuhashi, Y. 1982*b*. "Piecewise Interpolation Technique for Audio Signal Synthesis." *Journal of the Audio Engineering Society* 30(4):192–202.

Mitsuhashi, Y. 1982*c*. "Audio Signal Synthesis by Functions of Two Variables." *Journal of the Audio Engineering Society* 30(10):701–706.

Moorer, J. A. 1976. "The Synthesis of Complex Audio Spectra by Means of Discrete Summation Formulae." *Journal of the Audio Engineering Society* 24(9):717–727.

Moorer, J. A. 1977. "Signal Processing Aspects of Computer Music: A Survey." *Proceedings of the IEEE* 65(8):1108–1132. (Reprinted in *Computer Music Journal* 1(1):4–37, 1977.)

Moorer, J. A. 1979*a*. "The Use of Linear Prediction of Speech in Computer Music Applications." *Journal of the Audio Engineering Society* 27(3):134–140.

Moorer, J. A. 1979*b*. "About This Reverberation Business." *Computer Music Journal* 3(2):13–28.

Reinhard, P. 1981. "Distorsione non lineare della somma di due cosinusoidi: analisi dello spettro tramite matrici." *Atti del IV Colloquio di Informatica Musicale*, Pisa, pp. 160–183.

Risset, J.-C. 1969. "An Introductory Catalog of Computer Synthesized Sounds." Murray Hill, New Jersey: Bell Laboratories.

Risset, J.-C., and M. V. Mathews. 1969. "Analysis of Musical Instrument Tones." *Physics Today* 22(2):23–30.

Roads, C. 1978. "Automated Granular Synthesis of Sounds." *Computer Music Journal* 2(2):61–62. Revised and updated version forthcoming in C. Roads and J. Strawn, eds., *Foundations of Computer Music.* Cambridge, Massachusetts: MIT Press.

Roads, C. 1979. "A Tutorial on Non-linear Distortion or Waveshaping Synthesis." *Computer Music Journal* 3(2):21–34.

Rodet, X. 1980. "Time Domain Formant Wave-Function Synthesis." In *Spoken Language Generation and Understanding*, ed. J. G. Simon. Dordrecht: D. Reidel.

Rozenberg, M. 1979. "Microcomputer-controlled Sound Processing Using Walsh Functions." *Computer Music Journal* 3(1):42–47.

Rozenberg, M. 1982. "Linear Sweep Synthesis." *Computer Music Journal* 6(3):65–71.

Tempelaars, S. 1976. "The VOSIM Signal Spectrum." *Interface* 6:81–86.

Tempelaars, S. 1982. "Linear Digital Oscillators." *Interface* 11(2):109–130.

Truax, B. 1977. "Organizational Techniques for C:M Ratios in Frequency Modulation." *Computer Music Journal* 1(4):39–45.

Winham, G., and K. Steiglitz. 1970. "Input Generators for Digital Sound Synthesis" (Part 2). *Journal of the Acoustical Society of America* 47(2):665–666.

Xenakis, I. 1971. *Formalized Music.* Bloomington, Indiana: Indiana University Press.

35

**Xavier Rodet, Yves Potard,
Jean-Baptiste Barrière**
IRCAM
·31, rue Saint-Merri
F-75004 Paris, France

The CHANT Project: From the Synthesis of the Singing Voice to Synthesis in General

Introduction

The CHANT project was originally concerned with the analysis and synthesis of the singing voice. This work led to a complex program of voice *synthesis-by-rule*: CHANT. This program was enriched with a constantly expanding software environment, consisting of both analysis and composition programs. In time, broader aims than the synthesis of the singing voice imposed themselves. These aims centered on the search for models of the processes involved in the production of musical sound. Our present research encompasses the physical description of sound phenomena (the *sonic material*), the articulation of these phenomena (*organization*), and compositional issues.

This research is intended to transcend simulation. Our goal is to extrapolate new creative models for music on the basis of *knowledge models* developed using the synthesis-by-rule methodology. In this research, synthesis is the proof of both our understanding of sound phenomena, and of the music itself.

In this article we reexamine music synthesis in the following way. In the first part we reconsider the development of past synthesis techniques and programs. We explain our reasons for starting from a physical model of sound production—the voice—because of its generality and its complexity.

In the second part we present and compare two types of synthesis implementations inspired by the vocal model: one based on filters and another based on *formant wave functions*. (Those who are not concerned with the details of implementation problems, as well as readers without a scientific background, can skip this part.)

In the third part we describe the CHANT synthesis-by-rule program and methods for controlling this technique. Finally, we give examples of works realized with CHANT in the context of the rule-based FORMES system (Rodet and Cointe 1984).

From a Reconsideration of Synthesis Techniques and Programs to the Choice of a Production Model

A Reconsideration of Synthesis Techniques and Programs

Let us examine some of the reasons behind the development of the established digital sound synthesis techniques and programs.

The Imitation of Analog Techniques

Paradoxically, analog devices have often been simpler to use than many programs. Analog modules can be linked to each other by a simple cable. (This analogy does not work for subprograms because of complications with argument passing.) In systems that imitate analog synthesizers, effects are almost always obtained directly, without resorting to mysterious code, and control is achieved by such simple means as turning a knob. However, this approach makes meager use of the immense possibilities for controlling digital signals, and ignores the symbol processing capabilities of computer languages.

Speed of Calculation

This concern was particularly justified at the beginning of computer music when hardware was slow and not specialized for synthesis. But an emphasis on speed of calculation can have several negative consequences.

First, a technique that aims at rapidity is generally not related to the properties of perception. Such techniques may result in great difficulties in controlling the perceptual characteristics of sound, since they depend on the parameters of the synthesis method through a very complex and arbitrary set of relationships. Learning a synthesis method of this type is difficult and unjustified.

Second, a technique aimed at speed usually bears no relation to the mode of production of natural sounds. (There is no physical model.) This also makes it more difficult to use, because we cannot then use our knowledge of the relations between the variations of the mode of production and the corresponding variations of sound. Moreover, the development of electronic components now permits considerable computing power for a relatively low cost. The limit of possible calculations is therefore appreciably extended.

The "Patch/Note List/Function" Representation

This representation has several consequences. One of the difficulties lies in making explicit the intermediate levels of control between the patch and the note-list. A patch can be a fairly satisfactory description of an instrument or a synthesizer. But on the other hand, the patch languages that exist are weak in their ability to specify the elaborate control levels that resemble interpretation by an instrumentalist, for example, expressiveness, context-dependent decisions, timbre quality, intonation, stress, and nuances.

In these languages, to offer the real possibility of playing with sound, it is necessary to construct a very complex instrument controlled by a considerable number of parameters—to the point that writing a single note becomes an awesome task. Further, when the computation is performed on a sample-to-sample basis, the cost of calculation time must be added to the unwieldiness of the description.

Control functions have relatively slow variations, around 100 Hz on average. In the languages of the Music V family this type of control is also effected

by functions. But the latter are then no longer algorithmic descriptions, as is the patch. Therefore, correlations between parameters can no longer be taken into account. Moreover, their temporal scope is subject to the length of the note. This obliges a kind of acrobatic manipulation for the continuous control of parameters by means of notes (for example in the case of a legato) or the use of functions where the desired scope differs from the length of a note (for example, a crescendo over a whole phrase). In these languages, there seems to be a lack of intermediate control levels between the patch and the organizational level of the note. We want to be able to describe these intermediate levels in a programming language, enabling interactions between sound and perception, and between sonic material and musical organization.

These remarks imply that we have to make use of computer instruments that are at least as immediate in response as analog hardware—and even more so, since the software can provide an almost limitless "intelligence." We also have to try to take advantage of the specific richness of the various techniques by choosing to exploit their idiomatic qualities. At the same time, it is essential that users have a consistent formal system at their disposal to integrate different techniques, so as to eliminate the difficulties of access and understanding specific to each method.

Finally, we must be able to implement an interaction between interpretation and microsound organization. There should not be fixed sounds on the one hand, and an external structure organizing them on the other. On the contrary, the sounds must be formed as a function of their place in a certain context. Thus, sounds are simultaneously the objects and subjects of the organization.

A Voice Model, A Synthesis-by-Rule Methodology

These are the considerations that have led us to our choice of a production model: the voice, and our choice of a methodology: synthesis-by-rule. The choice of the voice as a model of production was imperative because of its extreme richness. By the wealth of its output and the variety of musical

Fig. 1. Log magnitude
spectrum of the transfer
function H1.

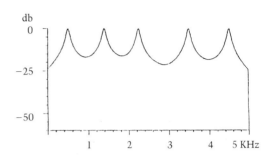

and linguistic uses to which it gives rise, the voice inspires a more general and fertile approach than the study of any other instrument—no matter how complex. It is the need to account fully for the complexity of the variations in the vocal model, and more particularly, in the resonator, which obliges us to reach a level of generality that has also enabled us to move toward quite different models.

A synthesis-by-rule methodology implements complex control levels, and constitutes a formalization of musical production and composition in terms of models that can be built up incrementally.

Description of the Working of the Vocal Apparatus: A Production Model

The sonic wave of the voice is produced by a stream of air breathed from the lungs into the vocal tract, through the larynx to the lips and nostrils. At various points, the wave is disturbed by sonic sources.

One source of disturbance is the vibration of the vocal cords, modulating the stream of air breathed out through the larynx. The sounds produced are quasi-periodic and are said to be *voiced*. A second source comes from a narrowing of the buccal cavity at certain points: the lips, tongue palate, and the glottis for whispered sounds. The stream of air becomes turbulent and produces an aperiodic sound known as a *fricative*. A third type of source is obtained through the interruption of the air stream by closing the buccal cavity with the lips or the tongue, and suddenly releasing them. The noise of an explosion is thus produced and the sound is known as a *plosive*.

The sounds that come from these sources are modified by the vocal tract itself which acts as a set of resonators by filtering certain frequencies to a greater or lesser extent; this is known as the *transfer function* of the vocal tract. During the production of a sentence the vocal tract is continually changing its shape and therefore its transfer function, consequently this function can only be defined at a given instant. Moreover, each type of source can act more or less independently, for a duration and with characteristics that also vary continuously. A spoken sentence is the end product of

this complex set of actions. The corresponding sound signal comes from successive phenomena, vowels and consonants that interact (coarticulate) in such a way that one cannot set a precise boundary between them (Rodet 1977; Sundberg 1978, 1979).

The production of speech, like that of numerous sounds or signals, is often represented by a model composed of a non-coupled source of excitation and a linear filter. However, it is desirable, if not essential that couplings be taken into consideration (Carré 1981; Weinreich 1977).

The filter $F1$, usually linear, is characterized by its transfer function $H1$, which varies continuously (Fig. 1). It takes into account the characteristics of the physical system that is perturbed or *excited* (such as the vocal tract), and its sonic radiation.

In the case of the voice, the model includes a periodic source P for the voiced sounds and a random source S for the fricatives or the plosives and for the breath. A source is characterized essentially by its amplitude spectrum (Fig. 2). It can also be described by means of a filter $F2$ that represents its envelope and by a source $P2$ (and $S2$) with a flat spectrum $X(f)$. The two filters $F2$ and $F1$ in series can then be connected in a single filter F. The spectrum of the resultant wave is then the product of the spectrum of the source by the gain of the filter: $Y(f) = X(f) \cdot H(f)$ (Fig. 3).

A glottal source is a good demonstration of a model of production (Fant 1970, 1973; Rothenberg 1981). But if we limit ourselves to a model of this type, we will only obtain a limited family of sources. For musical applications, the imagination must not

Fig. 2. Log magnitude
spectrum of the voiced
source P.

Fig. 3. Log magnitude
spectrum of the output
waveform.

Fig. 4. Representation of
the H parallel filter.

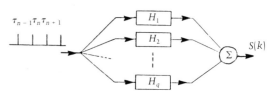

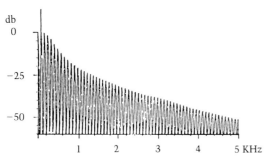

Fig. 3

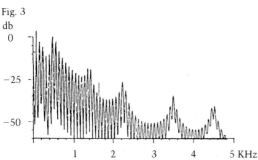

maxima of this type are well-represented in terms of a formant's center frequency, relative amplitude, and bandwidth.

Next we examine the details of two implementations of this synthesis technique, by digital filters and by formant wave functions.

The Chant Synthesizer

Digital Filter

A filter such as F can be represented by its z-transfer function:

$$H(z) = \frac{\beta_0 + \beta_1 z^{-1} + \ldots \beta_q z^{-q}}{1 + \alpha_1 z^{-1} + \ldots \alpha_p z^{-p}}$$

that includes p poles and q zeros. This is the case, for example, in linear prediction (Moorer 1977). The implementation of a digital filter of this type and the calculation of its parameters α and β present difficulties that we discuss later. Consequently, we can use another form:

$$H(z) = \sum_{i=1}^{l} c_i \frac{1 + d_i z^{-1}}{1 + a_i z^{-1} + b_i z^{-2}} \ .$$

The H filter is then presented as a set of parallel J cells (Fig. 4). Each cell is composed of a first-order filter (a zero) and of a section of the second order (two poles) in series, with a gain c_i. Each cell is implemented quite simply. The calculation of the parameters is also much less complex, and we can directly control the perceptually interesting characteristics of the envelope of the spectrum (Fig. 5). The parameters include: a and b, which determine the center frequency of a band Δf of the envelope of the spectrum and its local form (maximum and

be limited. It is therefore interesting to formalize this model in the spectral domain, then to include it in a more general model describing the spectrum of the source. This general model is controlled by spectral parameters, whose perceptual consequences can be easily forecast.

The vocal tract itself is a sort of tube about 17 cm long, of varying sections, branching towards the nasal tract. In a simplified fashion, it can be assimilated to a series of N resonators in series and M in parallel. Its gain or transfer function therefore usually presents N maxima, known as *formants*. The sharpness of these maxima is measured by their bandwidth at mid-height from the peak (−3 db).

The amplitude spectrum of the produced sonic wave presents maxima corresponding to the formants. The importance of these formants relates not only to the fact that they derive from the shape of the vocal tract at each moment (for each articulation) but also to their importance at the perceptual level. Because of the properties of the ear (in particular masking), the parts of the spectrum that present

Rodet et al.

Fig. 5. *Log magnitude of the different transfer functions of a cell.*

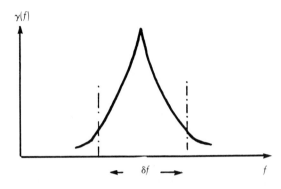

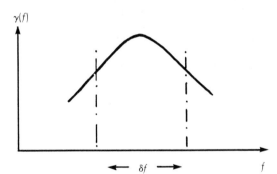

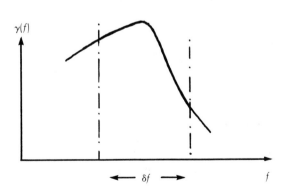

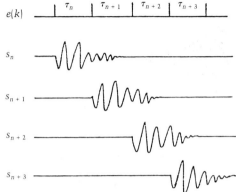

bandwidth), c, which controls the global amplitude of this zone, and d, which enables us to change the slope of the envelope.

Formant Wave Functions (FOF)

If the excitation is a series of impulses:

$$E(k) = \sum_{-\infty}^{+\infty} e_n(k)$$

when n indexes the impulses in turn, then the response S from the previous filter can be easily calculated as the sum of the responses $s_n(k)$ shifted from a period of the fundamental $T = 1/F0$. $F0$ is the fundamental frequency of the excitation and the response (Fig. 6). A response $s_n(k)$ is itself the sum of the J responses to the n parallel cells:

$$s(k) = \sum_{i=1}^{J} s_{n,i}(k)$$

where the $s_{n,i}(k)$ are termed *formant wave functions* (in French, *Forme d'Onde Formantique* or *FOF*) because they usually correspond to the formants or main modes of resonance of the system.

Fig. 7. A formant wave
function (FOF).

Fig. 8. Log magnitude
spectrum of a FOF:
$A(k)sin([\omega_c * k]) + \Phi$ for
different values of π/β. ω_c

$= 2500$ Hz, and $\alpha/\pi = 80$
Hz. Line 1: $\pi/\beta = 10$ msec;
line 2: $\pi/\beta = 1$ msec; line
3: $\pi/\beta = 0.01$ msec.

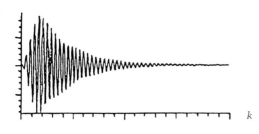

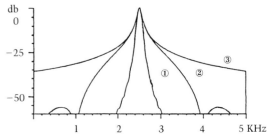

Variations of fundamental frequency are obtained by changing the durations of the fundamental periods $T = 1/F0$, that is, the beginnings of the successive FOFs. Variations of the envelope of the spectrum are obtained by changing the characteristics of each FOF.

Calculation of the FOF

The response to a unitary impulse, of a cell

$$C_i \frac{1 + d_i z^{-1}}{1 + a_i z^{-1} + b_i z^{-2}} = C_i \frac{1 + d_i z^{-1}}{(1 - r_i z^{-1})(1 - r_i \cdot z^{-1})}$$

is the FOF $s_i(k) = G \cdot e^{-\alpha k} \sin(\omega k + \Phi)$, with

$$\alpha = -\frac{1}{2} \log b_i;$$

$$\omega = \text{Arg } r_i;$$

$$\Phi = \text{arc} \left[\frac{\sin(\omega \cdot e^{-\alpha})}{d_i - a_i - \cos(\omega \cdot e^{-\alpha})} \right]; \text{ and}$$

$$G = \frac{c_i}{\sin(\Phi)}.$$

Thus a FOF is obtained simply as the product of a sinusoid by an exponential envelope. However, for natural sounds, the excitation is not a unitary impulse. In order to obtain a more precise control over the spectrum, we used the following FOF (Fig. 7):

$$s(k) = 0 \quad \text{for } k < 0$$

$$s(k) = \frac{1}{2} (1 - \cos[\beta k] \cdot e^{-\alpha k} \sin[\omega k + \Phi])$$
$$\text{for} \quad 0 \le k \le \pi/\beta$$

$$s(k) = e^{-\alpha k} \sin(\omega k + \Phi) \quad \text{for } \pi/\beta < k.$$

This is again a sinusoid multiplied by an envelope $A(k)$. This envelope is a damped exponential whose initial discontinuity is smoothed by multiplication by $1/2 (1 - \cos(\beta k))$ for a duration of π/β samples. One obtains thus an envelope of amplitude $A(k)$. This envelope has an attack of a duration of π/β samples and a general damping in $\exp(-\alpha k)$. The envelope has no first or second-order discontinuity, and it can be generated very simply by table lookup or by a multiplication by $C = \exp(-\alpha)$ for $\exp(-\alpha k)$.

The amplitude spectrum of this FOF (Fig. 8) presents a maximum and can be easily adjusted with the aid of the following parameters:

ω is the central frequency of the maximum
$\alpha\pi$ is the bandwidth at -3 db
β governs the skirt width or the slope of the attack

Finally, it is not difficult to adjust the amplitude of the signal produced, by means of the gain G (or, to avoid a multiplication, by the initial value of the exponential). The role of the initial phase is discussed later.

FOF Synthesizer

The structure of a FOF synthesizer is represented in Fig. 9. Its command parameters for each fundamental period are the following:

Center frequency $= 2\pi\omega_i$
Bandwidth $= BW_i$
Amplitude $= A_i$
Skirt width $= \pi/\beta_i$
Initial phase $= \Phi_i$

Rodet et al.

Fig. 9. Structure of a FOF synthesizer.

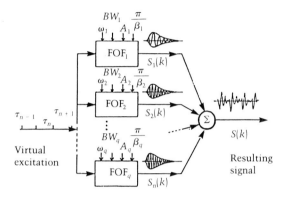

Virtual excitation

Resulting signal

The FOF method presents a number of advantages as far as the filters are concerned. The precision required in the calculation is at most that required at the output (for example, 16 bits). No risk of numerical overflow exists, and the cost of the calculations is fairly low except for very high fundamental frequencies. Finally, the calculation of the control parameters is simple.

We have used this method for the synthesis of a very great number of vocal, instrumental, and other sounds. The findings indicate that one can obtain synthesis of very high quality for a low calculation cost. It is possible, for example, to perform this synthesis technique in real-time on a signal-processing microprocessor.

Comparison of the FOF and the Filter Models

The parameters of the FOF synthesizer enable us to generate the same spectrum envelopes as an equivalent filter in parallel. Thanks to the parameter β governing the skirt widths, we can even generate forms that would require a filter of a higher order, or unique functions of excitation for each cell. (See later discussion entitled "Discussion of the Parallel Synthesis Model.")

Moreover, there is an interesting difference. We have always used within each FOF $s_{n,i}(k)$ a constant frequency ω (a variable frequency can produce in-

teresting "spectrum enlargement" effects). Since a continuously variable resonator like the vocal tract ought to be modeled by a continuously variable filter, therefore we have a ω within each FOF.

In practice, for vocal sounds and most instrumental sounds, the duration of each period is so short in relation to the speed of variation of ω that the difference is not perceptible. But in a filter the coefficients cannot be subject to discontinuity, and they have to be interpolated between each new value (whereas in FOF we need only a new value at each period, the FOF being continuous by construction).

The difference between the two methods appears when the bandwidth BW is very small and ω varies rapidly. The response of a cell in the filter is then almost a sinusoid whose center frequency evolves continuously. On the other hand, the $s_n(k)$ FOFs, triggered off at each period n, are almost sinusoids (with very weak damping if the bandwidth is very small) with frequencies that are each fixed but different from the preceding one. The spectrum then presents very dense partials giving a much richer sound than the quasi-sinusoid which comes out of the filter (Fig. 10).

This is an easy way of synthesizing a rich sound in a certain frequency band without having to specify each partial. We have, for example, synthesized cymbals in this way.

Discussion of the Parallel Synthesis Model

The parallel synthesis model (FOF and filters) previously described revealed itself as incomparably richer than might have been expected by listening to classical parallel-formant synthesizers. We discuss here some of its possibilities and certain implementation difficulties.

When the I cells are placed in parallel, one expects that the total complex gain will be the sum of that of the individual cells (or FOFs). This is not necessarily the case (Fig. 11), because some components may be opposites in phase and therefore cancel each other out. This mainly occurs between the center frequencies of two neighboring cells (Fig. 12), where one sees a "hole" (a zero) appearing in the spectrum.

Fig. 10. Comparison of the FOF and filter model outputs for small bandwidths and fast frequency variations. (a) FOF model. (b) Filter model.

Fig. 11. Comparison of the total complex gain with the sum of the individual FOFs. Note the differences caused by phase cancellations.

Fig. 12. (a) Presence of a "zero" (attenuation) between the center frequencies of two neighboring cells. (b) Corrected spectrum.

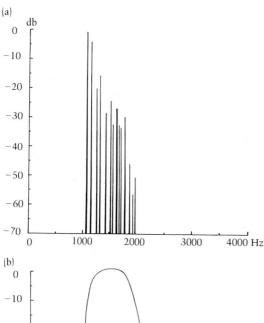

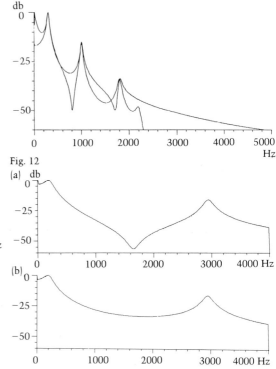

This problem can be cured by *dephasing* the response of one cell in relation to the other (Fig. 13). This is particularly easy in the FOF method since it requires that one simply position the initial phase ϕ of the sinusoid correctly in each cell.

For the filter model, we studied a great number of configurations of poles and zeros to dephase the cells in relation to one another. But we were obli-ged to discard the use of dephasing filters because they were either inadequate or too complex (which would be contrary to the simplicity that motivates the parallel model). On the other hand, we can use as many sources as there are cells and their dephasing is then simple (for example, it is the initial value of the index if one uses table lookup).

This is the solution that we chose for the implementation of CHANT on the Systems Concepts digital synthesizer (also known as the Samson Box) at the Center for Computer Research in Music and Acoustics (CCRMA) at Stanford University (Fig. 14). With an initial controllable phase, the generators can produce a flat spectrum and a limited periodic impulse.

This latter characteristic is also important because a parallel filter tends to have a higher gain than the series filter with the same characteristics in the frequency zone situated beyond the maxi-

Rodet et al.

Fig. 13. "Dephasing" the response of one cell in relation to another.

Fig. 14. Individual sources $e_i(t)$ for each cell of the parallel model.

Fig. 15. A set of impulses to vary the sizes of the odd and even harmonics. (a) Odd harmonics. (b) Even harmonics. (c) Sum of odd and even harmonics.

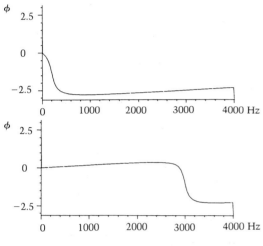

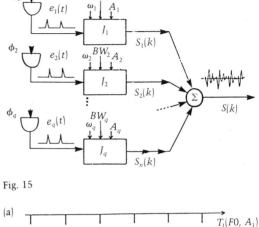

Fig. 15

mum frequency formant (Fig. 11). In effect, the gains of the cells are added, instead of being multiplied as in a series model. The problem does not arise in FOF thanks to the control of skirt widths by β, which controls the amplitude of the spectrum beyond the maximum frequency formant.

Granting an individual source to each cell is still desirable in order to control, in each frequency band, other characteristics of the spectrum such as inharmonicity and skirt width.

One may also vary the respective sizes of a particular class of partials in relation to another: for example the even and odd harmonics. Let us suppose that a source is composed of two sets of impulses T_1 and T_2 with respective frequencies $F0$ and $2F0$ and amplitudes A_1 and A_2 (Fig. 15). The spectrum corresponding to the first is a spectrum of $F0$, $2F0$, $3F0$ partials and to the second $2F0$, $4F0$, $6F0$ partials. The spectrum corresponding to the set $T_1 \cup T_2$ is the sum of the respective spectra of T_1 and T_2.

Thus, by summing these two spectra one can increase the intensity of the even partials if A_1 and A_2 are of the same sign, or decrease it (possibly to zero) if they are of opposite signs. In other words, the set of impulses to use, the sum of the sets 1 and 2, has a $2F0$ frequency and an amplitude that alternates successively between $A_1 + A_2$ and A_1. We have thus, by a simple control of the amplitude of the impulses, control of the even and odd partials. This is the case in each frequency band. (See "The CHANT Program," discussed later.)

Finally, in the case where the parallel filter is used for the processing of a signal, one can derive J signals that will serve as sources for J cells. By storing the original signal in a table and looking it up with dephased indexes, one creates an equivalent number of dephased sources. One can also introduce other variations (for example, amplitude variations), especially if each fundamental period can be detected with certainty (this can be tricky).

The Need for Floating-Point Arithmetic

We have referred to the difficulties presented by a series filter model. The first difficulty is inherent in the integer-based arithmetic used in most synthesizers. Already, with a single cell, one can easily encounter an auto-oscillating, and therefore unacceptable, filter (this is the case on the Samson Box for a "modifier" used in the two-pole mode). Moreover, from one cell to another, the noise inherent in the calculations increase, and numerical overflows are common.

With some effort, using judiciously calculated filter gains in a specific application, one can usually cure these problems. But then the model loses all its flexibility and generality. A specialist is required to carry out the adjustments and that means a considerable waste of time. Ideally, a computer instrument should be as flexible as possible and not confine the imagination of the musician within a labyrinth of calculations exactly at the point where new musical horizons open up.

The second difficulty is the computationally-intensive nature of the parameter calculations for a series filter, on the basis of data that the user can manipulate, such as frequencies, bandwidths, and amplitudes. These calculations require burdensome operations like division and exponentiation to be computed every 20 msec when the filter varies fairly quickly. Again, these calculations require a range and precision that only floating-point arithmetic can provide.

We do not deduce from this that the series model must be abandoned. Quite the contrary, because we have shown that the parallel model presents its own difficulties. But musical synthesizers must include very rapid floating-point arithmetic and the operations absolutely necessary to any modern computer. Present day technology allows this, in effect, for a reasonable cost that is declining year by year. Moreover, the extra cost (over fixed-point

arithmetic) is compensated for by the power and flexibility that the synthesizer gains.

Two other arguments plead in favor of floating-point arithmetic. First, one must correctly adjust the level of the audio signal for digital-to-analog conversion. Who has not suffered from saturated or inaudible sounds and lost a great deal of time in adjusting magical gain coefficients? In a synthesizer working to a large extent in floating-point arithmetic, an "empty" pass is enough to detect the maximum amplitude sample, to deduce the gain and to play (without human intervention) a sound whose level is optimally adjusted. This is the case in the CHANT program: the sound is never saturated or inaudible, and this is a significant factor in its productivity and pleasure.

The second argument relates to the calculation of the parameters, that is, all the calculations that precede the synthesis itself. These algorithms can be very complex, such as when emulating the refinements of traditional interpretation, and mastering all the details of a sound. These algorithms cannot be reduced to a few table lookups and interpolations. Moreover, the user must be free of all concern with the numerical range of the calculations and other overflows (the algorithms and the music are already quite complex enough). Consequently, parameter calculations must also use rapid floating-point arithmetic. We show later that these calculations also require sophisticated software.

With the aid of floating-point arithmetic, the computer can lend itself to the most extreme and unexpected uses. One of the merits of the CHANT program is that it accepts parameters that have, as far as possible, an immediate meaning. Moreover, one merely has to adjust the parameters at values that are not absurd from the physical and perceptual point of view to obtain a sound that is both expected and surprisingly rich.

The CHANT Program

General Description of the Program

The CHANT program was conceived as an interactive instrument. A distinction can be made between two modes of utilization, conditioned both by the type of sounds that the user desires to synthesize and by the user's experience. The first mode of utilization, which can be described as "basic," corresponds to the context of singing voice synthesis, starting with the basic rules defined in the program. The second mode, which can be described as "extended," corresponds to applications that demand either different or more developed controls than the basic ones implemented in the program, or that move from the vocal model toward other models, other "instruments," or other approaches (for example, additive synthesis).

In the first mode, the user simply specifies the values of the preexisting parameters, in the second mode the user has all the power of a programming language to specify algorithms to describe parameter evolutions, that is, to modify the basic rules or to create new rules.

In the basic version, CHANT includes about a hundred parameters. But many remain unchanged from one sound to another, so all parameters are consequently defined with default values, enabling immediate freedom of use. These parameters can be grouped together under the following headings:

Frequency of the fundamental
Random variations of the fundamental
Vibrato
Random variations of the vibrato
Spectrum: formants and fundamental
Slope of the spectrum
Automatic calculation of the spectrum
Intensity of the sound
Local envelope of the formants
Control over the synthesis

Each parameter can be defined either by a fixed value, that is, by a constant, or by a function of time (breakpoint functions) that associates a given value with a given time and consequently allows interpolation from one value to another.

These parameters and their values are stored in a file known as the *parameter file*. Other files may contain only functions, for example, complex functions calculated with tools in the CHANT environment and defined by a large number of points. The latter, known as *function files* can be called from a main file that describes all the calls.

Thus the data files can be used in modular fashion and constitute a network, sometimes of considerable complexity. In particular, by the interplay of factors and offsets applied to the functions, the files taken from the library can be used as models from which one progressively deviates by successive modifications and by the readjustment of values until the desired effect is obtained.

When CHANT is used in the "basic" mode (mainly voice synthesis), the user's work consists of editing a parameter file, either by directly defining the values or by modifying the values already defined if the user starts with a preexisting library file.

But these modifications can also be effected in an interactive mode at the last minute, right before starting the synthesis. In this case the user gives the program a parameter file and then only modifies particular values. The original file that was used as a model remains intact, but the modifications are preserved in an output file automatically produced by the program. This output file is therefore a replica of the input file, with the addition of the modifications inserted in the interactive mode. Hence, work can be stored and retrieved. The output file can be used as an input and remodified, or else it can be kept to trace each stage of the development. This demonstrates the special care taken to make CHANT an evolving instrument—with memory. These files are kept in a library of parameter and function files. This libary represents the first part of what we have called the CHANT environment, which also includes a catalog of programs and subprograms, consisting of tools for analysis, for function definition, and for rapid spectrum construction, among others.

Knowledge Models

The ability to save accumulated work springs from the same concerns as those that led us to envisage the definition in terms of schemas that are *knowledge models* of a given production. In order to be efficient, the definition of models, which is costly in experimentation time, must lead to knowledge that is easily accessible and can be reused.

This first level of intervention in CHANT could

be called the specification of a *data model*. The data controls the rules, the underlying algorithmic descriptions that form (by default in CHANT) a vocal model. But this standard model can also be modified by additions and/or deletions of rules and algorithms. This constitutes a second level of intervention in CHANT that could be called the specification of a *rule model* that we describe in a moment.

Let us now consider some of the rules specified for the vocal model, from fairly simple rules for the timbre of vowels, to more complex vocal rules that describe the relationship between timbre and amplitude.

Development of the Vocal Model

Specifying the vocal model consisted of precisely defining and realizing the timbres, in particular those of vowels, in the singing voice. This includes the frequency and amplitude of the vibrato, random variations of the fundamental frequency and of the vibrato, and relations between timbre and amplitude. At first, timbre is considered on the basis of a spectral envelope, which is itself defined in terms of center frequencies and amplitudes of the formants.

We represent the spectral envelope by its formants. This representation has shown itself to be particularly economical and informative, both at the level of the competence required for understanding the result of a spectral analysis (either analyzed by machine or by ear) and at the level of performance (synthesis). The formant frequencies were extracted by means of an original analysis with the phase vocoder, that is, by extracting the frequency and amplitude evolutions of each partial and by superimposing them to reveal their correlations and so deduce the formant frequencies. We also used more classical analysis tools offered by linear predictive coding.

Use of the data we developed for our vocal model is optional. One can also choose to have the bandwidths of the formants computed automatically, on the basis of the formant frequencies. This is done by following a parabola defined on the spectrum by three points; these points are themselves adjustable parameters.

Automatic calculation of the amplitude of the formants can be accomplished by simulating a filter series and, according to the frequency of each filter, fixing their amplitudes. Thus, when two or more formants approach each other their amplitudes are reinforced. A supplementary formant, known as a *complement*, can also be automatically assigned to modify the first formant and give more energy in the low register. This is, in a way, a "zeroth" formant.

Random variations in the fundamental (called *jitter*) are perceptually very important. By asking singers to produce sounds with absolutely no vibrato we were able to study the random and uncontrolled fluctuation of the frequency of the fundamental. In the analysis many irregularities were observed, although the variation is only of the order of $\pm 0.5\%$ from the fundamental frequency. Considerable variations in size were also observed. The random fluctuation of the fundamental follows a distribution close to $1/f$.

In the CHANT program this fluctuation is modeled by adding a term to the frequency of the fundamental. This term varies at random between limits given by the user, and is the sum of three components whose values are obtained by interpolation between independent, periodic random choices of frequency deviation. (Typical values for the three random periodicities are 0.05, 0.111, and 1.219 sec.) We distribute the excursions of the random fluctuations equally between the three components. The total fluctuation is typically situated between 1.1% and 3.7% from the fundamental for women's voices and between 2.0% and 5.7% for male voices.

Vibrato is traditionally defined as the more or less regular oscillation of the fundamental frequency around a center frequency that is perceived as a pitch. In CHANT, we distinguish between the amplitude of the vibrato—that is, deviation around the center frequency—from the frequency of the vibrato—that is, the *repetition rate* of this deviation and random variations of it. Vibrato is interesting from a timbral point of view, and it is important in the recognition of the identity of a singer. It

Fig. 16. (a) Log magnitude
spectrum of the vowel /a/
at a high amplitude.
(b) The same vowel at a
low amplitude.

(a)

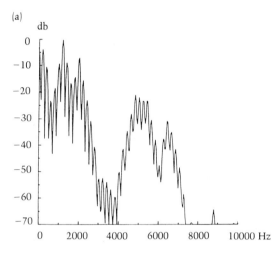

(b)

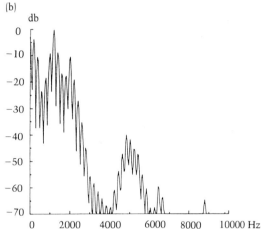

Fig. 16. (a) Log magnitude spectrum of the vowel /a/ at a high amplitude. (b) The same vowel at a low amplitude.

sweeps across vocal tract resonances corresponding to the formants and, consequently, reveals them to the ear. This is also why vibrato also plays an important role in interpretation.

Special care has also been given to the study of the relation between timbre and amplitude. When a vocalist sings loudly, the signal emitted from the vocal cords is completely different from that produced when the vocalist sings softly. It happens that this loud signal is much richer in high frequencies. The same difference exists between the notes at the top of a register and those at the bottom. We have modeled these effects by applying a corrective function to the amplitudes of the formants number 2–5.

This correction is, on the one hand, a function of the general amplitude demanded by the user, and on the other hand, a function of the position of the note in the register requested by the user. In CHANT, we define a *register* by the frequency that corresponds to the middle of the register desired. Thus, the same vowel synthesized at the same frequency will have different timbres depending on the choice of the frequency that defines the register.

Figures 16a and 16b show the spectrum of two sounds synthesized by the program. The fundamental is 300 Hz, the vowel is /a/. In Fig. 16a, the amplitude is at a maximum; in Fig. 16b it is much lower. The difference in the amplitude of the higher formants is noticeable.

The relation between timbre and amplitude is also perceptually important as an indication of the distance of a sound. If one applies a spectrum correction corresponding to a loud sound, while using a low amplitude for the synthesis, one hears the sound in the distance.

Finally, other controls have been defined to allow such things as tremolo, hoarseness, and balance between the fundamental and the first formant versus the higher formants.

The vocal model in CHANT has been specifically discussed elsewhere, so we will not enter in further details here. See Rodet and Bennett (1980) and Bennett (1981).

Model by Rules

The model just described is implemented in the program so as to answer to typical needs. But it is often necessary to go further towards less common uses. This is why we have designed CHANT to accept input from external subprograms that enable the definition of new correlations or rules. These subprograms are written directly in the implementation language of CHANT (or in any other available language) and are executed at a low frequency (typically 100 Hz), not at the sampling rate. All the parameters of the program are accessible in a simple manner.

These rules form the basis of the models that, ideally, should be both modular and context-sensitive. To illustrate this point, we present a few examples taken from two subprograms that are already complex. The first is an attempt to simulate a soprano voice with elements of phrasing and classical singing technique, and the second (using a voice inspired by Tibetan chant) includes consonant articulation and some original work on timbre.

Bel Canto Voice

For the soprano voice, we first emphasized the placing of the formants in a manner typical of the production of bel canto. On the basis of analysis performed with the phase vocoder on the same pitch interpreted by several singers, we were able to obtain precisely the frequencies of the first eight formants. Ultimately, we decided to keep the frequencies of the last six formants, and for the first two we revealed the following relationship between the frequencies of the formants and the pitch of the note. The first and the second formants are placed respectively on the first and second harmonics, except when the frequency so obtained is below a threshold fixed for both of them. This model produces a homogeneous vocal color over a large tessitura of about two octaves.

At this point, the task of modeling was concerned with the establishment of rules constraining the evolution of the various parameters of the source during staccatos.

In particular, these rules are concerned with describing the evolution of the following parameters:

Average pitch, described by the shape of an internal portamento

Vibrato, described by the increase and decrease of the pitch's amplitude and frequency

Energy, described by an envelope composed of three successive sinusoidal arches

Vocal effort, described linearly with the amplitude during the attack and the fall of a note only. (In the body of a note the effort continues to grow although the amplitude has stabilized.)

Tibetan Chant

In the work inspired by Tibetan chant, our main concern was to move away from the study of the conventional practices of Western music. Actually, until then the task of defining rules had mainly been concerned with bel canto, on voices which could be described as "trained," that is, tending to eliminate or to "regionalize" noise and randomness, except those expressive qualities that are very specific to Western music.

In the Tibetan chant work, we have emphasized several factors: the structure of a certain type of noise, separate control of the even and odd harmonics, and especially articulation, that is, consonant articulation. In the regular CHANT program, noise is controlled by formant-dependent parameters. That is, one sets up a noise bandwidth centered on the frequency of a formant (in this case a filter) and a noise amplitude. But in this example, noise has been approached by working mainly on random aspects, especially at the level of microfluctuations of the fundamental (different from jitter) and the frequencies of the formants.

For the timbre of the chanting, we have introduced the idea of another coefficient that provides separate amplitude controls for the even and odd harmonics, each controlled by an envelope and a random variation. This coefficient enables one to play with the *roughness* of the sound (already existing in the basic functioning of the program in another way) and also enables one to play with *fusion* and *fission* of the auditory image (McAdams 1984).

Articulation has been worked on intensively. Consonants have been modeled and constructed in the form of *transitions* from one vowel to another, affecting the amplitude, the fundamental, and the *formant trajectories*, that is, the frequency of each formant as a function of time.

Finally, rhythm and stress have been determined by rules describing the correlations between the length of the phonemes and local variations of vocal effort, fundamental frequency, and vibrato. This did not present any special difficulty once the definition of a transition was derived, apart from making CHANT more unwieldy to use. These rules are computationally inefficient and thus are not easy to use in musical applications. This type of difficulty suggests special procedures that we describe later.

A number of rules have also been defined that illustrate the power of the formant representation. In the practice of using CHANT, the formant representation suggested interesting ideas by offering specific cues or access to timbre control (Barrière 1983) and sound imaging (McAdams, forthcoming). These include the following:

Timbre fusion and fission by stretching or compressing formant frequencies and amplitudes

Granulation by different layers of random variations on formant frequencies, bandwidths, and amplitudes

Fusion and fission by playing between superimposition and remoteness of the FOF formants and of the noise formants (filters)

Spectral enrichment modulation, by different asynchronous levels of control of a curve that increases and decreases formant amplitudes

Reduction of formants to partials, by moving from a formant as a set of harmonics to a partial centered at the center frequency of the formant (crossing from harmonic to inharmonic)

Fusion and fission by concentrating or dispersing the formants of a spectral image into space

Transformation patterns between spectral envelopes by controlling the modes of transition/interpolation between their formants

Correlations between the abovementioned rules by several hierarchical levels of envelopes

Many of these rules have been generalized and are used extensively.

Models and Derivations

Our proposal, at what one could call the highest level, is therefore to construct models of laws and rules for all stages of musical production, from precomposition, to the choice of sonic materials, to performance. These models, in the form of data and algorithms, must describe as precisely as possible the sound and its evolution, as well as the structure in which it is placed and the dynamic interactions between sound and structure—between sonic material and organization. The idea of these models is not simply to imitate or simulate a given note or instrument in a given context, but rather to represent the formalization of any act or process, of a decision or a gesture, of a static or dynamic organization, or of a musical invariant in general.

These models must be viewed as *knowledge structures* or *knowledge schemes*, from which one deviates by successive modification or composition. They are in a way propositions in the quasi-logical sense of the term, and, consequently composers are not obliged to see their structure in depth. Composers can often content themselves with manipulating and assembling them, as they have always done in instrumental or vocal music. Thus, an understanding of the internal workings must not be made an essential prerequisite, but rather an optional endeavor (but not an occult science). In all cases, flexibility must be preserved.

Of course, it is not enough to be able to do everything in theory, it must be possible to do it simply and without having to rewrite everything for each application. In particular, a transition must be realized by a preexisting object that one manipulates symbolically and places "on" another object, or between two objects. This quasi-modular or symbolic processing derives almost automatically from the conception of models such as we have described. Thus, a transition is also in this sense a model to be placed in a context, without concern for the compatibility between two or several objects.

In the CHANT project, once the specific task of modeling was carried out, we then saw a need for a structure at the highest level to manage the models as objects or processes in a symbolic combination. This would enable both reciprocal modifications of the objects/processes "in context," and control at a still higher level.

These are the imperatives that led us to envisage a new program and a new language to control CHANT and other systems of synthesis. This program, known as FORMES (Rodet and Cointe 1984)

and implemented in the Lisp language, deals directly with problems relating to artificial intelligence. In particular, it deals with structures of knowledge, of constraints, and of parallelisms and transformations, that is, the algorithmic aspects of rule sequences, both at the horizontal level of temporal succession as well as at the vertical level of rule specification and combination.

FORMES provides a framework to manipulate and integrate models and rules as basic building blocks or functional objects with scheduling characteristics. FORMES is both an answer to questions arising in the course of CHANT's evolution, and a new direction evolving beyond these questions. CHANT extended the composition process and provided powerful tools for the composition of sonic material. FORMES starts where CHANT stops, in an attempt to process—with one set of tools—both synthesis and composition problems: sonic material and musical organization.

Conclusion

The CHANT program starts from but exceeds the study of vocal behavior. In any case, we do not consider the voice as a simple, single-faceted object. On the contrary, we have taken the voice as a starting point because of its richness and complexity. The issue at stake is principally musical but at the same time cognitive, as, in our opinion, the two aspects are intimately linked, particularly in the modeling process.

The sonic quality of the synthesis and the ease of use of the program make CHANT an exceptional instrument for computer music. Since its first implementation, it has been used in a wide variety of musical contexts by numerous composers, including Gerald Bennett (1981), Conrad Cummings, Jean-Baptiste Barrière (1983), Jonathan Harvey (1981; 1984), Jukka Tiensuu, Harrison Birtwistle, Kaija Saariaho (1983), Michel Tabachnik, Gerard Grisey, Alejandro Vinao, Tod Machover, and Marco Stroppa. A large number of models have been defined and used, taking special care at first to encompass all the traditional instruments. We have synthesized very good strings (contrabasses, violins, cellos),

winds (trumpets, oboes, clarinets, horns, flutes), percussion (drums, cymbals, gongs, gamelan, bells), and other instruments.

The definition of these models has allowed composers to place special emphasis on timbre, for example by defining imaginary hybrid instruments, or sophisticated interpolations between points in a timbre space. The synthesis-by-rule approach has also facilitated investigation into sounds that are quite removed from instrumental references, such as additive synthesis textures and inharmonic sound synthesis.

Although in permanent use at IRCAM, CHANT continues to be developed, enriched by new uses and new implementations on different machines. The first version of CHANT was written in the Sail language for a DEC PDP-10 by Xavier Rodet, Yves Potard, and Conrad Cummings at IRCAM and ran between 1979 and 1983. A portable version in Fortran was written in 1981 by Jean Holleville. This same Fortran version was ported from the PDP-10 to a DEC VAX-11/780 running the Unix operating system in 1983.

The entire library of user subprograms has since been translated into both Fortran and the C language. The rule-based knowledge embedded in these subprograms was transferred into FORMES (Rodet and Cointe 1984) by Jean-Baptiste Barrière and Xavier Rodet so that this knowledge base can also be used outside of CHANT with other synthesis devices.

With the help and support of John Gordon and John Chowning, CHANT has been running since 1981 in its filter version on the Systems Concepts digital synthesizer at CCRMA, Stanford University. The Fortran version is also running on a VAX-11/750 at the Electronic Music Studio in Stockholm. In 1983, a real-time filter version of CHANT was implemented by Xavier Rodet and Yves Potard on the 4X real-time digital sound processor at IRCAM.

Finally, in 1984 Yves Potard implemented a new version of CHANT on a Floating Point Systems FPS-100 Array Processor. This very fast implementation provides a combination of the FOF version and the filter version. Moreover, the sound source can be derived externally—for example, concrète sounds can be used. This makes possible processing and even cross-synthesis by combining the two models. CHANT has therefore, today, become a complete package of synthesis and processing.

References

Barrière, J.-B. 1983. "Chreode I: A Piece Using CHANT and FORMES." Presented at the International Computer Music Conference, October 1983, Rochester, New York.

Bennett, G. 1981. "Singing Synthesis in Electronic Music." In *Research Aspects of Singing*, ed. J. Sundberg. Publication 33. Stockholm: Royal Swedish Academy of Music, pp. 34–50.

Carré, R. 1981. "Couplage conduit vocal—source vocale." In *XIIème Journées d'études sur la parole*, Montreal, May, pp. 233–245.

Fant, G. 1970. *The Acoustic Theory of Speech Production*. The Hague: Mouton.

Fant, G. 1973. *Speech Sounds and Features*. Cambridge, Massachusetts: MIT Press.

Harvey, J. 1981. "Mortuos Plango, Vivos Voco: A Realization at IRCAM." *Computer Music Journal* 5(4):22–24.

Harvey, J. et al. 1984. "Notes on the Realization of Bhakti." *Computer Music Journal* 8(3):74–78.

McAdams, S. Forthcoming. "The Auditory Image: A Metaphor for Research on Psychological and Physical Research on Auditory Organizations." In *Cognitive Processes in the Perception of Art*, ed. R. Crozier and A. Chapman. Amsterdam: North-Holland Publishers.

Moorer, J. A. 1977. "Signal Processing Aspects of Computer Music: A Survey." *Proceedings of the IEEE* 65(8):1108–1137. Reprinted in *Computer Music Journal* 1(1):4–37.

Rodet, X. 1977. "Analyse du signal vocal dans sa representation amplitude-temps, Synthèse de la parole par règles." Thèse d'Etat. Université de Paris VI. Paris.

Rodet, X., and G. Bennett. 1980. "Synthèse de la voix chantée par ordinateur." In *Conferences des Journées d'études 1980*. Paris: Festival International du Son, pp. 73–91.

Rodet, X., and P. Cointe. 1984. "FORMES: Composition and Scheduling of Process." *Computer Music Journal* 8(3):32–50.

Rothenberg, J. 1981. "The Voice Source in Singing." In *Research Aspects of Singing*, ed. J. Sundberg. Publication 33. Stockholm: Royal Swedish Academy of Music, pp. 15–33.

Saariaho, K. 1983. "Using the Computer in a Search for New Aspects of Timbre Organization and Composition." Presented at the International Computer Music Conference, October 1983, Rochester, New York.

Sundberg, J. 1978. "Synthesis of Singing." *Swedish Journal of Musicology* 60(1):107–112.

Sundberg, J. 1979. "Perception of Singing." Speech Transmission Laboratory Quarterly Progress and Status Report 1-1979. Stockholm: KTH, pp. 1–48.

Weinreich, G. 1977. "Coupled Piano Strings." *Journal of the Acoustical Society of America* 62(6):1474–1484. Also published in 1979 as "Physics of Piano Strings." *Scientific American* 240:117–127.

Discography

Barrière, J.-B., ed. 1983. *IRCAM: un portrait—recherche et création*. IRCAM 0001. Paris: IRCAM.

36

Kevin Karplus

Computer Science Department
Cornell University
Ithaca, New York 14853

Alex Strong

Computer Science Department
Stanford University
Stanford, California 94305

Digital Synthesis of Plucked-String and Drum Timbres

Introduction

There are many techniques currently used for digital music synthesis, including frequency modulation (FM) synthesis, waveshaping, additive synthesis, and subtractive synthesis. To achieve rich, natural sounds, all of them require fast arithmetic capability, such as is found on expensive computers or digital synthesizers. For musicians and experimenters without access to these machines, musically interesting digital synthesis has been almost impossible.

The techniques described in this paper can be implemented quite cheaply on almost any computer. Real-time synthesis implementations have been done for Intel 8080A (by Alex Strong), Texas Instruments TMS9900 (by Kevin Karplus), and SC/MP (by Mike Plass) microprocessors. David Jaffe and Julius Smith have programmed the Systems Concept Digital Synthesizer at the Center for Computer Research in Music and Acoustics (CCRMA) to perform several variants of the algorithms (Jaffe and Smith 1983).

Not only are the algorithms simple to implement in software, but hardware realizations are easily done. The authors have designed and tested a custom n-channel metal-oxide semiconductor (nMOS) chip (the Digitar chip), which computes 16 independent notes, each with a sampling rate of 20 KHz.

Despite the simplicity of the techniques, the sound is surprisingly rich and natural. When the

This research was supported in part by the Fannie and John Hertz Foundation.

Computer Music Journal, Vol. 7, No. 2,
Summer 1983

plucked-string algorithm was compared with additive synthesis at Bell Laboratories, it was found that as many as 30 sine wave oscillators were needed to produce a similarly realistic timbre (Sleator 1981). The entire plucked-string algorithm requires only as much computation as one or two sine wave oscillators.

The parameters available for control are pitch, amplitude, and decay time. The pitch is specified by an integer that is approximately the period of the sound, in samples (periodicity parameter p). Amplitude is specified as the initial peak amplitude A. Decay time is determined by the pitch and by a decay stretch factor S.

The algorithms in this paper lack the versatility of FM synthesis, additive synthesis, or subtractive synthesis. They are, however, cheap to implement, easy to control, and pleasant to hear. For musicians interested primarily in performing and composing music, rather than designing instruments, these algorithms provide a welcome new technique. For those interested in instrument design, they open a new field of effective techniques to explore.

Wavetable Synthesis

One standard synthesis technique is the *wavetable synthesis* algorithm. It consists of repeating a number of samples over and over, thus producing a purely periodic signal. If we let Y_t be the value of the tth sample, the algorithm can be written mathematically as

$$Y_t = Y_{t-p}.$$

The parameter p is called the *wavetable length* or *periodicity parameter*. It represents the amount of memory needed and the period of the tone (in samples). The initial conditions of the recurrence relation completely determine the resulting timbre. Normally, a sine wave, triangle wave, square wave, or other simple waveform is calculated and loaded into the wavetable before the note is played. With a sampling frequency of f_s, the frequency of the tone is f_s/p.

The wavetable-synthesis technique is very simple but rather dull musically, since it produces purely periodic tones. Traditional musical instruments produce sounds that vary with time. This variation can be achieved in many ways on computers. The approach in FM synthesis, additive synthesis, subtractive synthesis, and waveshaping is to do further processing of the samples after taking them from the wavetable. All the algorithms described in this paper produce the variation in sound by modifying the wavetable itself.

What sort of modifications to the wavetable are useful? If no modification is done, the harmonic content is fixed, and the sound is purely periodic. To get an almost periodic output, the changes from period to period must be small. To keep the amount of computation and the number of memory accesses small, only one entry in the wavetable is changed for each sample output. Furthermore, since we have to look at a value in the wavetable each sample time, it makes sense to attempt to change that value. With the most recently read sample of the wavetable being the only one changed, the wavetable can be viewed as a delay line of length p. Figure 1 illustrates the general form of the algorithms from a delay-line standpoint.

Plucked-String Algorithm

The simplest modification, invented by Alex Strong in December 1978, is to average two successive samples. This can be written mathematically as

$$Y_t = \frac{1}{2} (Y_{t-p} + Y_{t-p-1}).$$

It turns out that this averaging process produces a slow decay of the waveform. The resulting tone of this algorithm has a pitch that corresponds to a pe-

riod of $p + \frac{1}{2}$ samples (frequency $f_s/(p + \frac{1}{2})$), and sounds remarkably like the decay of a plucked string. Since no multiplication is required (only adding and shifting), the algorithm is fast and easy to implement on microprocessors.

This recurrence can be viewed as a digital filter without inputs, as in Fig. 2. The naturalness of the sound derives largely from differing decay rates for the different harmonics. No matter what initial spectrum a tone has, it decays to an almost pure sine wave, eventually decaying to a constant value (silence). Later in the paper we will use digital filtering techniques to show that the decay time for the nth harmonic is roughly proportional to p^3/n^2.

As with any recurrence relation, initial conditions must be specified. In concrete terms, this amounts to preloading the wavetable with appropriate values. The initial values can form a sine wave, triangle wave, or any other desired waveform, just as for wavetable synthesis. To produce a realistic string sound, it is desirable to start the note with a lot of high harmonics. To accomplish this, the wavetable is filled with random values at the beginning of each new note. Since the samples in the wavetable are repeated, the randomness does not produce hiss or noise.

Without the decay algorithm, a random wavetable has essentially equal harmonics up to the Nyquist frequency, sounding like a reed organ. With decay, the higher harmonics decay rapidly, producing a plucked-string sound very similar to that of a guitar. The use of random initial load also has the advantage of giving each repetition of the same pitch a slightly different harmonic structure. This variation is small enough that the notes sound as if they come from the same instrument, but large enough that the notes don't sound like mechanical repetition. Of course, the wavetable can be copied to get truly identical notes.

One fast way to provide the initial randomness in the wavetable is to use *two-level randomness*. Mathematically, the initial conditions are

$$Y_t = \begin{cases} +A & \text{probability } \dfrac{1}{2} \\ -A & \text{probability } \dfrac{1}{2} \end{cases} \quad \text{for } -p \leq t \leq 0.$$

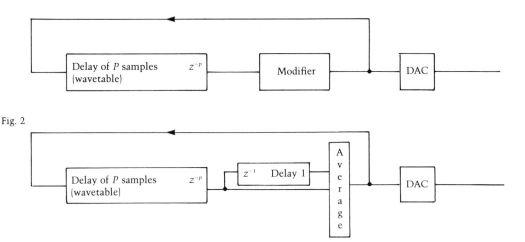

Fig. 2

The root-mean-square (rms) amplitude of the output is A, which is half the peak-to-peak amplitude. Using two-level randomness provides a signal about 5 db louder than using uniform random numbers between $-A$ and $+A$. Only a single bit of randomness is needed for each sample, so a feedback shift-register random-bit generator can be used (Knuth 1981, p. 29). A random-bit generator is simpler than a full random-word generator in either software or hardware.

There are some limitations on the values of the periodicity parameter p. If p is small, the variation between different initial conditions will be relatively large, resulting in poor control of amplitude. Also, since the pitch of a note is determined by p, and p must be an integer, not all frequencies are available. When p is large, the available frequencies are close together, but when p is small, they are fairly far apart. These effects, combined with the short decay times for small p, make p values less than about 32 undesirable. If the full range of a guitar is desired (up to about 880 Hz), this restriction requires sampling rates of at least 28.6 KHz. With some care in the choice of values for p, adequate performance can be achieved for sampling rates down to about 20 KHz. To get finer frequency resolution than is available by just changing p, it is often possible to vary the sampling rate, as well as the value of p.

After a note has been played, the wavetable is normally reloaded with random values before the next note is played. If the wavetable is not changed, the effect is that of a slur or tie. If p is unchanged, the note continues; if p is changed, the result is a slur between the two pitches. Frequent changes to p can be used to produce glissando and vibrato effects.

In digital filtering terms, preloading of the wavetable can be viewed as switching between an input burst and the feedback (see Fig. 3). By switching rather than adding, we avoid arithmetic overflow and eliminate the need for large word sizes. David James independently published a synthesis technique that has many similarities to ours (James 1978, p. 38). It also uses a digital filter excited by a noise burst. However, it provides only decaying amplitude, with no change in harmonic structure, and was intended for use as an excitation waveform for subtractive synthesis. His technique suffers from the usual digital filtering problem; it requires high-speed, high-precision arithmetic (particularly multiplication).

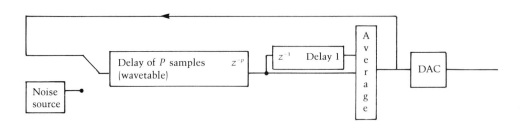

Fig. 4

Drum Algorithm

A simple variation of Strong's basic algorithm yields drum timbres. This was discovered by Kevin Karplus in December 1979. The simplest description of the drum variant is a probabilistic recurrence relation:

$$Y_t = \begin{cases} +\dfrac{1}{2}\,(Y_{t-p} + Y_{t-p-1}) & \text{probability } b \\[2mm] -\dfrac{1}{2}\,(Y_{t-p} + Y_{t-p-1}) & \text{probability } 1 - b. \end{cases}$$

Figure 4 shows the block diagram of the corresponding digital filter.

The parameter b is called the *blend factor*. With a blend factor of 1, the algorithm reduces to the basic plucked-string algorithm, with p controlling the pitch. With a blend factor of $\frac{1}{2}$, the sound is drumlike. Intermediate values produce sounds intermediate between plucked string and drum, some of which are quite interesting musically. A blend

factor of 0 negates the entire signal every $p + \frac{1}{2}$ samples. This drops the frequency an octave and leaves only odd harmonics of the new fundamental. For fairly high pitches, this is a rather odd timbre that we call a "plucked bottle." For lower pitches, the sound is harplike.

For $b \approx \frac{1}{2}$, the wavetable length does not control the pitch of the tone, as the sound is aperiodic. Instead, it controls the decay time of the noise burst. The decay time is roughly proportional to p. For fairly large p (200 or more) and a sampling frequency of 20 KHz, the effect is that of a snare drum. For small p (around 20), the effect is that of a brushed tom-tom. Intermediate values provide intermediate timbres, allowing smooth transition from one drum sound to another.

The initial wavetable can be filled with a constant (A), since the drum algorithm will create the randomness itself. For blends other than $b = \frac{1}{2}$, starting with a constant gives some buildup before the decay, while starting with randomness gives maximum amplitude initially. Blends near 1 require nonconstant initial loading of the wavetable, as little or no randomness is introduced. If b is restricted to 0, 1, or ½ (the most interesting values), then only a single random bit is needed for each sample. If arbitrary values are allowed for b, a more sophisticated random-number generator is required.

Modifications in the Basic Algorithm

Since the overall decay of a note is very roughly proportional to p^3, notes with a short wavetable (high pitch) decay very rapidly. There are several ways to make these notes last longer. The first method is to use a longer wavetable, but fill it with several copies of the same waveform. For example, if the wavetable is doubled in length, the frequency of the fundamental is dropped about an octave. However, if the first half of the wavetable is identical to the second half, only even harmonics will be present, so the note will sound an octave higher than the value of p would indicate. The nth harmonic of the sound we hear is the $2n^{th}$ harmonic of the fundamental pitch for the lengthened wavetable.

Since the decay time for the nth harmonic is roughly proportional to p^3/n^2, the decay time for the nth harmonic of such a doubled wavetable is proportional to $p^3/(2n)^2 = p^3/4n^2$, instead of $(p/2)^3/n^2 = p^3/8n^2$, as it would be if we used a wavetable of length $p/2$ directly. Note that if p is odd, it isn't possible to fill the buffer with two identical copies, so some of the "fundamental" pitch will remain. However, this small amount will not be noticeable until the note has decayed a long way. Odd values of p used this way can improve the tuning of high notes. The wavetable could also be filled with three, four, or more copies of the same waveform to get still higher notes. Making n copies of a waveform in a table of length p produces a note lasting about n times as long as using a table of length p/n. We call this technique the *harmonic trick*, since it allows us to get any of the first few harmonics of our fundamental pitch.

Decay stretching is a more general, more powerful, and more computationally expensive method for lengthening decay times. (It is still very cheap, since only random numbers are needed, not multiplication or additional table lookup.) The recurrence relation for stretching the basic plucked-string algorithm is

$$Y_t = \begin{cases} Y_{t-p} & \text{probability } 1 - \dfrac{1}{S} \\ + \dfrac{1}{2}\left(Y_{t-p} + Y_{t-p-1}\right) & \text{probability } \dfrac{1}{S}. \end{cases}$$

The new parameter S is called the *stretch factor*, and is always at least 1. The decay time of each overtone is approximately multiplied by S, when compared with the decay time for the same overtone in the basic algorithm. The pitch of the sound is also affected by S, as the period is now about $p + 1/2S$ instead of $p + ½$. The optimum choice for S depends on the sampling rate, p, and the effect desired. By choosing S proportional to p^{-1} or p^{-2}, the decay times for the nth harmonic can be made proportional to p^2/n^2 or p/n^2, instead of p^3/n^2, as they would be for a constant stretch factor. Note that for $S = 1$ the recurrence relation simplifies to the unstretched algorithm. For $S = \infty$ the sound does not decay; this is simple wavetable synthesis. Decay stretching can be used to solve the tuning problem caused by having $p + ½$ instead of p as the period of the basic algorithm. By making S proportional to p^{-1}, exact (just intonation) intervals can easily be tuned. Even simple approximations (such as doubling S for each higher octave) help with the tuning of intervals.

If nonrandom wavetable loads are used with large values of S (long decays), woodwindlike sounds can be produced. Strong has produced sounds that he refers to as a "plucked bassoon." More research is being done to determine appropriate initial wavetable loads and parameter settings. The "pluck" can be eliminated in a variety of ways; for example, by starting two strings exactly out of phase, then having them drift apart, or by using an external amplitude envelope. Whether realistic woodwind attacks are obtainable is currently unknown.

The recurrence relation for stretched drums is

$$
Y_t = \begin{cases}
+Y_{t-p} & \text{probability } b\left(1 - \dfrac{1}{S}\right) \\[2mm]
-Y_{t-p} & \text{probability } (1 - b)\left(1 - \dfrac{1}{S}\right) \\[2mm]
+\dfrac{1}{2}\,(Y_{t-p} + Y_{t-p-1}) & \text{probability } b\,\dfrac{1}{S} \\[2mm]
-\dfrac{1}{2}\,(Y_{t-p} + Y_{t-p-1}) & \text{probability } (1 - b)\,\dfrac{1}{S}.
\end{cases}
$$

Note that the stretch factor and blend factor are independent, so the algorithm can be implemented with two separate tests, and no multiplies are needed. For drums (b near ½), increasing S increases the "snare" sound, allowing smaller values of p to be used for the same duration. If $b = 1$, the recurrence simplifies to the stretched algorithm for string sounds. If $b = $ ½ and $S = \infty$, single-bit white noise is produced.

In many digital synthesizers, fast multiplies are available, but probabilistic algorithms like decay stretching are difficult to implement. On these machines, *multiplicative decay stretching* can be done:

$$
Y_t = cY_{t-p} + dY_{t-p-1}.
$$

To get an effect similar to the probabilistic decay-stretching algorithm, set $d = 1/2S$ and $c = 1 - d$. If $c + d < 1$, then there is an overall loss in the feedback loop, so decay times are reduced, and the signal eventually decays to zero, rather than just to a constant. David Jaffe has been experimenting with this algorithm at CCRMA (Jaffe and Smith 1983).

Shortening the decay times is more difficult than lengthening them. Use of multiplicative decay stretching, with $c + d < 1$, is one way to shorten decay times. Another possibility is to change the recurrence to one that smooths out the waveform faster. For example, we have experimented with the *1-2-1 weighting algorithm*:

$$
Y_t = \frac{Y_{t-p-1} + 2Y_{t-p} + Y_{t-p+1}}{4}.
$$

Unfortunately, the extra computation time this algorithm takes may increase the time per sample enough to offset the reduced number of samples

needed for the signal to decay. Decay stretching and the harmonic trick work just as well with this algorithm as with the basic plucked-string algorithm. It can also be modified to a drum algorithm, but there seems to be no advantage to this, since decay time for drums can be adequately controlled by varying p.

One advantage to the 1-2-1 weighting algorithm is that the frequency is f_s/p, rather than $2f_s/(2p+1)$. This allows better tuning, since consonant intervals are integer ratios of frequency.

Alan Siegel has suggested the following variation for reducing decay times:

$$
Y_t = \frac{Y_{t-p} + Y_{t-1}}{2}.
$$

This variant reduces decay times enormously for all the harmonics but is most noticeable in the higher harmonics. The resulting sound is still a plucked-string sound, but it is softer, more like a nylon string than a steel one. All the modifications to the basic algorithm can also be applied to this variation.

Generalizations of the Algorithms

Siegel's variant, multiplicative decay stretching, and the basic algorithm can all be viewed as variants of the *two-point recurrence*,

$$
Y_t = cY_{t-g} + dY_{t-h}.
$$

For stability, we need to have $c + d \leq 1$. So far, we've only investigated algorithms where g and h are near p or near 1. Many other possibilities (such as $g = 2h$) need exploring.

The 1-2-1 weighting algorithm is one of many possible three-point recurrences. Jaffe has been experimenting with others to get independent control of decay time and pitch. There is no reason (other than increased computational cost) not to explore recurrence relations with even more terms.

Probabilistic decay stretching can be generalized to probabilistic choice from any set of recurrence relations. In some cases, this can be used to get the effect of weighted averaging without multiplication (as in decay stretching). It can also produce wholly new sounds (as in the drum algorithms).

Hints for Implementation

On the Intel 8080A, four voices at a sampling rate of at least 10 KHz have been obtained (also, two voices at 20 KHz). By using a processor with a faster clock rate (Z80A or 8085), the sampling rate can be increased by a factor of about 2 with no change in the programs. On the TMS9900, two voices at 10 KHz or one voice at 20 KHz have been achieved. These times are for the basic string algorithms (except for the four-voice implementation, which involved a number of tricks). Drums, decay stretching, and the 1-2-1 weighting algorithm all are slower. These implementations and the Digitar chip (16 voices at 20 KHz) are described in a separate paper (Karplus and Strong 1983). Jaffe has programmed the Systems Concept Digital Synthesizer at CCRMA to implement 29 voices at 17 KHz.

There are many different ways to implement the recurrence relations for wavetable synthesis and the decay algorithms. The two most interesting algorithms are the *decreasing-counter* and *circular-buffer* techniques. For the decreasing-counter method, a wavetable is stored backward in sequential memory locations, with a pointer to the current value. As each sample is output, the pointer is decremented to get the next value. When the pointer is decreased below the bottom of the table, it is reset to the top.

Normally, the decreasing-counter technique is good for single-voice implementations only. Multiple voices cause difficulty with "balancing the loop" (keeping the sampling rate constant), since the pointer resettings occur at different times. Using a faster processor doesn't help, unless there is enough spare time in each sample to do both pointer resettings. A separate piece of hardware to resynchronize samples (a first-in-first-out [FIFO] buffer before the digital-to-analog converter [DAC]) would eliminate this problem. However, a two-voice implementation is possible using the decreasing-counter technique without extra hardware, if one voice is a plucked string and the other

is a drum. The same p value is used for both voices, sacrificing control of the drum timbre but allowing both pointers to be reset together.

One trivial variant of the basic algorithm replaces Y_{t-p-1} with Y_{t-p+1}, changing the nominal period to $p - \frac{1}{2}$. With a one-voice, decreasing-counter algorithm, this variant permits compensation to period p by using the extra time needed for restoring the pointer. If this extra time can be set to half the normal sample time, then the average sampling period is $1 + 1/2p$ times as long as the inner-loop time. This means that the frequency of the tone is

$$\frac{f_s}{\left(p - \dfrac{1}{2}\right)\left(1 + \dfrac{1}{2p}\right)} = \frac{f_s}{p - \dfrac{1}{4p}},$$

very near the desired frequency f_s/p. This trick, like the 1-2-1 weighting algorithm, allows easier tuning of consonant intervals.

The circular-buffer technique uses two pointers into an area of memory at least as large as p. The pointers are separated by p. The value is read from the position pointed to by the trailing pointer, output, then copied to the position pointed to by the leading pointer. Both pointers are then incremented around the buffer (with the first position coming immediately after the last one). Clever choice of the position and size of the buffer often allows the pointer wraparound to be done with no extra instructions. Multiple voices can be done by having several buffers with pointer pairs. If indexed addressing is used, the voices can share a common leading pointer, with different base addresses for the different voices. Alternatively, for two voices, three pointers can be used in a single larger buffer, with the middle pointer used as a trailing pointer for the first voice, and a leading pointer for the second voice. For a given amount of memory this allows a larger value of p for one voice, as long as the other voice has a small value of p.

Slurring works better with the circular-buffer technique than with the decreasing-counter technique. Increases in p merely tap more of the previous samples, instead of tapping undefined (though probably usable) values past the end of the table. With the circular buffer, slurring to a subharmonic (new p a multiple of its orginal value) is essentially the same as the harmonic trick, since no energy is introduced at the new fundamental. To slur a subharmonic, the algorithm first slurs to an intermediate note, waits about a period, and then slurs to the final pitch.

Average sampling rate can be increased by taking as much code as possible out of the innermost loop. For example, the harmonic trick is faster than decay stretching, because it only takes extra time during wavetable loading (between notes), not during notes.

Most software implementations require a timing counter to determine when to stop a note and read in new parameters. This counter could be decremented and tested on every sample to get very precise timing control. An alternative method is to subtract the buffer size every time the pointer wraps around. In the decreasing-counter technique, this is particularly attractive because there is plenty of spare time during the wraparound.

Using small word sizes (like 8 bits) makes round-off error a serious problem. In the algorithms described in this paper, round-off error is not random but rather a consistent rounding down of the samples. This effect significantly reduces the decay time of the fundamental frequency (compared to the theoretical decay time or to the decay time when the algorithm is computed with much larger word sizes). The effect can almost be eliminated by randomly adding 0 or 1 to $Y_{t-p} + Y_{t-p-1}$ before dividing by 2. This *dither* technique lengthens the final decay of the fundamental roughly back to its theoretical decay time, without appreciably lengthening the initial attack of the tone.

Since the round-off error is consistently in the same direction, it introduces a dc drift to the decay. This is not serious, because the algorithm is guaranteed not to cause arithmetic overflow (the usual danger with dc drift). Dithering reduces the drift considerably by converting it to a random walk, but does not entirely eliminate it. The dc component can cause clicks if a voice is silenced by being set to some constant value (such as 0). In a one-voice implementation, the simplest way to silence a voice without clicks is to stop sending new values to the DAC, letting it remain at the last value it received.

Another way to silence a note is to change p to a very small value (such as 2), producing almost instantaneous decay.

Analysis of the Plucked-String Algorithm

What makes the simple plucked-string algorithm sound so realistic? How can we predict how long notes will last? To answer these questions, we have to look at the decay of the overtones. From listening to the output of the algorithm, it is clear that the higher harmonics die very quickly, while the fundamental and the lower harmonics last a long time. Low notes last much longer than high notes.

It would be interesting to compare the theoretical analysis of our synthesis technique with an existing analysis of a guitar, lute, mandolin, or other string instrument. Unfortunately, we could not find a published analysis and did not have the tools to perform our own analysis. Some previous work has been done using physical models for synthesizing string sounds (Hiller and Ruiz 1971), but these models do not help to explain the high quality of the sound produced with our technique.

Before plunging into the mathematics, it's worth taking an informal look at what is happening to the harmonics. Essentially, one pass (p samples) takes what is in the wavetable and averages it with another copy delayed by one sample time. For sinusoids with long periods, one sample time is a very small phase difference, while for short periods it is a large difference. Averaging two sinusoids with a small phase difference decreases the amplitude slightly, while averaging two with a large phase difference (up to half a period) causes much more cancellation. Since the phase difference results from a time difference of one sample, it is always less than half a period for frequencies up to the Nyquist frequency.

The informal argument can be made more explicit if we give estimates of the decay rates of the harmonics (Jaffe and Smith 1983). However, by borrowing some techniques from digital-filter design, we can compute both the decay rates and the frequencies of the overtones accurately and see how good the simpler approximations are. If we view the algorithm as a digital filter with no input, the overtones and their decay rates correspond to poles in the z-transform of the impulse response of the filter. More information on z-transform techniques can be found in the literature (Moore 1978; Antoniou 1979). The decay time of a partial is inversely proportional to the log of the magnitude of the corresponding pole, and the frequency is proportional to the argument of the pole. Writing the location of pole in polar form as $ae^{i\omega}$ allows us to write the frequency and decay-time constant of the corresponding overtone:

$$f = \frac{f_s \omega}{2\pi}$$

$$D = \frac{-1}{f_s \ln a}.$$

The decay time is the time it takes for the partial to decay to $1/e$ of its initial amplitude. In audio work, the time it takes to decay 60 db is often used instead. To get the 60-db decay time, we multiply D by $\ln 1000 \approx 6.908$.

We can obtain the z-transform of the impulse response from the recurrence relations by using the standard techniques for digital filter analysis:

$$h(z) = \frac{\frac{1}{2}(z^{-1} + 1)z^{-p}}{1 - \frac{1}{2}(z^{-1} + 1)z^{-p}} = \frac{1 + z}{2z^{p+1} - z - 1}.$$

The poles of the z-transform are the roots of $2z^{p+1} - z - 1 = 0$. There is only one zero at $z = -1$ (corresponding to the Nyquist frequency $\frac{1}{2}f_s$). The roots are easy to approximate if we rearrange the equation to be $2z^{p+1/2} = z^{1/2} + z^{-1/2}$. Replacing z by $ae^{i\omega}$ gives us

$$2a^{p+1/2}e^{i\omega(p+1/2)} = a^{1/2}e^{i(\omega/2)} + a^{-1/2}e^{-i(\omega/2)}$$
$$= \sqrt{a + a^{-1} + 2\cos\omega} \cdot e^{i\theta}$$

for some angle θ. Looking at just the imaginary parts of the right-hand sides, we get

$$\sqrt{a + a^{-1} + 2\cos\omega}\,\sin\theta = (a^{1/2} - a^{-1/2})\sin\frac{\omega}{2}.$$

Approximations are easily found if we assume

that a is only slightly less than 1. This assumption is easily verified numerically. If $a = 1 - \varepsilon$, then

$$a + a^{-1} = 2 + \varepsilon^2 + \varepsilon^3 + \ldots \approx 2$$
$$a^{1/2} - a^{-1/2} = -\varepsilon^2/8 - \ldots \approx 0.$$

This gives us that $\sin\theta \approx 0$, so $e^{i\omega(p+1/2)} = e^{i\theta} \approx 1$, which we can solve for ω to get a first approximation of the frequency of the nth partial:

$$\omega = \frac{\theta + 2\pi n}{p + \frac{1}{2}} \approx \frac{2\pi n}{p + \frac{1}{2}}$$

Since $\sqrt{2 + 2\cos\omega} = 2\cos\omega/2$, the magnitude of the pole is $2a^{p+1/2} \approx 2\cos\omega/2$. Solving for a, we get an approximation for the decay time of the nth harmonic:

$$a \approx \left(\cos\frac{\omega}{2}\right)^{1/(p+1/2)} = \left(\cos\frac{2\pi n}{2p + 1}\right)^{1/(p+1/2)}$$

$$D \approx \frac{-1}{f_s \ln a} = \frac{p + \frac{1}{2}}{-f_s \ln\cos\frac{2\pi n}{2p + 1}}.$$

These estimates are the same as the ones obtained by less formal analysis. For large p and small n, they are quite accurate (for $p = 240$ and $n = 1$ the magnitude and frequency estimates are both correct to seven significant figures).

More accuracy can be obtained by using these estimates as starting values for iterative improvement. The simplest technique is to use a few iterations of Newton's method to improve the approximations for the poles:

$$z \leftarrow \frac{2pz^{p+1} + 1}{2(p + 1)z^p - 1}.$$

For a more intuitive grasp of the relationships between p, n, and decay time, it is worthwhile to expand the decay-time estimate in powers of n:

$$D \approx \frac{1}{f_s}\left(\frac{(2p + 1)^3}{4\pi^2 n^2} - \frac{2p + 1}{6}\right.$$
$$\left. - \frac{\pi^2 n^2}{15(2p + 1)} - \ldots\right).$$

Roughly speaking, decay time increases as p^3, and

decreases as n^{-2}. Appendix 1 provides a tabulation of decay-time constant, estimated-time constant, and the first term of the power series for various values of p and n. For most purposes, the first term of the power series is an accurate enough estimate of the decay time.

The frequency estimates for the overtones are purely harmonic. It is interesting to examine how much inharmonicity is actually present. This requires estimating θ somewhat more accurately. If we replace $a + a^{-1}$ by 2 as before, replace $a^{1/2}$ by $(\cos \omega/2)^{1/(2p+1)}$, and rearrange the equation involving $\sin \theta$, we get

$$\theta \approx \sin^{-1}\left(\frac{1}{2} \tan \frac{\omega}{2} \left(\left(\cos \frac{\omega}{2} \right)^{1/(2p+1)} - \left(\cos \frac{\omega}{2} \right)^{-1/(2p+1)} \right) \right).$$

Expanding by powers of ω gives

$$\theta \approx \frac{\omega^3}{16(2p+1)} - \frac{\omega^5}{128(2p+1)} + \cdots .$$

Plugging in our previous approximation for ω, computing θ, then recomputing ω gives us

$$\omega \approx \frac{4\pi n}{2p+1} - \frac{8\pi^3 n^3}{(2p+1)^5} - \cdots .$$

Appendix 2 tabulates the frequency of the pure harmonic, the improved estimate of ω, the frequency obtained by using Newton's method to refine the estimate of the pole, and the inharmonicity of the overtone. It can be seen that (except for small values of p) the overtones are almost pure harmonics.

The frequencies and decay times for the 1-2-1 weighting algorithm can be analyzed in a similar fashion. The partials are pure harmonics, and the decay times are about half the decay times for corresponding partials obtained using the basic algorithm.

Analysis of the Drum Algorithm

Since the drum algorithm produces aperiodic signals, we need to use different tools to analyze it. Instead of amplitudes of overtones, let's look at the rms amplitude. *Root-mean-square amplitude* is the square root of the expected value of the square of the amplitude $= \sqrt{E(Y_t^2)}$. Squaring the recurrence relation for the drum algorithm yields

$$E(Y_t^2) = \frac{1}{4} E(Y_{t-p}^2) + \frac{1}{4} E(Y_{t-p-1}^2) + \frac{1}{2} E(Y_{t-p}Y_{t-p-1}).$$

Since Y_{t-p} and Y_{t-p-1} have independent signs, $E(Y_{t-p}Y_{t-p-1}) = 0$. This reduces the recurrence relation to

$$E(Y_t^2) = \frac{1}{4} \left(E(Y_{t-p}^2) + E(Y_{t-p-1}^2) \right).$$

Note that for $-p < t \leq 0$, $E(Y_t^2) = A^2$. If we make the simplifying assumption that $E(Y_{t-p}^2)$ is approximately $E(Y_{t-p-1}^2)$, we get

$$E(Y_t^2) \approx \frac{1}{2} E(Y_{t-p}^2) = 2^{-\lfloor t/p \rfloor} A^2.$$

We can improve this estimate somewhat by changing our assumption that $E(Y_{t-p}^2)$ is nearly the same as $E(Y_{t-p-1}^2)$. If we instead assume that $E(Y_t^2)$ decays exponentially, we can express $E(Y_t^2)$ in the form $2^{\alpha t} A^2$. To compute α, we plug into the previous recurrence relation, getting

$$2^{\alpha t} A^2 = \frac{1}{4} \left(2^{\alpha(t-p)} A^2 + 2^{\alpha(t-p-1)} A^2 \right).$$

This can be simplified to

$$2^{\alpha p} = \frac{1}{4} \left(1 + 2^{-\alpha} \right).$$

Since $1 + 2^{-\alpha} \approx 2(2)^{-\alpha/2}$, we can conclude that

$$E(Y_t^2) \approx 2^{-2t/(2p+1)} A^2$$

and

$$\text{rms } Y_t \approx 2^{-t/(2p+1)} A.$$

This is not a complete analysis of the drum algorithm, since the absolute values of successive values are correlated, as are the absolute values of samples p apart. Experiments still need to be done to determine whether there is a perceptual difference between the drum algorithm and a Gaussian noise source with an exponentially decaying envelope.

Conclusions and Future Research

We have developed simple but powerful algorithms that can be implemented on a variety of different processors and synthesizers. They allow programmers and musicians to experiment with computer music using inexpensive equipment. The algorithms do not have the versatility of FM synthesis or additive synthesis, but provide surprisingly rich timbres. Readers interested in commercial application of these algorithms should contact the Office of Technology Licensing at Stanford University about licensing agreements.

In addition to the problems mentioned in the main body of the paper, there are still a lot of questions that need answering. For example, what sounds can be achieved by using the guitar decay algorithm as a digital filter to produce a tuned reverberator? Or by cross-coupling two strings at slightly different pitches? What about more complicated modifiers in the feedback loop (two delay-and-mix units instead of one, allpass filters, and so on)? What about locking together two voices (same initial load) with opposite amplitudes so that they cancel each other, then letting them drift apart by using independent probabilistic decay stretching? Some of these problems are examined by Jaffe and Smith (1983); others are being investigated with the Digitar chip.

Those interested in mathematical analyses could probably improve the current analyses a bit, and other variants have yet to be analyzed. A good approximation for the poles of the general two-point recurrence would be particularly welcome. It would also be interesting to convert the recurrence relations to differential equations, and to assign a physical interpretation. Techniques for taking the z-transform of a probabilistic algorithm are needed to perform a proper analysis of decay stretching.

References

Antoniou, A. 1979. *Digital Filters: Analysis and Design.* New York: McGraw-Hill.
Hiller, L., and P. Ruiz. 1971. "Synthesizing Musical Sounds by Solving the Wave Equation for Vibrating Objects." *Journal of the Audio Engineering Society* Part 1: 19(6):462–470; Part 2: 19(7):542–551.
Jaffe, D., and J. Smith. 1983. "Extensions of the Karplus-Strong Plucked-String Algorithm." *Computer Music Journal* 7(2):56–69.
James, D. 1978. "Real Time Synthesis Using High Speed Computer Networks." Ph.D. thesis, Massachusetts Institute of Technology.
Karplus, K., and A. Strong. 1983. "Implementations of the Digitar Algorithms." Unpublished manuscript.
Knuth, D. 1981. *The Art of Computer Programming: Volume 2, Seminumerical Algorithms.* 2nd ed. Reading, Massachusetts: Addison-Wesley.
Moore, F. R. 1978. "An Introduction to the Mathematics of Digital Signal Processing, Part II: Sampling, Transforms, and Digital Filtering." *Computer Music Journal* 2(2):38–60.
Sleator, D. 1981. Private communication.

Appendix 1: Decay-Time Constants

The decay time is the time (in seconds, sampling rate = 20 KHz) it takes for harmonic n to decay to $1/e$ of its initial amplitude, using the plucked-string algorithm (with periodicity parameter p). The first column in the table is a crude estimate of decay time, calculated from the first term of the power-series expansion (see the text):

$$\frac{(2p + 1)^3}{4\pi^2 n^2 f_s}.$$

The second column is the estimate from which the power series was derived:

$$\frac{p + \dfrac{1}{2}}{-f_s \ln \cos \dfrac{2\pi n}{2p + 1}}.$$

The third column is computed from the poles of the z-transform for the plucked-string algorithm (the roots of $2z^{p+1} - z - 1$). To compute the table, the poles were estimated by

$$\left(\cos \frac{2\pi n}{2p + 1} \right)^{2/(2p + 1)} e^{4\pi in/(2p + 1)}.$$

The estimates were then refined by iterating Newton's method until successive approximations differed by less than 10^{-6}. The log magnitude of the pole was divided by f_s to get the table entry.

Appendix 2: Frequencies of Overtones

The table in this appendix gives frequencies (in hertz, with a sampling rate of 20 KHz) for various overtones of the plucked-string algorithm. The first column is the simple harmonics of $1/(p + \frac{1}{2})$; the second is the improved estimate, including the n^3 correction term; the third is from Newton's method, using the second estimate as a starting point; the fourth is the deviation of the actual frequency from the pure harmonic (in cents). (Note: n is the number of the harmonic, and p is the periodicity parameter.)

p	n	first term	cos estimate	log |pole|
		good	better	best
2	1	0.0001583	0.0001064	0.0001443
3	1	0.0004344	0.0003704	0.0003861
4	1	0.0009233	0.0008442	0.0008538
4	2	0.0002308	0.0001285	0.0001736
30	1	0.2874748	0.2869659	0.2869670
30	2	0.0718687	0.0713582	0.0713592
30	3	0.0319416	0.0314284	0.0314295
60	1	2.2437082	2.2426996	2.2427001
60	2	0.5609271	0.5599176	0.5599182
60	3	0.2493009	0.2482901	0.2482906
60	4	0.1402318	0.1392190	0.1392196
120	1	17.7280674	17.7260590	17.7260592
120	2	4.4320169	4.4300080	4.4300082
120	3	1.9697853	1.9677757	1.9677760
240	1	140.9436443	140.9396359	140.9396361
240	2	35.2359111	35.2319025	35.2319026
240	3	15.6604049	15.6563960	15.6563961
240	4	8.8089778	8.8049683	8.8049685
240	8	2.2022444	2.1982317	2.1982319
240	15	0.6264162	0.6223924	0.6223925
240	30	0.1566040	0.1525322	0.1525324
240	60	0.0391510	0.0348608	0.0348610
240	120	0.0097878	0.0021007	0.0026590
480	1	1124.0365431	1124.0285347	1124.0285388
480	2	281.0091358	281.0011273	281.0011274
480	3	124.8929492	124.8849406	124.8849406
480	4	70.2522839	70.2442751	70.2442751
480	8	17.5630710	17.5550605	17.5550605

p	n	Harmonic	Corrected	Actual	Inharmonicity
2	1	8000.000	7747.338	7500.000	−111.7313
3	1	5714.286	5667.307	5642.389	−21.9205
4	1	4444.444	4431.073	4427.170	−6.7421
4	2	8888.889	8781.918	8507.279	−75.9665
30	1	655.738	655.737	655.737	−.0025
30	2	1311.475	1311.468	1311.468	−.0101
30	3	1967.213	1967.188	1967.187	−.0233
60	1	330.579	330.578	330.578	−.0002
60	2	661.157	661.157	661.157	−.0006
60	3	991.736	991.735	991.735	−.0015
60	4	1322.314	1322.312	1322.312	−.0026
120	1	165.975	165.975	165.975	.0000
120	2	331.950	331.950	331.950	.0000
120	3	497.925	497.925	497.925	−.0001
240	1	83.160	83.160	83.160	.0000
240	2	166.320	166.320	166.320	.0000
240	3	249.480	249.480	249.480	.0000
240	4	332.640	332.640	332.640	.0000
240	8	665.281	665.281	665.281	.0000
240	15	1247.401	1247.401	1247.401	−.0001
240	30	2494.802	2494.802	2494.802	−.0006
240	60	4989.605	4989.598	4989.596	−.0033
240	120	9979.210	9979.157	9965.363	−2.4038
480	1	41.623	41.623	41.623	.0000
480	2	83.247	83.247	83.247	.0000
480	3	124.870	124.870	124.870	.0000
480	4	166.493	166.493	166.493	.0000
480	8	332.986	332.986	332.986	.0000

37

David A. Jaffe and Julius O. Smith

Center for Computer Research in Music and
Acoustics (CCRMA)
Stanford University
Stanford, California 94305

Extensions of the Karplus-Strong Plucked-String Algorithm

Introduction

In 1979, an efficient computational model for vibrating strings, based on physical reasoning, was proposed by McIntyre and Woodhouse (1979). This model plays a crucial role in their recent work on bowed strings (McIntyre, Schumacher, and Woodhouse 1981; 1983), and methods for calibrating the model to recorded data have been developed (Smith 1983).

Independently, in 1978, Alex Strong devised an efficient special case of the McIntyre-Woodhouse string model that produces remarkably rich and realistic timbres despite its simplicity (Karplus and Strong 1983). Since then, Strong and Kevin Karplus have explored several variations and refinements of the algorithm, with an emphasis on small-system implementations. We have found that the Karplus-Strong algorithm can be used with equally impressive results on fast, high-power equipment. The availability of multiplies, for example, allows several modifications and extensions that increase its usefulness and flexibility. These extensions are described in this paper. The developments were motivated by musical needs that arose during the composition of *May All Your Children Be Acrobats* (1981) for computer-generated tape, eight guitars, and voice and *Silicon Valley Breakdown* (1982) for four-channel, computer-generated tape, both written by David Jaffe. Our theoretical approach and the extensions based on it have also been applied to the McIntyre-Woodhouse algorithm (Smith 1983).

David A. Jaffe is also affiliated with the Music Department at Stanford University, and Julius O. Smith is also affiliated with the Electrical Engineering Department there.

Computer Music Journal, Vol. 7, No. 2,
Summer 1983

The String-Simulation Algorithm

The Karplus-Strong plucked-string algorithm is presented in this issue of *Computer Music Journal*. From our point of view, the algorithm consists of a high-order *digital filter*, which represents the string; and a short *noise burst*, which represents the "pluck."[1] The digital filter is given by the difference equation

$$y_n = x_n + \frac{y_{n-N} + y_{n-(N+1)}}{2}, \qquad (1)$$

where x_n is the input signal amplitude at sample n, y_n is the output amplitude at sample n, and N is the (approximate) desired pitch period of the note in samples. The noise burst is defined by

$$x_n = \begin{cases} Au_n, & n = 0, 1, 2, \ldots, N-1 \\ 0, & n \geq N, \end{cases}$$

where A is the desired amplitude, and $u_n \in [-1,1]$ is the output of a random-number generator. The output y_n is taken beginning at time $n = N$ in our implementation.

Analysis of the String Simulator

Before proceeding to practical extensions of the algorithm, we will describe the theory on which many of them are based. Various concepts from digital filter theory are employed. For a tutorial introduction to digital filter theory, see the works by Smith (1982b) and Steiglitz (1974).

The input-output relation of Eq. (1) may be ex-

---

1. In some situations, the sound more closely resembles a string struck with a hammer or mallet than one plucked with a pick, but we will always use the term *pluck* when referring to the excitation.

pressed differently by means of *delay-operator* notation. We define the unit-sample delay operator d by the relation

$$d^k x_n \triangleq x_{n-k},$$

where x_n is an arbitrary signal, and k is an integer. (The symbol $\triangleq$ means "is defined as.") Thus, multiplying a signal by d^k delays the signal in time by k samples. In these terms, Eq. (1) becomes

$$y_n = x_n + \frac{d^N y_n + d^{N+1} y_n}{2}$$

$$= x_n + d^N \frac{1+d}{2} y_n.$$

Solving for y_n yields

$$y_n = \frac{x_n}{1 - \frac{1+d}{2} d^N}. \qquad (2)$$

We can convert linear delay-operator equations immediately to z-transform equations by replacing each time signal with its z-transform, and replacing d with z^{-1}. It is customary to denote a time signal in lowercase letters (e.g., x_n) and the corresponding z-transform in uppercase letters (e.g., $X(z)$). The *transfer function* of a (linear, time-invariant) digital filter is the z-transform of the output signal divided by the z-transform of the input. The transfer function of the string simulator is then found to be

$$H(z) \triangleq \frac{Y(z)}{X(z)} = \frac{1}{1 - \frac{1+z^{-1}}{2} z^{-N}}$$

$$= \frac{1}{1 - H_a(z) H_b(z)},$$

where

$$H_a(z) \triangleq \frac{1 + z^{-1}}{2}$$

$$H_b(z) \triangleq z^{-N}.$$

This form of the description is shown in Fig. 1. The feedback loop consists of a length N delay line $H_b(z)$ in series with a two-point average $H_a(z)$. Corresponding to this breakdown of the string simula-

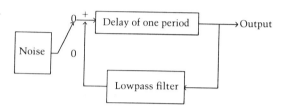

Fig. 1. Block diagram for the basic string simulator.

tor is the following set of difference equations:

$$v_n = y_{n-N}$$

$$w_n = \frac{v_n + v_{n-1}}{2}$$

$$y_n = x_n + w_n.$$

The *frequency response* of a digital filter is defined as the transfer function evaluated at $z = e^{j\omega T_s} = \cos(\omega T_s) + j \sin(\omega T_s)$, where T_s is the sampling period in seconds (T_s is the inverse of the sampling rate f_s), $\omega = 2\pi f$ is radian frequency, f is frequency in Hz, and $j = \sqrt{-1}$. The frequency response of the string simulator is then

$$H(e^{j\omega T_s}) = \frac{1}{1 - H_a(e^{j\omega T_s}) H_b(e^{j\omega T_s})},$$

where

$$H_a(e^{j\omega T_s}) = \frac{1 + e^{-j\omega T_s}}{2} = e^{-j\omega T_s/2} \cos(\omega T_s/2)$$

$$= e^{-\pi f T_s} \cos(\pi f T_s)$$

$$H_b(e^{j\omega T_s}) = e^{-j\omega N T_s} = e^{-j2\pi f N T_s}.$$

In this paper it is necessary to consider the amplitude response and phase delay of the feedback filters separately. The *amplitude response* is defined as the magnitude of the frequency response, and it gives the *gain* of the filter as a function of frequency. The *phase delay* is defined as minus the complex angle of the frequency response divided by radian frequency, and it gives the *time delay* (in seconds) experienced by a sinusoid at each frequency.

The amplitude response of each component filter is given by

$$G_a(f) \triangleq |H_a(e^{i\omega T_s})| = |\cos(\omega T_s/2)| = |\cos(\pi f T_s)|$$

$$G_b(f) \triangleq |H_b(e^{i\omega T_s})| = 1.$$

Thus the delay line H_b is lossless, and the two-point average H_a exhibits a gain that decreases with frequency according to the first quadrant of a cosine. We will assume hereafter that all frequencies are restricted to the Nyquist limit, that is, $|f| \leq f_s/2$. In this range, we have $|\cos(\pi f T_s)| = \cos(\pi f T_s)$.

It is convenient to define phase delay in units consisting of samples rather than seconds. The phase delays of H_a and H_b in samples are given by

$$P_a(f) \triangleq -\frac{\angle H_a(e^{i\omega T_s})}{\omega T_s} = \frac{1}{2},$$

$$P_b(f) \triangleq -\frac{\angle H_b(e^{i\omega T_s})}{\omega T_s} = N.$$

($\angle z$ denotes the complex angle of z). The two-point average has a phase delay equal to half a sample, and the delay line has a phase delay equal to its length.

Since the total loop consists of H_a and H_b in series, the loop gain and effective loop length are

$$loop\ gain = G_a(f)G_b(f) = \cos(\pi f T_s),$$

and

$$loop\ length = P_a(f) + P_b(f) = N + 1/2 \quad (samples)$$

for each sinusoidal frequency f Hz.

In synthesizing a single plucked-string note, we feed in N samples of white noise at amplitude A and listen to the output immediately afterward. It is equivalent to initialize the delay line H_b with sealed random numbers at time 0 and employ no input signal. Since the two-point average H_a is constantly changing the contents of the loop, the output signal is not periodic. It is close to periodic, however, and we use the term *period* in this loose sense. Each period of the synthetic string sound corresponds to the contents of the delay line at a particular time, and each period equals a somewhat lowpass version of the previous period. More precisely, a running two-point average of the samples comprising one period gives the next period in the output waveform. Since the effective loop length is $N + 1/2$ samples, the period is best defined to be

$NT_s + T_s/2$ sec. Experience shows this to correspond well with perceived pitch.

Decay of "Harmonics"

Since the signal is only quasi-periodic, it does not consist of discrete sinusoids. Essentially, we have many narrow "bands" of energy decaying to zero at different rates. When these energy bands are centered at frequencies that are an integer multiple of a lowest frequency, they will be referred to as *harmonics*. When the frequency components are not necessarily uniformly spaced, the term *partial* will be used to emphasize the possibility of inharmonicity. Consider, then, a partial at frequency f Hz circulating in the loop. On each pass through the loop, it suffers an attenuation equal to the loop-amplitude response, $G_a(f)G_b(f) = \cos(\pi f T_s)$; that is,

$$one\ period's\ attenuation = \cos(\pi f T_s).$$

Since the round-trip time in the loop equals $N + 1/2$ samples, the number of trips through the loop after n samples (nT_s sec) is equal to $n/(N + 1/2) = tf_s/(N + 1/2)$. Thus the *attenuation factor* at time $t = nT_s$ is given by

$$\alpha_f(t) \triangleq [\cos(\pi f T_s)]^{\frac{tf_s}{N + 1/2}}. \tag{3}$$

For example, an initial partial amplitude A at time 0 becomes amplitude $A\alpha_f(t)$ at time t seconds, where f is the frequency of the partial.

The *time constant* of an exponential decay is traditionally defined as the time when the amplitude has decayed to $1/e \approx 0.37$ times its initial value. The time constant at frequency f is found by equating Eq. (3) to e^{-t/τ_f} and solving for τ_f, which gives

$$\tau_f = \frac{-t}{\ln \alpha_f(t)} = -\frac{\left(N + \frac{1}{2}\right)T_s}{\ln \cos(\pi f T_s)} \quad (seconds). \tag{4}$$

For audio, it is normally more useful to define the time constant of decay as the time it takes to decay -60 db, or to 0.001 times the initial value. In this case, we equate Eq. (3) to 0.001 and solve for t. This value of t is often called t_{60}. Conversion from τ_f to

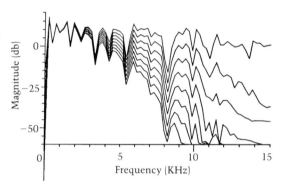

Fig. 2. Spectral evolution
during the first 16 periods.

$t_{60}(f)$ is accomplished by

$$t_{60}(f) = \ln(1000)\tau_f \approx 6.91\tau_f. \qquad (5)$$

For example, if a sinusoid at frequency f Hz has amplitude A at time 0, then at time $t_{60}(f)$ it has amplitude $A\alpha_f(t_{60}(f)) = A/1000$, or it is 60 db below its starting level.

The above analysis describes the attenuation due to "propagation" around the loop. It does not, however, incorporate the fact that sinusoids that do not "fit" in the loop are quickly destroyed by self-interference. This situation is analogous to making an actual string vibrate. Any signal may be "fed into" the string, but after the input ceases, the remaining energy quickly assumes a quasi-periodic nature. Thus, even though the loop is initialized with random numbers, after a very short time the primary frequencies present in the loop are those that have an integral number of periods in $N + 1/2$ samples. These frequencies are all multiples of the frequency whose period exactly matches the loop length $N + 1/2$. This lowest frequency provides the fundamental, or pitch frequency, of the note:

$$f_1 \triangleq \frac{1}{\left(N + \dfrac{1}{2}\right)T_s} = \frac{f_s}{N + \dfrac{1}{2}}. \qquad (6)$$

Setting f to the harmonic series beginning with f_1,

$$f_k = \frac{\omega_k}{2\pi} \triangleq k\frac{f_s}{N + \dfrac{1}{2}}, \quad k = 1, 2, \ldots, N/2, \qquad (7)$$

gives the decay factor at time t for the kth harmonic to be

$$\alpha_k(t) = [\cos(\pi f_k T_s)]^{f_1 t}. \qquad (8)$$

Similarly, the time constant per harmonic is given by

$$\tau_k \triangleq \frac{-t}{\ln \alpha_k(t)} = -\frac{1}{f_1 \ln \cos(\pi f_k T_s)} \quad (seconds). \qquad (9)$$

Figure 2 shows the spectral evolution during the first 16 periods of a note having a period of 128 samples. A 128 length Fast Fourier Transform (FFT) was computed every other period. Each curve in the figure is interpreted as the envelope of the har-

monic amplitudes, since a straight line is drawn from one harmonic amplitude to the next.

In certain extensions to the algorithm, H_a is other than a two-point average. In such a case, the attenuation factor of the kth harmonic after t seconds is approximately

$$\alpha_k(t) = G_a(f_k)^{\frac{t f_s}{N + P_a(f_k)}}, \qquad (10)$$

where we require $G_a(f) \leq 1$ for stability. The phase delay $P_a(f_k)$ of H_a may be used to create inharmonic spectra (Smith 1983). The spectrum is harmonic only when $P_a(f_k)$ is the same at all harmonic frequencies f_k.

Similarly, when H_a is more general, the time constant of decay for each harmonic becomes

$$\tau_k = -\frac{N + P_a(f_k)}{f_s \ln G_a(2\pi f_k T_s)} \quad (seconds). \qquad (11)$$

Having provided an analytic vocabulary, we now proceed to a detailed examination of our additions to the Karplus-Strong algorithm.

Tuning

The fact that the delay-line length N must be an integer causes tuning problems. Since the fundamental frequency is $f_1 = f_s/(N + 1/2)$, the allowed pitches are quantized, especially at high frequency. For large values of N (low pitches), the difference

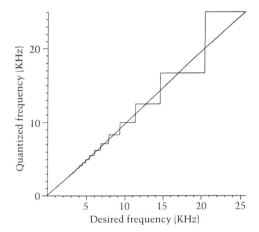

Fig. 3. Desired pitch versus resulting pitch for a 50-KHz sampling rate.

Quantized frequency (KHz)

Desired frequency (KHz)

between the pitch at N and $N + 1$ is very slight. However, for high pitches, N and $N + 1$ yield very different pitches and tuning becomes crude. Figure 3 shows the distortion in frequency for the sampling rate 50 KHz. For lower sampling rates, the curve is identical in form, and the distortion occurs at proportionately lower frequencies.

The key to a solution for this problem lies in the expression for loop length in terms of phase delay. The fundamental frequency is given by

$$f_1 = \frac{f_s}{N + P_a(f_1)},$$

where $P_a(f) = 1/2$ when the two-point average is used for H_a. To make up the difference between f_1 and the desired frequency, we need to introduce into the feedback loop a filter that can contribute a small delay without altering the loop gain. The filter we introduce has the difference equation

$$y_n = Cx_n + x_{n-1} - C_{y_{n-1}} \qquad (12)$$

and transfer function

$$H_c(z) \triangleq \frac{C + z^{-1}}{1 + Cz^{-1}},$$

where C is the only coefficient to be set. For stability, we must have $|C| < 1$. It can be shown that when the input x_n is bounded by 1, the output is bounded by $2|C| + 1$. The transfer function of the

whole string is now

$$H(z) \triangleq \frac{1}{1 - H_a(z)H_b(z)H_c(z)}.$$

The filter H_c is a first-order *allpass* filter, and as such it has a constant amplitude response. Indeed, the amplitude response is simply

$$G_c(f) \triangleq |H_c(e^{j\omega T_s})| = \frac{|C + e^{-j\omega T_s}|}{|1 + Ce^{-j\omega T_s}|} = 1.$$

The use of an allpass filter ensures that no modification of the decay rate will take place. The loop gain is $G_a(f)G_b(f)G_c(f) = \cos(\pi f T_s)$ as before.

We will select the phase delay of H_c so as to tune f_1 to the precise desired frequency. This requires only the ability to select phase delays between 0 and T_s sec, or one sample's worth.

The phase delay of the first-order allpass H_c is given by

$$\begin{aligned}
P_c(f) &\triangleq -\frac{\angle H_c(e^{j\omega T_s})}{\omega T_s} \\
&= \frac{-1}{\omega T_s} \angle \frac{C + e^{-j\omega T_s}}{1 + Ce^{-j\omega T_s}} \\
&= \frac{\angle(1 + Ce^{-j\omega T_s})}{\omega T_s} - \frac{\angle(C + e^{-j\omega T_s})}{\omega T_s} \\
&= \frac{1}{\omega T_s} \tan^{-1}\left(\frac{-C\sin(\omega T_s)}{1 + C\cos(\omega T_s)}\right) \\
&\quad - \frac{1}{\omega T_s} \tan^{-1}\left(\frac{-\sin(\omega T_s)}{C + \cos(\omega T_s)}\right). \qquad (13)
\end{aligned}$$

When the arguments to the arctangent above have magnitude less than unity, we can use the power-series expansion (Abramowitz and Stegun 1966),

$$\tan^{-1}(x) = x - \frac{x^3}{3} + \frac{x^5}{5} - \frac{x^7}{7} + \cdots, \quad |x| < 1.$$

Thus we can approximate the *low-frequency* phase delay by

$$\begin{aligned}
P_c(f) &\approx \frac{\sin(\omega T_s)}{\omega T_s(C + \cos(\omega T_s))} - \frac{C\sin(\omega T_s)}{\omega T_s(1 + C\cos(\omega T_s))} \\
&\approx \frac{1}{C + 1} - \frac{C}{1 + C} = \frac{1 - C}{1 + C}. \qquad (14)
\end{aligned}$$

A plot of the exact phase delay is given in Fig. 4 for

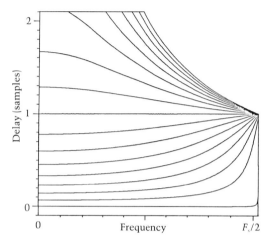

Fig. 4. Phase delay for the
fine-tuning allpass filter
$H_c(z) = (C + z^{-1})/$
$(1 + C z^{-1})$.

17 values of C equally spaced between -0.999 and
0.999. Note that delays between 0 and 1 sample can
be provided somewhat uniformly across the frequency axis. A delay of 0 samples corresponds to
$C = 1$, where the pole and zero of $H_c(z)$ cancel to
give $H_c(z) \equiv 1$. However, pole-zero cancellation on
the unit circle is not a good thing in practice, since
round-off errors may yield an unstable filter. Therefore, it is preferable to shift the range of one-sample
delay control to the region $\varepsilon \le P_c \le (1 + \varepsilon)$ for
some small nonnegative ε $(0 < \varepsilon \ll 1)$. It is best not
to shift very far, since the phase-delay curves are
less flat in the region beyond one sample's delay.

Note that the delay curves below the one-sample
level in Fig. 4 correspond to slightly flattened upper partials, while the delay curves above the one-
sample level correspond to slightly sharpened upper
partials. The timbre change due to slight systematic shifting of the upper partials, of an amount less
than one sample period, was found to be hardly noticeable. It may even be desirable as a source of subtle timbral variation. In any case, it is important to
get the perceived pitch right.

To tune the instrument precisely to a desired
fundamental frequency f_1, let P_1 equal f_s/f_1, the real
value for the period of the first partial, in samples,
which would give perfect tuning. Then, neglecting
resonant modes other than at f_1, we desire $N +$

$P_a(f_1) + P_c(f_1) = P_1$. The integer buffer length N
and the delay $P_c(f_1)$ required from the allpass filter
become

$$N \triangleq \text{Floor}(P_1 - P_a(f_1) - \varepsilon)$$

$$P_c(f_1) \triangleq P_1 - N - P_a(f_1), \tag{15}$$

where $\varepsilon > 0$ is the offset that shifts $P_c(f_1)$ into the
range $[\varepsilon, 1+\varepsilon]$, and $P_a(f_1)$ is the delay in samples due
to the filter H_a. In the simple case where H_a is a
two-point average, $P_a(f_1) = 1/2$.

We next solve for the filter coefficient in Eq. (13)
as a function of $P_c(f_1)$. Taking the tangent of both
sides, and using an identity for the tangent of a
difference leads to the quadratic equation in C,

$$C^2 \sin(\omega_1 T_s P_c(f_1) + \omega_1 T_s) + 2C \sin(\omega_1 T_s P_c(f_1)) + \sin(\omega_1 T_s P_c(f_1) - \omega_1 T_s) = 0,$$

where $\omega_1 \triangleq 2\pi f_1$. The solution is found, after some
manipulation (Mont-Reynaud 1982), to be

$$C = \frac{-\sin(\omega_1 T_s P_c(f_1)) \pm \sin(\omega_1 T_s)}{\sin(\omega_1 T_s P_c(f_1) + \omega_1 T_s)}.$$

We have introduced an extra root by producing a
quadratic equation. The previous approximation
Eq. (14) indicates that the $+$ sign should be taken.
Therefore, the final solution is

$$C = \frac{\sin(\omega_1 T_s) - \sin(\omega_1 T_s P_c(f_1))}{\sin(\omega_1 T_s P_c(f_1) + \omega_1 T_s)}$$

$$= \frac{\sin\left(\dfrac{\omega_1 T_s - \omega_1 T_s P_c(f_1)}{2}\right)}{\sin\left(\dfrac{\omega_1 T_s + \omega_1 T_s P_c(f_1)}{2}\right)} \tag{16}$$

which can be approximated, at low frequencies, by

$$C \approx \frac{1 - P_c(f_1)}{1 + P_c(f_1)}. \tag{17}$$

Although this technique provides a fairly precise
fundamental frequency, it does not guarantee an in-
tune *percept*, since the perceived pitch does not
always coincide with the fundamental frequency.
An additional mapping onto a perceptual tuning
dimension may be needed for the very high notes.
In our case, it was found that tuning the octaves
slightly stretched, as is done in piano tuning, gives
a more satisfying in-tune percept.

Jaffe and Smith

Decay-time Alteration

The basic algorithm naturally results in a shorter decay time for high pitches than for low pitches, reflecting the behavior of real strings. This is due to two effects. First, higher frequencies are more attenuated by the two-point average H_a; second, higher pitch means more trips through the attenuating loop in a given time. This may be seen in Eq. (3).

Unfortunately, the range of decay times between the high and low pitches is too extreme. The high-pitched notes die away so fast that only a click is perceived, while the low-pitched notes last for an unnaturally long time. In addition, the decay time of real strings varies with many factors such as tension, length, thickness, and material. Consequently, we have found it useful to add a means for altering the note duration. The ability to control decay time is essential for a realistic simulation as well as for musical flexibility.

On systems that have separate control of the sampling rate of each voice, sampling-rate change can be used to control decay time. On other systems, however, it is necessary to use other methods to alter decay time.

Decay Shortening

To shorten the decay time, a loss factor ρ can be introduced in the feedback loop. With the loss factor, the difference Eq. (1) for the string becomes

$$y_n = x_n + \rho \frac{y_{n-N} + y_{n-(N+1)}}{2} . \tag{18}$$

The amplitude envelope of a sinusoid at frequency f, previously given by Eq. (8), is now proportional to

$$\alpha_f(t, \rho) = |\rho \cos(\pi f T_s)|^{t_1 t} = |\rho|^{t_1 t} \alpha_f(t) .$$

Thus all partials are affected equally: the relative decay rates are unchanged.

Note that ρ cannot be used to lengthen the decay time, since the amplitude at 0 Hz would increase exponentially. In general, we must have $|\rho| \leq 1$ if the string is to be stable. Thus ρ is used to shorten the low-pitched notes to make them more compa-rable in duration with notes from a real string. With the loss factor operative, the decay-time constant for the fundamental frequency becomes

$$\tau_1(\rho) = - \frac{1}{f_1 \ln |\rho \cos(\pi f_1 T_s)|} . \tag{19}$$

Decay shortening produces a damped version of the algorithm, analogous to substitution of a soft material for the bridge of a string instrument.

Decay Stretching

To stretch the decay, the feedback average (H_a) can be changed to a two-point weighted average. This reduces the amount of loss at high frequencies. Thus, we replace $H_a(z)$ by

$$H_a(z, S) = (1 - S) + Sz^{-1}, \tag{20}$$

where S, the stretching factor, is between 0 and 1. The gain of this filter is

$$
\begin{aligned}
G_a(f, S) &= |(1 - S) + Se^{-j\omega T_s}| \\
&= \sqrt{((1 - S) + S \cos \omega T_s)^2 + (S \sin(\omega T_s))^2} \\
&= \sqrt{(1 - S)^2 + S^2 + 2S(1 - S) \cos \omega T_s}
\end{aligned}
\tag{21}
$$

With $S = 1/2$, $H_a(z, S)$ reduces to the previous case $H_a(z)$. For stability of the overall string, we must have $0 < S < 1$. If $S = 0$ or 1, the frequency-dependent term disappears, and the gain response is unity for all f; in this case, the initial white-noise burst circulates forever in the loop, producing harmonics that never decay. At intermediate values, $0 < S < 1$, the effective note duration (t_{60}) is finite, and it is minimum for $S = 1/2$. The amplitude trajectory and the decay-time constant for each partial can be obtained by substituting Eq. (21) into Eqs. (10) and (11), respectively.

For the greatest control, both the uniform-loss method and the weighted two-point-average method may be used for decay-time alteration. The resulting decay time is then a function of loss factor ρ and stretch factor S. Karplus and Strong (1983) describe a method of decay stretching that uses no multiplies.

Fig. 5. Phase delay for the
decay-stretching, one-zero
filter $H_a(z, S) = (1 - S) +$
$S z^{-1}$.

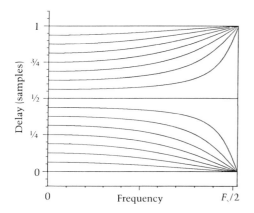

Note that for $S \geq 0$ the phase delay is quite flat over most of the frequency axis. Another point of interest is that since $G_a(z, S) = G_a(z, 1 - S)$, we may choose the case that yields the best phase delay curve for the fine-tuning allpass H_c.

Since the tuning calculation needs to be done only once per note, the precise form of Eq. (22) can be used for each new frequency without much computational expense.

Effect of Decay Stretching on Tuning

Changing S changes the effective loop length as a function of frequency, since it changes the phase delay of the overall loop. We must therefore compute $P_a(f_1)$ for use in Eq. (15) when fine tuning with the allpass filter H_c. The phase delay of the weighted two-point average is given by

$$P_a(f, S) \triangleq -\frac{\angle H_a(e^{i\omega T_s}, S)}{\omega T_s}$$

$$= -\frac{\angle((1 - S) + Se^{-i\omega T})}{\omega T_s}$$

$$= -\frac{1}{\omega T_s} \tan^{-1}\left(\frac{-S \sin(\omega T)}{(1 - S) + S \cos(\omega T)} \right), \quad (22)$$

and for low frequencies, relative to the sampling rate, we may use the approximation

$$P_a(f, S) \approx \frac{S \sin(\omega T_s)}{\omega T_s(1 - S) + S\omega T_s \cos(\omega T_s)}$$

$$\approx S, \qquad 0 \leq S \leq 1.$$

For $S = 1/2$, we have the basic string algorithm, and the phase delay of H_a is $1/2$, as given by the above approximation. For other values of S the approximation is always precise at $f = 0$. Figure 5 shows the true phase-delay curves of $H_a(z, S)$ as S is stepped uniformly through 17 values from 0 to 1.

Dynamics

The loudness of the signal output by the algorithm is a function of the amplitude of the input noise burst. However, this is an unsatisfactory control in simulating the timbral effect of dynamic level as it occurs in the case of a real string instrument. The effect of varying initial amplitude gives the impression of a change more in the distance between the listener and the apparent source than in dynamics. Since strings plucked hard have more energy in the higher partials than strings plucked lightly (due to nonlinearities becoming important), the dynamic simulation is based on modeling this difference in spectral balance. We therefore change the effective spectral bandwidth of a note to modulate its apparent intensity.

The bandwidth is controlled by means of a one-pole, lowpass filter applied to the initial noise burst (before it is fed into the string). This filter will be referred to as the *dynamics filter*. The difference equation of the dynamics filter is

$$y_n = (1 - R)x_n + Ry_{n-1},$$

and its transfer function is

$$H_d(z) \triangleq \frac{1 - R}{1 - Rz^{-1}}, \quad (23)$$

where R is a real number between 0 and 1, computed as a function of fundamental frequency f_1 and the desired dynamic level L. When a series of notes at pitch f_1 is played while R is moved gradually toward 1, a diminuendo is approximated in terms of both decreasing loudness and spectral bandwidth reduction.

We define the *dynamic level L* as a bandwidth be-

Jaffe and Smith

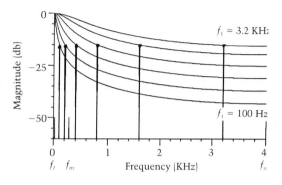

Fig. 6. Frequency response
of $H_a(z) = (1 - R)/$
$(1 - R\,z^{-1})$ computed at
dynamic level $L = 100$ for
six values of f_1.

tween 0 and $f_s/2$. If L is small, the spectrum is more lowpass filtered, corresponding to a softer dynamic level. Conversely, large L gives a bright spectrum corresponding to louder notes. It is not sufficient to use a fixed lowpass filter for all pitches, since low-pitched notes would then be louder than high-pitched notes. Rather, for a given dynamic level, R must be changed with pitch to yield a uniform perceived loudness. While this is a difficult problem in general, a good approximation is obtained by varying R so that the amplitude of the fundamental frequency is constant.

It remains to be shown how R is computed for a given pitch f_1 and dynamic level L. The main steps are as follows. First, a one-pole, lowpass filter is designed having bandwidth L. Second, the gain of this filter at a "middle" frequency is computed. Third, the dynamics filter is computed as a one-pole, lowpass filter having this gain at the desired fundamental f_1. The remainder of this section gives the equations needed for these steps.

The reference frequency f_m is chosen as the logarithmic middle (geometric mean) of the range to be used (a function of the particular musical context and the sampling frequency):

$$f_m = e^{(1/2)(\log(f_u) + \log(f_l))} = \sqrt{f_u f_l},$$

where f_u is the upper pitch limit $(< f_s/2)$, and f_l is the lower pitch limit.

The one-pole lowpass filter having bandwidth L is given by

$$H_L(z) \triangleq \frac{1 - R_L}{1 - R_L z^{-1}},$$

where

$$R_L \triangleq e^{-\pi L T_s}.$$

The substitution $R_L = e^{-\pi L T_s}$ is a somewhat standard approximate formula for mapping bandwidth to pole radius.

The gain of the lowpass filter H_L at the reference frequency is defined as

$$G_L \triangleq |H_L(e^{j2\pi f_m T_s})|$$

$$= \frac{1 - R_L}{|1 - R_L e^{-j2\pi f_m T_s}|}.$$

Now, for any desired fundamental frequency f_1, R is computed so as to provide gain $G_d(f_1) = G_L$. In other words, all fundamental frequencies are made to have the same amplitude. The value of R is found by solving

$$G_L = \frac{1 - R}{|1 - Re^{-j2\pi f_1 T_s}|}.$$

Squaring both sides of this equation and solving the resulting quadratic polynomial in R yield

$$R = \frac{1 - G_L^2 \cos(2\pi f_1 T_s)}{1 - G_L^2}$$

$$\pm 2G_L \sin(\pi f_1 T_s) \frac{\sqrt{1 - G_L^2 \cos^2(\pi f_1 T_s)}}{1 - G_L^2}.$$

We use whichever value is < 1 in magnitude to ensure stability.

A family of frequency-response curves for H_d is shown in Fig. 6 for six fundamental frequencies in octave steps from $f_1 = 100$ Hz to $f_1 = 3{,}200$ Hz. The dynamic level in each case is $L = 100$ Hz. A vertical line is drawn to each curve at the fundamental frequency to which it applies. The reference frequency f_m is set to 282.84 Hz (the geometric mean of $f_l = 20$ Hz and $f_u = f_s/2$), and the sampling rate is $f_s = 8{,}000$ Hz.

To add to the effect of simulated dynamics, it is sometimes helpful to do a bit of decay shortening on the low soft notes, using a loss factor ρ as described previously. It is also possible to simulate the spectral characteristics of soft notes by simply turning the output of the algorithm on late, after some of the high-frequency energy has died away. This latter method has the effect of diminishing the attack noise, corresponding to a milder pluck. For other decay-softening techniques, see the section entitled Varying the Character and Number of Attacks.

Rests and the Ends of Notes

In the case of a real string instrument, the player often plays two notes on the same string, playing the second note before the first has died away. The basic algorithm handles this without a problem for all but very high pitches, since the discontinuity at the beginning of the new note is perceived as a new pluck rather than as a click. (With a real instrument, there is a short time when the pick has muted the vibration for the previous note but has not yet set the string again into vibration, but this brief silence was not found to be necessary for realism in the synthetic model.) A problem arises, however, when there is a rest after a note. If the output of the algorithm is abruptly turned off (replaced by zeros), a discontinuity in the waveform results, causing a click.

Even if the note is allowed to decay for a very long time, a note turned off abruptly may cause a click because the feedback loop has unity gain at 0 Hz. To see this, note that $G_a(0) = \cos(0) = 1$. Thus the final value of the waveform is the mean of the initial noise burst. Since the pseudo-random-number sequence used to initially excite the filter has a mean of zero only in special cases or when an infinite number of samples is taken, the 0 Hz component can be significant. For uniform pseudorandom white noise at amplitude A, the statistical variance is $A^2/3$, which implies a variance in sample mean over N samples equal to $A^2/(3N)$. Thus the standard deviation of the mean in a length of N samples is $A/\sqrt{3N}$. As N decreases, the probability of having a large amount of energy at 0 Hz becomes greater. Karplus and Strong describe a technique they call "dithering" to handle this problem, but this technique was not economical in our context.

Our solution to the discontinuity problem is as follows: the loss factor ρ, as was discussed for de-

cay shortening, is set to a relatively small value in the last few milliseconds of the note. The duration of the decay is dependent on the loss factor chosen. A loss factor close to 1 simulates a string being damped with a soft material such as the flesh of the finger, while a smaller loss factor simulates damping with a hard material, such as a pick. It is useful to compute ρ as a function of a desired t_{60}. Substituting Eq. (19) into Eq. (5) and solving for ρ yields

$$\rho(t_{60}) = \frac{e^{-1/f\tau}}{|\cos(\pi f T_s)|}, \quad \tau \triangleq \frac{t_{60}}{\ln(1000)}.$$

For pitches above about 3 KHz, clicks can appear even at the onset of notes. Onset clicks can also occur when a pianissimo setting of the dynamics filter is used, since the masking effect of the onset noise burst is weakened by the dynamic filter. To alleviate this problem, it may be necessary to multiply the output of the algorithm by an exponential or linear envelope, rather than switching it on abruptly.

Glissandi and Slurs

A slur can be simulated by changing the order of the filter without reexciting it; that is, by changing the delay buffer length N. The result is analogous to a performer's refretting a string without replucking it (what guitarists call the "hammer-on" and "pull-off" technique). A rapid alternation of ascending and descending pitch changes gives a good left-hand-trill effect.

If the buffer length is gradually changed over time, a crude glissando results. For low pitches and high sampling rates, it can be quite smooth, but for higher pitches and lower sampling rates, the pitch quantization resulting from the integer-delay lengths becomes noticeable. In the upper range, the effect is similar to a glissando on a fretted instrument, where the pitch changes in discrete steps, and it can be musically useful. Of course, the synthetic quantization is not in semitone intervals.

A perfectly smooth glissando can be created by ramping C, the tuning coefficient, during the time between buffer-length changes. This technique can also be used to create vibrato.

Jaffe and Smith

Sympathetic String Simulation

In a real string instrument, sympathetic vibrations of other open strings, as well as resonances in the instrument body, give each pitch in the range of the instrument an individual character and thus give the instrument as a whole a distinctive identifiable character. In comparison, the basic form of the Karplus-Strong algorithm, like many instrument-simulation algorithms, has an excessive homogeneity of character throughout its range. One way to remedy this situation is to feed the output of the string into a body resonator. This technique has produced impressive results, but its discussion is beyond the scope of this paper (see Smith 1983). Another way to combat unnatural uniformity is to create the effect of an instrument with sympathetic strings, using a modified version of the basic algorithm.

Just as a sympathetic string is set into motion by the vibration of another string, the illusion of a sympathetically vibrating string can be created by exciting one copy of the string simulator by a small percentage of the output from another (plucked) string, tuned to a different pitch.

In the discussion that follows, the algorithm that is excited with the noise burst is referred to as the *plucked string* and the algorithm that is excited only by the plucked string is referred to as the *sympathetic string*. All partials of the plucked string that do not coincide with those of the sympathetic string will be highly attenuated. Thus the sympathetic string acts as a bank of very narrow bandpass filters with center frequencies at the partial frequencies of the sympathetic string. The partials of the plucked string that will strongly resonate are those for which

$$f_i = f_{k,}$$

where f_k is the frequency of the kth partial of the sympathetically resonating string, and f_i is the frequency of the ith partial of the plucked string.

A problem can arise after several successive noise bursts have excited the plucked string. The repeated reintroduction of energy into the sympathetic string may cause it to overflow. Therefore, it is essential

that a loss factor ρ, such as was introduced with reference to decay shortening, be used to provide energy dissipation.

The effect of several sympathetic strings can be created simply by a bank of parallel sympathetic strings, as defined above, each tuned to a different frequency. The resulting overall string-transfer function (omitting fine tuning and decay alteration for clarity) is then

$$H(z) = \cfrac{1}{1 - \cfrac{1+z^{-1}}{2} z^{-N}}$$

$$\left((1 - \gamma) + \gamma \sum_{i=1}^{M} \cfrac{1}{1 - \rho_i \cfrac{1+z^{-1}}{2} z^{-N_i}} \right),$$

where γ is the fractional part of the plucked-string signal sent to the sympathetic strings, M is the number of sympathetic strings, ρ_i is the loss factor for the ith sympathetic string, $N_i = f_s/f_i$ where f_i is the fundamental frequency of the ith sympathetic string, and f_s/N is the pitch of the plucked string and hence of the played note.

The sympathetic-string version of the algorithm is also helpful in creating a stereo or quadraphonic image. By distributing around the room the outputs of several banks of differently tuned sympathetic strings, all fed with the same plucked string, the effect of being inside a huge guitar can be created.

Attractive musical results have been created by replacing the plucked string with another computer instrument, so that the bank of sympathetic strings is used as a "reverberator." One can achieve the effect, for example, of a clarinet being played into an open grand piano with the pedal down.

Simulation of a Moving Pick

An effective means of simulating pick position is to introduce zeros uniformly distributed over the spectrum of the noise burst. This can quite accurately simulate the effect of plucking a string at varying distances from the bridge. The noise burst is filtered with a comb filter, H_e, having the difference equation

$$y_n = x_n - x_{n-\mu N},$$

where μ is the fraction of the string between the bridge and pluck point. When $\mu = 1/2$, the even harmonics are removed, and the effect is that of plucking a string at its midpoint. Similarly, when $\mu = 1/10$, every tenth harmonic is suppressed, and the effect is like plucking a tenth of the way up the string. With $\mu = 1/N$, the filter approximates a differentiator, creating a sharp *sul ponticello* sound. For the theory behind the simulation of pick location, see Smith's paper (1982a).

Varying the Character and Number of Attacks

Since the attack is very important in perception of timbre, it is advantageous to be able to alter its character. To give a noticeably more noisy attack, approximating the sound of a snap or "Bartók pizzicato," the duration of the noise burst x_n can simply be increased from $t_x = NT_s$ to some $t_x > NT_s$. Similarly, the attack can be subdued by making $0 < t_x < NT_s$, though for very small t_x the pluck illusion (as well as loudness) fades.

A variety of other methods can soften the attack. The string can be excited with a rich harmonic spectrum rather than a noise spectrum, or with some mixture of the two, with the sum of their amplitudes not exceeding 1. Another possibility is to lowpass filter the noise burst. Yet another way to soften the attack is to turn on the output of the algorithm late, after some of the high-frequency energy has been filtered out.

A realistic simulation of the up-and-down picking pattern characteristic of a mandolin tremolo has been created by using a one-pole, lowpass filter, H_l, to mellow the "up" picks while using the standard unfiltered noise burst for the "down" picks.

A crude simulation of instruments having multiple strings tuned in unison, such as the mandolin or bazooki, can be created by simply exciting the string with two successive noise bursts separated by a short amount of time, on the order of .05 sec. While multiple attacks can be achieved in this manner, the steady state fuses into a single note. In a real mandolin, the strings are never perfectly tuned, and the beating effect of the slightly mistuned strings is a strong recognition cue. A better mandolin simulation simply uses two parallel forms of the algorithm, differing in pitch by a few cents and excited at slightly different times.

Use of Other Filters in Feedback Loop

The use of filters other than a one-zero for H_a will give a different decay characteristic and, in turn, a different timbre. However, care must be taken that the amplitude response G_a does not reach unity near any partial frequency. Energy at any frequency f_k for which $G_a(f_k) = 1$ will never decay, and if $G_a(f_k) > 1$, the amplitude will grow exponentially until overflow.

For example, a one-pole filter with the pole between 0 and 1 gives a tone with the same attack and a more mellow decay than with a one-zero filter; that is, the higher partials decay more rapidly. Placing the pole at $z = Q$ and normalizing the peak-amplitude response of the one-pole filter to unity yield the transfer function

$$H_a(z) = \frac{1 - |Q|}{1 - Qz^{-1}},$$

where $|Q| < 1$ is required for stability of the one-pole filter. The transfer function of the whole string becomes

$$H(z) = \frac{1}{1 - z^{-N}\dfrac{1 - |Q|}{1 - Qz^{-1}}}$$

$$= \frac{1 - Qz^{-1}}{1 - Qz^{-1} - (1 - |Q|)z^{-N}}.$$

Thus the difference equation is

$$y_n = x_n - Qx_{n-1} + Qy_{n-1} + (1 - |Q|)y_{n-N}.$$

This version of the algorithm, with $0 \ll Q < 1$ is useful for pitches in the lower half of the range. In the upper range, the notes die away too fast to be of use. This is because the one-pole, lowpass filter, with $Q \gg 0$, filters out the high-frequency energy

Fig. 7. Block diagram containing algorithm exten-
sions discussed in this
paper.

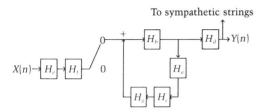

To sympathetic strings

$$f_k = \frac{k}{P_0 + P_g(f_k)} = \frac{kf_1 s(k)}{s(1)}$$

$$\Rightarrow \quad P_g(f_k) = \frac{s(1)}{f_1 s(k)} - P_0,$$

where P_0 is the length of the loop in the absence of
the allpass H_g (typically $P + 1/2$). Methods for designing allpass filters with prescribed phase delay
are reviewed by Smith (1983).

Summary

Figure 7 shows a block diagram of the string simulator with some of our revisions, where H_a is the
feedback lowpass filter, H_b is the delay line, H_c is
the allpass filter used for tuning, H_d is the lowpass
filter used to simulate dynamics, H_e is the comb filter that simulates pick position, H_f is the filter that
simulates the difference between "up" and "down"
picking, and H_g is the allpass filter used to simulate
string stiffness.

  The simulator provides a high degree of flexibility that begins to approach that of a skilled player
performing on a real musical instrument. Many aspects of a real string instrument have been simulated. Pitch can be precisely specified, and articulation can be finely tuned. An expressive vocabulary
is provided by a wide variety of performance nuances, including such "left-hand" techniques as
glissandi, slurs, and trills, as well as such "right-
hand" techniques as variation in dynamic level,
pick position, and attack characteristics. These parameters were found to be sufficient to create shaped
musical phrases. Furthermore, parameters such as
sustain time, body resonance, string flexibility,
bridge and pick hardness, and degree of sympathetic
string excitation, which, in the case of real instruments, are usually fixed at the time of instrument
construction, are available as performance parameters. It is important to point out that this variety is
at no time achieved at the expense of the integrity
of the basic sound. Rather, as is the case with a real
musical instrument, the diversity exists within the
bounds of a clearly defined sound domain.

in the loop much more drastically than does the
one-zero, lowpass filter. A technique similar to that
used in dynamics simulation could be used to compensate for this trend.

Simulation of Stiff Strings

The spectral components of the basic algorithm
that have significant amplitude are almost perfectly
harmonic after the attack noise has been filtered
away, corresponding, in the real world, to a perfectly flexible string. But since real strings always
have some degree of stiffness, it is desirable to alter
the spectrum of the algorithm accordingly. The theory of stiff strings (Morse 1976) indicates that stiffness creates a stretching of the partials according to
the approximate formula

$$f_k \approx kf_0 \left[1 + \delta + \left(\frac{1 + k^2 \pi^2}{8} \right) \delta^2 \right] \triangleq kf_0 s(k),$$

$$k = 1, 2, \ldots, \quad k^2 < \frac{4}{\pi^2 \delta^2},$$

where f_0 is near the fundamental frequency, and k
is the partial number. The parameter δ has been
called the *coefficient of inharmonicity*; if $\delta = 0$,
then perfect harmonicity results.

  This effect can be created, in principle, by introducing an allpass filter $H_g(z)$ in the string loop (Allen 1982) much as was done for the fine tuning of
pitch. The phase delay in samples desired for an all-
pass filter inserted in the feedback loop of a harmonic
string simulator tuned to f_1 is given by solving

Conclusion

The algorithm originated by Karplus and Strong and extended by the methods outlined here has proven very useful as a computer instrument. In the process of composing *May All Your Children Be Acrobats* and *Silicon Valley Breakdown*, it was found to be sufficiently flexible to allow for a wide range of musical expression and sufficiently idiosyncratic to maintain a characteristic identity. We expect that new refinements of the algorithm will continue to arise.

References

Abramowitz, M., and I. A. Stegun, eds. 1966. *Handbook of Mathematical Functions.* Washington, D.C.: National Bureau of Standards.

Allen, J. B. 1982. Private communication.

Jaffe, D. A. 1982. *Silicon Valley Breakdown.* Compact disk recording: *Dinosaur Music—Music by Chafe, Jaffe, and Schottstaedt.* CCRMA, 1986.

Karplus, K., and A. Strong. 1983. "Digital Synthesis of Plucked-String and Drum Timbres." *Computer Music Journal* 7(2):43–55.

McIntyre, M. E., and J. Woodhouse. 1979. "On the Fundamentals of Bowed String Dynamics." *Acustica* 43(2): 93–108.

McIntyre, M. E., R. T. Schumacher, and J. Woodhouse. 1981. "Aperiodicity in Bowed-String Motion." *Acustica* 49(1):13–32.

McIntyre, M. E., R. T. Schumacher, and J. Woodhouse. In press. "On the Oscillations of Musical Instruments." *Journal of the Acoustical Society of America.*

Mont-Reynaud, B. 1982. Private communication.

Morse, P. M. 1976. *Vibration and Sound.* New York: American Institute of Physics for the Acoustical Society of America. (Originally published in two editions [1936 and 1948].)

Smith, J. O. 1982a. "Synthesis of Bowed Strings." Paper presented at the Acoustical Society of America Conference, Chicago, Illinois. (Reprints available upon request.)

Smith, J. O. 1982b. "Introduction to Digital Filters." Typescript. (Copies available upon request.)

Smith, J. O. 1983. "Techniques for Digital Filter Design and System Identification with Application to the Violin." Ph.D. Diss., Electrical Engineering Department, Stanford University.

Steiglitz, K. 1974. *An Introduction to Discrete Systems.* New York: Wiley.

38

C. Cadoz, A. Luciani, and J. Florens

Association pour la création et la recherche sur les outils d'expression (ACROE) and Laboratoire d'Informatique Fondamentale et d'Intelligence Artificielle (LIFIA) ENSIMAG Boite Postale 68 38402 Saint Martin d'Heres, France

Responsive Input Devices and Sound Synthesis by Simulation of Instrumental Mechanisms: The Cordis System

Principles and Hypotheses

Since the development of programs like Music V (Mathews et al. 1969), digital synthesis of sound has become increasingly important. Moreover, spectacular progress in digital circuitry has accelerated the trend toward real-time synthesis. In the course of this development, the original premises have not been questioned, and hence, they remain fixed. We can characterize these premises schematically as processes of waveform and envelope table lookup, followed by signal processing, leading to audio conversion and the production of sound. The success of these principles in terms of synthesis precision and acoustical richness is evident.

Yet these same criteria are insufficient when considering the computer as a tool used by musicians, as a means of creation with no comparable predecessor. Other important considerations must be taken into account. An analysis of the quality of musician-machine interaction is one such criterion, as is an analysis of the languages we use to communicate with the machine. This article is addressed to the idea of developing new instrumental models for digital sound synthesis. These models take two forms:

Input devices that capture physical gestures and react to the gestures under program control
Sound synthesis techniques based on the simulation of physical sound producing mechanisms

Translated by Curtis Roads and Françoise Chadabe.

Computer Music Journal, Vol. 8, No. 3, Fall 1984

Creative Limits of Acoustic Synthesis

We use the term *acoustic synthesis* to mean a sound-generating process in which synthesis is carried out in acoustical terms: frequency, spectrum, waveform, amplitude, modulation, and so on. In this approach, creating sound objects specifiable in these terms is a goal in itself. It appears to us that this direction, even with improvements yet to come, imposes an inherent limit on the computer as a tool of musical creativity.

New Instrumental Models for Synthesis

Analysis in acoustic terms is a means of mastering the objective structure of sound but not its symbolic content. Our critique of this approach is based on the fact that its central goal is the sound object itself.[1] What we are discussing is the possibility of creating innovative and unheard-of sound structures loaded with meaning, without a return to the conditions of primitive instruments.

The traditional experience of composers, issuing instructions to instrumentalists, is based on intimate knowledge of the physical origins of the sound. The faculties of abstraction and creativity of the traditional composer are indissociable from an "instrumental knowledge" of sounds. We mean by "instrumental knowledge" something quite different from "knowledge of instruments." Instrumental knowledge results from experiences which, although they

1. We use the term *sound object* in a larger sense than that used by Pierre Schaeffer (1966). In Schaeffer's book, the notion of an object is associated with elementary sounds. In our use of this term, a complex sound structure can be an object.

are slightly specialized, are no less profound. These experiences include the observation of instruments in action. An even more obvious example is the daily experience of hearing sounds in our environment caused by our actions. From this stage, the process of instrumental knowledge is based on the confrontation of our actions with the acoustical properties of the objects we manipulate.

It is precisely when composers are placed before a digital synthesis machine—giving them access to unheard-of events—that this experience is lacking. We believe that new sounds have a chance of cognitive "survival" only if we can link them to events heard before. The possibility of linkage is very slim with regard to the potential variety of sounds that digital synthesis can produce. Hence, the point of view we adopt consists of viewing the computer no longer as a means of representing a sound object, but rather as a means of representing what produces it. In other words, we reject the sound object as a focus of study, and replace it by the instrument and its determinants—especially those determinants that establish the conditions for sonic and perceptual experimentation.

Multisensory Representation of the Instrument

We set forth two hypotheses here. One is that perception is, at all levels, an active process. It is an essentially cognitive process at the level of complex hearing, and an essentially physical process at the elementary level in which the sound is inscribed into a sensory/motor circuit where bodily and gestural action are correlated.

Our other hypothesis is that perception is global. Given an object's integrity, the whole of its manifestations constitute a totality. Distinguishing it by means of the senses corresponds to an analysis. In the case of sound objects, this analysis is carried out by acoustical processing.

Global perception is narrowly connected to three sensory/motor processes: hearing, seeing, and what we will call *gestural perception*, which covers touch and all proprioceptive sites. An immediate consequence of this is the following. In order to provide a primitive instrumental basis for making

music, we must set up an information-gathering configuration using three transducers capable of supporting each of these three sensory dimensions.

The two major components of an instrumental device are the following:

A transducer which is applied to the three principal sensory channels. This implies the necessity of building gestural, sonic, and visual computer peripherals.

A simulator of the actual instrument, which controls the relationship between the magnitudes of the different senses.

The rest of this article is divided into two parts which address these components. These parts cover the design of gestural devices, beginning with an analysis of instrumental gestures, and the design of the Cordis instrument simulator system.

Analysis of Instrumental Gestures

Excitation Gestures and Modulation Gestures

We must distinguish first of all between *excitation gestures* and *modulation gestures*. Excitation gestures are powered by energy. In all traditional instruments (except for instruments like the organ) the instrumentalists are themselves the source of the energy which is projected acoustically by the instrument. The excitation gesture permits this transfer of energy from the instrumentalist to the instrument. For example, the drawing of a bow on a violin string is an excitation motion.

Modulation gestures are accompanied by a weak expenditure of energy, which does not contribute to the acoustic energy in any significant way. This type of gesture has the function of modifying certain qualities in the instrument's structure. An example of a modulation gesture is the finger pressed on the neck of a violin to specify a pitch.

The Direction of Actions

From the mechanical point of view, the large number of independent actions within a system consisting of fingers, hands, wrists, arms, elbows,

Fig. 1. Instrumental ges-
tures generate retroactive
(or feedback) energy.

and so on, produces a great diversity of trajectories and gestural behaviors. We distinguish the following action groups:

Frontal action in which the acts of moving away or moving toward form an opposition
Vertical action in which the effects of gravity stand in opposition to a gesture or accentuate it
Lateral action in which the acts move from side to side.

The separation of these three cases is a simplification, of course. In reality, a single gesture can include combinations of two or three of these cases at once.

Modes of Manipulation

It is possible to separate two cases according to which contact with the manipulator is either permanent, or simply unilateral. In the first case, there is a permanent grasping of an element which follows all the evolutions of movement, for example, manipulations of a bow or a drum stick.

In the second case, which we characterize by the absence of grasping, the manipulator object is merely moved in a limited space in which the gesture is constrained, for example, the touch of a key on a keyboard.

We found it necessary to develop the idea of two phases of gesture, a *preparatory phase* and an *action phase*. Gesture is rarely just an execution; the nature of the preparation/action articulation is conditioned both by human motions and by the characteristics of the manipulated device. For example, grasping, when it occurs, is part of the preparatory phase.

Gesture-Transducers

The variables of motion are *force F* and *displacement X*. From a mechanical point of view, the relation between the instrumentalist and the instrument is a relation between two mechanical dipoles (Fig. 1).

The exchange of energy implies that F and X are

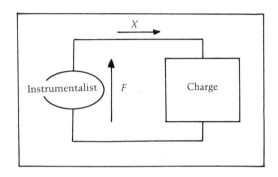

not null simultaneously. The relation between F and X depends on two dipoles. The instrumentalist receives feedback from the manipulated object. The excitation gesture is thus necessarily bilateral (emitter and receiver). Gestures generate *retroactive* or *feedback* energy corresponding to the situation in Fig. 1.

By contrast, a modulation gesture is not necessarily retroactive (or *reactive*) in its effect. In the ideal case, the exchange of energy in this type of gesture is nil. If F is not equal to zero, then X equals zero, or if F equals zero, then X is not equal to zero. Modulation imparts nonretroactive energy on the transducers. Most user-interfaces on computer systems correspond to this category. These include graphic tablets, potentiometers, joysticks, position sensors, and force sensors with strain gauges.

We have realized two prototypes of gesture-transducers with feedback. The essential limitation in these devices is that we have reduced the feedback effect to one degree of freedom. In any case, each of the prototypes corresponds to a different category of gesture according to our previous definitions.

In our first device, gestures may range up to 50 cm in width. The trajectory of the gesture is a linear, horizontal motion, and grasping is used. In our second device, gestures are at the scale of the finger (5 cm). The gesture's trajectory is a vertical line without grasping.

As a prelude to our description of the simulations of these instruments, we will mention that they

Fig. 2. Instrumental ges-
tures operate through a
transducer to an excitor
and to a vibrating
structure.

Fig. 3. Gesture-transducer
built by J. L. Florens.

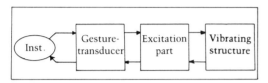

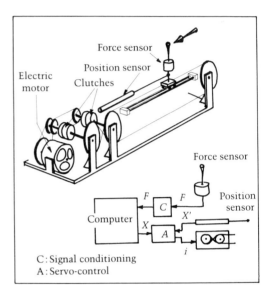

C: Signal conditioning
A: Servo-control

are organized into two parts: (1) an *excitation part*
and (2) a *vibration part*, or *vibrating structure*. The
excitation part is directly related to the gesture-
transducers. It is charged with the double function
of using gestural information from the sensors and
generating commands that define the mechanical
behavior of the transducer (see Fig. 2).

First Gesture-Transducer

This device was built by J. L. Florens (1978). It consists of a "stick" mounted on a carriage which
moves on two horizontal guides (Fig. 3).

A force sensor with strain gauges picks up the operator's pressures on the stick. An inductive position sensor picks up the displacement. The "return
motion" of the gesture is assured by a system consisting of a permanently turning motor and a set of
electrodynamic clutches under the control of a
computer which force the stick to return.

The models we have simulated respond to human force by returning to the starting position.
The calculated position is thus the start of a servo-
control integrated with the transducer. The effort
transmitted to the stick is only null when the command given by the position sensor is equivalent to
the one calculated by the model.

Second Gesture-Transducer

Conceived and realized during 1980, this device
consists of a unique key inspired by those of the
piano keyboard, but with a larger displacement—
about 5 cm (Fig. 4).

The conception of this device, mechanically
more dense than the first, and the use of new motor

and sensor elements, enable it to work quite differently from the other device. There is no vibration
or noise due to a constantly rotating motor. It has a
better response time, and the spatial precision of
the device is on the order of a dozen microns.

However, since the power produced by the motor
is less strong, there is a limit to the simulation.
From the perspective of return motion, the most
difficult thing to simulate is that of a perfectly rigid
obstacle. The magnitude of the applied force can
become very large in a very short time. This behavior is difficult to model on limited mechanical systems which are light and compact.

In contrast to the first system, this system can be
used in two complementary modes:

As force sensor with position-return
As a position sensor with force-return

From the point of view of the operator, the two situations are equivalent when a servo control is integrated with the system. Two variables, force and
displacement, come into play, and one cannot distinguish whether a gesture is effected as a displacement or as a force.

Fig. 4. Retroactive touch
transducer key. (a) Sche-
matic of operation. (b) Second version built January
1981.

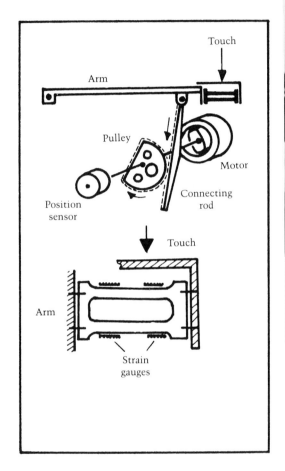

The Cordis Simulation System

Considering the efficacy of additive synthesis for the
production of sounds, one can imagine the immediate usefulness of retroactive gesture-transducers for
the control of real-time synthesizers. We must acknowledge a certain discrepancy between the concrete parameters of a gesture and the proper control
parameters for sound synthesis, though we think
this discrepancy can be made small. However,
between an instrument's excitation part and its
vibration part, there is such a small difference that
it does not justify a recourse to two distinct algorithms, a slow algorithm corresponding to gestures, and a fast algorithm corresponding to sound
synthesis.

The mechanical processes are based on the same
principles. This means that at the level of algorithmic simulation, there will also be no distinction between excitation and vibration parts. We have envisaged the Cordis system (Cadoz 1979) not as an
isolated synthesis device, but rather as a tool for the
exploration of different instrumental structures.
These instruments can be manipulated by different
gestures in a flexible manner by anyone.

Three stages of simulation were conceived:

Analysis of instrumental mechanisms
Choice of an appropriate algorithmic system to
  represent the instrumental mechanisms
Design of a computer language for describing an

instrument and for realizing it in programs that are transparent to the user

We next describe the decisions made in the Cordis system for the first two stages.

Mechanical Analysis of Instrumental Devices

An analysis of instruments in terms of excitation and vibration structures leads to a study of each of their parts and their interaction. The essential characteristics of vibrating bodies are strings, columns of air, rigid or flexible membranes, and solid or fluid volumes. These elements are, in general, associated with resonators that are described in terms of surface area, volume, and other measurements.

We assume that the vibrating structure is reducible to one or more of the following elements:

Vibrating line
Vibrating surface
Vibrating volume

Certain qualitative characteristics (e.g., the nature of the materials used) are reducible to a set of parameters. These may be tuned, yielding a great variety of instrument structures.

The excitation part also adopts a wide variety of forms. It can be developed to the complicated mechanisms of a piano, or reduced down to a single string. Examples of excitation parts include drumsticks, bows, piano and harpsichord actions, plectrums, and the flow of air channeled by the reeds.

The interaction between the excitation part and the vibration part of an instrument determines the nature of the energy exchange between them. We have considered two key modes for this exchange: *instantaneous exchange* and *extended exchange*. In instantaneous exchanges, the gesture ends at the moment when the vibration structure is excited, i.e., at the moment the sound manifests itself. The energy exchange takes place at a precise moment.

Within this instantaneous model, two submodels can be distinguished:

Percussion—the transfer of energy is dynamic and results in a shock
Plucking—the vibrating structure is displaced

from its resting position and then returns to its original position

In extended energy exchanges, the gesture and the emission of the sound are almost simultaneous. A typical case is friction on a bow, which can be modeled as a constant oscillation. We will examine other cases of extended exchanges later.

Simulation of Vibrating Structure

Our simulation of vibrating structures rests on three initial elements which can be described by linear differential equations: mass, elasticity (or stiffness), and friction.

The Vibrating String

The simulation of a vibrating string is relatively complex if one takes into account, in the general case, at least three types of string deformation: transverse, longitudinal, and rotational. One can simplify the problem by assuming that there is no mechanical interlocking between the three degrees of freedom.

The theoretical model we used describes a line segmented into a number of points. Each point possesses two unique and independent characteristics: (1) a direction of deformation and (2) a direction of propagation. The mechanical characteristics of the continuous line determining the modes of vibration are the following:

Mass
Length
Tension
Coefficients of resistance by air friction and by the internal material

The value of the mass of one point of material is equal to the mass of the line divided by the number of points. In order to represent the elasticity, it is necessary to interpose a springlike element between each point on the material, in the direction defined by two consecutive points. Elasticity, in its bidimensional definition, requires a distance calculation which burdens many of the algorithms. An

Cadoz et al.

important simplification is to consider the coupling unique in the direction $\overrightarrow{O\,X}$ and to neglect the others.

To make up for the loss of energy due to friction we introduce two variables: an internal friction parallel to the spring, and air friction introduced between each material point and the point on the axes $\overrightarrow{O_iX_i}$.

Friction is then defined as $F_f = Z * V_r$, with Z as the friction constant, V_r the relative speed between the two points, and F_f the force of the friction. Finally, the spring and friction encountered in connecting one endpoint of the line to a fixed origin will determine the various conditions at the extremities of the line, whether open line, closed line, or adapted impedance.

At our laboratory, T. Berberyan (1979) has calculated the behavior of a system corresponding to the case of a homogenous line (equal stiffness constant, equal masses, equal friction constant). We have obtained the fundamental characteristics of complex vibration, propagation, and reflection from the line's extremities. Ruiz (1970) pointed out the correspondence between this model and a real string at the level of wave propagation.

There are, however, differences between this model and a real string:

First, the number of sinusoidal components is equal to the number of points.
Second, the frequency relation of these components is harmonic only when the number of points is very large.

Limiting Case of a Line and a Single Element   The smallest vibrating component of this system is made of three basic elements: mass, spring, and friction (Fig. 5).

The displacement of the mass M due to the impulse of a force F_e is a damped sine wave, the parameters of which are connected to the mechanical constants K, M, and Z and to the excitation amplitude.

The smallest component meets our "concrete" criteria. Even at this level there is a complete, albeit simple, relation between an excitation and a sound event. The character of this sound event is predetermined, whereas the oscillator or the enve-

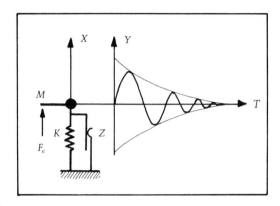

Fig. 6

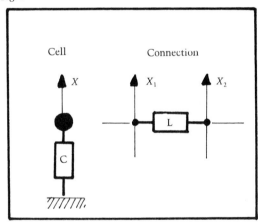

lope generator of digital sound synthesis is not predetermined. This component can be used as a unit of measure for what we call *structure complexity.* A combination of such components does not lead directly to a combination of the acoustical characters inherent in each component. This component constitutes the basic module of the vibrating structure. If we add to it a basic module connecting elasticity and friction, we obtain a system capable of realizing more complex vibrating objects. From this point on, we represent these two components with graphic symbols, as in Fig. 6.

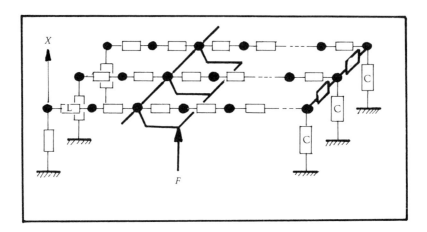

Simulating a Vibrating String We can simulate the behavior of three vibrating strings by exciting three components of force. These correspond to transverse, longitudinal, and rotational excitation. In order to do this, we have to use a sensor with three independent degrees of freedom. The parameters of each string can be chosen in such a way as to simulate the vibrations of a real string. The connection between each directional vibration can also be established between several points in the different strings. See Fig. 7 for the principles of this simulation.

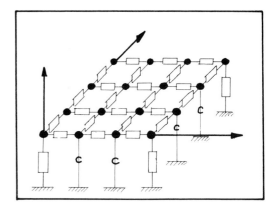

Representation of Surfaces and Volumes

Each element of surface or volume must be represented strictly by an element with six independent degrees of freedom, necessitating six position variables for each of them. The distance of the connecting elements has to be calculated in space. The algorithms are understandably complex.

In generalizing the method used for the string and neglecting the interactions between the independent degrees of freedom, we can construct surfaces or volumes by superimposing a two-dimensional network under a surface (Fig. 8) or a three-dimensional network around a volume (see Fig. 9).

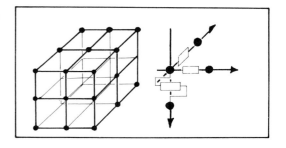

Fig. 10. Simulation of the
connection between the
excitation and vibrating
surface.

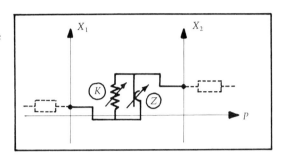

Conclusions on Vibrating

Two kinds of simulations of vibrating structures are possible: quantitative and qualitative. However, the essential interest in our research is first, to permit research and to establish, if it exists, a relation between the "geometry" of a structure and what in the obtained timbre is independent of the mode of excitation. Second, we hope to distinguish in the construction of sound what results from the mode of excitation—the excitation and the relation between the excitation and the vibrating structure.

Modeling the Excitation

Following the same line of analysis, the basic component of a vibrating structure for producing sound is a *cell*—a combination of mass, spring, and friction. However, because the excitation is not necessarily vibrating we have to take the mass, spring, and friction as subcomponents. We can apply the same hypotheses and simplifications for the material and nonconnecting components as before. The excitor may also include nonlinear or discontinuous connections, like the gap between the key and the hammer in the piano.

Modeling the Connection of the Excitation and Vibrating Structure

Our method of modeling the junction between the excitation and vibrating structures in an instrument will follow as we discuss algorithms for percussion, plucking, oscillation maintenance, and friction.

X_1 and X_2 are the two points between which we want to establish a connection. X_1 corresponds to the excitation and X_2 corresponds to the vibrating structure (Fig. 10).

This connection will be made by the "spring-friction" element which is set to different states according to the values of the stiffness constant K and the friction constant Z. If $K = Z = 0$, we have a state of no connection. The passage in a given state is determined by the conditions on the positions x_1 and x_2 of the points X_1 (belonging to the excitation E) and X_2 belonging to the vibrating structure S on the axes $\overrightarrow{O_1X_2}$ and $\overrightarrow{O_1X_2}$.

Percussion

The connection between the excitation and the vibrating structure has two states: connected or not. For example, we can compare x_1 and x_2 as in Fig. 10, where $x_1 < x_2$ implies connection, and $x_1 > x_2$ implies nonconnection.

Note that the connection between the two components at the time of impact involves an elasticity coefficient. This corresponds to the real situation where the elasticity coefficient is the result of the combined characteristics of each of the two components in contact.

In the case of percussion, the elasticity coefficient is derived from a third component—the connection—independent of the other two components. This yields a smaller number of parameters to define without changing the principle. It also enables us to study the connection apart from what it is connected to.

Plucking

We show two methods (out of several) for modeling the connection between the excitation and the vibrating structures in plucked string timbres.

Example 1

If $x_1 \geqslant x_2$ then the point X_1 leads to point X_2. If $x_2 \geqslant h$ the connection is broken. If $x_2 < h$ and $x_1 < x_2$, return to the first condition.

Here h is the parameter of control outside of the

Fig. 11. Modeling plucked
string synthesis: method
1.

Fig. 12. Modeling plucked
string synthesis: method
2.

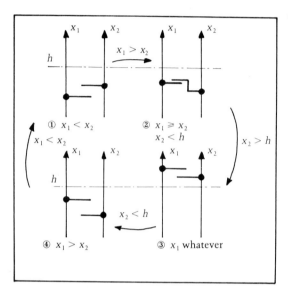

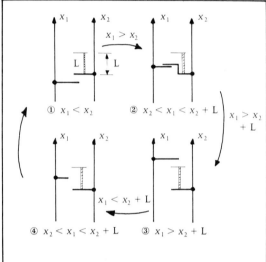

connection (Fig. 11). Since the movement of X_1 is slow and almost static, the vibration of S is completely determined by the initial conditions: a speed of zero, and initial elongation equal to h. The excitation variations vary only the speed of X_1 during the movement.

Example 2

The condition $x_2 \geq h$ is replaced by the more complicated relationship in which $x_2 - x_1 \geq h'$ (Fig. 12). With the almost static position of X_1, the elongation of X_2 at the time of a broken connection depends on the global stiffness of S seen from X_2. In this case, the potential energy is independent of the vibrating structure; it depends only on the connection.

Maintenance of Oscillation

Here we give a simple model to explain the friction of the bow. We are not dealing with the simulation of bowed strings but with what happens at the con-

tact of the rosined hair and the string. The point X_1 belonging to the excitor is displaced in a constant direction on a time field that is important for the variations of X_2 belonging to the vibrating structure. For the structure S to receive energy from E, the connection between X_1 and X_2 must be such that the applied force of X_2 is in the same direction as its displacement. We can approach this situation by considering two states for the connection:

A connection by viscous friction when the relative speed of X_1 in relation to X_2 is less than a threshold speed

A broken connection when the relative speed of X_1 is greater than the threshold speed.

We can demonstrate that S then receives from E an energy depending on the speed of X_1, and that the oscillation reaches a maximum amplitude depending on this speed.

This is a most rudimentary model of the bow/string connection. It does, however, present the essential characteristics of the energy relationship between gesture and vibration.

Friction

By friction, we denote roughly the general case of the vibration of the vibrating structure through continuous excitation. It is not as regular as simple viscous vibration or even bow friction. There is also rough friction characterized by an irregular connection between two elements. The parameters K and Z may then be random functions of x_1 and x_2.

Conclusions on Modeling the Connection of the Excitation and Vibration

We have defined so far a rather general system with these main features: the connection presents several conditional states defined by the values of the coefficients K and Z. The conditions are expressed by the variables x_1 and x_2 and characteristic parameters. They influence the separate values of x_1 and x_2, the value of the difference between x_1 and x_2, the sign of the difference, and their variations.

Algorithms of the Cordis System

The Cordis algorithms translate each of the elements defined previously into a computer program. Each algorithm attempted to meet the following constraints:

> Faithful representation of the model
> Modularity identical to the original structure
> Combinatorial properties similar to the one derived from mechanical analysis
> Efficiency with respect to computation time

The Cordis system consists of models of the linear elements: mass, spring, friction, and vibrating cell, and their interaction. The algorithms for discontinuous elements of connection will be presented later.

Mass

In our models, computation determines the behavior of a point subjected to some external action. The variables to be considered include force and position. Considering the algorithm as a device with input and output, we can take force as an input, and assume that position is the output. We have adopted the following convention. The elements that have a mass (called material elements) will have an input of force and a response of position. The different elements of connection are described according to this dual mode, enabling us to combine them easily.

For a value of force at each instant, the mass algorithm must give a corresponding position value:

$$F(t) = M * X''(t).$$

Here F is the applied force to the mass M, and X'' is the acceleration. After temporal sampling,

$$F(n) = M * X''(n).$$

The speed at instant n is

$$X'(n) = X(n) - X(n - 1).$$

Acceleration is defined as follows:

$$X''(n) = X'(n) - X'(n - 1)$$
$$X''(n) = X(n) - 2X(n - 1) + X(n - 2).$$

Therefore:

$$F(n) = M * [X(n) - 2X(n - 1) + X(n - 2)]$$
$$X(n) = F(n)/M + 2X(n - 1) - X(n - 2). \qquad (1)$$

The approximations introduced in the expressions X' and X'' do not significantly affect the response for typical excitations (Berberyan 1979).

Elasticity and Friction

If x_1 and x_2 are the respective positions of two material elements X_1 and X_2 connected by a spring or by friction, the forces applied to the stiffness K are the following:

$$\text{On } X_2 : F_{r2} = K * [x_1(n) - x_2(n)] \qquad (2)$$
$$\text{On } X_1 : F_{r1} = -F_{r2}(n).$$

For viscous friction of a constant value Z we have the following:

$$\text{On } X_2 : F_{f2}(n) = Z * \qquad\qquad (3)$$
$$[x_1(n) - x_1(n - 1) - x_2(n) + x_2(n - 1)]$$
$$\text{On } X_1 : F_{f1}(n) = -F_{f2}(n)$$

Combination of Elements

Imagine a simple system corresponding to an elementary vibrating cell (Fig. 6). The resultant of the forces $F(n)$ applied to the mass is

$$F(n) = F_e(n) + F_{r1}(n) + F_{f1}(n),$$

where F_e is the result of external forces. With the spring and friction grounded, we have $x_2(n) = 0$, for all n. If $M = 1$, Eqs. (1), (2), and (3) give us the following:

$$X(n) = (1 + K + Z)^{-1} * \{F_e(n) + (2 + Z) * [x(n - 1) - x(n - 2)]\}. \quad (4)$$

This is a new algorithm, but we cannot generate a new algorithm for every simulation. Thus, the computation of each element must remain independent of each other, which is contrary to the nature of the interaction between the elements.

We were led to assume a theory of causality between forces and displacements, considering that the positions at instant n are calculated with the forces defined at instant $n - 1$. We then have

$$x(n) = F(n - 1) + 2x(n - 1) - x(n - 2)$$
$$F(n - 1) = F_e(n - 1) + F_r(n - 1) + F_f(n - 1).$$

That is,

$$x(n) = F_e(n - 1) + \quad (5)$$
$$\{([2 - K] - Z) * x(n - 1)\} - [(1 - Z) * x(n - 2)].$$

Sequential computing by independent modules is possible through this approximation. Thus the general sequencing for all types of structures for each step of the computation is realized as follows. Compute the positions $x_i(n)$ for all material elements starting from the connecting forces $F_i(n)$ of all the connecting modules starting from the positions $x_i(n)$. Compute the connecting forces $F_i(n)$ of the connection models starting from the positions $x_i(n)$.

The Cell

Since we have a combinatorial system, we can speculate that it would be interesting to introduce elements at a higher level than the basic elements already introduced. Such a system, directed toward instrumental expression and activity, must be able to realize the simulations from gesture to sound in real time. In this context, speed is important. For the cell, the computation starting from the fundamental algorithms is as follows:

$$X(n) = F(n) + 2x(n - 1) - x(n - 2)$$
$$F_{r1}(n) = -K * x(n)$$
$$F_{f1}(n) = Z[x(n) - x(n - 1)].$$

This computation requires three multiplies, three additions/subtractions, and some data transfers. The rigorous expression (Eq. 4) needs one division, two multiplications, and three additions/subtractions. The integrated and approximated expression needs two multiplications and three additions/subtractions, and is therefore the fastest algorithm. Here a new compromise appears. The modularity necessary in the operative code is partly contrary to the speed of the algorithms.

The Cordis system offers modules corresponding to elementary algorithms and *primary modules*, which are integrated algorithms of simple, frequently-used structures such as the cell or the vibrating string. The system can also be used to specify other primary modules.

Examples of Simulation

Starting from a qualitatively determined model, the numerical values of the mechanical parameters were modified in the course of experimentation. The computation at the level of the exciter and programming of the retroactive gesture-transducer is done in real time. The computation of the vibrating structure produces sound, not computed in real time. The sound computation is based on stored gestures recorded by the computer.

Gestural Feedback from a Retroactive Input Device

With the first retroactive gesture-transducer, we have produced mostly qualitative simulations, since the behavior of the device did not enable us to attain precise conditions corresponding to real instrumental performance.

Percussion of a Mass upon a Fixed Obstacle

In the first example, that of a mass bumping into a fixed obstacle, the operator moves a shaft along the rectangular guides. The shaft behaves like a mass in a viscous environment. The value of the mass and the friction is modifiable. On a given abscissa, there is a simulated obstacle (invisible) with a programmable stiffness and friction. When the mass (the shaft) strikes the obstacle, the different aspects of the resulting collision are felt by the operator. We obtain different types of bouncing of the mass on the obstacle, from very rapid bouncing with great amplitude and no damping to a soft, completely damped bounce. This effect varies according to the values of the stiffness of the obstacle, its damping coefficient, its mass, and the speed of its movement.

Percussion of a Mass upon an Obstacle with an Elastic Connection to a Fixed Point

This example resembles a performer hitting a suspended gong. The obstacle is likely to move from its resting position. In addition to the phenomena described in the previous simulation, the operator perceives the return shock of the obstacle on the shaft. The operator may then accentuate or interfere with the movement of the obstacle depending on the instant when the obstacle is hit in its perpendicular movement.

Plucking of a String by a Plectrum

The string is represented by a vibrating cell and the plectrum is represented by a conditional elastic connection, described earlier in the section on "Plucking" with programmable stiffness. One of its endpoints is fixed to a shaft manipulated by an operator. Before the connection, the plectrum has its own behavior. When the distance between the shaft and the cell is lower than a given threshold, the connection is made. At first, the operator perceives a slight percussion of the shaft on the string. Then the operator feels a change in behavior of the shaft, in particular its new resistance to displacement, as a function of the cell stiffness. Beyond this new threshold the shaft releases the string. The operator

senses the disconnection and again feels the initial behavior of the shaft.

Other Types of Stimulation

Different situations were simulated without direct reference to existing instrumental mechanisms. The stick, held by the operator, was displaced in a positive or negative direction, or along a jagged line. We have simulated regularly spaced surfaces with simple shapes such as triangles, rectangles, and sinusoids of varying amplitude. If the amplitude of the surfaces is weak, the operator has the impression of moving along a rough surface. If the amplitude is higher, the operator can go over obstacles of various shapes, even though the movement of the stick is always rectilinear.

Sound Synthesis Examples

String Simulation

In order to simulate a string, the string is partitioned into a number N of masses realigned by $(N - 1)$ identical *elasticity/friction* linkages. A harmonic string is only obtained when N is very large. What is the influence of the number of masses on the sense of causality evoked in the listener? That is, for what value of N could one assume that one is hearing a string? On a series of 26 sounds in which N varies between 9 and 34 and where the excitation of the string is an "ideal" pluck, we have proven that the sense of causality evoked is very stable. Even when the sounds are inharmonic, the series evoked clearly a permanent sense of a "string" object when notes were played from high to low along a scale.

Modulation of Stiffness

The equivalent in the Cordis system of the common technique of frequency modulation is modulation of stiffness. This procedure corresponds in reality to instrumentalists' gestures when they modulate the stiffness or tension of a string or a skin.

In the Cordis system, modulation of stiffness is effectuated in real time on a non-retroactive stick by a manipulator. In this simulation, the important thing is the maintenance of the relation between variations of frequency and amplitude such that it is defined in a concrete instrumental situation and its coherence is translated concretely to sound. The obtained sound, whatever its acoustic complexity, has the particularity to immediately invoke a sense of natural gestural "play."

Simulation of Different Materials

Starting with a similar vibrating structure made up of masses and "elasticity-friction" elements in which all the coefficients are identical, we have varied the stiffness parameter of these linkage elements between two extremes K_m and K_n, following a geometric scale. The excitation is an "ideal" pluck. The series obtained consists of 20 sounds of different pitches. The listener perceives a progressive change in the instruments, interpreting this change as a change of material. The listener's perception of the gestural causality is modified by the change in the stiffness parameter. For example, a pluck is no longer perceived in the case of an object made of wood or glass.

Conclusions

We have posed, in the Cordis system, a basis for a study of instrumental relationships, viewing it as a prelude to musical creativity. Our purpose is not to realistically simulate, in a physical sense, musical instruments. Rather, it is to research the equilibrium between what, in a sound event, proceeds from the gesture and what proceeds from the instrument. This dissociation illuminates two points:

The notion of timbre can take on a well-defined meaning: everything in the sound that is a translation of the information contained in the instrument's structure. A question to pursue is therefore the parallel between different perceptual categories and different physical networks such as those we have defined.
The articulation of macroscopic dynamics is di-

rectly connected to the gestural information. The recording of gestural information allows us to examine aspects of composition. One research direction appears intriguing: research into the continuity of process between instrumental performance and composition.

As far as gestural control is concerned, we have seen the necessity for devices that are much more complex than those we have already utilized, but that impose even more limitations on instrument gesture activity. We are not interested in realistic representations, but in representations which allow us to study, in symbolic form, the relations between gesture and instrument, allowing a reduction in complexity if the characteristic qualities are preserved. This is our basis for research into new instruments and instrument/instrumentalist relations.[2]

Acknowledgments

This research has been sponsored by the French Ministry of Culture, Department of Music and Dance.

References

Berberyan, T. 1979. "Application des processus récursifs à la synthèse sonore." Grenoble: Rapport D. E. A., I. N. P.
Cadoz, C. 1979. "Synthese sonore par simulation des mécanismes vibratoires." Thèse de troisième cycle. Grenoble: I. N. P.
Florens, J. 1978. "Coupleur gestuel interactif pour la commande et le contrôle de sons synthétisés." Thèse de troisième cycle. Grenoble: I. N. P.
Mathews, M. et al. 1969. *The Technology of Computer Music*. Cambridge, Massachusetts: MIT Press.
Ruiz, P. 1970. "A Technique for Simulating the Vibrations of Strings with a Digital Computer." Master's thesis. Urbana: University of Illinois.
Schaeffer, P. 1966. *Traité des objets musicaux*. Paris: Editions du Seuil.

2. This paper was written in 1980. In 1982, we developed a real-time signal processor called Cordis-Temps-Reel or CTR. CTR allows real-time synthesis of sound by means of the simulation algorithms described in this paper.

39

Julius O. Smith

Center for Computer Research in Music and
Acoustics (CCRMA)
Department of Music, Stanford University
Stanford, California 94305 USA

Fundamentals of Digital Filter Theory

Introduction

Any medium through which a music signal passes, whatever its form, can be regarded as a filter. However, we do not usually think of something as a filter unless it can modify the sound in some way. For example, speaker wire is not usually considered a filter, but the loudspeaker is (unfortunately). The different vowel sounds in speech are produced primarily by changing the shape of the mouth cavity, which changes the resonances and hence the filtering characteristics of the vocal tract. The tone control circuit in an ordinary car radio is a filter, as are the bass, midrange, and treble boosts in a stereo preamplifier. Graphic equalizers, reverberators, echo devices, phase shifters, and speaker crossover networks are further examples of audio filters. There are also undesirable filters such as the uneven reinforcement of certain frequencies in a room with "bad acoustics." A well-known signal processing wizard is said to have remarked, "When you think about it, everything is a filter."

A digital filter is just a filter that operates on digital signals, such as sound represented inside a computer. It is a computation that takes one sequence of numbers (the input signal) and produces a new sequence of numbers (the filtered output signal). The filters mentioned in the previous paragraph are not digital only because they operate on signals that are not digital. It is important to realize that a digital filter can do anything that a real-world filter can do. That is, all the filters alluded to above can be simulated to an arbitrary degree of precision digitally. Again, a digital filter is only a formula for going from one digital signal to another. It may exist as an equation on paper, as a small loop in a computer subroutine, or as a handful of integrated circuit chips properly interconnected.

This material is based on lecture notes for a class given by the author at Stanford University in 1979. The support of the Hertz Foundation at that time is gratefully acknowledged. A longer version appeared in *Digital Audio Signal Processing*, ed. J. Strawn (Kaufmann, 1985).

This paper is in two parts. The first part presents a simple example of a digital filter and how it can be analyzed to find its gain and delay characteristics as a function of frequency. The second part is almost a glossary of fundamental terms in digital filter theory. It is intended to serve more as a reference than a tutorial. The interested reader is highly encouraged to explore the references (especially Rabiner and Gold 1975) for a more detailed treatment.

The Simplest Lowpass Filter

A lowpass filter does not affect low frequencies and rejects high frequencies. The gain (ratio of output amplitude to input amplitude) of the ideal lowpass filter is unity (1) for frequencies between 0 Hz and the *cutoff* frequency f_c Hz, and is 0 for all higher frequencies. This ideal gain versus frequency curve is shown in Fig. 1. The output spectrum is obtained by multiplying the input spectrum by the function shown.

The simplest (and by no means ideal) lowpass filter is given by the following so-called difference equation

$$y(n) = x(n) + x(n-1), \quad n = 0, 1, 2, \ldots \quad (1)$$

where $x(n)$ is the filter input amplitude at time (or sample) n, and $y(n)$ is the output amplitude at time n. The system diagram for this little filter is given in Fig. 2. The symbol "z^{-1}" means a delay of one sample; i.e., $z^{-1} x(n) = x(n-1)$.

Physically, Eq. (1) means

$$y(nT) = x(nT) + x[(n-1)T], \quad n = 0, 1, 2, \ldots (2)$$

where T is the sampling interval (in seconds). It is customary in digital signal processing to leave off T (set it to 1), so we will write the equation as in Eq. (1).

Let's write a computer subroutine to implement Eq. (1). In the computer, $x(n)$ and $y(n)$ are data arrays, and n is an array index. Since sound files are

Fig. 1. Gain versus fre-
quency specification for
the ideal lowpass filter.

Fig. 2. System diagram for
the simplest lowpass filter.

Fig. 3. "Black Box" representation of an arbitrary
filter.

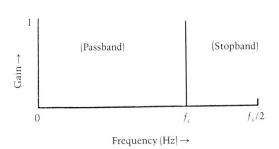

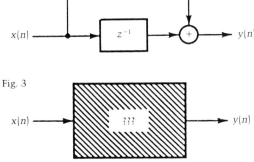

Fig. 3

usually larger than what the computer can hold in memory all at once, we must process the data in blocks of some reasonable size. Therefore, the complete filtering operation consists of two loops, one within the other. The outer loop fills the input array x and empties the output array y, while the inner loop does the actual filtering on the x array to produce y. Let M denote the block size (i.e., the number of samples processed on each iteration of the outer loop). In Pascal, the inner loop of the subroutine might appear as follows:

```
procedure SIMPLP(x, y :
  array[0..M] of real);
  var n : integer;
  for n := 1 to M do
  y[n] := x[n] + x[n - 1];
  end.
```

The outer loop might read something like "fill $x[1..M]$ from the input file," "call SIMPLP," and "write out $y[1..M]$." However, there is one more important statement whose absence will cause a "glitch" every M samples: After the call to SIMPLP, there must be the line "$x[0] := x[M]$;" to make $x[n - 1]$ valid in the first iteration of the next call to SIMPLP. (For the very first call to SIMPLP, $x[0] := 0$.)

You might suspect that since Eq. (1) is the simplest possible lowpass filter, that it is also somehow the worst possible lowpass filter. How bad is it? To answer this question, we must find the frequency response of this filter.

Finding the Frequency Response

Think of the filter expressed by Eq. (1) as a "black box" as shown in Fig. 3. We want to know the effect of this black box on the spectrum of $x(\cdot)$, where $x(\cdot)$ represents the entire input signal. Suppose we test its effect at each frequency separately. This is called sinewave analysis. Figure 4 shows an example of an input-output pair, for the filter of Eq. (1), at the frequency $f_s/4$ Hz. (The continuous-time waveform has been drawn through the samples for clarity.) Figure 4a shows the input, and Fig. 4b shows the output. The ratio of the peak output amplitude to the peak input amplitude is the filter *gain* at this frequency. From Fig. 4, we find that the gain is about 1.414 at frequency $f_s/4$.

The phase of the output minus the phase of the input is called the *phase response* of the filter. Figure 4 shows that Eq. (1) has a phase response equal to $-2\pi/8$ (minus one-eighth of a cycle) at the frequency $f_s/4$. Continuing in this way, we can input a sinusoid at each frequency (from 0 to $f_s/2$), examine the input and output waveforms as in Fig. 4, and record the peak-amplitude ratio (gain) and phase shift for each frequency on a graph. The resultant pair of plots, shown in Fig. 5, is called the *frequency response*. Note that Fig. 4 specifies the middle point of each graph in Fig. 5.

Not every black box can be characterized by a frequency response, however. What good is a pair of graphs such as shown in Fig. 5 if, for all input

Fig. 4. Input and output
signals for the simplest
lowpass filter. (a) Input
sinusoid at amplitude 1,
frequency $f_s/4$, and phase

0. (b) Output sinusoid at
amplitude $\sqrt{2}$, frequency
$f_s/4$, and phase $-\pi/4$
radians.

Fig. 5. Frequency response
of the simplest lowpass
filter. (a) Amplitude re-
sponse. (b) Phase response.

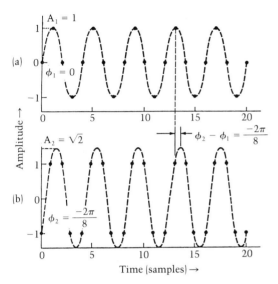

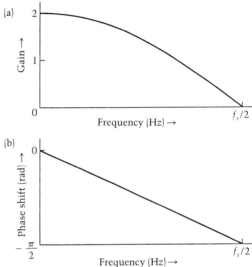

sinusoids, the output is 60 Hz hum? The sinewave analysis procedure for measuring frequency response is guaranteed to work only if the filter is *linear* and *time-invariant* (LTI). Linearity means that the output due to a sum of input signals equals the sum of outputs due to each signal alone. Time-invariance means that the filter does not change over time. LTI filters are guaranteed to produce a sinusoid in response to a sinusoid—and at the same frequency.

The previously described method of finding the frequency response involves physically measuring the amplitude and phase response for input sinusoids of every possible frequency. While it may be practical for a real black box, it is hardly useful for filter design. Ideally, we wish to arrive at a formula for the frequency response of the filter given by Eq. (1). Assuming Eq. (1) to be a linear time-invariant filter specification (which it is), let's take a few points in the frequency response by analytically "plugging in" sinusoids at a few different frequencies. Two graphs are required to fully represent the frequency response: gain versus frequency and phase shift versus frequency.

The frequency 0 Hz (often called DC for direct current) is always comparatively easy to handle when analyzing a filter. Since plugging in a sinusoid means setting $x(n) = A \cos(2\pi fnT + \phi)$, by setting the frequency $f = 0$ we obtain $x(n) = A \cos[2\pi(0)nT + \phi] = A \cos(\phi)$ for all n. Thus, the input signal is the same number ($A \cos \phi$) over and over again for each sample. It should be clear that the filter output will be $y(n) = x(n) + x(n-1) = A \cos(\phi) + A \cos(\phi) = 2A \cos(\phi)$ for all n. The gain at frequency $f = 0$ is therefore 2 which we get by dividing $2A$, the output amplitude, by A, the input amplitude. Phase is arbitrary at $f = 0$ Hz, so the phase response can be arbitrarily defined at this frequency. In all cases such as this where the phase response can be arbitrarily defined, we choose a value that preserves continuity. This means we must analyze at frequencies in a neighborhood of the arbitrary point and take a limit. We will compute the phase response at DC later using different techniques. It is worth noting, however, that at 0 Hz, phase is almost always defined to be zero.

The next easiest frequency to look at is half the

sampling rate, $f = f_s/2 = 1/(2T)$. In this case, the input x can be written as

$$x(n) = A \cos[2\pi(f_s/2)nT + \phi] = A(-1)^n \cos(\phi),$$

$$n = 0, 1, 2, \ldots$$

where the beginning of time was arbitrarily set at $n = 0$. Now with this input, the output of Eq. (1) is

$$y(n) = x(n) + x(n - 1) =$$

$$(-1)^n A \cos(\phi) + (-1)^{n-1} A \cos(\phi) = 0$$

The filter of Eq. (1) thus has a gain of 0 at $f = f_s/2$. Again the phase is not measurable, since the output signal is identically zero, and we will have to extrapolate the phase response from surrounding frequencies.

If we back off a bit, these results for gain response are obvious without any trigonometry. The filter of Eq. (1) is equivalent (except for a factor of 2) to a simple two-point average, $y(n) = [x(n) + x(n - 1)]/2$. Averaging adjacent samples in a signal is intuitively a lowpass filter because at low frequencies the sample amplitudes change slowly so that the average of two neighboring samples is very close to either sample, while at high frequencies the adjacent samples tend to have opposite signs and cancel out when added. The two extremes are frequency 0 Hz, at which the averaging has no effect, and half the sampling rate $f_s/2$, where the samples alternate in sign and exactly add to 0.

We are beginning to see that Eq. (1) may be a lowpass filter after all since we found a boost of about 6 db at the lowest frequency and a null at the highest frequency. (A gain of 2 may be expressed in db as $20 \log_{10}(2) \approx 6$ db, and a *null* or *notch* is another term for a gain of 0 at a single frequency.) Of course we only tried two out of an infinite number of possible frequencies.

Let's go for broke and plug the general sinusoid into Eq. (1), confident that trigonometry will see us through. After all, this is the simplest filter there is, right? We let $x(n) = A \cos(2\pi fnT + \phi)$ so that

$$y(n) = A \cos(2\pi fnT + \phi) + A \cos[2\pi f(n - 1)T + \phi].$$

Recall from the discussion surrounding Fig. 4 that only the peak-amplitude *ratio* and the phase *difference* between input and output sinusoids are needed

to measure the frequency response. The filter phase response does not depend on ϕ above (due to time-invariance), and so we can set ϕ to 0. Also, the filter amplitude response does not depend on A (due to linearity), so we can let $A = 1$. With these simplifications of $x(\cdot)$, the gain and phase response of the filter appear directly as the amplitude and phase of the output $y(\cdot)$. Thus, we input the signal

$$x(n) = \cos(2\pi fnT) = \cos(\omega nT)$$

where $\omega \overset{\Delta}{=} 2\pi f$ is radian frequency. (The symbol "$\overset{\Delta}{=}$" means "is defined as.") With this input, the output of the simple lowpass filter is given by

$$y(n) = \cos(\omega nT) + \cos[\omega(n - 1)T].$$

It is a fundamental fact that a sum of sinusoids at the same frequency, but different phase and amplitude, can always be expressed as one sinusoid at that frequency with a new phase and amplitude (Moore 1978a). Thus, $y(n)$ can be written in the form

$$y(n) = G(\omega)\cos[\omega nT + \Theta(\omega)],$$

where $G(\omega)$ is the filter gain response and $\Theta(\omega)$ is the phase response. Using various trigonometry identities (Abramowitz and Stegun 1965), we find

$$G(\omega) = 2\cos(\omega T/2), \quad |\omega| \leq \pi f_s$$

$$\Theta(\omega) = -\omega T/2.$$

We have completely solved for the frequency response of the simplest lowpass filter given in Eq. (1) using only high-school level math (although the derivation not shown here is somewhat lengthy). We found that an input sinusoid of the form $x(n) = A \cos(2\pi fnT + \phi)$ produces the output

$$y(n) = 2A \cos(\pi fT)\cos(2\pi fnT + \phi - \pi fT).$$

Thus, the gain versus frequency is $2 \cos(\pi fT)$ and the change in phase at each frequency is given by $-\pi fT$ radians. These functions are shown in Fig. 5.

An Easier Way

Fortunately, there are much more effective (and less arduous) methods for finding the gain and delay as a function of frequency. The basis for the improved techniques is *Euler's identity,*

$$e^{i\theta} = \cos(\theta) + j\sin(\theta), \quad j = \sqrt{-1}. \tag{3}$$

I shall refer to $e^{j\omega nT}$ as the *complex sinusoid.* It is normally easier to manipulate both *sine* and *cosine* simultaneously in this form than it is to deal with either sine or cosine separately. One may take the point of view that $e^{i\theta}$ is simpler and more fundamental than $\sin(\theta)$ or $\cos(\theta)$ as evidenced by the following identities (which follow immediately from Eq. (3)):

$$\cos\theta = \frac{e^{i\theta} + e^{-i\theta}}{2} \quad \sin\theta = \frac{e^{i\theta} - e^{-i\theta}}{2j}.$$

Consider again the simplest lowpass filter. This time let's do a complex sinewave analysis. For this, we test the filter response at frequency f by letting $x(n) = Ae^{j(2\pi fnT + \phi)}$. Again, because of time-invariance, the frequency response will not depend on ϕ, so let $\phi = 0$. Due to linearity, we may normalize A to 1. By virtue of Euler's relation and the linearity of the filter, setting the input to $x(n) = e^{j\omega nT}$ is physically equivalent to putting $\cos(\omega nT)$ into one copy of the filter, and $\sin(\omega nT)$ into a separate copy of the same filter. The signal path where the cosine goes in is the *real* part of the signal, and the other signal path is simply called the *imaginary* part. Thus, a complex signal in real life is just two ordinary signals side by side (one-quarter cycle out of phase at each frequency in the case of a complex sinusoid).

Using the normal rules for manipulating exponents, we find that the response of the simple lowpass filter to the complex sinusoid at frequency $\omega/2\pi$ Hz is given by

$$y(n) = x(n) + x(n-1) = e^{j\omega nT} + e^{j\omega(n-1)T}$$
$$= (1 + e^{-j\omega T})e^{j\omega nT} = (1 + e^{-j\omega T})x(n) \tag{4}$$
$$\triangleq H(e^{j\omega})x(n)$$

This derivation is clearly easier than the trigonometry approach which used tricky identities that few people would think of without staring at the answer for a good while. What is a little puzzling, however, is that the filter ends up looking like a frequency-dependent complex multiply. What does this mean? Well, in theory, it must somehow mean

a gain scaling and a phase shift. This is true and easy to see once the complex filter gain is expressed in *polar form,*

$$H(e^{j\omega}) \triangleq G(\omega)e^{j\Theta(\omega)}.$$

The gain versus frequency is given by the absolute value of H (the absolute value is just the radius in polar coordinates), and the phase shift in radians versus frequency is given by the complex angle of H (angle in polar coordinates). In other words, we must find

$$G(\omega) \triangleq |H(e^{j\omega})|,$$

which is the amplitude response, and

$$\Theta(\omega) \triangleq \angle H(e^{j\omega}),$$

which is the phase response. Note that for the lowpass of Eq. (1)

$$H(e^{j\omega}) = 1 + e^{-j\omega T} = (e^{j\omega T/2} + e^{-j\omega T/2})e^{-j\omega T/2} =$$
$$2\cos(\omega T/2)e^{-j\omega T/2}.$$

It is now easy to see that

$$G(\omega) = |2\cos(\omega T/2)e^{-j\omega T/2}| = 2\cos(\pi fT), \quad |f| \le \frac{f_s}{2},$$

and

$$\Theta(\omega) = -\omega T/2, \quad |f| \le \frac{f_s}{2}.$$

We have derived again the graph of Fig. 5 which shows the complete frequency response of Eq. (1). The gain of the simplest lowpass filter varies, as cosine varies, from 1 to 0 as the frequency of an input sinusoid goes from 0 to half the sampling rate. In other words, the amplitude response of Eq. (1) goes sinusoidally from 1 to 0 as ωT goes from 0 to π. It does seem somewhat reasonable to consider it a lowpass, and it is a poor one in the sense that it is hard to see which frequency should be called the cutoff frequency. We see that the spectral "rolloff" is very slow, as lowpass filters go, and this is what we pay for the extreme simplicity of Eq. (1). The phase response $\Theta(\omega) = -\omega T/2$ is linear in frequency, which gives rise to a constant time delay of $1/2$ samples irrespective of the signal frequency.

It deserves to be emphasized that all a linear

time-invariant filter can do to a sinusoid is scale its amplitude and change its phase:

> If a sinusoid $A_1 \cos(\omega nT + \phi_1)$ is input to a linear time-invariant filter, then the output signal (after start-up transients have died away) is a sinusoid at the same frequency $A_2 \cos(\omega nT + \phi_2)$. The only possible differences between the input and output are in their relative amplitude A_2/A_1 and relative phase $\phi_2 - \phi_1$. Any linear time-invariant filter may thus be completely characterized by its gain $G(\omega) = A_2/A_1$ and phase $\Theta(\omega) = \phi_2 - \phi_1$ at each frequency ω.

Mathematically, a sinusoid has no beginning and no end, so there really are no start-up transients in the theoretical setting. However, in practice, we must approximate eternal sinusoids with finite-time sinusoids whose starting time was so long ago that the filter output is essentially the same as if the input had been applied forever.

Tying it all together, the general output of a linear time-invariant filter with a complex sinusoidal input may be expressed as

$y(n) = (Complex\ Filter\ Gain)times(Input\ Circular$
$Motion\ with\ Radius\ A,\ Phase\ \phi)$

$\quad = (G(\omega)e^{i\Theta(\omega)})(A\ e^{i(\omega nT\ +\ \phi)})$

$\quad = (G(\omega)A)e^{i(\omega nT\ +\ (\phi\ +\ \Theta(\omega)))}$

$\quad = Circular\ Motion\ with\ Radius\ G(\omega)A,\ Phase$
$\quad \phi + \Theta(\omega).$

Basic Terms in Filter Theory

This section is a concise summary of elementary terms in digital filter theory. After some preliminary definitions, the notions of linearity, time-invariance, difference equations, transfer functions, and frequency response are introduced for the general finite-order, real, causal, linear, time-invariant, single-input, single-output digital filter. This section is quite terse and is intended mainly as a reference for those already at home with the ideas involved.

Definitions

All time is in *seconds* (sec) or *samples*. The continuous (or real) time variable is normally written t and the discrete (or integer) time variable n, with $t = nT$, where T is the sampling interval in seconds. Frequencies are either in cycles per second or radians per second. The name for cycles per second is *Hertz* (Hz). One cycle = 2π radians = 360 degrees, and therefore f Hz is the same frequency as $2\pi f$ radians per second. It is easy to confuse the two because both radians and cycles are pure numbers, so that both types of frequency are in physical units of inverse seconds (sec^{-1}). As an example, a sine wave with period τ (Greek "tau") seconds has frequency $f = (1/\tau)$ Hz, and radian frequency $\omega = 2\pi/\tau$ rad/sec. The sampling rate f_s is the reciprocal of the sampling period T. Note that since the sampling period is in seconds, the sampling rate has to be in Hz. One might often find it helpful, however, to think "seconds per sample" and "samples per second," where "samples" is a dimensionless quantity (pure number) thrown in for clarity. The phase of a signal will be written as ϕ as often as possible and will be in radian units. The amplitude of a signal can be thought of in any arbitrary units such as volts, sound pressure, and the like.

We represent the *time-waveform* of a signal as a real-valued function of an integer, corresponding to continuous amplitude versus discrete time. This means that for any sample (numbered n), the amplitude may take on any real value. The time-waveform may appear in your mind as a kind of bar graph that extends forever to the left and right.

By convention, $x(n)$ will denote the filter input amplitude at sample n, and the output will be called $y(n)$. This notation should be comfortable to anyone who has written a computer subroutine for processing samples of digitized sound. It could even be Fortran, except that lower case is significant here.

The term *sinusoid* will be used to mean a waveform of the type $A \cos(2\pi f nT + \phi) = A \cos(\omega nT + \phi)$, i.e., any delay ϕ of a sine or cosine at amplitude A and frequency f. A complex sinusoid is any waveform of the type $Ae^{i\omega nT + \phi}$.

We think of filters primarily in terms of their effect on the spectrum of a signal. This is appropriate because the ear (to a first approximation) converts the time-waveform from the eardrum into a neurologically encoded spectrum. Mathematically, the spectrum of a signal is the Fourier transform[1] of its time-waveform. Equivalently, the spectrum is the z transform evaluated on the unit circle $z = e^{i\omega T}$ (Papoulis 1977; Moore 1978b). We denote both the spectrum and the z transform of a signal by uppercase letters. For example, if the time-waveform is denoted $x(n)$, its z transform is called $X(z)$ and its spectrum is therefore $X(e^{i\omega T})$. The time-waveform $x(n)$ is said to "correspond" to its z transform $X(z)$, meaning they are transform pairs. This correspondence is often denoted $x(n) \leftrightarrow X(z)$, or $x(n) \leftrightarrow X(e^{i\omega T})$. (The double-arrow means "corresponds to.") Both the z transform and its special case, the (discrete-time) Fourier Transform, are said to transform from the *time domain* to the *frequency domain*.

We deal most often with discrete time nT (or simply n) but continuous frequency f. This is because the computer can represent only digital signals, and digital time-waveforms are discrete in time but may have energy at any frequency. On the other hand, if we are going to talk about FFTs (Fast Fourier Transforms), then we would have to "discretize" the frequency variable in order to represent spectra inside the computer.

When we wish to consider an entire signal as a "thing in itself," we write $x(\cdot)$ meaning the whole time-waveform $\{x(n), n = -\infty, \ldots, -1, 0, 1, \ldots, \infty\}$, or $X(\cdot)$ to mean the entire spectrum taken as a whole. Imagine for example that we have plotted $x(n)$ on a strip of paper that is infinitely long. Then $x(\cdot)$ refers to the complete picture while $x(n)$ refers to the nth sample point on the plot.

A real *filter* $\mathcal{L}_n$ is defined as any real-valued functional of a signal for each integer n. We express the input-output relation of the filter by $y(n) = \mathcal{L}_n\{x(\cdot)\}$,

1. More precisely, the discrete-time Fourier transform. The more commonly heard term, "Discrete Fourier Transform" (DFT), refers to the one which is discrete in both time and frequency (Moore 1978b). The "Fast Fourier Transform" (FFT) is a high-speed implementation of the DFT.

where $x(\cdot)$ is the entire input signal, and $y(n)$ is the output at time n.

Linearity and Time-Invariance

In everyday terms, the fact that a filter is *linear* means simply that (1) the amplitude of the output is proportional to the amplitude of the input, and (2) when two signals are added together and fed to the filter, the filter output is the same as if one had put each signal through the filter separately and then added the outputs. More precisely, a filter is said to be linear if for any pair of signals $x_1(\cdot)$, $x_2(\cdot)$ and for all constant gains g, we have

$$
\begin{aligned}
&1. \quad \mathcal{L}_n\{g\, x_1(\cdot)\} = g\, \mathcal{L}_n\{x_1(\cdot)\} \\
&2. \quad \mathcal{L}_n\{x_1(\cdot) + x_2(\cdot)\} = \mathcal{L}_n\{x_1(\cdot)\} + \mathcal{L}_n\{x_2(\cdot)\},
\end{aligned} \tag{5}
$$

for all n, then the filter is said to be linear. These two conditions are a mathematical statement of the previous definition. For g rational, property (2) implies property (1).

A filter is said to be *time-invariant* if shifting the input signal $x(\cdot)$ results in a corresponding shift of the output signal $y(\cdot)$, or,

$$
\mathcal{L}_n\{x(\cdot - N)\} = \mathcal{L}_{n-N}\{x(\cdot)\} = y(n - N), \tag{6}
$$

where $x(\cdot - N)$ is understood to denote the waveform $x(\cdot)$ shifted right (or delayed) by N samples.

Difference Equation, Causality, and Order

The *difference equation* for a general linear time-invariant (LTI) digital filter is given by

$$
\begin{aligned}
y(n) = {}&b_0\, x(n) + b_1\, x(n-1) + \cdots + b_{n_b} x(n - n_b) \\
&- a_1 y(n-1) - \cdots - a_{n_a} y(n - n_a)
\end{aligned} \tag{7}
$$

where x is the input signal, y is the output signal, and the constants $\{b_i,\ i = 0, 1, 2, \ldots, n_b\}$, $\{a_i,\ i = 1, 2, \ldots, n_a\}$ are called *difference equation coefficients*, or more simply, *filter coefficients*. When the a and b coefficients are real numbers, then the filter is said to be *real*.

Equation (7) represents only *causal* LTI filters. A

filter is said to be causal when the output does not depend on any "future" inputs. (In more colorful terms, a filter is causal if it does not "laugh" before it is "tickled.")

The *maximum time span*, in samples, used in creating each output sample is called the *order* of the filter. In (7), the order is the larger of n_b and n_a. Since n_b and n_a in (7) are assumed finite, (7) represents the class of *finite order* causal LTI filters.

Impulse Response and Stability

Any LTI filter may be represented in the time domain by its response to a specific signal called the *impulse*. The impulse is denoted as $\delta(n)$ and is defined for integer n by

$$\delta(n) \triangleq \begin{cases} 1, & n = 0 \\ 0, & n \neq 0 \end{cases}.$$

The *impulse response* of a filter is the response of the filter to $\delta(n)$ and is most often denoted $h(n)$. A filter is said to be *stable* if the impulse response $h(n)$ approaches zero as n goes to infinity.

Convolution and z-Transform

If $y(n)$ is the output of an LTI filter with input $x(n)$ and impulse response $h(n)$, then y is the *convolution* of x with h,

$$y(n) = x * h(n) \triangleq \sum_{i=0}^{n} x(i)h(n-i) = \sum_{i=0}^{n} h(i)x(n-i). \quad (8)$$

The last equality results from the fact that convolution is commutative, i.e., $x * h(n) = h * x(n)$.

The *z-transform* of the discrete-time signal $x(n)$ is defined to be

$$X(z) \triangleq \sum_{n=-\infty}^{\infty} x(n)z^{-n},$$

That $x(n)$ and $X(z)$ are transform pairs is expressed by writing $X(z) = Z\{x(n)\}$ or $X(z) \leftrightarrow x(n)$. As stated earlier, lower case denotes the time-waveform (signal) and upper case denotes the frequency-function (spectrum or z-transform). Note that transform-pair correspondence is between *entire waveforms* $X(\cdot)$

and $x(\cdot)$. Strictly speaking, it is incorrect to write $x(n) \leftrightarrow X(z)$, because we do not mean $X(z)$ is computed solely from the single sample $x(n)$. Nevertheless, this notation is very common in the signal processing literature. Where there should appear $(\cdot)$, there appears an indication of the time or frequency variable as it would appear inside a transform or summation.

The *convolution theorem* (Papoulis 1977) states that

$$x * y(n) \leftrightarrow X(z)Y(z). \quad (9)$$

In words, convolution in the time domain is multiplication in the frequency domain.

Transfer Function

Taking the z-transform of both sides of (8) and applying the convolution theorem gives

$$Y(z) = H(z)X(z) \quad (10)$$

where $H(z)$ is the z-transform of the filter impulse response. Thus, the z-transform of the filter output is the z-transform of the input times the z-transform of the impulse response. Accordingly, the *transfer function* $H(z)$ of a linear time-invariant discrete-time filter is defined to be the z-transform of the impulse response $h(n)$.

The *shift theorem* (Papoulis 1977) for z-transforms states that $x(n-k) \leftrightarrow z^{-k}X(z)$. Taking the z-transform of both sides of Eq. (7) and solving for $Y(z)/X(z)$, which equals the transfer function $H(z)$, yields

$$H(z) \triangleq \frac{Y(z)}{X(z)} = \frac{b_0 + b_1 z^{-1} + \cdots + b_{n_b} z^{-n_b}}{1 + a_1 z^{-1} + \cdots + a_{n_a} z^{-n_a}}. \quad (11)$$

Frequency Response and Polar Form

When z is restricted to the unit circle in the complex plane, i.e., $z = e^{j\omega T}$, the z-transform becomes the DFT, and therefore the transfer function becomes the ratio of the filter output spectrum divided by the input spectrum. Thus, the *frequency response* of a linear time-invariant digital filter is defined to be the transfer function, $H(z)$, evaluated on the unit circle, that is, $H(e^{j\omega})$.

The frequency response is a complex-valued function of a real variable $\omega = 2\pi f$. The response at frequency f Hz, for example, is $H(e^{j2\pi fT})$, where T is the sampling period in seconds.

Since every complex number can be represented as a magnitude and angle, the frequency response may be decomposed into two real-valued functions, the *amplitude response* and the *phase response*. Formally, we may define them as follows:

$$G(\omega) \triangleq |H(e^{j\omega})| \quad \Theta(\omega) \triangleq \angle H(e^{j\omega})$$

so that

$$H(e^{j\omega}) = G(\omega)e^{j\Theta(\omega)}. \tag{12}$$

Thus, $G(\omega)$ is the magnitude (or complex modulus) of $H(e^{j\omega})$, and $\Theta(\omega)$ is the phase (or complex angle) of $H(e^{j\omega})$. The real valued function $G(\omega)$ is called the filter amplitude response and it specifies the *amplitude gain* that the filter provides at each frequency. The function $G^2(\omega)$ is called the *power response* and it specifies the *power gain* at each frequency. The real function $\Theta(\omega)$ is the phase response and it gives the phase shift in radians that each input component sinusoid will undergo. If the filter input and output signals are $x(n)$ and $y(n)$ respectively, then

$$|Y(e^{j\omega})| = G(\omega)|X(e^{j\omega})|$$

$$\angle Y(e^{j\omega}) = \Theta(\omega) + \angle X(e^{j\omega}).$$

Phase Delay and Group Delay

The phase response of a filter $\Theta(\omega)$ gives the *radian* phase shift experienced by each sinusoidal component of the input signal. Sometimes it is more meaningful to consider *phase delay* (Papoulis 1977). The phase delay of an LTI filter $H(z)$ with phase response $\Theta(\omega)$ is defined by

$$P(\omega) \triangleq - \frac{\Theta(\omega)}{\omega}.$$

The phase delay gives the *time delay* in seconds experienced by each sinusoidal component of the input signal. For example, in filter $y(n) \leftarrow x(n) + x(n$

$- 1)$, the phase response is $\Theta(\omega) = -\omega T/2$ which corresponds to a phase delay $P(\omega) = T/2$ which is one-half sample. If the input to a filter with frequency response $H(e^{j\omega}) = G(\omega)e^{j\Theta(\omega)}$ is

$$x(n) = \cos(\omega nT),$$

then the output is

$$y(n) = G(\omega)\cos[\omega nT + \Theta(\omega)] =$$

$$G(\omega)\cos\{\omega[nT - P(\omega)]\},$$

and it can be seen that the phase delay expresses phase response as time delay.

In working with phase delay, care must be taken to ensure all appropriate multiples of 2π have been included in $\Theta(\omega)$. We defined $\Theta(\omega)$ simply as the complex angle of the frequency response $H(e^{j\omega})$, and this is not sufficient for obtaining a phase response which can be converted to true time delay. By discarding multiples of 2π, as is done in the definition of complex angle, the phase delay is modified by multiples of the sinusoidal period. Since LTI filter analysis is based on sinusoids without beginning or end, one cannot in principle distinguish between "true" phase delay and a phase delay with discarded sinusoidal periods. Nevertheless, it is convenient to define the filter phase response as a *continuous* function of frequency with the property that $\Theta(0) = 0$ (for real filters). This specifies a means of "unwrapping" the phase response to get a consistent phase delay curve.

A more commonly encountered representation of filter phase response is called the *group delay*, and it is defined by

$$D(\omega) \triangleq - \frac{d}{d\omega} \Theta(\omega).$$

For linear phase responses, the group delay and the phase delay are identical, and each may be interpreted as time delay.

For any phase function, the group delay $D(\omega)$ may be interpreted as the time delay of the *amplitude envelope* of a sinusoid at frequency ω (Papoulis 1977). The bandwidth of the amplitude envelope in this interpretation must be restricted to a frequency interval over which the phase response is approximately linear. While the proof will not be given here, it should seem reasonable when the process of amplitude envelope detection is considered. The narrow "bundle" of frequencies centered at the carrier frequency ω is translated to 0 Hz. At this point, it is evident that the group delay at the carrier frequency gives the slope of the linear phase of the translated spectrum. But this is a constant phase delay, and therefore it has the interpretation of true time delay for the amplitude envelope.

Poles and Zeros and Stability

We can write the general transfer function for the recursive LTI digital filter as

$$H(z) = g \frac{1 + \alpha_1 z^{-1} + \cdots + \alpha_{n_b} z^{-n_b}}{1 + a_1 z^{-1} + \cdots + a_{n_a} z^{-n_a}},$$

which is the same as Eq. (11) except that we have factored out the leading coefficient b_0 in the numerator (assumed to be nonzero) and called it g. (Here $\alpha_i = b_i/b_0$.) In the same way that $z_2 + 3z + 2$ can be factored into $(z + 1)(z + 2)$, we can factor the numerator and denominator to obtain

$$H(z) = g \frac{(1 - q_1 z^{-1})(1 - q^2 z^{-1}) \cdots + (1 - q_{n_b} z^{-1})}{(1 - p^1 z^{-1})(1 - p^2 z^{-1}) \cdots (1 - p_{n_a} z^{-1}).} \quad (13)$$

Assume that none of the factors cancel out. The (possibly complex) numbers $\{q^1, \ldots, q_{n_b}\}$ are the roots of the numerator polynomial. When z equals any of these values, the transfer function evaluates to 0. For this reason, the roots of the *numerator* polynomial of the filter transfer function are called the *zeros* of the filter. Similarly, when z approaches any root of the denominator polynomial, the magnitude of the transfer function becomes larger and larger, approaching infinity. Consequently, the *denominator* roots $\{p^1, \ldots, p_{n_a}\}$ are called the *poles* of the filter.

Notice that the n_b feedforward coefficients from the general difference equation, Eq. (7), give rise to n_b zeros. Similarly, the n_a feedback coefficients in Eq. (7) give rise to n_a poles. This illustrates the general fact that zeros are caused by adding a finite number of input samples together, and poles are caused by feedback. Recall that the filter order is the maximum of n_a and n_b. If $b_0 \neq 0$ in Eq. (11),

it then follows that the filter order is determined by the number of poles or zeros, whichever is greater.

As mentioned, a filter is said to be *stable* if its impulse response $h(n)$ decays to 0 as n goes to infinity. Unstable filters are to be avoided because they lead to overflow of the computer word, which can make pompoms out of your speakers. The physical counterpart of an unstable filter is something that will never stop quivering after you hit it with a hammer (or worse, begin to shake more and more violently like a washing machine with boots in it). In terms of poles and zeros, a filter is stable if and only if all the poles are inside the unit circle in the z-plane. This is because the transfer function is the z-transform of the impulse response, and if there is a pole outside the unit circle, then there is an exponentially increasing component of the impulse response.

Conclusion

Some basic concepts for the analysis and description of digital filters have been presented, including linearity, time-invariance, filter impulse response, difference equations, transfer functions, amplitude response, phase response, group delay, poles and zeros, filter stability, and the general use of complex numbers to represent signals and spectra.

Acknowledgments

I would like to express appreciation to Janet Coursey, David Jaffe, Andy Moorer, Andy Schloss, Ken Shoemake, and John Strawn for their helpful proofreading and suggestions. The figures in this paper are reprinted with permission from J. O. Smith (1985).

Bibliography

Abramowitz, M., and I. A. Stegun, ed. 1965. *Handbook of Mathematical Functions.* New York: Dover.
Bers, L. 1969. *Calculus.* New York: Holt, Rinehart, and Winston.

Smith

Bracewell, R. 1965. *The Fourier Transform and Its Applications*. New York: McGraw-Hill.

Churchill, R. V. 1960. *Complex Variables and Applications*. New York: McGraw-Hill.

Digital Signal Processing Committee, ed. 1979. *Programs for Digital Signal Processing*. New York: IEEE Press.

Gold, B., and C. M. Rader. 1969. *Digital Processing of Signals*. New York: McGraw-Hill.

Kailath, T. 1980. *Linear Systems*. Englewood Cliffs: Prentice-Hall.

Markel, J. D., and B. Gold. 1976. *Linear Prediction of Speech*. Berlin: Springer-Verlag.

Mathews, M. V. 1969. *The Technology of Computer Music*. Cambridge, Massachusetts: MIT Press.

Moore, F. R. 1978a. "An Introduction to the Mathematics of Digital Signal Processing, Part I." *Computer Music Journal* 2(1):38–47. Reprinted in *Digital Audio Signal Processing: An Anthology*. J. Strawn, ed. 1985. Los Altos: Kaufmann.

Moore, F. R. 1978b. "An Introduction to the Mathematics of Digital Signal Processing, Part II." *Computer Music Journal* 2(2):38–60. Reprinted in *Digital Audio Signal Processing: An Anthology*. J. Strawn, ed. 1985. Los Altos: Kaufmann.

Oppenheim, A. V., and R. W. Schafer. 1975. *Digital Signal Processing*. Englewood Cliffs: Prentice-Hall.

Papoulis, A. 1977. *Signal Analysis*. New York: McGraw-Hill.

Rabiner, L. R., and B. Gold. 1975. *Theory and Application of Digital Signal Processing*. Englewood Cliffs: Prentice-Hall.

Rabiner, L. R. 1978. *Digital Processing of Speech Signals*. Englewood Cliffs: Prentice-Hall.

Rosenbach, J. B., and E. A. Whitman. 1949. *College Algebra*. New York: Ginn.

Smith, J. O. 1985. "Introduction to Digital Filter Theory." In *Digital Audio Signal Processing: An Anthology*, J. Strawn, ed. Los Altos: Kaufmann.

Steiglitz, K. 1974. *An Introduction to Discrete Systems*. New York: Wiley.

40

Gérard R. Charbonneau
Institut d'Electronique Fondamentale
Laboratoire associé au CNRS
Bâtiment 220
Université Paris Sud
91405 Orsay CEDEX
France

Timbre and the Perceptual Effects of Three Types of Data Reduction

Introduction

Research conducted with the help of the computer in the last several years has allowed us to synthesize tones whose timbres are perceptually indistinguishable from those of many musical instruments. This success has often given us important information about the relationships between the psychological components of hearing and the physical attributes of sound. For musical purposes, an analysis/synthesis model of a real tone can be considered perfect if, when using data resulting from the analysis, we find that a resynthesized tone is perceptually indistinguishable from the real sound. Such a system can be realized, for example, by heterodyne filtering (Moorer 1973) or, better yet, with the phase vocoder (Portnoff 1976; Moorer 1978).

However, defining a tone completely in order to reproduce exactly a given timbre leads to a four-dimensional representation, with amplitude, frequency, time, and phase as physical parameters. Usually phase does not appear as a perceptibly significant parameter because in most cases it can be significantly perturbed—by a reverberant room, for example—without audible loss of information. Nevertheless, with only three physical dimensions, the amount of data necessary for an individual tone is still considerable since it consists of two time-varying functions (amplitude and frequency) for each partial. This is why additive synthesis, although capable of producing excellent results, is often considered by musicians to be not very useful, even if computations are done quickly by dedicated hardware, because the quantity of data is quite large even for a simple score.

Recently, multidimensional scaling techniques

(Shepard 1962a; 1962b; Kruskal 1964a; 1964b; Carroll and Chang 1970; Benzécri et al. 1973a; 1973b) have provided unambiguous evidence that timbre is a multidimensional attribute of sound (Plomp 1970; Wessel 1973; 1978; Miller and Carterette 1975; Grey 1977). This could justify a priori the necessity for a large amount of data to define this attribute. The analyses of timbre just cited, however, indicate that the identification of timbre is related to few psychological factors. All the details of the time-varying functions (for amplitude and frequency) are probably not significant for the perception of timbre.

Parallel to this development, the success of nonlinear synthesis techniques illustrated by frequency modulation (FM) synthesis (Chowning 1973) leads us to think that important simplifications can be made in the definition of sound without significant deterioration in timbre. By controlling a simple modulation index, we can simulate the timbre of different musical instruments in a very satisfactory (though discernible) manner. Data reduction is thus not only of obvious interest for the synthesis, transformation, or transmission of sound. It also permits a deeper understanding of the truly relevant features of hearing (specifically the invariable elements of sound perception).

We have experimented with data reduction in the three dimensions defining sound, namely amplitude, frequency, and time. In this article we will discuss three approaches: (1) data reduction for the time-varying amplitude functions of each partial, (2) data reduction for the time-varying frequency functions for each partial, and (3) prediction of the starting and ending times of each partial. We will discuss the results concerning discrimination of the various modifications of timbre for 16 isolated tones, which represent a wide range of the traditional nonpercussive orchestral instruments.

Table 1. The 16 reference tones provided by John Grey

Abbreviations	Reference Tones
BC	Bass clarinet
BN	Bassoon
EC	E-flat clarinet
EH	English horn
FH	French horn
FL	Flute
O1	Oboe
O2	Oboe, not the same player or instrument as O1
S1	Cello, played *sul ponticello*
S2	Same cello as S1, with normal bowing
S3	Same cello as S1, played muted *sul tasto*
TM	Muted trombone
TP	Trumpet
X1	Alto saxophone, played *mezzo forte*
X2	Same alto saxophone as X1, played piano
X3	Soprano saxophone

Stimuli

The stimuli used as sources for our simplifications were derived from 16 tones played at the pitch of E-flat above C3 (fundamental at approximately 311 Hz), with durations ranging from 280 to 400 msec. Grey (1975) and Grey and Moorer (1977) give a detailed description of the recording, analysis, and re-synthesis of these sounds. Briefly, each tone, after being analyzed with the heterodyne filter (Moorer 1973), is represented in the computer by a set of two time-varying functions (one for amplitude, the other for frequency) for each harmonic. We used the *line-segment approximations* described by Grey (1975), except for the clarinets, saxophones, oboes, trumpet, and French horn, for which we used Grey's *cut-attack approximations*. The 16 tones, which we will call *reference tones*, are listed with their abbreviations in Table 1.

Amplitude Data Reduction

We investigated first the possibility of reducing the data for specifying the amplitudes of the various partials of a tone. Multidimensional scaling studies

of timbre (cited earlier) clearly indicate that the major factor for identifying timbre is closely bound to the spectral composition of the sound. This spectral composition can be evaluated in many ways, however, including the bandwidth, the balance of energy between low and high frequencies, and even the relative harmonic or quasi-harmonic nature of the signal. It seems (see, for example, Plomp 1970; Grey and Gordon 1978) that one of the most important features of the spectrum is the shape of the spectral envelope. Thus we decided to keep the peak value of each harmonic in our amplitude transformation so that the spectral envelope is not changed significantly.

Taking the arithmetic mean of the amplitudes of all harmonics at each point in time, we arrived at an *amplitude mean curve* for each instrument, which we normalized to a peak amplitude of 1. Thus the description of the time-varying amplitudes for a tone is reduced to the following information:

One amplitude mean curve normalized to 1
A set of three values TS_i, TE_i, MAX_i ($i = 1, 2, ... N$) representing respectively the starting time, ending time, and peak amplitude of each of the N harmonics

Rebuilding the simplified tone consists of synthesizing the N harmonics with the same amplitude variation as that computed for the normed amplitude mean curve. For each harmonic, this curve is weighted in amplitude so that the peak value reached coincides with the maximum MAX_i and, in time, so that the ith harmonic starts at time TS_i and ends at time TE_i (Figs. 1 and 2). Thus from the 16 reference tones we drew a set of 16 *amplitude-simplified* tones. Despite the fact that the peak amplitude values are the same, the time at which the amplitude of a harmonic reaches its peak value is sometimes shifted substantially, as can be seen in Fig. 2.

Frequency Data Reduction

Our second area of investigation dealt with another dimension of sound: frequency. Again, our aim was to obtain a single variation curve from which it would be possible to derive by some simple transformation a frequency variation curve for each partial. After examination of spectrogram analyses of tones played on different instruments, it did not seem reasonable to compute a mean curve like the one calculated for amplitude. In fact, although quite different in detail, amplitude curves of the various components of a tone show common features, especially a common shape: they start from 0, grow to a maximum, and then decrease to 0. In this case, the mean curve reflects the shape of the different curves. On the other hand, frequency variation curves do not present, even for a single instrument, such a common, general form. Similarity in the local variations of the different harmonics seemed to be encountered most frequently (although this cannot be accepted as a generalization).

For this reason, we chose to take as our frequency reference curve the function corresponding to the variation of the fundamental frequency. In this kind of simplification, the choice of the fundamental harmonic is not imperative, and it is probably possible to obtain similar results with another harmonic. The fundamental harmonic presents an important advantage, however; in all the reference tones, it has a longer lifetime than the other harmonics. The time-varying frequency of each harmonic is obtained by multiplying each point of the frequency reference curve by the appropriate harmonic number between the starting and ending times of the harmonic under consideration (the frequency is set to 0 elsewhere). By using the fundamental, we avoid extrapolating the frequency variations at times when the harmonic does not exist. In this type of simplification, the resulting spectrum is strictly harmonic at any time, but the period of the waveform fluctuates in time like that of the fundamental frequency in the reference tone.

Thus the information relevant to frequency is reduced to the following data:

One frequency reference curve (the frequency function for the fundamental)

A set of two values, TS_i and TE_i, representing the starting and ending time of the ith harmonic (note that this information already exists in the amplitude simplifications)

This kind of reduction gives us a new set of 16 *frequency-simplified* tones.

Time Data Reduction

The third area of investigation concerned the reduction of information related to the starting (TS_i) and ending (TE_i) times of all the components of the sound. We intended to see whether the starting and ending times of each partial were critical. For this, we replaced the sets TS_i and TE_i by two functions of the harmonic number (one for the starting time, the other for the ending time) obtained by polynomial fitting. When the degree of the polynomial is higher, the fit is of course better, but the amount of data reduction is lowered.

As a measure of the goodness of fit, we computed the ratio

$$\frac{\text{standard error of the fit}}{\substack{\text{delay between first and last starting or} \\ \text{ending times}}}.$$

Preliminary tests showed that a fourth-degree polynomial, for which this ratio was less than 0.25 for

*Fig. 1. Data reduction of
the amplitude functions
for the trumpet tone. The
line-segment approxima-
tions of the reference tone
(Grey 1975) are shown at*

*the top; the lower plot
shows the amplitude-sim-
plified functions used in
one of the experiments described here.*

*Fig. 2. Data reduction of
the amplitude functions
for the flute tone. In the
amplitude-simplified form
(bottom), the times at*

*which several of the
harmonics reach their
peak values are shifted
considerably.*

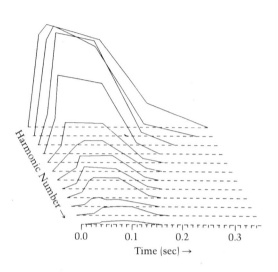

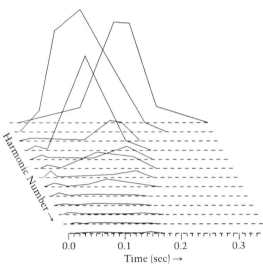

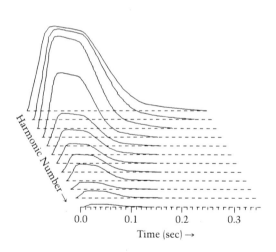

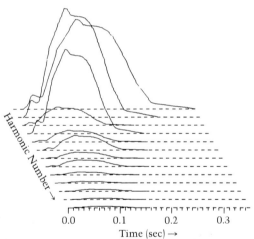

all of the reference tones, would produce satisfactory results for the purposes of the work described
here. Further work on the effects of changing the
order of the polynomial has yet to be done. The
choice of a fourth-degree polynomial gives a good
fit (Fig. 3) but does not permit accurate reproduction of strong irregularities such as the 65-msec

delay in the fourth harmonic of the soprano saxophone, for which the computed value turned out
to be 31 msec.

The degree of data reduction for this type of approximation can be measured as the ratio between
the number of starting or ending times (i.e., the
number of harmonics) and the number of coeffi-

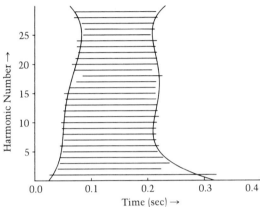

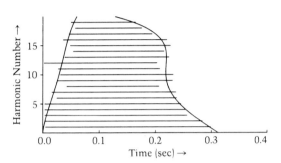

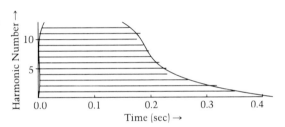

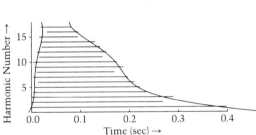

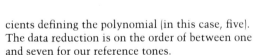

cients defining the polynomial (in this case, five). The data reduction is on the order of between one and seven for our reference tones.

We thus obtained a third set of 16 *time-simplified* tones as follows: for each instrument, we synthesized the sound, using the amplitude and frequency functions of the reference tone, but with TS_i and TE_i modified so that each component started and ended at the times predicted by the polynomial fitting.

Listeners and Procedure

The experiment compared the reference tone to a simplified tone produced by one of the three previously described methods. For each pair, there was a short warning tone (a double warning tone every fifth pair) preceding the reference tone by 2.5 sec;

then the simplified tone followed the reference tone after a 0.5-sec silence. Five seconds were provided for the judgment of the pair before the next pair was started. With 16 instruments and three kinds of simplification, there were 48 different stimuli, each one presented four times, thus making a set of 192 stimuli presented in random order. Twenty trials taken from this set were selected as practice trials for giving the maximum range of variation in the sounds before starting the experiment. The 212 trials were played back from the computer and recorded on a Sony 854-4 tape recorder.

Eighteen listeners at Stanford University participated in this experiment. They were musically sophisticated and active as performers or composers. Each listener was instructed to judge each pair as to how *discriminably different* the two sounds were in timbre, using the following scale:

0 — The tones are identical.
1 — Perhaps there is a slight difference.
2 — There is a slight difference of some kind.
3 — There is definitely a difference.

Table 2. Discriminability of 16 instruments for three different methods of data reduction

Results for 18 Listeners

Instruments	Amplitude						Proportion of Answers for the Simplifications in Frequency						Timing					
	0	1	2	3	4	5	0	1	2	3	4	5	0	1	2	3	4	5
BC	.139	.264	.361	.167	.069	.000	.569	.264	.083	.042	.042	.000	.667	.292	.042	.000	.000	.000
BN	.361	.444	.181	.000	.014	.000	.250	.361	.236	.097	.056	.000	.556	.333	.083	.014	.014	.000
EC	.083	.278	.375	.194	.069	.000	.597	.278	.111	.014	.000	.000	.306	.444	.139	.083	.028	.000
EH	.361	.403	.153	.056	.028	.000	.542	.375	.069	.014	.000	.000	.431	.417	.111	.028	.014	.000
FH	.278	.347	.278	.069	.028	.000	.083	.319	.250	.125	.222	.000	.556	.319	.083	.028	.014	.000
FL	.083	.167	.153	.264	.292	.042	.194	.264	.306	.167	.069	.000	.431	.319	.139	.083	.028	.000
O1	.139	.333	.236	.153	.139	.000	.292	.514	.139	.056	.000	.000	.417	.292	.208	.056	.028	.000
O2	.153	.347	.278	.153	.069	.000	.431	.375	.097	.042	.056	.000	.389	.417	.097	.083	.014	.000
S1	.167	.417	.208	.194	.014	.000	.194	.306	.333	.111	.056	.000	.514	.347	.111	.028	.000	.000
S2	.111	.083	.181	.306	.319	.000	.153	.278	.333	.222	.014	.000	.375	.361	.153	.056	.056	.000
S3	.444	.417	.125	.014	.000	.000	.653	.278	.028	.042	.000	.000	.583	.292	.125	.000	.000	.000
TM	.056	.153	.278	.306	.208	.000	.278	.264	.222	.111	.125	.000	.444	.347	.153	.042	.014	.000
TP	.042	.111	.208	.347	.278	.014	.222	.333	.264	.125	.056	.000	.444	.375	.139	.028	.014	.000
X1	.264	.500	.139	.042	.056	.000	.472	.375	.083	.028	.042	.000	.306	.333	.236	.097	.028	.000
X2	.069	.125	.250	.306	.250	.000	.486	.444	.042	.000	.028	.000	.375	.319	.194	.083	.028	.000
X3	.069	.111	.250	.250	.319	.000	.500	.347	.153	.000	.000	.000	.528	.250	.153	.069	.000	.000
ALL	.176	.281	.228	.176	.135	.003	.370	.336	.172	.075	.048	.000	.457	.341	.135	.049	.017	.000

NOTE: Table indicates the proportion of answers obtained for each instrument, each simplification, and each possible answer. For example, there is a 36.1% (.361) chance that the answer 0 will occur for the amplitude simplification of the English horn (EH). See text for an explanation of the answer ratings 0–5. Round-off error in the individual entries can result in a total probability of more than 100% in some cases.

4 — There is a considerable difference, but the instrument timbre is still recognizable.

5 — The timbral difference between the pair of tones is large enough to significantly alter the apparent instrumental sound.

Data sets were collected in a session of about one hour. Playback was done through an Altec 804-E speaker in a very dry room at a moderate but comfortable amplitude level for listeners.

Results and Discussion

For each combination of instruments and type of simplification, the data were averaged across all four repetitions for each of the 18 listeners. Table 2 shows the results. Although certain listeners were sometimes inconsistent in their judgments (for instance, one listener responded with 0, 1, 3, and 4 for the four presentations of the bass clarinet [BC] in the amplitude simplification), the cumulative results present a satisfactory distribution. We then calculated the mean answer and the estimated standard deviation for each instrument and for each kind of data reduction, as shown in Table 3. For 41 of the 48 stimuli, the mean answer is less than 2, which corresponds to a slight perceived difference.

It is interesting to note that the answer 5 never occurred except for the flute (FL) (three times) and the trumpet (TP) (one time), both with the amplitude simplification; these four answers were given by the same listener. None of the 18 listeners indi-

Charbonneau

Table 3. Mean answers and estimated standard deviations for each instrument in each of the three simplifications

	Results for 18 Listeners		
	Mean Answers and Estimated Standard Deviations for the Simplifications in		
Instruments	Amplitude	Frequency	Timing
BC	1.7639 ± .1304	.7222 ± .1254	.3750 ± .0669
BN	.8611 ± .0955	1.3472 ± .1329	.5972 ± .0962
EC	1.8889 ± .1228	.5417 ± .0813	1.0833 ± .1199
EH	.9861 ± .1178	.5556 ± .0813	.7778 ± .1013
FH	1.2500 ± .1199	2.0833 ± .1529	.6250 ± .1017
FL	2.6389 ± .1635	1.6528 ± .1387	.9583 ± .1273
O1	1.8194 ± .1484	.9583 ± .0958	.9861 ± .1243
O2	1.6389 ± .1331	.9167 ± .1293	.9167 ± .1149
S1	1.4722 ± .1219	1.5278 ± .1297	.6528 ± .0931
S2	2.6389 ± .1549	1.6667 ± .1219	1.0556 ± .1325
S3	.7083 ± .0872	.4583 ± .0883	.5417 ± .0838
TM	2.4583 ± .1355	1.5417 ± .1582	.8333 ± .1101
TP	2.7500 ± .1352	1.4583 ± .1341	.7917 ± .1045
X1	1.1250 ± .1218	.6389 ± .0955	1.0694 ± .1272
X2	2.5417 ± .1412	.7917 ± .1186	1.2083 ± .1266
X3	2.6389 ± .1458	.6528 ± .0866	.7639 ± .1127
ALL	1.8238 ± .0384	1.0946 ± .0331	.8273 ± .0282

cated that the timbre was no longer recognizable either in the frequency data reduction or for the time-simplified tones.

The three different simplifications are not equivalent for all instruments, however. Figure 4 shows that the results for the amplitude simplification are much more scattered, with a mean value generally higher than for the other two simplifications. In the amplitude simplification, we observe (see also Table 2) the results 0 or 1 in 75% of the answers for only 4 instruments (BN, EH, X1, S3). For this same discriminability, there are 9 instruments (BC, EC, EH, O1, O2, S3, X1, X2, X3) for the frequency simplification, and 12 instruments (BC, BN, EC, EH, FH, FL, O2, S2, S3, TM, TP, X3) for the time transformation. As can be seen in Table 3, none of the 16 instruments has a worst result for the time reduction; 3 have it for the frequency simplification (BN, FH, and S1) and the remaining 13 for the amplitude

reduction. Hence it appears that among the first three dimensions describing the sound space, the changes in the specification of amplitude are perceptibly the most important, followed by the frequency and temporal changes.

It is also interesting to study how differently the instruments react for a given simplification (Fig. 4). For the timing simplification, there is no evidence of systematic differences among the instruments. For the frequency simplification, all the instruments except for the French horn (FH) are divided into two groups. In the first group there are the three saxophones (X1, X2, X3), the two clarinets (BC, EC), the two oboes (O1, O2), the cello (played *sul tasto* (S3)), and the English horn (EH). These instruments are nearly unaffected by the frequency simplification. In the second group, we find the other two cellos (S1, S2), the trumpet (TP), the trombone (TM), the flute (FL), and the bassoon

Fig. 4. Mean discrimina-
tion of 16 instrument tones
for 18 listeners with simplification of data for amplitude, frequency, and
time (see Table 1 for explanation of abbreviations).

Amplitude

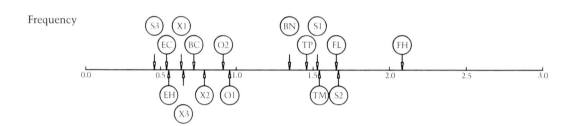

Frequency

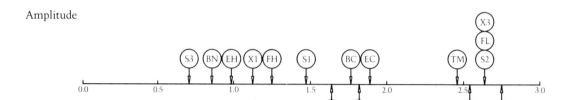

Time

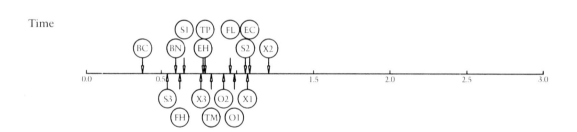

(BN). For this group, the frequency simplification still does not significantly affect the timbre recognition. The result for the French horn is undoubtedly related to the wide frequency fluctuations in the attack of all the harmonics of the reference tone.

For the amplitude simplification, there are also basically two groups. In the first group (S3, BN, EH, X1, FH, S1, O2, BC, O1, EC) the change introduced by the data reduction is barely perceived; for the second group (TM, X2, X3, FL, S2, TP) the difference is clearly discernible. The order of distribution along the amplitude-simplification plot of Fig.

4 depends mainly on the similarity of the amplitude curves of the various harmonics. For instance, the functions for the cello (S3) are quite similar in all the harmonics, while there is considerable difference in the functions for the soprano saxophone, the flute, and the trumpet.

Thus far we have not had any great success in relating the distribution of the tones in Fig. 4 to the multidimensional analysis performed by Grey. In particular, we expected a correlation between the distribution of the instruments along our amplitude axis (Fig. 4) and the second axis of Grey's multidimensional analysis (Grey 1977; Gordon and

Charbonneau

Grey 1978), which has been interpreted as being related to the overall amount of *spectral fluctuation* through time. Unfortunately, there is no evidence of such a correlation. For example, on the one hand, TP, FL, S2, and TM are at the end of Grey's second axis, which would indicate a strong spectral fluctuation, and the results are similar in our experiment. On the other hand, FL and X3 are very close on our axis, while they are on opposite ends of the axis in Grey's work.

In looking at these results, we have to remember that the specifications obtained for each instrument by the various types of simplification cannot be considered generally valid for all the notes playable on the instrument. It is an important property of timbre that the analysis of one instrumental note is rarely sufficient for synthesizing a note of differing pitch, intensity, or duration. It is usually easier to find common properties of a set of notes after the complex data has been simplified, however.

Conclusion

The simplifications that we have described shed new light on the problem of reducing the data necessary for synthesis of a tone with a given timbre. Moreover, with the amplitude and frequency simplifications, the description of the sound becomes very simple. Such a model fits very well indeed with nonlinear sound synthesis techniques, which are much more cost-effective than additive synthesis. In particular, waveshaping (LeBrun 1979) allows us to define a time-varying spectral envelope with a single index. In this kind of synthesis, the spectral envelope is described by the peak-amplitude values of the various harmonics, while the index is given by the amplitude mean curve.

The most interesting part of our experiment, however, seems to be in the psychoacoustic field. Although the simplified tones are not always identical to the reference tones, they are unexpectedly close. This demonstrates that little or no significant information has been lost. The results of the experiment do not contradict the importance of the spectral envelope in timbre recognition, as found in many studies (Plomp 1970; Grey 1977). They also

indicate that of the three dimensions of sound considered here, amplitude is probably the most sensitive.

Regarding the frequency dimension, it appears that inharmonicity (or quasi-periodicity) existing in natural sounds is not intrinsically significant with regard to the timbre of instruments playing continuous tones, such as the tones we studied. (This result would probably not be true for percussive sounds, in which inharmonicity can sometimes be very pronounced.) It is well known that a tone synthesized with constant frequencies is clearly discernible from the original (Grey 1975). This evident discriminability would lead us to think that the independent frequency variations observed in natural sounds are necessary for timbre recognition. Except for the French horn, however, which has strong inharmonicity in the attack, timbre recognition is not really affected by the frequency simplification. Hence the ear is much more sensitive to the frequency variations of all harmonics than to whether or not these variations are different for each harmonic.

The timing simplification has given the best results of the three data reductions we studied. This indicates that delays existing in natural sounds between the starting (or ending) times of all partials are important but probably not critical for the identification of timbre. In particular, irregularities such as the 65-msec delay in the fourth harmonic of the soprano saxophone are not really significant because, as we have already seen, the polynomial does not capture them completely (see also Fig. 3).

Some improvements can surely be made on the proposed methods of data reduction, especially concerning the frequency reference curve. It is possible that curves empirically obtained would give better results. On the other hand, more extensive data reduction can be done, for example by combining two (or all) of the three simplifications discussed here; but preliminary results suggest that doing so will affect the timbre even more than one might expect.

Acknowledgments

This research was conducted at Center for Computer Research in Music and Acoustics (CCRMA),

Stanford University. We would like to thank John M. Chowning and John M. Grey, who originated this research, and also John W. Gordon and John Strawn for their helpful collaboration. We are also indebted to the Stanford Artificial Intelligence Laboratory, whose facilities were used for this research.

References

Benzécri, J. P. et al. 1973a. *L'Analyse des données: la taxinomie*. Paris: Dunod.

Benzécri, J. P. et al. 1973b. *L'Analyse des données: l'analyse des correspondances*. Paris: Dunod.

Carroll, J. D., and J. J. Chang. 1970. "Analysis of Individual Differences in Multidimensional Scaling via an N-way Generalization of 'Eckart-Young' Decomposition." *Psychometrika* 35:283–319.

Chowning, John M. 1973. "The Synthesis of Complex Audio Spectra by Means of Frequency Modulation." *Journal of the Audio Engineering Society* 10:526–534. Reprinted in *Computer Music Journal* 1(2):46–54.

Gordon, John W., and John M. Grey. 1978. "Perception of Spectral Modifications on Orchestral Instrument Tones." *Computer Music Journal* 2(1):24–31.

Grey, John M. 1975. "Exploration of Musical Timbre." Technical Report STAN-M-2. Stanford, California: Stanford University Department of Music.

Grey, John M. 1977. "Multidimensional Perceptual Scaling of Musical Timbre." *Journal of the Acoustical Society of America* 61:1270–1277.

Grey, J. M., and J. W. Gordon. 1978. "Perceptual Effects of Spectral Modifications on Musical Timbres." *Journal of the Acoustical Society of America* 63:1493–1500.

Grey, J. M., and J. A. Moorer. 1977. "Perceptual Evaluations of Synthesized Musical Instrument Tones." *Journal of the Acoustical Society of America* 62:454–462.

Kruskal, J. B. 1964a. "Multidimensional Scaling by Optimizing Goodness of Fit to a Nonmetric Hypothesis." *Psychometrika* 29:1–27.

Kruskal, J. B. 1964b. "Nonmetric Multidimensional Scaling: A Numerical Method." *Psychometrika* 29:115–129.

LeBrun, M. 1979. "Digital Waveshaping Synthesis." *Journal of the Audio Engineering Society* 27:250–266.

Miller, J. R., and E. C. Carterette. 1975. "Perceptual Space for Musical Structures." *Journal of the Acoustical Society of America* 58:711–720.

Moorer, James A. 1973. "The Heterodyne Filter as a Tool for Analysis of Transient Waveforms." Memo AIM-208. Stanford, California: Stanford University Artificial Intelligence Laboratory.

Moorer, James A. 1978. "The Use of the Phase Vocoder in Computer Music Applications." *Journal of the Audio Engineering Society* 26:42–45.

Plomp, R. 1970. "Timbre as a Multidimensional Attribute of Complex Tones in Frequency Analysis and Periodicity Detection in Hearing." In *Frequency Analysis and Periodicity Detection in Hearing*, ed. R. Plomp and G. F. Smoorenburg. Leiden: Sijthoff.

Portnoff, M. R. 1976. "Implementation of the Digital Phase Vocoder Using the Fast Fourier Transform." *IEEE Transactions on Acoustics, Speech and Signal Processing* ASSP-24:243–248.

Shepard, R. N. 1962a. "The Analysis of Proximities: Multidimensional Scaling with an Unknown Distance Function. Part I." *Psychometrika* 27:125–140.

Shepard, R. N. 1962b. "The Analysis of Proximities: Multidimensional Scaling with an Unknown Distance Function. Part II." *Psychometrika* 27:219–246.

Wessel, David L. 1973. "Psychoacoustics and Music." *Bulletin of the Computer Arts Society* 30:1–2.

Wessel, David L. 1978. "Timbre Space as a Musical Control Structure." *Computer Music Journal* 3(2):45–52.

41

Paul Lansky
Music Department
Princeton University
Princeton, New Jersey 08540

Kenneth Steiglitz
Electrical Engineering and Computer
Science Department
Princeton University
Princeton, New Jersey 08540

Synthesis of Timbral Families by Warped Linear Prediction

Introduction

We will consider here the following problem faced by a composer using a digital computer for realization of a piece: that of how to generate sounds that are recognized as belonging to distinct families (such as strings, brass, etc.), while at the same time allowing for different instruments in each family (such as violin, viola, etc.) to be clearly distinguishable from one another. Since the composer obviously wants also to have more or less complete control over pitch, loudness, vibrato, and other features, the overall problem is quite complex.

In this article we will describe an approach to this problem that combines linear predictive coding and frequency warping and that was implemented and used for the performance of a "string" piece, *Pine Ridge*, written by P. Lansky. The method involves the following steps:

1. A few typical notes (perhaps a tune) played on one member of the family are recorded and digitized.
2. A linear predictive analysis is performed on the notes and the results stored in large-scale memory (e.g., on a disk). Each frame represents an all-pole synthesis filter with transfer function $1/D(z)$.
3. Synthesis is carried out with the general-purpose program Music 4BF (Howe 1975), which in effect acts as an orchestra. Each instrument is synthesized by use of the *frame filters* with transfer functions $1/D$

This paper was originally presented at the 1981 IEEE International Conference on Acoustics, Speech, and Signal Processing, 30 March to 1 April 1981, Atlanta, Georgia.

Computer Music Journal, Vol. 5, No. 3, Fall 1981

obtained in step 2 by linear predictive analysis, except that the excitation signals are determined by the instantaneous pitch requirements of the composer and the filters used have undergone frequency transformations to change the effective timbre of the instrument.

Recording and Digitization

The starting material for *Pine Ridge* was a tune of 10 notes lasting about 11 sec and played on a violin by Cyrus Stevens. Analog-to-digital conversion was done with a sampling rate of 14 KHz and 12 bits. This was the only sound used to produce the entire piece.

Linear Predictive Analysis

The covariance method (Markel and Gray 1976) (with no window) was used for the linear predictive analysis. Eighteen poles and 250-point (17.9 msec) frames were used. The original signal was pre-emphasized by the highpass filter with transfer function $(1 - z^{-1})$. The frames were not contiguous, but overlapped by 125 points, or 50%. That is, each new frame consisted of the last half of the previous frame followed by the first half of the next. This amount of overlap enabled us to use linear interpolation of predictor coefficients without instability.

As is well known, the covariance method can produce unstable frame filters. In this case, more than half the frames did have one or two poles outside the unit circle. One advantage of dealing with such a small amount of material is that it is not too expensive to factor every denominator $D(z)$. This was done and any poles at radius $R > 0.998$ were then moved to a radius of 0.998.

Excitation for Synthesis

A pitch contour was also obtained by use of the algorithm in "Pitch Extraction by Trigonometric Curve Fitting" (Steiglitz, Winham, and Petzinger 1975). Deviations in pitch as much as $\pm\frac{1}{3}$ of a semitone were observed. A semitone is a frequency ratio of $2^{1/12}$, or about 6%, so the observed vibrato was as much as $\pm 2\%$ in pitch. Furthermore, the higher formants of the linear predictive analysis moved in a way correlated with the pitch, possibly because the higher formants were tracking harmonics of the excitation signal. This suggested that the pitch contour associated with a particular note be incorporated in the synthesis so that the original correlation of pitch variation with formant motion would be preserved. We accomplished that by transposing the original pitch contour to the desired pitch and by using the transposed pitch contour with the frame filters that corresponded to the original pitch contour. Preserving the correlation between vibrato in pitch and formant structure seemed to improve the realism of the synthesis.

The excitation signal itself was obtained using the method described by Winham and Steiglitz (1970), in which a table lookup of a closed-form expression for a harmonic series was used with a flat spectrum. Its spectrum was then shaped by a 2-pole bandpass filter, always centered at the fundamental, with a bandwidth of about 1500 Hz. The resultant harmonic series descends in amplitude monotonically and is a gross approximation of the spectrum of a triangular waveform, which is probably a good source for a bowed instrument.

In addition to transposing the original pitch-tracking data, we also subjected the pitch to random deviations of ± 0.1 semitone. Seven such versions of each instrument, with different phases, were added to create the effect of an orchestral section rather than a single instrument.

Warping of the Synthesis Filter

In the Appendix to this article an efficient method is described for realizing the filter with transfer function

$$\frac{1}{D'(z)} = \frac{1}{D(A(z))},$$ (1)

where $A(z)$ is the transfer function of any causal filter. To transform (warp) the frequency axis we choose the all-pass function

$$A(z) = \frac{d + z^{-1}}{1 + dz^{-1}}.$$ (2)

If the original frame filter has the transfer function

$$\frac{1}{D(z)} = \frac{1}{1 + \sum_{i=1}^{L} b_i z^{-i}},$$ (3)

the transformed filter has the structure shown in Fig. 1, where the new coefficients are obtained by the simple calculation

$$b'_L = b_L$$
$$b'_i = b_i + db'_{i-1} \qquad i = L - 1,\dots,1$$ (4)
$$c_L = 1/(1 + db'_1)$$

and the function $B(z)$ is defined by

$$B(z) = A(z) - d.$$ (5)

$B(z)$ has no feed-through term, so the signal-flow graph in Fig. 1 has no delay-free loops and is therefore computable.

The effect of the transformation is to map the frequency axis by

$$\phi(\omega) = \omega - 2 \tan^{-1}\left(\frac{d \sin(\omega)}{1 + d \cos(\omega)}\right).$$ (6)

Therefore, if the original transfer function has a formant at $\omega = \omega_0$, the new transfer function will have one when $\phi(\omega) = \omega_0$. This shows that when $0 < d < 1$, formants are shifted up and when $-1 < d < 0$, formants are shifted down. To a second-order approximation in ω, $\phi(\omega)$ is linear at the origin, with slope

$$\phi'(0) = \frac{1 - d}{1 + d},$$ (7)

Fig. 1. The structure of the warped filter.

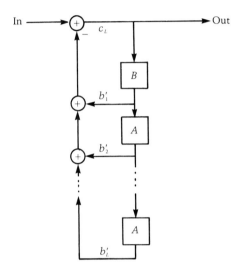

so for small ω, a formant at ω_0 will be shifted to approximately $[(1+d)/(1-d)]\omega_0$.

We can view the frequency-warping process as an approximate way of scaling the psychoacoustic size of the instrument. For example, in applying this technique to speech the lowering of a woman's vocal formants gives the impression of a larger but still feminine source, while raising the formants gives the distinct impression of a young girl's voice.

In the family of string instruments, a viola is tuned 7 semitones lower than a violin, a violoncello 19 semitones lower, and a double bass 27 semitones lower. We assumed that instrument sizes and formant structures are related in roughly this way and used the values of d obtained from

$$\frac{1+d}{1-d} = 2^{-7/12}, 2^{-19/12}, 2^{-27/12}, \tag{8}$$

$$d = -0.19946, -0.49958, -0.65259. \tag{9}$$

(If we know a pair of frequencies we wish to be related by the mapping, we can use Eq. (6) to find d precisely.)

As noted earlier, high formants obtained from linear predictive analysis of the violin tend to track the pitch harmonics. On synthesis of high violin notes, therefore, we shifted the formants (via the relation [6]) by the same ratio as the pitch so as to keep the high formants lined up with the pitch harmonics. This is not critical at lower pitches since the pitch harmonics are more closely spaced.

Conclusion

Pine Ridge gives the intended impression of performance by an ensemble of strings. There are some clear differences, however, which may or may not be musically significant. The diminuendi, for example, sound artificial because no attempt was made to change the excitation or formants with loudness.

A linear predictive analysis of a few notes of a musical instrument puts within easy reach a great deal of musically useful information. A flexible analysis—synthesis, combining a careful linear prediction with a synthesis program like Music 4BF—enables the composer to "play" real-sounding instruments with the computer. In this article we have described a method that allows alteration of the apparent size of such instruments in a methodical way. Much work remains to be done in applying the method to families of instruments other than strings and in refining the technique.

Appendix

A Note on Variable Recursive Digital Filters, by Kenneth Steiglitz [1]

Schüssler and Winkelnkemper [1970] note than when z is replaced by the low-pass-to-low-pass bilinear frequency transformation in the transfer function of a recursive digital filter, the resulting direct form structure has delay-free loops and is therefore not realizable without modification. John-

1. Reprinted from *IEEE Proceedings on Acoustics, Speech, and Signal Processing* 28:111–112, 1980. Copyright© 1980 by the Institute of Electrical and Electronics Engineers, Inc. Reprinted with permission.

son [1976, 1979] gives two methods for computing the new coefficients in a realization which is in direct form, except for a factor of the form $(1 + dz^{-1})^k$, where k is the difference between the degrees of the original denominator and numerator. In [Johnson 1976] he shows that the new coefficients of both the denominator and numerator can be produced at the taps of a network similar to the frequency-warping network in [Oppenheim et al. 1971; Oppenheim and Johnson 1972]. In [Johnson 1979] an FIR network is used to recompute the coefficients. (Mullis and Roberts [1976] discuss the recomputation of coefficients in a state variable realization.)

In this correspondence we describe another method for realizing the transformed transfer function, one which preserves the all-pass substructure inherent in the bilinear transformation, and which results in a very fast coefficient recomputation.

We consider the transformation

$$z^{-1} \rightarrow \frac{d + z^{-1}}{1 + dz^{-1}} = A(z)$$

and define

$$B(z) = A(z) - d = \frac{(1 - d^2)z^{-1}}{1 + dz^{-1}} .$$

Given the transfer function

$$\frac{N(z)}{D(z)} = \frac{\displaystyle\sum_{i=0}^{M} a_i z^{-i}}{1 + \displaystyle\sum_{i=1}^{L} b_i z^{-i}} ,$$

the transformed transfer function is

$$\frac{\displaystyle\sum_{i=0}^{M} a_i A(z)^i}{1 + \displaystyle\sum_{i=1}^{L} b_i A(z)^i} .$$

The numerator can be implemented as it stands, as described in [Schüssler and Winkelnkemper 1970]. We therefore concentrate on the denominator: the difficulty is caused by the constant term in the sum. The following algebraic manipulation decreases by 1 the degree of the offending sum:

$$\frac{1}{1 + \displaystyle\sum_{i=1}^{L} b_i A^i} = \frac{1}{1 + (B + d) \displaystyle\sum_{i=1}^{L} b_i A^{i-1}}$$

$$= \frac{c_1}{1 + c_1 d \displaystyle\sum_{i=2}^{L} b_i A^{i-1} + c_1 B \displaystyle\sum_{i=1}^{L} b_i A^{i-1}} .$$

where

$$c_1 = 1/(1 + db_1) .$$

If this is repeated L times, we get

$$\frac{1}{1 + \displaystyle\sum_{i=1}^{L} b_i A^i} = \frac{c_L}{1 + c_L B \displaystyle\sum_{i=1}^{L} b'_i A^{i-1}} .$$

Thus, we obtain the identity

$$1 + \sum_{i=1}^{L} b_i A^i = \frac{1}{c_L} + B \sum_{i=1}^{L} b'_i A^{i-1} .$$

Substituting $B = A - d$ and equating coefficients of like powers of A, we get the recursion relations

$$b'_L = b_L$$
$$b'_i = b_i + db'_{i+1} \qquad i = L - 1,...,1$$

and

$$c_L = \frac{1}{1 + db'_1} .$$

The transfer function B has no feedthrough term, so this form of the denominator is directly realizable [Fig. 1].

When the numerator and denominator of the original filter are of the same degree, Johnson's form has the advantage of having the same filtering complexity as the original filter, although both numerator and denominator coefficients must be recomputed, whereas the present method requires recomputation of only the denominator coefficients. In the case of an all-pole transfer function, such as might arise in linear predictive coding, both methods result in a structure requiring more arithmetic to implement than the original.

A real advantage of the present method is the fast coefficient recomputation: the new b's can be found with only L multiplications, L additions, and one division, in contrast with the techniques described by Johnson, which appear to require $O(L^2)$ steps. The method also works without change for any causal A; B is defined by subtracting the constant term from A.

Acknowledgment

This work was supported by NSF Grants ECS-7916292 and GK-42048, and U.S. Army Research Office-Durham Grants DAAG29-79-C-0024 and DAHCO4-75-G0192.

References

Howe, Hubert S., Jr. 1975. *Electronic Music Synthesis.* New York: Norton.

Johnson, D. H. 1976. "Application of Digital-Frequency Warping to Recursive Variable-Cutoff Digital Filters." In *IEEE Electronics and Aerospace Systems Convention. Proceedings.* New York: IEEE, pp. 154A–154E.

Johnson, D. H. 1979. "Variable Digital Filters Having a Recursive Structure." *IEEE Proceedings on Acoustics, Speech, and Signal Processing* 27:98–99.

Markel, J. D., and A. H. Gray, Jr. 1976. *Linear Prediction of Speech.* New York: Springer.

Mullis, C. T., and R. A. Roberts. 1976. "Roundoff Noise in Digital Filters—Frequency Transformations and Invariants." *IEEE Proceedings on Acoustics, Speech, and Signal Processing* 24:538–550.

Oppenheim, A. V., D. H. Johnson, and K. Steiglitz. 1971. "Computation of Spectra with Unequal Resolution Using the Fast Fourier Transform." *Proceedings of the IEEE* 59:299–301.

Oppenheim, A. V., and D. H. Johnson. 1972. "Discrete Representation of Signals." *Proceedings of the IEEE* 60:681–691.

Schüssler, W., and W. Winkelnkemper. 1970. "Variable Digital Filters." *Archiv für Elektronik und Uebertragungstechnik* 24:524–525. (Reprinted in Rabiner, L. R., and C. M. Rader, eds. 1972. *Digital Signal Processing.* New York: IEEE Press.)

Steiglitz, K., G. Winham, and J. Petzinger. 1975. "Pitch Extraction by Trigonometric Curve Fitting." *IEEE Proceedings on Acoustics, Speech, and Signal Processing* 23:321–323.

Winham, G., and K. Steiglitz. 1970. "Input Generators for Digital Sound Synthesis." *Journal of the Acoustical Society of America* 47 (2, Part 2):665–666.

42

Chris Chafe
Center for Computer Research in Music and
Acoustics
Department of Music
Stanford University
Stanford, California 94305

Bernard Mont-Reynaud
Systems Control Technology
P. O. Box 10180
Palo Alto, California 94303

Loren Rush
Center for Computer Research in Music and
Acoustics
Department of Music
Stanford University
Stanford, California 94305

Toward an Intelligent Editor of Digital Audio: Recognition of Musical Constructs

In this article, we present the view that computer-aided editing of music (in the form of digital audio) would greatly benefit from coordination with the musical properties of the signals involved. Simultaneous access to the low-level representations of the music in the signal and the higher-level constructs familiar to musicians would allow them to perform operations and transformations whose realization by signal processing techniques alone would range from cumbersome to unimaginable. In the cumbersome category might be such operations as "advance 15 sec and stop at the first G" or "play from the loudest point near 25 sec to the loudest point near 50 sec." In the barely imaginable category might be "start at the 17th measure" or "replay the violin part, this time transposed down a fifth and with the timbre of a clarinet, while preserving all stylistic features of the original."

This article and its companion, by Foster, Schloss, and Rockmore, address methods of analysis that make such operations imaginable and maybe even practical. Here, we will focus on higher-level approaches to the problem. The companion article, which follows this one, will focus on lower-level methods.

Background

Music recording and editing facilities utilizing large-scale, random-access storage media exist at several locations, including Soundstream (Easton 1976), Bell Laboratories, New York Institute of Technology (Kowalski and Glassner 1982), the Center for Computer Research in Music and Acoustics (CCRMA) (Rush and Mattox, forthcoming), the Institut de Recherche et Coordination Acoustique/Musique (IRCAM) (Haynes 1982), and the University of California at San Diego (UCSD) (Moore 1982). An elaborate system is also currently being developed at Lucasfilm (Abbott 1981; Moorer 1981; Snell 1981).

As the technology proliferates and production-oriented facilities become common, the need for efficient software tools for sound editing becomes more pressing. Most current software editing involves montage-like operations derived from sequential recording media (analog or digital tape), such as copying, mixing, cutting, and splicing, but also incorporates signal processing tools such as filtering, reverberation, and flanging. Editing processes are applied to sound segments delimited by their time boundaries, given as sample numbers or

This material is based on work supported by the National Science Foundation under Grant No. MCS-7923282.

Computer Music Journal, Vol. 6, No. 1, Spring 1982

seconds. In addition to auditory playback, which was the sole form of information retrieval in sequential media, software systems offer a variety of visual representations of the sound, which assist in pinpointing the timing data needed for the operations on sound segments. These visual navigational aids include waveform, amplitude, and spectral displays. To locate a point in the sound file, one moves to its general vicinity and then zooms in on the desired feature by moving forward or backward along a magnifiable time axis. Some software allows a limited amount of automatic assistance for this task in the form of segmentation based on the magnitude of the waveform (Rush and Mattox, forthcoming). However, relating the visual representation to the music remains a nontrivial matter; the specialized knowledge required does not always solve the more obscure cases.

It thus becomes important to investigate further software possibilities for automatic assistance with tasks of the type just described. Systems capable of meeting these objectives would have to include genuine signal recognition techniques such as have been developed for speech (Erman et al. 1980) or hydrophonics (Drazovich, Brooks, and Foster 1979). They would also need to incorporate a significant degree of knowledge about musical constructs, which is the aspect we will emphasize in this article.

Related Research

For the automatic locator needed for editing, the system navigates through a file of samples, putting up musical signposts for each event. The map it makes can then be used by the editor or converted into a score that matches the original. Obviously, the system can create lead sheets or other notation if no original score exists.

This last capacity for automatic transcription from sound has been the goal of other research. Transcription has posed an interesting problem in the fields of computer science, psychology, and signal processing, and the resulting research has expressed the particular concerns of each.

In J. A. Moorer's exploratory work in the field (Moorer 1975), a set of signal processing routines were implemented that detected and labeled notes from a guitar duet. The musical material was restricted to two voices that did not cross and did not include interval relationships of fifths or octaves. Note durations were converted into a score according to user-specified metric values. Instrument identification was not attempted because

> We do not know how people do this. It is often said that recognition is done on the basis of the attack transients and the steady-state harmonic amplitudes. This is easy to say but somewhat difficult to implement. The same instrument will exhibit widely varying harmonic amplitudes at different times, different loudnesses, and most certainly for different pitches [Moorer 1977, p. 38].

Confirming evidence for this statement can be found in a study of timbral variety in the cello (Chafe 1978), and a subsequent discussion of the complexities of modeling string instruments (Chafe, forthcoming).

H. C. Longuet-Higgins has approached the problem as a psychologist interested in the perception of melody. He has concentrated on both the kinds of surface inconstancies of rhythmic timings in real performance and the formulation of structures for naming note durations and pitches according to the surrounding context. A performer at an organ keyboard provides data in the form of frequency versus time note lists (Longuet-Higgins 1976). The values observed for note-to-note differences between performed durations agree with the values we found. For shorter durations there seems to be a variance of about 100 msec between any two notes performed as equals. Longuet-Higgins's program, in brief, is primed with some information about metric context and then processes the note list to make proper labelings. He feels that the structures for this transformation model the perceptual mechanisms at work, in partial analogy with Chomskyan linguistics (Longuet-Higgins 1978).

Longuet-Higgins's co-worker Steedman (1977) parses some melodic constructions from the note list as further cues to support perception of meter,

Fig. 1. A performance of this melody (from the final movement of Mozart's Piano Sonata in B-flat Major, K.333) was analyzed by the system described in this article. Certain rhythmic figures in the score added to the problem of extracting metric information from the raw note durations.

which was found to be necessary in our work toward an automatic "foot-tapper."

Piszczalski and co-workers (1981) report success in labeling pitch and duration by parsing frequency-domain signal processing output from the analysis of single-voice real performance data. They have developed an interactive laboratory setting for accomplishing score transcription within user-supplied metrical contexts (Piszczalski and Galler 1977).

Knowledge-Based Recognition

Our current work extends some of these capabilities in the domain of real performance. First, we make a digital recording of a performance of an acoustic musical instrument. Then the lower-level (signal processing) methods produce a note list that contains frequency and timing information (currently without rests). Using this note list, higher-level processing methods attempt to deduce the musical and notational contexts that have been supplied by hand in all of the previous systems.

The approach incorporates knowledge about musical signals into all levels of decision making. Knowledge is required at the "microtime" level, where the signal processing operates to determine the identity of individual musical notes. *Notes*, for our purposes, are the smallest musically meaningful events, and we need to label them according to instrumental source, timing, pitch, loudness, articulation, and so on. The signal processing must deal with notes that overlap, with reverberation, and with mechanical noise. A detailed treatment of the issues at this level is given by Foster, Schloss, and Rockmore. The rest of this discussion will focus on the higher-level aspects of the system, that is, on the musical knowledge-based processing of a note list generated by the signal processing.

Starting with the musical example in Fig. 1, the

Fig. 2. The raw note list, displayed in a frequency-versus-time plot, as determined by signal processing of the digitally

recorded performance (cf. Fig. 1). The raw note list contains all of the information input to the higher-level analysis sys-

tem. The example in Fig. 1 is broken into two different graphs: m. 1–12 (above) and m. 13–26 (below).

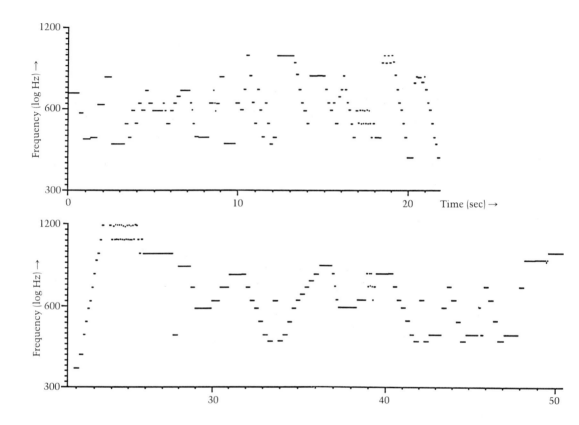

signal processing stage produces the raw data that are represented in the pitch-versus-time plot given in Fig. 2. The pianist gave us a pleasantly fluid rendition full of the kinds of real performance nuances that make the problem difficult. The piece is in 4/4 meter but contains several passages whose scored and/or performed rhythms are rather elusive. For example, the first half of the example consists of a sort of written-out accelerando in which the quarter-note unit is split into successively finer subdivisions, from eighth to triplet eighth, sixteenth, and finally a trill at the cadence. The real durations measured here do not allow discrimination between the scored values, so additional methods of gathering metric information are needed to

group the notes correctly. Elsewhere, trills must be distinguished from trill-like sixteenth note alternations (m. 10–11). And correct values have to be assigned across passages performed with tempo fluctuations, which are an essential ingredient of the style.

Anchoring to the Rhythm

If our example were played with machinelike precision, faithfully reproducing the duration proportions of the score, the problem of assigning a value (such as "eighth note") to each note would become quite simple. All we would need to know is the tempo of a quarter-note. For example, at M. M. 120 (beats per minute), an eighth-note's duration is 0.250 sec, a duration of 0.083 sec is immediately recognized as a triplet sixteenth, and so forth. It is commonly accepted that music played in this mechanical manner sounds very unnatural. In fact, musical examples generated with controlled random deviation from nominal durations still sound rhythmically artificial. Real data have much more complex patterns of temporal variation, and the ear-pleasing rhythmic "noise" arises from at least two sources. The instrument and human musculature are incapable of interacting and playing "perfectly," and this imparts short, note-to-note inaccuracies. Furthermore, the player always incorporates some amount of tempo fluctuation over both short and long note groups. Short groups of repeated note values always show some kind of nonuniformity, which can often be interpreted as a trend or gesture emphasizing some other feature (e.g., a trill). Longer groups, nominally phrases, contain sliding tempo changes that are constantly "going somewhere," particularly slowing down for cadences. The general notion is that timing deviations in real music are concentrated in certain spots and are not spread out in a random fashion over the entire piece.

The system must achieve some kind of mapping that allows reconstitution of the scored values from these "noisy" performed values. The inclusion of knowledge about scored rhythms is a successful approach. We know that eighteenth-century music is metrically consistent for long passages (whole movements are usually in one meter). This means that somewhere within the signal is a periodicity that we can tap our feet to, and that it forms a large grid spread over all rhythmic values of the example. Also, the meter must be deducible from a constrained set of acceptable choices.

First, we build a foot-tapper routine that catches this periodicity despite the vagaries of real performance. Our system's "foot" does not tap to the beat directly. Rather, it proceeds in several steps. The first is to mark certain structural points in the grid that will occur most often in multibeat intervals. We detect these points with a simple, powerful rule about the rhythmic style, in which adjacent note

durations are compared to find rhythmic accents. Figure 3 illustrates an aid to tuning the threshold according to which durations are distinguished by this rule. All sequential duration pairs in the score were labeled according to the relationships of their lengths (greater than, less than, or equal to). The real data were mapped into this representation on a note-to-note basis. For a given note pair, the relationship derived from the score was plotted in Fig. 3 according to the actual recorded lengths of the two notes. By charting the values along with a representation of the threshold, we came up with a good formula for distinguishing equal durations from nonequal ones. The same threshold has performed well in tests of different pieces. If the durations in a note pair are significantly distinguishable as short and long values in succession, then the latter one is marked as an *agogic accent*. Our rule goes through the list marking these accents. In the case of conjunct accented pairs, it marks only the last one. Rhythmic accents, marked "R" in Fig. 4, are labeled after the first pass with this rule. These new "anchor" points reliably outline a metric grid in all passages where notes have nonuniform values.

However, one large segment of the present example is left unmarked. A long string of running short notes (m. 7–10) leaves a large gap in our intended grid, because nothing satisfies the short/long distinction. This section is part of the written-out accelerando described above, and the grid must be accurately anchored to it in order to group its different subdivisions, which by virtue of their performed values appear identical. The technique we employed marks anchor notes by detecting melodic patterns that imply certain rhythmic accents. It checks for repeated pitches and scale-wise motion and as a side effect labels trills, collapsing the latter into a single duration. By making a pass over the full example with this rule, it marks the uniform-value passages. Elsewhere, new anchor points are marked or existing ones are confirmed (though we have been able to ignore this and other possible accent-weighting considerations). These new points are marked "M" in Fig. 4. We now have sufficient information about the performance to turn to matters of pitch and key.

Fig. 3. A graphic aid for studying the note-to-note differences of duration in the performance. This aid was developed to derive a suitable threshold for evaluating duration relationships. Each row and each column represents 0.025 sec. Every point in the square corresponds to a possible sequential pair of note durations in the performance. Each point is marked according to the relationship that was inferred from the original score: greater than (G), equal (E), or less than (L). The threshold level for determining the classification of equal or unequal note durations in the recorded data is marked by the fields of pluses and minuses, leaving a blank diagonal corridor of "equality" in the middle. The interactive program places a question mark next to any point placed incorrectly by the threshold setting. That is, for the threshold shown, there is only one point in this figure that will be incorrectly classified when the threshold is applied to the real data. The threshold setting shown in this figure is effective for different performances and agrees with the observations of Longuet-Higgins (1976).

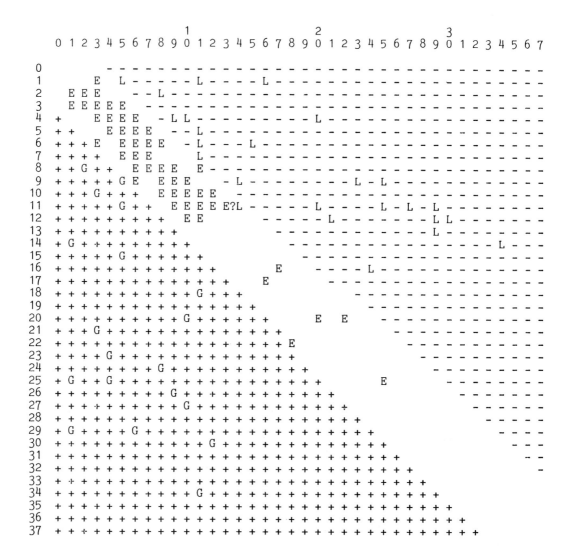

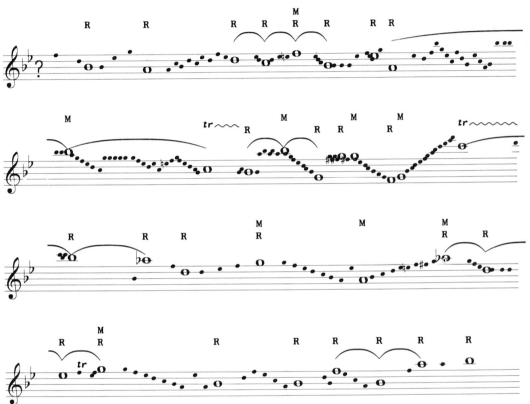

Determining Key and Clef

Figure 4 is displayed with the correct key signature,
clef, and pitch names. Our music navigator/editor
must recognize all significant attributes of a given
musical style and label notes in the terms most appropriate to a group of musicians concentrating on
production. Toward this end, our present system responds to harmonic structure and from this information represents the note list in the context of the
proper key. The Mozart example is interesting in
this respect because it completes a typical cycle of
local tonicizations from which the processing can
infer the correct key—rather than directly, as in a

trivial one-tonic excerpt. All music of the style in
question roves around a bit harmonically. For the
system to infer key properly as a listener does, it
should sense tonicizing implications of pitch relations and then the key-defining implications of the
temporary tonics.

Our key-recognizer supposes that the marked
rhythmic and melodic accent points are going to be
significant to the harmony. Since tonicizing pitches
are often accented in various ways, we gather the
accents that we already know about from earlier
passes. They are searched for important pitch relations and a list is made of all temporary tonicizations thus implied. These local tonics are then

weighted by frequency of occurrence and by their own key implications. From these statistics, a best-choice key is found; its third degree is then checked to see whether the mode is major or minor. The key choice is mapped onto a proper key signature, and all pitch names are assigned for agreement. Accidentals are added only to nonscale pitches (as long as the interval thus defined is melodically appropriate). For example, we allow the augmented second only in exceptional cases.

Pitch letter names are assigned to notes on the basis of the fundamental frequency data received via the raw note list. The example in Fig. 4 required no retuning or adaptive averaging techniques because it was played on a fixed-pitch instrument that was in close agreement with the frequency standard of the signal processing instrument. The worst difference between a measured frequency and its nearest standard pitch was 40 cents. An error of 50 cents would create ambiguities in pitch naming and require application of a technique for adapting to local frequency formations. Continuous-pitch instruments (strings, trombone, etc.) might require the more sophisticated algorithm, though initial trials with the flute and violin have been straightforward.

Thus, our signal processing routines have not named any incorrect octaves in the piano music, though this is a common error for some types of tones in other instruments (for example, overblown notes often have weak fundamentals). As needed, we can make corrections at this stage based on the context of the melodic contour. Stylistically uncharacteristic intervallic leaps are detected and brought back into line after it is affirmed that some energy was present in the melodically most correct octave (though it might not have been strong enough to convince the pitch detector in the first signal processing pass). Of course, there is a limit as to how much help higher-level routines can give the signal processing. There might be a few cases for which a mistake in note detection looks great musically.

The clef is determined simply by choosing the one (treble or bass) whose center best fits the average pitch of the example.

Table 1. The lengths of bridges in Fig. 5

Number	Average	Ratio	[Cluster Elements]			
28	0.986	1	[0.766	0.779 . . . 1.209	1.354]	
7	2.040	2	[1.976	1.988 . . . 2.084	2.144]	
2	3.815	4	[3.808	3.821]		

Determining Meter

The slurs between some accent points in Fig. 4 represent the first level of processing that will refine the metrical grid. These connections are established when adjacent pairs of accents are close to being evenly spaced in time, an indication that the segment was performed in an even tempo. We can connect these "simple bridges" to mark areas of local tempo stability, a first step toward deducing the metric relationships between values in performed rhythms. The next task is to propagate more bridges over the example, placing them so we can get a handle on tempo behavior between the rest of the anchor points.

Figure 5 shows the result of propagating bridges across the rest of the list. With the method used, the system looks ahead from simple bridges to see if it can extend to a note an equal bridge-width apart. Any remaining unconnected zones are examined in reverse on a second pass. The method of targeting ahead (or behind) for a particular time interval enables the system to ignore intervening syncopated accents and frees it to latch on to any note placed within a prescribed distance of the target. The resulting spans in Fig. 5 include only the three lengths of the original simple bridges, which by eye clearly stand in a ratio of 1 : 2 : 4. To make the system see these ratios as well, we invoke a cluster analysis of all bridge lengths. These values easily form distinct groups, and we find that their mean values are near the desired simple relationships. The result is listed in Table 1. The entries in the cluster column give the actual time values found in the real signal for the notes. The lengths were grouped by clustering. Then the groups were

MOZART PIANO SONATA

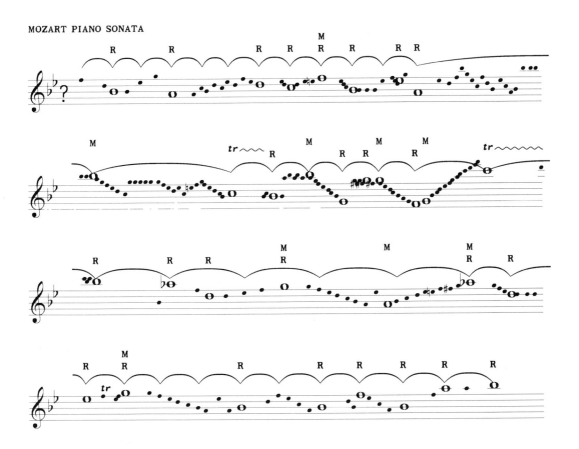

counted and averaged and their simple ratios determined by rounding. The simple 1:2:4 ratios reflect
the proportions that are easily visible by eye in Fig.
5. It is only coincidental that the tempo of the performance (ca. M. M. = 62) yields values in the clusters that are close to the resulting integer ratios.

Figure 6 gives some insight into the problem of
directly extracting rhythmic values from performed
durations. In Fig. 6(a), two identical rhythms from
different parts of the example are compared. Figure 7 is a graph of tempo fluctuations over the entire example. After integer ratios in the bridge
structure are found, a routine can be called that
normalizes these fluctuations. The note durations

spanned by each bridge are scaled (stretched or
compressed) so that the bridge span equals the integer value of all other spans in its cluster group.
Overall tempo fluctuations can thus be factored
out. Figure 6(b) shows the result of this method.

The most predominant bridge length is found in
Table 1. The corresponding period is an important
feature of the meter. Even if it does not turn out to
equal the beat or the bar (as in this example), it
does turn out to equal the unit that is conducted.
(In Fig. 1, this unit equals the half-note.)

All normalized note durations are first labeled according to their ratio with the conducted unit. Important sub- and superunit values are those that

Fig. 6. Two identical rhythms from different sections of the example in Fig. 1. (a) Raw data. The ticks (vertical bars) show 1-sec intervals. The dots above a tick are the dura- tion values recorded in m. 1–3; and below the tick, m. 16–18. (b) The same measures after normaliza- tion for tempo fluctuations (cf. Fig. 7).

Fig. 7. The tempo curve ob- served in the analysis of the example performance. The ordinate axis repre- sents a scale of beats per minute.

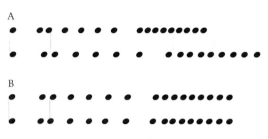

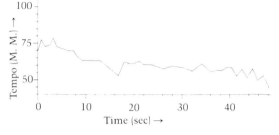

stand in duple or triple relationships to the con- ducted unit. All simple number ratios found are used to construct a latticelike ordering relating to the conducted unit (Fig. 8). From this structure we can determine the meter. The correct beat and meter values both correspond to one of these nodes and are identified by application of further style- based rules.

The next set of rules comprises a set of very par- ticular style-dependent heuristics, and here we will only trace the path that the example in Fig. 8 takes through them. The first rule categorizes the data as either slow or fast music by virtue of the overall complexity that shows up in the simple number ratios in Fig. 8. If it is fast, then durations fall into simpler relationships than for slow music; that is, double-dotted notes, half-notes tied to sixteenths, and the like do not tend to occur in fast time. Know- ing the likely tempo ranges for slow or fast eigh- teenth-century music, we can narrow down our choice of the beat node in the lattice. The current example is fast music according to our criteria, and we narrow down the choice of the beat to lie be- tween approximate bounds, in this case, M. M. 72 and M. M. 200 (see Fig. 8). Our best choice is at M. M. 124, which lies comfortably in the middle of this range, though the conducted unit at M. M. 62 might be considered close to a possibility. All oth- ers are well beyond the range. The rule is currently biased to use the median candidate, so we label the beat to be M. M. 124, or half of the conducted unit.

The last step is to pick the meter from a list of all stylistically acceptable possibilities. The list in- cludes duple (2, 4, 6, or 12) or triple numerators (3 or 9) over the denominators 2, 4, or 8. Some of the possible combinations never occur in eighteenth- century music; for example, 2/2, 12/2, 2/8. The du-

ple or triple decision can be made by checking the metric grid for the number of beats in its groups. The bridge ratios imply a choice of the duple list of numerators. The ratios of 4 : 2 : 1 are reevaluated as 8 : 4 : 2 in order to map them into the list of duple numerators. The denominator 4 is chosen because the subdivisions of the beat imply a quarter-note unit and appear as subbeat branches in Fig. 8. De- nominators of 8 or 2 would give improper subdivi- sions. The remaining possibilities are now 4/4 and 2/4 (8/4 does not exist), of which 2/4 is eliminated because the conducted unit never equals the bar in duple time. So, via several stylistically dependent rules, 4/4 is deduced as the meter and all durations are fit into the context.

Figure 9 illustrates the final labeling of the three- bar rhythm (1–3 and 16–18) from Fig. 6. The pro- portionally represented durations in Fig. 6(b) are as- sociated with ratio values corresponding to various nodes in Fig. 8. The ratios are finally used to get a common musical label for durations. The shortest proportions in Fig. 6(b) were all rounded to ratios of one-fourth of the conducted unit, since the con- ducted unit is now determined to be a half-note in 4/4 time. These shortest durations are labeled as eighth-notes in the notation of Fig. 9. Final items for transcription output (spacing, beaming, stem di- rection) are handled automatically by our resident manuscript program (Smith 1973).

Future Capabilities

The Mozart example demonstrates a basic capacity to parse a "noisy" performed rhythm for underlying metrical periodicities. Though this was accom-

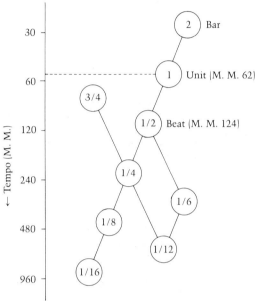

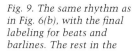

plished despite a few contradictory accents, it would probably need help in the face of very many more; certainly, a sequence of regularly spaced syncopated accents would lead to ambiguities. Orienting our research toward situations with multiple intermediate-level solutions, we are formulating a control structure with hypothesis formation and evaluation. Competing hypotheses will be tracked through until a best-fitting solution is decided upon. This is true as well for our approach to some of the lower-level problems that brute-force signal processing alone cannot solve. Signal processing will be directed by the control structure so that ambiguous note-detection situations can be refined in the context of confident ones. We consider the present example to be good evidence of the confidence that is achievable—one upon which we can assert our hypothesis formulations for all levels.

The control structure approach is akin to approaches that have been applied to artificial intelligence work in other domains. Complex signal processing allocation and feature recognition processes used in speech (Erman et al. 1980) and hydrophonics (Drazovich, Brooks, and Foster 1979) have provided a model for discussion of our current design work. As one would hope, considering the enormous human and machine resources these systems required in their design and construction, these systems are quite powerful. We are attempting to solve similar problems with much more modest means. The system we have described in this article can be summed up as a collection of modules that are strung together to test basic capacities and that can now serve as the building blocks for a "strategic analysis" approach. The study of new knowledge-based systems is made convenient by friendly qualities in the musical domain. Signals are clean, the answer can be known beforehand, and the data complexity can be tailored to any level of system expertise. This is seldom the case with speech or other real-world signals.

References

Abbott, C. 1981. "Microprogramming a Generalized Signal Processor Architecture." Paper presented at the 1981 International Computer Music Conference, 5–8 November 1981, Denton, Texas.

Chafe, C. 1978. "A Comparison of Timbres Inherent in Traditional Violoncello Playing." *Catgut Acoustical Society Newsletter* 29: 19–22.

Chafe, C. Forthcoming. "Modelling String Sound." In *Computer Music*, ed. C. Roads and J. Strawn. Cambridge, Massachusetts: MIT Press.

Drazovich, R., S. Brooks, and S. Foster. 1979. "Knowledge Based Ship Classification." Report to the Technical Workshop on the Application of Artificial Intelligence and Spatial Processing to Radar Signals for Automatic Ship Classification, February, New Orleans, Louisiana. (Contains unclassified information on knowledge-based recognition of acoustic signals in underwater surveillance.)

Easton, R. 1976. "Soundstream: The First Digital Studio." *Recording Engineer/Producer* 7(2):57–61.

Erman, L. et al. 1980. "The Hearsay-II Speech-Understanding System: Integrating Knowledge to Resolve Uncertainty." *Computing Surveys* 12(2):213–253.

Foster, S., W. A. Schloss, and A. J. Rockmore. 1982. "Toward an Intelligent Editor of Digital Audio: Signal Processing Methods." *Computer Music Journal* 6(1):42–51.

Haynes, S. 1982. "The Computer as a Sound Processor: A Tutorial." *Computer Music Journal* 6(1):7–17.

Kowalski, M., and A. Glassner. 1982. "The N.Y.I.T. Digital Sound Editor." *Computer Music Journal* 6(1):66–73.

Longuet-Higgins, H. C. 1976. "Perception of Melodies." *Nature* 263:646–653.

Longuet-Higgins, H. C. 1978. "The Perception of Music." *Interdisciplinary Science Reviews* 3(2):148–156.

Moore, F. R. 1982. "The Computer Audio Research Laboratory at UCSD." *Computer Music Journal* 6(1):18–29.

Moorer, J. A. 1975. "On the Segmentation and Analysis of Continuous Musical Sound by Digital Computer." Ph.D. dissertation, Stanford University. Also available as Department of Music Report STAN-M-3.

Moorer, J. A. 1977. "On the Transcription of Musical Sound by Computer." *Computer Music Journal* 1(4):32–38.

Moorer, J. A. 1981. "The Lucasfilm Audio Signal Processing Station." Paper presented at the 1981 International Computer Music Conference, 5–8 November 1981, Denton, Texas.

Piszczalski, M., and B. Galler. 1977. "Automatic Music Transcription." *Computer Music Journal* 1(4):24–31.

Piszczalski, M. et al. 1981. "Performed Music: Analysis, Synthesis, and Display by Computer." *Journal of the Audio Engineering Society* 29(1/2):38–46.

Rush, L., and J. Mattox. Forthcoming. "Mama Don't Allow No Tape Machine 'Round Here: The Digital Audio Production Facility." In *Computer Music*, ed. C. Roads and J. Strawn. Cambridge, Massachusetts: MIT Press.

Smith, L. 1973. "Editing and Printing Music by Computer." *Journal of Music Theory* 17(2):292–308.

Snell, J. 1981. "Real-Time Console for Live Performance of Computer Music and Recording Studios." Paper presented at the 1981 International Computer Music Conference, 5–8 November 1981, Denton, Texas.

Steedman, M. J. 1977. "The Perception of Musical Rhythm and Metre." *Perception* 6:555–569.

43

Scott Foster
Systems Control Technology
P. O. Box 10180
Palo Alto, California 94303

W. Andrew Schloss
Center for Computer Research in Music and
Acoustics
Department of Music
Stanford University
Stanford, California 94305

A. Joseph Rockmore
Systems Control Technology
P. O. Box 10180
Palo Alto, California 94303

Toward an Intelligent Editor of Digital Audio: Signal Processing Methods

Introduction

In this article, we will describe signal processing methods that have been developed for use in an automatic music analysis system. A companion article by Chafe, Mont-Reynaud, and Rush, also in this issue of the *Journal*, deals with higher-level issues, namely the recognition of musical constructs.

Unless one is willing to settle for a direct interface between musician and computer, such as the hardwired keyboard in the Xerox PARC system (Ornstein and Maxwell 1981), techniques must be developed to extract musical features from the sound itself. The approach of combining signal processing with knowledge engineering seems quite promising for music analysis. In contrast with many of the signals to which signal processing methods are applied, musical signals usually contain a great deal of order, chiefly in the form of quasi-periodicity (pitch and rhythm), and are not usually severely corrupted with random noise. By taking advantage of these features, one can construct mechanisms that provide musically significant descriptions of real data, such as tempo tracking ("foot-tapping"), meter analysis, attack characterization, pitch characterization (including vibrato), and timbre analysis. In this article and its

Computer Music Journal, Vol. 6, No. 1, Spring 1982

companion, sample results of some promising strategies for accomplishing these goals are presented.

In particular, we will concentrate on the problems of *primary segmentation*, that is, the first few passes through the data using little or no a priori knowledge. If we can mark the begin time for each new event in the music, the task of classifying and parameterizing each event is made easier. We have tried three approaches to this segmentation problem: (1) an amplitude thresholding method, (2) a linear predictive coding (LPC) method, and (3) a pitch detection method. While we will also discuss more advanced strategies, these are generally awaiting implementation and thus are not included in the examples.

Amplitude Thresholding Methods

The most straightforward approach to the segmentation of musical sound is amplitude thresholding. It seems reasonable to make a first pass through the data in the time domain, using a standard threshold technique. At the very least, this will provide a global signal detection facility, saving system resources for analyzing sound, not silence. At first, one might think that it would be possible to do much more than that. It turns out that there are rather severe limitations in applying this approach to real music.

A very simple amplitude threshold method will work well on synthesized data and, in many cases,

Fig. 1. A section from the
third movement of the
Piano Sonata in B-flat Major, K. 333, by Mozart.

Fig. 2. (a) Peak amplitude
plot of the Mozart example
given in Fig. 1. It is clear
that this plot obscures the
three descending notes at
point 2 (E-flat, D, C).
(b) This plot shows what
happens when the data
analyzed in Fig. 2(a) are
subjected to a highpass filter with a cutoff frequency
of 2230 Hz, thus eliminating the first three to five

harmonics. Suddenly the
three notes at point 2
spring into view (point 4),
and there seems to be
some hope of segmenting
the music. Unfortunately,
at point 3 there is a swell
that looks very much like
an attack but is not. To
distinguish between the
real attack at point 4 and
the spurious one at point 3
is very difficult.

on real data. We found it useful to operate on the
peak amplitude envelope, which is found by sliding
a window through the signal and plotting the maximum and minimum values in the window at each
point in time that they occur. It is necessary to
make the window large enough so that at least one
period of the waveform is contained in each window. This is a nonlinear method, but it gives a clear
view of the overall amplitude envelope and does
not smear time, as do the more standard types of
amplitude envelope estimation. In this way, we
take advantage of the nearly noise-free nature of periodic signals to maximize time resolution.

On real data, however, one comes to a point of
diminishing returns in the search for a heuristically
determined threshold value. Consider the short example given in Fig. 1. A peak amplitude plot of a
piano recording of this selection is given in Fig. 2(a).
It should be clear from the figure that it is difficult
to find a single threshold that will be low enough
to detect all notes but high enough to avoid spurious ones.

Unfortunately, many complex elements, such as
a legato playing style or room reverberation, can
confuse peak amplitude segmentation. For example,
the three descending notes at point 2 in Figs. 1 and
2(a) (E-flat, D, C) are obscured. Interestingly, the
original notation does not call for these three notes
to be overlapping, which they obviously are. This is
an example of the performer playing something
that differs subtly from what was written, although
one does not notice it aurally until it is pointed out
by the analysis. Even resonances within an instrument can cause problems. Figure 3 shows a plot of
the eighth-note D in the second measure of the
Mozart example (point 1 in Figs. 1 and 2[a]). What
seems to be a large amount of amplitude modulation (AM) at about 37 Hz is apparently caused by
beating of the D with the previous E-flat that is still
ringing. In some cases, such AM might complicate
the choice of a proper threshold.

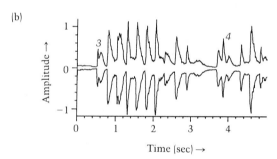

Figure 4, a three-dimensional plot of a section of
the same piano piece, suggests one way to get more
mileage out of this peak amplitude segmentation
approach. It is easy to see that the upper partials die
out much more rapidly than the fundamental.
Therefore, the upper harmonics will tend not to
overlap in time, making segmentation much easier.
Figure 2(b) shows what happens when the data plotted in Fig. 2(a) are first subjected to a highpass filter
with a cutoff frequency of 2230 Hz, thus eliminating the first three to five harmonics (the pitches in
the passage lie between 440 and 700 Hz). The three
notes at point 2 spring into view (point 4 in Fig.
2[b]), and there seems to be some hope of segmenting the music by means of amplitude thresholds.

It turns out that the battle has not yet been won.
At point 3 in Fig. 2(b), there is a swell that looks

Foster et al.

Fig. 3. A single note on the piano, lasting for about 0.24 sec. This is a close-up of point 1 (D natural) in Figs. 1 and 2(a). The large *amount of AM at about 37 Hz is apparently due to beating with the E-flat just before the D, which is still ringing.*

Fig. 4. Three-dimensional plot of a section of the piano piece shown in Fig. 1. It is easy to see that the upper partials die out much more rapidly than the fundamental and the first few harmonics. There- *fore, segmentation will be easier if the material is first highpassed (see Fig. 2[b]), thus eliminating the overlap in time of the lower spectral components.*

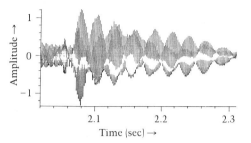

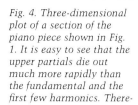
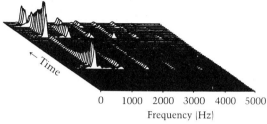

very much like an attack but is not. To distinguish between the real attack at point 4 and the spurious one at point 3 is very difficult. Even further processing, such as smoothing, *n*-point differencing of the signal, or various line segment approximation techniques (Strawn 1980), require a considerable amount of refinement to deal with these sorts of cases. It may be possible to reject double attacks caused by secondary swells using minimum duration criteria, but this is really correcting an error already made in the analysis. Furthermore, a duration of about 60 msec, which could be required to remove the spurious attack in Fig. 2(b), is in fact in the musically significant range. Fortunately, there are other methods (discussed in the following sections) that complement this approach.

Autoregressive Segmentation

As shown in the previous section, an instrument will ring through several notes in many musical contexts. Any attempt to segment by amplitude alone will result in missed events. The method explored here is the application of a segmenter that is based on an *autoregressive (AR) model* fit of the audio data (Makhoul 1975). This allows one to segment the data automatically and will succeed in cases where the standard "energy threshold" or amplitude-based segmenter will fail. This method is also applicable to instruments with inharmonic spectra, such as percussion instruments. This technique has never been applied before to musical data, and the results have proven its usefulness.

AR techniques such as this are regularly employed in the speech community to achieve LPC of speech (Markel and Gray 1976). A musical signal $y(t)$ is assumed to fit a pth-order autoregressive model of the form

$$y(t) = \sum_{i=1}^{p} a_i y(t - i) + u(t).$$

Usually, $u(t)$ is considered to be a white-noise driving function that is filtered with the a_i coefficients to yield a spectrum matching that of the music segment. For our application, we might hope to model the spectrum of the instrument well enough with the a_i's that the input $u(t)$ is just exactly the driving function used by the musician—a pair of pulses per period for a bowed instrument or an impulse for a plucked or percussive instrument. In practice, however, $u(t)$ contains a good deal of modeling error no matter how the a_i coefficients are calculated.

How to calculate the a_i's is a subject of great discussion in the spectral estimation field (see, for example, Burg 1975; Morf 1977). There are several ways to compute a so-called least-squares solution that minimizes $\Sigma u^2(t)$. Of course, no method can work well if the instrument is not well modeled as an AR process. Additionally, numerical problems can occur, since many sounds are best modeled with a_i's representing poles on or very near the unit circle (in the z-plane).

There are a number of recursive algorithms available with which one can efficiently estimate time-varying coefficients $a_i(t)$ from a sliding window of data. The coefficients can be calculated for most of the criteria in common use, and a variety of data windows are available, notably square and exponential windows.

Thus, these algorithms can "track" the $a_i(t)$ coefficients through the sound data. So now in addition to the sound data $y(t)$ we have p additional data streams $a_i(t)$. Suppose we reverse the sound data in time and define $y^*(t)$ as

$$y^*(t) = y(-t).$$

We can run this time-reversed data through the above process to yield the functions $a_i^*(t)$.

How are $a_i(t)$ and $a_i^*(t)$ related? For each time point t, $a_i(t)$ represents an AR model fit to the data prior to and including t. $a_i^*(-t)$ represents a similar model fitted to the data including and after the time point t. Of course, the $a_i^*(t)$ represents a different model, since the AR modeling was done in reverse. Fortunately, it is easy to calculate a set of "forward predicting" a_i's from the "backward predicting" a_i^*'s. Thus, we have a pair of comparable models that represent AR models before and after t. These models must now be compared to determine the likelihood that something happened at time point t.

One way to compare these two models is to run each model on the data for which the *other* model was fitted and look at the energy in the error signals. The total error energy should always be less for the model that was fitted to the data; this is guaranteed if we use an exact least-squares method. The error energy is likely to be very nearly the same if the models are similar—it is hoped that this will reflect the fact that nothing happened at time point t. On the other hand, if the sound data change in character at time t, say, with an abrupt attack or pitch change in some component of the sound, the models will be dissimilar and the "cross-computed" error energies will be large compared to the "fitted" error energies.

This algorithm has intuitive appeal but requires multiple passes through the sound data. We have implemented a simpler version, diagrammed in Fig. 5, which makes one pass. We did not experiment with a wide variety of estimation techniques or windows. Most of our runs were made using an extended least-squares recursive algorithm (Lee,

Friedlander, and Morf, in press) implemented in ladder form. This algorithm has an exponential window to "forget" older data. The time constant of this window can be adjusted from just a few samples to infinity. In the latter case, no windowing occurs—at each point in time an exact least-squares solution is available for all the data up to that point. In addition, this algorithm uses square roots internally, which provides improved numerical conditioning.

This method works amazingly well in cases in which the amplitude information alone is insufficient because the energy does not diminish enough to segment according to simple or even adaptive thresholding. Figures 6 and 7 show interesting cases with flute and cello in which this method has proven effective. Our most difficult example is a vibraphone with the sustain pedal down (Fig. 8). The AR segmenter was able to pick out the attacks, while the amplitude plot showed only a "wash" of energy throughout the run. We made the problem even harder by recording with the tremolo on and the sustain pedal down, which adds extreme amplitude modulation to the sound.

In more difficult passages, the AR segmentation and the amplitude-based segmentation methods can be complementary. This is because the AR model is not sensitive to amplitude changes, while the amplitude method is not primarily sensitive to pitch. That is, repeated attacks of one note are not detectable using the AR method unless the model changes significantly between the attack and steady-state portions of a note. This is not typical of many instruments and, as a result, the AR method will miss repeated attacks. A graphic example of this is the mistake of the player that is undetected in Fig. 8. However, amplitude segmentation is often possible in these cases, since repeated notes on most instruments involve a new attack. For example, on the piano, one must "let go" of a key in order to repeat it, which results in a new attack.

Pitch Segmentation

Along with attacks as cues to new events, a change in pitch corresponds to a new "note." The basic

Foster et al.

Fig. 5. Autoregressive (AR) segmentation procedure. The fit of two models is compared on current data at each point in time. One model is recursively track-ing the data, the other is recursively tracking older data. In practice, the "older" model is obtained via a delay of the current model. The likelihood function ℓ(t) at the bottom indicates whether the data immediately prior to t fit the same model as the sound data immediately after t.

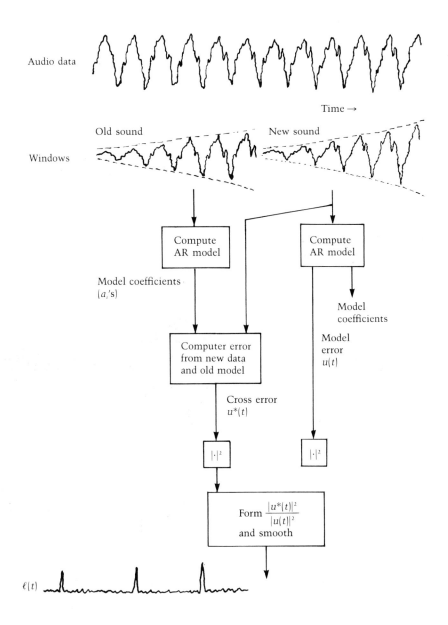

Fig. 6. Two notes played on a flute. Segmentation based on peak amplitude detection is not a good approach due to the

large amplitude variations. However, the AR segmenter detects the new note.

Fig. 7. Result of AR segmentation applied to a fragment of the "Sarabande" from the Suite for Unaccompanied Cello in D minor *by Bach. Note the difference between (top)*

the prescriptive notation (Seeger 1958) and what was played (middle). Also, note that detail from the trill is captured in the AR plot.

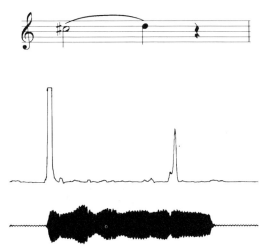

Written:

Played:

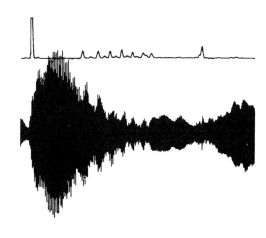

melodic structure is outlined by following pitch change. This is a reasonable way to segment and, in many forms of music, is the central parameter.

This technique could be called *adaptive attack detection*. The idea is that the attack of a note is easier to determine and characterize after the spectral components of the note have been determined. We can go to the middle (or loudest or clearest) part of a note and model the note as a summation of partials with an amplitude distribution that we can measure. We can then track this distribution *backward* in time to find the attack and its characteristics. As a by-product, we have an indication of the time-varying spectra of the note, which may be useful for identification or other purposes. The principal result, however, is that if the note is properly modeled and tracked, then the attack can be characterized with great precision even though it may be "swamped" by loud broadband signals or other pitches.

The corresponding routine in our system makes only one pass through the sound data. The data are processed in reverse in short time segments. The locations and amplitudes of the spectral peaks in each segment are estimated using the Fast Fourier Transform (Rabiner and Gold 1974; Oppenheim

and Schafer 1975). These are "clustered" to determine a pitch by an algorithm similar to the one described by Piszczalski and Galler (1979). The results from the pitch detector are compared over consecutive time frames until the existence of a certain pitch becomes definite. This test is based on consistency from the pitch detector as well as on the intensity level of the cluster.

Once a definite pitch is determined, subsequent time frames are analyzed for their fit to this pitch. The fit is determined as a weighted sum of the estimated amplitudes of those components in the frame that apparently belong to the pitch cluster

See Fig. 9 for an example of the pitch detection sequence.

Fig. 8. A major scale (two octaves) played on a vibraphone with the sustain pedal down and the motor on. The motor produces a very strong periodic tremolo (AM), which is clearly visible in the amplitude plot. The reason for performing this test with the motor on is that it creates an even more demanding situation for the segmenter. The global amplitude envelope (bottom) is entirely at odds with the actual attacks produced by the player, who is playing the scale with an accelerando such that the rate of attacks crosses the period of the tremolo. It is clear that any strict amplitude segmenter will segment according to the periodic AM of the tremolo and will completely miss the actual attacks, which are obscured since the notes ring over each other. Interestingly, the AR segmenter missed a note at point 1, which should be a G natural. This is because the player actually erred and repeated the previous F. We were puzzled by this omission, and had to listen to the example to confirm that the F was repeated. It is hard to hear this mistake because the ascending scale context is so strong and because the speed of the notes at the end of the flourish blurs the attacks significantly (the scale ends about six times faster than it starts). As mentioned in the text, the AR segmenter will miss repeated attacks on the same note.

Fig. 9. This waterfall-like display is produced by the pitch segmenter. The spectra of short time segments are displayed in a three-dimensional format, starting with the first E-flat in the score example and ending with the high G. The pitch detector clusters the peaks in each segment to determine pitch. When a note is detected, the pitch is "frozen" (except for minor fluctuations), and the cluster is tracked backward to find the attack. The attacks are marked with a spike over the third harmonic to make the pitch changes more obvious.

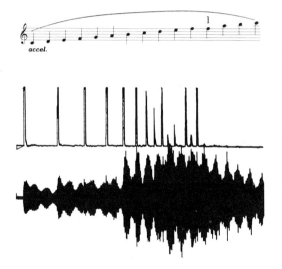

teristics of the note are well represented by the series of fits; the onset time can be determined by interpolating between frames to estimate when the fit drops to, say, one-half of its maximum value. See Fig. 9 for an example of the pitch detection sequence.

To cope with minor fluctuations in the fundamental pitch frequency, we track the pitch simultaneously while looking for the attack. This is done with a local pitch detection on each segment. Thus, we have a one-pass mechanism that accurately determines note onset times and that can not only handle but characterize moderate tremolo (amplitude variation) and vibrato (frequency variation) in the notes. It was this algorithm that provided the data input to the analysis discussed by Chafe, Mont-Reynaud, and Rush (1982).

Polyphonic Segmentation

How well do these segmentation ideas work when we try to transcribe polyphonic music? Clearly, if an entire orchestra is playing, we cannot at this juncture hope for a descriptive score for each player

(those with estimated frequencies near the expected partial frequencies). For most instruments, this fit parameter increases smoothly as the note "undecays." (Remember, we are processing the sound in reverse.) The fit then drops dramatically as the note "un-attacks." The dynamic amplitude charac-

from a single audio track. If only two voices are present, as in a violin duet, we can still expect ambiguities to occur. For instance, whenever the voices merge into unison (playing the same note) it may be impossible at the signal processing level to tell which is which following the unison.

The situation improves if we try to transcribe a small number of different instruments. For voices in dissimilar registers, it may be possible to separate them with conventional filtering methods. Consider the simple case of a piano and a sharp-cutoff, highpass/lowpass filter. We record a two-part melody, in which each hand is playing (at most) one note at a time. To separate the melodies, we try placing the filter cutoff frequency between the highest note in the bass melody and the lowest note in the treble melody. This may not always be possible. If the filter is a highpass, the upper melody comes through perfectly, of course. Interestingly, the lower voice also comes through substantially—and it still sounds low. The higher harmonics of the lower voice lie above the cutoff frequency and are not attenuated. These harmonics imply the low pitch, which is perceived even though no energy is present at the fundamental (pitch) frequency. If we now switch to a lowpass filter, we find that the upper voice is essentially eliminated, since all its harmonics are above the cutoff frequency. The upper harmonics of the lower voice are also attenuated, but the fundamental (at least) is not. Thus, the lower voice comes booming through accompanied only by the soft tapping of the hammers from the upper voice. This indicates that with only a high-performance, tunable, lowpass filter, we should be able to isolate the lowest voice in an ensemble at least well enough to segment it (mark start times and pitches). This could be done by slowly raising the cutoff frequency until the filter begins to pass significant energy from the segment in question.

Other tricks can be employed. The listener does not usually perceive that instruments are played at widely varying amplitude levels. Even though several voices may be sounding simultaneously, one voice (or group of like voices) will often stand out at each point in the music. This should help with detection and identification. Some instruments, such

as the piano, do not allow much input from the player in regard to the time-varying spectra of a single tone. Thus, spectral template matching is a suitable technique for identifying piano tones, whereas it is much less appropriate for most other instruments. After detection, the spectral template is useful for "hearing through" the piano to analyze the remaining sound. Since most of the energy in a piano tone is concentrated in narrow frequency bands, these bands can be masked or ignored during subsequent analysis. Suppose that the notes G and B-flat are sounding simultaneously, and the G has been located. The B-flat should be easy to detect by this method, since the B-flat harmonic frequencies do not overlap the G's frequencies significantly. This is essentially the technique used by Moorer (1975; 1977) to transcribe two simultaneous guitar melodies.

Unfortunately, a great deal of polyphonic music is played in harmonies where harmonics overlap to a large extent. Unisons and octaves are also common. These cases are more difficult and not amenable to this simple masking approach. A more sophisticated approach for dealing with these overlapping harmonics might be formulated as follows. Many instruments produce frequency modulated sound (vibrato) that is often distinctive and even regular. In perhaps most cases the harmonics are all modulated together; that is, they are "frequency locked." We may be able to track the pitch through these minor fluctuations accurately enough to enable a precise estimation of the strengths of the harmonic components. Now we repeat this procedure while tracking a different simultaneously sounding pitch. By comparing the results from these two passes, it may be possible to unravel the actual harmonic distributions played or at least to confirm the two pitch estimates.

Another useful trick in the polyphonic case is to focus the processing on the attacks. Two voices will rarely enter simultaneously, even if they are meant to. A short glimpse of the attack of one voice alone may be available. Again, some instruments have well-known attack characteristics; but many do not. Even if the attack cannot be recognized, it may be possible to tell which instrument is "speaking" early with a pitch analysis on the brief segment.

Pitch analysis and instrument identification are areas where knowledge of musical signals can be a great help in processing. We are currently experimenting with *pitch-synchronous harmonic estimation*. In this technique, we use pitch-tracking methods to provide a Fourier-series analysis with the window size set to be an integer multiple of the period. This allows a much more precise measurement of the harmonic component strengths than discrete Fourier transforms of arbitrarily blocked data. These results in turn can be used to characterize the evolution of the spectral content of the sound over very short intervals, such as one or two periods. This technique affords very high resolution for those segments that are *clean*; that is, a single periodic sound with no appreciable noise or interference. For these cases, it may be possible to use the spectral estimate versus time characterization to identify the source instrument (if it is unknown), or certain aspects of player performance, for instance, the position of the violinist's bow.

Conclusion

These strategies are typical examples of using knowledge about the target domain (music signals) to combine various basic methods into mechanisms with musically significant results. This "goal-oriented" processing approach contrasts with other research, which has tried to preserve all the musically relevant information through each stage of a hierarchical processing sequence (Moorer 1975; Piszczalski and Galler 1977). Nothing is lost until the end, when final decisions characterizing the sound are made. The trouble with this traditional approach is that the intermediate data can be much larger and more cumbersome than the original sound. To reduce this data volume, the system is forced to start making decisions. These reduce the amount of data, but information is always lost, especially when a bad decision is made.

We prefer the point of view of an evolving hypothesis that characterizes the original sound. The system makes decisions, but they are not necessarily final. The original sound is always retained and is reexamined in part from time to time to re-

fine the hypothesis. An effort is made to make the "easy" or "sure" decision first in order to build up a context for the "hard" decisions.

As we have indicated, a wide variety of situations is regularly encountered in musical signals. In many cases, good mileage can be obtained from the application of basic signal processing techniques. Unfortunately, for any given technique it is usually easy to find real data for which the technique gives ambiguous or incorrect results. It is therefore important to develop strategies that overcome these difficulties by invoking the various techniques at the appropriate times and combining the results in decisions that are consistent with the music domain.

Acknowledgments

We would like to acknowledge the assistance of Julius O. Smith and John Strawn. This work has been conducted jointly by Systems Control Technology, Inc. and the Center for Computer Research in Music and Acoustics at Stanford University, under the sponsorship of the National Science Foundation. This material is based on work supported by the National Science Foundation under Grant No. MCS-7923282.

References

Burg, J. P. 1975. "Maximum Entropy Spectral Analysis." Ph.D. dissertation, Stanford University Department of Geophysics.

Chafe, C., B. Mont-Reynaud, and L. Rush. 1982. "Toward an Intelligent Editor for Digital Audio: Recognition of Musical Constructs." *Computer Music Journal* 6(1):30–41.

Lee, D. T. L., B. Friedlander, and M. Morf. In press. "Recursive Square-Root Ladder Estimation Algorithms." *IEEE Transactions on Acoustics, Speech, and Signal Processing.*

Makhoul, J. 1975. "Linear Prediction: A Tutorial Review." *Proceedings of the IEEE* 63:561–580.

Markel, J. D., and A. H. Gray, Jr. 1976. *Linear Prediction of Speech.* New York: Springer-Verlag.

Moorer, J. A. 1975. "On the Segmentation and Analysis

of Continuous Musical Sound by Digital Computer."
Ph.D. dissertation, Stanford University Department of
Computer Science. Also available as Department of
Music Report STAN-M-3.

Moorer, J. A. 1977. "On the Transcription of Musical
Sound by Computer." *Computer Music Journal*
1(4):32–38.

Morf, M. et al. 1977. "Efficient Solution of Covariance
Equations for Linear Prediction." *IEEE Transactions on
Acoustics, Speech, and Signal Processing* ASSP-25:
429–433.

Oppenheim, A., and R. Schafer. 1975. *Digital Signal Processing.* Englewood Cliffs, New Jersey: Prentice-Hall.

Ornstein, S., and J. Maxwell. 1981. "MOCKINGBIRD: A
Composer's Amanuensis." Paper presented at the 1981
International Computer Music Conference, 5–8 No-
vember 1981, Denton, Texas.

Piszczalski, M., and B. Galler. 1977. "Automatic Music
Transcription." *Computer Music Journal* 1(4):24–31.

Piszczalski, M., and B. Galler. 1979. "Predicting Musical
Pitch from Component Ratios." *Journal of the Acoustical Society of America* 6(3):710–720.

Rabiner, L. R., and B. Gold. 1974. *Theory and Application of Digital Signal Processing.* Englewood Cliffs,
New Jersey: Prentice-Hall.

Seeger, C. 1958. "Prescriptive and Descriptive Music
Writing." *Musical Quarterly* 44(2):185–195.

Strawn, John M. 1980. "Approximation and Syntactic
Analysis of Amplitude and Frequency Functions for
Digital Sound Synthesis." *Computer Music Journal*
4(3):3–24.

Foster et al.

44

F. Richard Moore

Computer Audio Research Laboratory
Center for Music Experiment, Q-037
University of California, San Diego
La Jolla, California 92093 USA

A General Model for Spatial Processing of Sounds

Introduction

We perceive sounds in a spatial context. Without visual cues, we can often tell the direction or distance from which a sound comes. We also perceive things about the apparent acoustic environment of sounds, such as whether they seem to come from a reverberant cave or a padded cell. Multichannel recordings can portray the spatial characteristics of recorded sounds independent of listening conditions. In ways analogous to looking through windows, we can discern things about one acoustic environment through headphones or loudspeakers while we move about in another.

Ideally, spatial processing of sounds would allow us to have complete control over the acoustic environment heard through the loudspeakers. Each sound located within this heard environment could have a specified "size," direction, distance, and apparent motion. We can use computers to gain such control over the spatial characteristics of sounds, but for musical applications we must always specify the acoustic processing we believe will produce the intended psychological effect. Spatial processing therefore involves the simultaneous consideration of two sets of problems: the physical characteristics of a space to be simulated and the psychological characteristics of sounds presented to listeners over loudspeakers.

The work described in this article consists of (1) a conceptual model for representing the problem of spatial processing and (2) a description of an implementation of this model in the context of the Cmusic sound synthesis program (Moore 1982).

This work was described by the author in a talk presented at the International Computer Music Conference in Venice, Italy, in September 1982.

Computer Music Journal, Vol. 7, No. 3,
Fall 1983

Localization

Much attention has been paid to our ability to localize sounds. Roederer (1975) points out that, especially at high frequencies, intensity cues (amplitude differences between the sound waves arriving at our two ears) help us to determine the direction from which a sound comes. At lower frequencies, time cues also contribute to localization (Molino 1974). What distinguishes high from low? At a speed of about 335 m per second, it takes a sound wavefront about 500 μsec to travel the 17 cm or so between our ears. A 2000-Hz tone therefore has a wavelength about equal to our interaural distance. At frequencies below this, interaural time delay can be an important factor in localization.

For interaural time differences to be important, something must exist in our neural mechanism that *correlates* the signals coming into our two ears. Neural models of such crosscorrelators were proposed as early as 1959 (Licklider 1959), and physiological evidence for such mechanisms has since been found (Rose et al. 1969). Roederer also points out that the existence of such a crosscorrelation mechanism has implications for spatial control:

> It is easy to see that the location . . . will depend on the interaural time delay, which in turn depends on the direction of the incoming sound. Two tones, a mistuned interval apart, fed into *separate* ears, may "foul up" the crosscorrelator: The gradually shifting phase difference between the two tones . . . will be interpreted by this mechanism as a changing difference in the *time of arrival* of the left and right auditory signals, hence signaling to the brain the sensation of a (physically nonexistent) cyclically changing sound direction! This is why two pure tones forming a mistuned consonant interval, presented di-

chotically with headphones, gives the eerie sensation of a sound image that seems to be "rotating inside the head" [Roederer 1975].

For localization to occur, we must know not only the direction of a sound source but also its distance. In research based on earlier work by Gardner (1962) and Wendt (1961), Chowning (1977) demonstrated that the relative mixture of direct-to-reverberant sound is a powerful cue for determining the distance between sound source and listener. By combining simulated cues for angular location, distance, and velocity (i.e., Doppler shift) with artificial reverberation (Schroeder 1962) via the Music V program (Mathews et al. 1969), Chowning was able to create convincing illusions of moving sound sources.

Improvements in our understanding of the acoustics of rooms (Schroeder, Gottlob, and Siebrasse 1974) allowed Moorer (1979) to synthesize a concise yet powerful model for artificial reverberation. Following Schroeder's suggestions, Moorer based his processing model on a tapped-delay line filter (also known as a *finite-impulse response* [FIR] filter) to simulate the "early echo" response of a room followed by a bank of recirculating filters (also known as *infinite-impulse response* [IIR] filters) to produce the effect of dense global reverberation. Moorer used the data gathered by Gottlob (1975) and Schroeder to obtain "reasonable-sounding" values for the tap-delay and gain parameters of the delay-line filter, together with acoustic data on sound absorption, to obtain similar values for the comb filters. These all led to a loose but useful simulation of Boston's Symphony Hall, with suggestions for alternatives.

Psychophysics Versus Performance

To gain more general control over spatial characteristics of musical sound, we need a general way to obtain reasonable-sounding values for the processing algorithm. The work of Schroeder, Gottlob, and Siebrasse, on which Moorer's values are based, was oriented toward improving the subjective impression of the sound of concert halls. With spatial processing, however, we wish not to analyze but rather to synthesize the sound of a concert hall or some other acoustic environment. In terms of the *tapped-delay-plus-recirculating* (TDR) filter model, we must find ways to synthesize the gain, delay, and recirculation parameters according to a specified musical intent.

Direct manipulation of such psychophysical parameters as interaural time delay can lead to compelling illusions of sounds in space. Using headphones or biteboards (which a listener grasps with the teeth) to control relative head position, interaural time delays can be used to obtain TDR filter parameters. We would expect the results of such an approach to produce strong impressions of localization.

Unfortunately, the relative positions of listeners and sound sources in a concert situation is unpredictable. No two listeners in a concert hall hear exactly the same sound, rendering such factors as interaural time delay useless as control parameters for music intended to be heard under concert conditions. Even the relative amplitude of sound entering the two ears of each listener is likely to vary throughout the performance space.

Even though no two listeners in a concert hall hear the same thing, there is an invariance in their subjective perception—they all hear the same music, if from different vantage points. We are clearly able to compensate for our own vantage points, except under unusual conditions that fool the perceptual mechanism. (The failure of this compensation is the basis of most so-called illusions.) In the visual realm we compensate readily for the difference between size and distance, and we make similar sonic distinctions between loudness and intensity.

Since we cannot control psychophysical parameters directly in a concert, a practical model for spatial processing must be based on physical characteristics of the real or imaginary space or spaces to be simulated. This suggests modeling the playback situation itself, rather than the details of the listener's perception of it—the approach taken in this study. The model described here is based on the following elements:

The relevant characteristics of the listening

Fig. 1. An outer room enclosing an inner room. The circles on the periphery of the inner room represent holes in its walls (loudspeaker positions). A sound source is shown in the upper right quadrant. The small circle represents

the base of the radiation vector associated with this source, and the line points in the direction of greatest radiation (the length of the vector is proportional to the amplitude of radiation in that direction).

Fig. 2. Signal flow diagram of a basic TDR filter. A characteristic set of delays $(D[\cdot])$ and frequency-dependent gains $(G_\omega[\cdot])$ determine the operation of the tapped-delay (FIR) part *of the filter. The summed output of the delay taps is then further processed by a recirculating (IIR) filter R, which provides dense-echo reverberation.*

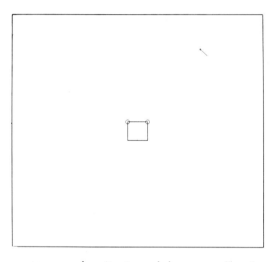

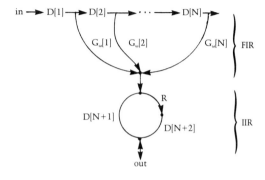

The *outer room* represents the illusory acoustic space from which the sounds emanate. The *inner room* represents an actual or intended performance space that holds listeners and loudspeakers. Loudspeakers are modeled as acoustic "windows" communicating with the illusory space outside the perimeter of the listening space. A particular set of "important" paths taken by the sound from sources located in the outer room to the loudspeakers is used to obtain time-varying TDR filter parameters. The TDR filter structure is extended to allow a separate tapped-delay section for every source location and for every sound channel (Figs. 2 and 3).

In practice, the numerous FIR stages can be collapsed into a single long delay with dynamic, movable taps, each with frequency-dependent gain.

For example, the inner room might be a living room with loudspeakers placed in each corner, while the outer room's specifications suggest the acoustic properties of a reverberant cathedral. From within the listening space, we listen through "holes" in the walls to sounds that exist in the outer room. Depending on proximity to the loudspeakers, each listener will hear these sounds from a slightly different perspective. Information is presented at each loudspeaker about all sound sources in the virtual outer room. The differences in perception among listeners in the inner room are analogous to perspective distortion. A sound moving along a circular path centered around the inner

space, such as its size and shape, as well as the number and placement of an arbitrary number of loudspeakers along its perimeter

The acoustic properties of the illusory space, including its size, shape, and sound-absorbing characteristics, specified independently of the characteristics of the listening space

The radiating characteristics of the sound sources themselves, including their positions within the illusory space and their directional characteristics, again specified independently of the properties of the space or spaces in which they occur

Uncontrollable aspects of the concert situation, such as the listeners' head positions, present no greater problem from the standpoint of this model than they do in a traditional concert. Each listener hears something different, but all listeners gain individual perspectives on the same illusion.

Overview of the Model

The present model represents the performance and illusory acoustic spaces as a room within a room (Fig. 1).

Fig. 3. Extended TDR filter structure for spatial processing. Time-varying (FIR$_i$(t)) filter stages (one per speaker channel per sound source location) with both dynamically movable taps and frequency-dependent gains form the multichannel "early echo image" of the sound. Each sound source transmits to each loudspeaker along a direct path plus as many reflected paths as there are distinct surfaces in the outer room. A monophonic version of the multichannel early echo image is used to drive the global reverberator, which has decorrelated multichannel output.

Fig. 4. Multiple radiation vectors and moving sources. The group of four radiation vectors in the upper left quadrant represents a radiating "surface" comprised of several directional sources (each source radiates, in general, a different version or component of the "same" sound). In the lower right quadrant, a sound path for a single moving source is depicted.

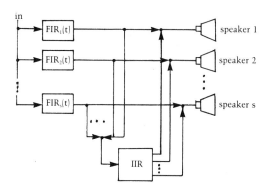

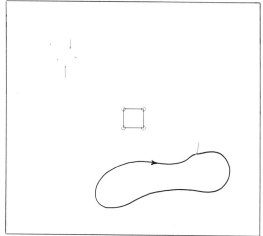

room would pass more closely to someone sitting close to a wall than to someone sitting in the center. After listening a while, however, all listeners should be able to agree on sound source locations regardless of where they sit in the inner room, at least as well as they could by listening through holes to actual sound sources moving about in a real outer room.

Sound sources may in general be located at any position in the outer room. Having more loudspeakers leads to a clearer depiction of the outer room. But even a small number of speakers can give the listener a great deal of information about the entire outer room and all sound source locations in it. Imagine, for example, that a performer in the outer room is walking in a circle around the inner room while beating on a tambourine. If we listen to the tambourine performance through two holes in the front two corners of the inner room (stereo), our ability to locate the sound will be excellent when it is in the front (the azimuth—or angle between the front-back line and a line pointing toward the sound source—lies between the two loudspeakers), less good when it is to the sides (outside the "cone" described by the lines drawn between the listener and the two loudspeakers), and ambiguous at the single point when it is directly behind the listeners.

Thus even two loudspeakers would do a fair job of representing the entire two-dimensional plane of locations in the outer room. More loudspeakers would sample the acoustic field of the outer room with greater spatial frequency, lessening source location ambiguity.

By specifying sound paths in the outer room separately from the characteristics of the listening space, we separate the intended percept from its manner of presentation. Thus a given spatial composition might exist in several versions: one for two loudspeakers in a small room (a living-room-stereo version), one for headphones, and one for eight channels of sound in a large room (a concert version). The sound paths themselves would be identical in each version, that is, the composition itself would be *invariant*. Only the inner room specification would vary according to intended presentation.

A sound source in the outer room is modeled as one or more radiation vectors, each with an adjustable position, directionality, magnitude, and field shape. A single radiation vector suffices for most sound sources. Multiple radiation vectors (Fig. 4) may be used to describe sound-radiating surfaces to an arbitrary degree of precision. Individual radiation vectors may have time-varying characteristics, allowing sounds to move in arbitrary paths through-

Fig. 5. Front-back distinctions in stereo. The direct
sound from one source is
obstructed in the left
channel, while the other is
not. While this case is too
simple to allow an audi-
tory distinction to be
made, more complex infor-
mation in the early echo
image of the sound gives
perceptible front-back
cues, even in stereo.

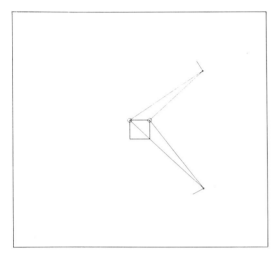

purely refractive source. Higher frequencies would tend to "beam" through the hole if it were large compared to a wavelength of the transmitted sound. Good loudspeaker design minimizes this effect, however, producing as faithfully as possible a far field (i.e., nondirectionally differentiated) representation of the acoustic field sampled at a point by an ideal microphone.

Details of the Model

The major features modeled are the following:

Loudspeaker placement in the listening space
Geometry of the virtual acoustic space
Radiation of sound sources into the virtual space
Early echo response of the virtual space
Global response of the virtual space

Loudspeaker Placement

Under normal circumstances it is impossible to create the illusion that the sound source is closer to the listener than the loudspeakers. Therefore, the shape of the inner room is determined by the shape of the performance hall and the location of the loudspeakers within it. For quadraphonic sound, the loudspeakers are normally considered to be at the four corners of a square (or other quadrilateral); for stereo they are normally at the front two corners of a square. For stereo headphones, the two loudspeakers are considered to be in the middle of the two side walls of a very small listening space (the size of one's head). In general, the loudspeakers are considered to lie at the vertices or along the perimeter of an arbitrary, closed polygon.

Virtual Acoustic Space

In two dimensions, the geometries of the inner and outer rooms are those of arbitrary, closed planar polygons. Each surface of the outer room is made an effective part of the acoustic space by being allowed to contribute to the early echo response. Because of the crudity of our spatial perception,

out the illusory space. In a real room, the number of radiated sound paths between source and destination is infinite. Restricting the model to two dimensions and including only the "important" sound paths results in the inclusion of only the direct paths from a source to each loudspeaker, plus one reflection from each wall of the outer room to each loudspeaker.

If the outside wall of the inner room is made absorptive (acoustically opaque), it is possible to minimize undersampling effects, emphasizing, for example, front-back distinctions even when only two front stereo loudspeakers are used (Fig. 5).

The outer room and radiation-vector specifications allow a complete description of the *perceptual effect* intended by the musician. Given the inner room specifications, computations for the requisite delays, attenuations, Doppler shifts, and so on can be made automatically from the specification of the desired perceptual effect.

The extent to which real loudspeakers are as acoustically transparent as holes in walls is questionable, of course. The infinite baffle loudspeaker model (which is basically just a hole in an infinite wall), allows sound to radiate hemispherically (on one side). This requires a hole that is small compared to the transmitted wavelengths, making it a

Fig. 6. Detailed radiation pattern for (x=0, y=0, θ=315°, amp=1, back=.1), in which the amplitude of the radiation in the direction opposite to 315° is one-tenth that of the forward radiation (−20 db) (a). Detailed radiation pattern for (x=0, y=0, θ=315°, amp=1, back=0), in which the amplitude of the radiation in the direction opposite to 315° is zero (−∞ db) (b). Detailed radiation pattern for (x=0, y=0, θ=315°, amp=1, back=1), in which the amplitude of the radiation in the direction opposite to 315° is equal to that of the forward radiation (−0 db) (c).

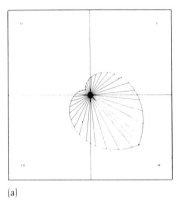

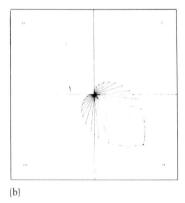

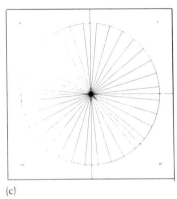

(a) (b) (c)

simple shapes such as squares and rectangles should usually suffice for the outer room.

The inner room polygon is determined not by the actual shape of the performance hall but by the location of the loudspeakers within it. Four speakers at the corners of a square 10 m on a side therefore define a square inner room 10 m on a side, regardless of the actual size and shape of the listening room. No particular allowance is made in this model for reverberant or other properties of the listening space, since matching and/or compensating for these is largely independent of the spatial characteristics of the illusory outer room.

Radiation Vectors

Sound sources are injected into the space by means of radiation vectors. A radiation vector **RV** is completely defined by the quintuple

$$RV = (x, y, \theta, amp, back),\qquad(1)$$

where

  x and y are the base of the vector (all coordinates are given in meters, with the origin (0, 0) in the center of the inner room);
  θ is the direction of the vector (an angle of 0 rad points to the right as viewed from above);
  amp is the length of the vector and is used to scale the amplitude of the source sound; and
  back is the relative amplitude of the radiation in the direction opposite to that of the vector.

Sound is considered to be radiated in a supercardiodal pattern principally in the direction of the vector but with smaller amplitude to the sides and back (see Fig. 6).

The *back* value given in the specification of the radiation vector varies between 0 and 1. A *back* value of 0 implies no back radiation and a strongly directional radiation pattern. A *back* value of 1 implies an omnidirectional radiation pattern. The supercardiodal shape of the radiation pattern is given by:

$$r(\phi) = scaler \text{ for } radiation \text{ in} \\ ray \text{ direction } \phi \\ = \left[1 + \frac{(back - 1)\,|\theta - \phi|}{\pi} \right]^2,\qquad(2)$$

where θ and *back* are defined as in Eq. (1). A single sound source emanates from one or more radiation vectors. Each radiation vector may be located anywhere outside the inner room in the space described by the outer room. Each radiation vector represents a source of sound in the virtual sound space.

Sound Paths

Sound sources radiate to each speaker channel in two ways: (1) by direct paths and (2) by reflected paths. There is exactly one potential direct path between each source and each speaker channel. For each source, there is also one potential reflected

Fig. 7. Direct radiation be-   radiation between a single
tween a single source and   source and four loud-
four loudspeakers (note   speakers (note cut
the cut path) (a). Reflected   paths) (b).

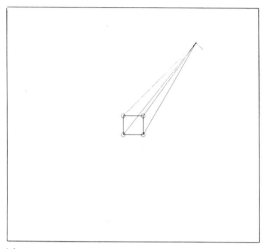

(a)

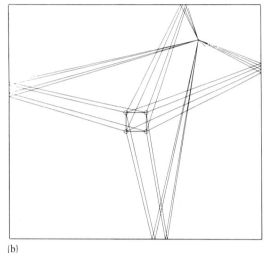

(b)

path to each speaker channel from each wall of the outer room. Thus a single source radiating sound to quad loudspeakers in a square outer room is modeled with four potential direct paths (one to each loudspeaker) and sixteen potential reflected paths (one from the source to each wall to each loudspeaker) (Fig. 7).

The shape of each path determines the following parameters:

Attenuation along the path due to distance
Frequency-dependent attenuation due to air absorption
Frequency-dependent attenuation due to reflection (absorption by the reflecting surface)
Absorption due to collision with the outer walls of the inner room (these are modeled as being completely absorptive)
Time delay due to the finite speed of sound transmission

The paths are calculated in the following manner. Each direct sound path is simply a straight line between the source and the loudspeaker. One reflection path is used for each wall of the outer room. Of the possible reflection paths from a given wall, the one chosen for this model is the *principal* reflection path, that is, the one that results in the great-

est amplitude at the loudspeaker position. The reflection point chosen is therefore the one that results in the shortest distance from source to wall to loudspeaker. This is the point at which the angles of sound incidence and reflection are equal. Such reflections are easily modeled by standard acoustic techniques involving virtual sources located on the opposite side of the reflecting wall.

Cut Factors

Modeling the outer wall of the inner room as completely absorptive yields good directional distinctions among various source locations. Therefore, a sound path is potential until it is determined whether it is obstructed by the inner room. An obstructed sound path is considered to be "cut" by the barrier, and to be completely absorbed at that point. We can define the *cut factor* for a sound path to have a value of 0 when the path is obstructed by a barrier and 1 when it is unobstructed. The cut factor can then be combined multiplicatively with the overall amplitude of the sound on a particular path.

Since the cut factors may dynamically vary for moving sound sources, flipping back and forth between 0 and 1 as ray paths change with changing source locations, some mechanism must be used to avoid clicks (due to stopping or starting the sound too abruptly). A simple method for dealing with this problem involves a linear interpolation between the 0 and 1 values as necessary to avoid clicks. A more sophisticated approach would be to model the refraction of the path around the edge of a cutting surface, but it seems unlikely that the computation involved would be justified on perceptual grounds.

Early Echo Pattern

The early echo pattern for each sound source is a collection of delays and frequency-dependent gains. At each moment, for each radiation vector, one potential direct path exists between the base of the vector and each loudspeaker. The cut factors determine whether the path is actually present or not. In addition, one potential path exists from each radiation source to each reflecting surface of the outer room to each loudspeaker. Thus the total number of sound paths included in this model is

$$N_{path} = N_{vec} N_{chan} (1 + N_{surf})$$ (3)

sound paths modeled, where

N_{path} is the total number of paths;
N_{vec} is the number of radiation vectors;
N_{chan} is the number of speaker channels; and
N_{surf} is the number of reflecting surfaces in the outer room.

For each of these paths, P_i, $i = 1, 2, \ldots, N_{path}$, we define a delay $D[P_i]$ and a frequency-dependent gain $G_\omega[P_i]$:

$$D[P_i] = \frac{Dist[P_i]}{c}$$ (4)

and

$$G_\omega[P_i] = \frac{Amp[P_i] Rad[P_i] Cut[P_i]}{1 + Dist[P_i]},$$ (5)

where

$Dist[\cdot]$ is the length of the path (the symbol $[\cdot]$ stands for the path argument);
c is the speed of sound;

$Amp[\cdot]$ is the amplitude scalar given in the radiation vector that is the source of the path;
$Rad[\cdot]$ is a "radiant," that is, an amplitude scaler for the direction of radiation ($= r(\phi)$ for the path); and
$Cut[\cdot]$ is the cut factor for the path (0 if cut and 1 if not).

A changing source position would likely cause a changing delay parameter, which would result in pitch shift as a side effect (shrinking delay values would shift the pitch up and vice versa). The magnitude of this pitch shift is precisely the same as that of a Doppler shift for a moving sound source. Since the TDR filter (with properly interpolated delay taps) provides such shifts automatically, no specification of Doppler shift is necessary for moving sounds with this model (they happen automatically!).

The complexity O_{dir} of the direct path computation is proportional to

$$O_{dir} \propto N_{vec} N_{chan}.$$ (6)

The complexity of the reflected path computation is then

$$O_{refl} \propto N_{vec} N_{chan} N_{surf},$$ (7)

where the factors are defined as above. The overall complexity of the computation involved is proportional to the total number of paths:

$$\begin{aligned} O_{tot} &= O_{dir} + O_{refl} \\ &\propto N_{vec} N_{chan} (1 + N_{surf}) = N_{path}. \end{aligned}$$ (8)

Since for each path P_i we must compute both $D[P_i]$ and $G_\omega[P_i]$ as defined above, the total amount of computation for this model is significant. If all radiation-vector elements are allowed to be time varying, for example, new values must in general be calculated at every sample.

Global Reverberation

The output of the dynamic TDR filters is further processed by the global reverberator, which simulates the dense reverberation of the outer room after the first 60 msec or so. The characteristics of the global reverberation may be obtained from specifi-

Fig. 8. Cmusic score example. This score produces a
sound that moves in a 10-
m-radius circle centered
about the point (32,22).

cations of the overall size and shape of the outer room and the reflective properties of its walls.

For the purposes of this model, the global reverberator accepts a single (monophonic) signal input consisting of the mixed outputs of all TDR filter signals. Parallel comb filters with frequency-dependent loop gains may be used to achieve dense echo. Output channels of the global reverberator (one for each loudspeaker) must be statistically decorrelated from each other in order to produce a good subjective effect (Schroeder 1980).

Implementation in Cmusic

The model has been implemented as a special unit generator in the Cmusic sound synthesis program. A special macro called SPACE allows an especially simple and direct control over the space unit generator. The initial implementation allows for simple room geometries and as much automatic operation as possible. Figure 8 shows a sample Cmusic score that moves a sound in a circle about an arbitrary point.

Conclusion

The Cmusic implementation described here is not a complete implementation of the spatial model, but it has been sufficient to test the hypothesis that the model yields convincing results. It produces convincingly localized sound images when used conservatively, such as with front sources in stereo. It also performs as well as expected under adverse conditions, such as with rear sources in stereo.

The main advantage of this model lies in its generality: from a physical specification of an intended perceptual effect, the model provides a tool with which to realize this effect computationally under given playback constraints. Either a change in the constraints, such as a change in the number or location of loudspeakers, or a more fundamental change in the method by which the computational structure is realized does not affect the intention or its specification. The problems of specification of the intended effect, realization of the computational

```
#include ⟨carl/cmusic.h⟩
set stereo;
{
{The following are all default values which are repeated
    here only to show what they are}
{specify outer room 100 meters square}
    set space = 50,50 −50,50 −50,−50 50,−50;
{specify inner room 6 meters square}
    set room = 3,3 −3,3 −3,−3 3,−3;
{specify speakers in front corners}
    set speakers = 3,3 −3,3;
{global reverb time = 3 seconds}
    set t60 = 3;
{overall scale factor for global reverb}
    set revscale = .15;
{stop computing when reverb tail under cutoff}
    set cutoff = −60dB;
}
ins 0 circ;
    seg b4 p5 f4 d 0;      {b4 = envelope}
    osc b2 p7 p8 f2 d;     {b2 = x}
    osc b3 p7 p8 f3 d;     {b3 = y}
    adn b3 b3 p10;         {p10 = y-offset}
    adn b2 b2 p9;          {p9 = x-offset}
    osc b1 b4 p6 f1 d;     {b1 = carrier}
{specify 1 radiation vector with x = b2, y = b3,
    theta = 0, amp = 1, and back = 1 (omni source)}
    SPACE(b1,1) b2 b3 0 1 0dB;
end;
SAWTOOTH(f1);
SINE(f2);
COS(f3);
ENV(f4);
{play a note on instrument circ:} note 0 circ 4
{p5 = main amplitude:} 0dB
{p6 = carrier frequency:} 1000Hz
{p7 = circle radius in meters:} 10
{p8 = circular motion period:} 2sec
{p9,p10 = x,y center of circle:} 32,22
;
sec;
{allow 3 seconds for reverb tail to die away}
ter 3;
```

means by which to produce this effect, and the playback constraints imposed in a given performance situation are neatly separated.

The model could readily be extended to three (or more) dimensions. Improvements in the computational structure are likely to follow from improvements in our understanding of both room acoustics and psychoacoustics.

References

Chowning, J. M. 1977. "The Simulation of Moving Sound Sources." *Computer Music Journal* 1(3):48–52.

Gardner, M. B. 1962. "Binaural Detection of Single-Frequency Signals in Presence of Noise." *Journal of the Acoustical Society of America* 34:1824–1830.

Gottlob, D. 1975. "Vergleich objektiver akustischer Parameter mit Ergebnissen subjektiver Untersuchungen an Konzertsälen." Ph.D. dissertation, Georg-August Universität.

Licklider, J. C. R. 1959. "Three Auditory Theories." In *Psychology: A Study of a Science*. Ed. I. S. Koch. New York: McGraw-Hill.

Mathews, M. V. et al. 1969. *The Technology of Computer Music.* Cambridge, Mass.: MIT Press.

Molino, J. 1974. "Psychophysical Verification of Predicted Interaural Differences in Locating Distant Sound Sources." *Journal of the Acoustical Society of America* 55:139.

Moore, F. R. 1982. "The Computer Audio Research Laboratory at UCSD." *Computer Music Journal* 6(1):18–29.

Moorer, J. A. 1979. "About This Reverberation Business." *Computer Music Journal* 3(2):13–28.

Roederer, J. G. 1975. *Introduction to the Physics and Psychophysics of Music.* New York: Springer-Verlag.

Rose, J. E. et al. 1969. "Some Possible Neural Correlates of Combination Tones." *Journal of Neurophysiology* 32:402.

Schroeder, M. R. 1962. "Natural Sounding Artificial Reverberation." *Journal of the Audio Engineering Society* 10:219–223.

Schroeder, M. R. 1980. "Toward Better Acoustics for Concert Halls." *Physics Today* 33(10):24–30.

Schroeder, M. R., D. Gottlob, and K. F. Siebrasse. 1974. "Comparative Study of European Concert Halls." *Journal of the Acoustical Society of America* 56:1195–1201.

Wendt, K. 1961. "The Transmission of Room Information." *Journal of the Audio Engineering Society* 9:282.

45

John Stautner and Miller Puckette
Experimental Music Studio
Massachusetts Institute of Technology
Cambridge, Massachusetts 02139

Designing Multi-Channel Reverberators

Introduction

We present here a methodology for the design of digital reverberators. Some properties of digital recursive networks that are useful for reverberation simulation are considered along with simplified assumptions of the behavior of sound in rooms. The method presented leads to a wide variety of possible reverberation networks, though only one such possibility is presented in detail.

These results have led to the design of some reasonable four-channel reverberators useful for computer music. While no attempt has been made to imitate the ambience of an existing room or concert hall, the methods described herein may lead to such applications when they are combined with a consideration of the perceptual importance of attributes of the soundfield in a real room.

Overview

In designing reverberators, we must attempt to account for both the early part of the reverberant response and the overall quality of the long-term response. It is very difficult to model exactly the long-term behavior of sound in an enclosure, but use of recursive delay networks can provide a satisfactory and practical approximation. Much can be said about the pattern of sound reflections during the first 100 msec or so of the reverberant response, however. It is convenient as well as perceptually meaningful to simulate these reflections directly by considering the configuration of the room to be modeled.

Both of these methods are present in our design procedure. First, we create a skeletal recursive network where each delay unit is assigned to a speaker. The output of a delay unit feeds a speaker

Computer Music Journal, Vol. 6, No. 1, Spring 1982

and also feeds one or more of the other delay units in the network. In this way, the echoes spread among the speakers and increase in density during the reverberant response. The feedback pathways are characterized with a feedback matrix, G, and ways of choosing G to yield a stable response are presented.

Next, a specific feedback matrix is chosen that gives a skeletal network appropriate for use with four output channels arranged in a square. Methods of simulating the early response and further refinements of the design procedure are introduced within the context of this particular example.

Finally, some hints for efficient computation are given, and excerpts of a sample Music 11 implementation are shown.

Model of the General Delay Network

A network of delays may be described as an extension of the comb filter (Fig. 1) whose system equation is usually written

$$y = z^{-\tau}(x + gy), \qquad (1)$$

where x is the input, y is the output, τ is the delay in samples, g is the feedback coefficient and $z = e^{i\omega}$. We may generalize this recursive network by replacing the delay with n delays in parallel, each with an input and an output signal. The feedback signal is replaced by n feedback signals, each of which is some combination of the output signals. If we denote the feedback signal to the ith delay unit as f_{i}, then we have

$$f_i = \sum_{j=1}^{n} g_{ij} y_j. \qquad (2)$$

If we adopt the language of matrices, the system equation becomes

$$Y = D(X + GY), \qquad (3)$$

where X is a vector whose components are the n

Fig. 1. A comb filter with
feedback coefficient g and
delay of τ samples.

Fig. 2. The network of
Fig. 1 generalized to vector
signals.

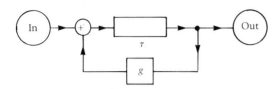

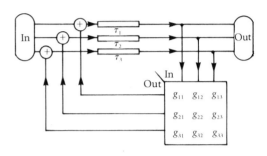

inputs, Y a vector of n outputs, G the matrix with the components in Eq. (2), and D a matrix of the form

$$D = \begin{bmatrix} z^{-\tau_1} & & & 0 \\ & z^{-\tau_2} & & \\ & & z^{-\tau_3} & \\ & & & \cdot \\ & & & & \cdot \\ 0 & & & & \cdot \end{bmatrix} \quad (4)$$

The form of the network is shown in Fig. 2.

The network may be modified by introducing other elements such as filters. For simplicity, however, we consider the stability and frequency response of the skeletal network shown. Additional elements will be useful later for imitating early echo patterns as an aid to directionality and enhancement of quality.

Iterating Eq. (3) gives the system function

$$Y = DX + DGDX + DGDGDX + \dots,$$

$$= D(I + (GD) + (GD)^2 + (GD)^3 + \dots)X,$$

or

$$Y = D(I + A + A^2 + A^3 + \dots)X, \quad (5)$$

where I stands for the identity matrix and A replaces GD for future convenience. The properties of this system function determine most of the qualities of the delay network.

Writing the system function in the form in Eq. (5) makes it clear that a condition for stability is that successive powers of A become smaller instead of larger. To develop sufficient conditions for this, let $|X|$ denote the vector norm of X (in real terms the root-mean-square [RMS] amplitude of the signal X), defined by

$$|X| = \sqrt{|X_1|^2 + |X_2|^2 + \dots + |X_n|^2}.$$

Then if for any reason we have

$$|AX| < k|X| \quad (6)$$

for all X and some positive $k < 1$, then the norms of the terms of the expression

$$X + AX + A^2X + A^3X + \dots$$

decrease exponentially. This implies convergence of the sum, which in turn implies the stability of the network. Since D is unitary, that is, has the property

$$|DX| = |X|,$$

we may rewrite Eq. (6) as

$$|GX| < k|X|. \quad (7)$$

That the condition in Eq. (7) is also sufficient for stability is also true but by no means obvious.

The simplest means of ensuring the truth of Eq. (7) is to let G take the form

$$G = U \begin{bmatrix} k_1 & & & 0 \\ & k_2 & & \\ & & \cdot & \\ & & & \cdot \\ 0 & & & & \cdot \end{bmatrix} \quad (8)$$

where none of the k's exceed k in Eq. (7), and U is unitary. Since we are presently assuming that G has real entries, we may write the condition that U be unitary as

$$\sum_{k=1}^{n} U_{ik}U_{jk} = \begin{cases} 1 & \text{if } i = j; \\ 0 & \text{otherwise.} \end{cases}$$

Stautner and Puckette

The simplest example of a unitary matrix is the identity, which gives parallel comb filters for the network. A nontrivial example is

$$U = \begin{bmatrix} \sin(r) & \cos(r) \\ -\cos(r) & \sin(r) \end{bmatrix}$$

for any r. Since the product of two unitary matrices is again unitary, matrices of the above form can be applied repeatedly to mix the outputs of pairs of delays, thus forming more complex networks.

Equation (3) may now be rewritten as

$$Y = \frac{D}{I - A} X, \qquad (9)$$

still in analogy to the comb filter. Since D consists only of delays, the numerator has no coloring effect. The denominator acts in much the same way as it does in the conventional comb filter. Multiplying Eq. (9) by $I - A$ gives

$$Y - AY = DX.$$

Since $|AY| < k|Y|$, we have

$$(1 - k)|Y| < |Y - AY| < (1 + k)|Y|.$$

Substituting DX for $Y - AY$, and using the fact that D is unitary,

$$\frac{1}{1 - k} > \frac{|Y|}{|X|} > \frac{1}{1 + k} .$$

This inequality gives an upper and lower bound on the frequency response of the network, taken as the ratio of the total RMS power of the speaker outputs Y to the RMS power of the input signals X. For a simple comb filter, these upper and lower bounds are nothing more than the peaks and troughs of the comb filter frequency response described by Schroeder (1962). When delays of various lengths are used in the general recursive network, however, the frequency response achieves these peaks and troughs at very irregular intervals in frequency, which removes the buzzy sound that comb filters give. The coloration is usually much less bothersome than that of the equivalent number of comb filters in parallel.

A Four-Channel Network

For most of the remainder of this discussion, we will assume the skeletal delay network given in Fig. 3, which is suitable for use in a four-channel playback environment where the speakers are arranged at the corners of a square. The feedback matrix G for this network is given by

$$G = \begin{bmatrix} 0 & 1 & 1 & 0 \\ -1 & 0 & 0 & -1 \\ 1 & 0 & 0 & -1 \\ 0 & 1 & -1 & 0 \end{bmatrix} \cdot g,$$

where

$$|g| < \frac{1}{\sqrt{2}} .$$

A source signal may be introduced at any point in this network, such as the end of one of the delays.

An advantage of this delay network is that the speaker outputs are mutually incoherent signals that are spatially responsive to the input channel of the source. Past research (Meyer, Burgtorf, and Damaske 1965) has shown that incoherent output signals are important to create a diffuse soundfield, which is characteristic of good concert hall reverberation (Beranek 1962; Schroeder, Gottlob, and Siebrasse 1974). Consider also the growth of the soundfield: if the input is a pulse in channel 1, we first hear an output pulse in channel 1, then in the adjacent channels, and finally in the diagonally opposite channel before the echo density grows and spreads among the four channels. This behavior acts as an additional cue of source position and of the physical extent of the simulated space.

Definition of Early Response

Much research has been done to determine the importance of the early response, which occurs roughly during the first 50–100 msec of the reverberation impulse response. Measurements and simulations of the early reflections in concert halls have demonstrated that time separation, frequency

Fig. 3. Basic feedback network with source intro-
duced in left front
channel.

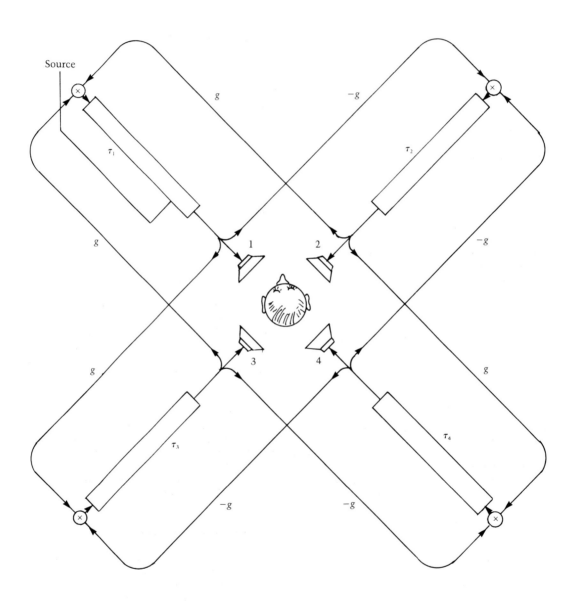

Fig. 4. Various pathways of
sound from source to lis-
tener. For objects, only the
first reflections of the
source signal from the objects are shown.

characteristics, and incident angle of the reflections
are important perceptual cues of reverberation (Jordan 1969; Barron 1971; 1974). The design of the reverberation network can be extended to simulate
the effect of these early reflections.

Ultimately, these results may be applied in the
design of reverberation networks that can simulate
the favorable properties of existing concert halls or
even aid in the design of new halls. Our purposes
here are not to carry out such a simulation, but
rather to find some guidelines for designing an early
response leading to a good sounding reverberator
suitable for general use. In doing this, we consider
a greatly simplified description of the behavior of
sound in rooms.

To model the early response, we simply add various proportions of the source signal directly into
the delay loops for each channel. The length of
each delay determines the amount of the early response that can be simulated for that channel and
direction.

Actual delays, amplitudes, and incident directions of the early reflections may be chosen by
defining a room of particular dimensions and employing the method of image sources to determine
the reflections from the walls (Moorer 1979). An
enhancement of this method is to define objects in
the room and consider reflections from them as
well.

The pathways of the sound rays for such a room
are shown in Fig. 4. The amplitude of the sound
pressure emanating from a simple source (point
source) drops as $1/distance$ when the distance is
greater than a few wavelengths or so. Near field
effects of actual sound radiators are generally very
complicated, so when the distance from the source
is less than a few wavelengths we can approximate
the amplitude of the sound pressure as being virtually unchanged.

Using these rules, we can find the amplitude of
the direct sound signal or of that ray traveling the
direct path from the source to the listener. In general, the attenuation of a ray coming from an image
source will be approximately

$$att = k^m/src\_to\_lis,$$

where k is the amplitude reflection coefficient of

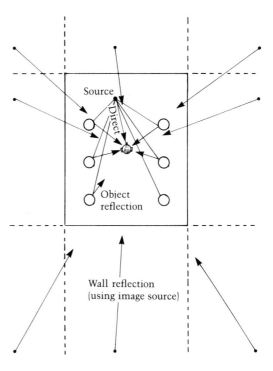

the walls, m is the number of walls the ray has
traversed, and src_to_lis is the distance from the image source to the listener position. The corresponding delay is

$$del = src\_to\_lis/VEL,$$

where VEL is the speed of sound. For objects, we
may consider only the first reflection of the sound
source from the object in order to simplify the calculations. As a further simplification, we will treat
all objects as either large and flat like walls or
cylindrical and with a given diameter.

Reflections from the large flat objects may be
treated as a single wall reflection, with the corresponding amplitude attenuation.

For the reflections from cylinders, we have the
following approximations for distances greater than
a few wavelengths from the cylinder:

$$att = q \cdot (1/src\_to\_obj) \cdot (1/\sqrt{obj\_to\_lis})$$

and

$$del = (src\_to\_obj + obj\_to\_lis)/VEL,$$

where q is some attenuation coefficient representing the overall reflection characteristics of the object, src_to_obj is the distance from the source to the object, and obj_to_lis is the distance from the object to the listener. Near field effects of sound scattering from cylinders are very complicated, and it is sufficient to approximate the amplitude attenuation when the distance from the object is less than a few wavelengths simply as

$$att = q \cdot (1/src\_to\_obj).$$

The choice of values for k and q in the above relationships is not critical but should be made reasonably. Typical values for k can be found by consulting an acoustics text (e.g., Beranek 1954); normally, the quantity given is the energy absorption coefficient. The amplitude attenuation k is related to the energy absorption coefficient by

$$k = (1 - absorption)^{1/2}.$$

Absorption coefficients normally vary with the frequency and type of material, but a typical value for plaster is 0.04 at 500 Hz, yielding

$$k = \sqrt{1 - 0.04} = 0.98.$$

Setting a value for q is less straightforward, since q is highly dependent on the size and shape of the object and also on its position relative to the source and listener positions. For now, we may arbitrarily estimate a value of about 0.2. A more detailed way of choosing this coefficient will be discussed later.

The speaker channels for the reflections are chosen simply to correspond to that quadrant around the listener in which the incident sound ray approaches. This in effect samples the space into four discrete directions.

By addition of these early reflections into the delay network, the echo density of the early response is increased substantially. Without this initial density of reflections, the early part of the simulated reverberation response would sound ragged, especially for impulsive sounds. On the other hand, if the early reflections are too dense, the resulting sound will be mushy. Furthermore, the directional

relationships of the reflections resemble the reverberation onset in a real room and contribute to the sense of spaciousness.

Long-Term Response

The choice of delay lengths gives at least a sense of the size of the room being modeled. As a rough guide, the lengths determine the interval between successive echoes, which is described statistically for real rooms by the mean free path of sound in the room. Shorter delays give more coloration (as do smaller rooms), which can be objectionable for long reverberation times.

Choosing incommensurate delay lengths is important to avoid flutter and achieve a smooth response. Schroeder suggests using lengths spanning a ratio of 1:1.5 (Schroeder 1962). Our longest delay lengths were typically about $^1\!/_{10}$ sec. If much longer delays are desired, it may be useful to add a flat network with short delays to improve echo density.

Another important part of the long-term response of room reverberation is the frequency-dependent effect of air absorption. To simulate this effect, we insert lowpass filters at the output of each delay. The cutoff frequencies of the filters depend on the length of each delay (Moorer 1979).

Additional Modifications

A richer and more realistic sounding reverberation can be obtained by simulating the frequency characteristics of the reflections from walls and objects. Most wall materials show the greatest energy absorption in the middle frequencies between 500 and 2000 Hz or higher. This effect can be conveniently simulated by using a lowpass or a bandstop filter.

Some typical absorption coefficients for hard surfaces given by Kuttruff (1973) indicate a gently rolling off lowpass-filter effect. To simulate this behavior, we calculate the corresponding amplitude attenuation coefficients and then normalize these values so the maximum amplitude is 1. An example of these values is shown in Table 1. A first-order IIR filter with its attenuation (att) at 2000 Hz

Table 1. Finding the filter characteristics to simulate wall reflections

Domain of measurement	Frequency (Hz)					
	125	250	500	1000	2000	4000
Energy absorption coefficients for hard surfaces (from Kuttruff 1973)	0.02	0.02	0.03	0.03	0.04	0.05
Resulting amplitude attentuation of reflected wave	0.99	0.99	0.985	0.985	0.98	0.975
Normalized values to model filter, using attenuation of 0.99	1	1	0.995	0.995	0.99	0.985

chosen to match that of the wall attenuation is sufficient to model this behavior. The normalizing factor found is then used as the amplitude coefficient k in the equations given previously. For image sources whose rays have traversed several walls, the filter attenuation at 2000 Hz can be set to $(att)^m$, and the amplitude coefficient becomes k^m as before.

The frequency behavior of reflections from cylinders may be summarized as follows. For sound of wavelengths larger than the diameter of the object, very little sound is reflected, and it is reflected in all directions. Sound of wavelengths smaller than the diameter tends to be reflected back toward the source from the object and shadowed on the side of the object away from the source.

We may conveniently separate this behavior into two cases: (A) a listener on same side of object as source and (B) a listener on the opposite side. These situations are labeled in Fig. 5. For our purposes, it is satisfactory to model these two situations using a highpass, first-order FIR filter and a second-order IIR bandpass filter respectively. In the backward-reflecting case, we choose the half-power point of the highpass filter at about

$$freq_{1/2\ power} (Hz) = 10 \cdot VEL/(\pi \cdot diameter)$$

and use an amplitude coefficient q of about

$$1/\sqrt{2\pi} \,.$$

In the forward-reflecting case, we choose a center frequency and bandwidth of the bandpass filter at about

$$center\_freq (Hz) = VEL/(\pi \cdot diameter)$$

$$bandwidth (Hz) = 0.3 \cdot center\_freq$$

and set q at about

$$1/\sqrt{20\pi} \,.$$

We stress that these choices of filter properties are approximate and serve only to enrich the characteristics of the early response. The filters used here are quite standard and are described in great detail by, for example, Oppenheim and Schafer (1975). Further detailed descriptions of the scattering and absorption of sound may be pursued by referring to Morse's work (1948).

It may serve equally well to use some entirely different criteria in choosing these properties. It is advantageous, however, to create a systematic method that can easily be extended to allow the introduction of several sources into the simulated acoustic space, each with its own particular reflection relationships related to its simulated position in the space.

A further improvement can be gained by continuously varying the delay lengths in a random way. This has the effect of shifting the resonant peaks in the frequency response and decreases the possibility of flutter. Usually, a variation of 1 msec or less a few times per second is sufficient to enhance the quality of the sound without introducing

Fig. 5. Simplified diagram
of scattering of sound from
a cylinder at low and high
frequencies. In case A, the

listener is on the same
side as the source. In case
B, the listener is on the opposite side.

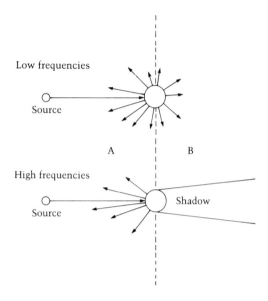

Low frequencies

Source

A   B

High frequencies

Source   Shadow

disturbing side effects. The reverberator design now stands as shown in Fig. 6.

Notes on Implementation

A program was written to design automatically a Music 11 reverberator using the preceding design methodology. The ROOM program takes as its input the dimensions of a rectangular room, coordinates and dimensions of objects in the room, a feedback matrix, a list of delay values, and a list of source locations. The output consists of Music 11 code to be used as part of a Music 11 orchestra file. An example of a reverberator with a single source in the left front channel implemented in this way is described in the section on sample Music 11 implementation.

More efficient use of memory space is obtained by avoiding the use of a delay for the source and reducing all delays of early reflections by a corresponding amount. This also has the effect of increasing the time window in which the early reflections can be calculated.

The reverberator design contains several optional branches around the statements that filter the early reflections and adds them into the delay. These branches become effective when the input source is not active, thereby eliminating unnecessary computation. This becomes very important in designing reverberators that allow several separate input sources.

A reverberator capable of handling several sources is a simple generalization of the single-source method. In our implementation, the ROOM program defines a set of early reflection characteristics for each source, corresponding to its simulated location. In practice, the calculation of early reflections in using a reverberator with many sources can become computationally intensive, but each additional source generally requires only a fractional amount of memory space compared to the amount of memory occupied by the delays. Furthermore, the use of conditional branches to avoid unnecessary computation, as described earlier, can greatly ease the matter.

In considering the various filter characteristics, we have assumed that filters of unity maximum gain are used in conjunction with an amplitude attenuation of the input signal. Further computational efficiencies can be achieved by scaling the filter coefficients by this attenuation value, thereby avoiding computationally costly multiplication of the signal prior to filtering.

Observations and Suggestions for Further Work

A long list of possible improvements springs to mind. We have only gone into detail about one possible network, and new possibilities are born with each unitary matrix (of which there are plenty for everybody).

There is still no easy way to gauge overall coloration in a complex network, and trial and error is still required to control it. Coloration is probably less for networks containing at least some long delays; but incorporating them makes it harder to control echo density.

Another problem arising for long reverberation times and pure tone bursts is a fluctuation in am-

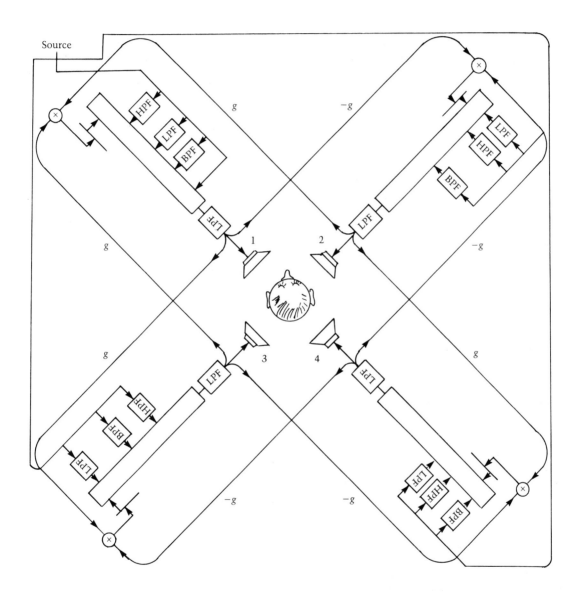

Source

plitude during the decay. This phenomenon is caused by the "excitation" of a small number of poles in the frequency response that create their own tones and beat against one another. This is a problem for every reverberator we have tried, and the only solution we can suggest is to arrange for the pole density to be so great that the beating is slower than the decay (i.e., for a reverberation time of 2 sec we need a pole density of two per Hertz). However, we are unable to think of any delay network resulting in a pole separation smaller in Hertz than the reciprocal of our total delay time in seconds. We strongly suspect that this is a fundamental limitation for reverberators. If that amount of space is not available, the best solution is to avoid using long reverberation times when the input is a pure tone burst.

A next step in the reverberation design procedure will be to allow for moving sources. This implies making extensions to the ROOM program in order to make it generate code that specifies the time-varying relationships of the early reflections as the source moves between two positions.

Further experiments using more than four channels would be worthwhile and could lead to an enhanced sense of acoustic ambience and greater realism. A study of the directional growth of reverberation in real rooms may help in choosing delay matrices for networks with many channels.

We also found that variation of the early response constraints, such as filter criteria, led to different qualities of reverberation, but we have no quantitative way of describing these relationships in perceptually meaningful terms. Some important research attacking these questions appears in the literature (Beranek 1962; Reichardt and Schmidt 1967; Barron 1971; 1974), and we would be interested in exploring simpler and more direct ways of defining the early response. Perhaps a statistical method of choosing the early reflection properties, combined with some perceptually meaningful constraints, can be found. Such a method may also lead to greater efficiency in computing the early response.

Conclusion

A methodology for the design and experimentation of reverberation networks has been presented. Some of the favorable properties of reverberators designed in this way are as follows:

1. The reverberant response is spatially sensitive to the location of the input source.
2. Several unique input sources may be added without significantly increasing the main memory space required.
3. A significant portion of the early room response characteristics may be modeled directly.
4. When a source signal is dormant, there is an increase in computational efficiency.

The methods we have presented are flexible enough to permit the design of stable recursive reverberators with an arbitrary number of output channels.

Acknowledgments

This work was supported by a grant from the M.I.T. Department of Humanities. We owe much to Barry Vercoe, whose initial insights led us to the present design, and to Roger Hale, who supplied us with additional ideas.

References

Barron, M. 1971. "The Subjective Effects of First Reflections in Concert Halls—the Need for Lateral Reflections." *Journal of Sound and Vibration* 15(4):475–494.

Barron, M. 1974. "The Effects of Early Reflections on Subjective Acoustic Quality in Concert Halls." Ph.D. thesis, Institute of Sound and Vibration Research, University of Southampton, England.

Beranek, L. 1954. *Acoustics*. New York: McGraw-Hill.

Beranek, L. 1962. *Music, Acoustics and Architecture.* New York: Wiley.

Jordan, V. L. 1969. "Room Acoustics and Architectural Acoustics Development in Recent Years." *Applied Acoustics* 2(1):59–81.

Kuttruff, H. 1973. *Room Acoustics*. New York: Wiley.

Meyer, E., W. Burgtorf, and P. Damaske. 1965. "Eine Ap-

Stautner and Puckette

paratur zur Electroakustischen Nachbildung von Schallfeldern, Subjektive Hörwirkungen beim Übergang Koharenz-Inkoharenz." *Acustica* 15(5):339–344.

Moorer, J. 1979. "About This Reverberation Business." *Computer Music Journal* 3(2):13–28.

Morse, P. M. 1948. *Vibration and Sound.* New York: McGraw-Hill.

Oppenheim, A., and R. Schafer. 1975. *Digital Signal Processing.* Englewood Cliffs, New Jersey: Prentice-Hall.

Reichardt, W., and W. Schmidt. 1967. "Die Wahrnehmbarkeit der Veranderung von Schallfeldparametern bei der Darbietung von Musik." *Acustica* 18(5):274–282.

Schroeder, M. R. 1962. "Natural Sounding Artificial Reverberation." *Journal of the Audio Engineering Society* 10(3):219–223.

Schroeder, M. R., D. Gottlob, and K. F. Siebrasse. 1974. "Comparative Study of European Concert Halls: Correlation of Subjective Preference with Geometric and Acoustic Parameters." *Journal of the Acoustical Society of America* 56(4):1195–1201.

Strang, G. 1976. *Linear Algebra and Its Applications.* New York: Academic.

Appendix—

Sample Music 11 Implementation

An example of a Music 11 reverberator designed with the aid of the ROOM program will be preceded here by a brief description of the unit generators used.

The Music 11 sound synthesis language computes samples of sound at two rates: the *control rate* and the *audio rate*. Typically, quantities that vary relatively slowly, such as amplitude envelopes or variable delay lengths, are calculated at the control rate, while actual waveform generation occurs at the faster audio rate. Variables updated at the control rate are represented as kN or lkN, where N is an integer and l indicates a variable local to the particular instrument. Similarly, audio rate quantities are designated by aN or laN. Constants are represented by iN. Global variables are values that can be passed between instruments and are designated by gkN for the control rate and gaN for the audio rate.

A delay space of the desired length in seconds is defined in the code by the **pipdef** statement. Any number of audio rate signals can be added into the delay using **pipad** statements up to the following **piprd** statement, which marks the end of the delay space and reads the audio rate samples from the delay. By using a **pipadv** statement, audio rate samples may be added into the delay space at a time-varying delay value determined by a control-rate variable.

Lowpass infinite-impulse response (IIR) filters are implemented using the **tone** unit generator, which takes the desired half-power point as an argument. The **reson** generator implements a second-order recursive filter with the desired center frequency and bandwidth between upper and lower half-power points. Finite-impulse response (FIR) filters are implemented by first delaying the input signal by one sample using the **delay1** unit generator and then adding the combined weights of the original signal and delayed signal. (In Fig. 7, both the filter coefficients and the amplitude attenuation factor appear in the implementation of the FIR filter; these constants are actually multiplied only once, and their combined product is then used for the audio rate calculations.)

The control-rate interpolating, random-number generator **randi** produces random straight-line segments between positive or negative random points lying within the given amplitude and occurring at the given frequency. These values are used to offset the feedback delay lengths slightly.

In the example presented later, the input signal is assumed to be generated in a sound-producing module or instrument occurring before the reverberator and is represented by the global audio-rate signal $ga1$. The global control rate variable $gk1$ is used as a flag to indicate whether the instrument is active or not in order to determine when the branches avoiding the early reflection calculations become effective. At the bottom of the reverberator, $ga1$ is set to zero to avoid recycling the last sample in the event that the sound-producing module has turned off at the end of a note.

Fig. 7. Music 11 implementation of a four-channel
reverberator with one
source. Music 11 unit gen-
*erators and statements are
in bold type, and com-
ments are denoted by a
semicolon.*

```
instr 13                                        ;Reverberation instrument
ga1     init    0                               ;Initialize source signal to 0
k1      randi   .001, 3.1, .06                  ;Interpolated random numbers to
k2      randi   .0011, 3.5, .9                  ;  jitter delay lengths. First arg
k3      randi   .0017, 1.11, .7                 ;  is max. range in ms, then cycle
k4      randi   .0006, 3.973, .3                ;  rate in Hz, then a seed.
la11    delay1  ga1                             ;Delay source by one sample for FIR filters
if gk1 = 0 kgoto nof11                          ;Skip unnecessary computation when source is off
a1      reson   ga1*.02286, 214.7, 64.411, 1    ;Early reflections for channel 1
a2      reson   ga1*.036248, 365, 109.5, 1      ;Bandpass filters
a3      reson   ga1*.027143, 219, 65.699, 1
a4      reson   ga1*.019974, 219, 65.699, 1
a5      tone    ga1*.070542, 9800               ;Lowpass filters
a6      tone    ga1*.061021, 10000
a7      tone    ga1*.05216, 9800
a8      tone    ga1*.046154, 9800
nof11:
        pipdef  .0683                           ;Pipe delay space for channel 1
if gk1 = 0 kgoto noa11                          ;If source is off, don't bother
        pipad   a1, .0006                       ;   adding in early reflections
        pipad   a2, .0001351
        pipad   a3, .0031383
        pipad   a4, .0046684                    ;Early reflections added into pipe
        pipad   a5, .0094834
        pipad   a6, .010068
        pipad   a7, .023716
        pipad   a8, .029589
noa11:                                          ;Feedback signal from channel 2 and 3 added
        pipadv  la2 + la3, .0663 + k1           ;  into time-varying delay.
la11    piprd                                   ;Read pipe output, channel 1.
if gk1 = 0 kgoto nof21                          ;Branch if source turned off
a1      =       ga1*.1014*.84379 − la11*.1014*.15621    ;Early reflections,
a2      =       ga1*.071322*.85075 − la11*.071322*.14925  ;  channel 2
a3      =       ga1*.055855*.85028 − la11*.055855*.14972
a4      tone    ga1*.03917, 10000
a5      =       ga1*.048756*.85015 − la11*.048756*.14985  ;Highpass FIR filter
a6      tone    ga1*.033955, 9800
a7      tone    ga1*.029319, 9800
a8      tone    ga1*.029319, 9800
a9      tone    ga1*.025974, 9800
nof21:
        pipdef  .0773                           ;Pipe delay, channel 2
if gk1 = 0 kgoto noa21                          ;Branch if source is dormant
        pipad   a1, .014705
        pipad   a2, .030699
        pipad   a3, .032913
        pipad   a4, .035149
        pipad   a5, .03897
        pipad   a6, .052999
```

Fig. 7 (cont'd)

```
        pipad   a7, .064321
        pipad   a8, .064321
        pipad   a9, .074434
noa21:
        pipadv  −la1 − la4, .0753 + k2                          ;Feedback from channels 1 and 4
la12    piprd                                                   ;Read pipe, channel 2
if gk1 = 0 kgoto nof31                                          ;Branch if source dormant
a1      reson   ga1*.024515, 210.57, 63.172, 1
a2      =       ga1*.08472*.84379 − la11*.08472*.15621
a3      =       ga1*.065767*.85015 − la11*.065767*.14985
a4      =       ga1*.055937*.85015 − la11*.055937*.14985
a5      tone    ga1*.034039, 10000
a6      =       ga1*.043571*.84647 − la11*.043571*.15353
a7      tone    ga1*.03061, 9800
a8      tone    ga1*.028892, 9800
nof31:
        pipdef  .0902                                           ;Pipe delay space, channel 3
if gk1 = 0 kgoto noa31                                          ;Branch if source dormant
        pipad   a1, .010752
        pipad   a2, .018758
        pipad   a3, .022562
        pipad   a4, .03701
        pipad   a5, .045961
        pipad   a6, .05096
        pipad   a7, .062167
        pipad   a8, .065731
noa31:
        pipadv  la1 − la4, .0882 + k3                           ;Feedback from channels 1 and 4
la13    piprd                                                   ;Read pipe output, channel 3
if gk1 = 0 kgoto nof41                                          ;Branch if source dormant
a1      =       ga1*.080287*.84379 − la11*.080287*.15621
a2      =       ga1*.071111*.85041 − la11*.071111*.14959        ;Early reflections,
a3      =       ga1*.057238*.85015 − la11*.057238*.14985        ;   channel 4
a4      =       ga1*.048448*.84985 − la11*.048448*.15015
a5      tone    ga1*.030297, 10000
a6      =       ga1*.042724*.84647 − la11*.042724*.15353
a7      tone    ga1*.022991, 9800
a8      tone    ga1*.021125, 9800
nof41:
        pipdef  .0991                                           ;Pipe delay space, channel 4
if gk1 = 0 kgoto noa41                                          ;Branch if source dormant
        pipad   a1, .028855
        pipad   a2, .033654
        pipad   a3, .041818
        pipad   a4, .053455
        pipad   a5, .057372
        pipad   a6, .05831
        pipad   a7, .090532
        pipad   a8, .098614
```

Fig. 7 (cont'd)

```
noa41:
         pipadv  la2 − la3, .0971 + k4          ;Feedback from channels 2 and 3
la14     piprd                                  ;Read pipe output, channel 4
i1       =      10.6301                         ;Distance of source from listener in meters
outq     la11 + ga1/i1, la12, la13, la14        ;Four channel reverb output, with source
                                                ;  in channel 1
la1      tone   la11*p4, 9000                   ;Lowpass filters to simulate air
la2      tone   la12*p4, 9000                   ;   absorption before signals are
la3      tone   la13*p4, 9000                   ;   fed back to pipes. p4 is feedback
la4      tone   la14*p4, 9000                   ;   coefficient "g" which controls reverb time
ga1      =      0                               ;Zero source signal before getting new samples
endin
```

VI

Signal Processing Hardware

Overview

Curtis Roads

Sometime in the summer of 1944 I was waiting for a train to Philadelphia . . . when along came von Neumann. Prior to that time I had never met this great mathematician, but I knew much about him and of course heard him lecture on several occasions. It was therefore with considerable temerity that I approached this world-famous figure, introduced myself, and started talking. Fortunately for me von Neumann was a warm, friendly person who did his best to make people feel relaxed in his presence. The conversation soon turned to my work. When it became clear to von Neumann that I was concerned with the development of an electronic computer capable of 333 multiplications per second, the whole atmosphere of our conversation changed from one of relaxed good humor to one more like the oral examination for the doctor's degree in mathematics. (Goldstine 1972)

The core function of digital signal processing (DSP) hardware is high-speed numerical calculation. Fast multiplication, addition, and memory access (also called *table lookup*) are central to the generation and the processing of digital sound (Moorer 1977; Snell 1977; Strawn 1985). In a digital audio system, a sound waveform is represented as an array of samples stored in memory. In order to mix two signals together, the system must read in a sample from each signal, add them, and write the sum back to memory (or to a digital-to-analog converter if sound output is desired). Multiplication is at the heart of amplitude control, since to shape the amplitude of a signal means to multiply it by an envelope function. Multiplication, addition, and memory access are also central to signal processing operations such as filtering.

DSP hardware falls into two categories: *application-specific* and *general-purpose*. An application-specific device performs a set task, such as frequency modulation synthesis, filtering, or computing fast Fourier transforms to determine the spectrum of an input signal. With such systems, the user can adjust certain parameters but the basic task remains fixed.

One of the major questions in designing music hardware is whether to tailor it for a particular application or to make it general-purpose and programmable. Many large manufacturers, such as Yamaha, prefer to design fixed-function custom chips for their own synthesizers. Occasionally these chips can be sold to other companies for use in different products. For example, IBM used Yamaha frequency modulation synthesis chips in its IBM PC Music Feature product.

At the other end of the spectrum are general-purpose DSP devices. A general-purpose DSP device is a type of programmable computer whose architecture is optimized to process sample data at high rates. DSP devices take advantage of the repetition inherent in signal processing operations. For example, if a signal sampled at 48 KHz is passed through a digital filter for 10 minutes, that filter will run through the same routine for each of the 28,800,000 input samples. One method of exploiting the repetitive nature of signal processing is by *pipelining* the flow of data through the device for extra speed. A pipelined architecture is one in which the processor is constructed in such a way that the execution of a new task can begin before a preceding task has been completed.

More and more, entire general-purpose DSP devices are being implemented on a single integrated circuit (chip) (Snell 1987). The DSP chips, which are not specifically designed for music applications, can be programmed for speech, sonar, seismic, or image processing. The chips usually depend on software to tailor them to the application at hand. Massively integrated circuits seem ideal for realizing the computer musician's goal of "Music V on a chip"—a reference to Max V. Mathews's flexible and extensible language Music V (Mathews 1969). After a generation of closed, "black box" instruments restricted to sampling or a single synthesis technique, this seems welcome indeed.

Another way of characterizing DSP systems is by whether they handle *fixed-point* or *floating-point* calculations. A fixed-point system handles only integers; a floating-point system can handle a much greater range of numbers, since it has provisions for decimal points and exponents, as in "scientific notation" (where, for example, 6.17×10^6 represents 6,170,000). A floating-point system is more complex, and is therefore usually more expensive. Floating-point computation is especially important in such audio applications as resonant (infinite-impulse-response) filters, where precision is of paramount concern (see articles 35 and 39 above).

The state of the art for hardware has come far since the summer of 1944, when 333 multiplications per second seemed astounding to John von Neumann. Through parallel processing, today's numerical engines can attain speeds in excess of 11 billion floating-point multiplications per second, or 11 gigaflops ("flop" means "floating-point operations per second") (Peled 1987). Machines capable of such speed are very expensive, however. For practical studio and onstage work, we must content ourselves with considerably less "horsepower" for some time to come.

The struggle to cope with limited computational resources is recounted in article 46. When he wrote that article ("Synthesizers I Have Known and Loved"), James Moorer had as much experience as anyone in the world with the programming of digital synthesizers. His thoughtful analysis is well worth reading for its insights into the special engineering requirements of music synthesizers. Careful study of this article will reveal how Moorer's critiques of the 4B and 4C synthesizers (developed at IRCAM) and of the Systems Concepts digital synthesizer led to his design of the Lucasfilm Audio Signal Processor, which is outlined in article 47.

The Audio Signal Processor (ASP) was a pioneering effort to bring the tradition-bound film sound industry into the digital age. The principles embodied in the ASP changed many people's notions of how audio would be manipulated in the future. Marketed as the SoundDroid, the device represented several new concepts: multitrack digital recording to disk, real-time mixing, random access to samples stored on disk, integration of sound synthesis with processing and mixing in one programmable unit, and graphics-based editing of music notation and audio samples.

Rapid advances in technology have made it possible for many users of small systems to benefit from the approach pioneered in the ASP at a much lower cost. Specifically:

- For signal processing, a single VLSI (very-large-scale integration) DSP chip can replace several large and expensive circuit boards full of SSI (small-scale integration) chips; several chips can be used in parallel to boost performance.

- For sample storage and recording, a compact Winchester disk drive with backup tape can replace a bulky and expensive removable drive. Optical disks, which can store large amounts of sample data, replace magnetic disks in some applications.

- For sound conversion, a single chip can perform high-quality digital-to-analog or analog-to-digital conversion in place of an entire circuit board full of parts.

- For interconnection with external devices, standard interfaces such as the AES/EBU (Audio Engineering Society/European Broadcast Union) serial digital audio protocol and MIDI (Musical Instrument Digital Interface) replace custom-built interface hardware.

- For host computer interaction, an inexpensive personal computer can replace a custom-engineered workstation.

As a result of these hardware economies, the market has expanded and a host of new audio processing products have been introduced to address it. But the ASP set new standards for digital audio processing, and thus it remains a landmark in the history of computer music.

S. Jerrold Kaplan's contribution, "Developing a Commercial Digital Synthesizer" (article 48), is a rare gem. This is the only time that an insider has retraced the circuitous path of product development in the pages of *Computer Music Journal*. Kaplan's frank observations bring the product-development process down to earth. To update his saga, it is worth noting that the musical power of the Synergy synthesizer he helped to create has been demonstrated in a series of recordings by composer Wendy Carlos, including *Digital Moonscapes* (CBS) and *Beauty in the Beast* (Audion).

The final article in this part deals with the increasingly important subject of VLSI circuits. A VLSI circuit is a tiny chip with hundreds of thousands of transistors on it. Mark Kahrs examines some of the issues in the designing of such a chip for music synthesis and sound processing. One of the distinguishing needs of a music processor is that musicians need to interact with it as it is running, possibly changing its function as a piece is played. Of particular interest in Kahrs's scheme is the attention given to real-time input of performance and score data.

References

Goldstine, H. 1972. *The Computer from Pascal to von Neumann.* Princeton University Press.

Mathews, M. V. 1969. *The Technology of Computer Music.* Cambridge, Mass.: MIT Press.

Moorer, J. A. 1977. "Signal Processing Aspects of Computer Music—A Survey." *Proceedings of the IEEE* 65(8): 1108–1137. Revised and updated version in J. Strawn, ed., *Digital Audio Signal Processing: An Anthology* (Los Altos, Calif.: Kaufmann, 1985).

Peled, A. 1987. "The Next Computer Revolution." *Scientific American* 257(4): 57–64.

Snell, J. 1977. "Design of a Digital Oscillator That Will Generate up to 256 Low Distortion Sine Waves in Real Time." *Computer Music Journal* 1(2): 4–25. Revised and updated version in C. Roads and J. Strawn, eds., *Foundations of Computer Music* (Cambridge, Mass.: MIT Press, 1985).

Snell, J. 1987. "General-Purpose High-Fidelity Affordable Real-Time Computer Music System." In J. Beauchamp, ed., *Proceedings of the 1987 International Computer Music Conference* (San Francisco: Computer Music Association).

Strawn, J. 1985. *Digital Audio Engineering: An Anthology.* Los Altos, Calif.: Kaufmann.

46

James A. Moorer
Center for Computer Research in Music and
Acoustics
Stanford University
Stanford, California 94305

Synthesizers I Have Known and Loved

Introduction

There are now several digital music processors in the world. Having used these processors, there are a number of things we have learned that have implications for future synthesizer design. The advantages and disadvantages of three different signal processors are discussed in this article: the 4C Machine at IRCAM, the Systems Concepts Digital Synthesizer, and the Stanford POLYCEPHALOS processor.

Disclaimer

The views expressed are strictly those of the author and are not meant to imply any criticism of the makers of the machines discussed, or of the companies or institutions to which they belong. Moreover, the 4C Machine was an ever-evolving part of a synthesizer research project, and most likely its problems have already been corrected. Nonetheless, it seems important to review what the problems were to help future designers avoid them.

Studio and Performance Considerations

There are many uses of digital sound processing, each demanding a slightly different processor architecture. In an attempt to introduce some order into the range of usages, let us define a few terms. We will categorize sound processors as being designed for performance or studio work. This does not necessarily mean that a studio device does not make music in real time, but only that the finished musical product does not happen all at once.

It is clear that for performance applications some input device, typically an organlike keyboard, must be provided to convey the musician's gestures to the synthesizer. The device may be monophonic or polyphonic and still be useful in performance, although solo performance makes more sense on a polyphonic device.

For a studio device a keyboard may still be important, but even more important is the ability to store and overlay multiple "passes" through the piece. We can immediately see that this categorization is not very rigid. For example, we might imagine a performance device that has a number of preprogrammed sections that may have even been typed in on a teletype keyboard and require little or no performer intervention. Likewise, as soon as we attach an organ keyboard to a studio machine we require the immediacy of response of a performance device.

We can argue back and forth about the merits of studio versus performance devices, and the tenor of such discussions often approaches a semireligious fervor, precipitating a calamitous drop in the amount of information exchanged. We shall attempt to avoid such a discussion here by dealing only with the architectural implications of each point of view.

The 4C Machine

The 4C Machine was designed at IRCAM by Pepino di Giugno. A discussion of this machine has been presented elsewhere (Moorer et al. 1979), so we will proceed with the assumption that the details of the architecture are available to the reader. The machine was designed as a performance device. It implements a number of phase accumulators, table lookups, multiply-accumulators, and various other functions. The internal state of the machine (i.e., the contents of all the parameter and control memories) is indirectly available through the UNIBUS. The entire device looks like memory to the PDP-11 (controlled by a small memory map, which allows a 1K-word "window" to be accessed at any one time). In some ways, this might seem like an ideal situation, since there is no delay between the execution of a memory write by the PDP-11 and the arrival of the data in the 4C memory. As it turns out, the blessing is mixed. It is important to understand that the 4C and the PDP-11 are independent, parallel machines with a shared memory but without a hardware means of synchronizing data updates. Thus the exact arrival time of a parameter value cannot be synchronized with a particular sample number. The 4C allows a single PDP-11 access every 2 μsec, but the access itself only takes a few hundred nanoseconds. This means that the PDP-11 will wait for a time that can vary between a fraction of a microsecond and somewhat over 2 μsec. This time delay depends on the relative phasing of the 4C clock period and the PDP-11 instruction cycle, which adds yet another degree of uncertainty to the timing. One might offer the counterargument that a few microseconds could not possibly make any difference perceptually, but such an argument is fallacious. Indeed, if the problem were limited to the fact that a particular note occurred a few microseconds earlier or later, there would certainly be no perceivable difference, but if this means that one channel of a stereo signal would lag or lead the other channel indeterminately, the perceived image would be moved toward the earlier signal, which could result in perceptual image shifts of many degrees. Likewise, relative micro shifts among the events within a note can be important. For instance, if we try to simulate a violin tone by putting one period of the steady-state into an oscillator wavetable, and then add a noise burst at the beginning to simulate the bow scratch, we find that the exact positioning of the noise burst is critical. Listeners seem to be able to distinguish a shift of just a few samples in the timing of the noise burst.

Another amusing problem arises when we consider doing amplitude envelopes. In this case, we wish to output a number of parameters over a period of time in response to a single keystroke, such as in the case of a piecewise-linear envelope. In the 4C, the way this is done is that each segment of the envelope is started with a current value, an increment, and a final value. For each sample, the current value and the increment are added and compared with the final value. If the final value has been passed, then it is substituted for the current value and the envelope "hangs" until the computer can issue the next segment. Meanwhile, one of the timers counts down the number of samples in the segment and then interrupts the PDP-11. The PDP-11 takes the interrupt, determines the number of the finished segment, and delivers the new increment, final value, and sample count. If we compute the data rate here, it may seem quite small. We have 32 envelope generators, each one of which might have 10 segments per second, for an average data rate of 320 new segments per second; since a segment requires three values (increment, final, and count), there would be a total of 960 parameters per second. This gives slightly over a millisecond per parameter, an easy rate to achieve even with the relatively slow PDP-11/34 computer. The problem is that this is an average rate; the *burst rate* is more important. In music, the parameter updates come in bursts of extremely high bandwidth such as occur at the beginnings of notes where a large amount of "setup" information must go out all at once. Likewise, during the attack portion of a note, the envelopes may be quite complex and require that a large number of parameters go out in a short time. It takes the PDP-11 numerous microseconds to take an interrupt and figure out what to do about it. If several segments reach their final values simultaneously, they will be forced to wait while the PDP-11 shuffles the parameters out one at a time at a rate much slower than the memory bandwidth of the computer. To quantify this more precisely, a memory cycle on a PDP-11 might be between 400 nsec and 1 μsec in length, whereas an instruction might require three to five memory cycles itself plus some execution time. On the PDP-11/34, a simple indexed MOV instruction might take 5 μsec. In addition, the instruction is not an isolated event. It is presumably part of a parameter loop and is thus followed by decrement-and-branch code of some kind, thus increasing the time for each parameter to 10 μsec or more.

Although the computer can read and write the parameters directly, this does not mean that it can transfer sample-time data to or from the machine. The problem is that the computer cannot readily be synchronized with the synthesizer to assure that it will transfer a sample every sample period. The PDP-11 cannot service interrupts fast enough to be able to take an interrupt, read one sample, and dismiss the interrupt without occasionally missing samples. We can argue that for a performance machine all the music should be synthesized so that there is no need to exchange sample-data streams with the computer, but this prohibits the use of prerecorded concrète sounds that might provide other musical material and rules out the usage of the machine in an all-digital studio environment. We would have to use analog overlays. The other counterargument is that when we run out of power on the 4C, there is nothing we can do but build another 4C (and possibly buy another PDP-11 to feed it). As will be described later with reference to the Systems Concepts Digital Synthesizer, the ability to extract the samples from the synthesizer and write them back onto the disk for further processing (such as overlaying) is crucial to the extensibility of a synthesizer.

Another problem is that the table length is currently set at 16K samples. This may sound like a lot when we consider the 512-word tables of the Music V world, but since the machine does no table interpolation, low tones often require enormous tables. Consider the problem of simulating the bottom octave of the piano by placing one period of the waveform into the oscillator table. We should perhaps explain here that the piano does not really exhibit a harmonic waveform, so the concept of a single period is not well defined. What we used was a fictional periodic waveform derived from the spectral envelope. The extremely large number of partials for these low tones (120 partials for G1) caused a most objectionable "buzz-saw" distortion for all but a full 16K wavetable. Needless to say, it defeats the purpose of having 32 oscillators if we are forced to eat the entire wavetable for one tone,

but this was the only way we found to obtain that particular sound. Indeed, the mere fact that the wavetable is loadable is, we consider, a significant advantage over many other synthesizer designs.

We might argue that simulating a tone with 120 partials on a music synthesizer is hard and that we should be content with the remaining spectrum of things that the synthesizer can do well, rather than try to squeeze things out of it that it was not designed for. We cannot argue this point, but can only counter that the desire to do this came from the musical need of a serious composer. This was a limitation that this composer reached in the course of trying to realize his piece. The whole point of these machines is to allow us to realize pieces previously unrealizable, and the success of the machine must be judged on the basis of how well it allows us to do so.

We can also argue that the new 64K random-access-memory (RAM) chips will allow us to use a much larger wavetable without any increase in the complexity of the device. This is of course true, but we also have to consider from where these wavetables come. Since PDP-11 memory cannot support many of these waveforms at the same time, they come in from the disk at about 1.6 μsec per 16-bit word for the modern storage module disk drives. It takes the PDP-11/34 about 8 μsec more to take this word and write it into the 4C memory. Thus to transfer 16K words takes a little over 150 msec. This assumes that the PDP-11 is completely dedicated to the task and is not doing anything else such as updating parameters in the synthesizer. Needless to say, we cannot change tables very often at that rate. We must be content with small tables that change relatively slowly.

In any machine with a small number of oscillators, some cleverness must be exercised with respect to the allocation of oscillators to notes. We may argue that 32 is not a "small" number of oscillators, since many analog synthesizers have fewer than a dozen oscillators. We have nothing to add to this argument. The problem is that it usually takes several oscillators to make up an instrument. There are two common ways of doing this. The first is "fixed" allocation, in which a certain group of oscillators is assigned once and for all to a particular "instrument." When a key is depressed this instrument is activated, and each time the instrument is activated the same group of oscillators is activated. We might have several copies of the instrument, so that as different keys are depressed different copies of the instrument are activated to produce polyphony. An alternative scheme is to have dynamic allocation such that when a key is depressed, a number of oscillators is assigned from the pool of currently free oscillators. It is clear that the dynamic scheme requires more computer overhead but is potentially more efficient in resource (i.e., oscillator) utilization, in that we could have a large number of possible instruments, only a small number of which could be realized at any one time. On the other hand, a fixed allocation allows the clever programmer to compile in-line code to update parameters in the instrument, thus minimizing the overhead on the host processor.

A problem that occurs with any synthesizer where the number of oscillators is small compared to the number of fingers on human hands (this value is normally taken to be 10 in the Northern Hemisphere) is that sooner or later we run out of instruments. We could argue that if we had 10 instruments we could never run out, but that depends on the instrument. Many instruments have a note duration that is independent of the duration of key depression, such as bells, tam-tam, or sustained piano. We must then find a way to "hurry up" the envelope decay to complete the note as soon as possible without creating a click in the sound, which would occur if the note were simply turned off. This is doubly tricky in that both the increment and the count must be changed to reasonable values. This usually requires reading the current value and doing some further arithmetic, then delaying the new note until the previous one has been terminated.

Another question that arises when we do manage to put down the 11th finger (two keys with one finger? nose? elbow?): what instrument do we flush to make room for the new note? Organ and commercial digital synthesizer manufacturers have solved this problem in a number of ways, and the consensus seems to be that we keep the lowest and the newest notes and everything after that is up for

grabs. Typically, the oldest note of those that remain is discarded. There does not seem to be any elegant solution for this, except to add more oscillators (which is the solution that I favor personally).

Another application of the performance synthesizer is to have the score preplanned and typed in ahead of time. The performer adjusts the tempo and various other parameters like tone qualities and spatial positions, but does not play the notes as such. There is a problem in adjusting the timing of a ramp that is already in progress. To speed it up or slow it down requires, as we have noted, that a calculation be made on the slope and the timing count to reflect the new duration of the note. Since the processor is not exactly synchronized with the synthesizer, this is generally not possible without introducing clicks of various sorts, not to mention the problem of doing all that arithmetic for 32 or more envelopes. One solution is to do envelopes differently. We don't need to store an envelope as a sequence of increment/final value/count triplets; we could just as well store a sampled version of the envelope in a wavetable and read it off just as we do for oscillators. This is not a new idea, since Music V and any number of other music programs work this way, but it solves much of the complexity of the tempo-change problem by introducing another problem: that of interpolation. It is clear that we cannot just jump from one sample of the envelope to the next, since that would surely introduce modulation distortion. As an example of this, the 4B Machine (Alles and di Giugno 1977) computed the envelopes at 2 kHz, which means that the envelope held its value for 8 samples before changing. (The 4C Machine runs at a sampling rate of either 16 kHz or 32 kHz or higher; the most common rate is 16 kHz, giving a 6.4-kHz audio bandwidth.) This did not make any difference in use of the envelope as a frequency ramp, since the frequency is integrated as the phase angle is accumulated, which is like putting a 6-db per octave noise filter on it, but noticeable chirps and whistles were produced when the envelope was used as an amplitude envelope. Experiments showed that the sampling rate of the envelope had to be at least half the signal sampling rate to eliminate the chirps. Most synthesizers are not built with interpolation in mind, but having noticed the numerous cases where it is useful, we would recommend that any future synthesizers at least offer it as an optional feature. Another problem with doing envelopes via sample-data table is that it forces the envelope to have uniform resolution throughout its duration. For a 10-sec note a 50-msec attack portion would certainly carry the bulk of the envelope activity, which would require that many points be wasted on the relatively stable steady-state portion of the envelope. We can imagine any number of ways to correct this (variable-rate envelope scanning; separate tables for attack, decay, and steady-state, etc.), but none of them stands out as being particularly better than any other one at this time. Likewise, the sample-data envelope introduces additional complexity if we imagine very long envelopes that would not fit entirely in any reasonable-length wavetable in one piece. We thus have the problem of transferring the envelope one hunk at a time and synchronizing the switching from one part to the next in the synthesizer. All of these problems can be solved, but all of them must be dealt with explicitly, either by ignoring them, building in more complexity, or limiting the scope of the synthesizer.

Most synthesizers are built on the assumption that a functional module has some number of inputs and one output. Examples might be adders and multipliers, both of which take two inputs and deliver one output, or oscillators that take in frequency and amplitude and produce a waveform. Unfortunately, this assumption is violated so often that we must mention it here. The most common violation is for some form of frequency modulation (FM) or vibrato. One example is the application of vibrato to an additive synthesis instrument. In additive synthesis, we use a number of sinusoidal oscillators with separate frequencies to produce a single sound. If they are harmonically related, then any vibrato term that is added into their frequencies must be multiplied by the harmonic number. This means that the output of a vibrato oscillator must be multiplied successively by 1, 2, 3, and so on. Here is a case of a single functional unit (a vibrato oscillator) that has a large number of outputs (one for each partial to be controlled). Other cases include application of vibrato to an FM instrument when the carrier and modulating frequencies are not equal. This arises in FM vowel sounds or string sounds, where the carrier(s) will be placed at the spectral locations of resonances in the original sound. Again, there is no particularly good solution for this except to increase the amount of hardware in our synthesizer. We might reason that since the vibrato is relatively slow, it should be possible to do this on the host computer. As we have pointed out, the host computer is usually completely occupied with feeding the synthesizer already, and any additional burden forces the process out of real time (which may be acceptable for studio work). Likewise, as mentioned with respect to any frequency envelope, the vibrato signal cannot just jump occasionally from one value to the next, but must glide smoothly (i.e., it must be interpolated) from one value to the other, which must be done either by ramp generators in the synthesizer or by compute power in the host processor.

There is another curious problem with the 4C Machine in the multiplier design. The multiplication is a strictly fractional operation, which means that both numbers are considered to be less than 1.0 in magnitude. This means that when we multiply two numbers together, the product is always smaller than the smallest of the two numbers. There is no way to make numbers bigger in the 4C Machine except to add them together. Since digital filter coefficients are often greater than 1.0 in magnitude, we have to take several additional add cycles to increase the magnitude of a number after a multiply. This also causes some loss of precision. Likewise, to do interpolation we must shift up the low-order bits of the table address by, say, 10 bits. This is only accomplished by adding this number to itself 10 times. The machine is thus sort of an "attenuation machine" with no convenient way to scale things up. Normalization is quite obtuse on the 4C Machine.

Another deficiency was that the synthesizer itself can not write into the 16K memory. Only the PDP-11 can. Consequently, it cannot do reverberation, phasing, or any long-time delay. This was an unfortunate oversight.

The Systems Concepts Digital Synthesizer

Although the Systems Concepts Digital Synthesizer was designed largely by Samson (forthcoming) as a studio and research machine, it has some limited performance capabilities as well. There are three logically separate direct memory access (DMA) channels: one for commands, one for sample-data input, and one for sample-data output. Although all three of these channels go through the same physical cable, they are logically separate data streams, the sample-data paths containing any number of audio channels.

In the Systems Concepts Digital Synthesizer, each command has an opcode that determines its function. Most of the commands just update a particular parameter in a particular functional module, but there are some additional commands for timing and miscellaneous control functions (e.g., stopping the machine). The synchronization and timing problems are thus solved by the inclusion of timing information in the command stream. The *linger* command takes a sample number or a number of samples as an argument and stops the interpretation of commands either until a specific, absolute sample number is reached or a given number of samples is counted. The generation of samples is largely independent of the processing of commands and proceeds unimpeded in the presence of a linger command. Consequently, there is no processor intervention each time an envelope segment reaches its final value, and parameters can be updated at memory speed rather than at processor speed. There is a 28-command FIFO that allows a high burst rate of commands (which are processed at 195 nsec each) while maintaining a somewhat lower average rate of memory access. This FIFO is both a blessing and a curse. The obvious benefit is that tremendously high command rates can be sustained because DMA access can go quite fast. The ultimate limit is therefore either the main memory size or the disk bandwidth; the modern storage-module drives can transfer at a maximum rate of about one command every 3 μsec. The curse is that since the commands contain timing information, those 28 commands in the FIFO might represent (hypothetically) a time span of as much as 30 min.

There is no way to update a parameter (for example, a frequency or an amplitude) without first inserting it into the FIFO behind all the other commands. There is no way to insert a command ahead of the FIFO, or to bypass the FIFO. Consequently, it is not reasonable to think of adjusting some parameter of an ongoing piece in real time, since any command we insert will not take effect until some unknown time in the future, depending on what commands are already in the FIFO. There is a solution, and that is to disable the timing entirely and treat the machine much like the 4C. In this mode, we would simply compile command lists without timing information (linger commands) at all, and do the timing in the computer, occasionally "burping" out groups of commands that are then interpreted immediately. This brings back all of the problems of the 4C and again places a substantial burden on the computer to keep up with all this.

Another consequence of the command structure is what we call the "merge" problem. Music is inherently a parallel process, with noninteracting notes happening at the same time and with each note being composed of a number of simultaneously emerging envelopes. Since there is only one DMA path for synthesizer commands, all these logically separate processes must be merged into a single command stream in time order. Although this merge is straightforward to implement, it is time-consuming (Loy 1981). Let us assume for demonstration purposes a simple model of M envelopes each containing exactly N points and no other parameters to be merged. The order of the computational complexity for the merge is between $N \log_2 M$ and NM, depending on the implementation. (A note on complexity theory: when we discuss the "order" of a computation, we are not specifically referring to adds, multiplies, table lookups, or whatever. We are merely saying that as we increase one of the parameters, the resulting time or cost increases by a certain amount. For example, if the complexity is N, then as we double N the complexity is doubled. We are not saying what the cost is, but only how it varies.) The most common methods of doing the merge in use today exhibit a compute time proportional to NM. In other words, no one has yet programmed one of the many possi-

Moorer

ble logarithmic-speed algorithms. It seems quite likely to me that the next big advance in music processors will be special-purpose hardware for doing this merge.

Notice that a consequence of the single command stream with embedded timing information is that keyboard performance is essentially ruled out. The pressing of a key is asynchronous, and the data (envelope control) for that note would have to be merged into the command stream, which is only possible for very simple (and musically trivial) command streams.

The sample-data DMA paths are very useful in that they assure that the machine is capable of overlaying many different runs to produce sounds of arbitrary complexity. Any sound in any number of channels may be routed back to the computer and stored on the disk for further processing. This is the only music processor known to me that has this capability. It has turned out to be enormously useful in debugging both the hardware and the software. We can use this feature as a kind of "scope probe" to tap the signal at various places throughout the processing and make it available for scrutiny, or to inject a known signal to trace the processing. Errors in the low-order bits are normally not audible but can nonetheless cause problems in certain cases when the signal gets amplified or recycled, as happens in digital reverberation. Without a write-back feature, we must depend entirely on our ears to detect hardware problems, and such a check will not necessarily detect low-order bit errors. These errors make a kind of "time bomb" that will be uncovered at some later date, usually the day of the concert. To our way of thinking, there is no reason why all medium- to large-scale synthesizers should not include this feature. It is one of the few sensible hedges against obsolescence available to the synthesizer maker. Even for the performance machine, it aids machine checkout so much that debugging a complex synthesizer is almost unthinkable without such a feature.

There is a problem with the implementation of the sample-data paths on this processor. Multiple channels are multiplexed into a single stream. That is, sample 1 of channel 1 is first; next comes sample 1 of channel 2, then sample 1 of channel 3. Af-

ter the first sample of all the channels goes by, the second sample for all the channels goes by, and so on. The problem is that this doesn't allow multiple asynchronous channels. There is thus another merge problem in the sample-data paths. Similarly, it is difficult to change the number of channels during a run. If the command to change the number of channels occurs on a different sample from that in which the first new sample appears in the merged sample-data stream, the channels will get out of synchronization, and a rotation of the channels will be observed. The command might get out of step by memory or disk interference, or by being preceded by a high-bandwidth burst of commands. Consequently, it is not reasonable to use this machine for doing a mixdown of a large number of independently timed sample-data streams. This limits its usage greatly for digital editing and mixing purposes. Again, probably the next big advance in this technology will be the development of merging hardware of some sort.

As with the 4C Machine, the assumption that processing elements have many inputs and few outputs is rampant and, indeed, one of the limiting factors in the Systems Concepts Digital Synthesizer is the lengths we go to to program around this fact. For instance, the current synthesis programs do much of the vibrato in software, and the vibrato information is merged into the command stream. The synthesizer provides the ramp, so that the host processor only calculates the vibrato at relatively wide intervals.

The POLYCEPHALOS Processor

As a research project into ways of circumventing many of the problems discussed in the previous designs, a small prototype processor is being built at Stanford (Fig. 1). This processor was not designed to be a full-scale synthesizer, but mostly a sound editing and mixing station of up to 8 simultaneous channels of audio to test out one potential solution to the merge problem. If the solution turns out to be a viable one, then we may contemplate more extensive implementations of this idea.

Since music is inherently a parallel process, the

Fig. 1. Partial block diagram of the POLYCEPHA-
LOS signal processor. An
internal data bus connects
the various processing elements. Micro code (not
shown) controls the flow
of information on the bus.
All data paths are 36 bits
wide, since the device was
designed to operate with
the FOONLY F2 processor,
which emulates the DEC-
System 10.

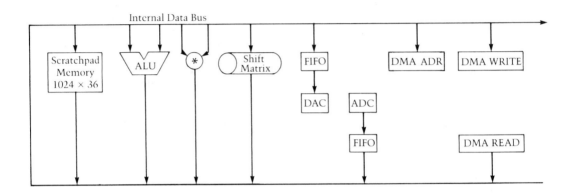

idea of the POLYCEPHALOS processor (POLY) is to build the parallel processes into hardware. The processor is a kind of micro-programmed computer that has eight different program counters (PCs) for its eight sequentially running programs. Each program does whatever is necessary to process a single sample for as many channels as it is handling, then it executes an instruction that increments the program number (i.e., moves to the next program). The next program will pick up at the instruction where it left off after its last sample and will process the next sample. For instance, the first program might do nothing but forward four samples from four locations in the scratchpad memory to the DACs and then clear these four locations (called OUTA, OUTB, OUTC, and OUTD in some music compilers). The next program might do a DMA access to bring out the next sample from a data stream in memory, scale it by some envelope, and add it into OUTA (for example). The next program might do a DMA access to some other address to bring out a pair of stereo samples and add them into OUTB and OUTC, and so on. One program might be sitting in an idle loop waiting for a key to be pressed, at which time it would start transferring samples into some output channels. Another program might be doing DMA accesses to forward OUTA, OUTB, OUTC, and OUTD back into main memory for further processing. Yet another program might be waiting until sample number 342254 to

start transferring another sample-data stream to the converter (digital mixing of asynchronous sources). In this scheme, the amount of compute time for each sample will vary. Consequently there must be some kind of buffer (FIFO) between the processor and the converters so that the converters can proceed at a steady rate.

Since the device is a computer, it can execute loops and conditional branches, and is entirely programmable. All control signals are derived from the micro code that is stored in read-write memory and is thus directly accessible. Since all the programs are entirely independent, they can handle completely separate audio materials in entirely different ways without interfering with one another. Each program might be dealing with a different number of channels and might be doing entirely different things (scaling, spatial location, filtering, DMA reading, DMA writing). The fact that each program can manage its own DMA addresses means that data streams do not have to be merged, but that each program can be reading independently from a different data stream. The merging happens as each program adds its output into OUTA, OUTB, OUTC, and OUTD (if that is what we have programmed it to do).

At first this might seem to be an ideal solution to the merge problem, but it does have limitations. For one, the number of parallel processes is quite small. One thousand twenty-four would be a better

Moorer

number. The other is that this machine has no bulk storage and consequently cannot do oscillators in any reasonable way. It could, of course, use the host computer's memory for that, but the bandwidth of the host memory is somewhat limited. The same is true for reverberation, time delays, phasing, and all other processes that use bulk memory. Note that for non-real-time applications use of the host memory for bulk memory still offers considerable speed advantage over doing the calculation in the host computer.

The omission of bulk memory was deliberate. First of all, we ran out of room on the wire-wrap board. Second, the device was designed to be a processor of natural sounds and a sound-stream-merging device and not a general-purpose synthesizer. The fact that it can do oscillation at all is somewhat serendipitous.

Next, introducing this hardware coroutining is not without cost. Of the 350 integrated circuits in the machine, probably 50 of them go to just that feature, and another 50 or so to the FIFO buffering for the converters. Somewhat less than a third of the machine is thus taken up by the introduction of this generality. The machine also runs somewhat more slowly than the synthesizers previously mentioned, since most of the signals have to run through an extra layer of gates related to the programmability of the machine.

In any case, the machine is an experiment to see if the anticipated advantages can be realized. After some experience with the machine, we anticipate publishing further results on its usefulness.

Summary

For future signal processors, some of the more important points stand out from consideration of the advantages and failings of previous synthesizers. Among these are the following:

1. The digital-to-analog converter (DAC) output path [or analog-to-digital converter (ADC) input path] should have some amount of buffering, which is commonly implemented with FIFO memories. This allows the synthesizer to be momentarily stopped without interrupting the flow of data to (or from) the converters. It also removes the restriction that the synthesizer take a constant amount of time to compute each sample. With suitable buffering, it need only take a constant amount of time on the average. The trade-off is that this introduces some amount of delay between synthesis and conversion of the output signal. If this delay is kept below a maximum of about 1 msec there will be no ill effects, and often even larger delays can be accommodated.

2. If any form of real-time control by the user is desired, then there must be a direct path to update parameters that bypasses any other update path that contains timing information. That is, in addition to whatever else is going on at the time we must be able to jam-load a parameter at any time. This means either eliminating timing information, as is done in the 4C Machine, or providing a secondary update path.

3. Some kind of synchronized sample-data writeback should be included, if only for diagnostic purposes.

References

Alles, H., and di Giugno, P. 1977. "A One-Card 64-Channel Digital Synthesizer." *Computer Music Journal* 1(4): 7–9.

Moorer, J. A., et al. 1979. "The 4C Machine." *Computer Music Journal* 3(3): 16–24.

Loy, D. G. 1981. "Notes on the Implementation of MUSBOX: a Compiler for the Systems Concepts Digital Synthesizer." *Computer Music Journal* 5(1): 34–50.

Samson, P. 1980. "A General-Purpose Digital Synthesizer." *Journal of the Audio Engineering Society* 28(3): 106–113.

Samson, P. Forthcoming. "Architectural Issues in the Design of the Systems Concepts Digital Synthesizer." In *Computer Music*, ed. C. Roads, J. Snell, and J. Strawn. Cambridge, Massachusetts: The MIT Press.

47

James A. Moorer
Lucasfilm Ltd.
P.O. Box 2009
San Rafael, California 94912

The Lucasfilm Audio Signal Processor

Introduction

The requirements of audio processing for motion pictures present several special problems that make digital processing of audio very desirable and also relatively difficult. The difficulties can be summarized as follows:

1. Large amounts of numerical computation are required, on the order of 2 million integer multiply-adds per second per channel of audio, for some number of channels.
2. The exact processing involved changes in real time but must not interrupt the flow of audio data.
3. Large input/output (I/O) capacity is necessary, simultaneous with numerical calculation and changes to the running program, on the order of 1.6 million bits per second per channel of audio.

To overcome these difficulties, the digital audio group at Lucasfilm is building a number of audio signal processors, the architecture of which reflects the special problems of audio.

Motivation: What Is the Problem?

The sound in motion pictures is usually divided into three and sometimes four categories: dialogue, music, and sound effects. Additionally, sound effects are sometimes divided into two further categories, *Foley effects* and *special effects*. Foley effects (after Jack Foley, who was with Universal Studios during the 1930s) are human nonvocal noises, such as footsteps. Special effects include pistol shots, explosions, and everything else.

Although dialogue is generally recorded at the set, it is most often not of suitable quality and must

Computer Music Journal, Vol. 6, No. 3, Fall 1982

be recreated in the studio. This entails an actor watching a print of the film and speaking the lines in synchrony with the film. The actor, however, usually hears little or no other sound cues, such as other voices, music, or sound effects while he or she is trying to speak the lines. Needless to say, it requires actors of substantial talent to give convincing performances under these conditions. Some actors are unable to do this, necessitating use of recordings from the set regardless of their quality.

Consider now the problem faced by dialogue editors. They are presented with stacks of recordings, some from a studio (an acoustically dead environment), some from a stage (which can be very reverberant), and some garbled or poorly recorded (with the actor facing away from the microphone, for instance). The editors must make all these recordings sound as if they are coming from the same environment and as if they are coming from the environment that the viewer is seeing on the screen. This consistency and apparent authenticity is usually accomplished with the use of ad hoc combinations of signal processing devices such as filters, reverberators, modulators, and other tools of the analog audio studio. The art of the dialogue editor lies in the skillful use of such equipment.

Sound effects production is a complete art in itself. Take the simple example of a "nose crunch." A real fist hitting a nose sounds a lot like someone hitting a side of beef. Sometime in the 1930s this was deemed to be insufficiently spectacular for movies, and since that time nose crunches (as well as all other sound effects) have been made by combining several sounds. There is a smack, sometimes taken from the sound of a pistol shot, and then a crunch, usually made by dropping a watermelon out of a second-story window. Other sounds, like the whizzing of the fist through the air, are added to produce the final sound. Often, signal processing is added, the most common forms probably being pitch shifting and phasing (feedback delay lines). Each sound must then be synchronized with the picture, which is typically done by splicing bits of

599

sound (with silence in between) into reels. As if this were not enough, the sound editors are generally doing this work while the film editors are still making changes in the movie. Needless to say, when a film editor decides to, for instance, delete three frames from a scene, the poor sound editor must go through every reel of sound for that scene and cut out three frames. This is not so bad in most cases, but if a scene that has a background noise (like a factory or a train) is lengthened, generally it means that that sound must be reedited (copied and spliced anew) to fit properly.

Each sound editor (of music, dialogue, sound effects) will then *mix down* (combine) several reels of sound into single, composite reels. Each editor shows up at the final mix session with a stack of reels of sound for each reel of film. This occasion is often the first on which anyone has heard the music, the dialogue, and the sound effects all together. It is usually scheduled for just a few months before the film's release, and much too late to change anything substantial. The final mix usually has several tracks of dialogue, several tracks of music, and several tracks of sound effects. The mixing boards for commercial film work are quite large—a 72-track mixing console is not unusual. A console of this size is operated by a team of two to six people. The most common arrangement is for the "head" mixer to handle the dialogue, while two other mixers handle the music and sound effects. Typically, the mixing consoles have no automation, so level and filter settings must be "rehearsed" in much the same way that musicians rehearse their performances. Balancing the various elements so that important aspects are brought out at the right times without distracting from the action on the screen is a delicate art.

If we gauge the number of reels of sound needed for every reel of film by multiplying the number of premixed reels by the number of reels that have gone into the premix and summing over all reels, we find that a complicated scene can entail as many as 130 separate reels or tracks of audio. Premixing is essential, then, as a way of reducing this to a manageable number, even at the cost of introducing additional noise during the copying process.

This is the way movie sound has been made, vir-

tually as long as there has been movie sound. What we wish to do here at Lucasfilm is to put a computer in the middle of all of this, so that each manipulation is precisely recorded and memorized and there can be complete (and semiautomatic) sharing of information among the different mixers, including the film editor. To this end, we have designed, built, programmed (Abbott 1981), and are currently debugging an audio signal processing station that we hope will be able to perform these tasks with great efficiency and clarity of sound.

This system can only affect the production of sound for the film. We cannot now expect to have a strong influence on how the sound is presented in the theater. (Obviously, to reap the benefits of digital processing fully, theater sound systems have to be thoroughly overhauled also.) Our aim is to reduce the tremendous amount of hand work (splicing and resplicing all those little pieces together) and consequently lower the cost of film production (at least in the sound department). With costs down, we hope funds will become available to bring new talent and creativity into the field.

This, then, is the background for our project. Since most of us on the team come from the computer music synthesis world, we have also embedded a great deal of music processing and synthesis capability into the system, with the feeling that when sound editors, particularly those involved with sound effects and music production, learn the true potential of the system, they will be seduced into using it more and more.

And In Signal Processing Terms . . .

The implications of this scenario for the signal processor are numerous. We plan to store the sound itself on standard 300-Mbyte disks. They offer several advantages, such as the fact that they are mature products that are easily available and easily maintained. The packs may be mounted and dismounted, giving us the flexibility we need in face of the startling realization that we cannot afford to keep all the sound for an entire movie on-line all the time. With a 50-KHz sampling rate, an entire 300-Mbyte disk pack, when formatted in a standard way (32 sectors per track at 512 bytes per sector), holds 42 min of monaural sound. Since the 70-mm print of a film uses six magnetic tracks, a single pack only holds between 6 and 7 min of six-track sound, and this is in finished form. Many, many disk packs have been used to produce these tracks. Until storage systems several orders of magnitude more dense (such as optical storage) are readily available, we must accept the need to mount and dismount large numbers of disk packs.

Sounds for movies vary from very short (pistol shots) to very long (background noise or music). During the mix-down process, deliberate steps must be taken to prevent these sounds from being scattered around the disks in unpredictable ways, which would require a great deal of head motion to recover them all. Since the disk rotates at 60 revolutions per second and each track contains 16 Kybtes, a mean transfer rate of about 980,000 bytes per second could theoretically be obtained (despite the fact that the burst rate is about 1.2 Mbytes per second). Since we only need 800,000 bytes per second to provide eight channels of audio at 50 KHz, some margin is provided for head motion, but then the buffer space must be quite large to allow large, contiguous transfers to proceed in an uninterrupted manner.

The processing of the signal can be easily formulated using digital techniques, since it consists mostly of various kinds of filtering. Each sound, however, usually has its own "private" processing that must be applied, which is different from the processing of other sounds that might be going on at the time. For example, we might have two simultaneous pieces of dialogue, one of which was recorded in a studio and the other of which was recorded on the set. When the sound is started, microcode must be loaded to perform the particular processing that is necessary for this sound and must be unloaded when the sound is done (or somewhat after the sound is done if, for instance, the reverberation is to persist after the sound). For the duration of a sound, the microcode for that sound typically does not change, but various parameters (loudness, filter frequencies) will often change slowly with time. This means that we must be able to load a bunch of microcode at or near a particular time without disturbing any other processing (microcode) that is happening at the time. Not all the microcode changes at once; more often, relatively small bits of it flow in and out of existence at various (precise) times.

The Audio Signal Processor

The audio signal processing station is a semimodular, self-contained unit composed of several major subassemblies. The control computer is a Motorola 68000 with Winchester disk, 1 Mbyte of main memory, and a high-resolution, bit-map, graphic display screen. The audio signal processor (ASP) is composed of two parts: the controller and up to eight digital signal processors (DSPs). The console is a stand-alone 68000 with a custom-built panel that has various kinds of control devices, such as slide potentiometers and knobs (Snell 1982). We allow up to seven independent control processors to forward updates (changes to microcode and parameter memories) to the ASP simultaneously. There is a priority system for arbitration of simultaneous requests. The remainder of this article will be concerned with the architecture of the ASP itself, since this is where any innovation in audio signal processing is to be found. Figure 1 shows the block diagram of the entire system.

A DSP is designed to handle 8 channels of audio at a sampling rate of 50 KHz. Since movie sound does not normally have a full 20-KHz bandwidth, we may be able to reduce the sampling rate to 35 KHz and thus increase the number of channels to 12. For professional music applications, however, 50 KHz is considered to be standard. Since up to eight DSPs can be connected to a single DSP controller, a maximum of 64 channels for an ASP is achievable. Each DSP is capable of a computation rate of about 18 million 24-bit integer multiply-adds per second, simultaneous with a sustained disk transfer rate of 6.4 million bits per second (800 Kbytes per second) and a sustained analog-to-digital or digital-to-analog converter (ADC or DAC) transfer rate of 6.4 million bits per second.

The DSP is a horizontally microcoded device with 4K 96-bit microcode words. The device is a

Fig. 1. Block diagram of
the Lucasfilm audio signal
processor (ASP) system.

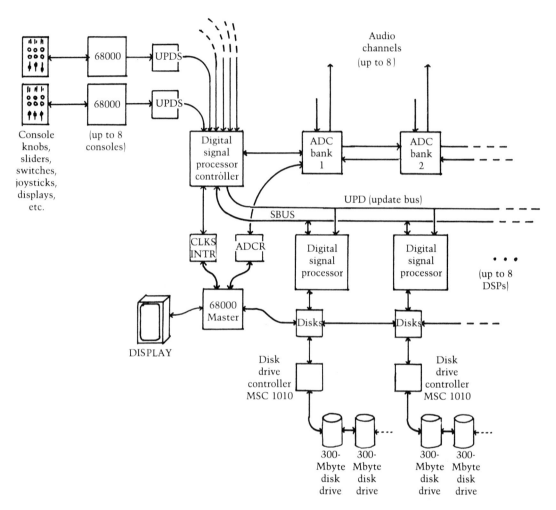

lock-step, synchronous machine with no branching. The instruction counter starts at zero, goes to a fixed limit, then returns to zero. It was designed this way for several reasons, not the least of which is that branching is not generally necessary in this kind of sample-at-a-time "stream" processing, as long as logic and decision-making capabilities are provided in some other way. Another reason is that with a number of DSPs in the system, it is very convenient to have them all working on the same sample at the same time. This greatly simplifies interprocessor communication. For computing recur-rence relations, such as those involved in digital filtering, it is perfectly clear that the "program" is the same for each sample. (Note: we cannot readily make use of the Fast Fourier Transform [FFT] for realizing these digital filters, since most of these filters have time-varying coefficients, and sometimes the rate of variation approaches the FFT frame rate. We are thus forced to use the time-domain recur-rence relation.)

Inside the DSP itself, there are separate func-tional units for dealing with each of the main prob-lems in this kind of device: (1) transferring data to

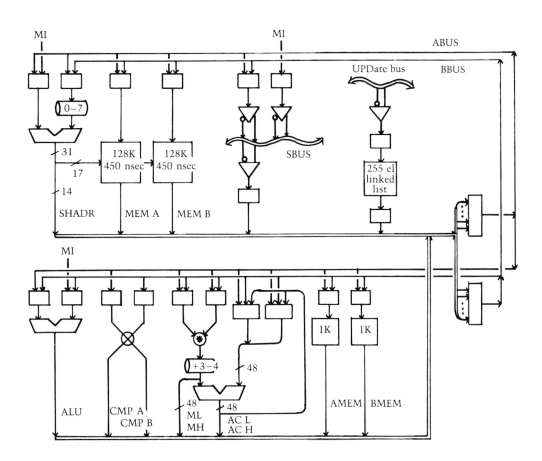

Fig. 2. Block diagram of
the digital signal processor
(DSP) subsystem of the
ASP.

MI   MI   ABUS

UPDate bus   BBUS

0–7

31

128K
450 nsec

128K
450 nsec

SBUS

255 el
linked
list

17

14

SHADR   MEM A   MEM B

MI

1K   1K

+3–4   48

48   48

ALU   CMP A
CMP B   ML
MH   AC L
AC H   AMEM   BMEM

and from the disks continously at near the max-imum rate, (2) effecting the required numerical cal-culation rate, (3) transferring data to and from the ADCs and DACs, and (4) handling the synchronous changes to microcode and parameters. In addition, extensive diagnostic aids are distributed throughout the machine, allowing it to be single-stepped and allowing readback of most of its internal registers.

The Numerical Engine

The heart of the numerical part of a DSP is the multiply-accumulate unit, the scratchpad memo-ries, and the busses. Figure 2 shows a block dia-gram of the DSP itself. There are two 24-bit busses, called the *ABUS* and the *BBUS*, which supply data to each of the arithmetic units. Each microinstruc-tion has two 4-bit fields that specify the source for each bus, and a number of bits saying which arith-metic unit input latches are to receive the contents of these busses. On each 50-nsec instruction, two 24-bit data are selected and forwarded, via the busses, to the input latches of some functional units. For ease of programming, the two 16-input multiplexers for the busses are identical. This makes the busses largely interchangeable, even though some of the combinations will be seldom

Fig. 3. Data flow through
the multiply-accumulate
unit.

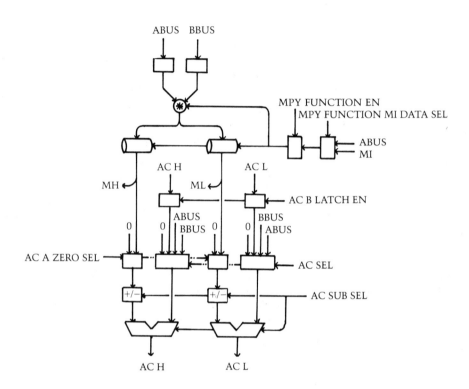

ABUS BBUS

MPY FUNCTION EN
MPY FUNCTION MI DATA SEL

ABUS
MI

AC H   AC L

MH   ML

AC B LATCH EN

0   0 ABUS   0   0 BBUS
          BBUS   ABUS

AC A ZERO SEL   AC SEL

AC SUB SEL

AC H   AC L

used. We did it this way because every time in the past that we have attempted to anticipate which paths would be used and which paths would not be used, further developments in signal processing techniques have invariably proved us wrong. After gaining some experience with the machine, we will be able to look back over our programs and ask which combinations have not been used. Then we may reduce the width of the selectors in future versions of the machine.

The multiply-accumulate unit consists of a 24-by-24-bit, signed/unsigned multiplier that develops a full 48-bit product, followed by a shifter that is capable of shifting left up to three places and right up to four places, followed by a 48-bit accumulator. This allows the partial products for a digital filter to be summed in double precision, permitting later truncation to single precision or the use of even higher precision. There are pipeline registers in the

multiplier so that a full multiply may be started every 50 nsec (that is, every instruction). If a multiply is started on instruction N, its results may be selected onto one of the busses on instruction $N + 2$, and the output of the accumulator may be selected on instruction $N + 3$. The output of the multiplier may be either added into or subtracted from the accumulator contents.

The Multiply-Accumulate Unit

The multiply-accumulate unit consists of a 24-by-24-bit, signed/unsigned integer multiplier, a 48-bit combinational shifter (three left to four right, signed or unsigned), and a 48-bit accumulator (adder and latch). Figure 3 shows the data flow through this unit. There are pipeline registers so that a new multiply-accumulate can be started every instruction (50 nsec). If the accumulate function is not needed, the direct multiplier output is available (to the bus multiplexers). The programmer may choose either the high-order or the low-order word, or may use the full 48-bit product. There are multiplexers on the accumulator input, so that three different functions may be selected: initialize to zero; accumulate (that is, use previous accumulator contents as input); and initialize to the contents of the ABUS and/or the BBUS. Similarly, the multiplier output can be inverted before it is accumulated to provide for subtraction as well as addition. If a multiply-accumulate is started on instruction N (that is, if instruction N specifies latching of either of the multiplier input latches), then the product may be selected into the bus multiplexers on instruction $N + 2$, and the accumulator output may be selected on instruction $N + 3$.

Although the shift amount is normally specified by a microinstruction, it may also be latched from the ABUS. This allows a limited form of data-dependent shifting, such as is needed for normalization or alignment of floating-point or block-floating-point operations. Since the shift matrix has only a very limited range, large shifts must be synthesized in other ways, such as with multiplication by powers of two. For normalization, we must first determine the position of the high-order bit. In this machine, this is most easily accomplished by the use of table lookups for large shift amounts or of the compare/exchange unit for lesser shift amounts.

The signed/unsigned feature of the multiplier allows simple extension to multiple precision operations. It also simplifies table interpolation, which is used extensively in variable-length delay lines, such as those used in audio "phasers" or reverberators. Multiple precision does not have direct application in garden-variety audio processing, but rather in certain exotic possibilities, such as linear prediction speech modification or deconvolution of room reverberation. In linear prediction, the filter itself can be easily realized in single precision, but the matrix inversion necessary for computing filter coefficients must be done in multiple precision for higher filter orders (such as order 45 or higher).

Since the DSP does not have a divide unit as

such, divides must be accomplished by other means. There are various schemes for doing this, but probably the most relevant is a reciprocal table for some number of the divisor bits, followed by some number of iterations of Newton's method for the low-order bits. Since the reciprocal is a seldom-used operation even in matrix processing, this is not expected to be a bottleneck, but merely an annoyance. We have found that for a 24-bit number, a 4096-word lookup table followed by one iteration of Newton's method gives us 23-bit accuracy for all but the smallest (i.e., less than 1/4096) numbers. In this range, the dynamic range of the reciprocal exceeds the word length of the machine. If numbers spanning this range are expected, then some more comprehensive method must be used.

The Logical Unit

Even in a stream machine without program branches, decision making is necessary. Decision making is done by (1) the compare/exchange unit or (2) the conditional execution of a microinstruction. A condition code set by a microinstruction specifies the condition, such as arithmetic-logic unit (ALU) output compared to zero, or the relation of the two compare/exchange inputs. All eight logical combinations, including unconditional TRUE and FALSE, are possible. The result of the OR of all the bits showing through the condition mask forms the condition. Based on this condition, the current instruction may be executed or not. Likewise based on this condition, the two inputs to the compare/exchange unit may be swapped. This latter feature is handy for control functions, such as filter frequencies that are being changed in real time. In this manner, we can specify a control function in piecewise-linear form, such that each segment has an increment, a current value, and a final value. When the current value passes the final value, the compare/exchange unit can be employed to substitute the final value. Similarly, other piecewise-linear functions, such as the absolute value of a number, can be simulated. Figure 4 shows the data flow in the compare unit.

The conditional execution of an instruction is

Fig. 4. Data flow in the compare unit.

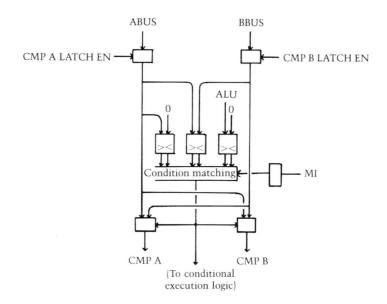

ABUS   BBUS

CMP A LATCH EN →   ← CMP B LATCH EN

ALU

0   0

Condition matching ← [ ] — MI

CMP A   CMP B

(To conditional
execution logic)

useful in several different ways. It can be used to reset loop variables such as the span, the increment, and the "twiddle" angle in an FFT calculation. It can be used to interrupt conditionally the host processor after a calculation is complete. In general, it is the "escape" from the lock-step of the computing engine.

The Arithmetic-Logic Unit

For performing all the other operations that are needed, such as Boolean functions, a general-purpose ALU is included. This provides AND, OR, and EXCLUSIVE-OR, as well as addition and subtraction operations. Furthermore, a second register is included for accumulation of high-order bits in multiple-precision operations (i.e., the carry bit is accessible), with optional sign-extension of either or both operands.

Main Memory

The main, bulk memory of the system is arranged in boards of two banks of 128K 24-bit words each.

Up to eight boards may be connected to each DSP. Each bank can be cycled simultaneously such that two 24-bit transfers may be accomplished each 450-nsec interval. Error detection and correction are pipelined with the memory cycle.

There are two addressing schemes for the main memory. The first is the DSP's address-calculation engine, consisting of a shift matrix and an adder, which provides two-dimensional addressing capabilities. This is most useful for table lookup with tables of power-of-two lengths. The shift matrix scales down the address such that the entire 24-bit range is reduced to correspond to the length of the table, then the origin of the table is added in to produce the final address. The high-order 17 bits of this combined number are used as the memory address, and the low-order 14 bits (24 bits plus a possible seven-position shift) are available to the multiplexers for interpolation. This makes operations such as delays quite simple. Likewise, special functions such as computing square root or arctangent can be accomplished with limited precision by table lookup and interpolation. For interpolation, we might store the function values in one memory bank and the differences between adjacent values in the other bank, so that the difference and the low-

606   *Moorer*

Fig. 5. Update queue
mechanism.

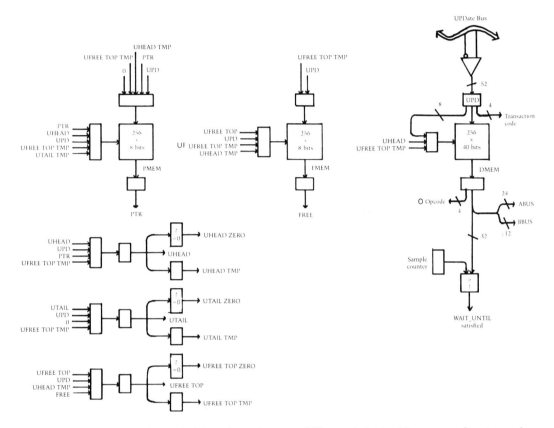

order address bits may be forwarded directly to the multiplier for the interpolation calculation.

The second addressing scheme is asynchronous and is not under the control of the DSP micro-engine. This is direct memory access (DMA) from the disk. There is a separate word count and memory-address counter for this data path. The DMA is operated on a *cycle-stealing* basis in that it uses cycles when the DSP is not referencing the memory.

In the normal mode of operation, we plan to use four memory boards for a total of 1 million 24-bit words of storage. This gives enough room for adequate disk buffering with some space left for delay lines and table lookups. With the 450-nsec cycle time, somewhat more than 120 memory references could be made in the 20-μsec sampling interval if we started a memory cycle at every available opportunity.

The Update System

Certainly the most unconventional part of the machine is the update queue (Fig. 5). This is a linked list, implemented in hardware, of triples (opcode, address, and data). The opcodes specify for the most part which memory is to be written, but one of the opcodes is critically important for timing updates: the WAIT_UNTIL code. In this operation, the address and data are taken as a single 32-bit number and compared to a sample number counter that is "incremented" automatically each time the DSP program counter is reset to zero (i.e., at the beginning of each sample calculation). The operation of the queue is as follows. Up to eight computers may give update transactions. A priority arrangement selects one transaction and forwards it to the specified DSP. The transaction code (different from the opcode) tells the disposition of this transaction. Some of the options are (1) insert at beginning of queue, (2) insert at end of queue, and (3) insert at specified address in queue (i.e., after a specified element of the queue). Normally, the master processor will insert at the end of the queue. At the end of the processing for a sample, all the DSPs will go into update mode. In this mode, triples are read from the head of the update queue (if it is non-empty) and the appropriate actions are taken at the rate of 50 nsec per update. If the operation code specified WAIT_UNTIL, then the datum is compared to the sample number. If the datum is greater than the sample number, then updates for that DSP will be halted, and the WAIT_UNTIL will not be removed from the queue. If the datum is less than or equal to the sample number, then the WAIT_UNTIL is removed from the queue and updates proceed as described above. When all the DSPs have either emptied their queues or have hit an unsatisfied WAIT_UNTIL, they will all simultaneously exit update mode and start again at instruction zero. If there are no updates to do, all DSPs will spend a total of three instruction times (150 nsec) in update mode. The point of this complexity is that the 68000 can forward changes to be made at a specific time to the DSP as fast as it can. When that time comes, the DSP will be held in update mode until all of those changes are made. The net result is that large amounts of changes can be made (up to 255 per DSP) that appear to happen entirely between two samples. This occurs quite often in the audio processing case, since each time a new sound is begun, it typically requires an amount of processing (filtering, reverberation, etc.) that must be commenced at the same time. This involves, as often as not, the "splicing" of new processing elements into the audio stream. As we might expect, there is a critical section problem here: if the splicing is done in the wrong order, discontinuities in the signal can

result. We solve this problem by making a group of updates into an indivisible unit so that updates are all effected at the same "time." Likewise, in order not to slow down the ASP, the changes are accumulated and effected at the natural rate of the ASP rather than at the somewhat slower rate of the controlling computer.

This update scheme has one problem, and that is with real-time manual intervention. What we have described above works quite well if the changes are known beforehand. If the changes are not known, such as when the operator is manipulating a potentiometer or some other input device, then the queue must be "short-circuited" so that the parameter changes may be introduced ahead of any timed updates that are already in the queue. This is why we allow updates to be entered at the beginning of the queue, thus going ahead of any WAIT_UNTIL that might delay its effect. Of the eight computers that can access the update queue, only one can be the *queue master* and insert WAIT_UNTIL instructions. All the others must insert untimed changes at the beginning of the queue. Otherwise, two computers that are not perfectly synchronized could insert WAIT_UNTILs that were not in order.

There is no substantial hardware limit to the rate at which updates can be forwarded to the DSP. The only limit is how fast the 68000 processors can deliver them, which is a maximum of about 100,000 updates per second, per 68000 processor. The DSP can handle more than 1,200,000 updates per second as a sustained maximum rate.

The SBUS

The SBUS is the catch-all for data transfer. It is used to communicate among DSPs and to send data to the DACs and read data from the ADCs. To communicate with other DSPs, one DSP merely writes a 24-bit word into its SBUS output port on instruction N. All other DSPs can then read this word on instruction $N + 2$. To communicate with a DAC, a DSP places the converter number (a 6-bit quantity) and an opcode into an SBUS function register, then provides a 24-bit datum to its SBUS output port. Automatically, the SBUS controller (a global resource) polls the first-in first-out (FIFO) for the named DAC. If there is room in its FIFO, the 16 bits in the middle of the 24-bit word are placed in that FIFO and the ASP proceeds. If the FIFO for the named DAC is full, indicating that the ASP is running ahead of the DAC, then the clock of the ASP will be held until the FIFO is no longer full. The situation with the ADCs is analogous. If the named ADC FIFO is empty, the ASP clock will be held. These FIFOs are 64 samples long, giving a maximum delay of 1.28 msec to the audio path.

Another SBUS feature, which we call the *bulletin board*, is a 256-element memory that may be written by an SBUS operation and may be read by any computer with an update bus (UPDS) interface. This provides a channel for certain kinds of feedback, such as the root-mean-squared (RMS) level of an audio signal or an overload condition of some kind. The controlling computers may also read back the current value of the sample counter and thus keep track of time.

Conclusions

The ASP, through its multiple data paths and unique architecture, is capable of the very high numerical computation rate required for processing many channels of high-quality digitized audio. Both synchronous and asynchronous data exchange proceeds at very high sustained rates without interfering with computation. Large blocks of program memory may also be changed without interference with the sample data stream. The device is ideally suited to large-scale, real-time audio processing applications, such as film sound mixing, special effects processing, and music synthesis.

Status of the Project

The prototype machine became operational in April 1982 and is functioning reliably at the full clock rate. All of the complex features, such as the DAC FIFO mechanism, the direct DMA path to the bulk memory system, and the 24-by-24-bit multiply followed by the 48-bit accumulate, function reliably

with a substantial amount of timing margin. The software, under development for more than a year, is now operational. We hope to turn the machine over to users very soon. As soon as this is done, we will begin building two more devices for our own in-house use.

Acknowledgments

The hardware was designed by James A. Moorer with the exception of the main memory board, which was designed by John M. Snell. The technicians who did the board preparation and final assembly were Charlie Keagle, Kris Handwerk, and Sharon McCormick. The project was started in April 1980 by George Lucas and it is entirely his foresight and vision that have enabled us to proceed.

References

Abbott, C. 1981. "Microprogramming a Generalized Signal Processor Architecture." Paper presented at the 1981 International Computer Music Conference, 5–8 November 1981, in Denton, Texas.

Samson, P. 1980. "A General-Purpose Digital Synthesizer." *Journal of the Audio Engineering Society* 28(3): 106–113.

Samson, P. Forthcoming. "Architectural Issues in the Design of the Systems Concepts Digital Synthesizer." In *Computer Music*, ed. C. Roads and J. Strawn. Cambridge, Massachusetts: MIT Press.

Snell, J. 1982. "The Lucasfilm Real-Time Console for Recording Studios and Performance of Computer Music." *Computer Music Journal* 6(3):33–45.

48

S. Jerrold Kaplan
Computer Science Department
Stanford University
Stanford, California 94305

Developing a Commercial Digital Sound Synthesizer

Introduction

In September 1978, a project was proposed: to design and build a high-quality all-digital keyboard synthesizer for the commercial market currently served mainly by analog devices. The proposal was motivated by the successful prototyping of a digital circuit that simulated 32 oscillators and provided convenient mechanisms for controlling their amplitude and frequency independently in real time with an inexpensive microprocessor. With a working example in hand, it seemed to everyone involved that the hard part was over. All that remained was to incorporate the device into a suitable package, program the desired features, and sell it. Initially, it was estimated that this process might take a few months.

Two and one-half years and nearly one million dollars later, the resultant product—the Synergy (from Digital Keyboards, Inc.)—is available for sale. In retrospect, the tremendous number of technological, design, and production difficulties encountered make the original estimates seem appallingly naive. Problems were encountered almost continuously that required original research, the development of novel techniques, and outright "hacks" to produce a marketable product. This article will outline some of the unanticipated pitfalls in designing a digital instrument for the commercial market and describe some of the solutions adopted.

Background

The Synergy is a fully digital, portable, keyboard-oriented synthesizer designed for use by profes-

Computer Music Journal, Vol. 5, No. 3, Fall 1981

sional musicians. It incorporates a velocity-sensing keyboard, two foot pedals, a joystick, a cartridge socket and a variety of switches, and potentiometers (pots) and light-emitting diodes (LEDs) for controlling the sound (Fig. 1). While the player has control over many parameters of the sound, the unit is primarily a preset machine. A read-only memory (ROM) containing data for 24 voices is included that can be assigned in various patterns to the keyboard by pressing switches. Additional voices can be accessed via external ROMs by inserting a cartridge in a slot much like in home video games. The main unique features of the machine are the use of the keyboard velocity to affect the spectrum of the sound as well as the amplitude (under player control), a built-in four-track event recorder (about 1800 notes), the ability to play multiple timbres simultaneously, stereo outputs, nonvolatile program storage, and realistic voices.

The heart of the machine is a circuit of 32 digital oscillators, based on a design by Hal Alles of Bell Laboratories (Alles 1979; 1980). The oscillators appear in the memory space of a Z-80 microprocessor, which is also interfaced to the keyboard and other input devices. The oscillator card requests data from the processor by issuing interrupts; all other devices are polled at regular intervals. The oscillators can be "patched" through a set of data-storage registers in a variety of ways and their outputs routed to one or both of a pair of 16-bit digital-to-analog converters (DACs).

The processing is controlled by software that resides in 24 Kbytes of ROM. Sixteen Kbytes of random-access memory (RAM) are used for variable data and sequencer storage (sequences are not retained). One Kbyte of complementary metal oxide semiconductor (CMOS) nonvolatile memory are used to save user "programs" and the state of the machine across power downs. Voice data reside in an additional 8 Kbytes of ROM. When external cartridges are used, they are bank-switched into the voice-data address space.

Fig. 1. The Synergy digital synthesizer.

ging real-time interrupt-driven software hampered program development.

Imitating the Accepted Technology

A peculiar characteristic of performing musicians is their ability to adapt positively to the limitations of their instruments. Players may use and ultimately come to depend on characteristics of their instruments that were quite incidental in the original design. This creates an obstacle to incorporating improvements or introducing a new technology to the musician: the designers (and, for that matter, the musicians themselves) may not appreciate which features of the existing instrument should be retained.

In the acoustic domain, breath noise can be a desirable (and controllable) part of sounds such as those of overblown flutes; the difficulty of properly tuning chimes and bells is a part of their characteristic charm. As an example in the electronic domain, performers now insist on the "fuzz-tone" effect originally produced by overloaded amplifiers. (Indeed, there is now one product on the market, called Tubes, that touts the superior ability of vacuum-tube amplifiers to distort in a desirable way.)

This effect is no less true of analog synthesists than of other musicians. Analog synthesists have adapted to the limitations of the technology and have come to expect their instruments to behave in particular ways. In designing a digital synthesizer, it rapidly became obvious that the product had to do a plausible job of imitating the major characteristics of the analog equipment that players were already used to, in addition to providing new capabilities. This put the development staff in the peculiar position of researching techniques for making a digital instrument sound and perform like an analog one.

Many of the features of analog equipment that performers are accustomed to are not so much intentional points of design as limitations of the technology. Primary among these drawbacks is the difficulty of accurately tuning analog oscillators over a wide frequency range. (Some analog synthesizers have a tuning cycle that allows the oscillators to be tuned automatically after their

While the initial hardware design was intended to be as general as possible so as not to commit the project to a particular instrument design, it was also intended to be produced inexpensively, so the specifications bounded the accepted data on the limits of human perception quite closely. It was discovered at several points during the development that these accepted data were inadequate for the requirements of the domain. As a result, some techniques not originally envisioned in the hardware design had to be added through additional software. Many of these problems dealt with extremely accurate frequency control and, interestingly enough, with using this control to introduce various forms of noncorrelated randomness into the sound.

Like the hardware, the software was designed to be quite general in order to facilitate diverse applications. Written in Fortran and Z-80 assembly language, virtually all communication between modules is accomplished via a shared common data structure. Just as the processor can inspect and adjust any parameter in the oscillators' memory through shared memory access, each program module can set or adjust any parameters in the common area. While this provided the required flexibility, it created severe debugging problems because of the lack of program modularity in the design. In the computing environment available during development, the nearly complete lack of tools for debug-

frequencies have drifted. This process may take several seconds.) Synthesists, however, rapidly discovered that playing *detuned* oscillators in unison provides a richness that is otherwise difficult to achieve. These "fat" sounds have become the standard in the commercial market, with each instrument known for a characteristic sound that depends on the nature and quality of its oscillators.

From the standpoint of developing a digital synthesizer, the accuracy of digital oscillators would appear to be their primary advantage over analog oscillators. This precision is essential for synthesizing convincing imitations of natural sounds and for providing the range of control needed for diverse timbres and effects. The problem is that it is precisely this accuracy that makes it difficult to imitate analog synthesizers. Nonetheless, the standard analog sounds must be included in any unit that intends to compete seriously in the marketplace.

Consequently, a variety of techniques were developed for adding carefully controlled "random" detuning and pitch fluctuations to the frequency of the oscillators. Close imitations of rich analog sounds became feasible. It was possible in the Synergy, however, to improve on this feature by giving the player precise control over the degree to which the oscillators could be put out of tune, thereby controlling the choruslike effects.

Several types of frequency control are available in the Synergy, although most are intrinsic to the individual voices and hence not under direct player control. The first is the frequency envelope itself. Each oscillator can have its own frequency envelope, expressed as up to 16 (value, time) pairs. The envelope values are scaled according to the base pitch of the note when started up. (The base pitch is determined by the key struck, the *transposition*, and *current tuning*.) In addition to their spectral control function, frequency envelopes can be used to introduce small variations in the pitch of the oscillators by creating *looping* envelopes (envelopes that cycle between specified points as long as the key is held down).

A second option is to defeat the scaling of the frequency envelopes so that the pitch deviations are specified in absolute Hertz. Providing a small, fixed offset has the effect of distorting the frequency rela-tionships between different notes (the tuning of the keyboard), resulting in subtle but natural *beating* throughout the keyboard range.

A time-varying pitch-control pot allows the player to set the desired depth of certain pitch changes. The pot is divided into two segments, with the center setting indicating no pitch variations. When the setting indicator is turned to the right, values read from a sine table are scaled and added to the pitch of the oscillators; when it is turned to the left, values from a modified random-number table are scaled and added to the pitch. The main function of this pot is vibrato (the sine table), a familiar control for synthesizer players. The random table creates discrete pitch fluctuations, which have various uses depending on the depth selected. At large settings, the pitches vary randomly up and down an octave from the struck note, giving the equivalent of the analog effect of routing noise through a sample-and-hold. At shallow depths, the deviations cause random beating against other notes and voices. When two identical voices are assigned to the same key with small pitch fluctuations, they create a chorus effect that can be further enhanced by (external) reverberation or delay lines. Two other pots are used to set the rate of pitch fluctuations (vibrato speed) and onset delay.

Normally, two notes started with the same vibrato depth will fluctuate in phase as they do, for example, on a vibraphone. In the Synergy, the voices are preset with a parameter that can also cause the vibrato to be independent on individual notes. This imitates the commonly heard sound of many instruments playing with vibrato independently, as in a string quartet. For additional naturalness, noncorrelated randomness can be added to the vibrato depth and rate. It was found through experimentation that the most natural effect was achieved by making inverse adjustments to the depth and rate, rather than by varying them both independently. When the rate increased (randomly), the depth decreased.

An additional form of frequency control is the *detuning parameter*. This allows the frequency of individual oscillators to be increased or decreased by a fixed, minute amount (measured in hundredths of Hertz). This is typically used for specific beating effects and the maximum range of the control is about 2.5 Hz. This detuning can also be "randomized," so that small pitch fluctuations occur about 25 times a second, up to a maximum depth. The effect is essentially that of skewing the phase periodically, which can create timbral variations and the perception of additional depth. Finally, the player can introduce pitch bending and "modulation" (actually just additional vibrato), by moving the joystick. On a typical voice, a variety of these options will occur simultaneously. The net effect is the kind of activity and variability characteristic of both natural instruments and analog synthesizers.

Negotiating Processing Constraints

Unfortunately, the need for extremely detailed frequency fluctuation and control was not adequately foreseen in the hardware design. While the oscillators were capable of producing the desired sounds, most of the computation required to control these effects had to be performed in the microprocessor. (By contrast, the frequency and amplitude-envelope computations were handled directly by the oscillators, which request points as required and ramp smoothly toward those values on their own.) The technique chosen to implement the needed frequency adjustment was a periodic interrupt driven by a timer on the oscillator circuit. Every 12 msec an interrupt is processed that recalculates the center frequencies of all active oscillators, taking into account the key, transposition, pitch bend, portamento, detuning, random detuning, vibrato, random pitch fluctuations, and global tuning (frequency envelopes are handled separately). The cost of this computation is substantial—the time required to process one such interrupt has a worst case of about 10 msec, although the expected case is about 5 msec. Several things were done to diffuse the potential impact on performance.

First, it was observed that there is sufficient processing power in the microprocessor to handle the demands placed on it. The potential performance problems occur when a variety of demands are made simultaneously and some must be deferred while others take precedence. As with highways and power grids, the solution to the implementation problem is to average the demand over time as much as possible. Consequently, the software was designed to dictate that strict priorities be observed when simultaneous demands occur. Normally, this would be as simple as implementing a version of priority interrupts. In this application, however, it is not sufficient simply to defer computations: many functions that can be delayed slightly in a given instance must ultimately be compensated by being expedited in the future. For example, to achieve a constant vibrato rate, it is acceptable to delay the computation of a sample by a few milliseconds as long as in the near future some sample is shortened by the same amount. Similarly, a sequencer event can be slightly late as long as a subsequent event is early by the same amount. Such functions could be characterized as locally elastic but globally fixed.

A strategy of allowing computations to be deferred was adopted subject to the ability to keep track of exactly how late that computation was. This was accomplished through the use of independent clocks (timers) on the oscillator board that are unaffected by computing loads on the microprocessor. Along with a locally noncritical event, a desired time for that event to occur is noted. When the event actually occurs, the true time is noted and compared to the desired time. The desired time of the subsequent event is then adjusted by this difference. Such computations eventually catch up to their global optimum.

This technique was found to be very successful in maintaining real-time response under unusually heavy computation loads. Perhaps the most critical example occurs when many notes are struck simultaneously from the keyboard (complex chords, for example). All processing not directly related to the selection of voices, oscillators, and envelope setup for the keys is immediately deferred. Interrupts are disabled and other routine processing is suspended. When the highest-priority event in the system is no longer a *key-down*, all pending oscillators are started up synchronously. This minimizes any "arpeggios" due to note-setup time and provides a crisp attack. With the critical processing complete, interrupts are reenabled and calculations such as frequency updates are allowed to catch up. Because this process is invoked mainly when a flurry of activity is taking place, the resulting delays are imperceptible.

Creating a Development Environment

One difficulty encountered at the outset of the project was the need for a *testbed* system to try out features and ideas and to create voices. It was clear that the Synergy could not simply be designed and implemented from scratch. Although several concepts for the design existed at the start, it was not yet clear which features were desirable (or for that matter would work at all).

Consequently, it was decided that a special development testbed would be designed in which we could test concepts relatively quickly and easily. The original version of this system was based on a Cromemco System 3 microcomputer (an S-100 bus, Z-80-type sytem), with dual floppy-disk drives, 64 Kbytes of RAM and an ADDS Regent 20 terminal. (The computer was later changed to a similar system from Industrial Micro Systems, for reasons of price and customer support.) A special panel with a variety of general-purpose input devices (32 sliders, 16 switches, 12 rotary pots, two foot switches, a variable foot pedal, a joystick, a bat-handle, return-to-center pot, and a velocity-sensing 61-key keyboard) was designed. S-100 bus-compatible oscillator and key/pot interfaces were fabricated, as well as a 16-bit DAC.

Initially, two software packages were written. The first was a program that allowed interactive control and display of data for the purpose of designing voices. The other was a performance program that allowed up to eight voices to be loaded at a time, assigned to the keyboard, and played in a performance-style setting, for evaluating features. Both of these programs made extensive use of the display, reassignment of the functions of the controls, and disk files.

The task of designing and building the testbed system, presumably an essential though indirect subgoal of the project, proved to be many times more difficult than designing and building the final product itself. Initial estimates of the effort required for the project tended to overlook the size and complexity of this task since it was regarded as somewhat tangential to the final result. This proved to be a serious planning oversight.

Compounding this problem was a management decision to attempt to market the testbed system directly. After about one year of development, the backers of the project were understandably anxious to see some positive evidence of results and to relieve the strain on their cash flow. Selling this system appeared to be an attractive way to make the project self-supporting, as well as to develop outside sources of input and expertise. There was evidence of considerable outside interest in the system and it appeared that several could be sold with minimal effort at a reasonable profit. In addition, all indications were that the system would produce a favorable image for the entire project. The system was named the General Development System (GDS) and marketed under the Crumar name (one of the project's backers—a well-known synthesizer manufacturer).

Marketing the GDS created the problem, unforeseen at the time, of committing the staff to a level of support and quality control that was unnecessary for internal purposes, as well as limiting the experimental role of the system. With outside users of the system, new features had to be compatible with existing ones; subsequent software versions could not make old files obsolete; marginal features could not be changed substantively or removed; a 200-page manual describing the system, and at least rudimentary marketing materials had to be written. The personnel devoted to the project (one full-time engineer, an assistant, and two part-time consultants), already spread quite thin, had to divert their attention to educating customers and marketing personnel, providing customer support, manufacturing the instruments, writing user documentation and advertising copy, staffing trade-fair booths, giving demonstrations, and handling inquiries.

An additional problem was that outside customers wanted to use the system for applications for which it was not originally intended. Existing features were designed mainly for a smaller, self-contained synthesizer; customers tended to regard the system as an integrated voicing and recording studio. This created substantial pressure, mainly from the marketing staff, to develop new features not directly related to the primary goals of the project.

For a variety of reasons, the commercialization of the development system was not entirely successful. Aside from the demands it made on scarce staff time, little was known about how to market a large digital synthesizer effectively. A limited promotional budget did not prove adequate to publicize the instrument very widely. In addition, several other superficially comparable units became available at the same time, some of which were aimed at more focused markets. A tension developed within the project over whether to put resources into further GDS development or plunge ahead with the Synergy. On the positive side, however, the availability of the GDS did improve the visibility of the project, provided useful feedback from sophisticated users, and fostered a favorable technical reputation for the design.

One thing that the staff gained from this experience was an appreciation for the quantity of support work required to create a product like the Synergy. Most of the effort expended on the project went to activities that did not seem directly related to design and production of the instrument. On the hardware side, a completely different processor, DAC, oscillator interface and key/pot interface boards, cabinets, and panels were required for the development system. On the software side, voicing, performance, oscillator and key/pot testing, file conversion, and voice ROM preparation programs were developed that do not appear at all in the Synergy. Display and graphics modules, disk-handling routines for voices, filters, sequences, and performance configurations were also incidental to the Synergy. Of the tens of thousands of lines of code written, only 24 Kbytes of compiled code actually reside in the final unit.

Handling Fundamental Limitations

Like any instrument, the Synergy has performance limitations. While these do not generally appear ex-plicitly to the player of the instrument, questions arose frequently during the software development as to how to handle situations where demands could be placed on the instrument that could not be fulfilled. Many potential features were very valuable in particular situations but taxed the capabilities of the instrument in others. For example, it is of obvious benefit to allow multiple timbres and polyphonic sequences to be recorded into individual tracks of the sequencer. If an attempt is made to play four tracks simultaneously, however, each of which requires nearly the full resources of the machine, clearly the performance will be degraded.

In the GDS, the design philosophy was to provide as wide a range of capabilities as possible, on the assumption that the user had a basic understanding of the processing limitations and would be sensitive to resource-allocation issues. The Synergy owner, however, cannot be assumed to be as knowledgeable. Consequently, three approaches were taken to the handling of limitations.

The first is that features that invite abuse were simply left out. For example, the ability to mix down sequencer tracks—available in the GDS—is not included in the Synergy.

The second is to make it more difficult to invoke features that may tax the capability of the machine. During initial use of the instrument, when a new player is becoming accustomed to its feel and characteristics, these features are unlikely to be encountered. As greater sophistication is developed, more advanced features will be explored when their effects on performance are easier to understand. For example, placing multiple voices on the keyboard in "unison" voice-assignment mode—where each key pressed starts a note for each active voice—normally limits the keyboard polyphonicity substantially (since there are only 32 oscillators and at most 16 notes active simultaneously). To put the instrument into this mode, a series of switches must be pushed in a given sequence. The novice user is unlikely to encounter this configuration without consulting the manual, which explains the characteristics of the feature. This is not to say that the machine is complex to operate. Quite the contrary—the primary use of the instrument is accomplished by pushing a single switch (to select a voice); it is then ready to play. (In fact, this can be preset so that when the instrument is powered up it does not even require this single action.) To use the many advanced modes and features of the instrument requires some knowledge, however.

The third approach to handling limitations is to degrade the performance of the instrument gracefully when limits are approached. Surprisingly, techniques were developed that blurred these boundaries without adversely affecting performance. Three examples will be mentioned here: the reallocation of active notes, the reassigning of voices, and the filtering of pitch-bend movements.

A problem in all synthesizers of limited polyphonicity is what to do when all oscillators/voice boards/note generators are occupied and a new key is depressed. The most obvious and least adequate scheme is simply to ignore the new key movement until such time as the resources are available to process it. Not only does this create a performance problem for the player, making it difficult or impossible to come in on cue, but it reverses the musical priority of events in that the newest note is likely to be where the listener's perception is focused. Given that an existing note must be terminated, it is preferable to abort notes that are less likely to be noticed. In the Synergy, each voice typically requires about 4 of the 32 oscillators for each active note. For a variety of reasons, these oscillators must be contiguously grouped in the oscillator circuit (i.e., they cannot be assembled out of oscillators' "garbage collected" from other notes). Consequently, in most situations the instrument is eight-note polyphonic. These eight notes may be shared among the keyboard and currently playing sequencer tracks. An interesting algorithm was found to be effective in deciding which notes to abort and restart when all existing notes are active and a new one is needed. The oldest but not lowest note is selected unless only one note of that voice is possible at that time. That is, the lowest active note cannot be preempted unless it is the only note of that voice currently allocated.

The justification for this scheme is that listeners are likely to perceive, in decreasing order of importance, (1) the newest notes, (2) the boundary (highest and lowest) notes (these seem to provide a sort

of context for the sound), and (3) the oldest notes. The least perceptual damage is done by taking the oldest interior notes. (In the implementation, however, the highest note is not exempted.) During an ascending arpeggio with the sustain pedal depressed, for example, the lowest note is retained while the top notes (usually seven) always sound. Experience indicates that this algorithm provides the illusion of a fully polyphonic keyboard. Even experienced players do not usually notice the aborted notes until they are pointed out. In part, this is because the notes are terminated only when a substantial amount of other activity is taking place. It is nearly impossible to hear them end; rather, it is their subsequent absence that may be noted.

A second issue in reallocation of notes is the problem of smoothly and efficiently redirecting the oscillators to their new frequencies. Several approaches to this problem were tried before one was selected as superior. Sweeping or jumping the frequency of sounding oscillators to their new pitches is inadequate for two reasons. First, it creates a noticeable effect not related to either the old or the new note. Second, it typically eliminates the attack characteristics of the new note, which are essential to preserving the desired timbre. Therefore, the process must involve some manipulation of the amplitudes. If the amplitude of a sounding note is ramped down too abruptly, an audible click will result. If it is aborted more slowly, however, a perceptible delay may be introduced between the key movement and the beginning of the sound. Neither of these conditions is acceptable to the performer. In short, the problem is to avoid clicks and get the new note started as soon as possible.

This is accomplished in the Synergy by beginning to ramp down the amplitudes of the sounding oscillators at a rate just below the perceptible click range as soon as the abort decision is made. While the amplitude is dropping, all the calculations required to restart the note at the new frequency are performed. When they are complete, the amplitude is usually considerably reduced, although by no means zero. The oscillators are then reset to their new frequencies and the direction of the amplitude ramps is (potentially) reversed at the attack rate of the new note and ramped back up to the first amplitude point of the new envelopes. Frequency and amplitude-envelope processing then proceeds as normal. The abrupt frequency change is masked quite effectively by the attack of the new note.

The selection of the abort rate and the time required to calculate the new frequencies are critical to tuning this process. If the abort rate is too fast, the note transitions are perceived as abrupt or noisy. If the amplitude of the oscillators is too high when the frequency transition occurs, the new attack is lost. This is particularly noticeable when the new note is being struck at the same pitch—it is not perceived as a new note at all. Fortunately, intermediate values exist, and the problem was solved effectively.

A similar problem occurs when voices are switched. Such transitions must be made smoothly and in a timely manner. In this instance, however, the techniques just described cannot be used because switching from one voice to another can require repatching the oscillators, which cannot be safely accomplished when any oscillator is sounding. Another complication is that different voices may require different numbers of oscillators, so it is advisable to repack completely the note groupings in the oscillator circuit when voices are changed. (This is done using a round-robin "greedy" heuristic.) If this reorganization is carried out promptly when a new voice is selected, existing notes are abruptly terminated. Sometimes, of course, this may be desirable; at other times it is not.

The approach adopted to this problem is to provide the user with a simple method for controlling the point at which repatching takes place. If a key is down (as distinct from sounding) when the new voice is selected, the repatching of the oscillators is delayed until all sounding oscillators complete their envelopes. If no key is down (although several notes may still be sounding) when the new voice is selected, existing notes are aborted and the new voice is available immediately.

A third performance issue is the tracking of the pitch-bend pot. Since the pots are polled at regular intervals and have a relatively low processing priority (keys are higher, as are oscillator service requests), several milliseconds may elapse between readings of the position of this control. Whereas this delay is not critical with regard to other pot functions (such as vibrato rate), the pitch must change smoothly and accurately in response to movements of the pitch bend. If the pitch of relevant notes is simply shifted to the new reading of the pot each time it is polled, the result is an unacceptable quantization of the pitch bending.

To smooth this quantization, a software "filter" is applied to the changing pitches. Current and final pitch-bend values are kept for each active note. Every 12 msec the distance from the current to the final pitch is halved until it arrives at the target value. Processing of the pitch-bend pot simply involves updating the final pitch-bend value for each note. This greatly smooths the pitch-bend updates and does not introduce objectionable response delays.

The design, implementation, and evaluation of techniques such as these proved to be one of the most time-consuming and difficult aspects of the project. What appeared to be details at the outset—such as how to deal with overbooking of the oscillators—turned out to be substantial engineering problems.

Providing an "Intelligent" Computing Environment

One of the by-products of using digital technology in a musical instrument is that the player becomes a (perhaps unwitting) computer user. The performer is interacting with a program that presents a *computing environment*, albeit with unusual input devices. Like other computer systems, this environment can adopt a variety of postures toward the user. It can (1) present itself as providing low-level tools (which may be abused), (2) provide protection against "dangerous" actions, (3) make heavy use of defaults, and (4) exhibit friendliness toward the user. Partly because of the background of the developers, the Synergy evolved as an "intelligent" performer aid that is cognizant of its own capabilities and the likely needs of its users and that is willing to make "judgments" when required. In spirit, it is modeled on the Interlisp programming environment, with its programmer's apprentice, Do-What-I-Mean (DWIM) facility, and other advanced user-support concepts.

In practice, this computing environment translates mainly into details such as deciding whether to start the sequencer tracks playing immediately or to provide a slight delay when the sequencer is turned on. If the player is trying to record, a delay is introduced to allow the player to position the hands on the keyboard; otherwise it begins immediately. If a key is down when a new voice is selected, existing notes are allowed to run their course rather than be terminated immediately. The reason for this is that the user is likely to hold a note explicitly if the musical focus is on the previous phrase; a complete lifting of hands is likely to indicate a shift of focus onto the subsequent events. After a recording is completed, the newly recorded track is set to play (rather than shut off) to facilitate immediate playback. If a "repeating" sequencer track is turned off while it is still playing, it is not actually terminated until it completes its current cycle. Most of these features are not obvious to unsophisticated players, yet provide flexibility for sophisticated players who are aware of them.

In some instances, typical artificial intelligence (AI) techniques were directly applied. The *floating-split* feature is a prime example of this: the processor computes an expected hand position for the performer's hands over the keyboard and uses the positions to adjust dynamically the keysplit so that each hand will play a particular voice. This feature represents a major advance over fixed, or programmable keysplit (also available on the instrument) in that the performer can move either hand into any range of the keyboard and have the appropriate voice track the movement. This feature provides a measure of freedom for the player in that the machine—rather than the player—keeps track of the appropriate keysplit location and provides a degree of flexibility not available in more traditional polytimbral voice-assignment schemes.

Another area of "intelligent" processing is the decision as to how the oscillators should be assigned when multiple voices are selected. (Due to real-time processing constraints, the number of oscillators assigned to each active voice must be deter-mined when the oscillators are patched, i.e., before they are actually played.) If the performer does not make any explicit indications, an algorithm attempts to distribute the resources fairly to the requested voices, taking into account such things as the number of oscillators required, whether a given voice appears in a sequencer track that is poised to play, how many event sources (four tracks plus the keyboard) are requesting that voice, and so on. The performer can override this decision by indicating (for instance) that only one note of a given voice is needed currently. This is accomplished by pressing a particular button before selecting the voice.

The software is aware of appropriate musical concepts in much the same way that a good word processor is aware of linguistic units such as words, sentences, and paragraphs. For example, a special technique is used to determine when a "chord" is played; that is, when a group of notes is struck within a small time window without any intervening events. This is used in features such as the *even* mode in the sequencer, in which an even (metronomelike) rhythm is substituted for the one actually played during recording. Groups of events designated as chords are played during the same time interval, whereas all other events are split up into separate intervals. Similarly, if the sequencer speed is substantially reduced on playback, the time intervals that actually occurred between notes when a chord was struck are compressed on playback to avoid unwanted arpeggios and maintain the original crispness. In effect, the sequencer "cleans up" the playing technique of the performer.

In several respects, the user can "customize" the environment in much the same way that a login "command file" does in larger interactive computer systems. Global parameters such as the "throw" of the pitch bend, tuning of the instrument, transpositions, and default voice settings are stored and recalled whenever the unit is powered up.

The computational environment also facilitates the detailed control required for features such as the *intelligent portamento*, which allows individual notes to slide in both directions simultaneously or at different times. The player indicates which note is to slide next by the order in which the keys are released; since only pedaled notes can portamento, this control technique has no audible effect on the performance.

Designing for Production

One aspect of the project not typically encountered in research settings is the consideration of production issues in the design. While the staff was sensitive to making the Synergy perform effectively from the user's standpoint, most were unaccustomed to considering maintenance and assembly problems. Techniques that are acceptable for constructing research prototypes proved to be problematic for a production environment. Fortunately, the primary engineer had experience in this area and was very helpful in providing guidelines for the rest of the staff.

At the outset of the project, a working, wirewrap prototype oscillator card existed. It ultimately developed that to achieve high performance several unusual practices were used in its construction. While these were legitimate for building a single example, they were likely to create difficulties for an assembly-line operation.

Perhaps the most serious of these difficulties was the assumption of minimum propagation delays for various chips. To achieve optimal speed, for example, a new address might be applied to a line before the previous data were read. It was assumed that the time required for the new address to propagate through the relevant portion of the circuit would not exceed the time required to read the old data. In general, the chip manufacturers warrant only maximum propagation-delay times, so there is no guarantee that subsequent versions of the chips will take as long to propagate as current ones.

A related problem is circuit design that is sensitive to particular brands of chips. There is an understandable temptation in designing high-performance circuitry to make use of the observed performance of chips rather than their published specifications. This can result in circuit designs that work with one manufacturer's chips but not with those of another, although the published specifications are the same. In research environments where one or a few working examples are required,

this may not be a serious problem. In a production environment, however, it may require discarding a substantial proportion of expensive components, not to mention testing them for actual performance.

Often the observed performance of components far exceeds the manufacturer's published documentation. Memory chips, for example, may outperform their specifications. Substantial overall product-performance improvements could be achieved by removing wait states from the instruction or data fetches. Faster memories may be prohibitively expensive and cheaper ones may prove to be adequate. Judgments were made on such shortcuts on a case-by-case basis.

Another problem is the availability of components. The market for integrated circuits is notoriously volatile. If a component is required that becomes difficult to obtain, production may have to be completely halted until a replacement can be found. Consequently, a distinct effort was made to avoid the use of obscure or scarce parts. (This is not typically a concern when one is constructing a small number of prototypes.) In general, components that were available from only a single manufacturer or source were avoided.

The changing cost of various components affected the design. Originally, it seemed advisable to use nonreprogrammable ROMs made from fixed masks. This was less expensive but had the dual drawbacks of a large initial start-up cost (to have the ROM masks made) and the requirement that the software be completely tested, debugged, and "frozen" in advance of test marketing. It developed that a surplus of erasable, programmable ROMs (EPROMs) forced the cost of these components below the cost of standard ROMs by production time, so these were selected instead. This took considerable pressure off the software-development group.

A factor in production-oriented design is durability. The unit should be able to survive moderate abuse and recover from momentary disruptions gracefully. This occasioned several changes to the circuitry so that the instrument would be capable of recovering from (for example) a large static discharge to the chassis without being powered down. Checks to be sure that timers assumed to be running synchronously are actually doing so are performed periodically and appropriate adjustments are made (such a problem delayed the launch of the space shuttle). The ability to force a complete software reset quickly from the front panel was included. (A second, more complex maneuver resets the entire machine to its factory state.) Abusing the prototypes was the source of some amusement for the development staff.

Care was taken to avoid the use of parts that would drift or require adjustment during initial manufacture or subsequent service. A source of some pride for the staff is that absolutely no adjustments of any kind are required: if the components function properly, all variability in the unit is handled automatically by the hardware and software.

The mechanical engineering—the physical design of the case, controls, and components—was also a complex task. The unit had to be configured to require little or no hand wiring. Not only must everything fit properly, but the design must take into account the dissipation of heat and the ease of initial construction and subsequent servicing. The spacing and positioning of controls for easy access also had to be considered carefully.

One unavoidable difficulty with both the hardware and the software is complexity. It takes a highly skilled technician several months of intensive training to understand the design and implementation sufficiently to make reasonable modifications to the instrument. Several attempts to train additional staff in the course of the project were unsuccessful. Consequently, it was essential that appropriate debugging tools be provided for the production staff along with the design. Since software is not particularly subject to incidental breakdown, this help consists mainly of special programs that perform hardware tests. A cartridge is being designed that will contain existing test routines that report their results by illuminating patterns of LEDs on the instrument panel. These programs check the operation of the oscillators, the values read from ROMs, and the physical devices (by reporting relevant data when they are moved), and will be distributed to nonfactory service centers.

Provisions for modification of the software (by changing ROMs) are also incorporated into the unit.

Most of these deal with compatibility with potential future software. Additional voice and special ROMs (such as sequence storage and retrieval interfaces) do not reference specific subroutine entry points explicitly. In addition, room was left for subsequent expansion of both ROM and RAM. A variety of "escapes" were included at strategic points in the code for executing programs that could be located in external ROMs. These might capture and/or simulate key/pot activity, interface with outboard equipment (such as other computers), or simply implement extended features (such as sequence editing or synchronization with an external source).

Conclusion

One consequence of marrying a new technology to an existing application is that the endeavor acquires characteristics from both. In developing the Synergy, a fully digital keyboard-oriented sound synthesizer for the commercial market, we found ourselves facing both the accelerated pace of high-technology development—where small lead times can make or break a product—and the skepticism and conservatism of performing musicians—where the demands of live performance require that an instrument be comprehensible, trusted, and responsive. To some degree, these goals conflicted: to constantly revise and polish the design would unacceptably delay the availability of the instrument, while to release it prematurely would tip our hand to our competitors and could create a poor reputation for our products.

The development process was a perpetual compromise between the various pressures in the project. Fortunately, common ground did exist for a consensus among the backers, in-house staff, and consultants, and with regard to the limitations of the available technology and adaptivity of the prospective market, that permitted the project to come to a successful engineering conclusion. Whether the resulting instrument will prove to be a commercial success remains to be seen. The promises of the project's originators have been substantially fulfilled at this time, however. A group of musical-instrument manufacturers and distributors find themselves going into the computer business, and a staff of hardware and software engineers have found a novel application for their skills.

Acknowledgments

The project owes its success to the dedication of many people. Hal Alles of Bell Laboratories, Murray Hill, New Jersey, provided the initial inspiration, motivation, and invaluable advice on both the hardware and software development. In addition, he is primarily responsible for the basic hardware design and low-level software routines, as described in two of his papers (1979, 1980). Kevin Doren was responsible for translating these concepts into a practical hardware design, as well as coordinating the efforts of the various people on the project and following up on innumerable details. Stoney Stockell provided support services for both hardware and software and developed the hardware test routines. Tom Piggot served as director of marketing and primary source of advice on features and design and contributed to the development of Synergy's voicings. Ernie and Dennis Briefel patiently provided backing and support during the lengthy development process. John Strawn wrote manuals and contributed technical advice. Jan Mattox and Chris Chafe developed voices for the instrument. Peter Nye aided in the software implementation. Mechanical engineering was performed by Chris Scafidi. Musical and design advice was also provided by Jeff Johnson, Randy Mcgrew, Bo Tomlin, Mike Bottiker, Christoph Franke, Klaus Schulze, Max Mathews, and Wendy Carlos. Responsibility for the instrument design, software implementation, and coordination of voicing and documentation efforts was carried by the author.

References

Alles, H. G. 1979. "An Inexpensive Digital Sound Synthesizer." *Computer Music Journal* 3(3):28–37.
Alles, H. G. 1980. "Music Synthesis Using Real Time Digital Techniques." *Proceedings of the IEEE* 68(4):436–449.

49

Mark Kahrs

Computer Science Department
University of Rochester
Rochester, New York 14627

Notes on Very-Large-Scale Integration and the Design of Real-Time Digital Sound Processors

Introduction

Since the 1960s, electronic components that make up digital systems have been packaged as tiny integrated circuits (ICs) or chips. There has been steady progress since that time in making the components smaller and thereby packing more components per chip. This has led to several generations of IC devices, from small-scale integration (SSI), with only a couple of components per chip, to medium-scale integration (MSI) and large-scale integration (LSI), with tens of thousands of components per chip (Myers 1980). As a result of improvements in the technology of chip fabrication, achievable circuit densities continue to grow higher. The present level of density extends into very-large-scale integration (VLSI).

The Present State of the Art

New digital sound processor technologies are made possible by the introduction of VLSI technology. In a recent survey of integrated circuits and signal processing, Hoff (1980) points out the increasing complexity that is coming with the introduction of VLSI technology. At the present time, chips like the Motorola MC68000, a 16-bit microprocessor with 68,000 transistors, are at the upper limit of today's mass production (Fig. 1). As the size of circuit features decreases more in the next few years, one can expect to see dramatic increases in chip density and functional capacity. Some estimates place as many

Computer Music Journal, Vol. 5, No. 2, Summer 1981

as one million logic gates per chip by 1990 (each logic gate may comprise several transistors).

There are five principal limitations in VLSI design: chip size, device density, circuit speed, complexity of device interconnects on the chip, and number of pinouts (the number of pins emanating from a chip's package). When designing a VLSI sound processor, one must consider various tradeoffs. For example, one can conserve on the number of pins used by adding multiplexers to the chip, allowing any one pin to be used for more than one purpose. The demands of real-time computation put an extra burden on digital processors. For such real-time processors, duplication of chip circuitry can increase the speed of signal-processing algorithms at the cost of additional "real estate" on the chip being dedicated to the parallel circuits.

Current Sound Processors

I began my research into VLSI and digital sound processors by considering existing processors implemented using MSI technology. The 4B Machine at the Institut de Recherche et Coordination Acoustique/Musique (IRCAM) (Alles 1976; 1980) and the Systems Concepts Digital Synthesizer (Samson 1980) were examined for ideas usable in a VLSI implementation.

The 4B is a multiplexed machine, that is, it runs fast enough to compute a number of voices of sound in the time between sample periods. Translating this machine into a single chip would not be a terribly difficult job. The machine does have a problem, however. When generating line segments for functions (e.g., envelope curves) the 4B allows timer interrupts to be set for the endpoints of the

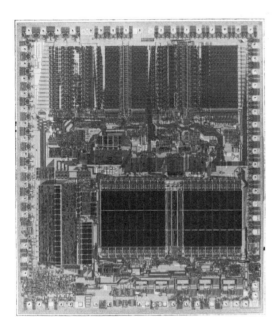

stop temporarily and allow processing of sound to take place. The problem arises when one must integrate a command stream that comes from diverse input sources such as knobs and keyboards being played by musicians. This *real-time input problem* must be solved if such processors are to be used in live performance. Designers of digital sound processors will face other problems that will come up as the designs become more refined.

Current Algorithms

As more processing power becomes available on each chip and as the complexity of what musicians want to accomplish with such chips increases, it becomes necessary to think about processors differently. Commonly used signal-processing algorithms can be committed to firmware, thus simplifying the software environment considerably. Rather than consider, What algorithms can I implement using this beast? the chip designer must consider, What algorithms should I implement in silicon? Therefore, the designer of any new digital sound processor must consider what algorithms the user wants to implement. These might include lattice filtering, convolution, waveshaping, additive synthesis, and other algorithms useful for sound generation. In the following sections, two VLSI architectures for music processing will be discussed that address the issues pointed out so far.

A Command-Stream Processor

The purpose of the command-stream processor is to solve the real-time input problem. One needs to be able to mix many external sources of commands and data into a single command stream. One immediate difficulty is the instability of analog components often used in input devices such as potentiometers. In particular, the reference levels of analog-to-digital converts (ADCs) tend to wander. Use of a *hysteresis register* is one way to solve this problem. The contents of this register are compared against the current input (which is masked) and will match if the masked bits equal the last known

line segments. This can put a considerable load on the host processor, which is feeding parameters from the score to the 4B to control the sound synthesis. In the case of the 4B the host computer is a slow LSI-11. The LSI-11 is constantly being interrupted and asked to supply more data; this is known as the *parameter-update problem*.

The Systems Concepts Digital Synthesizer is a large, pipelined processor built using MSI technology. It has 256 generators, 128 modifiers, and a mixing memory called *sum memory*. Unfortunately, the machine appears to be designed mainly for frequency modulation (FM) and additive synthesis, rather than as a truly general-purpose synthesizer. Attempts to use the machine for synthesis techniques other than additive and FM synthesis are sometimes successful, but implementation is somewhat contrived. As a stream processor, the Systems Concepts synthesizer has another problem. Commands to the synthesizer are read from memory and executed until a command is given to

Fig. 2. The internal bus is
a tri-state precharged bus.
The multiplier and adder
are latched, allowing operations to proceed while
computations are being
performed. There is one
multiplexer that connects
the coefficient ROM and
the register bank to the internal bus. The output of
the adder is connected to a
"breakpoint" detection circuit that detects the endpoints of line segments.
The time-tick bus is a serial input connected to a
global clock. The slot-ad-
dress bus contains the address broadcast by the slot
clock. When the slot of the
chip is recognized by the
slot recognition logic, one
byte from the FIFO is put
onto the central data bus.
The external world can
communicate by using the
latched "world" input.
This circuit has a "hys-
teresis" circuit that allows
for instability in ADCs
and other inputs.

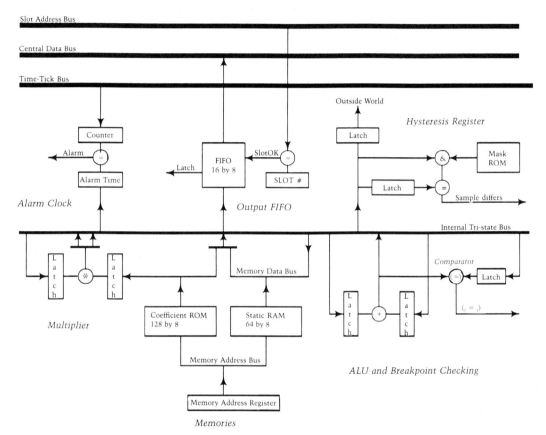

input. Such a sample can then be ignored. Thus the main processor doesn't have to be interrupted for a "new" value so often.

Samples gathered from these input devices (knobs, joysticks, etc.) usually must be scaled at some point in the processing. The command-stream processor can do this for the sound processor if it has its own on-chip multiplier. Then, in order to provide linear interpolation between endpoints of envelope line segments, an adder is also available on the command-stream-processor chip. The whole processor is controlled by a horizontal microprogram store. In such a scheme, a very wide (hence horizontal) control word directly controls the flow of internal signals within the processor. The control words are stored in a microprogram read-only-memory (ROM) implemented as a programmable logic array (PLA). PLAs are ubiquitous in VLSI design (Mead and Conway 1980). Most commonly, they are implemented as an array of AND/OR gates which the designer can selectively connect by changes in the metalization layer. The data paths for the command-stream processor are shown in Fig. 2.

In the implementation of the command-stream processor, note that the data paths are parallel

Fig. 3. This is a layout of
the command-stream-pro-
cessor chip without the input or output pads. The

area taken up is approx-
imately 3000 by 4000
microns.

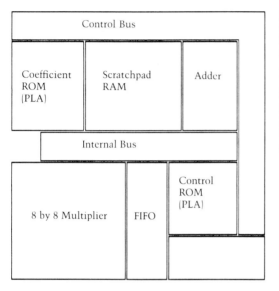

Control Bus		
Coefficient ROM (PLA)	Scratchpad RAM	Adder
Internal Bus		
8 by 8 Multiplier	FIFO	Control ROM (PLA)

rather than serial. Although the space consumed by the parallel circuits is larger than serial (Freeny [1975] states that parallel multipliers consume four times the space of serial multipliers), the payoff is speed. Serial circuits can be used effectively in signal processors (Jackson, Kaiser, and McDonald 1967; Lyon 1980), but I felt that the speed to be afforded by parallel design was worth the cost in chip space.

The implementation of this processor will be in n-channel metal-oxide semiconductors (NMOS) (Mead and Conway 1980). A layout of the chip is shown in Fig. 3.

A Sound Processor

So far, I have discussed ways to overcome the limitations in the bandwidth brought about by multiple, real-time command lists. In this section, I will discuss some considerations in the design of the signal processor that does the work of musical sound generation.

One can begin by considering exactly what al-

gorithms will be implemented using the sound processor. This is a synthesis machine, not to be used for sound analysis. By and large, the computational demands of analysis and synthesis machines differ. Analysis algorithms are mostly block algorithms. These require an entire array (block) of samples before processing can take place. Although such algorithms are useful, in this article I will not discuss processors that implement them. What kinds of synthesis algorithms would be implemented? There are at least three major techniques:

1. Additive synthesis. This involves combining many relatively simple signals (such as sine waves), each with its own frequency and amplitude envelopes, to form complex, evolving timbres (Moorer 1977).
2. Subtractive synthesis. This takes a spectrally rich waveform and filters the sound down into a less complex timbre (Markel and Gray 1976).
3. Nonlinear synthesis. This involves modulations of signals with each other (FM, waveshaping, etc.) to produce rich, evolving timbres (Chowning 1973; LeBrun 1979; Arfib 1979).

Additive synthesis, with its individual envelopes for each partial of a complex sound, can be computationally expensive. Subtractive synthesis techniques also make substantial demands. This arises, for example, in realizing the linear-predictive-coding (LPC) synthesis technique, often used for synthesizing speech sounds (Markel and Gray 1976). In the lattice implementation of LPC, a multiplier must be provided. In waveshaping, the principal demand is for a large lookup table and another multiply. (This table could also be used for artificial reverberation.) Clearly, a large lookup table is a necessary requirement for any synthesis processor. Note that the Systems Concepts synthesizer has an external memory of 128 Kbytes accessible through the modifiers. Although a large memory is desirable, its place is not on the processor chip. It is easier to buy the memory chips and put only the interface to the memory on the processor chip.

Many existing signal processors do not have branch instructions. This is often due to the com-

Fig. 4. In this rather conventional sound processor, notice that all the inputs from the common bus are latched. This one level of pipelining allows the computation to proceed in parallel throughout the chip. Notice also that the off-board memory could be quite large, which is the reason for placing it off the chip. External input is buffered in the external register. Note the bypasses on the inputs to the ALU and multiplier. This allows results from the common bus to be used immediately in the next step of computation.

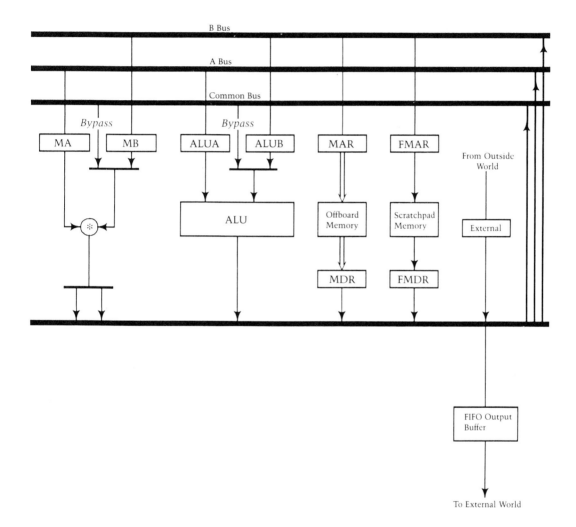

plexity of the machine architecture. This lack of branch instructions can prove to be a handicap in the implementation of algorithms such as matrix inversion or pitch extraction.

If the signal-processing lessons of the Digital Voice Terminal are of any help (Gold 1974), then the processor should have as much raw speed as possible. Pipelining within the processor is one way to achieve this. Multiple computation units that are spread across the task (such as found in the IBM Model 360/91) are another way to achieve higher execution speeds (Tomasulo 1967).

In Fig. 4, the data path of a rather ordinary sound processor that can be implemented in NMOS is given. Notice that the processor has an "outboard" memory and an internal multiplier. Once again, the processor is microprogrammed. This is more than a consideration for user programming of the control store. As processors get more complicated, it gets more difficult to design the processor to be logically correct. Using random logic only exacerbates this problem. The MC68000 is an example in which microprogramming was used to avoid bugs in the control section of the processor (Stritter and Tredennick 1979).

Each unit of the processor has latches on the input and the output so that processing may proceed without a wait for the results of a given operation (i.e., overlapped execution). The machine is synchronous, and results are latched when the execution unit finishes its action. Notice that the result bus can be connected directly to the execution units. This allows the current results on the bus to "bypass" the latches on the input side of the execution units.

The One-Voice One-Processor Doctrine

In the processor organizations discussed so far, it has been assumed that only one high-speed processor is available. With the advent of low-priced processors, lack of processor cycles should not be permitted to be a problem. Unfortunately, some of the problems of computer networking are then introduced. If we modify the existing architecture of the processor shown in Fig. 1 to have multiple processors, the interconnection of input modules and the sound processor modules becomes a problem. It's not sufficient just to restrict each sound-processor module to have one input module because one might want a single input device to affect many processors. A crossbar switch such as is shown in Fig. 5 would be ideal. Such a switch was used in C.mmp (Wulf and Bell 1972). C.mmp was composed of slightly modified DEC PDP-11/40 processors augmented with a writable control store. Up to 16 of these processors could be connected to

up to 16 shared memory modules through a 16 by 16 crosspoint switch (Jones and Schwartz 1980). Of course, C.mmp's problem is well known: the number of switches increases as the square of the number of inputs and the area increases likewise.

Another solution to the problem is to use a bus and grant the bus (arbitrate it). Suppose each of the processors is connected in a chain. Then each processor could pass the control token to the next processor when it was finished putting data on the bus. But of course then the sound processor must know which real-time input placed the data on the bus. Therefore, a new bus is needed that buses the processor ID of the input on the data bus. All processors can sample the bus to find out which input is there. The problem with this is that each processor must filter out the real-time requests on the data bus. This again introduces the parameter-update problem!

Other possible bus organizations include a time-division multiplexed (TDM) bus or an Ethernet-like network where each real-time input has a time slot (an address in the Ethernet scheme) and they communicate by broadcasting to the other processor (Metcalfe and Boggs 1976). Of course this too has its problems—the TDM bus requires that processors wait for the proper time slot. Ethernet was designed to be "unreliable" in the sense that it keeps retransmitting a message over the network until it receives an acknowledgment; it does not assume the message got through on the first transmission. Unfortunately, there is no upper bound on the time it can take a packet of information to be transmitted and received. Because of the basically slow rate of change (with respect to the processor) involved in parameter update, a TDM-bus scheme was used in the command-stream processor.

Notice that in Fig. 6 a new mixing processor has been added to the output of the three sound processors. There must be one mixing processor per channel of output sound. With a fast mixing processor, this could be simulated through the use of multiplexing, since even at a 50-KHz sampling rate for audio, the samples would have to be added at a rate of 20 μsec each, well within the range of the processor's speed.

Kahrs

Fig. 5. A musical crossbar processor (à la C.mmp) that allows the command stream to be directed to any sound processor. The problem with the network is the second-order nature of the connections (N by M).

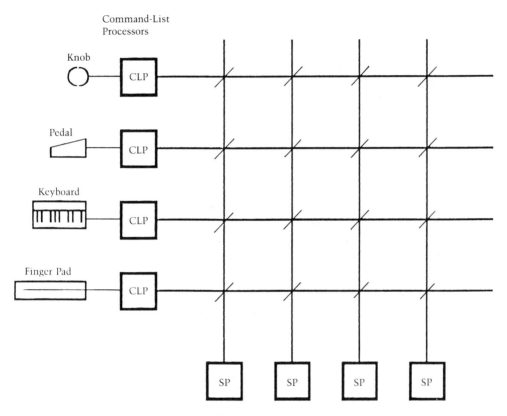

Command-List Processors

Knob

CLP

Pedal

CLP

Keyboard

CLP

Finger Pad

CLP

SP   SP   SP   SP

Sound Processors

Designing the Processor for the Algorithm Instead of Vice Versa

In the design of VLSI processors, a prominent concern is to design the processor for the algorithm. This is based on the belief that processors will decrease in cost, and that by customizing the processor for the algorithm speed can be obtained. An example of customizing the processor can be found in the work of Kung (1980). *Systolic algorithms* are formed by arrays of processors that communicate with their neighbors and form rectilinear arrays. For example, Kung has designed second-order filters, a convolution box, and a discrete-Fourier-transform (DFT) box. A special-purpose reverberation box could use a convolution box to implement reverberation using the impulse response of a hall. As more research is done into sound-generation algorithms, perhaps more of them can be placed into systolic form.

Conclusion

In this article, I have explored a tip of the VLSI iceberg. Computer music's high computational requirements are an ideal problem for VLSI technol-

Fig. 6. This figure demonstrates the connections of
the various chips in a
time-division multiplexed
system. Notice the addi-
tion of a score processor,
which generates com-
mands that are not depen-
dent on real-time inputs.
There is a global clock and
slot clock, which broad-
casts the current slot on
the slot bus. Data is gated
to the stream bus, which
then feeds the sound pro-
cessors. The sound pro-
cessors in turn feed
another sound processor
that acts as a mixer. A
DAC connects the signal
back to analog levels.

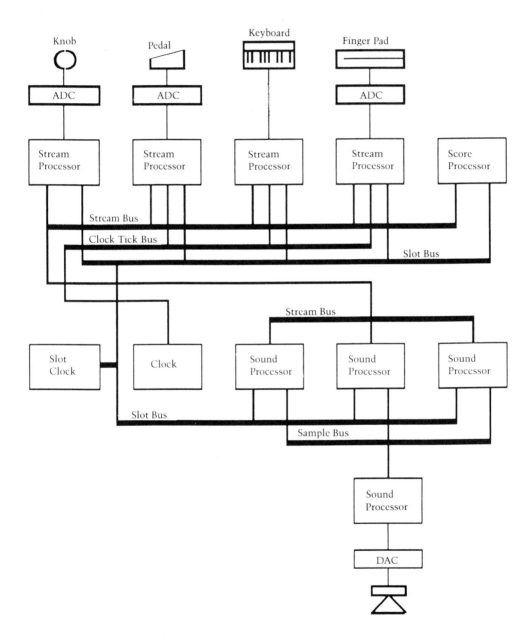

ogy to solve. Research is required in many areas. More research is needed into the structure of algorithms used by computer musicians, particularly the implementation of algorithms that are computationally expensive. Multiprocessor implementation of complex algorithms would be of considerable interest to VLSI designers. If computer musicians engage in a dialogue with VLSI designers, then profitable results for both sides will surely follow. I hope this article will start some of that dialogue.

Acknowledgments

Many of these ideas have been "in the air." I hope I haven't broken any feet by presenting them here. I appreciate the comments of John Snell, Peter Eastty, and Curtis Abbott, but I am solely responsible for this article's content. This clandestine research has been sponsored by the Sloan Foundation under grant 78-4-15 and by the Defense Advanced Research Projects Agency under contract number N00014-78-C-0164.

References

Alles, H. G. 1976. "A Portable Digital Sound Synthesis System." *Computer Music Journal* 1(4):5–9.

Alles, H. G. 1980. "Music Synthesis Using Real-time Digital Techniques." *Proceedings of the IEEE* 68(4):436–449.

Arfib, D. 1979. "Digital Synthesis of Complex Spectra by Means of Multiplication of Nonlinear Distorted Sine Waves." *Journal of the Audio Engineering Society* 27(10):757–768.

Chowning, J. M. 1973. "The Synthesis of Complex Audio Spectra by Means of Frequency Modulation." *Journal of the Audio Engineering Society* 21(7):526–534. Reprinted in *Computer Music Journal* 1(2):46–54.

Freeny, S. L. 1975. "Special-purpose Hardware for Digital Filtering." *Proceedings of the IEEE* 63(4):633–648.

Gold, B. 1974. "Parallel and Sequential Trade-Offs in Signal Processing Computers." In *National Telecommunications Conference of 1974*, pp. 491–495.

Hoff, M. E., Jr. 1980. "IC Technology: Trends and Impact on Digital Signal Processing." *Proceedings of the ICASSP*, pp. 1–6.

Jackson, L. B., J. F. Kaiser, and H. S. McDonald. 1967. "An Approach to the Implementation of Digital Filters." *IEEE Transactions on Audio and Electroacoustics* AU-16(3):413–421.

Jones, A., and P. Schwartz. 1980. "Experience Using Multiprocessor Systems—A Status Report." *Computing Surveys* 12(2):121–165.

Kung, H. T. 1980. "Special-purpose Devices for Signal and Image Processing: An Opportunity for VLSI." CMU Technical Report. Pittsburgh, Pennsylvania: Department of Electrical Engineering and Computer Science, Carnegie-Mellon University.

LeBrun, M. 1979. "Digital Waveshaping Synthesis." *Journal of the Audio Engineering Society* 27(4):250–265.

Lyon, R. F. 1980. "Signal Processing with VLSI." Unpublished ms.

Markel, J. D., and A. H. Gray, Jr. 1976. *Linear Prediction of Speech*. New York: Springer-Verlag.

Mead, C., and L. Conway. 1980. *Introduction to VLSI Systems*. Reading, Massachusetts: Addison-Wesley.

Metcalfe, R. M., and D. R. Boggs. 1976. "Ethernet: Distributed Packet-switching for Local Networks." *Communications of the ACM* 19(7):395–404.

Moorer, J. A. 1976. "The Synthesis of Complex Audio Spectra by Means of Discrete Summation Formulas." *Journal of the Audio Engineering Society* 24(9):717–727.

Moorer, J. A. 1977. "Signal Processing Aspects of Computer Music." *Computer Music Journal* 1(1):4–37.

Moorer, J. A. 1979. "About This Reverberation Business." *Computer Music Journal* 3(2):13–27.

Moorer, J. A. 1981. "Synthesizers I Have Known and Loved." *Computer Music Journal* 5(1):4–12.

Myers, G. 1980. *System Design with LSI Bit-slice Logic*. New York: Wiley Interscience.

Samson, P. 1980. "A General-Purpose Digital Synthesizer." *Journal of the Audio Engineering Society* 28(3):106–113.

Stritter, S., and N. Tredennick. 1979. "Microprogrammed Implementation of a Single Chip Microprocessor." In *11th Micro Proceedings*, pp. 8–16.

Tomasulo, R. M. 1967. "An Efficient Algorithm for Exploiting Multiple Arithmetic Units." *IBM Journal of Research and Development* January:25–33.

Wulf, W. A., and C. G. Bell. 1972. "C.mmp—A Multi Mini Processor." *Proceedings of the Fall Joint Computer Conference* 41:765–777.

VII

Music and Artificial Intelligence

Curtis Roads

Overview

Artificial intelligence (AI) research falls into two broad categories. The first is a scientific discipline (also known as cognitive science) devoted to the development of theories of human intelligence. The second category is an engineering discipline (also known as applied AI) devoted to the development of programs that exhibit intelligent behavior, whether of human or nonhuman quality. Music projects have engaged both the scientific and the applied aspect.

Article 50—written by one of the founders of AI, Marvin Minsky—is mainly concerned with cognitive science. Minsky attempts to provide answers to the query: Why do we like music? This seemingly naive question opens up a vast domain of inquiry into the nature of thought and emotion and the structure of the human brain. Minsky, whose "society of mind" theories (see Minsky 1987) have become well known, believes that human thought is the product of many different "agents" working together inside the brain. Since listening to music involves many agents with different strategies, Minsky proposes in his provocative essay several theories of listening.

The precise boundaries of AI are elusive, since they are related to our expectations for "intelligent behavior." In the early 1950s, adding thousands of numbers per second was considered the work of "giant brains." Today's expectations for intelligent behavior are much higher. As computers take on more and more tasks, the borderlines of AI seem to recede. To some people, "AI" represents what has not yet been achieved, regardless of what has been solved. But the fact is that computers can now perform many musical tasks that were once associated exclusively with naturally intelligent musicians (Roads 1985a).

As Karlheinz Stockhausen predicted in 1965 (see Stockhausen 1978), basic listening and performance skills are not major obstacles to automation. Rapid progress has been made in giving machines ears with which to listen to music. WABOT-2, the musical robot at the Tsukuba World Expo (Roads 1986), solicits song requests in spoken Japanese, sight-reads music, performs the music with two hands and two feet on an organ, accompanies a singer, and adjusts tempo and pitch to match the singer's performance. This demonstration robot makes a formidable statement about technology, but the musical applications of intelligent systems go far beyond traditional keyboard performance.

Morton Subotnick, George Lewis, and other composers increasingly use computer systems that can track pitch and tempo cues played by human musicians and can respond appropriately (Roads 1985b; Roads 1988). In the simplest case, the computer is asked to listen for a cue and then play a previously entered score. In other cases, however, the computer is asked to improvise along with human performers or other computer systems. "Computer bands" have been formed out of networks of interacting systems (Bischoff, Gold, and Horton 1978).

Several of the articles in part II demonstrate the attraction that algorithmic (or automated) methods of composition hold for composers. A musical style can be thought of as a set of rules that can be programmed to generate the forms and processes characteristic of that style. Likewise, AI techniques can make an important contribution to music theory. As John Rothgeb states in article 51, "It is part of the essence of theoretical studies . . . to render explicit that which has been inexplicit. . . . By symbolically representing the elements of musical notation and expressing in formal terms those operations believed to form the basis of inter-stratal relationships, the music theorist obtains something comparable to a generative grammar, with all of its advantages for the refinement and verification of theories." Rothgeb describes his pioneering work in solving problems of music theory by computer. In particular, Rothgeb used a computer program to transform unfigured bass notation (a bass line) into figured bass notation (a shorthand musical notation of a bass line and its harmonization used in the seventeenth and eighteenth centuries for keyboard music accompanied by a *basso continuo*).

AI techniques promise to circumvent the very problem they have made us most cognizant of—namely that the printed score is an incomplete basis for a musical theory. As Rothgeb states, "the notated score, even of the simplest traditional Western art music, is incomplete; the musical work as conceived by the composer and as produced by the sensitive performer deviates from the precision of the . . . printed score in countless subtle ways— most obviously with respect to temporal organization, but also with respect to even pitch and timbre." As the article by Johan Sundberg, Anders Askenfelt, and Lars Frydén shows, their research goal is to turn the art of interpretation into a science—that is, to teach computers how to play with more sensitivity to musical form and style. Specifically, Sundberg et al. investigate the effects of seven performance rules used in the computer-controlled synthesis of traditional and classical music. According to them, these rules could be useful in sound synthesis and in teaching student instrumentalists how to interpret scores.

For several years John Rahn has served as the editor of the Seattle-based journal *Perspectives of New Music*. His contribution to the present volume is an erudite response to three papers presented to an "Applications in Music Theory" session at a conference held by the Association for Computing Machinery. All three of those papers were published in *Computer Music Journal* (Smoliar 1980; Meehan 1980; Rothgeb 1980), and one of them (Rothgeb's) appears in this book. Rahn's reading of Rothgeb prompts him to discuss metatheory as it applies to music—i.e., What is a valid music theory? After offering a critique of Smoliar's computational model of Heinrich Schenker's (1956) hierarchical theory of tonal harmony, Rahn compares the proposals of Meehan (and his mentor Roger Schank) with the views of the anti-Schenkarian music theorist Eugene Narmour (1977).

Another application of AI techniques is digital audio signal processing (Strawn 1985). Until the development of AI techniques, signal processing was a primarily a numerical discipline. As signal processing takes on more difficult "signal understanding" tasks, increasing use is being made of symbolic techniques (such as pattern recognition) and of other AI methods.

A prime application of pattern recognition in computer music is the task of data reduction in an analysis/synthesis system. An analysis/synthesis system makes it possible to analyze a natural sound and then resynthesize it with a computer or a synthesizer. The musical power of an analysis/synthesis system is that, once the natural sound has been analyzed, the data can be subtly or radically modified in resynthesis, sometimes to great musical effect.

The problem with analysis/synthesis based on additive synthesis is that it generates tremendous amounts of frequency and amplitude data for each partial. Efficient storage and easy manipulation call for some form of data reduction. Charbonneau's article in part V discusses one approach to this problem. John Strawn's article in this part focuses on an automated system based on pattern-recognition algorithms. Strawn's system uses a formal grammar to recognize the salient features of the amplitude and frequency functions; it then creates much simpler approximations to these functions that preserve their salient features. The approximations require much less storage space.

Besides the creation of new options for computer musicians, another major goal of research in applied AI and music is to make life easier for musicians who use computers. Most of today's systems require musicians to descend to the computer's level in order to accomplish even simple musical tasks. To advance the state of the art, we need to bring computers up to our level by teaching them more about music and about interacting with musicians.

References

Bischoff, J., R. Gold, and J. Horton. 1978. "Music for an Interactive Network of Microcomputers." *Computer Music Journal* 2(3): 24–29. Reprinted in C. Roads and J. Strawn, eds., *Foundations of Computer Music* (Cambridge, Mass.: MIT Press).

Meehan, J. 1980. "An Artificial Intelligence Approach to Tonal Music Theory." *Computer Music Journal* 4(2): 60–65.

Minsky, M. 1987. *The Society of Mind.* New York: Simon and Schuster.

Narmour, E. 1977. *Beyond Schenkerism.* University of Chicago Press.

Roads, C. 1985a. "Research in Music and Artificial Intelligence." *ACM Computing Surveys* 17(2): 163–190.

Roads, C. 1985b. "Improvisation with George Lewis." In C. Roads, ed., *Composers and the Computer* (Los Altos, Calif.: Kaufmann).

Roads, C. 1986. "The Tsukuba Musical Robot." *Computer Music Journal* 10(2): 39–43.

Roads, C. 1988. "Interview with Morton Subotnick." *Computer Music Journal* 12(1): 9–18.

Rothgeb, J. 1980. "Simulating Musical Skills by Digital Computer." *Computer Music Journal* 4(2): 36–40.

Schenker, H. 1956. *Neue musikalische Theorien und Phantasien: Der freie Satz.* Vienna: Universal Edition.

Smoliar, S. 1980. "A Computer Aid for Schenkerian Analysis." *Computer Music Journal* 4(2): 41–59.

Stockhausen, Karlheinz. 1978. "Elektronische Musik und Automatik." In *Texte zur Musik: 1963–1970* (Cologne: DuMont-Schauberg).

Strawn, J., ed. 1985. *Digital Audio Signal Processing: An Anthology.* Los Altos, Calif.: Kaufmann.

50

Marvin Minsky

Artificial Intelligence Laboratory
Massachusetts Institute of Technology
Cambridge, Massachusetts 02139

Music, Mind, and Meaning

Why Do We Like Music?

Why do we like music? Our culture immerses us in it for hours each day, and everyone knows how it touches our emotions, but few think of how music touches other kinds of thought. It is astonishing how little curiosity we have about so pervasive an "environ-mental" influence. What might we discover if we were to study musical thinking?

Have we the tools for such work? Years ago, when science still feared meaning, the new field of research called *artificial intelligence* (AI) started to supply new ideas about "representation of knowledge" that I'll use here. Are such ideas too alien for anything so subjective and irrational, aesthetic, and emotional as music? Not at all. I think the problems are the same and those distinctions wrongly drawn: only the surface of reason is rational. I don't mean that understanding emotion is easy, only that understanding reason is probably harder. Our culture has a universal myth in which we see emotion as more complex and obscure than intellect. Indeed, emotion might be "deeper" in some sense of prior evolution, but this need not make it harder to understand; in fact, I think today we actually know much more about emotion than about reason.

Certainly we know a bit about the obvious processes of reason—the ways we organize and represent ideas we get. But whence come those ideas that so conveniently fill these envelopes of order? A poverty of language shows how little this concerns us: we "get" ideas; they "come" to us; we are "reminded of" them. I think this shows that ideas come from processes obscured from us and with which our surface thoughts are almost uninvolved. Instead, we are entranced with our emotions, which are so easily observed in others and ourselves. Per-

haps the myth persists because emotions (by their nature) draw attention, while the processes of reason (much more intricate and delicate) must be private and work best alone.

The old distinctions among emotion, reason, and aesthetics are like the earth, air, and fire of an ancient alchemy. We will need much better concepts than these for a working psychic chemistry.

Much of what we now know of the mind emerged in this century from other subjects once considered just as personal and inaccessible but which were explored, for example, by Freud in his work on adults' dreams and jokes, and by Piaget in his work on children's thought and play. Why did such work have to wait for modern times? Before that, children seemed too childish and humor much too humorous for science to take them seriously.

Why do we like music? We all are reluctant, with regard to music and art, to examine our sources of pleasure or strength. In part we fear success itself—we fear that understanding might spoil enjoyment. Rightly so: art often loses power when its psychological roots are exposed. No matter; when this happens we will go on, as always, to seek more robust illusions!

I feel that music theory has gotten stuck by trying too long to find universals. Of course, we would like to study Mozart's music the way scientists analyze the spectrum of a distant star. Indeed, we find some almost universal practices in every musical era. But we must view these with suspicion, for they might show no more than what composers then felt *should* be universal. If so, the search for truth in art becomes a travesty in which each era's practice only parodies its predecessor's prejudice. (Imagine formulating "laws" for television screenplays, taking them for natural phenomenon uninfluenced by custom or constraint of commerce.)

The trouble with the search for universal laws of thought is that both memory and thinking interact and grow together. We do not just learn about things, we learn *ways to think* about things; then we learn to think about thinking itself. Before long,

This is a revised and updated version of A.I. Memo No. 616. The earlier version will also appear in *Music, Mind, and Brain: The Neuropsychology of Music* edited by Manfred Clynes, and published by Plenum, New York.

our ways of thinking become so complicated that we cannot expect to understand their details in terms of their surface operation, but we might understand the principles that guide their growth. In much of this article I will speculate about how listening to music engages the previously acquired personal knowledge of the listener.

It has become taboo for music theorists to ask why we like what we like: our seekers have forgotten what they are searching for. To be sure, we can't account for tastes, in general, because people have various preferences. But this means only that we have to find the causes of this diversity of tastes, and this in turn means we must see that music theory is not only about music, but about how people process it. To understand any art, we must look below its surface into the psychological details of its creation and absorption.

If explaining minds seems harder than explaining songs, we should remember that sometimes enlarging problems makes them simpler! The theory of the roots of equations seemed hard for centuries within its little world of real numbers, but it suddenly seemed simple once Gauss exposed the larger world of (so-called) complex numbers. Similarly, music should make more sense once seen through listeners' minds.

Sonata as Teaching Machine

Music makes things in our minds, but afterward most of them fade away. What remains? In one old story about Mozart, the wonder child hears a lengthy contrapuntal mass and then writes down the entire score. (I do not believe such tales, for history documents so few of them that they seem to be mere legend, though by that argument Mozart also would seem to be legend.) Most people do not even remember the themes of an evening's concert. Yet, when the tunes are played again, they are recognized. Something must remain in the mind to cause this, and perhaps what we learn is not the music itself but a way of hearing it.

Compare a sonata to a teacher. The teacher gets the pupils' attention, either dramatically or by the quiet trick of speaking softly. Next, the teacher

presents the elements carefully, not introducing too many new ideas or developing them too far, for until the basics are learned the pupils cannot build on them. So, at first, the teacher repeats a lot. Sonatas, too, explain first one idea, then another, and then recapitulate it all. (Music has many forms and there are many ways to teach. I do not say that composers consciously intend to teach at all, yet they are masters at inventing forms for exposition, including those that swarm with more ideas and work our minds much harder.)

Thus *expositions* show the basic stuff—the atoms of impending chemistries and how some simple compounds can be made from those atoms. Then, in *developments*, those now-familiar compounds, made from bits and threads of beat and tone, can clash or merge, contrast or join together. We find things that do not fit into familiar frameworks hard to understand—such things seem meaningless. I prefer to turn that around: a thing has meaning only after we have learned some ways to represent and process what it means, or to understand its parts and how they are put together.

What is the difference between merely knowing (or remembering, or memorizing) and understanding? We all agree that to understand something we must know what it means, and that is about as far as we ever get. I think I know why that happens. A thing or idea seems meaningful only when we have several different ways to represent it—different perspectives and different associations. Then we can turn it around in our minds, so to speak: however it seems at the moment, we can see it another way and we never come to a full stop. In other words, we can *think* about it. If there were only one way to represent this thing or idea, we would not call this representation thinking.

So something has a "meaning" only when it has a few; if we understood something just one way, we would not understand it at all. That is why the seekers of the "real" meanings never find them. This holds true especially for words like *understand*. That is why sonatas start simply, as do the best of talks and texts. The basics are repeated several times before anything larger or more complex is presented. No one remembers word for word all that is said in a lecture or all notes that are played

in a piece. Yet if we have understood the lecture or piece once, we now "own" new networks of knowledge about each theme and how it changes and relates to others. No one could remember all of Beethoven's *Fifth Symphony* from a single hearing, but neither could one ever again hear those first four notes as just four notes! Once a tiny scrap of sound, these four notes have become a known thing—a locus in the web of all the other things we know and whose meanings and significances depend on one another (Fig. 1).

Learning to recognize is not the same as memorizing. A mind might build an *agent* that can sense a certain stimulus, yet build no agent that can reproduce it. How could such a mind learn that the first half-subject of Beethoven's *Fifth*—call it *A*—

prefigures the second half—call it *B*? It is simple: an agent A that recognizes *A* sends a message to another agent B, built to recognize *B*. That message serves to "lower B's threshold" so that after A hears *A*, B will react to smaller hints of *B* than it would otherwise. As a result, that mind "expects" to hear *B* after *A*; that is, it will discern *B*, given fewer or more subtle cues, and might "complain" if it cannot. Yet that mind cannot reproduce either theme in any generative sense. The point is that interagent messages need not be in surface music languages, but can be in codes that influence certain other agents to behave in different ways.

(Andor Kovach pointed out to me that composers do not dare use this simple, four-note motive any more. So memorable was Beethoven's treatment

that now an accidental hint of it can wreck another piece by unintentionally distracting the listener.)

If sonatas are lessons, what are the subjects of those lessons? The answer is in the question! One thing the *Fifth Symphony* taught us is how to hear those first four notes. The surface form is just *descending major third, first tone repeated thrice*. At first, that pattern can be heard two different ways: (1) *fifth and third in minor mode* or (2) *third and first, in major*. But once we have heard the symphony, the latter is unthinkable—a strange constraint to plant in all our heads! Let us see how it is taught.

The *Fifth* declares at once its subject, then its near-identical twin. First comes the theme. Presented in a stark orchestral unison, its minor mode location in tonality is not yet made explicit, nor is its metric frame yet clear: the subject stands alone in time. Next comes its twin. The score itself leaves room to view this transposed counterpart as a complement or as a new beginning. Until now, fermatas have hidden the basic metric frame, a pair of twinned four-measure halves. So far we have only learned to hear those halves as separate wholes.

The next four-measure metric half-frame shows three versions of the subject, one on each ascending pitch of the tonic triad. (Now we are sure the key is minor.) This shows us how the subject can be made to overlap itself, the three short notes packed perfectly inside the long tone's time-space. The second half-frame does the same, with copies of the complement ascending the dominant seventh chord. This fits the halves together in that single, most familiar, frame of harmony. In rhythm, too, the halves are so precisely congruent that there is no room to wonder how to match them—and attach them—into one eight-measure unit.

The next eight-measure frame explains some more melodic points: how to smooth the figure's firmness with passing tones and how to counterpoise the subject's own inversion inside the long note. (I think that this evokes a sort of sinusoidal motion-frame idea that is later used to represent the second subject.) It also illustrates compression of harmonic time; seen earlier, this would obscure the larger rhythmic unit, but now we know enough

to place each metric frame precisely on the afterimage of the one before.

Cadence. Silence. Almost. Total.

Now it is the second subject-twin's turn to stand alone in time. The conductor must select a symmetry: he or she can choose to answer prior cadence, to start anew, or to close the brackets opened at the very start. (Can the conductor do all at once and maintain the metric frame?) We hear a long, long unison F (subdominant?) for, underneath that silent surface sound, we hear our minds rehearsing what was heard.

The next frame reveals the theme again, descending now by thirds. (We see that it was the dominant ninth, not subdominant at all. The music fooled us that time, but never will again.) Then *tour de force*: the subject climbs, sounding on every scale degree. This new perspective shows us how to see the four-note theme as an appogiatura. Then, as it descends on each tonic chord-note, we are made to see it as a fragment of arpeggio. That last descent completes a set of all four possibilities, harmonic and directional. (Is this deliberate didactic thoroughness, or merely the accidental outcome of the other symmetries?) Finally, the theme's melodic range is squeezed to nothing, yet it survives and even gains strength as single tone. It has always seemed to me a mystery of art, the impact of those moments in quartets when texture turns to single line and forte-piano shames sforzando in perceived intensity. But such acts, which on the surface only cause the structure or intensity to disappear, must make the largest difference underneath. Shortly, I will propose a scheme in which a sudden, searching change awakes a lot of mental *difference-finders*. This very change wakes yet more difference-finders, and this awakening wakes still more. That is how sudden silence makes the whole mind come alive.

We are "told" all this in just one minute of the lesson and I have touched but one dimension of its rhetoric. Besides explaining, teachers beg and threaten, calm and scare; use gesture, timbre, quaver, and sometimes even silence. This is vital in music, too. Indeed, in the *Fifth*, it is the start of the subject! Such "lessons" must teach us as much about triads and triplets as mathematicians have learned about angles and sides! Think how much we can learn about minor second intervals from Beethoven's *Grosse Fuge in E-flat, Opus 133.*

What Use Is Music?

Why on earth should anyone want to learn such things? Geometry is practical—for building pyramids, for instance—but of what use is musical knowledge? Here is one idea. Each child spends endless days in curious ways; we call this *play.* A child stacks and packs all kinds of blocks and boxes, lines them up, and knocks them down. What is that all about? Clearly, the child is learning about space! But how on earth does one learn about time? Can one time fit inside another? Can two of them go side by side? In music, we find out! It is often said that mathematicians are unusually involved in music, but that musicians are not involved in mathematics. Perhaps both mathematicians and musicians like to make simple things more complicated, but mathematics may be too constrained to satisfy that want entirely, while music can be rigorous or free. The way the mathematics game is played, most variations lie outside the rules, while music can insist on perfect canon or tolerate a casual accompaniment. So mathematicians might need music, but musicians might not need mathematics. A simpler theory is that since music engages us at earlier ages, some mathematicians are those missing mathematical musicians.

Most adults have some childlike fascination for making and arranging larger structures out of smaller ones. One kind of musical understanding involves building large mental structures out of smaller, musical parts. Perhaps the drive to build those mental music structures is the same one that makes us try to understand the world. (Or perhaps that drive is just an accidental mutant variant of it; evolution often copies needless extra stuff, and minds so new as ours must contain a lot of that.)

Sometimes, though, we use music as a trick to misdirect our understanding of the world. When thoughts are painful we have no way to make them stop. We can attempt to turn our minds to other matters, but doing this (some claim) just submerges the bad thoughts. Perhaps the music that some call *background music* can tranquilize by turning under-thoughts from bad to neutral, leaving the surface thoughts free of affect by diverting the unconscious. The structures we assemble in that detached kind of listening might be wholly solipsistic webs of meaninglike cross-references that nowhere touch "reality." In such a self-constructed world, we would need no truth or falsehood, good or evil, pain or joy. Music, in this unpleasant view, would serve as a fine escape from tiresome thoughts.

Syntactic Theories of Music

Contrast two answers to the question, Why do we like certain tunes?

Because they have certain structural features.
Because they resemble other tunes we like.

The first answer has to do with the laws and rules that make tunes pleasant. In language, we know some laws for sentences; that is, we know the forms sentences must have to be syntactically acceptable, if not the things they must have to make them sensible or even pleasant to the ear. As to melody, it seems, we only know some features that can help—we know of no absolutely essential features. I do not expect much more to come of a search for a compact set of rules for musical phrases. (The point is not so much what we mean by *rule*, as how large a body of knowledge is involved.)

The second answer has to do with significance outside the tune itself, in the same way that asking, Which sentences are meaningful? takes us outside shared linguistic practice and forces us to look upon each person's private tangled webs of thought. Those private webs feed upon themselves, as in all spheres involving preference: we tend to like things that remind us of the other things we like. For example, some of us like music that resembles the songs, carols, rhymes, and hymns we liked in childhood. All this begs this question: If we like new tunes that are similar to those we already like, where does our liking for music start? I will come back to this later.

The term *resemble* begs a question also: What are the rules of musical resemblance? I am sure that this depends a lot on how melodies are "represented" in each individual mind. In each single mind, some different "mind parts" do this different ways: the same tune seems (at different times) to change its rhythm, mode, or harmony. Beyond that, individuals differ even more. Some listeners squirm to symmetries and shapes that others scarcely hear at all and some fine fugue subjects seem banal to those who sense only a single line. My guess is that our contrapuntal sensors harmonize each fading memory with others that might yet be played; perhaps Bach's mind could do this several ways at once. Even one such process might suffice to help an improviser plan what to try to play next. (To try is sufficient since improvisers, like stage magicians, know enough "vamps" or "ways out" to keep the music going when bold experiments fail.)

How is it possible to improvise or comprehend a complex contrapuntal piece? Simple statistical explanations cannot begin to describe such processes. Much better are the *generative* and *transformational* (e.g., neo-Schenkerian) methods of syntactic analysis, but only for the simplest analytic uses. At best, the very aim of syntax-oriented music theories is misdirected because they aspire to describe the sentences that minds produce without attempting to describe how the sentences are produced. Meaning is much more than sentence structure. We cannot expect to be able to describe the anatomy of the mind unless we understand its embryology. And so (as with most any other very complicated matter), science must start with surface systems of description. But this surface taxonomy, however elegant and comprehensive in itself, must yield in the end to a deeper, causal explanation. To understand how memory and process merge in "listening," we will have to learn to use much more "procedural" descriptions, such as programs that describe how processes proceed.

In science, we always first explain things in terms of what can be observed (earth, water, fire, air). Yet things that come from complicated processes do not necessarily show their natures on the surface. (The steady pressure of a gas conceals those countless, abrupt microimpacts.) To speak of what such things might mean or represent, we have to speak of how they are made.

We cannot describe how the mind is made without having good ways to describe complicated processes. Before computers, no languages were good for that. Piaget tried algebra and Freud tried diagrams; other psychologists used Markov chains and matrices, but none came to much. Behaviorists, quite properly, had ceased to speak at all. Linguists flocked to formal syntax, and made progress for a time but reached a limit: transformational grammar shows the contents of the registers (so to speak), but has no way to describe what controls them. This makes it hard to say how surface speech relates to underlying designation and intent—a baby-and-bath-water situation. The reason I like ideas from AI research is that there we tend to seek procedural description first, which seems more appropriate for mental matters.

I do not see why so many theorists find this approach disturbing. It is true that the new power derived from this approach has a price: we can say more, with computational description, but prove less. Yet less is lost than many think, for mathematics never could prove much about such complicated things. Theorems often tell us complex truths about the simple things, but only rarely tell us simple truths about the complex ones. To believe otherwise is wishful thinking or "mathematics envy." Many musical problems that resist formal solutions may turn out to be tractable anyway, in future simulations that grow artificial musical semantic networks, perhaps by "raising" simulated infants in traditional musical cultures. It will be exciting when one of these infants first shows a hint of real "talent."

Space and Tune

When we enter a room, we seem to see it all at once; we are not permitted this illusion when listening to a symphony. "Of course," one might declare, for hearing has to thread a serial path through time, while sight embraces a space all at once. Actually, it takes time to see new scenes, though we are not usually aware of this. That totally compelling sense that we are conscious of seeing every-thing in the room instantly and immediately is certainly the strangest of our "optical" illusions.

Music, too, immerses us in seemingly stable worlds! How can this be, when there is so little of it present at each moment? I will try to explain this by (1) arguing that hearing music is like viewing scenery and (2) by asserting that when we hear good music our minds react in very much the same way they do when we see things.[1] And make no mis-take: I meant to say "good" music! This little the-ory is not meant to work for any senseless bag of musical tricks, but only for those certain kinds of music that, in their cultural times and places, com-mand attention and approval.

To see the problem in a slightly different way, consider cinema. Contrast a novice's clumsy patched and pasted reels of film with those that transport us to other worlds so artfully composed that our own worlds seem shoddy and malformed. What "hides the seams" to make great films so much less than the sum of their parts—so that we do not see them as mere sequences of scenes? What makes us feel that we are there and part of it when we are in fact immobile in our chairs, helpless to deflect an atom of the projected pattern's predetermined destiny? I will follow this idea a little further, then try to ex-plain why good music is both more and less than sequences of notes.

Our eyes are always flashing sudden flicks of dif-ferent pictures to our brains, yet none of that sac-cadic action leads to any sense of change or motion in the world; each thing reposes calmly in its "place"! What makes those objects stay so still while images jump and jerk so? What makes us such innate Copernicans? I will first propose how this illusion works in vision, then in music.

We will find the answer deep within the way the

1. Edward Fredkin suggested to me the theory that listening to music might exercise some innate map-making mechanism in the brain. When I mentioned the puzzle of music's repetitious-ness, he compared it to the way rodents explore new places: first they go one way a little, then back to home. They do it again a few times, then go a little farther. They try small digressions, but frequently return to base. Both people and mice explore new territories that way, making mental maps lest they get lost. Mu-sic might portray this building process, or even exercise those very parts of the mind.

mind regards itself. When speaking of illusion, we assume that someone is being fooled. "I know those lines are straight," I say, "but they look bent to me." Who are the different I's and me's? We are all convinced that somewhere in each person struts a single, central self; atomic, indivisible. (And se-cretly we hope that it is also indestructible.)

I believe, instead, that inside each mind work many different agents. (The idea of societies of agents [Minsky 1977; 1980a; 1980b] originated in my work with Seymour Papert.) All we really need to know about agents is this: each agent knows what happens to some others, but little of what happens to the rest. It means little to say, "Eloise was unaware of X" unless we say more about which of her *mind-agents* were uninvolved with X. Think-ing consists of making mind-agents work together; the very core of fruitful thought is breaking prob-lems into different kinds of parts and then assign-ing the parts to the agents that handle them best. (Among our most important agents are those that manage these assignments, for they are the agents that embody what each person knows about what he or she knows. Without these agents we would be helpless, for we would not know what our knowing is for.)

In that division of labor we call *seeing*, I will sup-pose that a certain mind-agent called *feature-finder* sends messages (about features it finds on the ret-ina) to another agent, *scene-analyzer*. Scene-analyzer draws conclusions from the messages it gets and sends its own, in turn, to other *mind-parts*. For instance, feature-finder finds and tells about some scraps of edge and texture; then scene-analyzer finds and tells that these might fit some bit of shape.

Perhaps those features come from glimpses of a certain real table leg. But knowing such a thing is not for agents at this level; scene-analyzer does not know of any such specific things. All it can do is broadcast something about shape to hosts of other agents who specialize in recognizing special things. (Since special things—like tables, words, or dogs—must be involved with memory and learning, there is at least one such agent for every kind of thing this mind has learned to recognize.) Thus, we can hope, this message reaches *table-maker*, an agent specialized to recognize evidence that a table is in the field of view. After many such stages, descendants of such messages finally reach *space-builder*, an agent that tries to tell of real things in real space.

Now we can see one reason why perception seems so effortless: while messages from scene-analyzer to table-maker are based on evidence that feature-finder supplied, the messages themselves need not say what feature-finder itself did, or how it did it. Partly this is because it would take scene-analyzer too long to explain all that. In any case, the recipients could make no use of all that information since they are not engineers or psychologists, but just little specialized nerve nets.

Only in the past few centuries have painters learned enough technique and trickery to simulate reality. (Once so informed, they often now choose different goals.) Thus space-builder, like an ordinary person, knows nothing of how vision works, perspective, foveae, or blind spots. We only learn such things in school: millennia of introspection never led to their suspicion, nor did meditation, transcendental or mundane. The mind holds tightly to its secrets not from stinginess or shame, but simply because it does not know them.

Messages, in this scheme, go various ways. Each motion of the eye or head or body makes feature-finder start anew, and such motions are responses (by muscle-moving agents) to messages that scene-analyzer sends when it needs more details to resolve ambiguities. Scene-analyzer itself responds to messages from "higher up." For instance, space-builder may have asked, "Is that a table?" of table-maker, which replies (to itself), "Perhaps, but it should have another leg—there," so it asks scene-analyzer to verify this, and scene-analyzer gets the job done by making *eye-mover* look down and to the left. Nor is *scene-understander* autonomous: its questions to scene-analyzer are responses to requests from others. There need be no first cause in such a network.

When we look up, we are never afraid that the ground has disappeared, though it certainly has "dis-appeared." This is because space-builder remembers all the answers to its questions and never changes any of those answers without reason; moving our eyes or raising our heads provide no cause to exorcise that floor inside our current spatial model of the room. My paper on *frame-systems* (Minsky 1974) says more about these concepts. Here we only need these few details.

Now, back to our illusions. While feature-finder is not instantaneous, it is very, very fast and a highly parallel pattern matcher. Whatever scene-analyzer asks, feature-finder answers in an eye flick, a mere tenth of a second (or less if we have image buffers). More speed comes from the way in which space-builder can often tell itself, via its own high-speed model memory, about what has been seen before. I argue that all this speed is another root of our illusion: *if answers seem to come as soon as questions are asked, they will seem to have been there all along.*

The illusion is enhanced in yet another way by "expectation" or "default." Those agents know good ways to lie and bluff! Aroused by only partial evidence that a table is in view, table-maker supplies space-builder with fictitious details about some "typical table" while its servants find out more about the real one! Once so informed, space-builder can quickly move and plan ahead, taking some risks but ready to make corrections later. This only works, of course, when prototypes are good and are rightly activated—that is what intelligence is all about.

As for "awareness" of how all such things are done, there simply is not room for that. Space-builder is too remote and different to understand how feature-finder does its work of eye fixation. Each part of the mind is unaware of almost all that happens in the others. (That is why we need psychologists; we think we know what happens in our minds because those agents are so facile with "defaults," but we are almost always wrong.) True, each agent needs to know which of its servants can do what, but as to *how*, that information has no place or use inside those tiny minds inside our minds.

How do both music and vision build things in our minds? Eye motions show us real objects; phrases show us musical objects. We "learn" a room with bodily motions; large musical sections show us musical "places." Walks and climbs move us from room to room; so do transitions between musical sections. Looking back in vision is like recapitulation in music; both give us time, at certain points, to reconfirm or change our conceptions of the whole.

Hearing a theme is like seeing a thing in a room, a section or movement is like a room, and a whole sonata is like an entire building. I do not mean to say that music builds the sorts of things that space-builder does. (That is too naive a comparison of sound and place.) I do mean to say that composers stimulate coherency by engaging the same sorts of interagent coordinations that vision uses to produce its illusion of a stable world using, of course, different agents. I think the same is true of talk or writing, the way these very paragraphs make sense—or sense of sense—if any.

Composing and Conducting

In seeing, we can move our eyes; lookers can choose where they shall look, and when. In music we must listen *here*; that is, to the part being played now. It is simply no use asking *music-finder* to look *there* because it is not *then*, now.

If composer and conductor choose what part we hear, does not this ruin our analogy? When *music-analyzer* asks its questions, how can music-finder answer them unless, miraculously, the music happens to be playing what music-finder wants at just that very instant? If so, then how can music paint its scenes unless composers know exactly what the listeners will ask at every moment? How to ensure—when music-analyzer wants it now—that precisely that "something" will be playing now?

That is the secret of music; of writing it, playing, and conducting! Music need not, of course, confirm each listener's every expectation; each plot demands some novelty. Whatever the intent, control is required or novelty will turn to nonsense. If allowed to think too much themselves, the listeners will find unanswered questions in any score; about accidents of form and figure, voice and line, temperament and difference-tone.

Composers can have different goals: to calm and soothe, surprise and shock, tell tales, stage scenes,

teach new things, or tear down prior arts. For some such purposes composers must use the known forms and frames or else expect misunderstanding. Of course, when expectations are confirmed too often the style may seem dull; this is our concern in the next section. Yet, just as in language, one often best explains a new idea by using older ones, avoiding jargon or too much lexical innovation. If readers cannot understand the words themselves, the sentences may "be Greek to them."

This is not a matter of a simple hierarchy, in which each meaning stands on lower-level ones, for example, word, phrase, sentence, paragraph, and chapter. Things never really work that way, and jabberwocky shows how sense comes through though many words are new. In every era some contemporary music changes basic elements yet exploits established larger forms, but innovations that violate too drastically the expectations of the culture cannot meet certain kinds of goals. Of course this will not apply to works whose goals include confusion and revolt, or when composers try to create things that hide or expurgate their own intentionality, but in these instances it may be hard to hold the audience.

Each musical artist must forecast and predirect the listener's fixations to draw attention *here* and distract it from *there*—to force the hearer (again, like a magician) to ask only the questions that the composition is about to answer. Only by establishing such preestablished harmony can music make it seem that something is there.

Rhythm and Redundancy

A popular song has 100 measures, 1000 beats. What must the martians imagine we mean by those measures and beats, measures and beats! The words themselves reveal an awesome repetitiousness. Why isn't music boring?

Is hearing so like seeing that we need a hundred glances to build each musical image? Some repetitive musical textures might serve to remind us of things that persist through time like wind and stream. But many sounds occur only once: we must hear a pin drop now or seek and search for it; that is why we have no "ear-lids." Poetry drops pins, or says each thing once or not at all. So does some music.

Then why do we tolerate music's relentless rhythmic pulse or other repetitive architectural features? There is no one answer, for we hear in different ways, on different scales. Some of those ways portray the spans of time directly, but others speak of *musical things*, in worlds where time folds over on itself. And there, I think, is where we use those beats and measures. Music's metric frames are transient templates used for momentary matching. Its rhythms are "synchronization pulses" used to match new phrases against old, the better to contrast them with differences and change. As differences and change are sensed, the rhythmic frames fade from our awareness. Their work is done and the messages of higher-level agents never speak of them; that is why metric music is not boring!

Good music germinates from tiny seeds. How cautiously we handle novelty, sandwiching the new between repeated sections of familiar stuff! The clearest kind of change is near-identity, in thought just as in vision. Slight shifts in view may best reveal an object's form or even show us whether it is there at all.

When we discussed sonatas, we saw how matching different metric frames helps us to sense the musical ingredients. Once frames are matched, we can see how altering a single note at one point will change a major third melodic skip at another point to smooth passing tones; or will make what was *there* a seventh chord into a dominant ninth. Matching lets our minds see different things, from different times, together. This fusion of those matching lines of tone from different measures (like television's separate lines and frames) lets us make those magic musical pictures in our minds.

How do our musical agents do this kind of work for us? We must have organized them into structures that are good at finding differences between frames. Here is a simplified four-level scheme that might work. Many such ideas are current in research on vision (Winston 1975).

Feature-finders listen for simple time-events, like notes, or peaks, or pulses.

Measure-takers notice certain patterns of time-events like 3/4, 4/4, 6/8.

Difference-finders observe that the figure *here* is same as that one *there*, except a perfect fifth above.

Structure-builders perceive that three phrases form an almost regular "sequence."

The idea of interconnecting *feature-finders, difference-finders*, and *structure-builders* is well exemplified in Winston's work (1975). *Measure-takers* would be kinds of *frames*, as described in "A Framework for Representing Knowledge" (Minsky 1974). First, the feature-finders search the sound stream for the simplest sorts of musical significance: entrances and envelopes, the tones themselves, the other little, local things. Then measure-takers look for metric patterns in those small events and put them into groups, thus finding beats and postulating rhythmic regularities. Then the difference-finders can begin to sense events of musical importance; imitations and inversions, syncopations and suspensions. Once these are found, the structure-builders can start work on a larger scale.

The entire four-level *agency* is just one layer of a larger system in which analogous structures are repeated on larger scales. At each scale, another level of order (with its own sorts of things and differences) makes larger-scale descriptions, and thus consumes another order of structural form. As a result, notes become figures, figures turn into phrases, and phrases turn into sequences; and notes become chords, and chords make up progressions, and so on and on. Relations at each level turn to things at the next level above and are thus more easily remembered and compared. This "time-warps" things together, changing tone into tonality, note into composition.

The more regular the rhythm, the easier the matching goes, and the fewer difference agents are excited further on. Thus once it is used for "lining up," the metric structure fades from our attention because it is represented as fixed and constant (like the floor of the room you are in) until some metric alteration makes the measure-takers change their minds. *Sic semper* all Alberti basses, um-pah-pahs, and ostinati; they all become imperceptible except when changing. Rhythm has many other functions, to be sure, and agents for those other functions see things different ways. Agents used for dancing do attend to rhythm, while other forms of music demand less steady pulses.

We all experience a phenomenon we might call *persistence of rhythm*, in which our minds maintain the beat through episodes of ambiguity. I presume that this emerges from a basic feature of how agents are usually assembled; at every level, many agents of each kind compete (Minsky 1980b). Thus agents for 3/4, 4/4, and 6/8 compete to find best fits. Once in power, however, each agent "cross-inhibits" its competitors. Once 3/4 takes charge of things, 6/8 will find it hard to "get a hearing" even if the evidence on its side becomes slightly better.

When none of the agents has any solid evidence long enough, agents change at random or take turns. Thus anything gets interesting, in a way, if it is monotonous enough! We all know how, when a word or phrase is repeated often enough it, or we, begin to change as restless searchers start to amplify minutiae and interpret noise as structure. This happens at all levels because when things are regular at one level, the difference agents at the next will fail, to be replaced by other, fresh ones that then re-present the sameness different ways. (Thus meditation, undirected from the higher mental realms, fares well with the most banal of repetitious inputs from below.)

Regularities are hidden while expressive nuances are sensed and emphasized and passed along. Rubato or crescendo, ornament or passing tone, the alterations at each level become the objects for the next. The mystery is solved; the brain is so good at sensing differences that it forgets the things themselves; that is, whenever they are the same. As for liking music, that depends on what remains.

Sentic Significance

Why do we like any tunes in the first place? Do we simply associate some tunes with pleasant experiences? Should we look back to the tones and patterns of mother's voice or heartbeat? Or could it be that some themes are innately likable? All these

theories could hold truth, and others too, for nothing need have a single cause inside the mind.

Theories about children need not apply to adults because (I suspect) human minds do so much self-revising that things can get detached from their origins. We might end up liking both *Art of Fugue* and *Musical Offering*, mainly because each work's subject illuminates the other, which gives each work a richer network of "significance." Dependent circularity need be no paradox here, for in thinking (unlike logic) two things can support each other in midair. To be sure, such autonomy is precarious; once detached from origins, might one not drift strangely awry? Indeed so, and many people seem quite mad to one another.

In his book *Sentics* (1978), Manfred Clynes, a physiologist and pianist, describes certain specific temporal sensory patterns and claims that each is associated with a certain common emotional state. For example, in his experiments, two particular patterns (that gently rise and fall) are said to suggest states of love and reverence; two others (more abrupt) signify anger and hate. He claims that these and other patterns—he calls them *sentic*—arouse the same effects through different senses—that is, embodied as acoustical intensity, or pitch, or tactile pressure, or even visual motion—and that this is cross-cultural. The time lengths of these sentic shapes, on the order of 1 sec, could correspond to parts of musical phrases.

Clynes studied the "muscular" details of instrumental performances with this in view, and concluded that music can engage emotions through these sentic signals. Of course, more experiments are needed to verify that such signals really have the reported effects. Nevertheless, I would expect to find something of the sort for quite a different reason: namely, to serve in the early social development of children. Sentic signals (if they exist) would be quite useful in helping infants to learn about themselves and others.

All learning theories require brains to somehow impose "values" implicit or explicit in the choice of what to learn to do. Most such theories say that certain special signals, called *reinforcers*, are involved in this. For certain goals it should suffice to use some simple, "primary" physiological stimuli like eating, drinking, relief of physical discomfort.

Human infants must learn social signals, too. The early learning theorists in this century assumed that certain social sounds (for instance, of approval) could become reinforcers by association with innate reinforcers, but evidence for this was never found. If parents could exploit some innate sentic cues, that mystery might be explained.

This might also touch another, deeper problem: that of how an infant forms an image of its own mind. Self-images are important for at least two reasons. First, external reinforcement can only be a part of human learning; the growing infant must eventually learn to learn from within to free itself from its parents. With Freud, I think that children must replace and augment the outside teacher with a self-constructed, inner, parent image. Second, we need a self-model simply to make realistic plans for solving ordinary problems. For example, we must know enough about our own dispositions to be able to assess which plans are feasible. Pure self-commitment does not work; we simply cannot carry out a plan that we will find too boring to complete or too vulnerable to other, competing interests. We need models of our own behavior. How could a baby be smart enough to build such a model?

Innate sentic detectors could help by teaching children about their own affective states. For if distinct signals arouse specific states, the child can associate those signals with those states. Just knowing that such states exist, that is, having symbols for them, is half the battle. If those signals are uniform enough, then from social discourse one can learn some rules about the behavior caused by those states. Thus a child might learn that conciliatory signals can change anger to affection. Given that sort of information, a simple learning machine should be able to construct a "finite-state person-model." This model would be crude at first, but to get started would be half of the job. Once the baby had a crude model of some *other*, it could be copied and adapted in work on the baby's self-model. (This is more normative and constructional than it is descriptive, as Freud hinted, for the self-model dictates more than portrays what it purports to portray.)

With regard to music, it seems possible that we conceal, in the innocent songs and settings of our children's musical cultures, some lessons about successions of our own affective states. Sentically encrypted, those ballads could encode instructions about conciliation and affection, aggression and retreat; precisely the knowledge of signals and states that we need to get along with others. In later life, more complex music might illustrate more intricate kinds of compromise and conflict, ways to fit goals together to achieve more than one thing at a time. Finally, for grown-ups, our Burgesses and Kubricks fit Beethoven's *Ninths* to *Clockwork Oranges*.

If you find all this farfetched, so do I. But before rejecting it entirely, recall the question, Why do we have music, and let it occupy our lives with no apparent reason? When no idea seems right, the right one must seem wrong.

Theme and Thing

What is the subject of Beethoven's *Fifth Symphony*? Is it just those first four notes? Does it include the twin, transposed companion too? What of the other variations, augmentations, and inversions? Do they all stem from a single prototype? In this case, yes.

Or do they? For later in the symphony the theme appears in triplet form to serve as countersubject of the scherzo: *three notes and one, three notes and one, three notes and one, still they make four* (Fig. 2). Melody turns into monotone rhythm; meter is converted to two equal beats. Downbeat now falls on an actual note, instead of a silence. With all of those changes, the themes are quite different and yet the same. Neither the form in the allegro nor the scherzo alone is the prototype; separate and equal, they span musical time.

Is there some more abstract idea that they both embody? This is like the problem raised by Wittgenstein (1953) of what words like *game* mean. In my paper on frames (Minsky 1974), I argue that for vision, *chair* can be described by no single prototype; it is better to use several prototypes connected in relational networks of similarities and differences. I doubt that even these would represent musical ideas well; there are better tools in contemporary AI research, such as constraint systems,

Fig. 2. Introductory measures of the third movement of Beethoven's Symphony No. 5 in C Minor.

conceptual dependency, frame-systems, and semantic networks. Those are the tools we use today to deal with such problems. (See *Computer Music Journal* 4[2] and 4[3], 1980.)

What is a good theme? Without that bad word *good*, I do not think the question is well formed because anything is a theme if everything is music!

So let us split that question into (1) What mental conditions or processes do pleasant tunes evoke? and (2) What do we mean by *pleasant*? Both questions are hard, but the first is only hard; to answer it will take much thought and experimentation, which is good. The second question is very different. Philosophers and scientists have struggled mightily to understand what pain and pleasure are. I especially like Dennett's (1978) explanation of why that has been so difficult. He argues that pain "works" in different ways at different times, and all those ways have too little in common for the usual definition. I agree, but if pain is no single thing, why do we talk and think as though it were and represent it with such spurious clarity? This is no accident: illusions of this sort have special uses. They play a role connected with a problem facing any society (inside or outside the mind) that learns from its experience. The problem is how to assign the credit and blame, for each accomplishment or failure of the society as a whole, among the myriad agents involved in everything that happens. To the extent that the agents' actions are decided locally, so also must these decisions to credit or blame be made locally.

How, for example, can a mother tell that her child has a need (or that one has been satisfied) before she has learned specific signs for each such need? That could be arranged if, by evolution, signals were combined from many different internal processes concerned with needs and were provided with a single, common, output—an infant's sentic signal of discomfort (or contentment). Such a genetically preestablished harmony would evoke a corresponding central state in the parent. We would feel this as something like the distress we feel when babies cry.

A signal for satisfaction is also needed. Suppose, among the many things a child does, there is one that mother likes, which she demonstrates by making approving sounds. The child has just been walking *there*, and holding *this* just so, and thinking *that*, and speaking in some certain way. How can the mind of the child find out which behavior is good? The trouble is, each aspect of the child's behavior must result from little plans the child made before. We cannot reward an act. We can only reward the agency that selected that strategy, the agent who wisely activated the first agent, and so on. Alas for the generation of behaviorists who wastes its mental life by missing this plain and simple principle.

To reward all those agents and processes, we must propagate some message that they all can use to credit what they did; the plans they made, their strategies and computations. These various recipients have so little in common that such a message of approval, to work at all, must be extremely simple. Words like *good* are almost content-free messages that enable tutors, inside or outside a society, to tell the members that one or more of them has satisfied some need, and that tutor need not understand which members did what, or how, or even why.

Words like *satisfy* and *need* have many shifting meanings. Why, then, do we seem to understand them? Because they evoke that same illusion of substantiality that fools us into thinking it tautologous to ask, Why do we like pleasure? This serves a need: the levels of social discourse at which we use such clumsy words as *like*, or *good*, or *that was fun* must coarsely crush together many different meanings or we will never understand others (or ourselves) at all. Hence that precious, essential poverty of word and sign that makes them so hard to define. Thus the word *good* is no symbol that simply means or designates, as *table* does. Instead, it only names this protean injunction: Activate all those (unknown) processes that correlate and sift and sort, in learning, to see what changes (in myself) should now be made. The word *like* is just like *good*, except it is a name we use when we send such structure-building signals to ourselves.

Most of the "uses" of music mentioned in this article—learning about time, fitting things together, getting along with others, and suppressing one's troubles—are very "functional," but overlook much larger scales of "use." Curt Roads remarked that, "Every world above bare survival is self-constructed; whole cultures are built around common things people come to appreciate." These appreciations, represented by aesthetic agents, play roles in more and more of our decisions: what we think is beautiful gets linked to what we think is important. Perhaps, Roads suggests, when groups of mind-agents cannot agree, they tend to cede decisions to those others more concerned with what, for better or for worse, we call aesthetic form and fitness. By having small effects at many little points, those cumulative preferences for taste and form can shape a world.

That is another reason why we say we like the music we like. Liking is the way certain mind-parts make the others learn the things they need to understand that music. Hence liking (and its relatives) is at the very heart of understanding what we hear. *Affect* and *aesthetic* do not lie in other academic worlds that music theories safely can ignore. Those other worlds are academic self-deceptions that we use to make each theorist's problem seem like someone else's.[2]

2. Many readers of a draft of this article complained about its narrow view of music. What about jazz, "modern" forms, songs with real words, monophonic chant and raga, gong and block, and all those other kinds of sounds? Several readers claimed to be less intellectual, to simply hear and feel and not build buildings in their minds. There simply is not space here to discuss all those things, but:

1. What makes those thinkers who think that music does not make them do so much construction so sure that they know their minds so surely? It is ingenuous to think you "just react" to anything a culture works a thousand years to develop. A mind that thinks it works so simply must have more in its unconscious than it has in its philosophy.

2. Our work here is with hearing music, not with hearing "music"! Anything that we can all agree is music will be fine—that is why I chose Beethoven's *Fifth Symphony*. For what is music? All things played on all instruments? Fiddlesticks. All structures made of sound? That has a hollow ring. The things I said of words like *theme* hold true for words like *music* too: it does not follow that because a word is public the ways it works on minds is also public. Before one embarks on a quest after the grail that holds the essence of all "music," one must see that there is as significant a problem in the meaning of that single sound itself.

Acknowledgments

I am indebted to conversations and/or improvisations with Maryann Amacher, John Amuedo, Betty Dexter, Harlan Ellison, Edward Fredkin, Bernard Greenberg, Danny Hillis, Douglas Hofstadter, William Kornfeld, Andor Kovach, David Levitt, Tod Machover, Charlotte Minsky, Curt Roads, Gloria Rudisch, Frederic Rzewski, and Stephen Smoliar. This article is in memory of Irving Fine.

References

Clynes, M. 1978. *Sentics*. New York: Doubleday.

Dennett, D. 1978. "Why a Machine Can't Feel Pain." In *Brainstorms: Philosophical Essays on Mind and Psychology*. Montgomery, Vermont: Bradford Books.

Minsky, M. 1974. "A Framework for Representing Knowledge." AI Memo 306. Cambridge, Massachusetts: M.I.T. Artificial Intelligence Laboratory. Condensed version in P. Winston, ed. 1975. *The Psychology of Computer Vision*. New York: McGraw-Hill, pp. 211–277.

Minsky, M. 1977. "Plain Talk About Neurodevelopmental Epistemology." In *Proceedings of the Fifth International Joint Conference on Artificial Intelligence*. Cambridge, Massachusetts: M.I.T. Artificial Intelligence Laboratory. Condensed in P. Winston and R. Brown, eds. 1979. *Artificial Intelligence*. Cambridge, Massachusetts: MIT Press, pp. 421–450.

Minsky, M. 1980a. "Jokes and the Logic of the Cognitive Unconscious." AI Memo 603. Cambridge, Massachusetts: M.I.T. Artificial Intelligence Laboratory.

Minsky, M. 1980b. "K-lines: A Theory of Memory." *Cognitive Science* 4(2): 117–133.

Roads, C. ed. 1980. *Computer Music Journal* 4(2) and 4(3).

Winston, P. H. 1975. "Learning Structural Descriptions by Examples." In P. Winston, ed. 1975. *Psychology of Computer Vision*. New York: McGraw-Hill, pp. 157–209.

Wittgenstein, L. 1953. *Philosophical Investigations*. Oxford: Oxford University Press.

51

John Rothgeb
State University of New York
Binghamton, New York

Simulating Musical Skills by Digital Computer

Introduction

It was inevitable that the digital computer, an instrument of such enormous potential and accomplishment in the study of the natural and social sciences and the humanities, should be applied to the investigation of problems in the fine arts. Music is directly accessible to computational study; it is normally set down in the form of a notated score that can be represented almost completely in a code consisting of discrete symbols. It must be said at once, however, that the notated score, even of the simplest traditional Western art music, is incomplete; the musical work as conceived by the composer and as produced by the sensitive performer deviates from the precision of the printed or written score in countless subtle ways—most obviously with respect to temporal organization, but also with respect to even pitch and timbre.[2] Thus the score is at best an approximation of what can properly be designated as "the" composition.

To appreciate fully what this means, it is instructive to imagine or actually to experience a literal realization by synthesizer of, say, a Bach sonata for unaccompanied violin (to choose a particularly extreme example). The hearer of such a realization finds it almost impossible to "follow" the music, to "make sense" of it; and this has far less to do with the timbral inadequacies of the synthesizer's violin tone than with missing temporal and dynamic nuances. (The same music speaks eloquently on ancient phonorecords, despite their obvious timbral deficiencies.) But the printed score and its representation in an appropriate linear code, incompleteness notwithstanding, present a sufficiently detailed picture of the music's structure to render it accessible to analytic probing in a depth not approachable in many other art forms.

Tonal Music

Music theorists customarily group musical art works into classes defined on the basis of shared structural characteristics. Tonal music, or the class of tonal compositions, is one such class; twelve-tone music (indigenous to the twentieth century) is another. It is convenient, moreover, to distinguish between the compositions belonging to a given class and the language underlying those compositions; this distinction is often compared to that made in linguistics between the corpus of sentences in a language and the grammar according to which those sentences are produced and interpreted. (The analogy, although useful, is far from perfect; I shall not develop it further here.) Tonal music, comprising most of the music written between about 1650 and 1900, is especially suitable as an object for rigorous (and therefore computational) study for several reasons. First, its significance as a pinnacle in the history of art music in general is indisputable. Second, it has a highly constrained syntax embodying many known regularities: for ex-

This is an edited version of a paper appearing in *Proceedings of ACM 79.* Copyright 1979, Association for Computing Machinery, Inc.; reprinted by permission.

2. During the past three hundred years or so, the general trend in notating music has been to make the written score more and more explicit. At the same time, the interpretative responsibilities of the performer have increased (at least up until the first decades of the twentieth century), so that the written score of a Mahler symphony, however fully specified it may appear, is not an appreciably closer approximation to an orchestral performance than is the score of a Brandenburg Concerto by Bach.

ample, the class of intervals characterized as "dissonant," and the structural obligations incumbent upon such intervals, were firmly established long before 1650 and remained constant throughout the period of tonal music.[3] Finally, tonal compositions are structurally organized in terms of a series of strata (each stratum specifiable in its own musical notation) that relate to one another as simple to (more) complex.[4] This means that we can *explain* a tonal composition according to the venerable explanatory model wherein complex phenomena or configurations are related through known operations to simple and familiar ones. (This notion elucidates, among many other things, the basis of the art of musical variation as applied not only in works entitled "Theme and Variations" but also from phrase to phrase and bar to bar in the classical masterworks: variations which contrast markedly in notation and therefore in sonic qualities may share a common underlying stratum.) For convenience, I shall speak here occasionally of the *simple-to-complex array* or simply *array* of strata associated with a given composition.

Computer-Accessible Problems in Music Theory

In view of the characteristics of music representation and the nature of tonal music as already discussed and the capabilities of the digital computer, a wide range of possible computer applications in music theory comes to mind. Well-trained musicians have a thorough but inexplicit understanding of the elements and operations that make up the language we call *classical tonality*. It is part of the essence of theoretical studies, however, to render explicit that which has been inexplicit. The familiar result of such work is that new areas of

inexplicitness are exposed, and those areas are then subject to study and explication in their turn. By symbolically representing the elements of musical notation and expressing in formal terms those operations believed to form the basis of inter-stratal relations, the music theorist obtains something comparable to a generative grammar with all of its advantages for the refinement and verification of theories.

There are several avenues through which we may approach such research; they may be characterized in terms of the requirements we might impose on the theory to be tested. In the first place a theory might be required, in its computational implementation, to compose credible tonal music and only such music, starting from minimal axiomatic bases of some kind and applying the known operations to derive further steps in the simple-to-complex array. In principle, we could require the output of such a machine to include the *Goldberg Variations* and the *Hammerklavier Sonata* while excluding such conservative departures from classical tonal syntax as the milder pieces from Hindemith's *Ludus Tonalis*. (The exclusion clause is obviously necessary: trivial theories could be constructed that would generate authentic tonal pieces among countless arbitrary concatenations of notes.) A weaker requirement would be that the theory be capable, given an authentic tonal composition, of constructing the simple-to-complex array associated with it. Or, a theory could be designed to operate as a decision procedure: given an arbitrary musical score, does the composition specified belong to the class of tonal compositions, or not?

Investigations of each of these types have been proposed, but to my knowledge none has been brought to a satisfactory conclusion. Nor is this surprising, in view of the obvious complexity of the tonal language and of the compositional technique displayed by its greatest "native speakers." We might, therefore, want to consider possibly useful initial limitations of the foregoing experimental designs. For example, work is currently being done[5]

3. Indeed, the structural significance of the various intervals is a defining property of tonal music; the departure from established norms of the intervallic behavior thus became *the* salient feature of pitch organization in the "atonal" music of the early twentieth century.
4. The concept of structural strata was most fully and convincingly expounded by the Austrian music theorist Heinrich Schenker from about 1906 to 1935.

5. By Steven Haflich for a Ph.D. dissertation in progress at Yale University.

toward solution of the following problem: given level n in the simple-to-complex array (or possibly levels 0 through n), compute level $n + 1$ (or $n + m$, for some relatively small value of m). Alternatively, we could start with an extremely restricted corpus of music—initially even a single work—and, proceeding from an apparently correct rational reconstruction thereof, supplement the rules of procedure for moving from stratum n to stratum $n + 1$ with rule constraints appropriate to the particular style of composition under investigation.[6] In either case, the advantages afforded by the computational implementation for verification of the theory and in suggesting new lines of inquiry are both obvious and familiar.

The Unfigured-Bass Problem

I was originally invited to present this paper as a "pioneer" in the field of computational studies in music. That characterization can be considered accurate only if it is interpreted as indicating that the project that I undertook several years ago, and that I will now describe to you with merciful brevity, belongs properly to the prehistory of such endeavors (Rothgeb 1968).

The unfigured-bass problem can be fitted in a loose way into the schema of simple-to-complex arrays outlined previously in that it involves a progression from a less fully specified pitch structure to a more fully specified one. From the locution *unfigured bass*, you may correctly infer that there is such a thing as a *figured bass*; the latter entity is, in an important and interesting sense, more advanced in the array terminating in a tonal composition than the former. A figured bass, that is, a bass line with certain combinations of arabic numbers and musical accidental symbols adjoined either above or below it, specifies not only the bass voice of the composition with which it is associated but also the chords that accompany those bass notes and, to a considerable extent, the voice lead-

ing (horizontal progression) of the (as yet unwritten) voices above that bass. During the seventeenth and eighteenth centuries, the figured bass (or thoroughbass) was applied in practice as a kind of musical shorthand in notating all music accompanied by a *basso continuo*, normally played by cello, gamba, or bassoon together with a keyboard instrument. The keyboard player was expected to infer and supply chords and voice leading on the basis of the figures given; this was known as *realizing* the figured bass.[7]

Since a figured-bass realization as performed by a trained accompanist can also be written down in standard musical notation, the art of realizing such a bass is itself a skill that admits of simulation by computer. If the continuo bass was unfigured, as occasionally happened in the thoroughbass period, the accompanist was still required to provide a competent realization. The necessary musical skill in this case involves two distinct steps, to (1) infer appropriate figured-bass figures from the structure of the bass itself, and (2) realize the resulting figured bass in accordance with the conventional rules. It was the first step of this process that I endeavored to simulate computationally.

To supply appropriate figures for an unfigured bass is a nontrivial problem; although some latitude exists, an arbitrary assignment of figures would, in general, result in violations of tonal syntax. For example, the penultimate note of a "cadential" configuration must be set with a figure which determines a major triad or a "dominant-seventh"-type chord; other combinations of figures such as 6, $\frac{5}{3}$, $\frac{4}{3}$, and so forth, although in themselves possible in figured-bass realization, would be incorrect in such a context.

The problem of the unfigured bass was recognized by a number of eighteenth-century thoroughbass theorists and treated in some detail by a few. Among the more extended informal algorithms

6. This is the strategy employed by James L. Snell in his "Design for a Formal System for Deriving Tonal Music," Master's thesis, State University of New York, Binghamton, 1979.

7. With the demise of the *basso continuo* the figured bass disappeared from finished musical scores; but masters such as Mozart, Beethoven, Mendelssohn, and even Brahms continued to use it in sketching their compositions. It provided them with a record, for their own reference, of the basic harmonic and voice-leading content of compositions in progress. Figured bass remains today an indispensable pedagogical aid in the study of tonal harmony and voice leading.

for solving the unfigured-bass problem—that is, for determining appropriate figures from the organization of the bass itself—were those by Heinichen (1728) and Saint-Lambert (1707). One of the main computational aspects of my study, then, was the explication and testing, by computer, of the theories set down by those eighteenth-century authors.

It would far exceed time and space limitations to undertake an exhaustive description of the Heinichen and Saint-Lambert procedures for bass harmonization. For our purposes it is sufficient to state briefly the necessary components of a computational implementation of them. First, the computer must have access to an unfigured bass in a symbolic code readable by it. Second, computer programs must be defined in a suitable programming language; these programs must have the capability to examine the encoded bass, derive from it information of various kinds, and generate new symbolic code incorporating the computed figured-bass specifications.

The music-representation system adopted for this purpose was the code known as DARMS (digital alternate representation of musical scores), developed by Stefan Bauer-Mengelberg and his associates. DARMS is capable of representing all aspects of even very complex conventional musical scores, including stem-direction, beamings, dynamics, and expression marks. The unfigured-bass programs accept as input data relatively simple monophonic musical utterances, and it was not necessary to retain all of the information included in the musical notation; for example, stem-direction is irrelevant to the harmonization procedures, and therefore was not specified in the code.

The programs were written in the SNOBOL3 programming language, then one of the more sophisticated languages available for problems involving operations on data in the form of free character strings. They comprised a network of variable and constant terms (used for designating individual bass notes and musical-interval constants, respectively), one- and two-termed predicates, and one- and two-termed functions. The relation of these entities to bass-harmonization rules as formulated by the eighteenth-century theorists under consideration can best be shown with reference to a specific example. The first of Heinichen's "General Rules"

(his theory also includes "Special Rules," which will not concern us here) for assigning figures to an unfigured bass is stated as follows: "If the bass of a triad descends a semitone . . . [then] the next bass note has a 6th" (Heinichen 1728). Figure 1 illustrates the analysis of this rule into its component parts. The predicates (some of which were regarded as "primitive" and others as "defined") accept as arguments individual bass notes as represented in DARMS and/or musical interval names (with or without specification of interval quality and direction) and return truth values. The functions accept bass notes as arguments and return other bass notes. In general the functions enable the program to look forward and backward in the bass line, while the predicates answer questions about the mode of progression of the bass and about the figures already assigned to specific bass notes. The values returned by predicates determine the applicability or inapplicability of a given rule. The operation of the program, then, follows closely the logical structure of the individual rules.

The bass-harmonization procedures set forth by Heinichen and Saint-Lambert were completely formulated as computer programs and were tested for completeness and adequacy on input data derived from several standard figured-bass treatises of the eighteenth century. The programs were allowed to admit failure and print the message "undefined" when necessary; this permitted discrimination between a program's occasional inability to compute a figure (signaling incompleteness of the harmonization procedure under investigation) and the absence of a figure for reasons consistent with figured-bass practice, wherein the assignment of the figure $\frac{5}{3}$ was regarded as a "default" situation not requiring any explicit figure specification. The adequacy of a given solution was determined by fiat emanating from the investigator's intuitive grasp of figured-bass lore.

Results

As expected, both of the procedures tested were shown to be partially incomplete and to a certain extent inadequate. The deficiencies revealed in both procedures suggested certain refinements

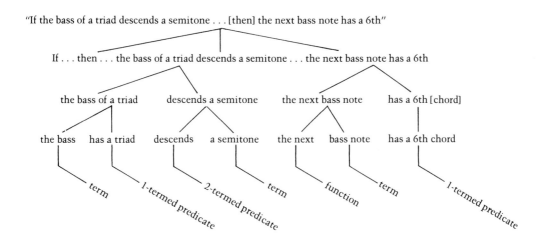

Fig. 1. Analysis of Heinichen's first "General Rule."

"If the bass of a triad descends a semitone . . . [then] the next bass note has a 6th"

If . . . then . . . the bass of a triad descends a semitone . . . the next bass note has a 6th

the bass of a triad   descends a semitone   the next bass note   has a 6th [chord]

the bass   has a triad   descends   a semitone   the next   bass note   has a 6th chord

term   1-termed predicate   2-termed predicate   term   function   term   1-termed predicate

which were incorporated in subsequent versions of the programs and which led to improved results. Nevertheless, it gradually became clear that general solutions to the unfigured-bass problem were probably inaccessible to procedures of the type represented by those of Heinichen and Saint-Lambert. The principal source of inadequacy seemed to be that such procedures did not allow for a sufficiently sophisticated analysis of the structure of the bass line; in particular, they failed to take into account the hierarchic, stratified character of the bass. As a result, they were unable to identify cadential configurations and to cope with the implications of compositional elaborations of a single harmony within the bass line.

Conclusions

The musical skill involved in assigning figures to an unfigured bass has not yet, to my knowledge, been fully explicated and computationally simulated. The study that I have briefly reported

constituted an initial step toward such a solution. The computer made a significant and well-defined contribution to the study by exposing deficiencies in the theories under investigation and in suggesting further lines of inquiry. Although I have not elected to follow them up systematically, there is no doubt that the experience of attempting to simulate a musical skill with the digital computer has made its mark on my way of thinking about musical problems of all kinds.

References

Heinichen, Johann David. 1728. *Der Generalbass in der Composition*, Dresden.

Rothgeb, John. 1968. "Harmonizing the Unfigured Bass: A Computational Study." Ph.D. dissertation, Yale University.

Saint-Lambert, Michel de. 1707. *Nouveau traité de l'accompagnement du Clavecin*, Paris.

52

John Rahn

Department of Music, DN-10
University of Washington
Seattle, Washington 98195

On Some Computational Models of Music Theory

On Some Assumptions of Music Theorists

John Rothgeb's pioneering 1968 Yale dissertation successfully showed that two early eighteenth-century theories about how to realize an unfigured bass were inadequate and incomplete, and suggested that the fault lay in the inadequacy of the general theory of music at that time. The example from that thesis in his present paper, "Simulating Musical Skills by Digital Computer" (1980), is a good example of a process now being described as constructing an "explicit text base" in a formal language equivalent to an "implicit text" in a natural language (van Dijk 1977).

But most of John Rothgeb's present paper is of a more discursive nature. I shall venture to criticize two methodological positions implicit in his text. Since both positions are subscribed to by many of the most venerable music theorists active in this field, it should be kept in mind that my attack is not so much on positions held by John Rothgeb as on the assumptions of a very reputable community of music theorists.

The prevailing image of the present intellectual epoch, perhaps soon to be supplanted, is that of the machine, interpreted in its widest sense to subsume formalizations of any kind. The work of Frege, Russell, Gödel, Hilbert, Carnap, and so many others laid the foundations of the current *civitas mentis machinosae*, leading naturally through Church's Thesis and Turing to such pervasive popular idioms as "it turns me on." To explicate something is, ultimately, to formalize it, that is, to make

it into a machine at whose mataphorically whirring and clicking parts we are happy to stare, and be enlightened. As a child of my epoch, this is my belief. But Schenker, who died in 1935, was something of an anachronism. His metaphors are overwhelmingly organic and the philosophy within which his theories swam was (insofar as it can be determined) an idealistic one. Although Schenker's philosophy has been compared to Hegel's and Goethe's, it was "essentialist" in the medieval sense, and similar in flavor to that of Plotinus or the Pseudo-Dionysios; and Schenker's epistemology was the ecstatic one of the mystic. *We* tend to assume that, in principle, a mechanical model of a theory can preserve all essential aspects of it, that whatever cannot be formalized is nugatory nonsense. Schenker would have fits at our presumption.

Since I cannot understand or cannot apply any aspects of Schenker's theory that are not (in principle) formalizable, I must consider formalizations of Schenker explications or even improvements of Schenker. Nevertheless a few brave souls—I am thinking of Gregory Proctor—have stood up to defend the integrity of Schenker's thought; and it is for their sake, and that of Truth, that I have here played angel's advocate.

Next, I will follow my demiurge by creating an entity called the *Metaphorical Fallacy*. Broadly speaking, this is the fallacy of carrying over to

This paper was delivered as a response at a SIGLASH session entitled "Computational Models of Music Theory" (chaired by Stephen Smoliar) at the National Conference of the Association for Computing Machinery, Detroit, 30 October 1979. That session contained John Rothgeb's "Simulating Musical Skills by Digital Computer," Stephen Smoliar's "A Computer Aid for Schenkerian Analysis," and James Meehan's "An Artificial Intelligence Approach to Tonal Music Theory." These three papers are also published in this issue of the *Computer Music Journal*.

Computer Music Journal, Vol. 4, No. 2, Summer 1980

whatever is being modeled inappropriate features of the structure being used as a model. Numerology is a familiar kind of instance of this fallacy: for example, reasoning that because planets and fingers (of one hand, usually) have the properties of being both natural and five, the first five partials, which also are both natural and five, are both cosmic and organic. More particularly relevant here is that version of the fallacy by which, when using the theories of one discipline to model those of another, we accept inappropriate basic features of the modeling theory as basic features of the theory being modeled.

When music theory was first formalized, it naturally took for its model the most highly developed and rigorous formalized theory in existence, which is formal logic (and its extension into axiomatic set theory and mathematics). Later on, especially in the heyday of formal linguistics, there were attempts to model music theory on linguistics, but the problems arising from these are a superset of the problems arising from the modeling by formal logic, to which we will momentarily restrict ourselves.

Michael Kassler may have been the first to make the analogy between a theorem (of, say, formal logic) and a piece of music (1963; 1968). This is a very fruitful analogy, as is Kassler's analogy between a derivation sequence and a musical analysis (viewed either generatively or analytically).

Deduction in a formalized theory, by given rules of inference, spells out how to get from one thing to another. If a piece of music can profitably be regarded as many things derived from fewer things, an analytic model of that piece in a formalized theory can make explicit (1) in what way or ways the many are derived from the few (rules of inference), and (2) in what order the derivations take place (shown by the order in the list of formulas in the "proof sequence" which is the analytic model of the piece). In theories whose only rules of inference are logical (that is, preserve truth of sentences under standard interpretations) any consistent theory must exclude at least one sentence (in fact, half of them); for if all sentences were provable, all would be true, and the use of negation in the theory proves the theory inconsistent. But a theory of mu-

sic can (*ceteris paribus*) only gain explanatory value by including all pieces of music, excluding none; the class of assertions provable in a musical theory is ideally the class of all pieces of music. Does this paradoxically make such an ideal music theory both inconsistent (for the above reasons) and vacuous (because unfalsifiable)?

Indeed not: if a theory is supposed under an intended interpretation to assert only statements that have some quality in common (e.g., truth, or grammaticality), it fails under either of two conditions. Some statements which are provable do not exhibit the given quality (inconsistency in logical theories), or some statements which exhibit the quality are not provable (incompleteness in logical theories). Identify this common quality with the true application of a predicate $C(x)$, where x represents any well-formed formula of the theory. In the case that $C(x)$ means "x is true," the rules of negation ensure that not all x's are C; but if $C(x)$ is to mean "x is a piece of music," or "x is a thing," then since every x may be C, no stigma is attached to a theory of music or of things in which every well-formed formula is provable. As the Dodo said of his Caucus-race, "*Everybody* has won, and *all* must have prizes." (In particular, such theories need not be "trivial," as is the case for inconsistent logical theories, nor need they be any more *ad hoc* than any other theory.)

In other words, in the intended interpretation of some kinds of theories, provability is not correlated with truth. Specifically, the theorems of a musical theory are pieces of music, not sentences; and pieces of music, unlike sentences (or at least, declarative sentences), are not either true or false under standard interpretation.

There remains the charge that such musical theories are vacuous because unfalsifiable—that they have, to use Karl Popper's term, no "empirical content." The theories Popper is concerned with are supposed to assert only general truths about the universe, or scientific facts; in order to be falsifiable they must exclude at least one singular existential statement. ("All swans are white," but "this swan is black.") These theories again are concerned with preserving truth, and as such come under the analysis just described.

The empirical value of a musical, nonexclusive

theory lies in its ability to present structural descriptions. Within one theory, it may be that the same piece of music can have many different descriptions (be derived in many different proof-sequences). (This would open the question, In what sense is this the same piece? for identity can be considered to be dependent on description.) Also, any given piece of music may be described in many different theories; for example, both "tonal" and "serial" descriptions are possible of both Schoenberg's Fourth Quartet, and of Mozart's G minor Symphony. *In analyzing a piece, the choice of a theory, and then of a description among those possible in the theory, should be made according to not logical or dogmatic but aesthetic criteria; the description that results should be the most musically satisfying description among the alternatives.* In music theory, then, unlike logic or grammar, the point lies not in whether the piece is generable, but in how it is generable; not in the product but the process.[2]

There are satellites to the primary Metaphorical Fallacy. In logic, it is logical to generate each theorem in the most efficient way, using fewest and simplest steps in the derivation sequence. It is only too easy (*dies atque noctes patet atri janua Ditis*) to carry this over fallaciously into the derivation of a piece of music, where the point is the beauty of the structure revealed in the music by the entire derivation sequence. The most beautiful structure is seldom shown in the most efficient sequence. The same fallacy can seduce music theorists into aiming for theories that are themselves of maximal formal beauty, rather than theories through which the music as modeled is most beautiful.

Smoliar's Model

Stephen Smoliar's admirable development of a detailed, working, computational model of the tonal theory of Heinrich Schenker as found in *Der Freie*

2. The preceding discussion is indebted to Section 1.41 of my 1974 Princeton University Ph.D. dissertation, "Lines (Of and About Music)." The dissertation also amplifies many of the surrounding assumptions and consequences with specific examples.

Satz (Schenker 1956) exemplifies what John Rothgeb so aptly described as ". . . part of the essence of theoretical studies . . . to render explicit that which has been inexplicit." Rothgeb continues: "The familiar result of such work is that new areas of inexplicitness are exposed, and those areas are then subject to study and explication in turn" (Rothgeb 1980). Hence my following remarks; only solid, detailed construction such as Smoliar's allows or even deserves, but above all, benefits from, detailed critical scrutiny.

The fuller specifics of this model must be gleaned from a series of papers authored or coauthored by Smoliar (Frankel, Rosenschein, and Smoliar 1976; 1978; Smoliar 1980). Perhaps the greatest virtues of the model lie in the accuracy with which it represents the Schenkerian transformations and in the clarity with which it presents the embedded levels. Perhaps the area most in need of further explication is, as Stephen Smoliar has himself remarked in an earlier paper, the relative order of the elements of two or more sequences (SEQs) that are directly derived from a simultaneity (SIM). By the definition of SIM, two SIM-related SEQs must begin concurrently; that is, the first elements of the two SEQs must begin together. But what is the relative order of the nth members of two SIM-related SEQs, where n is greater than one? If the two SEQs have the same number of elements, we might assume that each pair of nth elements starts concurrently. But, for one thing, two SIM-related SEQs (formally) may have different numbers of elements, and often must if they are to model music. And secondly, even if they do have the same number of elements, there are many musical situations requiring a model in which nth pairs do not start concurrently. Moreover, these same musical situations demand a model that reflects the specific partial order obtaining among pitch events modeled in this theory as elements of SIM-related SEQs.

It might help to represent the music as a matrix in two or more dimensions, in an appropriate computer language. It is arguable that even music that is not electronically generated requires at least five dimensions for adequate representation, of which only two are explicitly structured to some degree by Schenker's theories. Such a representation is not unknown in current compositional theory—Godfrey Winham, Igor Stravinsky, J. K. Randall, Hubert S. Howe, John Selleck, Paul Lansky, and others have used it. But, to my knowledge, no computer programs manipulating multidimensional arrays have been implemented for an analytic music theory, except Michael Kassler's 1975 model of Schenker's background and middleground structures, which manipulates two-dimensional arrays in APL (Kassler 1975).

I might add that there do exist recent analytic theories for tonal music that, unlike Schenker's, specify both the pitch and something of the time placement—in some of them, the exact time-span—of each sound in the music being modeled, obviating the original problem of specifying relative order. All of these theories are derived from but distinct from Schenker's: some of the published efforts along these lines are authored by Benjamin Boretz (1971), Arthur Komar (1971), Peter Westergaard (1975), Maury Yeston (1976), and myself (1979). Some idea of the degree of purely formal difference between one of these theories and Schenker's may be suggested by noting that, while Schenker's theory as correctly modeled by Smoliar is roughly comparable to the transformational component of a transformational grammar (without transformational grammar's morphophonemic and phrase structure components), my theory is roughly isomorphic to a "simple phrase structure grammar" (Bar-Hillel 1964; Chomsky 1971).

An analysis in the Smoliar model is, then, a sequence of treelike structures, such that the $n+1$th tree cannot in general be produced from the nth tree by the Post-production (i.e., Emil Post) kind of rewrite rules definitive of a simple phrase-structure grammar; rather, successive trees are "transformationally" related. The entire sequence of trees can be adequately represented by the terminal tree if and only if any possible terminal tree can be produced by only one sequence of trees using the defined transformations. This would seem to be a desideratum for such a theory. But even if this condition is fulfilled, it would be helpful to the human music theorist if the computer could, on a graphics display, run through each tree in the proof sequence in order. It would also be helpful to the average musician if the trees could each be represented in something like traditional music notation.

Finally, I would like to note Stephen Smoliar's implementation of a "macro-definition facility," inviting the construction of theoretical extensions tailored for particular pieces of music. Such a non-absolutist attitude is always refreshing.

Meehan's Proposal

The most provoking paper is James Meehan's "An Artificial Intelligence Approach to Music Theory" (1980), in which he proposes a marriage between Schank (Schank and Abelson 1977) and Narmour (1977). All my prejudices scream at me that this is impossible or, if possible, immoral, and that any progeny of such a union would be a real bastard of a music theory. This is the standard reaction, which I will call the "fuddy-duddy reaction," to any radical proposal, especially an interdisciplinary one. In this case the fuddy-duddy outrage is compounded because both members of the proposed nuptial couple, Schank and Narmour, are themselves polemical iconoclasts. Schank's work I am incompetent to judge. (It looks good.) Narmour's *Beyond Schenkerism* (1977) is extraordinarily ambitious in the quality of the issues it faces and the broad range of kinds of supporting arguments it uses. But to the extent that it has raised any controversy I find myself, with at least one other member of this panel, in the enemy camp which Narmour has constructed for us (Rothgeb 1978a; 1978b; Keiler 1978; Martin 1978).

Closer examination is necessary to determine to what extent, if any, these hostile prejudgments of James Meehan's proposal are justified. Moreover, if I put aside my prejudices, the bare possibility of such a radically different kind of music theory is utterly fascinating. At the very least, I have Meehan's paper to thank for pointing me in the direction of a discipline called *discourse theory*, which is currently emerging from a combination of the fields of linguistics (especially the formal examination of the semantics and pragmatics of natural and artificial languages), cognitive psychology, and artificial intelligence (Winograd 1977).

There is a whole slew of semiseparable issues here, broadly divisible into two parts: (1) How could Schank's approach work for music theory, if at all? and (2) Can some of Narmour's concepts be used or modified so as to be usable in a Schank-type music theory? In order to address the first issue I will have to pretend to understand what Schank is doing, and crave the reader's momentary indulgence and subsequent correction for any inaccuracies.

The initial simplification of Conceptual Dependency Theory is based on synonymy. According to Schank and Abelson, "The basic axiom of the theory is: For any two sentences that are identical in meaning, there should be only one representation," where "sentences" here can be construed as "explicit text sentences." They go on to say, "The meaning propositions underlying language are called conceptualizations" (1977). This leads to their concepts of "semantic primitives," "knowledge structures," and so forth. In order for this to be a simplification, meanings and sentences must be distinct, and it should turn out that a subsequent theory of discourse is simpler when based on these semantic constructions than when based on sentences, as is claimed by Schank and Abelson for "causal types," for example. Another crucial idea is that of conventional knowledge, or "frames," allowing an efficient structuring of lower-level data in various restricted contexts. An associated issue is that of the "top-down" nature of the process of understanding; that larger contexts crucially affect the structures of their contents. (This, at least, has long been a canon of music theory.)

I am trying to imagine two slices of music that

3. In view of Narmour's more recent theory of harmony, it is only fair to quote that assertion here: "Dissatisfaction with the misleading results of the old descriptive procedures—the naive associationism inherent in the roman-numeral analysis of harmonic function, the lifelessness of symbolizing form by letters or numbers (ABA, 4 + 4), the trivial results of analyzing melodic 'climax' according to curvilinear graphs (symmetrical vs. skewed shapes, etc.)—has resulted in a growing appreciation of the work of Heinrich Schenker" (Narmour 1977, p. 1).

are distinct yet have identical meaning. There are such: Beethoven's Fifth on Monday versus Beethoven's Fifth on Thursday; Beethoven's Fifth played at A 442 versus Beethoven's Fifth played at A 436; and so on. But musicians identify such "synonymous" musical utterances as "the same piece," or "the same fragment of music" (for a short, incomplete example). Precisely at the point where the "meaning" might be said to diverge, musicians start talking about the musical utterances as though they were distinct things. Thus, "Bruno Walter's interpretation of Mozart's G minor Symphony," and "George Szell's interpretation of Mozart's G minor Symphony;" they are in a real sense considered to be different pieces (Boretz 1971; Rahn 1974). It seems that our understanding of music is already structured so as to take advantage of any possible notion of synonymy.

What about Narmour's "style forms"? Can they function as Schankian "semantic primitives"? Narmour's definition of "style form" as quoted in Meehan's paper is, unfortunately, self-destructive. How can anything be locally defined without reference to its immediate context? To do it justice requires Narmour's Chapter 11 (1977), where (e.g., on page 173) it is made reasonably clear that a "style form" is a structure that has "achieved closure" so many times in so many pieces of music that it can be abstracted from its generating pool of compositions. The idea is as follows. When we next hear in a comparable context (style) the initial features of such a style form we will expect to hear it completed, although it often isn't, making possible a rich structure of once-expected but never-realized forms (Narmour's "shadowgraphs"). The idea of understanding a piece in terms of what it isn't is rather appealing, if you can accept such a severely limited set of might-have-been structure types and applications, so that the set of what the piece isn't can conceivably be finite, and also such an enormous amount of "shadow" data for processing even so. (Some finite numbers are too large for all practical purposes, even for computers, let alone people.)

This notion of style form would seem to shade into conventional knowledge of larger contexts ("frames"). We need to show that there is some set of smallest style forms in terms of which, moreover, a satisfactory theory of understanding of music can be constructed.

Here we must modify Narmour's formulations. His theory in *Beyond Schenkerism* is essentially a theory of melody only. A multivoice context is treated either as separate voices (no apprehension of the simultaneities) or as Roman-numeral-labeled chords in a conventional, Markov-chain kind of theory at best. Never is there a simultaneous grasp of linear and vertical relations, one crowning glory of the admittedly imperfect theories of Heinrich Schenker. Narmour's more recent extensions of his theory have been disappointing: a subsequent paper read in November 1978 at the National Conference of the Society for Music Theory in Minneapolis sadly reverted to a kind of pseudo-scientific nineteenth-century harmonic theory.

Let us assume some satisfactory extension of "style form" to contrapuntal situations, Herculean (even Augean) task though this may be. Let us substitute for this hypothetical and nonexistent satisfactory contrapuntal "style form" a sample style form described in what Narmour once asserted to be an outdated theory, namely the Roman-numeral theory.[3] Although in the Roman-numeral theory, the formula "dominant seventh—tonic" certainly qualifies as a "style form" on other counts; when we hear a dominant seventh, in practically any context, some part of our attention "expects" a tonic. I greatly fear that the subsequent Schankian theory, using this kind of thing as a primitive would, applied to Bach chorales, be the probabilistic obverse of the notorious statistical study of immediate chord-successions in the Bach chorales. But let us be charitable and assume the addition of transformations to allow the embedding of maximally probable successions as nonadjacent members of larger chord-strings. This attains the level of theory taught to most sophomore music majors in backward colleges.

The notion of representation remains intriguing, but the results of applying it may be disappointing. For example, many different kinds of musical fragments can be represented by the term *cadence*; others by *sequence*, and so on. These representations can even be considered to be relatively "context-free" (at least in the sense that a "style form" is free of its immediate (perhaps contradictory) context by virtue of its overwhelmingly consistent presence in confirming contexts in other places and pieces). But this road seems to lead to trivial musical analysis, since the abstraction required to obtain the representations leaves out almost everything of musical interest to the musically informed. There is perhaps a danger here: musically naive people, especially if recently exposed to a "music appreciation" course or some unsophisticated music theory, may indeed assent to the proposition that people do understand music in terms of such representations. In fact, any investigation of the understanding of music should concentrate on how music is understood *by those who understand it best*. To adopt any other approach is to trivialize the art object that is studied.

And yet, even the musically informed do "represent" music; a passage can be "zany," or "velvety," and so on, in our secret hearts. Such cross-domain metaphors are no longer very reputable in music criticism because of their lack of musical specificity if nothing else. More interesting is the kind of nonverbalizable "representation" that occurs, even in my listening mind, gathering each specific aspect of a performance into a whole that is greater than the sum of its parts, endowing every musical part with a strongly cast supporting role in the emergent "character" of that piece or performance. If these representations are *not* inherently nonverbalizable, a theory dealing with them would be both possible and most interesting.

The development of such a theory would encounter formidable obstacles even of a purely formal kind, since at the very least the language of the theory would be a pragmatic one, with apparatus similar to that of Montague's and others' extension for modal logics of Tarski's model theory (Apostel 1971; Cresswell 1973; van Dijk 1977). Such theories formalize intensional meanings as functions on some domain (e.g., possible worlds) with extensions as their values. Perhaps the artificial intelligence (AI) approach, a fullback typically so strongly task-oriented as to ignore all theoretical problems of less than crushingly immediate relevance, can make a first down through this defensive line.

References

Apostel, L. 1971. "Further Remarks on the Pragmatics of Natural Languages." In *Pragmatics of Natural Languages*, ed. Y. Bar-Hillel. New York: Humanities Press, pp. 1–34.

Bar-Hillel, Y. 1964. *Language and Information*. Reading, Massachusetts: Addison-Wesley.

Boretz, B. 1971. "Meta-Variations: Studies in the Foundations of Music Thought." Ph.D. dissertation, Princeton University.

Chomsky, N. 1957. *Syntactic Structures*. The Hague: Mouton.

Cresswell, M. J. 1973. *Logics and Languages*. London: Methuen. Distributed in the USA by Harper and Row, New York. (See especially the chapter on pragmatics.)

Frankel, R. E.; Rosenschein, S. J.; and Smoliar, S. W. 1976. "A LISP-Based System for the Study of Schenkerian Analysis." *Computers and the Humanities* 10:21–32.

Frankel, R. E.; Rosenschein, S. J.; and Smoliar, S. W. 1978. "Schenker's Theory of Tonal Music—Its Explication Through Computational Processes." *International Journal of Man-Machine Studies* 10:121–138.

Kassler, M. 1963. "A Sketch of the Use of Formalized Languages for the Assertion of Music." *Perspectives of New Music* 2:83–94.

Kassler, M. 1968. "A Trinity of Essays." Ph.D. dissertation, Princeton University.

Kassler, M. 1975. "Proving Musical Theorems I: The Middleground of Heinrich Schenker's Theory of Tonality." Technical Report Number 103, Basser Department of Computer Science, School of Physics, The University of Sydney, Sydney, Australia.

Keiler, A. 1978. "The Empiricist Illusion: Narmour's *Beyond Schenkerism*." *Perspectives of New Music* 17(1):161–195.

Komar, A. 1971. *Theory of Suspensions*. Princeton: Princeton University Press.

Martin, H. 1978. "*Beyond Schenkerism* by Eugene Narmour." *Perspectives of New Music* 17(1):196–210.

Meehan, J. 1980. "An Artificial Intelligence Approach to Tonal Music Theory." *Computer Music Journal* 4(2):61–65.

Narmour, E. 1977. *Beyond Schenkerism*. Chicago: University of Chicago Press.

Rahn, J. 1974. "Lines (Of and About Music)." Ph.D. dissertation, Princeton University.

Rahn, J. 1979. "Logic, Set Theory, Music Theory." *College Music Symposium* 19(1):114–127.

Rothgeb, J. 1968. "Harmonizing the Unfigured Bass: A Computational Study." Ph.D. dissertation, Yale University.

Rothgeb, J. 1978a. "Narmour's *Beyond Schenkerism*." *Journal of Research in Music Education* 26(4):281–286.

Rothgeb, J. 1978b. "Narmour's *Beyond Schenkerism*." *Theory and Practice* 3(2):28–42.

Rothgeb, J. 1980. "Simulating Musical Skills by Digital Computer." *Computer Music Journal* 4(2):36–40.

Schank, R. C., and Abelson, R. P. 1977. *Scripts, Plans, Goals, and Understanding*. Hillsdale, New Jersey: Erlbaum.

Schenker, H. 1956. *Neue Musicalische Theorien und Phantasien: Der Freie Satz*. Vienna: Universal Edition.

Smoliar, S. W. 1980. "A Computer Aid for Schenkerian Analysis." *Computer Music Journal* 4(2):41–59.

van Dijk, T. A. 1977. "Semantic Macro-Structures and Knowledge Frames in Discourse Comprehension." In *Cognitive Processes in Comprehension*, ed. Marcel Just and Patricia Carpenter. Hillsdale, New Jersey: Erlbaum. Distributed by Halsted (Wiley), New York.

Westergaard, P. 1975. *Introduction to Tonal Theory*. New York: Norton.

Winograd, T. 1977. "A Framework for Understanding Discourse." In *Cognitive Processes in Comprehension*, ed. Marcel Just and Patricia Carpenter. Hillsdale, New Jersey: Erlbaum.

Yeston, M. 1976. *The Stratification of Musical Rhythm*. New Haven: Yale University Press.

53

John Strawn

Center for Computer Research in Music and
Acoustics
Stanford University
Stanford, California 94305

Approximation and Syntactic Analysis of Amplitude and Frequency Functions for Digital Sound Synthesis

1. Introduction

Of the various models proposed and used for analyzing and synthesizing musical sound, additive
synthesis is one of the oldest and best understood.
In recent years, time-variant Fourier methods implemented as computer programs have made it
possible to analyze digitally a large variety of tones
from traditional musical instruments. Such research has led to a better understanding of the
physical and perceptual nature of musical sound as
well as improvements in techniques for digital
sound synthesis.

The heterodyne filter (Moorer 1973) and the
phase vocoder (Portnoff 1976; Moorer 1978) provide
time-varying amplitude and frequency functions for
each harmonic of a tone being analyzed. This
quickly leads to an almost unmanageable increase
in the amount of data used to represent the original
tone. The question of reducing the amount of data
without sacrificing tone quality is thus of potential
interest to hardware and software designers as well
as musicians and psychoacousticians.

Computer Music Journal, Vol. 4, No. 3, Fall 1980

One approach to data reduction has involved the
use of line-segment approximations (Risset 1969;
Beauchamp 1969; Grey 1975), in which an amplitude or frequency envelope is represented by a
relatively small number of line segments. Depending on the degree of reduction, tones resynthesized
using line-segment approximations often sound as
though they were produced by the original instrumental source and in many cases cannot be distinguished perceptually from the original tone.

There is still no definitive answer to the question
of how much data can be omitted without changing
the tone significantly. The ultimate goal would be
to use the smallest possible amount of data to produce a tone that would be perceptually indistinguishable from the (digital) recording of the
original tone (Strong and Clark 1967). Grey was unable to explore the question of the degree of
acceptable data reduction because at that time only
analog tape recordings could be digitized for analysis by computer at the Center for Computer Research in Music and Acoustics (CCRMA). Thus
the resynthesized tone could be discriminated from
the original tone merely by the absence of tape hiss.
Using the digital recording facility (Moorer 1977) it
is now possible to record traditional musical instruments at CCRMA in digital form.

An important problem in data reduction concerns the selection of features to be retained in the

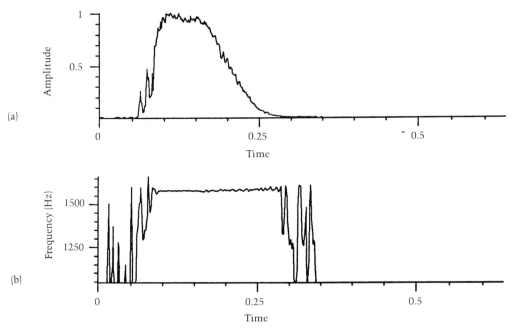

Fig. 1. (a) The amplitude-versus time function of the fifth harmonic of a single trumpet tone, analyzed by the heterodyne filter and normalized to a maximum amplitude of 1.0. The y-axis represents amplitude on an arbitrary linear scale. This function has been chosen as an interesting test case for investigating methods of approximation because of the large amount of noise in the trace and the presence of blips in the attack. Presumably such blips play an important role in the timbre of the note from which this function was derived. (b) The frequency-versus-time function for the same harmonic of the same tone as in (a). Both functions contain 230 points.

simplified representation of the amplitude and frequency waveforms. In this article, *feature* will be used in a very narrow sense to mean components of functions that are presumably important perceptually. An example of this would be the so-called blips which typically occur in brass tones, such as those shown in Fig. 1 (cf. Strong and Clark 1967; Moorer, Grey, and Strawn 1978). The central hypothesis of the work discussed here might be formulated as follows: it is possible to reduce time-varying amplitude and frequency functions derived from traditional instrument tones to some minimum number of line segments such that a digitally resynthesized tone using such line segments is perceptually indistinguishable (according to some suitable measure) from a digital recording of the original tone. Reducing the number of line segments further, that is, omitting some features, results in tones which can be distinguished from the original.

Various manual and automatic algorithms for generating line-segment approximations were used in previous research. In the first half of this paper we will review several algorithms from the literature on pattern recognition which have been developed for analyzing such diverse data as coastlines on maps (Davis 1977), electrocardiograms (Pavlidis and Horowitz 1974), chromosomes (Fu 1974), outlines of human heads (Kelly 1971), and gasoline blending curves (Stone 1961), but which have not yet been applied to musical problems. After discussing the difficulties inherent in such "low-level" techniques for the problem at hand, preliminary results from a syntactic, hierarchical scheme for analyzing amplitude and frequency functions will be presented. Since Grey concluded that it was necessary to retain time-varying information for both frequency and amplitude functions (1975), a method for analyzing both will be discussed.

The algorithms which will be outlined below draw extensively from the literature on approxima-

Fig. 2. The solid line represents a first-degree spline function a(t) as defined in Eq. (1), with m = 4. The function f(t) being approximated is shown as a dotted line. Each breakpoint of a_i is the same as a point in the original function, as specified in Eq. (3).

tion theory and pattern recognition. Considerations of time and space prevent a review of these topics here, except the mention of some standard texts (Davis 1963; Rosenfeld 1969; Duda and Hart 1973; Fu 1974; Tou and Gonzales 1974) which have proved useful.

The work presented in this article forms part of a larger research project investigating the role of timbre in the context of a musical phrase. For the purposes of this report, only individual tones from traditional orchestral wind instruments will be presented. The trumpet tone shown in Fig. 1 was analyzed using the heterodyne filter, but the phase vocoder will be used exclusively in future work. No matter which of the two analysis techniques are applied, the issues of approximation remain the same.

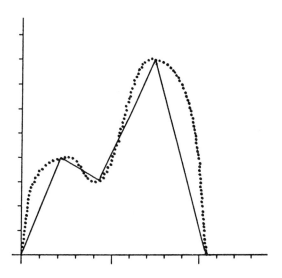

2. Line Segments

Formally speaking, the various approximations will be treated as first-degree splines. The following definition has been adapted from that of Cox (1971). Let $f(t)$ be a sampled function, where $t = \{t_0, t_1, t_2, \ldots t_{(n-1)}, t_n\}$ is a sequence of real numbers representing time defined at $t = qT$; T is some sampling period and $q = 0, 1, 2, \ldots n$. Then a first-degree spline *approximation* $a(t)$ to $f(t)$ is given by

$$a(t) = \begin{array}{ll} a_1(t) = g_1 + h_1(t - t_{a0}), & t \in \{t_{a0}, t_{a1}\} \\ a_2(t) = g_2 + h_2(t - t_{a1}), & t \in \{t_{a1}, t_{a2}\} \\ \cdots \\ a_m(t) = g_m + h_m(t - t_{a(m-1)}), & t \in \{t_{a(m-1)}, t_{am}\} \end{array} \quad (1)$$

where $m \leq n$, $t_0 = t_{a0}$ and $t_n = t_{am}$. $a(t)$ is also required to be continuous across $t_{a0} \leq t \leq t_{am}$, with continuity defined as

$$a_i(t_{ai}) = a_{i+1}(t_{ai}). \quad (2)$$

Any a_i is obviously continuous across $t \in \{t_{a(i-1)}, t_{ai}\}$.

Furthermore, one important restriction has been adopted and concerns the endpoints of the line segments used to approximate a function. Each endpoint is required to be the same as some data point in the original waveform (Fig. 2). In terms of the definition given above:

For every $i \in \{0 \leq i \leq m\}$ there exists $j \in \{0 \leq j \leq n\}$ such that

$$t_{ai} = t_j \text{ and } a(t_{ai}) = f(t_j). \quad (3)$$

The reasons for this restriction will become clear only at the very end of this paper. In the meantime, it will merely be mentioned again when appropriate.

Since the functions being approximated exist only in sampled form, such requirements as the existence of the nth-order derivative are satisfied by definition (see also Pavlidis and Maika 1974).

There is a considerable body of literature on the use of higher-order approximations, for example cubic splines. Line segments, however, have the advantage of being conceptually simple. The effect of changing the slope or intercept of a straight line is easy to conceptualize, but it is more difficult to correlate changes in higher-order polynomial coefficients with changes in the appearance of the approximation to some waveform. However, just such a one-to-one correspondence is essential in the feature-oriented work presented here. Cubic splines are also more complicated in that a change in any $a(t_i)$ will change all of the coefficients across the entire approximation since the slopes at each t_i

are required to be continuous. This criterion of continuity at a breakpoint is in fact ignored when working with line segments. Finally, the line-segment approach is currently implemented in most general-purpose music compilers as well as in most hardware devices for digital sound synthesis.

3. Error Norms

The most common measure of error is the square of the vertical distance (i.e., the distance parallel to the y-axis) between a function and an approximation to it. Duda and Hart (1973, p. 332) discuss a variation of this, in which the error is the *perpendicular* distance from a point $f(t)$ of the original function to the approximating line; Dudani and Luk (1977) present an algorithm for fitting a line to a set of points using this error norm. But according to Moorer (1980), experience has shown that using this error criterion does not improve the results of approximation for the class of waveforms under discussion here. Since it involves a considerable increase in computation time, this variation has not been tested in the work to be presented below.

Before various methods for approximating functions can be examined, three error norms need to be defined.

3.1 Maximum Error

The maximum error E_x is given by

$$E_x = \max_t \, [f(t) - a(t)]^2, \tag{4}$$

with $a(t)$ defined in Eq. (1). This is sometimes called the *uniform error norm* (Davis 1963, p. 133).

3.2 Sum-of-Squared Error

Pavlidis (1973) also calls this norm the *integral square error*:

$$E_n = \sum_{t=t_0}^{t_n} [f(t) - a(t)]^2. \tag{5}$$

3.3 Mean Squared Error

The mean squared error across each a_i is given by

$$E_m = \frac{\sum_{t=t_{a(i-1)}}^{t_{ai}} [f(t) - a(t)]^2}{t_{ai} - t_{a(i-1)}}. \tag{6}$$

The E_m norm is more tolerant of error across long line segments than the E_n and E_x norms.

4. Algorithms for Line-Segment Approximation

There are two basic approaches to solving the problem of approximation using splines. In the first, the number of segments is specified in advance and the algorithm is required to minimize some measure of error. The number of splines is changed in the other method until the measure of error lies as close as possible to, but still under, some predetermined threshold.

4.1 Minimizing Error: ADJUST

One method for minimizing error with a given number of line segments is presented by Pavlidis (1973). Since two typographical errors occurred in Eq. (3) of Pavlidis's article, (which should read $P_j = t_{i(j)} - M^k$), and since it forms an integral part of the procedures discussed in the next section, Pavlidis's algorithm will be discussed in some detail.

The algorithm, called *ADJUST* in the rest of this paper, is given in Fig. 3. For each iteration, the endpoints of successive segments (first the odd-numbered segments, then the even-numbered ones) are moved by some number M, always set to 1 in the work discussed in this paper; larger values of M could be specified for the first few iterations if the initial approximation were thought to be significantly different from the expected final solution. If the error of the approximation using the trial breakpoint is less than the original error, then the trial

Fig. 3. The algorithm AD-
JUST, modified from
Pavlidis's algorithm (1973),
in a quasi-ALGOL nota-
tion. The algorithm ac-
cepts as input some func-
tion to be approximated,
some initial approxima-
tion a(t) in the form given
in Eq. (1), M (the number
of points to move a breakpoint for each trial), and
iterationLimit (the max-
imum number of iterations
allowed). When the al-
gorithm has finished, ei-
ther iterationLimit has
been exceeded or the ap-
proximation has been ad-
justed so that any further
changes in the breakpoints
will cause some (local) error to increase. Error in
this algorithm refers to one
of the three error norms defined in Section 3 of the
text, although Pavlidis
originally designed this algorithm for the E_x and E_n
norms.

```
INTEGER iterationCount, start, stop, i;
BOOLEAN odd, breakPointChanged;

FOR iterationCount ← 1 STEP 1 UNTIL iterationLimit DO
  BEGIN "iteration loop"
  breakPointChanged ← FALSE;
  FOR odd ← TRUE, FALSE DO
    BEGIN "odd/even loop"
    IF odd THEN start ← 1 ELSE start ← 2;
    FOR i ← start STEP 2 UNTIL n DO
      BEGIN "step through segments"
      τ₁ ← t_{a(i-1)};
      τ₂ ← t_{ai}; COMMENT τ₁, τ₂ are the breakpoints for segment aᵢ,
      τ₃ ← t_{a(i+1)}; COMMENT τ₂, τ₃ are the breakpoints for segment a_{i+1};
      eᵢ ← error across (τ₁, τ₂);
      e_{i+1} ← error across (τ₂, τ₃);
      IF eᵢ ≠ e_{i+1} THEN
        BEGIN "try moving point"
        IF eᵢ > e_{i+1} THEN τ₂' ← τ₂−M ELSE τ₂' ← τ₂+M;
        eᵢ' ← error across (τ₁, τ₂');
        e_{i+1}' ← error across (τ₂', τ₃);
        IF MAXIMUM (eᵢ, e_{i+1}) > MAXIMUM (eᵢ', e_{i+1}') THEN
          BEGIN "accept moved point"
          t_{ai} ← τ₂';
          breakPointChanged←TRUE;
          END "accept moved point";
        END "try moving point";
      END "step through segments";
    END "odd/even loop";
  IF breakPointChanged = FALSE THEN DONE;
END "iteration loop";
```

breakpoint replaces the original breakpoint.
Pavlidis presents a proof to show that the algorithm
will converge in a finite number of steps, and (more
importantly) that no cycling is possible. It must be
emphasized that this algorithm is useful for finding
local minima, not some globally optimal solution.
Pavlidis states that the maximum error norm is to
be preferred for most applications, although the
sum-of-squared error and mean squared error
norms have also been used successfully in the work
presented here.

A note on the implementation of ADJUST: if
both endpoints of some a_i are points from the function being approximated, then e_i, for example, only
needs to be calculated using points $\tau_1 + 1$ through
$\tau_2 - 1$, because the points τ_1 and τ_2 cannot contribute
to the error. This represents a slight improvement
over Pavlidis's algorithm, which points out this
computational saving only for the beginning
endpoint.

The results of applying ADJUST to two test cases
are given in Fig. 4 and Table 1. The "worst" case (in
terms of computational time) is given if the breakpoints for the original approximation are all
gathered at one end of the function, in which case
ADJUST must spread the points out across the
function in the process of finding the optimal
approximation.

Fig. 4. Results of applying the algorithm ADJUST (given in Fig. 3) to the approximation of two test cases; further data is given in Table 1. The E$_n$ norm was used in all of the cases illustrated here.

(a) This test case consists of two diagonal lines, each corresponding to 24 units on the x-axis, separated by a horizontal line one unit in length. The original smooth diagonal lines have been modified by

adding quasi-random variations, the amplitude of which depends on the y-value of the original line. (b) Arbitrary, initial placement of four line segments approximating test case (a). (c) Approximation to test case (a), with four line segments, after algorithm ADJUST has reached a solution. (d) As in (c), but with 11 line segments. Perhaps if the breakpoints were distributed more evenly, the error could be reduced fur-

ther and the blip on the left-hand side might be avoided. But ADJUST converges onto a locally optimal solution, which is not necessarily optimal globally. (e) One-half of a sine wave, again spread across 49 units of the x-axis and with noise added as in (a). (f) Approximation to (e), with four line segments, after ADJUST has reached a solution. (g) As in (f), with 11 line segments.

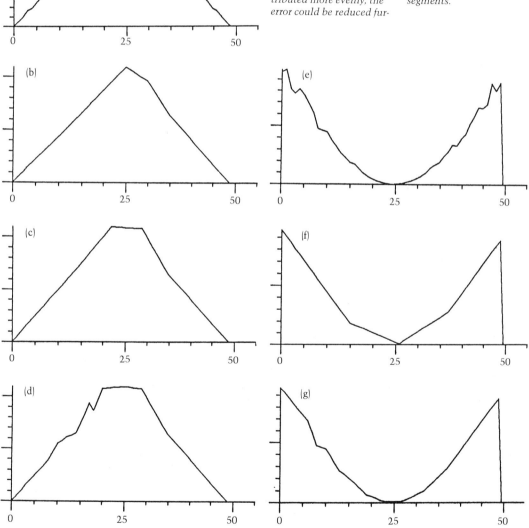

Table 1. Performance of the algorithm ADJUST for the test cases shown in Fig. 4

Corresponding Illustration in Fig. 4	Error (E_n)		Number of Iterations
	Initial	Final	
b, c	122.9	43.21	4
d	43.2	25.5	2
f	0.45	0.07	11
g	0.0205	0.0190	6

NOTE: *Initial error* refers to the error for the initial, arbitrary placement of the approximating line segments. E_n is calculated across the entire test case. Note that the function in Figs. 4(a)–4(d) varies from 0 to 24, whereas the half-period of the sinusoid in Figs. 4(f) and 4(g) does not exceed 1.0.

4.2 Initial Segmentation

Three algorithms (and a variant of one of them) for approximating a function with line segments will be discussed. The first two represent solutions to the problem, discussed above, of finding an approximation such that the error does not exceed some threshold, with no a priori restrictions on the final number of segments.

One widely used method, in which each line segment provides the least mean squared error approximation to all or part of a function, is not considered here because of the restriction of Eq. (3). Another interesting approach (Stone 1961; Phillips 1968; Pavlidis 1971) will be omitted here for the same reason.

4.2.1 Thresholding Sum-of-Squared Error

The sum-of-squared error norm was defined in Eq. (5). The method, as suggested by Pavlidis (1973), is quite simple. The endpoint for the approximating segment is incremented until the sum-of-squared error exceeds some threshold. The endpoint is then decremented by 1, a segment is established, and the process is repeated using the endpoint just found as the new initial point.

4.2.2 Split-and-Merge

Pavlidis and Horowitz (1974) developed a highly efficient algorithm, presented in Fig. 5. In the version to be discussed here, the error across each segment of the approximating function must not exceed some threshold. The initial line segments are first split into smaller line segments until the threshold requirement is satisfied (or the line segment consists of only two points). Neighboring line segments are then joined when possible by MERGE, that is when joining them will not violate the same threshold conditions. Finally, ADJUST is applied to the segmentation. The algorithm repeats until no changes are made to the breakpoints during an iteration.

In its original formulation, the split-and-merge algorithm returned to the SPLIT procedure ("start:" in Fig. 5[a]) after every iteration. But given the restriction of Eq. (3), SPLIT only needs to be invoked once (during the first pass) for the following reason. After SPLIT, the error across each segment is less than or equal to the threshold. MERGE likewise can only result in segments with error less than or equal to the threshold. For τ_2' in ADJUST (cf. Fig. 3) to be accepted as a breakpoint, e_i' and e_{i+1}' must be less than or equal to e_i and e_{i+1} respectively. But when ADJUST is invoked after MERGE, e_i and e_{i+1} must be less than or equal to the threshold. Thus MERGE and ADJUST cannot result in segments with an error greater than the threshold, so that there is no need to invoke SPLIT again.

4.2.3 "Case 2"

There is another version of the algorithm, called "Case 2" by Pavlidis and Horowitz (1974), in which the error across *all* of the segments must not exceed some threshold. For the maximum error norm, both cases are identical. When using the sum-of-squared error norm, however, the sum of the squared error across the *entire* function is examined. Modifications to the split-and-merge algorithm are necessary. This variation has been tested but will not be discussed here for reasons to be summarized in Section 4.3.

4.2.4 Curvature

There is yet another method, based on a measure of curvature (Symons 1968; Shirai 1973; 1978). In a study of human visual perception, Attneave (1954)

Fig. 5. The split-and-merge algorithm in a quasi-AL-GOL notation, after Pavlidis and Horowitz (1974). Procedure ADJUST is presented in Fig. 3. (a) Outline of the algorithm. (b) Procedure SPLIT. Assume that SPLIT has been initialized so that $t_{a1} = t_{an}$, that is, there is initially one line segment which covers the entire function f(t). (c) Procedure MERGE.

a) Split-and-Merge Algorithm
    start: breakPointChanged ← FALSE;
             invoke SPLIT
    loop1:   breakPointChanged ← FALSE;
             invoke MERGE
             invoke one iteration of ADJUST
             IF (breakPoint changed by ADJUST or MERGE) THEN GOTO loop1, ELSE DONE;

b) Procedure "SPLIT"
    $i \leftarrow 1$
    numberSegments ← 1;
    loop2:
    $\tau_1 \leftarrow t_{a(i-1)}$;
    $\tau_3 \leftarrow t_{ai}$; COMMENT τ_1, τ_3 are the breakpoints for segment a_i;
    $c_i \leftarrow$ error across (τ_1, τ_3);
    IF e_i > threshold THEN
        BEGIN "split a_i"
        IF maximum squared error across (τ_1, τ_3) occurs only once
            THEN $\tau_2 \leftarrow$ point halfway between (τ_1, τ_3)
            ESLE $\tau_2 \leftarrow$ point halfway between (first) two error maxima across (τ_1, τ_3);
        redefine segment a_i to extend from τ_1 to τ_2
        after a_i, insert a new segment to extend from τ_2 to τ_3
        renumber segments
        numberSegments ← numberSegments+1;
        breakPointChanged ← TRUE;
        END "split a_i"
    ELSE
        BEGIN
        COMMENT note that a_i may be split more than once if necessary;
        $i \leftarrow i + 1$
        IF i > numberSegments THEN DONE "SPLIT";
        END;
    GOTO loop2;

c) Procedure "MERGE"
    $i \leftarrow 1$;
    loop3:
    IF numberSegments = 1 THEN DONE "MERGE";
    $\tau_1 \leftarrow t_{a(i-1)}$;
    $\tau_3 \leftarrow t_{a(i+1)}$; COMMENT segments a_i and a_{i+1} lie between τ_1 and τ_3;
    $e_i \leftarrow$ error across (τ_1, τ_3);
    IF $e_i \leq$ threshold THEN
        BEGIN
        redefine segment a_i to extend from τ_1 to τ_3 (i.e. remove t_{ai} as a breakpoint)
        renumber segments
        breakPointChanged ← TRUE;
        numberSegments ← numberSegments − 1;
        END
    ELSE
        BEGIN
        $i \leftarrow i + 1$;
        IF $i \geq$ numberSegments THEN DONE "MERGE";
        END;
    GOTO loop 3;

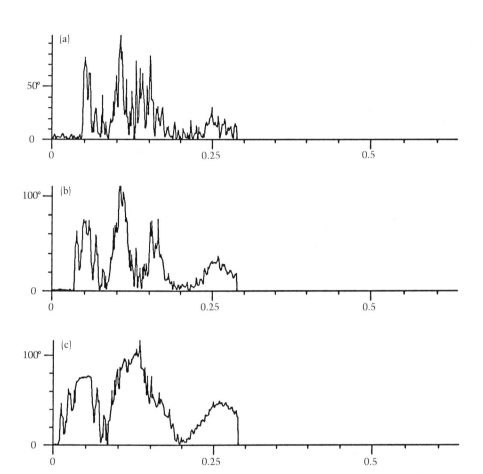

Fig. 6. (a) Curvature (in degrees) of the waveform shown in Fig. 1, with M (see text) set to correspond to approximately 12.5 msec. (b) As in (a), but with M ≈ 25 msec. (c) As in (a), with M ≈ 50 msec. In (a), even small variations in the original function result in large values of curvature. M in (c) is so large that the points of high curvature at t ≈ 0.1 sec and t ≈ 0.15 sec are missed.

found that the points on a curved line where its direction changes most rapidly were extracted by test subjects as endpoints for drawing an outline of the curve. Conversely, he found that an illustration can be satisfactorily reproduced by drawing straight lines between points of high curvature; the cat-drawing in his article has been widely reprinted (e.g., Duda and Hart 1973, p. 339).

Shirai defines curvature at a point P along a digitized function as the angle α between RP and PQ, where Q and R are points of the function a constant number of samples (called M by Shirai) away from P. In this method, then, the curvature at each point of the function to be approximated is calculated (Fig. 6), and breakpoints are assigned at points of high curvature. If RPQ is a straight line, $\alpha = 0°$; for a highly acute angle RPQ α approaches 180°.

It is important to choose an appropriate value for M. Too small a value will result in distortions in the approximation because features which are too small will cause large variations in curvature and thus be assigned breakpoints. If M is too large, sig-

Fig. 7. (a) Approximation to the waveform of Fig. 1, derived from the curvature shown in Fig. 6(b), with the threshold for establishing a breakpoint set at 60°.

The breakpoint which presumably should occur near t = 0.25 sec is missed. (b) As in (a), with a threshold of 30°. The breakpoint omitted in (a) is included, *along with a large amount of presumably extraneous points. The approximation in (a) comprises 32 segments; (b) has 77, both with a long segment for* *the initial silence. Choosing an appropriate threshold would be just as hard, if not harder, for the plots of curvature in Figs. 6(a) and 6(c).*

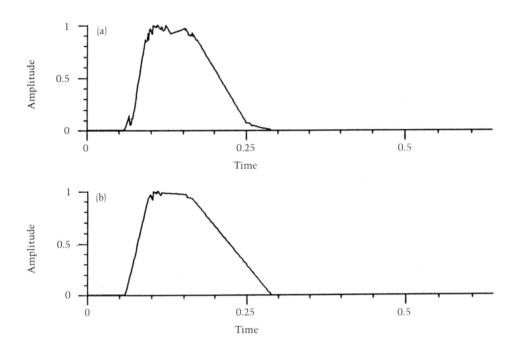

nificant points of high curvature will be missed (cf. Fig. 7).

Shirai suggests a thresholding scheme for assigning breakpoints according to curvature. This method undoubtedly works for the cases cited by Shirai, in which fairly smooth lines change direction only occasionally. But as is shown in Fig. 7, it seems difficult to find a single threshold which provides a useful approximation for the kinds of functions under consideration here. This method has also been found to be sensitive to the absolute values used to represent $f(t)$, especially for small M. Another problem occurs because the curvature near a probable breakpoint often does not reach a peak, but rather stays at a plateau; this happens, for example, at $t \approx 0.1$ sec in Fig. 6(b). Obviously only one point needs to be assigned—but which one? I have spent considerable time and effort in an attempt to derive heuristics for selecting only appropriate peaks of curvature, with no notable success to date. Perhaps a varying curvature threshold could be applied, but this has not yet been explored.

4.3 Summary

Three different analyses using the split-and-merge algorithm are presented in Fig. 8. As one would expect, the approximation using a very small threshold captures many details; as the threshold is increased, some details are lost and the overall shape of the waveform is emphasized.

Similar analyses have been conducted using the "Case 2" form of the split-and-merge algorithm as well as the thresholding algorithm of Section 4.2.1. The mean squared error and maximum squared error norms have likewise been explored. In general, using any combination of these algorithms and error criteria it is possible to produce results similar to those shown in Fig. 8. Each combination admittedly reacts to changes in the threshold in a unique

Fig. 8. Results of the split-and-merge algorithm in the form given in Fig. 5, using the sum-of-squared error norm given by Eq. (5). Recall that the maximum amplitude has been nor-

malized to 1.0. (a) A threshold of 0.001 yields 61 segments, some of which contain only two points of the original data. (b) Threshold = 0.01, re-sulting in 22 segments, a

few of which are still only two points long. (c) Twelve segments are found when the threshold = 0.05; the shortest segment now covers five points of the original data. When the

threshold is raised to 0.1 (not shown), the first blip in the attack is missed completely. See Section 4.3 for further discussion.

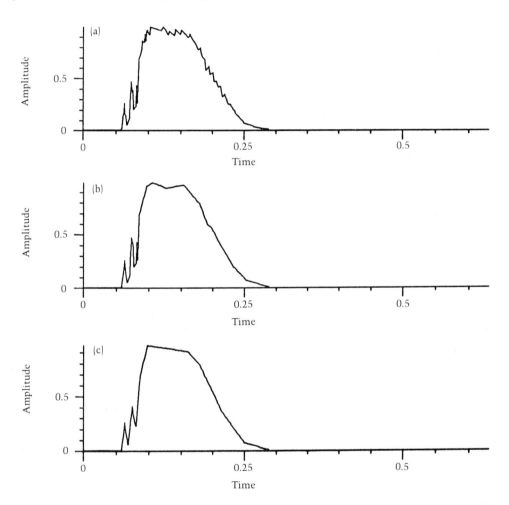

way, but it seems impossible to reach any general conclusion about the superiority of any algorithm or error norm for the purposes of the work outlined in the introduction to this article.

Rather, it has proven impossible to find a paradigm for controlling the threshold for the one waveform shown here so that the projected perceptually salient features (e.g., blips in the attack) can be retained or removed without concomitant, sig-

nificant changes in the rest of the waveform. If the threshold is large, then the analysis delivers the overall waveshape; with a small threshold, supposedly necessary details are retained along with presumably superfluous ones. (Moorer [1980] has suggested that the threshold could be dynamically adjusted according to some measure of randomness, but this approach has not yet been explored.)

In general, our experience has led to the conclusion that no single algorithm of this type will ultimately be sufficient for the systematic exploration of timbre and data reduction. None of these algorithms can take into account both global and local considerations, which seems to be a major drawback. Still, these methods will probably be useful in a wide variety of musical applications where such control is not a prime consideration.

5. Syntactic Analysis

Hierarchical syntactic analysis would seem ideal for mediating between global and local considerations. In the rest of this paper, then, such an approach will be presented.

5.1 Introduction

The method to be discussed draws extensively from the literature on pattern recognition through syntactic analysis, which is based on the similarities between the structures of patterns and (formal) languages. There are, of course, many other methods of pattern recognition, such as template matching, but they will not be discussed here.

In syntactic pattern recognition, a relatively small vocabulary of terminals, called *primitives*, is "parsed" according to the rules (productions) of a grammar to form higher-level nonterminals known as "subpatterns" and "features." Characteristic features are further grouped into patterns (or objects). A successful parse is equated with "recognition" of the pattern. Fortunately, many of the problems involved in pattern recognition by computer can be ignored here. A considerable body of literature is devoted, for example, to the question of finding lines in digitized pictures.

5.2 Primitives

One major advantage of syntactic analysis lies in the fact that a relatively small vocabulary of primitives can be used for constructing a wide variety of patterns. The choice of primitives is thus an impor-

tant issue. It would seem reasonable, for example, to require that the same primitives be used in the analysis of both amplitude and frequency functions even if it turned out that analysis of the two at higher levels followed different rules.

A generalized approach to primitive selection has not yet been found. Fu, however, gives the following two requirements to serve as guidelines:

> (i) The primitives should serve as basic pattern elements to provide a compact but adequate description of the data in terms of the specified structural relations (*e.g.*, the concatenation relation).
> (ii) The primitives should be easily extracted or recognized by existing nonsyntactic methods, since they are considered to be simple and compact patterns and their structural information not important (Fu 1974, p. 47).

Various kinds of primitives have been developed for different pattern-recognition applications. Fu gives many examples, such as Freeman's chain code and half-planes in the pattern space for representing arbitrary polygons. However, in light of the restriction (still to be justified) imposed in Eq. (3), it seems reasonable to use very small line segments connecting points of the original data as primitives for syntactic analysis.

For reasons discussed by Moorer (1976), the implementation of the phase vocoder used at CCRMA performs an averaging of the amplitude and frequency functions. At a sampling rate of, for example, 25.6 kHz, 32 samples of the original output (corresponding to 1.25 msec) might be averaged to form one output point. These averaged output points are perfectly suited to serve as breakpoints for line-segment primitives in syntactic analysis, and will be used as such in this paper.

5.3 Grammar

The choice of primitives having been made, the next step is to decide on a set of subpatterns and features, and to specify a grammar for parsing the primitives accordingly. Davis and Rosenfeld (1978) provide a grammar based on hierarchical relaxation methods. Briefly, a line-segment primitive is classified as having length x or $2x$, and as being horizontal, sloped upward, or sloped downward. The relaxation algorithm parses the primitives into longer line segments at a first hierarchical level; at the second level, peaks and valleys are formed from the line segments of the first level, and the final level expresses the whole function as a concatenation of valleys and peaks. There are productions in the grammar for combining not only two adjacent primitives, but also two primitives separated by another.

Pavlidis (1971) provides examples of a grammar which can be used to remove line segments of very short duration and to substitute in their place a single straight line. Grammars for finding more complex features such as the so-called "hats" (up-horizontal-down) or "cups" (down-horizontal-up) are given as well.

Having examined a large number of amplitude and frequency functions, it seemed reasonable to the author to specify three hierarchical levels for syntactic analysis. The first level attempts to remove very small features which one would ascribe to noise in the waveform, artifacts of the analysis procedure, and so on. The second reduces the waveform to its overall shape in terms of fairly long line segments, and the third classifies those line segments into parts of a note. The analysis system, which incorporates elements of the two methods just reviewed, will be presented in detail.

The primitives have already been specified as being very short line segments. Associated with each primitive is its duration and its slope, which are used to classify the line as *up*, *down*, or *horizontal*. The only relational operator between primitives is, coincidentally, the concatenation mentioned in the quote from Fu. Pattern recognition can often involve other operators such as *above* and *below* or *to the right*, which complicate the analysis significantly, but these will not be considered here.

5.3.1 Level 1a: lineSeg

The grammar for the first two hierarchical levels is presented in Fig. 9. There are two subdivisions of

Level 1. In the first, successive *microLineSeg* primitives (as they will be called) are combined into *lineSeg* as long as (1) the next microLineSeg is within the thresholds *DurThresh* and *YThresh* (defined in Fig. 9), or the direction of the first microLineSeg in the lineSeg being formed is the same as the direction of the next microLineSeg; and (2) including the next microLineSeg will not cause the duration of the lineSeg being formed to exceed some threshold $\Sigma YThresh$.

After a new lineSeg has been found, its duration is calculated as the sum of the durations of the constituent microLineSegs. The slope for the new lineSeg a_i is likewise calculated using the values of $f(t_{a(i-1)})$ and $f(t_{ai})$ at its beginning and endpoints. (This is known as a *synthesized attribute* of a_i [Knuth 1968]). A similar process takes place at the other hierarchical levels.

5.3.2 Level 1b: macroLineSeg

It proved advisable to insert a second subdivision into this hierarchical level in order to avoid occasional irregularities at Level 2. This is accomplished by the introduction of *macroLineSeg*, which are formed of one or more lineSeg, all with the same direction (up, down, or horizontal).

5.3.3 Level 2: featureLineSeg

The second hierarchical level uses a syntax with productions and conditions corresponding exactly to those of Level 1a. At this second level, macroLineSeg are combined into *featureLineSeg*, with thresholds chosen so that only the most striking elements of the function remain.

5.3.4 Level 3: Note

At the third level, featureLineSeg are assigned to the various parts of a note: attack, steady-state, and decay, as well as to any silence which might occur before the attack. Software has been written to search out the longest horizontal segment for which the amplitude (in an amplitude function) exceeds some silence threshold and the duration exceeds some minimum time threshold. Anything

Fig. 9. Grammar for the first two levels of hierarchical syntactic analysis. The conditional form is based on a model used by Pavlidis (1971). The complete hierarchy is shown in Fig. 11. At Level 1 the primitives (microLineSeg) are parsed into lineSeg and then the latter are combined when possible into macroLineSeg. The same syntax, but with different thresholds and corresponding changes in nonterminals, is used in Level 2 for combining macroLineSeg into featureLineSeg. A less formal version of the grammar is given in section 5.3 of the text.

Vocabulary:
V_N = lineSeg, macroLineSeg, featureLineSeg
V_T = microLineSeg

Abbreviations:

$\tau_L, f(\tau_L)$	beginning point of lineSeg (featureLineSeg in Level 2)
$\tau_{i-1}, f(\tau_{i-1})$	beginning point of microLineSeg a_i (macroLineSeg in Level 2)
$\tau_i, f(\tau_i)$	endpoint of microLineSeg a_i (macroLineSeg in Level 2)
D_{M1}	direction of first microLineSeg in lineSeg
D_M	direction of microLineSeg
D_{L1}	direction of first lineSeg in macroLineSeg
D_L	direction of lineSeg
D_{MA1}	direction of first macroLineSeg in featureLineSeg
D_{MA}	direction of macroLineSeg

Thresholds:
DurThresh
    duration of microLineSeg (macroLineSeg in Level 2)
ΣYThresh
    threshold for $abs[f(\tau_i)-f(\tau_L)]$, constrained to be $\geq$ YThresh
YThresh
    threshold for $abs[f(\tau_i)-f(\tau_{i-1})]$

Level	Condition	Production
1a	$\tau_i-\tau_{i-1} >$ durThresh $\vee$ $abs[f(\tau_i)-f(\tau_{i-1})] >$ YThresh $\vee$ $abs[f(\tau_i)-f(\tau_{i-1})] > \Sigma$YThresh	lineSeg ::= microLineSeg
	$\tau_i-\tau_{i-1} \leq$ durThresh $\wedge$ $abs[f(\tau_i)-f(\tau_{i-1})] \leq$ YThresh $\wedge$ $abs[f(\tau_i)-f(\tau_L)] \leq \Sigma$YThresh	lineSeg ::= lineSeg,microLineSeg
	$D_{M1}=D_M$ $\wedge$ $abs[f(\tau_i)-f(\tau_L)] \leq \Sigma$YThresh	lineSeg ::= lineSeg,microLineSeg
1b	$D_{L1}=D_L$	macroLineSeg ::= macroLineSeg,lineSeg
	(none)	macroLineSeg ::= lineSeg
2	$\tau_i-\tau_{i-1} >$ durThresh $\vee$ $abs[f(\tau_i)-f(\tau_{i-1})] >$ YThresh $\vee$ $abs[f(\tau_i)-f(\tau_{i-1})] > \Sigma$YThresh	featureLineSeg ::= macroLineSeg
	$\tau_i-\tau_{i-1} \leq$ durThresh $\wedge$ $abs[f(\tau_i)-f(\tau_{i-1})] \leq$ YThresh $\wedge$ $abs[f(\tau_i)-f(\tau_L)] \leq \Sigma$YThresh	featureLineSeg ::= featureLineSeg,macroLineSeg
	$D_{MA1}=D_{MA}$ $\wedge$ $abs[f(\tau_i)-f(\tau_L)] \leq \Sigma$YThresh	featureLineSeg ::= featureLineSeg,macroLineSeg

between the initial silence and the steady-state is classified as *attack*; everything after the steady-state is *decay*. If no steady-state is found, then as many successive up featureLineSeg as possible are grouped together following the initial silence to form the attack, and the remaining featureLineSeg are assigned to the decay. It should be emphasized that the *attack—steady-state—decay* terminology is used merely for convenience in labeling part of the syntactic analysis, with no semantic implications, at least at this stage.

5.4 Analysis of Amplitude Functions

Figure 10 shows an analysis of the waveform of Fig. 1 at every stage of the hierarchical analysis. None of these plots represents the ultimate form of the output from this method of analysis; further processing is envisioned, as will be discussed. However, by adjusting the thresholds properly, data reduction at, say, the lineSeg level (Fig. 10[a]) can be achieved which will probably be useful in a wide variety of cases.

The model for the analysis of an amplitude waveform assumes that the note will consist of the parts discussed above. This attack—steady-state—decay model has been widely used in commercial analog synthesizers. The fact that it appears here is merely coincidental. The class of waveforms for which this software has been optimized is restricted to waveforms derived from a limited set of test tones lasting, typically, one-quarter of a second or longer.

Ultimately these programs will be used to analyze two or three such notes played in succession, either separated by silence or connected in some way (legato, portato, etc). In fact, the software has already been implemented to handle such groups of notes. Briefly, the output of a given channel of the phase vocoder is first compared with an amplitude threshold. Notes are initially defined within the entire function as being separated by periods of silence. The hierarchical analysis is then performed on a note-by-note basis. Each period of silence is assigned to the note immediately following. The entire function is thus represented as a linked list

of notes followed by an optional silence. Each note, in turn, includes an optional initial silence, attack, decay, and optional steady-state. Within each note, the line segments at a given hierarchical level are represented as a linked list of records. A line segment at one hierarchical level also has pointers to one or more line segments at the next lower hierarchical level which the line segment at the higher level encompasses.

5.5 Analysis of Frequency Functions

This preliminary division of a function into notes incorporates the notion of *planning* originally formulated by Minsky (1963) but used here as developed by Kelly (1971). Planning is further applied to the analysis of the frequency functions produced by the phase vocoder, which is especially problematical at low amplitudes where the frequency traces varies widely (Fig. 1[b]). There is also the problem of *phase wraparound*, which occasionally produces characteristic spikes in the frequency trace. Before the frequency traces are submitted to syntactic analysis, these spikes are removed from the regions of the frequency trace bounded by the attack—steady-state—decay parts of the notes in the amplitude function. These same portions of the frequency trace are then analyzed syntactically using the grammar already given in Fig. 9. Details of the assignment of featureLineSeg to the parts of a note vary slightly for the frequency functions but the basic approach is the same. Fig. 11 shows the results of syntactic, hierarchical analysis of the frequency trace belonging to the same harmonic as the tone shown in Fig. 10. Obviously the thresholds are different for amplitude and frequency functions. Given the diverging abilities of the ear to discriminate frequency and amplitude, it would not be surprising if the higher-level analysis of frequency functions could eventually be simplified or modified somewhat.

An entire musical phrase is thus represented as a linked list of phase vocoder channel outputs. Each channel consists of an amplitude and frequency function. Each function in turn points to a linked

Fig. 10. Syntactic hierarchical analysis of the amplitude waveform shown in Fig. 1. (a) lineSeg, resulting from analysis of microLineSeg, with DurThresh = 0.01 sec, YThresh = 0.01, and ΣYThresh = 0.1. (b) lineSeg of the same direction have been combined into macroLineSeg. (c) featureLineSeg, with DurThresh = 0.1 sec, YThresh = 0.2, and ΣYThresh = 0.4. (d) Analysis of featureLineSeg into parts of a note. The "direction" of the straight line from t ≈ 0.1 sec to t ≈ 0.175 sec in (c) is analyzed as being diagonal (pointing downward) and therefore is not classified as belonging to a steady-state. There are 65 line segments in the approximation of (a), 19 line segments in (b), and 7 in (c).

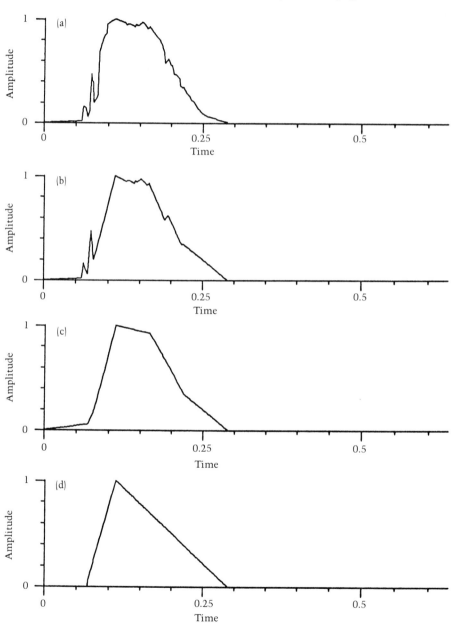

Fig. 11. Syntactic hierarchical analysis of the frequency function of Fig. 1(b). The vertical line extending to the x-axis on the right-hand side is an artifact of the display routine used for plotting; compare this with Fig. 1(b). (a) lineSeg, resulting from analysis with DurThresh = 0.01 sec, YThresh = 2, *and ΣYThresh = 5 (YThresh and ΣYThresh in Hertz). (b) lineSeg of the same direction have been combined into macroLineSeg. (c) featureLineSeg, with DurThresh = 0.1 sec, YThresh = 10, and ΣYThresh = 30. (d) Analysis of featureLineSeg into parts of a note. The "decay" slopes slightly down-* *ward because it is constrained to end at a point which occurs at the same time as the final point of the note found in the amplitude function. As stated in the text, however, use of the terms* attack, steady-state, *and* decay *is merely for the sake of convenience. The top-down parse allows such pre-* *liminary analysis to be refined considerably before arrival at a final set of breakpoints for such a function. There are 80 line segments in the approximation of (a), 46 line segments in (b), and 14 in (c).*

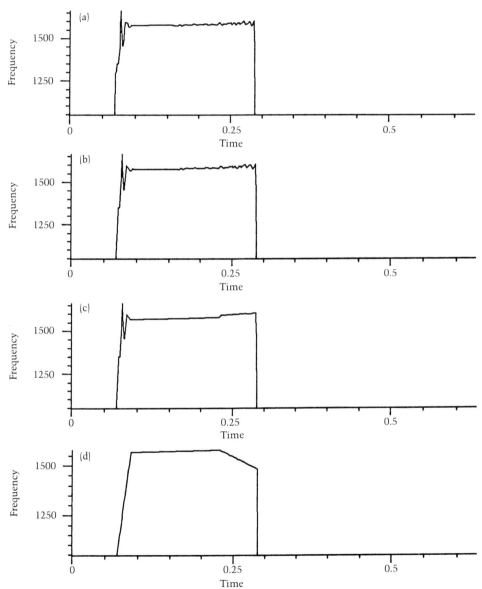

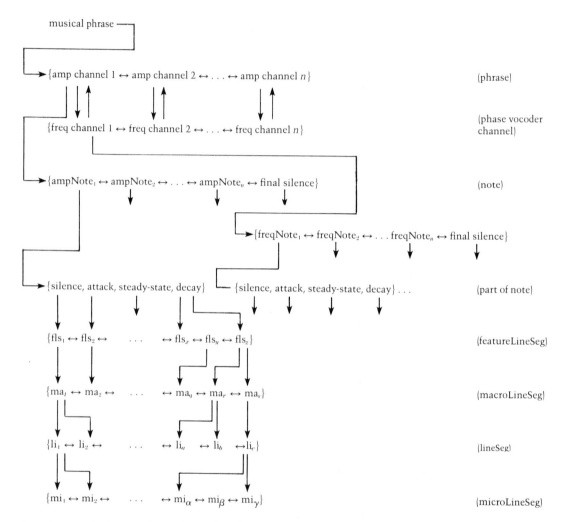

Fig. 12. Overview of the data structure used in the hierarchical syntactic analysis. Curly brackets are used to delineate a two-way linked list of records; the arrangement of pointers between hierarchical levels indicates one of many possible configurations. Names of the hierarchical levels are enclosed in parentheses.

list of notes which are individually analyzed in terms of the grammar presented here. The complete structure is summarized in Fig. 12.

5.6 Refinement: A Top-Down Parse

This "bottom-up" parse is only the beginning of a projected system, shown in Fig. 13. Once the at-tack, steady-state, and decay portions of the amplitude function have been found, they can be utilized in terms of planning as a guide for a "top-down" directed search for features to be included in the final set of breakpoints. The output would thus no longer be grouped according to attack, steady-state, or decay. Rather, it would consist of the breakpoints found and confirmed by the top-down analysis.

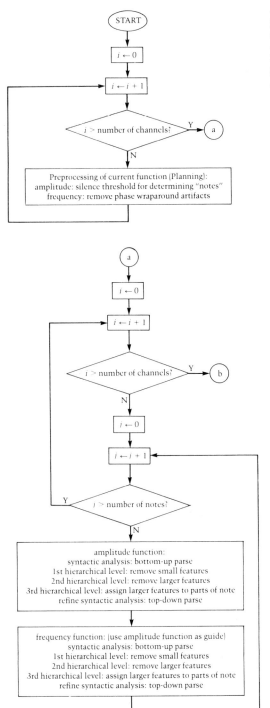

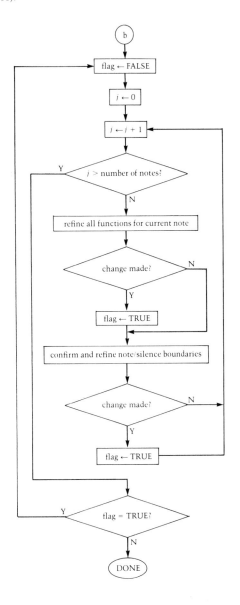

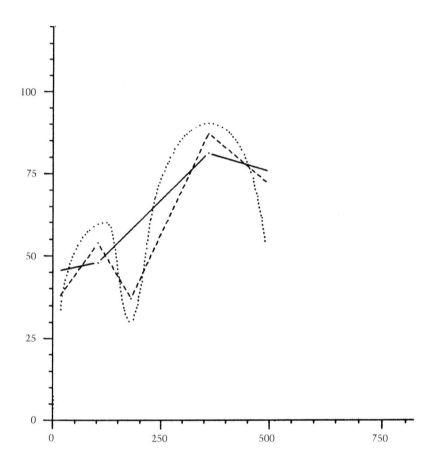

Consider the blips in the attack portion of the amplitude waveform analyzed in Fig. 10. A blip can be represented as a characteristic succession of line segments (e.g., up-down-up, or up-horizontal-down-up) at the lineSeg level. Such a pattern can easily be found using syntactic analysis. The juncture of "attack" and "steady-state" can be refined similarly, for example, by "tracking" to extend each part as far as possible (Shirai 1973) or, to include an initial "overshoot" at the beginning of the steady-state.

After each function is refined in this manner, the entire family of functions can be scanned to con-

firm the acceptability of various features for each note (cf. Fig. 13). For example, a flag can be set to retain a blip in an amplitude function only if the blip occurs at the same place in, say, more than two harmonics. The initial segmentation of the phase vocoder channel outputs into notes can likewise be confirmed by comparing all of the functions. It might happen that a spurious "silence" detected in some amplitude function would result in an erroneous initial division of one note into two. Such an error can be corrected at this stage.

This also provides, at long last, the justification

for requiring that all breakpoints in the approximation be identical to points of the original waveform (Eq. [3]). If the approximations at the various hierarchical levels could include other points, then a large amount of recomputation would be necessary every time a breakpoint were modified (Fig. 14). In other words, it seems reasonable at this stage to require that the analysis retain some of the low-level information, in the form of the original data points, at higher levels of the parse. This requirement may have to be modified later, however, if it turns out that a significant reduction in the final number of segments can be achieved by doing so.

Other methods from pattern recognition will probably prove useful in this work. Perhaps stochastic syntax analysis (Fu 1974) in the bottom-up parse would reduce the amount of refining to be done later. The Hough transform (Duda and Hart 1973; Iannino and Shapiro 1978) might also prove useful for deciding, for example, that four points defining two separated line segments a_i and a_{i+k}, $k > 1$, were actually colinear and that the entire function between them could be represented as a single line.

6. Summary and Conclusion

Various algorithms from the literature on approximation theory and pattern recognition have been shown to be useful for approximating waveforms in digital sound synthesis. A syntactic analysis scheme has also been presented which will ultimately be extended to a generalized parser for amplitude and frequency functions.

This work represents one aspect of the growing application of artificial intelligence (AI) techniques to musical problems. The syntax and data structure here could easily be extended to a system for instrument recognition similar to the speech-recognition system Hearsay (Erman and Lesser 1975; Erman 1976). A scheme for automatic transcription of music could also be derived which in turn could be used to drive a music-analysis system such as that developed by Tenney (1978). The syntactic analysis presented here will also be useful for approximating other time-varying waveforms in a wide variety of musical applications.

7. Acknowledgments

Dexter Morrill (Colgate University) provided the trumpet tone used as an example in this paper. In addition to assisting at every stage of this work, James A. Moorer (CCRMA) contributed considerably to the design and implementation of the syntactic analysis. I would also like to express my appreciation to my teachers and colleagues for their time, patience, and many helpful suggestions: John Chowning, John Grey, and Julius Smith (CCRMA); Barry Soroka (Stanford AI Project); and Curtis Roads.

References

Attneave, F. 1954. "Some Informational Aspects of Visual Perception." *Psychological Review* 61 : 183 – 193.

Beauchamp, James W. 1969. "A Computer System for Time-Variant Harmonic Analysis and Synthesis of Musical Tones." In *Music By Computer*, ed. Heinz von Foerster and James Beauchamp. New York: John Wiley and Son.

Cox, M. G. 1971. "An Algorithm for Approximating Convex Functions by Means of First-Degree Splines." *Computer Journal* 14 : 272 – 275.

Davis, Philip J. 1963. *Interpolation and Approximation.* New York: Blaisdell.

Davis, Larry S. 1977. "Shape Matching Using Relaxation Techniques." *Proc. 1977 IEEE Conf. on Pattern Recognition and Image Processing.* Rensselaer, New York, pp. 191 – 197.

Davis, Larry S., and Rosenfeld, Azriel. 1978. "Hierarchical Relaxation for Waveform Parsing." In *Computer Vision Systems*, ed. Allen R. Hanson and Edward M. Riseman. New York: Academic Press, pp. 101 – 109.

Duda, Richard O., and Hart, Peter E. 1973. *Pattern Classification and Scene Analysis.* New York: John Wiley and Son.

Dudani, Sahibsingh, and Luk, Anthony L. 1977. "Locating Straight-Line Edge Segments on Outdoor Scenes." *Proc. 1977 IEEE Conf. on Pattern Recognition and Image Processing.* Rensselaer, New York, pp. 367 – 377.

Erman, Lee D. 1976. "Overview of the Hearsay Speech Understanding Research." *SIGART Newsletter* 56 : 9 – 16.

Erman, Lee D., and Lesser, Victor R. 1975. "A Multi-Level Organization for Problem Solving using Many, Diverse, Cooperating Sources of Knowledge." In *Advance Pa-*

pers. Fourth International Conference on AI, Tbilisi, USSR, pp. 483–490.

Fu, K. S. 1974. *Syntactic Methods in Pattern Recognition.* New York: Academic Press.

Grey, John M. 1975. "An Exploration of Musical Timbre." Ph.D. thesis, Stanford University. Distributed as Department of Music Report No. Stan-M-2.

Iannino, Anthony, and Shapiro, Stephen D. 1978. "A Survey of the Hough Transform and its Extensions for Curve Detection." In *Proc. IEEE Conf. Pattern Recognition and Image Processing.* Chicago, 1978, pp. 32–38.

Kelly, M. D. 1971. "Edge Detection in Pictures by Computer Using Planning." *Machine Intelligence* 6:397–409.

Knuth, D. E. 1968. "Semantics of Context-Free Languages." *J. Mathematical Systems Theory* 2:127–146.

Minsky, Marvin. 1963. "Steps toward Artificial Intelligence." In *Computers and Thought,* ed. Edward Feigenbaum and Julian Feldman. New York: McGraw-Hill, pp. 406–450.

Moorer, James A. 1973. "The Heterodyne Method of Analysis of Transient Waveforms." Artificial Intelligence Laboratory Memo AIM-208. Stanford: Stanford University.

Moorer, James A. 1976. "The Use of the Phase Vocoder in Computer Music Applications." *Journal of the Audio Engineering Society* 26(1/2):42–45.

Moorer, James A. 1977. "Signal Processing Aspects of Computer Music: A Survey." *Proceedings of the IEEE* 65(8):1108–1137.

Moorer, James A. 1980. Personal communication.

Moorer, James A.; Grey, John M.; and Strawn, John. 1978. "Lexicon of Analyzed Tones. Part 3: The Trumpet." *Computer Music Journal* 2(2):23–31.

Pavlidis, Theodosios. 1971. "Linguistic Analysis of Waveforms." In *Software Engineering,* vol. 2, ed. Julius T. Tou. New York: Academic Press, pp. 203–225.

Pavlidis, Theodosios. 1973. "Waveform Segmentation through Functional Approximation." *IEEE Transactions on Computers* C-22(7):689–697.

Pavlidis, Theodosios, and Horowitz, Steven L. 1974. "Segmentation of Plane Curves." *IEEE Transactions on Computers* C-23(8):860–870.

Pavlidis, Theodosios, and Maika, A. P. 1974. "Uniform Piecewise Polynomial Approximation with Variable Joints." *Journal of Approximation Theory* 12:61–69.

Phillips, G. M. 1968. "Algorithms for Piecewise Straight Line Approximations." *Computer Journal* 11:211–212.

Portnoff, M. R. 1976. "Implementation of the Digital Phase Vocoder Using the Fast Fourier Transform." *IEEE Transactions on Acoustics, Speech, and Signal Processing* ASSP-24:243–248.

Risset, Jean-Claude, and Mathews, Max V. 1969. "Analysis of Musical-Instrument Tones." *Physics Today* 22(2):23–30.

Rosenfeld, Azriel. 1969. *Picture Processing by Computer.* New York: Academic Press.

Shirai, Yoshiaki. 1973. "A Context-Sensitive Line Finder for Recognition of Polyhedra." *Artificial Intelligence* 4(2):95–119.

Shirai, Yoshiaki. 1978. "Recognition of Real-World Objects Using Edge Cue." In *Computer Vision Systems,* ed. Allen R. Hanson and Edward M. Riseman. New York: Academic Press, pp. 353–362.

Stone, Henry. 1961. "Approximation of Curves by Line Segments." *Mathematics of Computation* 15:40–47.

Strong, William, and Clark, Melville. 1967. "Synthesis of Wind-Instrument Tones." *Journal of the Acoustical Society of America* 41(1):39–52.

Symons, M. 1968. "A New Self-organising Pattern Recognition System." *Conference on Pattern Recognition.* Teddington, pp. 11–20.

Tenney, James (with Polansky, Larry). 1978. *Hierarchical Temporal Gestalt Perception in Music: A "Metric Space" Model.* Toronto: York University.

Tou, Julius T., and Gonzales, Rafael C. 1974. *Pattern Recognition Principles.* Reading, Massachusetts: Addison-Wesley.

54

Johan Sundberg
Department of Speech Communication
and Music Acoustics
Royal Institute of Technology (KTH)
S-100 44, Stockholm, Sweden

Anders Askenfelt
Department of Speech Communication
and Music Acoustics
Royal Institute of Technology (KTH)
S-100 44, Stockholm, Sweden

Lars Frydén
Conservatory of the Swedish Radio
Edsberg, Sweden

Musical Performance: A Synthesis-by-Rule Approach

Introduction

The musical act of converting a string of note signs into a sequence of tones is by no means a simple one-to-one translation. If this task is left to a computer, the result is generally very poor from a musical point of view.

The complexity of musical performance has been recognized for a long time. Seashore (1938) measured the actual durations of the tones in several musical performances of the same song. Among other things, he found that in none of the singers was there "a slightest approach to an even time for a measure." Also, he found that musicians tend to show a modest degree of reproducibility as regards the performance of a given piece of music. Later investigations reporting on measurements of timing in performed music have confirmed this observation (Bengtsson and Gabrielsson 1977).

These findings may seem almost trivial to anybody acquainted with music listening. We all know that a piece of music can be played in a number of different ways, all of which are musically excellent. And yet, the musician's freedom is by no means unlimited; there is a large class of performances that are musically unacceptable. This implies the existence of rules that state how a string of notes normally should be converted into a sequence of sounds.

Computer Music Journal, Vol. 7, No. 1,
Spring 1983

If players violate one or more of these rules, they run the risk of being classified as poor musicians.

These rules seem to be scientifically interesting. An important task of scientific research is to eliminate mystery originating from lack of knowledge. Some of the mystery surrounding music can be eliminated if some of the discrepancies typically observed between the notated and the played version of a piece of music can be explained by means of a set of "pronunciation" rules. Moreover, the rules would mirror certain aspects of the auditory and cognitive processing of the musical sounds involved in listening. Thus, pronunciation rules could reveal part of the intra- and extramusical basis of musical communication. From the point of view of practical application, the rules would be useful in digital synthesis of music and in musical pedagogy.

Method

To explore the rules that a musician normally must obey in playing a piece of music, we can choose either measurements or *synthesis-by-rule*. The reason why we have chosen the synthesis-by-rule strategy is that we assume the rules are numerous and that they interfere with one another. Also, the pedagogical and artistic experience of one of the authors (Frydén) had generated a number of hypotheses as regards such rules.

As in a previous study of musical performance focusing on singing (Sundberg 1978), a computer-

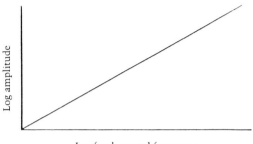

Fig. 1. Schematic illustration of a typical relationship between fundamental frequency and overall amplitude in musical instruments.

controlled vowel synthesizer was used (MUSSE; see Larsson 1977). MUSSE can generate one part only. The complexity of the synthesis was reduced to an absolute minimum, with the only variables being fundamental frequency and amplitude. An advantage of this simplicity was that a minimum of synthesis parameters required control by rule. The basic assumption was that any acoustic variable that can be varied in musical performance is varied by the performer for the purpose of musical expression. The timbre resembled that of a woodwind instrument. The pitch frequency changed in steps in accordance with the equal-tempered scale, and there was a very slight vibrato. The amplitude could be changed in steps of ¼ db. The duration was controlled with a time unit corresponding to 8–12 msec, depending on the tempo, which, according to findings by van Noorden (1975) is accurate enough for such an experiment.

The computer programs used for controlling the synthesizer were (1) a notation program (Askenfelt and Elenius 1977) by means of which the melody can be written in ordinary notation on the computer screen and (2) a text-to-speech program written by Carlson and Granström (1975). The input information is the melody as written in ordinary music notation. This information is then translated into "vowel sounds" possessing duration, pitch, frequency, and amplitude. The rules are triggered by specific sequences of durations and/or pitches, that is, by information contained in the input notation.

Rules

Rule 1: Amplitude and Pitch

In almost every musical instrument, the amplitude increases somewhat with the fundamental frequency, as is illustrated schematically in Fig. 1. If this is not modeled in a performance, the sound gives a peculiar, lifeless impression. Sound Examples 1a, 1b, and 1c demonstrate amplitude increases of 0, 8, and 4 db per octave pitch-frequency rise. (See Soundsheet Examples, *CMJ* 7[1].)

Rules 2–4 affect the duration of the individual note, either by lengthening or by shortening it. It should be noted that therefore no corrections are made with regard to the durations of adjacent notes. Thus, the effect of rule 1 is that the entire "time-table of tone departures" is perturbed.

Rule 2: Duration and Note Value

Rule 2 deals with notes of various values. If a piece of music is played with exactly the durations that are theoretically specified in the notation, the result is rigid, as in Sound Example 2a. In Sound Example 2b and 2c, we have introduced a rule that increases the contrasts between durations slightly. In short, the rule works as something like a "perverse tax system," where the tax rate is high for the poorest and zero for the wealthiest. If we exaggerate this rule, the result is as in Sound Example 2b. The mechanical character obtained with nominal note durations is replaced by lack of rhythmic balance. A more moderate quantity of the rule gives the version in Sound Example 2c.

Rule 3: Duration and Pitch Increase

Rule 3 simply states that the duration of each note be decreased by 3% as soon as the following note has a higher pitch. In sequences of rising pitches, this rule has the effect of increasing the tempo somewhat. Sound Examples 3a, 3b, and 3c demonstrate the effect. In the first version (3a), the rule is not applied; in the second (3b) it is exaggerated; and

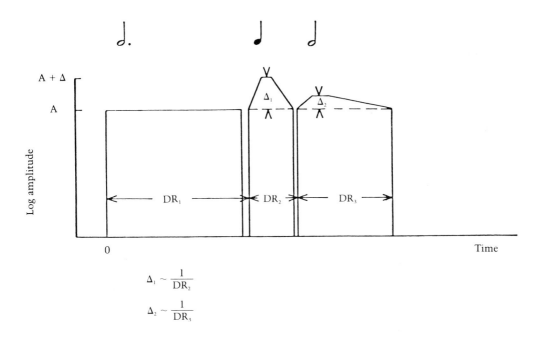

Fig. 2. Schematic illustration of the accents used in the rule system: the amplitude increase is inversely proportional to the duration of the note and is completed during a tenth of this same duration. The increased amplitude value is maintained for 40 msec, after which the amplitude gradually decreases to its initial value, which is reached at the end of the note. The figure also illustrates the two categories of notes that receive the accents. A = constant amplitude; DR = duration; Δ = accent; and V = peak of accent.

in the third (3c) the 3% perturbation is present, in accordance with our formulation of rule 3.

Rule 4: Duration and Leaps

Our next rule, rule 4, has the effect of increasing the duration of all tones that terminate a melodic leap. The quantity is 3% for tones terminating a leap of a minor or major third, 6% for leaps wider than fifths, and 5% for intermediate intervals. Sound Examples 4a, 4b, and 4c are played without the rule (4a), with the rule exaggerated (4b), and then with the rule quantity of rule 4 (4c) respectively.

Rule 5: Pauses and Leaps

In instrumental music, particularly that played on bowed instruments, wide melodic leaps are often performed with a very short pause just between the two tones. This is the effect of rule 5, which decreases the amplitude of the tone to zero during the last 30 or 40 msec of its duration, depending on the width of the leap; the fourth being the boundary. The effect of this rule is illustrated in Sound Examples 5a, 5b, and 5c, where the first version is played without this rule (5a), the second version is played with the rule exaggerated (5b), and the third version (5c) is played with rule 5 as described above.

Rule 6: Accents and Note-Value Contrasts

Rule 6 marks contrasts in note value by *accents*, that is, small and very rapid increase-decrease gestures in the amplitude. Rule 6 adds an amplitude increment proportional to the duration of the tone. The details of the accent used are illustrated schematically in Fig. 2. The rule adds such an accent to two types of notes, as is indicated in the figure. One is a short note surrounded by longer notes. The other case is a note terminating a specific pattern of changes

Fig. 3. Schematic illustration of rule 7, by which
amplitude contrasts be-
tween adjacent tones are
decreased. A = amplitude.

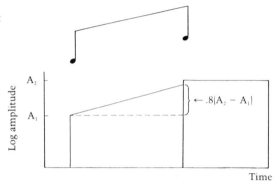

in durations: a decrease followed by an increase.
This rule has a clear effect, particularly on the short
notes after a dotted note. Sound Examples 6a, 6b,
and 6c illustrate this by presenting a melody first
without the rule (6a), then with the rule exaggerated (6b), and then with rule 6 (6c).

Rule 7: Amplitude Continuity

If tones of differing amplitudes follow each other,
the melodic continuity may be disturbed. Rule 7
states that the last amplitude reading of a tone be
corrected by a quantity corresponding to 80% of
the decibel difference between it and the following
note (Fig. 3). The effect is demonstrated in Sound
Examples 7a and 7b, where a piece is first played
without the rule (7a), and then with rule 7 as just
described (7b).

In Sound Examples 1–7, the effect of one rule at
a time has been demonstrated. Sound Example 8
presents two different performances of a piece of
music. In example 8a, none of the rules are used,
and in example 8b, all seven rules are applied.

Evaluation

An opinion commonly encountered is that random
variations, as opposed to variations effected according to rules, occur in musical performance. An informal experiment was made in which all of our
rule-controlled deviations from nominal tone durations were multiplied by a random number between
0 and 1. Thus, there was no system in the deviations from the nominal tone durations. As expected,
the results demonstrated that randomized deviations often work quite well, but in cases of "bad
luck" an embarrassing lack of rhythmic balance occurs. This demonstrates the axiom that in an ideal
performance all that can be perceived serves a musical purpose.

The rules presented here do not appear to improve
the musicality of a performance to any appreciable
extent if they are applied only one at a time. According to our hypothesis, however, the effect of an individual rule is dependent on the effects of other

rules. Therefore, it is the summed effect of all rules
that will improve the performance; hence, they
should be tested together.

A listening tape was prepared, in which different
melodies were presented in pairs of performances.
In each pair, one version was nominal, with no
changes in durations or amplitudes, while in the
other, all rules were used. The musical excerpts are
listed in the Appendix. Each of the excerpts was
chosen so as to demonstrate clearly the effect of at
least one of our 7 rules. Thirteen different examples
were recorded on the tape. The tape was presented
via headphones to nine musically experienced
judges who were asked to tell which performance
of each pair they preferred. The results are shown
in Table 1.

It can be seen from Table 1 that most examples
were liked better by more than half of the jury
when played in accordance with the rule system.
Still, the scores are low in some cases. One cause of
some low scores seemed to be an artifact, though.
In tuning the pauses occurring between tones separated by a leap, we listened on loudspeakers. Thus,
the reverberation time of the listening room was
certainly influencing our work. In the listening
test, on the other hand, headphones were used,
eliminating room reverberation. The effect of this
was that the pauses sounded too long, and this hurt
the musical acceptability of some examples that
contained many leaps, such as the Nursery tune
and Geistliches Lied. The examples chosen in order

Table 1. Result of listening experiment in which nine musical experts compared the musical quality of performances

Rule	Example		Preference
1	Händel:	*Sonata*	9
	Mozart:	*Alla Turca*	6
2	Schubert:	*Sonata*	4
	Tegnér:	Nursery tune	5
3	Jularbo:	Dance music	5
	Mozart:	*Alla turca*	6
4	Bach:	*Bourrée*	8
	Bach:	*Courante*	8
5	Bach:	Geistliches Lied	5
	Bach:	*Gavotte*	8
6	Traditional:	*Happy Birthday*	5
	Bellman:	*Hvila vid denna källa*	3
7	Schubert:	*Fruehlingstraum*	7
	Bach:	*Sarabande*	8

Note: The rule number indicates which rule which was particularly highlighted by the example. The preference numbers indicate how many of the experts preferred the rule-controlled performance. The examples are specified in the Appendix.

to demonstrate clearly the sharpening of durational contrasts and the marking of certain notes with accents (rules 2 and 6) resulted in close to 50% preference or even lower. Future research efforts should be directed at investigating the reason for these low scores.

In examining the results of the listening experiment (Table 1), it may be observed that excerpts from music of the baroque era are rated higher than excerpts from more recent music. The possibility cannot be excluded that the reason for this is that our rules fit baroque music better than more recent music. We believe, however, that the reason is that our examples from the classical, post-baroque periods are more dependent on the harmonic progressions underlying the melody; such examples are likely to suffer more from the fact that, as yet, we have introduced no rules dealing with the harmonic context.

Discussion

Our general experience during work with the rules was that the magnitude of the effects (e.g., the magnitude of the durations that are added to notes terminating leaps) is very critical. If the magnitude is too great, the effect is almost embarrassing, as the reader might have observed in listening to the exaggerated versions of the sound examples. We found that the optimum magnitude yielded an effect that was barely noticeable: it was scarcely possible to tell what physical reality the rule affected. It was impossible to "diagnose" the rule. A typical example is the sharpening of the note-value contrasts. If the magnitude is too great, it is easy to hear that the short notes are too short; and when the magnitude is correct, the diagnosis is nearly impossible to make, yet the rule has achieved a clear effect, namely elimination of the lifeless, mechanical character of the performance. It is probably revealing that these effects are not marked explicitly in the musical score.

Rules for Different Musical Styles

There are certainly more rules for musical performance than the seven presented in this paper. Presumably, some of the as yet missing rules take into account the harmonic aspects of the music, as mentioned. All present rules operate with a time window of two or three notes, and there must be rules operating on longer strings of notes. Also, there would be different rule systems for different musical styles. The rules discussed here have been tested mainly on examples selected from eighteenth- and nineteenth-century compositions. Their effects on other repertoires remain to be tested. If the rules reflect pure conventions developed within music, then the rules' generality can be expected to be restricted. If, on the other hand, the rules reflect extramusical reference systems, such as listeners' associations with physical movement (e.g., a scale upward would be associated with climbing uphill by many listeners), then the rules would possess a greater generality. This question is left open for future investigation based on a more complete system of performance rules.

Another important point: we have not tried to model the multitude of choices that are available to professional musicians and that allow them to play the same piece in many different ways, all equally acceptable from a musical point of view. The rules do, however, leave room for some musical liberties. One would be to allow for variations in the magnitude of the rules' effects. Another possibility would be to mark in the score the performer's interpretation of the music. We could then formulate rules that operated on these marks. (Musicians often adopt a similar practice.)

Violating the Rules

We do not believe that our performance rules must always be obeyed in a good performance. On the contrary, such a rule-controlled performance might be boring in the long run. We believe that musicians can and should violate one or more of the performance rules in order to communicate something in particular. Evidently, the perceptual effects of such violations of a rule system depend on the rule system being well known by both players and audience.

According to the results of the listening test (Table 1), our rules seem to contribute to the musical acceptability of performance of a melody. An interesting question is then what the origin of these rules might be. We believe that some of the rules are derived from the human voice. The reduction of amplitude steps at tone boundaries and the general growth of amplitude with fundamental frequency may be examples of this derivation. A possible interpretation of these rules would be that they serve the purpose of making the performance slightly more similar to singing.

Other rules are likely to have a psychoacoustic origin. The principle of lengthening the note that terminates a leap might reflect certain effects studied by van Noorden (1975); a melody may split into two quasi-simultaneous melodies (fission) if wide leaps occur in rapid tempo. This fission might be avoided if the tone terminating the leap were lengthened.

There may also be purely psychological founda-tions for some of the rules. Lacking any kind of data at this point, we are free to speculate. For instance, the increase in tempo during sequences of rising intervals may have a psychological origin; a rising interval may possess an "activating" connotation that the player should stress by increasing the tempo. Also, pitch rises are often combined with an increased tempo in excited speech. Again, these last-mentioned attempts to interpret the rules are no more than speculation. The point is that our 7 rules probably have a foundation of some kind that may be independent of music. We believe that further research on the foundations of performance rules will be interesting and rewarding.

Conclusions

From this research, we conclude the following. First, it is possible to improve the musical acceptability of a performance by applying a limited set of pronunciation rules. Second, these rules can be discovered by means of an analysis-by-synthesis approach. Third, such an approach enables us to formulate new hypotheses as to how our present set of rules should be extended, thus contributing to knowledge about and scientific understanding of music.

References

Askenfelt, A., and K. Elenius. 1977. "Editor and Search Programs for Music." *Speech Transmission Laboratory—Quarterly Progress and Status Report* 4/1977. Stockholm: KTH.

Carlson, R., and B. Granström. 1975. "A Phonetically Oriented Programming Language for Rule Description of Speech." In *Speech Communication*, Vol. II, ed. G. Fant. Stockholm: Almqvist and Wiksell, pp. 245–253.

Bengtsson, I., and A. Gabrielsson. 1977. "Rhythm Research in Uppsala." In *Music Room Acoustics*. Publication 17. Stockholm: Royal Swedish Academy of Music, pp. 19–56.

Larsson, B. 1977. "Music and Singing Synthesis Equipment (MUSSE)." *Speech Transmission Laboratory—Quarterly Progress and Status Report* 1/1977:38–40. Stockholm: KTH.

Seashore, C. 1938. *Psychology of Music.* New York: McGraw-Hill.

Sundberg, J. 1978. "Synthesis of Singing." *Swedish Journal of Musicology* 60(1): 107–112.

van Noorden, L. P. A. S. 1975. "Temporal Coherence in the Perception of Tone Sequences." *Druk vam Voorschooten* (Diss.).

Appendix: Origin of the Melody Excerpts Used in the Evaluation Test

Parentheses indicate abbreviated titles used in Table 1.

J. S. Bach: *Gavotte* from *Partita in E major for violin solo,* BMV 1006
Courante from *Suite in D major for cello solo,* BMV 1012
Bourrée from *Suite in C major for cello solo,* BMV 1009
Sarabande from *Suite in C minor for cello solo,* BMV 1011
Dir, dir, Jehova . . . (Geistliches Lied), BMV 452

C. M. Bellman: *Hvila vid denna källa,* Fredmans Epistlar, no. 82

G. F. Händel: *Sonata in E major for violin and continuo,* op. 1 : 15

K. Jularbo: *Livet i Finnskogarna* (Dance music)

W. A. Mozart: *Alla Turca* from *Sonate für Klavier in A major,* K 331

F. Schubert: *Fruehlingstraum* from *Winterreise,* op. 89 : 11, D 911
Sonata for Violin and Piano, op. posth. 137 : 1, D 384

A. Tegnér: *Eckorn satt i granen* (Nursery tune)

Traditional: *Happy Birthday*

Name Index

Subject Index

definition of, 199
Digitar chip, 467, 473
Direct memory access, 337
Direct time lock, 213
Direct-to-hard disk recording. *See* Workstations
Discourse theory, 666
Discrete Fourier transform, 624
Discrete uniform probability distribution, 359
Discrete variables, 353
Disk storage requirements for digital audio, 600
Dissonance, theory of, 12
Distribution functions, 353
Doppler Shift effect, simulation of, 112, 232, 563, 566
Dorian Wind Quintet, 35
Dr. T's Echo Plus software, 211
Dreamsong (M. McNabb), 65, 101
Drum machines, 179, 218
  E-mu Drumulator, 306
  Linn drum, 218
  Yamaha RX-11, 206
Drum synthesis, 467, 470
DSP. *See* Digital signal processing
DuPont, 78
Durchkomponieren (through composing), 126
DX-Android program, 217
DX/TX Editor program, 216, 218
Dyaxis digital audio system, 231
Dynamic spectrum, 427

E text editor program, 292
E-mu Drumulator, 306
Early echo patterns in reverberation, 560
Early reaction to computer music, 8
Eastern Anatolia, 27
Eastman School of Music, 67
Echoes (J. Chadabe), 143
Eckorn satt i granen (A. Tegner), 699
Ecole Normale Superieure, 67
Economy in Music, 132
Ed sound editor program, 256
Editing digital audio. *See* Editing sound
Editing sound, 208, 232, 537, 586. *See also* Workstations; Sound editors
  automated, 65
Editors, sound. *See* Sound editors
Editors, score. *See* Score editors
EDSND program, 102, 277
Education, MIDI applications in, 214
Electric Sonata for Four-Channel Tape (L. Hiller), 78, 79
Electroacoustics, 351

Electronic Arts company, 220
Electronic Music Studio, Stockholm, 464
Electronic music, 35
  ensembles, 63
  problems with, 51–52
Electronic wind instruments, 203
Elektronische Musik, 64
EMS. *See* Electronic Music Studio, Stockholm
E-mu company, 215–6
Encapsulated PostScript, 229
ENIGMA kernel, 228
Ensembles
  Arch Ensemble, 45
  Dorian String Quartet, 35
  L'Itineraire, 73
  Maple Sugar Group, 46
  New York Philharmonic, 51
  WQXR String Quartet, 79
Ensoniq Mirage sampler, 215–216
Entropy in Music, 133
Entry delay, 123
Envelopes
  ADSR, 208
  definition in FORMES, 20
  definition in Pla, 288
  line segment approximations of, 671–691
Epicurean concept of randomness, 365
EPSCO, 5
Equalization, 17. *See also* Filters
Ergodic Markov chains, 383
Error correction, 17
Error norms in line segment approximation, 673
Essay (G. M. Koenig), 399
Ethernet, 628
Eulerian gamma function, 367
Event spaces in probability theory, 382
Event streams, 296
Event vectors with Markov chains, 385
Evolution, concepts of, 45
Exhaustive trials, 364
Exponential distribution, 366
EZ-Score Plus program, 225

FAIL programming language, 342
Fanfare (P. Lansky), 43
Farey series, 137
Fast Fourier transform, 33, 91, 215–216, 554, 585, 602
  "twiddle" angle calculations in, 641, 652, 667
Feedback delay lines, 599
Feedback signals, 569

Fender-Rhodes Chroma hybrid synthesizer, 218, 306
Festival de Musiques Experimentales de Bourges, 153
FFT. *See* Fast Fourier transform
Figured bass, 635, 659
File format conversion, 220
Film, relation to new music, 49
FILS sound file, 149
Filters, 342, 468, 601
 comb, 569, 576, 111, 116, 190, 436
 coefficients of, 14
 design of, 434–435, 452
 digital, 427
 finite impulse response filters, 435, 560–563, 575
 group delay in, 517
 heterodyne, 671, 673
 infinite impulse response, 347, 435, 575, 586, 560–563
 linearity of, 515
 lowpass, 510
 phase delay in, 517
 poles and zeros in, 518
 reverberators made with, 20
 time-invariance of, 515
 transfer function of, 516
Finale score editor program, 203, 225, 228
 keyboard split in, 228
Finite impulse response filters, 435, 560–563, 575
Finite state grammars. *See* Grammars
FIR filters. *See* Finite impulse response filters
Firelake (K. Jones), 382
Fission in melodies, 698
Fixed waveform synthesis, 264, 429
Fixed-point arithmetic, 347, 585
Flanging, 111, 211
Flavor System in Lisp, 292, 306, 406
Flavors Band music language, 295, 304
Floating point systems FPS-100 Array processor, 464
Floating-point arithmetic, 17, 457, 585
Floating-split keyboard, 619
Flops (floating-point operations per second), 586
Flowers (J. Chadabe), 143
FM. *See* Frequency modulation
FOF. *See* Formant-wave-function synthesis
Foil music language, 47
Foley effects, 599
Folk Images (P. Lansky), 38, 40
Folk music, 38
FOONLY F2 computer, 664
Foot-tapper routine, 541, 549
Force II computer, 197
Form in music, 238

Formal grammars, 238
Formal languages, 387–388
Formalism in composition, 64
Formant synthesis, 101, 107, 417, 427, 452, 462
Formant-wave-function synthesis, 434, 449, 453
Forme d'Onde Formantique, 453
FORMES language, 296, 464, 73, 405–423, 238
 calculation tree in, 409
 examples of, 412, 420–423
 interprocess communication in, 410
 monitors in, 415–416
 process definition in, 408
 portability of rules in, 410
Fortran programming language, 6, 16, 26, 224, 225, 285, 365, 464, 611
Forums, in electronic mail, 205
Foundations of Computer Music (book), xi
Fourier analysis, 431
 time-variant, 671
Fourier series, 270
Fourier transform, 14, 15, 101, 107. *See also* Fast Fourier transform
Fourth Quartet (A. Schönberg), 665
Frame systems, 648, 650
Frames in granular synthesis, 429
French horn, 35
Frequency domain, 427
Frequency modulation (FM), 42, 65, 68, 70, 101, 107–111, 137, 149, 208, 237, 243, 264, 333, 342, 427, 437, 441, 467, 585, 593, 624–626
 complex, 101, 445
 double-modulator, 150
 oscillators, 311
 patching, 216
Fricative vocal sound, 451
Frog Peak Music, 225
Front panel emulation, 218
FSK synchronization, 212
Function definition, 279
Fundamental bass, theory of, 12
Future Travel (D. Rosenboom), 48

G minor Symphony (W. A. Mozart), 665, 667
Gamma distribution, 362, 366, 376
Gauss-LaPlace distribution, 361, 366, 371, 376
Gaussian noise, 476
Gcomp sound editor program, 277
General Development System digital synthesizer, 615
Generative syntactic analysis, 646
Genpatch ST software, 219

Modem, 205
Modes
  melodic, 101
  in MIDI. *See* Musical Instrument Digital Interface
  of production in composition, 399
  of selection in Flavors Band, 299
  statistical, 367
Modifiers, 333, 334
Moments Newtoniens (J. -C. Risset), 71–72
Monochromal synthesizers, 427
Monte Carlo processes, 78
Moog, R. A., company, 143
Moore's Law, 194
Mortuos Plango, Vivos Voco (J. Harvey), 64, 91–93
Motion pictures, audio for, 599
Motorola DSP 56000, 231
Motorola MC68000 microprocessor, 21–22, 199, 601, 623
Motorola MC68020 microprocessor, 199
Motorola MC68030 microprocessor, 199
Mouse, 199
  as musical instrument, 222
Moving pick, simulation of, 491
Mrdangam, 46
MSI. *See* Medium-scale integration of circuits
MSS program, 237
Multimedia spectacles, 64
Multichannel reverberators, 569
Multidimensional cyclic arrays, 36
Multiplication
  high-speed, 585–586
  parallel, 626
Multiplicative synthesis, 439
Multiply-accumulators, 589
MUS10. *See* Music 10 language
MUSBOX program, 117
Music I synthesis language, 5
Music II synthesis language, 6
Music III synthesis language, 6
Music IV synthesis language, 3, 6, 35, 71, 79, 102
Music IVB synthesis language, 6
Music 4BF synthesis language, 6, 71
Music V synthesis language, 3, 8, 9, 11, 67, 72, 91, 103, 264, 287, 312, 319, 338, 390, 344, 450, 591
  note lists in, 336
  on a chip, 585
Music 10 synthesis language, 8, 9, 19, 72, 102, 105, 149, 287, 312, 319
  I-only code in, 319
Music 11 synthesis language, 8, 9, 278, 312, 569, 576
  implementation of four-channel reverberation in, 579

Music 360 synthesis language, 8, 71
Musical Dice Game (W. A. Mozart), 79
Musical Instrument Digital Interface (MIDI), xi, 178, 206, 237, 243
  1.0 specification, 181
  adapters and THRU boxes, 201
  bandwidth problems, 190–191
  channel commands, 198
  channels in, 184–187
  commands in, 184–187
  control of concert hall acoustics, 212
  file format, 220
  graphics, 243
  IN port, 183
  interfacing to computers, 190–192
  international MIDI Association, 182, 192, 213
  Japan MIDI Standards Association, 192
  keyboard controller, 203
  LAN-to-MIDI converter, 179
  Manufacturers MIDI Association, 192
  matrix switches, 202
  messages, 179
  mode select commands, 185–186
  modes in, 184–187
  mono mode, 185
  omni mode, 185
  OUT port, 183
  physical specification, 182
  poly mode, 185
  possible improvements to, 193
  programming environments, 224
  sample format, 179
  sequencers, 209, 233
  SMPTE-to-MIDI converters, 180, 213
  standard, 586
  system common commands, 186, 198
  system exclusive commands, 186, 191, 198
  system real time commands, 186
  time code, 179, 213
  THRU port, 182, 201
  THRU boxes, 199
Musical intelligence, 58–59
Musical Offering (J. S. Bach), 651
Musical redundancy, 649–650
  Musical style, 38
  specification of, 295
Musical understanding, 668
Music analysis, 691
Music and expectations, 649
Musicdata, 189

Rock musicians, 8
Roland MPU-401 MIDI interface, 187, 243, 248
Roland SBX-80 synchronizer, 243, 248
Roland synthesizers, 218
Roman numeral theory, 668
ROOM program, 576
Rotations (D. Morrill), 95
Roughness, control of in sound synthesis, 150
Rubato, produced by a probability distribution, 367

S sound editor program, 14, 91, 102, 149, 151, 277
S-100 bus, 615
SAIL programming language, 13–14, 285, 338
SalMar Construction, 144
Sample reading and writing, 342
Samplers. *See* Synthesizers and samplers
Sample space, in probability theory, 352
Sample storage, 586
Sample-and-hold units, 17
Sampling rates for digital audio, 601
Samson Box. *See* Systems Concepts Digital Synthesizer
Scales, 223
Sced score editor, 256, 265
Scheduling algorithms, 237
Scheduling among processes, 339
Scheduling synthesis events, 614
Scheduling theory, 344
Schools
  California Institute of Technology, 5
  Carnegie-Mellon University, 20
  Dartmouth College, 73
  Eastman School of Music, 67
  Ecole Normale Supérieure, 67
  Harvard University, 7
  High School of Music and Art, New York, 35
  Massachusetts Institute of Technology, 5, 13, 16, 29,
    206, 224, 239, 569, 578, 639
  Musikhochschule Köln, 26
  New York Institute of Technology, 537
  Princeton University, 6, 16, 35, 68, 665
  Queen's University, 277
  Queen's College, City University of New York, 35
  Stanford University, 3, 64, 71, 91, 101–102, 225, 237,
    432, 611, 671
  State University of New York at Albany, 143
  State University of New York at Binghamton, 657
  University of California, Los Angeles, 48
  University of California, Santa Barbara, 16, 232
  University of California, San Diego, 537
  University of Delaware, 214
  University of Illinois, 7, 45, 64, 75
  University of Indiana, 237
  University of Michigan, 48
  University of Paris VI, 405
  University of Paris VIII, 65, 169
  University of Paris-Sorbonne, 131
  University of Rochester, 623
  University of Toronto, 255, 263
  University of Washington, 663
  University of Western Ontario, 206
  Yale University, 663
Scope, in music score editors, 237, 255
SCORE program, 102, 225
Score copying, 213
Score editors, 225–229
  Deluxe Music Construction Set program, 203, 221,
    225–226
  Finale score editor program, 203, 225, 228
  Gcomp, 277
  HB Music Engraver, 225
  High Score program, 203, 228
  MIDIMac sequencer software, 218, 221
  Mockingbird score editor program, 239
  MUZACS score editor, 239
  Nightingale score editor program, 203, 226, 229
  Personal Composer program, 225, 237, 243
  Pla, 292
  PREFORMES, 224
  Professional Composer program, 221, 225, 226
  Sced score editor, 256, 265
  scope in, 237, 255
  Scriva, 259, 265
  Steinberg Pro-24 sequencer, 219, 231
  Treed score editor, 260
Score formats, 336
Score score input language, 285, 287
Score transcription from numeral listings, 402
Scot score input language, 285
Scratchpad memory in the Lucasfilm ASP, 603
Scriva score editor, 259, 265
SCSI hard disk, 231
Search algorithms in composition, 157
Segments 1–7 (G. M. Koenig), 399
Segments 99–105 (G. M. Koenig), 399
Semantic approaches to musical scope, 255, 261
Semantic primitives, 667
Sensors of an instruments, 9
Sentic significance, 651
Sequencers, 65, 179, 215–216, 229–231, 243
  Bisequencer program, 173

Superscore program, 225
Synthworks program, 217
Total Music program, 230
TX-Android, 217
Upbeat program, 205, 220, 222
Waves interactive soundfile editor, 277
Solo (J. Chadabe), 143
Sonata form, as a teaching machine, 640–645
Sonata for piano in A major (W. A. Mozart), 699
Sonata for violin and piano (F. Schubert), 699
Sonata in E major for violin and continuo (G. F. Handel), 699
Sorting algorithms in composition, 157
Sound Composition Systems MIDI performer, 187
Sound conversion, 586. *See also* Analog-to-digital converters; Digital-to-analog converters
Sound editors
  Ed, 256
  EDSND, 102, 277
  Gcomp, 277
  MacMix, 232
  S, 14, 91, 102, 149, 151, 277
  Softsynth, 216, 221
  Waves, 277
Sound Designer program, 215–216
Sound Droid digital audio workstation, 586
Sound
  as a side effect, 132
  editing, 277, 537, 586, 595, 600, 277
  fetishism, 30
  file manipulation, 149, 151, 231–232
  laboratory applications, 213
  materials, 63
  objects, 263
  paradoxes, 70–71
  spatialization, 427
Sound synthesis languages
  4CED, 311–331
  Cmusic, 277–8, 559, 567
  Music I, 5
  Music II, 6
  Music III, 6
  Music IV, 3, 6, 35, 71, 79, 102
  Music IVB, 6
  Music 4BF, 6, 71
  Music V, 3, 8, 9, 11, 67, 72, 91, 103, 264, 287, 312, 319, 338, 390, 344, 450, 591
  Music 10, 8, 9, 19, 72, 102, 105, 149, 287, 312, 319
  Music 11, 8, 9, 278, 312, 569, 576, 579

Music 360, 8, 71
Sound synthesis techniques
  additive synthesis, 15, 101, 105, 208, 264, 342, 346, 427
  amplitude modulation, 113, 342, 346
  CHANT synthesis program, 97, 405, 427, 449–465
  cross-synthesis, 97
  formant synthesis, 101, 107, 417, 427, 452
  formant wave-function synthesis, 451
  frequency modulation, 42, 65, 68, 70, 101, 107–111, 137, 149, 208, 237, 243, 264, 333, 342, 427, 437, 441, 467, 585, 593, 624–626
  granular synthesis, 381, 429
  Karplus-Strong plucked string and drum algorithm, 215, 427, 467, 481
  nonlinear distortion synthesis, 73, 626. *See also* Waveshaping synthesis
  piano tones, synthesis of, 326
  singing synthesis, 449–465
  string instrument synthesis, 493
  subtractive synthesis, 435, 626
  synthesis by rule, 407, 427, 449, 693
  two-input nonlinear transformation synthesis, 445
  vocal synthesis. *See* Linear predictive coding; Formant wave-function synthesis
  VOSIM, 264, 402, 432
  Walsh function synthesis, 432
  waveshaping synthesis, 73, 264, 342, 346, 437. *See also* Nonlinear distortion synthesis
  wavetable synthesis, 24, 467
Sound synthesizers. *See* Synthesizers and samplers
Soundstream, Inc. 537
Southworth Music Systems, 220, 225, 230, 231
Space grammars, 388–396
Space-builders, 648
SPAM (Signal Processing and Mixing) program, 282
Spatialization of sound, 52–53, 112–113, 427, 559–568. *See also* Doppler shift effect, simulation of; Panning
Special effects in film and video sound, 599
Spectral analysis, 91
  of chords, 69
Spectral estimation, 551–554
Spectral fusion, 107
Spectral pitch, 70
Spectrum and timbre, relations between, 137
Speculum Musicae ensemble, 39
Splicing of audio signals, 599
Spline approximations, 673
Split and merge algorithm, 677
SSI. *See* Small-scale integration of circuits